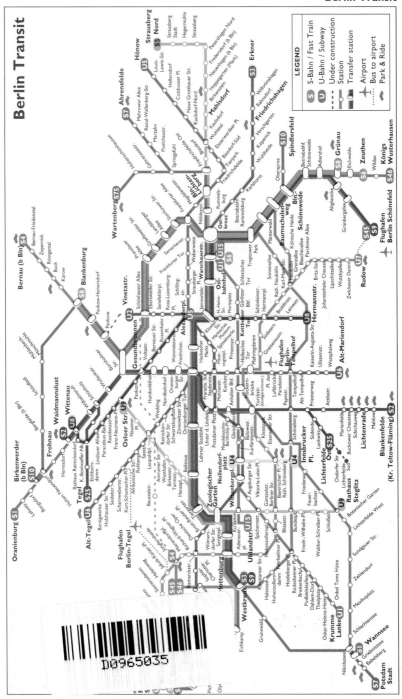

Berlin Transit

LEGEND

- **S** S-Bahn / Fast Train
- **U** U-Bahn / Subway
- Under construction
- Station
- Transfer station
- Airport
- Bus to airport
- Park & Ride

D0965035

Munich Transit

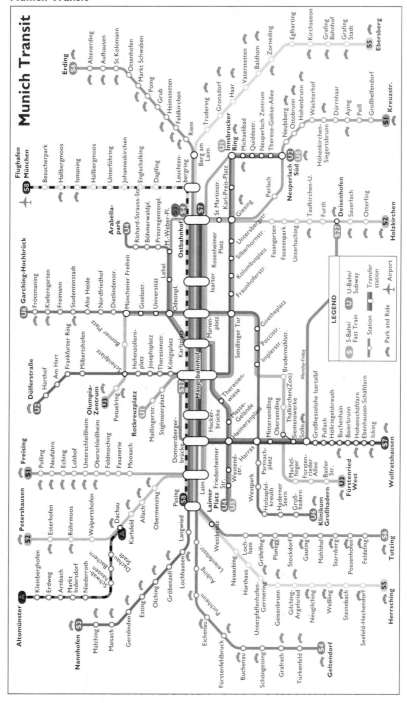

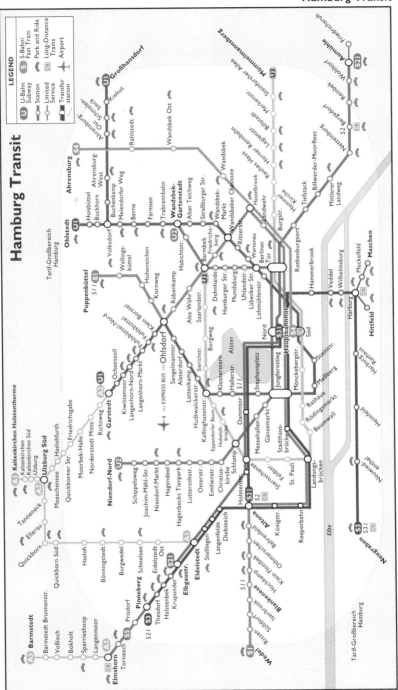

Hamburg Transit

Frankfurt Transit

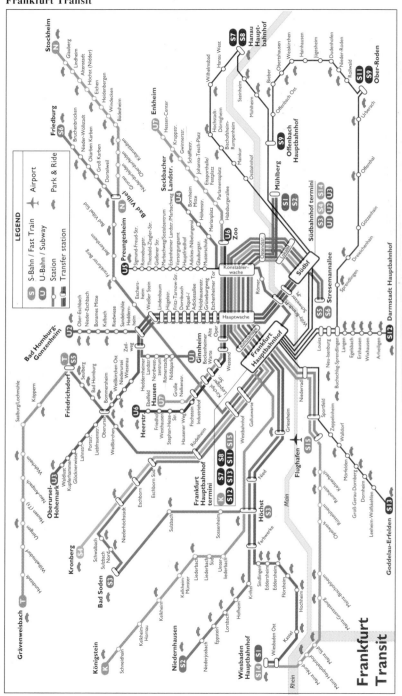

◼ Let's Go writers travel on your budget.

"Guides that penetrate the veneer of the holiday brochures and mine the grit of real life."

—The Economist

"The writers seem to have experienced every rooster-packed bus and lunar-surfaced mattress about which they write."

—The New York Times

"All the dirt, dirt cheap."

—People

◼ Great for independent travelers.

"The guides are aimed not only at young budget travelers but at the independent traveler; a sort of streetwise cookbook for traveling alone."

—The New York Times

"Flush with candor and irreverence, chock full of budget travel advice."

—The Des Moines Register

"An indispensible resource, *Let's Go*'s practical information can be used by every traveler."

—The Chattanooga Free Press

◼ Let's Go is completely revised each year.

"Only *Let's Go* has the zeal to annually update every title on its list."

—The Boston Globe

"Unbeatable: good sightseeing advice; up-to-date info on restaurants, hotels, and inns; a commitment to money-saving travel; and a wry style that brightens nearly every page."

—The Washington Post

◼ All the important information you need.

"*Let's Go* authors provide a comedic element while still providing concise information and thorough coverage of the country. Anything you need to know about budget traveling is detailed in this book."

—The Chicago Sun-Times

"Value-packed, unbeatable, accurate, and comprehensive."

—Los Angeles Times

Let's Go Publications

Let's Go: Alaska & the Pacific Northwest 2000
Let's Go: Australia 2000
Let's Go: Austria & Switzerland 2000
Let's Go: Britain & Ireland 2000
Let's Go: California 2000
Let's Go: Central America 2000
Let's Go: China 2000 **New Title!**
Let's Go: Eastern Europe 2000
Let's Go: Europe 2000
Let's Go: France 2000
Let's Go: Germany 2000
Let's Go: Greece 2000
Let's Go: India & Nepal 2000
Let's Go: Ireland 2000
Let's Go: Israel 2000 **New Title!**
Let's Go: Italy 2000
Let's Go: Mexico 2000
Let's Go: Middle East 2000 **New Title!**
Let's Go: New York City 2000
Let's Go: New Zealand 2000
Let's Go: Paris 2000
Let's Go: Perú & Ecuador 2000 **New Title!**
Let's Go: Rome 2000
Let's Go: South Africa 2000
Let's Go: Southeast Asia 2000
Let's Go: Spain & Portugal 2000
Let's Go: Turkey 2000
Let's Go: USA 2000
Let's Go: Washington, D.C. 2000

Let's Go *Map Guides*

Amsterdam	New Orleans
Berlin	New York City
Boston	Paris
Chicago	Prague
Florence	Rome
London	San Francisco
Los Angeles	Seattle
Madrid	Washington, D.C.

Coming Soon: *Sydney* and *Hong Kong*

Let's Go

2000

GERMANY

Max Hirsh
Editor

Kirstin E. Butler
Associate Editor

Benjamin E. Lytal
Associate Editor

Researcher-Writers

Emily Brott   Benjamin Morgan

Claudia Grégoire

Rebecca Hardiman   Nathaniel Popper

Lucy Ives   Filip Wojciechowski

St. Martin's Press 🙢 New York

HELPING LET'S GO If you want to share your discoveries, suggestions, or corrections, please drop us a line. We read every piece of correspondence, whether a postcard, a 10-page email, or a coconut. Please note that mail received after May 2000 may be too late for the 2001 book, but will be kept for future editions. **Address mail to:**

> **Let's Go: Germany**
> **67 Mount Auburn Street**
> **Cambridge, MA 02138**
> **USA**

Visit Let's Go at **http://www.letsgo.com,** or send email to:

> **feedback@letsgo.com**
> **Subject: "Let's Go: Germany"**

In addition to the invaluable travel advice our readers share with us, many are kind enough to offer their services as researchers or editors. Unfortunately, our charter enables us to employ only currently enrolled Harvard students.

Maps by David Lindroth copyright © 2000, 1999, 1998, 1997, 1996, 1995, 1994, 1993, 1992, 1991, 1990, 1989, 1988 by St. Martin's Press.

Distributed outside the USA and Canada by Macmillan.

ISBN: 0-312-24468-1

First edition
10 9 8 7 6 5 4 3 2 1

Let's Go: Germany is written by Let's Go Publications, 67 Mount Auburn Street, Cambridge, MA 02138, USA.

Let's Go® and the thumb logo are trademarks of Let's Go, Inc.
Printed in the USA on recycled paper with biodegradable soy ink.

HOW TO USE THIS BOOK

For 40 years, *Let's Go* has been jockeying to stay on top of Germany as it's grown, changed, and unified. In 2000, we're hand-picking web addresses and the latest trip-hop clubs, yet we've still got all the tips you wouldn't know you needed until you landed in Frankfurt. You'll find restaurant write-ups, car-pooling services, streetcars that will take you to swimming pools, and all the gritty details you need to thrive and travel without a hitch. How to use this book? Ideally, you should read it from cover to cover and memorize everything. Yet we're sensitive to the fast pace of the new millennium, and we've made an accessible compilation you can hold in the palm of your hand.

As you plan your odyssey, sift through towns you're interested in by looking at their introductions and sights sections. Or, if you can't stay for 20 years, our new **Discover** section outlines tours that take you straight to Germany's best, from discos to fairy-tale castles. Before you lose yourself in either escape, read through our **Essentials** section, 40 pages of hard information on bank cards, railpasses, contact lenses, and how to call home. If all that window-shopping leaves you feeling cheap, or if the in-flight movie is crap, we've provided a rich **History and Culture** section, explaining the life of a country as charmingly problematic as any. Of course, if you read the literature section before you depart, you could be reading the latest translation of one of the hot German authors we've singled out for merit.

Aside from reading our book, don't discount its uses as fashion accessory. Its brightly colored cover will do wonders next to your toiletries kit, and our bold fonts and new format will make other travelers salivate. Just so you don't overdo the tourist look when flashing *Let's Go* in public, remember that the book is divided into regional **chapters** for quick reference, with Berlin at the beginning and the rest of the country following in clockwise geographic order. Each town includes an **Orientation and Practical Information** section that offers everything from train times to internet access. After that comes **Accommodations, Food, Sights,** and **Entertainment;** the content of those sections is ranked according to quality and value. Entries with a ▨ are really super; we'd print these entries in red if we weren't saving colored ink for our transit maps. If someone is so impressed with your travel guide that they want to talk to you, refer to our **Appendix** to learn a little *deutsch*, or impress them with its useful weather, distance, and communications information.

Besides being better than all the guides from that "other century," *Let's Go: Germany 2000* includes intensified coverage of Berlin and Germany's other major cities, balanced by expanded information on the country's best hiking trails. It may be hard to put this book down. But remember that like any good drug, your guidebook should be a pleasure, not a habit. No matter how beautiful our cover is, leave it in your bag sometimes—it might not match your outfit. After all, it's your vacation. Go get 'em.

CONTENTS

MAPS

COLOR INSERT MAPS

Germany: Chapters

DENMARK
Baltic Sea
North Sea

SCHLESWIG-HOLSTEIN
pp. 528–546

Rostock
MECKLENBURG-VORPOMMERN
pp. 547–571

HAMBURG
pp. 514–527

NETHER-LANDS
Bremen

NIERDERSACHSEN (LOWER SAXONY) AND BREMEN
pp. 465–513

Hannover

BRANDENBURG
pp. 140–151

POLAND

Potsdam
BERLIN
pp. 87–139

SACHSEN-ANHALT
pp. 185–206

NORDRHEIN-WESTFALEN
pp. 427–464

Düsseldorf

Köln (Cologne)

Bonn

Leipzig
SACHSEN (SAXONY)
pp. 152–184

Dresden

HESSEN
pp. 399–426

THÜRINGEN
pp. 207–229

BEL.

Frankfurt

CZECH REPUBLIC

RHEINLAND-PFALZ AND SAARLAND
pp. 375–398

LUX.

Heidelberg

Nürnberg (Nuremberg)

FRANCE

Stuttgart

BADEN-WÜRTTEMBERG
pp. 321–374

BAYERN (BAVARIA)
pp. 230–320

München (Munich)

AUSTRIA

Freiburg

SWITZERLAND

RESEARCHER-WRITERS

Emily Brott   *Bonn, Frankenland, Köln, Hessen, Rheinland-Pfalz, Sächsische Schweiz, Thüringen*
Bisecting Germany's midriff, Emily cut an intrepid diagonal from the Eastern extremes of Sachsen to the idyllic valleys of the Rheinland. Caught in a rainstorm early on, Emily took shelter in the fairy-tale grottoes of Saalfeld, expanding our coverage of the bucolic trails lacing the Thüringer Wald. She then returned to her former haunts in central Hessen, splicing her write-ups with a healthy apprecia-tion for *Bratwurst* and *Bananenweizen*. Never at a loss for company, Emily was last seen heading for the sunnier climes of Madrid by way of Amsterdam.

Claudia Grégoire   *Allgäu, Baden-Württemberg, Frankfurt, Saarland*
Seduced by the warmth of German hospitality and the steam of thermal baths, Claudia bared it all in the sultry climes of Baden-Württemberg. Beginning her adventure in Frankfurt, Claudia hunted down the most cost-effective ways to enjoy Germany's money-driven business center. From the banks of the Main to the shores of the Bodensee, Claudia went on to discover towering abbeys and soaring peaks, stopping off at hip spots to rest and frolic in between hiking jaunts.

Rebecca Hardiman   *Bayern*
Lean mean hiking machine Rebecca took Bavaria by storm, leaving *Kur*-seeking tourists and hordes of schoolchildren in her dust. Diving from the alpine heights of Berchtesgaden to the punky depths of Munich's underworld, Rebecca scoured the landscape with a nose for bargains and hidden delights. Though illness prevented her from completing her route, Rebecca's hyper-efficient researching and volumi-nous write-ups never ceased to amaze us.

Lucy Ives   *Berlin, Bayern, Brandenburg, Niedersachsen, Schleswig-Holstein*
Tearing across Germany on the longest itinerary in recent memory, Lucy was, well, simply amazing. Whether she was giving us the low-down on the perils of the *Watt* or the cruise factor of one of Berlin's sketchier clubs, Lucy managed to cap-ture the elusive essence of the land of the Teutons. Breaking hearts left and right, Lucy cast off the cloying doilies of her Frisian admirers and rejected the advances of Viking scrubs in Schleswig. Through it all, Lucy's flair for the absurd and astute eye combined to craft seven tomes of insightful prose. Bravo.

Benjamin Morgan   *Hamburg, Mecklenburg-Vorpommern, Niedersachsen, Nordrhein-Westfalen*
Determined not to let a backpacker's budget deter him, Ben did Germany in style. From the faded glitter of the Baltic seacoast to the insomniac streets of Hamburg, Ben "trendy-pants" Morgan walked the walk and talked the talk into the hottest bars and coolest clubs in Germany, always making sure to leave time to scope out that new internet café down the block. Fortunately, Ben's stylishness extended to his writing, leaving us salivating for more with each successive copybatch.

Nathaniel Popper   *Bayern*
This savvy Switzerland researcher-writer jumped the border to give us the skinny on Augsburg and the Frankenland. Shedding his hiking gear and *Schwyzertütsch* vocabulary, Nathaniel dove into the underbelly of Germany's largest *Land*, ren-dering a stellar account full of curiosity and enthusiasm.

Filip Wojciechowski   *Berlin, Kassel, Niedersachsen, Sachsen, Sachsen-Anhalt, Spreewald*
Filip struggled with the dialectic of work and play from the Marx-riddled streets of Chemnitz to the gritty dancefloors of Berlin. Struck by a mysterious illness in the *Hauptstadt*, he continued undeterred, rising to the spooky heights of the Harz and intellectual lows of Göttingen. Filip overcame adoring *Schulmädchen* to deliver six monolithic copybatches, each stuffed with his trademark wit and irony.

ACKNOWLEDGMENTS

TEAM GERMANY THANKS: Our R-Ws. Waka and Marshall for Axis Pod antics, Haunted Chair and Special Drawer, Knecht Ruprecht, *Bills, Bills, Bills*, Telnet vs. Eudora, Snivelitch, Gribble, and *Nonstop to Tokyo*. Thanks also to Peter Burgard and Eric Rentschler of the Department of Germanic Languages and Literatures at Harvard University, Melissa and Matt for kick-ass design, Helga Brenner-Khan at the GNTO in New York, Rose Schwartz at Deutsche Bahn, The Harvard *Advocate*, Kurt Müller, Katie Mannheimer, Jamie Jones, John Fiore, and Anne Chisholm.

MAX HIRSH THANKS: Kirstin first and foremost, for your hard work, integrity, and thoughtfulness. Your concern for the book (and insights on contemporary R&B) kept me going. Thank you, Ben, for chats on the back porch and for being a Danish robot. Thanks also to Nia for coming to visit; Andy for keeping it real, sort of; Anna for *kompot* and tea; Landi and John for late-night runs to IHOP; Annie for suggesting Karl-Marx-Allee; Nadia for letters; Carrots; und meine Schwester, obwohl sie immer noch so klein ist.

KIRSTIN E. BUTLER THANKS: Max, whose professionalism and encyclopedic knowledge of all things deutsch never ceased to amaze. It was, of course, your CD collection for which I truly reserved my respect. Ben, with whom I share a middle initial and for whom I will always be amused. Die Familie Butler, die mir alles beigebracht hat. My Max, who made this summer possible.

BENJAMIN E. LYTAL THANKS: First I wanna thank God, then Sam Lytal & Co., then the fire escape and the private eyes-32: Annie, who untaught me the very madness, and Nadia, for being the North Star. But most DJ Max 1999, for all parts of the party and all the sidewalk squares between here and Calvin, and Kirstin, who everyday dressed better than me but never mentioned it. And finally the kitchen table for its loyalty in all hard moments, and Mandy for the same but in spades, plus feeding me.

Editor
Max Hirsh
Associate Editors
Kirstin E. Butler, Benjamin E. Lytal
Managing Editor
Benjamin Paloff

Publishing Director
Benjamin Wilkinson
Editor-in-Chief
Bentsion Harder
Production Manager
Christian Lorentzen
Cartography Manager
Daniel J. Luskin
Design Managers
Matthew Daniels, Melissa Rudolph
Editorial Managers
Brendan Gibbon, Benjamin Paloff, Kaya Stone, Taya Weiss
Financial Manager
Kathy Lu
Personnel Manager
Adam Stein
Publicity & Marketing Managers
Sonesh Chainani, Alexandra Leichtman
New Media Manager
Maryanthe Malliaris
Map Editors
Kurt Mueller, Jon Stein
Production Associates
Steven Aponte, John Fiore
Office Coordinators
Elena Schneider, Vanessa Bertozzi, Monica Henderson

Director of Advertising Sales
Marta Szabo
Associate Sales Executives
Tamas Eisenberger, Li Ran

President
Noble M. Hansen III
General Managers
Blair Brown, Robert B. Rombauer
Assistant General Manager
Anne E. Chisholm

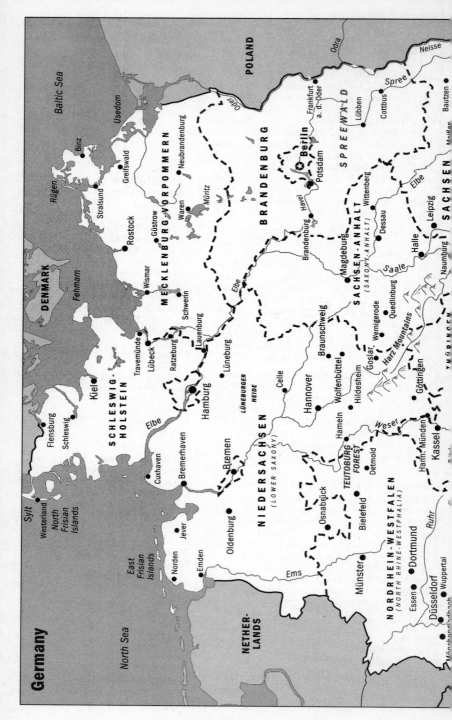

Germany

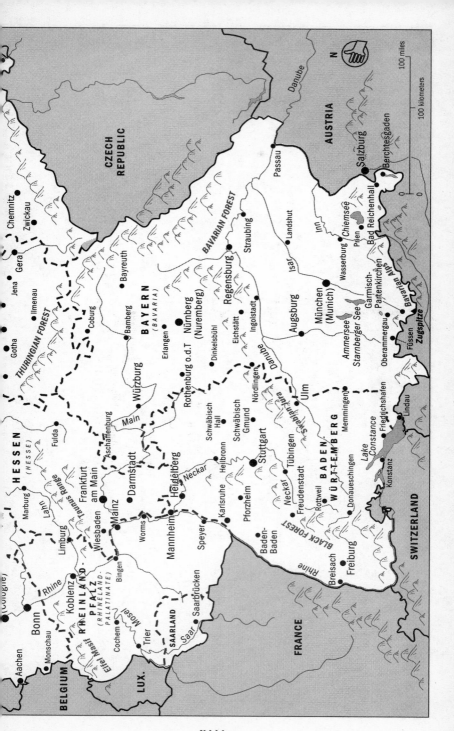

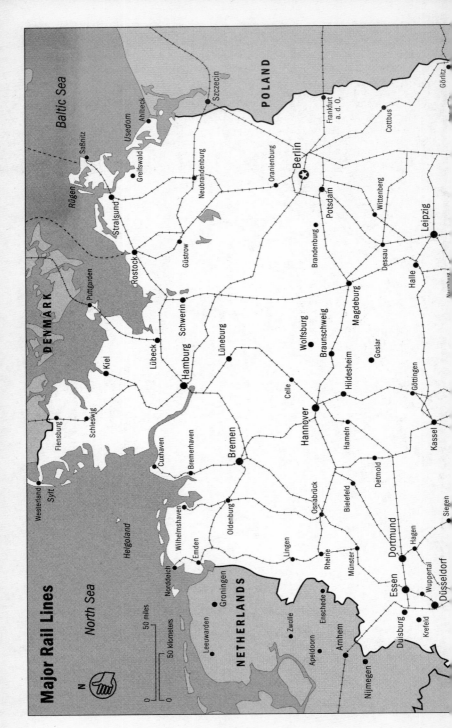

Major Rail Lines

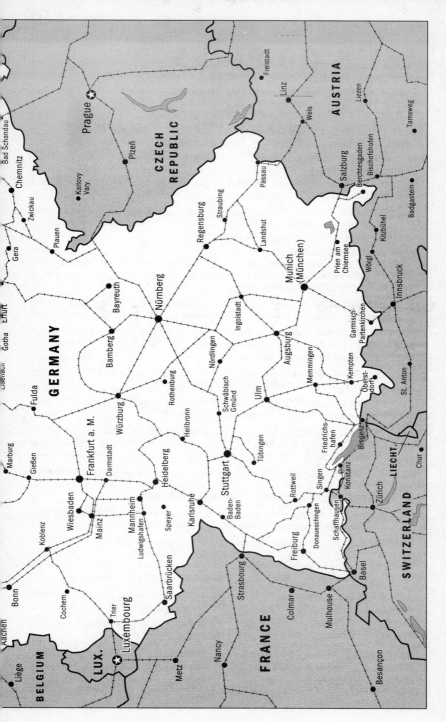

LET'S GO PICKS

BEST ACCOMMODATIONS: Reconciling human living space with mass tourism, the **Bauhaus** architectural school (p. 190) in Dessau offers single and double rooms. The friendly **Station Hostel** (p. 430) in Cologne has a great location.

BEST ALPINE RESORT: Find everything but stress in **Oberstdorf** (p. 258), where cable cars await to whisk you to the peaks of the Allgäu Alps. In the nearby Bavarian Alps, **Ramsau** (p. 268) offers an open-air inhalatorium and ice-skating in winter.

BEST BIERGARTEN: No, it's not in Munich! Sip beer and watch the Donau slide by at Regensburg's 800-year-old **Wurstküche** (p. 287), which features *Wurst* and sauerkraut as good as the atmosphere.

BEST BEACHES: Germans flock to the ritzy resort of **Sylt** (p. 545), but if you want to avoid the crowds, **Amrum** (p. 546) may be for you. On the Baltic Sea, **Rügen** (p. 561) combines beaches, chalk cliffs, and hiking.

BEST CASTLES: Neuschwanstein (p. 261), the model for Disneyland's castle, towers over the Alps. **Schloß Moritzburg** (p. 164), with its hunting lodge interior, drips with decadent masculinity, but for something literally decadent, visit the ruins of Heidelberg's crumbling **Schloß** (p. 326).

BEST CATHEDRAL: The towers of the Dom at **Cologne** (p. 433) take High Gothic style to a higher level, but the abbey of **Ottobeuren** (p. 257) is our Baroque favorite.

BEST HIKING TRAIL: The 168km **Rennsteig** (p. 222) runs from Eisenach all the way to Bavaria, hitting countless villages and intersecting with the **Goethewanderweg** (p. 222), which makes an ideal day hike.

BEST LATE-NIGHT SNACKS: Dance. Afterwards, even at four in the morning, munch Turkish pastries at Berlin's **Melek Pastanesi** (p. 107).

BEST NEW YEAR'S PARTY: Dresden will throw a free bash in its Altmarkt (p. 161), but the obvious place to be is **Brandenburg Gate** (p. 108).

BEST PLACES TO DANCE: SO36 (p. 138) in Berlin draws a friendly, eclectic crowd. Avoid Dresden's **DownTown** (p. 162) if you can't dance; try Munich's city of discos, **Kunstpark Ost** (p. 254), if its museums have numbed your attention span.

BEST RELICS OF THE GDR: Thrill to the concrete pomposity along **Straße der Nationen** (p. 173) in Chemnitz, the city formerly known as Karl-Marx-Stadt. In Berlin, **Karl-Marx-Allee** (p. 119) is prime for a parade of Western tourists.

BEST BATHTIME: Backpackers will feel refreshingly out of their element after a bath and pink-towel nap in Baden-Baden's **Friedrichsbad** (p. 352).

BEST FASHION: Do the lemming with the Pied Piper–costumed tour guides of **Hameln** (p. 479). The "night watchman" tour in **Rothenburg** (p. 297) is equally embarrassing, but at least it's in the dark so no one will see you. For less medieval digs, Düsseldorf's **Königsallee** (p. 449) is Germany's strutting fashion capital.

BEST KITSCH: The train leading to **Oybin** (p. 172) is reminiscent of a cheesy amusement park, and the *Biergarten* flaunts miniature moving dwarves and hikers.

BEST BIRD-WATCHING: The tourist office at **Waren** (p. 550) leads early morning excursions to the rare bird and marsh preserves of **Müritz national park**.

BEST UNDISCOVERED COUNTRY: Dessau (p. 188), home to the Bauhaus architectural school, was the fount of modern design; **Wittenberg** (p. 185), home of Luther and his many monuments, wants to be your Protestant fix; and **Wörlitz** (p. 191) is surrounded by an artificial landscape designed by its visionary prince. All three bide their time in a quiet corner of Sachsen-Anhalt.

DISCOVER
GERMANY

In between Germany's Alpine wonderlands and seaside resorts, medieval cities and cosmopolitan metropolises form one of the most prosperous belts in all of Europe. Each of the country's historically distinct cities and regions pulls Germany in its own direction: Munich, for example, revels in beer-drenched tradition, while Berlin steps to a cutting-edge beat. For those who think blisters make the best souvenirs, there's hiking, biking, and skiing in the Bavarian Alps, the Black Forest, and the Harz Mountains. But outdoor Germany isn't all forest—salty beaches abound on the North and Baltic seacoasts, while some stretches of the balmy Bodensee (Lake Constance) are warm enough to support tropical vegetation and southern European tan lines. The traveler in Germany could easily spend weeks in the romantic canyons and medieval castles of Bavaria or in dynamic urban centers like Frankfurt and Dresden, never imagining the scenery that awaits a few hours away. Even a sprawling city like Hamburg offers picturesque sailing only a subway ride from a nightlife where everything—and we mean everything— is for sale.

Germany's millennia of history have endowed many cities with stunning cathedrals and clusters of half-timbered facades; but for a preview of the next millennium, head to Berlin, a city whose conflicted past and future lend it a compelling fervor. Many attractions are made doubly rich by the stories surrounding them: a boat ride down the craggy Rhine Valley evokes the drama of the legendary Lorelei siren, while touring the opulent chambers of Neuschwanstein castle provides a glimpse of Mad King Ludwig's eccentric tastes. After the museums close, the best beer awaits in the hippest clubs on the continent. Discover Germany in 2000.

WHEN TO GO

Temperatures and airfares rise in July and August along with the number of tourists. In winter months, some German hostels hibernate, and museum hours may be abbreviated. The cloudy, temperate months of May, June, and September are the best time to go, as there are fewer tourists and the weather is pleasant. But bear in mind that most schools go on *Klassenreise* (extended field trips) in June, and that youth hostels may be inundated with schoolchildren. Germans head to vacation spots *en masse* with the onset of school vacations in early July; airports and train stations are jammed and the traffic on the Autobahn can be measured in meters per hour. The staggering of vacation periods among the federal states has alleviated the crunch, but you should still avoid trekking across Germany the day after school lets out. Winter sports gear up in November and continue through April; high season for skiing hits mid-December to mid-January and February to March. See the **Appendix** (p. 572) for further holiday and festival information. For a primer on **Y2K events**, see **Apocalypse 2000**, p. 37. For more specific weather information, see **Climate**, p. 578.

SUGGESTED ITINERARIES

BEST OF GERMANY (3 WEEKS) Enter Germany at its center, **Berlin** (p. 87). The capital's enormous cultural and historical treasures, not to mention its chaotic nightlife, sprawl over an area eight times the size of Paris. Save time for a daytrip to the neoclassical splendors of nearby **Potsdam** (p. 140). If Berlin is too intense for you, **Dresden** (p. 153) won't help much. With its jumping nightlife and exquisite palaces and museums, the city is neatly counterpointed by a trip to **Weimar** (p. 208). The most thoroughly rebuilt city in Eastern Germany, Weimar rests solidly on the cultural heritage of Goethe, the Bauhaus architectural movement, and Germany's first liberal constitution. Continue your trip to Germany's past in **Rothenburg** (p. 297), a medieval city that deserves to be as kitschy as it wants to be. **Munich** (p. 231), takes bucolic merriment to a frothy head as the capital of Bavaria; the condition of its excellent museums and jovial beer halls both bear witness to its prosperity. Continuing south, the castles of **Neuschwanstein, Hohenschwangau,** and **Linderhof** make up the fairy-tale triumvirate of Mad King Ludwig's **royal castles** (p. 261). Head west into Baden-Württemberg to live out your favorite Grimms fairy tales in the **Black Forest** (p. 360); from the winding alleys of **Freiburg** (p. 353) to the mountain-top lakes at **Titisee** and **Schluchsee** (p. 362), the region can't fail to impress. To the north, **Heidelberg** (p. 322) is home to Germany's oldest, most prestigious, and most scenic university, sitting below the brooding ruins of the city's castle. Next stop: **Koblenz** (p. 377), gateway to the Rhine and Mosel. Take a daytrip to the **Lorelei** cliffs of the **Rhine Valley** (p. 381) and embark on a side-trip to the wine-growing **Mosel Valley** (p. 386). Next, saunter northward to **Cologne** (p. 428), site of Germany's largest and perhaps most poignant cathedral and home to a pounding nightlife. Much further north, reckless **Hamburg** (p. 514), Germany's largest city after Berlin, fuses the burliness of a port town with cosmopolitan flair, while the stolid townhouses of **Lübeck** (p. 528) recall an earlier age when the town was capital of the Hanseatic league.

VALLEY TOUR (1 WEEK) The famous valleys of Rheinland-Pfalz and Baden-Württemberg are tightly grouped, suggesting an excellent bike or bus tour. Trains are often less convenient, but it is possible to travel to the area's major towns and then make daytrip excursions into the valleys. Start off in **Stuttgart** (p. 337) and spend a day walking the nearby fountains of the Schloßgarten or partying on Königstraße. Then move on to Germany's most popular Uni-town, **Heidelberg** (p. 322), taking time to look at the city's famed castle from the Philosophenweg trail across the Neckar. Heidelberg is a perfect base for daytrips down the **Neckar Valley** (p. 328), a miraculously untouristed stretch of the river that weaves between lookout castles and thickly forested hills. Take a train from Heidelberg to **Bingen** (p. 384), from where you can explore the legendary Lorelei cliffs of the **Rhine Valley** (p. 381). From Bingen, ferry across the Rhine to touristy **Rüdesheim** (p. 382), or stay aboard and trundle down the entire castle-lined gorge. Stop off for a visit to the famed wineries of **Bacharach** (p. 382), or continue on to the **Lorelei** cliffs (p. 381), a towering section of the river difficult to navigate and renowned for its mythical siren, who lured sailors onto the rocky crags that line the shore. Consider spending the night below the Lorelei in **St. Goar,** or move on to **Koblenz** (p. 377), where the Mosel and Rhine rivers converge at the **Deutsches Eck** peninsula, a memorial to the foundation of the Teutonic state. From Koblenz, the **Mosel Valley** (p. 386) is at your fingertips. Not as staggeringly steep as the cliffs of the Rhine, the valley is also less touristed, and its vineyards are too dense to bear commercial cheapening. Be sure to sample the fruity vines of **Cochem** (p. 387), or take a detour into the shaded valley where **Burg Eltz** (p. 388), one of the oldest intact medieval castles, keeps watch. At the end of the Mosel's most scenic stretch sits the ancient city of **Trier** (p.

390), littered with Roman ruins from the city's tour of duty as a capital of the Holy Roman Empire.

ROMANTIC ROAD & ROYAL CASTLES (1 WEEK)

Officially dubbed the Romantic Road by German tourist officials in 1950, the route between Würzburg and Füssen has since become the most heavily touristed area in the country. **Würzburg** (p. 301) is home to the Residenz, one of the largest Baroque palaces in Germany. Continue to **Rothenburg** (p. 297); venturing behind its ancient ramparts is like stepping into the 16th century. **Dinkelsbühl** (p. 299), to the south, pulls the same medieval tricks. Everything is old in **Nördlingen** (p. 300), a town built in a 15-million year old crater whose bell tower has rung daily for the past 500 years. Further along on the Lech River, the abbey of **Ottobeuren** (p. 257) is the topographical and architectural climax of the Baroque style. Where the Lech tumbles down from the Alps, **Füssen** (p. 269) enchants with its castle and ancient fortifications, and is an ideal base for excursions to the **Royal Castles** (p. 261). Alpine getaways of mad King Ludwig, the castles are the product of eccentric Romantic imagination with money to burn. **Schloß Neuschwanstein** (p. 261), the castle upon which Walt Disney modeled the Magic Kingdom, towers above the Pöllat Gorge, recreating "the true style of German knights" with more success than any animated film could. While the nearby **Schloß Hohenschwangau** (p. 261) has perhaps a slightly more realistic medieval style, its personable interior is done in competing Biedermeier and Oriental styles. **Schloß Linderhof** (p. 262), placed deep in one of the Alps wildest valleys, comprises a Rococo palace with Renaissance gardens that are themselves enclosed by an English park. For tips on travel between the castles, see p. 263.

NORTHERN GERMANY (1-2 WEEKS)

This tour surveys regions popular with vacationing Germans but generally overlooked by foreign tourists. Begin your exploration in **Hannover** (p. 466), the host of **EXPO 2000,** the first world exposition of the new millennium. After a glimpse of the future, head for the rolling plains of the **Lüneburger Heide** and its eponymous gateway, **Lüneburg** (p. 493). Germany's largest port, **Hamburg** (p. 514) hosts a befuddling mix of students, strippers, and sailors. Next stop: **Sylt** (p. 545), whose majestic dunes and rideable surf make the island Germany's premier beach resort. Travelers with a bit more time should head for **Amrum** (p. 546), Sylt's less commercial sibling to the south, and **Schleswig** (p. 541), home to the remains of a Viking settlement and a superb collection of Expressionist paintings and Jugendstil design. Otherwise, high-tail it to **Lübeck** (p. 528). The city's legacy as a Hanseatic powerhouse funded one of the most beautiful Old Towns in Germany. After crossing the former East-West divide, head to **Rostock** (p. 553), the northeast's largest city and a hopping university town. Admire the Gothic spires of **Stralsund** (p. 559) on your way to **Rügen** (p. 561). Once the summer digs of Berlin's pre-war glitterati, the island boasts isolated beaches and the stunning chalk cliffs of **Jasmund national park** (p. 564). Back on the mainland, **Waren** (p. 550) is the gateway to the **Müritz,** Germany's largest freshwater lake. The surrounding national park hosts some of the best hiking and birdwatching opportunities in the country. If you've tired of the country, fear not—the urban hedonism of **Berlin** (p. 87) is less than two hours away.

HIKING TOUR (2 WEEKS)

From the white beaches in the north to the forested mountains bordering Austria and Switzerland, Germany offers hiking that can be historic, challenging, and breathtaking, usually all at once. Begin a hike around Germany in its witch-haunted heart, the **Harz mountains** (p. 196). Between hikes, freshen up in Goethe's favorite get-away, **Wernigerode** (p. 199), now the unofficial capital of the Harz. Next, ride across to **Saxon Switzerland** (p. 165) and the towering peaks of the Czech frontier; backpack between towns or do daytrips from **Dresden** (p. 153). Before heading to Bavaria, spend some time on the trails Goethe loved in the **Thuringian Forest** (p. 222). Hike the centuries-old

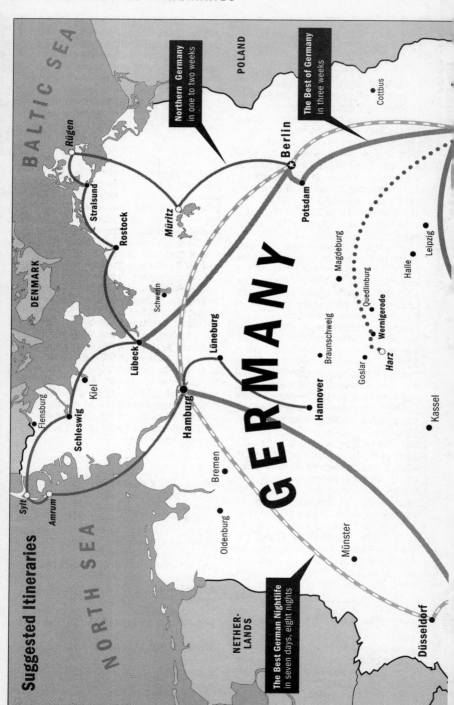

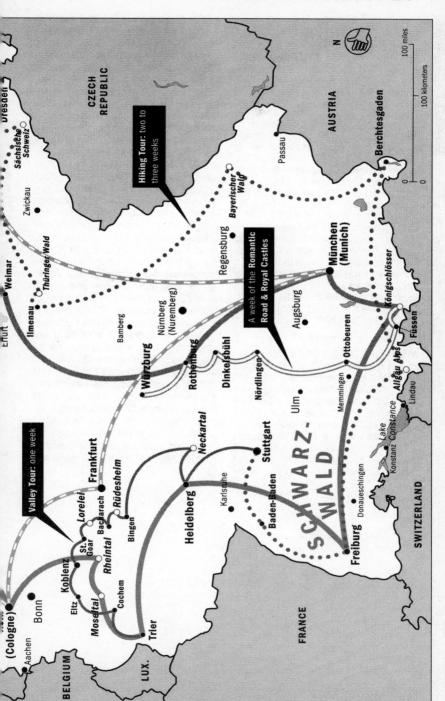

Rennsteig through these time-worn hills; consider using **Erfurt** (p. 218) as a base of operations. A favorite of German tourists, the **Bavarian Forest** (p. 289) is the largest range of wooded mountains in Central Europe. It offers miles and miles of trails dotted by monastic ruins and kitschy tourist towns; work out of the centrally located rail hub, **Zwiesel** (p. 289). In Bavaria's southwestern corner, climb up to Hitler's mountain retreat at **Berchtesgaden** (p. 266), at the eastern end of the Bavarian Alps, or cool off in the nearby **Königssee**. Hard-core hikers head east to the **Allgäu Alps** (p. 256), where **Oberstdorf** (p. 258) offers cable-car access to heady Alpine trails. The trails around **Immenstadt** and **Bühl** (p. 257) offer various levels of difficulty, while the less ambitious can soak in the refreshing **Alpsee**. The immense **Black Forest** (p. 360) makes a fitting climax to any scenic tour of Germany; access its trails from the city of **Freiburg** (p. 353), at the forest's center, or from **Stuttgart** (p. 337) or **Baden-Baden** (p. 351), near the northern edges of the forest.

NIGHTLIFE TOUR (7-10 DAYS) Germany's nightlife scene is one of the most varied and extensive in all of Europe. Any tour of the country should include at least a few nights at the Biergarten; but Germany isn't all beer and *Schnitzel*, as a trip to one of the country's too-hip-for-their-own-good dance clubs will prove. Begin your downfall in **Berlin** (p. 132), the epicenter of Teutonic debauchery and the undisputed capital of techno. Get your feet wet in one of the relaxed *Kneipen* along Oranienburger Str.; move on to Kreuzberg and Mitte's techno clubs or, if that's not your scene, to the cutting-edge hard-core raging in Prenzlauer Berg; and round off the night in any number of the capital's after-hours "chill-out" bars. Berlin also boasts the largest **gay and lesbian scene** in continental Europe (p. 137), with venues ranging from the super-chill to the super-cruisey. Take your pick. Once you've regained consciousness, hop on a train to **Dresden** (p. 161) for a taste of Eastern Germany's rapidly evolving nightlife scene. If Berlin is the herald of all things cutting edge and illicit, then **Munich** (p. 251) is the guardian of Germany's most respected ritual, i.e. the mass consumption of beer. Despite its traditional appearance, the Bavarian metropolis still manages to foster impressive punk and gay scenes (p. 254). If money is what you want, head to the fashion-conscious economic capital, **Frankfurt** (p. 408), where only the super-rich and super-pretty will make it past the bouncer. Or high-tail it to **Cologne** (p. 437) to indulge in a few (dozen) rounds of *Kölsch*. If you have time, stop off in **Düsseldorf** (p. 455) and pay homage to what is reputed to be the longest bar counter in the world, with 500 pubs stretching across the Old Town. Last stop: **Hamburg** (p. 525), where everything—and we mean *everything*—is for sale. Indulge in the pleasures of the flesh along the Reeperbahn, Germany's most notorious legalized prostitution strip, or chill with the happy student crowd in the Sternschanze. Phew. All tired out? Oh, hell—go back to Berlin and start over.

HISTORY AND CULTURE

A decade after the fall of the Berlin Wall, Germans are still trying to fashion themselves a new identity for the 21st century. After centuries of war, fragmentation, occupation, and division, Germany now finds itself a wealthy nation at the forefront of both European and global politics. Yet, bound by an ignoble past, Germans are hesitant to draw upon historical precedent as a source of unity and pride. Indeed, what may be the most striking aspect of contemporary German culture is the contrast among average Germans' intransigent sense of order and an embrace of the American-influenced global pop culture that distances the nation from the notoriety of its wartime belligerence and inhumanity. It is this enigmatic juxtaposition between modern Germany's loyalty to its cultural institutions and its desire to annihilate its ignominious position in world history that the next few pages attempt to explore.

Despite its long history of reactionary politics, Germany has been a perennial wellspring of revolutionaries and innovators—for better and for worse. One of the first heroes of German history, **Charlemagne** (Karl der Große) unified post-Roman Europe under relatively enlightened rule. **Martin Luther** went from small-town German monk to one of the most influential figures in Western history when he authored his *95 Theses*, spawning the Protestant Reformation. Communist pioneers **Karl Marx** and **Friedrich Engels** equipped the revolutionary groundswell of 19th-century Europe with an ideology that precipitated the major conflicts of the second half of the 20th century. And one of the most horrifying figures in history, **Adolf Hitler** forever tainted Germany's international reputation with his expansionist dreams of a greater Germany and genocidal race theories. This last image, of course, indelibly colors all subsequent German history, as Germany has become irreversibly linked to the Holocaust in the world's mind. As historians are fond of pointing out, Germans must grapple with the fact that the same country that produced Goethe, Kant, and Beethoven was also the breeding ground of Hitler, Goebbels, and Mengele.

To combat this incongruous legacy, Germans these days are busy trying to further integrate themselves into the economic and political institutions of the international future, while still coming to terms with the problems brought on by the remarkably quick reunification of the country ten years ago. In the wake of Europe's most recent revolutions, Germany's pivotal role between East and West is even more important than it was during the Cold War, yet efforts to provide leadership on the Continent have been hampered by Germany's internal identity crises. Nevertheless, Germany assumes an increasingly assertive role in the global community, and while the country's prospects for the future continue to be elusive, Germany enters the next millennium more unified and stable than ever before.

HISTORY

Entering into the fray surrounding German history can feel a little like wine tasting in the Moseltal: every historian will tout a different theory as the most salient. One of the longest-running historical debates is over the question of a *Sonderweg*, the idea that German history has been on a particular—and divergent—path from the rest of Western history since its very origin. *Sonderweg* theory arose largely through historiographers' constant search for a version of German history that can explain the Holocaust. Even the starting point of German history is a debatable issue, as it wasn't until 1871 that Germany became a unified nation. Nominally speaking, "German" history didn't begin until 90 BC, when the Roman author Posidonius first applied the word to the peoples that migrated from Southern Scandinavia to central Europe around 1000 BC. That's where we pick up the story.

EARLY GERMAN HISTORY: 58 BC-1517

AD 9
Chief Hermann leads Germanic tribes to victory over the Romans in the Teutoburg forest

800
Charlemagne crowned emperor of Holy Roman Empire

843
Treaty of Verdun splits the Empire into three kingdoms, marking off the territory that would become Germany

1356
Hanseatic League founded; the Golden Bull splits authority between archbishops and electors in choosing the emperor

German history of the first millennium is more rightly considered prehistory, as the notion of a German nation didn't come to fruition until the 19th century. However, the clans of peoples in the region now known as Germany became a real political entity much earlier, when they were forced to defend and define themselves against the powerful **Roman Republic.** After many years of war with the "barbaric" German tribes the Empire had, by 58BC, expanded its borders to the Rhein. Allied Germanic tribes, under the leadership of **Hermann,** earned themselves the sobriquet **"Teuton"** when they scored a great upset against the Romans in the Teutoburg Forest (see p. 459). The battle, which most likely took place near what is now Osnabrück, is recognized as the **first assertion of true Germanic culture.** Five centuries of often antagonistic relations preceded a series of successive pillages of Rome by Germanic tribes. This resulted in the seizure of the city by the Ostrogoths and the end of the Roman Empire in 476. Still, Christianity continued to take hold and German peoples appropriated many of the later Roman church institutions.

While the southern German tribes were busy moving upon their well-heeled Roman neighbors, **the Franks** expanded their power into the Rhein Valley. Three centuries later under the rule of **Charlemagne** (whom Germans know as Karl der Große), nearly all of the Germanic kingdoms of Europe were united. Pope Leo III crowned Charles **Holy Roman Emperor** on Christmas Day in the year 800, inviting comparisons between the emerging Europe and the erstwhile Roman Empire. Charlemagne initiated administrative reforms and cultural advancements; under his rule, monasteries became centers of learning and knowledge preservation, and commerce within Europe and with the Arab and Byzantine worlds was revived. This Dark Age "renaissance" soon came to an end, however, as invasions from outsiders, weak infrastructure, and disputes over inheritance after Charlemagne's death prompted the Treaty of Verdun in 843, which split the empire into three kingdoms. A leader of the Frankish kingdom, **Otto I,** pushed the Franks' borders east to the Oder River, earning him the renewed title of Holy Roman Emperor in 962. Over the next half millennium, the would-be German lands were further dismantled into a feudal society by internecine disputes. Still, in the 12th and 13th centuries, the kingdoms continued to expand in a fever of political competition. The **Hohenstaufen** family is the closest the emerging German nations could claim as a dynasty during this period, with **Friedrich I (Barbarossa) and Friedrich II** as the most prominent Teutons among the clan. Still, the grand aspirations of a succession of regional princes, prominent among whom was **Heinrich der Löwe** (Henry the Lion), maintained the state of decentralization.

Despite the continued existence of the Holy Roman Empire, quarrels between the church and political leadership arose repeatedly throughout the next several centuries until the signing of the **Golden Bull of 1356,** which declared that seven electors—three archbishops and four secular leaders—would approve the selection of each emperor. Large-scale bribing of these electors ensued, clearing the way for the ascent of the **House of Habsburg,** which occupied the throne for the next five centuries with the support of its Austrian domains. Under the Habsburg leadership, the German nation began to define itself a little more clearly; the **Hanseatic League** banded a number of German merchant towns together in 1358, and outlying areas of the still-alive Holy Roman Empire, including Italy, slipped out of the Habsburgs' control entirely.

THE REFORMATION AND
THE THIRTY YEARS WAR: 1517-1700

On All Saints' Day 1517, **Martin Luther,** a monk and professor of Biblical studies at the University of Wittenberg (p. 185), posted his **Ninety-Five Theses** on the door of the city's castle church. Luther took issue with the Roman Catholic Church for the extravagance of the papal court in Rome and its practice of selling **indulgences**—gift certificates for the soul that promised to shorten the owner's stay in purgatory. He insisted that salvation came only through God's grace, not through paying fees to clergy. The repercussions of the **Protestant Reformation** could not have been anticipated even by the movement's founder. Luther's greatest cultural contribution to the Reformation was a **new translation of the Bible,** a document whose publication singlehandedly crystallized the fragmentary German dialects into a standard, literary High German language.

The German electoral princes soon adopted Lutheranism, captivated by hopes of stemming the flow of money to Rome without the threat of descending to Hell. Armed conflicts soon erupted. The disturbances quickly became more than just religious conflicts; the serfs rebelled during the **Peasants' Wars** in 1524-1525. Reacting against the **Junker** class of noble landholders, the peasants demanded their rights. The ensuing chaos exceeded the bounds of Luther's initial objectives, and he called upon the princes to crush the bands of peasants. But Lutheranism as a political movement continued to spread throughout Europe. The Habsburg Emperor **Karl V,** the most powerful leader since Charlemagne, declared his intention to uproot the subversive doctrine and destroy those who professed it. However, in the 1555 **Peace of Augsburg,** Karl granted individual princes the right to choose the religion practiced in their respective territories, an arrangement that led to a number of absurd overnight conversions and further divided the empire.

Karl's successors did not keep the bargain. When Archduke Ferdinand of Austria tried to impose Catholicism on Bohemia, the Protestant inhabitants rebelled, leading to the instigatory **Defenestration of Prague** in 1618, when the unsuspecting papal legate was hurled out of a window and had his fall broken by a pile of steamy horse dung. The **Thirty Years War** (1618-48) that ensued was a catastrophic setback in Germany's development.

1517
Martin Luther posts his *95 Theses,* inaugurating the Protestant Reformation

1618-1648
Thirty Years War between Protestants and Catholics wipes out about a third of Germany's population. With the Peace of Westphalia, Germany becomes a land of overwhelming territories and a decentralized system of government

At least one-third of the Holy Roman Empire population was wiped out, towns were laid to waste, and famine gripped the population in the longest and bloodiest conflict ever to embroil Europe. The **Peace of Westphalia,** which ended the war, served as the *de facto* constitution of the empire until its abolition in 1806; it granted 300 princes the right to elect the emperor. The Habsburg's imperial administration was dismantled, and although the Holy Roman Empire lingered nominally for another 150 years, it was a dead institution, leaving Germany with power divided among the various regional monarchs.

THE RISE OF BRANDENBURG-PRUSSIA: 1700-1862

1709
Friedrich the Great establishes Berlin as the capital of Prussia

1806
Napoleon creates the Confederation of the Rhine

1815
Congress of Vienna pushes Napoleon out and establishes the German Confederation

1848
Frankfurt National Assembly drafts Germany's first liberal constitution

The war indirectly benefited the leaders of **Brandenburg-Prussia.** Friedrich II—known as **Friedrich the Great**—envisioned and executed the consolidation of the heartland of the rising Prussian state. Friedrich is remembered in German history as an enlightened despot, the initiator of administrative and military reform as well as a patron of the arts. When Maria Theresa became empress of the Habsburg domains in 1740, Friedrich seized the opportunity to snatch the prosperous province of Silesia. By the end of the **Seven Years War** in 1763, Prussia was recognized as one of Europe's great powers. Friedrich II and his nephew joined forces with Russia and Austria to begin to **partition Poland** in 1772 and to link Brandenburg to Prussia physically for the first time, piecing together a kingdom for the Habsburg's dynastic rivals, the **Hohenzollern.**

These skirmishes paled in comparison to the havoc wreaked by France in the wake of the French Revolution. **Napoleon** conquered and disbanded what remained of the Holy Roman Empire and created a subservient **Confederation of the Rhine** in 1806. Despite incorporating hundreds of thousands of German soldiers, Napoleon's armies were bogged down in Russia, and a general rebellion known as the **Wars of Liberation** ejected Napoleon from German territory (see Jena, p. 214). The 1815 **Congress of Vienna** partially restored the pre-war German state system by creating the Austrian-led **German Confederation.** In 1834, Prussia sponsored the **Zollverein,** a customs union that linked most German territories—except Austria—in a free trade zone.

In 1848, revolution broke out again in France, and discontent spread rapidly to other parts of Europe. The German Confederation agreed to let an elected assembly decide the future of the confederation. The **Frankfurt National Assembly** drafted a liberal constitution, and invited **Friedrich Wilhelm IV** of Prussia to serve as emperor. Yet he spurned the offer, saying that he would not accept a cardboard Bürger King crown with limited powers of authority. The assembly disbanded, and the ensuing revolt in Frankfurt was crushed by the Prussian army (see p. 406). Subsequent economic growth heralded the coming of industrialism.

THE SECOND REICH: 1862-1914

In 1862, Prussian King Wilhelm I appointed a worldly aristocrat named **Otto von Bismarck** as chancellor. The originator and greatest practitioner of *Realpolitik* ("the ends justify the means"), Bismarck exploited a remarkably complex series of alliances and compromises that were more than once dissolved in favor of more violent tactics. Blood and iron, Bismarck liked to point out, were paramount to the creation of a strong and unified German nation. To prove the consolidating effect of war, he fought Denmark in 1864 and seized control of Northern Schleswig. The fallout from this dispute led to conflict with Austria, which Prussia quashed in 1866 at Sadowa. Bismarck made it clear that Prussia would now dominate German affairs, voiding the current constitution and thereby excluding Austria. In 1867, he disbanded the Confederation and replaced it with the Prussian-dominated **North German Confederation.** Bismarck realized that France would never willingly acquiesce to a fully united Germany under Prussian domination. Through a series of trivial diplomatic slights he suckered France into a misguided declaration of the **Franco-Prussian** war in 1870; the technologically superior Prussian army and its allies swept through France and trounced the French army, capturing Emperor Napoleon III. Parisians declared a republic and vowed to carry on the fight. Bismarck gleefully besieged Paris and had Wilhelm crowned **Kaiser of the German Reich** at the Palace of Versailles. With France thus disposed of, Bismarck was free to found the **German Empire** on his own terms in 1871. He presented German liberals with an offer they couldn't refuse: unification in exchange for an authoritarian monarchy. The so-called conservative empire garnered popular support by promoting an aggressive nationalism.

Germany underwent breakneck **industrialization** in the last decades of the 19th century. In the space of fewer than 40 years, one of the lagging nations in Europe developed the most advanced industrial base on the continent, yet retained an anachronistic political system unaccommodating to the newer liberal ideals; Bismarck came to power in a political climate still controlled by the **Junker** class of noble, landed aristocracy. Many historians have attributed Germany's problems in the early 20th century to this belated industrialization and despotism.

By the 1870s, reformist sentiment had gained ground in Germany. Led by a burgeoning trade union movement and the **August Bebel**-founded **Social Democratic Party** (*Sozialdemokratische Partei Deutschlands*—SPD), working-class radicalism began to pose a serious threat to the reactionary order, while the Catholic church threatened the authority of Prussia's secular institutions by affirming its ultimate loyalty to the Pope. To consolidate power, Bismarck engaged in a long series of initiatives that alternatively revolved around reforms and repression (known as the **Kulturkampf**). Bismarck pioneered social welfare programs such as unemployment insurance for the working class, but harshly repressed trade unions and the Social Democrats with the **Anti-Socialist Laws** of 1878. His 1879 **Alliance of Iron and Rye** brought together the two leading conservative forces in society—the industrialists and the agrarian aristocrats. By appeasing potential radical factions with these welfare-like programs and alliances, Bismarck quelled revolt. Facing mounting problems with his own constitution and disputes with the new Kaiser Wilhelm II, Bismarck resigned in 1890.

Such rapid transitions produced tremendous social friction. The numbers of the proletariat exploded, but protectionist tariffs kept food absurdly expensive. Germany accelerated its pattern of foreign adventurism in part to quell unrest at home—a policy derisively known as **"Flucht nach vorn"** (escape forward). Bismarck's successors realized the need for a German navy that

1864–71
Bismarck's wars of unification assert Germany's strength throughout the continent

1871
Wilhelm I crowned Kaiser of a unified Germany, heralding the Second Reich

After an initial lag, Germany pursues industrialization and colonization with a vengeance

1880s
Bismarck quells dissent, but is eventually crushed under a political system of his own making

1907
Increasing international tension prompts Britain, France, and Russia to form the Triple Entente

could compete with Britain in the race for overseas colonies, even though Germany's sense of imperialism, like its industrialization, came later than all of its European peers. Yet disputes over colonial issues left Germany diplomatically isolated in Europe, and tension between Germany and its neighbors rose. Germany flaunted the most powerful army in the world at the turn of the century, prompting Britain, France, and Russia to unite as the **Triple Entente**. Meanwhile, democratic opposition began to pose a challenge within the regime itself. For the Kaiser and the elites who supported him, it became clear that dramatic and militaristic action would be required for self-preservation.

WORLD WAR I: 1914-1918

1914
Europe erupts in war, with Germany and Austria-Hungary allied as the Central Powers

Trench and submarine warfare result in unprecedented casualties

1918
WWI concludes with the Treaty of Versailles, with Germany under conditions of heavy reparations

On the eve of WWI, Europe was caught in a complex web of alliances in which a minor dispute could easily escalate into full-blown continental war. As Russia's rail network modernized, German generals saw their window of opportunity closing; they were strongly inclined to mobilize at the first sign of a crisis. That crisis broke out in 1914, when a Serbian nationalist assassinated the Habsburg heir to the Austrian throne, **Archduke Franz-Ferdinand,** in Sarajevo.

Austria marched on Serbia. Russia came to the aid of its Slavic brethren. Almost the entire Reichstag, including the Social Democratic delegates (who despised the Russian Czar), voted to prepare for war to defend their Austrian allies, forming the **Central Powers.** The decision provoked a politically-desirable rush of nationalist sentiment, receiving popular support from a young generation of Germans. After Russia ignored an ultimatum to rescind their advance, Germany entered the war on the side of Austria, prompting France to mobilize. The German General Staff had designed the **Schlieffen Plan** to win a war on two fronts: a lightning thrust through Belgium would deliver a knock-out blow to France, whereupon Germany could turn to the east and defeat the Russian Czar before he could prepare his backward army; however, the one-two was not so easily executed. Germany then declared war on France and demanded that Belgium allow its army to cross its frontier. Belgium refused. Britain, which was treaty-bound to defend Belgian neutrality, declared war on Germany. Germany quickly advanced through Belgium and northern France, and suddenly virtually all of Europe was at war.

After advancing within 50km of Paris, the German offensive stalled at the **Battle of the Marne.** Four years of agonizing **trench warfare** ensued. The slaughter was staggering, magnified by new weapons such as machine-guns, tanks, planes, flame-throwers, and poison gas. Germany's policy of unrestricted submarine warfare on all ships entering European waters provoked the United States into entering on the side of France and Britain. After England checked the imperial navy, a naval blockade rapidly choked Germany. Coupled with the industrial capacity and fresh armies of the U.S., the blockade allowed the Entente to emerge victorious.

THE WEIMAR REPUBLIC: 1918-1933

In late 1918, with the German army on the brink of collapse, riots and mutinies broke out on the home front. On November 9, 1918, Social Democratic leader **Philipp Scheidemann** declared a republic in Berlin, with **Friedrich Ebert** as its first president. France insisted on a harsh peace in the **Treaty of Versailles** (signed, symbolically and punishingly, at the spot of Wilhelm's coronation), which imposed staggering reparation payments, reduced the German army to 100,000 men, and ascribed the blame for the war to Germany. The new republican government had little choice but to accept the treaty, as the continuing Allied blockade was starving the country. Even before a constitution was drawn up, the republic was stuck with the stigma of the humiliating treaty; because the Kaiser had promised a smashing victory right up to the end, Germans were psychologically unprepared for defeat. And because of the sudden and desperate transition to parliamentary government, Germany's political structure was itself in a precarious state.

Building on this unsettled sentiment, the newly formed **Communist Party** (*Kommunistische Partei Deutschlands*—KPD), led by **Karl Liebknecht** and **Rosa Luxemburg,** launched a revolt in Berlin that found some support (see p. 89). The Republic crushed the revolution by appealing to bands of right-wing army veterans called **Freikorps,** who in turn launched their own coup d'état under **Wolfgang Kapp.** Workers, however, didn't share in the revolutionary fervor: they demonstrated support for the new republic through a general strike, organizing a force of 50,000-80,000 against the coup. The republic emerged bruised but intact. Its leaders drew up a constitution in **Weimar;** chosen for its legacy as the birthplace of the German Enlightenment, it now gave its name to a period of intense cultural activity between the world wars (p. 208).

Outstanding war debts and the burden of reparations produced the staggering hyperinflation of 1922-23. Germany had not found itself so close to collapse since 1871. The Republic achieved stability with help from the American **Dawes Plan,** which reduced the amount of war reparations, and an age of relative calm and remarkable artistic production ensued. However, the old, reactionary order still clung to power in many segments of society. When an Austrian corporal named **Adolf Hitler** was arrested for treason after the abortive 1923 **Beer Hall Putsch** uprising in Munich, his unsuccessful march to a patriotic monument, he was not deported (on the grounds that he "believed he was German") and received the minimum sentence of five years—of which he served only 10 months. During his time in jail, Hitler wrote *Mein Kampf* and decided that his party, the National Socialist German Workers Party (*Nationalsozialistische deutsche Arbeiterspartei*—NSDAP), also known as the **Nazis,** would have to seize power by constitutional means. Two aspects of the Weimar constitution, intended to establish a perfectly representative and functional democracy, expedited this process. Pure proportional representation encouraged a spectrum of political parties and discouraged stable governments,

1918
Weimar Republic founded in the midst of political chaos and cultural renaissance

1920
Communist Party uprising quashed in Berlin

1922–23
Hitler stages unsuccessful Beer Hall Putsch; Germany suffers in conditions of hyperinflation

Late 1920s
Nazis gain power during a period of extreme political vulnerability

while the infamous **Article 48** (drafted by sociologist Max Weber) gave the chancellor power to rule by decree during crises, creating the potentiality of a monarchical—or dictatorial—state.

The Nazi party expanded its efficient, faithful bureaucracy and nearly quadrupled its membership to 108,000 by 1929. Even so, it was still a fringe party in 1928, receiving only 2.6% of the vote. But when the Great Depression struck in 1929, 25% of the population was unemployed within months. Membership in the NSDAP exploded to more than a million by 1930—the **SA** *(Sturmabteilung)*, its paramilitary arm, grew as large as the German army. The Nazis campaigned on an anti-Semitic, xenophobic platform; Hitler failed in a presidential bid against the nearly senile war-hero Hindenburg in 1932, but parliamentary elections made the Nazis the largest party (winning 37% of the seats) in the *Reichstag*. After various political maneuvers, President Hindenburg reluctantly appointed Hitler chancellor of a coalition government on January 30, 1933. Hitler had taken over Germany.

THE THIRD REICH: 1933-45

1933
Hitler consolidates power, declaring himself *Führer* of the Third Reich

1935
Racial Purity Laws enacted, depriving Jews of German citizenship and prohibiting intercourse between "Aryans" and Jews

1938
Jewish property destroyed during *Kristallnacht*

Although Hitler now held the most powerful government post, the Nazi party, though the largest single party in the coalition government, had difficulty obtaining a majority in the *Reichstag*. Within two months of taking control, Hitler convinced the ailing and aging Hindenburg to dissolve the *Reichstag* and call new elections, allowing Hitler to invoke Article 48 and to rule by decree for seven weeks. During this reign of terror, he curtailed freedom of the press, authorized his special security arms (the Special State Police, known as the **Gestapo,** the **SA** Storm Troopers, and the **SS** Security Police) as auxiliary police, and brutalized opponents. Politically astute, he seized the opportunity of the mysterious Reichstag fire one week prior to the elections, declaring a state of emergency in order to round up opponents, many of whom were relocated to newly built **concentration camps.** In the ensuing election on March 5, 1933, with 44% of the votes, the Nazis once again fell short of a majority. Nonetheless, they arrested and browbeat enough opposing legislators to pass an **Enabling Act** making Hitler legal dictator of Germany, authorized to ban all opposition and rule by decree indefinitely. Characteristic humility led Hitler to place himself as the successor to the two previous *Reichs:* the Holy Roman Empire (800-1806) and the German Empire.

Vilifying the Weimar government as soft and ineffectual, Hitler's platform played on a variety of German anxieties that had accumulated since 1918; these ideas drew strength from notions of anti-Semitism and German racial superiority. Wounded pride over WWI losses and the failing economy ensured a receptive public. Aided by **Joseph Goebbels,** his propaganda chief, Hitler exploited self-promotion to an insuperable degree; Nazi rallies were masterpieces of political demagoguery, and the iconography of Hitler and the Nazi emblem, the **swastika,** embellished everything from match covers to fingernails of loyal teeny boppers. *Heil Hitler* and the right arm salute became the legally obligatory greeting.

One of the government's first acts was to institute a boycott of Jewish businesses and to expel Jews from professions and the civil service. In 1934, after Hindenburg's death, Hitler appropriated the presidential powers for himself. The following year, the first of the anti-Semitic **Racial Purity Laws** deprived Jews of German citizenship. After a respite during the 1936 Berlin Olympics, an ironically international gesture, the program resumed in earnest on November 9, 1938, with **Kristallnacht** (Night of Broken Glass). In that evening alone, Nazis destroyed thousands of Jewish businesses, burned synagogues, killed nearly 100 Jews, and sent at least 20,000 to concentration camps.

Hitler directed his wrath at Jews, gypsies, communists, Social Democrats, gays, lesbians, artists, free-thinkers, and the disabled, as well as anyone who demonstrated any sympathy toward these groups. The momentum of the Third Reich played off of the Weimar era's uncertainty. A massive program of industrialization restored full employment, though productivity was hardly innocent: Geman business was mounting a war effort. Hitler abrogated the Versailles Treaty, thus freeing Germany from reparations payments and instigating rearmament. Next, he stared down the Western Allies and annexed Austria—the infamous **Anschluß.** He then demanded territorial concessions from Czechoslovakia, on the grounds that it served as a home to thousands of ethnic Germans. British Prime Minister Neville Chamberlain assured Hitler in the notorious 1938 **Munich Agreement** that Britain would not interfere with this hostile takeover. Hitler's foreign policy was dominated by one of the fundamental tenets of Nazi ideology: the necessity of acquiring **Lebensraum** (living space) from the "inferior" Slavs in the East as a first step toward his messianic goal of expansion. The Allies had allowed German aggression until war was inevitable.

WORLD WAR II: 1939-1945

On September 1, 1939, German tanks rolled across the eastern border into Poland. Britain and France, bound by treaty to defend Poland, immediately declared war on Germany but did not attack. Having secretly divided up Eastern Europe between themselves and the Germans under the **Molotov-Ribbentrop pact,** the Soviet Union likewise did not respond to the German invasion. Germany's new tactic of mechanized **Blitzkrieg** (literally, "lightning war") quickly crushed Poland. In a month, Poland was vanquished, and Hitler and Stalin carved it between them. On April 9, 1940, Hitler overran Denmark and Norway. A month later, the *Blitzkrieg* roared through the Ardennes Forest of Luxembourg and quickly overwhelmed Belgium, the Netherlands, and France, but the Nazis failed to bomb London into submission in the aerial struggle of the **Battle of Britain.** Preparations for a cross-channel invasion were shelved as Hitler turned his attentions to Russia. The German **invasion of the USSR** in June 1941 ended the Hitler-Stalin pact. Despite the Red Army's overwhelming manpower, the German invasion came close to success due to the pathetic state of the Soviet corps. At the peak of his conquests in late 1941, Hitler held an empire stretching from the Arctic Circle to the Sahara Desert, from the Pyrenees to the Urals.

The Soviets suffered extremely high casualties, but the *Blitzkrieg* faltered in the Russian winter and Hitler sacrificed thousands of German soldiers in his adamant refusal to retreat. The bloody battle of **Stalingrad** was the critical turning point in the East. Hitler had already committed a fatal error when he declared war on the United States after ally Japan bombed Pearl

1939
Axis and Allied powers meet in the second global clash of the century

Germany invades and occupies most of Europe with its lightning offensive

1945
World War II concludes with the Allied defeat of Germany

Harbor. His attempt to save Mussolini in North Africa led to the Nazi's first battlefield defeats, and soon Germany was retreating on all fronts. The Allied landings in Normandy on **D-Day** (June 6, 1944) preceded an arduous, bloody advance across Western Europe. The Third Reich's final offensive, the **Battle of the Bulge,** failed in December 1944. In March 1945, the Allies crossed the Rhein. The Red Army overcame bitter resistance and took Berlin in April 1945. With Red Army troops overhead, Hitler married Eva Braun just prior to killing himself in his bunker. The Third Reich, which Hitler had boasted would endure for 1000 years, had lasted only 12.

THE HOLOCAUST

1942–45
"Final Solution," the attempted extermination of European Jewry, kills six million Jews in concentration and labor camps

By the outbreak of the War, societal persecution of the Jews was virtually complete in scope. Jews and Christians of Jewish heritage were barred from serving in any public capacity and wore the Star of David patch as a reminder of their lost citizenship. In the years before 1939, **pogroms** became increasingly frequent, and Jews were already being herded into ghettos. Hitler's racial ideology, the central plank of the Nazi platform, was that the German *Volk* was meant to triumph or perish forever. He made no secret of his desire to exterminate all Jews, who, associated with internationalism, communism, pacifism, and democracy, represented the scourge of German nationalism.

Early in the war German **SS** troops invading eastward massacred whole towns of Jewish inhabitants. But as the war progressed, institutions of mass execution were developed for their efficiency. The **"Final Solution to the Jewish problem,"** the Nazis' horrific designation for the genocide of European Jewry, called for an appalling expansion of the persecution, deprivation, and deportation to which Jews had been subjected since the first days of the *Reich*. The mass gassing of Jews in specially constructed **extermination camps** began only in 1942. Seven full-fledged extermination camps, **Auschwitz, Buchenwald** (p. 213), **Chelmno, Treblinka, Majdanek, Sobibor,** and **Belzec,** plus dozens of nominal "labor" camps such as **Bergen-Belsen** (p. 496), **Dachau** (p. 255), and **Sachsenhausen** (p. 122) were operating before war's end. Nearly six million Jews, two-thirds of Europe's Jewish population, mostly from Poland and the Soviet Union, were gassed, shot, starved, worked to death, or killed by exposure. Five million other victims—prisoners of war, Slavs, gypsies, homosexuals, the mentally retarded, and political opponents—also died in Nazi camps. The atrocities of the Nazi years reach beyond the scope of tragedy into the realm of inconceivable horror.

How much did the average German know about the Holocaust? No one can say for sure, but it is certain that the vicious persecution of Jews in pre-war Germany was evident for all to see. And as the records of elaborate killing procedures were studied following the war, it was clear that the vastly efficient bureaucracy of genocide was far from ignorant.

As the living memory of the Holocaust slowly fades, the aging remains of concentration camps become the most crucial, tangible testimony to the events of half a century ago. Just as a monument can lose its power to shock by becoming too familiar to passersby, so can the existence of "museums" and tours trivialize what occurred at the camps. If you choose to visit one, keep in mind that while some treat these grounds as just another sight, many visitors come with a knowledge of the camp's past or haunted by the memory of a loved one who perished there.

OCCUPATION AND DIVISION: 1945-1949

Germans call their defeat in the Second World War *Nullstunde*—"Zero Hour"—the moment at which everything began again. Unlike WWI, Germany's battlefield defeat was total and indisputable. In July 1945 the United States, Great Britain, and the Soviet Union met at **Potsdam** to partition Germany into zones of occupation: the east under the Soviets, the west under the British and Americans, and Berlin under joint control. The economy was in shambles. Most cities had been bombed into ruin. More than five million German soldiers and civilians died in the war, and millions remained in POW camps. All German territory east of the Oder and Neisse rivers—a quarter of the nation's land—was confiscated and placed under Soviet and Polish administration, while the coal-rich Saarland was put under French control. Ten to twelve million ethnic Germans were expelled from Eastern Europe and the Baltics; more than two million perished during the exodus. As the details of the Nazi genocidal project became public, "German" became synonymous with "barbaric."

The Allied program for the **Occupation**—demilitarization, democratization, and de-Nazification—proceeded apace, but growing animosity between the Soviets and the Western allies made joint control of Germany increasingly difficult. De-Nazification proceeded in quite disparate ways in East and West, paving the way for total division in 1949. Blaming the structures of bourgeois capitalism for the Nazi nightmare, the Soviets pursued former Nazis within their occupation zones. The Allies, however, prosecuted Nazis individually, some as part of the international spectacle of the **Nuremberg trials,** yet often so inadequately that many retained their posts. In anticipation of the coming Cold War, many former Nazis were recruited by American intelligence units to act as spies. In 1947, the Western Allies merged their occupation zones into a single economic unit known as **Bizonia** (later Trizonia, after a French occupation zone was carved out of the British and American zones). The Western Allies began rebuilding their zone along the lines of a market economy with the aid of huge cash infusions from the American **Marshall Plan.** The Soviets, who suffered immeasurably more in the war than the U.S. or Britain, had neither the desire nor the spare cash to help the East rebuild—they plundered it instead, as allowed by the Potsdam agreement. The Soviet Union carted away everything that wasn't fixed in concrete and a lot of things (such as factories and railroads) that were. The Western Allies ceased their contribution to the East in 1948 and then effectively severed the East's economy from the West's by introducing a new hard currency to Bizonia, the **Deutschmark.** Although the imposition of the new Mark seemed draconian at the time, most historians agree that it was the single greatest cause of the eventual stabilization of West Germany. The *Wirtschaftswunder* (economic miracle), led by economist **Ludwig Erhard,** built it into

1945
The Allies and Soviets convene at the Potsdam Conference to divide Germany into occupation zones

1945
Nuremberg war trials prosecute Nazis for war atrocities

1949
Soviet forces blockade Berlin

Soviet and Allied relations deteriorate, pulling the nation in both directions until the seams split. The Cold War, FRG, and GDR are born the world's fourth-largest economy during the 1950s and 60s. The currency reform dispute was the proximate cause of the **Berlin Blockade** and the ultimate **division of Germany** in 1949.

THE FEDERAL REPUBLIC OF GERMANY

1949
Allied powers oversee the drafting of the Basic Law, establishing individual rights and a republican form of government

1949
Konrad Adenauer becomes the Federal Republic's first chancellor

1950s
FRG makes an overnight recovery from post-war ruins to economic power, necessitating the importation of thousands of foreign workers

The Federal Republic of Germany (*Bundesrepublik Deutschland*—FRG) was established as the provisional government of Western Germany on May 24, 1949. The new government set up camp in the sleepy university town of **Bonn**. A **Basic Law**, drawn up under the direction of the Western Allies, safeguarded individual rights and established a system of Federal States with freely elected parliamentary assemblies. Although similar in many ways to the Weimar constitution, the Basic Law featured several significant departures: it made the chancellor responsible to Parliament, banned anti-democratic parties, renounced militarism, and emasculated the presidency. The tripartite government of the FRG (with emphasis on the legislative and judicial, rather than executive, branches) was also a clear case of Allied adoption. One of the most visionary paragraphs of the Basic Law was the one that established a Right of Asylum, guaranteeing refuge to any person fleeing persecution. Ratification of the Basic Law, however, did not restore German sovereignty; the Allies retained the right to claim supreme authority over the country.

As the only party untainted by the Third Reich, the **Social Democratic Party** (*Sozialdemokratische Partei Deutschlands*—SPD) seemed poised to dominate postwar German politics. Another new party, the **Free Democratic Party** (*Freidemokratische Partei*—FDP), assembled bourgeois liberals and professionals along with several former Nazis. Although the FDP remained small, it acquired power as a coalition partner. A third party, the **Christian Democratic Union** (*Christlich Demokratische Union*—CDU), managed to unite Germany's historically fragmented conservatives and centrists under a nondenominational platform. With former Köln Mayor **Konrad Adenauer** at the helm, a relative political veteran, the CDU won a small majority of *Bundestag* seats in the Federal Republic's first general election in mid-1949.

Adenauer, 73 years old when he assumed office, was perhaps the federal republic's greatest chancellor. He unflaggingly pursued the integration of Germany into a unified Europe and, at the same time, the return of German national self-determination. He achieved both of these aims, first in 1951 with West Germany's entrance into the European Coal and Steel Community—the precursor of the modern European Union (EU)—and then in 1955 when the Western Allies recognized West German sovereignty. Adenauer's federal republic, in fact, was one of the charter members of the European Economic Community in 1957. The idealistic Adenauer also helped to restore the self-esteem and purpose of his defeated people without rekindling nationalism. The speedy recovery of the economy secured the future dominance of the German economy and of the CDU party. Rebuilding progressed rapidly; Germany achieved full employment by the late 1950s and soon began recruiting thousands of foreign **Gastarbeiter** (guest workers). Despite SPD opposition, Adenauer aligned Germany with NATO (North Atlantic Treaty Organization) in a common defense bloc when the Occupation Statute expired in 1955.

The SPD, whose fortunes seemed so promising in 1945, wandered in the electoral wilderness without any bread crumbs for over 20 years. The party's Marxist rhetoric prevented it from expanding beyond a working-class base. In 1961, the SPD jettisoned Marx and found a dynamic young leader in **Willy Brandt,** the charismatic former Berlin mayor who had worked in the anti-Nazi resistance. Germany's first postwar recession in 1967 badly hurt the CDU and the 1969 *Bundestag* elections launched the SPD into power. With Brandt as chancellor, the **Social-Liberal Coalition** of the SDP and FDP enacted a number of overdue reforms in education, governmental administration, social security, and industrial relations. Its most dramatic policy innovation, however, was in foreign relations. Under the old **Hallstein Doctrine,** the Federal Republic cut ties to any government that recognized the German Democratic Republic, driving a wedge between West Germany and the entire Eastern Bloc. Yet through Brandt's **Ostpolitik** (Eastern Policy), the Federal Republic actively sought improved relations with East Germany, the Soviet Union, and other Eastern Bloc nations—a policy symbolized by the famous image of a tearful Brandt dropping to his knees in front of a Polish war memorial. Brandt and his foreign minister **Walter Scheel** concluded several important treaties, including an agreement **normalizing relations** with the GDR. The treaty didn't ensure complete diplomatic relations; nonetheless, Brandt received the Nobel Peace Prize in 1971 for arranging it.

After Brandt resigned in the wake of a 1974 spy scandal, Social Democrat **Helmut Schmidt** became chancellor. Under Schmidt, West Germany racked up an economic record that was the envy of the industrialized world. Nevertheless, persistent structural problems in heavy industry contributed to **mounting unemployment** and dissatisfaction with the SPD in the late 1970s. In 1982, new partners FDP and CDU formed a government under Christian Democrat **Helmut Kohl** after FDP leader **Hans-Dietrich Genscher** abruptly abandoned the Social-Liberal coalition. Kohl's government pursued a policy of welfare state cutbacks, tight monetary policy, and military cooperation with the U.S.

At the same time, a new political force emerged in Germany: the **Green Party** *(die Grünen).* By fighting for disarmament and environmentalism and rejecting traditional coalition politics, the Greens won a surprisingly large following. In 1984, **Richard von Weizsäcker** of the CDU was elected to the symbolic post of president. He urged Germans to shoulder fully their moral responsibility for the Third Reich—an implicit rebuke of politicians like Kohl who spoke of "the grace of late birth."

THE GERMAN DEMOCRATIC REPUBLIC

When Soviet troops occupied Eastern Germany, a cadre of German Communists who had spent the war in exile came close on their heels. Even before the surrender was signed, these party functionaries began setting up an apparatus to run the Soviet occupation zone. The first party licensed to operate in the Soviet sector was the **German Communist Party** *(Kommunistische*

1970s
Through a policy of *Ostpolitik,* the Federal Republic adopts a friendly neighbor attitude toward the GDR

1980s
The Greens, an environmentally-conscious political party, find a niche amidst an increasingly capitalist economy

1949
Modeled upon Soviet Communism, the Socialist Unity Party forms a one-party dictatorship

Partei Deutschlands) under **Wilhelm Pieck** and **Walter Ulbricht,** but versions of the Western parties were established shortly afterwards. At first, the German Communists pledged to establish a parliamentary democracy and a distinctively "German path to socialism." However, their dependence on Moscow quickly became apparent. Through some fancy political maneuverings the Social Democrats were forced to join the KPD in a common working-class anti-fascist front, the **Socialist Unity Party** (*Sozialistische Einheitspartei Deutschlands*—SED).

In Berlin, the SPD was permitted to operate freely, and the SED was soundly defeated at the ballot box. The Soviets responded by not holding any more freely contested elections, and future elections required voters to approve or reject a "unity list" of pre-selected candidates that ensured SED dominance. On October 7, 1949, a People's Congress selected by such methods declared the establishment of the **German Democratic Republic** (*Deutsche Demokratische Republik*—GDR) under Pieck, with the national capital in Berlin. Although the first constitution of the GDR guaranteed civil liberties and paid lip service to parliamentary democracy, these were empty promises. Real power lay in the hands of the SED's *Politbüro* and the party's secretary. Although the SPD was nominally an equal partner in the SED, some 200,000 SPD members were purged. Economic, religious, and journalistic regimentation drove GDR citizens to seek refuge in West Germany.

After Stalin's death, political conditions relaxed a bit in the GDR, though the nationalization of industry proceeded without hesitation. Impossibly high work goals, worsened by an exodus of workers to the West, led to a **workers' revolt** across the GDR on June 17, 1953, which was ruthlessly crushed with the aid of Soviet tanks. In response to the FRG's normalization of relations with the Western powers, the GDR was recognized by the USSR in 1954 and became a member of the **Warsaw Pact** in 1955.

In 1961, when the tally of *Republikflüchtige* (illegal emigrants) from East to West Germany reached 3 million, the GDR decided to remedy the exodus of skilled young workers to the Federal Republic; although borders to the West had been sealed off, escape through Berlin remained a possibility. On the night of August 12-13, the first, rudimentary barriers of the **Berlin Wall** were laid. The regime called it an "anti-fascist protective wall," but Berliners knew which way the guns were pointed. The time was right for Ulbricht to launch his hard-line **New Economic System** and to establish the GDR's **second constitution** in 1968. This document jettisoned most constitutional rights, already ignored in practice, and abandoned all pretense of parliamentary democracy.

Ulbricht's iron grip on power was broken in 1971 when he ran afoul of his Soviet patrons. His replacement, **Erich Honecker,** returned East Germany to unquestioning subservience to the Soviet Union and eliminated the possibility of reform. Relations with the West improved remarkably during the era of Willy Brandt's **Ostpolitik,** and many Westerners were permitted to visit relatives in the GDR for the first time. Despite the scars of the war and the shortcomings of central planning, East Germans enjoyed the highest standard of living in the Eastern Bloc by the late 1970s, yet still lagged far behind their Western neighbors in both productivity and quality. The secret police, the **Stasi,** maintained a network of agents that strove to monitor every citizen; one in seven East Germans was a paid informant.

With the ascension of the *glasnost*-minded **Mikhail Gorbachev** to the leadership of the USSR in 1985, reform began to spread throughout the Eastern Bloc—except in the GDR, which ignored the liberalizing reforms. Nevertheless, discontent over the increasingly apparent economic disparities between East and West as well as the alarmingly high level of pollution in East German cities continued to pose a challenge to the SED's grip on power. The foundation for *die Wende* (the turning or the change), as the sudden toppling of the GDR is referred to in Germany, began in May 1989 when Hungary dismantled the barbed-wire border with Austria, giving some 55,000 East Germans an indirect route to the West. By October, Czechoslovakia tolerated a flood of GDR citizens into the West German embassy; thousands emigrated. On October 6, while on a state visit to celebrate the GDR's 40th birthday, Gorbachev publicly reprimanded Honecker and announced that the USSR would not interfere in the GDR's domestic affairs. Dissident groups such as **Neues Forum** (New Forum) began to operate more freely, organizing massive **anti-government demonstrations** *(Demos)*, which started in Leipzig and spread to Dresden, Berlin, and other cities. The East Germans demanded free elections, freedom of press, and freedom of travel. Faced with rising pressure, Honecker resigned. His successor, **Egon Krenz,** promised reforms. Meanwhile, tens of thousands of GDR citizens—largely young professionals—continued to flee via Czechoslovakia, which completely opened its border with West Germany. The entire GDR Politbüro resigned on November 8, and a day later, a Central Committee spokesperson announced the **opening of all borders to the West,** including the Berlin Wall.

REUNIFICATION AND ITS AFTERMATH: 1989-THE PRESENT

The opening of the Wall marked the **Wende,** the most symbolically significant turning point for Germans since the end of WWII. However, the fall did not immediately herald the demise of the GDR or the Communist regime. Elected four days after the opening of the wall, East German Prime Minister **Hans Modrow** pledged to hold free elections. The constitution was re-written to remove references to the SED's leading role, but the party remained in power and the *Stasi* continued to operate despite intense pressure. Honecker was whisked away to the USSR and the SED renamed itself the **Party of Democratic Socialism (PDS),** whose initials, critics joked, really stood for *Pack deine Sachen* ("pack your bags"). The year 1990 began with another ecstatic celebration on top of the Berlin Wall, but the apparent community belied a furious political struggle going on in both Germanies. In the East, opposition parties took shape and assumed positions in the existing government, while the West's political parties scrambled to assert their influence; eventually, all of them linked up with like-minded parties in the GDR in preparation for March **elections.** The SPD was crippled by its expressed reluctance about the prospect of reunification, which inhibited it

1989
Fall of the Berlin Wall

1990
The *Wende.* Germany reunifies

East Germany is absorbed into the FRG

The socialist net is pulled out, and a reunified but unprepared Federal Republic experiences its worst recession

Foreign workers bear the brunt of discrimination and resentment during economic hardship

1990s
Helmut Kohl and his political party, the CDU, ride the roller-coaster of public opinion

1998
Gerhard Schröder takes over the chancellorship following Kohl's 16-year tenure

from making allies in the East. Buoyed by Kohl's success at getting Moscow to assent to unification, the CDU-backed **Alliance for Germany** emerged the winner. In the East, a broad coalition government of non-Communist parties authorized **economic and social union** with the Federal Republic. On the day of the *Währungsunion*, July 1, 1990, GDR citizens exchanged their worthless Ostmarks for mighty Deutschmarks. The signing of the **Four-Plus-Two Treaty** by the two Germanies and the four occupying powers on September 12, 1990, signaled the **end of a divided Germany.**

Despite the designation *Wiedervereinigung* (reunification), East and West Germany did not unify on an equal basis to create a new nation-state. Rather, East Germany was absorbed into the institutions and structures of the Federal Republic, leading some to call the union *der Anschluß* (annexation). Under the Basic Law's paragraph 23, any territory had the power to accede, or simply declare themselves ready to be consumed by, the FRG. This was a fast route to nominal unity, and after a great deal of debate, it was the one Germany took. On **October 3, 1990,** the Allies forfeited their occupation rights, the GDR ceased to exist, and Germany became one united, sovereign nation for the first time in 45 years. Germans now distinguish between East and West with the labels **"new federal states"** and **"old federal states."**

Immediately following the quick pace of events in 1989-90, nationalistic euphoria blurred the true state of matters for Germans on both sides of the wall. The collapse of East Germany's inefficient industries and institutions led to massive unemployment and the Federal Republic's worst-ever recession. Many Westerners resented the inflation and taxes brought on by the cost of rebuilding the new federal states, while Easterners had to give up the generous social benefits communism afforded them. A rightward-moving political climate in the West pulled the East with it, restricting social programs not only in welfare but also in areas such as abortion.

In the years following, economic frustrations led to the scapegoating of foreigners, especially asylum-seekers from Eastern Europe and the *Gastarbeiter*, many of whom had been living in Germany for decades. German law does not automatically grant citizenship to children born in Germany; parentage is considered the determining factor. This has become a more and more troubling point as the children of immigrants grow up in Germany, speak only German, know no other home, but are defined as aliens. The violent attacks on foreigners reached horrible proportions in 1992 and 1993, when wide-scale assaults were launched against immigrants in Mölln and Rostock, resulting in numerous deaths. Soon after, the liberal Asylum Law was repealed. Fortunately, violence has decreased significantly since the early 1990s.

After the dramatic fall of the Berlin Wall in 1989, Kohl and his CDU seemed insurmountable. Carrying their momentum into the first all-German elections, the CDU scored a stunning victory. After that, however, Kohl's popularity plummeted to the point where, during one visit, Eastern voters pelted him with rotten vegetables, and his party failed to carry his own state in state elections. The CDU bounced back in 1994, only to be resoundingly ousted in 1998 by the left-wing parties.

Europe, or more specifically the new Germany's place in it, remains the big political question. The burden of the past makes everyone, including Germans themselves, nervous about Germany's participation in international military operations, highlighted most recently by the **Kosovo** crisis, in which Germany played a pivotal role in negotiating a peace accord. A persistent feeling among Germans now is that they should stay out of foreign policy, acting instead as a large, benign economic machine at the heart of the European Union. But Germany is not Switzerland; such a neutral stance may not always be possible for the most populous and economically powerful nation in Europe. Yet most questions surrounding Germany's larger role in world affairs remained unanswered at the close of the 20th century.

THIS YEAR IN GERMANY

The fall 1998 elections unseated Kohl after 16 years as chancellor; in his place, **Gerhard Schröder** led the SPD to victory as the largest party in the Bundestag; to achieve a majority, however, Schröder formed a coalition with the Greens, and propelled long-time environmental politician **Joschka Fischer** to the post of secretary of state. This distinct leftward shift led to the reopening of a number of old debates. In January, Fischer announced the government's intention to **shut down all of Germany's remaining nuclear reactors.** The declaration caused much friction in Europe, as France and the UK demanded billions in reparations for the nuclear reprocessing contracts that were effectively canceled by the government's new energy policy. The progressive climate also spawned heated debate over Germany's contentious **citizenship laws,** which have been criticized as outdated given Germany's increasingly multicultural demographics. Measures to extend citizenship to non-Germans were strongly opposed by the CDU, who feared diminished returns at the ballot box in the wake of the enfranchisement of the several million Turks residing permanently in Germany. This year also marked the **fiftieth anniversary of the founding of the Federal Republic,** accompanied by appropriately well-tempered celebrations of the FRG's democratic institutions. Anxiety surrounded the Bundestag's move to Berlin, which restored the city's role as political capital of Germany for the first time in more than 50 years and inaugurated the much-anticipated **Berlin Republic.**

1999
The national government moves back to Berlin after 55 years' absence

1999
Fiftieth anniversary of the founding of the German Republic.

FURTHER READING

Great overviews for those seeking a broader education in German history from its beginnings to the present include Mary Fulbrook's *Concise History of Germany* and Hagen Schulze's *Germany: A New History.* Gordon Craig's *Germany 1866-1945* provides a definitive history of those years. Detlev Peukert's *The Weimar Republic* is a thorough examination of the major trends of the interwar period, while Craig's *The Germans* offers an excellent general picture of modern German society. For an in-depth look at postwar German history, pick up Henry Ashby Turner's *The Two Germanies Since 1945* or Peter J. Katzenstein's *Policy and Politics in Western Germany.* Ralf Dahrendorf's *Society and Democracy in Germany* is a great treatment of "the German Question," while Fulbrook's *Anatomy of a Dictatorship: Inside the GDR, 1949-1989* offers a concise retrospective of the East German state.

CULTURE

Germany, the Germans like to say, is the land of *Dichter und Denker*—poets and philosophers. Playwright Bertolt Brecht, with inspired cynicism, claimed that a truer epithet was land of the *Richter und Henker*—judges and hangmen. While such a scathing inversion may seem a bit too harsh, it reveals the flawed romantic premises upon which the original phrase rests. The German word *Kultur* has always echoed with immediate political connotations. Invoked by Bismarck as a means of wresting political control from the Catholic Church, the word again became charged with nationalism during the Third Reich, when it was used to refer to a celebrated myth of a shared Nordic character. Despite such occasionally militaristic tendencies, the humanities in Germany have had an enormous influence on the development of artistic, literary, and musical trends in all of Europe and the world.

VISUAL ART

It was the late 8th- and 9th-century Frankish emperor **Charlemagne** who first marshaled Germanic drawing boards in a big way, commissioning Romanesque churches and illuminated manuscripts by the dozen. Although German painting during the late Gothic period was fairly successful, it consisted mainly of religious icons painted on wall panels. Little changed until Renaissance painters like **Matthias Grünewald** and **Hans Holbein the Younger** brought a strong sense of realism to the form. Their set also took up portraiture, as did the singularly prolific **Lucas Cranach**—who also brought historical and mythological themes to German art (see p. 212). The most exciting and enduring work of this time was done by **Albrecht Dürer,** master of the woodcut. His *Adam and Eve* still peppers advertisements today and his *Self-Portrait at 20,* one of the first self portraits in Europe, painted in 1500, famously resembles a humanist messiah.

Soon the **Protestant Reformation** ushered in a long period of turmoil. While **Baroque** and **Rococo,** movements appropriated from France and Italy, made their architectural marks, the visual arts suffered from discontinuity and conflict brought on by the Thirty Years War. However, in the 19th century German critics encouraged **Romantic** painting (and rebuffed Neoclassicism) by advocating a return to traditional German masterworks—divinely inspired and individually interpreted. This idea easily bled into the expressive landscapes of **Philipp Otto Runge** and **Caspar David Friedrich.** Like much Romantic art, Friedrich's melancholy paintings of chalk cliffs (see **Rügen,** p. 564), and ancient ruins (see **Eldena,** p. 568) seem to be inspired by man's longing and loneliness in the face of nature (see also **Berlin,** p. 126).

In the 20th century, German art exploded. **German Expressionism** recalled the symbolist tendencies of Viennese **Jugendstil** (Art Nouveau) and French Fauvism (see **Schleswig,** p. 542). Its deliberately anti-realist aesthetics intensified colors and the respresentation of objects to project deeply personal emotions. **Die Brücke** (The Bridge) was the earliest Expressionist group, founded in Dresden in 1905 (see **Berlin,** p. 126). Its artists, especially the celebrated **Ernst Ludwig Kirchner,** used jarring outlines and deep color planes inspired by the primitivism of **Emil Nolde** to make paintings and sculptures that were loud and aggressively expressive.

A 1911 exhibition in Munich entitled **Der Blaue Reiter** (The Blue Rider), led by Russian emigré **Wassily Kandinsky,** marked the rise of a second expressionist school. Kandinsky's contribution was a series called *Improvisations.* Painted in 1910-11, they are considered the some of the first totally **non-representational** paintings in Western art. Other members include **Franz Marc,** of "Blue Horses" fame, and **Paul Klee,** whose primitive style has remained influential throughout the century.

World War I and its aftermath interrupted the flow of German art movements. Artists became increasingly bold and political in reaction to the rise of Fascism. **Max Beckmann** painted severely posed figures whose gestures and symbolism expressed a tortured view of man's condition. **Max Ernst** started a **Dadaist** group expressing artistic nihilism with collage and composition in Köln. **Kurt Schwitters,**

on the other hand, remained Dada until death. The grotesque, satirical works of **Otto Dix** walked a tightrope between Expressionism and Dada before embracing the **Neue Sachlichkeit** (New Objectivity), a movement that sought to come to terms with the rapid modernization of the times through matter-of-fact representation. A New Sobriety made sense after the nationalist pomp of Bismarckian years and the self-indulgence of Expressionism. **Georg Grosz** and **John Heartfield** brought a sharp edge to *Neue Sachlichkeit* with their almost violent collage and sketch satires of their increasingly fascist surroundings. The smaller German **Realist** movement devoted itself to bleak, critical works such as the social reform posters of **Käthe Kollwitz** (see **Berlin**, p. 127, and **Moritzburg**, p. 164). Sculptor **Ernst Barlach** infused realism with religious themes, inflaming Nazi censors (see **Güstrow**, p. 551).

The rise of Nazism drove most artists and their work into exile. Themes of *Blut und Boden* (Blood and Soil) dominated Nazi visual arts, depicting the mythical union of folkish blood and German soil through idealized images of workers, farmers, and soldiers of the "master race." In 1937, the Nazi's famous **Entartete Kunst** (Degenerate Art) exhibit placed pieces by Kandinsky, Kirchner, and other masters—which Goebbels had stolen from museums—next to paintings by psychotics, sending a clear message to all artists in Germany.

After the war, German art made a quick recovery. In **East Germany**, state-supported **socialist realism** dominated the scene. Leipzig in particular became prominent for its paintings thematizing class struggle and socialist economic advances. While Realism reigned in the East, **abstraction** dominated West German art. As time went on, installations, "actions," and other art pieces that combined new technologies, especially video, edged out painting, although **Sigmar Polke** and a few other masters kept the medium alive. Polke was a member of the **Junge Wilde,** a group of late 1970s neo-expressionists that also included **Anselm Kiefer.** Kiefer commented on Nazism and the **Holocaust** with rare irony, first in symbolic photography and later on huge canvases. He also studied with **Josef Beuys** and his **constructivist sculpture** school at Düsseldorf (see p. 455). Along with Düsseldorf, Berlin and München stand as centers of contemporary art in Germany—Berlin alone offers many times more government funding for the arts than all of the United States. The hottest (or at least the biggest) thing to see in contemporary German exhibitions is **documenta,** a summer-long exhibition of art from around the world that takes place every five years; the next event, documenta XI, will draw hordes to Kassel from June 8 through September 15, 2002.

ARCHITECTURE AND DESIGN

Long ago, German architecture and design began to pave the way for a thriving tourist industry. Churches and romantic castles around the country manifest stunning Romanesque, Gothic, and Baroque styles, all made possible by Germany's unique history and geography. The **Romanesque** period, spanning the years 1000 to 1300, arose from direct imitation of Roman ruins. Outstanding Romanesque cathedrals can be found along the Rhein at Speyer, Trier, Mainz, and Worms. Note that in German a cathedral is a **Dom** or **Münster.** Such cathedrals often feature a cloverleaf floor plan, numerous towers, and sometimes a mitre-like steeple.

The **Gothic** style, with its pointed rib vaulting, gradually replaced the Romanesque form between 1300 and 1500. Stained glass windows fill otherwise gloomy interiors with artificially divine light, evoking a gothic sense of otherworldly salvation. Gothic cathedrals often take the form of a cross, facing east so that the morning sunrise will shine down onto the altar. Notable Gothic cathedrals dominate the skylines of Regensburg and Magdeburg; the cathedral at Köln is one of the most famous structures in Germany. Gothic style was also often employed in brick structures such as those at Lübeck, Stralsund, and Greifswald.

Secular architecture at the end of the Middle Ages is best remembered through the **Fachwerk** (half-timbered) houses that still dominate the Altstädte of many German cities. The **Renaissance** influence can be found in southern Germany; see the Augsburg Rathaus (p. 296) and the Heidelberg Schloß (p. 326). By 1550, Lutheran reforms had put a damper on the unrestrained extravagance of cathedrals in the north, while the Counter-Reformation in the Catholic south spurred a splendid new **Baroque** style. Based on an Italianate idiom, the 18th-century German Baroque sought to achieve an impression of fluidity and contrast, achieved through complex forms and sinuous contours. The **Zwinger** in Dresden (p. 160) is a magnificent example. Baroque eventually achieved a fanciful extreme with **Rococo**, as exemplified by **Schloß Sanssouci** at Potsdam (p. 142). Versailles' decadent precedent exerted a strong influence on Bavarian castles, notably at **Herrenchiemsee** (p. 271) and the **Königsschlößer** (p. 261).

Eventually this exuberance ran its course and the late 18th century saw an attempt to bring Greco-Roman prestige to Germany in the form of **Neoclassical** architecture. This was in part spurred on by contemporary archaeological digs at Pompeii and the pomp of **Karl Friedrich Schinkel**, state architect of Prussia. The **Brandenburger Tor** and the buildings along **Unter den Linden** in Berlin (p. 108) were products of this new, simpler period. For more on Schinkel, see p. 123.

The **Maltidenhöhe** buildings at Darmstadt (p. 412) are products of a much more modern movement, that of **Jugendstil**, which derived its name from the Munich magazine *Die Jugend*, and spanned the decades before and after the turn of the century. The style was strongly influenced by *art nouveau*. In the 1920s and early 30s, a new philosophy emerged with **Walter Gropius,** who began his career with several sensational buildings featuring clean forms, flat roofs, and broad windows, all made possible by new concrete-and-steel construction techniques. In 1919, Gropius founded the **Bauhaus** school in Weimar (p. 211). A ground-breaking school of design, Bauhaus combined theoretical training in the new principles of efficiency with exposure to the realities of mass production. "Form follows function" was its oft-quoted principle. The school moved to Dessau in 1925 (p. 190) where Gropius designed its new facility; it quickly became a symbol of the modern style.

Hitler disapproved of the new buildings. He named a design school reject, **Albert Speer,** as his minister of architecture, and commissioned ponderous, neoclassical buildings appropriate to the "thousand-year Reich." Many were intended for public rallies, such as the **congress hall** and **stadium** at Nürnberg (p. 309) and the **Olympic Stadium** at Berlin (p. 117). After the war, gloomy—but perversely fascinating—Soviet architecture began to clutter East Germany, reaching a high-point with the 365m high **Fernsehturm** (TV tower) in Berlin (p. 113). For the serious fetishist of Stalinist architecture, Karl-Marx-Allee is rich in **Plattenbauten,** the dispassionate pre-fab apartment buildings that can be found throughout East Germany (p. 119). In all of Germany, reconstruction of war-torn Altstadt architecture fostered a revival of old forms, and in the West economic prosperity and new materials led to a widespread commercialization and modernization.

LITERATURE

As soon as chivalry took hold in Germany, a strong lyric poetry dealing with unrequited love emerged, best represented by **Walter von der Vogelweide.** That genre, called **Minnesang**, marked a high point in medieval literature, but by the mid-13th century the chivalric ideal of love without satisfaction was wearing thin, and the anonymous **lyric ballad** became popular with a new, less elite public that was feeling the influences of Renaissance Italy. By the late 15th century, the best minds of Germany were thinking about the **Reformation,** and poetry took a more serious turn. **Martin Luther** produced his translation of the **Bible** in the 1530s, in the process setting the groundwork for a written form of modern German as well as the creation of the lumbering **protestant hymn.**

What Luther did for language, **Martin Opitz** did for poetics a century later, insisting that word accent and metrical stress coincide and that meter have regular stresses. Although sometimes constraining, these new linguistic rules allowed German literature to adopt foreign forms, and during the chaos of the Thirty Years War many poets, such as **Andreas Gryphius,** found solace in an intense religious life that could be recorded in structured meter. The first significant German novel, **Hans J.**

C. von Grimmelshausen's roguish epic *Simplicissimus*, was written in this period. Ultimately, however, the Reformation and the Thirty Years War fragmented Germany and stunted political development such that German literature had no equivalent to the French *grand siècle*. Often, Germany simply imitated France. **Gotthold Ephraim Lessing,** who admired Shakespeare, rebelled against this humiliating posturing by writing plays that broke with the French adherence to the Aristotelian unities of time, place, and motive with plays like *Nathan der Weise*, which is set in the Middle East and features a plot several days in length (see p. 492).

In the mid-18th century, a sentimental, unusually personalized poetry arose, and soon the literary giant **Johann Wolfgang von Goethe** was writing his early poetry (see p. 406). Goethe's lyrics possessed a revolutionary immediacy and drew on rediscovered folk songs and ballads. His novel *Die Leiden des jungen Werthers* eschewed formula and drew the attention of Europe to the budding **Sturm und Drang** (Storm and Stress) movement, which would influence early Romantic literature. Goethe later turned to the *Bildungsroman* (novel of educational development) and themes of classicism and orientalism. His masterpieces are numerous; his retelling of the **Faust** legend is often considered the pinnacle of a German literature that had moved from the provincial to the center of Europe's attention by the time Goethe died in 1832. His friendship with **Friedrich Schiller** (see p. 345) was crucial to the molding of German literature, and their adopted base of Weimar (p. 211) and the surrounding region are full of literary history (see **Thüringer Wald,** p. 222).

In the early 19th century, **Romanticism** began to flower, with **Novalis** as its great poet. The movement continued to mature with the 1805 publication of *Des Knaben Wunderhorn*, an influential collection of popular folk tales, and the more celebrated collection by the **Brothers Grimm,** *Grimms' Fairy Tales*, followed in 1812. The **novella,** usually a story based on a reported event, served as a primary vehicle for new tales; **Heinrich von Kleist** (see **Berlin,** p. 120) and **Ludwig Tieck** were its chief practitioners. **E.T.A. Hoffmann** wrote ghost stories that were later analyzed by Freud (see **Bamberg,** p. 315). At the same time, **Johann Christian Friedrich Hölderlin** was writing a unique, myth-laden poetry until he succumbed to an insanity that had been haunting him for years and moved to a tower in Tübingen (p. 348), where he lived out the rest of his life, composing neat quatrains on the four seasons.

The romantic attempt to transcend the limitations of practical life eventually turned to gritty, sometimes ironic resignation. A rush of realistic political literature exploded around the time of the revolutions of 1848. **Heinrich Heine** was the finest of the **Junges Deutschland** (Young Germany) movement and also one of the first German Jews to achieve literary prominence (see **Düsseldorf,** p. 454). From self-exile in France, he wrote telling satires as well as romantic poems like *Die Lorelei* (see p. 381), while **Georg Büchner** wrote several strikingly modern plays, *Woyzeck* among them, which was later prized by both Expressionists and Marxists. Another social dramatist, **Gerhart Hauptmann,** achieved great influence around the turn of the century, and **Theodor Fontane** wrote realist novels which commented on Prussian society.

Opposite this *fin-de-siècle* realism, the **Symbolist** movement of the early 20th century concentrated on fleeting, sonorous image-poems; the **George-Kreis** (George Circle), led by critic and poet **Stefan George,** combined passions for literature and stylishness. The spirituality of **Hermann Hesse** showed an Eastern flair; his 1922 quasi-Buddhist novel *Siddhartha* became a paperback sensation in the 1960s. **Thomas Mann** carried the modern novel to a high point with *Der Zauberberg* (The Magic Mountain) and *Doktor Faustus*, two allegorical recountings of Germany's fateful history (see **Lübeck,** p. 532). Also vital to this period were German-language writers living in Austria-Hungary, among them **Rainer Maria Rilke** and **Franz Kafka**.

In the years before WWI, Germany produced a violent strain of Expressionist poetry that partially mirrored developments in painting. This poetry was well suited to depict the horrors of war, although several of its finest practitioners were killed in battle. The **Weimar era** was filled with surprisingly lively artistic production. Its most famous novel was **Erich Maria Remarque's** *Im Westen nichts Neues* (All Quiet on the Western Front), a blunt, uncompromising account of war's hor-

GÜNTER GRASS: LITERARY SUPERSTAR

Considered Germany's most celebrated contemporary writer, Günter Grass was born in Danzig (now Gdańsk, Poland) in 1927. In the immediate postwar period, he quickly came to prominence in the literary group Gruppe 47. His brilliant "Danzig Trilogy" (*The Tin Drum, Cat and Mouse,* and *Dog Years*) looked at the Nazi experience from the periphery, treating World War II as it came to the townspeople of Danzig. While Grass' early novels scandalized the German public at their first printing, they are now part of most university curricula. Grass continues to write against the grain, especially through his political essays. Since 1989, he has consistently professed a strong, and increasingly isolated, criticism of German unification. In his 1990 *Two States—One Nation?* Grass argues that with Auschwitz, Germany lost for all time the right to reunify. His millenial *My Century* is scheduled to be published in English in December 1999.

rors which became embroiled in the political turmoil of the era. **Bertolt Brecht's** dramas and poems present humankind in all its grotesque absurdity (see **Berlin,** p. 114); his *Dreigroschenoper* (Three-Penny Opera) was set to music by **Kurt Weill** (see **Dessau,** p. 190). The years of the Third Reich were more about burning books than publishing them; the Nazi attitude toward literature was summed up by Goebbels: "Whenever I hear the word 'culture,' I reach for my gun."

While the prolific literature of the Weimar period seemed to succeed WWI almost effortlessly, the second World War left Germany's artistic consciousness in shambles. Some thinkers, such as **Theodor Adorno** (see **Philosophy,** below), even questioned the propriety of writing certain types of literature after the **Holocaust** had so tragically called human consciousness into question. To nurse German literature back to health, several writers joined to form **Gruppe 47,** named after the year of its founding. The group included many who would become world-class writers: **Günter Grass** and (more peripherally) the poet **Paul Celan.** Much of the ensuing literature dealt with the problem of Germany's Nazi past; the novels of Grass and **Heinrich Böll** and the poetry of **Hans Magnus Enzensberger** turned a critical eye to post-war West Germany's repressive, overly organized tendencies.

The state of letters in the **GDR** was largely determined by the waxing and waning of government control. Many expatriate writers, particularly those with Marxist leanings from before the war (such as Brecht), returned to the East with great hopes. But the communist leadership was not interested in eliciting free artistic expression. The combination of personal danger, the burden of censorship, and simple disillusionment led many immensely talented writers to emigrate, including **Ernst Bloch, Uwe Johnson, Sarah Kirsch,** and **Heiner Kipphardt.** In the 70s and 80s, some East German writers were able to publish in the West, though not at home, and took that option as a middle ground. **Christa Wolf,** one of the most prominent German women writers, voluntarily remained in the GDR. Radical GDR playwright **Heiner Müller** shocked audiences with his disgusted protagonists and stripped-down scenarios of Beckett-esque plays such as *Hamletmaschine.* Since reunification, there has been a period of artistic anxiety and occasional malaise; in the former East, many authors are caught up in controversies over complicity with the *Stasi.* The new world of global capitalism has filled the shelves of German bookstores with translations of American best-sellers, pushing many works by German authors to the side. For happening German literature, look for **W. G. Sebald, Monika Maron, Peter Schneider,** or, straight from Oprah's book club, **Bernhard Schlink.**

PHILOSOPHY

Germany's philosophical tradition—one of the most respected in the world—is often very difficult reading. In 1517, **Martin Luther** defied the Catholic church, arguing against papal infallibility by claiming that only scripture was holy and that the individual should have a direct relationship with God. **Gottfried Wilhelm Leibnitz** thought of God as a metaphysical watchmaker who set the individual's body and soul in motion like two synchronized clocks. He also developed a **calculus** independent of Newton.

Immanuel Kant, the foremost thinker of the **German Enlightenment**, argued that ethics can be rationally deduced. While Kant sought to reconcile empiricism and rationalism, **Johann Gottlieb Fichte** spearheaded the new **German idealist** movement from Jena. Idealism stressed the importance of a postulated spirit or *Geist* in interpreting experience. Also in Jena, **Georg W. F. Hegel** added a dialectical twist to idealism, proposing that world history as well as the development of the individual consciousness could be understood through discerning conflicts of thesis and antithesis that would lead to a new synthesis. The two thinkers were laid to rest side by side in a Berlin cemetery (see p. 114). Hegel's view of world history would, after some distortion, eventually provide a theoretical backing for German nationalism. Meanwhile, **Johann Gottfried Herder** pushed for romantic nationalism, asserting that the spirit of a nation could be found in its folklore and peasant traditions. **Karl Marx** turned Hegel's dialectic around, asserting that class conflict was the stage on which world history was made—and the rest is history.

Similarly controversial, **Friedrich Nietzsche,** influenced by pessimist *par excellence* **Arthur Schopenhauer,** scorned the mediocrity of the hypocritical Christian masses. He propogated the idea of the *Übermensch*, a super-man so wise and self-mastered that he could enjoy life even to the point of eternal repetition. Later, Nietzsche went insane after hugging a horse, and for ten years he lay in bed while his sister contorted his works to fit her husband's **anti-Semitic** ideologies.

Max Weber accurately announced that we are trapped in a bureacratic iron cage and spoke out against the archaic, retarding affect of noble **Junker** society on German agriculture. **Edmund Husserl** inaugurated the philosophy of **phenomenology,** which occupied great German philosophers for decades. Phenomenology emphasizes the observation of pure consciousness stripped of metaphysical theories or scientific assumptions. **Martin Heidegger,** Husserl's successor at Freiburg and sometime Nazi, went his own way with *Being and Time*. This confusing, cumbersome book details the importance for man to understand what it means to question the meaning of life in a world where one-sided technical development has led to a crisis of **existential alienation.**

While Heidegger was comfortable with Hitler, the members of the **Frankfurt School,** progenitors of **Critical Theory** and erstwhile Marxists in the tradition of **Walter Benjamin,** fled to Columbia University in New York. **Theodor Adorno** and **Max Horkheimer** returned to Frankfurt after the war; their *Dialectic of Enlightenment* explores the merits of a civilizing process that seemingly culminates in fascism. The most celebrated post-war exponent of the school, **Jürgen Habermas,** has criticized German re-unification, citing the danger of joining two nations that have been forced to adopt two very different cultures.

FILM

The newborn medium of film exploded onto the German art scene in the **Weimar era** thanks to numerous brilliant directors. These early German films persist as central elements of all film study. *Das Cabinet des Dr. Caligari* (The Cabinet of Dr. Caligari), an early horror film directed by **Robert Wiene,** plays out a melodrama of autonomy and control against brilliantly expressive sets of painted shadows and tilted walls. **Fritz Lang** produced a marvelous succession of films, including *M., Dr. Mabuse der Spieler*, and *Metropolis*, a dark and brutal vision of the techno-fascist city of the future. **Ernst Lubitsch** also produced silent classics, while **F.W. Murnau's** *Nosferatu* crystallized German pathologies of "the other" in his portrayal of the Dracula legend. Meanwhile, **Josef von Sternberg** extended the tradition into sound with his satiric and pathetic *Der blaue Engel* (The Blue Angel), based on Heinrich Mann's novel *Professor Unrath*, which starred the inimitable **Marlene Dietrich.** Relics of German film's heyday are on display at the former **UFA** studio grounds in Potsdam and Babelsberg (p. 145).

Heeding Hitler's prediction that "without motor-cars, sound films, and wireless, (there can be) no victory for National Socialism," propaganda minister **Joseph Goebbels** became a masterful manipulator. Most **Nazi films** fell into two categories: political propaganda and escapism. *Der Ewige Jude* (The Eternal Jew) and *Jud Süss* (Jew Süss) glorified anti-Semitism. The frighteningly compelling propaganda films of **Leni Riefenstahl,** including *Triumph des Willens* (Triumph of the Will), which documented a Nürnberg Party Rally (p. 309), and *Olympia*, an account of the 1936 Olympic Games (p. 117), took the art of the documentary to new heights.

Film continued to be one of the most vigorous artistic media in the latter half of the 20th century. The late 60s and the 70s saw the greatest flood of cinematic excellence. The renaissance began in 1962 with the **Oberhausen Manifesto,** a declaration by independent filmmakers demanding artistic freedom and the right to create the new German feature film; within a few years, the government was granting subsidies to a constellation of young talents. Meanwhile, **Rainer Werner Fassbinder** made fatalistic films about individuals corrupted or defeated by society, including an epic television production of Alfred Döblin's mammoth novel *Berlin Alexanderplatz*. Fassbinder's film *Die Ehe der Maria Braun* (The Marriage of Maria Braun) and **Volker Schlöndorff's** *Die Blechtrommel* (The Tin Drum, based on Günther Grass's novel) brought the new German wave to a wider, international audience. **Margarethe von Trotta** focused mainly on women and politics, notably in her film *Die bleierne Zeit* (Marianne and Juliane). **Wolfgang Petersen** directed *Das Boot* (The Boat), one of the greatest war films ever made. **Werner Herzog's** works, including *Nosferatu*, drew inspiration from the silent films of the 20s in an attempt to recall German cinema's golden age. **Wim Wenders'** "road films," such as *Alice in den Städten* (Alice in the Cities) and the award-winning *Paris, Texas*, examine unconventional relationships and the freedom of life on the road. In 1984, **Edgar Reitz,** one of the Oberhausen signatories, created the 15-hour epic *Heimat* (Home). The film met with overwhelming approval for its questioning of national and regional identities.

East German film was subject to more constraints than other artistic media due to the fact that all films had to be produced under the aegis of the state-run German Film Corporation (DEFA). Just after the war, directors in the Soviet Occupation Zone produced several internationally acclaimed films, among them **Wolfgang Staudte's** *Die Mörder sind unter uns* (The Murderers are Among Us), about a Nazi war criminal who evades detection and goes on to lead the good life, **Kurt Maetzig's** *Ehe im Schatten* (Marriage in the Shadows), and **Erich Engel's** *Affaire Blum* (The Blum Affair). **Slatan Dudow** produced the first of DEFA's films, *Unser täglich Brot* (Our Daily Bread), a paean to the nationalization of industry, and went on to make one of the best East German films, *Stärker als die Nacht* (Stronger than the Night), which tells the story of a communist couple persecuted by the Nazis. After a brief post-Stalinist thaw, few East German films departed from the standard format of socialist heroism or love stories. **Egon Günther's** 1965 film *Lots Weib* (Lot's Wife), an explicitly feminist exploration of marital breakdown and divorce, was one notable exception. The next year saw three major films, Maetzig's *Das Kaninchen bin ich* (The Rabbit is Me), **Frank Vogel's** *Denk bloß nicht, ich heule* (Just Don't Think I'm Crying), and **Frank Beyer's** *Spur der Steine* (Track of Stones). Beyer later made the critically acclaimed *Jakob der Lügner* (Jacob the Liar), which was nominated for an Oscar. Another promising director, **Konrad Wolf,** produced such films as *Ich war neunzehn* (I was Nineteen), *Goya*, and *Sonnensucher* (Sun Seekers), the last of which was not permitted to be released until 14 years after its completion. The GDR also devoted a healthy portion of its filmmaking resources to **documentaries,** with **Winfried Junge, Volker Koepp,** and **Jürgen Böttcher** making significant contributions to the genre. A handful of these films managed to critique the prevailing political situation, although the majority of directors concocted unremarkable films glorifying the Soviet Union and the SED and denouncing the Federal Republic and the United States.

MUSIC

Because Germany traces its origins to the Holy Roman Empire, the earliest forms of music that appeared in German lands were religious. Compositions were originally written for the church, with their sole purpose being the worship of God. A tradition of secular music began in the 12th century with the **Minnesänger,** German troubadours whose technique of singing poetry passed gradually to the **Meistersänger** of the 14th and 15th centuries. After advancing through five ranks from apprentice to *Meister* (master), commoners organized themselves into guilds; their instrumental counterparts were the town-pipers, whose own guilds heralded the modern orchestra. **Polyphony,** the musical phenomenon in which more than one melodic and rhythmic line operates simultaneously within a piece, developed during this period. Luther's new **German translation of the Bible** in the 16th century ushered in a reformation of the musical world as well. The German *cantata* and *oratorio* (sacred and secular forms, respectively) gained ascendancy because they were finally composed in the language of the homeland. **Michael Praetorious** was a music theorist and composer whose settings of Lutheran chorales provide important examples of the first German hymns. At the turn of the century, **Dietrich Buxtehude** wailed on his organ, adding more settings to the German canon. Another musical form, the passion, came into being; the work thematized a saint's transcendance. **Johann Pachelbel** (best known for his Canon in D) worked in these new musical modes.

Johann Sebastian Bach was the stand-out in a long line of musically successful Bachs. His organ works construct worlds whose meticulous symmetries and regularities reflect a careful spiritual order. In mid-career he produced more secular works; the *Brandenburg Concerti* are famous for their imaginative exploration of the contrast between solo instruments and the chamber orchestra in the Baroque concerto. In 1723, Bach's appointment as cantor of Leipzig's largest church, the *Thomaskirche,* caused him to return to Lutheran religious music (see *Thomaskirche,* p. 181). During his appointment here, Bach composed over 200 cantatas, with the requisite one per week just to keep his job. Both his *St. Matthew* and *St. John Passions* were composed during this time, as were his famous Easter and Christmas oratorios; they consist of arias and choruses based on Biblical texts. Bach and his contemporary **Georg Friedrich Händel** composed during the Baroque period of the 17th century, which was known for its extravagant decoration and popularized the theme-and-variation idiom. Händel is the man behind every ad campaign that uses the Hallelujah Chorus; his 1742 work **The Messiah** has made its way to more audiences than the composer could have imagined.

The 19th century was an era of German musical hegemony. **Ludwig van Beethoven's** symphonies and piano sonatas bridged Classicism and Romanticism (see p. 442). He pushed classical forms to their limits as he focused on rhythmic drives, extremes of musical elements, and intense emotional expressionism. His monumental *Ninth Symphony* and late string quartets were written in the 1820s after he was completely deaf. The ethereal work of **Felix Mendelssohn-Bartholdy** is well represented by his overture to *A Midsummer Night's Dream.* Immigrant **Franz Liszt** pushed piano music and the symphonic form into still further reaches of unorthodox harmony and arrangement (see p. 212). The second generation of Romantic composers included **Johannes Brahms,** who imbued Classical forms with rich Romantic emotion.

Richard Wagner was perhaps the most influential German composer after Beethoven. He composed many of the world's best-known operas—*Tannhäuser, Die Meistersinger, Der Ring des Nibelungen*—in an attempt to revolutionize the form of opera; his vision of **Gesamtkunstwerk** (total work of art) unified music and text, poetry and philosophy. Through the reappearance of a *Leitmotiv,* a musical figure that would appear throughout an entire piece, Wagner would give signature sound to dramatic action. The composer's works were highly nationalistic in their celebration of Germanic legend, and were easily exploited by German-Aryan supremacists.

The unstable economy of the Weimar Republic and the anti-Romantic backlash encouraged smaller, cheaper musical forms such as jazz. A new movement of *Gebrauchsmusik* (utilitarian music) engendered music for amateur players and film scores. Austrian **Arnold Schönberg** and his disciples **Anton Webern** and **Alban Berg** mastered the possibilities of 12-tone composition (using a scale based on 12 notes) and explored the expressions of dissonance. In 1921, Berg's opera **Wozzeck** set author Georg Büchner's harrowing tale of insanity to a jarring score. **Paul Hindemith** headed a group of Neoclassicists influenced by the *Neue Sachlichkeit* and the emphasis on craftsmanship introduced by the *Werkbund* and *Bauhaus*. They embraced the older, variational forms (such as the sonata) most suited to the abstract aesthetic of the time. **Carl Orff,** Hitler's favorite composer, is most noted for his eclectic *Carmina Burana*, a resurrection of bawdy 13th-century lyrics with a bombastic score. Music hall works prior to WWII bred satiric operettas with songs of the political avant-garde. **Kurt Weill's** partnership with Bertolt Brecht produced such masterpieces of the genre as *Die Dreigroschenoper* (Three-Penny Opera). The immediate post-war period was not conducive to much musical experimentation, and schmalzy *Schlager* tended to dominate. A number of exiled musicians (like the reknowned chanteuse **Lotte Lenya**) returned to Germany after the war and briefly revitalized the otherwise unremarkable music scene.

The current state of German musical tastes is dismally transnational; Germans are more likely to listen to the Backstreet Boys or Britney Spears than their own countrymen. Nonetheless, German artists continue to make significant contributions to both the national and global music scene. Apart from **Nena's** apocalyptic 80s hit *99 Luftballons* and, more recently, **Rammstein's** frightening tune *Du hast,* Germany is best known internationally for having pioneered **techno,** an umbrella term for various kinds of electronic music. In addition to **hardcore** and **gabber,** whose hard-hitting beats (upwards of 200 bpm) inspire fury on the international dancefloor, techno has also spawned genres more conducive to crossover; outgrowths such as **house** and **jungle,** developed mainly in the United States and England, juxtapose techno with more established genres like hip-hop and funk. More recently, **ambient** and **trance,** less bass-heavy, more serene forms of electronica, have become quite popular in Germany, with artists like Berlin-based **Mijk van Dijk** receiving international attention. Techno's most pronounced manifestation is the annual **Love Parade** in Berlin (see p. 135), when DJs such as **Dr. Motte** (the parade's founder), **Da Hool,** and **Phil Fuldner** induce hundreds of thousands of Germans to drop ecstasy and get down.

Apart from techno, Germany enjoys a modest rock scene, with such noteable acts as **Die Ärtzte** and **Die fantastischen Vier.** Further afield, **Blümchen** has gained infamy for her bizarre combination of cutesy girl rock and ear-splitting techno beats. Influenced by American musical trends, Germans have also begun to dabble in hip-hop and rap, ranging from the comically adolescent girl group **Tic Tac Toe** to the cannabis-inspired tracks of the Hamburg-based hip-hop act **Fünf Sterne Deluxe.** One of the most prolific homegrown labels is undoubtedly **3p,** which from its base in Frankfurt bills itself as the number one source of *deutsche Soulmusik*. Under its aegis, numerous hip-hop and rap stars, among them **Sabrina Setlur, Xavier Naidoo,** and **Illmatic,** have come to the forefront of the German charts.

MEDIA

British dailies, such as the *Times* and *Guardian,* are widely available at newsstands in most cities. The *International Herald Tribune* and the European edition of the *Wall Street Journal* are the most common U.S. papers. American and British armed forces maintain English-language radio stations in Western Germany. German speakers can keep track of things with German language papers both in print and on the web. Stay in touch with world events with the informative, Hamburg-based weekly *Der Spiegel* (www.spiegel.de), one of the world's leading newsmagazines. *Die Zeit* (www.zeit.de) is a left-leaning weekly. The *Frankfurter*

Allgemeine (www.faz.de) is a stodgy, more conservative daily. Munich's *Süddeutsche Zeitung* (www.sueddeutsche.de) is one of the country's best newspapers, though the reactionary tabloid *Bild* (www.bild.de) is far more popular. Coming at you from Berlin are the liberal *Berliner Tagesspiegel* (www.tagesspiegel.de) and the leftist *Tageszeitung* (www.taz.de). For a different spin on the news, check out the PDS' neo-communist daily *Neues Deutschland*.

German television has expanded in the last 15 years. In addition to the three government-run channels (ARD, ZDF, and a third regional channel), Germans can now receive more than 30 channels, including the popular private networks RTL, SAT1, and Pro7. English speakers have access to numerous U.S. and British stations, including CNN, NBC, and BBC. For an entertaining peek at pop culture, watch German MTV and its homegrown counterpart VIVA, or tune into Germany's highest-grossing soap, *Gute Zeiten, Schlechte Zeiten* (Good Times, Bad Times).

FOOD AND DRINK

German food gets bad press. Although it is not as compelling as other European cuisines, *Deutsche Küche* has a 'robust' charm. Meat-and-potato lovers especially will find the food in Germany hearty and satisfying. And if the local food is not to your taste, Germany's cities offer a wide variety of quality ethnic restaurants. Be careful when ordering from a German menu if you don't speak the language; ingredients such as *Aal* (eel), *Blutwurst* (blood sausage), and *Gehirn* (brains) are not uncommon, and may necessitate an acquired taste.

Vegetarians should not be afraid of entering this land of carnivores. Since the 1970s, vegetarianism has steadily gained popularity in Germany, with a recent rise due to the fear of mad cow disease. Approximately one-fifth of Germany's population now eats little or no meat. Vegetarian restaurants abound in most cities, and vegetarian and *Biokost* (health foods) supermarkets are much more prevalent than in the rest of Europe. As most vegetarian fare relies heavily on cheese, vegans may have a more difficult time finding non-dairy options. For more information, see **Dietary Concerns** (p. 81).

The typical German **Frühstück** (breakfast) consists of coffee or tea with *Brötchen* (rolls), several kinds of bread, butter, marmalade, *Wurst* (cold sausage), *Schinken* (ham), *Eier* (eggs), and *Käse* (cheese). **Mittagessen** (lunch) is usually the main meal of the day, consisting of soup, broiled sausage or roasted meat, potatoes or dumplings, and a salad or *Gemüsebeilage* (vegetable side dish). **Abendessen** or **Abendbrot** (supper) is a re-enactment of breakfast, only beer replaces coffee and the selection of meat and cheese is wider. **Dessert** after meals is uncommon, but many older Germans indulge in a daily ritual of **Kaffee und Kuchen** (coffee and cakes), a snack analogous to English "tea-time," at 3 or 4pm.

Germany's bakeries produce an impressive range of quality **Brot** (bread). *Vollkornbrot* is whole-wheat (which has a completely different meaning in Germany) and *Roggenbrot* is rye bread. *Schwarzbrot* (black bread) is a dense, dark loaf that's slightly acidic. Go to a *Bäckerei* (bakery) and point to whatever looks good. Generally they sell you the whole loaf; for half, ask for *ein Halbes*. German bread does not contain preservatives and will go stale the day of its purchase.

Beer and wine (see below) are the meal-time **beverages.** *Saft* (juice), plain or mixed with mineral water, is an alternative. Germans do not guzzle glasses of water by the dozen as Americans do, although they will sip a (small) glass of carbonated mineral water. If you ask for *Wasser* in a restaurant, you get mineral water, which isn't free. For tap water, ask for *Leitungswasser* and expect funny looks.

With very few exceptions **restaurants** expect you to seat yourself. If there are no tables free, ask someone for permission to take a free seat (ask *Darf ich Platz nehmen?*, pronounced "DAHRF eesh PLAHTS nay-men"). In traditional restaurants, address waiters *Herr Ober*, and waitresses (but no one else) as *Fräulein* (pronounced "FROY-line"). In a less formal setting, just say *hallo*. At the table, Germans eat with the fork in the left hand and the knife in the right and keep their hands above or resting on the table. While eating, it is polite to keep the tines of your fork pointing down at all times. When you're finished, pay at the table. Ask the server *Zahlen, bitte* (TSAH-len, BIT-teh: "check, please"). Taxes *(Mehrwert-steuer)* and service are always included in the price, but it is customary to leave a little something extra, usually by rounding up the bill by a Mark or two.

Eating in restaurants at every meal will quickly drain your budget. One strategy is to stick to the daily *prix-fixe* option, called the *Tagesmenü*. A cheaper option is to buy food in **grocery stores**. German university students eat in cafeterias called **Mensen**. Some *Mensen* (singular *Mensa*) require a student ID (or charge higher prices for non-students), while some are open only to local students, though travelers often evade this requirement by strolling in as if they belonged. In smaller towns, the best budget option is to stop by a *Bäckerei* (bakery) for bread and garnish it with sausage purchased from a butcher *(Fleischerei* or *Metzgerei)*.

Besides bread, the staples of the German diet are *Wurst* (sausage, in dozens of varieties; see p. 227), *Schweinefleisch* (pork), *Rindfleisch* (beef), *Kalbfleisch* (veal), *Lammfleisch* (lamb), *Huhn* (chicken), and *Kartoffeln* (potatoes). Sampling the various **local specialties** around Germany gives a taste of the diverse culinary tradition. In **Bavaria**, *Knödel* (potato and flour dumplings, sometimes filled with meat) are quite popular, as is *Weißwurst*, a sausage made with milk. Thüringen and northern Bavaria are famed for their succulent grilled *Bratwurst*, the classic, roasted sausage slathered in mustard and eaten with potatoes or bought from a street vendor and clasped in a roll. Southwestern Germany is known for its *Spätzle* (noodles), and *Maultaschen* (pasta pockets) are also popular in **Swabia**. German *Pfannkuchen* (pancakes) are quite heavy and come with a range of toppings. *Kaiserschmarren* is a chopped-up pancake with powdered sugar. **Hessians** do amazing things with potatoes, like smothering them in a delectable *grüne Soße* (green sauce). The North and Baltic seacoasts harvest an assortment of seafood delights, including *Krabben* (shrimp) and *Matjes* (herring; see p. 543).

No summary of food in Germany would be complete without mentioning the tremendous contribution the Turkish population has made to the culinary scene. When Turks began emigrating to West Germany in the early 1960s, the indigenous palate was revitalized by such now-ubiquitous delights as the *Döner Kebab*, thin slices of lamb mixed with cucumbers, onions, and red cabbage in a wedge of *Fladenbrot*, a round, flat, sesame-covered bread (see **What's a Döner?**, p. 107). Asking for a *Döner mit Soße* adds a deliciously piquant garlic sauce. Other well-known Turkish dishes include *Börek*, a flaky pastry filled with spinach, cheese, or meat; and *Lahmacun* (sometimes called *türkische Pizza*), a smaller, spicier version of Italy's staple fast food. Turkish restaurants and fast food *Imbiße* also proffer delicious *Kefir* (flavored yogurt drinks) and, for dessert, *Baklava*.

BEER

Where does the German begin? Where does it end? May a German smoke? The majority says no ... But a German may drink beer, indeed as a true son of Germania he should drink beer.

—Heinrich Heine

Germans have brewed frothy malt beverages since the 8th century BC, and they've been consuming and exporting them in prodigious quantities ever since. The state of Bavaria alone contains about one-fifth of all the breweries in the world. The Germans drink more than 150 liters of beer per person every year, more than any other country. According to legend, the German king Gambrinus invented the modern beer recipe when he threw some hops into fermenting malt. During the Middle Ages, monastic orders refined the art of brewing, imbibing to stave off starvation during long fasts. It wasn't long before the monks' lucrative trade caught the eye of secular lords, who established the first *Hofbrauereien* (court breweries).

The variety of German beers boggles even the most sober mind. Most beer is **Vollbier,** containing about 4% alcohol. **Export** (5%) is also popular, and stout, tasty

DAS REINHEITSGEBOT: GERMANY'S BEER PURITY LAW

One of the most despised characters in medieval Germany was the shoddy brewer who tried to cut costs by substituting lesser grains for the noble cereal at the heart of beer—barley. In 1516, Duke Wilhelm IV of Bavaria decreed that beer could contain only pure water, barley, and hops. As a result, German beer is world-famous, but it also contains no preservatives and will spoil relatively quickly. Wilhelm's Purity Law *(Reinheitsgebot)* has endured to this day, with minor alterations to permit the cultivation of Bavaria's trademark wheat-based beers. The law even applies to imports—none of the filler-laden products of the major American breweries can be imported into Germany. But with the arrival of the European Union, the law was challenged by other European countries, who saw it as an unfair trade barrier. Now the "impure" foreign beers are being admitted to the market, but to the joy of drinkers worldwide, the German breweries have all reaffirmed their full commitment to the *Reinheitsgebot*.

Bockbier (6.25%) is brewed in the spring. **Doppelbock** is an eye-popping concoction reserved for special occasions. Ordering *ein Helles* will get you a light-colored beer, while *Dunkles* can look like anything from Coca-Cola to molasses.

Although generalizations are difficult, the average German beer is maltier and more "bread-like" than Czech, Dutch, or American beers. (An affectionate German slang term for beer is *flüßiges Brot*, "liquid bread.") Among the exceptions is **Pils**, or Pilsner, which is most popular in the north. Its characteristic clarity and bitter taste come from the addition of extra hops. From the south, especially Bavaria, comes **Weißbier**, also known as **Weizenbier**, a smooth, refreshing brew. Despite the name, *Weißbier* is not white, but a rich brown. The term *Weizenbier* refers to a lighter wheat beer, while **Hefeweizen** is wheat beer with a layer of yeast in the bottom. **Flaschenbier** is bottled beer, while **Bier vom Faß** (or **Faßbier**) comes from the tap.

Sampling local brews numbers among the finest of Germany's pleasures. In Köln, one drinks smooth **Kölsch**, an extraordinarily refined, light-colored beer; a Düsseldorf specialty is **Altbier**, a darker top-fermented beer. Berliners are partial to **Berliner Weiße**, a lighter beer; ordering it *mit Schuß* adds a shot of raspberry or woodruff syrup. On hot summer days, lightweight drinkers and children prefer **Radler**, a mix containing half beer and half lemon-lime soda. **Diesel** is a mixture of *Bier* and cola that will get your engine started.

The variety of places to drink beer is almost as staggering as the variety of brews. The traditional **Biergarten** consists of outdoor tables under chestnut trees; sometimes food is served as well. The broad leaves of the trees originally kept beer barrels cool in the days before refrigeration, until—according to one legend—an enterprising brewer figured out that they could do the same thing for beer drinkers. The **Bierkeller** is a subterranean version of the *Biergarten*, where local breweries dispense their product. To order *ein Bier*, hold up your thumb, not your index finger. Raise your glass to a *Prost*, (Cheers) and drink (for more on beer halls in Munich, see **Beer, Beer, and more Beer**, p. 251). Another option for beer drinking is the **Gaststätte**, a simple, local restaurant. It's considered bad form to order only drinks at a *Gaststätte* during mealtimes, but at any other time, friends linger for hours over beers. Many *Gaststätten* have a *Stammtisch* (regulars' table), marked by a flag, where interlopers should not sit. The same group of friends may meet at the *Stammtisch* every week for decades to drink, play cards, and chill; keep in mind that your visa has an expiration date. **Kneipen** are bars where hard drinks are also served.

WINE AND SPIRITS

Although overshadowed by Germany's more famous export beverage, German wines win over connoisseurs and casual drinkers alike. Virtually all German wines are white, though they vary widely in character. Generally, German wines are sweeter and taste fresher than French, Mediterranean, or Californian wines. Because Germany is the northernmost of the wine-producing countries, the quality of a vineyard's produce can vary considerably with the climate.

The cheapest wines are classified as *Tafelwein* (table wine), while the good stuff (which is still pretty affordable) is *Qualitätswein* (quality wine). The label *Qualitätswein bestimmter Anbaugebiete*, or *Q. b. A.*, designates quality wine from a specific cultivation region. *Qualitätswein mit Prädikat* (quality wine with distinction) denotes an even purer wine derived from a particular variety of grape. The *Prädikat* wines are further subdivided according to the ripeness of the grapes when harvested; from driest to sweetest, they are *Kabinett*, *Spätlese*, *Auslese*, *Beerenauslese*, *Trockenbeerenauslese*, and *Eiswein*. The grapes that produce the *Trockenbeerenauslese* are left on the vine well into winter until they have shriveled into raisins and begun to rot—no kidding.

The major concentrations of viticulture lie along the Rhein and Mosel valleys, along the Main River in Franconia, and in Baden. Of the dozens of varieties, the most famous are *Riesling*, *Müller-Thurgau*, *Sylvaner*, and *Traminer* (source of *Gewürztraminer*). In wine-producing towns, thirsty travelers can stop by a *Weinstube* to sample the local produce. In Hessen, the beverage of choice is *Äppelwoi* or *Äpfelwein* (apple wine), a hard cider similar in potency to beer. After a meal, many Germans aid their digestion by throwing back a shot of *Schnapps*, distilled from fruits. *Kirschwasser*, a cherry liqueur from the Schwarzwald, is the best known and probably the easiest to stomach, but adventurous sorts can experiment with the sublimely tasty *Black Haus*, a delectable, 100 proof, blackberry *Schnapps* also from the Schwarzwald, which will get you *Haus*ed in a most delightful fashion. Each year, unsuspecting tourists are seduced into buying little green bottles of *Jägermeister*, one of Germany's numerous (and barely palatable) herb liqueurs.

SOCIAL LIFE

An afternoon of relaxation in a park or cafe will teach you more about Germany than one spent in a museum. Many Germans know Americans and Britons only through contact with soldiers, who haven't always made the best impression. Anti-Americanism is a powerful sentiment among young Germans concerned by the American military's role as a global police force. If you are sensitive to this concern, you will find that most Germans have a passionate interest in the U.S. Despite anti-American sentiments, Germans are obsessed with Americana, and English words and American popular culture pervade German media and fashion.

Take the time to actually meet people. Although Germans may seem reserved or even unfriendly, they are not as stand-offish as they first appear. Europeans in general are sincerely interested in other lands and cultures, but have a very strong sense of their own cultural background; if you insult or belittle it, you'll only seem arrogant (and rude). Above all, don't automatically equate the American, Canadian, British, Australian, etc. way with "better."

Germans are incredibly frank and will not hesitate to register their disapproval. To the uninitiated this may come across as confrontational, but it stems more from an intense honesty than anything else. Many Germans consider effusive chumminess insincere and superficial, and Americans are often perceived as disingenuous for being overly friendly.

The Byzantine rules surrounding German etiquette make Ann Landers look like a gas station attendant. However, it is important to note that many of these precepts do not apply to people under 30 and in larger urban areas. In general, Germans are much more formal than Americans and Australians, and incredibly big on punctuality. An invitation to a German home is a major courtesy; you should bring something for the hostess. Among the older generations, be careful not to use the informal *du* (you) or a first name without being invited to do so. *Du* is appropriate when addressing fellow students and friends at a youth hostel, or when addressing children. In all other circumstances, use the formal *Sie* for "you," as in the question *Sprechen Sie englisch?*

Only waitresses in traditional restaurants are addressed as *Fräulein*; address all other women as *Frau* (followed by a name). Always ask if someone speaks English before launching into a question. Better yet, try to learn a little German and don't be afraid to test your talents. The language is related to English, and you can learn the pronunciation system and some useful phrases in about 15 minutes (see **Appendix**, p. 574). In any case, learn at least two phrases: **bitte** (please; BIT-teh) and **danke** (thank you; DAHNK-eh).

Everything you've heard about the Germans' compulsive abidance of the law is true. The first time you see a German standing at an intersection in the pouring rain, with no cars in sight, waiting for the "walk" signal, you'll know what we mean. Jaywalking is only one of the petty offenses that will mark you as a foreigner (and subject you to fines); littering is another. Many tourists also do not realize that the bike lanes marked in red between the sidewalk and the road are not for pedestrian use. The younger generation takes matters much less seriously. The **drinking age** is 16 for beer and wine and 18 for hard liquor, although both are skimpily enforced; driving under the influence, however, is a severe offense.

APOCALYPSE 2000. Germany has something for every New Year's palate. Throughout the guide we list numerous events, along with a festival table in the appendix (p. 572). For the short list of highlights, look no further.
Berlin justifies its newly earned status as country capital (p. 127).
Hannover gets virtual in the New Year (p. 467).
Oberammergau presents the Passion Play, starring the man, Himself (p. 263).

ESSENTIALS

FACTS FOR THE TRAVELER

A fun and inexpensive trip to Germany requires preparation. For better or worse, there is a sprawling industry designed to help you and other travelers. The many organizations listed below, especially national tourist offices, will send daunting mounds of literature; dive in and plan a trip tailored to your specific interests. Resist the urge to see everything, as a madcap schedule will detract from your enjoyment. If you try to see Berlin, Munich, and Köln in a week, you'll come away with only vague memories of train stations, youth hostels, and night clubs. Make sure to use the information provided by *Let's Go* and other sources to assemble your support system, both in terms of what you bring and the arrangements you make. It's been said that all you really need are time and money, but on a budget voyage you don't want to waste either due to lack of planning.

DOCUMENTS AND FORMALITIES

 THE EUROPEAN UNION AND THE TRAVELER. Traveling between the 15 member states of the **European Union (EU)** has never been easier, especially for EU citizens. Citizens of EU member states need only a valid state-issued identity card to travel within the EU, and have right of residence and employment throughout the Union, though some regulations do apply (see **Visas and Work Permits**, p. 41). Freedom of mobility within the EU was established on May 1, 1999; henceforth, with the exception of the UK, Ireland, and Denmark, border checks will be abolished at internal EU borders. However, travelers should always carry a passport or EU member-issued identity card as police controls may still be carried out. Over the next five years, immigration and visa policies will start to be made on a Union-wide basis.

The 15 member states of the EU are: Austria, Belgium, Denmark, Finland, France, Germany, Greece, Ireland, Italy, Luxembourg, the Netherlands, Portugal, Spain, Sweden, and the United Kingdom. More information on the EU can be found at its official site, www.europa.eu.int.

GERMAN EMBASSIES AND CONSULATES ABROAD

The German embassy or consulate in your home country can supply legal information concerning your trip, arrange for visas, and direct you to a wealth of other information about tourism, education, and employment in Germany.

Australia: Embassy: 119 Empire Circuit, Yarralumla, Canberra, ACT 2600 (tel. (02) 6270 1911; fax 6270 1951); **Consulates: Melbourne,** 480 Punt Rd., South Yarra, VIC, 3141 (tel. (03) 9828 6888; fax 9820 2414); **Sydney,** 13 Trelawney St., Woollahra, NSW. 2025 (tel. (02) 9328 7733; fax 9327 9649).

Canada: Embassy, 1 Waverly St., Ottawa, ON K2P OT8 (tel. 613-232-1101; fax 594-9330; email 100566.2620@compuserve.com). **Consulates: Montréal,** 1250 René-Lévesque Ouest, Suite 4315, H3B 4X1 (tel. 514-931-2277; fax 931-7239).

Ireland: Embassy, 31 Trimleston Ave., Booterstown, Blackrock, Co. Dublin (tel. (012) 69 30 11; fax 269 39 46).

New Zealand: Embassy, 90-92 Hobson St., Thorndon, Wellington (tel. (04) 473 6063; fax 473 6069).

ENTRANCE REQUIREMENTS.
Passport (p. 40). Required for citizens of Australia, Canada, Ireland, New Zealand, South Africa, the U.K., and the U.S.
Visa (p. 41). Required only for citizens of South Africa.
Work Permit (p. 41). Required for all foreigners planning to work in Germany.
Driving Permit (p. 74). Required for non-EU citizens planning to drive.

South Africa: Embassy, 180 Blackwood St., Arcadia, Pretoria, 0083 (tel. (012) 427 8900; fax 343 9401). **Consulate: Cape Town,** 825 St. Martini Gardens, Queen Victoria St., 8001 (tel. 021 424 2410; fax 24 94 03).

U.K.: Embassy, 23 Belgrave Sq., London SW1X 8PZ (tel. (020) 78 24 13 00; fax 78 24 14 35). **Consulates: Manchester,** Westminster House, 11 Portlant St., M60 1HY (tel. (0161) 237 5255; fax 237 5244); **Edinburgh,** 16 Eglinton Crescent, EH12 5DG, Scotland (tel. (0131) 337 2323; fax 346 1578).

U.S.: Embassy, 4645 Reservoir Rd. NW, Washington, D.C. 20007-1998 (tel. 202-298-4000; fax 298 4249; www.germany-info.org). **Consulates: New York,** 871 U.N. Plaza, New York, NY 10017 (tel. 212-610-9700; fax 940-0402 or 610-9702); **Los Angeles,** 6222 Wilshire Blvd., Ste. 500, LA, California 90048 (tel. (323) 930-2703; fax 930-2805); other consulates in Atlanta, Boston, Chicago, Detroit, Houston, Miami, San Francisco, and Seattle.

EMBASSIES AND CONSULATES IN GERMANY

All embassies moved back to Berlin in summer 1999. For the latest information, call the **Auswärtiges Amt,** in Berlin at (030) 20 18 60.

Australia: Embassy, Berlin, Friedrichstr. 200, 10117 (tel. (030) 880 08 80). **Consulate, Frankfurt,** Grunebrückweg 58-62, 60311 (tel. (069) 273 90 90; fax 23 26 31).

Canada: Embassy, Berlin, Friedrichstr. 95, 12th fl., 10117 Berlin (tel. (030) 20 31 20; fax 20 31 25 90). **Consulates, Düsseldorf,** Benrataerstr. 8, 40213 (tel. (0211) 172 170). **Hamburg,** ABC-Str. 45, 20354 (tel. (040) 35 55 62 95; fax 35 55 62 94). Munich, Tal 29, 80331 (tel. (089) 219 95 70).

Ireland: Embassy, Berlin, Ernst-Reuter-Pl. 10, 10587 (tel. (030) 34 80 08 22; fax 34 80 08 63). **Consulates, Hamburg,** Feldbrunnerstr. 43, 20148 (tel. (040) 44 18 62 13). **Munich,** Mauerkircherstr. 1a, 81679 (tel. (089) 98 57 23).

New Zealand: Embassy, Berlin, Friedrichstr. 60, 10117. **Consulate, Hamburg,** Zürich-Dom-Str. 19, 20095 (tel. (040) 442 55 50).

South Africa: Embassy, Berlin, Friedrichstr. 60, 10117. **Consulates, Berlin,** Douglasstr. 9, 14193 (tel. (030) 82 50 11 or 825 27 11; fax 826 65 43). **Frankfurt,** Cerberstr. 33 (tel. (069) 719 11 30). **Munich,** Sendlinger-Tor-Pl. 5, 80336 (tel. (089) 231 16 30).

U.K.: Embassy, Berlin, Unter den Linden 32-34, 10117 (tel. (030) 20 18 40; fax. 20 18 41 58). **Consulates, Düsseldorf,** Yorckstr. 19, 40476 (tel. (0211) 944 80). **Frankfurt,** Bockenheimer Landstr. 42, 60323 (tel. (069) 170 00 20; fax 72 95 53). **Hamburg,** Harvestehuder Weg 8a, 20148 (tel. (040) 448 03 20; fax 410 72 59). **Munich,** Bürkleinstr. 10, 80538 (tel. (089) 21 10 90). **Stuttgart,** Breite Str. 2, 70173 (tel. (0711) 16 26 90).

U.S.: Embassy, Berlin, Neustädtische Kirchstr. 4-5 (tel. (030) 238 51 74; fax 238 62 90). **Consulates, Düsseldorf,** Kennedydamm 15-17, 40476 (tel. (0211) 47 06 10). **Frankfurt,** Siesmayerstr. 21, 60323 (tel. (069) 753 50; fax 74 89 38). **Hamburg,** Alsterufer 27, 20354 (tel. (040) 41 17 10; fax 41 76 65). **Leipzig,** Wilhelm-Seyfferth-Str. 4, 04107 (tel. (0341) 21 38 40). **Munich,** Königinstr. 5, 80539 (tel. (089) 288 80).

PASSPORTS

REQUIREMENTS. Citizens of Australia, Canada, Ireland, New Zealand, South Africa, the U.K., and the U.S. need valid passports to enter Germany and to re-enter their own country. Returning home with an expired passport is illegal, and may result in a fine.

PHOTOCOPIES. It is a good idea to photocopy the page of your passport that contains your photograph, passport number, and other identifying information, along with other important documents such as visas, travel insurance policies, airplane tickets, and traveler's check serial numbers, in case you lose anything. Carry a set of copies in a safe place apart from the originals and leave another at home.

LOST PASSPORTS. If you lose your passport, immediately notify the local police and the nearest embassy or consulate of your home country. To expedite its replacement, you will need to show identification and proof of citizenship. With the proper information in hand, you may be able to claim a replacement in under a week; otherwise, a replacement may take weeks to process. In an emergency, ask for immediate temporary traveling papers that will permit you to re-enter your home country. Your passport is a public document belonging to your nation's government. You may have to surrender it to a foreign government official, but if you don't get it back in a reasonable amount of time, inform the nearest mission of your home country.

NEW PASSPORTS. All applications for new passports or renewals should be filed several weeks or months in advance of your planned departure date—remember that you are relying on government agencies to complete these transactions. Most passport offices offer emergency passport services for an additional fee. Citizens residing abroad who need a passport or renewal should contact their nearest embassy or consulate.

Australia: Citizens must apply for a passport in person at a post office, passport office, or overseas diplomatic mission. Passport offices are located in Adelaide, Brisbane, Canberra, Darwin, Hobart, Melbourne, Newcastle, Perth, and Sydney. New adult passports cost AUS$126 (for a 32-page passport) or AUS$188 (64-page), and a child's is AUS$63 (32-page) or AUS$94 (64-page). Adult passports are valid 10 years and child passports 5 years. For more information, call toll-free (in Australia) 13 12 32, or visit www.dfat.gov.au/passports.

Canada: Application forms are available at all passport offices, Canadian missions, many travel agencies, and Northern Stores in northern communities. Passports cost CDN$60, plus a CDN$25 consular fee, are valid for 5 years, and are not renewable. For more information, contact the Canadian Passport Office, Department of Foreign Affairs and International Trade, Ottawa, ON, K1A 0G3 (tel. (613) 994-3500; www.dfaitmaeci.gc.ca/passport). Travelers may also call 800-567-6868 (24hr.); in Toronto, (416) 973-3251; in Vancouver, (604) 586-2500; in Montreal, (514) 283-2152.

Ireland: Citizens can apply for a passport by mail to either the Department of Foreign Affairs, Passport Office, Setanta Centre, Molesworth St., Dublin 2 (tel. (01) 671 1633; fax 671 1092; www.irlgov.ie/iveagh), or the Passport Office, Irish Life Building, 1A South Mall, Cork (tel. (021) 27 25 25). Obtain an application at a local Garda station or post office, or request one from a passport office. Passports cost IR£45 and are valid 10 years. Citizens under 18 or over 65 can request a 3-year passport that costs IR£10.

New Zealand: Application forms for passports are available in New Zealand from most travel agents. Applications may be forwarded to the Passport Office, P.O. Box 10526, Wellington, (tel. 0800 22 50 50; www.govt.nz/agency_info/forms.shtml). Standard processing time in New Zealand is 10 working days for correct applications. The fees are adult NZ$80, child NZ$40. Children's names can no longer be endorsed on a parent's passport—they must apply for their own, which are valid for up to 5 years. An adult's passport is valid 10 years.

South Africa: South African passports are issued only in Pretoria. However, all applications must be submitted or forwarded to the applicable office of a South African consulate. Tourist passports, valid 10 years, cost around SAR80. Children under 16 must be issued their own passports, valid 5 years, which cost around SAR60. Time for completion of an application is normally 3 months or more from the time of submission. For further information, contact the nearest Department of Home Affairs Office (www.southafrica-newyork.net/passport.htm).

United Kingdom: Full passports are valid 10 years (5 years if under 16). Application forms are available at passport offices, main post offices, and many travel agents. Apply by mail or in person to one of the passport offices in London, Liverpool, Newport, Peterborough, Glasgow, or Belfast. The fee is UK£31, children under 16 UK£11. The process takes about 4 weeks, but the London office offers a 5-day, walk-in rush service; arrive early. The U.K. Passport Agency can be reached by phone on (0870) 521 04 10; more information is available at www.open.gov.uk/ukpass/ukpass.htm.

United States: Citizens may apply for a passport at any federal or state courthouse or post office authorized to accept passport applications, or at a U.S. Passport Agency, located in most major cities. Refer to the "U.S. Government, State Department" section of the telephone directory or the local post office for addresses. Passports are valid 10 years (5 years if under 18) and cost US$60 (under 18 US$40). Passports may be renewed by mail or in person for US$40. Processing takes 3-4 weeks. For more information, call the U.S. Passport Information's 24-hour recorded message (tel. 202-647-0518) or look on the web at http://travel.state.gov/passport_services.html.

VISAS AND WORK PERMITS

VISAS. Citizens of **Australia, Canada, Ireland, New Zealand,** the **U.K.,** and the **U.S.** need only a passport to stay in Germany for up to 90 days within six months. Those seeking an extended stay, employment, or student status should obtain a visa and a residence permit. Citizens of **South Africa** need a visa to enter Germany. Contact the nearest German Consulate General (see p. 39).

STUDY AND WORK PERMITS. Admission as a visitor does not include the right to work, which requires a work permit, and entering Germany to study requires a special visa. Student visas require proof of financial independence and admission to a German academic institution. These procedures can take up to three months. For more information, see **Alternatives to Tourism,** p. 81.

IDENTIFICATION

When traveling, always carry two or more forms of identification on your person, including at least one photo ID. A passport combined with a driver's license or birth certificate usually serves as adequate proof of identity and citizenship. Many establishments, especially banks, require several IDs before cashing traveler's checks. Never carry all your forms of ID together, however; you risk being left entirely without ID or funds in case of theft or loss. It is useful to carry extra passport-size photos to affix to the various IDs and railpasses you may acquire.

STUDENT AND TEACHER IDENTIFICATION. The **International Student Identity Card (ISIC)** is the most widely accepted form of student identification. Flashing this card garners discounts on sights, theaters, museums, accommodations, and meals, as well as student rates on train, ferry, bus, and airplane transportation. and other services. Present the card wherever you go, and ask about discounts even when none are advertised. The international identification cards are preferable to institution-specific cards because the tourism personnel in Germany are taught to recognize the former. For U.S. cardholders abroad, the ISIC also provides insurance benefits, including US$100 per day of in-hospital sickness for a maximum of 60 days, and US$3000 accident-related medical reimbursement for each accident (see **Insurance**, p. 56). In addition, cardholders have access to a toll-free 24hr. ISIC helpline whose multilingual staff can provide assistance in medical, legal, and financial emergencies overseas (tel. 800-626-2427 in the U.S. and Canada; elsewhere call collect (020) 8666 9025).

Many student travel agencies around the world issue ISICs, including STA Travel in Australia and New Zealand; Travel CUTS in Canada; USIT in Ireland and Northern Ireland; SASTS in South Africa; Campus Travel and STA Travel in the U.K.; and Council Travel, STA Travel, and via the web (www.counciltravel.com/idcards/index.htm) in the U.S. The card is valid from September of one year to December of the following year and costs AUS$15, CDN$15, or US$20. Applicants must be at least 12 years old and degree-seeking students of a secondary or post-secondary school. Because of the proliferation of phony ISICs, many airlines and some other services require additional proof of student identity, such as a school ID card or a signed letter from the registrar attesting to your student status that is stamped with the school seal. The **International Teacher Identity Card (ITIC)** offers the same insurance coverage and similar but limited discounts. The fee is AUS$13, UK£5, or US$20. For more information on these cards, contact the **International Student Travel Confederation (ISTC)**, Herengracht 479, 1017 BS Amsterdam, Netherlands (from abroad, call 31 20 421 28 00; fax 421 28 10; email istcinfo@istc.org; www.istc.org).

YOUTH IDENTIFICATION. The International Student Travel Confederation also issues a discount card to travelers who are under 25 but not students. Known as the International Youth Travel Card (IYTC; formerly the GO25 Card), this one-year card offers many of the same benefits as the ISIC, and most organizations that sell the ISIC also sell the IYTC. A brochure of discounts is free when you purchase the card. To apply, you will need either a copy of a birth certificate and a passport-sized photo with your name printed on the back, passport, or valid driver's license. The fee is US$20.

CUSTOMS

 THE EUROPEAN UNION AND THE TRAVELER. There are **no customs** at internal EU borders (travelers arriving in one EU country from another by air should take the blue channel when exiting the baggage claim), and travelers are free to transport whatever legal substances they like across the Union, provided they can demonstrate that it is for personal (i.e. non-commercial) use. In practice, this means quantities in excess of 800 cigarettes, 10L of spirits, 90L of wine (60L of sparkling wine) and 110L of beer—quite enough for most people. Correspondingly, on June 30, 1999, **duty-free** was abolished for travel among EU member states. Those arriving in the EU from outside will still have a duty-free allowance. January 1, 1999 saw the launch of the euro, a common currency for 11 of the EU nations (see **The Euro,** p. 44).

CUSTOMS: ENTERING GERMANY

Don't mention the war!
—Basil Fawlty (John Cleese)

Upon entering Germany, you must declare certain items from abroad and pay a duty on the value of those articles that exceed the allowance established by Germany's customs service. Keeping receipts for purchases made abroad will help establish values when you return. It is wise to make a list, including serial numbers, of any valuables that you carry with you from home; if you register this list with customs before your departure and have an official stamp it, you will avoid import duty charges and ensure an easy passage upon your return. Be especially careful to document items manufactured abroad. For information on a **Value Added Tax** refund, see **Taxes** (p. 48).

Unless you plan to import a BMW or a barnyard beast, you will probably pass right through the customs barrier with minimal to-do. Germany prohibits or restricts the importation of firearms, explosives, ammunition, fireworks, controlled substances, many plants and animals, lottery tickets, and obscene literature or films. To prevent problems with transporting **prescription drugs,** make sure that the bottles are clearly marked, and carry a copy of your prescription to show customs officials. When dealing with customs officers, do your utmost to be polite and look responsible.

Travelers may "import" gifts and commodities for personal use into Germany. For EU citizens, "personal use" is interpreted relatively freely, see **The European Union and the Traveler** (p. 42) for information. For non-EU citizens however, regulations are as follows: travelers may import 200 cigarettes, 100 cigarillos, 50 cigars, or 250g of smoking tobacco; 1L of spirits stronger than 44 proof, 2L of weaker spirits, or 2 liters of wines or liqueur; 50g of perfume and 0.25L toilet water; 500g of coffee and 200g of extracts. The total value of personal use goods cannot exceed DM350. You must be 17 or over to import tobacco and alcohol products. There are no regulations on the import or export of currency.

CUSTOMS: GOING HOME

Upon returning home, you must declare all articles acquired abroad and pay a **duty** on the value of articles that exceed the allowance established by your country's customs service. Goods and gifts purchased at **duty-free** shops abroad are not exempt from duty or sales tax at your point of return; you must declare these items as well. "Duty-free" merely means that you need not pay a tax in the country of purchase. For more specific information on customs requirements, contact the following information centers:

Australia: Australian Customs National Information Line (tel. 1 300 363 263; www.customs.gov.au).

Canada: Canadian Customs, 2265 St. Laurent Blvd., Ottawa, ON K1G 4K3 (tel. 613-993-0534 or 24hr. automated service 800-461-9999; www.revcan.ca).

Ireland: Collector of Customs and Excise, Custom House, Dublin 1 (tel. (01) 679 27 77; fax 671 20 21; email taxes@revenue.iol.ie; www.revenue.ie/customs.htm).

New Zealand: New Zealand Customhouse, 17-21 Whitmore St., Box 2218, Wellington (tel. (04) 473 6099; fax 473 7370; www.customs.govt.nz).

South Africa: Commissioner for Customs and Excise, Private Bag X47, Pretoria, 0001 (tel. (012) 314 99 11; fax 328 64 78).

United Kingdom: Her Majesty's Customs and Excise, Custom House, Nettleton Road, Heathrow Airport, Hounslow, Middlesex TW6 2LA (tel. (020) 8910 3602 or 8910 3566; fax 8910 3765; www.hmce.gov.uk).

United States: U.S. Customs Service, Box 7407, Washington D.C. 20044 (tel. 202-927-6724; www.customs.ustreas.gov).

MONEY

If you stay in hostels and prepare your own food, expect to spend anywhere from $25-50 per person per day. Hotels start at about $25 per night; a basic sit-down meal costs at least $6. Transportation and alcohol will increase these figures. Don't sacrifice your health or safety for a cheaper tab. If you plan to travel for more than a couple of days, you will need to keep handy a larger amount of cash than usual. Carrying money around, even in a money belt, is risky but necessary. Personal checks from home probably won't be accepted no matter how many forms of identification you have, and even traveler's checks may not be acceptable in some locations (see **Traveler's Checks,** p. 45). Members can cash personal checks at AmEx offices worldwide.

CURRENCY AND EXCHANGE

The **deutsche Mark** or **Deutschmark** (abbreviated DM) is the unit of currency in Germany. It is one of the most stable and respected currencies in the world; indeed, in most markets in Eastern Europe, "hard currency" means U.S. dollars and Deutschmarks exclusively. One DM equals 100 Pfennig (Pf). Coins come in 1, 2, 5, 10, and 50Pf, and DM1, 2, and 5 amounts. Bills come in DM5, 10, 20, 50, 100, 200, 500, and 1000 denominations, though DM5 bills are now rare. Although some (especially Americans) may think of minted metal disks as inconsequential pieces of aluminum, remember that a DM5 coin can easily buy you a meal. To make sure you're not getting duped, only accept bills with an embedded silver strip.

 THE EURO. On January 1, 1999, 11 countries of the European Union, including Germany, officially adopted the **euro (€)** as their common currency. Euro notes and coins will not be issued until January 1, 2002; until then, the Euro will exist only in electronic transactions and traveler's checks. On June 1, 2002, the Deutschmark will be entirely withdrawn from circulation and the euro will become the only legal currency in Germany. *Let's Go* lists all prices in Deutschmarks, as these will still be most relevant in 2000. However, all German businesses must by law quote prices in both currencies.

Travelers who will be passing through more than one nation in the euro-zone should note that exchange rates between the 11 national currencies were irrevocably fixed on January 1, 1999. Henceforth, banks and exchange kiosks will be obliged to interchange euro-zone currencies at the official rate and with **no commission,** though they may still charge a nominal service fee. Euro-denominated traveler's checks can also be used throughout the 11 euro nations and exchanged commission-free.

The currency chart below is based on published exchange rates as of August 1999.

THE DEUTSCHE MARK (DM)

US$1 = DM1.84	DM1 = US$0.55
CDN$1 = DM1.23	DM1 = CDN$0.82
UK£1 = DM2.97	DM1 = UK£0.34
IR£1 = DM2.48	DM1 = IR£0.40
AUS$1 = DM1.17	DM1 = AUS$0.86
NZ$1 = DM0.97	DM1 = NZ$1.03
SAR1 = DM0.30	DM1 = SAR3.32
€1 = DM1.96	DM1 = €0.51

As a general rule, it's cheaper to exchange money in Germany than at home. However, converting some money before you go will allow you to zip through the airport while others languish in exchange lines. It's a good idea to carry enough Deutschmarks to last for the first 24 to 72 hours of a trip to avoid getting stuck with no money after banking hours or on a holiday.

Watch out for commission rates and check newspapers for the standard rate of exchange. Banks generally have the best rates. A good rule of thumb is only to go to banks or tourist offices and exchange kiosks that have at most a 5% margin between their buy and sell prices. Since you lose money with each transaction, convert in large sums. Also, using an ATM card or a credit card (see p. 45) will often get you the best possible rates.

If you use traveler's checks or bills, carry some in small denominations (US$50 or less), especially for times when you are forced to exchange money at disadvantageous rates. However, it is good to carry a range of denominations since charges may be levied per check cashed.

TRAVELER'S CHECKS

All German banks cash traveler's checks, though the prevalence of ATMs (see below) may be a more convenient option. Large department stores and businesses in Germany will accept the checks for purchasing products, but for smaller stores and rural areas, you will need to cash the checks into Deutschmarks first. Traveler's checks are one of the safest means of carrying funds, since they can be refunded if stolen. Several agencies and banks sell them, usually for face value plus a small percentage commission. (Members of the American Automobile Association, and some banks and credit unions, can get American Express checks commission-free; see **Driving Permits and Insurance**, p. 74). **American Express** and **Visa** are the most widely recognized. If you're ordering checks do so well in advance, especially if you're requesting large sums. You can have checks issued directly in Marks.

Many agencies provide additional services such as toll-free refund hotlines abroad, emergency message services, and stolen credit card assistance. In order to collect a **refund for lost or stolen checks,** keep your check receipts separate from your checks and store them in a safe place or with a traveling companion. Record check numbers when you cash them, leave a list of check numbers with someone at home, and ask for a list of refund centers when you buy your checks. Never countersign your checks until you are ready to cash them, and always bring your passport with you when you plan to use the checks.

American Express: Call (0130) 85 31 00 in Germany; 800 251 902 in Australia; in New Zealand (0800) 441 068; in the U.K. (0800) 52 13 13; in the U.S. and Canada 800-221-7282. Elsewhere, call U.S. collect 1-801-964-6665; www.aexp.com. Checks can be purchased for a small fee (1-4%) at American Express Travel Service offices, banks, and American Automobile Association offices. AAA members (see p. 74) can buy checks commission-free. American Express offices cash their checks commission-free (except where prohibited by national governments), but often at slightly worse rates than banks. *Cheques for Two* can be signed by either of two people traveling together. The booklet *Traveler's Companion* lists travel office addresses and stolen check hotlines abroad.

Citicorp: Call 800-645-6556 in the U.S. and Canada; in Germany, call the London office at 44 20 7508 7007. Traveler's checks in 7 currencies. Commission 1-2%. Guaranteed hand delivery of traveler's checks when a refund location is not convenient.

Visa: Call 800-227-6811 in the U.S.; in the U.K. (0800) 895 078; from elsewhere, call 44 1733 318 949 and reverse the charges. Any of the above numbers can tell you the location of the nearest office.

CREDIT CARDS

Credit cards are generally accepted in Germany, and major credit cards—**MasterCard** and **Visa**—can be used to extract cash advances in Deutschmarks from associated banks and teller machines throughout Germany. **Eurocard,** which is affiliated with MasterCard, is preferred in Germany, and is more widely accepted than Visa. Credit card companies get the wholesale exchange rate, which is generally 5% better than the retail rate used by banks and other currency exchange establishments. **American Express** cards also work in some ATMs, as well as at AmEx offices and major airports. All such machines require a **Personal Identification Number (PIN).** You must ask your credit card company for a PIN before you leave; without it, you will be unable to withdraw cash with your credit card out-

ESSENTIALS

Money From Home In Minutes.

If you're stuck for cash on your travels, don't panic. Millions of people trust Western Union to transfer money in minutes to 165 countries and over 50,000 locations worldwide. Our record of safety and reliability is second to none. For more information, call Western Union: USA 1-800-325-6000, Canada 1-800-235-0000. Wherever you are, you're never far from home.

www.westernunion.com

WESTERN UNION | MONEY TRANSFER

The fastest way to send money worldwide.

side your home country. If you already have a PIN, check with the company to make sure it will work in Germany. Credit cards offer an array of other services, from insurance to emergency assistance. Check with your company to find out what is covered.

CREDIT CARD COMPANIES. Visa (U.S. tel. 800-336-8472), **MasterCard,** and **Euro-card** (both U.S. tel. 800-307-7309) are issued in cooperation with individual banks and some other organizations. **American Express (AmEx)** (tel. 800-843-2273) has an annual fee of up to US$55, depending on the card. Cardholder services include the cashing of personal checks at AmEx offices, a 24-hour hotline with medical and legal assistance in emergencies (tel. 800-554-2639 in U.S. and Canada; from abroad call U.S. collect 1-202-554-2639), and the American Express Travel Service. Benefits include assistance in changing airline, hotel, and car rental reservations, baggage loss and flight insurance, sending telegrams, and holding mail at one of the more than 1,700 AmEx offices around the world.

Visa TravelMoney (in Germany call (0800) 810 99 10) is a system allowing you to access money from any Visa ATM, common throughout Germany. You deposit an amount before you travel (plus a small administrative fee) and withdraw up to that sum. The cards give you the safety of not having to carry too much cash, the same favorable exchange rate for withdrawals as a regular Visa, and are especially useful if you plan to be traveling through many countries. Check with your local bank to see if it issues TravelMoney cards. **Visa Road Cash** (tel. 1-877-762-3227; www.roadcash.com) issues cards in the U.S. with a minimum US$300 deposit.

CASH CARDS

24-hour ATMs (Automated Teller Machines) are widespread in Germany. Practically all German cities and towns provide cash machine services, and withdrawing funds directly in German currency (your bank statements will read in your home currency) is convenient. Depending on the system that your home bank uses, you can probably access your own personal bank account whenever you need money. ATMs get the same wholesale exchange rate as credit cards. Despite these perks, do some research before relying too heavily on automation. There is often a limit on the amount of money you can withdraw per day (usually about US$500, depending on the type of card and account), and computer networks sometimes fail. If you're traveling from the U.S. or Canada, **memorize your PIN code in numeral form** since machines elsewhere often don't have letters on their keys. Also, if your PIN is longer than four digits, ask your bank whether the first four digits will work, or whether you need a new number. Also inquire as to the amount your bank will charge for each transaction.

The two major international money networks are **Cirrus** (U.S. tel. 800-4-CIRRUS (424-7787)) and **PLUS** (U.S. tel. 800-843-7587). To locate ATMs in Germany, use www.visa.com/pd/atm or www.mastercard.com/atm; both web pages will indicate which money network is used at a given machine.

 ATM ALERT. All Automated Teller Machines require a four-digit **Personal Identification Number (PIN),** which credit cards in the United States do not always carry. In this event, ask your credit card company to assign one before you leave. Without this PIN, you will be unable to withdraw cash with your credit card abroad.

GETTING MONEY FROM HOME

American Express: Cardholders can withdraw cash from their checking accounts at any major AmEx office and many of its representatives' offices, up to US$1000 every 21 days. AmEx also offers Express Cash at any of their ATMs in Germany. Express Cash withdrawals are automatically debited from the cardmember's checking account or line of credit. To enroll in Express Cash, cardmembers should call 800-CASH NOW (227-4669) in the U.S.; outside the U.S. call collect 1-336-668-5041. The AmEx national number in Germany is 336 63 93 11 11.

Western Union: Travelers from the U.S., Canada, and the U.K. can wire money abroad through Western Union's international money transfer services. In the U.S., call 800-325-6000; in the U.K., (0800) 833 833; in Canada, 800-235-0000; in Germany, 19 33 33 28. The rates for sending cash are generally US$10 cheaper than with a credit card, and the money is usually available at the place you're sending it to within an hour.

U.S. State Department (U.S. citizens only): In emergencies, U.S. citizens can have money sent via the State Department. For US$15, they will forward money within hours to the nearest consular office, which will disburse it according to instructions. The office serves only Americans in the direst of straits; non-American travelers should contact their embassies for information on wiring cash. Check with the State Department or the nearest U.S. embassy or consulate for the quickest way to have money sent. or contact the Overseas Citizens Service, American Citizens Services, Consular Affairs, Room 4811, U.S. Department of State, Washington, D.C. 20520 (Tel. 202-647-5225; nights, Sundays, and holidays 647-4000; fax (on demand only) 647-3000; travel.state.gov.)

TIPPING AND BARGAINING

Germans generally round up DM1-2 when tipping. However, tipping is not practiced as liberally as it is elsewhere—most Germans only tip in restaurants and bars, or when they are the beneficiary of a service, such as a taxi ride. Note that tips in Germany are not left lying on the table, but handed directly to the server when you pay. If you don't want any change, say *Das stimmt so* (DAHS SHTIMT ZO). Germans rarely bargain except at flea markets.

TAXES

Most goods and services bought in Germany will automatically include a Value Added Tax **(VAT)** of 15%. In German, this is called the *Mehrwertsteuer* (MwSt). Non-EU citizens can usually get the VAT refunded for large purchases of goods (not services). At the point of purchase, ask for a Tax-Free Shopping Cheque, then have it stamped at customs upon leaving the country or at a customs authority. (You will have to present the goods, receipt, and cheque.) The goods you have purchased must remain unused until you leave the country.

SAFETY AND SECURITY

EMERGENCY TELEPHONE NUMBERS	Police: 110 Fire/Ambulance: 112 Medical emergency: 115

Germany is on par with the rest of Western Europe when it comes to safety. Violent crime is rare, with incidents largely confined to urban areas. German modes of conduct are on the reserved side, so crime is more likely to be encountered in the form of theft, rather than assault. After reunification, incidents of crime against foreigners in Eastern Germany were more frequent, largely as a result of economic depression (see **Reunification and its Aftermath**, p. 21). Former GDR citizens are now more acclimated to travelers' presence, but right-wing groups maintain an uncomfortable presence in disadvantaged areas.

BLENDING IN

Tourists are particularly vulnerable to crime because they often carry large amounts of cash and are not as street savvy as locals. To avoid unwanted attention, try to blend in as much as possible—avoid clothing emblazoned with name brands and university logos. Western styles are the norm in Germany, though,

Violent crime is less common in Germany than in most countries, but it exists, especially in big cities like Frankfurt and Berlin, as well as economically depressed regions of the East. Most of Germany's neo-Nazis and skinheads subscribe to the traditional skinhead uniform of flight jackets worn over white shortsleeve shirts and tight jeans rolled up high to reveal high-cut combat boots. Skinheads also tend to follow a shoelace code, with white supremacists and neo-Nazis wearing white laces, while anti-gay skinheads wear pink laces. Left-wing, anti-Nazi "S.H.A.R.P.s" (Skinheads Against Racial Prejudice) also exist; they favor red laces.

despite the image of a *lederhosen*-clad native. The gawking camera-toter is a more obvious target than the low-profile traveler. Familiarize yourself with your surroundings before setting out; if you must check a map on the street, duck into a café or shop. If you are traveling alone, be sure that someone at home knows your itinerary, and **never admit that you're traveling alone.**

EXPLORING

Find out about unsafe areas from locals or, from the manager of your hotel or hostel. You may want to carry a **whistle** to scare off attackers or attract attention; memorize the emergency number of the city or area (see above). Whenever possible, *Let's Go: Germany* warns of unsafe neighborhoods and areas, but there are good general tips to follow. When walking at night, stick to busy, well-lit streets and avoid dark alleyways. Do not attempt to cross through parks, parking lots, or other large, deserted areas. Buildings in disrepair, vacant lots, and unpopulated areas are all bad signs. The distribution of people can reveal a great deal about the relative safety of the area; look for children playing, women walking in the open, and other signs of an active community.

GETTING AROUND

If you are driving, make sure to learn local driving signals and signs (see **Getting Around: By Car**, p. 73). Wearing a seatbelt is the law in Germany, and children should sit in the rear seat; children under 40lbs. (17kg) should ride only in a specially-designed carseat, available for a small fee from most car rental agencies. Study route maps before you hit the road. If you plan on spending a lot of time on the road, you may want to bring spare parts. For long drives in desolate areas invest in a cellular phone and a roadside assistance program (see p. 74). Be sure to park your vehicle in a garage or well-traveled area. The legal cut-off for blood alcohol levels in Germany is 0.08%. German police strictly enforce driving laws.

Let's Go does not recommend **hitchhiking** under any circumstances, particularly for women—see **Getting Around**, p. 71 for more information. Germany has **Mitfahrzentralen**, however, which are a regulated system for ride shares (see **Getting Around: By Car**, p. 73).

SELF DEFENSE

There is no sure-fire set of precautions that will protect you from all the situations you might encounter while traveling. A good self-defense course will give you concrete ways to react to different types of aggression. **Impact, Prepare, and Model Mugging** can refer you to local self-defense courses in the United States (tel. 800-345-5425) and Vancouver, Canada (tel. 604-878-3838). Workshop (2-3 hours) start at US$50 and full courses run US$350-500. Both women and men are welcome.

FURTHER INFORMATION

The following government offices provide travel information and advisories by telephone or on their websites:

Australian Department of Foreign Affairs and Trade. Tel. (02) 6261 1111. www.dfat.gov.au.

Canadian Department of Foreign Affairs and International Trade (DFAIT). Tel. 800-267-8376 or (613) 944-4000 from Ottawa. www.dfait-maeci.gc.ca. Call for their free booklet, *Bon Voyage...But.*

United Kingdom Foreign and Commonwealth Office. Tel. (020) 7238 4503. www.fco.gov.uk.

United States Department of State. Tel. 202-647-5225; http://travel.state.gov. Call 202-512-1800 for their publication, *A Safe Trip Abroad.*

FINANCIAL SECURITY

PROTECTING YOUR VALUABLES

Don't keep all your valuables in one place. **Photocopies** of important documents allow you to recover them in case they are lost or filched. Label every piece of luggage both inside and out. **Don't put a wallet with money in your back pocket.** Never count your money in public and carry as little as possible. If you carry a purse, buy a sturdy one with a secure clasp, and carry it crosswise on the side, away from the street with the clasp against you. Secure packs with small combination padlocks which slip through the two zippers. A **money belt** is the best way to carry cash, available at most camping supply stores. A nylon, zippered pouch with a belt that sits inside the waist of your pants or skirt combines convenience and security. A **neck pouch** is equally safe, although far less accessible. Refrain from pulling out your neck pouch in public; if you must, be very discreet. Avoid keeping anything precious in a fanny-pack (even if it's worn on your stomach): your valuables will be highly visible and easy to steal. Keep some money separate from the rest to use in an emergency or in case of theft.

CON ARTISTS AND PICKPOCKETS

Among the more colorful aspects of large cities are **con artists.** Con artists and hustlers often work in groups, and children are among the most effective. They possess an innumerable range of ruses. Be aware of certain classics: sob stories that require money, rolls of bills "found" on the street, mustard spilled (or saliva spit) onto your shoulder distracting you for enough time to snatch your bag. Be especially suspicious in unexpected situations. Do not respond or make eye contact, walk away quickly, and keep a solid grip on your belongings. Contact the police if a hustler is particularly insistent or aggressive.

In city crowds and especially on public transportation, **pickpockets** are amazingly deft at their craft. Also, be alert in public telephone booths. If you must say your calling card number, do so very quietly; if you punch it in, make sure no one can look over your shoulder.

ACCOMMODATIONS AND TRANSPORTATION

Never leave your belongings unattended; crime occurs in even the most demure-looking hostel or hotel. If you feel unsafe, look for places with either a curfew or night attendant. *Let's Go* lists locker availability in the hostels and train stations of larger cities, but you'll need your own **padlock.** Lockers are useful if you plan on sleeping outdoors or don't want to lug everything with you, but don't store valuables in them. Most hotels also provide lock boxes free or for a minimal fee.

Be particularly careful on **buses,** carry your backpack in front of you where you can see it, don't check baggage on trains, and don't trust anyone to "watch your bag for a second." Thieves thrive on **trains;** professionals wait for tourists to fall asleep and then carry off everything they can. When traveling in pairs, sleep in alternating shifts; when alone, use good judgement in selecting a train compartment: never stay in an empty one, and use a lock to secure your pack to the luggage rack. Keep important documents and other valuables on your person and try to sleep on top bunks with your luggage stored above you or in bed with you.

If you travel by **car,** try not to leave valuable possessions—such as radios or luggage—in it while you are away. If your tape deck or radio is removable, hide it in the trunk or take it with you. Similarly, hide baggage in the trunk.

DRUGS AND ALCOHOL

A meek "I didn't know it was illegal" will not suffice. Remember that you are subject to the laws of the country in which you travel, not to those of your home country, and it is your responsibility to familiarize yourself with these laws before leaving. If you carry insulin, syringes, or any other **prescription drugs** while you travel, it is vital to have a copy of the prescriptions themselves and a note from a doctor, both readily accessible at country borders. **Avoid public drunkenness;** it can jeopardize your safety and earn the disdain of locals. The drinking age in Germany is 16 for beer and wine and 18 for spirits, although it is skimpily enforced. The maximum permissible blood alcohol level while driving in Germany is 0.08%.

Needless to say, **illegal drugs** are best avoided altogether; the average sentence for possession outside the U.S. is about seven years. Buying or selling narcotics may lead to a prison sentence. In 1994, the German High Court ruled that while possession of marijuana or hashish was still illegal, possession of "small quantities for personal consumption" was not prosecutable. Each *Land* has interpreted the quantities involved in "personal consumption" differently, with possession of 3 to 30 grams *de facto* decriminalized at publication time. The more liberal areas, notably Berlin and Hamburg, tend toward the higher end of this spectrum, while the more conservative states of Bayern and Eastern Germany afford less leniency. Those interested should find out what the latest law is, including what quantities of possession are acceptable in the various *Länder*, before filling a backpack with hash bricks.

The worst thing you can possibly do is carry drugs across an international border; not only could you end up in prison, you could be blessed with a "Drug Trafficker" stamp on your passport for the rest of your life. If arrested, call your country's consulate. Embassies may not be willing to help those arrested on drug charges. Refuse to carry even an apparent nun's excess luggage onto a plane; you're more likely to wind up in jail for possession of drugs than in heaven.

HEALTH

Germany has no exceptional health issues. No vaccinations are required for a visit, unless you're traveling from a region which is currently infected. Check with the German embassy or consulate and with your travel agent if you're coming from an area with health issues, such as Latin America, Africa, or Asia; an inoculation against yellow fever is the most likely requirement. Longer stays may require other certification (see **AIDS, HIV, and STDs,** p. 55).

Common sense is the simplest prescription for good health while you travel. Travelers complain most often about their feet and their gut, so take precautionary measures: drink lots of fluids to prevent dehydration and constipation, wear sturdy, broken-in shoes and clean socks, and use talcum powder to keep your feet dry. To minimize the effects of jet lag, "reset" your body's clock by adopting the time of your destination as soon as you board the plane.

Obtain a full supply of any necessary medication before the trip, since matching a prescription to a foreign equivalent is not always easy, safe, or possible. To get a prescription filled in Germany you must go to an *Apotheke;* a *Drogerie* sells only toilet articles. Most German cities have a rotating all-night pharmacy schedule to ensure that services are available 24 hours a day. Refer to the **Practical Information** section of each particular city for the location of a convenient pharmacy. In dire straits, check the front door of the *Apotheke* nearest a city's train station for a schedule of rotating all-night pharmacies. Carry up-to-date, legible prescriptions or a statement from your doctor, especially if you use insulin, a syringe, or a narcotic. While traveling, keep all medication with you in your carry-on luggage.

BEFORE YOU GO

Preparation can help minimize the likelihood of contracting a disease and maximize the chances of receiving effective health care in the event of an emergency. For minor health problems, bring a compact **first-aid kit**, including bandages, aspirin or other pain killer, antibiotic cream, a thermometer, a Swiss army knife with tweezers, moleskin, decongestant for colds, motion sickness remedy, medicine for diarrhea or stomach problems (Pepto Bismol or Immodium), sunscreen, insect repellent, burn ointment, and a syringe for emergency medical purposes (get a letter of explanation from your doctor). **Contact lens** wearers should bring an extra pair, a copy of the prescription, a pair of glasses, extra solution, and eyedrops. Those who use heat disinfection might consider switching to chemical cleansers for the duration of the trip.

In your **passport,** write the names of any people you wish to be contacted in case of a medical emergency, and also list any **allergies** or medical conditions you want doctors to be aware of. Allergy sufferers might want to obtain a full supply of any necessary medication before the trip. Carry up-to-date, legible prescriptions or a statement from your doctor stating the medication's trade name, manufacturer, chemical name, and dosage.

While Germany has no vaccination requirements for foreigners entering the country from developed areas (see above), you should take a look at your immunization records before you go. Travelers over two years old should be sure that the following vaccines are up to date: MMR (for measles, mumps, and rubella); DTaP or Td (for diptheria, tetanus, and pertussis); OPV (for polio); HbCV (for haemophilus influenza B); and HBV (for hepatitus B). Check with a doctor for guidance through this maze of injections.

USEFUL ORGANIZATIONS

The U.S. **Centers for Disease Control and Prevention (CDC)** (tel. 888-232-3299; www.cdc.gov) is an excellent source of information for travelers around the world and maintains an international fax information service for travelers. The U.S. **State Department** (http://travel.state.gov) compiles Consular Information Sheets on health, entry requirements, and other issues for all countries of the world. For quick information on travel warnings, call the **Overseas Citizens' Services** (tel. (202) 647-5225; after-hours 647-4000). To receive the same Consular Information Sheets by fax, dial (202) 647-3000 from a fax and follow the recorded instructions.

For detailed information and tips on travel health, including a country-by-country overview of diseases, check out the **International Travel Health Guide,** Stuart Rose, MD (Travel Medicine, $20). Information is also available at **Travel Medicine's** website (www.travmed.com).For general health information, contact the **American Red Cross.** The ARC publishes *First-Aid and Safety Handbook* (US$5) available by calling or writing to the American Red Cross, 285 Columbus Ave., Boston, MA 02116-5114. (Tel. 800-564-1234. Open M-F 8:30am-4:30pm.)

MEDICAL ASSISTANCE ON THE ROAD

Germany has generally excellent medical care. Most doctors speak English, and the hospital system is largely public; private practices are smaller clinics, and less common.

EU citizens in possession of an E11 form can get free first aid and emergency services. If you are concerned about being able to access medical support while traveling, contact one of these two services: **Global Emergency Medical Services' (GEMS)** (tel. 800-860-1111; fax 770-475-0058; www.globalems.com) *MedPass* provides 24-hour international medical assistance and support coordinated through registered nurses who have online access to your medical information, your primary physician, and a worldwide network of screened, credentialed English-speaking doctors and hospitals. Subscribers also receive a personal medical record that contains vital information in case of emergencies, and GEMS will pay for medical evacuation if necessary. Prices start at about US$35 for a 30-day trip and run up to about $100 for annual services. The **International Association for Medical Assistance to Travelers (IAMAT)** has free membership and offers a directory of English-speaking doctors around the world who treat members for a set fee schedule, as well as detailed charts on immunization requirements, climate, and sanitation. Chapters include: **U.S.,** 417 Center St., Lewiston, NY 14092 (tel. 716-754-4883; fax 519-836-3412; email iamat@sentex.net; www.sentex.net/~iamat); **Canada,** 40 Regal Road, Guelph, ON N1K 1B5 (tel. 519-836-0102) or 1287 St. Clair Avenue West, Toronto, ON M6E 1B8 (tel. 416-652-0137; fax 519-836-3412); **New Zealand,** P.O. Box 5049, Christchurch 5 (fax (03) 352 4630; email iamat@chch.planet.org.nz).

Doctors may expect you to pay cash for immediate health services. If your regular **insurance** policy does not cover travel abroad, you may wish to purchase additional coverage. With the exception of Medicare/Medicaid, most health insurance plans cover members' medical emergencies during trips abroad; check with your insurance carrier. See **Insurance,** p. 56).

MEDICAL CONDITIONS

Those with medical conditions may want to obtain a **Medic Alert** identification tag (US$35 the first year, $15 annually thereafter), which identifies the condition and gives a 24-hour collect-call information number. Contact the Medic Alert Foundation, 2323 Colorado Ave., Turlock, CA 95382 (tel. 800-825-3785; www.medicalert.org). Diabetics can contact the **American Diabetes Association,** 1660 Duke St., Alexandria, VA 22314 (tel. 800-232-3472), to receive a copy of the article "Travel and Diabetes" and a diabetic ID card, which carries messages in 18 languages explaining the carrier's diabetic status. If you are **HIV** positive, contact the Bureau of Consular Affairs, #4811, Department of State, Washington, D.C. 20520 (tel. 202-647-1488; auto-fax 647-3000; travel.state.gov).

ENVIRONMENTAL HAZARDS

Heat exhaustion, characterized by **dehydration** and salt deficiency, can lead to fatigue, headaches, and wooziness. Avoid heat exhaustion by drinking plenty of clear fluids and eating salty foods, like crackers. Always drink enough liquids to keep your urine clear. Alcoholic beverages are dehydrating, as are coffee, strong tea, and caffeinated sodas. Wear a hat, sunglasses, and a lightweight longsleeve shirt in hot sun. If you are prone to **sunburn,** bring sunscreen with you and apply it liberally and often. If you are planning on spending time near the water or in the snow, you are at risk of getting burned, even through clouds. Protect your eyes with good sunglasses. If you get sunburned, drink more fluids than usual and apply calamine or an aloe-based lotion.

A rapid drop in body temperature is the clearest warning sign of **overexposure to cold.** Victims may also shiver, feel exhausted, have poor coordination or slurred speech, hallucinate, or suffer amnesia. Seek medical help, and *do not let hypothermia victims fall asleep*—their body temperature will continue to drop and they may die. To avoid hypothermia, keep dry, wear layers, and stay out of the wind. In wet weather, wool and synthetics such as pile retain heat. Most other fabric, especially cotton, will make you colder. When the temperature is below freezing, watch for **frostbite.** If a region of skin turns white, waxy, and cold, do not rub the area. Drink warm beverages, get dry, and slowly warm the area with dry fabric or steady body contact, until a doctor can be found. Travelers to **high altitudes** must allow their bodies a couple of days to adjust to lower oxygen levels in the air before exerting themselves. Alcohol is more potent at high elevations. High altitudes mean that ultraviolet rays are stronger, and the risk of sunburn is therefore greater, even in cold weather.

PREVENTING DISEASE

INSECT-BORNE DISEASES

Many diseases are transmitted by insects—mainly mosquitoes, fleas, ticks, and lice. Be aware of insects in wet or forested areas, while hiking, and especially while camping. **Mosquitoes** are most active from dusk to dawn. Use insect repellents, such as DEET. Wear long pants and long sleeves, and buy a mosquito net. Wear shoes and socks, and tuck long pants into socks. Soak or spray your gear with permethrin, which is licensed in the U.S. for use on clothing. Natural repellents can be useful supplements: taking vitamin B-12 pills regularly can eventually make you smelly to insects, as can garlic pills. Calamine lotion or topical cortisones may stop insect bites from itching, as can a bath with a half-cup of baking soda or oatmeal. **Ticks**—responsible for Lyme and other diseases—can be particularly dangerous in rural and forested regions. Pause periodically while walking to brush off ticks using a fine-toothed comb on your neck and scalp. Do not try to remove ticks by burning them or coating them with petroleum jelly.

Tick-borne encephalitis, a viral infection of the central nervous system, is transmitted during the summer by tick bites, and also by consumption of unpasteurized dairy products. The disease occurs most often in wooded areas. Symptoms can range from nothing to headaches and flu-like symptoms to swelling of the brain (encephalitis). A vaccine is available in Europe, but the immunization schedule is impractical for most tourists, and the risk of contracting the disease is relatively low, especially if you take precautions against tick bites.

Lyme disease, also carried by ticks, is a bacterial infection marked by a circular bull's-eye rash of 2in. or more that appears around the bite. Other symptoms include fever, headache, tiredness, and aches and pains. Antibiotics are effective if administered early. Left untreated, Lyme can cause problems in joints, the heart, and the nervous system. If you find a tick attached to your skin, grasp the tick's head parts with tweezers as close to your skin as possible and apply slow, steady traction. If you remove a tick within 24 hours, you greatly reduce your risk of infection.

FOOD- AND WATER-BORNE DISEASES

Prevention is the best cure: be sure that everything you eat is cooked properly and that the water you drink is clean. Germans' compulsive tendencies extend into the culinary realm, and most food is prepared under strictly-monitored sanitary conditions. Use your own judgment when it comes to *Imbiß* (fast food) fare—some establishments are cleaner than others. German tap water is generally safe to drink except in the most polluted areas of the former GDR, though most Germans prefer bottled mineral water.

Traveler's diarrhea results from drinking untreated water or eating uncooked foods. It can last three to seven days. Symptoms include nausea, bloating, urgency, and malaise. Eat quick-energy, non-sugary foods with protein and carbohydrates to keep your strength up. Over-the-counter remedies (such as Pepto Bismol or Immodium) may counteract the problems, but they can complicate serious infections. The most dangerous side effect of diarrhea is dehydration; the simplest and most effective anti-dehydration formula is 8 oz. of water with a ½ tsp. of sugar or honey and a pinch of salt. Soft drinks without caffeine or salted crackers are also good. Down several of these remedies a day, rest, and wait for the disease to run its course. If you develop a fever or your symptoms don't go away after four or five days, consult a doctor. If children develop traveler's diarrhea, consult a doctor immediately.

OTHER INFECTIOUS DISEASES

Rabies is transmitted through the saliva of infected animals. It is fatal if untreated. Avoid contact with animals, especially strays. If you are bitten, wash the wound thoroughly and seek immediate medical care. Once you begin to show symptoms (thirst and muscle spasms), the disease is in its terminal stage. If possible, try to locate the animal that bit you to determine whether it does indeed have rabies. A rabies vaccine is available but is only semi-effective. Three shots must be administered over one year.

Hepatitis B is a viral infection of the liver transmitted through the transfer of bodily fluids, by sharing needles, or by having unprotected sex. A person may not begin to show symptoms until many years after infection. The CDC recommends the Hepatitis B vaccination for health-care workers and sexually active travelers. Vaccination consists of a 3-shot series given over a period of time, and should begin 6 months before traveling.

Hepatitis C is like Hepatitis B, but the modes of transmission are different. Intravenous drug users, those with occupational exposure to blood, hemodialysis patients, or recipients of blood transfusions are at the highest risk, but the disease can also be spread through sexual contact and sharing of items like razors and toothbrushes, which may have traces of blood on them.

AIDS, HIV, AND STDS

Acquired Immune Deficiency Syndrome (AIDS) is a continuing problem around the world. The World Health Organization estimates that there are around 30 million people infected with the HIV virus; women now represent 40% of all new HIV infections.

The easiest mode of HIV transmission is through direct blood-to-blood contact with an HIV-positive person; *never* share intravenous drug, tattooing, or other needles. The most common mode of transmission is sexual intercourse. Health professionals recommend the use of latex condoms. Since it isn't always easy to buy condoms when traveling, take a supply with you before you depart for your trip. Germany can require the screening of incoming travelers, primarily those planning extended visits for work or study. For more information on AIDS, call the **U.S. Centers for Disease Control's** 24-hour hotline at 800-342-2437. In Europe, contact the **World Health Organization,** Attn: Global Program on AIDS, Avenue Appia 20, 1211 Geneva 27, Switzerland (tel. (44 22) 791 21 11; fax 791 31 11), for statistical material on AIDS internationally. Council's brochure, *Travel Safe: AIDS and International Travel*, is available at all Council Travel offices and at their website (www.ciee.org/study/safety/travelsafe.htm).

Sexually transmitted diseases (STDs) such as gonorrhea, chlamydia, genital warts, syphilis, and herpes are easier to catch than HIV, and some can be just as deadly. **Hepatitis B** and **C** are also serious sexually-transmitted diseases (see **Other Infectious Diseases,** above). It's a wise idea to examine your partner's genitals before you have sex. Warning signs for STDs include: swelling, sores, bumps, or blisters on sex organs, rectum, or mouth; burning and pain during urination and bowel movements; itching around sex organs; swelling or redness in the throat, flu-like symptoms with fever, chills, and aches. If these symptoms develop, see a doctor immediately. When having sex, condoms may protect you from certain STDs, but oral or even tactile contact can lead to transmission.

WOMEN'S HEALTH

Women traveling in unsanitary conditions are vulnerable to **urinary tract** and **bladder infections,** common and severely uncomfortable bacterial diseases that cause a burning sensation and painful and sometimes frequent urination. To try to avoid these infections, drink plenty of clean water and juice rich in vitamin C, and urinate frequently, especially after intercourse. Untreated, these infections can lead to kidney problems, sterility, and even death. If symptoms persist, see a doctor.

Women are also susceptible to **vaginal yeast infections,** a treatable but uncomfortable illness likely to flare up in hot and humid climates. Wearing loosely fitting trousers or a skirt and cotton underwear will help. Yeast infections can be treated with an over-the-counter remedy like Monostat or Gynelotrimin; an *Apotheke* can hook you up with the German equivalents, which are stronger, in many cases, than their American counterparts. Bring supplies from home if you are prone to infection, as they may be difficult to find on the road. Some travelers opt for a natural alternative such as plain yogurt and lemon juice douche if other remedies are unavailable. Women on the pill should bring enough to allow for possible loss or extended stays. Bring a prescription, since forms of the pill vary a good deal. **Contraceptive devices** are in plentiful supply.

Women seeking an **abortion** while abroad should contact the **International Planned Parenthood Federation,** European Regional Office, Regent's College Inner Circle, Regent's Park, London NW1 4NS (tel. 44 20 7487 7900; fax 7487 7950), for more information.

For further reading on women's health and travel, peruse *Handbook for Women Travellers*, by Maggie and Gemma Moss (Piatkus Books, US$15).

INSURANCE

Travel insurance generally covers four basic areas: medical problems, property loss, trip cancellation/interruption, and emergency evacuation. Although your regular insurance policies may well extend to travel-related accidents, consider purchasing travel insurance if the cost of potential trip cancellation/interruption is greater than you can absorb.

Medical insurance often covers costs incurred abroad; check with your provider. **Medicare does not cover foreign travel.** Canadians are protected by their home province's health insurance plan for up to 90 days after leaving the country; check with the provincial Ministry of Health or Health Plan Headquarters for details. **Homeowners' insurance** (or your family's coverage) often covers theft during travel and loss of travel documents up to US$500.

ISIC and **ITIC** provide basic insurance benefits, including US$100 per day of in-hospital sickness for a maximum of 60 days, US$3000 of accident-related medical reimbursement, and US$25,000 for emergency medical transport (see **Identification, p. 41**). Cardholders have access to a toll-free 24-hour helpline whose multilingual staff can provide assistance in medical, legal, and financial emergencies overseas. (Tel. 800-626-2427 in the U.S. and Canada; elsewhere call the U.S. collect 1-713-267-2525.) **American Express** (tel. 800-528-4800) grants most cardholders automatic car rental insurance (collision and theft, but not liability) and ground travel accident coverage of US$100,000 on flight purchases made with the card. Prices for travel insurance purchased separately generally run about US$50 per week for full coverage, while trip cancellation/interruption may be purchased separately at a rate of about US$5.50 per US$100 of coverage.

INSURANCE PROVIDERS. Council and **STA** (see p. 67) offer a range of plans that can supplement basic insurance coverage. Other private insurance providers in the **U.S. and Canada** include **Access America** (tel. 800-284-8300; fax 804-673-1491); **Berkely Group/Carefree Travel Insurance** (tel. 800-323-3149 or 516-294-0220; fax 294-1095; info@berkely.com; www.berkely.com); **Globalcare Travel Insurance** (tel. 800-821-2488; fax 781-592-7720; www.globalcare-cocco.com); and **Travel Assistance International** (tel. 800-821-2828 or 202-828-5894; fax 202-828-5896; email wassist@aol.com; www.worldwide-assistance.com). Providers in the **U.K.** include **Campus Travel** (tel. (01865) 258 000; fax (01865) 792 378) and **Columbus Travel Insurance** (tel. (020) 7375 0011; fax 7375 0022). In **Australia,** try **CIC Insurance** (tel. 9202 8000).

PACKING

Though German climate is temperate, planning trips to the northernmost islands, ascending the Bavarian Alps or expecting the inevitable shower are cause for particular packing consideration. **Pack light:** a good rule is to lay out only what you absolutely need, then take half the clothes and twice the money. Don't forget the obvious things: it's always a good idea to bring a rain jacket (Gore-Tex is a miracle fabric that's both waterproof and breathable), a warm jacket or wool sweater, and sturdy shoes and thick socks. Remember that wool will keep you warm even when soaked through, whereas wet cotton is colder than wearing nothing at all. You may also want to add one all-black ensemble and a nicer pair of shoes for clubbing if you have the room. If you are doing a lot of hiking, see **Camping and Hiking Equipment,** p. 62.

LUGGAGE

If you plan to cover most of your itinerary by foot, a sturdy **frame backpack** is unbeatable. **Internal-frame packs** mold better to your back, keep a lower center of gravity, and can flex adequately on difficult hikes that require a lot of bending and maneuvering. **External-frame packs** are more comfortable for long hikes over even terrain—like city streets—since they keep the weight higher and distribute it more evenly. Look for a pack with a strong, padded hip belt to transfer weight from your shoulders to your hips. Good packs cost anywhere from US$150 to US$500. Before you leave, pack your bag, strap it on, and imagine yourself walking uphill on hot asphalt for three hours; this should give you a sense of how important it is to pack lightly. Organizations that sell packs through mail-order are listed on p. 62.

Toting a **suitcase** or **trunks** is fine if you plan to live in one or two cities and explore from there, but a very bad idea if you're going to be moving around a lot. Make sure suitcases have wheels and consider how much they weigh even when empty. Hard-sided luggage is more durable but more weighty and cumbersome. Soft-sided luggage should have a PVC frame, a strong lining to resist bad weather and rough handling, and its seams should be triple-stitched for durability. In addition to your main vessel, a small backpack, rucksack, or courier bag may be useful as a **daypack** for sight-seeing expeditions; it doubles as an airplane **carry-on.** An empty, lightweight **duffel bag** packed inside your luggage may also be useful. Once abroad, fill your luggage with purchases and keep your dirty clothes in the duffel.

SLEEPSACKS

Some youth hostels require that you rent their sheets, but you can avoid linen charges by making the requisite sleepsack yourself: fold a full size sheet in half the long way, then sew it closed along the open long side and one of the short sides. Sleepsacks can also be bought at any Hostelling International outlet store. In some areas of Bavaria, the Thüringer Wald, and the Sächsiche Schweiz, hostels are at high altitudes; it can be useful to use a sleepsack in addition to the linen provided.

WASHING CLOTHES

Let's Go: Germany provides information on laundromats, called *Wäschereien,* in the **Practical Information** listings for larger cities, but it's cheaper to use a sink. Bring a bar or tube of detergent soap, a small rubber ball to stop up the sink, and a travel clothes line.

ELECTRIC CURRENT

In Germany, electricity is 220 volts AC, enough to fry any 110V North American appliance; sockets only accept a two-prong plug. Visit a hardware store for an adapter (which changes the shape of the plug) and a converter (which changes the voltage). Don't make the mistake of using only an adapter unless appliance instructions explicitly state otherwise.

CONTACT LENSES

Machines which heat-disinfect contact lenses will require a small converter (about US$20) to 220 volts AC (see above). Consider switching temporarily to a chemical disinfection system, but check with your lens dispenser to see if it's safe to switch; some lenses may be damaged by a chemical system. Contact lens supplies may be expensive and difficult to find; bring saline and cleaner for your entire vacation.

FILM

Film in Germany is of excellent quality and available at photo shops and drug stores; the same businesses usually process and develop film. If you're not a serious photographer, you might want to consider bringing a **disposable camera** or two rather than an expensive permanent one. Despite disclaimers, airport security X-rays *can* fog film, so either buy a lead-lined pouch, sold at camera stores, or ask the security to hand inspect it. Always pack it in your carry-on luggage, since higher-intensity X-rays are used on checked luggage.

OTHER USEFUL ITEMS

No matter how you're traveling, it's always a good idea to carry a first-aid kit including sunscreen, insect repellent, and vitamins (see **Health,** p. 51). Other useful items include: an umbrella; sealable plastic bags; alarm clock; waterproof matches; sun hat; needle and thread; safety pins; sunglasses; pocketknife; plastic water bottle; compass; towel; padlock; whistle; rubber bands; flashlight; cold-water soap; earplugs; electrical tape; tweezers; garbage bags; a small calculator for currency conversion; a pair of flip-flops for the shower; a money-belt for carrying valuables; deodorant; razors; tampons; and condoms (see **AIDS, HIV, and STDs,** p. 55).

FURTHER READING

The Packing Book, by Judith Gilford. Ten Speed Press ($9).

Backpacking One Step at a Time, Harvey Manning. Vintage ($15).

ACCOMMODATIONS

HOSTELS

In 1908, a German named Richard Schirmann, believing that life in industrial cities was harmful to the physical and moral development of Germany's young people, built the world's first **youth hostel** in Altena—a budget dormitory that would bring travel within the means of urban youth. Germany has been a leader in hosteling

ever since, and Schirmann is something of a mythical figure. Some hostels are housed in stunning castles, others in run-down barracks far from the city center. Hostels are generally dorm-style accommodations, often in single-sex large rooms with bunk beds, although some hostels do offer private rooms for families and couples. Whatever the locale, a bed in a hostel will average around DM20-30. They sometimes have kitchens and utensils for use, bike or moped rentals, storage areas, email terminals, and laundry facilities. There can be **drawbacks:** some hostels close during certain daytime "lockout" hours, have a curfew, don't accept reservations, impose a maximum stay, or, less frequently, require that you do chores. There's often little privacy and you may run into more screaming pre-teen groups than you care to remember. Many hostels require sleepsacks (see **Packing,** p. 57). Sleeping bags are usually prohibited for sanitary reasons, but almost all hostels provide sheets and blankets for a fee, usually about DM5.

Hostelling in Germany is overseen by **Deutsches Jugendherbergswerk (DJH)** Postfach 1462, 32704 Detmold, Germany (tel. (05231) 740 10; fax 74 01 84). DJH has recently initiated a growing number of **Jugendgästehäuser,** youth guest-houses that are generally more expensive, have more facilities, and attract slightly older guests. DJH has absorbed hundreds of hostels in Eastern Germany with remarkable efficiency, though some still lack the truly sparkling facilities of their western counterparts. Still, Germany currently has about **600 hostels**—more than any other nation on Earth. DJH publishes *Jugendherbergen in Deutschland* (DM14.80), a guide to all federated German hostels, available at German bookstores and major train station newsstands, or by writing to DJH.

The **DJH webpage** (http://www.djh.de), has pictures, prices, addresses, and phone numbers for almost every hostel in Germany. Contact information can also be found on most Germany cities' official webpages, listed under the tourist office in the **Practical Information** section of many cities in this guide. **Eurotrip** (http://www.eurotrip.com/accommodation/accommodation.html) has information and reviews on budget hostels and several international hostel associations. Also check out the **Internet Guide to Hostelling** (http://www.hostels.com), which provides a directory of hostels around the world in addition to endless hostelling and backpacking tips.

For their various services and lower rates at member hostels, hostelling associations, especially **Hostelling International (HI),** are worth joining. HI hostels are scattered throughout Germany, and many accept reservations via the International Booking Network (tel. 02 9261 1111 from Australia, 800-663-5777 from Canada, (01629) 581 418 from the U.K., (01) 301 766 from Ireland, (09) 379 4224 from New Zealand, 800-909-4776 from U.S.; www.hiayh.org/ushostel/reserva/ibn3.htm) for a nominal fee. To join HI, contact one of the following organizations in your home country.

Australian Youth Hostels Association (AYHA), 422 Kent St., Sydney NSW 2000 (tel. (02) 9261 1111; fax 9261 1969; email yha@yhansw.org.au; www.yha.org.au). 1-year membership AUS$44, under 18 AUS$13.50.

Hostelling International-Canada (HI-C), 400-205 Catherine St., Ottawa, ON K2P 1C3 (tel. 800-663-5777 or 613-237-7884; fax 237-7868; email info@hostellingintl.ca; www.hostellingintl.ca). 1-yr. membership CDN$25, under 18 CDN$12; 2-yr. CDN$35.

An Óige (Irish Youth Hostel Association), 61 Mountjoy St., Dublin 7 (tel. (01) 830 4555; fax 830 5808; email anoige@iol.ie; www.irelandyha.org). 1-yr. membership IR£10, under 18 IR£4, families IR£20.

Youth Hostels Association of New Zealand (YHANZ), P.O. Box 436, 173 Cashel St., Christchurch 1 (tel. (03) 379 9970; fax 365 4476; email info@yha.org.nz; www.yha.org.nz). 1-yr. membership NZ$24, ages 15-17 NZ$12, under 15 free.

Hostelling International South Africa, P.O. Box 4402, Cape Town, 8000 (tel. (021) 24 2511; fax 24 4119; email info@hisa.org.za; www.hisa.org.za). 1-yr. membership SAR50, under 18 SAR25, lifetime SAR250.

ESSENTIALS

Youth Hostels Association of England and Wales (YHA), 8 St. Stephen's Hill, St. Albans, Hertfordshire AL1 2DY, England (tel. (01727) 855 215 or 845 047; fax 844 126; email yhacustomerservices@compuserve.com; www.yha.org.uk). 1-yr. membership UK£11, under 18 UK£5.50, families UK£22.

Hostelling International Northern Ireland (HINI), 22-32 Donegall Rd., Belfast BT12 5JN, Northern Ireland (tel. (01232) 324 733 or 315 435; fax 439 699; email info@hini.org.uk; www.hini.org.uk). One-year membership UK£7, under 18 UK£3, families UK£14.

Scottish Youth Hostels Association (SYHA), 7 Glebe Crescent, Stirling FK8 2JA (tel. (01786) 891 400; fax 891 333; email info@syha.org.uk; www.syha.org.uk). 1-yr. membership UK£6, under 18 UK£2.50.

Hostelling International-American Youth Hostels (HI-AYH), 733 15th St. NW, Suite 840, Washington, D.C. 20005 (tel. 202-783-6161 ext. 136; fax 783-6171; email hiayhserv@hiayh.org; www.hiayh.org). 1-yr. membership US$25, over 54 US$15, under 18 free.

 NO OLD PEOPLE ALLOWED—SORRY POPS. HI-affiliated hostels in **Bayern (Bavaria)** generally do not admit guests over age 26, although families with young children are usually allowed even if parents are over 26.

HOTELS AND PRIVATE ROOMS

The cheapest hotel-style accommodations are places with **Pension, Gasthof, Gästehaus,** or **Hotel-Garni** in the name. Breakfast *(Frühstück)* is almost always included. Hotels are quite expensive in Germany: rock-bottom for singles is DM30, for doubles DM40-45; in large cities, expect to pay at least DM50 per night for a single and DM90 for a double. Budget European hotels might come as a rude shock to pampered North American travelers: a bathroom of your own is a rarity and costs extra when provided. Hot showers may also cost extra.

The best bet for a cheap bed is often a private room *(Privatzimmer)* in a home. Private rooms are much, much quieter than hostels, and will bring you in direct contact with the local population. Costs generally run DM20-50 per person, and usually include warm and personal service. Rooms are reserved through the local tourist office or through a private **Zimmervermittlung** (room-booking office), either for free or for a DM2-8 fee. This option works best if you have a rudimentary knowledge of German, since homeowners prefer to lay down a few household rules before handing over keys for the night. Travelers over 26 who would otherwise pay senior prices at youth hostels will find these rooms within budget range.

LONGER STAYS

Those planning to remain in Germany for an extended period of time should contact the local **Mitwohnzentrale,** an accommodation-finding office, in the city where they plan to stay. Throughout Germany, *Mitwohnzentralen* match apartments with apartment seekers; look under the **Practical Information** listings of individual cities. The stay can last anywhere from a few days to eternity, depending on the availability of apartments and the price you are willing to pay. Also check postings in universities, where student housing can offer lodging and utilities for DM200-300 per month.

Another option is a home exchange. These offer the traveler various types of homes (houses, apartments, condominiums, villas—even castles in some cases), plus the opportunity to live like a native and cut down dramatically on accommodation costs. Once you join or contact one of the exchange services listed below, it is up to you to decide with whom you would like to exchange homes. Most companies have pictures of member's homes and information about the owners. A great site listing many exchange companies can be found at www.aitec.edu.au/

~bwechner/Documents/Travel/Lists/HomeExchangeClubs.html. Home rentals, as opposed to exchanges, are much more expensive. However, they can be cheaper than comparably-serviced hotels.

HomeExchange, P.O. Box 30085, Santa Barbara, CA 93130 (tel. 805-898-9660; email admin@HomeExchange.com; www.homeexchange.com).

Intervac International Home Exchange, c/o Helge and Dieter Guenzler, Verdiweg 2, 70771 Leinfelden-Echterdingen, Germany (tel. (0711) 754 60 69; fax (0711) 754 28 31; email intervacgue@t-online.de; www.intervac.com). Offers 11,000 home exchanges in 50 countries.

The Invented City: International Home Exchange, 41 Sutter St., Suite 1090, San Francisco, CA 94104 (tel. 800-788-2489 in the U.S. or (415) 252-1141 elsewhere; fax 252-2171; email invented@aol.com; www.invented-city.com). For US$75, you get your offer listed in 1 catalog and unlimited access to the club's database containing thousands of homes for exchange.

CAMPING AND THE OUTDOORS

Germans love the outdoors, and their enthusiasm is evidenced by the 2,600 campsites that dot the outskirts of even the most major cities. Though the offerings in Germany are generally rather tame in comparison to those in Switzerland, Austria, or other more mountainous areas, the facilities for outdoor activities in Germany are among the best maintained in the world. Most are accessible by public transportation and include showers, bathrooms, and a restaurant or store. Often, however, campgrounds resemble battlegrounds, with weary travelers and screaming children vying for tiny grassy plots. Camping costs DM3-10 per person with additional charge for tents and vehicles.

Blue signs with a black tent on a white background indicate official sites. **Deutscher Camping-Club (DCC)**, Mandlstr. 28, 80802 München (tel. (089) 380 14 20), and **Allgemeiner Deutscher Automobil-Club (ADAC)** (see **Getting Around: By Car,** p. 73) have specific information on campgrounds, and the National Tourist Office distributes a free map, *Camping in Germany*, with a list of campgrounds (see p. 85).

Hiking trails wind through the outskirts of every German city, and a national network of long-distance trails links the whole country together. The Black Forest and the Bavarian Alps are especially well-traversed, as are the Harz Mountains and Saxon Switzerland. Alpine clubs in Germany provide inexpensive, simple accommodations in splendid settings. The **German Alpine Association**, Von-Kahr-Str. 2-4, 80997 München (tel. (089) 14 00 30; fax 140 03 11), maintains more than 14,000km of trails in the Alps and 252 huts open to all mountaineers. They also offer courses and guided expeditions.

USEFUL PUBLICATIONS AND WEB RESOURCES

For information about camping, hiking, and biking, contact the publishers listed below to receive a free catalogue. Campers heading to Europe should consider buying an **International Camping Carnet**. Similar to a hostel membership card, it's required at a few campgrounds and provides discounts at others. It is available in North America from the **Family Campers and RVers Association** and in the U.K. from **The Caravan Club** (below), and can usually be purchased at associated campsites.

Automobile Association, TBS Frating Distribution Centre, Colchester, Essex, CO7 7DW, U.K. (tel. (01206) 25 56 78; www.theaa.co.uk). Publishes *Camping and Caravanning: Europe* (UK£9). They also offer road atlases of Germany.

The Caravan Club, East Grinstead House, East Grinstead, West Sussex, RH19 1UA, U.K. (tel. (01342) 32 69 44; www.caravanclub.co.uk). One of the most detailed English guides to campsites in Europe. Members receive a 700-page directory and handbook, discounts and a monthly magazine (£27.50).

CAMPING AND HIKING EQUIPMENT

Good camping equipment is both sturdy and light. Camping equipment is generally more expensive in Australia, New Zealand, and the U.K. than in North America.

Sleeping Bag: Most good sleeping bags are rated by "season," or the lowest outdoor temperature at which they will keep you warm ("summer" means 30-40°F at night and "four-season" or "winter" often means below 0°F). Sleeping bags are made either of down (warmer and lighter, but more expensive, and miserable when wet) or of synthetic material (heavier, more durable, and warmer when wet). Prices vary, but range from US$80-210 for a summer synthetic to US$250-300 for a good down winter bag. **Sleeping bag pads,** including foam pads (US$10-20) and air mattresses (US$15-50), are essential, cushioning your back and neck and insulating you from the ground. Bring a **"stuff sack"** or plastic bag to store your sleeping bag and keep it dry.

Tent: The best tents are free-standing, with their own frames and suspension systems; they set up quickly and only require staking in high winds. Low-profile dome tents are the best all-around. Tent sizes can be somewhat misleading: 2 people *can* fit in a two-person tent, but will find life more pleasant in a 4-person. If you're traveling by car go for the bigger tent, but if you're hiking, stick with a smaller tent that weighs no more than 5-6 lbs. (2-3kg). Good 2-person tents start at US$90, 4-person tents at US$300. Seal the seams with waterproofer, and make sure it has a rain fly. Other tent accessories include a **battery-operated lantern**, a **plastic groundcloth**, and a **nylon tarp.**

Backpack: A **waterproof backpack cover** will prove invaluable. Otherwise, plan to store all of your belongings in plastic bags inside your backpack.

Boots: Be sure to wear water-repellent hiking boots with good **ankle support** which are appropriate for the terrain you plan to hike. Your boots should fit snugly and comfortably over one or two wool socks and a thin liner sock. Breaking in boots properly before setting out requires wearing them for several weeks; doing so will spare you from painful and debilitating blisters.

Other Necessities: Raingear in two pieces, a top and pants, is far superior to a poncho. **Synthetics,** like polypropylene tops, socks, and long underwear, along with a pile jacket, will keep you warm even when wet. When camping in autumn, winter, or spring, consider bringing along a **"space blanket,"** which helps you to retain your body heat and doubles as a groundcloth (US$5-15). Plastic **canteens** or water bottles keep water cooler than metal ones do, and are virtually shatter- and leak-proof. Large, collapsible **water sacks** will significantly improve your lot in primitive campgrounds and weigh practically nothing when empty, though they are bulky and heavy when full. Bring **water-purification tablets** for when you can't boil water. Though most campgrounds provide campfire sites, you may want to bring a small **metal grate** or **grill** of your own. For those places that forbid fires or the gathering of firewood (this includes virtually every organized campground in Germany), you'll need a **camp stove.** The classic Coleman stove starts at about US$40. You will need to purchase a **fuel bottle** and fill it with propane to operate it.

The mail-order and online companies listed below offer lower prices than many retail stores, but a visit to a local camping or outdoors outlet will give you a good sense of an item's look and weight.

Campmor, P.O. Box 700, Upper Saddle River, NJ 07458-0700 (U.S. tel. 888-226-7667, outside U.S., call 1-201-825-8300; email customer-service@campmor.com; www.campmor.com).

Discount Camping, 880 Main North Rd., Pooraka, South Australia 5095, Australia (tel. (08) 8262 3399; fax 8260 6240; www.discountcamping.com.au).

Recreational Equipment, Inc. (REI), Sumner, WA 98352 (tel. 800-426-4840 or 253-891-2500; www.rei.com).

YHA Adventure Shop, 14 Southampton St., London, WC2E 7HA, U.K. (tel. (01718) 36 85 41).

WILDERNESS SAFETY

Stay warm, stay dry, and stay hydrated. The vast majority of life-threatening wilderness situations result from a breach of this simple dictum. On any hike, however brief, you should pack enough equipment to keep you alive in the event of disaster. This includes **raingear, hat** and **mittens, a first-aid kit, a reflector, a whistle, high energy food,** and extra **water.** Dress in warm layers of **synthetic materials** designed for the outdoors, or **wool.** Pile fleece jackets and Gore-Tex raingear are excellent choices. Never rely on **cotton** for warmth. This "death cloth" will be absolutely useless should it get wet. Make sure to check all equipment for any defects before setting out, and see **Camping and Hiking Equipment,** above, for more information.

Check **weather forecasts** and pay attention to the skies when hiking. Whenever possible, let someone know when and where you are going hiking. Do not attempt a hike beyond your ability—you may be endangering your life. See **Health,** p. 51 for information about outdoor ailments such as heatstroke, hypothermia, rabies, and insects, as well as basic medical concerns and first-aid.

For further information, consult *How to Stay Alive in the Woods,* Bradford Angier (Macmillan, US$8).

ENVIRONMENTALLY RESPONSIBLE TOURISM. The idea behind responsible tourism is to leave no trace of human presence behind. A campstove is the safer (and more efficient) way to cook than using vegetation, but if you must make a fire, keep it small and use only dead branches or brush rather than cutting vegetation. Make sure your campsite is at least 150 ft. (50m) from water supplies or bodies of water. If there are no toilet facilities, bury human waste (but not paper) at least four inches (10cm) deep and above the high-water line, and 150 feet or more from any water supplies and campsites. Always pack your trash in a plastic bag and carry it with you until you reach the next trash can. For more information contact one of the organizations listed below.

Earthwatch, 680 Mt. Auburn St., Box 403, Watertown, MA 02272 (tel. 617-776-0188; fax 926-8532; email info@earthwatch.org; www.earthwatch.org).

Ecotourism Society, P.O. Box 755, North Bennington, VT 05257-0755 (tel. 802-447-2121; email ecomail@ecotourism.org; www.ecotourism.org/tesinfo.html).

Ecotravel Center: www.ecotour.com.

National Audobon Society, Nature Odysseys, 700 Broadway, New York, NY 10003 (tel. 212-979-3066; email travel@audobon.org; www.audobon.org).

Tourism Concern, Stapleton House, 277-281 Holloway Rd., London N7 8HN, England (tel. (020) 7753 3330; www.gn.apc.org/tourismconcern).

KEEPING IN TOUCH

MAIL

SENDING MAIL TO AND RECEIVING MAIL IN GERMANY

Airmail letters under 1 oz. between North America and Germany take 7 to 10 days and cost US$0.90 or CDN$0.95. Allow at least 4-6 days from Australia (postage AUS$1 for up to 20g) and 3 days from Britain (postage $0.30 for up to 20g). Envelopes should be marked "air mail" or "par avion" to avoid having letters sent by sea. Follow the instructions below to arrange pick-up of letters sent to you by friends and relatives while you are abroad.

General Delivery: Mail can be sent to Germany through **Poste Restante** (the international phrase for General Delivery; **Postlagernde Briefe** in German) to almost any city or town with a post office. Address *Poste Restante* letters to: Postlagernde Briefe, für <u>Mary Jones</u>, Hauptpostamt, D-70001 Stuttgart, Germany. The mail will go to a special desk in the central post office unless you specify a post office by street address or postal code. As a rule, it is best to use the largest post office in the area, and mail may be sent there regardless of what is written on the envelope. When picking up your mail, bring a form of photo ID, preferably a passport. There is generally no surcharge; if there is a charge, it shouldn't exceed the cost of domestic postage. If the clerks insist that there is nothing for you, have them check under your first name as well. *Let's Go: Germany* lists postal codes and post offices in the **Practical Information** section for every city and town.

American Express: AmEx's travel offices throughout the world will act as a mail service for cardholders if you contact them in advance. Under this free **Client Letter Service,** they will hold mail for up to 30 days and forward upon request. Some offices will offer these services to non-cardholders (especially those who have purchased AmEx Travelers Cheques), but you must call ahead to make sure. Check the **Practical Information** sections; Let's Go lists AmEx office locations for most large cities. A complete list is available free from AmEx (tel. 800–528-4800).

If regular airmail is too slow, **Federal Express** (U.S. tel. 800-247-4747; UK (0800) 123 800; Australia 13 26 10; Ireland (1800) 535 800; South Africa 011 923 8000; New Zealand (0800) 733 339) can get a letter from New York to Berlin in two days for a whopping US$25.50; rates among non-U.S. locations are prohibitively expensive. (London to Berlin, for example, costs upwards of £25.) By **U.S. Express Mail,** a letter from New York will arrive within two to three days and cost US$21.

Surface mail is by far the cheapest and slowest way to send mail. It takes one to three months to cross the Atlantic and two to four to cross the Pacific—appropriate for sending large quantities of items you won't need to see for a while. When ordering books and materials from abroad, always include one or two **international Reply Coupons (IRCs)**—a way of providing the postage to cover delivery. IRCs should be available from your local post office and those abroad (US$1.05).

SENDING MAIL HOME FROM GERMANY

Aerogrammes, printed sheets that fold into envelopes and travel via airmail, are available at post offices. It helps to mark letters *mit Luftpost*, though *par avion* is universally understood. Most post offices will charge exorbitant fees or simply refuse to send aerogrammes with enclosures. Airmail from Germany averages 7 to 10 days, although times are more unpredictable from smaller towns.

To send a postcard to an international destination within Europe costs DM1 and to any other international destination via airmail costs DM2. Within Germany, postcards require DM1. Sending a letter (up to 50g) to another European country costs DM3 and to anywhere else in the world via airmail costs DM6.

TELEPHONES

CALLING GERMANY FROM HOME

To call Germany direct from home, dial:

1. The **international access code** of your home country. **Access codes** include: Australia 0011, Ireland 00, New Zealand 00, South Africa 09, U.K. 00, U.S. 011.
2. 49 (Germany's country code).
3. The city code (see the city's **Practical Information** section) and local number. City codes are sometimes listed with a zero in front (e.g., 030), but after dialing the country code, drop initial zero (with an access code of 011 49, e.g., 011 49 30)

CALLING HOME FROM GERMANY

A calling card is probably your best and cheapest bet. Calls are billed either collect or to your account. **MCI WorldPhone** also provides access to MCI's Traveler's Assist, which gives legal and medical advice, exchange rate information, and translation services. Other phone companies provide similar services to travelers. To obtain a calling card from your national telecommunications service before you leave home, contact the appropriate company below.

USA: AT&T (tel. 888-288-4685); **Sprint** (tel. 800-877-4646); or **MCI** (tel. 800-444-4141).

Canada: Bell Canada **Canada Direct** (tel. 800-565-4708).

U.K.: British Telecom **BT Direct** (tel. (800) 34 51 44).

Ireland: Telecom Éireann **Ireland Direct** (tel. 0800 250 250).

Australia: Telstra **Australia Direct** (tel. 13 22 00).

New Zealand: Telecom New Zealand (tel. (0800) 000 000).

South Africa: Telkom South Africa (tel. 09 03).

To call home with a calling card, contact the Germany operator for your service provider by dialing:

AT&T: Tel. (0800) 2255 288.

Sprint: Tel. (0800) 8880 013.

MCI WorldPhone Direct: Tel. (0800) 888 8000.

Canada Direct: Tel. (0800) 888 0014.

BT Direct: Tel. (0130) 80 0144.

Ireland Direct: Tel. (0800) 180 0027.

Australia Direct: Tel. (0130) 80 0061.

Telecom New Zealand Direct: Tel. (0130) 80 0064.

Telkom South Africa Direct: Tel. (0800) 180 0027.

Wherever possible, use a calling card for international phone calls, as the long-distance rates for national phone services are often exorbitant. German **Telefonkarten** (see below) can be used for direct international calls. Although incredibly convenient, in-room hotel calls invariably include an arbitrary and sky-high surcharge (as much as US$10).

If you do dial direct, you must first insert a *Telefonkarte*, then dial 00 (the international access code for Germany), and then dial the country code and number of your home. **Country codes** include: Australia 61; Ireland 353; New Zealand 64; South Africa 27; U.K. 44; U.S. and Canada 1.

The expensive alternative to dialing direct or using a calling card is using an international operator to place a **collect call.** An English-speaking operator from your home nation can be reached by dialing the appropriate service provider listed above, and they will typically place a collect call even if you don't possess one of their phone cards.

CALLING WITHIN GERMANY

You can always be sure of finding a **public phone** *(Telefonzelle)* in a post office. Additionally, phones are located at all train and bus stations, on ICE trains, and on nearly every other street corner. Most public phones only accept telephone cards, though restaurants and bars sometimes have coin-operated phones. Telephones in transport hubs and near major attractions sometimes give you the option of paying by **credit card.** You can pick up a **Telefonkarte** (phone card) in post offices, at a *Kiosk* (newsstand), or at selected Deutsche Bahn counters in major train stations.

The cards come in DM12, DM24, and DM50 denominations. If you purchase a card at a *Kiosk*, the salesperson will insert it in a machine to show you the balance.

To place **inter-city calls**, dial the **Vorwahl** (area code), including the first zero that appears in the code, followed by the **Rufnummer** (telephone number). There is no standard length for telephone numbers. The smaller the city, the more digits in the city code, while telephone numbers tend to have three to ten digits. The **national information number** is 11 833. For **international information**, call 118 34. **Phone rates** tend to be highest in the morning and afternoon, lower in the evening, and lowest after 9 p.m. and on Sundays and holidays. *Let's Go: Germany* lists **phone codes** at the end of each **Practical Information** section throughout the guide.

EMAIL AND INTERNET

While Germany lagged behind the U.S. and UK for many years in the internet arena, more and more German citizens and companies are coming to rely on email and the web as a means of communication. Most German cities as well as a surprising number of smaller towns have at least one **internet café**, where patrons can check email, surf the web, and sip cappuccinos to the tune of DM3-7 per half hour. In addition, some German universities have banks of computers hooked up to the internet in their libraries, though ostensibly for student use. *Let's Go: Germany* lists internet access after post offices in the **Practical Information** section. For advice on traveling with the use of the internet, see the **World Wide Web**, p. 86.

Many web-based email providers offer **free email accounts**; check out Hotmail (www.hotmail.com), RocketMail (www.rocketmail.com), or Yahoo! Mail (www.yahoo.com) to subscribe. Most providers are funded by advertising and some may require subscribers to fill out a questionnaire. Almost every internet search engine has an affiliated free email service.

Travelers who have the luxury of a laptop with them can use a **modem** to call an internet service provider. Long-distance phone cards specifically intended for such calls can defray normally high phone charges. Check with your long-distance phone provider to see if they offer this option.

GETTING THERE

BY PLANE

When it comes to airfare, a little effort can save you a bundle. If your plans are flexible enough to deal with the restrictions, courier fares are the cheapest. Tickets bought from consolidators and standby seating are also good deals, but last-minute specials, airfare wars, and charter flights often beat these fares. The key is to hunt around, be flexible, and persistently ask about discounts. Students, seniors, and those under 26 should never pay full price for a ticket.

DETAILS AND TIPS

Timing: Airfares to Germany peak between June and September, and holidays are also expensive periods in which to travel. Midweek (M-Th morning) round-trip flights run US$40-50 cheaper than weekend flights. Return-date flexibility is usually not an option for the budget traveler; traveling with an "open return" ticket can be pricier than fixing a return date when buying the ticket and paying later to change it.

Route: Round-trip flights are by far the cheapest; "open-jaw" (arriving in and departing from different cities) and round-the-world, or RTW, flights are pricier but reasonable alternatives. Patching one-way flights together is the least economical way to travel. Flights between capital cities or regional hubs will offer the most competitive fares; Frankfurt will generally be the least expensive destination.

Boarding: Whenever flying internationally, pick up tickets for international flights well in advance of the departure date, and confirm by phone within 72 hours of departure. Most airlines require that passengers arrive at the airport at least 2 hours before departure. 1 carry-on item and 2 pieces of checked baggage is the norm for non-courier flights. Consult the airline for weight allowances.

Fares: Round-trip fares to Western Europe from the U.S. range from US$400-600 (during the off season) to US$700-1000 (during the summer). Round-trip flights from the UK to Frankfurt are a comparative snip at UK£100-180.

BUDGET AND STUDENT TRAVEL AGENCIES

A knowledgeable agent specializing in flights to Germany can make your life easy and help you save, too, but agents may not spend the time to find you the lowest possible fare—they get paid on commission. Students and under-26ers holding **ISIC and IYTC cards** (see **Identification,** p. 41), respectively, qualify for big discounts from student travel agencies. Most flights from budget agencies are on major airlines, but in peak season some may sell seats on less reliable chartered aircraft.

Campus/Usit Youth and Student Travel, 52 Grosvenor Gardens, London SW1W 0AG (in the U.K., call (0870) 240 10 10, worldwide call 44 20 7730 8111; www.usitcampus.co.uk). Other offices include: 19-21 Aston Quay, O'Connell Bridge, **Dublin** 2 (tel. (01) 677 8117; fax 679 8833); New York Student Center, 895 Amsterdam Ave., **New York,** NY, 10025 (tel. 212-663-5435; email usitny@aol.com). Additional offices in Cork, Galway, Limerick, Waterford, Coleraine, Derry, and Belfast.

Council Travel (www.counciltravel.com). U.S. offices include: 273 Newbury St., **Boston,** MA 02116 (tel. (617) 266-1926); 1160 N. State St., **Chicago,** IL 60610 (tel. 312-951-0585); 10904 Lindbrook Dr., **Los Angeles,** CA 90024 (tel. 310-208-3551); 205 E. 42nd St., **New York,** NY 10017 (tel. 212-822-2700); 530 Bush St., **San Francisco,** CA 94108 (tel. 415-421-3473); 1314 NE 43rd St. #210, **Seattle,** WA 98105 (tel.

206-632-2448); 3300 M St. NW, **Washington, D.C.** 20007 (tel. 202-337-6464). **For U.S. cities not listed,** call 800-2-COUNCIL (226-8624). Also 28A Poland St. (Oxford Circus), **London,** W1V 3DB (tel. (020) 7287 3337).

CTS Travel, 44 Goodge St., **London** W1P 2AD (tel. (020) 7635 0031; fax 7637 5328; email ctsinfo@ctstravel.com.uk; www.cts.com).

STA Travel, 6560 Scottsdale Rd. #F100, Scottsdale, AZ 85253 (tel. 800-777-0112; fax 602-922-0793; www.sta-travel.com). A student and youth travel organization with more than 150 offices worldwide. Ticket booking, travel insurance, railpasses, and more. **U.S.** offices include: 297 Newbury Street, **Boston,** MA 02115 (tel. 617-266-6014); 429 S. Dearborn St., **Chicago,** IL 60605 (tel. 312-786-9050); 7202 Melrose Ave., **Los Angeles,** CA 90046 (tel. 323-934-8722); 10 Downing St., **New York,** NY 10014 (tel. 212-627-3111); 4341 University Way NE, **Seattle,** WA 98105 (tel. 206-633-5000); 2401 Pennsylvania Ave., Ste. G, **Washington, D.C.** 20037 (tel. 202-887-0912); 51 Grant Ave., **San Francisco,** CA 94108 (tel. 415-391-8407). In the **U.K.,** 6 Wrights Ln., **London** W8 6TA (tel. (020) 7938 4711 for North American travel). In **New Zealand,** 10 High St., **Auckland** (tel. (09) 309 04 58). In **Australia,** 222 Faraday St., **Melbourne** VIC 3053 (tel. (03) 9349 2411).

Travel CUTS (Canadian Universities Travel Services Limited), 187 College St., **Toronto,** ON M5T 1P7 (tel. 416-979-2406; fax 979-8167; www.travelcuts.com). 40 offices across Canada. Also in the **U.K.,** 295-A Regent St., **London** W1R 7YA (tel. (020) 7255 1944).

Wasteels, Victoria Station, London, U.K. SW1V 1JT (tel. (020) 7834 7066; fax 7630 7628; www.wasteels.dk/uk). A huge chain in Europe, with 203 locations. Sells the BIJ Wasteels tickets, which are discounted (30-45% off regular fare) 2nd class international point-to-point train tickets with unlimited stopovers (must be under 26).

Other organizations that specialize in finding cheap fares include:

Cheap Tickets (tel. 800-377-1000) flies worldwide to and from the U.S.

Travel Avenue (tel. 800-333-3335) rebates commercial fares to and from the U.S. and offers low fares for flights anywhere in the world. They also offer package deals, which include car rental and hotel reservations, to many destinations.

COMMERCIAL AIRLINES

The commercial airlines' lowest regular offer is the **APEX** (Advance Purchase Excursion) fare, which provides confirmed reservations and allows "open-jaw" tickets. Generally, reservations must be made 7 to 21 days in advance, with 7- to 14-day minimum and up to 90-day maximum-stay limits, and hefty cancellation and change penalties (fees rise in summer). Book peak-season APEX fares early, since by May you will have a hard time getting the departure date you want.

Although APEX fares are probably not the cheapest possible fares, they will give you a sense of the average commercial price from which to measure other bargains. Specials advertised in newspapers may be cheaper but have more restrictions and fewer available seats. Popular carriers to Germany include:

Deutsche Lufthansa (tel. 800-645-3880 in the U.S. and 800-563-5954 in Canada; www.lufthansa.com), is Germany's premier airline and offers flights to the most cities, but fares tend to be high.

Icelandair (tel. 800-223-5500; www.centrum.is/icelandair), has last-minute offers and a standby fare from New York to Luxembourg. Reservations must be made within 3 days of departure.

KLM (tel. 800-374-7747; www.klm.com), is Dutch airline, with services throughout Europe and several North American cities.

LTU (tel. 800-888-0200; www.ltu.com), offers very reasonable rates to a number of German cities, including Frankfurt, Hamburg, and Düsseldorf. Service is only out of Miami, Orlando, Ft. Myers, and Los Angeles.

Martinair (tel. 800-627-8462), offers one-way only standby fares from New York to Amsterdam (you're responsible for the ticket home).

OTHER CHEAP ALTERNATIVES

AIR COURIER FLIGHTS

Couriers help transport cargo on international flights by guaranteeing delivery of the baggage claim slips from the company to a representative overseas. Generally, couriers must travel light (carry-ons only) and deal with complex restrictions on their flight. Most flights are round-trip only with short fixed-length stays (usually one week) and a limit of a single ticket per issue. Most of these flights also operate only out of the biggest cities, like New York. Generally, you must be over 21 (in some cases 18), have a valid passport, and procure your own visa, if necessary. Groups such as the **Air Courier Association** (tel. 800-282-1202; www.aircourier.org) and the **International Association of Air Travel Couriers,** 220 South Dixie Hwy., P.O. Box 1349, Lake Worth, FL 33460 (tel. 561-582-8320; email iaatc@courier.org; www.courier.org) provide their members with lists of opportunities and courier brokers worldwide for an annual fee.

FURTHER READING

Air Courier Bargains, Kelly Monaghan. The Intrepid Traveler (US$15).

Courier Air Travel Handbook, Mark Field. Perpetual Press (US$10).

CHARTER FLIGHTS

Charters are flights a tour operator contracts with an airline to fly extra loads of passengers during peak season. They can sometimes be cheaper than flights on scheduled airlines, some operate nonstop, and restrictions on minimum advance-purchase and minimum stay are more lenient. However, charter flights fly less frequently than major airlines, make refunds particularly difficult, and are almost always fully booked. Schedules and itineraries may also change or be cancelled at the last moment (as late as 48 hours before the trip, and without a full refund), and check-in, boarding, and baggage claim are often much slower. As always, pay with a credit card if you can, and consider traveler's insurance against trip interruption.

Discount clubs and **fare brokers** offer members' savings on last-minute charter and tour deals. Study their contracts closely; you don't want to end up with an unwanted overnight layover. **Travelers Advantage,** Stamford, CT (tel. 800-548-1116; www.travelersadvantage.com; specializes in European travel and tour packages ($US60 annual fee).

STANDBY FLIGHTS

To travel standby, you will need considerable flexibility in the dates and cities of your arrival and departure. Companies that specialize in standby flights don't sell tickets but rather the promise that you will get to your destination (or near your destination) within a certain window of time (anywhere from 1-5 days). You may only receive a monetary refund if all available flights which depart within your date-range from the specified region are full, but future travel credit is always available.

Carefully read agreements with any company offering standby flights, as tricky fine print can leave you in the lurch. To check on a company's service record, call the Better Business Bureau of New York City (tel. 212-533-6200). It is difficult to receive refunds, and clients' vouchers will not be honored when an airline fails to receive payment in time.

Airhitch, 2641 Broadway, 3rd fl., New York, NY 10025 (tel. 800-326-2009 or 212-864-2000; fax 864-5489; www.airhitch.org) and Los Angeles, CA (tel. 310-726-5000). In Europe, the flagship office is in Paris (tel. 01 47 00 16 30) and the other one is in Amsterdam (tel. (020) 626 32 20). Flights to Europe cost US$159 each way when departing from the Northeast, $239 from the West Coast or Northwest, $209 from the Midwest, and $189 from the Southeast. Travel within the USA and Europe is also possible, with rates ranging $79-139.

TICKET CONSOLIDATORS

Ticket consolidators, or **"bucket shops,"** buy unsold tickets in bulk from commercial airlines and sell them at discounted rates. The best place to look is in the Sunday travel section of a major newspaper, where many bucket shops place tiny ads. Call quickly, as availability is typically extremely limited. Not all bucket shops are reliable establishments, so insist on a receipt that gives full details of restrictions, refunds, and tickets, and pay by credit card.

FURTHER READING: BY PLANE

Consolidators FAQ (www.travel-library.com/air-travel/consolidators.html).

Consolidators: Air Travel's Bargain Basement, Kelly Monaghan. Intrepid Traveler (US$8).

The Worldwide Guide to Cheap Airfare, Michael McColl. Insider Publications (US$15).

Discount Airfares: The Insider's Guide, George Hobart. Priceless Publications (US$14).

The Official Airline Guide, an expensive tome available at many libraries, has flight schedules, fares, and reservation numbers.

Travelocity (www.travelocity.com). A searchable online database of published airfares. Online reservations.

Air Traveler's Handbook (www.cs.cmu.edu/afs/cs.cmu.edu/user/mkant/Public/Travel/airfare.html).

TravelHUB (www.travelhub.com). A directory of travel agents that includes a searchable database of fares from over 500 consolidators.

BY TRAIN

European trains retain the charm and romance their North American counterparts lost long ago. Nevertheless, bring food and a water bottle; the on-board café can be pricey, and train water undrinkable. Lock your compartment door and keep your valuables on your person.

Many train stations have different counters for domestic and international tickets, seat reservations, and information—check before lining up. Even with a railpass, reservations are often required on major lines, and are advisable during the busier holiday seasons; make them at least a few hours in advance at the train station (US$3-10). Use of many of Europe's high speed or quality trains (such as EuroCity and InterCity) requires a supplementary expenditure for those traveling with German railpasses.

For overnight travel, a tight, open bunk called a **couchette** is an affordable luxury, but watch your luggage. (About US$20; reserve at the station several days in advance.) Germany and the EU offer youth ticket discounts and youth railpasses. (See **Getting Around,** below.)

BY FERRY

Travel by boat is a bewitching alternative favored by Europeans but often overlooked by foreigners. Most European ferries are comfortable and well-equipped. Check in at least two hours early for a prime spot and allow plenty of time for late trains and getting to the port. Fares jump sharply in July and August. Ask for discounts; ISIC holders can often get student fares, and Eurail passholders get many reductions and free trips; check the brochure that comes with your railpass. You'll occasionally have to pay a small port tax (under US$10).

Ferries in the **North** and **Baltic Seas** are reliable and go everywhere. Ferries run from Hamburg, Kiel, Travemünde, Rostock, and Saßnitz to England, Scandinavia, Poland, the Baltic States, and Russia. Those content with deck passage rarely need to book ahead. If you really have travel time to spare, **Ford's Travel Guides,** 19448 Londelius St., Northridge, CA 91324 (tel. 818-701-7414; fax 701-7415) lists **freighter companies** that will take passengers worldwide. Ask for their *Freighter Travel Guide and Waterways of the World* (US$16, plus US$2.50 postage if mailed outside the U.S.).

GETTING AROUND

BY TRAIN

"In Germany, the trains run on time." It's a cliché, almost a joke, and not infallibly true. At the same time, it brings up an important truth about getting around in Germany—if the trains aren't perfect, they do go almost everywhere a traveler would want to, with the exception of some very rural areas. In fact, the train system's obligation to run lines to inaccessible areas, even at a loss, is written into Germany's Basic Law. Averaging 120km per hour and connecting some 7,000 locations, the **Deutsche Bahn** network is Europe's best, and also one of the most expensive, although many discount opportunities exist (see below). The German Rail webpage (www.bahn.de) is excellent; to check out times and prices go directly to http://bahn.hafas.de.

S-Bahn trains are commuter rail lines that run from a city's center to its suburbs; they are frequently integrated with the local subway or streetcar system. **RE** (RegionalExpress) and the slightly slower **RB** (Regionalbahn) trains include a number of rail networks between neighboring cities. **IR** (InterRegio) trains, covering larger networks between cities, are speedy and comfortable. **D** trains are foreign trains that serve international routes. **EC** (EuroCity) and **IC** (InterCity) trains zoom along between major cities every hour 6am-10pm. Even the IC yields to the futuristic **ICE** (InterCityExpress) trains, which approach the luxury and kinetics of an airplane and run at speeds up to 280km per hour. You must purchase a **Zuschlag** (supplement) to ride an ICE, IC or EC train. (DM7 when bought in the station, DM9 on the train.)

Most German cities have a **main train station;** in German, **der Hauptbahnhof.** Unless otherwise noted, this is the location referred to when *Let's Go* gives directions "from the station." In train stations, yellow signs indicate departures *(Abfahrt),* and white signs indicate arrivals *(Ankunft).* The number under *Gleis* is the track number.

Second-class travel is pleasant, and compartments are excellent places to meet people of all ages and nationalities. Larger train stations have different counters for domestic tickets, international tickets, seat reservations, and information; check before lining up. On major lines, reservations are advisable even if you have a railpass; make them at least a few hours in advance at the train station.

Most European and German railpasses are best purchased before you leave home. Contact a domestic **budget travel agency** (see p. 67). Alternatively, contact Deutsche Bahn through their web page (www.bahn.de), or, once in Germany, by calling their toll-free hotline (tel. (0180) 599 66 33).

GERMAN RAILPASSES

DEUTSCHE BAHN PASS. Designed for tourists, the German Railpass allows unlimited travel for four to 10 days within a four-week period. Non-Europeans can purchase German Railpasses in their home countries and—with a passport—in major German train stations. A second-class Railpass costs US$196 for 5 days of unlimited travel and $306 for 10. The **German Rail Youth Pass,** for tourists under 26, is US$156 for 5 days and $198 for 9. The second-class **Twin Pass,** for two adults traveling together, is US$294 for 5 days and $459 for 10.

BAHNCARD. A great option for those making frequent and extensive use of German trains for more than one month, the Bahncard is valid one year and entitles you to a 50% discount on all trains. Passes are available at major train stations and require a passport-sized photo. A **second-class** pass is DM260; a pass for those aged 17-22 or over 60, or any student under 27, is DM130; students under 17 pay DM65.

YOUTH, STUDENT, AND DISCOUNT FARES. Travelers under 26 can purchase **TwenTickets,** which knock 20-60% off fares over DM10; be sure to let your ticket agent know your age. A **Schönes-Wochenende-Ticket** offers a fantastic deal for weekend trips. For a single price of DM35, up to five people receive unlimited travel on any of the slower trains (*not* ICE, IC, EC, D, or IR) from 12:01am Saturday until 2am on Monday. Single travelers often find larger groups who are amenable to sharing their ticket, either free or for a fraction of the purchase cost. The **Guten-Abend-Ticket** provides an excellent deal for long-distance night travel and entitles its holders to travel anywhere (*not* on InterCityNight or CityNightLines) in Germany between 7pm and 2am. Second-class tickets are DM59, with ICE surcharge DM69; first-class DM99, with ICE surcharge DM109; Friday and Sunday DM15 extra.

EUROPEAN RAIL PASSES

There are two primary international European railpasses: the **Eurailpass** and the **Europass.** They are a good deal for travelers looking to cover a lot of ground in very little time. Ideally conceived, a railpass allows you to jump on any train in a given portion of Europe, go where you want whenever you want, and change your plans at will. In practice, it's not so simple. You still must stand in line to pay for supplements, seat reservations, and couchette reservations, as well as to have your pass validated when you first use it. More important, railpasses don't always pay off. For ballpark estimates, consult the **DER Travel** (www.dertravel.com) or the **RailEurope** railpass brochure (www.raileurope.com) for prices of **point-to-point** tickets. Add them up and compare with railpass prices. It may turn out that for a tour of Germany, Deutsche Bahn Passes, not Eurail or Europass, are a better option.

Eurailpasses and Europasses can be purchased only by non-Europeans almost exclusively from non-European distributors. These passes must be sold at uniform prices determined by the EU, so no one travel agent is better than another as far as the price itself is concerned. However, some agents tack on a US$10 handling fee. Also, agents often offer different perks with purchase of a railpass, so shop around. Under both pass plans, children 4-11 pay half of adult prices.

EURAILPASS. Eurailpasses are valid in Austria, Belgium, Denmark, Finland, France, Germany, Greece, Hungary, the Republic of Ireland, Italy, Luxembourg, the Netherlands, Norway, Portugal, Spain, Sweden, and Switzerland. With your railpass you will receive a timetable for major routes and a map with details on possible ferry, steamer, bus, car rental, and hotel, and **Eurostar.**

> **Eurail Saverpass:** Unlimited 1st-class travel for those traveling in a group of 2-5. 15 days US$470; 21 days $610; 1 month $1072; 2 months $1072; 3 months $1324.
>
> **Eurail Youthpass:** Unlimited 2nd-class travel for those aged 12-25. 15 days US$388; 21 days $499; 1 month $623; 2 months $882; 3 months $1089.
>
> **Youth Flexipasses:** 2nd-class travel for those under 26. Days can be distributed over 2months: 10 days (US$458), 15 days (US$599). Children 4-11 pay half price, and children under 4 travel free.

EUROPASS. With a Europass you can travel in France, Germany, Italy, Spain, and Switzerland for five to 15 days within a window of two months. Second-class youth tickets begin at US$233 and increase incrementally by US$29 for each additional day of travel. With purchase of a first-class adult ticket, starting at US$348, you can buy an identical ticket for your traveling partner at a 40% discount. You can add associate countries for a fee; call for information. Be sure to plan your itineraries in advance before buying a Europass; you may be fined if you cut through a country you haven't purchased. Europasses are not appropriate if you like to take lots of side trips—you'll waste rail days.

PURCHASING A RAILPASS. You'll find it easiest to buy a Eurailpass before you arrive in Europe; virtually any travel agency handling Europe can sell them (see **Budget Travel Agencies,** p. 67), as does **Rail Europe,** 500 Mamaroneck Ave., Harrison, NY 10528 (in the U.S. tel. 800-438-7245; fax 800-432-1329; in Canada tel. 800-361-7245; fax 905-602-4198; www.raileurope.com). If you're stuck in Europe and unable to find someone to sell you a Eurailpass, call an American railpass agent, who can send a pass by express mail. Eurailpasses are not refundable once validated, and you can get a replacement for a lost pass only if you have purchased insurance on it under the Pass Protection Plan (US$10).

INTERRAIL PASS. Travelers who have resided in Europe for more than six months and plan to travel through more than one country should consider Inter-Rail Passes. For information and ticket sales in Europe, contact **Student Travel Center,** 24 Rupert St., 1st fl., London, W1V 7FN (tel. (020) 74 37 01 21, 74 37 63 70 or 74 37 81 01; fax 77 34 38 36; www.student-travel-centre.com). Tickets should be purchased in your country of residence and are available from travel agents and at larger train stations.

> **Under 26 InterRail Card:** 14 days or 1 month of unlimited travel within 1, 2, 3 or all of the 7 zones into which InterRail divides Europe. If you buy a ticket which includes your country of residence, you must pay 50% of the fare for travel within your country. UK£159-259.

> **Over 26 InterRail Card:** unlimited 2nd-class travel in 20 countries (Austria, Bulgaria, Croatia, Czech Republic, Denmark, Finland, Germany, Greece, Hungary, Republic of Ireland, Luxembourg, Netherlands, Norway, Poland, Romania, Slovakia, Slovenia, Sweden, Turkey, and Yugoslavia) for 15 days or 1 month. UK£215-275.

BY BUS

Germany does have a few regions that are inaccessible by train, and some bus lines fill the gaps. Bus service between cities and to outlying areas run from the local **Zentralomnibusbahnhof (ZOB),** which is usually close to the main train station. Buses are often slightly more expensive than the train for comparable distances. Railpasses are not valid on any buses other than a few run by Deutsche Bahn.

Europe's largest coach operator is **Eurolines,** 4 Cardiff Rd., Luton LU1 1PP (tel. (08705) 143 219; fax (01582) 400 694; in London, 52 Grosvenor Gardens, Victoria (tel. (01582) 404 511); email welcome@eurolines.uk.com). A **Eurolines Pass** offers unlimited 30-day (under 26 and over 60 UK£159; 26-60 UK£199) or 60-day (UK£199/£249) travel between 30 major cities. Eurolines also offers **Euro Explorers,** seven travel loops through Europe with set fares and itineraries.

BY CAR

Cars offer speed, freedom, access to the countryside, and an escape from the town-to-town mentality of trains. Unfortunately, they also insulate you from the *esprit de corps* of rail traveling. Although a single traveler won't save by renting a car, four usually will. If you can't decide between train and car travel, you may benefit from a combination of the two; Rail Europe and other railpass vendors offer rail-and-drive packages for both individual countries and all of Europe.

German road conditions are generally excellent, with the exception of a few secondary roads in the former GDR that have yet to be renovated. Yes, there is no set speed limit on the **Autobahn,** or German highway; only a recommendation of 130km per hour (81mph) exists. Germans drive *fast*. Make a point to learn local driving signals and signs, and watch for signs indicating right-of-way (usually designated by a yellow triangle). The Autobahn is indicated by an intuitive "A" on signs; secondary highways, where the speed limit is usually 100km per hour, are accompanied by signs bearing a "B." Germans drive on the right side of the road, and it is illegal to pass on the right, even on superhighways. In cities and towns, speeds hover around 30-60kph (31mph).

Before setting off, know the laws of the countries in which you'll be driving. The **Association for Safe International Road Travel (ASIRT)** can provide more specific information about road conditions. Contact them at 5413 West Cedar Lane 103C, Bethesda, MD 20814 (tel. 301-983-5252; fax 983-3663; email asirt@erols.com; www.asirt.org). Germans use unleaded gas almost exclusively; prices run around DM7 per gallon, or about DM1.80 per liter.

MITFAHRZENTRALEN

These agencies are indicated in the **Getting There and Getting Around** or **Practical Information** sections of cities throughout the guide. *Mitfahrzentralen* pair up drivers and riders, who pay the agency a fee for the match and then negotiate the payment agreement with their driver. They provide a safe option for travel, as both the vehicle and driver must be registered with the office.

DRIVING PERMITS

Driver's licenses for most countries are valid in Germany for one year, after which a German license is required. Though it's not mandatory, it's strongly advised that you have an **International Driving Permit (IDP)**. In case you're in a situation (e.g. an accident or being stranded in a smaller town where the police speak less English), the IDP is an excellent idea; information on the card is printed in ten languages, including German. The IDP, valid for one year, must be issued in your home country before you depart; AAA affiliates cannot issue IDPs valid in their own country. You must be 18 years old to receive the IDP. An application for an IDP usually needs to include one or two photos, a current local license, an additional form of ID, and a fee.

Australia: Contact the Royal Automobile Club (RAC) or the National Royal Motorist Association (NRMA) if in NSW or the ACT (tel. (08) 9421 4298; www.rac.com.au/travel). Permits AUS$15.

Canada: Contact any Canadian Automobile Association (CAA) branch office in Canada, or write to CAA, 1145 Hunt Club Rd., Suite 200, K1V 0Y3 Canada. (tel. (613) 247-0117; fax 247-0118;www.caa.ca/CAAInternet/travelservices/internationaldocumentation/idp-travel.htm). Permits CDN$10.

Ireland: Contact the nearest Automobile Association (AA) office or the Irish Automobile Association, 23 Suffolk St., Blackrock, Co. Dublin (tel. (01) 677 9481). Permits IR£4.

New Zealand: Contact the Automobile Association (AA) or their main office at Auckland Central, 99 Albert St., Auckland (tel. (09) 377 4660; fax 302 2037; www.nzaa.co.nz.). Permits NZ$8.

South Africa: Contact the Automobile Association of South Africa at P.O. Box 596, Johannesburg, 2000 (tel. (011) 799 1000; fax 799 1010). Permits SAR28.50.

U.K.: Visit your local AA Shop, contact AA Headquarters (tel. (0990) 448 866), or write to the Automobile Association, International Documents, Fanum House, Erskine, Renfrewshire PA8 6BW (tel. (990) 500 600). Permits UK£4.

U.S.: Visit any American Automobile Association (AAA) office or write to AAA Florida, Travel Related Services, 1000 AAA Drive (mail stop 100), Heathrow, FL 32746 (tel. 407-444-7000; fax 444-7380). Permits US$10.

CAR INSURANCE

Third-party insurance is mandatory to drive in Germany. Most gold and platinum credit cards cover standard insurance; otherwise check to make sure that your regular car insurance will carry over onto your rental car. If you rent, lease, or borrow a car, you will need a **green card,** or **International Insurance Certificate,** to prove that you have liability insurance. Obtain it through the car rental agency; most include coverage in their prices—although if your credit card provides insurance, you'll want to turn down the offer provided by the rental agency. If you lease a car, obtain a green card from the dealer. Verify whether your auto insurance applies abroad; even if it does, you will still need a green card to certify this to foreign officials. If you have a collision abroad, the accident will show up on your domestic records if you report it to your insurance company. Rental agencies may require you to purchase theft insurance in countries that they consider to have a high risk of auto theft. Ask your rental agency about Germany.

If you belong to the Australian or American AAA, the British AA, or the Canadian CAA, you are eligible for roadside assistance, discounts on some forms of car insurance, and other road services from the German motor club equivalent, **Allgemeiner Deutscher Automobil Club (ADAC),** Am Westpark 8, 81373 Munich (tel. (089) 767 60). All cities have an ADAC branch.

RENTALS

You can **rent** a car from a U.S.-based firm with European offices, from a European-based company with local representatives, or from a tour operator which will arrange a rental for you from a European company at its own rates. Multinationals offer greater flexibility, but tour operators often strike better deals. Expect to pay DM130-180 per week, plus 16% tax, for a teensy car. Reserve well before leaving for Germany and pay in advance if at all possible. It is always significantly less expensive to reserve a car from the U.S. than from Germany. Always check if prices quoted include tax, unlimited mileage and collision insurance; some credit card companies cover this automatically. Ask about discounts and check the terms of insurance, particularly the size of the deductible. Non-Europeans should check with their national motoring organization (like AAA or CAA) for international coverage. Ask your airline about special fly-and-drive packages; you may get up to a week of free or discounted rental. Minimum age to rent in Germany is usually 21. At most agencies, all that's needed to rent a car is a U.S. license and proof that you've had it for a year. Rent cars in Europe from the following agencies:

Sixt, tel. (0180) 523 22 22; www.sixt.com.

Auto Europe, 39 Commercial St., P.O. Box 7006, Portland, ME 04101 (tel. 888-223-5555; fax 800-235-6321; www.autoeurope.com).

Avis, tel. 800-331-1084 in U.S. and Canada; in U.K., (0990) 900 500; in Australia, 800-225-533; www.avis.com.

Budget, tel. 800-472-3325 in the U.S.; in Canada, 800-527-0700; in the U.K., (0800) 181 181; in Australia, 13 2727; www.budgetrentacar.com.

Europe by Car, 1 Rockefeller Plaza, New York, NY 10020 (tel. 800-223-1516, 212-581-3040; www.europebycar.com).

Europcar, 145 Avenue Malekoff, 75016 Paris (tel. 800-227-3876 in the U.S.; 800-227-7368 in Canada; 145 00 08 06 in France; www.europcar.com).

Hertz, tel. 800-654-3001 in the U.S.; in Canada, 800-263-0600; in the U.K., (0990) 996 699; in Australia, 13 30 39; www.hertz.com.

LEASING

For trips longer than 17 days, **leasing** can be cheaper than renting; it is often the only option for those under 21. The cheapest leases are agreements to buy the car and then sell it back to the manufacturer at a prearranged price. As far as you're concerned, though, it's a lease and doesn't entail enormous financial transactions. Leases generally include insurance coverage and are not taxed, though they may include a VAT. Expect to pay at least US$1200 for 60 days. Contact **Auto Europe** or **Europe by Car** (see above).

SPECIFIC CONCERNS

WOMEN TRAVELERS

Women exploring on their own inevitably face additional safety concerns, but it's easy to be adventurous without taking undue risks. German cities, especially, offers services—from women-only taxi services to **Frauenzentrum** (women's centers)—that cater to women's traveling needs; these resources are listed in the **Practical Information** section. Moreover, German standards of public behavior are fairly reserved, and harassment is less common than in other parts of Europe.

Still, German women inhabit a less central political and economic position, and the *Wende* is only slowly changing this cultural reality. Many vestiges of a patriarchal government remain, both real and symbolic. For example, women have been able to serve in the Federal Republic's armed services since the induction of the **Basic Law** (see p. 18), which retains the possibility of female military service, but only in medical and musical capacity. It was not until 1999 that the Defense Ministry announced that women might soon be able to serve in guard duty capacity within the army, and a German woman appeared before the European Court of Justice to challenge the ban against combat duty. For more information on feminist initiatives, visit the local *Frauenzentrum* and *Frauenbuchladen* (women's bookstore).

If you are concerned about safety, you might consider staying in hostels which offer single rooms that lock from the inside or in religious organizations that offer rooms for women only. Communal showers in some hostels are safer than others; check them before settling in. Stick to centrally located accommodations and avoid solitary late-night treks or subway rides. When traveling, always carry extra money for a phone call, bus, or taxi. **Hitchhiking** is never safe for lone women, or even for two women traveling together. Choose train compartments occupied by other women or couples; ask the conductor to put together a women-only compartment if he or she doesn't offer to do so first. Look as if you know where you're going and consider approaching older women or couples for directions if you're lost or feel uncomfortable.

Generally, the less you look like a tourist, the better off you'll be. Wearing a conspicuous **wedding band** may help prevent unwanted overtures. Some travelers report that carrying pictures of a "husband" or "children" is extremely useful to help document marriage status. Even a mention of a husband waiting back at the hotel may be enough in some places to discount your potentially vulnerable, unattached appearance.

In cities, you may be harassed no matter how you're dressed. Your best answer to verbal harassment is no answer at all; feigned deafness, sitting motionless and staring straight ahead at nothing in particular will do a world of good that reactions usually don't achieve. The extremely persistent can sometimes be dissuaded by a firm, loud, and very public *Laß mich in Ruhe!* ("Leave me alone!"; LAHSS MEECH IN ROOH-eh). You can often rebuff a harasser by calling attention of passersby to his behavior. Don't hesitate to seek out a police officer or a passerby if you are being harassed.

Memorize the emergency numbers in Germany—**police: 110** and **ambulance: 112.** *Let's Go: Germany* lists other emergency numbers (including rape crisis lines) in the **Practical Information** listings of most cities. Carry a **whistle** or an airhorn on your keychain, and don't hesitate to use it in an emergency. An **IMPACT Model Mugging** self-defense course will not only prepare you for a potential attack, but will also raise your level of awareness of your surroundings as well as your confidence (see **Self Defense**, p. 49). Women also face some specific health concerns when traveling (see **Women's Health**, p. 55).

FURTHER READING

A Journey of One's Own: Uncommon Advice for the Independent Woman Traveler, Thalia Zepatos. Eighth Mountain Press (US$17).

Adventures in Good Company: The Complete Guide to Women's Tours and Outdoor Trips, Thalia Zepatos. Eighth Mountain Press (US$7).

Active Women Vacation Guide, Evelyn Kaye. Blue Panda Publications (US$18).

Travelers' Tales: Gutsy Women, Travel Tips and Wisdom for the Road, Marybeth Bond. Traveler's Tales (US$8).

A Foxy Old Woman's Guide to Traveling Alone, Jay Ben-Lesser. Crossing Press. (US$11).

TRAVELING ALONE

There are many benefits to traveling alone, among them greater independence and challenge. On the other hand, any solo traveler is a more vulnerable target of harassment and street theft. Lone travelers need to be well-organized and look confident at all times. If questioned, never admit that you are traveling alone. Maintain regular contact with someone at home who knows your itinerary.

A number of organizations supply information for solo travelers, and others find travel companions for those who don't want to go alone. A few are listed here.

Connecting: Solo Traveler Network, P.O. Box 29088, 1996 W. Broadway, Vancouver, BC V6J 5C2, Canada (tel. 604-737-7791; email info@cstn.org; www.cstn.org). Bi-monthly newsletter features solo travel tips, single-friendly tips and travel companion ads. Annual directory lists holiday suppliers that avoid single supplement charges. Advice and lodging exchanges facilitated between members. Membership US$25-35.

Travel Companion Exchange, P.O. Box 833, Amityville, NY 11701 (tel. 516-454-0880 or 800-392-1256). Publishes the pamphlet *Foiling Pickpockets & Bag Snatchers* (US$4) and *Travel Companions,* a bi-monthly newsletter for single travelers seeking a travel partner. Subscription US$48.

FURTHER READING: TRAVELING ALONE

Traveling Solo, Eleanor Berman. Globe Pequot (US$17).

The Single Traveler Newsletter, P.O. Box 682, Ross, CA 94957 (tel. 415-389-0227). 6 issues US$29.

OLDER TRAVELERS

Senior citizens are eligible for a wide range of discounts on transportation, museums, movies, theaters, concerts, restaurants, and accommodations in Germany. If you don't see a reduced price listed, ask, and you may be delightfully surprised. Furthermore, Germany's excellent public transportation systems make most places easily accessible for older travelers. Agencies for senior group travel are growing in enrollment and popularity. These are only a few:

ElderTreks, 597 Markham St., Toronto, ON, Canada, M6G 2L7 (tel. 800-741-7956 or (416) 588-5000; fax 588-9839; email passages@inforamp.net; www.eldertreks.com).

Elderhostel, 75 Federal St., Boston, MA 02110-1941 (tel. 617-426-7788 or 877-426-8056; email registration@elderhostel.org; www.elderhostel.org). Programs at colleges, universities, and other learning centers in Germany on varied subjects lasting 1-4 weeks. Must be 55 or over; spouse can be of any age.

The Mature Traveler, P.O. Box 50400, Reno, NV 89513 (tel. 775-786-7419 or 800-460-6676). Soft-adventure tours for seniors. Subscription $30.

ESSENTIALS

ESSENTIALS

FURTHER READING

No Problem! Worldwise Tips for Mature Adventurers, Janice Kenyon. Orca Book Publishers (US$16).

A Senior's Guide to Healthy Travel, Donald L. Sullivan. Career Press. (US$15).

Unbelievably Good Deals and Great Adventures That You Absolutely Can't Get Unless You're Over 50, Joan Rattner Heilman. Contemporary Books (US$13).

BISEXUAL, GAY, AND LESBIAN TRAVELERS

Many bisexual, gay, and lesbian visitors to Germany are surprised to find a more acceptable environment than in their home country. While homophobic attitudes persist in rural areas as well as in ultraconservative Bavaria, Germans are generally more tolerant of homosexuality than Americans and Britons, though not quite as accepting as the Dutch. The German word for gay is *Schwul*, which refers exclusively to men; for lesbians, it's *Lesbe*. *Let's Go* provides information on local bisexual, gay, and lesbian culture in **Practical Information** listings and **Entertainment and Nightlife** sections of city descriptions. The epicenter of gay life in Germany, and possibly all of Europe, is Berlin (see p. 137). Other major centers include Hamburg, Frankfurt, Köln, and München. While tolerance is still very much a new concept in Eastern Germany, fairly prominent gay scenes have developed in Leipzig and, to a lesser extent, Dresden. Women should look for *Frauencafés* and *Frauenkneipen*. It should be stressed that while such cafés are for women only, they are *not* for lesbians only. The local *Frauenbuchladen* (women's bookstore) is a good resource. There are dozens of regional and national gay and lesbian organizations; two of the largest are the **Bundesverband Homosexualität (BVH)**, Greifswalder Str. 224, 10405 Berlin (tel. (030) 441 24 98), and the **Schwulenverband Deutschland (SVD)**, Friedrichstr. 165, 10117 Berlin (tel. (030) 201 08 04). Listed below are contact organizations, mail-order bookstores and publishers which offer materials addressing some specific concerns.

Gay's the Word, 66 Marchmont St., London WC1N 1AB (tel. (020) 7278 7654; email gays.theword@virgin.net; www.gaystheword.co.uk). The largest gay and lesbian bookshop in the U.K. Mail-order service available. No catalogue of listings, but they will provide a list of titles on a given subject.

Giovanni's Room, 345 S. 12th St., Philadelphia, PA 19107 (tel. 215-923-2960; fax 923-0813; email giophilp@netaxs.com). An international feminist, lesbian, and gay bookstore with mail-order service which carries the publications listed below.

International Gay and Lesbian Travel Association, 4331 N. Federal Hwy., Suite 304, Fort Lauderdale, FL 33308 (tel. 954-776-2626 or 800-448-8550; fax 954-776-3303; email IGLTA@aol.com; www.iglta.com). An organization of more than 1,350 companies serving gay and lesbian travelers. Call for travel agents, accommodations, and events.

International Lesbian and Gay Association (ILGA), 81 rue Marché-au-Charbon, B-1000 Brussels, Belgium (tel./fax (02) 502 24 71; email ilga@ilga.org; www.ilga.org). Not a travel service. Provides political information, such as homosexuality laws of individual countries.

FURTHER READING

Spartacus International Gay Guide. Bruno Gmünder Verlag. (US$33).

Damron Men's Guide, Damron's Accommodations, and The Women's Traveller. Damron Travel Guides (US$14-19). For more information, call 415-255-0404 or 800-462-6654 or check their website (www.damron.com).

Ferrari Guides' Gay Travel A to Z, Ferrari Guides' Men's Travel in Your Pocket, Ferrari Guides' Women's Travel in Your Pocket, and Ferrari Guides' Inn Places. Ferrari Guides (US$14-16). To order, call 602-863-2408 or 800-962-2912 or check their website (www.q-net.com).

TRAVELERS WITH DISABILITIES

Germany provides very competent services, information and accessibility to facilities for travelers with disabilities, **Behinderte** or **Schwerbehinderte.** Both national and regional tourist boards provide directories on the accessibility of various accommodations and transportation services.

Germany's excellent public transportation systems make most places easily accessible for travelers with disabilities, and many public transport systems are wheelchair-accessible. The international wheelchair icon or a large letter "B" indicates access. Intersections in major cities have audible crossing signals for the blind. Those with disabilities should inform airlines and hotels of their disabilities when making arrangements for travel; some time may be needed to prepare special accommodations. Call ahead to restaurants, hotels, parks, and other facilities to find out about the existence of ramps, the widths of doors, the dimensions of elevators, etc. All ICE, EC, and IC trains are equipped for wheelchair accessibility, and you can request free seat reservations. Rail is probably the most convenient form of travel for disabled travelers in Europe; for more information, contact Deutsche Bahn (see **Getting Around: By Train,** p. 71). Guide dog owners should be aware that Germany requires evidence of rabies vaccination from a licensed veterinarian at least 30 days but not more than 12 months before entering the country. A notarized German translation of this certificate is required. Hertz, Avis, and National car rental agencies have hand-controlled vehicles at some locations.

The following organizations provide information that might be of assistance:

Mobility International USA (MIUSA), P.O. Box 10767, Eugene, OR 97440 (tel. 541-343-1284 voice and TDD; fax 343-6812; email info@miusa.org; www.miusa.org). Sells *A World of Options: A Guide to International Educational Exchange, Community Service, and Travel for Persons with Disabilities* (US$35).

Moss Rehab Hospital Travel Information Service (tel. 215-456-9600; www.mossresourcenet.org). A telephone and internet information resource center on international travel accessibility and other travel-related concerns for those with disabilities.

Society for the Advancement of Travel for the Handicapped (SATH), 347 5th Ave., #610, New York, NY 10016 (tel. 212-447-1928; fax 725-8253; email sath-travel@aol.com; www.sath.org). Advocacy group publishing the quarterly travel magazine *Open World* (free for members or US$13 for nonmembers). Also publishes a wide range of information sheets on disability travel facilitation and accessible destinations. Annual membership US$45, students and seniors US$30.

Directions Unlimited, 720 N. Bedford Rd., Bedford Hills, NY 10507 (tel. 800-533-5343; in NY 914-241-1700; fax 241-0243; email cruisesusa@aol.com). Specializes in arranging individual and group vacations, tours, and cruises for the disabled. Group tours for blind travelers.

FURTHER READING

Wheelchair Through Europe, Annie Mackin. Graphic Language Press (760-944-9594; email niteowl@cts.com).

Global Access (www.geocities.com/Paris/1502/disabilitylinks.html) has links for disabled travelers in Germany.

MINORITY TRAVELERS

Germany has a significant minority population composed mainly of about two million Turks. In addition, there are about a million residents from the former Yugoslavia, facing increasing hostility, a number of Romany-Sinti people (also known as Gypsies). Eastern Germany also has about 100,000 Vietnamese residents. All the same, conspicuously non-German foreigners may stand out in less-traveled parts of both the East and West.

In certain economically depressed regions, tourists of color or members of certain religious groups may feel threatened by the small, but vocal neo-Nazi groups. While they represent only a fraction of the population, Neo-Nazi skinheads in the large cities of former East Germany, as well as in Western Germany, have been known to attack foreigners, especially non-whites. In these areas, common sense will serve you best. Keeping abreast of news of any such attack and then keeping away from the area in which it happened is perhaps the best (and only) real strategy for avoiding trouble.

RELIGIOUS TRAVELERS

It is impossible to discuss religion in contemporary Germany without hearing a multitude of voices of past and present: the voices of Holocaust survivors, the voices of neo-Nazis, the voices of courageous East German pastors who led the peaceful resistance against the Communists, and the voice of the modern Basic Law which states that "freedom of faith and conscience as well as freedom of religious or other belief shall be inviolable. The undisturbed practice of religion shall be guaranteed." The total Jewish population in Germany today is approximately 40-50,000. The largest Jewish congregations are in Berlin and Frankfurt, which together are home to more than 10,000 Jews. An influx of foreign workers has brought with it a strong Islamic population; today, almost two million Muslims, mostly from Turkey, live in Germany. For information, contact these organizations.

Protestant: Kirchenamt der evangelischen Kirche in Deutschland, Herrenhäuser Str. 12, 30419 Hannover (tel. (0511) 279 60; fax 279 67 07; email ekd@ekd.de).

Catholic: Katholisches Auslandssekretariat der Deutschen Bischofskonferenz Tourismus und Urlauberselsorge, Kaiser-Friedrich-Str. 9, 53113 Bonn (tel. (0228) 91 14 30; fax 911 43 33).

Muslim: Islamische Gemeinschaft Berlin, Gesslerstr. 11, 10829 Berlin (tel./fax (030) 788 48 83; email mohammed.herzog@igdmb.de).

Jewish: Jewish community centers in each of the following cities: **Berlin,** Fasanenstr. 79-80 (tel. (030) 880-280); **Bonn,** Tempelstr. 2 (tel./fax (0228) 21 35 60); **Frankfurt,** Westendstr. 43, 60325 (tel. (069) 740 72 15; email yg.ssn@online.de); **Munich,** Reichenbachstr. 27, 80469 (tel. (089) 202 40 00; fax (089) 201 46 04).

TRAVELERS WITH CHILDREN

Family vacations require that you plan ahead and often that you slow your pace. When deciding where to stay, remember the special needs of young children; if you pick a hostel or a small hotel, call ahead and make sure it's child-friendly. If you rent a car, make sure the rental company provides a car seat for younger children. Consider using a papoose-style device to carry a baby on walking trips. Be sure that your child carries some sort of ID in case of an emergency or if he or she gets lost, and arrange a reunion spot in case of separation when sight-seeing.

Restaurants often have children's menus and discounts. Virtually all museums and tourist attractions also have a children's rate. Children under two generally fly for 10% of the adult airfare on international flights, but this does not necessarily include a seat. International fares are usually discounted 25% for children from two to 11. Finding a private place for breast feeding is often a problem while traveling, so pack accordingly.

FURTHER READING

Backpacking with Babies and Small Children, Goldie Silverman. Wilderness Press (US$10).

Take Your Kids to Europe, Cynthia W. Harriman. Globe Pequot (US$17).

The MCI WorldCom Card.

The easy way to call when traveling worldwide.

The MCI WorldCom Card gives you...

- Access to the US and other countries worldwide.
- Customer Service 24 hours a day
- Operators who speak your language
- Great MCI WorldCom rates and no sign-up fees

For more information or to apply for a Card call:

1-800-955-0925

Outside the U.S., call MCI WorldCom collect (reverse charge) at:

1-712-943-6839

COUNTRY	WORLDPHONE TOLL-FREE ACCESS #
Argentina (CC)	
To call using Telefonica ■	0800-222-6249
To call using Telecom ■	0800-555-1002
Australia (CC) ◆	
To call using AAPT ■	1-800-730-014
To call using OPTUS ■	1-800-551-111
To call using TELSTRA ■	1-800-881-100
Austria (CC) ◆	0800-200-235
Bahamas	1-800-888-8000
Belgium (CC) ◆	0800-10012
Bermuda ÷	1-800-888-8000
Brazil (CC)	000-8012
British Virgin Islands ÷	1-800-888-8000
Canada (CC)	1-800-888-8000
Cayman Islands	1-800-888-8000
Chile (CC)	
To call using CTC ■	800-207-300
To call using ENTEL ■	800-360-180
China ÷	108-12
For a Mandarin-speaking Operator	108-17
Colombia (CC) ◆	980-9-16-0001
Collect Access in Spanish	980-9-16-1111
Costa Rica ◆	0800-012-2222
Czech Republic (CC) ◆	00-42-000112
Denmark (CC) ◆	8001-0022
Dominican Republic	
Collect Access	1-800-888-8000
Collect Access in Spanish	1121
Ecuador (CC) ÷	999-170
El Salvador	800-1767

COUNTRY	WORLDPHONE TOLL-FREE ACCESS #
Finland (CC) ◆	08001-102-80
France (CC) ◆	0800-99-0019
French Guiana (CC)	0-800-99-0019
Guatemala (CC) ◆	99-99-189
Germany (CC)	0-800-888-8000
Greece (CC) ◆	00-800-1211
Guam (CC)	1-800-888-8000
Haiti ÷	193
Collect Access in French/Creole	190
Honduras ÷	8000-122
Hong Kong (CC)	800-96-1121
Hungary (CC) ◆	00▼800-01411
India (CC) ÷	000-127
Collect Access	000-126
Ireland (CC)	1-800-55-1001
Israel (CC)	
BEZEQ International	1-800-940-2727
BARAK	1-800-930-2727
Italy (CC) ◆	172-1022
Jamaica ÷	Collect Access 1-800-888-8000
(From Special Hotels only)	873
(From public phones)	#2
Japan (CC) ◆	To call using KDD ■ 00539-121▶
To call using IDC ■	0066-55-121
To call using JT ■	0044-11-121
Korea (CC)	To call using KT ■ 00729-14
To call using DACOM ■	00309-12
To call using ONSE	00369-14
Phone Booths ÷	Press red button, 03, then ●
Military Bases	550-2255
Lebanon	Collect Access 600-MCI (600-624)

COUNTRY	WORLDPHONE TOLL-FREE ACCESS #
Luxembourg (CC)	0800-0112
Malaysia (CC) ◆	1-800-80-0012
To call using Time Telekom ■	1-800-18-0012
Mexico (CC) Avantel	01-800-021-8000
Telmex ▲	001-800-674-7000
Collect Access in Spanish	01-800-021-1000
Monaco (CC) ◆	800-90-019
Netherlands (CC) ◆	0800-022-9122
New Zealand (CC)	000-912
Nicaragua (CC)	Collect Access in Spanish 166
(Outside of Managua, dial 02 first)	
Norway (CC) ◆	800-19912
Panama	108
Military Bases	2810-108
Philippines (CC) ◆	To call using PLDT ■ 105-14
To call using PHILCOM	1026-14
To call using Bayantel	1237-14
To call using ETPI	1066-14
Poland (CC) ÷	00-800-111-21-22
Portugal (CC) ÷	800-800-123
Puerto Rico (CC)	1-800-888-8000
Romania (CC) ÷	01-800-1800
Russia (CC) ◆ ÷	
To call using ROSTELCOM ■	747-3322
(For Russian speaking operator)	747-3320
To call using SOVINTEL ■	960-2222
Saudi Arabia (CC) ÷	1-800-11
Singapore	8000-112-112
Slovak Republic	(CC) 00421-00112
South Africa (CC)	0800-99-0011
Spain (CC)	900-99-0014

Worldwide Calling Made Easy

The MCI WorldCom Card, designed specifically to keep you in touch with the people that matter the most to you.

www.wcom.com/worldphone

Please cut out and save this reference guide for convenient U.S. and worldwide calling with the MCI WorldCom Card.

And, it's simple to call home or to other countires.

1. Dial the WorldPhone toll-free access number of the country you're calling from (listed inside).

2. Follow the easy voice instructions or hold for a WorldPhone operator. Enter or give the operator your MCI WorldCom Card number or call collect.

3. Enter or give the WorldPhone operator your home number.

4. Share your adventures with your family!

COUNTRY		WORLDPHONE TOLL-FREE ACCESS #
St. Lucia ÷		1-800-888-8000
Sweden (CC) ◆		020-795-922
Switzerland (CC) ◆		0800-89-0222
Taiwan (CC) ◆		0080-13-4567
Thailand ★		001-999-1-2001
Turkey (CC) ◆		00-8001-1177
United Kingdom	(CC) To call using BT ■	0800-89-0222
	To call using CWC ■	0500-89-0222
United States (CC)		1-800-888-8000
U.S. Virgin Islands (CC)		1-800-888-8000
Vatican City (CC)		172-1022
Venezuela (CC) ÷ ◆		800-1114-0
Vietnam ●		1201-1022

(CC)	Country-to-country calling available to/from most international locations.
÷	Limited availability.
▼	Wait for second dial tone.
▲	When calling from public phones, use phones marked LADATEL.
■	International communications carrier.
★	Not available from public pay phones.
◆	Public phones may require deposit of coin or phone card for dial tone.
●	Local service fee in U.S. currency required to complete call.
►	Regulation does not permit Intra-Japan calls.
❖	Available from most major cities

MCI WorldCom Worldphone Access Number

MCI WORLDCOM.sm

How to take Great Trips with Your Kids, Sanford and Jane Portnoy. Harvard Common Press (US $10).

Have Kid, Will Travel: 101 Survival Strategies for Vacationing With Babies and Young Children, Claire and Lucille Tristram. Andrews and McMeel (US$9).

Adventuring with Children: An Inspirational Guide to World Travel and the Outdoors, Nan Jeffrey. Avalon House Publishing ($15).

Trouble-Free Travel with Children, Vicki Lansky. Book Peddlers (US$9).

DIETARY CONCERNS

Although Germany is unapologetically carnivorous, vegetarianism has become increasingly popular in the last ten years (see **Food and Drink,** p. 33). Mad cow disease, growing health consciousness, and a blooming alternative scene have all contributed to a decline in meat consumption. Vegetarian restaurants have proliferated in larger cities, while health food shops, such as the well-known **Reformhaus,** provide a large selection of vegetarian and vegan products. *Let's Go: Germany* makes an effort to identify restaurants that offer vegetarian and vegan choices. Many of these establishments are ethnic restaurants; traditional German restaurants often offer no genuinely vegetarian dishes. For more information about vegetarian travel, contact:

European Vegetarian Union, Hildegund Scholvien, Friedhofstr. 12, 67693 Fischbach (tel. (06305) 272; fax (06305) 52 56; email scholvien@folz.de).

Vegetarian Association of Germany, Blumenstr. 3, 30159 Hannover (tel. (0511) 363 20 50; fax (0511) 363 20 07; email www.comlink.apc.org/vbd/).

North American Vegetarian Society, P.O. Box 72, Dolgeville, NY 13329 (tel. 518-568-7970; email navs@telenet.com; www.cyberveg.org/navs/). Publishes *Transformative Adventures,* a global guide to vacations and retreats (US$15).

Vegans International, c/o Heidrun Leisenheimer, Rosenheimer Landstr. 33a, 85521 Ottobrunn.

For historic and political reasons, few Jews live in Germany, and the kosher offerings are correspondingly small. Travelers who keep kosher should contact synagogues in larger cities for information on kosher restaurants; your own synagogue or college Hillel should have access to lists of Jewish institutions across the nation. If you are strict in your observance, you may have to prepare your own food on the road.

The Jewish Travel Guide lists synagogues, kosher restaurants, and Jewish institutions in more than 80 countries. Available from Vallentine-Mitchell Publishers, Newbury House 890-900, Eastern Ave., Newbury Park, Ilford, Essex, U.K. IG2 7HH (tel. (020) 8599 8866; fax 8599 0984). It is available in the U.S. ($16) from ISBS, 5804 NE Hassalo St., Portland, OR 97213-3644 (tel. 800-944-6190).

FURTHER READING

The Vegetarian Traveler: Where to Stay if You're Vegetarian, Jed Civic. Larson Publishers. (US$16).

Europe on 10 Salads a Day, Greg and Mary Jane Edwards. Mustang Publishing. (US$10).

ALTERNATIVES TO TOURISM

STUDY

Foreign study programs vary tremendously in expense, academic quality, living conditions, degree of contact with local students, and exposure to culture and language. Most American undergraduates enroll in programs sponsored by U.S. universities, and many college offices give advice and information on **study abroad.** Ask for the names of recent participants in the programs and get in touch with them. Even basic language skills might be sufficient to allow direct enrollment in German universities, which—because they are publicly funded—are far cheaper than those in North America (and vastly cheaper than a study abroad program).

Studying in Germany requires a passport (see p. 40) and usually a student visa and resident permit (see **Visas and Work Permits,** p. 41). Sometimes a summer abroad program will not require a visa. An **International Student Identity Card (ISIC)** is highly recommended (see p. 41).

Deutscher Akademischer Austauschdienst (DAAD), 950 3rd Ave., 19th fl., New York, NY 10022 (tel. 212-758-3223; email daadny@daad.org; www.daad.org); in Germany, Kennedyallee 50, 53175 Bonn. Information on language instruction, exchanges, and the wealth of scholarships for study in Germany. The place to contact if you want to enroll in a German university; distributes applications and the valuable *Academic Study in the Federal Republic of Germany.*

Goethe-Institut, Helene-Weber-Allee 1, 80637 München (tel. (089) 15 92 10; fax 15 92 14 50; mailing address Postfach 190419, 80604 München; email for adult students esb@goethe.de; for students under 26 esj@goethe.de; www.goethe.de), runs numerous German language programs in Germany and abroad; it also orchestrates high school exchange programs in Germany. For information on these programs and on their many cultural offerings, look on the web or contact your local branch (**Australia,** Canberra, Melbourne, Sydney; **Canada,** Montreal, Toronto, Vancouver; **Ireland,** Dublin; **New Zealand,** Wellington; **U.K.,** Glasgow, London, Manchester, York; **U.S.,** New York, Washington, D.C., Boston, Atlanta, San Francisco, Los Angeles, Seattle) or write to the main office. 8-week intensive summer course DM2940, with room DM3740.

FURTHER READING

Academic Year Abroad. Institute of International Education Books (US$45).

Vacation Study Abroad. Institute of International Education Books (US$40).

Peterson's Study Abroad Guide. Peterson's (US$30).

WORK

With unemployment in Western Germany still hovering over 10%, and rates even higher in the former GDR, Germany's days as a mecca for unskilled foreign workers are over. Millions of *Gastarbeiter* (guest workers) and former GDR citizens relocated in western Germany compete for positions, flooding an already tight bureaucracy and job market. Moreover, wading through the morass of German bureaucracy to obtain work permits can be disheartening, and the government takes documentation quite seriously, without which you will find the search impossible. However, if you are lucky enough to find work in Germany, take comfort in pay: wages are notably high, even among retail service industries.

There are often ways to make the search easier. Fluency in German will make employers much more likely to consider you. Friends in Germany can help expedite work permits or arrange work-for-accommodations swaps. EU citizens can work in Germany provided they have an EU residency permit *(EU-Aufenthaltserlaubnis);* if your parents were born in an EU country, you may be able to claim dual citizenship or at least the right to a work permit. For U.S. citizens and other non-Europeans, you will need to obtain a residency permit *(Aufenthaltserlaubnis)* and work permit *(Arbeitserlaubnis).*

The German government maintains a slew of federally run employment offices, the *Bundesanstalt für Arbeit,* throughout the country. The *Bundesanstalt* tends to treat EU citizens with specific skills more favorably than those from other countries. The youth division is a bit more welcoming for foreign students ages 18-30 seeking summer employment; jobs frequently involve manual labor. Contact the central office before March, and be able to work for at least two months. With the proper certification and an offer in hand, you will be referred to a local employment office *(Arbeitsamt)* who will issue another work permit for your particular position. In recent years, private employment agencies have cropped up, although the unofficial monopoly is still in the federal office.

The best tips on jobs for foreigners often come from other travelers, so be alert and inquisitive. Newspaper listings are another start. During the summer especially, the German tourist industry relies on students and illegal immigrants to blow the bellows at hotels, hostels, and resorts. Other fields such as fast food, agriculture, and nursing (for which you will need further health certification), and generally sectors involving skilled building labor, are friendlier to travelers. Ask around at pubs, cafés, restaurants, and hotels. Be sure to be aware of your rights as an employee; should a crafty employer try to refuse payment at the end of the season, it'll help if you have a written confirmation of your agreement. Consider work teaching English. Post a sign in markets or learning centers stating that you are a native speaker, and scan the classifieds of local newspapers.

If you are a full-time student at a U.S. university, the simplest way to get a job in Germany is through work permit programs run by the **Council on International Educational Exchange (Council)** and its member organizations. For a US$225 application fee, Council can procure three- to six-month work permits and a handbook to help you find work and housing. No matter what your employment, make sure that you are covered by some type of health insurance (see p. 56).

AU PAIR

Accord Cultural Exchange, 750 La Playa, San Francisco, CA 94121 (tel. 415-386-6203; fax 386-0240; email leftbank@hotmail.com; www.cognitext.com/accord), offers au pair jobs to people aged 18-29 in Germany. Au pairs work 5-6 hours a day, 30 hours a week, plus 2 evenings of babysitting. Light housekeeping and childcare in exchange for room and board plus US$250-400 per month salary. Program fees US$750 for the summer, US$1200 for the academic year. US$40 application fee.

interExchange, 161 Sixth Ave., New York, NY 10013 (tel. 212-924-0446; fax 924-0575; email interex@earthlink.net) provides information on international work and au pair positions in Germany.

Childcare International, Ltd., Trafalgar House, Grenville Place, London NW7 3SA (tel. (020) 8906 3116; fax 8906 3461; email office@childint.demon.co.uk; www.childint.demon.co.uk) offers au pair positions in Germany. Provides information on local language schools. The organization prefers a long placement but does arrange summer work. UK£80 application fee.

TEACHING ENGLISH

International Schools Services, Educational Staffing Program, P.O. Box 5910, Princeton, NJ 08543 (tel. 609-452-0990; fax 452-2690; email edustaffing@iss.edu; www.iss.edu). Recruits teachers and administrators for American and English schools in Germany. All instruction in English. Applicants must have a bachelor's degree and two years of relevant experience. Nonrefundable US$100 application fee. Publishes *The ISS Directory of Overseas Schools* (US$35).

Office of Overseas Schools, A/OS Room 245, SA-29, Dept. of State, Washington, D.C. 20522-2902 (tel. 703-875-7800; fax 875-7979; email overseas.school@state.gov; state.gov/www/about_state/schools/). Maintains a list of schools abroad and agencies that arrange placement for Americans to teach abroad.

ESSENTIALS

AGRICULTURE

Willing Workers on Organic Farms (WWOOF), c/o Miriam Wittmann, Postfach 210259, 01263 Dresden, Germany (email fairtours@gn.apc.org; www.phdcc.com/sites/wwoof). Membership ($10 or DM30) in WWOOF allows you to receive room and board at a variety of organic farms in Germany in exchange for chores.

FURTHER READING

Work Your Way Around the World: The Authoritative Guide for the Working Traveler, Susan Griffith. Peterson's (US$18). The Germany-specific information provides an incredibly thorough tour through the tangle of Germany's employment bureaucracy.

VOLUNTEERING

Volunteer jobs are readily available almost everywhere, and you may receive room and board in exchange for labor. You can sometimes avoid the high application fees charged by the organizations that arrange placement by contacting the individual workcamps directly.

Service Civil International Voluntary Service (SCI-VS), 814 NE 40th St., Seattle, WA 98105 (tel./fax 206-545-6585; email sciivsusa@igc.apc.org). Arranges placement in workcamps in Europe for those over 18. Local organizations sponsor groups for physical and social work. Registration fees US$50-250, depending on the camp location.

Volunteers for Peace, 1034 Tiffany Rd., Belmont, VT 05730 (tel. 802-259-2759; fax 259-2922; email vfp@vfp.org; www.vfp.org). A nonprofit organization that arranges speedy placement in 2-3 week workcamps in Germany comprising 10-15 people. Most complete and up-to-date listings provided in the annual *International Workcamp Directory* (US$15). Registration fee US$195. Free newsletter.

ESSENTIALS

FURTHER READING: VOLUNTEERING

International Jobs: Where They Are, How to Get Them, Eric Kocher and Nina Segal. Perseus Books (US$16).

How to Get a Job in Europe, Robert Sanborn. Surrey Books (US$22).

The Alternative Travel Directory, Clayton Hubbs. Transitions Abroad (US$20).

Work Abroad, Clayton Hubbs. Transitions Abroad (US$16).

International Directory of Voluntary Work, Victoria Pybus. Vacation Work Publications (US$16).

Teaching English Abroad, Susan Griffin. Vacation Work (US$17).

Overseas Summer Jobs 1999, Work Your Way Around the World, and *Directory of Jobs and Careers Abroad.* Peterson's (US$17-18 each).

OTHER RESOURCES

TOURIST OFFICES

For detailed information on any aspect of traveling in Germany, contact the **German National Tourist Office** in your home country or visit their website at www.germany-tourism.de, which includes suggested itineraries and links to over 50 major cities. The office will send you heaps of maps and brochures on Germany's 16 *Länder* and outdoor activities.

Canada: 175 Bloor Str. East, North Tower, Suite 604, Toronto, ON M4W 3R8 (tel. 416-968-1570; fax 416-968-1986; email germanto@idirect.com).

U.K.: P.O. Box 2695, London W1A 3NT (tel. (020) 7317 0908; fax (020) 7495 6129; email German_National_Tourist_Office@compuserve.com).

U.S.: 122 East 42nd St., Chanin Bldg., 52nd Floor, New York, NY 10168-0072 (tel. 212-661-7200; fax 661-7174; email gntony@aol.com).

USEFUL PUBLICATIONS

The publications we list here should be useful in preparing for your trip. For books on Germany's culture and history, see **Further Reading,** p. 23. For information on German newspapers, see **Media,** p. 32.

A Traveller's Wine Guide to Germany, Kerry Brady Stewart. Traveller's Wine Guides, 1997. (U.S.$17.95). Exactly what it says it is, by a well-known oenophile.

Atlantik-Brücke, Adenauerallee 131, 53113 Bonn. Devoted to promoting mutual understanding (hence "Atlantic Bridge"), it publishes *These Strange German Ways*—a must for any American planning on living in Germany—as well as *Meet United Germany, German Holidays and Folk Customs,* and *Speaking Out: Jewish Voices from United Germany.* Order the books from the Hamburg office (tel. (040) 600 70 22).

Culture Shock! Germany, published by Graphic Arts Publishing Company, P.O. Box 10306, Portland, OR 97296-0306 (tel. 503-226-2402). A readable low-down on living in Deutschland that isn't afraid to hold your hand.

Germany by Bike, Nadine Slavinski. Twenty tours throughout the *Länder,* with general information on getting your bike ready for the *Tour de...Deutschland.*

Wicked German, Howard Tomb. Workman, 1992 (U.S.$4.95). A little guide to everything your really didn't need to know how to say in German.

TRAVEL BOOK PUBLISHERS

Hippocrene Books, 171 Madison Ave., New York, NY 10016 (tel. (212-685-4371; orders 718-454-2366; fax 454-1391; email contact@hippocrenebooks.com; www.netcom.com/~hippocre). Publishes travel reference books, travel guides, foreign language dictionaries, and language learning guides. Free catalog.

Hunter Publishing, 130 Campus Dr., Edison, NJ 08818-7816 (tel. 800-255-0343; email kimba@mediasoft.net; www.hunterpublishing.com). Has an extensive catalogue of travel books, guides, language learning tapes, and quality maps, and the *Charming Small Hotel Guide to Germany* (US$15).

Rand McNally, 150 S. Wacker Dr., Chicago, IL 60606 (tel. 800-234-0679 or 312-332-2009; fax 443-9540; email storekeeper@randmcnally.com; www.randmcnally.com), publishes a number of comprehensive road atlases (each US$10).

THE WORLD WIDE WEB

Most tourist offices and many services and museums in Germany have web sites and email addresses. *Let's Go* lists web and email addresses for tourist offices in larger cities, which often have English versions—look for a Union Jack icon in many cases. Some make room reservations possible through the web; almost all have up-to-date information on how to do so by fax or phone. In addition to the many web sites listed throughout this chapter, there are several general sites useful for planning a trip to Germany.

German Embassy and German Information Center (www.germany-info.org), provides comprehensive information on all aspects of traveling to Germany.

Deutsche Welle (www.dwelle.de/english), broadcasts international news from a German perspective, in English.

Deutsche Telekom (www.teleauskunft.de), finds German addresses and phone numbers

Microsoft Expedia (expedia.msn.com), has everything you need to make travel plans on the web: compare flight fares, look at maps, make reservations. FareTracker, a free service, sends monthly mailings about the cheapest fares to any destination.

Shoestring Travel (www.stratpub.com), an alternative to Microsoft's monolithic site, is a budget travel e-zine that features listings of home exchanges and accommodations information.

Foreign Language for Travelers (www.travlang.com), offers a crash course in German.

Let's Go (www.letsgo.com), is where you can find our newsletter, information about our books, up-to-the-minute links, and more.

FURTHER READING

How to Plan Your Dream Vacation Using the Web. Elizabeth Dempsey. Coriolis Group (US$25).

Nettravel: How Travelers Use the Internet, Michael Shapiro. O'Reilly & Associates. (US$25).

Travel Planning Online for Dummies, Noah Vadnai. IDG Books. (US$25).

BERLIN

Now is the time to see Berlin. Plans are underway to transform it from the Allied-bombed and Allied-occupied city of the post-WWII years into a sparklingly whole metropolis which will once again serve as Germany's capital, irreversibly changing the city's identity. What has always made Berlin a remarkable city is its ability to flourish in times of adversity, and the bureaucratic structure that Bonn's corps of civil servants promises to bring with it may end Berlin's Phoenix-like existence. For once the construction sites become finished buildings, abandoned apartments are restored to their former glory, and the population settles down into a more conservative stance befitting a capital city, very little will be left of the chaotic atmosphere upon which Berlin thrived during the 20th century. During the Weimar Republic and again during the 40 years when the divided city personified the unde-clared Cold War, Berlin's struggles forced its inhabitants to innovate. Raised in the shadow of global conflict, Berliners responded with a glorious storm of cultural activity and the sort of free-for-all nightlife you might expect from a population that had its back against the wall. With the collapse of the Berlin Wall in 1989, the city suddenly gained the opportunity to reinvent itself. Communist governments fell across Eastern Europe, and Berlin found itself in a unique position, straddling the border of two distinct but no longer separate worlds. Almost overnight, it became a gateway—*the* gateway—between East and West. Yet at the same time, its two halves were forced to fuse, forming a complex, decentralized metropolis.

Greater Berlin and Environs

The task of reuniting the twin cities is proving to be a difficult one. Plagued by a divisive West-versus-East mentality intensified by the rapidity of reunion, Berliners from both sides of the former divide are palpably less enthusiastic about sharing "their" city a decade after the myopically euphoric reunification. High unemployment rates, skyrocketing rents, and Berlin's infamous reputation as an *ewige Baustelle*—perpetual construction site—have conspired against the Berliners' initial thrill of reestablishing their city as one of the continent's most prominent cultural and political centers. Nonetheless, the city continues to gain momentum from its omnipresent and chaotic ambivalence toward the future. The threat of nuclear holocaust taught Berliners to live like there was no tomorrow, and this penchant for shortsighted excess continues to manifest itself in all aspects of the city's existence, from its ridiculously grandiose building endeavors to the party-til-dawn atmosphere that reigns in its smoky nightclubs.

Now, as East and West Germany attempt to stitch themselves together, the result will be a new city for a new millennium, redefining Berlin as Germany's cultural center—or so the tourist brochures say. Yet at the heart of the city's current problems is an inability to draw upon a legacy with which to create an innovative, yet historically endowed, national capital. For many people who lived through the horrors of WWII, massive construction plans to turn Berlin into a center of intercontinental import are still overwhelmingly redolent of the fascist era; after all, the last man to attempt to exalt the city's virtues was Albert Speer, Hitler's chief architect. Nearly as worrisome is the tendency to attempt to replicate other cities in order to achieve parallel fame. A few years ago, the influential newsmagazine *Der Spiegel* derided this peculiarly German propensity, warning that "Berlin should stop trying to imitate other metropolises such as London and Paris," for "the thirst for glory of a city is even more dangerous than the thirst for glory of an individual."

The juxtaposition of the melancholy of a tumultuous past and the exhilaration of being on the cutting edge is reflected in Berlin's architecture. For now, the city is a fascinating mish-mash of GDR apartment blocks and designer boutiques, decaying pre-war buildings and gleaming (yet empty) office complexes. As Weimar decadent Karl Zuckmayer wrote, "Berlin tasted of the future, and for that one happily accepted the dirt and the coldness as part of the bargain." The hope is that as the city is rebuilt, its past will not be dismantled.

HIGHLIGHTS OF BERLIN

■ To see the churned-up center of the world's largest construction site, head to **Potsdamer Platz** (p. 111), where multinational corporations are busily reworking the heart of pre-war Berlin.

■ Stroll the **Straße des 17. Juni** and **Unter den Linden** to enjoy the green serenity of the massive **Tiergarten** as well as the imperial pomp of the **Siegessäule** (p. 115) and **Brandenburg Gate** (p. 108).

■ Though little of the **Berlin Wall** remains, a visit to **Checkpoint Charlie** (p. 118) quickly recalls the days of the Cold War. To view the longest surviving stretch of the Wall, head to the **East Side Gallery** in Friedrichshain (p. 119).

■ Vast holdings of art and artifacts are on display at the museum complexes of **Dahlem, Museuminsel,** the **Kulturforum,** and **Schloß Charlottenburg** (p. 122).

■ Berlin's notorious **nightlife** centers on the districts of **Kreuzberg, Prenzlauer Berg,** and **Mitte,** with the beginnings of a scene sprouting up in **Friedrichshain** (p. 132).

HISTORY

PRUSSIAN KINGDOM TO WORLD WAR I

Berlin took its time to attain international importance. Populated since the Stone Age, the first mention of a settlement called **Cölln** appeared in 1237. Despite political and economic links, it was not until 1709 that the five towns by the river Spree united into the city of Berlin, capital of the Prussian kingdom. In the 18th century,

Berlin flourished under the progressive rule of **Friedrich II** (the Great), and intellectuals such as **Gotthold Ephraim Lessing** and **Moses Mendelssohn** made the growing city a center of Enlightenment thought. Nonetheless, Berlin was little more than an ornate garrison town, as Friedrich's penchant for military pomp and circumstance (as well as young officers) turned the city into a series of grandiose parade grounds devoid of civilians. The city suffered a decline in the 19th century, during which time it was conquered by Napoleon and later beset by revolution in 1848. In 1871, Berlin became the capital of the German Empire established after Bismarck's wars, but the absence of centralized rule in Germany up to this point proscribed the city's status. Imperial Berlin never became the center of the new nation in the same way that Paris was for France or London for Britain. Munich and Frankfurt remained cultural and commercial rivals, and many Germans felt little affection for the Prussian capital. It was not until the end of WWI and the establishment of the first German Republic that Berlin became the undisputed center of national life.

REVOLUTION AND WEIMAR CULTURE

WWI and the Allied blockade brought about near-starvation conditions in Berlin. A popular uprising led to the Kaiser's abdication and **Karl Liebknecht's** declaration of a socialist republic, with Berlin as capital. Locally, the revolt—led by Liebknecht and **Rosa Luxemburg**—turned into a full-fledged workers' revolution that wrested control of the city for several days. The Social Democratic government enlisted the aid of radical right-wing mercenaries, the **Freikorps,** who brutally suppressed the rebellion and murdered Liebknecht and Luxemburg. Political and economic instability continued until 1923, when chancellor Gustav Stresemann's economic plan and generous loans from the United States improved the situation. Meanwhile, Berlin had become one of the major cultural centers of Europe. Expressionist painting flourished, **Bertolt Brecht** developed revolutionary new theater techniques, and artists and writers from all over the world flocked to the city. The city's "Golden Twenties," however, ended abruptly with the 1929 economic collapse. With 10% of Germany's unemployed living in Berlin, the city erupted with bloody riots, radicalization, political chaos, and the ascent of the Nazis.

CAPITAL OF THE THIRD REICH

When Hitler took power on January 30, 1933, traditionally left-wing **"Red Berlin"** was not one of his strongholds. He consolidated his control over the city through economic improvements and totalitarian measures and found plenty of supporters for the savage anti-Semitic pogrom of November 9, 1938, known as **Kristallnacht.** Berlin was hit extremely hard during WWII; Allied bombing and the Battle of Berlin leveled one-fifth of the city. With almost all healthy men dead or gone, it was Berlin's women, known as the **Trümmerfrauen** (rubble women), who picked up the broken pieces of the city, creating numerous artificial hills out of the tons of rubble strewn across the defeated capital. The pre-war population of 4.3 million sank to 2.8 million. Only 7,000 members of Berlin's once-thriving Jewish community of 160,000 survived the Holocaust.

After the war, the Allies took control of the city, dividing it into French, British, American, and Soviet sectors under a joint **Allied Command.** On June 16, 1948, the Soviets withdrew from the joint Command and demanded full control of Berlin. Ten days later, they began an 11-month blockade of most land and water routes into the Western sectors. The population would have starved were it not for a massive Allied airlift of supplies known as the **Luftbrücke** (air bridge). On May 12, 1949, the Soviets ceded control of West Berlin to the Western Allies.

A DIVIDED CITY

On October 5, 1949, the Soviet-controlled German Democratic Republic was formally established, with East Berlin as its capital. The city was thus officially divided. Dissatisfaction was great in East Berlin, and it manifested itself in the **work-**

ers' uprising of June 17, 1953, when widespread popular demonstrations were crushed under Soviet tanks. One result of the repression was an increase in the number of *Republikflüchtige* ("Republic-deserters") who emigrated to West Berlin—200,000 in 1960 alone. On the morning of August 13, 1961, the East German government responded to this exodus of its most talented citizens with the almost instantaneous construction of the **Berlin Wall,** which stopped virtually all interaction between the two halves of the city. The 165km Wall, or "anti-fascist protective barrier," as the East German government termed it, separated families and friends, sometimes even running through people's homes. In the early 1970s, a second wall was erected parallel to the first; the space in between them became known as the **Todesstreifen** ("death strip") as East German border guards were ordered to shoot any trespassers. The Western Allies responded to West Berlin's isolation by pouring millions into the city's reconstruction; to emphasize the glories of capitalism, the commercial center around Kurfürstendamm was created and nurtured to become *das Schaufenster des Westens* (the shop-window of the West).

West Berlin remained under joint French, British, and American control. Although there was an elected mayor, final say rested with the Allied commander-in-chief. The city was not officially a part of the Federal Republic of Germany but had "special status." Although Berlin adopted the resolutions of the Federal Parliament, the municipal Senate still had to approve them, and the Allies retained ultimate authority over the city right up until German reunification in 1990. One perk of this special status was the exemption of West Berliners from military conscription. Thousands of German artists, punks, homosexuals, and left-wing activists moved to Berlin to escape the draft and formed an alternative scene without parallel anywhere in the world. The West German government, determined to make a Cold War showcase of the city, subsidized its economic and cultural life, further enhancing its vitality.

THE WALL OPENS

On November 9, 1989—the 71st anniversary of the proclamation of the Weimar Republic, the 66th anniversary of Hitler's Beer Hall *Putsch,* and the 51st anniversary of *Kristallnacht*—a series of popular demonstrations throughout East Germany, riding on a decade of discontent and a year of rapid change in Eastern Europe, culminated in the opening of the Berlin Wall. The image of jubilant Berliners embracing beneath the Brandenburg Gate that night provided one of the most memorable images of the century. Berlin was officially reunited (and Allied authority ended) along with the rest of Germany on October 3, 1990, to widespread celebration. Since then, the euphoria has evaporated. Eastern and Western Berliners have discovered that they don't really like each other as much as they once imagined. Resignation to reconstruction has taken the place of the biting criticism and tasteless jokes that were standard immediately after reunification. Eastern Berlin remains politically volatile and economically disadvantaged, though the situation has improved somewhat in the past few years. The city is slowly knitting itself back together, but it will be years before residents on both sides of the divide consider themselves citizens of the same city.

After a decade of planning, the *Bundestag* finally made the move from Bonn to Berlin in 1999, thus restoring Berlin to its pre-war status as the locus of German political power. What this bodes for the 21st century remains to be seen.

■ ORIENTATION

Berlin is an *immense* conglomeration of what were once two separate and unique cities: the former East, which contains the lion's share of Berlin's landmarks and historic sites, as well as an unfortunate number of pre-fab concrete socialist architectural experiments, and the former West, which functioned for decades as a small, isolated, Allied-occupied state and is still the commercial heart of united

Berlin. The situation is rapidly changing, however, as businesses and embassies move their headquarters to Potsdamer Platz and Mitte.

The commercial district of Western Berlin lies at one end of the huge **Tiergarten** park and is centered around **Bahnhof Zoo** and **Kurfürstendamm** (Ku'damm for short). It is marked by the bombed-out **Kaiser-Wilhelm-Gedächtniskirche,** adjacent to the boxy tower of the **Europa-Center,** one of the few "skyscrapers" in Western Berlin. A star of streets radiates from Breitscheidplatz; toward the west run **Hardenbergstraße, Kantstraße,** and the great commercial boulevard of modern Berlin, the renowned and reviled Kurfürstendamm. About a kilometer down Kantstr. lies **Savignyplatz,** one of many pleasant squares in **Charlottenburg** home to cafés, restaurants, and *Pensionen.* Further afield, the regal splendor of **Schloß Charlottenburg** and its surrounding grounds hark back to the city's imperial past. Southeast of the Ku'damm, **Schöneberg** is a pleasant residential neighborhood renowned for its café culture and as the traditional nexus of the city's gay and lesbian community. Further south, **Dahlem** houses Western Berlin's largest university and museum complex amidst opulent villas.

The grand, tree-lined **Straße des 17. Juni** runs west-east through the Tiergarten to end at the triumphant **Brandenburg Gate,** which opens out onto **Pariser Platz,** a site of landmark public addresses. Heading south from the Brandenburg Gate and the nearby **Reichstag,** Ebertstraße runs haphazardly through the construction sites to **Potsdamer Platz.** Toward the east, the gate opens onto **Unter den Linden,** Berlin's most famous boulevard and the site of many historic buildings. The *Linden's* broad, tree-lined throughway empties into socialist-realist **Alexanderplatz,** the center of the East's growing commercial district and the home of Berlin's most visible landmark, the **Fernsehturm.** Southeast of Mitte lies **Kreuzberg,** a district home to an incongruous mix of radical leftists, Turks, punks, and homosexuals. Once confined to West Berlin's outer limits, Kreuzberg today finds itself bordering reunited Berlin's city center, a fact that is slowly pushing rents up and alternative types out as civil servants from Bonn descend on the area in a wave of gentrification.

Northeast of the city center, **Prenzlauer Berg,** a former working class suburb-turned-squatter's paradise, rumbles with as-yet-unrestored pre-war structures and a sublime café culture. Southeast of Mitte, **Friedrichshain** is emerging as the latest center of Berlin's counterculture and nightlife, though the area suffers from its heavy concentration of pre-fabricated apartment complexes.

The **Spree River** snakes its way from west to east through the center of Berlin; it forms the northern border of the Tiergarten and splits just east of Unter den Linden to close off the **Museuminsel** (Museum Island). The windswept waters of the Wannsee, Tegeler See, and Heiligensee lap against the city's west side and are connected by narrow canals.

If you're planning to stay more than a few days in Berlin, the blue-and-yellow **Falk Plan** (available at most kiosks and bookstores) is an indispensable and convenient city map that includes a street index and unfolds like a book (DM11). Dozens of streets and subway stations in Eastern Berlin were named after Communist heroes and heroines. Many, but not all, have been renamed in a process only recently completed; be sure that your map is up-to-date.

SAFETY WARNING! Although Berlin is by far the most tolerant city in Germany in every respect, the economic chaos caused by reunification has, unfortunately, unleashed a new wave of right-wing extremism, particularly in the outer boroughs of Eastern Berlin. While it is unlikely that you will come into contact with neo-Nazi skinheads, it is important for people of color as well as gays and lesbians to take precautions when traveling in the eastern suburbs or on the S-Bahn late at night; in particular, **Bahnhof Lichtenberg** is not a pleasant place to be. Also be aware that all skinheads are not alike: if you run into gangs of shaved-head, leather-toting types in Schöneberg or Kreuzberg, they're more likely to be radical leftists or homosexuals.

▣ GETTING THERE AND AROUND

Berlin surveys the Prussian plains from the northeastern corner of Germany and is rapidly becoming the hub of the national rail network. About three hours southeast of Hamburg by train and eight hours north of Munich, Berlin has a web of rail and air connections to most other European capitals. The city is well-connected to Eastern European countries—Prague is five hours by rail, Warsaw six hours. Almost all European airlines, Western or Eastern, have frequent service to one of Berlin's three airports.

LONG DISTANCE TRANSPORTATION

Flights: Berlin's airport authority has consolidated its telephone service. For information on all 3 airports, call (0180) 500 01 86. **Flughafen Tegel** is Western Berlin's main airport. Take express bus #X9 from Bahnhof Zoo, bus #109 from "Jakob-Kaiser-Platz" on U-Bahn #7, or bus #128 from Kurt-Schumacher-Platz" on U-Bahn #6. **Flughafen Tempelhof,** Berlin's smallest airport, is used for intra-German travel and flights within Europe. U-Bahn #6 to "Platz der Luftbrücke." **Flughafen Schönefeld,** southeast of Berlin, is used for intercontinental flights as well as travel to the former Soviet Union and developing countries. S-Bahn #45 or 9 to "Flughafen Berlin Schönefeld" or bus #171 from "Rudow" on U-Bahn #7.

Train Stations: While construction continues on the *Megabahnhof* of the future at Lehrter Stadtbahnhof, trains to and from Berlin are serviced by **Zoologischer Garten** (almost always called **Bahnhof Zoo**) in the West and **Ostbahnhof** (formerly the Hauptbahnhof) in the East. Most trains go to both stations, although some connections to cities in the former GDR only stop at Ostbahnhof. Quite a number of trains also connect to **Schönefeld** airport. A number of trains also make stops at **Oranienburg, Spandau,** and **Potsdam** before entering the city. If coming in late at night, it is preferable to arrive at Bahnhof Zoo, as the area around Ostbahnhof can be a little unsavory.

Connections: One per hour to: Leipzig (2hr., DM58); Dresden (2hr., DM59); Rostock (2¾hr., DM75); Hamburg (2½hr., DM88); Frankfurt (4hr., DM207); Köln (4¼hr., DM190); Munich (7½hr., DM249). **International connections:** Stockholm (15hr.), Copenhagen (7½hr., DM188), Amsterdam (6½hr., DM203), Brussels (7½hr., DM217), Paris (11hr., DM287), Zurich (9hr.), Rome (21hr.), Vienna (11½hr., DM217), Budapest (12hr.), Prague (5hr., DM127), Kraków (10½hr., DM52), Warsaw (6hr., DM50), and Moscow (27hr.). Times and prices change frequently—check your route at the computers located in the train stations.

Information: Deutsche Bahn Information (tel. (0180) 599 66 33). Be prepared for a long wait. Also long lines at the *Reisezentrum* in **Bahnhof Zoo** (open daily 4:45am-11pm) and **Ostbahnhof.** Both stations have recently installed computers, but there are lines for these, too—*arrive early.* There are two different types of computer: large squat ones to plan itineraries, and tall thin ones to purchase tickets. All computers can be operated in English or German. For **recorded information** about departures and arrivals (in German) there are several lines depending on the direction of your destination: Hamburg, Rostock, Stralsund, Schwerin, and Scandinavia (tel. 01 15 31); Magdeburg, Frankfurt, Hannover, and Köln (tel. 01 15 32); Frankfurt (tel. 01 15 33); Leipzig, Nürnberg, and Munich (tel. 01 15 34); Dresden, Czech Republic, Slovakia, Austria, and Hungary (tel. 01 15 35); and Poland, Baltic States, and Ukraine (tel. 01 15 36). For information in **English,** check the helpful staff at EurAide (see **Tourist Offices,** p. 94).

Buses: ZOB, the central bus station (tel. 301 80 28), is by the *Funkturm* near Kaiserdamm. U-Bahn #2 to "Kaiserdamm" or S-Bahn #4, 45, or 46 to "Witzleben." Check *Zitty* and *Tip* for deals on long-distance buses, or call **Gulliver's** travel agency (tel. 78 10 21). Buses aren't comfortable, but they are often much cheaper than the train. Paris (10hr., DM109 one-way); and Vienna (10½hr., DM79 one-way).

Mitfahrzentralen: City Netz, Joachimstaler Str. 17 (tel. 194 44; fax 882 44 20) has a computerized **ride-share** database. U-Bahn #15 or 9 to "Kurfürstendamm." To Hamburg DM12, Frankfurt DM17, Munich DM18. Open M-F 9am-8pm, Sa-Su 9am-7pm. **Branch**

office: Südstern 2 (tel. 693 60 95), in Kreuzberg. U-Bahn #7 to "Südstern." Open M-F 10am-8pm, Sa-Su 10am-4pm. **Mitfahrzentrale Zoo** (tel. 31 03 31), on the U-Bahn #2 platform at Bahnhof Zoo. Open M-F 9am-8pm, Sa-Su 10am-6pm. **Mitfahrzentrale Alex,** (tel. 241 58 20 or 241 58 21) in the Alexanderplatz U-Bahn station between lines #2 and 8, specializes in Eastern Europe. Open M-W and F 10am-6pm, Th 10am-8pm, Sa-Su 11am-4pm. The **Mitfahrtelefon für Schwule and Lesben,** Yorckstr. 52 (tel. 194 20 or 216 60 21), matches gay and lesbian drivers and passengers. U-Bahn #7 to "Yorckstr." Open M-F 9am-8pm, Sa-Su 10am-4pm. Berlin has many small *Mitfahrzentralen;* check *Zitty, Tip,* or *030* for addresses and phone numbers.

Hitchhiking: *Let's Go* does not recommend hitchhiking as a safe mode of transportation. Remember that it is illegal to hitch at rest stops or anywhere along the highway. Those heading west and south (Hannover, Munich, Weimar, Leipzig) take S-Bahn #1 or 7 to "Wannsee," then bus #211 to the Autobahn entrance ramp. Those heading north (Hamburg, Rostock) ride S-Bahn #25 to "Hennigsdorf," then walk 50m to the bridge on the right, or ask anyone in the area for the location of the *Trampenplatz.* Both have crowds, but someone gets picked up every few minutes.

GETTING AROUND

Public Transportation: The **BVG** *(Berliner Verkehrsbetriebe)* is the most efficient transportation system in the world. While most reconstruction and expansion of the pre-war transit grid has been completed, the BVG's mascot, **Max,** an inimitably affable cartoon mole, alerts travelers to disruptions in service. In most cases, the worst inconvenience is that you'll wait an extra 20min.

Orientation and Basic Fares: It is impossible to tour Berlin on foot—fortunately, the extensive **bus, Straßenbahn** (streetcar), **U-Bahn** (subway), and **S-Bahn** (surface rail) systems of Berlin will get you to your destination safely and relatively quickly. Berlin is divided into 3 transit zones. **Zone A** encompasses downtown Berlin, including Tempelhof airport. Almost everything else falls into **Zone B,** while **Zone C** contains the outlying areas, including Potsdam and Oranienburg. An AB ticket is the best deal, as you can buy regional Bahn tickets for the outlying areas. A single ticket for the combined network (*Langstrecke* AB or BC, DM3.90; or *Ganzstrecke* ABC, DM4.20) is good for 2hr. after validation. Children under 6 accompanied by an adult travel free; children under 14 pay a reduced fare.

Special Passes: With the high cost of single tickets, it almost always makes sense to buy a transit pass. A **Tageskarte** (AB DM7.80, ABC DM8.50) is valid from the time of cancellation until 3am the next day. A **Gruppentageskarte** (AB DM20, ABC DM22.50) allows up to 5 people to travel together on the same ticket. The **WelcomeCard** (DM29) is valid on all lines for 72hr. The **7-Tage-Karte** (AB DM40, ABC DM48) is good for 7 days of travel. For longer stays, an **Umweltkarte Standard** (AB DM99, ABC DM120) is valid for one calendar month. **Bikes** require an additional reduced fare ticket and are permitted on the U-Bahn and S-Bahn but not on buses and streetcars.

Purchasing Tickets: Buy tickets from *Automaten* (machines), bus drivers, or ticket windows in the U- and S-Bahn stations. When using an *Automat,* make your selection before inserting money; note that the machines will not give more than DM20 change. Inspections have increased severely in the past two years, and the cost of cheating is steep (DM60). *All tickets must be cancelled in the validation box marked "hier entwerten" before boarding.*

Maps and Information: The **Liniennetz** map can be picked up for free at any tourist office or subway station. The BVG also issues an excellent **Atlas** of the entire city (DM9.50). For more information, visit the **BVG Pavillon** in the bus parking lot outside Bahnhof Zoo (tel. 25 62 25 62; open daily 6:30am-8:30pm) or the **BVG Kundenbüro** at "Turmstr." station on U-Bahn #9 (open M-F 6:30am-8:30pm, Sa 9am-3:30pm). Or call the BVG's **information line** (tel. 194 49; open daily 6am-11pm) or check them on the **internet** (email auskunft@bvg.de; www.bvg.de).

Night Transport: U- and S-Bahn lines generally do not run from 1-4am, although most S-Bahn lines run once an hour during weekend nights. The **U9** and **U12** run all night Friday and Saturday. (The U12 line, which only runs F-Sa night, combines the Ruhleben-Gleisdreieck leg of the U2 with the Gleisdreieck-Warschauer Str. leg of the U1.) Most regular lines start their final runs by 12:15am. There is an extensive system of **night buses** centered on Bahnhof Zoo that run about every 20-30min.; pick up the free *Nachtliniennetz* map at the BVG pavilion. All night bus numbers are preceded by the letter **N**.

Ferries: Stern und Kreis Schiffahrt, Puschkinallee 16-17 (tel. 536 36 00; fax 53 63 60 99), operates ferry services along the Spree April-Oct. Ferries leave from locations throughout the city, including the Spreebogen, Friedrichstr., Museuminsel, the Dom, and the Nikolaiviertel. Five ferries run daily 10:30am-4:30pm; fares depend on distance traveled (DM3.50-22). Pleasure cruises also available. *Berlin Kombi-Tageskarte* is valid on all regularly scheduled services. For further information, contact the tourist office or BVG Pavillon.

Taxis: Tel. 26 10 26, 21 02 02, or 690 22. Call at least 15min. in advance. Women may request a female driver. Trips within the city usually cost less than DM20.

Car Rental: The **Mietwagenservice,** counter 21 in Bahnhof Zoo's *Reisezentrum* (see above), represents Avis, Hertz, Europacar and Sixt. Open daily 4:45am-11pm. Most companies also have offices at Tegel Airport.

Auto Clubs: ADAC Tel. (0180) 222 22 22. 24hr. breakdown service for members.

Bike Rental: Hackescher Markt Fahrradstation, downstairs at the "Hackescher Markt" S-Bahn stop. Also try the red trailer off the **Lustgarten,** which rents bikes for DM5 per day. S-Bahn #3, 5, 7, 75, or 9 to "Hackescher Markt" for both locations.

◪ PRACTICAL INFORMATION

TOURIST OFFICES

Since being privatized, the tourist offices no longer provide the range of free services and information that they once did. However, they sell a useful city **map** (DM1) on which sights and transit stations are clearly marked. They book same-day hotel **rooms** for a DM5 fee—though room prices start at DM50 and rise to stratospheric heights. A free list of hotels and *Pensionen* is available, but most of the rooms aren't really budget options. Tourist offices also have free copies of the city magazines *030* and (for gays and lesbians) *Siegessäule* and *Sergej*, which have reasonably good entertainment listings. The monthly magazine *Berlin Programm* (DM2.80) lists museums, sights, some restaurants and hotels, and opera, theatre, and classical music schedules. The city's main English-language magazine, *Berlin* (DM3.50), has good listings for classical music and opera but little else. Dig *deutsch?* You're better off buying *Tip* or *Zitty*, which have the most comprehensive listings for film, theater, concerts, clubs, and discos (DM4 each). For comprehensive information on the **internet,** check out www.berlin.de.

Berlin Tourismus (tel. 25 00 25; fax 25 00 24 24) isn't the office you want to visit once you arrive, but it is nonetheless a useful resource for planning a trip; they'll send information and reserve **rooms.** Write to Berlin Tourismus Marketing GmbH, Am Karlsbad 11, 10785 Berlin. Other tourist offices do not give out phone numbers, so all telephone inquiries should be directed to this office.

■ **EurAide,** in Bahnhof Zoo. Facing the *Reisezentrum,* go left and down the passage on your right. In English, French, and Spanish, the heroic representatives dole out comprehensive travel information, make train reservations, find places to crash, and much, much more. Free. Arrive early—the office can get packed with twentysomethings, and they don't accept phone calls. Open daily 8am-noon and 1-6pm.

Europa-Center, entrance on Budapester Str. From Bahnhof Zoo, walk along Budapester Str. past the Kaiser-Wilhelm-Gedächtniskirche; the office is on the right (5min.). Helpful staff speaks fluent English. Open M-Sa 8am-10pm, Su 9am-9pm.

Brandenburger Tor, S-Bahn #1, 2, or 25 or bus #100 to "Unter den Linden." Open daily 9:30am-6pm.

A.S. Airport-Service, at Tegel airport, near the Haupthalle exit opposite Gate O. Open daily 5am-10:30pm.

Infopoint Dresdner Bank, Unter den Linden 17. Open M, W, and F 8:30am-2pm, Tu and Th 8:30am-2pm and 3:30-6pm.

CITY TOURS

Berlin Walks (tel. 301 91 94; email berlin_walks@compuserve.com) offers a range of English-language walking tours, including tours of **Infamous Third Reich Sites, Jewish Life in Berlin,** and **Prenzlauer Berg.** Their **Discover Berlin Walk** is one of the best ways to get acquainted with the city; the guides' competence and passion for Berlin are remarkable. Tours last 2-3hr. and meet at 10am at the taxi stand in front of Bahnhof Zoo; in summer, the Discover Berlin Walk also meets at 2:30pm. All tours DM15.

Insider Tour enjoys a reputation of providing a very thorough historical narrative and hits all the major sights. Tours last 3½hr. and leave from the McDonald's by Bahnhof Zoo late March to Nov. daily at 10am and 2:30pm (DM15).

Terry's Top-Hat Tour is heavy on information but with a more personal touch. Tours leave daily at 10am and 3pm from the Neue Synagoge on Oranienburger Str., near the intersection with Tucholskystr. Take S-Bahn #1, 2, or 25 to "Oranienburger Str." DM10, under 14 free.

Dr. Bartholdy (tel. 283 23 48) offers a unique and interesting way to discover Berlin. Without a guide, you and fellow travelers will be sent on a quest to find Dr. Bartholdy, discovering a different side of Berlin in the process. The **Dächer und Keller** (roofs and cellars) tour equips you with a bike and sends you through the back alleys of some of Berlin's most interesting neighborhoods (F-Sa at 3pm, DM10), while the **Waterways** tour puts you in a kayak and leads you through Berlin's labyrinthine canals (Sa at 3pm, DM20). Both tours meet at Oranienburger Str. 83. Take S-Bahn #1, 2, or 25 to "Oranienburger Str."

Bus tours are offered by various companies in English and German, leaving roughly hourly from the Ku'damm near the Europa-Center and Gedächtniskirche.

BUDGET TRAVEL

STA, Goethestr. 73 (tel. 311 09 50), offer the standard budget travel services. U-Bahn #2 to "Ernst-Reuter-Platz." Open M-W and F 10am-6pm, Th 10am-8pm.

Kilroy Travels, Hardenbergstr. 9 (tel. 313 04 66; fax 312 69 75), across from the Technische Universität, two blocks from Bahnhof Zoo. The friendly staff will help you navigate through the intricacies of European planes, trains, and buses. **Branch offices** at: Takustr. 47 (tel. 831 50; fax 832 53 76; U-Bahn #1 to "Dahlem-Dorf"), Nollendorfpl. 7 (tel. 216 30 91; fax 215 92 21; U-Bahn #1, 15, 2, or 4 to "Nollendorfplatz"), Mariannenstr. 7 (in Kreuzberg; tel. 614 68 22; fax 614 99 83; U-Bahn #1, 15 or 8 to "Kottbusser Tor"), Georgenstr. 3 (in Mitte; S-Bahn #1, 2, 25, 3, 5, 7, or 75 or U-Bahn #6 to "Friedrichstr."). All open M-F 10am-6pm, Sa 11am-1pm.

EMBASSIES AND CONSULATES

Berlin's construction plans include a new complex to house foreign dignitaries. While most embassies have moved to their new homes, the locations of the embassies and consulates remain in a state of flux. For the latest information, call the **Auswärtiges Amt Dienststelle Berlin** at 20 18 60 or visit their office on the Werderscher Markt. (U-Bahn #2 to "Hausvogteiplatz.")

Australian Embassy: Friedrichstr. 200 (tel. 880 08 80). U-Bahn #2 or 6 to "Stadtmitte." Also try Uhlandstr. 181-183 (tel. 880 08 80; fax 88 00 88 99). U-Bahn #15 to "Uhlandstr." Open M-F 9am-noon.

Canadian Embassy: Friedrichstr. 95 (tel. 20 31 20; fax 20 31 25 90)., on the 12th floor of the International Trade Center. S-Bahn #1, 2, 25, 3, 5, 7, 75 or 9 or U-Bahn #6 to "Friedrichstr." Open M-F 8:30am-12:30pm and 1:30-5pm.

Irish Consulate: Ernst-Reuter-Platz 10 (tel. 34 80 08 22; fax 34 80 08 63). U-Bahn #2 to "Ernst-Reuter-Platz." Open M-F 10am-1pm.

New Zealand Embassy: Friedrichstr. 60. U-Bahn #6 to "Oranienburger Tor."

South African Consulate: Douglasstr. 9 (tel. 82 50 11 or 825 27 11; fax 826 65 43). S-Bahn #7 to "Grunewald." Open M-F 9am-noon.

U.K. Embassy: Unter den Linden 32-34 (tel. 20 18 40; fax 20 18 41 58). S-Bahn #1, 2, 25, 3, 5, 7, 75 or 9 or U-Bahn #6 to "Friedrichstr." Open M-F 8:30am-5pm.

U.S. Citizens Service: Clayallee 170 (tel. 832 92 33; fax 831 49 26). U-Bahn #1 to "Oskar-Helene-Heim." Open M-F 8:30am-noon. Telephone advice available M-F 9am-5pm; after hours, a machine gives emergency instructions.

U.S. Consulate: Neustädtische Kirchstr. 4-5 (tel. 238 51 74; fax 238 62 90). S-Bahn #1, 2, 25, 3, 5, 7, 75 or 9 or U-Bahn #6 to "Friedrichstr."

GENERAL SERVICES

Currency Exchange: The best rates are usually found at offices that exclusively exchange currency and traveler's checks. The **Wechselstube** at Joachimstaler Str. 1-3 (tel. 882 10 86), near Bahnhof Zoo, has good rates and no commission. Open M-F 8am-8pm, Sa 9am-3pm. **Geldwechsel,** Joachimtaler Str. 7-9 (tel. 882 63 71), has decent rates and no commission. **ReiseBank,** at Bahnhof Zoo (tel. 881 71 17; open daily 7am-10pm) and Ostbahnhof (tel. 296 43 93; open M-F 7am-10pm, Sa 7am-6pm, Su 8am-4pm), is conveniently located in both major train stations, but has poorer rates. **Berliner Bank** is in Tegel Airport. Open daily 8am-10pm. You can also change money at most **post offices,** which cash traveler's checks for DM6 per check. **Berliner Sparkasse** and **Deutsche Bank** have branches everywhere; their ATMs usually accept Visa and MC (as long as you know your PIN). Sparkasse changes cash for free, but charges a 1% commission on traveler's checks (with a DM7.50 minimum). **Citibank** has branches with **24hr. ATMs** at Kurfürstendamm 72, Wittenbergpl. 1, Wilmersdorfer Str. 133, and Karl-Marx-Allee 153. There's also a Citibank **ATM** at Tegel Airport.

American Express: Main Office, Uhlandstr. 173 (tel. 88 45 88 21). U-Bahn #15 to "Uhlandstr." Mail held, banking services rendered. No commission for cashing AmEx traveler's checks. On F and Sa, expect out-the-door lines of travelers carrying *Let's Go.* Open M-F 9am-5:30pm, Sa 9am-noon. **Branch offices,** Bayreuther Str. 23 (tel. 21 49 83 63). U-Bahn #1, 15, or 2 to "Wittenbergplatz." Traveler's checks cashed and sold, mail held. Open M-F 9am-6pm, Sa 10am-1pm. Also at Friedrichstr. 172 (tel. 20 17 40 12). U-Bahn #6 to "Französische Str." Open M-F 9am-5:30pm, Sa 10am-1pm.

Luggage Storage: In **Bahnhof Zoo.** Lockers DM2 per day, larger lockers DM4. 72hr. max. If all the lockers at Zoo are full, check your luggage at the center near the post office for DM4 per piece per day. Open daily 6am-11pm. Also at **Ostbahnhof** (lockers DM2 per day, larger DM4, 72hr. max.), **Bahnhof Lichtenberg,** and **Alexanderplatz** (lockers DM2 per day, 24hr. max.).

Lost Property: Zentrales Fundbüro, Platz der Luftbrücke 8 (tel. 69 95). **BVG Fundbüro,** Fraunhofer Str. 33-36 (tel. 256 230 40). U-Bahn #2 to "Ernst-Reuter-Pl." For items lost on the bus, streetcar, or U-Bahn. Many, many umbrellas. Open M-Tu and Th 9am-3pm, W 9am-6pm, F 9am-2pm. **Fundbüro Berlin,** Mittelstr. 20 (tel. 29 72 96 12), at the Schönefeld airport train station. S-Bahn #45 or 9 to "Flughafen Berlin-Schönefeld."

Bookstores: Marga Schoeler Bücherstube, Knesebeckstr. 33 (tel. 881 11 12), at Mommsenstr., between Savignyplatz and the Ku'damm. S-Bahn #3, 5, 7, 75, or 9 to "Savignypl." Large selection of books in English includes politics, history, poetry, lit crit, and fiction. Open M-W 9:30am-7pm, Th-F 9:30am-8pm, Sa 9:30am-4pm. The **British Bookshop,** Mauerstr. 83-84 (tel. 238 46 80), by Checkpoint Charlie. U-Bahn #6 to "Kochstr." An artfully stocked addition to Berlin's English book club, with well-chosen literature and history sections and English-language newspapers and mags. Open M-F 10am-7pm, Sa 10am-4pm. **Literaturhaus Berlin,** Fasanenstr. 23 (tel. 882 65 52), is in an old mansion complete with garden and readings of German and international literature. U-Bahn #15 to "Uhlandstr." Their resident bookstore, **Kohlhaas & Co.** (tel. 882 50

44), has lots of German paperbacks, and excellent Judaica and Nazi history sections. Open M-F 10am-8pm, Sa 10am-4pm.

Libraries: Staatsbibliothek Preußischer Kulturbesitz, Potsdamer Str. 33 (tel. 26 61), and Unter den Linden 8 (tel. 210 50). 3.5 million books—one for every Berliner—but not all are stored on site. Lots of English-language newspapers. The Potsdamer Str. library was built for West Berlin in the 1960s, after the Iron Curtain went down on the original **"Staabi"** on Unter den Linden, next to the Humboldt-Universität (see p. 110). Now Berliners can choose between them—so can you. Both open M-F 9am-9pm, Sa 9am-5pm.

Cultural Centers: Amerika Haus, Hardenbergstr. 22-24 (tel. 31 50 55 70). Library includes English-language books, videos, and day-old editions of *The New York Times.* Occasionally hosts readings by visiting American authors. Offices open M-F 8:30am-5:30pm. Library open Tu and Th 2-8pm, W and F 2-5:30pm. **British Council,** Hardenbergstr. 20 (tel. 31 10 99 10), is next door, on the first floor of the Berliner Bank building. Open M-F 9am-12:30pm and 2-5pm. Library open M and W-F 2-6pm, Tu 2-7pm.

Language Instruction: Goethe-Institut, Schönhauser Str. 20 (tel. 25 90 63; fax 25 90 64 00), is the best known and the most expensive. Take S-Bahn #1 to "Feuerbachstr." All levels of German available. Office open M-Th 9am-5pm, F 9am-3pm. DM1690 for 4 weeks, DM3140 for 8 weeks; 25hr. of instruction per week. The magazines *Tip* and *Zitty* are filled with ads for other schools and private tutors—check the classifieds under "Unterricht" and shop around.

Laundromat: Wasch Centers at various locations: **Leibnizstr. 72,** in Charlottenburg; U-Bahn #7 to "Wilmersdorfer Str." **Wexstr. 34,** in Schöneberg; U-Bahn #9 to "Bundesplatz." **Bergmannstr. 109,** in Kreuzberg; U-Bahn #7 to "Gneisenaustr." **Behmstr. 12,** in Mitte; S-Bahn #1, 2, or 25 or U-Bahn #8 to "Gesundbrunnen." **Jablonskistr. 21,** in Prenzlauer Berg; U-Bahn #2 to "Eberswalder Str." Wash DM6 per 6kg, soap included. Dry DM2 for 30min. All open daily 6am-11pm. **Waschcenter Schnell und Sauber, Uhlandstr. 61;** U-Bahn #15 to "Uhlandstr." **Torstr. 15,** in Mitte; U-Bahn #8 to "Rosenthaler Platz." **Oderberger Str. 1,** in Prenzlauer Berg; U-Bahn #2 to "Eberswalder Str." **Mehringdamm 32,** in Kreuzberg; U-Bahn #6 to "Mehringdamm." **Str. der Pariser Kommune 22,** in Friedrichshain; S-Bahn #3, 5, 7, 75, or 9 to "Ostbahnhof." Wash DM6 per 6kg. Open daily 6am-11pm.

Emergency: Police, Platz der Luftbrücke 6 (tel. 110). U-Bahn #6 to "Platz der Luftbrücke." **Ambulance** and **Fire,** tel. 112.

Crisis Lines: American Hotline tel. (0177) 814 15 10. Crisis and referral service. **Sexual Assault Hotline,** tel. 251 28 28. Open Tu and Th 6-9pm, Su noon-2pm. **Schwules Überfall** (gay bashing), tel. 216 33 36. Hotline and legal help. Open daily 6-9pm. **Schwulenberatung** (gay men's counseling), tel. 194 46. **Lesbenberatung** (lesbian counseling), tel. 215 20 00. **Drug Crisis,** tel. 192 37. Open M-F 8:30am-10pm, Sa-Su 2-9:30pm. **Frauenkrisentelefon** (women's crisis line), tel. 615 42 43. Open M and Th 10am-noon, Tu-W and F 7-9pm, Sa-Su 5-7pm. **Deutsche AIDS-Hilfe,** Dieffenbachstr. 33 (tel. 690 08 70). **Berliner Behindertenverband,** tel. 545 87 99. Information and advice for the handicapped. Open M-F 8am-4pm. English spoken at most crisis lines.

Pharmacies: Europa-Apotheke, Tauentzienstr. 9-12 (tel. 261 41 42), near the Europa-Center and Bahnhof Zoo. Open M-F 9am-8pm, Sa 9am-4pm. **Münz-Apotheke,** Münzstr. 5 (tel. 241 10 83), just off Alexanderplatz. Open M-F 8am-6:30pm, Sa 9am-1pm. Closed pharmacies post signs directing you to the nearest open one. For information about **late-night pharmacies,** call 011 89.

Medical Assistance: The American and British embassies have a list of English-speaking doctors. **Emergency Doctor** (tel. 31 00 31 or 192 42) and **Emergency Dentist** (tel. 89 00 43 33). Both available 24hr.

Post Offices: Budapester Str. 42, opposite the Europa-Center near Bahnhof Zoo. **Poste Restante** should be addressed: Postlagernd, Postamt in der Budapester Str. 42, 10787 Berlin. Open M-Sa 8am-midnight, Su 10am-midnight. Branch office at **Tegel Airport** (tel. 417 84 90). Open daily 6:30am-9pm. **Postamt Friedrichshain,** Str. der Pariser Kommune 8-10, 10243 Berlin, near Ostbahnhof. Open M-F 7am-9pm, Sa 8am-8pm.

Neighborhood branches are everywhere (usually open 9am-6pm, Sa 9am-noon); look for the little yellow *POST* signs.

Internet Access: Alpha, Dunckerstr. 72 (tel. 447 90 67), in Prenzlauer Berg. U-Bahn #2 to "Eberswalder Str." Open daily 3pm-midnight. DM12 per hour. **Cyberb@r,** Joachimstaler Str. 5-6, near Bahnhof Zoo. On the second floor of the Karstadt Sport department store. DM5 per 30min. **Free internet access** available in the **Info Box** on Potsdamer Platz (p. 124), but it's almost always impossible to find a free computer. For the trendiest internet joint, see **Website,** p. 106.

PHONE CODE	030

▕ ACCOMMODATIONS

Even though tourists mob Berlin during the summer, same-day accommodations aren't impossible to find thanks to the ever-growing hosteling and hotel industry; but as always, it's best to call ahead. Reservations are a must if you're arriving on a weekend. If you plan on visiting during the **Love Parade,** book your room at least three weeks in advance as most hostels tend to fill up very quickly (see p. 133).

For a DM5 fee, **tourist offices** will find you a room in a hostel, *Pension,* or hotel. Be prepared to pay at least DM70 for a single and DM100 for a double. There are also over 4000 **private rooms** available in the city; the overwhelming majority are controlled by the tourist offices. Expect to pay DM80 for singles, DM100 for doubles, plus a single-night surcharge of DM5. For that price, there's a wide spectrum of locations, comfort levels, and amenities. Press for details, and be sure that they know your language abilities (if any). They often prefer to fill up the *Pensionen* first, so you may have to ask for private rooms.

Although most accommodations are in Western Berlin, the office does have some listings for private rooms in the Eastern half of the city. The tourist offices have the pamphlet "Accommodations, Youth Hostels, and Camping Places in Berlin," which lists hostels and inexpensive guest houses and hotels in English and German (DM2).

For longer visits (more than 4 days), the various **Mitwohnzentralen** can arrange for you to housesit or sublet someone's apartment. Prices start at DM40 for a single, DM70 for a double, and DM80-100 for a two-person apartment. For longer stays, expect to pay DM500-800 per month for a studio. The fee decreases relative to the price the longer you stay. **Home Company Mitwohnzentrale,** Joachimstaler Str. 17 (tel. 194 45) is the biggest, and the staff speaks English. (U-Bahn #9 or 15 to "Kurfürstendamm." Open M-F 9am-6pm, Sa 11am-2pm.) **Erste,** Sybelstr. 53 (tel. 324 30 31; fax 324 99 77), tends to be less chaotic. (U-Bahn #7 to "Adenauerplatz." Open M-F 9am-8pm, Sa 10am-6pm.) **Mitwohnzentralen** usually require you to pay up front unless you have, or can find a friend who has, a German bank account. Keep fees in mind—for short stays (less than a month) the standard commission is 20% of the final sum while for longer stays the rate is usually 25%, although the monthly prices are lower. Leases in Berlin start at any time—you don't need to wait for a new calendar month.

HOSTELS AND DORMITORY ACCOMMODATIONS

Hostels in Berlin fall into three categories: HI-affiliated, state-owned *Jugendherbergen* and *Jugendgästehäuser;* large, privately-owned hostels; and smaller, more off-beat private hostels. **HI hostels** can be a great, cheap sleep, but it's often very difficult to get a place, as they fill quickly with German school groups. Also note that state-run hostels invariably impose a **curfew,** putting a damper on late-night forays into Berlin's nightlife. Most HI hostels are for members only, though you can usually get a nonmember's stamp (DM6 extra) and spend the night. To purchase an **HI card,** head to Tempelhofer Ufer 32 (tel. 264 95 20), where the staff issues membership cards (DM30) and reserves spots in the myriad hostels. (Open M, W, and F 10am-4pm, Tu and Th 1-6pm. U-Bahn #1, 15, or 2 to "Gleisdreieck.")

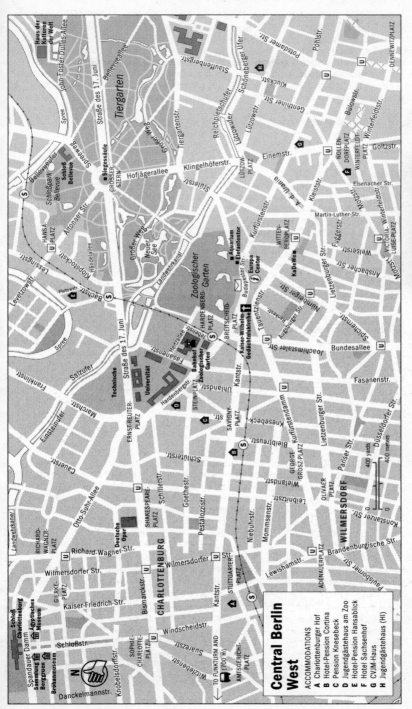

BERLIN

Central Berlin West

ACCOMMODATIONS
A Charlottenburger Hof
B Hotel-Pension Cortina
C Pension Knesebeck
D Jugendgästehaus am Zoo
E Hotel-Pension Hansablick
F Hotel Sachsenhof
G CVJM-Haus
H Jugendgästehaus (HI)

If you're looking for a more party-ready crew, shack up at one of the large, well-equipped **private hostels,** which have a mostly non-German clientele. These centers of youthful hipness are located near the train stations and major nightlife areas and have a guest turnover rate of about two days, so you'll never be bored—unless you tire of hearing more English spoken than German. For more adventurous travelers, the **smaller independent hostels,** though often less central and with fewer amenities, are a better choice. These establishments offer a more relaxed atmosphere as well as a respite from the backpacking crowd.

> ❗ Unless otherwise noted, all hostel accommodation prices are *per person.*

MITTE

 Circus, Rosa-Luxemburg-Str. 39-41 (tel. 28 39 14 33; fax 28 39 14 84; email circus@mind.de). U-Bahn #2 to "Rosa-Luxemburg-Platz." Close to Alexanderplatz, Circus makes a heroic effort at hostel hipness, offering cheap internet access and a disco ball in the lobby. 5-6 bed dorms DM25, quads DM27, triples DM30, doubles DM35, singles DM45. Spacious apartment with kitchen and private bath DM160. Sheets DM3. Bike rental DM12 per day. 24hr. reception. No curfew. Reservations in summer are a must and should be reconfirmed 1 day before arrival. Wheelchair accessible. The same walking tour that leaves the Backpacker at 9am and 2pm departs from Circus 30min. later.

Clubhouse Hostel, Johannisstr. 2 (tel. 28 09 79 79). S-Bahn #1, 2, or 25 to "Oranienburger Str." or U-Bahn #6 to "Oranienburger Tor." Great location in the center of the Oranienburger Str. club and bar scene. 8-10 bed dorms DM25, 5-7 bed dorms DM30, doubles DM40. Breakfast DM5. Internet access DM1 per 5min. 24hr. reception and bar. No curfew. Call at least 2-3 days ahead. Wheelchair accessible.

The Backpacker/Mitte, Chausseestr. 102 (tel. 262 51 40 or 28 39 09 65; fax 28 39 09 35; email backpacker@snafu.de; www.backpacker.de). U-Bahn #6 to "Zinnowitzer Str." Look for the giant orange sign on the wall outside. Ever striving to excel, the Backpacker has rooms with themes like "Garden of Eden" and "Under the Sea." The décor may be unique, but this is *not* a little slice of Berlin so much as a central resting place for those on a whirl-wind tour of Europe seeking the company of other English-speakers. The staff provides information on nightlife and is eager to help with travel and sight-seeing plans. 5- to 6-bed room DM25, quads DM28, triples DM30, doubles DM38. Sheets DM5. Laundry DM5 per load. Bikes DM10-12 per day. A thorough walking tour leaves the hostel daily at 9am and 2pm (6hr., DM10). No curfew. Reception 7am-10pm.

BAHNHOF ZOO

Jugendgästehaus am Zoo, Hardenbergstr. 9a (tel. 312 94 10; fax 401 52 83), opposite the Technical University *Mensa.* Bus #145 to "Steinplatz," or take the short walk from the back exit of Bahnhof Zoo straight down Hardenbergstr. Within spitting distance of Bahnhof Zoo. Lace curtains and a wearing wood-panelled interior in a 19th-century apartment building. Classy, though a little worse for the years; improvements for Y2K are in the works. It's on the 5th floor; ride up in the elevator. Small dorms (4-8 beds) DM35, over 26 DM40. Singles DM47, over 26 DM52; doubles DM85, over 26 DM95. Reception 9am-midnight. Check-in 10am. Check-out 9am. Lockout 10am-2pm. No curfew. No reservations accepted, but call in the morning to see if there's room. Grab a bite to eat at the adjacent Café Hardenberg (see p. 106).

SCHÖNEBERG—TIERGARTEN

Jugendgästehaus (HI), Kluckstr. 3 (tel. 261 10 97 or 261 10 98; fax 265 03 83). From Bahnhof Zoo, take bus #129 (direction: "Hermannplatz") to "Gedenkstätte," or U-Bahn #1 to "Kurfürstenstr.," then walk up Potsdamer Str., go left on Pohlstr., and right on Kluckstr. The *Gästehaus* to end all *Gästehäuser* is HI's most magnificent fortress, complete with café, conference rooms, and patriotic landscape murals. An abstract 8m conceptual "DJH" archway stands before it. While the "art" out front recalls the dark ages of

60s modernism, the 4- and 5-bed rooms are clean and contemporary. DM34, over 26 DM43. Sheets and breakfast included. Key deposit DM10. Lockers and laundry facilities. Bike rental DM15 per day, students DM10. Internet access. 24hr. reception. Curfew midnight; stragglers admitted every 30min. 12:30-6am. Lockout 9am-1pm; ring the bell later. Reservations strongly recommended.

Studentenhotel Berlin, Meininger Str. 10 (tel. 784 67 20; fax 788 15 23). U-Bahn #4 to "Rathaus Schöneberg." Walk toward the Rathaus on Freiherr-vom-Stein-Str., cross Martin-Luther-Str. and turn right on Meininger Str. Rooms have that old-time monk-cell feel to them, but you'll have to be a creative soul to find the antique glory in this 60s institutional high-rise. Same day rooms often available if you call from the station. Quads DM37, doubles DM43, singles DM59. Breakfast included. Reception M and Th-Su 8am-10pm, Tu-W 8am-midnight. Check-in by 10pm.

CVJM-Haus, Einemstr. 10 (tel. 264 91 00; fax 261 43 08). U-Bahn #1, 15, 2, or 4 to "Nollendorfplatz." Young men: it's fun to stay at the German YMCA, despite the Christian institutional atmosphere. Palpably wholesome interior, all in tranquil blue. Popular with school groups. Conveniently located one block from Nollendorfplatz's gay nightlife. DM40 per person for singles, doubles, and dormitory rooms. Quiet time 10pm-7am and 1-3pm. Breakfast included. Reception 8-11am and 4-9pm. You can get a key for curfew-free revelry. Book ahead.

Jugendgästehaus Feurigstraße, Feurigstr. 63 (tel. 781 52 11; fax 788 30 51). U-Bahn #7 to "Kleistpark," or bus #204 or 348 to "Kaiser-Wilhelm-Platz." An unadorned brown stucco building in a busy district full of book stores and supermarkets. 4- and 6-bed rooms that won't cramp your style. 200 beds. Good location for the bars and clubs of Schöneberg. Dorms DM38 (DM27 after August), doubles DM45, singles DM55. Breakfast included. Sheets DM5 if staying fewer than 3 nights, otherwise free. 24hr. reception. Call ahead.

KREUZBERG

Die Fabrik, Schlesische Str. 18 (tel. 611 71 16; fax 617 51 04; email info@diefabrik.com). U-Bahn #1 or 15 to "Schlesisches Tor" or night bus #N65 to "Taborstr." *Pension qua* hostel with lush green interior in a beautifully converted factory within walking distance of Kreuzberg's mad nightlife. Surprisingly comfortable "sleep-in" deal puts you up in a 15-bed dorm for DM30. Quads DM36, triples DM40, doubles DM47, singles DM66. Breakfast in the café downstairs DM10. Bike rental DM20 per day. 24hr. reception. Reserve or call ahead. Curfew? Rage all night, little pumpkin.

FRIEDRICHSHAIN

Odyssee, Grünberger Str. 23 (tel. 29 00 00 81; www.hostel-berlin.de). U-Bahn #5 to "Frankfurter Tor" or S-Bahn #3, 5, 6, 7, 75, or 9 or U-Bahn #1 or 15 to "Warschauer Str." In the center of the quickly growing Friedrichshain pub and club scene. 8-bed dorms DM24, 6-bed dorms DM26, quads DM32, doubles DM36. Breakfast DM5. Internet access DM3 per 15min. 24hr. reception. Bar open until dawn. No curfew. Always reserve ahead.

Frederik's Hostel, Str. der Pariser Kommune 35 (tel. 29 66 94 50 or 29 66 94 51; fax 29 66 94 52; email hostel@frederiks.de; www.frederiks.de). Take U-Bahn #5 to "Weberwiese" or S-Bahn #3, 5, 7, 75 or 9 to "Ostbahnhof." From the U-Bahn, exit on Karl-Marx-Allee and turn left on Str. der Pariser Kommune; the hostel will be on the right. From Ostbahnhof, walk to the farthest exit along the train tracks. Once downstairs, with your back to station, walk straight along Str. der Pariser Kommune; the hostel will be on the left side of the street (10min.). The building was originally a Jewish girls' school, but now backpackers enter to grow in wisdom; if you endure the 6-floor hike and mushy shower room floors, so can you. Rooms have high ceilings and large windows from which to observe the revelers at the adjacent *Biergarten* and karaoke club. 7-bed dorms DM22, 4-6 bed dorms DM25-27, triples DM29, doubles DM35, singles DM49. Sheets DM4. Kitchen facilities. Internet access. 24hr. reception.

PRENZLAUER BERG

Lette'm Sleep Hostel, Lettestr. 7 (tel. 44 73 36 23; fax 44 73 36 25). U-Bahn #2 to "Eberswalder Str." The cleverly named Lette'm Sleep is the first hostel to open up in Prenzlauer Berg, a few blocks from Kollwitzplatz. The hostel redefines the expressions "laid-back staff" and "relaxed atmosphere." 3-6 bed dorms DM26-35. Internet access DM1 per 5min. Kitchen facilities. Call ahead. Wheelchair access.

TEGEL

Jugendherberge Ernst Reuter (HI), Hermsdorfer Damm 48-50 (tel. 404 16 10; fax 404 59 72). S-Bahn #25 to "Tegel" or U-Bahn #6 to "Alt-Tegel," then bus #125 or night bus #N25 (direction: "Frohnau/Invalidensiedlung") to "Jugendherberge." Distant from the center in a placid suburb, on the edge of the forest. Lots of school groups necessitate reservations. 6-bed rooms DM28, over 26 DM35. Breakfast and sheets included. DM8 for laundry facilities. Curfew 1am, but someone is always at the reception. Key deposit DM20. Closed Dec.

Jugendgästehaus Tegel, Ziekowstr. 161 (tel. 433 30 46; fax 434 50 63). S-Bahn #25 to "Tegel" or U-Bahn #6 to "Alt-Tegel," then bus #222 or night bus #N22 to "Titusweg." On the north end of town by the Tegel parks. Old brick outside, new and bright inside with linoleum halls. No English spoken. 3-8 bed dorms DM37.50. Breakfast and sheets included. Reception 7:30am-11pm. No curfew. Reservations are a must.

Backpacker's Paradise, Ziekowstr. 161 (tel. 433 86 40). S-Bahn #25 to "Tegel" or U-Bahn #6 to "Alt-Tegel," then bus #222 or night bus #N22 to "Titusweg." Next to the Jugendgästehaus Tegel. It's the next best thing to rolling a doobie in your VW van. DM10 gets you a blanket and thermal pad under a tent; add DM3 for a summer camp-like cot. Campfire every night. Officially under 27 only, but rules are made for conformists, and they aren't into that sort of thing here. Breakfast buffet DM3. Washing machines DM5. 24hr. reception. No reservations needed. Open late June-Aug.

ELSEWHERE IN BERLIN

Jugendgästehaus Nordufer, Nordufer 28 (tel. 45 19 91 12; fax 452 41 00). U-Bahn #9 to "Westhafen," left over the bridge and left onto Nordufer for about 15min. Away from the center, but on the pretty, blue, swimmable Plötzensee. Some singles, but mostly quads. DM37.50. Breakfast buffet and sheets included. Reception 7am-5pm; ring the bell at other times. No curfew. Swim in the adjacent pool for DM4, students DM3.

Jugendgästehaus am Wannsee (HI), Badeweg 1 (tel. 803 20 35; fax 803 59 08). S-Bahn #1 or 7 to "Nikolassee." From the main exit, cross the bridge and head left on Kronprinzessinweg; Badeweg will be on your right after 5min. 30min. from the center, but Wannsee has its own charm. The tan tile floors, open spaces, white plaster walls, and bright red trim are reminiscent of a municipal swimming pool. 62 4-bed rooms. Toilets shared between 2 rooms, showers among 6. Large groups of jolly kids make it virtually impossible to get a room without booking 2 weeks in advance. Members only. DM34, over 26 DM42. Breakfast and sheets included. Key deposit DM20.

HOTELS AND PENSIONEN

Many small *Pensionen* and hotels are within the means of budget travelers, particularly since most establishments listed in *Let's Go* are amenable to *Mehrbettzimmer*, where extra beds are moved into a large double or triple. However, these benefits are really only for groups of three or more; hotels will not usually allow random individuals to crash together (lest an orgy spontaneously erupt). Most affordable hotels are in Western Berlin; the hotels in Mitte are ridiculously expensive, and other areas in the East still lack the facilities to support many visitors. The best places to find cheap rooms is Charlottenburg, especially around Savignyplatz and Wilmersdorfer Str.

TIERGARTEN

Hotel-Pension Hansablick, Flotowstr. 6 (tel. 390 48 00; fax 392 69 37). S-Bahn #3, 5, 7, 75, or 9 to "Tiergarten." Somewhat pricey, but it's an absolute *Jugendstil* pearl, from the decorative ceilings to the marble entrance and lamps gracing the cobblestone streets in front. All rooms have bath, hair dryer, phone, and cable TV. Some have patios from which you can watch ferries on the Spree. Few places like this survived WWII, so call, write, or fax ahead for reservations. Singles DM150, doubles DM175-215. In the low season (July-Aug. and mid-Nov. to Feb.) singles DM135, doubles DM155-195. Extra bed in the big doubles DM55. 5% discount if you mention *Let's Go.* July-Aug. same-day specials are available but without the *Let's Go* discount. 24hr. reception.

CHARLOTTENBURG

🐾 **Pension Berolina,** Stuttgarter Pl. 17 (tel. 32 70 90 72; fax 32 70 90 73). S-Bahn #3, 5, 7, 75, or 9 to "Charlottenburg" or U-Bahn #7 to "Wilmersdorfer Str." Simple, spartan rooms, but the prices get two thumbs up. Singles DM50, doubles DM60, triples DM70, quads DM80, quints DM90. Shared bathrooms. Breakfast DM8. Reservations recommended.

Hotel-Pension Cortina, Kantstr. 140 (tel. 313 90 59; fax 31 73 96). S-Bahn #3, 5, 7, 75, or 9 to "Savignyplatz." High-ceilinged, bright, convenient, and hospitable. Singles DM60-90, doubles DM90-150. More expensive rooms have private showers. Dorm-style accommodation DM35-60, depending on the time of year and the size of the group. Breakfast included. 24hr. reception.

Pension Knesebeck, Knesebeckstr. 86 (tel. 312 72 55; fax 313 95 07). S-Bahn #3, 5, 7, 75, or 9 to "Savignyplatz." Just north of the park. Friendly, large *Alt-Berliner* rooms with faux Baroque stylings come with couches and sinks. Singles DM75, with shower DM85; doubles DM110-120, with shower DM130-140; big *Mehrbettzimmer* DM50-60 per person. Cheaper in winter. Hearty buffet-style breakfast included. Laundry machines DM8. 24hr. reception. Phone reservations must be confirmed by fax or letter.

Charlottenburger Hof, Stuttgarter Pl. 14 (tel. 32 90 70; fax 323 37 23). S-Bahn #3, 5, 7, 75, or 9 to "Charlottenburg" (across the street) or U-Bahn #7 to "Wilmersdorfer Str." Slick but expensive *Pension* with Miró, Klee, and Dalí on the walls. Spotless rooms with phones and TVs, plus a peaceful guest lounge with funky black chairs. Singles DM80-120, doubles DM110-160, quads DM160-220. Shower, bathroom, and TV in all rooms. Nov.-Dec. 20-30% winter discounts. Breakfast in the adjoining **Café Voltaire** DM6 (see **Food,** p. 106). Laundry DM5. Sometimes has same-day space.

SCHÖNEBERG-WILMERSDORF

Hotel Sachsenhof, Motzstr. 7 (tel. 216 20 74; fax 215 82 20). U-Bahn #1, 15, 2, or 4 to "Nollendorfplatz" Small, well-furnished rooms in the middle of Nollendorfplatz's gay night-life scene. Singles DM57, with shower DM65; doubles DM99-116, with shower DM146, with bath (including an adorable bathtub with feet) DM126-156; DM30 per extra bed. Breakfast DM10. 24hr. reception. Call for reservations between 7am and 11pm.

Hotel-Pension München, Güntzelstr. 62 (tel. 857 91 20; fax 85 79 12 22). U-Bahn #9 to "Güntzelstr." Bright 3rd floor *Pension* with balconies and art by contemporary Berlin artists. Clean, white-walled rooms with TVs and phones. Singles DM66-70, with shower DM95-110; doubles DM80-90, with bath DM115-130. Breakfast DM9. Written reservations are best as the hotel has many admirers.

Frauenhotel Artemesia, Brandenburgische Str. 18 (tel. 873 89 05; fax 861 86 53; email frauenhotel-berlin@t-online.de). U-Bahn #7 to "Konstanzer Str." Pricey, but a rare bird—an immaculate, elegant hotel for women only, the first of its kind in Germany. Rooms celebrate famous women in Berlin's history, while an outdoor terrace provides a damn fine view of Berlin. The **Speiseraum** upstairs serves breakfast (M-F 7:30-10:30am, Sa-Su 8-11:30am) and evening drinks (5-10pm) to an all-female crowd. Singles DM109, with shower DM148; doubles DM170, with bath DM198; extra beds DM40 per person.

Summer rates: singles DM89-125, doubles DM145-165. Children under 8 free. Breakfast included. Come on your birthday and stay the next three nights for free! Alternatively, try to get the "last-minute, same-day" specials, with singles from DM79 and doubles from DM129 (without breakfast). Reception 7am-10pm.

KREUZBERG

Pension Kreuzberg, Großbeerenstr. 64 (tel. 251 13 62; fax 251 06 38). U-Bahn #6 or 7 or night bus #N19 to "Mehringdamm." Decently priced rooms, small but well decorated with things abstract in an old but grand building close to the Kreuzberg scene. Watch your head in the doorway to the bathroom. Singles DM75, doubles DM98, *Mehrbettzimmer* DM44 per person. Breakfast included. Reception 8am-10pm.

Hotel Transit, Hagelberger Str. 53-54 (tel. 789 04 70; fax 78 90 47 77). U-Bahn #6 or 7 or night bus #N19 to "Mehringdamm." Party hard and crash gently in this stylin' *Pension*. Big-screen MTV lounge with bar open 24hr. Rooms adorned with sleek, faux Bauhaus furnishings and showers. If you anticipate a hangover, you can request breakfast at noon or later. Singles DM90, doubles DM105, triples DM140, quads DM180. Their "Sleep-In" deal allows you to share a *Mehrbettzimmer* for DM33. Breakfast included. 24hr. reception.

CAMPING

Deutscher Camping-Club runs the following campgrounds in Berlin; both are adjacent to the imaginary line tracing the site of the Berlin Wall. Written reservations can be made by writing the Deutscher Camping-Club Berlin, Geisbergstr. 11, 10777 Berlin. Otherwise, call in advance. Both sites charge DM9.70 per person, DM4.60 per child, DM7.20 per tent, and DM12.70 for trailers.

Dreilinden (tel. 805 12 01). S-Bahn #7 to "Griebnitzsee," then walk back between the station and lake. A city campsite, surrounded on 3 sides by the vestiges of the Berlin Wall. The remains of a stretch of the *Autobahn* which fell into disuse after 1949 can be seen through the trees. The site's bar is an old border checkpoint. Open March-Oct.

Kladow, Krampnitzer Weg 111-117 (tel. 365 27 97). U-Bahn #7 to "Rathaus Spandau," then bus #135 (direction: "Alt-Kladow") to the end. Switch to bus #234 to "Krampnitzer Weg/Selbitzer Str.," then follow Krampnitzer Weg 200m. A store and restaurant complement the relaxed atmosphere by a swimmable lake. Open year-round.

◨ FOOD

Berlin's cuisine has joined the melting pot; delectable international culinary options save the *Wurst*-weary traveler from the ubiquitous pig by-products of other German cities. Many offerings from German cuisine are quite tasty, but Berlin's most notable home-grown option is the sweet **Berliner Weiße mit Schuß,** a concoction of wheat beer with a shot of syrup. *Rot* (red) is the most popular variety, made with fruity *Himbeer* (raspberry) syrup; *grün* (green) is less palatable to the uninitiated, consisting of a lemony syrup with a piney aftertaste called *Waldmeister.*

A lot of typical Berlin food is Turkish, and almost every street has its own Turkish *Imbiß* or restaurant. The *Imbiß* stands are a lifeline for the late-night partier; most are open ridiculously late, some 24 hours. The *Döner Kebab,* a sandwich of lamb and salad, has cornered the fast-food market, with *Falafel* running a close second. Either makes a small meal for DM3-5. A second wave of immigration has brought quality Indian and Italian restaurants to Berlin.

There is no clear distinction between *Kneipen,* cafés, and restaurants; indeed, cafés often have better food, a livelier atmosphere than restaurants, and much more reasonable prices. The leisurely breakfast is a gloriously civilized institution in Berlin cafés, often served well into the afternoon, sometimes 24 hours. Berliners read the paper and linger over their fruity, fatty breakfasts; join them and relax with *Milchkaffee.*

Aldi, Plus, Edeka, and Penny Markt are the cheapest supermarket chains, followed by the pricier Bolle, Kaiser's, and Reichelt. Supermarkets are usually open Monday to Friday 9am-6pm and Saturday 9am-4pm, though some chains like Kaiser's are open until as late as 8pm on weekdays. At Bahnhof Zoo, Ullrich am Zoo, below the S-Bahn tracks, and Nimm's Mit, near the *Reisezentrum*, have longer hours. (Open daily 6am-10pm.) The best open-air market fires up Saturday mornings on Winterfeldtplatz, though almost every neighborhood has one. For cheap vegetables and enormous wheels of *Fladenbrot*, check out the kaleidoscopic Turkish market in Kreuzberg, along Maybachufer on the Landwehrkanal, every Friday. Arrive early for the best produce. Take U-Bahn #8 to "Schönleinstr."

CHEAP EATS IN MITTE

Cafeteria Charlottenstraße, Charlottenstr. 55 (tel. 203 09 23 40). U-Bahn #6 to "Französische Str." or U-Bahn #2 or 6 to "Stadtmitte." At the Hochschule für Musik, near the Gendarmenmarkt. Meals DM2.55 for students, DM4.50 for others. Salads and grill items also available. Open M-F 9am-2:45pm.

Mensa der Humboldt-Universität, Unter den Linden 6, in the back of the university's main building. The cheapest *Mensa* in Berlin, conveniently located for sight-seeing in Eastern Berlin. Full meals DM2.50. Student ID required. Open M-F 11:30am-2:30pm.

Käse-König, under the *Fernsehturm* near the Alexanderpl. S-Bahn station. S-Bahn #3, 5, 7, 75, or 9 or U-Bahn #2, 5, or 8 to "Alexanderplatz." *Incredibly* cheap German food served in a GDR-style canteen to a mix of students and *Bauarbeiter* (construction workers). Gobble up a *Bockwurst* (DM1), Schnitzel (DM2.70), or go for a "healthy" salad (DM2). Wash it all down with the generically labelled "Bohemian beer" (DM1.50). Open M-F 9am-6:30pm, Sa 9am-6pm.

AROUND ORANIENBURGER STRASSE

Trattoria Ossena, Oranienburger Str. 65 (tel. 283 53 48). S-Bahn #1, 2, or 25 to "Oranienburger Str." Surrounded on all sides by Oranienburger Straße's myriad cafés, Ossena serves more substantial fare than the rest in the form of delicious Italian pastas and enormous pizzas. Most meals under DM20, many (especially pizzas) large enough to feed two. Try the *Pizza Treccose* (artichokes, ham, and mushrooms; DM14.80) or the *Lasagne con verdura* (vegetarian lasagna; DM14). Open daily from 5pm.

Mendelssohn, Oranienburger Str. 39 (tel 281 78 59). S-Bahn #1, 2, or 25 to "Oranienburger Str." This swank locale serves Macedonian fare in a candlelit setting. Try the *Musaka* (DM12.80), a creamy layered dish of meat and potatoes, or the *Kifli* (DM5.50), a doughy pastry stuffed with goat cheese. Open M-F after 11am, Sa-Su after 9am. Kitchen opens at noon.

Beth Café, Tucholskystr. 40 (tel. 281 31 35), just off Auguststr. S-Bahn #1, 2, or 25 to "Oranienburger Str." Kosher restaurant in the heart of the Scheunenviertel. Serves inexpensive Israeli specialties and a generous selection of kosher wines. Try the falafel (DM4.70) or a bagel with lox and cream cheese (DM4). Other dishes DM5-15. Open M-Th and Su 11am-10pm; F 11am-5pm, in winter 11am-3pm.

Taba, Chausseestr. 106 (tel. 282 67 95). U-Bahn #6 to "Zinnowitzer Str." Indulge in great quesadillas (DM13.50), *empanadas* (DM11.50), or burritos (DM13). On Wednesday, all entrees are DM10. Open W-Su from 7pm.

Village Voice, Ackerstr. 1a (tel. 282 45 50). U-Bahn #8 to "Rosenthaler Platz." Café-bar/bookstore trying hard for NYC hipness. American literature and inexpensive tex-mex fare. Tacos DM9, nachos DM7.50. Café open M-F 11am-2am, Sa-Su noon-2am. Bookstore open M-F 11am-8pm, Sa noon-4pm.

AROUND KURFÜRSTENDAMM

Mensa TU, Hardenbergstr. 34 (tel. 311 22 53). Bus #145 to "Steinpl.," or walk 10min. from Bahnhof Zoo. The mightiest of Berlin's *Mensen* (behold its gigantic neon sign), serves decent food, including rather good vegetarian dishes. Meals DM4-5 for students, others DM6-7. Cafeteria downstairs has longer hours and slightly higher prices. *Mensa* open M-F 11:15am-2:30pm. Cafeteria open M-F 8am-7:45pm.

Café Hardenberg, Hardenbergstr. 10 (tel. 312 33 30). Opposite the TU's *Mensa,* but with a lot more atmosphere. Funky music, artsy interior, and students. Order breakfast (DM5-12) day or night, and eggs and taters could arrive at your table in a sizzling skillet. Less dramatic, but equally good, salads and pasta dishes DM5-13. Good for a few drinks (grog DM4.50). Open M-F 9am-1am, Sa-Su 9am-2am.

Website, Joachimstaler Str. 41 (tel. 88 67 96 30; www.vrcafe.de). U-Bahn #9 or 15 to "Kurfürstendamm." Berlin's trendiest cybercafé offers two levels of smoky, black-lit internet access and virtual reality stations to a mix of cyber-hip Germans and homesick Americans (DM7 per 30min.). Pasta, salads, and omelettes under DM20. Breakfast (DM8-16) served all day. Snacks DM5-7. Open M-Sa 10am-late.

Restaurant Marché, Kurfürstendamm 14-15 (tel. 882 75 78), a couple of blocks down from Bahnhof Zoo and the Gedächtniskirche. Run by the ubiquitous Mövenpick restaurant company, this place styles itself as a French marketplace and provides self-service cafeteria comfort for non-German speakers. The colorful, very Euro cafeteria area is full of fresh produce, salads, grilled meats, pour-it-yourself wines, and hot pastries (DM12-25). Free ice water! Bar and terrace upstairs. Open daily 8am-midnight.

KaDeWe, Tauentzienstr. 21-24 (tel. 212 10). U-Bahn #1, 15, or 2 to "Wittenbergplatz." Satiate every desire in the 6th-floor food emporium of this tremendous department store. Beautiful stands heaped with cabbage and caviar. An entire wing devoted just to tinned fish. The prices? Ah, but such a joy! Open M-F 9:30am-8pm, Sa 9am-4pm.

Filmbühne am Steinplatz, Hardenbergstr. 12 (tel. 312 65 89). This café at one of Berlin's independent cinemas has an eclectic and extensive but generally inexpensive menu. The "Harry & Sally Breakfast" (DM28.50) serves two...or three or four. Vegetarian entrees DM13. Open M-Sa 9am-3am, Su 9am-2am. Films daily are often subtitled rather than dubbed (DM11, Mondays DM8.50). Call 312 90 12 for film info.

CHARLOTTENBURG

Schwarzes Café, Kantstr. 148 (tel. 313 80 38; fax 215 29 54). S-Bahn #3, 5, 7, 75, or 9 to "Savignypl." Knotty interior full of trendy young folks. Dark walls and dapper waiters compliment a bar stocked to the gills. It's not so cool to pay DM4.20 for 0.2L of apple juice—but hey, they have breakfast at all hours (DM8.50-17). Open daily 11am-3am.

Der Ägypter, Kantstr. 26 (tel. 313 92 30). S-Bahn #3, 5, 7, 75, or 9 to "Savignyplatz." It's the one with King Tut's death mask blazing on the front. A little pricey (vegetarian entrees DM14-18), but where else can you get authentic Egyptian food in Berlin? Those who can't afford to eat here drool over the handicrafts on sale in the window before heading to the falafel (DM4) place next door. Open daily after 6pm.

Café Voltaire, Stuttgarter Platz 14 (tel. 324 50 28). S-Bahn #3, 5, 7, 75 or 9 to "Charlottenburg," or U-Bahn #7 to "Wilmersdorfer Str." Café-bistro-gallery with a talkative crowd and Jackson Pollock imitations on the walls. Features an extensive menu of salads, omelettes, and baguettes along with great breakfasts (DM6-8; served 5am-3pm). Open daily 24hr.

SCHÖNEBERG

Baharat Falafel, Winterfeldtstr. 37. U-Bahn #1, 15, 2, or 4 to "Nollendorfplatz." Perhaps the best falafel in Berlin. Five plump chick-pea balls in a fluffy pita, covered with veggies and heavenly sesame, mango, or chili sauce, for DM5-6. Bright shop with Arab pop and watercolors depicting selfless falafel balls leaping into waiting pita. Wash down the sacrifices with fresh juices (DM3-6). Open daily 11am-2am. Closed last week in July.

Café Belmundo, Winterfeldtstr. 36 (tel. 215 20 70), opposite Baharat Falafel. U-Bahn #1, 15, 2, or 4 to "Nollendorfplatz." Nights are for the young, days for a slightly older clientele reading the newspaper. Sunday breakfast buffet (DM14) until 3pm. Salads and pasta DM5-10. Good selection of reasonably priced drinks. Open daily 9am-1am. Kitchen open 11am-11pm.

Sushi am Winterfeldtplatz, Goltzstr. 24 (tel. 215 49 30). U-Bahn #1, 15, 2, or 4 to "Nollendorfplatz." Standing-room only Japanese cuisine in the heart of Schöneberg. Try the fresh sushi à la carte (DM3-8) or filling lunch platters (including miso soup) for DM15-19. Open M-Sa noon-midnight, Su 3pm-midnight. Delivery until 1hr. before closing.

Bua Luang, Vorbergstr. 10a (tel. 781 83 81). U-Bahn #7 to "Kleistpark." Mild to spicy Thai food in a quiet residential section of Schöneberg. Feast on the hefty noodle dishes (DM10) or on the delectably spicy Masaman curried tofu (DM8). Order out or try to find a spot in the tiny café. Open daily 2pm-midnight.

WHAT'S A DÖNER?

When this question was posed to Germany's *Döner* dealers, their response was utter bafflement. After all, everyone knows what a *Döner Kebab* is—chunks of spit-roasted lamb stuffed in a toasted Turkish *Fladenbrot* topped with vegetables and garlic sauce. Yet where does the name come from? Vendors in northern Germany unanimously insisted that it comes from Berlin and told us not to get any ideas about this being authentic Turkish food. But we learned that the German "Dön" comes from the Turkish word meaning "to turn," and that the meat is thus named a *Döner* because it revolves as it cooks. A *Döner* by any other name simply would not be the same.

KREUZBERG

Amrit, Oranienstr. 202-203 (tel. 612 55 50). U-Bahn #1 or 15 to "Görlitzer Bahnhof." Possibly Berlin's best Indian restaurant, in the thick of Kreuzberg's bar scene. Fabulous vegetarian dishes like Palak Paneer (DM11) as well as delectably spicy meat entrees; try the Chicken Saag (DM13.50). English menu available. Open M-Th and Su noon-1am, F-Sa noon-2am.

Tibet-Haus, Zossener Str. 19 (tel. 694 89 48). U-Bahn #7 to "Gneisenaustr." This smallish restaurant grooves to the beat of sitar music and Eastern spices. Himalayan delights such as mountain mushrooms roasted in paprika sauce (DM11.50) pique the diner's culinary interest. Tasty chicken with spiced spinach (DM11). Open daily noon-midnight. No toilets. Take-out available.

Melek Pastanesi, Oranienstr. 28 (tel. 694 89 48). U-Bahn #1, 15, or 8 to "Kottbusser Tor." Delicious Turkish pastries sold around the clock. A favorite hangout for sugar-deprived late-night partygoers. 100g baklava DM1.40.

Die Rote Harfe, Oranienstr. 13 (tel. 618 44 46), on Heinrichplatz. U-Bahn #1 or 15 to "Görlitzer Bahnhof." Leftists and grizzled types eating solid German food. Menu changes daily; most meals DM5-17, salads DM9-12. Open daily 2pm-late.

Café Abendmahl, Muskauer Str. 9 (tel. 612 51 70). U-Bahn #1 or 15 to "Görlitzer Bahnhof." While some of the *Ecce Homo* decorative motifs are a touch overbearing, the restaurant's delicious vegetarian and fish dishes are a favorite of gay and lesbian Berliners. Substantial salads DM9.50-16.50. Open daily after 6pm.

Café V, Lausitzer Pl. 12 (tel. 612 45 05). U-Bahn #1 or 15 to "Görlitzer Bahnhof." Berlin's oldest vegetarian restaurant. Try the *Tofu-Würstchen* breakfast with scrambled eggs and tomato sauce (DM10.50). Pizzas DM10.50-13, salads DM8.50 and up. Open daily 10am-2am.

PRENZLAUER BERG

Die Krähe, Kollwitzstr. 84 (tel. 442 82 91), off Kollwitzpl. U-Bahn #2 to "Senefelderplatz." Check out the psychedelic "crow" tapestry. Bright crowd orders from changing weekly menu; tasty breakfasts under DM10, crunchy salads DM12. The popular Sunday buffet lets you load up until you burst for DM13.50. Open M-Th 5:30pm-2am, F-Sa 5:30pm-3am, Su 10:30am-2am.

Ostwind, Husemannstr. 13 (tel. 441 59 51). U-Bahn #2 to "Senefelderplatz." Chinese food that seeks to bridge the cultural divide between East and West. Prenzlauer hipsters indulge in the dim sum or *Shao-Lin Min* (noodles with tofu, lotus, broccoli, and carrots; DM13.90). Open M-Th 6pm-1am, F-Sa 10am-1am.

Café-Restaurant Miró, Raumerstr. 29 (tel. 44 73 30 13). U-Bahn #2 to "Eberswalder Str." Generous portions of attractive and delectable Mediterranean cuisine. Breakfast DM7-11. Soups DM5, large appetizers DM8.50-15.50, salads DM7.50-16. Open 10am-late. Kitchen closes at midnight.

Osswald, Göhrener Str. 5 (tel. 442 74 50). U-Bahn #2 to "Eberswalder Str." A perfect place for breakfast, dinner, or a late-night drink, the restaurant/bar caters to locals and a few lucky tourists who read *Let's Go*. Simple but tasty dishes at great prices. Su breakfast buffet served until 5pm (DM12). Open daily 9am-4am.

Café Restauration 1900, Husemannstr. 1 (tel. 442 24 94), at Kollwitzplatz. U-Bahn #2 to "Senefelderplatz." Alternative interior with black and white drawings on a street decorated in Potemkin-village 19th-century style. Decent food at decent prices. Open M-Sa 11am-2am, Su 10am-2am. Kitchen open until midnight.

🕾 SIGHTS

Berlin's sights are spread out over an area eight times the size of Paris. For a guide to the city's major neighborhoods, see **Orientation**, p. 90. Below, the sights are organized by *Bezirk* (district), beginning with Mitte and spiraling outward. Areas farther from the center are grouped together in **Outer Districts.** Many of central Berlin's major sights lie along the route of **bus #100,** which travels from Bahnhof Zoo to Prenzlauer Berg, passing the Siegessäule, Brandenburg Gate, Unter den Linden, the Berliner Dom, and Alexanderplatz along the way. To add an element of thrill to your sightseeing expedition, climb up to the second floor of the double-decker bus, and sit in the very first row: the view is unbeatable, and you'll feel like you're on an amusement park ride. Buying individual tickets every time you reboard the bus can get pricey; consider investing in a day pass (DM7.80) or a 7-day pass (DM40), as it's impossible to see everything on foot (see **Getting Around,** p. 93).

MITTE

Formerly the heart of Imperial Berlin, much of Mitte languished in disuse and disrepair during GDR days. Now that the government is back in town, the district is once again living up to its name ("Mitte" means center), as embassies and national institutes pour back into the area's rapidly-renovating streets.

UNTER DEN LINDEN

The area between the Brandenburg Gate and Alexanderplatz is best reached by taking S-Bahn #1, 2, or 25 to "Unter den Linden" and heading east; alternatively, bus #100 runs the length of the boulevard every 4-6 minutes.

BRANDENBURGER TOR. For decades a barricaded gateway to nowhere, today the Brandenburg Gate is the most powerful emblem of reunited Berlin. Standing directly in the center of the city, it opens east onto Unter den Linden and west onto the Tiergarten and Straße des 17. Juni. Built during the reign of Friedrich Wilhelm II as an image of peace to replace its crumbling medieval predecessor, the gate became a symbol, *the* symbol, of the Cold War East-West division. The images broadcast around the world of East and West Berliners dancing together atop the Wall were all filmed at the Brandenburg Gate, since this section of the wall was the only part with a flat top—everywhere else, the top is curved, preventing would-be escapers from getting a good grip.

PARISER PLATZ. The Brandenburger Tor opens eastward onto Unter den Linden, once one of Europe's best-known boulevards and the spine of old Berlin. All but a few of the venerable buildings near the gate have been destroyed, although a massive reconstruction effort centered around the gate has already

BERLIN

Mitte

ACCOMMODATIONS
A Circus
B Clubhouse Hostel

Volkspark
Friedrichshain

Friedenstr.
Palisadenstr.
Karl-Marx-Allee
Lichtenberger Str.
STRAUSBERGER PLATZ
Blumenstr.
Singerstr.
Karl-Marx-Allee
Prenzlauer Berg
Molistr.
Otto-Braun-Str.
Prenzlauer Allee
Torstr.
ROSA-LUXEMBURG-PLATZ
Grunerstr.
Alexanderstr.
ALEXANDER-PLATZ
Holzmarktstr.
Spree
Michaelkirchstr.
Schillingstr.
MICHAEL KIRCHPLATZ
Köpenicker Str.
Brückenstr.
Jannowitzbrücke
Heinrich-Heine-Str.
Sebastianstr.
Märkisches Museum
Alte Jakobstr.
Waldeckpark
Former Berlin Wall
Lindenstr.
Zimmerstr.
Kochstr.
Checkpoint Charlie
Friedrichstr.
Markgrafenstr.
Niederkirchnerstr.
Abgeordnetenhaus von Berlin
Martin-Gropius-Bau
Stresemannstr.
Linkstr.
Infobox
Führerbunker
Voßstr.
Wilhelmstr.
Mauerstr.
Glinkastr.
Behrenstr.
Mohrenstr.
Russia
Deutscher Dom
Französische Str.
GENDARMEN-MARKT
Französische Str.
Konzerthaus
St. Hedwigs-Kathedrale
Deutsche Guggenheim Berlin
Charlottenstr.
Georgenstr.
Deutsche Staatsbibliothek
Humboldt Universität
Unter den Linden
Neue Wache
Deutsche Staatsoper
Oberwallstr.
BEBEL-PLATZ
WERDER-SCHER MARKT
Staats rat
Schloßplatz
Breite Str.
Nikolaiviertel
Mühlendamm
Fischerinsel
Spree
Palast der Republik
Zeughaus
Altes Museum
MARX-ENGELS-FORUM
Berliner Dom
Alte Nationalgalerie
Pergamon-Museum
Bode-museum
Neue Synagoge
Oranienburger Str.
Tucholskystr.
Gr. Hamburger Str.
Alter Jüdischer Friedhof
Dircksenstr.
HACKESCHER MARKT
Karl-Liebknecht-Str.
Spandauer Str.
Rotes Rathaus
Marienkirche
Fernsehturm
Nikolaikirche
Ephraim-Palais
Knoblauchhaus
ROSENTHALER PLATZ
Rosenthaler Str.
Augustr.
Linienstr.
Torstr.
Oranienburger Str.
Johannisstr.
Friedrichstr.
Chausseestr.
Bertolt-Brecht-Haus
Dorotheenstädtischer Friedhof
Hannoversche Str.
Oranienburger Tor
Albrechtstr.
Reinhardtstr.
Marienstr.
Schumannstr.
Luisenstr.
Deutsches Theater
Georgenstr.
Friedrichstr.
Reichstag
Hotel Adlon
PARISER PLATZ
Brandenburger Tor
Dorotheenstr.
Scheidemannstr.
Schiffbauerdamm
PLATZ VOR DEM NEUEN TOR
Hamburger Bahnhof
Heidestr.
Humboldt hafen
Former Berlin Wall
Invalidenstr.
Moltkestr.
Spree
Alt-Moabit
Straße des 17. Juni
Kongreßhalle
PLATZ DER REPUBLIK
Sowjetisches Ehrenmal
John-Foster-Dulles-Allee
Entlastungstr.
Tiergarten
Bellevuestr.
Lennéstr.
POTSDAMER PLATZ
Potsdamer Str.
Sigismundstr.
Stauffenbergstr.
Staatsbibliothek
Neue National-galerie
Gemälde-galerie
Kulturforum
Philharmonie
Musik-instrumenten-museum
Kunstgewerbe-museum
KEMPER-PLATZ
Tiergartenstr.
Str. der Pariser Kommune
Mühlenstr.
Ostbahnhof
Schillingbrücke
Stralauer Allee
400 yards
400 meters
N

revived such pre-war staples as the **Hotel Adlon,** once the premier address for all visiting dignitaries and celebrities.

RUSSIAN EMBASSY. Rebuilding the edifices of the rich and famous wasn't a huge priority in the workers' state; one exception, however, is the imposing **Palais Unter den Linden 7.** The seat of the Russian embassy since 1831, the building was rebuilt to house Soviet comrades after the war, evidenced by the magnificent hammer-and-sickle engravings upstairs. With the end of the Cold War, the *palais* has reverted to being just another embassy, and the huge bust of Lenin that once graced its red star-shaped topiary was quietly removed in 1994.

AROUND FRIEDRICHSTRASSE. Beyond Friedrichstr., many neighboring 18th-century structures have been restored to their original splendor, though the excesses of the GDR days continue to mar the landscape. As the principal thoroughfares of downtown East Berlin, the intersection of Friedrichstr. and Unter den Linden became a proletarian showcase of glitzy hotels and restaurants named after other Communist capitals. From the architectural terror rises the stately **Deutsche Staatsbibliothek** (state library), whose shady, ivy-covered courtyard and café provide a pleasant respite from the surrounding landscape. *(Unter den Linden 8. Tel 210 50. Library open M-F 9am-9pm, Sa 9am-5pm. Café open M-F 9am-6pm, Sa 10am-4pm.)*

HUMBOLDT-UNIVERSITÄT. Just beyond the Deutsche Staatsbibliothek is the H-shaped main building of the Humboldt-Universität, whose hallowed halls have been filled by the likes of Hegel, Einstein, the Brothers Grimm, and Karl Marx. In the wake of the post-1989 internal ideological *Blitzkrieg*, in which "tainted" departments were radically revamped or simply shut down, international scholars have descended upon the university to take part in its dynamic renewal. Nevertheless, or perhaps consequently, Marx and Lenin's greatest hits are available for cheap from the book vendors outside. *(Unter den Linden 6. Tel. 209 30.)* Near the university, the statue of **Friedrich the Great** atop his horse stands in the middle of the boulevard. The designer despised Fred; rumor has it that he placed the emperor's visage on the horse's behind. Ah, sweet myth.

NEUE WACHE. The new guard house was designed by Prussian architect Karl Friedrich Schinkel in unrepentant Neoclassical style. During the GDR era, it was known as the "Monument to the Victims of Fascism and Militarism," and, ironically, was guarded by goose-stepping East German soldiers. After reunification, the building closed briefly but was reopened in 1993 as a war memorial. Buried inside are urns filled with earth from the Nazi concentration camps at Buchenwald and Mauthausen as well as from the battlefields of Stalingrad, El Alamein, and Normandy. A copy of Käthe Kollwitz's sculpture *Mutter mit totem Sohn* (mother with dead son) fills the interior with a heavy atmosphere evocative of the atrocities of war. *(Unter den Linden 4. Open daily 10am-6pm.)*

BEBELPLATZ. It was here on May 10, 1933 that Nazi students burned nearly 20,000 books by "subversive" authors such as Heinrich Heine and Sigmund Freud—both Jews. A plaque in the center of the square is engraved with Heine's eerily prescient 1820 quote: *Nur dort wo man Bücher verbrennt, verbrennt man am Ende auch Menschen.* ("Wherever books are burned, ultimately people are burned as well.") The building with the curved facade is the **Alte Bibliothek.** Once the royal library, it is now home to the Humboldt's law faculty. On the other side of the square is the handsome **Deutsche Staatsoper,** fully rebuilt after the war from original sketches by Knobelsdorff, the same architect who designed Schloß Sanssouci in Potsdam (see p. 142). The distinctive blue dome at the end of the square belongs to the **St.-Hedwigs-Kathedrale.** Built in 1773 as the first Catholic church erected in Berlin after the Reformation, it was burnt to a crisp by American bombers in 1943. Designed after the Roman Pantheon, the church was rebuilt in the 1950s in high atheist style, such that the interior resembles a socialist nightclub more than a house of worship. On Wednesdays at 3pm, its massive organ erupts with rather frightening tunes. *(Cathedral open M-F 10am-5pm, Sa 10am-4:30pm, Su 1-5pm. Free.)*

ZEUGHAUS. Once the Prussian army's hall of fame and military museum, the heavily ornamented building has calmed down a bit to become the **Museum of German History** (see **Museums,** p. 123). The exhibits are currently housed in the **Kronprinzenpalais** across the street while the Zeughaus undergoes renovations. *(Unter den Linden 2. Tel. 20 30 40; fax 230 45 43.)*

GENDARMENMARKT

Berlin's most impressive ensemble of 19th-century buildings is a few blocks south of Unter den Linden on the **Gendarmenmarkt,** also known as the French Quarter after it became the main settlement for Protestant Huguenots in the 18th century. Take U-Bahn #2 to "Französische Str." or U-Bahn #2 or 6 to "Stadtmitte." During the last week of June and the first week of July, the square transforms into an outdoor stage for open-air classical concerts; call 53 43 53 43 for details, or stop by one of the discount ticket offices for last-minute deals (see p. 127).

DEUTSCHER DOM. Gracing the southern end of the square, the square houses **Fragen zur deutschen Geschichte,** a Bundestag-sponsored exhibition which traces German political history from despotism to fascism to democracy. *(Gendarmenmarkt 5. Tel. 22 73 21 41. Open Tu-Su 10am-7pm. Free.)*

FRANZÖSISCHER DOM. At the opposite end of the square from the Deutscher Dom. Built in the early 18th century by French Huguenots, the Dom is now home to a restaurant and a small museum chronicling the Huguenot diaspora. The tower offers an interesting panorama of the surrounding construction sites. *(Gendarmenmarkt 5. Tel. 229 17 60. Museum open Tu-Sa noon-5pm. DM3, students DM2. Restaurant open daily noon-1am. Tower open daily 9am-7pm.)*

KONZERTHAUS AM GENDARMENMARKT. Located between the two churches. Designed by Karl Friedrich Schinkel in 1819 (see p. 26), the Konzerthaus was badly damaged in air attacks toward the end of WWII. It reopened in 1984 as the most elegant concert venue in Berlin and hosts a variety of performances from chamber music to concerts by international orchestras (see p. 128). *(Gendarmenmarkt 2. Tel. 203 09 21 01.)*

POTSDAMER PLATZ

No longer in geographic limbo, Potsdamer Platz is accessible by S-Bahn #1, 2, or 25 or U-Bahn #2 to "Potsdamer Platz."

POTSDAMER PLATZ. Caught in the death strip between the two walls during the Cold War, Potsdamer Platz was the commercial and transport hub of pre-war Berlin. The square was built under Friedrich Wilhelm I in an approximation of Parisian boulevards with the primary purpose of moving troops quickly. Having gained notoriety in the 1990s as the world's largest construction site, current plans aim to restore Potsdamer Platz to its position as the commercial heart of reunited Berlin. The construction was supposed to conclude by 2000, but the date has been pushed back to 2004. To find out more about the future of the square, visit the **Infobox,** the shiny red structure near the subway station (see **Museums,** p. 124).

FÜHRERBUNKER. Near Potsdamer Platz, unmarked and inconspicuous, lies the site of the bunker where Hitler married Eva Braun and then ended his life (or so the government would like to believe). In macabre irony, the actual bunker site is now a playground (behind the record store at Wilhelmstr. 92); tourists looking for it often mistakenly head for the visible bunker at the southern edge of Potsdamer Platz. Plans to restore the bunker were shelved amid fears that the site would become a shrine for the radical right.

LUSTGARTEN AND MUSEUMINSEL

After crossing the Schloßbrücke over the Spree, Unter den Linden passes by the **Museuminsel** (museum island), home to four major museums and the **Berliner Dom.**

BERLIN

SPECTACULAR WRECKAGE Berlin's skyline is spiked with the narrow bodies of cranes, the streets are covered with little mountains of bricks and debris, and on windy days curtains of dust rise from the empty lots of construction sites. Berlin is, and undoubtedly always will be, an unfinished city. Since the decision to move the national capital back from Bonn, there has been a push to restore Berlin's bombed-out and bullet-riddled edifices to their pre-war glory as well as to make room for the hoards of bureaucrats and foreign diplomats streaming into the city. Climb the lookout deck at Potsdamer Platz and you'll see a full square mile of gargantuan foundations and cranes busily dipping and tugging truck-sized blocks from lot to lot. At nearby Museuminsel, two of Berlin's best museums are swaddled in scaffolding to purge them of 50 years of GDR-style neglect. Posh Unter den Linden suffers the same fate to the tune of concrete-pounding jackhammers and sandblasters. Berlin has been subjected to architectural terror many times before, from the lofty militarist plans of Friedrich the Great to the fascist whims of Hitler's urban planning henchman, Albert Speer; but it's clear that the sheer scale of the nascent capital's plans will dramatically change the city's fate. This period of flux is probably more exciting than what the end product will be. Berlin is at its best with most of its bricks still unmortared.

Take S-Bahn #3, 5, 7, 75, or 9 to "Hackescher Markt" and walk toward the Dom; alternatively, pick up bus #100 along Unter den Linden and get off at "Lustgarten." For information on the **Altes Museum, Pergamon, Bodemuseum,** and **Alte Nationalgalerie,** see **Museums,** p. 122.

ALTES MUSEUM. Across the Lustgarten from Unter den Linden. The museum was created by Schinkel, who envisioned Berlin as the "Athens on the Spree." The tubby granite bowl in front was supposed to adorn the main hall, but it didn't fit through the door. The **Lustgarten,** a pleasant collection of trees and benches, is being redesigned to look as it did in the 19th century. The park was scheduled to reopen in October 1999.

BERLINER DOM. Next door to the Altes Museum. The beautifully bulky, multiple-domed cathedral proves that Protestants can go overboard as much as Catholics. Built during the reign of Kaiser Wilhelm II, the cathedral recently emerged from 20 years of restoration after being severely damaged by an air raid in 1944. The ornate gold- and jewel-encrusted interior, with its distinctively Protestant idols (Calvin, Zwingli, and Luther), is stunning, if tacky to non-believers. *(Open daily 9am-7:30pm. Admission to Dom DM5, students DM3. Comprehensive admission to the Dom, tower, and galleries DM8, students DM5. Free organ recitals W-F at 3pm. Frequent concerts in summer; buy tickets in the church or call 20 26 91 36 for more information.)* There's also the **Kaiserliches Treppenhaus** upstairs, with exhibits of period art and imperial booty. *(Open M-Sa 9am-8pm, Su noon-8pm. Free.)*

SCHLOSSPLATZ. Across the street from the Lustgarten. Known as Marx-Engels-Platz during the days of the GDR, the square houses the glaring, amber-colored **Palast der Republik,** where the East German parliament met. In 1990, city authorities discovered that the building was full of asbestos and shut it down; a current reconstruction project aims to make it carcinogen-free. The problems associated with the building are further complicated by the fact that the entire square used to be the site of the **Berliner Schloß,** the Hohenzollern family palace. Remarkably, the palace survived the war, only to be demolished by GDR authorities in the 1950s in censure of its royal excess. The **Staatsrat,** currently the temporary office of the federal chancellor, resides on the site—look for the modern building with a slice of the palace facade embedded in the middle. The East German government preserved this section because **Karl Liebknecht** proclaimed a German socialist republic from its balcony. The newest plans for the site call for the *Palast*'s demolition and the reconstruction of the Schloß's facade with a modern entertainment center behind it, but whether this will materialize is anybody's guess. In the meantime, the square is a huge construction site and is practically inaccessible to the public.

MARX-ENGELS-FORUM. Across the Liebknecht-Brücke on the right-hand side of the street stands a memorial consisting of steel tablets dedicated to the world-wide workers' struggle against fascism and imperialism. The exhibit is dwarfed by a huge statue of a seated Santa Claus-like Marx and a standing Engels that has become a popular jungle gym for visiting tourist children. The park and the street behind it used to be collectively known as the Marx-Engels-Forum; the park has not been renamed, while the street is now called Rathausstr.

ALEXANDERPLATZ AND NIKOLAIVIERTEL

On the other side of Museuminsel, Unter den Linden becomes Karl-Liebknecht-Str., and leads into the monolithic **Alexanderplatz.** Take S-Bahn #3, 5, 7, 75, or 9 or U-Bahn #2, 5, or 8 to "Alexanderplatz."

ALEXANDERPLATZ. Formerly the frantic heart of Weimar Berlin, the plaza was transformed in East German times into an urban wasteland of fountains and pre-fab office buildings, including some concrete-block classics. In the 1970s, the East German government made a concession to the People's implacable craving for bright lights by erecting some enormous neon signs, giving the area the superficial trappings of a Western metropolis: "Chemical Products from Bitterfeld!" and "Medical Instruments of the GDR—Distributed in All the World!" Although nearly all the buildings have been thoroughly sanitized, their dreary demeanor remains.

FERNSEHTURM. The TV tower, the tallest structure in Berlin at 365 meters, is a truly awkward piece of design intended to show off the new heights achieved through five-year plans. The project proved to be somewhat of a flop when it was discovered that the sun's reflection on the tower's amber-tinted windows creates a shadow that looks very much like a crucifix (known as the *Papsts Rache*—the Pope's revenge). The view from the top (the spherical node 203m up the spike) is magnificent. An elevator whisks tourists up and away. *(Tel. 242 33 33. Open daily March-Oct. 9am-1am; Nov.-Feb. 10am-midnight. DM9, under 17 DM4.)*

NIKOLAIVIERTEL. A carefully reconstructed Altstadt deriving its name from the Nikolaikirche, the Nikolaiviertel consists of a series of narrow, winding streets that are popular and crowded. Among the two dozen historic buildings is the **Knoblauchhaus,** home to a small museum documenting the life and times of architect Eduard Knoblauch. *(Poststr. 23. Tel. 238 09 00. Open Tu-Su 10am-6pm. DM5, students DM2.50.)* Nearby is the **Ephraim-Palais,** at the corner of Poststr. and Mühlendamm. The Nazis used this Rococo building as a sports museum; it now houses a collection of contemporary art from the era of Friedrich the Great. *(Open Tu-Su 10am-6pm. DM3, students DM1.)*

SCHEUNENVIERTEL AND ORANIENBURGER STRASSE

Northwest of Alexanderplatz lies the **Scheunenviertel,** once the center of Berlin's Orthodox Jewish community. Take S-Bahn #1, 2, or 25 to "Oranienburger Str." or U-Bahn #6 to "Oranienburger Tor." Prior to WWII, Berlin never had any ghettos. Jews lived throughout the city, though during the war they were deported to ghettos in Poland. Wealthier and more assimilated Jews tended to live in Western Berlin while Orthodox Jews from Eastern Europe settled in the Scheunenviertel. Although evidence of Jewish life in Berlin dates back to the 13th century, the community was expelled in 1573 and not invited back for 100 years. Today the Scheunenviertel is better known for its outdoor cafés and punk clubs than for its historical significance as Berlin's Jewish center, but the past few years have seen the opening of several Judaica-oriented bookstores and kosher restaurants.

NEUE SYNAGOGE. This huge, "oriental-style" building was designed by Berlin architect Eduard Knoblauch. The synagogue, which seated 3,200, was used for worship until 1940, when the Nazis occupied it and used it for storage. Amazingly, the building also survived *Kristallnacht*—the SS torched it, but a local police chief, realizing that the building was a historical monument, ordered the Nazis to extinguish the fire. The synagogue was destroyed by bombing, but its restoration, largely financed by international Jewish organizations, began in 1988. The temple's beautiful, gold-laced domes were rebuilt and opened to the public in 1995. The interior houses an exhibit chronicling the synagogue's history in addition to temporary exhibits on the history of Berlin's Jews. To enter, you must pass through a metal detector. *(Oranienburger Str. 30. Tel 28 40 13 16. Open M-Th and Su 10am-6pm, F 10am-2pm. Museum DM5, students DM3. Entry to the dome DM3, students DM2.)*

ALTER JÜDISCHER FRIEDHOF. Destroyed by the Nazis, the site now contains only the restored gravestone of the Enlightenment philosopher and scholar Moses Mendelssohn; the rest is a quiet park. In front, a plaque marks the site of the **Jüdisches Altersheim,** the Jewish old-age home which after 1942 served as a holding place for Jews before their deportation to concentration camps. *(At the end of Große Hamburger Str., near the intersection with Monbijoustr.)*

JÜDISCHE KNABENSCHULE. Next to the cemetery, another plaque marks the location of Berlin's oldest **Jewish school,** where Moses Mendelssohn taught. Mendelssohn, who was known as "the German Socrates," translated the Hebrew Bible into German and supported interaction between Berlin's Jewish and non-Jewish communities. Corresponding with his humanist outlook, the school's enrollment was half-gentile, half-Jewish. The building was reopened as a school in 1992; its student body is still half-and-half.

OTHER SIGHTS. Berlin's **first synagogue** opened in 1714 near the corner of Rochstr. and Rosenstr. Remarkably, this synagogue was not destroyed on *Kristallnacht* because of the presence of a post office that had been renting space in the building; however, it was later bombed during the war, never to be reconstructed. The spot is marked by a huge construction site. The former **Jewish welfare office** was located at Rosenstr. 2-4. In the adjacent park, a terra cotta memorial was erected in October 1995 on the 54th anniversary of the first deportation of Berlin's Jews.

OTHER SIGHTS IN MITTE

BERTOLT-BRECHT-HAUS. If any single man personifies the maelstrom of political and aesthetic contradictions that is Berlin, it is **Bertolt Brecht,** who called the city home. "There is a reason to prefer Berlin to other cities," the playwright once declared, "because it is constantly changing. What is bad today can be improved tomorrow." Brecht lived and worked in the house near the intersection with Schlegelstr. from 1953 to 1956. If you understand German, take the guided tour, given in flamboyant Brechtian style. The **Brechtforum** on the second floor sponsors exhibits and lectures on artistic and metropolitan subjects; pick up a schedule. *(Chausseestr. 125. Tel. 283 05 70 44. U-Bahn #6 to "Zinnowitzer Str." Entrance only with a tour. Tours every 30min. Tu-W and F 10am-noon, Th 10am-noon and 5-7pm, and Sa 9:30am-2pm. Tours every hour Su 11am-6pm. DM4, students DM2.)*

DOROTHEENSTÄDTISCHER FRIEDHOF. Directly adjacent to Brecht's house, the cemetery contains the graves of a host of German luminaries, including Brecht and his wife, Helene Weigel. Fichte and Hegel are buried side by side a few yards away; both graves are often festooned with flowers from admirers (or pillaged by frustrated students). A map of the cemetery is located at the end of the entrance path, next to the chapel on the right. *(Open May-Aug. daily 8am-8pm; Feb.-April and Sept.-Nov. 8am-6pm; Dec.-Jan. 8am-4pm.)*

TIERGARTEN

In the center of Berlin, the lush **Tiergarten** is a relief from the neon lights of the Ku'damm to the west and the din and dust of construction work to the east. Stretching from Bahnhof Zoo to the Brandenburg Gate, the vast landscaped park was formerly used by Prussian monarchs as a hunting and parade ground. Today Berliners use the park to blow off steam, as the Tiergarten is filled with strolling families by day and cruising gay men at night. **Straße des 17. Juni** bisects the park from west to east, connecting Ernst-Reuter-Platz to the Brandenburg Gate. The thoroughfare is the site of many demonstrations and parades throughout the year, including the infamous Love Parade (see p. 135).

SIEGESSÄULE. In the heart of the Tiergarten, the slender 70m victory column, topped by a gilded statue of winged victory, commemorates Prussia's humiliating defeat of France in 1870. In 1938, the Nazis moved the monument from its former spot in front of the Reichstag to increase its height and make it more impressive. Climb the monument's 285 steps to the top for a panorama of the city. *(Großer Stern. Tel. 391 29 61. Take bus #100, 187, or 341 to "Großer Stern." Open April-Nov. M 1-6pm, Tu-Su 9am-6pm. DM2, students DM1.)*

SOWJETISCHES EHRENMAL. At the eastern end of the Tiergarten stands the Soviet Memorial (yes, you're still in Western Berlin) guarded by a pair of red star-emblazoned tanks, the first two to enter Berlin in 1945. *(Bus #100 to "Platz der Republik" and walk down Entlastungsstr. to Straße des 17. Juni.)*

THE REICHSTAG

Just to the north of the Brandenburg Gate sits the imposing, stone-gray Reichstag building, former seat of the parliaments of the German Empire and the Weimar Republic, and current home of Germany's governing body, the Bundestag. In 1918 Philipp Scheidemann proclaimed a German republic from one of its balconies with the words *"es lebe die deutsche Republik"* ("long live the German Republic"). His move turned out to be wise, since two hours later Karl Liebknecht, in the Berliner Schloß a few kilometers away on Unter den Linden, announced a German Socialist Republic on the site that later supported the parliament of the GDR. Civil war followed in Berlin and much of the rest of Germany. The government fled to Weimar to draw up a new constitution, but over the course of the next decade the Reichstag became the fractured center of the economically troubled Republic. As the Republic declined, Nazi members showed up to sessions in uniform, and on February 28, 1933, a month after Hitler became Chancellor, fire mysteriously broke out in the building. The event provided a pretext for Hitler to declare a state of emergency, giving the Nazis broad powers to arrest and intimidate opponents before the upcoming elections. The infamous end result was the Enabling Act, which established Hitler as legal dictator and abolished democracy. A conceptual monument outside recalls the 96 members of the Reichstag executed by the Nazis.

In the summer of 1995, the Reichstag metamorphosed into an artsy parcel, when husband-and-wife team **Christo** and **Jeanne-Claude** wrapped the dignified building in 120,000 yards of shimmery metallic fabric. After the wrapping was torn down, the building was restored to its former glory, and then some: a giant glass dome was constructed around an upside-down solar cone that powers the building. Most recently, the long-awaited move of Germany's parliament from Bonn to Berlin was executed in several stages throughout the summer and fall of 1999. At press time a schedule for tours of the new Bundestag had not yet been set; call for the latest information. *(Tel. 22 73 14 30, 22 73 14 31, 22 73 14 32, or 22 73 14 33.)*

CHARLOTTENBURG

The borough of Charlottenburg, one of the wealthiest areas in Berlin, includes the area between the Ku'damm and the Spree river. Like many of Berlin's neighborhoods, it was once a separate town.

BERLIN

KURFÜRSTENDAMM

Stretching several kilometers from Bahnhof Zoo, **Kurfürstendamm** (**Ku'damm** for short) is Berlin's biggest and fanciest shopping strip, lined with designer boutiques, department stores, and pricey hotels. For more on the Ku'damm's consumer delights, see **Shopping**, p. 132.

BAHNHOF ZOO. During the city's division, West Berlin centered around Bahnhof Zoo, the only train station in the world to inspire a rock album stadium tour (the U2 subway line runs through the station). The station is surrounded by a tourism-oriented district of currency exchange booths, drunks, peep shows, and department stores.

ZOOLOGISCHER GARTEN. Across Bahnhof Zoo and through the corral of bus depots, the renowned Zoo is one of the best in the world, with many animals displayed in open-air habitats instead of cages. The second entrance across from Europa-Center is the famous **Elefantentor,** Budapester Str. 34, a delightfully decorated pagoda of pachyderms. *(Open May-Sept. daily 9am-6:30pm; Oct.-Feb. 9am-5pm; March-April 9am-5:30pm. DM13, students DM11.)*

AQUARIUM. Next door to the Zoo is the excellent Aquarium, which houses broad collections of insects and reptiles as well as endless tanks of wide-eyed, rainbow-colored fish. Its pride and joy is its 450kg **Komodo dragon,** the world's largest reptile, a gift to Germany from Indonesia. Check out the psychedelic jellyfish tanks, filled with many translucent sea nettles. *(Budapester Str. 32. Open daily 9am-6pm. Aquarium DM12, students DM10. Combination ticket to the zoo and aquarium DM21, students DM17, children DM10.)*

KAISER-WILHELM-GEDÄCHTNISKIRCHE. Nicknamed "the rotten tooth" by Berliners, the shattered church stands as a sobering reminder of the destruction caused during WWII. The decapitated tower, its jagged edges silhouetted against the sky, is one of Berlin's most striking sights. Built in 1852 in a Romanesque-Byzantine style, the church has an equally striking interior, with colorful mosaics covering the ceiling, floors, and walls. The ruins house an exhibit showing what the church used to look like, as well as shocking photos of the entire city in ruins just after the war. Don't let the cold gray exterior of the adjacent modern church deter you. The enormous octagon-shaped building, erected in the late 1950s, is coated on all eight sides with deep blue stained-glass windows, and the effect from the interior is spectacular. In the summer, Berlin's many touts, foreigners, and young people often gather in front of the church to hang out, sell less-than-legal watches, and play bagpipes and sitars. *(Tel. 218 50 23. Exhibit open M-Sa 10am-4pm. Church open daily 9am-7pm.)*

SCHLOSS CHARLOTTENBURG

Tel. 32 09 11. Take bus #145 from Bahnhof Zoo to "Luisenpl./Schloß Charlottenburg" or U-Bahn #7 to "Richard-Wagner-Platz." and walk about 15min. down Otto-Suhr-Allee. Altes Schloß open Tu-F 9am-5pm, Sa-Su 10am-5pm. DM8, students DM4. Schinkel-Pavilion open Tu-Su 10am-5pm. DM3, students DM2. Belvedere open April-Oct. Tu-Su 10am-5pm; Nov.-March Tu-F noon-4pm and Sa-Su noon-5pm. DM3, students DM2. Mausoleum open April-Oct. Tu-Su 10am-noon and 1-5pm. DM3, students DM2. Schloßgarten open Tu-Su 6am-9pm. Free. Ticket to entire complex DM15, students DM10, under 14 free. Family card DM25.

The broad, bright Baroque palace commissioned by Friedrich I for his second wife, Sophie-Charlotte, drapes its yellow walls over a carefully landscaped park on the northern edge of Charlottenburg. The Schloß's many buildings include the **Neringbau** (or **Altes Schloß**), the palace proper, which contains many rooms filled with historical furnishings; the **Schinkel-Pavilion,** a museum dedicated to Prussian architect Karl Friedrich Schinkel; **Belvedere,** a small building housing the royal family's porcelain collection; and the **Mausoleum,** the final resting spot for most of the family. The **Galerie der Romantik,** a state museum housing Berlin's first-rate collection of German Romantic paintings, is located in a side wing (see **Museums,** p. 122). Seek out the **Schloßgarten** behind the main buildings, an elysium of small lakes, footbridges, fountains, and carefully planted rows of trees.

OTHER SIGHTS IN CHARLOTTENBURG

OLYMPIA-STADION. At the western edge of Charlottenburg, the olympic stadium is one of the most prominent legacies of the Nazi architectural aesthetic. It was erected for the 1936 Olympic Games, in which Jesse Owens, an African-American, triumphed over the Nazis' racial theories by winning four gold medals. Hitler refused to congratulate Owens because of his skin color, but there's now a Jesse-Owens-Allee to the south of the stadium. Film buffs will recognize the complex from Leni Riefenstahl's infamous Nazi propaganda film *Olympia*. *(U-Bahn #2 to "Olympia-Stadion (Ost)" or S-Bahn #5 or 75 to "Olympiastadion." DM1. Open daily in summer 8am-8pm, in winter 8am-3pm.)*

FUNKTURM. Erected in 1926 to herald the radio age, the Funkturm is the Fernsehturm's marginally less impressive twin. Though not as touristed than its Alexanderplatz sibling, the tower offers a stunning view of the city atop its 200m-tall observation deck. Inside, the **Deutsches Rundfunkmuseum** chronicles the history of German broadcasting, including an exhibit dedicated to the world's first television transmission, made here in 1931. *(Tel. 30 38 39 99. Take S-Bahn #45 or 46 to "Witzleben" or U-Bahn #2 to "Kaiserdamm." Panorama deck and museum open daily 10am-11pm. DM5.)*

GEDENKSTÄTTE PLÖTZENSEE. Housed in the terrifyingly well-preserved former execution chambers of the Third Reich, the memorial exhibits documents death sentences of "enemies of the people," including the officers who attempted to assassinate Hitler in 1944. More than 2,500 people were murdered within these red brick walls. Still visible are the hooks from which victims were hanged. The stone urn in front of the memorial contains soil from Nazi concentration camps. English literature is available at the office. *(Hüttigpfad. Tel. 344 32 26. Off the main road where the bus stops, down Emmy-Zehden-Weg on Hüttigpfad. Take U-Bahn #9 to "Turmstr.," then bus #123 (direction: "Saatwinkler Damm") to "Gedenkstätte Plötzensee." Open daily 9am-5pm. Free.)*

SCHÖNEBERG AND WILMERSDORF

South of the Ku'damm, Schöneberg and Wilmersdorf are pleasant, middle-class residential districts noted for their shopping streets, lively cafés, and good restaurants. The birthplace of Marlene Dietrich and the former stomping grounds of Christopher Isherwood, Schöneberg is home to the more affluent segments of Berlin's gay and lesbian community (see **Gay and Lesbian Berlin,** p. 137).

RATHAUS SCHÖNEBERG. West Berlin's city government convened here until the Wall fell in 1989. On June 26, 1963, 1.5 million Berliners swarmed the streets beneath the windowless tower to hear **John F. Kennedy** reassure them of the Allies' commitment to the city. Kennedy's speech ended with the now-famous words, "All free men, wherever they may live, are citizens of Berlin. And therefore, as a free man, I take pride in the words: *Ich bin ein Berliner.*" Of course, every German understood what Kennedy meant, but for the grammar buffs out there, the prez *did* say he's a jelly doughnut. Today, the fortress with the little Berlin bear on top is home to Schöneberg's municipal government as well as an exhibit on the life of former mayor and federal chancellor Willy Brandt. *(John-F.-Kennedy-Pl. Tel. 787 60. U-Bahn #4 to "Rathaus Schöneberg." Rathaus open daily 9am-6pm. Exhibit open daily 9am-1pm.)*

BAYERISCHER PLATZ. In 1993, a conceptual art exhibit was set up along the streets surrounding the square. If you look closely, you'll notice some of the street signs have black-and-white placards above them stating some of the Nazi edicts against Berlin's Jews. A number of these signs can be seen on **Grunewaldstr.** *(U-Bahn #4 or 7 to "Bayerischer Platz.")*

FEHRBELLINER PLATZ. The Wilmersdorf square was erected by the Nazis as a vision of the fascist architectural future. These gruesomely regular, prison-like blocks were meant to be model apartment houses; try to imagine a city full of them. *(U-Bahn #1 or 7 to "Fehrbelliner Platz.")*

GRUNEWALD. In summer, clear your head in the Grunewald, a 745-acre birch forest. While there, visit the **Jagdschloß,** a restored royal hunting lodge housing a worthwhile collection of European paintings, including works by Rubens, van Dyck, and Cranach. *(Am Grunewaldsee 29. Tel. 813 35 97. U-Bahn #1 or 7 to "Fehrbelliner Pl.," then bus #115 (direction: "Neuruppiner Str.") to "Pücklerstr." Walk west 15min. along Pücklerstr. until you see the castle. Open Tu-Su 10am-5pm. DM4, students and seniors DM2.)*

KREUZBERG

Indispensable for a sense of Berlin's famous *alternative Szene*, or counter-culture, is a visit to Kreuzberg, an area loaded with cafés, clubs, and bars. Kreuzberg has long been proud of its diverse population and liberal leanings: this is the place to see anti-Nazi graffiti and left-wing revolutionary slogans (in English, Turkish, Russian, Spanish, and German). During President Reagan's 1985 visit to Berlin, authorities so feared protests from this quarter that they cordoned the whole Kreuzberg district off without warning—an utterly unconstitutional measure. Much of the area was occupied by *Hausbesetzer* (squatters) in the 1960s and 70s. A conservative city government decided to forcibly evict the illegal residents in the early 80s, provoking riots and throwing the city into total consternation.

■**HAUS AM CHECKPOINT CHARLIE.** A strange, fascinating exhibition on the site of the famous border crossing point with an uneasy mixture of blatant Western tourist kitsch and didactic Eastern earnestness, the Haus am Checkpoint Charlie is one of Berlin's most popular tourist attractions. On the ground floor, flashiness is the order of the day; an expensive snack bar is crammed against a ticket desk covered with postcards, mugs, posters, books, and "Communist" baubles. Right by the door stands the car in which Johannes Ehret smuggled his girlfriend across the border in 1988. Upstairs you can find out everything you've ever wanted to know about the Wall or various ways of escaping over it (e.g. in a hot-air balloon or in loudspeakers), while studying the history of human rights struggles throughout the world. Documentaries and dramas about the Wall are screened daily in the rooms upstairs. *(Friedrichstr. 44. Tel. 251 10 31. U-Bahn #6 or bus #129 to "Kochstr." Museum open daily 9am-10pm. DM8, students DM5. Films M-F at 5:30 and 7:30pm, Sa-Su at 4:30, 6, and 7pm.)*

AROUND MEHRINGDAMM. For a look at Kreuzberg's new, somewhat gentrified face, take the U-Bahn to "Mehringdamm" and wander around. The area around **Chamissoplatz,** bordered by Bergmannstr. and Fidicinstr., features an especially large number of old buildings and second-hand shops as well as excellent used music shops (see **Shopping,** p. 132). On the other side of Mehringdamm, the **Viktoriapark** contains Kreuzberg's namesake, a 66m hill featuring Berlin's only waterfall, albeit artificial. At night, many cafés and clubs line **Gneisenaustraße,** which heads west from the intersection with Mehringdamm. *(U-Bahn #6 or 7 to "Mehringdamm.")*

ORANIENSTRASSE. The cafés and bars on Oranienstraße boast a more radical element; the May Day parades always start on Oranienplatz, and the area was the site of frequent riots in the 1980s. The anarchists and left-wing radicals share the neighborhood with an odd mix of traditional Turkish families as well as a sizeable portion of Berlin's gay and lesbian population. The scene at night is pretty crazy; see **Nightlife,** p. 134. *(U-Bahn #1 or 15 to "Kottbusser Tor" or "Görlitzer Bahnhof.")*

EASTERN KREUZBERG. The **Landwehrkanal,** a channel bisecting Kreuzberg, is where Rosa Luxemburg's body was thrown after being murdered by the Freikorps in 1919 (see p. 13). The tree-dotted strip of the canal near Kottbusser Damm, **Paul-Linke-Ufer,** may be the most graceful street in Berlin, with its shady terraces and old facades. *(U-Bahn #8 to "Schönleinstr.")* The east end of Kreuzberg near the site of the Wall is home to Turkish and Balkan neighborhoods, with a corresponding wealth of ethnic restaurants popular with radicals, students, and shabby genteel gourmets. A punkier element crops up further east near **Schlesisches Tor.** At the end of Kreuzberg, the **Oberbaumbrücke** spanning the Spree was once a border crossing into East Berlin; it now serves as an entrance to Friedrichshain's nightlife scene. *(U-Bahn #1 or 15 to "Schlesisches Tor.")*

FRIEDRICHSHAIN AND LICHTENBERG

EAST SIDE GALLERY. The longest remaining portion of the Wall, the 1.3km stretch of cement and asbestos slabs also serves as one of the world's largest open-air art galleries. The murals are not the remnants of Cold War graffiti, but rather the efforts of an international group of artists who gathered here in 1989 to celebrate the end of the city's division. The scrawlings of later tourists have been added to their work. Occasionally, wall-peckers nibble at the edges of the gallery, trying to knock off a chunk for posterity. *(Along Mühlenstr. Take S-Bahn #3, 5, 6, 7, 75, or 9 or U-Bahn #1 or 15 to "Warschauer Str." and walk back toward the river. Open 24hr.)*

█KARL-MARX-ALLEE. The cornerstone of the East German *Nationales Aufbauprogramm* (national construction program), Karl-Marx-Allee became the socialist realist showcase of the infant Communist government in the early 1950s, when it was known as Stalinallee. Billed as Germany's "first socialist road," the ludicrously broad avenue, widened in the 1960s to accommodate grandiose military parades, is flanked by scores of pre-fabricated gems, climaxing with the "people's palaces" at Strausberger Platz. *(U-Bahn #5 to "Strausberger Platz.")*

FORSCHUNGS- UND GEDENKSTÄTTE NORMANNENSTRASSE. In the suburb of Lichtenberg stands perhaps the most hated and feared building of the GDR regime—the headquarters of the East German secret police, the **Staatssicherheit** or **Stasi.** On January 15, 1990, a crowd of 100,000 Berliners stormed and vandalized the building to protest the continued existence of the police state. The building once contained six million individual dossiers on citizens of the GDR, a country of only 16 million people. Since a 1991 law returned the records to their subjects, the "Horror-Files" have rocked Germany, exposing informants—and wrecking careers, marriages, and friendships—at all levels of society. The exhibit displays the offices of Erich Mielke (the loathed Minister for State Security from 1957-1989), surveillance equipment employed by the Stasi, and loads of Stasi kitsch (including innumerable Lenin busts). The present-day museum, memorial, and research center contains fascinating artifacts, but the history and anecdotes are only written in German. Lichtenberg suffers from severe unemployment and has become a somewhat dangerous haven for squatters. When visiting the memorial, be cautious among the remaining emblems of GDR misery. *(Ruschestr. 103, Haus 1. Tel. 553 68 54. U-Bahn #5 to "Magdalenenstr." From the station's Ruschestr. exit, walk up Ruschestr. and take a right on Normannenstr.; it's Haus #1 in the complex of office buildings. Open Tu-F 11am-6pm, Sa-Su 2-6pm. DM5, students DM3.75.)*

PRENZLAUER BERG

Northeast of Mitte lies Prenzlauer Berg, a former working-class district largely neglected by East Germany's reconstruction efforts. Many of its old buildings are falling apart; others still have shell holes and embedded bullets from WWII. The result is the charm of age and graceful decay, slightly less charming for local residents with bad plumbing and no phones. Don't be surprised, however, at the mind-blowing rate of gentrification underway here; Prenzlauer Berg is one of the most sought-out locales for ex-Kreuzbergers fleeing rent increases. Fancy shops and restaurants are popping up left and right, disturbing this neighborhood's reputation as a mellow, low-key retreat for artists and students. Unlike the loud, raucous scene in Kreuzberg and Mitte, Prenzlauer Berg is more sedate and cerebral—

which is not to say that it isn't lively. The streets here are studded with hip but casual cafés and bars frequented by an ever-burgeoning crowd. To reach Kollwitz-platz and Husemannstr., take U-Bahn #2 to "Senefelderplatz."

KOLLWITZPLATZ. The heart of Prenzlauer Berg's café scene, Kollwitzplatz centers around a statue of the square's namesake, visual artist **Käthe Kollwitz** (see **Museums,** p. 127). The monument has been painted a number of times in past years in acts of affectionate rather than angry vandalism, most notably with big pink polka-dots.

HUSEMANNSTRASSE. Just off Kollwitzplatz, Husemannstr. is particularly representative of the Prenzlauer Berg ambience. Lined with hip bars and cafés, it is also home to **Museum Berliner Arbeiterleben um 1900,** a meticulously accurate reproduction of a working-class family's apartment at the turn of the century. Though closed at press time, the museum was scheduled to reopen in early 2000. *(Husemannstr. 12. Tel 442 25 14. Open M-Th 10am-3pm. Free.)*

JÜDISCHER FRIEDHOF. Berlin's Jews found slightly remote Prenzlauer Berg ideal, slowly gravitating there during the 19th and early 20th centuries. The Jewish cemetery on Schönhauser Allee contains the graves of composer Giacomo Meyerbeer and painter Max Liebermann. *(Open M-Th 8am-4pm, F 8am-1pm. Men must cover their heads before entering the cemetery.)* Nearby stands the **Synagoge Rykestraße.** One of Berlin's loveliest synagogues, it was spared on *Kristallnacht* due to its inconspicuous location in a courtyard. *(Rykestr. 53.)*

CARL-ZEISS-GROSSPLANETARIUM. One of the last great feats of East Berlin's city planners, the planetarium opened in 1987 as the most modern facility of its kind in the GDR, and it remains one of the best in Germany. Operated by the vintage 1980s *Cosmorama* projector, the planetarium is an example of East German know-how at its best. *(Prenzlauer Allee 80. Tel. 42 18 45 12. S-Bahn #4, 8, or 85 to "Prenzlauer Allee." Shows in English W and Su at 3:30pm. DM8, students DM6.)*

OUTER DISTRICTS

The city districts listed below are accessible in about 20 minutes from the center of Berlin by public transportation and make good afternoon or daytrips. For excursions to Potsdam, see **Brandenburg** (p. 140).

WANNSEE

Most Berliners think of the town of Wannsee, on the lake of the same name, as the beach. Wannsee has long stretches of sand along the Havelufer-Promenade, and the roads behind the beaches are crowded with vacation villas. To reach the lake, take S-Bahn #1 or 7 to "Wannsee" or "Nikolassee" and walk 15 minutes to the beach. On summer weekends, a special bus shuttles bathers from the train station.

HAUS DER WANNSEE-KONFERENZ. The reputation of the charming village of Wannsee is indelibly tarnished by the memory of the notorious **Wannsee Conference** of January 20, 1942. Leading officials of the SS completed the details for the implementation of the "Final Solution" in the **Wannsee Villa,** formerly a Gestapo intelligence center. In January 1992, the 50th anniversary of the Nazi death-pact, the villa reopened as an excellent museum with permanent Holocaust exhibits and a documentary film series. The villa is discomfitingly lovely, and its grounds offer a dazzling view of the Wannsee. *(Am Großen Wannsee 56. Tel. 805 00 10. Take bus #114 from the S-Bahn station to "Haus der Wannsee-Konferenz." Open M-F 10am-6pm. Free.)*

KLEISTGRAB. Along the shores of the Kleiner Wannsee, the brilliant young author **Heinrich von Kleist** and his terminally ill companion committed suicide in 1811. A small grave marks the site of their demise. *(Bismarckstr. 3, below the Wannseebrücke.)*

PFAUENINSEL. Friedrich Wilhelm II built a *trompe l'oeil* "ruined" castle as a private pleasure house on the banks of Peacock Island; here, he and his mistress could romp undisturbed for hours. A flock of the island's namesake fowl roams about the gardens surrounding the castle. *(Take bus #316 or A16 from the S-Bahn station to "Pfaueninsel" and hop on the ferry. Ferry operates May-Aug. 8am-8pm, April and Sept. 9am-6pm, March and Oct. 9am-5pm, Nov.-Feb. 10am-4pm. DM2, students and seniors DM1.)*

GLIENICKER BRÜCKE. At the southwestern corner of the district, the bridge crosses the Havel into Potsdam and what was once the GDR. Closed to traffic in Cold War days, it is famed as the spot where East and West once exchanged captured spies. The most famous such incident traded American U-2 pilot Gary Powers for Soviet spy Ivanovich Abel. To continue on the other side of the bridge, see p. 145. *(Bus #116 from the S-Bahn station (direction: "Glienicker Brücke (Potsdam)" to the end.)*

WANNSEE CRUISES. Two ferry companies run boats from the Wannsee waterfront just behind the park to the right of the S-Bahn station. **Stern und Kreis** (tel. 803 87 50) and **Reederverband** (tel. 434 89 80) both set sail once or twice an hour, though the ferries' leisurely clip means that they're meant more as pleasure cruises than as an efficient means of transport. *(Most cruises run DM10-12.)*

DAHLEM AND STEGLITZ

A southern suburb with small streets and shop windows, Dahlem is a quiet residential neighborhood home to affluent professionals as well as the sprawling **Freie Universität**, one of Berlin's three universities. The district also houses one of Berlin's most prestigious museum complexes (see p. 126). Next door to Dahlem, **Steglitz** is an unremarkable suburb noted for its busy shopping district (U-Bahn #9 to "Schloßstr.") as well as its exquisite botanical garden (see below).

BOTANISCHER GARTEN. One of the best botanical gardens in the world, the Botanischer Garten features traditional hot houses, but they're not afraid to experiment here: entire forests and fields of wildflowers unfold before the visitor's eyes. The resulting scents are *dee*-vine. *(Königin-Luise-Str. 6. Tel. 83 00 61 27. S-Bahn #1 to "Botanischer Garten." Follow the signs from the S-Bahn station. Open May-July 9am-9pm, April and Aug. 9am-8pm, March and Oct. 9am-7pm, Nov.-Jan. 9am-4pm, Feb. 9am-5pm. Last admittance 30min. before closing. DM6, students DM3; Abendkarte, valid 2hr. before closing, DM3, students DM1.)*

TREPTOW

The powerful **Sowjetisches Ehrenmal** (Soviet War Memorial) is a mammoth promenade built with marble taken from Hitler's Chancellery. Take S-Bahn #4, 6, 8, 85, or 9 to "Treptower Park." The Soviets dedicated the site in 1948, honoring the millions of Red Army soldiers who fell in what Russians know as the "Great Patriotic War." Massive granite slabs along the walk are festooned with quotations from Stalin, leading up to colossal bronze figures in the socialist realist style, symbolically crushing Nazism underfoot. It's quite moving, despite the pomp. Buried beneath the trees surrounding the monument are the bodies of 5,000 unknown Soviet soldiers who were killed during the Battle of Berlin in 1945. The memorial sits in the middle of **Treptower Park,** a spacious forest ideal for morbid picnics. Also in the park is the **Figurentheater,** Puschkinallee 15a, full of figures with wooden expressions on their faces who perform *Märchen* (fairy tales). The neighborhood adjoining the park is known for its pleasant waterside cafés.

SPANDAU

Spandau is one of the oldest parts of Berlin and in many respects remains a separate city. Take U-Bahn #7 to "Altstadt Spandau." Many of the old buildings have been restored, though unfortunately they are now surrounded on all sides by car dealerships.

ZITADELLE. Encircled by waters once considered impregnable, the star-shaped enclosure was the anchor of Spandau in medieval days. During WWII, the Nazis used the fort as a chemical weapons lab, and in 1945 the Allies employed the *Zita-*

delle as a prison to hold war criminals before the Nürnberg trials. Despite its grim name and past, the citadel is now a sort of wistful ghost town filled with old field-cannons, statues, a **medieval history museum,** and fields of grass on its ramparts. The thickly fortified **Juliusturm,** dating to circa 1200, is Spandau's unofficial symbol. *(Am Juliusturm. Tel. 339 12 12. Take U-Bahn #7 to "Zitadelle." Open Tu-F 9am-5pm, Sa-Su 10am-5pm. DM4, students DM2.)*

OTHER SIGHTS. Spandauers defiantly constructed a somewhat unremarkable **Rathaus** from 1911 to 1913 (at a cost of DM3.5 million) in a futile effort to stave off absorption into Berlin. Take U-Bahn #7 to "Rathaus Spandau." **Spandau Prison** was demolished after its last inmate, Hitler's deputy Rudolf Hess, committed suicide in 1987 at age 93. Hess, a devoted party member from the beginning (he participated in the Beer Hall Putsch and took dictation for Hitler's *Mein Kampf*) was an unrepentant Nazi until his death. Lately this unsavory character has made a controversial comeback as a latter-day idol for neo-fascist groups; to Berlin's credit, the local anti-Hess response has been even stronger.

ORANIENBURG AND SACHSENHAUSEN

The small town of Oranienburg, just north of Berlin, was home to **KZ Sachsenhausen,** a Nazi concentration camp in which more than 100,000 Jews, communists, intellectuals, gypsies, and homosexuals were killed between 1936 and 1945. The **Gedenkstätte Sachsenhausen,** Str. der Nationen 22 (tel. (03301) 80 37 15), was opened by the GDR in 1961. Parts of the camp have been preserved in their original forms, including the cell block where particularly "dangerous" prisoners were kept in solitary confinement and tortured daily, and a pathology department where Nazis performed medical experiments on inmates both dead and alive. Only the foundations of Station Z (where prisoners were methodically exterminated) remain, but the windswept grounds convey the horrors that were committed here. A GDR slant is still apparent; the main museum building features Socialist Realist stained-glass windows memorializing "German Anti-Fascist Martyrs." The museums, however, have been totally overhauled recently. The main one hosts special shows of Holocaust-related art, as well as a fascinating permanent exhibit (in English and German) on the history of anti-Semitic practices throughout the world. To get to Sachsenhausen, take S-Bahn #1 (direction: "Oranienburg") to the end (40min.). The camp is a 20-min. walk from the station; follow the signs. (Open April-Sept. Tu-Su 8:30am-6pm; Oct.-March Tu-Su 8:30am-4:30pm. Last entry 30min. before closing. Free.)

🏛 MUSEUMS

Berlin is one of the world's great museum cities, with collections of art and artifacts encompassing all subjects and eras. The **Staatliche Museen Preußischer Kulturbesitz (SMPK)** runs the four major complexes—Charlottenburg, Dahlem, Museuminsel, and the Kulturforum—that form the hub of the city's museum culture. Since these museums are government-run, their prices are standardized; a single admission costs DM4, students DM2. A *Tageskarte* (DM8, students DM4) is valid for all SMPK museums on the day of purchase; the *Wochenkarte* (DM25, students DM12.50) is valid for the whole week. The first Sunday of every month offers free admission. Smaller museums deal with every subject imaginable, from sugar to tarts. **Artery Berlin** is a comprehensive art guide, including museum exhibitions and galleries, as well as a map, available at many museums for DM3.50. **Berlin Programm** also lists museums and some galleries (DM2.80).

MUSEUMINSEL (MUSEUM ISLAND)

Museuminsel holds the treasure hoard of the former GDR in four separate museums. Designed to look like ancient Athens, the island's faux temples are separated from the rest of Mitte by the murky Spree. Many of the museums are undergoing extensive renovation, and both the **Alte Nationalgalerie** and **Bodemuseum** remain closed until 2001 and 2004, respectively. Take S-Bahn #3, 5, 7, 75 or 9 to "Hacke-scher Markt" or bus #100 to "Lustgarten." Unless otherwise noted, all Museuminsel museums are open Tuesday through Sunday 9am to 6pm. All museums offer free **audio tours** in English.

PERGAMONMUSEUM. One of the world's great ancient history museums from the days of the empire when Western archaeology was king and Heinrich Schlie-mann traversed the world, pillaging the debris of ancient civilizations and reas-sembling it at home. The scale of its exhibits is mind-boggling: giant rooms can barely contain the entire Babylonian Ishtar Gate (575 BC), the Roman Market Gate of Miletus, and the majestic Pergamon Altar of Zeus (180 BC). The museum also houses extensive collections of Greek, Assyrian, Islamic, and Far Eastern art. *(Kupfergraben. Tel. 203 55 00. Tours of Pergamon altar daily at 11am and 3pm. Tageskarte required for entry. Last entry 30min. before closing.)*

ALTE NATIONALGALERIE. Closed for renovations until 2001, the museum's col-lection of 19th-century German as well as French Impressionist painters is cur-rently housed in the Altes Museum (see below).

ALTES MUSEUM. At the far end of the Lustgarten, the Altes Museum's galleries are surprisingly untouristed. The lower level contains a permanent collection of ancient Greco-Roman decorative art, including a particularly fine slew of Greek vases. Upstairs, the greatest hits of the Alte Nationalgalerie languish in exile while the Galerie is being refurbished. *(Lustgarten. Tageskarte valid as long as the Alte National-galerie collection remains.)*

AROUND MITTE

DEUTSCHE GUGGENHEIM BERLIN. Located in a newly renovated building across the street from the Deutsche Staatsbibliothek (see p. 110). A joint venture between the Deutsche Bank and the Guggenheim Foundation in New York, the museum features changing exhibits of contemporary avant-garde art. *(Unter den Lin-den 13-15. Tel 20 20 93 13. Open daily 11am-8pm. DM8, students DM5; M free.)*

DEUTSCHES HISTORISCHES MUSEUM. Permanent exhibits trace German his-tory from the Neanderthal period to the Nazis, while rotating exhibitions examine the last 50 years. Large quantities of GDR art in the "painting-of-a-happy-faced-worker" vein. Until renovations of the Zeughaus are completed in 2002, the museum is housed in the Kronprinzenpalais across the street. *(Unter den Linden 2, in the Zeughaus. Tel. 20 30 40. S-Bahn #3, 5, 7, 75, or 9 to "Hackescher Markt." Open Th-Tu 10am-6pm. Free.)*

SCHINKELMUSEUM. Nineteenth-century French and German sculpture and an exhibit on the life and work of the famous Prussian architect Karl Friedrich Schinkel. The church housing the museum was built in 1824-30 based on Schinkel's designs; destroyed in WWII, it was restored in 1987. *(Werderscher Markt, on the corner of Oberwallstr. Tel. 20 90 55 55, south of Unter den Linden. U-Bahn #2 to "Hausvogtei-platz." Open Tu-Su 10am-6pm. SMPK prices.)*

MÄRKISCHES MUSEUM. A beautiful building on the banks of the Spree housing a collection of primeval and early Berlin history and lots of applied art. Demon-stration of automatophone W and Su at 3pm. *(Am Köllnischen Park 5, at the corner of Märkisches Ufer. Tel. 30 86 60. U-Bahn #2 to "Märkisches Museum." Open Tu-Su 10am-6pm. DM5, students DM2.50; W free.)*

HANFMUSEUM. The first museum in Germany dedicated to the study of mari-juana, the museum hosts exhibits on the cultivation and cultural significance of everyone's favorite topiary. *(Mühlendamm 5. Tel 24 72 02 33. U-Bahn #2 to "Klosterstr." Open Tu-F 10am-8pm, Sa-Su noon-8pm. DM5.)*

■INFOBOX. Sponsored by Potsdamer Platz investors, the Infobox brings everything you ever wanted to know about Europe's largest construction site just a click of the mouse away. *(Leipziger Platz 21. Tel. 226 62 40. S-Bahn #1, 2, or 25 or U-Bahn #2 to "Potsdamer Platz." Open daily 9am-7pm. Tours every hour on the hour 10am-4pm. Free.)*

KULTURFORUM

The **Tiergarten-Kulturforum**, on Matthäikirchplatz (tel. 20 90 55 55 for all museums), is a complex of museums at the eastern end of the Tiergarten, near the *Staatsbibliothek* (see **Sights**, p. 110) and Potsdamer Platz. Right now its location is less than ideal; the area near Potsdamer Platz is Europe's biggest construction site, and finding your way around is quite a task. Hop on S-Bahn #1, 2, or 25 or U-Bahn #2 to "Potsdamer Platz" and walk down Potsdamer Str.; the museums will be on your right. All museums are open Tu-Su 10am-6pm and have SMPK prices.

■GEMÄLDEGALERIE. One of Germany's most famous museums, and rightly so. It houses a stunning and enormous collection by Italian, German, Dutch, and Flemish masters, including works by Rembrandt, Bruegel, Vermeer, Raphael, Titian, Botticelli, and Dürer.

KUNSTBIBLIOTHEK/KUPFERSTICHKABINETT. A stellar collection of lithographs and drawings by Renaissance masters, including Goya, many Dürers, and Botticelli's fantastic illustrations for the *Divine Comedy*. Tours Su at 3pm.

KUNSTGEWERBEMUSEUM. A plethora of plates, jugs, and china more or less trace a millennium's advances in dining technology. Hey, if you put it behind glass and shine spotlights on it, it's art.

AROUND THE TIERGARTEN

NEUE NATIONALGALERIE. This sleek building, designed by Mies van der Rohe, now gives quantity its own quality in a collection devoted to large art displays. Billboard-sized paintings and sculptures heavy enough to make Atlas cry fill the first two floors. The permanent collection includes works by Kokoschka, Barlach, Kirchner, and Beckmann, but these are often put away to make room for special exhibits that wouldn't fit through the door in any other museum. An SMPK *Tageskarte* will get you into the permanent exhibit, but two-thirds of the museum is occupied by special exhibitions *(Potsdamer Str. 50. Tel. 266 26 62 or 266 26 56. Just past the Kulturforum. DM12, students DM6. Open Tu-F 10am-6pm and Sa-Su 11am-6pm.)*

MUSIKINSTRUMENTEN-MUSEUM. Fittingly next door to the Philharmonic's bumpy yellow home, this is a fascinating museum for anyone even remotely interested in classical music. Musical instruments from every period, 16th-century virginals to pianolas. Includes acoustic exhibitions of period instruments. *(Tiergartenstr. 1. Tel. 25 48 10. S-Bahn #1, 2, or 25 or U-Bahn #2 to "Potsdamer Platz." Open Tu-F 9am-5pm, Sa-Su 10am-5pm. DM4, students DM2. Tours Sa at 11am. DM3.)*

RAABGALERIE. A well-kept gallery with thoughtful exhibitions of famous and not-so-famous 20th-century artists. *(Potsdamer Str. 58. Tel. 261 92 17. U-Bahn #2 to "Mendelssohn-Bartholdy-Park." Open M-F 10am-7pm, Sa 10am-4pm.)*

BAUHAUS-ARCHIV MUSEUM FÜR GESTALTUNG. A building designed by Bauhaus founder Walter Gropius that houses an exhibit devoted to the school's development along with a collection of paintings featuring Kandinsky and Klee. *(Klingelhöferstr. 14. Tel. 254 00 20. Bus #100 or 187 to "Stülerstr." Open M and W-Su 10am-5pm. DM5, students DM2.50; M free.)*

HAMBURGER BAHNHOF/MUSEUM FÜR GEGENWART. Berlin's foremost collection of contemporary art features works by Beuys, Kiefer, Twombley, and Warhol, all housed in a converted 19th-century train station. *(Invalidenstr. 50-51. Tel. 397 83 11. S-Bahn #3, 5, 7, 75, or 9 to "Lehrter Stadtbahnhof" or U-Bahn #6 to "Zinnowitzer Str." Open Tu-F 10am-6pm, Sa-Su 11am-6pm. DM8, students DM4; first Su of the month free. Tours Sa-Su at 3pm.)*

KREUZBERG

MARTIN-GROPIUS-BAU. Walter Gropius' uncle Martin designed this neo-Renaissance wedding cake as a museum for and tribute to the industrial arts. The building alone is worth the price of admission, and the temporary exhibits of modern art and history are top-notch. The year 2000 promises a slew of millennium-related exhibitions. *(Niederkirchnerstr. 7. Tel. 25 48 60. S-Bahn #1, 2, or 25 to "Anhalter Bahnhof" or U-Bahn #2 to "Mendelssohn-Bartholdy-Park." Open Tu-Su 10am-8pm. Admission varies.)*

TOPOGRAPHIE DES TERRORS. Built on top of the ruins of a Gestapo kitchen, the area used to be the site of the notorious Gestapo headquarters at Prinz-Albrecht-Str. (now Niederkirchnerstr.). The very comprehensive exhibit (in German) details the Nazi party's rise to power and the atrocities that occurred during the war. English guides are available, but you don't need to understand the captions to be moved by the photographs. *(Behind the Martin-Gropius-Bau, at the corner of Niederkirchnerstr. and Wilhelmstr. Tel. 25 48 67 03. S-Bahn #1, 2, or 25 to "Anhalter Bahnhof" or U-Bahn #6 to "Kochstr." Open Tu-Su 10am-6pm. Free.)* The adjacent **Prinz-Albrecht-Gelände,** a deserted wasteland near the site of the Wall, contains the ruins of Gestapo buildings. *(Open 10am-dusk. Free.)*

DEUTSCHES TECHNIKMUSEUM. Souvenirs from Autobahn speed-devils, medieval printing presses, WWI fighting planes, and an historic brewery filled with historic empties. Combined admission with a yard of antique locomotives down the street. *(Trebbiner Str. 9. Tel. 25 48 40. U-Bahn #1, 15, or 2 to "Gleisdreieck" or U-Bahn #1, 15, or 7 to "Möckernbrücke." Open Tu-F 9am-6pm, Sa-Su 11am-6pm. DM4, students DM2; first Su of the month free.)*

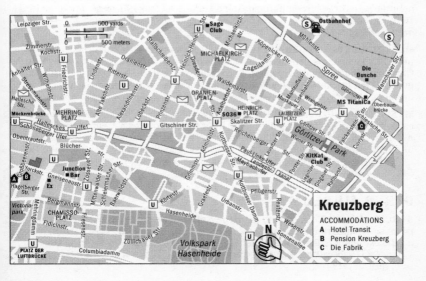

Kreuzberg

ACCOMMODATIONS
A Hotel Transit
B Pension Kreuzberg
C Die Fabrik

SCHLOSS CHARLOTTENBURG

The wide-flung wings and surrounding neighborhood of **Schloß Charlottenburg** (tel. 32 09 11) are home to a number of excellent museums. Take bus #145 from Bahnhof Zoo to "Luisenpl./Schloß Charlottenburg" or U-Bahn #7 to "Richard-Wagner-Platz" and walk about 15 minutes down Otto-Suhr-Allee. For more on the Schloß and its grounds, see **Sights** (p. 116).

■**ÄGYPTISCHES MUSEUM.** This stern Neoclassical building contains a famous collection of ancient Egyptian art, dramatically lit for the full Indiana Jones effect. The most popular item on display is the stunning 3,300-year-old bust of **Queen Nefertiti** (1350 BC), thought by many to be the most beautiful representation of a woman in the world. (*Schloßstr. 70. Tel. 20 90 55 55. Across Spandauer Damm from the palace. Open Tu-Su 10am-6pm. SMPK prices.*)

■**SAMMLUNG BERGGRUEN.** Five floors off a central spiralling staircase offer a comprehensive overview of Picasso's life's work. The bottom floor also exhibits works that influenced Picasso, including late French impressionist paintings and African masks. (*Schloßstr. 1. Tel. 326 95 80. In an identical building across the street from the Egyptian museum. Open Tu-F 10am-6pm, Sa-Su 11am-6pm. SMPK prices.*)

GALERIE DER ROMANTIK. The museum holds the Prussian crown's dynamic collection of 19th-century art. The unquestioned show-stealers are the beautiful, bleak landscapes by early 19th-century Prussian artist Caspar David Friedrich, with infinite, looming skies and seas and tiny human figures placed precariously in their midst. (*Tel. 20 90 55 55. In the palace's Neuer Flügel. Open Tu-F 10am-6pm, Sa-Su 11am-8pm. SMPK prices.*)

BRÖHANMUSEUM. Features two floors of *Jugendstil* and Art Deco furniture, housewares, and paintings in the sleekest of surroundings. Pieces date from 1889 to 1939. (*Schloßstr. 1a. Tel. 321 40 29. Next door to the Berggruen. Open Tu-Su 10am-6pm. DM8, students DM4.*)

DAHLEM

The **Staatliche Museen Preußischer Kulturbesitz Dahlem** complex looms near the Freie Universität. Take U-Bahn #1 to "Dahlem-Dorf" and follow the *Museen* signs. Several globe-spanning museums cram into one enormous building, plus another across the street; unfortunately, some are closed for renovations until 2001. Pick up a map at the entrance; the museums are laid out very strangely. *All have SMPK prices.*

MUSEUM EUROPÄISCHER KULTUREN. A hop away from the main Dahlem complex, this museum is dedicated to artifacts of lower- and middle-class life from Germany and the rest of Europe from the past 400 years. The exhibit on post-war pop culture is charming—never thought you'd see *Garbage Pail Kids* in a museum, eh? (*Im Winkel 6-8. Tel. 20 90 55 55. Open Tu-F 10am-6pm, Sa-Su 11am-6pm.*)

MUSEUM FÜR VÖLKERKUNDE. Fascinating collections of tools, artifacts, musical instruments, weapons, and clothing from Africa, Polynesia, Central and South America, and Southeast Asia. The Polynesian exhibit climaxes with a giant display of ornately decorated boats, many of which you can climb into. Play the *baláfon* (xylophone) in the African section. (*Lansstr. 8. Tel. 20 90 55 55. Open Tu-F 10am-6pm, Sa-Su 11am-6pm. Free admission first Su of the month.*)

OTHER MUSEUMS

BRÜCKE MUSEUM. Along with the Neue Nationalgalerie, this is *the* Expressionist museum in Berlin, with wildly colorful works by adherents of the Expressionist *Brücke* school. (*Bussardsteig 9. Tel. 831 20 29. Take U-Bahn #1 or 7 to "Fehrbelliner Pl." then bus #115 (direction: "Neuruppiner Str.") to "Pücklerstr." Open M and W-Su 11am-5pm. DM6, students DM3.*)

KÄTHE-KOLLWITZ-MUSEUM. A marvelous collection of works by one of Germany's most prominent modern artists, much of it focusing on the themes of war and poverty. *(Fasanenstr. 24. Tel. 882 52 10. U-Bahn #15 to "Uhlandstr." Open M and W-Su 11am-6pm. DM8, students DM4.)*

ZUCKERMUSEUM. A cultural history of sugar explores its uses, such as sculpture, records, and alcohol. Yum. *(Amrumer Str. 32. Tel. 31 42 75 74. U-Bahn #9 to "Amrumer Str." Open M-W 9am-5pm, Th 3-8pm, Su 11am-6pm. DM4.50, students DM2, or a solemn oath never to buy into the myth of cavities.)*

⧉ ENTERTAINMENT

Berlin has one of the most vibrant cultural scenes in the world: exhibitions, concerts, plays, and dance performances abound. Despite recent cutbacks, the city still has a generously subsidized art scene, and tickets are usually reasonable, especially with student discounts. Numerous festivals celebrating everything from Chinese film to West African music spice up the regular offerings.

Reservations can be made by calling the box office directly. Always ask about student discounts; most theaters and concert halls offer up to 50% off, but only if you buy at the *Abendkasse* (evening box office), which generally opens one hour before performance. Numerous other ticket outlets charge commissions and do not offer student discounts. There are also ticket counters in all **Karstadt** department stores (general tel. 80 60 29 29; fax 80 60 29 22), and in the **KaDeWe** department store, Tauentzienstr. 21 (tel. 217 77 54), on Wittenbergplatz. All offices charge a 15-18% commission. Remember that while most theaters do accept credit cards, most other ticket outlets don't. Most major theaters and operas close from mid-July to late August.

Hekticket (tel. 230 99 30; fax 23 09 82 30), on Hardenbergstr. next to the gigantic Zoo-Palast cineplex. Sells last-minute tickets for half-price. Tickets available for shows advertised in the window. Open M-F 9am-8pm, Sa 10am-8pm, Su 4-8pm.

PUTTIN' ON THE OLD BIRTHDAY SUIT
As the up-and-coming capital of Germany, Berlin refuses to be left by the wayside for the turn of the century. As if it wasn't already exhibitionistic enough, the city is calling its antics **Berlin: Open City.** From the summer of 1999 until January 1, 2000, it will attempt to reveal itself in a typically brilliant and unsubtle fashion. For starters, 10 sightseeing routes have been staked out aimed at putting the constantly changing construction site that is Berlin into an historical context that can be understood by the average walking tour fiend. Behind the rest of the flap of the (metaphoric) trench coat are a series of exhibitions. **Gesammelte Räume—Gesammelte Träume** (Collected Rooms—Collected Dreams), at the Martin-Gropius-Bau, from November 19, 1999 to February 6, 2000, will chronicle the last 40 years of German art with more than 700 works. At the Neue Nationalgalerie, the excessively self-explanatory **The 20th Century—A Century of Art in Germany** will bare the Teutonic soul in paintings, sculptures, video, and plenty of other media. Then there's the **50th Berliner Festwochen,** dedicated to key composers of the 20th century (Sept. 1-Oct. 4, 2000). For information, call 25 48 91 00. For tickets, phone 25 00 25. The Kulturforum, with its mixture of visual and audio art, joins the chorus Dec. 30, 1999 to Jan. 2, 2000 with its very own **millennial art festival.** The other flap of the trench coat will come flying open at Brandenburger Tor, when Berlin unveils its ▨**Welcome 2000 New Year's Eve Party,** at which revelers will be taken "around the world in 24 hours" with TV screens broadcasting the antics of every other metropolis on the planet. The turnout on Friedrichstraße will be a bit more nostalgic, but no less raucous, with its **Golden Twenties** celebration.

Berliner Festspiele, Budapester Str. 48-50 (tel. 25 48 92 50; www.berliner festspiele.de). Tickets for a variety of shows, concerts, and events. Open M-F 10am-6pm, Su 10am-2pm.

Berlin Ticket, Potsdamer Str. 96 (tel. 23 08 82 30; fax 23 08 82 99). Reservations only by phone.

Theater & Konzertkasse City Center, Kurfürstendamm 16, at the corner of Joachimstaler Str. (tel. 882 65 63; fax 882 65 67).

Theaterkasse Centrum, Meineckestr. 25 (tel. 882 76 11; fax 881 33 32). Open M-F 10am-6:30pm, Sa 10am-2pm.

CONCERTS, OPERA, AND DANCE

Berlin reaches its musical zenith during the fabulous **Berliner Festwochen,** lasting almost the entire month of September and drawing the world's best orchestras and soloists. The **Berliner Jazztage** in November also brings in the crowds. For more information and tickets (which sell out months in advance), call or write to Berliner Festspiele (see above). In mid-July, the **Bachtage** offer an intense week of classical music, while every Saturday night in August, the **Sommer Festspiele** turns the Ku'damm into a multi-faceted concert hall with punk, steel-drum, and folk groups competing for attention.

Look for concert listings in the monthly pamphlets *Konzerte und Theater in Berlin und Brandenburg* (free) and *Berlin Programm* (DM2.80), as well as in the biweekly *Zitty* and *Tip*. The programs for many theaters and opera houses are also listed on huge posters in U-Bahn stations. Tickets for the *Philharmonie* and the *Oper* are often impossible to acquire through conventional channels without writing months in advance. Try standing out in front before performances with a small sign saying *Suche Karte* (I seek a ticket)—invariably a few people will try to unload tickets at the last moment. Remember that concert halls and operas close for a few weeks during the summer months.

Berliner Philharmonisches Orchester, Matthäikirchstr. 1 (tel. 25 48 81 32; fax 25 48 81 35; email kartenbuero@philharmonic.sireco.de). Take S-Bahn #1, 2 or 25 or U-Bahn #2 to "Potsdamer Platz" and walk up Potsdamer Str. The big yellow asymmetrical building, designed by Scharoun in 1963, is as acoustically perfect within as it is unconventional without. The *Berliner Philharmoniker,* led for decades by the late Herbert von Karajan and currently under the baton of Claudio Abbado, is one of the world's finest orchestras. It is well-nigh impossible to get a seat; check an hour before concert time or write at least 8 weeks in advance. The *Philharmonie* is closed from the end of June until the start of September. Tickets start at DM14 for standing room, DM26 for seats. Box office open M-F 3:30-6pm, Sa-Su 11am-2pm.

Konzerthaus (Schauspielhaus Gendarmenmarkt), Gendarmenmarkt 2 (tel. 203 09 21 01). U-Bahn #2 or 6 to "Stadtmitte." The opulent home of Berlin's symphony orchestra. Last-minute tickets are somewhat easier to come by. Box office open M-Sa noon-6pm, Su noon-4pm. The orchestra goes on vacation from mid-July to mid-Aug., but the *Deutsches Kammerorchester* continues to perform chamber music in the *Kleiner Saal.* Order tickets by writing to Deutsches Kammerorchester, Suarezstr. 15, 14057 Berlin; or call 325 42 29; or fax 32 60 86 10.

Komische Oper, Unter den Linden 14 (tel. 20 26 03 60; fax 20 26 02 60; www.komischeoper.line.de). U-Bahn #6 to "Französische Str," or S-Bahn #1, 2, 25 to "Unter den Linden." Its reputation was built by the famous post-war director Felsenstein, but in recent years zany artistic director Harry Kupfer has revitalized the opera with clever stagings of the classics. Program ranges from Mozart to Gilbert and Sullivan. Tickets DM15-94. 50% student discounts almost always available 2hr. before performance. Box office open M-Sa 11am-7pm, Su 1pm until 1½hr. before performance.

Tanzfabrik, Möckernstr. 68 (tel. 786 58 61). U-Bahn #7 to "Yorckstr." Turn left on Yorckstr., then right onto Möckernstr. Modern dance performances and a center for dance workshops. Box office open M-Th 10am-noon and 5-8pm, F 10am-noon. Tickets DM15. Occasional weekend performances start at 8 or 8:30pm.

Deutsche Oper Berlin, Bismarckstr. 35 (tel. 341 02 49 for info, 343 84 01 for tickets). U-Bahn #2 to "Deutsche Oper." Berlin's best and youngest opera, featuring newly commissioned works as well as all the German and Italian classics. Student discounts available 1 week or less before performance. Tickets DM15-140. Box office open M-Sa 11am until 1hr. before performance, Su 10am-2pm. Evening tickets available 1hr. before performance. For tickets, write to Deutsche Oper Berlin, Richard-Wagner-Str. 10, 10585 Berlin; or fax 343 84 55. For program information, write to Deutsche Oper Berlin, Bismarckstr. 35, 10627 Berlin. Closed July-Aug.

Deutsche Staatsoper, Unter den Linden 7 (tel. 20 35 45 55; fax 20 35 44 83; www.staatsoper-berlin.org). U-Bahn #6 to "Französische Str." Eastern Berlin's leading opera company, with sets and costumes on a big, bold scale, led by Daniel Barenboim (also the conductor of the Chicago Symphony Orchestra). Ballet and classical music, too, although the orchestra fluctuates between good and mediocre. Tours daily at 11am. Tickets DM18-35. 50% student discount. Box office open M-F 10am-6pm, Sa-Su 2pm-6pm, and 1hr. before performance. Closed mid-July to mid-Aug.

THEATER

Theater listings are available in the monthly pamphlets *Kultur!news* and *Berlin Programm*, as well as in *Zitty* and *Tip*. They are also posted in most U-Bahn stations. In addition to the best German-language theater in the world, Berlin also has a lively English-language theater scene. Look for listings in *Zitty* or *Tip* that say *in englischer Sprache* (in English) next to them. There are a number of privately run companies called "off-theaters" that feature occasional English-language plays. As with concert halls, look out for summer closings (*Theaterferien* or *Sommerpause*); see the introduction to **Entertainment,** p. 127, for box office information. There is an international **theater festival** in May.

Deutsches Theater, Schumannstr. 13a (tel. 28 44 12 25). U-Bahn #6 or S-Bahn #1, 2, 25, 3, 5, 7, 75, or 9 to "Friedrichstr." or bus #147 to "Albrechtplatz." Walk north on Friedrichstr., turn left on Reinhardtstr., and then right on Albrechtstr., which curves into Schumannstr. The word has spread to Western Berlin: this is the best theater in the country. Max Reinhardt made it great 100 years ago, and it now has innovative productions of the classics and newer works. The repertoire runs from Büchner to Mamet to Ibsen. Box office open M-Sa 11am-6:30pm, Su 3-6:30pm. Tickets DM15-25. The **Kammerspiel des Deutschen Theaters** (tel. 28 44 12 26) has smaller, controversial productions. Tickets DM15-40, but 50% student discounts often available. Box office open M-Sa noon-6pm, Su 3-6pm.

Hebbel-Theater, Stresemannstr. 29 (tel. 25 90 04 27 or 25 90 04 36; email tickets@hebbel-theater.de). U-Bahn #1, 15, or 6 to "Hallesches Tor." The most avant of the avant-garde theaters in Berlin, drawing cutting-edge talent from all over the world. Order tickets by phone M-Su 4-7pm or show up 1hr. before performance.

Berliner Ensemble, Bertolt-Brecht-Pl. 1 (tel. 282 31 60 or 28 40 81 55). U-Bahn #6 or S-Bahn #1, 2, 25, 3, 5, 7, 75, or 9 to "Friedrichstr." The famous theater established by Brecht is undergoing a renaissance. Hip repertoire, including Heiner Müller and some young American playwrights, as well as Brecht's own plays. Also some premieres. Tickets DM12-40, 50% student discount available. 1hr. before performance. Box office open M-Sa 11am-6pm, Su 3-6pm.

Maxim-Gorki-Theater, Am Festungsgraben 1 (tel. 20 22 10). U-Bahn #6 or S-Bahn #1, 2, 25, 3, 5, 7, 75, or 9 to "Friedrichstr.", or bus #100, 157, or 348 to "Deutsche Staatsoper." Excellent contemporary theater with wonderfully varied repertoire—everything from Schiller to Albee. Tickets DM5-25. Box office open M-Sa 1-6:30pm, Su 3-6:30pm., and 1hr. before performance.

BERLIN

Die Distel, Friedrichstr. 101 (tel. 204 47 04; fax 208 15 55). U-Bahn #6 or S-Bahn #1, 2, 25, 3, 5, 7, 75, or 9 to "Friedrichstr." During GDR days, this was a renowned cabaret for political satire—but reunification has taken the bite out of some of the jokes. Box office open M-F noon-6pm and 2hr. before performance.

Vagantenbühne, Kantstr. 12a (tel. 312 45 29). U-Bahn #2 or 9 or S-Bahn #3, 5, 7, 75, or 9 to "Zoologischer Garten." This off-beat hole-in-the-wall near the Ku'damm—the oldest private theater in Berlin—presents a healthy balance of contemporary German plays as well as such existentialist favorites as Sartre's *No Exit*. Tickets DM16-32, students DM12. Box office open M 10am-4pm, Tu-F 10am-7pm, Sa 2-7pm.

Friends of Italian Opera, Fidicinstr. 40 (tel. 691 12 11). U-Bahn #6 to "Platz der Luftbrücke." The name is a joking reference to the mafia in *Some Like It Hot,* and belies its role as Berlin's leading English-language theater. The stage is home to the renowned Berliner Grundtheater company as well as a grab-bag of English-language performances with a penchant for the grotesque, ranging from Tennessee Williams to Katherine Anne Porter. Tickets DM15-20. Box office opens at 6:30pm. Most shows at 8pm.

FILM

Berlin is a movie-loving town; it hosts the international **Berlinale** film festival (Feb. 9-20, 2000), and on any night in Berlin you can choose from 100 different films, many in the original languages. *O.F.* next to a movie listing means original version (i.e., not dubbed); *O.m.U.* means original version with German subtitles. Check *Tip, Zitty,* or the ubiquitous *Kinoprogramm* posters plastered throughout the city. Numerous cineplexes offer the chance to see dubbed Hollywood blockbusters. **UCI Kinowelt Zoo-Palast,** Hardenbergstr. 29a (tel. 25 41 47 77), near Bahnhof Zoo, is one of the biggest and most popular, with more than a dozen screens. Mondays, Tuesdays, or Wednesdays are *Kinotage* at most movie theaters, with prices reduced a few Marks. Bring a student ID for discounts.

Arsenal, Welserstr. 25 (tel. 219 00 10). U-Bahn #1, 15, or 2 to "Wittenbergplatz." Run by the *Freunde der deutschen Kinemathek,* the founders of the *Berlinale,* Arsenal showcases independent films as well as the occasional classic. Frequent appearances by guest directors make the theater a popular meeting place for Berlin's filmmakers.

Odeon, Hauptstr. 116 (tel. 78 70 40 19). U-Bahn #4 to "Rathaus Schöneberg." Odeon's venue is a mixture of mainstream American and British films with a pseudo-leftist slant. Reduced admission Tu-W. All films in English.

Filmkunsthaus Babylon, Rosa-Luxemburg-Str. 30 (tel. 242 50 76). U-Bahn #2 to "Rosa-Luxemburg-Platz." Shows classics and art films, often in their original languages. DM8, students DM7.

Babylon-Kino, Dresdener Str. 126 (tel. 61 60 96 93). U-Bahn #1, 15, or 8 to "Kottbusser Tor." The other branch of the Babylon plays offbeat comedies in English with German subtitles. Reduced admission Tu-W. Wheelchair accessible.

Freiluftkino. The summer brings a host of outdoor film screenings to Berlin. Two venues show films in English: **Freiluftkino Hasenheide** (tel. 62 70 58 85), at the Sputnik in Hasenheide park, screens anything from silent films to last year's blockbusters. U-Bahn #7 or 8 to "Hermannplatz." **Freiluftkino Kreuzberg,** Mariannenpl. 2 (tel. 24 31 30 34), screens avant-garde contemporary films. U-Bahn #1, 15, or 8 to "Kottbusser Tor." DM10 for either theater. Reduced admission M and W.

Blow Up, Immanuelkirchstr. 14 (tel. 442 86 62). S-Bahn #4, 8, or 85 to "Greifswalder Str." Explosive and entertaining—see *Unzipped* followed by a fashion show, or catch them when they're showing the eternally cool Bogey flicks. The theater always screens something in English. DM9, Tu-W DM7.

◪ SWIMMING

Berlin is very concrete-intensive; come summer, it's like a big ol' furnace. Though a fair amount of clothing comes off on the city's dance floors, the place to see the most skin and be cool in every way is in one of Berlin's fab *Freibäder* and *Sommerbäder*. Outdoor pools are generally open from May to August. In addition, Berlin is home to dozens of surprisingly clean lakes. In winter, the city's myriad *Schwimmbäder* keep Berliners from frowning too hard by lulling them into a climate-controlled state of relaxation. A dip in a municipal pool costs DM6, students DM4. For more information, contact the **Berliner Bäder-Betriebe's** service hotline at (01803) 10 20 20.

Sommerbad am Insulaner, Munsterdamm 80 (tel. 79 41 04 13). S-Bahn #2 or 25 to "Priesterweg." Beautiful outdoor pool beneath one of Berlin's towering *Trümmerberge*, hills made out of the rubble left behind by WWII. Idyllic, except when someone toting a beer belly and speedos walks by. Relive your childhood under one of the showering mushrooms.

Sommerbad Wilmersdorf, Forckenbeckstr. 114 (tel. 897 74 11). U-Bahn #4, 45, or 46 to "Hohenzollerndamm." Members of both sexes divest themselves of their clothing and cell phones all too willingly. The shady trees, trampoline, and pool-side *Imbiß* make up for the cliquishness.

Freibad Olympiastadion, Olympischer Pl. (tel. 30 06 34 40). S-Bahn #5 or 75 to "Olympiastadion" or U-Bahn #2 to "Olympia-Stadion (Ost)." Olympic-sized pool with a diving board the height of the Tower of Babel. Have your very own Riefenstahlian adventure alongside the sporty types who work out here.

Schwimmhalle Fischerinsel, Fischerinsel 11 (tel. 201 39 85). U-Bahn #2 to "Spittelmarkt." Just a few blocks from Mitte's historic sights, the indoor pool complex features a sauna and bistro. Open M 6:30am-4pm, Tu and F 6:30am-10pm, W 9am-10pm, Th 6:30am-4pm, Su 10am-7pm. Wheelchair accessible.

Strandbad Wannsee, Wannseebadweg 25 (tel. 803 56 12). S-Bahn #1 or 7 to "Nikolassee." Berlin's Coney Island, though (slightly) more subdued. Play with the giant chess pieces or bear all in the *FKK* (nudist) section. Open June-Aug. 8am-8pm, April-May and Sept. 10am-6pm.

Freibad Müggelsee, Fürstenwalder Damm 838 (tel. 648 77 77). S-Bahn #3 to "Rahnsdorf," then hike through the woods. Sandy beach with volleyball courts and an ever-popular nudist section along Berlin's largest lake. Open June-Aug. 8am-8pm, mid-April to May 10am-7pm.

■ SHOPPING

When Berlin was a lonely outpost in the Eastern Bloc consumer wilderness, Berliners had no choice but to buy native. Thanks to the captive market, the city accrued a mind-boggling array of things for sale: if a price tag can be put on it, you can buy it in Berlin. The high temple of the consumerist religion is the seven-story **KaDeWe department store** on Wittenbergplatz at Tauentzienstr. 21-24 (tel. 212 10), the largest department store in mainland Europe. The name is a German abbreviation of "Department Store of the West" *(Kaufhaus des Westens);* for the tens of thousands of product-starved East Germans who flooded Berlin in the days following the opening of the Wall, KaDeWe *was* the West—prompting warnings such as, "OK now, we're going in. Just act normal," as intrepid children stood on the threshold of consumerism. Even Westerners would do well to follow the advice, with the saccharine and pervasive materialism on display alternatively proving awe-inspiring and sickening. (Open M-F 9:30am-8pm, Sa 9am-4pm.) The food department, on the sixth floor, has to be seen to be believed (see **Food,** p. 104).

Two shopping districts have received a major face-lift in recent years. The **Kurfürstendamm,** near Bahnhof Zoo, has almost every kind of shop imaginable as well as a half-dozen monolithic department stores. The **Ku'damm Eck,** at the corner of Joachimstaler Str., and **Ku'damm Block,** near Uhlandstr., are the most notable areas. **Bleibtreustr.** has stores closer to the budget traveler's reach. **Friedrichstraße** is the commercial hub of Eastern Berlin. In particular, the **Friedrichstadtpassagen** are proof of just how much the area has changed in the past decade; flashy restaurants and clothing shops now stand where soldiers once guarded the entrance to the Soviet sector of the city. In addition, the newly opened **Daimler-Benz** complex on **Potsdamer Platz** offers more than 100 new shops and a multitude of restaurants, cafés, and pubs.

Theodore Sturgeon astutely observed that "90% of everything is crap," and the **flea markets** that regularly occupy Berlin are no exception. Nevertheless, you can occasionally find the fantastic bargain that makes all the sorting and sifting worthwhile. The market on **Straße des 17. Juni** probably has the best selection of stuff, but the prices are higher than those at a lot of other markets. (U-Bahn #2 to "Ernst-Reuter-Platz." Open Sa-Su 10am-5pm.) **Winterfeldtplatz,** near Nollendorfplatz, overflows with food, flowers, and people crooning Dylan tunes over their acoustic guitars. (Open W and Sa mornings.) The market on **Oranienburger Straße** by Tacheles offers works by starving artists and a variety of other nonsensical Dada delights. (Open Sa-Su 8am-3pm.) Closer to Hackescher Markt, Oranienburger Str. is also home to a number of trendy shoe and clothing stores. The **Hallentrödelmarkt,** Nostitzstr. 6-7 in Kreuzberg, aims to help the homeless of Berlin. (U-Bahn #6 or 7 to "Mehringdamm." Open Tu 5-7pm, Th 11am-1pm, Sa 11am-3pm.) Other markets are located near **Ostbahnhof** in Friedrichshain (S-Bahn #3, 5, 7, 75, or 9 to "Ostbahnhof"; open Sa 9am-3pm, Su 10am-5pm), and on **John-F.-Kennedy-Platz** in Schöneberg (U-Bahn #4 to "Rathaus Schöneberg"; open Sa-Su 8am-4pm). There is a typical German *Fußgängerzone* (pedestrian zone) on **Wilmersdorfer Str.,** where bakeries, *Döner* joints, trendy clothing shops, and department stores abound. (U-Bahn #7 to "Wilmersdorfer Str." or S-Bahn #3, 5, 7, 75, or 9 to "Charlottenburg.") For the latest in club gear, check out the trendy **Hennes & Mauritz** clothing chain (H&M for short), scattered throughout the city; convenient locations are **Kurfürstendamm 20,** near Bahnhof Zoo; **Friedrichstr. 79,** near Unter den Linden; and **Schönhauser Allee 78** in Prenzlauer Berg.

Zweite Hand ("second-hand"; DM3.80), an aptly named newspaper appearing at newsstands on Tuesdays, Thursdays, and Saturdays, consists of ads for anything anyone wants to resell, from apartment shares and plane tickets to silk dresses and cats; it also has good deals on **bikes. Bergmannstraße,** in Kreuzberg, is a used clothes and cheap antique shop strip. Take U-Bahn #7 to "Gneisenaustr." **Made in Berlin,** Potsdamer Str. 106, generally has funky second-hand stuff, all quite cheap. Get your leather jacket here. (U-Bahn #1 or 15 to "Kurfürstenstr.") A larger selection of used clothes, albeit with less consistent quality, awaits at **Checkpoint,** Mehringdamm 59. Hop on U-Bahn #6 or 7 to "Mehrngdamm."

Berlin's largest music store is the enormous **Saturn,** Alexanderpl. 8 (tel. 24 75 16), located right outside the train station. Most CDs are DM25-30. (Open M-F 9am-8pm, Sa 9am-4pm. U-Bahn #2, 5, or 8 or S-Bahn #3, 5, 7, 75, or 9 to "Alexanderplatz.") If you're looking for used CDs or LPs, snoop around the streets near the "Schlesisches Tor" U-Bahn stop (lines #1 and 15). A variety of used CDs and records are bought and sold at **Cover,** Turmstr. 52 (tel. 395 87 62), but they're particularly into pop and top-40s music. (U-Bahn #9 to "Turmstr." Open M-F 10am-8pm, Sa 10am-4pm.) To complete (or start) your trance, techno, house, and acid collection, head to **Flashpoint,** Bornholmer Str. 88. (Tel. 44 65 09 59. S-Bahn #1, 2, 25, 4, 8, or 85 to "Bornholmer Str.")

◪ NIGHTLIFE

Berlin's nightlife is absolute madness, a teeming cauldron of debauchery that runs around the clock and threatens to inflict coronaries upon the faint of heart. Bars, clubs, and cafés typically jam until at least 3am and often stay open until daylight; on weekends, you can dance non-stop from Friday night until Monday morning. From 1am to 4am, take advantage of the **night buses** and **U-Bahn #9 and 12,** which run all night on Fridays and Saturdays; normal transit service resumes after 4:30am. The best sources of information about bands and dance venues are the bi-weekly magazines *Tip* and the superior *Zitty* (both DM4), available at all news-stands, or the free *030,* distributed in cafés and bars.

In Western Berlin, the best places to look are **Savignyplatz, Nollendorfplatz,** and particularly **Kreuzberg.** The Ku'damm is best avoided at night, unless you enjoy frat-ernizing with drunken businessmen, middle-aged tourists, and dirty old men who drool at the sight of strip shows. The area west of Zoo, especially **Savignyplatz,** is rife with cafés and bars as well as a few venues for live music. The main focus of Schöneberg nightlife is around **Nollendorfplatz,** encompassing café-*Kneipen* on Winterfeldtplatz, Akazienstr., and Goltzstr.; the area is also the traditional center of Berlin's **gay scene** (see **Gay and Lesbian Berlin,** p. 137). Pushing up against the remains of the Wall is the center of the **Kreuzberg** *Szene.* The beat in Eastern Kreuzberg is wild; in the midst of the heavily Turkish neighborhoods along Oranienstr. between U-Bahn #1 and 15 stops "Kottbusser Tor" and "Görlitzer Bahnhof," you'll find a menagerie of radically alternative clubs that range from laid-back to breathtakingly salacious. Farther east lies Schlesisches Tor, home to a more punkish heap of bars, as well as the floating club and café aboard the **MS Sanssouci.** On the opposite bank of the Spree in **Friedrichshain,** several clubs have jumped off the capitalist bandwagon and headed East; check out the latest venues along Simon-Dach-Str. and Gabriel-Max-Str. (S-Bahn #3, 5, 6, 7, 75, or 9 or U-Bahn #1, 12, or 15 to "Warschauer Str.")

Berlin's best clubs are also located in Eastern Berlin. While Kreuzberg tries to defend West Berlin's reputation as the dance capital of the world, its alterna-charm has become a tad passé as clubs flee to the east and north. At present, **Pots-damer Platz** and the intersection of **Oranienburger Str.** and **Friedrichstr.** are the clear leaders in the nightclub scene. German teenagers still often choose the dinosaur-like clubs of West Berlin, but the real cutting-edge action is almost exclusively lim-ited to the East. In Mitte, the area around **Oranienburger Str.** (not to be confused with Kreuzberg's Oranienstr.) is particularly lively at night. Trendy bars abound, and prices are relatively high. Further afield, **Prenzlauer Berg** and **Friedrichshain** both host Berlin's newest alternative clubs and are the breeding ground of many of today's international dance music stars.

If at all possible, try to hit (or, if you're prone to bouts of claustrophobia, avoid) Berlin during the **Love Parade,** usually held in the second weekend of July (see **The Love Parade,** p. 135), when all of Berlin just says "yes" to everything. Though there is much speculation as to whether the Love Parade will take place in Berlin next year (a move to Paris seems imminent), most cannot imagine the parade happen-ing anywhere else. It's also worth mentioning that Berlin has **de-criminalized mari-juana possession** of up to eight grams. Smoking in public, however, has not been officially accepted, though it's becoming more common in some clubs. *Let's Go* does not recommend puffing clouds of hash smoke into the face of police officers.

BARS AND CLUBS

This is the section of *Let's Go: Germany* where we dance.

SAVIGNYPLATZ

Quasimodo, Kantstr. 12a (tel. 312 80 86). S-Bahn #3, 5, 7, 75, or 9 to "Savignyplatz." This unassuming basement pub with attached *Biergarten* is one of Berlin's most inte-gral jazz venues, drawing big names and lively crowds. It's totally dead until 10pm when the shows begin. (An extraordinary fact: the men's bathroom here is lit by fluo-rescent "black light" bulbs. Why is this extraordinary? Because human urine glows under fluorescent light!) Cover depends on performance, ranging from free to DM40. Concert tickets available from 5pm or at Kant-Kasse ticket service (tel. 313 45 54; fax 312 64 40). Club open daily from 8pm.

SCHÖNEBERG

Metropol, Nollendorfpl. 5 (tel. 217 36 80). U-Bahn #1, 15, 2, or 4 to "Nollendorfplatz," or night buses #N5, N19, N26, N48, N52, or N75. 650,000 watts of light! 35,800 watts of sound! A mob of Berlin's teenagers convinced that they are very cool! Berlin's largest disco is decked out in extravagant ancient Egyptian motifs. Commercialism at its best. F top 40, Sa dance/techno. Things usually get going around 10pm. Sometimes big-time concerts take place between dances. Concert ticket prices vary; call 215 54 63 for information and prices. Open M-F 11am-3pm and 3:30-6pm. Cover F-Sa DM15.

Café Bilderbuch, Akazienstr. 28 (tel. 78 70 60 57). U-Bahn #7 to "Eisenacher Str." This sophisticated jazzy café teleports its clientele into a world of flappers and speakeasies. Chill on the plush sofas with the over-30 crowd while sipping a fruity *Berliner Weiße mit Schuß* (DM4.50), or tango the night away at one of the café's biweekly *Tanztees*. The tasty brunch baskets, served around the clock, culminate in the sumptuous Sunday buffet (DM15). Open M-Sa 9am-2am, Su 10am-2am.

KREUZBERG

For a map of Kreuzberg's bars and clubs, see **Sights,** p. 118.

◼ **SO36,** Oranienstr. 190 (tel. 61 40 13 06; www.SO36.de). U-Bahn #1, 12, or 15 to "Görlitzer Bahnhof" or night bus #N29 to "Heinrichplatz" or N8 to "Adalbertstr." Berlin's only *truly* mixed club, with a clientele of hip heteros, gays, and lesbians grooving to a mish-mash of wild genres. Loud music, huge dance floor, and friendly people—just don't assume that what you see is what you get. Mondays are "electric ballroom," a trance party featuring Berlin's up-and-coming DJs and TV screens filled with anime. Th hip-hop, reggae, punk, or ska. Weekends run the gamut from techno to live concerts. For other nights, see **Gay and Lesbian Berlin,** p. 138. Open after 11pm. Cover varies.

KitKat Club, Glogauer Str. 2 (tel. 611 38 33). U-Bahn #1, 12, or 15 to "Görlitzer Bahnhof" or night bus #N29. Lascivious? The word loses its meaning here. Erotic? This implies innuendo, a quality which has no place on this dance floor. Sex. SEXSEXSEX. People with varying degrees of clothing, some copulating, some just digging the cool trance music in the jaw-dropping fluorescent interior, leave their inhibitions outside. Go latex! On Thursdays, the club cross-dresses as the **Fuck-Naked Sex Party** for some serious homoerotics (men only!). Not for the faint of heart Open W-Su after 11pm. Cover DM10-20. The after-hours party (Su 8am-7pm) is popular, free, and more fully clothed.

Ex, Mehringhof, Gneisenaustr. 2a (tel. 693 58 00). U-Bahn #6 or 7 to "Mehringdamm" or night bus #N4, N19, or N76. A bar, performance space, and club run by a leftist collective in a steel and concrete courtyard. Also a site for political meetings and (primarily) lesbian events, as well as an anarchist bookstore. The commies cook up an Indian storm bound to cause an intestinal revolution. Open Tu-F noon-2am, Sa-Su til late.

Junction Bar, Gneisenaustr. 18 (tel. 772 76 77). U-Bahn #7 to "Gneisenaustr." or night bus #N4 or N19 to "Zossener Str." Funk, soul, jazz, and hip-hop on the weekends accompany American-style breakfast served until 2:30am. Shows at 7:30, 8:30, and 9:30pm weeknights, and DJ parties after 1am. Open daily after 6pm.

Sage Club, Brückenstr. 1. U-Bahn #8 to "Heinrich-Heine-Str." or night bus #N8. One of the latest entries in Berlin's fast-paced dance club arena, Sage Club has dealt a one-two punch to its Kreuzberg competitors in cornering the techno and house market. Bring your lycra and pleatherwear, or at least enough hair gel to make up for those dirty sneakers. Get into the groove, boy, Th-Su from 11pm. Cover DM10-25.

Café Morena, Wiener Str. 60 (tel. 611 47 16). U-Bahn #1, 12, 15, or 8 to "Görlitzer Bahnhof." The crowd may be a little on the loud side, but that's what happens when you

THE LOVE PARADE Every year during the second weekend in July, the Love Parade brings Berlin to its knees—its trains run late, its streets fill with litter, and its otherwise patriotic populace scrambles to the countryside in the wake of a wave of West German teenagers dying their hair, dropping ecstasy, and getting down *en masse*. What started in 1988 as a DJ's birthday party with only 150 people has mutated into an annual techno Woodstock, the world's only 1.5 million-man rave, and a massive corporate event. A huge "parade" takes place on Saturday afternoon, involving a snail-paced procession of tractor-trailers loaded with blasting speakers and topped by gyrating bodies that slowly works it from Ernst-Reuter-Platz to the Brandenburg Gate. The city-wide party turns the Straße des 17. Juni into a riotous dance floor, and the Tiergarten into a garden of original—and sometimes quite creative—sin. To celebrate the licentious atmosphere, the BVG offers a "No-Limit-Ticket," useful for getting around from venue to venue during the weekend's **54 hours of nonstop partying** (DM10, condom included). Unless you have a fetish for tall people's hairy and sweaty armpits, the best way to see and enjoy the parade is to be up high (literally, of course)—the porta-potties are supreme watch towers. Club prices skyrocket for the event as the best DJs from Europe are imported for a frantic weekend of beat-thumping madness. It's an experience that you'll never forget, unless you consume something that leaves you in a hazy cloud of oblivion. Keep an ear out for updates on the 2000 event; although past Love Parades have been held in the Tiergarten, the authorities might move it after environmentalists raised concerns about the 750,000 liters of urine (and undetermined amounts of other bodily fluids) which the park must absorb every year. Rumor has it that the Love Parade may move to Paris next year, but fans unanimously proclaim that Berlin should remain the party venue. Check out the parade's official website (www.loveparade.de) for the latest news. Regardless of the locale, the techno world trembles in eager anticipation of next year's incarnation.

BERLIN

have happy "hour" every day from 7-8pm and midnight-2am. Long drinks DM7, cocktails DM10. "American-style" bagel and burger platters DM14-15. Open M-Th and Su 9am-4am, F-Sa 9am-5am.

ORANIENBURGER STRASSE-MITTE

Tresor/Globus, Leipziger Str. 126a (tel. 229 06 11 or 612 33 64). U-Bahn #2 or S-Bahn #1, 2, or 25 or night bus #N5, N29 or N52 to "Potsdamer Platz." One of the most rocking techno venues in Berlin, packed from wall to wall with enthusiastic ravers. Its 2 dance floors, both sporting rapidly blinking lights and floor-shaking bass, are enough to bring out the epileptic in all of us. **Globus** chills with house, while **Tresor** rocks to techno beats. Open W and F-Sa 11pm-6am. Cover W DM5, F DM10, Sa DM15-20.

WMF, Johannisstr. 19. S-Bahn #1, 2, or 25 to "Oranienburger Str." or U-Bahn #6 to "Oranienburger Tor." So you want more techno, eh? WMF has it all, from drum 'n bass to house. Sundays feature *GMF*, a gay tea dance. Open Th-Su after 11pm. Cover DM15.

Kalkscheune, Johannisstr. 2 (tel. 28 39 00 65). S-Bahn #1, 2, or 25 to "Oranienburger Str." or U-Bahn #6 to "Oranienburger Tor." Across from WMF, the two clubs occasionally host parties together. Kalkscheune plays anything from hip-hop to house and techno; call ahead to see what's on. Cover DM5-15.

Roter Salon, Rosa-Luxemburg-Pl. (tel. 30 87 48 02). U-Bahn #2 to "Rosa-Luxemburg-Platz" The club is notable because it doesn't play any electronica...well, almost none. M drum 'n bass, Tu salsa, W tango, F-Sa vary, Su happy 60s tunes. Cover DM7-12.

Tacheles, Oranienburger Str. 53-56 (tel. 282 61 85). U-Bahn #6 to "Oranienburger Tor" or S-Bahn #1, 2, or 25 to "Oranienburger Str." or night bus #N6 or N84. A playground for artists, punks, and curious tourists staying in the nearby hostels. Housed in a bombed-out department store and the adjacent courtyard, Tacheles plays host to several art galleries, bars, and vicious raves. The owners have staved off ambitious plans to convert the area into office buildings for several years. Open M-Su 24hr.

Hackesche Höfe, Rosenthaler Str. 40-41. S-Bahn #3, 5, 7, 75, or 9 to "Hackescher Markt." One of the few successful attempts at revitalizing northern Mitte, the Hackesche Höfe is a series of interconnected courtyards containing restaurants, cafés, clubs, galleries, shops, apartments, and a movie theater. The lively sound of *klezmer* bands vie with street performers for the attention of passersby, while the low-key **Oxymoron** club (tel. 28 39 18 85) offers daily jazz concerts to a thirtysomething crowd. Open M and W-Sa after 11pm, Tu after 8:30pm, Su after 10pm. Concerts DM15-20.

Café Silberstein, Oranienburger Str. 27 (tel. 281 28 01). S-Bahn #1, 2, or 25 to "Oranienburger Str." Post-everything decor offers sushi, ambient music, and a hipper than hip clientele. Popular student club Th-Su. Open M-F after 4pm, Sa after noon.

PRENZLAUER BERG

🦍 **Bibo Bar,** Lychener Str. 17 (tel. 443 97 98). Take U-Bahn #2 to "Eberswalder Str." and walk along Danziger Str. to Lychener Str., or hop on S-Bahn #4, 8, or 85 to "Prenzlauer Allee" and walk along the street of the same name; turn right onto Danziger Str. and then right again on Lychener Str. DJs change daily, but they're always as crazy and mixed (in every sense) as the bar's clientele, who spend long nights (and days) boozing it, dancing wildly, and discussing *das Leben* on the crowded sofas. Drinks DM8-12. Open 5pm-late.

KulturBrauerei, Knaackstr. 97 (tel. 44 05 67 56). U-Bahn #2 to "Eberswalder Str." Enormous party space located in a former East German brewery. Seven dance spaces, as well as an outdoor stage and café, host a variety of concerts and parties throughout the year. Because the venues include everything from hard-core *Ostrock* and disco to techno, reggae, and *Schlager*, it's best to call ahead. Well-known as a concert venue. Open Tu and Th-Su after 10pm. Cover DM3-5, more for special events.

Subground, in the **Pfefferberg** club, Schönhauser Allee 176 (tel. 44 38 31 16). U-Bahn #2 to "Senefelderplatz" or night bus #N58. As the name suggests, this club is at ground level. Less mobbed than other clubs, with DJs spinning a varied mix of drum 'n bass, jungle, and dub, as well as healthy quantities of techno and British house. Open Th-Sa after 11pm. Cover DM10.

Icon, Cantianstr. 15 (tel. 44 33 27 62). U-Bahn #2 to "Eberswalder Str." Great space with psychedelic lights. Famed for its Friday reggae/hip-hop and Sa drum 'n bass parties. Open from 11pm, but things really get going around 1-2am. Cover DM10.

Duncker, Dunckerstr. 64 (tel. 445 95 09). U-Bahn #2 to "Eberswalder Str." A small, alternative club keeping up the true spirit of Prenzlauer Berg. Music ranges from bizarre 80s selections to dub and industrial. The club also hosts concerts by up-and-coming punk and rock groups. Garden with grill in back. Cover DM5-10; Th usually free.

FRIEDRICHSHAIN

Intimes, Boxhagener Str. 107 (tel. 29 66 64 57). U-Bahn #5 to "Frankfurter Tor." Greek joint that's also an evening spot. Meals run DM11-20, except on Wednesdays, when all dishes are only DM7! Open daily from 10am. Kitchen open M-Th and Su 10am-midnight, F-Sa 10am-1am.

Maria am Ostbahnhof, Str. der Pariser Kommune 8-10 (tel. 29 00 61 98). S-Bahn #3, 5, 7, 75, or 9 to "Ostbahnhof" (surprise, surprise). Extremely popular. Evenings at Maria's usually begin with concerts, followed by DJs spinning techno later on. Open W-Sa 10pm-late. Cover DM5, more for special events.

TREPTOW

🏄 **Insel der Jugend,** Alt-Treptow 6 (tel. 53 60 80 20). S-Bahn #4, 6, 8, or 9 to "Treptower Park," then bus #166, 167, or 265 or night bus #N65 to "Alt-Treptow." Located in the Spree river, *Insel der Jugend* (island of youth) is not just for kids. 3 fiercely decorated floors of dancing have the feel of a fishbowl with fluorescent silver foil and netting all over the place; you'll have the memory of a goldfish if you linger too long on the side. Top 2 floors spin reggae, hip-hop, ska, and house (sometimes all at once), while the frantic techno scene in the basement claims the casualties of the upper floors. An outdoor patio overlooking the trees and river serves as a peaceful venue for smokers. Open W after 7pm, Th after 9pm, F-Sa after 10pm. Cover Th-Sa DM5-15.

GAY AND LESBIAN BERLIN

Berlin is one of the most gay-friendly cities on the continent. During the Cold War, thousands of homosexuals flocked to Berlin to take part in its left-wing activist scene as well as to avoid West Germany's *Wehrpflicht* (mandatory military service). Even before the war, Berlin was known as a gay metropolis, particularly in the tumultuous 1920s. Traditionally, the social nexus of gay and lesbian life has centered around **Nollendorfplatz** and the surrounding **"Schwuler Kiez"** (gay neighborhood) of **Schöneberg.** Christopher Isherwood lived at Nollendorfstr. 17 while writing his collection of stories *Goodbye to Berlin*, later adapted as the musical *Cabaret.* The city's reputation for tolerance was marred by the Nazi persecutions of the 1930s and 40s, when thousands of gay and lesbian Berliners were deported to concentration camps. A marble pink triangle plaque outside the Nollendorfplatz U-Bahn station honors their memory. With the fall of the Wall, Berlin's *Szene* was once again revitalized by the emergence of East Berlin's heretofore heavily oppressed homosexual community, and many of the new clubs that have opened up in the past few years are situated in the eastern half of the city.

The boisterous history of homosexuality comes out at the **Schwules Museum,** Mehringdamm 61 (tel. 693 11 72). Take U-Bahn #6 or 7 to "Mehringdamm." (Open W and F-Su 2-6pm, Th 2-9pm. DM7, students DM4.) **Spinnboden-Lesbenarchiv,** Anklamer Str. 38 (tel. 448 58 48), tends toward culturally hip lesbian offerings, with exhibits, films, and all kinds of information about current lesbian life. Take U-Bahn #8 to "Bernauer Str." (Open W and F 2-7pm.) **Lesbenberatung,** Kulmer Str. 20a (tel. 215 20 00), offers a library, movie screenings, and counseling on lesbian issues. Take U-Bahn #7 to "Kleistpark." (Open M-Tu, and Th 4-7pm, F 2-5pm.) The gay information center **Mann-o-Meter,** Motzstr. 5 (tel 216 80 08), off Nollendorfplatz, gives out information on nightlife, political activism, and gay or gay-friendly living arrangements (DM30-75 a night). They also offer informal monthly tours for those new to the Berlin scene on the third Friday of every month at 9pm. Take U-Bahn #1, 15, 2, or 4 to "Nollendorfplatz." (Open M-F 5-10pm, Sa-Su 4-10pm.)

For up-to-date events listings, pick up a copy of the amazingly comprehensive *Siegessäule* (free), named after one of Berlin's most prominent phallic monuments. Less in-depth but also useful is *Sergej*, a free publication for men. **Prinz Eisenherz Buchladen,** Bleibtreustr. 52 (tel. 313 99 36), stocks gay-themed books, many in English. They also sell the travel guide *Berlin von Hinten* (Berlin from Behind), which costs a hefty DM19.80 but has extensive information on gay life in English and German. (Bookstore open M-F 10am-7pm, Sa 10am-4pm.) **Lilith Frauenbuchladen,** Knesebeckstr. 86 (tel. 312 31 02), is a women's bookstore with a focus on lesbian issues. (Open M-F 10am-6:30pm, Sa 10am-4pm.) **Marga Schoeller Bücherstube,** Knesebeckstr. 33 (tel. 881 11 22), offers women's issues books in English. All three bookstores can be reached by taking S-Bahn #3, 5, 7, 75, or 9 to "Savignyplatz." *Blattgold* (DM5 from women's bookstores and some natural food stores) has information and listings for women on a monthly basis. Most *Frauencafés* listed are not exclusively lesbian, but do offer an all-female setting.

The second half of June is the high point of the annual queer calendar of events, culminating in the ecstatic, champagne-soaked floats of the **Christopher Street Day (CSD)** parade, a six-hour long street party drawing more than 250,000 revelers. The weekend before CSD sees a smaller but no less jubilant **Lesbisch-schwules Stadtfest** (street fair) at Nollendorfplatz. Exact dates had not been set for either event by press time; contact Mann-o-Meter for up-to-date information.

SCHÖNEBERG

Café Berio, Maaßenstr. 7 (tel. 216 19 46). U-Bahn #1, 15, 2, or 4 to "Nollendorfplatz." Bright, charming café caters to an easy-going crowd of gays and lesbians. Perfect for brunch or an early evening drink. Outdoor seating in summer. Open daily 8am-1am.

Anderes Ufer, Hauptstr. 157 (tel. 78 70 38 00). U-Bahn #7 to "Kleistpark." A quieter, more relaxed *Kneipe* away from the club scene. Occasional exhibits by local artists adorn the brightly painted interior. Open M-Th and Su 11am-1am, F-Sa 11am-2am.

Connection, Fuggerstr. 33 (tel. 218 14 32). U-Bahn #1, 15, or 2 to "Wittenbergplatz." Sketchy, sketchy, sketchy. The name says it all. Find your soul mate (well, one-night stand) in the above-ground disco, then head downstairs to the dimly lit, labyrinthine **Connection Garage.** You get the picture. Open M-Th 10pm-1am, F-Sa 10pm-6am, Su 2pm-2am. Cover DM12 including first drink. Men only.

ORANIENSTRASSE

Most bars and clubs on and around Oranienstraße lie between Lausitzer Platz and Oranienplatz. Take U-Bahn #1, 12, 15, or 8 to "Kottbusser Tor" or U-Bahn #1, 12, or 15 to "Görlitzer Bahnhof." After hours, night bus #N29 runs the length of the strip.

Flammende Herzen, Oranienstr. 170 (tel. 615 71 02). Pleasant café frequented by Kreuzberg's gay and lesbian community. People-watch outside or chill in the flaming orange interior. Drinks DM4-8; order at the bar. Open daily from 11am.

Rose's, Oranienstr. 187 (tel. 615 65 70). Voluptuous interior that's perpetually packed with people. The mixed gay and lesbian clientele kicks it amidst suspended fluffy red hearts and outrageously painted walls. Margaritas DM8. Open daily 10pm-6am.

Café Anal, Muskauer Str. 15. Spirited alternative gay and lesbian bar in east Kreuzberg. The decor hovers between Salvador Dalí and Pee-Wee's Playhouse: shiny gold ceiling, stuffed-pumpkin light fixtures, plump multi-colored cushions in corner nooks, seashell-shaped canopy. M women only. Open summer daily from 6pm; winter from 8pm.

Schoko-Café, Mariannenstr. 6 (tel. 615 15 61). Lesbian central; a café with a cultural center upstairs, billiards, and dancing every second Saturday of the month (10pm). Open M-Th and Su 5pm-1am year-round, plus F-Sa from noon in the summer.

SO36, while usually a mixed club (see p. 134), sponsors 4 predominantly queer events. The largest is **Hungrige Herzen** (Wednesdays after 10pm), a jam-packed gay and (somewhat) lesbian trance and drum 'n bass party. Delightful drag queens make the rounds with super-soakers to cool off the flaming crowd. **Café Fatal** (Sundays), has a more relaxed atmosphere, with ballroom dancing from 5pm followed by the obligatory *Schlagerkarusell* at 10pm. The third Friday in every month heralds the coming of **Jane Bond,** a wild party for lesbians and drags (10pm-late), while the second Saturday in the month brings **Gayhane,** a self-described "HomOrientaldancefloor" for a mixed crowd of Turks and Germans. The club also regularly invites famous gay and lesbian performers.

ELSEWHERE IN KREUZBERG AND FRIEDRICHSHAIN

Die Busche, Mühlenstr. 12. U-Bahn #1, 12, or 15 or S-Bahn #3, 5, 6, 7, 75, or 9 to "Warschauer Str." East Berlin's largest queer disco serves up an incongruous rotation of techno, top 40, and, yes, *Schlager.* Very cruisey. Open W and F-Su from 9:30pm. The party gets going around midnight. It *really* gets going around 3am. Cover DM6-10.

SchwuZ, Mehringdamm 61 (tel. 693 70 25). U-Bahn #6 or 7 to "Mehringdamm." Café *cum* club in southern Kreuzberg with a mostly male clientele. The relaxed *Kneipe* facade belies the intense dance floor scene inside. Th ballroom and tango from 8pm; F-Sa house, techno, and top 40 from 11pm. Cover DM5-15.

MS TitaniCa, on the MS Sanssouci boat off Göbenufer in the Spree River (tel. 611 12 55). U-Bahn #1 or 15 to "Schlesisches Tor." MS Sanssouci's gently swaying café transforms into a swinging lesbian party the first Friday of the month from 8:30pm.

PRENZLAUER BERG

Café Amsterdam, Gleimstr. 24 (tel. 231 67 96). S-Bahn #4, 8, or 85 or U-Bahn #2 to "Schönhauser Allee." To the beat of chill house music, Amsterdam's clientele down cheap drinks, play pool, or challenge one another to a game of backgammon or Monopoly. Drink specials: M shot of vodka DM1.50; Tu shot of tequila DM1.50. Open daily 4pm-6am.

BRANDENBURG

Surrounding Berlin on all sides, the *Land* of Brandenburg is overshadowed by the sprawling metropolis within it. The infamous Hohenzollern family emerged from the province's forests to become the wealthy and powerful rulers of Prussia, leaving their mark on the region by constructing more than 30 stunning palaces. Fancy castles and the legacy of riches attract folks to Brandenburg, but the pastoral lakes, forests, and canals that surround them are just as enticing. The entire region is an easy commute from Berlin, allowing it to provide a soul-saving break from the overloaded circuits of the non-stop metropolis.

HIGHLIGHTS OF BRANDENBURG

■ **Potsdam,** with **Schloß Sanssouci** as its crowning glory, stands in regal contrast to the grit of nearby Berlin (p. 140).

■ The winding canals of the swampy **Spreewald** make for a sort of rural Venice, with locals using the slow-moving rivers as streets (p. 147). **Lübbenau** is an excellent base for exploring the woods and waterways (p. 149).

POTSDAM

Visitors disappointed by Berlin's distinctly unroyal demeanor can get their Kaiserly fix by taking the S-Bahn to nearby Potsdam, the glittering city of Friedrich II (the Great). While his father, Friedrich Wilhelm I (a.k.a. "the Soldier King"), wanted to turn Potsdam into a huge garrison of tall, tall men he had kidnapped to serve as his toy soldiers, the more eccentric Friedrich II beautified the city. Although most of downtown Potsdam was destroyed in a 20-minute air raid in April 1945, the castle-studded **Schloßpark Sanssouci** still stands as a monument to Friedrich II's (sometimes dubious) aesthetic taste. In a second spurt of high heels, powder, and gilt, Potsdam served as Germany's "Little Hollywood" from 1921 until WWII, when the suburb of **Babelsberg** was one of the capitals of the nascent film industry. As the site of the 1945 **Potsdam Conference** during which the Allies divvied up D-land, Potsdam's name became synonymous with Germany's defeat. After serving for 45 years as the home of Communist Party fat cats, the 1,000-year-old city finally recovered its traditional elitism in 1991 when Brandenburgers restored its status as the *Land's* capital.

⚹ PRACTICAL INFORMATION

Trains: S-Bahn #7 runs from Potsdam-Stadt to Berlin's Bahnhof Zoo (30min., DM4.20). Hourly trains also run to Magdeburg (1½hr., DM32), Dessau (1½hr., DM30), and Leipzig (2hr., DM46).

Public Transportation: Potsdam lies in Zone C of Berlin's BVG transit network. For frequency and ticket prices, see **Getting Around,** p. 93.

Bike Rental: City Rad (tel. 61 90 52 or 270 27 29), 100m from the Potsdam-Stadt station on Bahnhofstr. DM20 per day, DM35 for 2 days. Open May-Sept. M-F 9am-7pm, Sa-Su 9am-8pm.

Tourist Office: Friedrich-Ebert-Str. 5 (tel. 27 55 80; fax 275 58 99). Between the streetcar stops "Alter Markt" and "Platz der Einheit"; all streetcars from the Potsdam-Stadt station go to one of the two stops. To get to the tourist office, go across the Lange Brücke and make a right onto Friedrich-Ebert-Str. The office provides a usable city map and books **rooms** for a DM5 fee. Rooms DM20-40 per person. Private bungalows DM35-50 per person. For accommodations information, call 275 58 16. Open April-

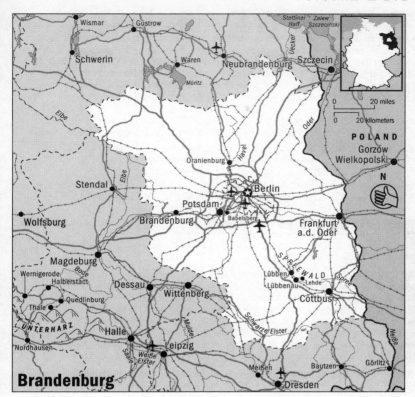

Wismar
Güstrow
Schwerin
Waren
Neubrandenburg
Szczecin
Stettiner Zalew
Haff. Szczecinski
Uecker
Müritz
Elbe
Havel
Oder
POLAND
0   20 miles
0   20 kilometers
Gorzów
Wielkopolski
N
Oranienburg
Stendal
Berlin
Elbe
Potsdam
Babelsberg
Wolfsburg
Brandenburg
Frankfurt
a.d. Oder
Magdeburg
Bode
SPREEWALD
Wernigerode
Halberstadt
Lübben
Lehde
Spree
Dessau
Lübbenau
Cottbus
Thale
Quedlinburg
Wittenberg
Nordhausen
UNTERHARZ
Halle
Mulde
Schwarze Elster
Neiße
Saale
Leipzig
Weiße
Elster
Meißen
Bautzen
Görlitz
Brandenburg
Dresden

BRANDENBURG

Oct. M-F 9am-8pm, Sa 9am-6pm, Su 9am-4pm; Nov.-March M-F 10am-6pm, Sa-Su 10am-2pm. A **branch office,** Brandenburger Str. 18 (tel. 275 58 88; fax 275 58 89), focuses on concerts, festivals, and plays. Open M-F 10am-7pm, Sa 10am-2pm.

Tours: The tourist office offers 3hr. **bus tours** from the **Filmmuseum,** Schloßstr. 1. Tours leave Tu-Su at 11am. DM39 with admission to Sanssouci castle (students DM30), DM25 without. Alternatively, **Berlin Walks** (see p. 95) offers tours of Potsdam that leave from the taxi stand outside Berlin's Bahnhof Zoo W and Sa at 9am. DM26, students DM19. **City Rad** (see above) offers 3-4hr. **bike tours** Sa at 11:30am. DM15, not including bike rental.

Post Office: Platz der Einheit, 14476 Potsdam. Open M-F 9am-6pm, Sa 9am-noon.

PHONE CODE	0331

▐ ACCOMMODATIONS AND CAMPING

Potsdam has no hostel—the closest is in Wannsee (see **Berlin,** p. 120), 10 minutes away by S-Bahn. Hotels are scarce, but the tourist office finds private rooms. It also offers a list of campgrounds in the Potsdam area. **Campingplatz Sanssouci-Gaisberg,** An der Pirschheide 41 (tel. 556 80), offers camping on the scenic banks of Templiner See. Take regional train #94 or 95 to "Bahnhof Pirschheide," and head down the lakeside road. (DM9.50 per person, DM3.90 per child. Tents DM2.50-10. Bungalows DM45-70. Open April-Oct.)

FOOD

Bright, renovated **Brandenburger Str.**, the local pedestrian zone, encompasses most of the city's restaurants, fast-food stands, and grocery shops. The cafés near Brandenburger Tor are lovely but pricey. Similarly, the **Holländisches Viertel** (see **Sights,** below) is lined with chic little cafés where you can have a civilized afternoon glass of wine or coffee. The merchants at the **flea market** on Bassinplatz include a number of farmers with fresh produce and fake Levi's. (Open M-F 9am-6pm.)

Pizza Jungle, Friedrich-Ebert-Str. 22 (tel. 270 12 87), around the corner from Mittelstr. Serves sandwiches (DM4.50), pizzas (DM5), and pasta (DM4). Open Tu-F 11am-8pm.

Eat & Read, Mittelstr. 41 (tel. 270 62 70). The menu is short but sweet so you'll have time for your book in this pocket-sized café. Feast on fresh pasta and sandwiches (DM6.50-14.50). Beer DM5. Open Tu-F 11am-6pm, Sa-Su 10am-6pm.

Ebert 86, Friedrich-Ebert-Str. 86 (tel. 270 63 22), serves *Döner,* falafel, and salads in a deli with Bauhaus-inspired stools. Most meals under DM5. Open daily until 1am.

▦ ♪ SIGHTS AND ENTERTAINMENT

A good investment for sightseeing is a **day ticket,** valid and available at all castles in Potsdam. (DM20, students DM15.)

PARK SANSSOUCI. Designed half in the Baroque style—straight paths intersect at topiary and statues of nude nymphs in geometrically pleasing patterns—and half in the rambling, rolling style of English landscape gardens, the 600-acre park is Friedrich II's testament to the size of his treasury and the diversity of his aesthetic tastes. It doesn't all necessarily match, but it's exciting to wander through the wheat fields at the center of the park and then get lost among the rose trellises later on. For information on the park's myriad attractions, visit the **Info Center** at the windmill behind Schloß Sanssouci. *(Tel. 969 42 00. Open M-F 10am-5pm, Sa-Su 11am-4pm.)*

SCHLOSS SANSSOUCI. At the other end of the park's long, long **Hauptallee** (central path) stands the main attraction, the Versailles-esque Schloß Sanssouci, atop a landscaped hill that defies all of nature's intentions. Built by Georg Wenzeslaus von Knobelsdorff in 1747, the yellow palace is small and airy, adorned with richly decorated depictions of Bacchus and other Greek gods. Friedrich used to go here to escape his wife and drown his sorrows (*sans souci* is French for "without cares"). Unfortunately, visits today are not always carefree; reunification has made this truly beautiful sight accessible, and thousands of tourists from East and West are making up for lost time. Tours of the castle in German (strictly limited to 40 people) leave every 20 minutes, but the final tour (5pm) usually sells out by 2pm during the high season. Come early. If you want an English-language tour, go on the one led by the tourist office, but note that it includes only the main Schloß (although you're free to wander around afterwards).

Inside, the style is cloud-like French Rococo (Friedrich was an unrepentant Francophile until his dying day)—all pinks and greens with startlingly gaudy gold trim. A high point is the steamy, tropical **Voltairezimmer,** decorated with colorful, carved reliefs of parrots and tropical fruit. Voltaire never stayed at the palace, though; the room was only built in his honor. The library reveals another of Friedrich's eccentricities: whenever he wanted to read a book, he had five copies printed, one for each of his palaces—*en français,* of course. By the way, the **Ruinenberg** (hill of ruins) the castle overlooks is fake: Friedrich liked the look of what was left of the Roman Forum, so he decided to bring it closer to home. In a macabre reunification gesture, Friedrich's remains, spirited away in 1945 to a salt mine near Tübingen to save them from the Red Army, were brought back to the grounds in 1991. He's buried to the right of the Schloß in a plot of grass under six plain flagstones. *(Tel. 969 41 90. Streetcar #96 or 98 to "Schloß Sanssouci." Open April-Oct. daily 9am-5pm; Feb.-March 9am-4pm; Nov.-Jan. 9am-3pm. DM10, students DM5, or free with a day ticket.)*

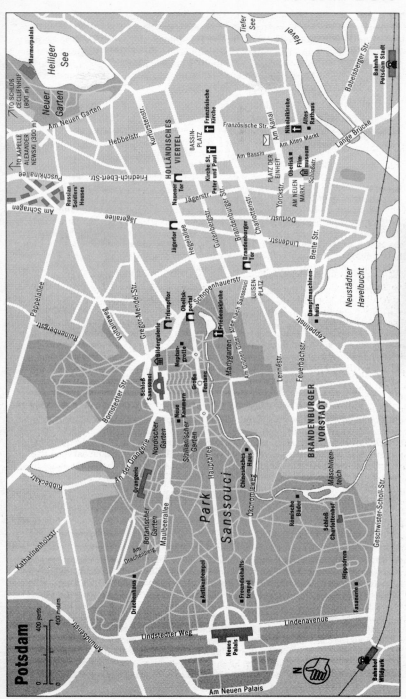

Potsdam

BRANDENBURG

NEUES PALAIS. At the opposite end of the park is the largest of the four royal castles, the 200-room Neues Palais, which was built by Friedrich to demonstrate Prussia's power and, incidentally, to house his guests. Inside is the 19th-century **Grottensaal,** a reception room whose ribbed walls glitter with seashells, and the **Schloßtheater,** which has occasional summer performances of plays, ballets, and concerts. *(Tel. 969 42 55. Open M-Th and Su April-Oct. 9am-5pm; Nov.-March 9am-4pm. DM6, students DM4. Tours DM2 extra.)*

AROUND THE PARK. Next door to the Neues Palais lies the **Bildergalerie,** whose collection of Caravaggio, van Dyck, and Rubens (some of them copies—but still impressive) recently opened after extensive restoration with gorgeous results. *(Tel. 969 41 81. Open mid-May to mid-Oct. Tu-Su 10am-noon and 12:30-5pm; closed 4th Wednesday of each month. DM4, students DM2, or free with a day ticket.)* On the other side of Schloß Sanssouci lie the **Neue Kammern,** which served as the guest house and recital hall for the dilettante king. *(Open mid-May to mid-Oct. M-Th and Sa-Su 10am-noon and 12:30-5pm; April to mid-May and mid-Oct. to early-Nov. Sa-Su only 10am-5pm. DM5 with a tour, DM4 without, students DM2.)* The former ball and festival rooms are lavishly decorated; check out the Hohenzollern porcelain collection in a huge gold-trimmed closet room. Romantic **Schloß Charlottenhof,** whose park surroundings were a Christmas gift from Friedrich Wilhelm III to Friedrich Wilhelm IV, melts into landscaped gardens and grape arbors at the south of the park. Nearby lie the **Römische Bäder** (Roman baths). Overlooking the park from the north, the pseudo-Italian **Orangerie-schloß** is famous for its 67 dubious Raphael imitations—they replace originals swiped by Napoleon. *(Open mid-May to mid-Oct. 10am-12:30pm and 1-5pm. Closed 4th Thursday of every month. DM6, students DM3.)* The most "exotic" of the park's pavilions is the gold-plated **Chinesisches Teehaus,** complete with a rooftop Buddha toting a parasol. Inside, get a glimpse of the 18th-century *chinoiserie* porcelain or sip tea in the café. *(DM2.)* For some relative plainness, visit the **Friedenskirche** at the east entrance to the park. Friedrich Wilhelm IV and his wife Elizabeth are "encrypted" below the glittering mosaics. *(Free organ concerts W and Sa at 4pm.)*

BRANDENBURGER TOR. A smaller, vanilla cousin of Berlin's sits amid the traffic flowing through Luisenplatz. From here, Brandenburger Str. leads down to the 19th-century **Kirche St. Peter und Paul,** Bassinplatz (tel. 280 49 42), Potsdam's only Catholic church.

HOLLÄNDISCHES VIERTEL. Friedrich's attempt to import Dutch craftsmen in order to beautify the city produced the Dutch Quarter around Friedrich-Ebert-Str. The Dutch didn't like Potsdam much and departed after a few years, leaving their houses behind. The neighborhood fell into disrepair until 1990, when some savvy entrepreneurs came on the scene and converted it into a posh row of shops and restaurants.

NIKOLAIKIRCHE. Toward the waterfront on Friedrich-Ebert-Str., the impressive dome of the Nikolaikirche rises above its neighbors. On closer inspection, the dome and the granite cube it sits on don't seem to match. The interior was renovated à la GDR with glass and sound-tiles that somehow lessen the aesthetic impact. *(Am Alten Markt. Tel. 270 86 02. Open M 2-5pm, Tu-Sa 10am-5pm, Su 11:30am-5pm. Vesper music Su at 5pm.)*

NEUER GARTEN. Nuzzling the Heiliger See, Potsdam's second park contains several royal residences. The most worthwhile is **Schloß Cecilienhof,** built in the image of an English Tudor manor. Exhibits document the **Potsdam Treaty,** signed at the palace in 1945. It was supposed to be the "Berlin Treaty," but the capital was too bombed out to house the Allies' head honchos. Visitors can see the tacky rooms in which the Allied delegates stayed. *(Tel. 969 42 44. Open Tu-Su 9am-noon and 12:30-5pm. DM8 with a tour, DM6 without, students DM4.)* The garden also contains the **Marmorpalais,** a stunning heap of marble, as well as various "ancient" monuments such as an Egyptian pyramid and Greek temple, which were actually used for food storage. *(Marmorpalais open April-Oct. Tu-Su 10am-5pm; Nov.-March Sa-Su 10am-4pm. To get to the Neuer Garten, ride bus #694 to "Cecilienhof," or streetcar #96 to "Platz der Einheit," then streetcar #95 to "Alleestr.")*

RUSSISCHE KOLONIE. In the beginning of the 19th century, General Yorck brought 500 Russian soldiers to Prussia, and Friedrich Wilhelm III, a great fan of Russian culture and handsome soldiers, discovered that many of them had singing talent. Unfortunately, by the 1820s, only 12 of the original group were left—the rest died of homesickness. To mitigate the depressing atmosphere, Friedrich III built each soldier an ornate wooden house. The nearby onion-domed **Kapelle Alexander Newski,** designed by Karl Friedrich Schinkel, was also intended as compensation. *(Streetcar #92 (direction: "Kapellenberg") to the end and walk south along Nedlitzer Str.)*

OTHER SIGHTS. Potsdam has two other palace-parks. **Schloßpark Glienicke** contains a casino as well as its namesake, **Schloß Glienicke,** a less-than-stunning yellow-green affair built by Schinkel in 1828 for Prince Karl of Prussia. Berliner Str. leads through to the **Glienicker Brücke** (a.k.a. "The James Bond Bridge"), which used to be swallowed up by the death strip between the GDR and West Berlin. Until 1989, it was used for the exchange of spies, at which time it was known rather ironically as the "Bridge of Unity." *(Take streetcar #93 (direction: "Glienicker Brücke") to the end and walk back across the bridge.)* Nearby, **Park Babelsberg** houses its own Schinkel palace, **Schloß Babelsberg,** as well as the **Flatowturm,** a tower overlooking the park and surrounding Havel river. *(S-Bahn #7 to "Babelsberg.")*

🏛 MUSEUMS

FILMMUSEUM. Housed in an old Orangerie that once held Friedrich's stables, the film museum documents Babelsberg's glory days as a film mecca with artifacts like Marlene Dietrich's costumes and a silent film archive. *(Tel. 27 18 10. On the corner of Breite Str. and Schloßstr. Open Tu-Su 10am-6pm. DM4, students DM2. Movies M-F from 2pm, Sa-Su from 3pm. DM7, students DM5.)*

FILMSTADT BABELSBERG. Back in the Golden Age of European cinema, the **UFA-Fabrik** in Babelsberg was *the* German studio, giving Marlene Dietrich, Hans Albers, and Leni Riefenstahl their first big breaks; in addition, Fritz Lang made *Metropolis* here. Tragically, apart from the films, few memorials of this era remain. The Disneylandish Filmstadt Babelsberg, built on the UFA lot, makes a feeble attempt to commemorate the greats of early German cinema, dishing out family fun of the worst sort in the form of video arcades and gift shops. Say hi to the glitzy stars of *Gute Zeiten, Schlechte Zeiten,* Germany's favorite prime time soap opera. *(August-Bebel-Str. 26-52. Tel. 721 27 50. Hop on S-Bahn #7 to "Babelsberg," then take bus #690 or 692 to "Ahornstr." Open April-Nov. daily 10am-6pm. DM25, students DM18.)*

BRANDENBURG

One-thousand-year-old Brandenburg has long been reluctant to wield its power; even when it was capital of the province to which it lends its name, it allowed Berlin civic freedom. When Albrecht the Bear built the town's cathedral in 1165, the surrounding city became the region's political epicenter. The city's industry took off during the 19th century, when the Brennabor bicycle factory and the Lehmann toy factory first began churning out their wares. Today, Potsdam has officially usurped Brandenburg's political limelight, as its flashy palaces outshine Brandenburg's quieter good looks, leaving the town to fade gently into obscurity. Reconstruction of the decaying buildings is proceeding slowly, and the winding cobblestoned streets are wistfully quiet. Anyone who is a fan of elegant roof tiling and strange, meandering canals can happily take up residence in this small town.

⛴ PRACTICAL INFORMATION. Two routes run to Brandenburg from Berlin: hop on trains heading toward Magdeburg and Hannover (DM11), or take S-Bahn #3 or 7 to "Potsdam-Stadt," then change to RB #33 (40min., DM7). The **tourist office,** Hauptstr. 51 (tel. 194 33; fax 22 37 43; email info@stadt-brb.de; www.stadt-brb.de), is just off Neustädter Markt. From the train station, walk along Große Gartenstr., follow it turning right onto Jakobstr. until it turns into Steinstr., and head left on

Hauptstr. Or take streetcar #1, 2, or 9 from the station to "Neustädter Markt." The immensely helpful staff will answer questions and book **rooms** for free. Private rooms run DM30 for singles, DM40 for doubles. The office also runs city **tours** and distributes free maps and brochures in English. (Open M-W and F 9am-7pm, Th 9am-8:30pm, Sa 10am-2pm.) The **telephone code** is 03381.

▌ ACCOMMODATIONS AND CAMPING. The **Jugendherberge "Walter Husemann" (HI),** Havelstr. 7 (tel./fax 52 10 40), sits on a tiny island right across from the Dom's Domlinden entrance. Bus B also stops near here; get off at "Domlinden," and walk one block toward the Dom to Havelstr., which is on your right opposite the Dom. The rustic streamside locale and old volleyball nets in back transcend backwaterhood; this is charm, *Ossi* style. When the hostel is booked, they've been known to provide overflow housing in tents outside for DM12 per night. (DM18, over 26 DM23. Members only. Breakfast included. Reception 7-9am and 5-7pm. Curfew 10pm, but you can get a key. No English spoken. Closed Dec. 19-Jan. 4.) For cushier digs, head to **Pension Engel,** Große Gartenstr. 37 (tel. 20 03 93; fax 20 03 94), across the streetcar tracks from the train station. The *Pension* features basic, quiet rooms with phone and TV as well as a restaurant downstairs. (Doubles DM90-100, triples DM105-165.) Or try **Pension Blaudruck,** Sternstr. 21 (tel. 22 57 34; fax 52 42 22). Call ahead because it's got so much character—and so few rooms. (Singles DM40, doubles DM80.) **Campingplatz Malge** (tel. 66 31 34) is in the middle of the woods, but only 20 minutes away from the city center. Take Bus B from Neustädter Markt; ask the driver to let you off at the campground. (DM6.50 per person. DM6-10 per tent. 2- and 4-person bungalows DM15-20. Showers included. Reception 9am-8pm. Open April-Oct.)

▐ FOOD. Inexpensive restaurants line the pedestrian area of **Hauptstraße,** which also features a **Spar supermarket,** Hauptstr. 39 (open M-F 8am-6pm, Sa 7-11am), and an open-air **farmers' market** (open daily 8am-6pm) behind the Katharinenkirche. For longer hours, head to **Nimm's mit,** in the train station behind the bike racks as you exit. (Open M-F 6am-10pm, Sa-Su 8am-10pm.) Delicious, starchy meals await at the appetizingly named **Kartoffelkäfer** (potato beetle), Steinstr. 56 (tel. 22 41 18). It's a short walk from Neustädter Markt, or take bus #9 to "Steinstr./Kino." Substantial meals cost about DM8; *very* substantial meals run DM10-18. **Blaudruck Café und Weinkeller,** Steinstr. 21 (tel. 22 57 34) has piles of appealing blue fabric and somewhat pricey meals (DM8-18). Follow the barrels to the wine cellar for a DM6 glass of the good stuff. **Pizzeria #31,** Steinstr. 31 (tel. 22 44 73) offers large and very large pizzas for under DM10. Wash down all that nummy dough with cheap beer. (DM2.70. Open M-Sa 11am-2:30pm and 5-10pm, F-Sa 11am-2:30pm and 5-11pm.)

▐ SIGHTS. Brandenburg is surrounded by lush greenery and water. The river Havel, dotted with rowboats, flows gently by the **Dom St. Peter und Paul,** Burghof 11 (tel. 20 03 25), begun in Romanesque style in 1165, completed in Gothic style, and currently being refashioned in late-20th-century-construction-site style, with red bricks swaddled in green netting, and hairy construction workers temporarily replacing the removed gargoyles. Before this modern overhaul, architect Friedrich Schinkel couldn't resist adding a few touches: the "Schinkel-Rosette" and the window over the entrance. The cathedral's many wings fold off from the center into darkness, ending in little rooms like the 1235 frescoed, crypt-like **Bunte Kapelle.** (Open M-Tu and Th-F 10am-4pm, W 10am-2pm, Sa 10am-6pm, Su 11am-6pm.) The **Dommuseum** inside displays an array of vestments and local-history treasures. (Open Tu-Sa 10am-4pm, Su noon-4pm. DM3, students DM2.) To get to the Dom from Neustädter Markt, walk down Neustädtische Fischerstr. for 10min., or take bus A or B to "Domlinden." Back on Neustädter Markt, the **St. Katharinenkirche,** built at the end of the 14th century, is a beautiful example of *Backstein* (glazed brick) Gothic, now pockmarked by war damage. The carved altar dates back to 1474. (Open daily 11am-6pm.) Also near the Markt, the 14th-century **Steintorturm**

(tel. 20 02 65) on Steinstr. holds a town history museum and a steep stairway that knots its way to the parapet lookout like a small intestine. The summit offers an excellent vantage point for surveying Brandenburg and its many construction sites, but the stairs aren't much fun for anyone with an irrational fear of being digested by a tower-shaped monster. A monument outside the tower commemorates soldiers who died in WWII. (Tower open Tu-F 9am-5pm, Sa-Su 10am-5pm. DM4, students DM2, family pass DM8.) For 500 years, a 6m statue of the legendary hero **Roland** has stood in front of the **Rathaus**—the GDR-era was just a ripple in time to this medieval symbol of free commerce. Several remaining towers from the 12th-century city walls add historic flavor to the Altstadt and the streets around **Neustädter Markt.** Incidentally, Neustadt (new town) is a relative term—it was founded in 1196.

SPREEWALD (SPREE FOREST)

The Spree River splits apart about 100km southeast of Berlin and branches out over the countryside in an intricate maze of streams, canals, meadows, and primeval forests stretching over 1000 square kilometers. This is the home of the legendary **Irrlichter,** German wood sprites who light the waterways for travelers who lose their way and lead those who refuse to pay to their deaths. Smart travelers now outwit the Irrlichter by warding them off with brightly colored travel guides.

Folklore, tradition, and wildlife blossom in tiny villages and towns first settled in the Middle Ages. Hire a barge, rent a paddle boat, or take to the trails by foot or bicycle to see why locals insist that the Spreewald—not Amsterdam, Stockholm, or St. Petersburg—is the true "Venice of the North." Although the Spreewald lacks the urbanity of its Italian cousin, its canals are in just as constant use: farmers row to their fields and noisy children paddle home from school. The fields and forests teem with owls, kingfishers, otters, and foxes, animals known to most Europeans only through textbooks or television documentaries. In contrast to the streets of Berlin or the concrete monuments of other East German cities, the Spreewald is strikingly idyllic.

The forest was hit hard by history; Prussian monarchs cut down the trees to make furniture, and occasionally burned historical buildings to settle disputes over their political competence. The GDR era was particularly insensitive to the well-being of the trees—"the People" apparently preferred factories. However, reunification has brought the mixed blessing of greater environmental protection and hordes of forest-trampling tourists. The Spreewald is now recognized as a *Biosphärreservat* (a biosphere nature reserve) by the U.N. Some sections of the forest are closed to the public; other sections are closed during mating and breeding seasons, but not tourist season. Guided tours are offered by reservation, camping spots abound, bicycles can be rented everywhere, and excellent hiking trails and footpaths weave their way through the peaceful forest. Each local tourist office has information on these leisure activities. They won't let you forget, however, that the forest is protected by the government; tourists are urged to be environmentally responsible.

Lübben and **Lübbenau,** two tiny towns that open up into the labyrinths of canals that snake through the forest, are the most popular tourist destinations and lie within daytrip range of Berlin. The **Sorbs,** Germany's native Slavic minority, originally settled the Spreewald region and continue to influence its cultural identity (see **The Absorbing Sorbs,** p. 168).

LÜBBEN (LUBIN)

A good base for excursions in the Spreewald, Lübben attracts scores of tourists eager to explore its hiking trails or paddle through the maze of canals which link the city to its neighbors. Pack your backpack, chomp on some juicy *Gurken* (cucumbers, the region's specialty), and get ready for an adventure.

BRANDENBURG

⚄ PRACTICAL INFORMATION. Lübben is located along the Cottbus-Berlin rail line, making the city easily accessible by **train**. The tiny station is a gateway to Berlin (1hr., 1 per hour, DM15), Cottbus (30min., 1 per hour, DM10), and nearby Lübbenau (10min., every 30min., DM4.60). Rent **bikes** at the station for DM10 per day (open daily 7am-9pm) or at the tourist office. (DM1.50 per hour, DM10 per day. ID deposit required.) For a **taxi** call 37 16. The **tourist office** (Spreewaldinformation), Ernst-von-Houwald-Damm 15 (tel. 30 90; fax 25 43), spreads Spreewald love. From the station, head right on Bahnhofstr., then make a left on Luckauer Str., cross the two bridges, and you'll be on Ernst-von-Houwald-Damm. The office is on the right, next door to the castle tower. The staff finds **rooms** for a DM5 fee (DM10 over the phone). The office charges DM2.50 for a good **map,** but it's worth avoiding a mapless meander through town. During winter months and after hours, the office posts a list of private rooms just outside the entrance. (Office open M-F 10am-6pm, Sa 10am-4pm, Su 10am-1pm.) The **post office,** 15907 Lübben, awaits at Poststr. 4. The **telephone code** is 03546.

⚃ ACCOMMODATIONS AND CAMPING. The **Jugendherberge Lübben (HI),** Zum Wendenfürsten 8 (tel./fax 30 46), is located in the middle of a wheat field on the outskirts of town. Although in the middle of nowhere, the hostel itself is a dream, with cozy 4- to 10-bed rooms, nightly entertainment (watching cows stumble into electric fences), and a hip regular crowd of sharply dressed *Schulmädchen.* To get there, follow Bahnhofstr. to its end and turn left onto Luckauer Str. Turn right onto Burglehrstr. before the big crossing and right again onto Puschkinstr. Follow it until it splits, take the road on your left, and walk straight for miles. (DM21, over 26 DM26. Sheets DM6. Reception 9am-7pm. No curfew—not that it really matters.) It takes a good 30 minutes to reach **Spreewald-Camping Lübben** (tel. 70 53; fax 18 18 15). From the station, turn right on Bahnhofstr., left on Luckauer Str., right on Burglehrstr., and continue along the footpath to the campground. (DM6 per person; DM5-8 per tent. 4-person cabins DM30. Reception 7am-10pm. Open mid-March to Oct.) If you think your body deserves more than a bed in a dorm or tent, try **Pension Klauß,** Wiesenweg 8 (tel. 72 88). From the station, bear right and follow Bahnhofstr. until it ends. Turn left onto Luckauer Str., left again onto Lindenstr., and go straight. Count the bridges; after you have crossed four of them, look out for Wiesenweg, which should appear on your left just behind a gas station. Comfortable rooms urge you to forget about nature, stretch out, and turn on the TV. (DM35 per person. Breakfast included. Call ahead if you plan to arrive after 8pm.)

⚅ FOOD. While you're in Lübben, be sure to sample the Spreewald's particular pickled delicacies, famous throughout Germany. **Gurken Paule,** Ernst-von-Houwald-Damm, is an outdoor stand offering the freshest of the Spreewald's unique assortment: *Salzdillgurken* (salty), *Senfgurken* (mustard), and *Gewürzgurken* (spicy). Expect to pay about DM0.30 per pickle, or DM5 for a jar. (Open daily 9am-6pm.) For something warm, visit **Goldener Löwe,** Hauptstr. 14 (tel. 73 09), which serves a variety of fish dishes and local specialties like the simple but mouth-watering *Quark mit Leinöl, Zwiebeln und Kartoffeln* (cottage cheese with onion and potatoes; DM9). The walls are decorated by paintings of Spreewald sprites and other legendary beings, including a portrait of the *Irrlichter.* (Open 10am-10pm.)

⚁⚄ SIGHTS AND HIKING. The Altstadt's architectural pride is the newly restored **Paul-Gerhardt-Kirche,** named for the most famous German hymn writer since Martin Luther. (Open May-Aug. W 10am-noon and 3-5pm.) Gerhardt is buried inside. The entrance to Lübben's lush green park, **Der Hain,** is at the end of Breite Str. Most of Lübben's attractions, however, lie outside the town in the surrounding forests—grab a bike, boat, or your own two feet and start exploring. The **Fährmannsverein Lübben/Spreewald,** Ernst-von-Houwald-Damm 15 (tel. 71 22), offers **boat trips** exploring different regions of the Spreewald (open daily 9am-4pm; 1½-

8hr., DM4-5 per hour). Trips depart from the Strandcafé Lübben after 9am; boats leave when full. Make a left out of the tourist office and the café will be on your left. The **Fährmannsverein "Flottes Rudel,"** Eisenbahnstr. 3 (tel. 82 69), offers boat and barge trips with picnics starting daily at 10am. Alternatively, rent a **boat** at **Bootsverleih Gebauer** (tel. 71 94) on Lindenstr. From the tourist office, go straight and turn right just before the bridge. (Boat rentals from DM7 per person per hour. Everyone must know how to swim. Lifejackets provided for children. ID required. Open daily April-Sept. 9am-7pm; Oct.-March 10am-7pm.)

LÜBBENAU (LUBNJOW)

Tiny Lübbenau is the most famous and perhaps the most idyllic of the Spreewald towns. For many tourists (and there are tons), the village serves as a springboard for trips into the kingdom of the *Irrlichter*. The winding streets of the town center open directly onto the wooded paths and villages of the upper forest. The landscape here is much denser than that around Lübben, and it is intricately interwoven with canals.

⚡ PRACTICAL INFORMATION. Lübbenau lies 13km past Lübben on the Berlin-Cottbus line. **Trains** depart for Berlin (1½hr., 1 per hour, DM15.30), Cottbus (1hr., 1 per hour, DM9.60), and Lübben (10min., every 30min., DM 4.60). For a **taxi** call 31 43. **Kowalski,** Poststr. 6 (tel. 28 35), near the station, rents **bikes.** (Open M-Sa 9am-6pm. DM10 per day.) Rent your own **paddle boat** at **Manfred Franke,** Dammstr. 72 (tel. 27 22). From the station, turn right down Bahnhofstr. and left at the next intersection. (Open April-Oct. daily 8am-7pm. DM3-6 per hour.) The **tourist office,** Ehm-Welk-Str. 15 (tel. 36 68; fax 467 70), at the end of Poststr., provides maps and finds **rooms** (DM25-45) for a DM5 fee. (Open M-F 9am-4pm.) In an **emergency,** call 81 91 or 22 22. The **telephone code** is 03542.

▮▯ ACCOMMODATIONS AND FOOD. Even though the closest hostel is in Lübben (10min. by train), finding a room isn't a problem in friendly Lübbenau. Check for *Zimmer frei* signs or ask for the *Gastgeberverzeichnis* brochure at the tourist office. **Pension Erlenhof,** Lindenstr. 5 (tel. 460 73), is the cheapest *Pension* around. From the train station, turn left onto Bahnhofstr. and go straight until Wiesengrund pops up on your right. Take a right and then a quick left onto Lindenstr. (25min. Singles DM40, doubles DM70. Call ahead.) Directly on the road to Lehde, **Campingplatz "Am Schloßpark"** (tel./fax 35 33) offers 300 plots for tents with cooking and bathing facilities on site, as well as a store with soap, soup, pickles, and other necessities. (DM7 per adult, DM3.50 per child. Tents DM5-8. Bungalows DM55 for up to 4 people, DM14 for trailer spots. Bikes DM10 per day, boats DM25 per day. Reception 7am-10pm.)

For cheap food and pickles, beets, and beans by the barrel, check out the snack bars and stands along the harbor. Toward the campgrounds, **Café-Garten** (tel. 36 22), on the Lehde stream, is a self-service outdoor café with potato salad (DM2.50) and pike filet. (DM10.20. Open daily 9am-10pm.) In town, **Spreewald Idyll,** Spreestr. 13 (tel. 22 51), serves regional specialties like *Grützwurst* with potatoes (DM12.60), fish dishes (DM8-25), and salads (DM4-10).

▦▮ SIGHTS AND HIKING. The Altstadt is a 10-minute trot from the station. Go straight on Poststr. until you come to the marketplace dominated by the Baroque **Nikolaikirche.** The carved stone pillar in front served as an 18th-century crossroads post marking the distance in *Stunden* (hours), an antique measurement equalling one hour's walk. (Open M-F 2-4pm.) The requisite **Schloß** is now a handsome (but terrifically expensive) hotel and restaurant. The lush castle grounds are open to the public and shelter the **Spreewaldmuseum,** which offers an overview of the Spreewald and its unique customs. (Open April to mid-Sept. Tu-Su 10am-6pm; mid.-Sept. to Oct. 10am-5pm. DM3, students DM2.)

BRANDENBURG

There are two main departure points for **gondola tours** of the forest: the **Großer Hafen** and the **Kleiner Hafen;** follow the signs from the town center or from the train station. The Großer Hafen offers a larger variety of tours, including two- and three-hour trips to Lehde (DM8-9, children DM4). Longer trips (4-8hr.) cost around DM5 per hour. The boats take on customers starting at 9 or 10am and depart when full, continuing throughout the day. (2-9hr. DM8-17. No English tours, but hilarious if you speak German and can decipher the dialect.) From the Kleiner Hafen, at the end of Spreewaldstr., tours leave daily from 9am on and last 1½ to 10 hours. **Genossenschaft der Kahnfährleute,** Dammstr. (tel. 22 25), is the biggest boat tour company. (Open April-Oct. daily 9am-6pm.) Round-trips to Lehde last three hours and cost DM9 (children DM4.50); a 9hr. tour of the forest costs DM17 (children DM7).

It's only a hop and a paddle from Lübbenau to **Lehde,** a UNESCO-protected landmark and the most romantic village in the Spreewald, accessible only by foot, bike, or boat. On foot, it's a 15-minute trek; follow the signs from the Großer Hafen. If you're partial to water, take a boat from the harbor. Check out the **Freilandmuseum,** where things remain as they were when entire Spreewalder families slept in the same room and newlyweds spent their honeymoons heaving in the hay. (Open April-Oct. daily 10am-6pm. DM6, students and seniors DM4.) Just before the bridge to the museum, lies **Zum Fröhlichen Hecht,** Dorfstr. 1 (tel. 27 82), a large café, restaurant, and *Biergarten.* Sit upstairs on the wooden benches for a view of the languidly passing boats. Try *Kartoffeln mit Quark* (potatoes with sour curd cheese) in a special Spreewald sauce (DM10.50) or pickles with a side order of *Schmalz* (lard; DM1.70), another Spreewald "specialty." Say a prayer for your heart, and dig in. (Open daily 10am-5pm.)

COTTBUS (CHOŚEBUZ)

The second-largest city in Brandenburg, Cottbus looms to the east of the Spreewald near the Polish border. The city lacks the small-town charm of the Spreewald, but at the same time it falls way short of being a happening metropolis. The redeeming features, however, are the parks and gardens which surround this otherwise mediocre city. Cottbus's vibrant Sorb community makes itself visible through bilingual street signs and frequent celebrations of traditional Sorb festivals, which fill the capitalist-wannabe streets with colorful traditional costumes, music, and dance.

■ **ORIENTATION AND PRACTICAL INFORMATION.** Direct **trains** to Berlin (2hr., 2 per hour, DM33) and Leipzig (2hr., every 2hr., DM41) and **bus** lines to nearby hamlets make Cottbus the nexus for touring southeastern Brandenburg. The **bus station** is a 15-minute walk from the train station. Make a left out of the train station, head up the stairs, hang a right onto Bahnhofstr., and then a left on Marienstr. Or take streetcar #1 from the train station to "Marienstr." (two stops, DM1.30); the bus station is on the right. The **tourist office,** Karl-Marx-Str. 68 (tel. 242 54; fax 79 19 31), like many things in the town, is situated in a mall. The staff books **rooms** for a DM5 fee. Make a left out of the train station, head up the stairs and turn left over the bridge; then follow Bahnhofstr. until it becomes Karl-Marx-Str. at the intersection with Berliner Str. (Open M-F 9am-6pm, Sa 9am-2pm.) **Schenker,** Friedrich-Ebert Str. 15 (tel. 330 95), rents **bikes** from DM5. (Open M-F 9am-6pm, Sa 9am-noon.) The **telephone code** is 0355.

■ **ACCOMMODATIONS AND FOOD.** Cottbus's youth hostel, **Jugendherberge am Klosterplatz,** Klosterpl. 3 (tel. 225 58; fax 237 98), has clean and modern 3- to 10-bed rooms conveniently located near the Klosterkirche. From the train station, take streetcar #1 or 3 to "Stadthalle" and head up Berliner Str. toward the Altstadt; take a left on Wendestr., and go around the church. (DM20, over 26 DM25. Nonmembers DM30. Breakfast included. Reception M-F 8am-1pm and 7-9pm.) The **Pension** next door, Klosterpl. 2-3 (tel. 225 58; fax 237 98), is in an historic building embedded in the town wall. (Singles DM50-90; doubles DM85, with shower DM85-130. Breakfast included.) The **Wendisches Café,** August-Bebel-Str. 82 (tel. 253 27) serves local specialties like *Plinse* and *Kartoffelpuffer* (DM4.50-7. Open M-F 1:30-midnight, Sa-Su 2:30pm-midnight.) Romantic atmosphere and a beer await at **Café Altmarkt,** Altmarkt 10. (Tel. 310 36. Open daily 9am-1am.) On the other side of town, **Café Baum,** Marienstr. 6 (tel. 311 20), to the right of the bus station, serves all four food groups: coffee, wine, beer, and ice cream. (Open M-Tu, Th, and F 9am-late, W 6pm-late, Sa-Su 2pm-late.) For cheap eats, *Imbiß* stands line Spremberger Str. near the Altmarkt.

◙ ♫ SIGHTS AND ENTERTAINMENT. Cottbus, like most East German cities, was severely scarred by WWII. Fortunately, GDR tract housing has not penetrated the Altstadt, which is liberally sprinkled with historic buildings. Heading down Berliner Str., the church on the left is the **Klosterkirche** (tel. 248 25). Built in 1300 by Franciscan monks, it is the oldest church in Cottbus. (Open W and F 10am-4:30pm.) The **Altmarkt** lies a bit farther down Berliner Str. The **Niederlausitzer Apotheke,** Altmarkt 21 (tel. 239 97), first started dealing drugs in 1573. The shop still sells herbal teas and other potions, but the back offers a museum with a poison chamber. (Store open Tu-F 10am-5pm. Obligatory tours Tu-F 11am and 2pm, Sa-Su 2 and 3pm or by appointment. DM4, students DM2.) At the eastern end of the Altmarkt, Sandower Str. leads to the **Oberkirche St. Nikolai,** the largest church in the region and home to frequent concerts by local orchestras. (Open M-Sa 10am-5pm, Su 1-5pm. Tickets DM12, students DM6.) Sorbian culture buffs can head to the **Wendisches Museum,** Mühlenstr. 12 (tel. 79 49 30), down Spremberger Str., which houses Sorbian folk art and costumes, including the distinctive headdresses. (Open Tu-F 8:30am-5pm, Sa-Su 2-6pm. DM2, students DM1.) Farther down Spremberger Str. lies the petite **Schloßkirche.** The Huguenots who rebuilt it had no delusions of grandeur. At the end of the street, the Altstadt transmogrifies into the Neustadt. The 1908 cherub-sprinkled **Staatstheater Cottbus,** Karl-Liebknecht-Str. 23 (tel. 782 40), is Europe's only extant example of late-*Jugendstil* architecture. The program includes works by Verdi, Goethe, and Brecht; call 237 61 for tickets. (Ticket office open Tu-F 10am-6pm, Sa 10am-noon.)

While the inner city is somewhat congested, Cottbus is surrounded by a beautiful landscape. The riverside panorama leads to **Schloß Branitz** (tel. 75 15 21), a Baroque castle built in 1772 by Prince Hermann von Pückler-Muskau, a globetrotter with a love of nature and larger-than-life architecture. From the Altstadt, follow Spremberger Str. to Str. der Jugend, bear left at Bautzner Str., turn left at Stadtring, and right at Gustav-Hermann-Str., which leads to the park. (Open April-Oct. daily 10am-6pm; Nov.-March Tu-Su 10am-5pm.) The **Schloßpark** is perhaps the most impressive of the multitude of parks surrounding the city. A total of 100 hectares of green paradise is open to tourists. Sculptures, flowerbeds, tiny bridges, and fountains dot the marvelous landscape, with a few Egyptian pyramids thrown in for good measure.

BRANDENBURG

SACHSEN (SAXONY)

Sachsen is known primarily for Dresden and Leipzig, the largest cities in Eastern Germany after Berlin, but the entire region offers a fascinating historical and cultural diversity that reveals a great deal about life in the former East. The castles around Dresden attest to the bombastic history of Sachsen's decadent electors, while the socialist monuments of Chemnitz and the formless architecture of other major cities depict the colorless world of the GDR. On the eastern edge of Sachsen, the mountain ranges of the Sächsische Schweiz and the Zittauer Gebirge provide a respite from the aesthetic violence done by East Germany's city planners. Sachsen is also home to the Sorbs, Germany's only national minority, whose historical presence has infused a Slavic air to many of the region's eastern towns.

HIGHLIGHTS OF SACHSEN

■ **Dresden** is one of Germany's most compelling cities. Its sights, museums, and galleries will make you gasp, while the nightlife will leave you speechless (p. 153).
■ **Leipzig** fostered East Germany's biggest anti-government demonstrations in 1989. A key trade city, it harbors an edgy *Uni*-culture and Europe's largest train station (p. 176).
■ Climbing, hiking, and skiing abound in the **Sächsische Schweiz** (p. 165).

Sachsen (Saxony)

DRESDEN

Dresden pulses with a historical intensity that is both vicious and sublime. The city was one of the cultural capitals of pre-war Germany and oversaw many key movements in European history, from the meetings of Goethe, Schiller, and Beethoven in Gottfried Körner's estate to the architectural revisionism of the 1920s. Sadly, no matter where you go, you will be unable to forget the Allied bombings of February 1945, which claimed over 50,000 lives and destroyed 75% of the city center. Warming up to the efforts of reunification, Dresden today engages visitors with spectacular ruins in the midst of world-class museums and partially reconstructed palaces and churches, featuring the exemplary Baroque designs of city architect Matthäus Daniel Pöppelmann. Reconstruction is scheduled for completion by 2006, the city's 800-year anniversary. However, the expectant energy driving present-day Dresden is not built solely on nostalgic appeals to the past; revitalization and reinvention go hand in hand. Dresden enters the new millennium as a young, dynamic metropolis propelled by a history of cultural turbulence.

▉ GETTING THERE AND GETTING AROUND

TRANSPORTATION

Flights: Dresden's airport (tel. 881 33 60, 881 33 62, or 881 33 70) is 9km from town. **Airport City Liners** buses leave both stations for the airport every hr. (DM8); call 251 82 43 for schedules and information.

Trains: From the **Dresden Hauptbahnhof** (tel. (0180) 599 66 33, or use the computerized schedule center in the main hall), travelers shoot off to Leipzig (1½hr., 34 per day, DM33), Berlin (2hr., 20 per day, DM52), Munich (8hr., 24 per day, DM148), Frankfurt am Main (6hr., 11 per day, DM136), Budapest (11hr., 4 per day, DM125), Kraków (7hr., 3 per day, DM52), Paris (15hr., 15 per day, DM269), Prague (3hr., 7 per day, DM38), and Warsaw (8hr., 9 per day, DM55). Another station, **Bahnhof Dresden Neustadt**, sits on the other bank of the Elbe and bears a striking resemblance to its mate; trains leave for Bautzen (1hr., 1 per hour, DM15), Görlitz (2hr., 1 per hour, DM29), Zittau (2½hr., 1 per hour, DM29), and other Eastern cities.

Ferries: The **Sächsische Dampfschiffahrt** (tel. 86 60 90, schedule information 866 09 40) grooves with a restaurant, band, and dancing. Ships travel up and down the Elbe from Seußlitz in the north to the Czech border town Děčín in the south. Ferries to Pillnitz (2hr., DM22) and Meißen (2hr., DM26). Day pass DM28.

Public Transportation: Dresden is sprawling—even if you only spend a few days here, familiarize yourself with the major bus and streetcar lines. **Punch your ticket as you board.** DM2.70; 4 or fewer stops DM1.60. Day pass DM8; weekly pass DM24, students DM18 (student ID required). Tickets and maps are available from friendly *Fahrkarten* dispensers at major stops and from the **Verkehrs-Info** stands outside the Hauptbahnhof or at Postplatz (both open M-F 7am-7pm, Sa-Su 8am-6pm), as well as at Albertplatz and Pirnaischer Platz (open M-F 7am-7pm, Sa-Su 8am-4pm). Most major lines run every hour after midnight. Dresden's **S-Bahn** network reaches from Meißen (DM7.70) to Schöna by the Czech border (DM7.70). Buy tickets from *Automaten* in the Hauptbahnhof and validate them in the red contraptions; insert the ticket and press *hard*. Harder.

Taxis: Tel. 459 81 12 or 21 12 21.

Car Rental: Sixt-Budget, An der Frauenkirche 5 (tel. 864 29 72; fax 495 40 74), in the Hilton Hotel by the Frauenkirche. Open M-F 7am-8pm, Sa 8am-noon. **Europacar** (tel. (0180) 580 00) in the Hauptbahnhof near the Prager Str. exit. Open M-F 7am-9pm, Sa 8am-7pm, Su 9-11am. Offices also at Bahnhof Neustadt, to the left of the station and up the stairs. Open M-F 7:30am-6pm, Sa 8am-noon, Su 9-11am.

Bike Rental: Tel. 461 32 85. In the Hauptbahnhof near the luggage storage. DM10 per day. Open M-F and Su 6am-10pm, Sa 6am-9pm.

Mitfahrzentrale: Antonstr. 41 (tel. 194 40). From Bahnhof Neustadt, walk 400m along the train tracks to the right of the station. DM0.10 per km plus finder's fee. Berlin

SACHSEN

DM21. Frankfurt am Main DM45. Munich DM43.50. Call 1-2 days in advance. Rides to Western Germany are easiest to get. Open M-F 9am-7pm, Sa-Su 10am-2pm.

Hitchhiking: *Let's Go* does not recommend hitchhiking as a safe mode of transportation. Hitchers stand in front of the *"Autobahn"* signs at on-ramps; otherwise they are heavily fined or smacked by oncoming traffic. To Berlin: streetcar #3 or 13 to "Liststr.," then bus #81 to "Olter." To Prague, Eisenach, or Frankfurt am Main: bus #72 or 88 to "Luga," or bus #76, 85, or 87 to "Lockwitz."

⚜ ORIENTATION

The capital of Sachsen, Dresden stands on the Elbe River 60km northwest of the Czech border and 200km south of Berlin. The city of half a million people is a major transportation hub between Eastern and Western Europe.

Dresden is bisected by the Elbe. The **Altstadt** lies on the same side as the Hauptbahnhof; **Neustadt,** to the north, escaped most of the bombing, paradoxically making it one of the oldest parts of the city. Many of Dresden's main tourist attractions are centered between the **Altmarkt** and the Elbe. From there it's a five-minute stroll to the banks of the Neustadt. Five immense bridges (Marienbrücke, Augustbrücke, Carolabrücke, Albertbrücke, and the "Blue Wonder" Loschwitzbrücke) connect the city's two halves.

⁊ PRACTICAL INFORMATION

Tourist Office: Two locations: one on **Prager Str.,** just across from the Hauptbahnhof, and another on Theaterplatz in the **Schinkelwache,** a small building in front of the Semper-Oper. (Tel. 49 19 20; fax 49 19 21 16. Both offices open M-F 10am-6pm, Sa-Su 10am-2pm.) The staff books rooms and hand out free maps. Consider buying a **Dresden Card,** which provides 48hr. of public transit and free or reduced entry at many museums (DM26). There are several special hot-lines for **general information** (tel. 49 19 21 00), **room reservations** (tel. 49 19 22 22), **city tours** (tel. 49 19 22 30), and **advanced ticket purchases** (tel. 49 19 22 33).

Currency Exchange: ReiseBank, in the main hall of the Hauptbahnhof. Open M-F 7:30am-7:30pm, Sa 8am-noon and 12:30-4pm, Su 9am-1pm. 2.5-4.5% commission for currency exchange, depending on the amount; DM7.50 for traveler's checks. Other banks on Prager Str. After hours, the self-service exchange machine in the Hauptbahnhof will do, but the rates are poor.

American Express: Hoyerswerdaer Str. 20 (tel. 80 70 30), in Neustadt near Rosa-Luxemburg-Platz. Money sent, mail held, and other standard AmEx offerings. Open M-F 7:30am-6pm.

LOCAL SERVICES

Luggage Storage and Lockers: At both train stations. Lockers DM2-4. 24hr. storage DM4 per piece. Open M-F 6am-10pm, Sa 6am-9pm.

Bookstore: Das Internationale Buch, Kreuzstr. 4 (tel. 495 41 90), directly behind the Kreuzkirche. English books on the 2nd floor. Open M-F 9am-7pm, Sa 9am-2pm.

Library: Haupt- und Musikbibliothek, Freiberger Str. 33-35 (tel. 864 82 33), in the World Trade Center. From the Hauptbahnhof, bear left and follow Ammonstr. up to Freiberger Str. A conveniently located library with tons of info, maps, and books about Dresden and Sachsen, plus a cool café. Open M-F 10am-7pm, Sa 10am-2pm.

Women's Center: Frauenzentrum "sowieso," Angelikastr. 1 (tel 804 14 70). Open M 9am-1pm, Th 3-7pm. Telephone advice W 3-5pm (general) and 7-10pm (lesbian issues). *Frauenkneipe* (women's bar) open Th-Sa from 7pm.

Gay and Lesbian Organizations: Gerede-Dresdner Lesben, Schwule und alle Anderen, Prießnitzstr. 18 (tel. 464 02 20; 24hr. hotline 802 22 70). From Albertpl., walk up Bautzner Str. and turn left onto Prießnitzstr. Open Tu 10am-noon and 3-5pm, Th 3-5pm.

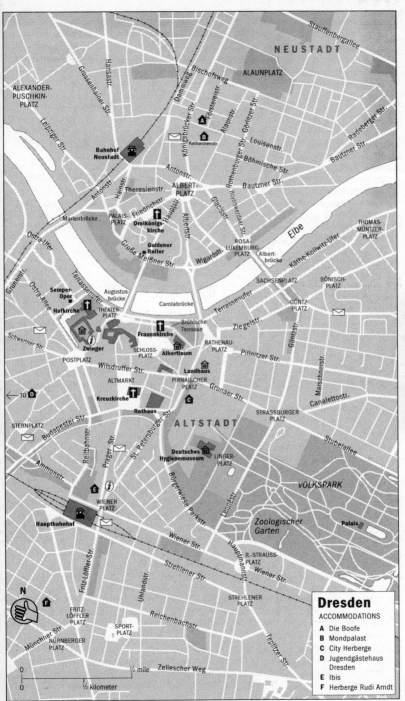

SACHSEN

Dresden

ACCOMMODATIONS

A Die Boofe
B Mondpalast
C City Herberge
D Jugendgästehaus
  Dresden
E Ibis
F Herberge Rudi Arndt

Laundromat: Groove Station, Katharinenstr. 11-13. A laundromat and much, much more. Wash your clothes (DM5, dry DM3, cup of coffee included) while shopping for leather, tattoos, piercings, drinks, or *Erektionsbekleidung* (condoms). Open Su-F 11am-2am, Sa 10am-late. **Öko-Express,** on Königsbrücker Str., right next to Albertplatz. DM3.50-5 per load. Open M-Sa 6am-11pm. Also at **Jugendherberge Rudi Arndt** (see **Accommodations,** p. 156) in the cellar. DM3-4 per load.

EMERGENCY AND COMMUNICATIONS

Emergency: Police, tel. 110. **Ambulance and Fire,** tel. 112.

Pharmacy: Apotheke Prager Straße, Prager Str. 3 (tel 490 30 14). Open M-F 8:30am-7pm, Sa 8:30am-4pm. When closed, a sign on the door indicates the nearest open pharmacies.

Post Office: The **Hauptpostamt,** Königsbrücker Str. 21/29, 01099 Dresden (tel. 819 13 70), is in Neustadt. Open M-F 8am-7pm, Sa 8am-1pm. **Postamt 72,** St. Petersburger Str. 26, is near the tourist office. Open M-F 8:30am-8pm, Sa 8:30am-noon.

Internet Access: Upd@te, Louisenstr. 30 (tel. 804 87 47). Close to Die Boofe (see **Accommodations,** p. 156). Speedy ISDN connections will make you bless modern technology. Keep in touch with the world for a mere DM10 per hour. Open M-F noon-8pm, Sa noon-2pm.

PHONE CODE	0351

▶ ACCOMMODATIONS AND CAMPING

If there's one thing that attests to Dresden's status as a city on the rise, it's the state of its accommodations. New hotels and hostels are constantly being planned, built, and opened, but come the weekend, it's hard to get a spot in anything with a good location. A 110-bed ship located at Leipziger Str. 57 was to have been opened in September 1999, a 10-minute walk from the train station in Neustadt. For information, or to reserve rooms, inquire at Rudi-Arndt (see below). Prices are likely to be DM25, over 26 DM30. In regular hotels, though, the reservation situation is just the opposite. The excess of available rooms means that you can often find same-day deals at some of the hotels on Prager Str. The tourist offices can also facilitate stays in private rooms and provide information on other accommodation options.

Mondpalast Backpacker, Katharinenstr. 11-13 (tel./fax 804 60 61), a 10min. walk from Bahnhof Neustadt, above Groove Station and DownTown (see p. 162). From Bahnhof Neustadt, walk down Antonstr. and turn left onto Königsbrücker Str. Cross the street and turn right on Katharinenstr.; the hostel is 100m ahead. A hostel created by backpackers for backpackers, located in the heart of the Neustadt scene but soundproofed for sweet dreams. The artfully decorated theme rooms, huge kitchen, absence of a curfew, and the brand-newness of the whole shebang make it a backpacker's paradise. 8-bed rooms DM25, 4-6 bed rooms DM27, doubles DM31 per person. Sheets DM5. Key deposit DM10. Internet access DM12 per hour. Breakfast DM8. 24hr. reception. Call ahead.

Hostel Die Boofe, Louisenstr. 20 (tel. 801 33 61; fax 801 33 62). Named after the caves in which Saxon hikers have taken rest for hundreds of years, Die Boofe has facilities that are even more sleep-friendly than the caves. A renovated apartment building set back in a small courtyard, this new hostel offers 54 beds in immaculate rooms in the middle of Neustadt. 2-5 bed rooms DM27. Sheets DM5. Breakfast DM8. Doubles DM39.50, sheets and breakfast included. Bike rental DM10 per day. 24hr. reception. Reservations recommended.

Jugendherberge Dresden Rudi Arndt (HI), Hübnerstr. 11 (tel. 471 06 67; fax 472 89 59). Streetcar #5 (direction: "Südvorstadt") or 3 (direction: "Plauen") to "Nürnberger Platz." Continue down Nürnberger Str., turn right onto Hübnerstr.; the hostel is at the first corner on the right. Or, from the Hauptbahnhof, walk down Fritz-Löffler-Str., bear right onto Münchener Str., turn right onto Eisenstuckstr. and walk up two blocks. Central, comfortable, and pacific with a laid-back staff. Crowded 3- to 5-bed rooms don't detract from the convenience. DM25, over 26 DM30. HI members only. Sheets DM5. Check-in 3pm-1am. Curfew 1am. Reservations recommended.

Jugendgästehaus Dresden (HI), Maternistr. 22 (tel. 49 26 20; fax 492 62 99), formerly the Hotel-Kongress-Business-Center, is now an authentic glimpse into pre-fab hotel living. Go out the Prager Str. exit of the Hauptbahnhof and turn left, following the streetcar tracks along Ammonstr. to Freiberger Str. Turn right and take another quick right onto Maternistr. Newly renovated with more than 400 beds, the hostel attracts lots of school groups. Rooms with washbasins DM33, over 26 DM38 per person; with private shower DM40, over 26 DM45. Single room DM15 extra. Breakfast and sheets included. Check-in after 4pm, check-out 9:30am. No curfew. Wheelchair accessible.

Pension Raskolnikoff, Böhmische Str. 34 (tel. 804 57 06), right above the restaurant and gallery of the same name. The *Pension* offers a good location in Neustadt, spacious rooms, 6 of them newly renovated, and reasonable rates. Double DM75, DM12 for every extra person. Call ahead.

City-Herberge, Lignerallee 3 (tel. 485 99 00; fax 485 99 01). From the Hauptbahnhof, walk up St. Petersburger Str., crossing over and using the right sidewalk. Turn right at Lignerallee. Central location with access to most major streetcar and bus lines. Practically a hotel, the rooms are crisp and well-appointed, though you have to share a bathroom. The grandiose breakfast buffet makes waking up a treat. May-June and Sept.-Oct. singles DM70, doubles DM100; all other times singles DM60, doubles DM80. Breakfast included. Reservations recommended.

Ibis Hotel, Prager Str. (tel. 48 56 66 61). Three huge hotel skyscrapers on Prager Str., just across the street from the Hauptbahnhof, offer summer same-day specials that are a good bargain for people traveling in pairs. Suites are appointed with TV, phone, and shower or bath. Doubles May-June and Sept.-Oct. DM130, DM110 all other times. Apartments (DM145-175) are a good deal for families. 24hr. reception.

Camping: Campingplatz Altfranken, Otto-Harzer-Str. 2 (tel. 410 24 00; fax 410 24 80). Thanks to the recent incorporation of Altfranken into Greater Dresden, the campground is no longer outside the city, and is now conveniently located next to a bus stop. From the Hauptbahnhof, take streetcar #17 (direction: "Gorbitz") to Tharandter Str., then bus #90 all the way to Altfranken. DM10 per tent. 24hr. reception.

FOOD

Unfortunately, the surge in Dresden tourism has yielded an increase in food prices, particularly in the Altstadt. The cheapest eats are at supermarkets or *Imbiß* stands along Prager Str. The Neustadt area, between Albertplatz and Alaunplatz, spawns a new bar every few weeks and clearly rules the roost of quirky ethnic and student-friendly restaurants. The free monthly *Spot*, available at the tourist office, details culinary options.

Raskolnikoff, Böhmische Str. 34 (tel. 804 57 06). A Dostoevskian haunt in a ramshackle pre-war brownstone. Hidden beneath a sign for *Galerie Raskolnikoff*. Russian and Afghan fare (DM8-20), from goat cheese (DM6) to flaming kippers (DM14.50) to *Srasi* (potato pockets with mushrooms, DM12.50). Open daily 10am-2am.

El Perro Borracho, Alaunstr. 70 (tel. 803 67 23). A tiny sparkle of sunny Spain under the heavy German sky. Try the tasty "mix & match" tapas and wash them down with sangría. All main courses DM12. Buffet breakfast before 4pm on weekends (DM10). Special deals for large groups. Open M-F 11:30am-1am, Sa-Su 10am-1am.

Café Aha, Kreuzstr. 7 (tel. 492 33 79), across the street from the Kreuzkirche. Come here if you need a refill of idealism. The restaurant celebrates healthy food produced by ecologically sound means. Each interesting dish (DM8-20) promotes the idea of "fair trade"; the café changes its menu monthly to introduce foods from developing countries who can't compete in the capitalist world market. Open daily 10am-midnight.

Planwirtschaft, Louisenstr. 20 (tel 801 31 87). One of the new and trendy restaurants in Neustadt. The orange interior and neon lights remind you that you are as alive as the German specialties you feel in your stomach. Try the pork chop with fried eggs and potatoes (DM14.50) or choose from a selection of fresh salads (DM7.50-13.50). English menu available. Open M-Th and Su 9am-1am, F-Sa 9am-3am.

Blumenau, Louisenstr. 67 (tel. 802 65 02). A busy place filled with cigarette smoke at night but quiet in the morning. One of the cheapest restaurants in Dresden. Menu changes unpredictably but most dishes run DM6-10; indulge in a portion of flatbread with caviar (DM15). Breakfast (DM5-11) served until 4pm. Open daily 10am-3am.

👁 SIGHTS

ALTSTADT

From the banks of the Elbe, the **electors of Sachsen** once ruled nearly all of central Europe. Destroyed during WWII and partly rebuilt during Communist times, the Altstadt carries the city's legacy as one of the Continent's major cultural centers. Presently a gigantic restoration project, slated for completion in 2006, aims to reestablish Dresden as one of Germany's most beautiful cities. Most of Dresden's celebrated sights are located near **Theaterplatz.**

ZWINGER. The extravagant collection of Friedrich August I, a.k.a August the Strong, Prince Elector of Saxony and King of Poland, is housed in this magnificent palace, designed by August's senior state architect, Matthäus Daniel Pöppelmann. Now championed as one of the most successful examples of Baroque design, the Zwinger complex once rivaled the Louvre. Today, hordes of tourists flock to view the Zwinger's array of decadent gates and pavilions. Some of the statues lining the palace grounds are still charred, though workers are busy sandblasting everything back to aesthetic perfection. The northern wing of the palace, a later addition, was designed by Gottfried Semper, revolutionary activist and master architect. Today the Zwinger is home to some of Dresden's finest museums (see **Museums,** p. 160).

SEMPER-OPER. Semper's famed opera house reverberates with the same robust style as the northern wing of the Zwinger palace. Its painstaking restoration has made it one of Dresden's major attractions. The interior is open for tours almost daily. Check the main entrance for tour times (usually mid-day) or call 491 17 05. *(DM9, students DM6, and it's worth every penny.)*

DRESDENER SCHLOß. Standing across from the Zwinger, the residential palace of Sachsen's Electors and emperors was ruined in the Allied firebombing of February 13, 1945, but now its restoration is nearly complete. Once the proud home of August the Strong, it features a display on the Renaissance and Baroque eras of the palace and the history of its reconstruction. The 100m tall **Hausmannsturm** hosts an exhibition of photographs picturing the destruction of the city in the February bombings and offers an excellent view of the city. *(Open Tu-Su 10am-6pm. DM5, students and seniors DM3.)* The **Katholische Hofkirche** (Catholic royal church) used to be connected to the Schloß. Ever-dependable August the Strong didn't fail in making himself a part of the church's history, this time by converting to Catholicism in order to obtain the Polish crown. Oh, and by donating his heart. It now occupies a little case stored safely in the church's crypt. *(Open M-Th 9am-5pm, F 1-5pm, Sa 10:30am-4pm, Su noon-4pm. Free.)* The **Fürstenzug** (Procession of Electors) along Augustusstr. is a mammoth (102m) mural made of 24,000 tiles of Meißen china which depicts the rulers of Saxony from 1123 to 1904. If you've been mistaking Friedrich the Earnest for Friedrich the Pugnacious, you may want to stop in here for a history lesson. Where's August the Strong? Why, in the middle of course.

FRAUENKIRCHE. Currently a massive cube of scaffolding covered in construction workers, the Frauenkirche was once Dresden's most famed silhouette until it collapsed after the bombings. For years the ruin remained a testament to the futility and horror of war. The reconstruction of the church began in 1994 and is the most complicated and expensive project of its kind in Germany. The ruin was carefully taken apart and each stone examined and catalogued, so that the new structure will be built with both new and original parts. Standing 25m tall at the moment, the building is scheduled to be completed by 2006.

BRÜHLSCHE TERRASSE. Running along the river, the Brühlsche Terrasse offers a prime photo opportunity of the Elbe. Within its casements alchemist Johann Friedrich Böttger was imprisoned by August the Strong until he finally solved the secret recipe for porcelain in 1707. Böttger had originally promised to produce gold, but had to settle for dainty teacups and cow-shaped creamers instead. The same Meißen china (see p. 163) which comprises the Fürstenzug (above) was Böttger's invention, and made for a booming German trade in porcelain.

KREUZKIRCHE. This church on the Altmarkt was the sight of the first Protestant celebration of communion in Dresden. Now the fourth church to be erected on the site, its rough plaster interior serves as a reminder of the war's devastation. Climb to the top for a bird's eye view of the colossal jigsaw puzzle of downtown Dresden. *(Open summer M-Tu and Th-F 10am-5:30pm, W and Sa 10am-4:30pm, Su noon-4:30pm; winter M-F 10am-4:30pm, Sa 10am-3:30pm, Su noon-4:30pm. Free. Tower closes 30min. before the church. DM2, children DM1.)* The church is also the home of the world-famous **Kreuzchor,** a boys' choir founded in the 13th century. *(Concerts Sundays at 6pm. DM2.)*

NEUSTADT

On the other end of the magnificent **Augustusbrücke,** the city *Let's Go* of its history and enjoys the present. A few worthwhile sights float in a sea of socialist architectural oddities and the area's busy cultural life.

GOLDENER REITER. A gold-plated statue of August the Strong is located near the former *Straße der Befreiung* (Liberation Street, referring to when Soviet troops overran Eastern Germany at the conclusion of WWII), now renamed **Hauptstraße** (Main Street) in a surge of nomenclatural genius. August's nickname was reputedly an homage to his remarkable (some might say unseemly) virility; legend has it he fathered 365 kids, though the official tally is 15.

DREIKÖNIGSKIRCHE. Near Hauptstr., the Church of the Magi is one of the oldest structures in the city. Inside, check out the *Dresden Danse Macabre*, a 12.5m Renaissance monument, below the organ. *(Open daily 10am-6pm. Free.)*

At the other end of Hauptstr., **Albertplatz** is surrounded by handsome 19th-century mansions, and marks the center of the Neustadt bar and restaurant scene.

ELSEWHERE IN DRESDEN

Dresden continues to surprise and impress farther away from the city center. Virtually untouched by the bombings, the outskirts of the city reverberate with spontaneity and local traditions. While the banks of the Elbe are perfect for a scenic stroll, the colorful architecture of the handsome mansions and villas is also well worth a visit.

SCHILLERHÄUSCHEN. This tiny cottage was where Beethoven first heard Schiller's "Ode an die Freude," which he later adapted for the finale of his Ninth Symphony. The house once belonged to Gottfried Körner, a well-to-do art patron who supported some of the greats during their stays in Sachsen. The *Häuschen* features a small museum of Schiller memorabilia. *(Schillerstr. 19., north of Körnerpl. in Loschwitz. Tel. 46 86 60. Open May-Oct. Sa-Su 1-5pm. DM1, students and seniors DM0.50.)*

BLAUES WUNDER. A 19th-century suspension bridge connecting Blasewitz and Loschwitz, the Blaues Wunder was the only bridge the Nazis didn't destroy on the eve of the Soviet invasion at the end of WWII. Take streetcar #1 (direction: "Tolkewitz") or 6 (direction: "Niedersedlitz"). **Körnerplatz,** on the Loschwitz side, remains one of Dresden's prettiest squares, with its artist colony ambience still partially intact. Beyond Körnerplatz is the **Schwebebahn** (overhead railway). The vintage construction offers stunning views of Dresden and the Elbe. *(DM4, DM6 return. Departs every 10min.)*

SCHLACHTHOFRINGE. The Schlachthofringe (Slaughterhouse Circle) is an original 1910 housing complex in a more dismal part of Dresden, commandeered during WWII as a camp for prisoners of war. Novelist Kurt Vonnegut was imprisoned here during the bombing of Dresden, inspiring his masterpiece *Slaughterhouse Five*. Take streetcar #9 (direction: "Friedrichstadt") to the last stop and walk up (don't do this at night). On the way, you'll pass one of Dresden's architectural oddities, the former **Zigarettenfabrik** (cigarette factory). Keep an eye out for its brown, stained glass dome. Built in 1907, it was modeled on a tobacco factory in Turkey, and now occasionally houses discos.

🏛 MUSEUMS

As reconstruction of the Zwinger and the Dresdner Schloß progresses, Dresden's museum exhibits are gradually moving back to their pre-war homes. If you're going to visit the Albertinum, the *Alte Meister* collections, or the Zwinger, it may be worthwhile to invest in the *Tageskarte* (DM12, students and seniors DM7), which covers one-day admission to the Albertinum museums, the Schloß, most of the Zwinger and a number of other sights. Purchase it at any of the major museums.

ZWINGER

Gemäldegalerie Alte Meister, Semper Wing. From the front portal, walk through the main courtyard to the building across the way; the museum is on the left. A world-class collection of paintings from 1500 to 1800. Cranach the Elder's luminous "Adam" and "Eve" paintings (see p. 24), and Rubens's erotically charged "Leda and the Swan" are only a few of the masterpieces. The Canaletto collections commemorate the magnificence of 18th-century Dresden. *(Tel. 491 46 19. Open Tu-Su 10am-6pm. DM7, students and seniors DM4. Tours F and Su at 4pm DM1.)*

Rüstkammer, across from the *Alte Meister* in the Semper Wing. An exhibit of the royal court's toys, including the knightly apparel that Sachsen electors donned for jousting tournaments. Most of the intricately decorated weapons would have been far too pretty to take into battle. What appears to be a collection of midget armor is, in fact, that of the Wettin (Windsor) family's toddlers. *(Tel. 491 46 19. Open Tu-Su 10am-6pm. DM3, students and seniors DM2, covered by admission to the Gemäldegalerie Alte Meister.)*

Porzellansammlung, entry across from the *Residenzschloß*. The "show-and-tell" centerpiece of Dresden, it traces Sachsen's porcelain industry through outlandishly delicate knick-knacks. Makes you feel like a bull in a china shop. *(Tel. 491 46 22. Open Su-W and F-Sa 10am-6pm. DM3, students and seniors DM2.)*

Mathematisch-physikalischer Salon, in the corner of the Zwinger courtyard closest to Postplatz. Europe's oldest "science museum" boasts a collection of historical scientific instruments—globes, clocks, atlases, etc. *(Tel. 491 46 60. Open Su-W and F-Sa 10am-6pm. DM3, students DM2. Not included in the Tageskarte.)*

ALBERTINUM

▧ Gemäldegalerie der Neuen Meister. Out with the *alt*, in with the *neu!* A solid ensemble of German and French Impressionists, including many Renoirs and Gauguins, leads into a collection of Expressionists and *Neue Sachlichkeit* modernist works hard to match. Check out Otto Dix's renowned "War" triptych and other works by Germany's finest 20th-century artists (see p. 24). *(Tel. 491 47 30. Open Su-W and F-Sa 10am-6pm. DM7, students and seniors DM4; includes admission to Grünes Gewölbe.)*

Grünes Gewölbe, on the second floor of the *Albertinum*. Provides a dazzling collection of the completely gratuitous refinements possessed by the House of Sachsen. A carved cherry pit with 185 tiny heads might be the most decadent miniature ever. *(Open Su-W and F-Sa 10am-6pm. Included in the admission to the Gemäldegalerie der Neuen Meister.)*

ELSEWHERE IN DRESDEN

Stadtmuseum. Located in the 18th-century **Landhaus,** the museum tells the story of the city since its beginnings in the 13th century, with special documentation of the 1945 fire bombings. Early history just can't compete with the collection of memorabilia from the Communist period, though: happy children flash their teeth in big bright smiles, propaganda posters make you love Stalin, and the 80s fashion collection will bring tears to your eyes. Across the wall, pictures, demonstration posters, and secret police files examine the more heroic side of the kitschy socialist era. *(Wilsdruffer Str. 2, near Pirnaischer Platz. Tel. 49 86 60. Open May-Sept. M-Tu, Th, and Sa-Su 10am-6pm, W 10am-8pm; Oct.-April daily 10am-6pm. DM4, students DM2.)*

Verkehrsmuseum. Dresden's transport museum rolls through the history of German transportation, from carriages to bullet trains and BMWs. Bizarre photographs of nude women decorate the hallways. The rest remains purely technical. *(Augustusstr. 1., in front of the Frauenkirche. Tel. 864 40. Open Tu-Su 10am-5pm. DM4, students and seniors DM2.)*

Museum zur Dresdner Frühromantik. A small museum celebrating the German cultural accomplishments of the late 18th and early 19th centuries. All you ever wanted to know about Weber, Kleist, Friedrich, Wagner, and the Schumanns. *(Hauptstr. 13. Tel. 804 47 60. Open W-Su 10am-6pm. Last entry 5:30pm. DM3, students DM1.50.)*

Karl-May-Museum. Dresden's Wild West. Karl May is a writer whose books about the 19th-century American West continue to charm generations of European children with Indians, buffaloes, and German cowboys who save the day. Includes a small exhibit devoted to the author. *(Karl-May-Str. 5. Take streetcar #4 (direction: "Weinböhle) to "Schildenstr." Tel. 837 30 10. Open Tu-Su 10am-4pm. DM8, children DM4.)*

Deutsches Hygienemuseum. This ill-named museum long celebrated the health and cleanliness of GDR Germans. Now that the Party's over, it exhibits models of our guts. *(Lingnerpl. 1. Tel. 484 60. Open Tu and Th-F 9am-5pm, W 9am-8:30pm, Sa-Su 10am-5pm. DM5, students and seniors DM3.)*

🎵 🎭 ENTERTAINMENT AND NIGHTLIFE

Dresden's nightlife scene is young and dynamic. Ten years ago, the area north of Albertplatz was but a maze of gray streets lined with tired, crumbling buildings, but Neustadt is the thudding heart of this fast-paced city. This lively neighborhood, where cool kids of every flavor come to shop during the day and partake in the *Szene* at night, comprises almost a full kilometer, roughly bounded by Königsbrücker Str., Bischofsweg, Kamenzerstr., and Albertplatz. At last count over 50 bars were packed into this area; *Kneipen Surfer* provides a list and description of every one. Peruse the back of *SAX* (DM2.50 at the tourist office, or ask to see one at any bar) to see what concerts and dances are coming up.

For centuries, Dresden has been a focal point of theater, opera, and music. The superb **Semper-Oper** premiered many of Strauss and Wagner's greatest, but tickets are hard to come by. From mid-July to September, many theaters close and students head for the hills, consequently diminishing the offerings. To help fill the gap, the **Filmnächte am Elbufer** (Film Nights on the Elbe) festival in July and August offers an enormous movie screen against the illuminated backdrop of the Altstadt. Most shows start at 9:30 or 10pm (DM10). Dresdeners will welcome the **year 2000** in style. Elaborate parties are still being planned, but it is expected that the frenzy will culminate at the free ■**Partypower auf dem Altmarkt** with music, dancing, fireworks, and megaliters of champagne.

CONCERTS, OPERA, AND DANCE

Sächsische Staatsoper (Semper-Oper), Theaterpl. 2 (tel. 491 17 30). See opera's finest in the most majestic of environs. The box office unloads tickets for DM5-20 1hr. before performances, but you have to get lucky; otherwise, call ahead or go to the tourist office for tickets (DM10-140). 50% student and senior discounts. Box office at Schinkelwache open M-F 10am-6pm, Sa 10am-1pm, and 1hr. before performance.

Kulturpalast, Am Altmarkt (tel. 486 60). Home to the **Dresdner Philharmonie** (tel. 486 63 06) as well as other small music groups and dance ensembles. Box office at Schloßstr. 2. Main entrance open M-F 9am-6pm, Sa 10am-2pm.

Staatsoperette Dresden, Pirnaer Landstr. 131 (tel. 207 99 29). Musical theater from Lerner and Loewe to Sondheim. DM10-34. Discounted shows Tu and Th. Ticket office open M 11am-4pm, Tu-F 11am-7pm, Sa 4-7pm, Su 1hr. before curtain.

THEATER AND CABARET

Schauspielhaus, Ostraallee 47 (tel. 491 35 67; box office tel. 491 35 55). Produces classics from Kleist to Shakespeare. Tickets DM25-40. Box office open M-F 10am-6:30pm, Sa 10am-2pm, and 1hr. before the show.

Schloßtheater, in the Dresdener Schloß (see p. 158; tel. 491 35 55). This small ensemble performs German classics in the Schloß. Tickets are available through the Schauspielhaus (see above) and the tourist office.

projekttheater dresden, Louisenstr. 47 (tel. 804 30 41). Experimental theater with an international twist in the heart of the Neustadt. So cool they don't use capital letters. Tickets DM20, students DM15. Box office opens at 8pm, shows at 9pm.

Die Herkuleskeule, Sternpl. 1 (tel. 492 55 55). Cabaret with an angry political outlook revels in blasting U.S. culture. Occasional special guests. Tickets M-Th and Su DM15-25, F-Sa DM20-30. Student discounts M-Th. Box office open M-F 1:30-6pm and 1hr. before performance.

Theater Junge Generation, Meißner Landstr. 4 (tel. 429 12 20). Shakespeare, opera, fairy tales, and more. Tickets DM10-14, 15-50% student discount. Tickets available M-Sa 10am-noon, extra hours W 2-6pm, F 2-7:30pm, and 1hr. before curtain.

Puppentheater der Stadt Dresden, in the Ufa-Palast on Prager Str. (tel. 496 53 70; fax 496 53 71). Children's performances during the day for young and old. DM6, children DM4, family ticket (up to five people) DM18. Occasional evening performance geared more toward adults DM12, students DM10. Box office open 30min. before shows on weekdays, 45min. before shows on weekends.

BARS AND CLUBS

Scheune, Alaunstr. 36-40 (tel. 804 55 32). From Albertpl., walk up Königsbrücker Str. and turn right onto Katharinenstr. Take a left on Alaunstr.; the club is on the other side of the street. The granddaddy of the Neustadt bar scene, in a former youth center. The culturally eclectic dance floor invites you to disco to West African roots and Baltic and Yiddish piano songs. Check *SAX* for what's happening. Frequent concerts. Club opens at 8pm. Cover varies.

AZ Conni, Rudolf-Leonhard-Str. 39 (tel. 804 58 58). From Albertpl., follow Königsbrücker Str. until the traffic lights. Turn left, walk under the railway bridge, and take a quick right. The club is 100m ahead. The club occupies an old kindergarten, but that doesn't stop the action from getting pretty naughty. The first floor is a nook-filled bar, and the second is a dance floor. Tu and Th are dance nights, and weekends frequently bring in concerts. Open daily 9pm until late. Cover varies.

■ **DownTown,** Katharinenstr. 11-13 (tel. 802 88 01), below the Mondpalast hostel (see **Accommodations,** p. 156). *The* place to shake your booty and indulge in Dresden's neon techno scene. One of the few night venues capable of convincing skeptics that some Germans *can* dance. Very popular straight, gay, and lesbian scene. In the upstairs **Groove Station** (see **Laundromat,** p. 154), patrons numb themselves with drinks before getting tattooed and/or pierced. F house and techno, Sa funk and occasional live music. M is *Valentinos Wunderbar,* a popular gay and lesbian party. Open 10pm-5am. Cover DM7, students DM5.

Die Tonne, Am Brauhaus 3 (tel. 802 60 17), boasts an offering of "cool drinks and hot jazz" for slightly more refined (read: twenty-something) entertainment. Fr is salsa night. Performances most nights at 9pm. Open daily 6pm-1am. Cover DM8-20; free M.

Studentenklub Bärenzwinger, Brühlischer Garten 1 (tel. 495 14 09), not far from the Albertinum. Head toward the Carolabrücke, but make a sharp left down a little hill just before reaching the streetcar stop. Students congregate in this bizarre tunnel under the Brühlsche Terrasse to nurse cheap drinks and partake in the disco action. Over 18 only. Bring student ID for discounts. Tu, F, and Sa are usually dance. Open Tu-Th and Su 8pm-1am, F-Sa 9pm-3am for live shows and dancing. Cover DM8-12.

Queens, Görlitzer Str. 3 (tel. 803 16 50). A popular gay bar. Drinks, music, and occasional special entertainment. F 70s/80s night. Open daily after 8pm.

Titty Twister, Kippsdorfer Str. 100 (tel. 316 01 50). Take streetcar #4 (direction: "Laubegast") to "Gottleubaer Str." The decor and the ambience are inspired by Tarantino's "classic" *From Dusk 'Til Dawn*. Beer, pool, vampires, and dancers (no, not Salma Hayek). Frequent live music. Open daily 7pm-3am. Cover DM8-10 for live shows and special parties.

NEAR DRESDEN: MEISSEN

Just 30km from Dresden, Meißen sits on the banks of the Elbe as yet another testament to the frivolity of August the Strong. In 1710, the Saxon elector developed a severe case of *Porzellankrankheit* (the porcelain "bug"—an affliction that continues to manifest itself in tourists today) and turned the city's defunct castle into a porcelain-manufacturing base. Those visitors who would otherwise feel little affinity for the craft indulge in a couple of glasses of Meißen's fine wines and soon find themselves toasting the beauty of "white gold" (china, not cocaine). Meißen has a distinct aesthetic advantage over its comrade Dresden; its medieval nooks and crannies were barely scathed by WWII.

The narrow, romantic alleyways of the Altstadt climb up to the **Albrechtsburg** (tel. 47 07 10), a castle and cathedral overlooking the city. (Open March-Oct. daily 10am-6pm; Nov.-Feb. 10am-5pm. Last entry 30min. before closing. DM6, students DM3.) From the train station, walk straight onto Bahnhofstr. and follow the banks of the Elbe to the Elbbrücke. Cross the bridge, continue straight to the Markt and turn right onto Burgstr. At the end of Burgstr., on Schloßstr., you'll find the stairs that lead to the right up to Albrechtsburg. If the bridge is closed, use the railway bridge and walk along the river towards the Elbbrücke. Follow Elbstr., continue straight to the Markt, and follow the original directions from here on. Alternatively, board a bus at the Markt to save yourself the walk up the hill. The castle foundations were first built in 929 to protect the area's Sorb population (see **The Absorbing Sorbs**, p. 168). The interior was lavishly redecorated in the 15th century, and once again when porcelain profits started pouring in. The fantastically decorated rooms also house an extensive medieval sculpture collection. Next door dwells the **Meißener Dom,** an early Gothic cathedral which ensures that its visitors get their money's worth with four priceless 13th-century **statues** by the Naumburg Master, a triptych by Cranach the Elder, and the beautiful metal grave coverings of the Wettins. (Open April-Oct. daily 9am-6pm; Nov.-March 10am-4pm. Last entry 30min. before closing. DM3.50, students DM2.50. Organ concerts May-Oct. daily at noon; DM4.)

Meißen's porcelain factory was once more tightly guarded than KGB headquarters for fear that competitors would discover its secret techniques. Porcelain was first discovered here in 1707, and today anyone can tour the **Staatliche Porzellan-Manufaktur** at Talstr. 9 (tel 46 82 07). The **Schauhalle** serves as a museum where visitors can peruse finished products (DM9, students DM7), but the real fun lies in the high-tech tour of the **Schauwerkstatt** (show workshop), which shows people working on different steps of the porcelain-manufacturing process. (Open daily 9am-6pm. DM5. English tapes available.) Meißen's Gothic **Rathaus** stands alongside the **Frauenkirche,** whose porcelain bells chatter every 15 minutes over the main market square. (Church open May-Oct. daily 10am-noon and 1-4pm.)

A puffed, almost hollow pastry, the *Meißener Fummel* owes its origin to August the Strong. One of his couriers was a spirited sort whose penchant for Meißen wine became known to the king. To keep tabs on his bacchanalian behavior, August ordered the Meißen bakers' guild to create an extremely fragile biscuit. The courier was to protect the *Fummel* from damage while delivering messages.

SACHSEN

Many Altstadt bakeries still sell this puffery. For less fluff, try **Zum Kellermeister**, Neugasse 10 (tel. 45 40 88). Most *Schnitzels* run DM6-12. (Open M-F 11am-9pm.) The farmer's **market** is on the Markt. (Open Tu-F 8am-5pm.) During the last weekend of September, Meißen frolics in merriment during its annual **wine festival.**

Meißen is an easy daytrip from Dresden by train (45min., DM7.70) or scenic cruise (round-trip DM25). The **tourist office**, Markt 3 (tel. 45 44 70; fax 45 82 40), is across the Markt from the church. Pick up maps or find a room in a private home (DM25-55) for a DM4 fee. (Open April-Oct. M-F 10am-6pm, Sa-Su 10am-3pm; Nov.-March M-F 9am-5pm.) Meißen's **Jugendherberge**, Wilsdrufferstr. 28 (tel. 45 73 01), is a crap shoot—its 45 beds are often booked. Should they have space, they'll put you up in a crowded five-bed room. From the station, cross the Elbe footbridge and take Obergasse to the end where it meets Plosenweg. Turn left and continue uphill until you see the small Edeka Markt; the hostel is across the street. An infrequent bus (line C/C; direction: "Dr.-Donner-Str.") runs from the train station up the steep hill. (DM18. Breakfast included. Sheets DM5. Reception M-F 7am-noon and 4-8pm, Sa-Su 4-8pm.) The **postal code** is 01662. The **telephone code** is 03521.

NEAR DRESDEN: MORITZBURG

Never one to be bashful about leaving his mark on the Saxon landscape, August the Strong tore down a little palace in 1723 and replaced it with ■**Schloß Moritzburg,** his titanic hunting lodge of ribaldry. The immense Schloß lounges arrogantly at the end of Schloßallee on an island in an artificial lake. Inside, lavish rooms and leering deer skulls commemorate the courtly hunting penchant, while the ornately embossed and painted leather wallpaper sets the standard for masculine, animal-killing prowess. A must-see is a portrait of one of Moritzburg's most "beautiful" oxen ever. To get to the Schloß from the *Schmalspurbahn* train station, join the pilgrimage out to the left and turn right on Schloßallee. (Tel. 873 18. Open April-Oct. daily 9am-5:30pm; Nov.-Dec. and Feb.-March Tu-Su 10am-5pm; Jan. open only Sa-Su 10am-5pm. DM7, students DM5.) Near the Schloß, the smaller **Fasanenschlößchen** was built by the great-grandson of August the Strong, Friedrich August III. Outside, sculptures of moose in tremendous pain remind you that this, too, is a hunting lodge. Unfortunately, the Fasanenschlößchen is closed indefinitely for repairs; ask the tourist office for information. From Schloß Moritzburg, follow Meißner Str. right until Große Fasanenstr.; the Fasanenschlößchen appears on the left. Farther down Große Fasanenstr., the structure peeking out of the forest is the **Leuchtturm** (lighthouse), which once served as a backdrop to the mock sea battles of the not-so-easily-amused princes. Moritzburg is also surrounded by extensive parks in addition to a huge gaming reserve and the **Sächsisches Langestüt** ("Saxon Stud-Farm"), where animals procreate almost as frequently as did August the Strong—that's over 300 children (see p. 159).

As the meeting place of *Brücke* artists from 1909 to 1911 (see p. 24), Moritzburg developed a rich art tradition. It continued to serve as a summer residence for many artists who came back to frolic in the waters. One of Germany's most-celebrated 20th-century artists, **Käthe Kollwitz** (see p. 24), resided in the region for a time: after Kollwitz's home in Berlin was bombed near the end of WWII, Prince Ernst Heinrich offered her a place of retreat here. Though Kollwitz passed away in 1945, only one year after her arrival, her house now holds the **Käthe-Kollwitz-Gedenkstätte**, Meißner Str. 7 (tel. 828 18). The museum showcases her powerful sculptures, woodcuts, and drawings, starkly and beautifully depicting the cruelty of war and poverty. Pictures and excerpts from her letters and diaries help fill in the gaps about the remarkable woman. (Open April-Oct. Tu-Su 11am-5pm. DM3.50, students DM2.)

The fastest way to Moritzburg from Dresden is by **bus** #326 (direction: "Radeburg") from Bahnhof-Neustadt to "Moritzburg, Schloß" (25min., DM5.20). The return trip runs from "Moritzburg, Markt" on Marktstr., parallel to Schloßallee. The most scenic route (but also the slowest, bumpiest, and noisiest) is the 110-year-old *Schmalspurbahn* (narrow-gauge railway) which leaves from Radebeul-Ost, accessible by S-Bahn to Meißen. (30min., 4 stops. S-Bahn and train DM7.40, students DM5.) Moritzburg's **tourist office**, Schloßallee 3b (tel. 854 10; fax

854 20), provides information on guided **tours** of the *Schloßpark*, concerts in the Schloß, horse-and-carriage rentals, and books rooms (DM30-40 per person) for a DM2 fee. (Open May-Oct. M-F 10am-5pm, Sa-Su noon-4pm; Nov.-April M-F 10am-5pm.) Eating in Moritzburg cries out for one thing: a picnic. The classical gardens behind the castle provide the perfect backdrop, and they never close. If you forget your basket, there's the **Edeka** supermarket, Schloßallee 13. (open M-F 8am-6pm, Sa 8-11am), or **Zum Dreispitz**, Schloßallee 5 (tel. 822 00), which offers *Sächsische* meat and mushroom dishes for DM10-20. (Open daily 11am-midnight). The **telephone code** is 035207.

PILLNITZ

August the Strong must have led a happy life. Among his many castles (almost as numerous as his mistresses), the magnificent gardens of **Schloß Pillnitz** (tel. 261 32 60) produce a singularly fantastic effect. The strongman inherited the nearly 300-year-old castle in 1694 and generously passed it on to Countess Cosel a few years later—who says *diamonds* are a girl's best friend? The Countess lived there from 1713 to 1715 until August decided to imprison her in the more poorly furnished Burg Stolpen and began the extensive remodeling that gave the complex its characteristic look. The turrets of the **Bergpalais** and **Wasserpalais** (modeled on Chinese architectural forms) swim in an amazing setting, surrounded on one side by the Elbe, and on the other by gardens in English, Chinese, and just plain decadent styles. The residences now house Dresden's **Kunstgewerbemuseum** (arts and crafts museum), some modern art displays, and lots of porcelain amidst the sumptuously sensual and suggestively salacious summer-like colors of the courtly rooms. Outside, brilliantly colored flowers heighten the mystical effect of the architecture. Concerts also take place in the garden during the summer; call for info. (Museum open May-Oct. 9:30am-5:30pm. *Bergpalais* and *Kunstgewerbemuseum* closed Mondays, *Wasserpalais* closed Tuesdays. DM3, students and seniors DM2. Grounds open daily May-Oct. 10am-6pm, Nov.-April 10am-4pm.) To reach Pillnitz from Dresden, take streetcar #1 (direction: "Tolkewitz") or 6 (direction: "Niedersedlitz") to "Schillerpl.," then jump on bus #85 and continue to Pillnitz. Alternatively, **Weiße Flotte** can get you there by boat. (2hr. DM22, children DM15.) Head straight through the main garden to the "Alte Wache" **tourist office** for maps, information, and tours. (Open daily 10am-6pm.)

SÄCHSISCHE SCHWEIZ (SAXON SWITZERLAND)

One of Eastern Germany's most beloved holiday destinations, the Sächsische Schweiz has become Germany's hottest national park since reunification. The region is "Swiss" because of the stunning landscape—striking sandstone cliffs emerge from dense vegetation, providing trails with an unusual intimacy, while sumptuous summits and excellent hiking beckon adventurous tourists. The national park is divided into two regions, the *vorderer Teil* and the *hinterer Teil;* both are easily accessible from the south with Dresden's S-Bahn #1, which runs along the Elbe River. The **Wanderwege** (footpaths) coil up the hills into the heart of the park, connecting all towns in the area in a spidery web. Vibrant, dense greenery and lovely landscapes make this uniquely beautiful yet inexpensive region a must-see for those convinced that Eastern Germany comes only in shades of gray. Visitors can obtain further information from the **Tourismusverband Sächsische Schweiz,** Am Bahnhof 6, 01814 Bad Schandau (tel./fax (035022) 49 50), or from the **Nationalpark-Verwaltung,** An der Elbe 4, 01814 Bad Schandau (tel. (035022) 900 60; fax 900 66). If you plan to explore more than one town in the region in a day, be sure to ask at a **Deutsche Bahn** information desk about the **Tageskarte** (DM8) and **Familientageskarte** (DM12), which allow unlimited travel on the S-Bahn, buses, and many of the ferries in the Sächsische Schweiz for a 24-hour period.

RATHEN AND WEHLEN

Upstream from Dresden, just around the first bend in the Elbe, the magnificent sandstone begins. The first cliffs are called *Die Bastei* and were once the roaming grounds of—you guessed it—August the Strong, King of Poland and Elector of Saxony. Closest to Dresden lies **Wehlen,** and on the other end of the Bastei you'll find **Rathen.** To get to Wehlen, hop on S-Bahn #1; from the Bahnhof, take the **ferry** (DM1.30, children DM0.90). A **tourist office** (tel. (035024) 704 14) in the Rathaus on the market finds rooms for free, and a list of accommodations is posted outside. (DM20-25. Open M-F 9am-6pm, Sa 9am-2pm.) There's not much in Wehlen apart from the trails to Rathen. One of the paths climbs up onto the Bastei and was a favorite of August the Strong's; look for the *Höllengrund an Steinern Tisch,* his mammoth dining table. The other path—shorter, easier, but much less impressive—is along the Elbe (45min.).

Once in Rathen, you'll find much more to do. Because of its location on the edge of the **Sächsische Schweiz national park,** hiking trails of all lengths and difficulties abound. Rathen also boasts the **Felsenbühne,** one of the most beautiful open-air theaters in Europe, with 2000 seats carved into a cliff and stone pillars looming over the stage. (Open 8am until 2hr. before rehearsal/event and 1hr. after rehearsal/event until 8pm.) To get there, walk into town from the ferry landing and take the first left; follow signs for "Felsenbühne." Tickets and schedules are available from the **Theaterkasse,** on the way to the theater. (Tel. 77 70; fax 77 735. DM6-39). A **tourist office** (tel./fax 704 22), upstairs in the *Gästeamt,* gives advice on hiking options and finds private rooms (DM25-35) for free. (Open M-F 9am-noon and 2-6pm, Sa 9am-2pm, closed Saturdays in winter.) The **telephone code** is 035024.

There are several options for accommodations. The most comfortable is the pricey **Gästehaus Burg Altrathen,** up the ramp near the ferry landing (tel. 700 37; fax 700 38), in a castle perched above the Elbe. (Singles DM40-45, doubles DM70-90, both with private shower.) For thriftier patrons, a *Bergsteigerzimmer* ("mountain climber's room") has a mattress for DM25. Alternatively, retreat back across the river on a ferry to the S-Bahn station, or continue on two hours to **Hohnstein.**

HOHNSTEIN

The small village of **Hohnstein** ("high stone" in old Saxon—the town sits atop a high, stony ridge), with its grand forest vistas on all sides, is linked to Rathen by two beautiful hikes through one of the national park's most stunning valleys. To get here from Rathen, follow the shorter (2hr.), more challenging path of the red stripe (the trail, not a Maoist paramilitary cadre), or the longer (3hr.) path of the green stripe. Or take the S-Bahn to "Pirna," and then bus #236 or 237 from the Bahnhof to "Hohnstein Eiche" (DM5.20).

The town encircles the **Naturfreundehaus Burg Hohnstein,** Am Markt 1 (tel. 812 02; fax 812 03), a fortress that holds a history and nature museum, lookout tower, café-restaurant, garden, and hostel. The hostel offers singles, quads, and titanic 6- to 18-bed rooms for the same price per person. (DM26-37, non-HI members DM33-37. DM1.20 tax per day. DM2 fee for stays under 3 days. Breakfast and sheets included. Reception open daily 7am-8pm.) The **Museum der Geschichte des Burg Hohnstein,** (tel. 809 87 or 812 02), also housed in the Naturfreundehaus, covers the history of the *Burg* with exhibits of medieval armor, weapons, and anti-fascist resistance in Dresden and the Sächsische Schweiz. The museum commemorates Konrad Hahnewald, the beloved father of Hohnstein's *Jugendherberge* (now the Naturfreundehaus) and later the first political refugee of the Hohnstein concentration camp. (Open daily April-Oct. 9am-5pm. DM2, ages 6-16 DM1, under 6 and patrons of the Naturfreundehaus free.) The **tourist office,** Rathausstr. 10 (tel. 194 33; fax 868 10), in the Rathaus, doles out information on the *Burg* and surrounding trails and finds rooms for free. (Open M and W-F 9am-noon and 12:30-5pm, Tu 9am-noon and 12:30-6pm.) The **telephone code** is 035975.

KÖNIGSTEIN

The next stop on the Dresden S-Bahn journey into the hills and dales of the Sächsische Schweiz is **Königstein**. The **Sächsische Dampfschiffahrt** boats also alight on these shores. Above the town looms the impressive **fortress,** whose huge walls are built right into the same stone spires that made the Sächsische Schweiz famous. (Open daily April-Sept. 9am-8pm; Oct. 9am-6pm; Nov.-March 9am-5pm. DM7, students and seniors DM5. English pamphlets at the information office within the castle.) Replete with drawbridges and impenetrable stone walls, this castle belongs on the list of legendary royal abodes. An oft-exploited retreat for the kings of Sachsen during times of civil unrest and marital discord (the Sachsen electors tended to flee faster than the French), it was later converted into a feared state prison; Nikolai Bakunin and **August Bebel** (see p. 11) were imprisoned here. During the Third Reich, it was used by the Nazis to stash stolen art, and between 1949 and 1955 it served as a juvenile correctional center. The complex now houses museums for everything from weapons to porcelain. The unobstructed view from the fortress is worth sweating for—from the city, it's a 40-minute struggle straight up from town; follow the signs to the well-worn uphill path. The cheesy **Festungs Express** tours Königstein as it drags up tourists too tired to make the trek. (Runs April-Oct. 9am-6pm. One-way DM4, children DM2; round-trip DM6, children DM3. Tickets available on board.) Rides leave from Reißigerplatz regularly, just to the right down Bahnhofstr. from the S-Bahn station. Paths also lead from the town up to the challenging 415m **Lilienstein,** hiked by August the Strong in 1708. To get there, take the ferry (DM1.30) and the first right after getting off. Stay on this paved road until you see a sign for "Lilienstein" marked with a blue stripe. The steep 2km hike takes 1½ hours.

The **tourist office,** Schreiberberg 2 (tel. 682 61; fax 688 87), two blocks uphill from the Festungs Express stop, books rooms (DM25-45), but in summer it's wise to call ahead. In addition to housing a brand-new **post office,** the office has a list of available rooms, vacation houses, and *Pensionen;* prices are listed in the window when they're closed. (Open April-Oct. M-F 9am-noon and 2-6pm, Sa 9am-noon; Nov.-March M-F 9am-noon and 3-5pm, Sa 9-10:30am.) Königstein's **Naturfreunde Jugendherberge,** Halbestadt 13 (tel. (035022) 424 32), is a lot nicer than most hostels but also more expensive—the stunning one- to four-bed rooms have private showers, and out back an enormous chess board beckons you to play. To get there, take the ferry across the river and turn right. The hostel will appear on your right after about 10 minutes. (DM40-90. Breakfast included. Reception daily 6am-10pm.) The **campground** (tel. 682 24) is on the banks of the Elbe about 10 minutes upstream from the station in the shadow of the fortress. It has washing facilities, a small supply shop, and a playground. (DM7.30 per person, DM6 per tent.) Fresh fruits and vegetables are sold at an open market on Tuesdays and Thursdays in the town's streets. The **telephone code** is 035021.

BAD SCHANDAU

The biggest town in the Sächsische Schweiz, Bad Schandau takes advantage of its location between the two halves of the national park by offering plenty of hiking opportunities. Bad Schandau is also amply connected to the rest of Sachsen, with the **S-Bahn** to Dresden (50min., every 30min., DM7.70), and **trains** running to Bautzen (2hr., every 2hr., DM16.20) and Prague (2hr., DM30.60). From the train station, take the **ferry** (7:30am-9:30pm, every ½hr., DM1) and walk uphill to the Markt where you'll find the **tourist office,** Markt 12 (tel. 900 30). The staff finds rooms (DM25-30), suggests hikes, and offers city tours and trips to the Czech Republic. (Open M-F 9am-6:30pm, Sa 9am-4pm.) **Adler Apotheke,** Dresdner Str. 2 (tel. 425 08), provides **pharmacy** services. (Open M-F 8am-12:30pm and 1:30-6pm, Sa 8:30am-noon.) Take the solar-powered **Kirnitzschtalbahn train** to the unimpressive **Lichtenhain waterfall,** nonetheless a favorite starting point for full-day hikes on the **Schrammsteine.** (May-Oct. every 30min., DM6.) To rent a **bike,** try the **Fahrradverleih,** Poststr. 14. (Tel. 428 83. Open M-F 9am-noon and 2-6pm, Sa 9am-noon. DM15 per day with ID.) The closest youth hostel is 40 minutes away, but there are plenty of private rooms to be found in town, and the rest of the Sächsische Schweiz isn't far off at all. In a town that closes down before 11pm, **Sigl's,** Kirnitzschtalstr. 17 (tel. 407 02), a bar-bistro, offers food and a wide selection of beers until 2am. The **telephone code** is 035022.

OBERLAUSITZ (UPPER LUSATIA)

In this part of Europe, "easternmost" was once a euphemism for boring and underdeveloped. On the cusp of two former Warsaw Pact neighbors, Oberlausitz works hard to overcome the negative image brought upon it by many years of economic stagnation prior to reunification. During GDR times, the Politburo *apparatchiks* let much of the region's magnificent Medieval, Renaissance, and Baroque architecture decay, but as in much of Eastern Germany, Oberlausitz is currently undergoing extensive restoration in pursuit of its former shine. The area around Bautzen is an excellent example of the early results of the rapid changes that have quickly transformed the region into a worthwhile tourist destination.

BAUTZEN (BUDYŠIN)

Bautz'ner *Senf* (mustard): sausage in Germany just wouldn't be the same without it. But mustard pilgrims aren't the only folks who flock to Bautzen; with ancient towers on a hill high above the Spree River, a large population of Germany's sole national minority, the Sorbs, and a collection of crumbling Medieval, Baroque, and Art Nouveau architecture, Bautzen has proven itself a stalwart, millennium-old cultural capital. Despite the bilingual street signs, Bautzen's character is very German, and there's no shortage of *Wurst* to go with your *Senf.*

◪┏ **PRACTICAL INFORMATION AND ACCOMMODATIONS.** Bautzen is a one-hour **train** ride from Dresden (1 per hour, DM14.80). The **tourist office,** Hauptmarkt 1 (tel. 420 16; fax 53 43 09), offers listings of accommodations and books **rooms** in hotels, *Pensionen,* and private homes (DM19-30). The staff also offer **city tours.** From the train station, walk straight through Rathenauplatz and bear left onto Bahnhofstr. Keep left on Postplatz and walk onto Karl-Marx-Str. Follow it straight until you see the Holiday Inn; before reaching it, cross the street near the artsy fountain. Up ahead on your right will be a tall white tower marking the beginning of Reichenstr. Follow Reichenstr. to the Hauptmarkt, which is the center of

---

THE ABSORBING SORBS The Sorbs are a Slavic minority stemming from tribes who streamed into the Niederlausitz and Oberlausitz areas between the Spreewald and Lusatian mountains during the 6th and 7th centuries. Sorbian is similar to Czech and Polish and is divided into two basic dialects: Niedersorbisch (Low Sorbian) spoken in and around Cottbus, and Obersorbisch (High Sorbian) spoken in the Bautzen region. Since the crystallization of the Sorb nationalist movement in 1848, small Sorbian-speaking communities totalling about 75,000 members have maintained their regional identities. Under Hitler's *Reich,* Sorbian was ruthlessly suppressed in a program of liquidation initiated in 1937. After the war, a law was enacted to assure the protection and promotion of the Sorbs' culture and language, and a special bureau was created to guarantee Sorbians civil rights in the German constitution. The Sorbs enrich German culture with their ornamental Easter eggs, their *Osterreiten* (Easter rides) organized in various towns, and their traditional style of celebrating marriage and weddings. Dance and music abound during the festival of *Zapust,* which lasts from the end of January to the beginning of March. January 25 marks the *Vogelhochzeit* (birds' wedding), during which children in costume represent birds grateful for seeds left by their human friends in order to celebrate a marriage.

Bautzen's Altstadt. The tourist office is located to the right of the Rathaus, the big yellow building towering over the Markt. (Open April-Oct. M-F 10am-6pm, Sa-Su 10am-3pm; Nov.-March M-F 10am-5pm, Sa-Su 10am-3pm. Tours W at 2pm, Sa and Su at 11am.) At the ancient defense-tower-turned-**Jugendherberge (HI),** Am Zwinger 1 (tel. 40 34 7), experience real Saxon hospitality (and great *Sächsische* accents) while sleeping in 2-, 3-, 4-, or 20-bed rooms. From the Hauptmarkt, go up Kornstr., and stick with it as it jogs right and turns into Schulerstr.; the hostel is to your right after you go through the Schülertor. (DM18, over 26 DM23. Breakfast included. Reception M-F 7am-8pm, Sa-Su 6-8pm. No lockout. Curfew 10pm, but you'll get a key.) If you don't dig the hostel scene, reserve a room at **Pension Stephan's,** Schloßstr. 1 (tel. 475 90; fax 475 91). From the Hauptmarkt, take Große Brudergasse; near the *Wasserturm* (water tower), turn right onto Predigergasse. Stephan's is the green building on the corner of Schloßstr. This family-run *Pension* is centrally located and features rooms with private bath and TV. (Singles DM60, doubles DM100. Breakfast included. Call ahead.) To find out more about Sorb culture, visit the **Sorbische Kulturinformation** office, Postpl. 2 (tel. 421 05; fax 428 11). The staff has information on cultural events and **homestays** with the local Sorb population. (Open M-F 10am-6pm.) For a **taxi** call 422 22. The **AVIS** office at the train station **rents cars.** The **post office,** 02625 Bautzen, is located on Postplatz. (Open M-F 8am-6pm, Sa 9am-noon.) The **telephone code** is 03591.

🍴 **FOOD.** If you think forks and knives are overrated and you like monks, devils, and candles, try **Mönchshof,** Burglehn 1 (tel. 49 01 41). Medieval cuisine (DM7-25) and a great atmosphere make the restaurant worth a visit. (Open M-Sa 11:30am-1am, Su 11:30am-11pm. Reservations recommended. To experience the German take on natural healing, visit **Zur Apotheke,** Schloßstr. 21 (tel 48 00 35). The restaurant prepares a wide range of meals rich in herbs (DM12-20), which unlike most medicines are very tasty. (Open daily from 11:30am-late.) With a decor heavy on gangsta motifs, **Al Capone's,** Schülerstr. 4 (tel. 49 10 10), bangs out pizzas (DM9-12) and pastas. (DM9-14. Open M 5pm-midnight, Tu-Su 11:30am-2pm and 5pm-midnight.) **Wjelbik,** Kornstr. 7 (tel. 420 60), serves tasty Sorbian specialities. Try the *Sorbische Stulle,* a traditional pork dish (DM13), or relish a hefty veggie dish. (DM16-17. Open daily 11am-11pm.) The Hauptmarkt hosts a twice-weekly **market** (Tu 8am-1pm, Sa 7-11am). **Optimal,** right around the corner from Rechnerstr. on Ressnerstr., fills all of your grocery needs. (Open M-F 9am-6pm, Sa 9am-noon.)

🏛 **SIGHTS.** The **Stadtmuseum,** Kornmarktstr. 1 (tel. 498 50), specializes in the regional and cultural history of Bautzen. The museum also displays a collection of wood carvings and copper engravings from the 15th through 17th centuries. (Open W-Su 10am-5pm. DM3, children and students DM2.) The **Reichenturm,** up Kornmarktstr. on Reichenstr., is the leaning tower of Bautzen. It was built in 1490, with a Baroque top added in 1715. It deviates exactly 1.44m from the perpendicular. The view is marvelous. (Open daily April-Oct. 10am-5pm. Last entrance at 4:30pm. DM2, students DM1.50, under 12 years DM1. Tours DM10.) A block away, at the intersection of Wendischer Graben and Wendische Str., lies the **Alte Kaserne** (old barracks), an elegant building designed by Dresden master Gottfried Semper to accommodate unappreciative 19th-century troops, now home to offices.

Left from the Reichenturm down Reichenstr. is the **Hauptmarkt.** The grand yellow building is the 13th-century **Rathaus,** with the Fleischmarkt behind it alongside the Gothic **Dom St. Petri.** (Open June-Sept. M-Sa 10am-4pm, Su 10am-1pm; May and Oct. M-Sa 10am-3pm, Su 10am-1pm; Nov.-April M-F 11am-noon.) Built in 1213, the Dom has been Eastern Germany's only *Simultankirche* (simultaneously Catholic and Protestant church) since 1524. The division of the church was a remarkably peaceful compromise, although until 1952 a 4m-high fence in the middle of the church was what kept it peaceful. Behind the cathedral sits the ornate red-and-gold **Domstift,** housing the **Domschatz** (cathedral treasury), a phenomenal collection of jewel-studded gowns, icons, and gold regalia. Ring to get in. (Open M-F

SACHSEN

10am-noon and 1-4pm. Free.) Follow An der Petrikirche downhill from the cathedral until you see the **Nikolaiturm** down the hill on your right. Crossing under the gate, check out the face carved above the entrance. Locals claim that this is a likeness of a former mayor, who was bricked alive into the tower as retribution for opening the city to Hussite attackers in the 16th century. Heading back through Nikolaiturm, take a right onto Schloßstr. and walk through the Matthiasturm. The **Sorbisches Museum,** Ortenburg 3 (tel. 424 03), which the intriguing history and culture of the Sorbs. Displays include samples of their writing, life-sized costumes, the area's special Easter eggs, and those mysterious *Dudelsacks* (bagpipes), which look like psychedelic water-filtration devices. (Open April-Oct. daily 10am-5pm; Nov.-March 10am-4pm. DM3, students and children DM2.)

From the Nikolaiturm or the Sorbisches Museum, follow the **Osterweg** path around the city walls and along the Spree, taking in the views of the 1480 **Mühlbastei** (mill tower), the 1558 **Alte Wasserkunst** (old water tower), and the spire of the 1429 **Michaeliskirche.** On the other side of the fortress lies the brown-shingled **Hexenhäusrl** (witches' cottage). This small wooden structure, the oldest house in the area, was the only home in the area to survive two devastating fires. The villagers subsequently shunned the inhabitants as witches, though the fire was actually averted by a well inside the house.

GÖRLITZ

The easternmost town in Germany, Görlitz has changed little since Napoleon trudged through it on the way to his unsuccessful invasion of Russia. Many of the elegant pastel Renaissance and Baroque homes of former mayors still stand. In fact, Görlitz was one of the only German towns to survive WWII completely unharmed. Dark, tired, and unattractive during Communist times, Görlitz's buildings are quickly regaining their long-forgotten splendor as a result of a massive restoration project underway throughout the city. With historic buildings competing for attention on every corner, straightforward rail connections, and easy access to major bus routes, Görlitz is an excellent starting point for exploring Oberlausitz.

Most of Görlitz's central sights are located around the **Obermarkt.** From the train station's main north exit, go straight down **Berliner Straße,** Görlitz's attractive pedestrian zone. The street intersects **Postplatz,** home to a central fountain surrounded by a motley collection of flowers; the darkly stained **Frauenkirche,** a late Gothic cathedral built in 1431; and the **post office,** a recent project of the restoration workers. The **Dicker Turm,** a squat gray tower with 5m-thick walls, stands tall and proud at Marienplatz, located right past the *Karstadt* department store.

Follow Steinstr. to reach the **Obermarkt.** Across the square sits the **Dreifaltigkeitskirche.** Originally a 13th-century Franciscan monastery, the church bears marks of frequent expansion. Walking past it down Brüderstr. leads to the **Untermarkt.** Here stands the **Rathaus,** burdened by a clock-face in which a sculptured head yawns with the passing of each minute. On the corner opposite the Rathaus is the **Ratsapotheke,** a Renaissance building from 1550 that still has an astrology and astronomy chart painted on its crumbling surface—the confluence of tweaked clocks is indicative of Görlitz's position on the 15-degree meridian, the center point of the Central European time zone. Don't miss the **Peterskirche** down Peterstr. from the Untermarkt. Its brightly adorned interior, speckled with gilded suns and clocks, is enough to impress even the most jaded tourists. Enter on the backside. (Open M-F 10:30am-4pm, Sa 10:30am-5pm, Su 11:30am-5pm.) Don't miss the view (or a stroll) across the river to the tower painted with an enormous head.

Trains chug to Bautzen (50min., 1 per hour, DM12), Dresden (2hr., 1 per hour, DM29), and Zittau (50min., 1 per hour, DM9.80). Travelers heading to Poland can catch connections to Warsaw (1 per day, DM27.40) and Wrocław (1 per day, DM16.80). The **tourist office,** Obermarkt 29 (tel. 475 70; fax 47 57 27), sells maps and finds **rooms** (DM30-40) in private homes for free. (Open M-F 10am-6:30pm, Sa 10am-4:30pm, Su 10am-1pm.) For a **taxi,** call 40 08 00. The **telephone code** is 03581.

Görlitz's **Jugendherberge (HI),** Goethestr. 17 (tel./fax 40 65 10), is one of the coolest hostels for miles around. Take the south exit *(Südausgang)* of the train station, bear left up the hill, turn right onto Zittauer Str., and continue until Goethestr. just past the **Tierpark.** Turn left, and the hostel is ahead on the right (15min.). Enter the gate up the stairs to reach the entrance on the right. The huge stained-glass windows are almost as brilliantly colorful as the comforters (we exaggerate—*nothing* is as colorful as the comforters). Accordions and guitars are supplied for guests' use; you can also rent skis and grills. Rooms have two to eight beds; some family rooms are available. (DM21, over 27 DM26. Breakfast included. Reception M-F 7am-9:30pm, Sa-Su 7-10am and 4-9:30pm. No lockout. Curfew 10pm, but you can get a key.)

Many cost-effective *Imbiß* options line Berliner Str., while the nooks and crannies of the Altstadt shelter numerous restaurants; see the beer glass key on the city map at the tourist office. **Destille,** Nikolaistr. 6 (tel. 40 53 02), directly across from the Nikolaiturm and down the street from St. Peter, serves *Soljanka* soup with toast (DM5) to the many locals who flock to its wooden tables. They also weigh patrons down with a hefty farmer's omelette, served with ham and potatoes. (DM10. Open daily 11:30am-11:30pm.) The immaculate seafood restaurant **Gastmahl des Meeres,** Struvestr. 2 (tel. 40 62 29), whips up Alaskan fish for DM11.90. (Open M-Sa 11am-10pm, Su 11am-3pm.) Two **Edeka supermarkets** make hunting for groceries easy: the one at Steinstr. 1 is in the Altstadt; enter from the Obermarkt. (Open M-F 8am-6:30pm, Sa 8am-noon.) The second, Goethestr. 17, is a few doors down from the hostel. (Open M-F 8am-7pm, Sa 8am-1pm.) The **post office** is at Gasthofstr. 29. (Open daily 9am-noon and 2:30-8pm.) The **postal code** is 92828. The **telephone code** is 03581.

ZITTAUER GEBIRGE (ZITTAU MOUNTAINS)

In a sliver of Germany wedged between the Czech Republic and Poland rise the rocky cliffs of the Zittauer Gebirge. Once a favorite spot of medieval monks, these beehive-shaped mountains are the conquests of choice for skiers, hikers, and landscape lovers. The sublime surroundings were a fountain of inspiration for Romantic artists like Ludwig Richter. But matters have not always been so picture-perfect: in 1491, the region was the scene of the vicious **Bierkrieg** (beer war), when the citizens of Görlitz protested Zittau's success as a beer-brewing town by destroying barrels of the beverage. The horror! More recently, the workers and local forests of this region have been reeling from a nasty socialist hangover plaguing much of Eastern Germany; as inefficient factories are shut down, many residents remain unemployed.

ZITTAU

At the crossroads of three nations—Poland, the Czech Republic, and Germany—Zittau has served as a trading and cultural center for many years. Under the rule of the Bohemian kings, Zittau took on a dominant role in Oberlausitz; it later came to dominate the vital yarn and thread industries. Most of the interesting sights lie in the **Altstadt.** From the train station, follow Bahnhofstr. through Haberkornplatz where it turns into Bautzner Str., and continue down the street to Johanniskirchplatz. The recently renovated exterior of the **Johanniskirche** shelters the dilapidated interior, which is currently being reconstructed. (Open M-F 10am-6pm, Sa-Su 10am-4pm.) From the church, walk directly down Bautzner Str. to the grand **Marktplatz.** The Renaissance-style **Rathaus** was designed by Prussian architect Friedrich Schinkel in 1843 (see p. 26.) Heading left down Johannisstr., you'll come across the late Gothic **Klosterkirche** and the adjoining **Stadtmuseum** (tel./fax 51 02 70), housed in a former 13th-century Franciscan monastery stocked with tourist-friendly medieval torture devices. (Open Tu-Su 10am-noon and 1-4pm. DM3, students DM2.) Nearby, the recently-restored **Museum der Kirche zum Heiligen Kreuz,** Frauenstr. 23, houses extremely rare 15th- and 16th-century tapestries the life of Christ. (Tu-Su 10am-5pm. DM7, students and seniors DM4.) To inspect the clerical treasures, follow Klosterstr. from the Klosterkirche until Theanterring; then take a right. The church museum is at the corner of Theaterring and Frauenstr.

Trains roll in from Dresden (1½hr., every 2hr., DM29) and Görlitz (1hr., 1 every hr., DM9.80). The **tourist office,** Markt 1 (tel. 75 21 37; fax 75 21 61), on the first floor of the Rathaus near the left side entrance, provides city maps and a room-finding service for free. (Rooms DM25-45. Open M-F 8am-6pm, Sa 9am-1pm, Su 1-4pm.) A **pharmacy, Johannis Apotheke,** Johannisstr. 2 (tel. 51 21 64), has emergency services listed on the door. (Open M-F 8am-6pm, Sa 8am-noon.) The **post office,** 02763 Zittau, is at Haberkornpl. 1. (Open M-F 7:30am-7pm, Sa 8am-1pm.) **Deutsche Bank,** Bautzner Str. 20, is just down the street. (M-Th 8:30am-6pm, F 8:30am-1pm.) Head up Johannisstr. from the tourist office for the old-fashioned beer-and-sauerkraut **Kloster Stüb'l,** Johannisstr. 4-6 (tel. 51 25 76). Try the *Abernmaunke mit Brotwurscht und Sauerkroattch* (evening meal with sausage and sauerkraut; DM8.50) or pay more for a "medieval meal" you eat with your hands. (Open M-Th 11am-10pm, F-Sa 11am-midnight.) The **Savi Café and Bar** (tel. 70 82 97), on Bautzner Str. across from the Hotel Dreiländereck, serves light but filling dishes in a relaxed, modern atmosphere. Myriad cafes and pastry shops in the Markt and along Johannisstr. provide tasty delights. The **telephone code** is 03583.

OYBIN

The neighboring spa town of Oybin is a love-child of beauty and kitsch that will make everyone smile. The surrounding scenery is sublime, with pine-forested hills punctuated by imposing mounds of twisted, eroded sandstone. At the top of the cliffs outside the town are the ruins of a high Gothic fortress and cloister built in the 14th century. In the summer, concerts are held in the halls of the **cathedral.** To get there, head up the stairs to the left of the church and across from the tourist office. (Cathedral DM5, under 16 DM2.) There's good hiking and more stone on the other side of the village. Kitsch is king at ▓**Märchenspiele,** a small *Biergarten* next to the train station which brings fairy tales to life with delightfully corny moving miniature dwarves and hikers. (Open M-Th and Sa-Su 10:30am-5:30pm. DM2, 5-6 DM1, under 5 free.)

To get to Oybin, hop on the Mr. Rogers-esque **Schmalspurbahn,** an adorable circa-1890 train just outside the Zittau train station (45min., 3-4 per day, DM5.40). To sleep over, stop by the **tourist office,** Hauptstr. 15, and get a cheap private room (DM18-22) or an elaborate vacation apartment (DM40-80). They also have free hiking maps. (Open M-F 10am-5pm, Sa noon-4pm, Su 2-4pm; when closed, a list of accommodations is posted next to the door.) The **telephone code** is 035844.

CHEMNITZ

Though Chemnitz ceased to be known as Karl-Marx-Stadt in 1990, the gigantic stone bust of the philosopher continues to tower over the city center. Oh, but how cruel is the world . . . what torture it must be for the petrified head of Papa Marx to have its eyes fixed on young people indulging in capitalist practices at the nearby McDonald's. Apparently history likes to play tricks on those who claimed to have understood her nature. East German planners rebuilt the post-war city with a decidedly Soviet, monolithic air, and while Chemnitz attempts to shake off its image as a gray industrial town, it does so with mixed success. The city's position on the German cultural map cannot withstand competition from nearby Dresden and Leipzig; Chemnitz feels both trapped in the past and all its Brave New World appeal. So, does Marx win in the end? Let's call it a draw.

▓ **ORIENTATION AND PRACTICAL INFORMATION.** To begin your search for that socialist dynamism, head straight down Georgstr. or Carolastr. from the Hauptbahnhof; after a block, you'll come to **Straße der Nationen,** the city's north-

THE GREATEST BUDGET SOUVENIR EVER—
CASTLES FOR DM1! Many travelers like to buy postcards of castles and happily shell out a few Marks for pretty little pictures of royal abodes. Some travelers, however, prefer to buy their own castle. The state of Sachsen has more royal palaces than it knows what to do with (about 1000), and has begun a novel pilot program to market some of these treasured historical fortifications for a mere DM1. There is, sadly, a slight drawback. Those who purchase the castles must renovate them—40 years of GDR neglect has produced a terrible state of disrepair. The cost of renovation tacks another DM7-20 million onto the purchase costs. Still, the opportunities for those who want to buy something by which to remember their travels in Germany are spectacular. Schloß Gaußig, about 10km from Bautzen, has a newly renovated ballroom with all the posh adornments one could ever hope for. Its dining room is a *Jägermeister's* fantasy, with deer antlers lining the walls. Nearby, Schloß Milkel comes with a mausoleum and the remains of ancient royalty. Schloß Lichtenwanlde, 10km from Chemnitz, is also up for grabs. Response to the offer has been rather slow, so the opportunity to purchase your very own bit of royalty should endure for a while.

south axis. To your right, on the north end of the boulevard lies a quiet neighborhood of old houses that centers on the **Brühl,** a serene pedestrian zone. The **tourist office,** Bahnhofstr. 6 (tel. 690 68; fax 690 68 30), is located across from the train station. The staff finds **private rooms** (DM25-40) for a DM3 fee. (Open M-F 9am-6pm, Sa 9am-1pm.) For a **taxi,** call 194 10. Down Carolastr., to the left along Str. der Nationen, looms the **post office,** 09009 Chemnitz. (Open M-F 8am-6pm, Sa 8am-2pm.) The **telephone code** is 0371.

▐▌▐▌ ACCOMMODATIONS AND FOOD. Accommodations in Chemnitz are relatively expensive, and the youth hostel is way out of town and virtually inaccessible by public transportation. Deciding whether or not it's worth staying in Chemnitz is difficult, especially since nearby Augustusburg beckons with its hostel-in-a-castle (see p. 174). If you do stay, it'll cost you. **Pension Art Nouveau,** Hainstr. 130 (tel. 402 50 71; fax 402 50 73), offers singles from DM65 and doubles from DM90, breakfast included. For a quick bite, swing by the market next to the Rathaus, which is always full of *Imbiße.* For something more, stop by the *Brühl,* or **Bogart's,** Hartmannstr. 7d (tel. 63 14 60), which serves a healthy vegetable platter (DM12) as well as tasty blueberry shakes. (DM5; open daily 4pm-3am.) A well-supplied **Nimm's mit supermarket** awaits in the train station. (Open M-F 6am-9:45pm, Sa-Su 7am-9:45pm.) It's also remarkably easy to find cheap eats of the fast food variety along Str. der Nationen.

▨ SIGHTS. Chemnitz begins building up to its socialist crescendo along ▨**Str. der Nationen;** every street corner boasts statues of frolicking children or happily scrubbed workers. But nothing outshines the **bust of Karl Marx,** an enormous concrete chunk that bears the likeness of the city's adopted philosopher—although Chemnitz was called Karl-Marx-Stadt for almost 40 years, Marx never lived here.

To escape all that bewildering concrete pomposity, check out Chemnitz's two museums. The last moment of pain will be walking down the oversized steps leading down to **Theaterplatz**—it seems that egalitarian ideas made an assumption that, theoretically speaking, the entire population of the city could be using the steps at the same time. The square is located halfway down Str. der Nationen and houses the **König-Albert-Museumsbau,** which contains the **Städtische Kunstsammlungen Chemnitz** (municipal art collection) and the **Museum für Naturkunde Chemnitz** (natural history museum). The art museum features a nice sampling of 19th- and 20th-century German art, as well as a huge collection of paintings and woodcuts by local Expressionist Karl Schmidt-Rotluff. (Open Tu and Th-F 11am-5pm, W 11am-7:30pm. DM4, students and seniors DM2.) Farther north, you'll find a peaceful park and the **Schloß complex,** Schloßberg 12 (tel. 488 45 01). To reach the castle, dash to Str. der Nationen from the train station and turn right, take a left onto Elisenstr., which merges with Müllerstr., which in turn leads to Schloßberg on the right. The castle that stood here was destroyed in the Thirty Years War; the **Schloßbergmuseum** occupies a reconstructed building that approximates the old structure. (Open Tu-F 11am-5pm, Sa-Su 11am-6pm. DM4, students DM2.) The goods reside upstairs in the **Stadtgeschichte** (city history) display, which documents the history of Chemnitz from its 12th-century foundation to the present. Particularly intriguing are the posters advertising Hitler's *Entartete Kunst* (Degenerate Art) exhibit, on display in Chemnitz at the outset of WWII, and the collections of Communist kitsch from the Karl-Marx-Stadt days.

🎭 **ENTERTAINMENT AND NIGHTLIFE.** Chemnitz has developed quite an eclectic nightlife scene; look for the free magazine *Blitz* for the latest nightlife information. Check out the **Chemnitz opera** or take in a play at the **Schauspielhaus.** Schedules and information for both are posted on Theaterplatz. (Opera tickets DM10-30, 50% student discount. Box office open M-F 10am-6pm, Sa 2-6pm.) If high culture's not for you, shake it at **Fuchsbau,** Carolastr. 8 (tel. 67 17 17), where local cats head for disco, techno, and jazz. (Open W-Su after 9pm.)

NEAR CHEMNITZ: AUGUSTUSBURG

A night at the lively castle in Augustusburg facilitates recovery from the exhaustion of post-industrialist, post-Marxist, monochromatic Chemnitz. The princely mountaintop hamlet can be reached by bus #T-244 or T-245 (direction: "Schloßberg") from the Chemnitz *Busbahnhof,* down Georgstr. from the train station. (45min., operates 7am-7pm. DM4.90.) The bus stop is at the foot of the path leading to the castle. The Renaissance **hunting lodge** of the Saxon electors is perched 1500m above the town with a mesmerizing 360-degree panorama of the surrounding **Erzgebirge** mountains—look for the Czech Republic on the horizon. (Schloß open daily May-Oct. 9am-6pm; Nov.-April 10am-5pm.) The obligatory guided tour of the royal playhouse leads through the **Brunnenhaus** (well house) and the intimate **Schloßkapelle** (church chapel), the only Renaissance chapel left in Sachsen. The altar is graced by a Lucas Cranach painting, portraying the dour Herzog August, his wife Anna, and their 14 pious children. (Tours every hour at 30min. past the hour. DM4, students DM2.50.) Also check out the **Motorradmuseum** (motorcycle museum), the **Museum für Jagdtier- und Vogelkunde des Erzgebirges** (hunting and game museum), and the **Kutschenmuseum** (carriage museum). A day pass for all museums costs DM10 (students DM6). Tickets for individual museums can also be purchased separately. The real treat of a visit to Augustusburg is the **Jugendherberge (HI)** (tel. (037291) 202 56). Located inside the castle, the hostel boasts domed ceilings, animal skins on the walls, and a supreme view of the surrounding mountains. Narrow and crooked stone stairways lead from the spacious bunk-bed rooms to the romantic doubles (two mattresses tucked together in an alcove). The ambience really is medieval—you are the prince or princess of the castle, and the screaming schoolchildren your lowly serfs. The part of the hostel in which the hostel guests usually reside is currently under restoration, so if you arrive before March 2000 you'll have to make do with a room in the big house opposite the bus stop. (DM26, students DM21. Breakfast included. Reception 7am-8pm, check-in after 3pm.)

ZWICKAU

Zwickau is best known as the motor city of East Germany. For more than 35 years, the city's Sachsenring-Auto-Union produced the GDR's ubiquitous consumer car, the tiny *Trabant.* An ill-engineered, two-cylinder plastic jalopy, the *Trabi* was Communist industry's inferior answer to the West's *Volkswagen,* and, like cockroaches, the wheezing little cars persist. Officially, the city would prefer to play up its more genteel distinctions, such as its active artistic tradition, which launched composer Robert Schumann and a couple of members of the *Brücke* painting school into the world. But it may be a losing battle: the tinny whine of a *Trabi* laboring uphill is never far from the ears of a visitor.

The dusky-colored, four-story **Robert-Schumann-Haus** stands at Hauptmarkt 5 (tel. 21 52 69). The museum plays up the Romantic composer's childhood in Zwickau before his life as a "globe-trotting" celebrity. It also devotes several parts of the display to Schumann's wife, Clara Wieck, one of the most accomplished pianists of her day; today, Clara is eternalized as "the woman on the DM100 bill." No mention here of Schumann's later insanity, although the less-than-flattering busts of the composer hint that all was not well. Musicians perform both Robert and Clara's works in the *Klavierhalle* monthly from September through April; contact the museum for dates. (Museum open Tu-Sa 10am-5pm. DM5, students and seniors DM3. Concerts DM15, students and seniors DM10.)

Amid a smattering of Schumann memorabilia and a dark, imposing **cathedral** at the nearly renovated Hauptmarkt, Zwickau's unique offering is its **Automobilienmuseum**, Walter-Rathenau-Str. 51 (tel. 332 22 32). Head north from Dr.-Friedrichs-Ring on Römerstr., which becomes Walther-Rathenau-Str., to the out-of-the-way building past the auto factory (20min.). Over a dozen *Trabant* models are on display, prompting wonder at the design's invulnerability to innovation over the years. The sight of the last *Trabi* ever produced (in 1991) in all of its pink splendor and emblazoned with the words, *"Trabant:* Legend on Wheels," is enough to make even the most ardent Cold Warrior misty-eyed. (Open Tu-Th 9am-noon and 2-5pm, Sa-Su 10am-5pm. DM5, students and seniors DM3.50.) Though many find it puzzling, the *Trabi* has a devoted following of worshippers, many of whom come to Zwickau every year in mid-June to participate in the *Trabantfahrertreffen.* In 1999, 1,200 drivers and 30,000 spectators showed up to celebrate Zwickau's infamous lovechild, and 12 couples chose the event as the perfect place to exchange wedding vows. To consecrate your own union, or just ogle cars, check with the tourist office for the dates of this year's *Trabi* hoedown.

Located in the middle of the busy Sachsen-Thüringen rail network, Zwickau is easily reached by **train** as a daytrip from Leipzig (1½hr., 13 per day, DM22), Dresden (2hr., 26 per day, DM35), or Altenburg (40min., 17 per day, DM12). Its oldest attractions and most beautiful streets are confined to a circular region in the Altstadt, bounded by a bustling three-lane roundabout called **Dr.-Friedrichs-Ring.** For a **taxi** call 21 22 22. Zwickau's **tourist office**, Hauptstr. 6 (tel. 83 52 70; fax 29 37 15), lies in the center of the circle. From the **Hauptbahnhof,** head along the left fork, which becomes Bahnhofstr., until it ends at Humboldtstr. Turn right, and then quickly left on Schumannstr., which leads across the Ring. The street resumes as Innere Plauensche Str., a pedestrian zone, which leads to the Marienkirche. Hang a right to the Markt; the office is right behind the Burger King. If possible, try to arrive at **Zwickau-Zentrum,** a new underground train station 100m from the tourist

JAMES BOND'S NEW CAR? Even though the official anthem of the *Trabi* owners starts with the words "It's amazing what you can do/with some scissors and some glue," the notorious cars of the former GDR are quickly establishing their poistion among other cult, vintage, and otherwise legendary vehicles. The engineers who in the early days of the GDR tried to develop an affordable counterpart to the West German *Volkswagen* clearly failed, creating instead what is often referred to as "the bastard son of a water pump and a motorcycle." Today, just as in the days of the Party, the merits of the 601 model are the subject of controversy and often vigorous dispute. Similarly, the *Trabi's* plastic body is simultaneously the object of awe and ridicule. Technically absurd or not, the East German *Seifenkiste* (soap box) is gaining more supporters by the day. Many from the world of show biz are switching from their Aston Martins and Rolls Royces to this economic limousine—Bono, the vocalist of the pop band U2, to name just one. Controversies aside, those fluent in the ways of the market hold on to their *Trabis;* after all, when demand rises and supply falls . . .

office. The staff provides maps and books **rooms** (from DM35) for free. (Open M-F 9am-6:30pm, Sa 9am-4pm.) The main **post office,** Humboldtstr. 3, 08056 Zwickau, is just outside the Ring near the intersection with Humboldtstr. (Open M-F 9am-noon and 2-6pm, Sa 9-11am.) The **telephone code** is 0375.

The monthly *Stadtsreicher*, free at the tourist office, lists the major events in the area, ranging from shows to bars to food. Just outside the Ring lies **Dönerhaus,** Schumannstr. 10 (tel. 29 88 09), an upscale *Imbiß* serving Turkish fare. (Meals DM4.50-8. Open M-Sa 10am-11pm, Su 3-11pm.) To imbibe some spirits and GDR nostalgia, head to **Roter Oktober,** at the corner of Leipziger Str. and Kolpingstr. Toast the hammer and sickle if you really feel like getting crazy (or beaten up). (Open M-F 5pm-1am, Sa 7pm-1am, Su 9am-1pm and 6-11pm.) The **Markt** hosts food stands (Th-F 8am-6pm). Other cheap dining options can be found along the Hauptmarkt and Innere Schneeberger Str. during the day, while the **SPAR supermarket,** across from the Schumannhaus, fills your grocery bags. (Open M-F 8am-6:30pm, Sa 8am-noon.)

LEIPZIG

Leipzig jumps out from the calm Eastern German landscape in a fiery blaze of nowNowNOW. The *Uni*-culture, spawned by more than 20,000 students, creates an aura of youthful vitality as it did when Goethe, Nietzsche, and Leibniz stalked these ivory towers. At the same time, Leipzig has been an important artistic center for centuries. The echoes of musical genius emanate from the top-notch Gewandhaus Orchester founded by Felix Mendelssohn in 1850 in the spirit of Bach and Wagner, both of whom preceded him as residents of this city. Goethe revered Leipzig for its cultivated inhabitants; the city even inspired him to set a pivotal scene from *Faust* here. Leipzig has been a site of repeated popular upheaval: first in the "Wars of Liberation," in which the city kicked Napoleon out of Germany in the 1813 Battle of Leipzig, again in the revolutions of 1830 and 1848, and, most recently, in 1989, when Leipzig gained fame as Germany's *Heldenstadt* (city of heroes) for its role as the crucible of *die Wende*, the sudden toppling of the Communist regime. Leipzig's half-millennium tradition as a *Messestadt* (fair city) gave prominence to the German dialect spoken in this area, which became the basis of modern *Hochdeutsch* (standard German), and now continues to accord international verve (and money) to the city. This boom town is bursting with style as it charges through the transformations of the *neue Bundesländer*, resolutely resisting threats to the student-hipster vibe by self-serving capitalists and speculators.

▐ GETTING THERE AND GETTING AROUND

Flights: Flughafen Leipzig-Halle (English information tel. 224 11 56), in Schkeuditzgasse, about 20km from Leipzig. International service throughout Central Europe. An **airport city liner bus** leaves Goethestr. next to the tourist office every 30min. during the day, every hour at night. DM10, round-trip DM16.

Trains: Leipzig lies on the Berlin-Munich line, with regular InterCity service to Frankfurt. Trains zoom to Halle (20min., 2-3 per hour, DM9.40), Dresden (1½hr., 1 per hour, DM26), Berlin (2-3hr., 1 per hour, DM46), Frankfurt (5hr., every 2 hours, DM90), and Munich (7hr., 1 per hour, DM113). Information counter on the platform near track 15, or ask at one of the counters in the huge and hugely helpful *Reisezentrum* at the entrance of the station.

Public Transportation: Streetcars and buses cover the city; the hub is on Platz der Republik, in front of the Hauptbahnhof. Your best bet for tickets is either five 1hr. tickets for DM11, or a day card, valid all day after 10am, for DM6. After midnight, night buses (1 per hour) provide transportation along the most trafficked routes. All night buses leave from the Hauptbahnhof. Tickets are available from the tourist office, vending machines, and drivers.

Taxis: Tel. 48 84, 98 22 22, or 42 33.

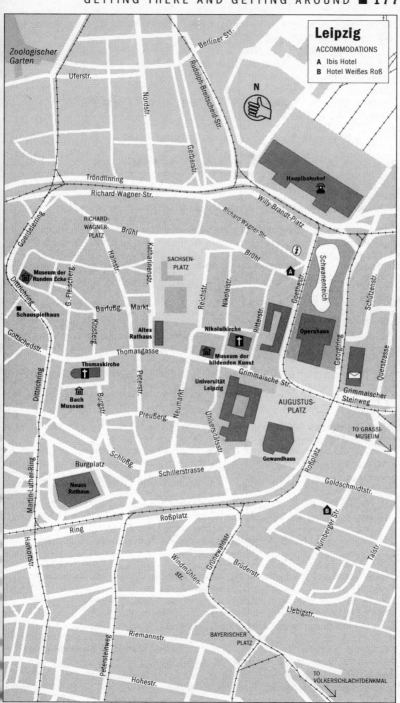

Leipzig

ACCOMMODATIONS
A Ibis Hotel
B Hotel Weißes Roß

SACHSEN

Car Rental: Sixt-Budget and **Avis** both have counters at the Hauptbahnhof's *Reisezentrum*. Open M-F 7am-9pm, Sa-Su 8am-6pm. More offices are at the airport.

Mitfahrzentrale: Goethestr. 7-11 (tel. 194 40), just past the tourist office, organizes rideshares. Dresden DM16, Berlin DM22, Munich DM44, Prague DM29. Open daily 7am-9pm. Call ahead.

Hitchhiking: *Let's Go* does not recommend hitchhiking as a safe mode of transportation. Hitchers going to Dresden and Prague take streetcar #3, 6, or 8 (direction: "Sommerfeld") to "Paunsdorfer Allee," and turn left down Paunsdorfer Allee to the *Autobahn* interchange. To Berlin, take streetcar #16 (direction: "Messegelände") to "Essener Str.," switch to bus #86, get out at Sachsenpark, and walk to the *Autobahn*.

⊡ ORIENTATION AND PRACTICAL INFORMATION

Much of what Leipzig offers to its guests is located in the ringed **Innenstadt,** but you'll have to leave the comforting sight of the huge, metal university tower for nightlife and any untouristed underground scenes. It's a 10-minute walk from the main train station on the north edge of the Innenstadt to **Augustusplatz,** the **Gewandhaus,** the university, and the main post office. The cavernous **Hauptbahnhof** is a sight in itself—its curved-beam roofs enclose Europe's largest train station and recall the grander days of rail travel. The station was recently renovated to include a three-story underground shopping center as crassly American as apple pie. (Most shops open M-Sa 9am-8pm.)

TOURIST SERVICES

Tourist Office: Leipzig Information, Richard-Wagner-Str. 1 (tel. 710 42 60; fax 710 42 71; email lipsia@aol.com). Walk across Willy-Brandt-Platz in front of the station and turn left at Richard-Wagner-Str. Among the gorgeous brochures, there's a useful free map of the center and suburbs with a street name index. They book **private rooms** and rooms in *Pensionen* for free, and sell tickets.

Tours: The tourist office leads bus tours daily at 10:30am (in German; 2hr.; DM20, students and seniors DM16) and 1:30pm (in German and English; 2½hr.; DM28, seniors DM20, students DM16). Themed walking tours depart daily. Some guides are English-speaking (2hr., DM10-15). For more information and departure times, call 710 42 80.

Budget Travel: Kilroy Travels Germany, Augustuspl. 9 (tel. 211 42 20), in the university courtyard. Open M-F 10am-7pm, Sa 10am-1pm.

Consulate: U.S., Wilhelm-Seyferth-Str. 4 (tel. 21 38 40). Entrance on Wächstr. behind the Museum der bildenden Künste. Available in emergencies M-F 8am-7pm.

Currency Exchange: Dresdner Bank, Goethestr. 3-5, just off Augustuspl. Open M-Th 9am-6:30pm, F 9am-4pm. Several **ATMs.**

American Express: Bergpl. 2 (tel. 997 00 22), on the 2nd floor of a building just behind the Neues Rathaus. The office acts strictly as a travel agency, and does not exchange money or issue traveler's checks. The **airport branch** (tel. 22 41 850) offers all services. Office open M-F 9:30am-6pm, branch open M-F 9am-6pm, Sa-Su 8am-noon.

LOCAL SERVICES

Library: British Council, Katharinenstr. 1-3 (tel. 140 64 10), near the Markt, stocks a reading room with English books a-plenty. Open M and W-F 1-6pm, Tu 1-8pm. Or check out the **Amerika-Haus Bibliothek** (tel. 213 84 25), in the U.S. consulate (see **Consulate,** above). Open Tu 4-7pm, W-F 2-5pm.

Gay and Lesbian Resources: AIDS-Hilfe, Ossietzkystr. 18 (tel. 232 31 26; counseling 194 11), features a popular café (Tu and Th 3-9pm). Also offers the updated **Queer Stadtplan,** a map of gay and lesbian nightlife. Office open M-Th 10am-6pm and F 10am-1pm. Counseling M, W 1-6pm and Tu, Th 1-9pm.

Mitwohnzentrale: Tel. 194 30, in the same office as the **Mitfahrzentrale** (see p. 153). Arranges long-term accommodation. Open 7am-9pm.

(see p. 153)

Women's Resources: Frauenkultur, Braustr. 17 (tel. 213 00 30), is a center for art, meetings, and relaxation. Office open M-F 8am-2pm. Women's café W 6-11pm.

■ **Laundromat: Maga Pon,** Gottschedstr. 11 (tel. 960 79 22), takes the cake as the jazziest laundromat in Sachsen—it doubles as a hep-cat bar and restaurant, so come in your coolest clothes (unless you want to wash them). Wash DM6, dry DM1. Open daily 9am-late.

EMERGENCY AND COMMUNICATIONS

Emergency: Police, tel. 110. **Fire** and **Ambulance,** tel. 112.

Pharmacies: Löwen-Apotheke, Grimmaische Str. 19 (tel. 960 50 27). Open M-F 8am-8pm, Sa 8am-4pm. Posts a list of open pharmacies.

Internet Access: see **Café le bit,** p. 180.

Post Office: Hauptpostamt 1, 04109 Leipzig (tel. 212 25 88), across from Augustuspl. on Grimmaische Str. Open M-F 8am-8pm, Sa 9am-4pm.

PHONE CODE	0341

⌐ ACCOMMODATIONS AND CAMPING

If there is one reason not to stay in Leipzig, it's the disastrous state of the budget accommodations scene. The development and renovation of the Innenstadt has provided a great new hangout, but it has also chased accommodations cheaper than DM100 a night way out into the suburbs. The best alternative to the over-crowded hostel is a private room (from DM40 for a single and DM70 for a double) or a cheap *Pension.* Ask for help at the tourist office, or consult **Leipziger Allerlei,** a listing of all of the accommodations in town.

Jugendherberge Leipzig Centrum (HI), Volksgartenstr. 24 (tel. 245 70 11; fax 245 70 12). Its name is a leftover from an earlier and better location; the hostel is actually a 15min. streetcar ride from the city. Take streetcar #17, 37, or 57 (direction: "Thekla" or "Schönefeld") to "Löbauer Str." Walk past the supermarket along Löbauer Str. and take a right onto Volksgartenstr. Bureaucracy like in Weber's textbooks: a long list of rules ensures that everyone gets equal treatment. The hostel's inflexible curfew precludes any late-night jaunts. DM24, over 26 DM29. Breakfast included. Sheets DM6. Reception 2:30-11pm. Curfew 1am.

Hotel Weißes Roß, Roßstr. 20 (tel. 960 59 51). Take the streetcar to "Augustusplatz," and walk down Roßpl. until it curves to the left. Go through the portal just to the left of center of the large, curving apartment building; the hotel is 100m straight ahead. Nothing decadent or four-star about this place, but it's very close to the city, and given the hostel's strict curfew, it's worth considering. Singles DM60, with private shower DM70. Doubles DM95, with private shower DM110. Reception M-F 2-8pm. Reservations strongly recommended.

ETAP Hotel Leipzig, Föpplstr. 7 (tel. 245 84 01). Take streetcar #17, 37, or 57 (direction: "Schönefeld" or "Thekla") to "Löbauer Str.," then bus #55 or 84 (direction: "Mockau-West") to "Braunstr." (30min.). Remotely located but near public transportation and damn cheap for a hotel. Rooms are equipped with private showers and TV. Singles and doubles are both DM54—a great bargain for two. Breakfast DM8.90. Reception 6:30-10am and 5-8pm.

Hotel Ibis, Brühl 69 (tel. 218 60; fax 218 62 22). From the Hauptbahnhof, cross the street and head a block down Goethestr. Take a right onto the Brühl. If you run out of budget options, the Ibis is a 2min. walk from the train station, and in summer offers a per-room special price of DM89.90. Rooms normally DM125. Breakfast DM15. 24hr. reception.

Camping: Campingplatz Am Auensee, Gustav-Esche-Str. 5 (tel. 465 16 00), in the nearby suburb of Wahren. A budgetary *deus ex machina* in the absence of hostels. From the station, take streetcar #11 or 28 (direction: "Wahren") to "Rathaus Wahren." Turn left at the Rathaus, and follow the twisting main road for 10min. DM8 per person, DM5 per car, DM12 for caravans. Small tent-huts function as 2-bed bungalows. Small hut DM30, large hut with shower DM60. Reception M-Sa 6am-9:30pm, Su 6am-8:30pm.

FOOD

Budget meals are not as hard to find in Leipzig as budget rooms, but it's still no cakewalk. The Innenstadt is well-supplied with *Imbiß* stands, bistros, and restaurants for consumption on the go. A **Kaiser's supermarket** pops up on the Brühl, near Sachsenplatz. (Open M-F 7am-8pm, Sa 7am-4pm.) There's a **market** on Sachsenplatz on Tuesdays and Fridays. You'll also find a daily **market** just south of the Innenstadt near Bayerischer Platz.

Maître, Karl-Liebknecht-Str. 62 (tel. 391 33 63), treads the fine line between bar, café, and restaurant. Take streetcar #11 or 28 (direction: "Markleeberg Ost," or "Markleeberg West," respectively) to "Arndtstr." In the morning, choose from Swedish, Finnish, or Spanish breakfast options; later on, try one of the quiches (DM5.75-6.50) or salads (DM6-13). Breakfast buffet Su 10am-2:30pm (DM11.80). Open M-F 9am-1am, Sa 2pm-1am, Su 10am-midnight.

Ashoka, Georgiring 8-9 (tel. 961 48 19), to the right of the Hauptbahnhof. Chill to sitar music while consuming orgasmically good Indian food. Luncheon buffet M-F noon-3pm (DM14.90). Dinner DM13-25. Open M-F noon-3pm and 5pm-midnight, Sa-Su noon-midnight.

Bagel Brothers, Nikolaistr. 42 (tel. 980 33 30), between the Hauptbahnhof and the Nikolaikirche, smears cream cheese on light and fluffy bagels. Bagel with flavored cream cheese DM2.90. Gorge yourself at the Sunday morning all-you-can-eat breakfast (9:30am-3pm). DM9.90 for the first hour of the feast, DM2 each additional half hour. Open M-Th 7am-11pm, F 7am-2pm, Su 10am-9pm.

Café le bit, Kohlgartenstr. 2 (tel. 998 20 00), right off Friedrich-List-Platz. Heading toward the train station on Georgiring, turn right on Schützenstr., which becomes Rosa-Luxemburg-Str. and leads straight there (10min. from the station). Cyberfreaks email or browse while drinking themselves silly in the cyber-hip surroundings. First 30min. free; DM2 each additional 15min. The bar menu includes great crepes (DM3-8.50). Open M-F 8:30am-3am, Sa 10am-late, Su 10am-1am.

Eck-Café, in the university complex just off Grimmaische Str., across from the *Mensa.* Probably as close as you will ever get to being a Leipzig University scholar, since the *Mensa* is only open to students. Freshly prepared daily specials for about DM3. Open Oct.-Feb. and April-Aug. M-Th 9am-9pm, F 9:30am-4pm.

Alexandrina, Körnerstr. 27 (tel. 213 18 88), a store front on Karl-Liebknecht-Str. Follow directions to Maître and backtrack a bit toward town. An ideal location for satisfying the late-night cravings of patrons at the many nearby bars, but it merits a trip out of the city center anytime. A friendly staff fixes up delectable kebabs (DM4.50) and fantastic falafel (DM3.50). You never knew *Imbiß* stands could live so large.

Dreiundzwanzigstunden, corner of Emilienstr. and Petersteinweg. A 5min. walk from the Innenstadt; head down Petersteinweg from Roßplatz. This self-service restaurant heaps on the German food at great prices. *Schnitzel* (DM5.50-7.50), breakfasts (DM7). Open daily 6am-5am.

SIGHTS

INNENSTADT. Leipzig's historic city center suffered from both WWII bombings and from the poorly planned architectural creations of the post-war era. The heart of the city beats on at the **Marktplatz,** a colorful, cobblestoned square guarded by the slanted 16th-century **Altes Rathaus,** with its elegant **clock tower** showing four bright-blue faces. Inside, a grand festival hall runs above the **Stadtgeschichtliches Museum Leipzig** (tel. 96 51 30), which offers a straightforward look at Leipzig's history. *(Open Tu 2-8pm, W-Su 10am-6pm. DM5, students DM2.50.)*

AUERBACHS KELLER. Leipzig's most famous restaurant. Tucked inside the Mädlerpassage, it was in this 16th-century tavern that Mephisto tricked some drunkards in Goethe's *Faust*, before disappearing in a puff of smoke. The entrees don't quite make the budget range (DM25-30), but it's still worth taking a peek. *(Grimmaische Str. 2-4. Tel. 21 61 00. From the Markt, head away from the Rathaus, and you'll see the Keller ahead. Open daily 11:30am-midnight.)*

THOMASKIRCHE. A little farther down the street from the *Keller* stands the church in which Bach spent the last 27 years of his career. Though it's undergoing massive renovations for the Bach Festival (July 21-30, 2000), it is open to the public. Performances of the **Thomaschor,** one of Europe's most prestigious boys' choirs, take place Friday at 6pm, Saturday at 3pm and Sunday during services. *(Church open daily in summer 9am-6pm, in winter 9am-5pm.)*

NIKOLAIKIRCHE. The 800-year-old Nikolaikirche witnessed the birth of Bach's St. John Passion as well as the GDR's peaceful revolution. The sandstone exterior, an unfortunate product of 19th-century *fin-de-siècle* malaise, hides a truly exceptional interior. The ceilings and columns feature a majestic array of pinks and greens—not your usual flavor for a church, but the late 18th-century renovation was, after all, inspired by the not-so-usual French Baroque school.

In 1989, the church became the gathering point for what would become a truly revolutionary political engagement. What began as regular Monday meetings at the Nikolaikirche turned into massive weekly demonstrations *(Montagdemos)*, in which ever-growing numbers of Leipzigers called for an end to the Communist government's policies. On October 7, 1989, the nerves of the Communist government erupted in a display of police violence against unarmed citizens. Despite the heightened security measures, over 70,000 people showed up at the church for the demonstration on Monday, October 9. For reasons that remain unclear, the armed forces allowed the protest to pass without a response. The following Monday demonstration drew 120,000 emboldened citizens, and on October 18, SED party chief Erich Honecker resigned. *(On Nikolaistr., just a bit past the Thomaskirche in the direction of the university. Church open M-Sa 10am-6pm, Su after services. Free.)*

UNIVERSITÄT LEIPZIG. The former Karl-Marx-Universität lies on Universitätsstr. Its "sharp tooth" tower, a steel and concrete behemoth, displaced the centuries-old Universitätskirche and other popular buildings following a wave of faculty protests in 1968. Since the beginning of 1999 it stands empty, as the tower's design has proven increasingly unstable over the years.

VÖLKERSCHLACHTDENKMAL. Outside the city ring, the memorial remembers the 400,000 soldiers engaged in the 1813 Battle of Nations—a struggle that turned the tide against Napoleon and determined many of Europe's current national boundaries. The monument, overlooking a large pool, is an absolutely massive pile of sculpted brown rock that all but conclusively proves that Kaiser Wilhelm had a very small penis. A dizzying 500 steps spiral up in a nearly windowless, one-person-wide passage to the very top of the monument; on clear days, you can see the Harz mountain range. *(Tel. 878 04 71. Streetcar #15 or 21 from the Hauptbahnhof (direction: "Meusdorf") to "Völkerschlachtdenkmal" (20min.). Open daily May-Oct. 10am-5pm; Nov.-April 9am-4pm. To climb to the top DM5, students DM2.50.)*

LEIPZIGER MESSEGELÄNDE. Finished in 1996, the trade grounds consist of five mammoth halls all clustered around an arched main building that resembles the Biosphere. The building hosts trade fairs nearly non-stop throughout the year, but the futuristic buildings themselves are more worth seeing than the yuppies networking inside. Ask the tourist office for more information. *(S-bahn #16 or 21 to "Messegelände.")*

SACHSEN

🏛 MUSEUMS

Leipzig's museums rely upon the compelling cultural endowments of the city's past to fill its hallowed halls. From remembering the days of Bach to documenting the struggle against the Communist regime, the museums acknowledge Leipzig's unique position on Germany's cultural landscape.

MUSEUM DER BILDENDEN KÜNSTE LEIPZIG. Since WWII, Leipzig's fine arts museum was housed in the pre-war supreme court building—until the court recently decided to reoccupy, leaving the museum homeless. Until the new building on Sachsenplatz is completed in 2002, the museum is making do with the third floor of an old trade hall. Although presentation is a bit jumbled, the core of the collection is still on display, including some works by Rubens, interesting paintings dating back to the late Middle Ages, and an excellent collection of 19th-century German paintings. *(Grimmaische Str. 1-7, just behind the Altes Rathaus. Tel 21 69 90. Open Tu and Th-Su 10am-6pm, W 1-9:30pm. DM5, students and seniors DM2.50.)*

MUSEUM DER "RUNDEN ECKE". One of the more thought-provoking museums in the new *Bundesländer*. Housed in the regional headquarters of the East German Ministry for State Security, or *Stasi*, the museum presents a stunningly blunt exhibit on the history, doctrine, and tools of the secret police. Displays also chronicle the triumph of the resistance that overthrew the Communist regime. On the night of December 4, 1989, the people of Leipzig took over the *Stasi* building; inside, they found some 50,000 letters seized over the last 40 years and entire floors devoted to documentation of the actions of suspected resistors. Even more disturbing, perhaps, are the mountains of paper-pulp which were found outside, indicating that much of what went on inside the building will never be known. *(Dittrichring 24. Tel. 961 24 43. Open W-Su 2-6pm. Free.)*

JOHANN-SEBASTIAN-BACH-MUSEUM. A chronicle of Bach's time in Leipzig from 1723 to 1750. It was during this period that Bach wrote his masterpieces the St. John Passion and Mass in H minor. The composer is buried across the street from the museum in the Thomaskirche (see p. 181). The *Sommersaal* hosts concerts Wednesday at 3pm. *(Thomaskirchhof 16. Tel. 96 44 10. Open daily 10am-5pm. DM4, students and seniors DM2.50. Tours daily at 11am and 3pm; price depends on the size of the group. Concerts DM20, students and seniors DM15.)*

GRASSIMUSEUM. The museum is home to three smaller museums. The largest of the three, the **Museum für Völkerkunde** (anthropology museum), has a huge collection of clothing, religious objects, artwork, and just about everything else documenting the lives and customs of people around the world. *(Open Tu-F 10am-5:30pm, Sa-Su 10am-5pm.)* The university's **Musikinstrumenten Museum** exhibits over 5000 instruments, some dating back to the 16th century. While most are too pretty to be touched, some can be tried out in the "sound laboratory." *(Open Tu-Sa 10am-5pm, Su 10am-1pm.)* Enter the courtyard to find the **Museum des Kunsthandwerk** (arts and crafts museum). The permanent collection contains 60,000 objects from the medieval age to the present. *(All 3 museums located at Johannispl. 5-11. Tel 21 42. Walk past the university and down Grimmaischer Steinweg. Open Tu and Th-Su 10am-6pm, W noon-8pm. Each museum DM5, students DM3. Combination ticket to all three museums DM9, students DM6.)*

🎭 ENTERTAINMENT

The patrons that frequent the super-cool, slightly artsy cafes scattered around Leipzig also support a throbbing theater and music scene. Be forewarned: most theaters, musical and otherwise, take a *Sommerpause* in July and August, during which there are no performances. The musical offerings are top-notch, particularly at the **Gewandhaus-Orchester,** a major international orchestra since 1843. Some concerts are free, but usually only when a guest orchestra is playing; otherwise buy tickets (DM7-60; 20% student discount) at the *Gewandhaus* **box office,** Augustuspl. 8 (tel. 126 12 61), next to the university. (Open M 1-6pm, Tu-F 10am-

6pm, Sa 10am-2pm.) Leipzig's **Opera** (tel. 126 10) receives wide acclaim and gives Dresden's *Semper* company a run for its money. Tickets run DM18-60, with a 30% student discount, except for premieres. Head to the ticket counter at Augustuspl. 12 for more information. (Reservations by phone daily 8am-8pm. Counter open M-F 10am-8pm, Sa 10am-4pm, and 1½hr. before performances.) The **Bachfest 2000**, July 21-30, 2000, will bring the two companies to the streets for free performances.

The opera house is also the entry point to Leipzig's diverse **theater** scene: it hosts the experimental **Kellertheater** (tel. 126 12 61; fax 126 13 00) in its basement. Renowned for its theater, Leipzig has unleashed a wave of experimental plays in the wake of the latest revolution. The **Schauspielhaus**, Bosestr. 1 (tel. 126 80), just off Dittrichring, produces the classics, including offerings from Euripides, Heiner Müller, and Brecht. (Box office open M-F 10am-6pm, Sa 10am-1pm and 1½hr. before performance. Tickets DM10-30. Student discount 30-50%.) The cabaret scene is centered in the understated **academixer**, Kupgergasse 6 (tel. 960 48 48), run by the Leipzig student body. (Open M-F 10am-6pm, Sa 10am-1pm.) Also check out the more brash **Gohglmohsch**, Markt 9 (tel. 961 51 11), and the **Leipzig Pfeffermühle**, Thomas Kirchhof 16 (tel. 960 32 53). Leipzig offers documentaries and short films at its annual late Octover **film festival** (call 980 39 21 for information, or ask at the tourist office). **Kino im Grassi**, Täubchenweg 2d (tel. 960 48 38) and **naTo**, Karl-Liebknecht-Str. 46 (tel. 391 55 39), show indy films, usually subtitled.

NIGHTLIFE

Free magazines *Fritz* and *Blitz* fill you in on nightlife, but the superior *Kreuzer* (also sold at newsstands, DM2.50) puts these to shame. **Barfußgäschen,** a street just off the Markt, serves as the see-and-be-seen bar venue for everyone from students to *schicki-mickis* (Yuppies). **Markt Neun, Steel, Gohglmohsch** (whose cobblestones are covered in summer with outdoor seating from all sides), and **Spizz** start to fill up between 8 and 10pm and remain packed into the wee hours.

Karl-Liebknecht-Straße is just as *Szene*-ic without being quite as claustrophobic as Barfußgäschen. Take streetcar #11 (direction: "Markkleeburg-Ost") to "Arndtstr." During the day, **Boom Town** and **Mrs. Hippie** fill that extra space in your pack with used or otherwise funked-out clothing. At night, bars along the street pour drinks for Irish lovers (**Killiwilly** at #44), Francophiles and Francophones (**Maître** at #62, see **Food**, p. 180), tough art-house film types (**naTo** at #46, see **Entertainment**, above), caffeine addicts (**KAHWE** at the corner of Arndtstr. and Karl-Liebknecht-Str.), and everyone else (**Weißes Rössel** right next door). Most are open during the day for three-martini lunches, but nighttime revelry kicks off around 8pm.

Moritzbastei, Universitätsstr. 9 (tel. 702 59 13; tickets tel. 70 25 90), next to the university tower. Leipzig university students spent eight years excavating this series of medieval tunnels so they could get their groove on. A chill atmosphere presides over the multiple bars and dance floors, enhanced by frequent concerts. **Café Barbakan** (open M-F after 10am, Sa after 2pm), an **open-air movie theater** (screenings June-Aug. M-Tu and Th-Sa at 10pm, weather permitting), and the outdoor terrace and *Biergarten* (open in nice weather M-F 11:30am-midnight, Sa-Su 2pm-midnight) provide respite from the wild music scene. Things kick off after 9pm, with a particularly salacious scene for the jam-packed, Wednesday night *"Papperlapop"* disco. Cover DM4-7 for discos, slightly more for concerts. Bring student ID for discount.

Distillery (tel. 963 82 11), at the corner of Kurt-Eisner-Str. and Loßinger Str. Streetcar #5 or 16 (direction: "Lößing") to the "K.-Eisner-Str./A.-Hoffman-Str." stop. Distillery is to the left at the dead end on Kurt-Eisner-Str. F special parties, Sa two floors of pulsing house and techno. MTV was here recently=trendy. Things usually get going after 11pm. Cover DM10-15.

Jam, Große Fleischergasse 12 (tel. 961 74 32). About as commercial and top-10 as discos can get, but with one saving grace: the building was the former *Stasi* headquarters. Techniques of intimidation continue to prevail as people try to find out as much as possible about each other. Fridays feature a *Flirtparty,* while Saturdays are just too crazy to have a theme. Every second Sunday hosts a gay and lesbian party. Cover DM12-14, including a few drinks.

RosaLinde, Lindenauer Markt 21 (tel. 484 15 11). Streetcar #17 or 57 (direction: "Böhlitz-Ehrenberg") to "Lindenauer Markt." Described by some as the enter of the gay and lesbian scene, it features a disco Friday and Saturday nights in addition to its daily bar. Tuesday amply entertains with the raucous *Travesti-Show.* Open daily after 8pm.

Kutsche (tel. 211 43 74), on Brandenburger Str., by the station. Less commercial than RosaLinde, the gay bar features a darkroom in the basement. Though no longer a disco, it still gets pretty naughty, especially upstairs. Wednesdays hosts the *Kennenlernen-Party,* a mad pick-up scene. Monthly theme parties. Open daily after 7pm. No cover.

SACHSEN-ANHALT

Sachsen-Anhalt's endless, mesmerizing grass plains offer one of the more tranquil landscapes in Eastern Germany. The fact that the region suffers from the highest unemployment rate in Germany doesn't seem to slow down the rapid process of reconstruction and modernization underway. Sachsen-Anhalt contains a number of worthwhile destinations including Wittenberg, the city of Martin Luther and cradle of the Protestant Reformation; Magdeburg, home to a splendid Gothic cathedral where the first Holy Roman Emperor is buried; and the witch-haunted Harz Mountains, a popular hiking region. The grand cathedrals filling the skyline attest to the region's former importance, while the many construction sites mushrooming across the *Land* point toward its future.

HIGHLIGHTS OF SACHSEN-ANHALT

■ **Martin Luther,** the instigator of the Reformation, posted his *95 Theses* on a church in **Wittenberg.** The city still celebrates its native Jesus Christ superstar and has recently been blessed with a Hundertwasser-designed high school (p. 185).

■ The original **Bauhaus** demonstrates principles of the merger of form and function, imbuing the city of **Dessau** with design-school hipness (p. 188).

■ The castle-spotted **Harz mountains** offer tons of outdoor fun (p. 196). Walk in Goethe's footsteps to the top of the **Brocken** (p. 198) or visit the half-timbered towns of **Quedlinburg** (see p. 200) and **Wernigerode** (see p. 199).

WITTENBERG

Wittenberg does everything in its power to milk Martin Luther for what he's worth; in 1938, the town even went so far as to rename itself **Lutherstadt Wittenberg.** Luther claimed that the town was the source and fount of his life's work: he preached, taught, married (a scandal to the Catholic clergy), raised children, and led the Protestant Reformation in this picturesque town. The city's fondest memories are of Luther nailing the *95 Thesen* to the Schloßkirche in 1517 and of his scandalous (and exceptionally contrived) wedding, a made-for-TV event that the town reenacts every June. The infamous "Luther Year," 1996, witnessed the 450th anniversary of Martin Luther's death—an unparalleled tourist extravaganza. If you missed it, don't worry. Martin's remains still remain; although he died in Eisleben in 1546, his body was buried directly beneath the pulpit of the Schloßkirche.

Luther managed to hang onto his celebrity status in the officially atheistic GDR; he was, after all, a harsh critic of Catholic wealth, inciting early bourgeois revolutions. He also had a presence in the civil sphere, and for many East Germans the image of Luther risking his life to nail up his *95 Thesen* became an emblem of courageous resistance. A successor of Luther at the Schloßkirche pulpit, Pastor Friedrich Schorlemmer, was a key player in the 1989 revolution. Since that time, religious pilgrims have returned in full force to Luther's city. The slow shuffle of Scandinavian church groups has pushed up *Schnitzel* prices while giving a fresh gleam to the architectural remnants. The huge new projects planned for the Expo 2000 spearhead an attempt to widen the spectrum of tourist attractions. Nothing, however, can compete with **Luthers Hochzeit,** a yearly event bringing more than 100,000 visitors to tiny Wittenberg (June 16-18, 2000). Theatrical performances, music, and dancing will turn the city into one of the best medieval festivals to take place in Germany at the break of the millennium. For more information about the event, contact the Kulturamt (tel. 49 66 22).

◪ ORIENTATION AND PRACTICAL INFORMATION. Wittenberg makes an excellent daytrip from Berlin or Leipzig. **Trains** leave for Berlin (1½hr., every 2hr., DM39), Dessau (30min., 1 per hour, DM10), Magdeburg (1½hr., 6 per day, DM22), and Leipzig (1hr., every 2hr., DM16). Instead of disembarking at the less-than-central Hauptbahnhof, get off at Wittenberg-Elbtor. Walk straight down Elbstr., hook a left at the second intersection (Schloßstr.), and walk for five minutes to the Schloß. Directly across the street, the brand new **tourist office,** Schloßpl. 2 (tel. 49 86 10; fax 49 86 11), provides maps and books **rooms** (DM25-75) for a DM3 fee. (Open March-Oct. M-F 9am-6pm, Sa 10am-3pm, Su 11am-4pm; Nov.-Feb. M-F 10am-4pm, Sa 10am-2pm, Su 11am-3pm.) **Tours** leave daily at 2pm from the Schloßkirche (DM10). The **regional tourist office,** Mittelstr. 33 (tel. 40 26 10; fax 40 58 57), by the Lutherhalle, has provides information about cultural events, and the staff is eager to welcome you to scenic Sachsen-Anhalt. (Open April-Oct. daily 9:30am-5:30pm; Nov.-March M-F 9:30am-5:30pm.) Rent **bikes** at **M&B Fahrradladen,** Coswiger Str. 21 (tel. 40 28 49), for DM8 per day. The **pharmacy** on Marktplatz, where painter Lucas Cranach pushed drugs to support his art habit, posts a rotating schedule of all-night pharmacies. (Open M-F 8am-6:30pm, Sa 9am-noon.) **Sparkasse,** Markt 20, has several **ATMs.** (Open M-F 8:30am-6pm, Sa 9am-1pm.) The **post office,** 06886 Wittenberg, is near the Lutherhalle on the corner of Friedrichstr. and Fleischerstr. (Open M-F 8am-6pm, Sa 9am-noon.) The **telephone code** is 03491.

⌐ ACCOMMODATIONS. The **Jugendherberge (HI)** (tel./fax 40 32 55), located in the castle, is haunted by the ghosts of the Reformation and the rabid kids who tear through the place every summer. Cross the street from the tourist office and walk straight into the castle's enclosure, then trek up the spiraling stairs to the right. All rooms sport snazzy new bunk beds and closets as part of a renovation campaign that has also left the bathrooms immaculate. There are a few doubles and quads and a number of spacious 10- to 18-bed rooms. (DM21, over 26 DM26. Breakfast included. Sheets DM6. Reception 5-10pm. Lockout 10pm, but keys are available for a DM10 deposit. Reservations recommended, but the hostel sometimes offers floor space for a reduced rate if it's full.) While not centrally located, **Gästehaus Wolter,** Rheinsdorfer Weg 77 (tel. 41 25 78), sings sweet lullabies with its truly homey ambience, complete with playground, family dog, sunny rooms with TV, and spotless bathrooms. Ride bus #302, 314, or 315 to "Elbedruckerei," walk in the direction of the bus, take the first right, and veer right on Rheinsdorfer Weg. If this sounds confusing, call Frau Wolter and she will happily pick you up from town. (Singles DM35; doubles DM70-90. Breakfast included. 24hr. reception.)

◨◪ FOOD AND ENTERTAINMENT. A number of delectable delights at low cost lie along the Collegienstr.-Schloßstr. strip, and a **City-Kauf supermarket** waits across from Coswiger Str. 15, about 20m from the tourist office. (Open M-F 8am-6:30pm, Sa 8am-12:30pm.) **Bosphorus,** Collegienstr. 64 (tel. 41 15 90), cooks up a filling, spicy *Döner Kebab* platter with a cucumber-tomato salad (DM10); tasty vegetarian entrees, such as falafel (DM4), provide a cheap respite from the tyranny of *Schnitzel.* (Open daily 9am-10pm.) Get Guinness on tap at the **Irish Harp Pub,** Collegienstr. 71 (tel. 41 01 50), where live English and Irish music rumbles on Saturdays. (Open daily 3pm-3am. Cover DM7.) Members of Wittenberg's artsy theater crowd occasionally burst into song or soliloquy at **Vis à Vis,** Sternstr. 14 (tel. 40 67 65), a cozy alternative establishment with an almost entirely vegetarian menu (main courses DM10) and tea specialities that add flavor to the lively atmosphere. The staff puts up musical productions, and local bands rock the house on weekends. (Open M-Th and Su 3pm-1am, F-Sa 3pm-2am.) Theater buffs get their fix at the **Mitteldeutsches Landestheater,** which puts on a variety of contemporary plays; buy tickets at Collegienstr. 74. (Tel. 40 20 85 or 40 20 86. Box office open M-F 10am-12:30pm and 1-5:30pm.)

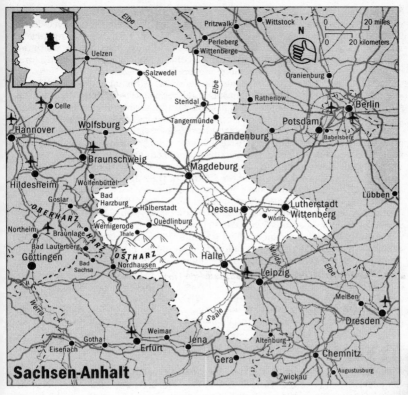

Sachsen-Anhalt

🔲 **SIGHTS.** Wittenberg's sights provide unending adulation of the eminently historical Luther. Plan your sight-seeing around **Collegienstr.**; the street is less than 1.5km long and encompasses all the major sights. The **Lutherhalle,** Collegienstr. 54 (tel. 40 26 71), to which Martin moved in 1508, houses a museum chronicling the history of the Reformation and also features paintings analogizing Luther to geese; while the metaphor may seem strained (Luther was a dumpy man, not a goose), the representation is supposed to symbolize his triumph in the face of adversity encountered in the fallout over his *95 Thesen.* Luther's ground-breaking translation of the Bible, considered a model of the German language, an original **Gutenberg Bible,** and many angry responses to the feisty minister's theses are also on display. An obnoxious tourist's graffiti has also been preserved: Russian Czar Peter the Great scribbled his name above the door when he stopped by in 1702. (Open April-Sept. Tu-Su 9am-6pm; Oct.-March Tu-Su 10am-5pm. DM7, students DM4.) Turn right from the Lutherhaus and stroll down to Lutherstr. to behold the elm tree under which Luther defiantly burned a papal bull (a decree of excommunication, not a Catholic beast).

At the end of Mittelstr. on the Marktplatz lies the **Stadtkirche St. Marien,** known for its dazzling altar painted by pharmacist and hometown art genius **Lucas Cranach the Elder.** The interior is a blend of Protestant severity and Catholic adornments, and bears eloquent testimony to the iconoclastic tradition begun here in 1522. (Open May-Oct. M-Sa 9am-5pm, Su 11am-5pm; Nov.-April M-Sa 10am-4pm, Su 11am-4pm.) Cranach lived in Wittenberg for most of his life. His home, **Cranachhof,** can be found at Markt 4. Under renovation until March 2000, the courtyard of the building is used as a lively open-air performance space; inside, the **Galerie im**

Cranach-Haus hosts some interesting modern art exhibitions. (Opening times and admission fees vary, but the gallery is usually open Tu-Sa 10am-6pm, Su 1-6pm.) Wittenberg's elegant white **Rathaus** dominates the Markt with its imposing facade. Matching statues of Luther and Reformation hero Philip Melanchthon share the square with the **Jungfernröhrwasser,** a 16th-century well whose refreshing (and potable) waters still flow through original wooden pipes.

Farther down Schloßstr., the **Schloßkirche,** crowned by a sumptuous Baroque cupola, holds a copy of the complaints that Luther nailed to its doors. At the front of the church, the man who fought to translate the scriptures into the common man's tongue is interred, ironically, under a Latin plaque. Also featured are the graves of Wittenberg's other important dead folks: Prince Electors Friedrich the Wise and Johann the Steadfast, and Reformation hero Philip Melanchthon the non-adjectivally monikered. In the 1840s, it was arranged that 15 people would check that old Luther was really buried here. The crypt was opened in secret for fear that failure to find Luther would discredit the church. Happily, they found the remains—or so they said. A sumptuous view of the surrounding countryside can be had atop the castle's enormous **tower.** (Church open May-Oct. M 2-5pm, Tu-Sa 10am-5pm, Su 11:30am-5pm; Nov.-April M 2-4pm, Tu-Sa 10am-4pm, Su 11:30am-4pm. Free. Tower open daily noon-5pm. DM2, students DM1.)

Recently, Wittenberg gained a new and unusual tourist attraction. A group of students at the local high school thought it would be fun to have the architect **Friedensreich Hundertwasser,** famous for his radical ideas, redesign their boring, pre-fab school building in his characteristically eccentric style. Apparently Hundertwasser thought it was a good idea as well, because Wittenberg now has what is perhaps the funkiest-looking high school in all of Germany. Follow Sternstr. out of the city center and turn right onto Schillerstr; the **Hundertwasser-Schule** is on the left. Shouldn't every building have trees growing from its roof?

DESSAU

The Bauhaus is undoubtedly the most significant architectural movement of the 20th century, and it was in Dessau, from 1925 to 1932, that its ideals and practices found a home. The Bauhaus art school was (and remains) a school of architecture and design where Bauhaus masters Walter Gropius, Hannes Meyer, László Moholy-Nagy, and their students struggled with aesthetic representations of modernity and attempted to reconcile human living space with 20th-century industrialization and urbanism. Hannes Meyer described their results perfectly when he said, "Building is *not* an aesthetic process." What he meant, and as Mies van der Rohe said, is that form follows function, where functionality consists not merely of pragmatic requirements, but also of the body and soul's needs. In short, the Bauhaus sought a unity of the human, the material, and the aesthetic. Though Dessau was not transformed in these short years, the masters did leave behind a number of stunning buildings. Unfortunately, Dessau *was* totally made over by WWII bombings; many Bauhaus buildings were obliterated, while others survived with considerable damage. It is appropriate and fortunate that Dessau has had more success in its post-war reconstruction than other former GDR cities. Though it has its share of run-down, faceless apartment blocks, much of Dessau's residential areas is lush and attractive, and its commercial areas are sleek and modern.

The history of Dessau stretches back into antiquity. Founded as a medieval fortress in 1341, Dessau became one of the first German Renaissance settlements. With the backing of Princess Henrietta Katharina von Oranien, Dessau flourished as a thriving center of cultural and economic importance. Dessau's famed Prince Leopold invented the method of marching in step, and introduced it into his regiment, thus creating a model for the Prussian army and stereotypes about German militarism. Dessau prides itself on a unique civic culture and its two major historical offspring. Moses Mendelssohn, one of the greatest German-Jewish philoso-

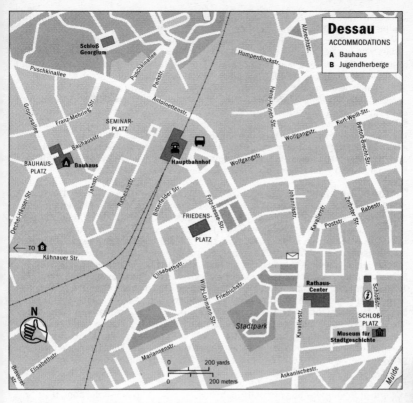

Dessau
ACCOMMODATIONS
A Bauhaus
B Jugendherberge

phers and a fervent proponent of religious tolerance in the 19th century, lived in Dessau, as did the greatly admired modern composer Kurt Weill, whose critical theater encouraged artistic resistance against Nazism.

■ **ORIENTATION AND PRACTICAL INFORMATION. Trains** depart for Berlin (2hr., 1 per hour, DM33), Leipzig (1hr., every 2hr., DM15), and Wittenberg (35min., every 2hr., DM10). Rent **bikes** at **Fahrradverleih Dieter Becker und Sohn,** Coswiger Str. 47. (Tel. 216 01 13. Open M-F 9am-noon and 2-6pm, Sa 9am-noon. DM10-12 per day.) The **Fahrradverleih am Wörlitzer Bahnhof,** Unruhstr. 10 (tel. 221 32 34), also puts wheels in motion. (Open M-F 9am-6pm. DM15 per day.) The **tourist office,** Zerbster Str. 2c (tel. 204 14 42; fax 204 11 42), finds **private rooms** (from DM30) for a DM5 fee and books hotel rooms for free; call or fax 220 30 03 for reservations. Take streetcar #1 or 2 from the train station's main exit to "Hauptpost." The office sits across the street from the huge *Rathaus-Center* signs. Walk toward the center and veer left on Ratsgasse. Take the first right; the office is on your left. The staff also sells the **Dessau Card,** a three-day ticket that allows up to one adult and one child unlimited access to all buses and streetcars in Dessau, as well as entry to most sights and museums. (DM15. Office open M-F 9am-7pm, Sa 9am-1pm.) **Tours** depart from the tourist office. (April-Oct. Sa at 10am. DM10, children DM1.50.) The **post office,** 06844 Dessau, is at the corner of Friedrichstr. and Kavalierstr. (Open M-F 8am-7pm, Sa 8am-noon.) The **Cyberb@r** on the top floor of the Karstadt in the Rathaus-Passage mall provides **internet access.** (Open M-F 9:30am-8pm, Sa 9:30am-4pm. DM5 for 30min.) The **telephone code** is 0340.

⬛ ACCOMMODATIONS. Dessau offers a unique opportunity to spend a night in the famous ⬛**Bauhaus** school building (tel. 650 83 18). Theory and practice converge in the functional and aesthetically pleasing singles (DM30) or doubles (DM50). They usually have free spaces, but call ahead (ask for Frau Oede) for reservations. Otherwise, knock on the door of room 318. For directions from the station, see **Sights,** below. The **Jugendherberge (HI),** Waldkaterweg 11 (tel. 61 94 52), is a 25-minute walk from the train station through suburban Dessau. Exit from the smaller *Westausgang* of the station through the underground tunnel, make a left onto Rathenaustr. and follow it to the end; at the intersection, zig-zag across and follow Kühnauer Str. for 10 minutes until you cross Kiefernweg. About 50m farther, a small path on the right (Waldkaterweg) leads to the hostel's woodsy entrance. The rooms are small and spartan, with metal beds and only a few chairs as furniture. (DM21, over 26 DM26. Breakfast included. Sheets DM6. Reception M-F 8am-4pm and 7:30-9:30pm, Sa-Su 6-9pm. Check-out 9am.)

⬛ FOOD. Affordable restaurants are difficult to come by in Dessau. The stunningly hip ⬛**Klub im Bauhaus** (tel. 650 84 44) in the Bauhaus school basement is a delightful place to indulge in angsty pretense over a light meal. To feel like the coolest cat ever, order the *Anarchistenfrühstück* (anarchist's breakfast)—a pot of coffee, some bread, and a *Karo* cigarette (DM4). For something less revolutionary, the spaghetti with pesto, feta cheese, and tomatoes (DM8) is enough savory food to make you wish they had doggie bags in Germany. The silver and black Bauhaus furniture completes the sensory experience. (Open M-F 8am-midnight, Sa 10am-midnight, Su 10am-6pm.) The **Ratskeller,** Zerbster Str. 4 (tel. 221 52 83), across the street from the Rathaus-Center, serves up Milchreis (DM10.80), the Dessau specialty that is best described as rice pudding with sugar and cinnamon. They've also got a tasty veggie and potato dish for DM14. (Open daily 11:30am-midnight.) The gleaming expanse of the newly built Rathaus-Center satisfies every craving for mall life, and the bakeries, produce stands, and **Tip supermarket** inside provide an easy end to the harrowing search for cheap eats. (Open M-F 8am-8pm, Sa 8am-4pm.) **Kiez Café,** Bertolt-Brecht-Str. 29a (tel. 21 20 32 or 21 20 37), just off Kurt-Weill-Str., is a good locale for a nightcap in the company of students. The café is a one-stop-shop for all your cultural needs, with a photo lab/dark room, theater, art studios, a cinema (DM7, students DM5), and **internet access.** (DM6 per hour. Café open M-Th and Su 8pm-1am, F-Sa 8pm-2am.)

⬛ SIGHTS. The Bauhaus began in Weimar in 1919, but the conservative local oligarchy pressured it to leave. The school toted its theory of constructive and artistic unity to Dessau in 1925; in 1932 the school fled yet again to the more brash Berlin before being exiled from the country in 1933 by the Nazis. Despite the necessity of remaining itinerant to avoid total dissolution, the Bauhaus masters inspired an architectural renaissance that attained its aesthetic zenith with the sleek skyscrapers of America's metropoli. After the war, as Dessau rebuilt, city planners perversely translated the shapely Bauhaus legacy into building-block-shaped monotony. Since 1977, the **Bauhaus,** Gropiusallee 38 (tel. 650 82 51), has housed a design school for international architecture. The school currently decorates its sparsely linear walls with the works of legendary alumni Gropius, Klee, Kandinsky, and Brandt. To get there from the station, turn left and go up the steps, then head left over the railroad tracks. Veer left at the first street onto Kleiststr., then right onto Bauhausstr. Or take bus E or K to "Bauhaus." The building is open for self-guided tours and there are rotating exhibits on Bauhaus themes in the hallways. There is also a special exhibit in the north space. (Building open 24hr. Free. Exhibition open Tu-Su 10am-5pm. DM5, students DM3.)

Taking a left from the Bauhaus entrance, a right on Gropiusallee, and a left on Ebertallee brings you to the **Kurt-Weill-Zentrum,** Ebertallee 63 (tel./fax 61 95 95), located in the former house of designer and painter Lyonel Feininger. The center has been restored to its original splendor, thus providing lucid insight into the

S A C H S E N - A N H A L T

school's musings. Occasional concerts honor the wacky Weill. (Open Tu-F 10am-5pm, Sa-Su noon-5pm. DM5, students DM3.) In addition, the annual **Kurt Weill festival** (Feb. 18-Mar. 5, 2000), this year celebrating the 100th anniversary of the conductor's birth, puts to practice the famous *Verfremdungseffekt*, a device that makes spectators feel drunk or confused. *Prost!* The Zentrum is the first in the row of the three famous Bauhaus *Meisterhäuser;* Georg Muche and Oskar Schlemmer each resided in house number two, and the third served as home to Kandinsky and Klee. Both houses are being restored and should be completed by 2000.

Several more spectacular Bauhaus buildings are scattered around town. To find them, pick up a copy of *Bauhaus Bauten in Dessau* (DM1) at the tourist office. Carl Fieger's **Kornhaus,** at the end of Elballee off Ebertallee, was designed as a modern-day fun house, with a beer hall, café, dance floor, and two terraces. To get a peek at the **Laubenganghäuser** on Peterholzstr., hop on streetcar #1 (direction: "Dessau-Süd") and hop off at "Damaschkestr." These were designed, in the true Bauhaus spirit, to be efficient, attractive housing tenements. Take a left onto Mittelring and behold an entire residential neighborhood in Bauhaus style. The house at Mittelring 38 is the **Moses-Mendelssohn-Zentrum** (tel. 850 11 99), which includes a museum about the philosopher's life and work as well as an exhibit on Jewish life in Dessau. (Open M-F 10am-5pm, Sa-Su noon-5pm. DM3, children DM2.)

Dessau also has its share of ornate, old-school architecture. From the Bauhaus, make a right on Gropiusallee to reach **Schloß Georgium,** Puschkinallee 100 (tel. 61 38 74), home to the **Anhaltische Gemäldegalerie.** Set in the midst of carefully tended formal gardens, the 17th-century country estate displays a range of lesser-known Old Masters' paintings from the 16th to the 19th century, while the tired exterior encases a couple of Lucas Cranach the Elder's star paintings. (Open Tu-Su 10am-5pm. DM5, students DM3. Gardens open 24hr.) **Schloß Mosigkau,** Knobelsdorffallee 3 (tel. 52 11 39), about 20 minutes from central Dessau, was built in 1752 as a summer hangout for Princess Anna Wilhelmine. Furnished in opulent Baroque style, the castle displays works by such masters as Rubens and van Dyck. Take bus D or L (direction: "Kochstedt") to "Schloß Mosigkau." (Open May-Sept. Tu-Su 10am-6pm; April and Oct. Tu-Su 10am-5pm; Nov.-March Tu-F 10am-4pm, Sa-Su 11am-4pm. DM5, students DM3.50.) If Dessau really floats your boat, visit the **Museum für Stadtgeschichte,** Schloßplatz 3a (tel. 220 96 12), in the Johannbau. The museum hosts off-beat exhibits on Dessau's history and contemporary political and cultural concerns. (Open Tu-Su, 10am-5pm. DM4, students DM2.)

WÖRLITZ

Prince Leopold III Friedrich Franz of Anhalt-Dessau is a local hero in Wörlitz, and both tourists and natives pronounce his name with a deep reverence and affection. Tourists relish the heavenly weekend destination he created, while natives are thankful for the tourist *Deutschmarks* drawn in by his estate. An eager traveler, Prince Franz encountered Enlightenment ideas during his trips to England, Italy, and France, and, convinced of their relevance, decided to put them into practice in his summer residence, the tiny village of Wörlitz. Driven by the desire to add an element of aesthetic perfection to the otherwise mundane life of his peasants, he commissioned the construction of a 112-hectare "English Garden," the first of its kind in mainland Europe. Jewels of classical and neo-Gothic architecture, fake antique ruins, and charming little bridges scattered throughout the beautifully landscaped park make Wörlitz a rewarding daytrip from Wittenberg or Dessau.

Though it appears natural, all of the area surrounding Wörlitz has been artificially landscaped according to the fancy of Prince Franz. A number of different parks, of which ■**Wörlitzer Park** is the largest, are strategically placed within a half an hour of one another. The village of Wörlitz is integrated into the park, reflecting an interesting choice—most aristocrats laid their parks out in such a way as to feel separated from, rather than a part of, the local community. The **Wörlitzer See** and a web of canals necessitate the use of ferries, which transport tourists between the more interesting sections of the park. (Ferries run daily in summer 9:30am-6:30pm. DM1, students DM0.50.) While it seems that something unusual lurks behind every tree, there are a few sights in particular that shouldn't be missed. **Schloß Wörlitz,** in the northeast corner of the village, is the first neo-classical building on the European mainland. Built between 1769 and 1773 by Prince Franz's close friend and travel companion Friedrich Wilhelm von Erdmannsdorff, the palace once again proves the prince's affection for his people. Virtually a part of the village, the location of the Schloß demonstrates the ruler's fascination with the ways of the English aristocracy, which did not separate itself from the commoners the way the German nobility did. The interior hosts a collection of antique furniture and Wedgewood ceramics. (Obligatory tours May-Sept. M 1-6pm, Tu-Su 10am-6pm; April-Oct. M 1-4:30pm, Tu-Su 10am-4:30pm. DM6, students DM3.)

Across the lake from the Schloß stands the appropriately named **Gotisches Haus,** Prince Franz's private retreat. Modelled on a Gothic Venetian church with English Tudor accents, the building seems worthy of a fairy-tale prince. While you can stare at the brick walls as long as you want for free, entry is possible only with a guided tour. (Tours May-Sept. M 1-6pm and Tu-Su 11am-6pm; April-Oct. M 1-4:30pm and Tu-Su 11am-4:30pm. DM5, students DM2.) Back in the village, the tower of the Romanesque **Kirche St. Petri** offers a beautiful view of the surrounding area. (Open Tu-Sa 11am-5pm, Su 11:30am-5pm. DM2, students DM1.)

After burning so many calories roaming the park, retreat to the village to pacify your empty stomach. **Grüner Baum,** Neuer Wall 103 (tel. 222 14), offers cheap *Bratwurst* (DM6.50) and goulash (DM8.90) as well as a great selection of home-made cakes in a shady garden. (Open daily 11am-9pm.) If potatoes in abundance is your idea of heaven, don't miss **Kartoffelkäfer,** Neue Reihe 149a (tel. 205 09). Start the potato feast with a bowl of potato soup (DM4.60), continue with a potato soufflé with herbs and mushrooms (DM13), and finish off with potato pancakes with apple sauce (DM4.80). Pure bliss. (Open daily 11am-11pm.)

Wörlitz is 18km from Dessau and 23km from Wittenberg. Regular **buses** connect the town with both cities. In Wittenberg, bus #348 leaves from Mauerstr., close to the intersection with Neue Str. (40min., 10 per day M-F); in Dessau, buses depart from bus platform #7 in front of the train station. (35min. 12 per day M-F, 5 per day Sa-Su. One-way DM4, round-trip DM6.) Disembark at the "Neue Reihe" stop. Rent **bikes** at the shop on Grabengasse, on the eastern side of the village. (Open M-Tu and Th 8am-noon and 2-6pm, W 8am-noon, F 8am-noon and 2-5pm.) The **tourist office,** Neuer Wall 103 (tel./fax 202 16), is down the street from the bus stop; follow the signs. The staff hand out maps of the park and book **private rooms** (from DM35) for free. (Open March-Oct. daily 10am-6pm; Nov.-Feb. M-F 9am-4pm.) A **tour** of the park leaves daily at 1:30pm from in front of the Schloß. (May-Sept. DM5, students DM2.) The **post office,** 06786 Wörlitz, is near the intersection of Erdmannsdorffstr. and Försterg. (Open M-F 2:30-5pm.) The **telephone code** is 034905.

HALLE

Halle an der Saale, the town saved by Katrin's drumming in the climactic scene of Brecht's *Mother Courage*, emerged from WWII relatively unscathed, although sometimes it's hard to tell in the dull physical landscape. Three months after the war came to a close, occupying Americans swapped Halle for a bit of Berlin under the terms of the Yalta agreement, and in the post-war decades, it served as Sachsen-Anhalt's political and industrial capital. Although several thousand workers have lost their jobs since reunification, adding a grim edge to the town, efforts are being made to salvage Halle's former beauty from the cascade of modern buildings that dominates its streets. While the Neustadt, an immense district of housing projects built under the Communist regime, stands untouched by capitalist evolution, the Altstadt boasts some historic beauty. The Moritzburg fortress' meager but well-chosen offerings of 20th-century avant-garde art, the lively university culture, and the contemporary theater scene all accompany Halle into the new millennium.

◢ ORIENTATION AND PRACTICAL INFORMATION. Halle is divided into several districts; most significant are the GDR-style **Neustadt** and the historical **Altstadt,** separated by the scenic Saale River. Come nightfall, Neustadt is not so secure, as political extremists (both right and left) reportedly roam this area. The train station as well as major streetcar termini are located in the Altstadt. If you haven't come to see the dingy and gray GDR-era housing, stick with the safer, brighter Altstadt areas—you'll still get your share.

Although most of Halle is walkable, streetcars efficiently cover the town (single ticket DM2.50, day pass DM7). The system is easy to use, and all stops are clearly marked, though be wary of possible route changes while tracks are being replaced. The main street is **Große Ulrichstr.;** moving away from the **Marktplatz,** it becomes Geiststr., then Bernburger Str.

The **tourist office** (tel. 202 33 40; reservations tel. 202 83 71; fax 50 27 98) is in the Roter Turm, on Marktplatz. From the main station, leave from the E.-Kamieth-Str. exit and head right to the buses, streetcars, and pedestrian tunnel to town. Follow the pedestrian tunnel and take a left on the pedestrian street Leipziger Str. past the Leipziger Turm to Marktplatz (15min.). Or take streetcar #4 (direction: "Heide/Hubertusplatz") or 7 (direction: "Kröllwitz") four stops to "Markt." The office hands out city maps, sells tickets, offers a number of pamphlets on cultural events, and finds **rooms** (DM35-50) for a DM5 fee. (Open M-F 10am-8pm, Sa 10am-2pm; May-Sept. also Su 10am-2pm.) **Tours** leave from Marktplatz. (M-Sa at 2pm. DM8.50, students and seniors DM5.) You can **exchange money** at several banks near Marktplatz, including **Deutsche Bank,** which has a 24-hour **ATM.** (Open M, Tu, and Th 9am-6pm, W and F 9am-3pm.) The **Weiberwirtschaft women's agency,** Robert-Franz-Ring 22 (tel. 202 43 31), complements meetings and lectures with a hotline and café. (Office and help-line open M-F 10am-4pm; café Tu and F 4pm-midnight.) For advice on all things queer, contact **BBZ "Lebensart,"** Schmeerstr. 22 (tel. 202 33 85). The **post office,** 06108 Halle, is at the corner of Hansering and Große Steinstr., five minutes from the Marktplatz. (Open M-F 8am-6pm, Sa 9am-noon.) The **telephone code** is 0345.

⌐ ACCOMMODATIONS. Hotels and *Pensionen* are generally far above the budgetary means of simple traveling folk, but the tourist office lists **private rooms.** Halle's **Jugendherberge (HI),** August-Bebel-Str. 48a (tel./fax 202 47 16), rests in a newly restored mansion north of the market. To get there, it's either a five-minute walk straight down August-Bebel-Str. from the *Opernhaus* on Universitätsring or a ride on streetcar #7 (direction: "Kröllwitz") to "Puschkinstr.," two stops from the Markt. Follow Geiststr. one block, turn right onto Puschkinstr., and take a right onto August-Bebel-Str. at the Hong Kong restaurant. Walk two blocks down; the hostel is on your left. The quiet residential location, proximity to the city center, and hardwood elegance of the common areas elicit that sublime feeling of youth hostel joy. Most rooms have six beds, though some doubles are available. Ask for room #7—it has a balcony. (DM23, over 26 DM28. Breakfast included; dinner DM7. Sheets DM6. Reception 5-11pm, but someone is usually there during the day. Curfew 11pm, but you can get a key. Call ahead.)

◻ FOOD. Affordable sit-down restaurants are a difficult find in Halle, but coffeehouses, ice cream parlors, and cafés line Leipziger Str. and Marktplatz. Between Marktplatz and Moritzburg, cafés cater to a lively student crowd. Halle also boasts several outdoor **markets** and cheap **supermarkets. EDEKA** is on Leipziger Str., approximately one block from the train station. (Open M-F 8am-8pm, Sa 8am-4pm.) **Café Nöö,** Große Klausstr. 11 (tel. 20 21 65 1), at the end of the street facing Domstr., is far töö green-tinted and cööl to say nöö töö. Occupying the ground floor of a building filled with social change and environmental groups, the café serves affordable breakfast (DM4.90-6.50, with coffee DM9) and salads (DM6.40-7.20), with a daily international menu that allows you to forget the evils of the world for a while. Vote Green! (Open M-Th 8am-1am, F 8am-2am, Su 4:30am-8:30am and 10am-2am.) At **Café & Bar Unikum,** Universitätsring 23 (tel. 202 13 03), there's serious hipster *Uni*-action going on amidst smoke and modern art. Cheap salads (DM4.50-6.30), sandwiches (DM3.30-3.90), and daily specials. (DM4.50-10) adorn the menu. (Open M-Th 8am-1am, F 8am-2am, Sa 4pm-midnight, Su 6am-1am.) Local flavor suffers an identity crisis at **Zur Apotheke,** Mühlberg 4a, off Mühlgasse between the Dom and Moritzburg fortress, with Thüringer morsels served in Sachsen-Anhalt. (DM6-13. Open M-Th 9am-1am, F-Sa 9am-2am, Su 9am-1am.)

⚙ SIGHTS. Central Halle revolves around the **Marktplatz,** which bustles with traffic, vegetable stands, and three-card monte con artists. At its center stands the **Roter Turm,** a 400-year-old bell tower. A number of popular myths surround the origin of the tower's name; some credit the copper roof, while others say the architect was a commie. The most gruesome version relates that after it was built (1418-1506), the blood of the people being executed on the adjoining gallows splattered onto the tower, lending it a grisly tinge. Across from the tower lies the **Marktkirche unsere lieben Frauen,** whose altar is adorned with a triptych painted by Lucas Cranach's disciples. The organ on which Händel began his musical studies swings above the altar; the stops were silent for over 100 years until recent renovations. (Open M-Tu, Th-F 10am-noon and 3-6pm, W 3-6pm, Sa 10am-noon and 3-5pm. Free 30min. organ concerts Tu and Th at 4pm.) Just to the right of the church is the red 16th-century **Marktschlößchen,** an unassuming, rather small castle overlooking the Marktplatz. The **Galerie Marktschlößchen,** Markt 13 (tel. 202 91 41), features works of lesser-known contemporary European artists. (Open M-F 10am-7pm, Sa-Su 10am-6pm.) The second floor houses the **Musikinstrumentensammlung des Händel-Hauses,** with an impressive collection of keyboard instruments, as well as three majestic music boxes, on display. (Open W-Su 1:30-5:30pm. DM2, students DM1, Th free.)

An 1859 centennial memorial to composer Georg Friedrich Händel decorates the Marktplatz, but the most important Händel shrine remains his familial home. The outstanding **Händelhaus,** Große Nikolaistr. 5 (tel. 50 09 00), is a short walk from the market down Kleine Klausstr. (Open M-W and F-Su 9:30am-5:30pm, Th 9:30am-9pm. DM4, students and seniors DM2, Th free.) If you call ahead, you can also get a cassette tour which covers the composer's career. From Händel's home, the **Dom** is a five-minute walk down Nikolaistr. (Open M-Sa 2:30-4pm.) This ancient complex, begun in 1250, remains a significant repository of religious relics. Today the church's most treasured offerings, renovations permitting, are 17 life-size figures by Peter Schroh from the 16th century. Witness the annual **Händel-Festspiele** (June 2-11, 2000), a celebration of Baroque music and one of its greatest masters. Tickets are available from the tourist office.

To reach the white-washed **Moritzburg fortress,** go around the far side of the Dom and head downhill, then turn right on Schloßburgstr. and walk up the hill. The **Staatliche Galerie Moritzburg** (tel. 281 20 10) occupies most of the 15th-century giant. The largest art museum in Sachsen-Anhalt focuses mostly on 19th- and 20th-century German painters. Halle's once-extensive Expressionist collection—including works by Max Beckmann, Paul Klee, and Oskar Kokoschka—offended Hitler, who drew heavily from this museum to furnish the infamous exhibit of *Entartete Kunst* (degenerate art) that toured Nazi Germany. Although much of the collection was either burned or sold off by the Nazis, the salvaged works remain an impressive monument to artistic freedom. Lyonel Feininger, Bauhaus headmaster and Expressionist painter, lived part-time in the tower at the entrance from 1929 to 1931 while completing his series of paintings of Halle; two still remain in the museum. (Open Tu 11am-8:30pm, W-Su 10am-6pm; last entry 30min. before closing. DM5, students DM3, Tu free.)

🎵🖼 ENTERTAINMENT AND NIGHTLIFE. Halle's swiftly growing theater scene produces the classics as well as contemporary German plays. Pick up a free copy of the city magazines *Fritz* and *Blitz* at the tourist office or in cafes and bars to find out what's going on.

Halle hosts a number of organ concerts in the **Konzerthalle,** Kleine Brauhausstr. 26. (Tel. 221 30 26. Box office open M 10am-1pm and 3-6pm, Tu and Th 3-6pm, F 10am-1pm. Tickets DM12-38, students DM8-29.) Completed in 1990, the **Neues Theater,** Große Ulrichstr. 50 (tel. 205 02 22), features a wide palate of works—everything from Schiller, Shakespeare, Molière, and Brecht to Halle's own home-grown playwrights. (Box office open M-Sa 10am-8:30pm and 1hr. before performance. DM10-25, students DM7-15. No performances mid-July to Sept.)

Halle's satirical theater, **Die Kiebitzensteiner,** (tel. 202 39 81), in the Moritzburg fortress' south tower, is tucked beneath the fortress and serves as a contemporary forum for criticism, holding spicy and engaging performances. **Kiebitzkeller,** the restaurant downstairs, offers snacks and spirits for nightly performances. (Theater open Tu-Sa from 7pm. Ticket office open Tu-Sa 5-8pm and 1hr. before shows. Restaurant opens at 6pm on evenings of performances.) **Kleines Thalia Theater,** (tel. 20 40 50), on Thaliapassage off Geiststr., premieres avant-garde theater productions as well as kiddie shows. (Box office open Tu and F 10am-noon and 1-4pm, W 10am-noon, Th 10am-noon and 1-6pm, and 1hr. before performances. DM12, children and students DM7.) **Turm** (tel. 202 37 37), in the northeast tower of the Moritzburg fortress, hosts the city's *Studentenklub* for Halle's literary set. The music is a mishmash of disco, punk, funk, blues, techno, and rock performed by local bands. A *Biergarten* and grill are outside. (Open daily 6-10pm.) Foreign students with ID (18 and over) are welcome. (Open Su, Tu, and sometimes Th from 8:30pm. Disco W and F-Sa from 10pm.) **Pierrot,** Großer Sandberg 10 (tel. 290 32 31), just off Leipziger Str., is a popular gay and lesbian bar and disco. Wednesday hosts a singles party, while Thursday features house and techno. (Open M-Th and Su 6pm-late. F-Sa disco after 8pm. Sa cover DM5.)

NAUMBURG

The town of Naumburg squats in the beautiful scenery of the Saale river valley, beckoning visitors with its medieval flavor. One of East Germany's 12 "model cities," Naumburg has been saved from destruction and blessed with a phenomenal cathedral. Careful restoration has revealed a colorful city center, reminiscent of Naumburg during its medieval days of glory, when its reputation as a trade city was rivaled only by Frankfurt am Main.

⚑ ORIENTATION AND PRACTICAL INFORMATION. Naumburg is an excellent sidelight during a visit to Leipzig (30min. by express train; those travelling on the cheap should take the 1½hr. local train via Großkorbetha, DM14.80), Halle (45min., 1 per hour, DM12), Weimar (45min., 31 per day, DM12), or Erfurt (30min., 31 per day, DM16.20). There are two competing **tourist offices** in Naumburg. One is on the market square at Markt 6. (Tel. 20 16 14; fax 26 60 47. Open M-F 9am-6pm, Sa 9am-1pm.) The other is near the entrance to the Dom at Steinweg 15. (Tel./fax 20 25 14. Open daily 10am-5pm.) Both are stocked with brochures and books on Naumburg and the surrounding region, and the office on the Markt arranges private **rooms** (from DM32) for free. To reach the Altstadt, head down Markgrafenweg from the train station, bearing right until you reach the end of the street. To the left is a winding cobblestoned path that leads uphill to the town proper. At the top of the path a sign points to the Dom; follow it until the cathedral's huge towers poke above the rooftops to guide you. There is an **ATM** on Markgrafenweg, immediately to the right as you exit the train station. The **telephone code** is 03445.

⌨ ACCOMMODATIONS AND FOOD. To reach Naumburg's **Jugendgästehaus,** Am Tennispl. 9 (tel./fax 70 34 22), from the Marktplatz, follow Wenzelsstr. out of the old walled city to Bürgergartenstr., which appears slightly to the right at the end of Wenzelsstr., then go straight until you see signs for the hostel (30min.). A monument to good old Eastern hosteling, this hostel is slowly being remodeled out of its current GDR standard. Double rooms with attached bath (and larger dorms without) all come with breakfast. (Dorms DM24 per person, over 26 DM29; doubles DM27, over 26 DM32. Sheets DM6. Reception 5-10pm.) Cheap meals await at the Markt and the Holzmarkt areas. For a chic cup of coffee or light meal, try **Engelgasse 3** (tel. 20 07 70)—"What's the address?" you might wonder. To get there, face the Rathaus from the Markt, and walk all the way around the building. A café, used book store, and art gallery, it has the retro, feel-good, funky style of renowned Leipzig illustrator Thomas Müller, further enhanced by omnipresent posters, menus, paintings, and postcards featuring the artist's work. Almost all of the ingredients on the menu come from small area farms, a *Brötchen* with *Bratwurst* or goat's milk gouda will run DM4.90-DM5.90. (Open M-W 11am-7pm, Th-F 11am-11pm, Sa 11am-4pm.) Another culinary surprise is **China-Garten,** Rosbacher Str. 4 (tel. 30 90), at the end of Markgrafenweg. The restaurant flaunts lacquer trim, mirrors, and Asian instrumental pop. The lunch specials (DM9-14) are the best deal—tons of food plus a big veggie-stuffed spring roll. (Open daily 11:30am-2:45pm and 5:30-11:30pm.)

■ **SIGHTS.** A true relic, the **Naumburger Dom** undoubtedly merits a pilgrimage if only to gaze upon the lovely Uta, one of 12 striking stone figures put in place in 1250 as the Dom was being completed. (Open April-Sept. M-Sa 9am-6pm, Su noon-6pm; Nov.-Feb. M-Sa 9am-4pm, Su noon-4pm; March and Oct. M-Sa 9am-5pm, Su noon-5pm. DM6, students and seniors DM4. DM10 fee to take photos or use video cameras inside.) Uta is considered to be one of the best examples of realism between classical times and the Renaissance. Too humble to carve his name in the cathedral's stone, the artist is remembered today simply as the *Naumburger Meister* (the Naumburg master). The sculptures of the double-chinned Eckehard and Snow-White-esque bride Uta were nearly taken from the Dom as reparations payments to the French after WWII. The removal proved to be effectively impossible, so Naumburg kept its treasures. The helpful staff at the front desk provides English pamphlets on request; English tours are also available.

The rest of Naumburg has recovered amazingly well from its 45 years as a backwater Red Army post. A jaunt past the Dom on Steinweg leads to Naumburg's bright, lively **market.** Just off the market square is the **Wenzelskirche,** the Dom's earnest runner-up. Its peeling walls provide a solemn backdrop for a few paintings by Cranach the Elder and an impressive 18th-century organ that received Bach's approval. (Open May-Sept. daily 10am-6pm; March-April and Oct. daily 10am-5pm; Nov.-Feb. M-Sa 9am-4pm, Su 10am-4pm. Tours Th at 2pm and Sa at 10am. Free. Organ concerts May-Oct. W and Sa-Su at noon. DM2.) Lest you think Naumburg functions solely as a bastion of religious relics, Nietzsche, Fichte, and the world-famous founder of Egyptology, Richard Pelsius, all lived in Naumburg for parts of their illustrious lives. In spite of the pious monuments, Nietzsche spent some of his formative years here from 1850 to 1858 (before he shaved his Kurt Cobain-esque hairdo and cultivated the bushy moustache) and returned in 1890 to visit his mother, who wouldn't let little Friedrich leave because he was too darn crazy. The **Nietzsche-Haus,** Weingarten 18 (tel. 20 16 38), off Jakobstr., has a well-presented display on Nietzsche's life, plus a second floor full of esoteric temporary exhibits. (Open Tu-F 2-5pm, Sa-Su 10am-4pm. DM3, students DM1.50.) The brand-new **Stadtmuseum Naumburg,** Grochlitzer Str. 49 (tel. 70 35 03), contains exhibits detailing the history of the town. (Open Tu-Su 10am-5pm. DM4, children under 14 free.)

HARZ MOUNTAINS

Heinrich Heine wrote that even Mephistopheles stopped and trembled when he approached the Harz, the devil's dearest mountains. It's easy to see why Heine—as well as Goethe, Bismarck, and a host of others—fell in love with these mist-shrouded woodlands. Germany's 45-year division allowed the Harz Mountains to flourish in an artificial time warp. Since the region straddled the Iron Curtain, both East and West declared much of it off-limits, sparing it from development.

Now that the armed border guards have gone, visitors have taken their places and multiplied like mosquitoes; hikers and spa-fiends alike rush to these misty, rugged hills in the heart of the restored nation. The range stretches from the northwestern **Oberharz** to the wind-sheltered valleys of the south and Wernigerode in the east. Throughout the Harz, historic villages compete with the lush, natural beauty of the mountains and valleys. In summer, the foliage offers great biking and strik-

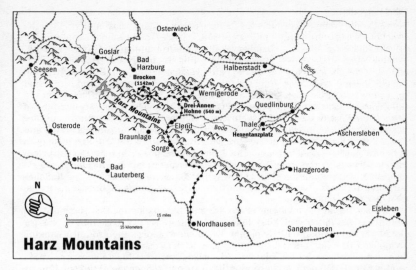

Harz Mountains

ing hiking, while the first snow signals the beginning of the skiing, skating, and tobogganing season. The **Ostharz,** untouched by the deforming winds of capitalism, is endowed with gorgeous scenery and half-abandoned castles. The **Harzquerbahn** and **Brockenbahn,** antique, narrow-gauge railways, steam through the gorgeous scenery from Nordhausen to **Wernigerode,** pass through the unfortunately named towns of **Sorge** and **Elend** (Sorrow and Misery), reach a 540m peak on **Drei Annen Hohne,** and chug along to **Brocken,** the Harz's highest peak (1142m). Trains run regularly in summer from 8:30am to 8:30pm. Schedules are available at most tourist offices, on the web at www.hsb-wr.de, and in the free monthly pamphlet *Brocken Tips,* which lists events and activities in Wernigerode, Goslar, and Quedlinburg. For more on cultural happenings and hiking tips, pick up a free copy of *Harz-Blick 43* at any Harz tourist office.

The easiest way to travel between the Ostharz and Oberharz is by **bus** lines between Bad Harzburg, the region's transportation hub, and Wernigerode. A **train** from Wernigerode to Bad Harzburg connects through Halberstadt and Vienenburg (1¾hr., 1 per hour, DM19.20). From Bad Harzburg, regular buses continue to Torfhaus and Braunlage. A more strenuous and interesting way involves a little jaunt through the woods. Torfhaus, Braunlage, Schierke, Elend, and Drei Annen Hohne all lie within a day's hike of one another. The **regional tourist office** in Goslar (p. 477) and the **regional bus station** in Wernigerode offer a wealth of information for navigating the region. Pick up a copy of the *Fahrplan der Verkehrs- und Tarifgemeinschaft Ostharz* (DM3) for a comprehensive list of bus and rail lines in the Ostharz. A similar *Fahrplan* is available for the buses in the Goslar Landkreis, which runs all over the *Oberharz.* Always be prepared for bad weather here, especially sudden and violent rainstorms. Travelers should call the **Braunlage Wetterstation** at (05520) 13 20 for summertime (April-Oct.) weather conditions. (Open 5:30am-11pm.) During the winter months (Nov.-March), call **Schneetelefon** at (05321) 340 40 or 200 24.

If possible, dive into the Harz to join in the immense regional celebration of **Walpurgisnacht** (April 30). The hedonistic festivities, immortalized by Goethe, center around legendary **witches** who sweep through the sky on broomsticks to land on **Brocken,** the Harz's highest peak. The legendary witches dance with the devil until midnight, at which point the May King cleans house. For more on regional sorcery, see **Raising Hell! Witchcraft in the Harz,** p. 202.

TORFHAUS

Tourists only come to Torfhaus for its near-perfect hiking trails and to climb the Brocken, at 1142m the Harz's tallest mountain. Since Goethe's first ascent in 1777, pilgrims have trampled the **Goetheweg,** the 16km round-trip trail to the summit. Though much of the path is littered in parts, it is still lovely and historically interesting, occasionally following the old patrol road along the Iron Curtain. To get to the Goetheweg, walk away from the bus stop (toward Braunlage) and turn left at the yellow *Altenau—8km* sign. The Brocken peak (2½hr. from Torfhaus) is now a full-fledged tourist trap. The **Brockenmuseum** inside the electronic warfare post of the former East German state security service houses an information counter where you can buy hiking maps. (Open daily 9:30am-5pm in summer. DM3, students DM2.) From the top of the Brocken, trails head to the Ostharz, leading to Schierke and Drei Annen Hohne. The **Schmalspurbahn,** a train that transports less nimble tourists to and from the Brocken to Wernigerode, runs regularly, takes a long time, and costs a lot. (1hr. One-way DM26, round-trip DM42.) The **National-parkhaus Torfhaus,** Torfhaus 21 (tel./fax 263), sells maps of Brocken's trails. (DM7.80. Open daily 9am-5pm.)

Torfhaus lies at the midpoint of **bus** #63 and 422 connecting Bad Harzburg and Braunlage. **Ski-Verleih** (tel. 203), near the bus stop, rents cross-country skis for DM20 per day. (Open daily 8am-5pm when snow adorns the ground.) Walking away from Bad Harzburg, turn right at the *Altenau-8km* sign for the **Jugendherberge (HI),** Torfhaus 3. (Tel. 242; fax 254. DM23, over 26 DM28. Members only. Ski rentals from DM10 per day. Reception 12:15-1pm, 4:30-5pm, and 6:15-7pm. Curfew 10pm.) The **postal code** is 38667. The **telephone code** is 05320.

BRAUNLAGE

The ideal stop for hikers working the trails around the Brocken, Braunlage provides a needed rest from other excessively cute Harz villages. The town amply compensates for its lack of architectural panache with kilometers of excellent trails and the luxury of spas at backpacker prices. Packed with spa connoisseurs in summer and skiers in winter, Braunlage is also a likely bus stop for those traveling from the Oberharz to the Ostharz.

⚄ PRACTICAL INFORMATION. Buses cruise from Bad Harzburg (40min., DM6) and Torfhaus (20min., DM4) to Braunlage. Disembark at the "Von-Langen-Str." stop in the center of town. To get to the **tourist office,** Elbingeröder Str. 17 (tel. 194 33), backtrack on Herzog-Wilhelm-Str. and make a right onto Elbingeröder Str. You'll think you're entering a spaceship, but it's actually an enormous interactive electronic board that indicates which hotels and pensions are full (red light) and which have vacancies (green light). A brochure of the town with a hotel list (on paper) is also available for luddites. (Open M-F 7:30am-12:30pm and 2-5pm, Sa 9:30am-noon.) The **Post-Apotheke,** Marktstr. 5 (tel. 930 20), is the local **pharmacy.** (Open M-F 8am-1pm and 3-6pm, Sa 8am-1pm.) The **post office,** 38700 Braunlage, is at Marktstr. 16. (Open M-F 9am-noon and 2:30-5:30pm, Sa 9am-noon.) The **telephone code** is 05520.

▓▓ ACCOMMODATIONS AND FOOD. The view through the wall of windows in the dining room of Braunlage's **Jugendherberge (HI),** Von-Langen-Str. 28 (tel. 22 38; fax 15 69), provides reason enough to crash in its ideal location. The hostel often fills with school groups, so call ahead. From the bus stop, follow Von-Langen-Str. uphill for 15 minutes. (DM21, over 26 DM26. Breakfast included. Sheets DM5.70. Reception 1-10pm.) Braunlage has so many *Pensionen* (from DM30) and vacation homes (from DM25) you won't believe your eyes. Check out the electronic board at the tourist office or roam the streets. **Rhodos,** Elbingeröder Str. 3 (tel. 22 23), whips up Greek specialties (DM10-20) and pizzas. (DM8.50-13.50. Open daily 11:30am-3pm and 5pm-midnight.) Pick up **groceries** at **Penny Markt,** Marktstr. 22 (open M-F 8am-7pm, Sa 8am-3pm), and fresh produce next door at **Fruchthaus Möller,** Marktstr. 21. (Open M-F 9am-1pm and 3-8pm, Sa 9am-1pm.)

⚠️🏃 HIKING AND ENTERTAINMENT. The **Wurmbergseilbahn** chair lift (tel. 725) is an exhilarating way to approach the hiking paths around Braunlage. Take the lift to the top (17min.) to access the hiking trail to the Brocken (3hr.) Alternatively, disembark at the *Mittelstation* to reach the **Schierke** (2½hr.). The lift departs from the mountain base at the huge parking lot behind the ice rink; from the tourist office, turn left, then take the first right to its end. (Open May-Oct. 9am-5:20pm. One-way to the top DM8, round-trip DM13. To Mittelstation DM5, round-trip DM8.) When winter hits, cower inside the enclosed lift on your way up the slopes. (Open Dec.-Jan. daily 8:40am-4:40pm; Feb.-April 9am-5:10pm. Day pass for open-air cabins and ski lifts DM32, for enclosed cabins and lifts DM35.) Rent **skis at Horst Bähr,** Harzburger Str. 23 (tel. 627) for DM20 per day, or try **Café Zur Seilbahn** at the chair lift station. (Tel. 600. Open daily 9am-5pm. DM25 per day.) An **ice rink** (tel. 21 91) on Harzburger Str. fulfills the need for winter sports year-round. (Open Tu and Th-F 10am-noon and 2-4pm; W and Sa 10am-noon, 2-4pm, and 8-10pm; Su 10am-noon, 1:30-3:30pm, and 4-6pm. DM5.50, with *Kurkarte* DM5. Skate rental DM4.50.) The **Kurmittelhaus,** Ramsenweg 2 (tel. 22 41), and the adjacent **Hallen- und Freizeitbad** (tel. 27 88) soak, steam, massage, and mud-pack the weary into clean, relaxed, well-adjusted personalities. (Kurmittelhaus open M-F 7:30am-noon and 2-5pm. Baths open M-W and F 9am-12:30pm and 2-6:30pm, Th 9am-12:30pm and 2-8:30pm, Sa 9am-6:30pm, Su 9am-5pm; Tu women only. Sauna DM15; pool DM9.)

WERNIGERODE

Wernigerode was one of Goethe's secret spots in the hills, and though the 20th century has plastered the town with many gray, block-shaped buildings, Wernigerode's Altstadt seems untouched by the passage of time. Unquestionably the capital of the Harz, the half-timbered town is crowned with one of the most magnificent castles in the region. Riders of the **Querbahn** visit the town en route to Brocken, the Harz's highest peak; others come to enjoy the wide pedestrian areas lined with well-preserved architectural treats. Wernigerode is the natural crossing point from Western to Eastern Harz, making it the region's most touristed town.

🛈 ORIENTATION AND PRACTICAL INFORMATION. To reach Wernigerode from Magdeburg, change **trains** at Halberstadt (30min., 1 per hour, DM7.60); trains also run directly from Halle (2hr., every 2hr., DM31), and a **bus** travels from Bad Harzburg. The town has two **train stations. Wernigerode-Westentor** is the next-to-last stop on the *Harzquerbahn* and close to the city center—head up Mittelstr., and then right on Bahnhofstr. to arrive at the Markt. The antique steamer also stops at the main **Bahnhof Wernigerode,** next to the regional **bus terminal.** To get to the Marktplatz and the tourist office from the train station, walk up Albert-Bartels-Str., which is right by the bus station, and make a right at the big intersection onto Breite Str., which leads to the pedestrian zone. The **tourist office,** Nikolaipl. 1 (tel. 63 30 35; fax 63 20 40; www.harztourist.de), will be on your right on Nicolaipl. around the corner from the Rathaus. The staff books **rooms** (from DM35) in private homes or hotels. The office also sells a small town guide with an excellent pull-out map. (DM3. Open May-Oct. M-F 9am-7pm, Sa 10am-4pm, Su 10am-3pm; Oct.-April M-F 9am-6pm, Sa-Su 9am-3pm.) **Tours** depart from the tourist office. (Tu at 10:30am, W-Th at 2pm, Sa at 10:30am and 2pm, Su at 2pm. DM5.) There is a **Deutsche Bank** near the tourist office, at the corner of Kohlmarkt and Breite Str. (Open M, Tu, and Th 8:30am-1pm and 2-6pm, W 8:30am-1pm, F 8:30am-2pm.) **Exchange currency** at the **post office,** Marktstr. 14, 38855 Wernigerode. (Open M-F 8am-6pm, Sa 8am-noon.) There is a **pharmacy,** Rathaus-Apotheke, on Nikolaipl. (Open M-F 8am-6:30pm, Sa 9am-1pm.) The **telephone code** is 03943.

🍴🛏 ACCOMMODATIONS AND FOOD. To reach Wernigerode's **Jugendgäste-haus,** Friedrichstr. 53 (tel. 63 20 61), from the Westerntor station, go right on Unter den Zindeln and turn right on Friedrichstr. (25min.). From the station, take bus #1,

4, or 5 to "Kirchstr." The hostel is on the corner of Friedrichstr. and Kirchstr. Rooms have been refurbished and sport modern facilities. The friendly staff serves a fresh breakfast buffet. (DM21, over 26 DM27. Breakfast included. Sheets DM6. Reception noon-9pm.) **Spar,** on Breite Str. near the Rathaus, takes care of all your **grocery** needs. (Open M-W and F 8:30am-6pm, Th 8:30am-7pm, Sa 8am-1pm.) There's also a **farmer's market** in the pedestrian zone (Tu and Th 10am-5pm). **Euro-grill,** Westernstr.6 (tel. 60 55 65), just off the Markt, serves salads (DM3-6) that are visual and gastronomical feasts. Better yet, they only charge DM4 for a *Döner;* on Saturday, it's a mere DM3.50. **Café Casa Nova,** Breite Str. 89 (tel. 63 30 60), serves delicious pizzas. (DM4-12. Breakfast DM5-7. Open daily 11am-8pm.)

◙ SIGHTS. Wernigerode's **Schloß** (tel. 55 30 30), on its looming perch in the wooded mountains above town, is a plush and pompous monument to the Second Reich. Though the place was maintained by the GDR as a museum of feudalism, its guiding spirit was much more recent. Graf Otto, one of Bismarck's flunkies, hosted Kaiser Wilhelm I here for wildly extravagant hunting expeditions. The perfectly preserved **Königszimmer** guest suite, where the *Kaiser* stayed, oozes inbred, masculine luxury down to the deep green and gold brocaded wallpaper in the bedroom. The other regal rooms include a chapel, two drawing rooms, and the jaw-dropping **Festsaal,** featuring a sky-high inlaid wooden ceiling, panoramic murals of glorious Teutonic dukes, and the heaped wealth of the ducal table service. (Open May-Oct. daily 10am-6pm; Nov.-April Tu-F 10am-4pm, Sa-Su 10am-6pm. Last entry 30min before closing. DM8, students DM7; DM1 additional for a tour.) The flower-trimmed terrace sports a vista of the **Brocken,** the Harz's tallest and supposedly most haunted mountain. Ride up to the Schloß on the bumpy **Bimmelbahn** (tel. 60 40 00), a train that leaves from the clock at the intersection of Teichdamm and Klintgasse behind the Rathaus. (May-Oct. daily every 20min. 9:30am-5:30pm; Nov.-April every 45min. 10:30am-5:50pm. One-way DM3, under 10 DM2.) To walk it, take the gravel Christianalweg path or follow the white brick road marked "Burgberg" and ascend the wooded park to the castle (30min. from town center).

Back in town, the renovated **Rathaus** dominates the Marktplatz with its steep spire and sharply pitched roof. Small figurines of saints, virgins, miners, and other Wernigerode notables decorate the facade of the 500-year-old building. Walk around the Altstadt for a nearly lethal dose of half-timbered architecture. The **Krummelsche Haus,** Breite Str. 72, is so completely covered with ornate wood carvings that the original *Fachwerk* is hardly visible. The **Älteste Haus,** Hinterstr. 48, is the oldest house in the city, having survived fires, bombs, and various acts of God since its construction in the early 15th century. The **Kleinste Haus,** Kochstr. 43, is 3m wide and the door is only 1.7m high. (Open daily 10am-4pm. DM1.) The **Normalste Haus,** Witzestr. 13, has no distinguishing traits.

QUEDLINBURG

Quedlinburg is a model tourist destination. Intrinsically historical, the town comes complete with spires, castles, torture chambers, and half-timbered houses that look as though they've been around since 919, when Heinrich I waited in the market square for the news that he'd been chosen as emperor. In 1994, the city was crowned by UNESCO as one of the world's most important cultural treasures. Quedlinburg has been neglected for the past 50 years, but locals are busy painting and patching. Unfortunately, navigational difficulties will no doubt survive the renovations: the tiny alleys, bends, kinks, and crazily oblique intersections are the price of Quedlinburg's historic charm.

◪ ORIENTATION AND PRACTICAL INFORMATION. Trains arrive every hour from Thale (10min., DM3) and Magdeburg (1½hr., DM20). There are also regular **buses** that depart from the train station to most Harz towns. Rent **bikes** at the **Fahrradverleih** at the station. (Tel. 51 51 18. DM15 per day, mountain bikes DM20.)

Quedlinburg's **tourist office,** Markt 2 (tel. 773 00; fax 77 30 16), books **rooms** (from DM25) for free, sells museum tickets, and offers an invaluable map. (Open May-Sept. M-F 9am-7pm, Sa 10am-4pm; March-April, Oct., and Dec. M-F 9am-6pm, Sa 10am-3pm; Nov. and Jan.-Feb. M-F 9am-5pm.) **Tours** leave from the tourist office. (April-Oct. daily 10am and 2pm; Nov.-March daily 10am.) **Exchange money** or use the **ATM** in the **Deutsche Bank,** Am Markt 3. (Open M 8:30am-4pm, Tu and Th 8:30am-6pm, W and F 8:30am-1:30pm.) The **post office,** 06484 Quedlinburg, stands at the intersection of Bahnhofstr. and Turnstr. (Open M-F 8am-6pm, Sa 8:30am-noon.) The **telephone code** is 03946.

▚▞ ACCOMMODATIONS AND FOOD. There is no hostel in Quedlinburg, but the abundance of private rooms makes finding a cheap bed easy. Look for *Zimmer Frei* signs, inquire at the tourist office, or try **Gästehaus Biehl,** Blankenburger Str. 39 (tel./fax 70 35 38). Head up Marktstr. from the Markt and turn left onto Marschlingerhof, which becomes Blankenburger Str. Rooms have TV and showers. (Singles DM35, doubles DM60. Breakfast included. Call ahead.) Culinary delights await on every corner in town. On the way to the castle, grab a local brew at the **Brauhaus Lüdde,** Blasistr. 14 (tel. 70 52 06). The interior is a high-ceilinged, circular, wooden brewing hall with a bar, filled with shiny copper brewing kettles. Try the light *Pilsner* (DM3.90) or the nutty *Lüdde-Alt* (DM3.30). Tasty snacks and meals run DM12. (Open M-Th 11am-midnight, F-Sa 11am-1am, Su 11am-10pm.) **Pasta Mia,** Steinbrücke 23 (tel. 21 22), faces the Marktplatz and serves inexpensive pizzas (DM8-14) and pastas. (DM9-15. Open M-Sa 11am-10pm.) Twice a week, local farmers sell their harvest on the Marktplatz (W 7am-5pm, Sa 7am-noon).

◉ SIGHTS. Heinrich I died within the original walls of the **Schloßberg,** an old Saxon stronghold, in 936. The current 13th-century structure has been a favorite residence-in-exile for the ruling family's widows and inconvenient relatives. The castle complex consists of three parts: the museum, the garden, and the church. The **Schloßmuseum** (tel. 27 30) depicts city history from the Paleolithic era until the present, all according to good old Marxist historiography. (Open May-Sept. Tu-Su 10am-6pm; Oct.-April Tu-Su 9am-5pm. DM5, students DM3.) Several rooms, decorated according to 17th- and 18th-century fashion. Loiter in the gardens around the Schloß, or walk down the castle path past an impressive row of houses cramped together on the hillside. (Grounds open May-Oct. 6am-10pm; Nov.-April 6am-8pm.)

Underneath the castle, the **Lyonel-Feininger-Galerie,** Finkenherd 5a (tel. 22 38), is tucked away in a smart, modern white house. Inside is an *Angst*-heavy collection of Feininger's bleak landscapes and portraits vivisected by characteristic fracture lines, as well as temporary exhibits featuring works by contemporary artists. (Open Tu-Su 10am-noon and 1-6pm.) The unavoidable stone statue of **Roland** guards the ivy-covered **Rathaus** after nearly four centuries underground: the statue was smashed and buried as punishment for the people after a failed insurrection in the mid-14th century. The neighboring **Benediktikirche** graces the Markt with its 13th-century base; the twisting Solomonic columns of the altar are truly exceptional. (Open daily 10am-4pm.) The **Schreckensturm,** at the end of Neuendorf, served as Quedlinburg's 14th-century S&M torture palace. The **Wipertikirche** (tel. 77 30 12), a squat, mostly rebuilt Romanesque church a short walk from the Schloß, stands guard over the 1,000-year-old crypt, resting on the site of Heinrich I's court. (Open daily 11am-5pm.)

THALE

Above the dramatic front of Thale's flowing rivers, jagged cliffs, and splendid mountainside scenery lurks a region of myths, legends, witches, and demons. Like most towns in the Harz, Thale boasts that Goethe fancied its **Bodetal** valley—hence the *Goetheweg*. The peaks on either side of the valley are the sites around which the regions rich folklore centers—lucky for us that Germany's witches just happened to do their thing in the middle of lush mountain forests, the peaks of which offer spectacular views.

◪ ORIENTATION AND PRACTICAL INFORMATION. Trains leave for Thale from Quedlinburg (10min., 2 per hour, DM3). **Buses** depart to many Harz towns from the bus station next to the train station. Across the street from the train station, the **tourist office**, Rathausstr. 1 (tel. 25 97 or 22 77; fax 22 77), books **rooms** (DM25-40) for free. (Open May-Oct. M-F 9am-6pm, Sa-Su 9am-3pm; Nov.-April M-F 9am-5pm.) A **Sparkasse**, on Bahnhofstr. **exchanges money.** The **Hubertus-Apotheke,** Poststr. 15, is to the left as you exit the train station. (Open M-F 8am-6pm, Sa 8am-noon.) The **post office,** Poststr. 1, 06502 Thale, lies across from the pharmacy. (Open M-F 9am-6pm, Sa 9am-noon.) The **telephone code** is 03947.

◪◪ ACCOMMODATIONS AND FOOD. Thale's **Jugendherberge (HI),** Bodetal-Waldkater (tel. 28 81, fax 916 53), deserves a lofty laud; its cavernous two- to six-bed rooms look out into the mountains and the running river below. Follow the directions to the cable car station, but instead of taking a right over the bridges, keep walking along the river on Hubertusstr. (DM22, over 26 DM 27. Sheets DM6. Breakfast included. Dinner DM7. Reception 3-6pm and 8-10pm.) The hostel's cafeteria has lunch and dinner specials (DM7-9). Otherwise, the many food stands on Hexentanzplatz can fill your need for cheap eats. Straight ahead of the Sparkasse, Karl-Marx-Str. provides each according to his needs with shops, restaurants, and amusements. The **Wolf und Sohn supermarket** (open M-F 7:30am-1pm and 2:30-6pm, Sa 7:30-11am) and the **J. Goethe** bakery fill the gaps for the needier ones. Thale goes crazy every year on April 30 for **Walpurgisnacht,** but only go if you dare commit yourself to an orgy of sin.

◪◪ SIGHTS AND HIKING. Legend dates Thale's cultic history back to prehistoric times, when a sorceress named **Watelinde** led pagan rituals that forced incorrigible youths down a path of destruction in the fast-lane lifestyle of witchery. A few thousand years later a Harz resident named **Hilda** got lost in the woods for a couple of years—her reappearance was, by all accounts, a touch sketchy. Watelinde freaked out at the sight of Hilda and begged God to save her from the frightening countenance before her. Amidst explosive thunder and lightning, a whirlwind threw poor Watelinde into some rocks, which now comprise the nifty **Hexentanzplatz.** Amidst the celebrated spot of splattering are statues of demonic and ghoulish creatures adorned with parasitic animals. A witch bending over a rock in a provocative pose will distort every image of witches you might have picked up from Halloween decorations. Walk down the hill from the Hexentanz-

RAISING HELL! WITCHCRAFT IN THE

HARZ German ritualism is not limited to beer drinking. In prehistoric times, nomadic German tribes who weren't concerned about public infamy would gather atop the highest neighborhood mountain on the eve of April 30 to celebrate the wedding anniversary of Wodan and Freja (Nordic gods who controlled the seasons). In celebrations that would make most decadents blush, shepherds and farmers danced naked around live human and animal sacrifices in hopes of receiving a good harvest. The pagan rituals persisted into the modern era; Charlemagne and other zealous missionaries weren't enamored of the blasphemous celebrations, so they attempted to usurp the occasion by proclaiming the events of April 30 to May 1 **Walpurgisnacht,** in memory of St. Walpurga. Even Charlemagne's efforts to quiet the madness failed; the festivities later came to celebrate witchcraft and the devil. In 1484, Pope Innocent VIII decided to put a vicious end to the infernal games. A crusade against witchcraft over the next century tortured and slaughtered more than 7,000 "witches." The campaign brought activity to a halt until Goethe's interest in witchcraft and things Faustian inspired historical societies to spring up in this century and spread the myths of devilish delight anew. Today, the most vexing *Hexen* you'll likely encounter will be grumpy *Pension* owners who will curse you with nasty showers and stale *Brötchen*.

platz and to the wildly entertaining **Walpurgishalle,** a museum commemorating the Harz's history of witchcraft through displays of Thale's cultic ceremonies. (Open May-Sept. daily 9am-5pm; Oct.-April 9am-1pm. DM2, students DM1.) Next to the museum is the impressive **Harzer Bergtheater Thale** (tel. 23 24), a huge, outdoor amphitheater, with performances vacillating between the sublime (anything from operas to Goethe's *Faust*) and the infernal (live performances by German *Schlager* stars). Shows run sporadically May-Sept. (Tickets DM15-32; 30% discount for students.) Ascend to the Hexentanzplatz either by following the adventure-filled **Winde** that begins by the hostel (30min.)—on foggy days its teeming life and poor visibility are reminiscent of Yoda's cave in the Dagobah system—or by means of the **Kabinenbahn,** a cable car that crosses the Bodetal to Hexentanzplatz. The ride offers spectacular views of the valley and adds an element of adventure to the trip by dramatically stopping every so often for no apparent reason, except perhaps to make you realize why, after the *Goethezeit* was well over, the valley was dubbed the "Grand Canyon of Germany." The **Roßtrappe,** the rocky peak across the valley from the Hexentanzplatz, can be reached by hiking up Präsidentenweg and then up Esselsteig; the trail starts a bit up-river from the chair lift station in the valley. Or take the **Sessellift.** (Lift open in summer daily 9:30am-6pm; in winter Sa-Su 10am-4:30pm. Round-trip in the Kabinenbahn DM8, children DM6. Round-trip in the chair lift DM6, children DM4. Combination ticket for both DM12, children DM8.) Both cable cars depart from a station in the valley. From the tourist office, walk diagonally through the park, turn right onto Hubertusstr. and cross the bridges on the right.

MAGDEBURG

Magdeburg has four claims to fame: it has a spectacular cathedral, it's the birthplace of 18th-century composer Georg Phillipp Telemann, and it was devastated in both the Thirty Years War and WWII. On May 10, 1631, one of the most gruesome battles of the Thirty Years War decimated the city after Protestant town leaders refused to cut a deal with Catholic troops; and as a major industrial center, it was a prime Allied target in WWII. After the war, Magdeburg was rebuilt GDR-style—blessed with enviably broad boulevards and parks but cursed by concrete, cookie-cutter apartment blocks. In the months before reunification, Magdeburg had the good luck to triumph over Halle, becoming the new capital of Sachsen-Anhalt. Now, the gentrification fairies have arrived. Magdeburg offers its visitors a cathedral and historical sites, all set in a cosmopolitan shopping district. With renovations almost complete, Magdeburg increasingly resembles its sister-in-Domness, Köln, with a vibrant university and cultural *Szene* surrounding the center.

◪ ORIENTATION AND PRACTICAL INFORMATION. Magdeburg is conveniently configured for pedestrians. Most sights and museums are located on Otto-von-Guericke-Str. and Breiter Weg, parallel streets that lie less than 10 minutes away from the train station via Ernst-Reuter-Allee. **Streetcars** shuttle between the major attractions. (Single ticket DM2.40; day pass DM5; for up to two adults and three kids, DM7; for up to five adults, DM9.) **Trains** connect Magdeburg with Berlin (1½hr., 1 per hour, DM40) and Hannover (1½hr., 2 per hour, DM37). The **tourist office,** Alter Markt 12 (tel. 194 33; fax 540 49 10; email mi@magdeburg.de; www.magdeburg.de), is on the main market square. From the station, head straight on Ernst-Reuter-Allee and turn left at the second intersection onto Breiter Weg; turn right onto the market. Pick up a free copy of *Dates* magazine for a schedule of cultural activities and nightlife. The **Zimmervermittlung** (tel. 540 49 04), in the same office, finds **rooms** (DM25-75). The **Kartenvorverkauf** (tel. 540 49 02) sells tickets to shows, concerts, and other cultural events in town. (Office open M-F 10am-6pm, Sa 10am-1pm; the *Zimmervermittlung* and *Kartenvorverkauf* have the same hours, minus a lunch break from 1-1:45pm.) **Tours** leave daily from the office at 11am (DM5). A 24-hour **ATM** squats outside the main doors of the **Karstadt** department store on Breiter Weg. For a **taxi,** call 73 73 73 or 56 56 56. **Courage,** Pors-

SACHSEN-ANHALT

estr. 14 (tel./fax 404 80 89), is the local center for **women's resources. Internet access** is available in **Cyberb@r** (see **Food,** below) and **Orbit Cybercafé** (see **Entertainment,** p. 206). The **post office,** 39104 Magdeburg, sits in a late Gothic hulk on Breiter Weg. (Open M-F 7am-6pm.) The **telephone code** is 0391.

⌐ ACCOMMODATIONS AND CAMPING. The **☒Jugendherberge Magdeburger Hof,** Leiterstr. 10 (tel. 532 10 10; fax 532 10 20), hides a renovated interior in an ugly pre-fab exterior. All rooms have showers and toilets, and the furniture is simple but tasteful. The hostel is a mere two minutes from the station and even closer to the main sights and museums. Follow the streetcar tracks to the right from the train station until you pass the bus station and walk up the stairs under the cement covering; the hostel is 30m down on the right. (DM32, over 26 DM37. Breakfast and sheets included. Supplement for a single DM10, for a double DM5 per person. Reception 2-10pm.) Camp at **Campingplatz Am Barleber See** (tel. 50 32 44). Take streetcar #10 (direction: "Barleber See") to the end, continue down the main street and cross below the highway bridge. (Tent DM5. Reception 7am-9pm. Open May-Sept.)

⌐ FOOD. Many of the cheaper restaurants crowd the streets around the intersection of **Breiter Weg** and **Einsteinstr.** in **Hasselbachplatz.** This was the only section of the downtown to survive the bombing. The **Alter Markt** proffers a bounty of cheap food like half-roasted chickens (DM3.50) and *Bratwurst.* (Open M-F 8am-5pm, Sa 7am-noon.) The **Karstadt Restaurant-Café,** Breiter Weg 128, across from the market, offers **groceries** and a complete self-service cafeteria on the second floor. (Open M-F 9am-8pm, Sa 9am-4pm.) Next door, the **Cyberb@r** brings the **internet** to Magdeburg. (Same hours as the restaurant. DM4 per 30min.) **Ratskeller** (tel. 568 23 23), in the Alter Markt, is a historical set-up in the basement of the Baroque Rathaus. Play your cards right and this can be the best food deal in Magdeburg: while *à la carte* dinners are prohibitively expensive, the restaurant offers two special deals. Each weekday features a different *Stammesse* (lunch special) from 11am to 3pm, including an entree, starch, and dessert for a delightful DM8-10. Get there by 1pm if you can. The other sweet deal occurs daily: from 5 to 7pm, all items on the menu are available at *Ratsherrenpreise,* i.e. half the normal price plus DM2. (Open M-Sa 11am-11pm, Su 11am-9pm.) Enjoy lighter meals or a cup of coffee (DM2.60) next door at **Marietta Kaffeehaus,** Breiter Weg 23. (Tel. 544 04 06. Open M-F 8am-10pm, Sa 10am-10pm.) **Mausefalle,** Breiter Weg 224 (tel. 543 01 35), at the north end of Hasselbachplatz, attracts a young crowd, particularly students. The big wall over the bathroom doors is decorated with old newspaper clippings and vintage car memorabilia. Solid spaghetti dishes run DM10-14, salads DM12-15. (Open M-F 8:30am-3am, Sa-Su 11am-3am.) A **Spar supermarket** stands north of the intersection of Breiter Weg and Julius-Brenner-Str. (Open M-F 7:30am-7pm, Sa 7:30am-2pm.)

◼ SIGHTS. Dominated by modern grays and beiges, Magdeburg's urban neutrality offers no challenge to the city's few dazzling sights. The main landmark and city symbol is the sprawling **Magdeburger Dom** (tel. 541 04 36), adjacent to the square on Breite Str. In fact, the Dom was famed as the largest cathedral in the nation until reunification forced it to yield that honor to Köln. But there's nothing second-rate about the spectacle of the wide courtyard quadrangle with the cathedral's twin dark towers spearing the skies above. At the front lies an inconspicuous tomb, the 973 grave site of Otto I, the second Holy Roman Emperor (after Charlemagne). Local ghost stories credit the Kaiser's spectral guardianship with preservation of the Dom during the destruction of 1631 (Catholic raiders) and 1945 (B-17 bombers). Ernst Barlach's famous wooden memorial to the victims of WWI, originally designed for the spot it now occupies, was removed by the Nazis, fortuitously spending the war years stored safely in Berlin's Nationalgalerie. (Open in summer M-Sa 10am-6pm, Su 11:30am-6pm; in winter M-Sa 10am-4pm, Su 11:30am-4pm. Free. Tours M-Sa 10am and 2pm, Su 11:30am and 2pm. DM6, students DM3.)

The ancient **Kloster unser lieben Frauen,** Regierungsstr. 4/6 (tel. 56 50 20), lies near the Dom between many faceless apartments. An 11th-century nunnery, it now serves as a museum for visiting exhibitions and as a concert hall. The grounds around the cloister still shimmer in sheltered tranquility; sit and cogitate on the benches or on the remains of stone walls. (Open Tu-Su 10am-5pm. DM4, students and seniors DM2. Café open Tu-Su 10am-6pm.) Heading away from the Dom and crossing Breiter Weg on Danzstr., the **Kulturhistorisches Museum,** Otto-von-Guerike-Str. 68-73 (tel. 53 65 00), will pop up on your left. As the building houses both a history and natural science museum, visitors can view everything from a potato bug model 15 times the bug's actual size to an exhibit on the city's history from the Stone Age (check out the mammoth hairs) to the demonstrations that led to the *Wende* in 1989. (Open Tu-Su 10am-5pm. DM4, students DM2.) The ruins of the **Johanniskirche,** almost on the Elbe behind the Alter Markt, stand as a memorial to the 1945 bombing. The skeletal remains of the central church, including the empty

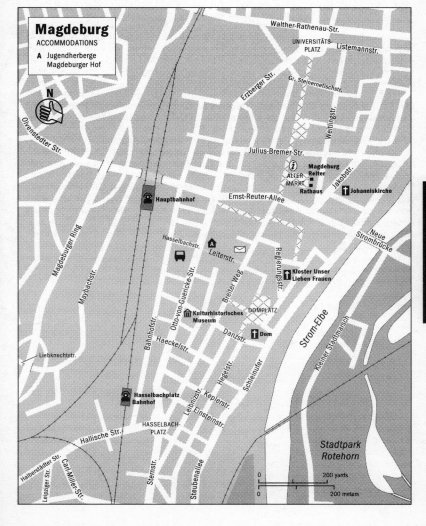

Magdeburg

ACCOMMODATIONS

A Jugendherberge
Magdeburger Hof

SACHSEN-ANHALT

stained-glass window frames, are slowly being rebuilt and the church is due to reopen in late 1999. Across from the Johanniskirche rises the clock tower of the elegantly proportioned 17th-century **Rathaus.** On the Marktplatz in front of the Rathaus is a replica of the **Magdeburger Reiter** (built in 1240), the oldest free-standing equestrian figure in northern Europe, built in 1240 (now there's something to boast about). The original rides into the sunset at the Kulturhistorisches Museum.

■ ■ **ENTERTAINMENT AND NIGHTLIFE.** Magdeburg's cultural scene is packed. The magazine *Dates* and the pamphlet *Stadtpass* provide extensive infor-mation about what's going on in theaters, cinemas, and concert halls. The **Theater Magdeburg,** Universitätspl. 9 (tel. 540 64 44 and 540 65 55), is located at the corner of Breiter Weg and Erzberger Str. Its **Großes Haus** hosts big-name operas, ballets, and plays, while the **Podiumbühne** is somewhat more experimental. (Box office open Tu-F 10am-7:30pm, Sa 10am-2pm, and 1hr. before performance. Closed mid-July to early Sept.) The **Freie Kammerspiele,** Otto-von-Guericke-Str. 64 (tel. 598 82 26), puts on modern interpretations of the classics. (Tickets available M-Th 4-6pm, F 2-6pm, and 1hr. before performances. Closed mid-July until early Sept.) **Die Kugelblitze,** Breiter Weg 200 (tel. 540 68 80), a cabaret around the corner from the youth hostel, was well known during the GDR era, and the last eight years have fed its sardonic sensibility. (Performances start around 8pm. DM20, students and seniors DM10.)

For bars, restaurants, and the inexpensive sport of people-watching, there are three superior areas in Magdeburg: **Hasselbachplatz** (see **Food,** p. 204); **Sudenburg,** along Halberstädter Str. and its cross streets (S-Bahn #1 or 10 or bus #53 or 54 to "Eiskellerplatz" or "Ambrosiusplatz"); and **Diesdorfstr.** (S-Bahn #1 or 6 to "Westring" or "Arndtstr."). As well prepared for emergencies as its namesake pre-decessor, the **Feuerwache** (fire station), Halberstädter Str. 140 (tel. 60 28 09), answers calls for theater, art exhibits, and concerts while serving as a winter café and a casual summer beer garden. (Open daily 7pm-midnight.) From Halberstädter Str., take a right on Heidestr., where **Orbit Cybercafé,** Heidestr. 9 (tel. 620 98 35), beams you up to a land with funky decorations, drinks of all sorts, occasional live DJs, and **internet access.** (Open M-F 6pm-1am, Sa-Su 6pm-2am. DM5 per hour.) The clientele at **Layla,** Lessingstr. 66 (tel. 731 70 28), gulp down pints of Guinness in a chill setting. (Open M-Th 11am-1am, F 11am-2am, Sa 10am-2am, Su 10am-1am.)

SACHSEN-ANHALT

THÜRINGEN

Aptly known as the "Green Heart of Germany," Thüringen is a hilly and mostly pastoral land with the Thüringer Wald (Thuringian Forest) at its center. Around the forest, a necklace of shining historic cities—among them Weimar, Jena, Erfurt, and Eisenach—is strung together by a direct east-west rail line. South of these cities are the hills and highlands of the forest, bisected by the historic Rennsteig hiking trail. Echoes of Thüringen are heard throughout Europe's cultural canon: Goethe, Schiller, Luther, and Wagner all left their mark on this landscape, which in turn left its mark on their work. Bach was another who found inspiration in the region, and Thüringen honors him by declaring this Bach Year 2000. Relatively unknown to foreigners, and refreshingly free of mass tourism, Thüringen is the perfect destination for an authentic and dazzling German experience.

HIGHLIGHTS OF THÜRINGEN

■ For those fascinated by Goethe, the city of **Weimar** (p. 208) and the town of **Ilmenau** (p. 222) are not to be missed.
■ **Jena** (p. 214) and **Erfurt** (p. 218) are the two most happening cities in Thüringen, with a cosmopolitan feel and an active student life.
■ Cultured out? On the outskirts of **Saalfeld** are the **Feengrotten,** the world's most colorful grottos (p. 224).

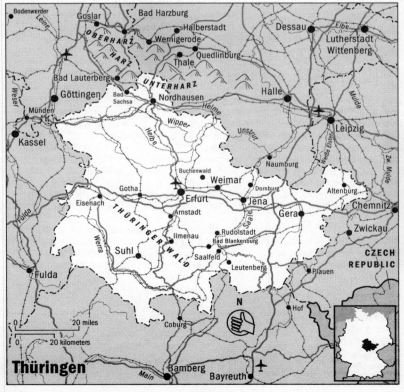

Thüringen

WEIMAR

Weimar thrives on the laurels of daring cultural achievement: intellectual energy resonates through the city of Goethe, Schiller, and the philosopher Johann Gottfried von Herder, grandfather of the Romantics. Weimar expanded the boundaries of the avant-garde into the 20th century, spawning both the Bauhaus architectural movement and the Weimar Republic's liberal constitution.

Yet Weimar is poised for the new millennium. Due to the distinction of being Europe's cultural capital in 1999, Weimar is now one of the most thoroughly rebuilt and renovated of former East German cities. While the cultural hype from last year's extravaganza has died down, the effects persist: revamped sites prevail, while budget stores and restaurants remain scarce. Exploring Weimar, you may find yourself in awe of this wonderland of ritzy hotels, fancy restaurants, and expensive shops. But with four solid hostels and a few cheap places to eat, visiting this beautiful city on a budget isn't impossible.

▌ GETTING THERE AND GETTING AROUND

Weimar is near the center of Germany, well-situated on the Dresden-Frankfurt and Berlin-Frankfurt rail lines. Its intelligently designed bus system runs through two nerve centers: the train station and the central Goetheplatz.

Trains: DB trains head to Erfurt (15min., 4 per hour, DM7.60), Jena (20min., 2 per hour, DM9.80), Eisenach (1hr., 3 per hour, DM19.40), Leipzig (1½hr., every 2 hours, DM24.40), Dresden (3hr., 1 per hour, DM65), and Frankfurt (3hr., 1 per hour, DM78).

Public Transportation: Weimar operates an extensive **bus network,** with most buses running until midnight. If you buy tickets from the driver, you'll pay an inflated price (DM2.50); instead, buy tickets at the train station. Open M 5:15am-8:30pm, Tu-Fr 6am-8:30pm, Sa 7am-5:30pm, Su 8:30am- 8:30pm. DM12 for 8 tickets.

Taxis: Tel. 90 36 00 or 90 39 00.

▌ ORIENTATION AND PRACTICAL INFORMATION

Weimar's center is located to the west of the Ilm River and south of the train station. To get to **Goetheplatz** from the station, head down Carl-August-Allee to Karl-Liebknecht-Str, (15 min.); the **Markt** and **Herderplatz** lie just east down side streets.

Weimar offers two principal **discount cards:** the **WeimarCard** (DM25, students DM20) and the **Sammelkarte** (DM25, students DM15, children DM10). The WeimarCard is valid for 72 hours of local transportation, entry to many of Weimar's museums, and discounts on city tours. For students, seniors, children, and disabled travelers, a better idea than the WeimarCard is the Sammelkarte, which yields entry into 11 different museums. Both cards can be purchased at either the tourist office or the **Stiftung Weimar Klassik,** Frauentorstr. 4 (tel. 54 50 or 54 51 02).

Tourist Office: The seriously modern and efficient **Weimar Information,** Marktstr. 10 (tel. 240 00; fax 24 00 40), is within view of the city's Rathaus. The office books **rooms** in for a DM5 fee. **Walking tours** leave the office daily at 11am and 2pm (DM12, students DM8), or go it alone with a walking-tour brochure available in various languages (DM1.50). Open M-F 10am-7pm, Sa-Su 10am-4pm.

Currency Exchange: Four banks are spread out on Schillerstr. and Frauentorstr., but beware—none are open between 4pm Friday and 8:30am Monday.

Laundry: SB-Waschsalon, on Graben a few blocks down from Goetheplatz. Wash DM6 per load. Dry DM1 for 15min. Iron DM1 per 10min. Open M-Sa 8am-10pm; last wash at 8:30pm.

Pharmacy: Bahnhof-Apotheke, Carl-August-Allee 14 (tel. 543 20), near the train station Evening hours as well as a *Notdienst* (emergency) buzzer and a list of night pharmacies. Open M-F 7:15am-7pm, Sa 9am-noon.

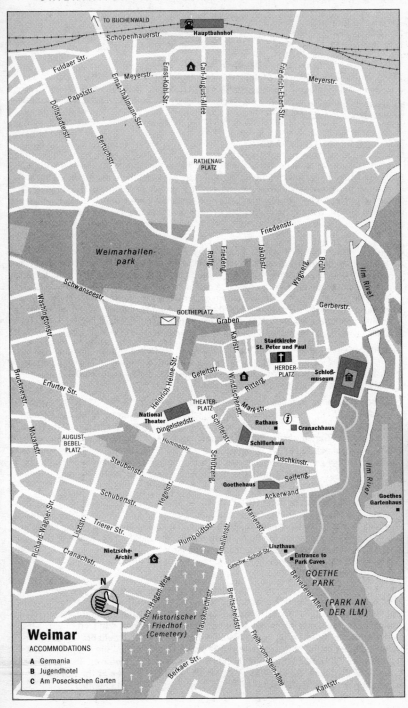

TO BUCHENWALD

Schopenhauerstr.

Hauptbahnhof

Fuldaer Str.

Meyerstr.

Papststr.

Ernst-Thälmann-Str.

Carl-August-Allee

Friedrich-Ebert-Str.

Meyerstr.

Döllstädter Str.

Bertuchstr.

RATHENAU-
PLATZ

Friedenstr.

Rollg.

Friedeng.

Jakobstr.

Wagnerg.

Brühl

Ilm River

*Weimarhallen-
park*

Schwanseestr.

Washingtonstr.

GOETHEPLATZ

Graben

Gerberstr.

**Stadtkirche
St. Peter und Paul**

Karlstr.

Geleitstr.

HERDER-
PLATZ

**Schloß-
museum**

Bruckerstr.

Erfurter Str.

Heinrich-Heine-Str.

Windischenstr.

Ritterg.

Markstr.

Mozartstr.

THEATER-
PLATZ

**National
Theater**

Dingelstedtstr.

Schießstr.

Rathaus

Cranachhaus

AUGUST-
BEBEL-
PLATZ

Hummelstr.

Schützeng.

Schillerhaus

Puschkinstr.

Steubenstr.

Hegelstr.

Schützeng.

Goethehaus

Seifeng.

Ackerwand

Ilm River

**Goethes
Gartenhaus**

Schubertstr.

Trierer Str.

Humboldtstr.

Marienstr.

Amalienstr.

Liszthaus

**Entrance to
Park Caves**

Richard-Wagner-Str.

Lisztstr.

Cranachstr.

**Nietzsche-
Archiv**

Geschw.-Scholl-Str.

*GOETHE
PARK*

Theo-Hagen-Weg

Hauskncehtstr.

Breitscheidstr.

*(PARK AN
DER ILM)*

Belvederer Allee

N

*Historischer
Friedhof
(Cemetery)*

Berkaer Str.

Freih.-von-Stein-Allee

Kantstr.

Weimar

ACCOMMODATIONS

A Germania
B Jugendhotel
C Am Poseckschen Garten

THÜRINGEN

Women's Resources: Frauenzentrum, Schopenhauerstr. 21 (tel. 87 11 82), often hosts a **Frauencafé** from 2-6pm, and serves "women's breakfast" once a month at 10am. Call for dates. Office open daily 2-6pm, usually longer, depending on what's planned.

Emergency: Police, tel. 110. **Fire and Ambulance,** tel. 112.

Post Office: Mail postcards of Goethe and Schiller from the **train station,** Goethepl. 7-8, 99423 Weimar (tel. 23 13 63). Open M-F 8am-6:30pm, Sa 9am-1pm.

PHONE CODE	03643

▶ ACCOMMODATIONS

Thanks to the city's three youth hostels and the "youth hotel," finding a cheap place to stay in Weimar is now easier than in many Eastern cities. Private accommodations are available through the tourist office (see above). Remember that prices vary according to location, not comfort; a room near the city center may cost DM50, while many of the nicer rooms in Weimar's southern suburbs go for DM25-30.

▓ **Jugendhotel Hababusch,** Geleitstr. 4 (tel. 85 07 37; email yh@larry.scc.uni-weimar.de; www.uni-weimar.de/yh). Smack in the middle of the sights, the Hababusch is run by a bunch of architecture students, and it shows: check out the upside-down sink turned into overhead lighting in the bathroom. A café is scheduled to open on the ground floor this year. From Goethepl., follow Geleitstr.; after it takes a sharp right, you'll come to a statue on your left. The entrance to Hababusch is hard to see; it's tucked in the ivied corner behind the statue. DM15 for a shared bedroom, doubles DM20 per person. DM20 key deposit. No breakfast, but access to a full kitchen. 24hr. reception.

Jugendherberge Germania (HI), Carl-August-Allee 13 (tel. 85 04 90; fax 85 04 91). Within spitting distance of the train station, this hostel has convenience written all over it. Walk straight downhill 2min.; it will be on the right. DM24, over 26 DM29. Sheets DM7. Lockout 10am-2pm. 24hr. reception.

Jugendherberge Am Poseckschen Garten (HI), Humboldtstr. 17 (tel. 85 07 92), is situ-ated near the city center, although fairly distant from the train station. Take bus #6 from the station (direction: "Merketal") to "Poseckscher Garten." Make a right onto Am Poseckschen Garten, then a left onto Humboldtstr.; the hostel is immediately on your left. A big turn-of-the-century brownstone with 8- to 10-bed rooms. The hostel tends to fill with school groups due to its proximity to cultural attractions, so come early. DM25, over 26 DM30. Breakfast included. Lunch and dinner DM8 each. Reception 7am-12:30am. Lockout 10am-2pm. Curfew 12:30am.

Jugendgästehaus Maxim Gorki (HI), Zum Wilden Graben 12 (tel. 85 07 50; fax 85 07 45). Take bus #8 from the station (direction: "Merketal") to "Wilder Graben." A con-verted villa in a tranquil Weimar suburb. Careful: buses stop running in this direction early, and the walk back from downtown is poorly lit. DM25, over 26 DM30. Sheets DM7. Breakfast included. 24hr. reception. No curfew.

◖ FOOD

The last few years of building and preparation for the cultural capital celebration wreaked havoc with many restaurants, especially those that catered to the prole-tariat and budget traveler. If you look hard enough, you can still find cheap eats, but look (and look and look) you must. For not-so-expensive delights, try the daily **produce market** at the Marktplatz (open M-F 8am-5pm, Sa 8am-noon), or the **Rewe grocery store,** in the basement of the *Handelhaus zu Weimar* on Theaterplatz. (Open M-F 7am-8pm, Sa 7am-4pm.) There is also another **Rewe** at the intersection of Frauenplan and Steubenstr. (Open M-F 7am-8pm, Sa 8am-12:30pm.)

Mensa: Bauhaus-Universität, Marienstr. 13/15, just across the footpath in front of the Bauhaus building. Also accessible from Park an der Ilm. Flee the omnipresent Goethe and Schiller in this sanctuary of modernism, and fraternize with the German students in smoky ambience. Downstairs you can get coffee and pay cheap-ish prices in the cafeteria. Upstairs, in the **Mensa,** grab the grub for DM3-5. Cafeteria open M-F 7am-7pm, Mensa opens at 11am.

Borsalino Ristorante Pizzeria, Frauentorstr. 17 (tel. 505 144), serves superlative Italian food and ice cream. Pizzas (DM7.50), pasta (DM8.50), and milkshakes (DM4). Open daily 10am-1am.

Anatolia, Frauenplan 15 (tel. 51 71 93). Ruminate on the immortals while noshing a *Döner Kebab* (DM5) and a view of Goethe's house. Open daily 9am-9:30pm.

Gerber III (see **Entertainment and Nightlife**). This ultra-funky bar-like joint almost always has a pot of something cooking on a back burner (DM2-3). No bibs, mashed peas, or tiny plastic-coated spoons. Stop by weekdays noon-1:30pm and daily in the evenings to see what's on.

FrischBack, at Theaterpl., between Schillerstr. and Schützergasse. A glorified bakery, FrischBack also serves delicious sandwiches (DM4) and fresh, tasty salads (DM4.80). Open M-F 7am-7pm, Sa 7am-6pm, and Su 8am-6pm.

■ SIGHTS

Despite a healthy dose of pre-modern attractions and left-overs from the time of the Weimar Republic, the real deal in Weimar is Johann Wolfgang von Goethe (see p. 27). The egotistical poet might not be surprised by crowds of insistent tourists who flock to his adopted home of Weimar to dwell upon him and his friend, collaborator, and rival **Friedrich Schiller.**

GOETHEHAUS. While countless German towns leap at any excuse to build memorial *Goethehäuser* (proclaiming Goethe slept here, Goethe went to school here, Goethe once asked for directions here), Weimar features the real thing. The Goethehaus and Goethe-Nationalmuseum show off the immaculately preserved private chambers where the poet entertained, wrote, studied, and ultimately died after spending 50 years in Weimar. It's jammed to the bursting point with busts, paintings, and sculptures from Goethe's 50,000-piece art collection. To get the most out of the largely unlabeled exhibits, pick up the handy English guide "Goethe's House on the Frauenplan at Weimar" (DM3) at the desk. *(Frauenplan 1. Open mid-March to midOct. Tu-Su 9am-7pm; mid-Oct. to mid-March Tu-Su 9am-4pm. DM8, students and seniors DM5, children DM2.50.)*

BAUHAUS-MUSEUM. This slick testament to the elegance of Modernism features historical artifacts about, and works produced by the Bauhaus school of design and architecture (see p. 26). Weavings, sculptures, prints, furniture, books, toys, and other nifty objects bear eloquent testimony to the breadth of the school's philosophy and undertakings. *(Am Palais, across from the Deutsches Nationaltheater. Tel. 54 60. Open April-Oct. Tu-Su 10am-6pm; Nov.-March Tu-Su 10am-4:30pm. DM5, students and seniors DM3.)*

PARK AN DER ILM. Flanking the river, the park was landscaped by Goethe. Of particular note are the fake ruins built by the Weimar shooting club and the *Kubus,* a huge black cube that is used as a theater and as a movie screen, complete with hammer and sickle. Perched on the park's far slopes is Goethe's **Gartenhaus,** the poet's first Weimar home and later his retreat from the city. It's also the site where Goethe put the moves on a certain *Fräulein* Christiane Vulpius, who later became *Frau* Goethe. Indicative of Weimar's commitment to Goethe-tourism, two replicas of the Goethehaus have been built to satisfy tourists who are merely interested in the house's architecture. *(Gartenhaus on Corona-Schöfer-Str. Open mid-March to mid-Oct. M and W-Su 9am-7pm; mid-Oct. to mid-March M and W-Su 9am-4pm. DM5, students and seniors DM2.50.)*

THÜRINGEN

NIETZSCHE-ARCHIV. Nietzsche spent the last three wacky years (1897-1900) of his life in this house; he was pretty far gone by the end, as is painfully evident from the cross-eyed glares emanating from the myriad pictures and busts. The archive was founded by Nietzsche's sister Elisabeth, a woman whose misunderstandings set the stage for the Nazis' cynical distortion of her brother's philosophy—she gave Hitler a tour of the house in 1932. *(Humboldtstr. 36. Open mid-March to mid-Oct. Tu-Su 1-6pm; mid-Oct. to mid-March 1-4pm. DM4, students and seniors DM3.)*

HISTORISCHER FRIEDHOF. South of the town center, Goethe and Schiller lie in rest together at the cemetery, where twisted black metal crosses protrude from a jungle of unkempt wild-flowers and weeds. Goethe arranged to be sealed in an air-tight steel case. Schiller, who died in an epidemic, was originally buried in a mass grave, but Goethe later combed through the remains until he identified Schiller and had him interred in a tomb. Skeptics argued for a long time that Goethe was mistaken, so a couple of "Schillers" were placed side by side. In the 1960s, a team of Russian scientists determined that Goethe was right after all. *(Cemetery open March-Sept. 8am-9pm; Oct.-Feb. 8am-6pm. Tomb open daily mid-March to mid-Oct. M and W-Su 9am-7pm; mid-Oct. to mid-March M and W-Su 9am-4pm. DM4, students and seniors DM3.)*

SCHILLERS WOHNHAUS. Sitting a neighborly distance from Goethe's pad, this was Schiller's home during the last three years of his life after he resigned from his academic chair at Jena. Showcasing the backgrounds to *The Maid of Orleans* and *William Tell*, both written here, the house offers original drafts and early editions of plays and a detailed biographical chronicle of its owner's life. *(Schillerstr. 12. Open mid-March to mid-Oct. M and W-Su 9am-7pm; mid-Oct. to mid-March M and W-Su 9am-4pm. DM5, students DM3.)*

DEUTSCHES NATIONALTHEATER. On Hummelstr., one block away from Schiller's erstwhile home, Schiller and Goethe are reconciled in bronze before the Deutsches Nationaltheater, which first breathed life into their stage works. The theater is the epicenter of Weimar's cultural and political spheres—in addition to operating as a first-run venue for their plays, it was also the locale from which the Weimar Constitution emerged in 1919. *(Am Palais. Tel. 75 53 34; fax 75 53 21.)*

WITTUMPALAIS. Here Goethe, Schiller, and Herder sat at the round table of their patron, Duchess Anna Amalia. Under the same roof, the **Wielandmuseum** documents the life and works of the extraordinary duchess. *(Am Palais 3. Open mid-March to mid-Oct. daily 9am-7pm, mid-Oct. to mid-March daily 9am-4pm. DM6, students DM4.)*

FRANZ-LISZT-HAUS. The composer spent his last years here. The instruments and furnishings are supposedly original, but given Liszt's torrid love life, the single bed seems improbable. *(Marienstr. 17. Open mid-March to mid-Oct. Tu-Su 9am-1pm and 2-7pm; mid-Oct. to mid-March Tu-Su 10am-1pm and 2-4pm. DM4, students and seniors DM3.)*

LUCAS-CRANACH-HAUS. The prolific 16th-century painter spent his last days behind this colorful Renaissance facade. Closed to the public except for an **art gallery** of fairly hip modern paintings, photos, and sculptures by still-to-be-discovered talents. *(On the Marktplatz. Gallery open Tu-F 10am-6pm, Sa 11am-3pm.)*

SCHLOSSMUSEUM. The first floor is a major-league Lucas Cranach fest; the second floor is a minor-league collection of 19th- and 20th-century German works, along with a Rodin sculpture and one of Monet's Rouen cathedral paintings. *(Burgpl. 4, to the left of the Marktplatz. Open April-Oct. Tu-Su 10am-6pm; Nov.-March Tu-Su 10am-4:30pm. DM6, students and seniors DM3.)*

OTHER SIGHTS. The cobblestoned **Marktplatz,** straight down Frauentorstr., spreads out beneath the neo-Gothic **Rathaus,** which is closed to the public. Cranach rests in the churchyard of the **Jakobskirche,** Am Jakobskirchhof 9. *(Open M-F 11am-3pm, Sa 10am-noon.)* Down Jakobstr., the **Stadtkirche St. Peter und Paul** features Cranach's last triptych altarpiece. *(Open M-Sa 10am-noon and 2-4pm, Su after services* *until noon and 2-3pm. Free.)* The church is also called the **Herderkirche,** in honor of philosopher and linguist Johann Gottfried von Herder, who preached here regularly in the 1780s. The church's interior is at odds with its solemn exterior: dazzlingly colorful coats of arms painted on all the balconies give the hall a festive air.

ENTERTAINMENT AND NIGHTLIFE

Weimar's nightlife is stuck in a pretty hard spot. With the more active rave culture of Erfurt to the west and Jena's *Uni*-culture to the East, the city is left with just a few cozy student clubs. When something cool does happen, the Bauhaus-Universität's *Mensa* has posters and bulletin boards directing you to what's going down (see **Food,** p. 210). The **Studentenklub Kasserturm** is in an old medieval tower on Goe- theplatz opposite the main post office. With a disco up top and a groovy beer cellar below, this is the oldest student club in Germany and a good place to chill. (Open M-Sa 8pm-late. Disco W and Sa. Cover varies.) The **Studentenklub Schützengasse,** on Schützengasse, has a beer garden outside. (Open M, W-Th, and Su 7:30pm-late, Tu and Fr-Sa 9pm-late. Disco Tu, Fr, and Sa. Cover DM3-6.) **Gerber III,** Gerberstr. 3, is a former squatters' house that now shelters all things leftist; a club, café, climbing wall, movie theater, and bicycle repair shop are all under the roof. The building is something mom would be proud of…if mom's an anarchist. Stop by and pick up the detailed *Gerberei* pamphlet for details on what's happening. Weimar also has a growing gay scene: **AIDS-Hilfe** (tel. 85 35 35), Erfurter Str. 17, holds a popular gay café. (Tu-Sa from 8pm.) They also host a gay "safe sex" party on the last Friday of every month.

NEAR WEIMAR: BUCHENWALD

Two hundred fifty thousand Jews, Gypsies, homosexuals, communists, and political prisoners were imprisoned and murdered by the Nazis at the labor camp of Buchenwald during WWII. Now a memorial to those who suffered there, the compound comprises a vast expanse of gravel with the former location of the prison blocks marked by the number they were assigned during the war. Around the perimeter remain the more permanent buildings of the camp, such as the SS officers' quarters and the crematorium. The stark ugliness of the site and the horror of its history are in wrenching contrast to the beauty of the natural surroundings: the view from the compound of the surrounding countryside is breathtaking.

Death claimed members of many groups at Buchenwald. A plaque near the former commandant's horse stable matter-of-factly states that an estimated 8,000 Soviet prisoners were executed by firing squad in the little space before the war's end. Many Jews were sent here, but after 1942, most were deported to Auschwitz. For the most part, Buchenwald served to detain and murder political enemies of Nazism and prisoners of war. Soviet authorities used the site from 1945 to 1950 as an internment camp in which more than 28,000 Germans, mostly Nazi war criminals and opponents of the Communist regime, were held; 10,000 died of hunger and disease. An exhibit detailing the Soviet abuses opened in 1997. In the woods behind the museum rests a cemetery with the graves of both the victims and perpetrators of the Soviet abuses.

The **Nationale Mahnmal und Gedenkstätte Buchenwald** (tel. (03643) 43 00) has two principal sights: the **KZ-Lager** and the **Glockenturm.** The former refers to the remnants of the camp, while the latter is a solemn monument overlooking Weimar and the surrounding countryside. The museum in the large storehouse building at the KZ-Lager documents both the history of Buchenwald (1937-1945) and the general history of Nazism, including German anti-Semitism. A moving installation by Polish artist Józef Szajna features thousands of photos of inmates pasted onto large silhouettes of human figures. Just outside the museum lies a brutally ironic symbol: the charred stump of the **Goethe-Eiche** (Goethe oak), left standing in the middle of the camp to commemorate Buchenwald's former role as a get-away for Germany's greatest cultural figure. The memorial stones recently embedded in the ground around block #22 read, in English, German, and Hebrew: "So that the generation to come might know, the children, yet to be born, that they too may rise and declare to their children." The camp **archives** are open to anyone searching for records of family and friends between 1937 and 1945. Call ahead to schedule an appointment with the curator (tel. (03643) 43 01 54).

A 20-minute walk away, on the other side of the hilltop from the KZ-Lager, are the GDR-designed **Mahnmal** (memorial) and **Glockenturm** (bell tower). A path leads through the woods, emerging at a two-way fork in the road. Head right, walking past the parking lot and bus stop. Keep going as the street curves left. The memorial consists of a series of carved blocks depicting stylized scenes of violence and oppression. Left from these blocks looms the somber bell tower with no marking other than an immense "MCMXLV" carved on each side. Behind the tower unfolds a commanding view of the surrounding countryside, overseen by the slightly awkward **Plastikgruppe,** a sculpture of ragged, stern-jawed socialist prisoners claiming their freedom.

The best way to reach the camp is by bus #6 from Weimar's train station or from Goethepl. Check the schedule carefully; only buses marked with a "B" or "EB" make the trip to Buchenwald (M-F 1 per hour, Sa-Su every 2hr.). There is an information center near the bus stop at Buchenwald. (Camp and information booth open Tu-Su May-Sept. 9:45am-5:15pm; Oct.-April 8:45am-4:15pm.) On your way back to Weimar, catch the bus by the parking lot near the Glockenturm.

JENA

Once home to the country's premier university, Jena still triggers intellectual fireworks in the German historical consciousness. Under the stewardship of literary greats Schlegel, Novalis, Tieck, and Hölderlin, Jena first transplanted the Romantic movement to German soil. It was here that philosophers Fichte and Schelling argued for a new conception of intellectual and political freedom, and here, in 1806, that a then-unknown junior philosophy professor named Georg Wilhelm Friedrich Hegel wrote the epoch-making *Phenomenology of Spirit.* Today, the university bears the name of Friedrich Schiller, who, in 1789, graced its halls with his lectures on the ideals of the French Revolution. True to its 19th-century tradition, Jena remains a campus town, albeit an increasingly Westernized one. Students keep the city youthful and left-leaning, and Jena's dearth of touristy sightseeing is made up for by its dynamism and forward-looking spirit.

7 ORIENTATION AND PRACTICAL INFORMATION. Jena lies in the Saale Valley, 25km east of Weimar by **train** (30min., 3 per hour, DM10). Trains between Dresden and Erfurt stop at **Bahnhof Jena-West,** while trains on the Berlin-Munich line stop at the more distant **Jena Saalbahnhof,** 15 minutes north of the center. Most of the city is connected by a bus and streetcar system that uses the "Zentrum" stop on Löbdergraben as its hub. (Single ride DM1.70; 6 rides DM10.20). From Saalbahnhof, turn left down Saalbahnhofstr. and take a right on Saalstr. to get to the center of town, or take bus #15. From Bahnhof Jena-West, head toward Westbahnhofstr. until it becomes Schillerstr. Turn left up Schillerstr. to the towering university building. Rent **bikes** at **Kirscht Fahrrad,** Löbdergraben 8 (tel. 44 15 39), near the "Zentrum" bus stop. (Open M-F 9am-7pm, Sa 9am-4pm. DM15 per day.) **Jena-Information,** Johannisstr. 23 (tel. 194 33), on Eichpl., hands out free maps and books **rooms** (DM30-45) for a DM6 fee. (Open M-F 9am-6pm, Sa 9am-2pm.) The **Goethe-Apotheke** (tel. 45 45 45) is conveniently located on Weigelstr., just north of Eichpl.; a sign lists emergency **pharmacy** information. (Open M-F 8am-8pm, Sa 8am-4pm.) The **post office** is at Engelpl. 8, 07743 Jena. (Open M-F 9am-6:30pm, Sa 8am-1pm.) The **telephone code** is 03641.

⌐⌐ ACCOMMODATIONS AND FOOD. Jena's budget accommodations aren't nearly as robust as its alternative culture. The **IB-Jugendgästehaus,** Am Herrenberge 3 (tel. 68 72 30), is the safest bet. Take bus #10 or 13 (direction: "Burgau") to "Zeiss-

Werk." Go right on Mühlenstr. up the hill until it turns into Am Herrenberge. (DM32. Sheets DM7. Reception M-F 24hr., Sa 5-8pm, Su after 6pm.) After five years in India, the owners of **Taj of India,** Wagnergasse 7 (tel. 42 03 33), developed a taste for subcontinental food, and today they invite you to an oasis of authenticity. Daily specials (DM7-10) are served with Basmati rice, *raita*, and salad, including plenty of vegetarian options. (Open Tu-Th 11:30am-2pm and 5:30-11pm, F-Sa 5:30-11pm, Su noon-11pm.) A crunchier clientele frequents **Café Immergrün,** Jenergasse 6 (tel. 44 73 13). Just off Fürstengraben, the fresh and friendly café is an unofficial environmental center. Vegetable and meat dishes with rice or baguette run DM3-8. (Open M-Sa 11am-1am, Su 3pm-late.) The **market** on the Markt provides fresh produce. (Open Tu and Th-F 10am-6:30pm.) The huge, round, metal eyesore of a university provides its students with very cheap meals in the ground floor **Mensa.** (Full meals DM2.50-5. Open M-Th 8am-3:30pm, F 8am-3pm, Sa 11am-2pm.) Check out the less regimented **Café Turmeck** next door. (Same hours as *Mensa.*)

■ **SIGHTS.** The **Romantikerhaus,** Unterm Markt 12a (tel. 44 32 63), just off the old market square, once bubbled with the raw creative energy of the Romantic period. Owned by philosopher and fiery democrat Johann Fichte, it later hosted the poetry and philosophy parties of the Romantics. Now it's a curious museum where first-edition books and portraits scattered around the interior are interspersed with big stenciled quotes of great thinkers on the walls. At the center of the museum's strangeness, the **Kritische Guillotine** (critical guillotine) remains frozen in mid-chop of a pile of books. A few blocks to the southwest sits **Schillers Gartenhaus,** Schiller's swank summer home on Schillergäßchen (tel. 93 11 88), just off (you guessed it!)

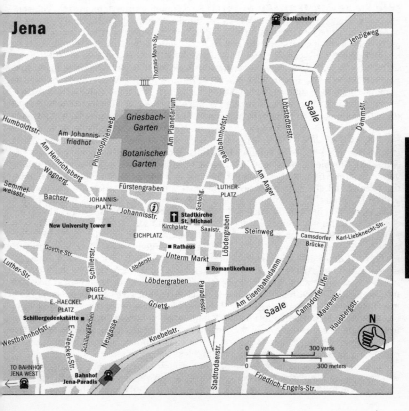

THÜRINGEN

Schillerstr. Another museum where the furniture, including a standing desk, looks like it *could* have been used by Schiller—who knows? A helpful brochure in English brings some history to these recently renovated rooms and delightful sculpture garden. (Open May-Oct. Tu-Su 11am-3pm; Sept.-April Tu-Sa 11am-3pm. DM2, students and seniors DM1.) Jena's most visible structure is neglected as a tourist sight: the cylindrical, 24-story new university tower. A product of the East German architectural imagination, it looks like a Buck Rogers-inspired vision of the future. A competing, capitalist vision of what's to come is the **Goethe-Galerie,** an enclosed shopping mall off Leutragraben. (Open daily 9am-midnight.)

Off Eichpl., the **Stadtkirche St. Michael** presides proudly over **Luther's tombstone.** He's not resting here, though the stone was intended for him; the folks at the Stadtkirche claim it was held up in shipping during a war, while back at the grave site in Wittenberg, tour guides mutter something under their breath about 17th-century plundering. The 16th-century church is unusually frightening outside, but the interior is graceful and light. Closed for renovations in 1999, the church was scheduled to reopen in 2000. Up Weigelstr. and left down Fürstengraben lies the **Botanischer Garten** (open dawn-dusk), and the row of statues of the university's distinguished faculty—notice that teachers and students of **Marx** are given particularly large statues. But there's one glaring exception—Marx's intellectual godfather and Jena's most famous professor, Hegel, has no bust at all. In fact, the only mention of him in the entire city is a piddly plaque on the back of the Romantikerhaus. The **Zeiss-Planetarium,** Am Planetarium 5 (tel. 88 54 88), the world's oldest, offers a rollicking good time for stargazers. (Open Tu-Sa 10am-4pm.)

🎭🎵 **ENTERTAINMENT AND NIGHTLIFE.** Extending from Johannisstr., **Wagnergasse** is shaping up as Jena's funkiest area, filled with bars and restaurants. The university energy has clearly been funneled in this direction, and numerous trendy cafés and clothing stores line the street. At the end of the strip lies the **Studentenhaus Wagner,** Wagnergasse 26 (tel. 93 06 80 or 93 06 81), the source of the funk, as it were. The university-sponsored hang-out doubles as a performance space for plays, readings, live music, and movie screenings. (Open M-F 11am-1am, Sa-Su 7:30pm-1am.) **Kassablanca,** Felsenkellerstr. 13a (tel. 282 60), sponsors a mind-boggling array of discos, concerts, and political discussions. The club hosts everything from freestyle to house. (Usually open W and F-Sa after 10pm. Cover DM5-8.)

NEAR JENA: DORNBURG

One of the more majestic summer estates in Thüringen lies 10 minutes north of Jena. The **Dornburger Schlösser** (tel. 222 91) are three royal palaces, running the gamut from medieval to Baroque, perched along a white chalk cliff. First in line is the **Altes Schloß,** the oldest and homeliest castle, built in 937 when the Kaisers still visited Dornburg. The first German parliament met here; later, the building was used as a prison by both the Nazi and Communist regimes. The interior is closed to the public. The summer residences of the Grand Duke of Sachsen-Weimar-Eisenach, the **Renaissanceschloß** and the **Rokokoschloß** preside majestically and frivolously (respectively) over the magnificent rose gardens where Goethe practiced his horticultural skills while writing letters to his lover, Charlotte von Stein. He was, of course, ambidextrous. (Open W-Su March-Oct. 9am-6pm; Nov.-Feb. 10am-4pm.) Inside the whitewashed, 16th-century Renaissance castle, the plain royal belongings are spiced up with stories about Goethe's frequent visits to the palaces. One look inside the lush chambers of this 1740 Rococo pleasure palace will reveal why Goethe chose its ornate, luxurious, and window-filled rooms for 19 of his 20 visits to Dornburg. Visitors partake in the pleasure of gliding along the slick main hall in slippers provided to protect its plum-tree wood. The gilded decorations and porcelain collection fall somewhere between priceless treasures and gaudy kitsch.

Dornburg also has an abundance of roses, which are celebrated during the last weekend in June with the **Rosenfest,** marking the anniversary of King Karl August's lavish birthday parties held here a century ago. The townspeople elect a rose queen on Saturday who then leads a procession around the town on Sunday, distributing roses to spectators. Locals don their party hats again during the last week in August to celebrate **Goethe's birthday.**

The castles are a 15-minute climb up a very steep hill. From the train station, head toward the castles and turn right on Am Born; the stairs are up the hill on the left. When you reach the main road, turn right and continue upward. To reach Dornburg from Jena, hop on one of the hourly **trains** from either Jena Saalbahnhof or Bahnhof Jena-Paradies, on Kahlaische Str., a five-minute walk from Bahnhof Jena-West. The **post office** on the Markt also sells **groceries.** (Open M-F 8am-1pm and 3-5pm, Sa 8-10am.) The **telephone code** is 036427.

ALTENBURG

Altenburg's fame and hilltop castle are literally built upon a house of cards. Famous for its role as the world's only *Skatstadt*, Altenburg revels in its card-playing glory and savors its status as the birthplace of the card-game *Skat*. Not surprisingly, the city is also the home of a centuries-old playing cards manufacturing industry, but it is the unique museums, scenic parks, and charming Altstadt that make Altenburg a pleasant daytrip.

⊿ ORIENTATION AND PRACTICAL INFORMATION. A web of rail-lines connects Altenburg with Zwickau (40min., 1 per hour, DM12), Leipzig (45min., 1 per hour, DM12), Chemnitz (1hr., DM16.20), and Weimar (2½hr., DM30). To reach the **tourist office,** Moritzstr. 21 (tel. 59 41 74; fax 59 41 79), turn left from the train station and walk to the end of Wettiner Str., then turn right onto Gabelentzstr. Follow it past the *Schloß* until Burgstr. emerges on your right. Turn left from Burgstr. down Weibermarkt, which becomes Moritzstr. The tourist office books **rooms** for free, provides maps with information in English, and leads **tours** in English and German on Mondays at 10am and 3pm. (Open M-F 9:30am-6pm, Sa 9:30am-noon.) When closed, the office posts available rooms in the window. Altenburg's **postal code** is 04600. The **telephone code** is 03447.

⌐⌐ ACCOMMODATIONS AND FOOD. Altenburg lacks a youth hostel, but booking a private room through the tourist office may cost less than DM30 per person. *Pensionen* also offer rooms for DM35 through the tourist office. While the restaurants in the Markt are a bit pricey, the **food markets** throughout the town soften the budget sting. (Most open M-F 8am-6pm, Sa 8am-noon.) The less expensive restaurant scene resides close to the Schloß driveway. **Schloß-Café,** Rosa-Luxemburg-Str. 6 (tel. 50 28 36), serves a selection of *Thüringer* specials (DM4.50-12.50) in addition to dark, caffeineated liquids. (Open daily 11am-midnight.) The *Biergarten* and restaurant **Kulisse,** Theaterpl. 18 (tel. 50 09 39), has a weird cow-themed menu (*Kuh-*lisse) that features moderately interesting barfare. (Most meals DM8-15. Open M-Th 4pm-midnight, F-Sa 4pm-2am, Su 4pm-1am.) For **groceries,** visit **EMarkt,** at the intersection of Rosa-Luxemburg-Str. and Johann-Sebastian-Bach-Str. (Open M-F 8am-6pm, Sa 8-11am.)

◑ SIGHTS. The wide cobblestoned footpath leading up to the looming **Schloß** winds from Theaterplatz in the heart of town. A massive sand-colored enclosure, the castle was begun in the 11th century and expanded over the next 700 years. The architecture ranges from a humbly squatting 11th-century guard tower called the **Flasche** (bottle) to the dazzlingly Gothic 15th-century **Schloßkirche.** The church organ, the **Trostorgel,** was given a thumbs-up by Bach after a trial performance in 1730. Unfortunately, the only way to view the inside of the church, its organ, and some of the castle's gems is through guided **tours** which leave from the second floor of the museum every hour, on the hour. Adjacent to the church is a museum that cunningly combines Altenburg's two claims to fame in one neat package: the **Schloß-und-Spielkartenmuseum.** (Church and museum open Tu-Su 9:30am-5:30pm;

THÜRINGEN

last entry 5pm. DM5, students DM2.50.) The Schloß amply entertains with its huge, hanging portraits of the dukes of Sachsen-Gotha-Altenburg. The **Waffenmuseum** section sports ornately gilded muskets and jagged-edged Bavarian cavalry sabres; the **Stadtgeschichte** (city history) displays, which have yet to recover from their socialist days, place Altenburg in the middle of all rebellious proletarian activities. You'll find a full house in the **Spielkarten** wing, occupying gorgeous, Rococo-ceilinged rooms jammed with excellent playing-card displays, representing more than 400 years of international gaming history. The most occult elements of the exhibit are the extra-large 15th-century Florentine tarot cards, each the size of a hand. The cards of the former GDR are fascinatingly comical—meant to indoctrinate the incorrigible, frenzied school groups who make life in hostels hell, they come in four suits: the October Revolution, solidarity, anti-Fascism, and the triumph of Communism. Presumably, no kings, queens, or jacks in this set. Leon Trotsky as *Schwarzer Peter?*

Altenburg's ace in the hole is a hidden cultural treasure: the **Lindenau-Museum** at Gabelentzstr. 5 (tel. 25 10). It possesses an unexpectedly sophisticated collection of cutting-edge modern paintings and some representatives of major movements of the past, including many works from the GDR. The museum also boasts an ultra-suave café, where you can skat it up at tables surrounded by plaster casts of antique sculptures. (Museum and café open Tu-Su 10am-6pm. DM7, students and seniors DM3.) Altenburg also has a couple of parties up its sleeve: the highlight of the **Skatbrunnenfest**, during the first weekend in May, is an attempt by four skinny boys to re-enact the statue located near the Markt's *Skatbrunnen* (skat fountain). There are equally lively attractions at the **Schloßfest** in mid-July and the **Altstadtfest** during the first weekend in October.

ERFURT

The capital of Thüringen, Erfurt has been renovated far more thoroughly and ingeniously than most towns and cities of the GDR. By day, the city offers a stunning cathedral, museums, and a handful of churches; by night, its collection of bars, clubs, and restaurants keeps its many students entertained and well-fed. Though not a cultural powerhouse like Dresden or Eisenach, Erfurt has a dynamic political history: Napoleon based his field camp here for more than a year, Konrad Adenauer lived here before WWII, and, more recently, West German Chancellor Willy Brandt met here in 1970 with East German leader Willi Stoph, commencing the long and arduous process of East-West reconciliation.

■ ORIENTATION AND PRACTICAL INFORMATION

Erfurt lies in the heart of Thüringen, only 15 minutes from Weimar and fittingly referred to as the gateway to the Thüringer Wald. The train station stands south of the city center. Head straight down Bahnhofstr. to reach the **Anger**—the main drag—and then the Altstadt, which is bisected by the **Gera River**. Across the river down Schlößerstr. lies the **Fischmarkt**, dominated by the **Rathaus**. From the square, Marktstr. leads left to the **Domhügel**, home to Erfurt's cathedral.

Trains: Trains chug to Weimar (15min., 4 per hour, DM7.60), Leipzig (2hr., 13 per day, DM32), Dresden (3hr., every 2hr., DM64), and Frankfurt (2½hr., 1 per hour, DM72).

Public Transportation: Buses and **streetcars** run through the pedestrian zones. DM2 per trip. Five trips DM7.50. Children and dogs 50% discount. Validate your ticket on board. Most streetcars and buses stop just before 1am.

Taxis: tel. 511 11 or, for those with bad memories, 555 55 or 66 66 66.

Bike Rental: Velo-Sport, Juri-Gagarin-Ring 72a (tel./fax 56 23 540). From the train station, take a right on Bahnhofstr. and walk left on Juri-Gagarin-Ring for about 3min. From DM15 per day. Open April-Sept. M-F 10am-7pm, Sa 9am-4pm; Oct.-March M-F 10am-7pm, Sa 9am-2pm.

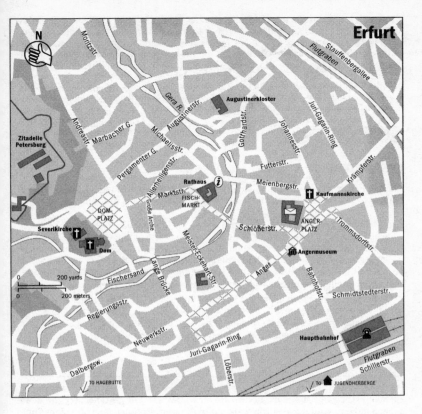

Tourist Office: Erfurt Fremdenverkehrsamt, Fischmarkt 27 (tel. 664 00; fax 664 02 90) down the street to the left of the Rathaus. Pick up a copy of the monthly *Erfurter Magazin* with a worthy map in the center, and for nightlife either *Takt* or *Fritz*. Maps of the Thüringer Wald are also available. The staff reserves tickets and books **rooms** (DM25-50) for a DM5 per person fee. Open M-F 10am-7pm, Sa-Su 10am-4pm. Two-hour **Tours** of the city in German depart from the office Sa and Su at 1pm (DM6, students DM3).

Currency Exchange: ReiseBank, in the train station. Money transfers, phonecards, and cash advances on credit cards. Nice hours, but somewhat stiff rates. Open M 8am-1pm and 1:30-4pm, Tu-F 8am-7:30pm, Sa 9am-1pm and 1:30-4pm. Close to the train station, and with better rates and a **24hr. ATM,** is **Deutsche Bank,** on the corner of Bahnhofstr. and Juri-Gagarin-Ring. Open M, W, and F 9am-4pm, Tu and Th 9am-6pm.

Laundry: SB Waschsalon, across the street and to the left as you exit the train station. Open daily 6am-11pm. DM6 per load.

Pharmacy: Apollo-Apotheke, Juri-Gagarin-Ring 94 (tel. 24 11 66) has a wide selection; all-night pharmacy listings are posted in the window. From the train station, go right on Bahnhofstr. to Juri-Gagarin-Ring. Take a left; the pharmacy should be just ahead. Open M-F 7:30am-7pm, Sa 8am-1pm.

Gay and Lesbian Resources: At the **AIDS-Hilfe,** Windhorststr. 43a (tel. 346 22 97). On the edge of the city park near the train station the rainbow flag flies over a house filled with a library, archive, and café. Counseling Tu-W 10am-3pm and Th noon-5pm. **Café SwiB** open W, F, and Su 7pm-midnight. Pick up *Buschlunk*, Thüringen's ultra-thorough, ultra-helpful monthly gay and lesbian magazine.

Women's Resources: Brennessel Frauenzentrum, Meister-Eckehart-Str. 5 (tel. 565 65 10; fax 565 65 11), in the center of the city, offers information and counseling, overnight stays, a café, sauna, and programs for lesbians. Open M-F 9am-5pm; events usually 8pm-midnight.

Emergency: Police, tel.110. **Fire and Ambulance,** tel 112.

Post Office: The main post office, 99084 Erfurt, the focal point of the Anger, occupies an ornate beast of a building probably larger than some of the punier European countries. Open M-F 8am-7pm, Sa 9am-1pm.

PHONE CODE	0361

▶ ACCOMMODATIONS

Though Erfurt has two youth hostels, they are far from central and cater predominantly to children. Your best bet is to use the tourist office's room-finding service.

Jugendherberge Karl Reiman (HI), Hochheimer Str. 12 (tel. 562 67 05; fax 562 67 06). From the station, take streetcar #5 (direction: "Steigerstr.") to the last stop. Backtrack a little, and turn left onto Hochheimer Str.; the hostel is on the left corner at the first intersection. DM24, over 27 DM29. Breakfast included. Lunch and dinner DM8 each. Sheets DM7. Reception 6-9am and 3-10pm. Curfew midnight. Wheelchair accessible.

Haus der Jugend "Hagebutte," Hagebuttenweg 47 (tel./fax 655 15 32), is nestled deep in the forests of pre-fab apartment buildings that sprouted south of the city in the last 40 years. Take streetcar #6 (direction: "Wiesenhügel") to "Färberwaidweg." Cross the tracks and walk parallel to them along Mispelweg. Go left at the first footpath and walk 100m uphill. DM15, over 27 DM30. Sheets DM5. Breakfast DM6. 24hr. reception.

▶ FOOD

Cheap food in Erfurt is hard to come by, though the region's specialty, *Thüringer Bratwurst*, is sold at stands all over the city (DM2-3). For **groceries,** try the **Rewe supermarket,** to your right as you walk out of the train station (open M-W 6am-7pm, Th-F 6am-8pm, Sa 7am-1pm), or the more central **König am Anger,** at the intersection of Anger and Lachsgasse. (Open M-F 8am-7pm, Sa 8am-2pm.) There is also a **market** for fresh fruits and vegetables on Domplatz. (Open M-Sa 7am-2pm).

Ristorante Don Camillo, Michaelisstr. 29 (tel. 260 11 45), has delicious, moderately priced Italian food in a setting worthy of a higher price bracket. Pizzas (DM8.50) and pastas from DM10. Open daily 11:30am-3pm and 5:30pm-1am.

Kurdischer Döner Kebab, Meienbergstr. 21. This stand is noteworthy for its clean, sit-down facilities and fresh, quality ingredients. *Döner* DM5. Open daily 11am-midnight.

▶ SIGHTS

MARIENDOM. The mammoth cathedral completely dominates the view from the marketplace at its perch on the **Domhügel,** impressing even the most ardent heathen. Today the church is a Gothic extravaganza, though its Romanesque foundation dates back to 1154. Inside, the most impressive part of the cathedral is the 15th-century **Hochchor** in the eastern wing; the **altar** is fully 17m high, embellished with miniature oil paintings, intricate carvings, and a painting by Lucas Cranach. The 15 **stained glass windows** rise higher than the altar and are about halfway through a massive cleaning that will make them brighter than they've been in centuries. (*Domplatz. Open May-Oct. M-F 9-11:30am and 12:30-5pm, Sa 9-11:30am and 12:30-4:30pm, Su 2-4pm; Nov.-April M-F 10-11:30am and 12:30-4pm, Su 2-4pm. Free.*)

SEVERIKIRCHE. The muted sandstone interior of this church proves less impressive than its turrets would lead one to believe. However, the enormous Baroque organ appendages scream with flying golden angels, sunbursts, flames, and a pastel palate of fake marble. *(Next to Mariendom. Open May-Oct. M-F 9-11:30am and 12:30-5pm, Sa 9-11:30am and 12:30-4:30pm, Su 2-4pm; Nov.-April M-F 10-11:30am and 12:30-4pm, Su 2-4pm. Free.)*

ANGER. Erfurt's wide pedestrian promenade, the Anger, is one of the most attractive shopping areas in Eastern Germany. The architecture lining the street—most of it 19th-century Neoclassical or *Jugendstil*—is for the most part fascinating, though some GDR-era behemoths mar the cityscape. Across from the post office lies **House #6,** where Russian Czar Alexander I stayed when he came to Erfurt to meet with Napoleon in 1808. The **Angermuseum** in an immaculate yellow mansion, is dedicated to displaying a collection of medieval religious art from around Erfurt. Don't miss the room designed and painted by Expressionist Erich Heckel in 1922. The bold colors and primitive style tell the tale of the artist's development in mural form. *(Anger 18. Tel. 562 33 11. Open Tu-Su 10am-6pm. DM3, students DM1.50)*

KAUFMANNSKIRCHE. At the end of the Anger sits the church where Bach's parents tied the knot. Outside, feet planted firmly on a pedestal decorated with scenes from his days here, a squat **Martin Luther** casts an indifferent stare over the street. *(Open M-Sa 9am-7pm, Su 11am-5pm.)*

AUGUSTINERKLOSTER. Martin Luther spent 10 years as a Catholic priest and Augustine monk in this cloister. Needless to say Luther got his way, and a Protestant college now occupies the site. Its **library** has one of Germany's most priceless collections, including a number of early bibles with personal notations by Luther himself. During WWII, the books were moved to make room for a bomb shelter. When U.S. bombers destroyed the library in February 1945, 267 people lost their lives, but the books remained unscathed. *(From the tourist office, cross the Krämerbrücke, turn left on Gotthardstr., and cut left through Kirchengasse. Hourly tours April-Oct. Tu-Sa 10am-noon and 2-4pm, Su after 11am; Nov.-March Tu-Sa 10am, noon, and 2pm. The cloister usually won't lead a tour if fewer than 6 people show up, so you may get bumped back an hour or more. DM5.50, students DM4.)*

KRÄMERBRÜCKE. The quietly babbling **Gera** flows down Marktstr. and provides the *raison d'être* for one of Erfurt's most interesting architectural attractions. Completely covered by small shops, the medieval bridge dates back to the 12th century. In the 1400s, the bridge was part of a great trade-route running from Kiev to Paris. Even more fascinating is the view from underneath—take one of the paths leading off the bridge to get a glance up from the water's edge. At the far end of the bridge from the tourist office, the **tower** of the **Aegidienkirche** is open for those interested in some vigorous stair-climbing and a different perspective on the city. *(Tower open sporadically M-Sa, but always Su noon-6pm. DM2.)*

STADTHALTEREI. It was from this massive Baroque building that the Communists ruled the city. Here, in a small salon on the second floor, Napoleon had breakfast with Goethe in 1808. Goethe later wrote that Napoleon spent the entire time chastising him for his gloomy tragedies—which the French emperor seemed to know inside and out—while Goethe listened passively. Both understood themselves to be immortals. Goethe also realized, however, that Napoleon's immortality was backed by an army. The building is not open to the public, but the exterior still merits a gawking.*(Bear right at the end of the Anger and follow Regierungstr. to have a look.)*

OTHER SIGHTS. From the Domplatz, Marktstr. leads down to the **Fischmarkt,** bordered by restored guild houses with wildly decorated facades. Overlooking the space is the brazenly neo-Gothic **Rathaus,** whose collection of stunning paintings depicts mythical narratives, including portrayals of Faust and Tannhäuser.

THÜRINGEN

🎵🎭 ENTERTAINMENT AND NIGHTLIFE

Erfurt's 220,000 inhabitants manage a fairly indulgent nightlife. The area near Domplatz and the Krämerbrücke between **Michaelisstraße, Marbacher Gasse,** and **Allerheiligenstraße** glows at night with cafes, candlelit restaurants, and bars. While the opera house is closed, a victim of stringent German safety regulations, the **Theater Erfurt** puts on regular shows at the nearby **Schauspielhaus.** The **ticket office** (tel. 223 31 55), Dalbersweg 2, is in the green house just down the street from the opera house. (Office open Tu-F 10am-1pm and 2-5:30pm, Sa 10am-1pm, Su 10am-noon, and 1hr. before performance; Sept.-March closed Su. Ask about student discounts. Tickets can also be purchased at the tourist office.) Just off Domplatz, the **Theater Waidspeicher** (tel. 598 29 24) charms all with a marionette and puppet theater, and cabaret crops up on weekends. (Box office at Dompl. 18. Open Tu-F 10am-2pm and 3-5:30pm. Puppet shows DM10-15, cabaret DM17-21.)

The **Double b,** Marbacher Gasse 10 (tel. 211 51 22), near Domplatz, functions as a hybrid Irish pub, German beer garden, and Amsterdam café; all the cool cats in Erfurt show up there to chill in the fiercely hip vibe. (Open M-F 8am-midnight, Sa-Su 9am-1am.) The **Studentenclub Engelsburg,** Allerheiligenstr. 20-21 (tel. 24 47 70), just off Marktstr., is down with the disco and moderate punk scene, especially at the frat-like musical grotto within. Live bands from Erfurt and the surrounding area offer their talents in the party room. (Open July-Sept. W and Sa 9pm-1am, Su 10pm-midnight; Oct.-June W-Sa 9pm-1am. Cover DM8, students DM4.) Erfurt also feeds a very healthy electronic music scene. Much of it is underground, but to find out what's up, stop by **Pure,** Johannesstr. 18a (tel. 643 09 55), a record store that has fliers for every concert going on between Eisenach and Leipzig. (Open M-F 11am-8pm, Sa 11am-2pm.)

THÜRINGER WALD (THURINGIAN FOREST)

"The area is magnificent, quite magnificent...I am basking in God's world," wrote Goethe in a letter from the Thüringer Wald more than 200 years ago. Goethe's exuberant exclamation is still accurate; the time-worn mountains make for perfect skiing during winter and excellent hiking, camping, and walking in summer. Cradled within these mighty hills, the region's towns and villages have cultivated and inspired many German composers, philosophers, and poets; Goethe and Schiller wrote some of their most brilliant poetry on these slopes.

Snaking through the forest, the **Rennsteig** has been a renowned hiking trail for centuries. While history books date the trail to 1330, locals claim that it was first trodden by prehistoric hunter-gatherers. During the years of East-West division, much of the trail was closed because of its potential as an escape route. Now hikers wander the length of the 168km, 5-day trek from Hörschel near Eisenach south into Bavaria. The **tourist office** in Erfurt (p. 219) sells guides and maps for an extended jaunt. If you're thinking about taking on the Rennsteig, reserve trail-side huts well in advance. Write or call **Gästeinformation Brotterode,** Bad-Vibeler-Platz 4, 98599 Brotterode (tel. (036840) 33 33), for more information.

ILMENAU AND THE GOETHE TRAIL

Surrounded by the spectacular beauty of the Thüringer Wald, Ilmenau is a pleasant, friendly, and well-kept town, proud of its native ingenue, Johann Wolfgang von Goethe. The author first worked in Ilmenau as a government minister responsible for mining under the Duke of Weimar; later, he came back to the area as a poet in search of inspiration. Today the town capitalizes on Goethe and his fame to draw visitors, vaunting the sights he frequented about town in addition to the stunning 18.5km 🚶**Goethewanderweg** (Goethe Trail), marked by the author's overflourished "g" monogram.

The trail starts from the market area to the right of the **Amtshaus,** which hosts the **Goethe-Gedenkstätte,** Am Markt 1 (tel. 20 26 67 or 60 01 06), a museum devoted to the author and his works. (Open May-Oct. daily 9am-noon and 1-4:30 pm; Nov.-April 10am-noon and 1-4pm. DM2, students and seniors DM1.) Facing the Amts-haus, bear left on Obertorstr. and take it up the hill to the graveyard on Erfurter Str. Follow the "g" signs to the grave of **Corona Schröter,** the first actress to portray Goethe's renowned *Iphigenia.* Continue to follow the signs out of the graveyard and back to Erfurter Str. Veer left at the double headed sign, keeping the play-ground on your right. The trail leads to Neue Marienstr.; from there, it's a 4km hike to **Schwalbenstein,** an impressive outcropping upon which Goethe wrote Act IV of *Iphigenia.* At this point, practically every rock, stone, and pebble gains fame: Goethe observed this tree in 1779, Goethe reclined on this rocky ledge in 1782, etc. About 10km into the trail (much of which is uphill) the **Goethehäuschen** rests on the **Kickelhahn,** where the poetry the author scratched on the walls in his youth is on display. Farther along (11km) lies the **Jagdhaus Gabelbach** (tel. 20 26 26), the hunting house of Duke Karl August that Goethe frequented in summer. The lodge features a display of the author's scientific experiments as well as some of his drawings. (Open W-Su March-Oct. 9am-5pm; Sept.-Feb. 10am-4pm. DM4, students DM3.) The hike ends in **Stützerbach,** where the local glass-works magnate often hosted the poet. The house is now the **Goethehaus,** but as a nod to the patron there are demonstrations of traditional **glass-blowing.** (Open W-Su March-Oct. 9am-5pm, Nov.-Feb. 10am-4pm. DM4, students DM3.)

Ilmenau can be reached by **train** or **bus** from Erfurt (1hr., 1 per hour, DM15). Ilmenau also makes a good starting point for a hike along the 168km-long ▨**Rennsteig;** take bus #300 (direction: "Suhl") to "Rennsteigkreuzung" (DM3.30). Cutting across a good swath of southern Thüringen, the Rennsteig links gorgeous scenery and traditional villages that lie scattered along the path. Pick up a map and ask for more information at the **tourist office,** Lindenstr. 12. (Tel. 20 23 58 or 621 32; fax 20 25 02.) From the station, walk down Bahnhofstr. to Wetzlarer Pl. and follow the pedestrian zone until it becomes Lindenstr. (15min.). The staff provides hiking maps and books **rooms** (DM20-45) for a DM2 per-person fee. (Open M-F 9am-6pm, Sa 9am-noon.) The **post office,** Poststr., 98693 Ilmenau, is uphill from Wetzlarer Pl. (Open M-F 8am-5:30pm, Sa 9am-noon.) The **telephone code** is 03677.

Jugendherberge Ilmenau, Am Stollen 49 (tel. 88 46 81; fax 88 46 82), offers a shower and bathroom for each spacious four-bed room. From the station, take a left at August-Bebel-Str., crossing the tracks and veering right on the path along

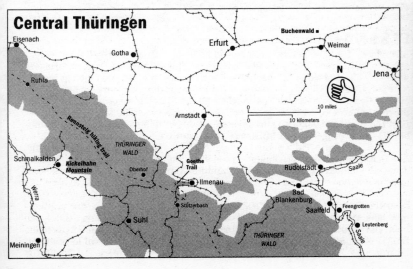

Central Thüringen

the tracks. After the sharp right curve, cross the bridge on your left, and continue on the trail until it merges with Am Stollen. (DM25, over 26 DM30. Breakfast included. Reception 10am-10pm. Key deposit DM20.) **Die Arche,** Str. des Friedens 28 (tel. 89 41 11), is a café featuring international cuisine as well as a shop for African and Indian trinkets. The walls on the bottom floor are covered with teas and herbs, while the top floor gives out on a colorful garden. Immerse yourself in the cloud of exotic scents, and enjoy a pot of tea—there are 170 options. (Cup DM2.50, pot DM5. Open M-F 10am-6pm, Sa 9am-2pm, Su 1-6pm.) **Zur Post,** Mühltor 6 (tel. 67 10 27), on Wetzlarer Pl., offers regional specialties at excellent prices (DM9-14). Try the *Thüringer Rostbrätel.* (Pork roast with fried potatoes, DM10. Open M-F 8:30am-midnight, Sa-Su 11am-midnight. Kitchen closes 11pm.) Head to the **farmer's market** on the Markt for fresh produce. (Tu and F 8am-6pm.)

SAALFELD

The **Saalfelder Feengrotten** (fairy grottos; tel. 550 40) are renowned for their captivating mineral-stained caves and spring-fed pools. The peculiar formations of the long, delicate stalagmites and stalactites provided the inspiration for Siegfried Wagner, son of composer Richard Wagner, to design the Bayreuther Festspiele set for one of his father's operas. (See p. 314. Grottos open March-Oct. daily 9am-5pm; Nov. Sa-Su 10am-3:30pm; Dec.-Feb. daily 10am-3:30pm. DM7.) **Trains** head to Jena (1hr., 2 per hour, DM19) and Ilmenau via Arnstadt (1½hr., 1 per hour, DM20). Free **buses** to the Feengrotten run hourly from the tourist office (May-Sept. daily 10am-4pm). Rent **bikes** at **City-Rad-Shop,** Schloßstr. 6. (Tel. 51 14 65. Open M-F 9am-noon and 1-7pm, Sa 9am-1pm. DM10 per day. ID required.) To get to the **tourist office** (tel./fax 339 50) from the train station, take Bahnhofstr., which turns into Puschkinstr., across the Saale river. Bear left onto Saalstr., which leads to the Markt; the office is on the opposite side of the square. The staff sells hiking maps and finds **rooms** (DM30-45) for free. (Open M-F 9am-6pm, Sa-Su 10am-2pm.) Ask for a free map of the **Historischer Wanderweg,** a trail leading through quiet back streets to Saalfeld's major sights. Stop along the way at the **Heimatmuseum** (tel. 59 84 71) on Brudergasse. Housed in a renovated Franciscan monastery, the museum documents Thüringen's rich history from the Middle Ages to the present with scale models and period costumes. The exhibit also showcases an impressive collection of modern art by local artists. (Open Tu-Su 10am-5pm. DM3.50, students and seniors DM2.) Budget accommodation in Saalfeld is limited; your best bet is the tourist office. For fresh picnic food, head to the **farmer's market** on the Markt. (Tu, Th, and Sa 8am-6pm.) The **telephone code** is 03671.

EISENACH

Birthplace of Johann Sebastian Bach and home-in-exile for Martin Luther, Eisenach boasts impressive humanist credentials. The writings of Marx and Engels were so well received in Eisenach that the duo called the local communist faction "our party." Adolf Hitler is said to have called the idyllic Wartburg "the most German of German castles," and he fought a pitched (and unsuccessful) battle with the local church to replace its tower's cross with a swastika. More recently, the East German regime tapped into old associations by dubbing its "luxury" automobile the *Wartburg.* This year, Eisenach celebrates Bach Festival week (July 21-30, 2000) with concerts and a permanent exhibition in the Bachhaus (p. 227). It's fitting that Eisenach—this romantic, rationalist, conservative, radical, democratic, despotic bundle of contradictions—should be home to one of Germany's most treasured national symbols.

◪ **ORIENTATION AND PRACTICAL INFORMATION.** Frequent **train** connections link Eisenach to Erfurt (1hr., 3 per hour, DM14.80) and Weimar (1hr., 3 per hour, DM19.50), Kassel (1½hr., 1 per hour, DM27), and Göttingen (2hr., 1 per hour, DM35). Eisenach's **tourist office,** Markt 2 (tel. 67 02 60), has plenty of information on Wartburg, offers daily city tours (2pm, DM5), and books **rooms** (DM30-40) for free. From the train station, walk on Bahnhofstr. through the arched tunnel, and angle left until you turn right onto the pedestrian Karlstr. (Open M 10am-12:30pm and 1:15-6pm, Tu-F 9am-12:30pm and 1-6pm, Sa-Su 10am-2pm.) Rent a **bike** at **Schmidt Fahrrad,** Johannispl. 12 (tel. 21 49 24; open M-F 10am-6pm, Sa 10am-1pm), or go for a ride on Eisenach's **buses** (2 trips DM2.40). For a **taxi,** call 22 02 20. The **Ost-Apotheke,** Bahnhofstr. 29 (tel. 20 32 42), has a list of night **pharmacies.** (Open M-F 8am-6pm, Sa 8am-noon.) Send your Wartburg postcard from the **post office** on the Markt, 99817 Eisenach. (Open M-F 8am-6pm, Sa 8am-noon.) The **telephone code** is 03691.

■■ **ACCOMMODATIONS AND FOOD. Jugendherberge Arthur Becker (HI),** Mariental 24 (tel. 74 32 59; fax 74 32 60), fills a comfortable old villa fairly far from the center, a bit beyond the Schloß. From the train station, take Bahnhofstr. to Wartburger Allee, which runs into Mariental. Walk down the street until the hostel

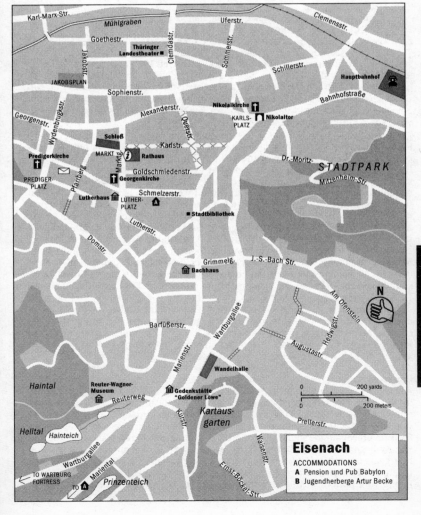

Eisenach

ACCOMMODATIONS

A Pension und Pub Babylon
B Jugendherberge Artur Becke

THÜRINGEN

comes up on your right, past the pond (35min.); alternatively, take bus #3 (direction: "Mariental") to "Lilienstr." About 100m past the bus stop, signs point the way up the sloping drive to the right. The hostel will be closed Jan.-June 2000 for complete renovation, but come July it should be sparkling and new. (DM22, over 26 DM26. Breakfast included. Sheets DM7. Reception 4-9pm. Curfew 10pm, but you can get a key.) Eisenach also offers one excellent, very central *Pension:* **Gasthof Storchenturm**, Georgenstr. 43 (tel. 21 52 50; fax 21 50 82), fills a secluded courtyard next to a park with a restaurant, *Biergarten*, and several clean and quiet rooms, all with showers. The restaurant's red bean soup (DM7.80) will beat any Texas chili. (Singles DM45, doubles DM70. Breakfast DM7.50. Restaurant open 7am-1am.) The nearest **camping** is at **Am Altenberger See** (tel. 21 56 37; fax 21 56 07), offering showers, a sauna, and a view of the lake in the hamlet of Eckartshausen. From the Eisenach station, take the **bus** to "Bad Liebenstein" and tell the driver your destination. (14 departures daily M-F; 7:43am, 1:43pm, and 5:23pm on weekends.) About 10km from town, the campground offers 13 cabins. (DM7 per person. Tent DM5. Car DM2. Reception 8am-1pm and 3-10pm.)

For **groceries** head to the **Edeka** on Johannispl. (Open M-F 7am-7pm, Sa 7am-2pm.) There's another **supermarket** in Eisenach's train station. (Open M-F 5:30am-8pm, Sa-Su 8am-8pm.) Near the train station, **Café Moritz,** Bahnhofstr. 7 (tel. 74 65 75), raises your daily caloric intake with Thüringer specialities (around DM8), served outside if the weather permits. (Open May-Oct. M-F 8am-9pm, Sa-Su 10am-9pm; Nov.-April M-F 8am-7pm, Sa-Su 10am-7pm.) For large and delicious ice cream cones with a mini-Dickman (a chocolate-covered marshmallow) on top (DM3), pay a visit to **Dänishe Eiscreme.** They also sell a melange of crepes and Danish waffles. From Marktplatz, walk down Karlstr. and veer right onto Querstr. (Open M-F 11am-6pm, Sa 11am-3pm.)

■ **SIGHTS.** High above Eisenach's half-timbered houses, **Wartburg fortress** lords over the northwestern slope of the rolling Thüringer Wald. In 1521, this much-hyped castle sheltered Martin Luther after his excommunication. To thwart the search, Luther grew a beard and spent his 10-month stay disguised as a noble named Junker Jörg. Burning the midnight oil working on his landmark German translation of the Bible, the reformer was visited by the devil; by Luther's account, it only took a toss of an ink pot to dispel the Beast. The perceptive traveler can't help but marvel at how often the Prince of Darkness and Luther's paths crossed during Luther's travels. Later pilgrims took the fable literally and mistook a smudge of stove grease for the blessed ink spot, gutting the wall (now a big hole) in their search for a souvenir. (Open March-Oct. daily 8:30am-5pm; Nov.-Feb. 9am-3:30pm. Admission to the whole complex DM11, students and children DM6, seniors and the disabled DM8. Admission to museum and Luther study DM6 and DM5 respectively.)

Petty vandalism aside, the Romanesque Wartburg is notable for the peaceful character of its history. Aside from sheltering Luther, it was a haven for the 12th-century *Minnesänger*, the originators of German choral music. The mural that inspired Wagner's *Tannhäuser*, a depiction of a 12th-century battle of musicians, adorns a wall in one of the castle's restored chambers. Like many of the more dazzling chambers in Wartburg, the mural room is a product of 19th-century imagination, not medieval reality. The Romantics' obsession with Wartburg began in 1777 when Goethe fell in love with the place and convinced some backers in the nobility to restore the interior as a museum. As a general rule, anything you see that's frayed and restrained-looking is old; anything shiny and ornate (unfortunately, the vast majority of the castle) is the product of the 19th-century fan club. The castle's **Festsaal** preserves the memory of the 1817 meeting of 500 representatives of university fraternities who threw a party, got inspired, and formed Germany's first bourgeois opposition (ruthlessly crushed two years later); a copy of the flag they toasted still hangs in the room. From the walls of Wartburg's courtyard, trace the line of your path through the countryside below. The view is spectacular—if you turn to the side opposite Eisenach, you can see the Thüringer Wald and all the way

TO WURST OR NOT TO WURST

Wurst is believed to be the very foundation of German national identity. "To *wurst* or not to *wurst*," pondered an anonymous 11th-century German poet. Shakespeare later failed to convey the existential dilemma obvious to connoisseurs of all things German when he paraphrased the credo in *Hamlet*. Arrogant English-speaking folks continue to believe that *Wurst* can be translated literally as "German sausage" and often indulge in what may seem a cheap and simple meal, oblivious to the true nature of the *Wurst*.

The only comprehensive categorization of different kinds of *Wurst* is said to have been included in the lost pages of Aristotles' Politics. While no one is sure how many types are currently available, four main varieties of *Wurst* can be distinguished:

Thüringer Bratwurst: The direct ancestor of the American "hot dog" comes cupped in a flaky Brötchen, doused in mustard. Also known as a *Roster* or *Thüringer Brat*, this zesty sausage puts the sickly pink American frank to shame. It's said to be a natural aphrodisiac, not to mention a possible cure for impotence.

Rheinländer Wurst: The *Rheinländer* is of religious significance to obscure tribal groups inhabiting Western Germany. Legend has it that on special occasions Rheinlanders grab a naked, greasy *Wurst* in their bare hands, alternately biting the meaty mass and a roll. It is not known whether they bathe or observe any social norms.

Bavarian Weißwurst: In the Middle Ages the *Weißwurst* was an essential element of a popular medical practice. Known for its cleansing properties, it guarantees a stomach-buckling experience, and was regarded as a perfect treatment for all sorts of digestive disorders. Now that universal aesthetic and moral standards are finally imposing themselves on the German *Volk*, a medically indifferent and safer version (but still rich in vitamin B6!) prevails.

Frankfurter: This *Wurst* is produced following a secret recipe in a gruesome and morally dubious process which involves stuffing the front legs of a pig into sheep intestines. Though not chemically addictive, each *Frankfurter* comes with a legally mandated warning against frequent consumption, as prolonged use has been known to induce mental instability and increased perspiration.

across the former East-West border to Hessen. The first floor of the tower is a deep dungeon dating from darker days.

The Wartburg sits on the south side of Eisenach; the foot of the hill can be reached by a stroll down **Wartburgerallee** from the train station. A number of city-sponsored **tour buses** run between the train station and the castle. (Hourly 9am-5pm. One-way DM1.50, round-trip DM2.50.) For the more adventurous, there are a number of well-cleared **footpaths** up the incline—hiking downhill is a blast. Arriving at the medieval stronghold after a 30-minute hike through rich-smelling pines and lilacs, you'll wipe your sweat and feel like a pilgrim. If you weigh 60kg (132 lbs.) or less, you can opt for a donkey ride for the last stretch (DM5). When eastern Germany was East Germany, West Germans were issued special visas that allowed them to visit the castle and nothing else, but those visas were hard to come by; these days, legions of sightseers are making up for lost time. On weekday mornings during the summer, expect crowds of schoolchildren; on weekday afternoons, crowds of German pensioners; on weekends, just be prepared for crowds. The interior of the castle can be visited only with a tour, and the wait may be more than an hour. To kill the time, grab an English-language pamphlet when you buy your ticket; alternatively, hike around the rich woods and grounds without spending a *Pfennig*.

Back at the base of the mountain, the **Bachhaus**, Frauenplan 21 (tel. 793 40; fax 79 34 24), where Johann Sebastian stormed into the world in 1685, recreates the family's living quarters. Downstairs are period instruments such as a clavichord, a spinet, and a beautifully preserved "house organ" from 1750, about the size of a telephone booth, with a little stool for the player. Roughly every 40 minutes, one of the museum's guides tunes up for a musical tour, including anecdotes about Bach's life, and spellbinding musical interludes—you can join the tour at any stage. Turn off Wartburgallee down Grimmelgasse to reach the house. (Open April-Sept. M noon-5:45pm, Tu-Su 9am-5:45pm.; Oct.-March M 1-4:45pm, Tu-Su 9am-4:45pm. DM5, students DM4.) The **Reuter-Wagner-Museum,** Reuterweg 2 (tel. 74 32 93; fax 74 32 940), below the fortress, is dedicated to the joint memory of writer Fritz and composer Richard. (Open Tu-Su 10am-5pm. DM4, students and seniors DM2.) Town life centers on the pastel **Markt,** bounded by the tilting dollhouse of a **Rathaus** and the latticed **Lutherhaus,** Lutherpl. 8. (tel. 298 30), young Martin's home in his school days. (Open April-Oct. daily 9am-5pm; Nov.-March daily 10am-5pm. DM5, seniors and the disabled DM4, students DM2.) "Communist performance car" is not an oxymoron at the **Automobilbaumuseum,** Rennbahn 6-8 (tel. 772 12), where shiny chitty-chitty-*Wartburgs* are on glorious display. (Open Tu-Su 10am-5pm. DM4, students, seniors, and children DM2.) Leave from the station's *Ausgang Nord,* and veer left; after an eight-minute walk, the museum is on the right.

GOTHA

Like many towns in the former GDR, Gotha suffered from widespread decay and disrepair. Today, however, it has made itself a pretty face with which to greet visitors coming to admire its handful of impressive sites. The part of town immediately surrounding the lively **Marktplatz** and extensive castle grounds is an island stripped of evidence of the socialist excesses. Less recently, Gotha has been involved in history more colorful than communist shades of gray. Prince Albert, one of the Dukes of Sachsen-Coburg-Gotha, married Queen Victoria of England, and hence Queen Elizabeth and Prince Charles are direct descendants of this house—the royal family's name of "Windsor" is a product of a name change during WWI, when Germany was "out of fashion." The birth of the Social Democratic Party in Gotha made Marx hopping mad, furthering his revolutionary career. When Charlemagne visited the city, he spent only a day—since then the town has accumulated enough history and culture to make you want to stay a bit longer.

⚠ ORIENTATION AND PRACTICAL INFORMATION. Gotha is connected by frequent **trains** to Erfurt (20min., 2 per hour, DM7.60) and Eisenach (20min., 2 per hour, DM7.60). The city is built around the four sides of **Schloß Friedenstein** and its grounds. To get to the castle from the **train station,** take Bahnhofstr. and turn left onto Parkallee. The entrance to the **Schloß** is on the far side of the park grounds. From there you'll be looking down on the **Hauptmarkt,** a collection of 17th-century homes and businesses set on a steep incline. At the far end of the Hauptmarkt and to the right is the **Neumarkt,** the most bustling part of town. To get to the **tourist office,** Blumenbachstr. 1-3. (tel. 85 40 36; fax 22 21 34), face the **Rathaus** entrance and go left down the narrow Hützelsgasse until you see the welcoming "i." Get information on the Schloß and nearby Thüringer Wald (ask about the *Rennsteig* hiking trail), or book a private **room** (DM35-40) for free. (Open M-F 10am-5pm, Sa 10am-noon.) City **tours** leave on Wednesday at 11am and on Saturday at 2pm from the steps of the Rathaus. (May-Oct.; DM5, students DM2.50.) The tourist office also sells the Gotha **Touristenticket** (DM9.50) which knocks a mark or two off the price of most attractions and is good for one free trip on Gotha's bus system and the *Thüringer Waldbahn,* which leads from the train station into hiking country. Unless you plan to use the *Waldbahn,* don't bother; Gotha is small enough to see on foot. The **postal code** is 99867. The **telephone code** is 03621.

▐▐ ACCOMMODATIONS AND FOOD. The place to stay in Gotha is the **Pension Am Schloß,** Bergallee 3a (tel. 85 32 06). Centrally located, the pension is a small house that boasts beautifully furnished rooms and a small kitchen for guests. Unfortunately, the bargain is so good that it's tough to get a room. Call between 10am-8pm, though, and give it a try. (DM35-48. Breakfast included.) If that fails,

Gotha's **Jugendherberge (HI),** Mozartstr. 1 (tel. 85 40 08), rests on the corner of the Schloßpark. From the station, walk two blocks straight ahead; the beige hostel is on the right. Explore your musical side with accordion (DM5) or acoustic guitar (DM3) rentals. In the hallway, schoolchildren crowd the 80s arcade games, relics from the pre-Nintendo era. (DM15, over 26 DM20. HI members only. Breakfast DM6, lunch DM8, dinner DM6. Sheets DM7. Reception 3-10pm. Curfew 9pm, but guests over 18 can get a key.)

Load up on edible booty at the market, which fills the Hauptmarkt and Neumarkt (open M-F 8am-6pm, Sa 8am-1pm), and picnic in the palace gardens for an aesthetically pleasing bargain. **Ciao Ciao,** Querstr. 12, serves pizza (from DM6), pasta (from DM7), and delicious ice cream delights. (Open M-Sa 9:30am-11pm, Su 1-10pm.) Another solid option is **Kuhn and Kuhn,** Hühnersdorfstr. 14, a few blocks down from the castle and adjacent to the Buttermarkt. They offer café fare as well as German standards (DM7.50-14) until the wee hours. (Open daily 5pm-1am.)

■ **SIGHTS.** Gotha's city-planning, history, and tourist attractions are all dominated by the imposing **Schloß Friedenstein.** Rumored to once have had as many rooms as the year has days, the building is enormous. It served as a center of the Enlightenment in Germany, and Voltaire spent quite a bit of time here. Goethe, too, had only good things to say about the castle. (Open April-Oct. daily 10am-5pm; Nov.-March daily 10am-4pm. Tickets to the Schloß and all other museums below DM12, seniors DM10, students DM5.)

The **Schloßmuseum** (tel. 823 40) captures the eclectic intellectual curiosity of the Enlightenment. The men in the castle found inspiration in all directions: Greece, Egypt, inwards into anatomy, even into mechanics, and the galleries of the museum reflect this. Upstairs, the splendor of the royal apartments contrasts strikingly with the castle's spartan exterior; follow the red carpets that lead through the 16 fully restored, lavishly furnished ducal rooms. The Rococo *Festsaal,* decorated with colorful crests from around the duchy, houses the original royal silver service. Other highlights include beautifully inlaid walls and the royals' bedroom cabinets.

Also in the palace are the **Museum für Regionalgeschichte,** a series of rooms devoted to Thüringen's early history, and the **Kartographisches Museum,** the world's first museum of maps. The Renaissance and early Mercator maps are especially fascinating: watch the continents slowly, awkwardly take shape. The palace also provided a place for Konrad Eckhof to flourish. The "father of German drama," Eckhof worked at making theater as realistic as possible, a bit of a contradiction, considering that the **Eckhoftheater,** located inside the palace and still in use today, is full of optical illusions and tricks to make it seem bigger than it is. The theater and small theater museum are part of Schloßmuseum. Tickets for plays are available through the tourist office (DM35-60). The rest of the palace's splendor resides in its gardens, one of the largest in Europe; the **Orangerie** is especially stunning.

The rest of Gotha's history has managed to slip out of preservation's hands. The **Haus am Tivoli,** at the intersection of Cosmartstr. and Am Tivoli, was where August Bebel and others organized the Social Democratic Party (SPD). The modern SPD is the largest political party in Germany and is currently in control of the federal government. The house was the site of an extensive display during the GDR, including the fully preserved room where all the action went down. The bourgeoisie has stormed back, though, and the house is now closed indefinitely. A similar story goes for the **Cranach-Haus,** Hauptmarkt 17. The wife of the famous painter was born here, and they lived shortly in the house; now all to be seen is the exterior undergoing renovation.

THÜRINGEN

BAYERN (BAVARIA)

Bayern is the Germany of Teutonic myth, Wagnerian opera, and fairy tales. From the tiny villages of the Wald and the Baroque cities along the Danube to Mad King Ludwig's castles perched high in the Alps, the region beckons to more tourists than any other part of the country. Indeed, when most foreigners conjure up images of Germany, they are imagining Bavaria, land of beer gardens, smoked sausage, and *Lederhosen*. This is in part a relic of Germany's 45-year division, which shifted Western perceptions southward and prevented iconoclastic Berlin from acting as a counterweight to more strait-laced Bavarian cities. Though mostly rural, Catholic, and conservative, this largest of Germany's federal states nurtures flourishing commerce and industry, including such renowned companies as the Bayerische Motorwerke (BMW).

However, these popular images of Bavaria present a somewhat inaccurate image of the whole of Germany, as the region's independent residents have always been Bavarians first and Germans second. It took wars with France and Austria to pull Bayern into Bismarck's orbit, and it remained its own kingdom until 1918; local authorities still insist upon using the *Land*'s proper name: *Freistaat Bayern* (Free State of Bayern). In a plebiscite, Bayern was the only state to refuse to ratify the Federal Republic's Basic Law, and the ruling CDU still abides by a long-standing agreement not to compete in Bavarian elections (instead, a related party, the

Christian Social Union, represents the center-right). The insistent preservation of its unique tradition and history, amply demonstrated by the impenetrable dialect spoken in the region, animates the wildest stereotypes about German culture.

> **!** **REMINDER.** HI-affiliated hostels in Bayern generally do not admit guests over age 26, although families and groups of adults with young children are usually allowed even if adults are over 26.

HIGHLIGHTS OF BAYERN

■ Brimming with beers, swathed with lush green parks, loaded with museums, and blessed with Germany's most well-oiled tourist industry, **Munich** deserves its great reputation among budget travelers. Make reservations early for **Oktoberfest** (Sept. 16-Oct. 1, 2000), or try out one of the city's dozens of outdoor beer gardens (p. 250).
■ Like all great visionaries, King Ludwig II was a nut. His **Königsschlösser** (royal castles), enormous getaway castles in the Bavarian Alps, now perch in the mountains near Füssen (p. 261).
■ The South of Bayern borders the spectacular Alps. For high-altitude fun, head to either the **Bavarian Alps** (p. 256) or the **Allgäu Alps** (p. 256).
■ Haunted by its many associations with Germany's Nazi past,**Nürnberg** is captivating and solemn, with many Nazi-era ruins still visible (p. 304).
■ The **Romantische Straße** (p. 296) snakes through western Bavaria, linking **Würzburg** to **Füssen** by way of well-touristed towns (p. 296).

MÜNCHEN (MUNICH)

The capital and cultural center of Bayern, Munich is a sprawling, relatively liberal metropolis in the midst of solidly conservative southern Germany. The two cities of Munich and Berlin are emblematic of the poles of German character. Munich, exuding a traditional air of merriment, stands in sharp contrast to Berlin, which thrives on its sense of fragmented avant-garde and is characterized by its dizzying reconstruction.

Munich unabashedly displays West German postwar economic glory. World-class museums, handsome parks and architecture, a rambunctious arts scene, and an urbane population collide to create a city of astonishing vitality. Even in the depths of winter, citizens meet in outdoor beer gardens to discuss art, politics, and (of course) *Fußball*. An ebullient mixture of sophistication and earthy Bavarian *Gemütlichkeit* keeps the city awake at (almost) all hours. *Müncheners* party zealously during *Fasching* (Jan. 7-March 7, 2000), Germany's equivalent of Mardi Gras, and during the legendary Oktoberfest (Sept. 16-Oct. 1, 2000).

HISTORY

Although Munich revels in its cushy Southern German location, the city was actually founded by a Northerner, Heinrich the Lion, in 1158. Named after the city's famous monk residents, Munich came under the rule of one of Europe's most stalwart dynasties, the **Wittelsbachs,** who controlled the city under strict Catholic piety from 1180 until the 18th century, when Napoleon's romp through Europe turned the city into a Napoleonic kingdom and ushered in the Bavarian Golden Age. At this time, "enlightened" absolutists rationalized state administration, promoted commerce, and patronized the arts. Ludwig I and Maximilian I contributed immensely to the expansion and evolution of the city, while its most famous king, **Ludwig II,** began his flight toward head-in-the-clouds extravagance. In 1871, after Bismarck's successful wars solidified Prussian dominance of Germany, Ludwig presided over the absorption of Bayern into the greater *Reich;* the process was facilitated by Bismarck's generous funding of Ludwig's loony architectural

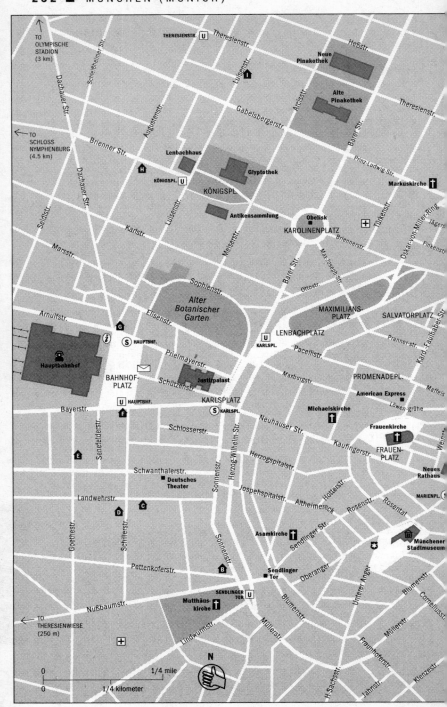

TO
OLYMPISCHE
STADION
(3 km)

Scheißheimer Str.

Dachauer Str.

THERESIENSTR. [U] Theresienstr.

Luisenstr.

Neue
Pinakothek

Heßstr.

Arcisstr.

Alte
Pinakothek

Theresienstr.

Augustenstr.

Gabelsbergerstr.

Barer Str.

TO
SCHLOSS
NYMPHENBURG
(4.5 km)

Brienner Str.

Lenbachhaus

Glyptothek

Prinz-Ludwig-Str.

KÖNIGSPL. [U]

[H]

KÖNIGSPL.

Markuskirche [†]

Dachauer Str.

Luisenstr.

Karlstr.

Meiserstr.

Antikensammlung

Obelisk
KAROLINENPLATZ

Barer Str.

Max-Joseph-Str.

Brennerstr.

[+]

Türkenstr.

Ottostr.

Oskar-von-Miller-Ring

Jägers

Finkenstr.

Serdlstr.

Marsstr.

Arnulfstr.

Hauptbahnhof

Elisenstr.

Sophienstr.

Alter
Botanischer
Garten

MAXIMILIANS-
PLATZ

SALVATORPLATZ

Kard.-Faulhaber-Str.

[G]

[i]

[S] HAUPTBHF.

LENBACHPLATZ

[U]
KARLSPL.

Pacellistr.

Pranner-str.

Mäffeis

BAHNHOF-
PLATZ

Prielmayerstr.

Schützenstr.

Justizpalast

Maxburgstr.

PROMENADEPL.

American Express

Löwen-grube

[U] HAUPTBHF.

KARLSPLATZ

[S] KARLSPL.

Michaeliskirche [†]

Frauenkirche [†]

Bayerstr.

[F]

Senefelderstr.

Schlosserstr.

Neuhauser Str.

Herzog-Wilhelm-Str.

Herzogspitalstr.

Kaufingerstr.

FRAUEN-
PLATZ

Weinstr.

[E]

Schwanthalerstr.

Deutsches
Theater

Sonnenstr.

Jospehspitalstr.

Hoterstr.

Neues
Rathaus

MARIENPL. [S]

Landwehrstr.

[D] [C]

Altheimereck

Rosenstr.

Rosental

Goethestr.

Schillerstr.

Pettenkoferstr.

[B]

Sendlinger Str.

Asamkirche [†]

Oberanger

Unterer Anger

[+]

Münchener
Stadtmuseum [🏛]

Blumenstr.

Cornelius

Nußbaumstr.

SENDLINGER
TOR [U]

Matthäus-
kirche [†]

Sonnenstr.

Sendlinger
Tor

Blumenstr.

Müllerstr.

Fraunhoferstr.

TO
THERESIENWIESE
(250 m)

[+]

Lindwurmstr.

Müllerstr.

Klenzestr.

H.-Sachsstr.

Jahnstr.

N

0   1/4 mile

0   1/4 kilometer

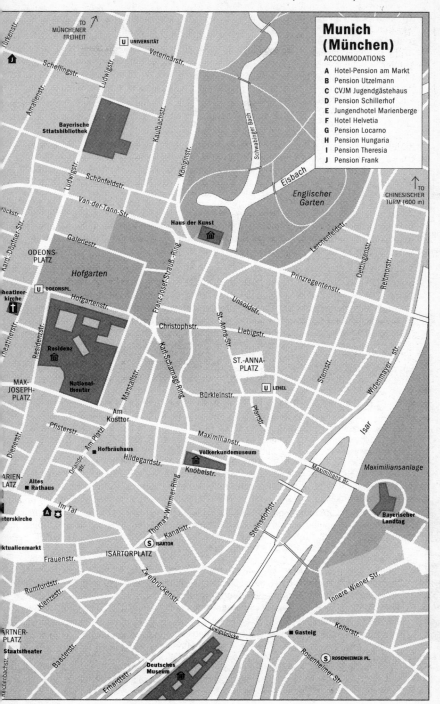

Munich (München)

ACCOMMODATIONS

A Hotel-Pension am Markt
B Pension Utzelmann
C CVJM Jugendgästehaus
D Pension Schillerhof
E Jungendhotel Marienberge
F Hotel Helvetia
G Pension Locarno
H Pension Hungaria
I Pension Theresia
J Pension Frank

projects. Munich rose to become a cultural powerhouse, rivalling hated Berlin (a city that *Müncheners* regarded as a glorified garrison town), with artists flocking to its burgeoning scene.

The Golden Age came to an abrupt end with Germany's defeat in WWI. Weimar Munich was an incubator for reactionary and anti-Semitic movements: **Adolf Hitler** found the city such fertile recruiting ground for the new National Socialist German Workers Party (Nazis) that he later called it "the capital of our movement." In 1923, Hitler attempted to overthrow the municipal government and lead a march on Berlin to topple the Weimar Republic. His **Beer Hall Putsch** was quickly quashed and its leaders arrested, but evidence of his movement's eventual success still haunts the city: Neville Chamberlain's attempted appeasement of Hitler over the Sudetenland is remembered as the **Munich Agreement,** and the Nazis' first concentration camp was constructed just outside the city at Dachau.

Despite Munich's fortuitous location deep inside the German air defenses, Allied bombings destroyed the city. By 1944, less than 3% of the city center remained intact; since then, much of it has been rebuilt in the original style. When Munich hosted the **1972 Olympics,** it was hoped that its tattered image would at last be restored. The city went to great lengths to revolutionize itself: it pedestrianized big chunks of the city center, extended the subway system, and brought the city's resources to their current, modernized status. But a tragic attack by the Palestinian terrorist group *Black September* during the Games led to the death of 11 Israeli athletes in a police shoot-out, dashing Munich's hopes.

Though Munich's history appears to speak otherwise, the city was and is now an indulgent, celebratory place. Today's riotous upheavals are of a much less threatening variety. Consider a recent protest, 20,000 citizens strong, over—what else?—beer. The issue at hand in this first-time "Bavarian beer garden revolution" was the **Waldwirtschaft beer garden,** which can accommodate 2,000 customers but has only 100 parking places. Numerous neighborhood complaints had finally led to a draconian court decision mandating a 9:30pm closing time for the beer garden. After *Müncheners* marched on Marienplatz in good revolutionary spirit a few years back, the court reversed its decision and they won back a half hour—enough time to chug at least one more *Maß*.

▄ GETTING THERE AND AROUND

Flights: Flughafen München (tel. 97 52 13 13). S-Bahn #8 runs to the airport and from the Hauptbahnhof every 20min. DM14 or 8 stripes on the *Streifenkarte*. Alternatively, a **Lufthansa shuttle bus** runs between the Hauptbahnhof and the airport (45min.), with a pickup at the "Nordfriedhof" U-Bahn stop in Schwabing. Buses leave from Arnulfstr., on the northern side of the train station every 20min. 6:50am-7:50pm. Buses return from Terminal A *(Zentralbereich)* and Terminal D every 20min. 7:55am-8:55pm. One-way DM15, round-trip DM25.

Trains: Munich's **Hauptbahnhof** (tel. 22 33 12 56) is the transportation hub of Southern Germany, with connections to Füssen (2hr., 1 per hour, DM36), Frankfurt (3½hr., 1 per hour, DM113), Köln (6hr., 1 per hour, DM173), Hamburg (6hr., 1 per hour, DM224), Berlin (7½hr., 1 per hour, DM183), Innsbruck (2hr., 1 per hour), Salzburg (1¾hr., 1 per hour), Zürich (5hr., every 2 hr., DM110), Vienna (5hr., 1 per hour, DM103), Prague (8½hr., 6 per day, DM97), Amsterdam (9hr., 1 per hour, DM245), and Paris (10hr., DM193). For schedules, fare information, and reservations call tel. (0180) 599 66 33. Open 6am-10:30pm. **EurAide** (see **Tourist Offices,** p. 236), in the station, provides free train information in English. **Reisezentrum** information counters open daily 6am-11:30pm. Reservation desk open 7am-9pm.

Public Transportation: MVV, Munich's public transport system, runs M-F 5am-12:30am, Sa-Su 5am-2:30am. Eurail, InterRail, and German railpasses are valid on the S-Bahn but *not* on the U-Bahn, streetcars, or buses. Buy tickets at the blue *MVV-Fahrausweise* vending machines and validate them in the boxes marked with an "E" *before entering the platform.* Payment is made on an honor system, but disguised agents check for tickets sporadically; if you plan to jump the fare or don't validate correctly, bring along an extra DM60 for the fine. **Transit maps** and **maps of wheelchair accessible stations** can be picked up in the tourist office or EurAide and at MVV counters near the subway entrance in the train station.

Prices: Single ride tickets DM3.50 (valid for 3hr.). *Kurzstrecke* (short trip) tickets cost DM1.80 and can be used for 2 stops on the U-Bahn or S-Bahn, or for 4 stops on a streetcar or bus. A *Streifenkarte* (11-strip ticket) costs DM15 and can be used by more than 1 person. Cancel 2 strips per person for a normal ride, or 1 strip per person for a *Kurzstrecke*. Beyond the city center, cancel 2 strips per additional zone. A **Single-Tageskarte** (single-day ticket) is valid for one day of unlimited travel until 6am the next day (DM9). A **Partner-Tageskarte** (DM12.50) can be used by 2 adults, 3 children under 18, and a dog. The **3-Day Pass** (DM21) is also a great deal. The best public transportation deal is the **München Welcome Card,** available at the tourist office and in many hotels, which is valid for 3 days of public transportation for DM29; a group ticket for up to 5 people runs DM42. The card includes a 50% discount on many of Munich's museums and on Radius bike rental (see below). Passes can be purchased at the MVV office behind tracks 31 and 32 in the Hauptbahnhof. Children under 15 pay reduced fares, and children under 4 ride free.

Taxis: Taxi-Zentrale (tel. 216 11 or 194 10) has large stands in front of the train station and every 5-10 blocks in the central city. Women can request a female driver.

Car Rental: Flach's Leihwagen, Landsberger Str. 289 (tel. 56 60 56), rents cars for DM60-112 per day. Open M-F 8am-8pm, Sa 9am-noon. **Swing,** Schellingstr. 139 (tel. 523 20 05), rents from DM45 per day. **Avis** (tel. 550 12 12), **Europcar/National** (tel. 550 13 41), **Hertz** (tel. 550 22 56), and **Sixt Budget** (tel. 550 24 47) have offices upstairs in the Hauptbahnhof.

Bike Rental: Radius Bikes (tel. 59 61 13), at the far end of the Hauptbahnhof, behind the lockers opposite tracks 30-31. DM10 per 2hr., DM30 per day, DM75 per week. Mountain bikes 20% more. Deposit DM100, passport, or credit card. Students and Eurailpass holders receive a 10% discount. Open April to early Oct. daily 10am-6pm. **Aktiv-Rad,** Hans-Sachs-Str. 7 (tel. 26 65 06), rents 'em at DM18 per day. U-Bahn #1 or 2 to "Fraunhofer Str." Open M-F 9am-1pm and 2-6:30pm, Sa 9am-1pm.

Mitfahrzentrale: McShare Treffpunkt Zentrale, Klenzestr. 57b and Lämmerstr. 4 (tel. 194 40). Walk out the "Arnulfstr." exit of the train station and cross the street, then walk left of the Hypo-Vereinsbank down Pfefferstr., and take a right down Hirtenstr. and a right on Lammerstr. Matches McDrivers and McRiders. Heidelberg DM34, Frankfurt DM41, Berlin DM54. Open daily 8am-8pm. At the same location, **Frauenmitfahrzentrale,** Klenzestr. 57b, arranges ride shares for women only. U-Bahn #1 or 2 to "Fraunhofer Str.," then walk up Fraunhofer Str. away from the river and turn right. Open M-F 8am-8pm. **Känguruh,** Amalienstr. 87 (tel. 194 44), is in the Amalien-passage near the university. Open M-F 9am-6:30pm, Sa 9am-3pm, Su 10am-7pm.

Hitchhiking: *Let's Go* does not recommend hitchhiking as a safe mode of transportation. Those looking to share rides scan the bulletin boards in the **Mensa,** Leopoldstr. 13. Otherwise, hitchers try *Autobahn* on-ramps; *those who stand behind the blue sign with the white auto may be fined.* Hitchers going to Salzburg take U-Bahn #1 or 2 to "Karl-Preis-Platz." For Stuttgart, take streetcar #17 to "Amalienburgstr." or S-Bahn #2 to "Obermenzing," then bus #73 or 75 to "Blutenburg." To Nürnberg and Berlin, take U-Bahn #6 to "Studentenstadt" and walk 500m to the Frankfurter Ring. To the Bodensee and Switzerland, take U-Bahn #4 or 5 to "Heimeranpl.," then bus #33 to "Siegenburger Str."

✈ ORIENTATION

Munich rests on the banks of the Isar in the middle of south-central Bayern. Mad King Ludwig's castles and the Bavarian Alps are only a short trip through the squalor of Munich's industrial outskirts.

A map of Munich's center looks like a skewed circle quartered by one horizontal and one vertical line. The circle is the main traffic **Ring,** which changes its name

BAYERN

again and again as it bounds the city center. Within it lies the lion's share of Munich's sights. The east-west and north-south thoroughfares, in turn, cross at Munich's epicenter, the **Marienplatz** (home to the **Neues Rathaus**), and meet the traffic ring at **Karlsplatz** (called **Stachus** by locals) in the west, **Isartorplatz** in the east, **Odeonsplatz** in the north, and **Sendlinger Tor** in the south. The **Hauptbahnhof** is just beyond Karlsplatz outside the Ring in the west. In the east beyond the Isartor, the **Isar** flows by the city center, south to north. To get to Marienplatz from the station, go straight on Schützenstr. to the yellow buildings of Karlsplatz. Continue straight through Karlstor to Neuhauser Str., which becomes Kaufingerstr. before it reaches Marienplatz (15-20min.). Or take S-Bahn #1-8 (two stops from the Hauptbahnhof) to "Marienplatz."

To the north, at Odeonsplatz, the giant **Residenz** palace sprawls over a hefty piece of downtown land; **Ludwigstraße** stretches north from there toward the university district. **Leopoldstraße,** the continuation of Ludwigstr., reaches farther toward **Schwabing**. This district, also known as "Schwabylon," is student country; it lies to the west of the maddeningly mobbed Leopoldstr. **Türkenstr., Amalienstr., Schellingstr.,** and **Barerstr.** meander through the funk. To the east of Schwabing sprawls the **Englischer Garten**; to the west is the **Olympiazentrum,** the hyper-modern complex constructed for the 1972 games, surrounded by the verdant **Olympiapark**. Farther west sits the posh **Nymphenburg,** built around the eponymous **Schloß Nymphenburg**. Southwest of Marienplatz, **Sendlinger Str.** leads past shops to the Sendlinger Tor. From there, Lindwurmstr. proceeds to Goetheplatz, from which Mozartstr. leads to **Theresienwiese,** the site of the Oktoberfest.

Several publications help to navigate around Munich. The most comprehensive one (in English) is the monthly *Munich Found,* available at newstands and bookshops; it provides a list of services, events, and museums. The tourist office distributes the encyclopedic *Monatsprogramm,* with a list of city events in chronological order. The bi-weekly *in München* (free) gives a more intensive insider's look at the Munich *Szene,* providing detailed movie, theater, and concert schedules. *Prinz* is the hip and hefty monthly with endless tips on shopping, art, music, film, concerts, and food. EurAide's free publication *Inside Track* provides updated information in English on train connections as well as basic tips on getting started in Munich; it's available at EurAide (see below) or at the *Reisezentrum* in the main hall of the station.

▣ PRACTICAL INFORMATION

TOURIST OFFICES

Main Office: Fremdenverkehrsamt (tel. 23 33 02 57; fax 23 33 02 33; email Munich_Tourist_Office@compuserve.com; www.munich-tourist.de), located on the front (east) side of the train station, next to ABR Travel on Bahnhofpl. Although friendly and helpful, this office is usually inundated with tourists, and the staff rarely answers the phone. They do speak English, but for more in-depth questions, EurAide (see below) will probably better suit your needs. The tourist office books **rooms** for free with a 10-15% deposit and sells excellent English city maps (DM0.50). You can also purchase the **München Welcome Card** here, which offers free public transportation and reduced admission to many sights (single-day ticket DM12, 3-day ticket DM29). The English/ German young people's guide *München Infopool* (DM1) lists beer gardens and gives tips on cycling, sightseeing, and navigating the confusing public transportation system. Call for **recorded information** in English on museums and galleries (tel. 23 91 62) or sights and castles (tel. 23 91 72). Open M-Sa 9am-10pm, Su 10am-6pm. A **branch office** (tel. 233 03 00) in the *Zentralgebäude* at the airport, provides general information but does not reserve rooms. Open M-Sa 8:30am-10pm, Su 1-9pm. An **even smaller office** roosts just inside the entrance to the Neues Rathaus on Marienpl. (tel. 23 33 02 72 or 23 33 02 73), offering free brochures and city maps (DM0.50). A counter on the opposite side of the room sells tickets for concerts and performances. Open M-F 10am-8pm, Sa 10am-4pm.

■ **EurAide in English** (tel. 59 38 89; fax 550 39 65; email euraide@compuserve.com; www.cube.net/kmu/euraide.html), along track 11 (room 3) of the Hauptbahnhof, near the Bayerstr. exit. Delve into the intricacies of Munich with one sound byte from EurAide's Alan R. Wissenberg, savior of frazzled English-speaking tourists. A nearly omniscient American, he points you in the right direction and books **rooms** for a DM7 fee. Also sells train tickets and offers the "Two Castle Tour," an outing to the *Königsschlösser* (see **Tours,** below). Open June-Oktoberfest daily 7:45am-noon and 1-6pm; Oct.-April M-F 7:45am-noon and 1-4pm, Sa 7:45am-noon; May daily 7:45am-noon and 1-4:30pm.

TOURS

Munich Walks (tel. (0177) 227 59 01; email 106513.3461@compuserve.com). Native English speakers give guided historical walking tours of the city with 2 different slants: the comprehensive introductory tour of the Altstadt hits all the major sights (May-Aug. daily 10:30am, also M-Sa 2:30pm; April and Oct. daily 10:30am; Nov. to late Dec. daily 10am), while a more specialized tour visits haunting Nazi sites (May-Aug. Tu, Th, Sa 10:30am; April Sa 2:30pm; Sept.-Oct. Tu, Th, Sa 2:30pm). The 2½hr. tours cost DM15, under 26 DM12, under 14 free with an adult. Both tours leave from outside the EurAide office in the train station.

Mike's Bike Tours (tel. 651 42 75; email Mike@bavaria.com). Ponder the "Eunuch of Munich," "hunt" lions, have lunch at a *Biergarten* in the Englischer Garten, and see the sights of the city. Mike and his gaggle of supremely funny tour guides lead small groups through Munich's cycling paths. Tours leave from the Altes Rathaus by the Spielzeugmuseum. The 4hr., 6.5km city tour includes a lunch break and runs April to early Oct. daily 11:30am and 4pm; March and late Oct. daily 12:30pm. DM31. The 6hr., 16km. tour includes 2 beer garden breaks. (June-Aug. daily 12:30pm. DM45.) All prices include bike rental and rain gear.

Radius Bikes (see **Getting There and Around,** p. 235) gives daily 2½hr. guided bike tours of the city. Tours meet in front of shop April-Oct.4 10:30am, May 16-Sept. 6 also 2:30pm. DM19 including bike, DM12 if you have a bike. Self-guided tour info DM5.

Spurwechsel Bike Tours (tel. 692 46 99). Entertaining German-speaking tour guides lead a 15km cycling spree around the Altstadt, Schwabing, and Englischer Garten, with a pause at the Chinesischer Turm beer garden for a pretzel and *Weißbier* feast. 2hr. DM22. Tours meet M, W, F, Su, and holidays at the Marienpl. fountain.

Panorama Tours, Arnulfstr. 8 (tel. 54 90 75 60 for day excursions, tel. 55 02 89 95 for city excursions; email GLMUC@aol.com). Offers staid bilingual **bus** tours that leave from the train station's main entrance on Bahnhofplatz. 1hr. tour in an open-air double-decker May-Oct. daily 10, 11, 11:30am, noon, 1, 2:30, 3, and 4pm. DM17, children DM8. A 2hr. tour leaves daily at 10am and 2:30pm; Tu-Su, the 10am tour goes to the Residenz or the Olympic Park, while the 2:30pm tour visits the Peterskirche, the Olympic Park, or the Nymphenburg Palace. DM30, children DM15. Hotel pick-up available. 10% off day excursions with Eurailpass. Open M-F 7:30am-6pm, Sa 7:30am-noon, Su 7:30-10am.

Two Castle Tour: For those who want to enter the magical realm of Mad King Ludwig II (see p. 261), two options await: **Panorama Tours** offers a 10½hr. bus excursion (in English) to Schloß Linderhof leaving April-Oct. daily 8:30am; Nov.-March Tu, Th, and Sa-Su 8:30am. DM78; with Eurailpass, InterRail, or German Railpass DM68; with ISIC DM59; Schloß admission not included. Book in advance. **EurAide** leads an English-speaking half-bus, half-train *Schloß*-schlepp that includes Neuschwanstein and an extra stop at the Rococo Wieskirche. Meet June-July Wednesday at 7:30am by track 11 in front of EurAide. DM70; with Eurailpass, InterRail, or flexipass DM55. Admission to castles not included, but EurAide will get you a DM1 discount. For those who'd like to catch an extra 45min. of sleep, a tour to Schloß Linderhof and Neuschwanstein leaves June-July every Wednesday at 8:15am in front of EurAide. DM78. Or drop by EurAide for train and public bus schedules to see the castles on your own (see **Hypertravel to the Castles,** p. 263).

CONSULATES

Canada: Tal 29 (tel. 219 95 70). S-Bahn to "Isartor." Open M-Th 9am-noon and 2-5pm, F 9am-noon and 2-3:30pm.

Ireland: Mauerkircherstr. 1a (tel. 98 57 23). Streetcar #20 or bus #54 or 87. Open M-F 9am-noon and 1-4pm.

South Africa: Sendlinger-Tor-Pl. 5 (tel. 231 16 30). U-Bahn #1, 2, 3 or 6 to "Sendlinger Tor." Open M-F 9am-noon.

U.K.: Bürkleinstr. 10 (tel. 21 10 90), 4th floor. U-Bahn #4 or 5 to "Lehel." Open M-F 8:45-11:30am and 1-3:15pm.

U.S.: Königinstr. 5 (tel. 288 80). Open M-F 8-11am. For a recording on visa information, call (0190) 27 07 89; to speak to an official, call (0190) 91 50 00 M-F 7am-8pm.

LOCAL SERVICES

Budget Travel: Council Travel, Adalbertstr. 32 (tel. 39 50 22), near the university, sells ISICs. Open M-F 10am-1pm and 2-6:30pm. **abr Reisebüro** (tel. 12 04 46) is located in the train station and sells train tickets and railpasses. Open M-F 9am-6pm and Sa 10am-1pm.

Currency Exchange: ReiseBank (tel. 551 08 37). 2 locations: one in front of the main entrance to the train station on Bahnhofplatz (open daily 6am-11pm); and around the corner from EurAide at track 11 (open M-Sa 7:30am-7:15pm, Su 9:30am-12:30pm and 1-4:45pm). Those with *Inside Track,* available at EurAide, get a 50% discount on commission if cashing US$50 or more in U.S. traveler's checks. All cash transactions DM5. Western Union services.

American Express: Promenadeplatz 6 (tel. 29 09 00; 24hr. hotline (0130) 85 31 00), in the Hotel Bayerischer Hof. Holds mail and cashes traveler's checks. Open M-F 9am-5:30pm, Sa 9:30am-12:30pm. **Branch** office at Kaufingerstr. 24 (tel. 22 80 13 87), by the Frauenkirche. Open M-F 9am-5:30pm, Sa 10am-1pm.

Luggage Storage: At the **train station** (tel. 13 08 50 47) and **airport** (tel. 97 52 13 75). Staffed storage room *(Gepäckaufbewahrung)* in the main hall of the train station. Open daily 6am-11pm. DM4 per piece per calendar day. Lockers opposite tracks # 16, 24, and 28-36. DM2-4 per 24hr.

Lost and Found: Fundamt, Ötztaler Str. 17 (tel. 23 34 59 00). U-Bahn #6 to "Partnachplatz." Open M and W-F 8:30am-noon, Tu 8:30am-noon and 2-5:30pm. For items lost on the S-Bahn contact **Fundstelle im Ostbahnhof** (tel. 12 88 44 09). Open M-F 8am-5:30pm, Sa 8am-11:45pm. Or try the **Deutsche Bahn Fundbüro,** Landsberger Str. 472 (tel. 13 08 58 59). S-Bahn to "Passing." Open M and W-F 8am-noon, Tu 8am-noon and 12:30-3pm.

Mitwohnzentrale: An der Uni (tel. 286 60 66), in the tunnel passage of U-Bahn #3 and 6 at the "Universität" stop, has apartments available for 1 month or more. Open M-F 10am-6pm, Sa 11am-1pm. **City Mitwohnzentrale,** Klenzestr. 57b (tel. 194 40), lists apartments and houses throughout Germany.

Bookstores: Anglia English Bookshop, Schellingstr. 3 (tel. 28 36 42), offers reams of English-language books in a gloriously chaotic atmosphere. U-Bahn #3 or 6 to "Universität." Open M-F 9am-6:30pm, Sa 10am-2pm. **Words' Worth,** Schellingstr. 21a (tel. 280 91 41), farther down, carries obscure English novels as well as a full range of classic literature. Open M-Tu and F 9am-6:30pm, W-Th 9am-8pm, Sa 10am-2pm.

Libraries: Many of Munich's city libraries have a hefty English section. **Bayerische Staatsbibliothek,** Ludwigstr. 16 (tel. 28 63 80), the largest university library in all German-speaking countries, has 6.5 million books and endless magazines and newspapers. Open M-F 9am-7:30pm, Sa 9am-4:30pm. **Universitätsbibliothek der Universität,** Geschwister-Scholl-Platz 1 (tel. 21 80 24 28). Open Dec.-July M-Th 9am-8pm, F 9am-4pm; Aug.-Nov. M-Th 9am-7pm, F 9am-noon. **The Bookshelf,** Blumenstr. 36 (tel. 61 62 27), is an English lending library. U-Bahn #1 or 2 to "Sendlinger Tor." Open M, W, F 3-6pm, Sa 11am-1pm.

Cultural Centers: Amerika Haus, Karolinenpl. 3 (tel. 552 53 70), is the cultural extension of the consulate. U-Bahn #2 to "Königsplatz." Cultural resources and advice for Americans wishing to teach, a library for reading and research, and language courses. Open Tu-F 1-5pm. **British Council,** Rosenheimer Str. 116b, Haus 93 (tel. 290 08 60).

Gay and Lesbian Resources: Gay services information (tel. 260 30 56). **Lesbian information** (tel. 725 42 72). Open F 6-10pm. Also for lesbians, **Lesbentraum LeTra,** Dreimühlenstr. 23 (tel. 725 42 72). Open Th 1:30-4pm; telephones open Th 7-10pm. See also **Gay and Lesbian Munich,** p. 254.

Women's Resources: Kofra Kommunikationszentrum für Frauen, Baaderstr. 30 (tel. 201 04 50). Job advice, tons of magazines, lesbian politics, and books. Open M-F 4-10pm. **Frauentreffpunkt Neuperlach,** Oskar-Maria-Graf-Ring 20-22 (tel. 670 64 63). An environmentally conscious women's café and shop. Open Tu and Th-F 10am-1pm, W 10am-1pm and 3-6pm. **Lillemor's Frauenbuchladen,** Arcisstr. 57 (tel. 272 12 05), is a women's bookstore and center for women's events. U-Bahn #2 to "Max-Joseph-Platz." Open M-F 10am-6:30pm, Sa 10am-2pm. **Fraueninfothek,** Johannispl. 12 (tel. 48 48 90). Open M 10am-1pm, Tu 10am-1pm and 2-5pm, Th 2-5pm.

Disabled Resources: Info Center für Behinderte, Schellingstr. 31, has a list of Munich resources for disabled persons. Open M-W 8am-noon and 2-6pm, Th 8am-noon and 2-4pm, F 8am-noon.

Ticket Agencies: Advance tickets for concerts in the Olympiapark and soccer games are available at the **Kaufhof** department store (tel. 260 32 49) on Marienplatz, 3rd floor, or at Karlsplatz, ground floor (tel. 512 52 48). Both open M-W and F 11am-6:30pm, Th 11am-8:30pm, Sa 9am-2pm. **Hertie Schwabing,** Leopoldstr. 82, (tel. 33 66 59) 4th floor, sells tickets for smaller rock, pop, and theater events. Open M-F 9am-6:30pm, Sa 9am-2pm. To order **tickets by phone** call **München Ticket** (tel. 54 81 81 81).

Laundromat: City SB-Waschcenter, Paul-Heyse-Str. 21, near the station. Take a right on Bayerstr., then left on Paul-Heyse-Str. for 1½ blocks. Wash DM6, soap included. Dry DM1 per 10min. Open daily 7am-11pm. **Münz Waschsalon,** Amalienstr. 61, near the university. Wash DM6.20, soap DM1. Dry DM1 per 10min. Open M-F 8am-6:30pm, Sa 8am-1pm. **Waschcenter,** Landshüter Allee 77. U-Bahn #1 to "Rotkreuzplatz." Wash DM6. Dry DM1 per 15min. Open 24hr. *Bring change for laundromats.*

Swimming Pools: Pool season is May to mid-Sept. Choose among 16 local dives. **Müllerisches Volksbad,** Rosenheimer Str. 1 (tel. 23 61 34 29), has Art Nouveau indoor pools and steam baths. S-Bahn to "Isartor." Open M 10am-5pm, Tu and Th 8am-7:30pm, W 6:45am-7:30pm, F 8am-8:45pm, Sa 8am-5:30pm, Su 9am-6pm. The outdoor, heated **Dantebad,** Dantestr. 6 (tel. 15 28 74), in Neuhausen, is excellent and much less crowded—hardly hellish. Streetcar #20 or 21 to "Baldurstr." Open daily 8am-7:30pm. **Westbad,** Weinburger Str. 17 (tel. 88 54 41), offers indoor and outdoor pools, a sauna, tanning booths, water slides, and a large green lawn (DM15). From Karlsplatz, streetcar #19 to "Am Knie/Westbad." **Nordbad,** Schleißheimer Str. 142 (tel. 23 61 79 41), has similar offerings plus a whirlpool for DM5. U-Bahn #2 to "Hohenzollernplatz."

EMERGENCY AND COMMUNICATIONS

Emergency: Police, tel. 110. **Ambulance** and **Fire,** tel. 112. **Emergency medical service,** tel. 59 44 75.

Rape Crisis Line: Frauennotruf München, Güllstr. 3 (tel. 76 37 37).

AIDS Hotline: Tel. 520 73 87 or 520 74 12 (M-Th 8am-3pm, F 8am-noon); or 194 11 (M-Sa 7-10pm).

Pharmacy: Bahnhof-Apotheke, Bahnhofpl. 2 (tel. 59 41 19 or 59 81 19), on the corner outside the train station. Open M-F 8am-6:30pm, Sa 8am-2pm. 24hr. service rotates among the city's pharmacies—call 59 44 75 for recorded information (German only).

Medical Assistance: Klinikum Rechts der Isar, clinic across the river on Ismaninger Str. U-Bahn #4 or 5 to "Max-Weber-Platz." STD/AIDS tests are free and anonymous at the **Gesundheitshaus,** Dachauer Str. 90 (tel. 520 71). Open M-Th 8-11am and 1-2pm, F 8-11am. U.K. and U.S. consulates carry lists of English-speaking doctors.

Post Office: Bahnhofplatz, 80335 Munich (tel. 59 90 87 16). Walk out of the main train station exit and it's the large yellow building directly across the street. Open M-F 7am-8pm, Sa 8am-4pm, Su 9am-3pm. **Postamt 31** (tel. 552 26 20), up the escalator in the train station, sells stamps and phone cards and mails letters, but doesn't mail packages or exchange money. Open M-F 7am-8pm, Sa 8am-4pm, Su 9am-3pm.

Internet Access: Times Square Internet Café, Bayerstr. 10a, located on the south side of the train station. The café offers beer (DM4.50-5.50), salads (DM7-16), and other specials (DM10-20). 15min. Internet access DM4.50. See also **Internet-Café,** p. 245.

PHONE CODE	089

▪ ACCOMMODATIONS AND CAMPING

Munich's accommodations usually fall into one of three categories: seedy, expensive, or booked solid. During times like Oktoberfest, there is only the last category. In summer, the best strategy is to start calling before noon or to book a few weeks in advance. Most singles (without private bath) run DM55-85, doubles DM80-120. If you're planning an extended stay in Munich, call the *Mitwohnzentrale* (p. 238) or try bargaining with a *Pension* owner. Remember: **Bavarian HI hostels do not accept guests over age 26.** The enforcement of this rule varies. At most of Munich's hostels you can check in all day, but try to start your search well before 5pm.

Don't even think of sleeping in any public area, including the Hauptbahnhof; police patrol frequently all night long. A few options for the roomless do exist: the Augsburg youth hostel (see p. 295) is 30 to 45 minutes away by train (until 11:20pm, 2-3 per hour, DM10), but be mindful of the 1am curfew. Alternatively, throw your luggage into a locker, party until 5am, and return to re-evaluate the hotel lists afterward.

HOSTELS

▪ **Jugendlager Kapuzinerhölzl** ("The Tent"), In den Kirschen 30 (tel. 141 43 00; fax 17 50 90). Streetcar #17 from the Hauptbahnhof (direction "Amalienburgstr.") to "Botanischer Garten" (15min.). Go straight on Franz-Schrank-Str. and left at In den Kirschen; The Tent is on the right. Night streetcars run at least once an hour all night. Spontaneous merrymaking around a bonfire at night; random films in English. Sleep with 400 fellow "campers" under a big circus tent on a wooden floor. DM14 gets a foam pad, multiple wool blankets, bathrooms, a rudimentary breakfast, and enthusiastic management. Actual "beds" DM18. Camping available for DM7 per tent plus DM7 per person. Includes a super deal on public transportation—rent a *Grüne Karte* that covers everything in the *Innenraum* (DM4 per day), or a *Partner-Tageskarte* good for 5 people for 1 day (DM13) or 3 days (DM33). Wash DM4. Lockers provided. Internet access DM2 per 15min. 24hr. reception. Bike rental DM10 per day. Free city tours (W 9am). Kitchen facilities. Passport required as deposit. Reservations only for groups over 10, but rarely full. Open mid-June to Aug.

▪ **Euro Youth Hotel,** Senefelderstr. 5 (tel. 59 90 88 11; fax 59 90 88 77). From the Bahnhofsplatz exit of the Hauptbahnhof, make a right on Bayerstr. and a left on Senefelderstr.; the hotel will be on the left. Offers an outlandishly friendly and well-informed English-speaking staff loaded with brochures. DM29; doubles and triples DM36, with shower DM45. Breakfast buffet DM8. Sleek bar open daily 8pm-2am; happy hour 8-9pm (drinks DM6.50). Wash and dry DM3. 24hr. reception. No curfew or lockout.

Jugendherberge München (HI), Wendl-Dietrich-Str. 20. (tel. 13 11 56; fax 167 87 45). U-Bahn #1 (direction "Westfriedhof") to "Rotkreuzplatz." Cross Rotkreuzplatz heading toward the Kaufhof department store, then go down Wendl-Dietrich-Str; the entrance is ahead on the right. The most "central" of the HI hostels (3km from the city center). Safes in the reception area—*use them,* and keep keys with you *at all times.* Big dorm (37 beds) for men only DM24; 4- to 6-bed coed rooms DM29. Breakfast and sheets included. Mandatory DM20 key deposit. DM50 deposit for use of safes. Check-in starts at 11am, but the lines form before 9am. 24hr. reception. Reservations only accepted a week in advance; if you get one, arrive by 6pm or call ahead. No curfew.

Jugendherberge Pullach Burg Schwaneck (HI), Burgweg 4-6 (tel. 793 06 43; fax 793 79 22), in a castle 12km outside the city center. S-Bahn #7 (direction: "Wolfrats-hausen") to "Pullach" (20min.). From the station, walk in the direction of the huge soccerfield down Margarethenstr. and follow the signs (8min.). Clean rooms with green furniture are quiet and well-kept. Soccer games in the castle courtyard. 6- to 8-bed rooms DM22, quads DM25, doubles DM34.50, singles DM36.50. Breakfast and sheets included. Dinner DM8. Reception 4-11pm. Curfew 11:30pm. Try to make reservations 7:30-10am.

4 you münchen, Hirtenstr. 18 (tel. 552 16 60; fax 55 21 66 66), 200m from the Hauptbahnhof. Exit at Arnulfstr., go left, quickly turn right onto Pfefferstr., then hang a left onto Hirtenstr. Ecological youth hostel with restaurant and bar, hang-out areas, a playroom, and wheelchair-accessible everything. 12-bed dorms DM24, 4-, 6-, or 8-bed dorms DM29, doubles DM38, singles DM54. Over 27 15% surcharge. Key deposit DM20. Breakfast buffet DM7.50. Sheets DM5. In their adjoining hotel, singles with bath run DM79; doubles with bath DM110, extra bed DM49. Breakfast included. Reception 24hr., except 1:30-3pm and 7-7:30pm. Reserve be4 you arrive—without good 4tune, acquiring a bed is a 4midable task.

Jugendgästehaus Thalkirchen, Miesingstr. 4 (tel. 723 65 50 or 723 65 60; fax 724 25 67; email BineMunich@aol.com). U-Bahn #1 or 2 to "Sendlinger Tor," then U-Bahn #3 (direction: "Fürstenrieder West") to "Thalkirchen." Take the Thalkirchner Platz exit and follow Schäftlarnstr. toward Innsbruck and bear right around the curve, then follow Frauenbergstr. and head left on Münchner Str.; follow the street as it curves left. Somewhat crowded and distant, but the rooms are comfortable. 2- to 15-bed rooms DM32, singles DM37. Sheets and breakfast included. Bike rental DM22 per day, DM90 per week. Reception 7am-1am. Check-in 2pm-1am. Curfew 1am. Call weeks in advance.

Jump In, Hochstr. 51 (tel. 48 95 34 37), a new, small, private place founded by a brother and Pointer Sister team tired of impersonal hostels. S-Bahn #1-8 to "Rosenheimer Pl.," then take the Gasteig exit to the left and walk left on Hochstr. (10min.). Or streetcar #27 or bus #51 to "Ostfriedhof." Supremely amicable and delightfully informal. Easily accessible location, but rather spartan rooms. Mattresses on the floor DM29, real beds DM35; doubles DM39. Wash DM3. Reception 10am-1pm and 5-10pm. No curfew.

Jugendhotel Marienberge, Goethestr. 9 (tel. 55 58 05; fax 55 02 82 60), less than a block from the train station. Take the "Bayerstr." exit and walk down Goethestr. Open only to women under 26. Staffed by merry nuns. The rooms in this Catholic hostel are spacious, cheery, and spotless. 6-bed dorms DM30, triples DM30, doubles DM35, singles DM40. Breakfast included. Kitchen and laundry facilities. Wash DM2, dry DM2. Reception 8am-midnight. Curfew midnight, before you turn into a pumpkin.

CVJM Jugendgästehaus, Landwehrstr. 13 (tel. 552 14 10; fax 550 42 82; email muenchen@cvjm.org). Take the Bayerstr. exit from the train station, head straight down Goethestr. or Schillerstr., and take the 2nd left onto Landwehrstr.; it's on the right. Central location with modern rooms and showers in the hall. Triples DM40, doubles DM43, singles DM50. Co-ed rooms for married couples only. Over 27 16% surcharge. Breakfast included. Reception 8am-12:30am. Curfew 12:30am. Reservations by mail, phone, fax, or email must arrive before 4pm. Nifty 50s-decorated restaurant offers pizza (DM7), soups, and salads Tu-F 6:30-10pm. Closed during Easter and Dec. 20-Jan. 7.

Haus International, Elisabethstr. 87 (tel. 12 00 60; fax 12 00 62 51). U-Bahn #2 (direction: "Feldmoching") to "Hohenzollernplatz," then streetcar #12 (direction: "Romanplatz") or bus #33 (direction: "Aidenbachstr.") to "Barbarastr." It's the 5-story beige building behind the BP gas station. Pleasantly clean dorms overlook a busy street. Quints DM40; quads DM43; triples DM46; doubles DM52, with shower DM72; singles DM55, with bath DM85. Lunch and dinner available (DM10-14). Free indoor pool (score!), small beer garden, TV room, and newly renovated disco. 24hr. reception. Reservations recommended in summer.

CAMPING

Munich's campgrounds are open from mid-March to late October.

Campingplatz Thalkirchen, Zentralländstr. 49 (tel. 723 17 07; fax 724 31 77). U-Bahn #1 or 2 to "Sendlinger Tor," then #3 to "Thalkirchen," and change to bus #57 (20min.). From the bus stop, cross the busy street on the left and take a right onto the footpath next to the road. The entrance is down the tree-lined path on the left. Well-run, crowded grounds with jogging and bike paths. TV lounge, groceries, and a restaurant (meals DM3-8). DM8.40 per person, DM2.50 per child under 14. Tent DM5.50-7. Car DM8.50. Showers DM2. Wash DM7, dry DM0.50 per 6min. Curfew 11pm.

Campingplatz Obermenzing, Lochhausener Str. 59 (tel. 811 22 35; fax 814 48 07). S-Bahn #3, 4, 5, 6, or 8 to "Passing," then exit toward track 8 and take bus #76 to "Lochhausener Str." Head up Pippinger Str. in the direction the bus was driving, then left on Obere Mühlstr. and right on Lochhausener Str. (5min.); it's on the left. On the noisy *Autobahn,* but friendly and well kept. DM7.80 per person, DM4 per child under 14. Tent DM7.50. Car DM6. Showers DM2. Reception 7:30am-noon and 3-8pm.

HOTELS AND PENSIONEN

While Munich—reputedly a city of 80,000 guest beds—has a surplus of dirt-cheap (and often dirty) accommodations, it is often a better idea to crash in a hostel. A clean room in a safe area costs at least DM55-65 for a single and DM80-100 for a double. Always call ahead. Call a few months in advance for Oktoberfest rooms, as some hotels are booked for the entire two weeks by early summer.

NEAR THE HAUPTBAHNHOF

Hotel Helvetia, Schillerstr. 6 (tel. 590 68 50; fax 59 06 85 70), at the corner of Bahnhofsplatz, next to the Vereinsbank, to the right as you exit the station. One of the friendliest hotels in all of Munich. Beautiful rooms, most with phones. Singles DM55-65, doubles DM68-90, triples DM99-120. Breakfast included. Also caters to backpackers with new hostel-like dorms: 10-bed DM22, 4- to 6-bed DM26 per person. Rates rise 10-15% during Oktoberfest. Breakfast DM7. Sheets DM4. 24hr. reception.

Hotel-Pension Utzelmann, Pettenkoferstr. 6 (tel. 59 48 89; fax 59 62 28). From the train station walk 4 blocks down Schillerstr. and go left on Pettenkofer; it's at the end on the left (10min.). Nostalgic, elegant rooms with upholstered furniture and oriental rugs. Singles DM50, with shower DM95, with bath DM125; doubles DM95, with shower DM110, with bath DM145; triples DM123, with shower DM150, with bath DM175; quads DM160, with shower DM180. DM5 for hall showers. Breakfast included. Reception 7am-10pm.

Hotel Kurpfalz, Schwanthaler Str. 121 (tel. 540 98 60; fax 54 09 88 11; email hotel-kurpfalz@munich-online.de; www.munich-hotels.com). Exit on Bayerstr. from the station, turn right and walk 5-6 blocks down Bayerstr., veer left onto Holzapfelstr., and make a right onto Schwanthaler Str. (10min.). Or streetcar #18 or 19 to "Holzapfelstr." (3 stops) and walk from there. The hotel's Sevdas brothers will win you over with their smiley proficiency in Americana. Satellite TVs, phones, and hardwood furniture in all rooms. Singles from DM79, doubles from DM99, triples (doubles with cots) DM165. All rooms have private bath. Breakfast buffet included. Free email access. 24hr. reception.

Pension Locarno, Bahnhofplatz 5 (tel. 55 51 64; fax 59 50 45). From the train station's main entrance walk left across Arnulfstr. past the subway exit; the *Pension* is to your left. Plain rooms, all with TV and phone. Helpful owners. Singles DM55-75, doubles DM85, triples DM125, quads DM140. Breakfast included. DM5 less without breakfast. Mention *Let's Go* for DM5 discount. Reception 7:30am-midnight; locked at 10pm, but your key opens the door 24hr.

Pension Schillerhof, Schillerstr. 21 (tel. 59 42 70; fax 550 18 35). Exit onto Bahnhofplatz from the train station, turn right, and walk 2 blocks down Schillerstr. Unpretentious, tidy rooms with TV. Singles DM60-80, doubles DM90-120. Extra bed DM20. Oktoberfest surcharge DM25-40 per person. Breakfast included. Reception 6am-10pm.

Pension Hungaria, Briennerstr. 42 (tel. 52 15 58). From the train station, go left onto Dachauer Str., right on Augustenstr., and across and to the right on Briennerstr.; it's the 2nd building to your left (10min.). Or U-Bahn #1 to "Stiglmaierpl."; take the Brienner Str./Volkstheater exit, and it's on the next corner at Augustenstr. Oriental rugs, comfortable furnishings, and small travel library. Singles DM58, doubles DM85, triples DM110, quads DM120. Breakfast included. Showers DM3. Oktoberfest surcharge DM10 per room. 24hr. reception 2 floors up.

Pension Central, Bayerstr. 55 (tel. 543 98 46; fax 543 98 47). 5 min. from the Bayerstr. exit of the train station on the right. The unattractive exterior belies the qualities within—just like Quasimodo. Singles DM50-60, with bath DM70-85; doubles DM85-115, with bath DM120-130. 24hr. reception.

SCHWABING/UNIVERSITY/CITY CENTER

Pension Frank, Schellingstr. 24 (tel. 28 14 51; fax 280 09 10; www.city-netz.com/pensionfrank). U-Bahn #3 or 6 to "Universität." Take the Schellingstr. exit, then the first right onto Schellingstr.; it's 2 blocks down on the right. Curious combination of scruffy backpackers, student groups, and dolled-up (second-rate) fashion models. Fabulous location for café and bookstore aficionados. 3- to 6-bed rooms DM40 per person, singles DM55-65, doubles DM95. Single beds in shared rooms almost always available. Hearty breakfast included. Reception 7:30am-10pm.

Pension am Kaiserplatz, Kaiserplatz 12 (tel. 34 91 90). Located a few blocks from nightlife central—good location if you doubt your own sense of direction after a couple of beers. U-Bahn #3 or 6 to "Münchener Freiheit." Take the escalator to Herzogstr., then left; it's 5 blocks to Viktoriastr. Take a left at Viktoriastr.; it's at the end of the street on the right (10min.). Sweet owner offers elegantly decorated, high-ceilinged rooms. Singles DM59; doubles DM85, with shower DM95; each additional person DM40; 6-bed rooms DM160-170. Breakfast included. Reception 7am-9pm.

Pension Geiger, Steinheilstr. 1 (tel. 52 15 56; fax 52 31 54 71). U-Bahn #2 to "Theresienstr." Take the Augustenstr. S.O. exit, and walk straight down Theresienstr. towards Kopierladen München. Take a right on Enhuberstr. and a left on Steinheilstr.; enter through the double doors on the right (5min.). Family-run *Pension* decorated in soft, bright colors with comfortable sofas. Singles DM50, with shower DM75; doubles DM90, with shower DM98. Hall showers DM2. Reception (2 floors up) 8am-9pm. Arrive by 6pm or call. Closed Dec. 24-Jan. 31.

Pension Theresia, Luisenstr. 51 (tel. 52 12 50; fax 542 06 33). U-Bahn #2 to "Theresienstr." and take the Augustenstr./Technische Univ. exit, head straight down Theresienstr., and take the second right onto Luisenstr.; the entrance is in the passageway left of the Dahlke store. Cheery red carpets and an elegant dining room complement the well-maintained rooms. Singles DM52-69; doubles DM88-115, with shower DM95-125; triples DM123-150; quads DM144-184. Breakfast included. Reception (2nd floor) 7am-10pm. Reservations by phone or fax.

Hotel-Pension am Markt, Heiliggeiststr. 6 (tel. 22 50 14; fax 22 40 17), smack dab in the city center. S-Bahn #1-8 to "Marienplatz," then walk through the Altes Rathaus and turn right down the little alley behind the green Heiliggeist church. Aging photographs recall celebrities who graced the hotel's small but shipshape rooms—recognize anyone? Singles DM62-64, with shower DM110; doubles DM110-116, with shower DM150-160; triples DM165, with shower DM205. Breakfast included.

◧ FOOD

The vibrant **Viktualienmarkt,** two minutes south of Marienplatz, is Munich's gastronomic center, offering both basic and exotic foods and ingredients. It's fun to browse, but don't plan to do any budget grocery shopping here. (Open M-F 9am-6:30pm, Sa 9am-2pm.) Located on every corner, the ubiquitous **beer gardens** (see **Beer, Beer, and More Beer,** p. 251) serve savory snacks along with booze, yet since the time of King Ludwig I, skinflints have been permitted to bring their own food

BAYERN

to many of the gardens. To make sure that your fixings are welcome, ask a server or check for tables without tablecloths, as bare tables usually indicate self-service *(Selbstbedienung)*. To stick your fangs into an authentic Bavarian lunch, grab a *Brez'n* (pretzel) and spread it with *Leberwurst* or cheese (DM4-5). *Weißwürste* (white veal sausages) are another native bargain, served in a pot of hot water with sweet mustard and a soft pretzel on the side. Don't eat the skin of the sausage; instead, slice it open and devour the tender meat. *Leberkäs*, also a *Münchener* lunch, is a slice of a pinkish, meatloaf-like compound of ground beef and bacon which, despite its name and dubious appearance, contains neither liver nor cheese. *Leberknödel* are liver dumplings, usually served in soup or with *Kraut*; *Kartoffelknödel* (potato dumplings) and *Semmelknödel* (made from white bread, egg, and parsley) are eaten along with a hearty chunk of German meat. Those not interested in chowing down on all things meaty can head to Munich's scrumptious and healthy vegetarian cafes.

Tengelmann, Bayerstr. 5, straight ahead from the main station, is most convenient for **grocery** needs. (Open M-F 8:30am-8pm, Sa 8am-4pm.) **HL Markt** at Rotkreuzplatz is larger and provides a little more variety. Take U-Bahn #1 to "Rotkreuzpl." (Open M-F 8:30am-8pm, Sa 8am-4pm.) *Munich Found* (DM4) lists a few restaurants, while *Prinz* (DM5) offers a fairly complete listing of restaurants, cafés, and bars in Munich. Fruit and vegetable **markets** are held throughout the city, with many on Bayerstr. just a few blocks from the train station.

NEAR THE UNIVERSITY

The university district off **Ludwigstraße** is Munich's best source of filling meals in a lively, unpretentiously hip atmosphere. Many restaurants and cafés cluster on **Schellingstr., Amalienstr.,** and **Türkenstr.** Ride U-Bahn #3 or 6 to "Universität." **Plus supermarket,** Schellingstr. 38, provides cheap **groceries.** (Open M-F 8:30am-7pm, Sa 8am-3pm.)

Mensa, Arcisstr. 17, to the left of the Pinakothek just below Gabelsbergstr. on Arcisstr. U-Bahn #2 to "Königsplatz." Serves large portions of cheap food (DM3-5.50) and offers at least one vegetarian dish. Student ID required. Buy your token from booths in the lobby before getting your meal. Open M-Th 8:30am-4:15pm, F 8:30am-2:30pm; during vacations open M-F 8am-4pm.

Türkenhof, Türkenstr. 78 (tel. 280 02 35), has a pseudo-Turkish menu. Immensely popular with the low-key student population. Smoky and buzzing from noon 'til night. Variable daily menu with numerous veggie options. Creative entrees DM10-15. Open M-Th and Su 11am-1am, F-Sa 11am-2am.

Schelling Salon, Schellingstr. 54 (tel. 272 07 88). Bavarian *Knödel* and billiard balls. Founded in 1872, this pool joint has racked the balls of Lenin, Rilke, and Hitler. Breakfast DM5-9, *Wurst* DM6-7. A free **billiard museum** displays a 200-year-old Polish noble's table and the history of pool back to the Pharaohs. Restaurant and museum open M-Tu and Th-Su 6:30am-1pm.

News Bar, Amalienstr. 55 (tel. 28 17 87), at the corner of Schellingstr. Trendy café teeming with younguns. Crepes DM12-14, pasta with pesto DM12, freshly pressed juice DM5. Open daily 7:30am-1am.

IN THE CENTER

Munich's touristy interior suffers from an overabundance of high-priced eateries, but there are some good options for the budget traveler.

Valentinmusäum Café (tel. 22 32 66), in the Valentinmusäum in the Isartorturm. S-Bahn #1-8 or Streetcar #18 or 20 to "Isartor." This curious nook in the bowels of the city's western tower serves up thick mugs of hot milk with honey (DM4.20) and savory *Apfelstrudel* with vanilla ice cream (DM9.40) in a comical and characteristically Valentin atmosphere. Must pay entrance fee for museum to get in. Open M-Tu and F-Sa 11am-5:30pm, Su 10am-5:30pm.

Shoya, Orlandostr. 5 (tel. 29 27 72), across from the Hofbräuhaus. The most reasonable Japanese restaurant in town. Fill up on rice dishes (DM13-19), teriyaki (DM8-16), sushi (DM5-30), and meat and veggie dishes (DM4-16). Open daily 10:30am-midnight.

La Fiorentia Trattorina Pizzeria Café, Goethestr. 41 (tel. 53 41 85), a few blocks from the train station, specializes in generating exquisite, mouth-watering fragrances. Salivating pizza-lovers from the nearby medical university transform the café into an Italian culinary festival on weekday afternoons. Calzones DM11.50, pizza DM7-12.80, *Maß* DM8.60.

Beim Sendlmayr, Westenriederstr. 6 (tel. 22 62 19), off the Viktualienmarkt. Anyone craving a *Weißwurst* will love this slice of Bavaria. Specials DM7-25. Beer DM5.60 for 0.5L. Open daily 9am-10pm. Kitchen open M-F 11am-9pm, Sa 8am-4pm.

Marché, Altheimer Eck 14 (tel. 23 08 79 19). The top floor of this monstrous eatery offers cafeteria-style food displays and a make-your-own-pizza bar. Downstairs, customers are given food cards before entering the area decorated as a mini-Munich and filled with buffet and food stations where chefs prepare every food imaginable. You'll get a stamp for each item you take; pay on the way out. Great vegetarian selections. Top floor open 11am-10pm, bottom floor open 8am-11pm between Karlsplatz and Marienplatz.

ELSEWHERE IN MUNICH

Internet-Café, Nymphenburger Str. 145 (tel. 129 11 20), on the corner of Landshuter Allee. U-Bahn #1 to "Rotkreuzplatz." With the addition of 12 terminals, this is an average Italian joint turned hopping, electronic haven—a Neuromancer's paradise. Unlimited free Internet access as long as you order pasta (DM9.50) or pizza (DM7.50-10). Open daily 11am-4am. **Another location,** Altheimer Eck 12 (tel. 260 78 15), sits in the city center between Marienplatz and Karlsplatz in the pedestrian zone *Arcade-Passage.* Same stuff, different hours—daily 11am-1am.

Schwimmkrabbe, Ickstattstr. 13 (tel. 201 00 80). U-Bahn #1 or 2 to "Fraunhoferstr.," then walk 1 block down Baaderstr. to Ickstattstr. Locals flock to this family-run Turkish restaurant. Try the delicious *Etli Pide* (lamb and veggies wrapped in a foot-long bread with salad; DM16). Filling appetizers DM6-14. Hearty dishes DM15-20. Belly-dancing darlings on F and Sa nights. Open daily 5pm-1am. Reserve on weekends.

VEGETARIAN RESTAURANTS

Gollier, Gollierstr. 83 (tel. 50 16 73). U-Bahn #4 or 5 or S-Bahn #7 or 27 to "Heimeranplatz." Serves delicious homemade pizzas, casseroles, and crepes (DM6-19). Food to go from DM3.50. Lunch buffet DM13. Open M-F noon-3pm and 5pm-midnight, Sa 5pm-midnight, Su noon-midnight.

Café Ignaz, Georgenstr. 67 (tel. 271 60 93). U-Bahn #2 to "Josephsplatz." Earth-friendly café with a nutritious, inexpensive menu. Yogurt with fresh fruit DM6.50. Carrot juice DM5.50. Dinners (pasta, quiche, and stir-fry dishes) DM13.50-16. English menu available. Daily lunch buffet DM15. Open M-F 8am-10pm, Sa-Su 9am-10pm.

buxs, Frauenstr. 9 (tel. 22 94 82), on the southern edge of the Viktualienmarkt on the corner of Westenriederstr. Tasty, artful pastas, salads, soups, and bread. Self-serve everything, with a weight-based charge at the end. Be careful; an average plate of this high-quality food can easily cost DM20. Open M-F 11am-8:30pm, Sa 11am-3:30pm.

🔭 SIGHTS

MARIENPLATZ. Munich's Catholic past has left many marks on the city's architecture. Numerous, often mightily impressive, sacred stone edifices prickle the area around Marienplatz, a major S-Bahn and U-Bahn junction as well as the social nexus of the city. An ornate 17th-century monument dedicated to the Virgin Mary, the **Mariensäule** was built to commemorate the fact that the amazing and powerful Swedes did not destroy the city during the Thirty Years War. Thanks, Thor. The onion-domed towers of the 15th-century **Frauenkirche** are one (well, maybe two) of Munich's most notable landmarks. *(Towers open April-Oct. M-Sa 10am-5pm. DM4, students DM2, under 6 free.)*

RATHAUS. At the neo-Gothic **Neues Rathaus,** the Glockenspiel chimes with a display of jousting knights and dancing coopers. According to legend, the barrelmakers coaxed townspeople out of their homes, singing and dancing, to prove that the Great Plague had passed. *(Daily 11am, noon, and 5pm.)* At bedtime (9pm), a mechanical watchman marches out and the Guardian Angel escorts the *Münchner Kindl* (Munich Child, the town's symbol) to bed. Don't miss the rooster perched above the knights; he crows three times after the bells stop tolling. *(Tower open M-F 9am-7pm, Sa 9am-7pm, Su 10am-7pm. DM2.50, under 15 DM1.50, under 6 free.)* On the face of the **Altes Rathaus** tower, to the right of the Neues Rathaus, are all of Munich's coats of arms since its inception as a city—with one noble gap. When the tower was rebuilt after its destruction in WWII, the local government refused to include the swastika-bearing coat of arms from the Nazi era.

PETERSKIRCHE. The 11th-century Peterskirche represents Munich's ritual past; its golden interior was Baroquified in the 18th century. More than 300 steps scale the tower, christened *Alter Peter* by locals. *(Rindermarkt and Petersplatz. Open M-Sa 9am-7pm, Su 10am-7pm. DM2.50, students DM1.50, children DM0.50.)*

MICHAELSKIRCHE. Ludwig II of Bayern (of crazy castle fame) rests peacefully with 40-odd other Wittelsbachs entombed in the crypt of the 16th-century Jesuit Michaelskirche. The construction of the church, designed to emphasize the city's loyalty to Catholicism during the Reformation, almost bankrupted the state treasury. Father Rupert Mayer, one of the few German clerics who spoke out against Hitler, preached here. *(Neuhauser Str. Crypt open M-F 9:15am-4:45pm. DM2, students and children under 16 DM1.)*

ASAMKIRCHE. A Rococo masterpiece, the Asamkirche is named after its creators, the Asam brothers, who promised God that they would build a church if they survived the wreckage of their ship. Rocks at the bottom of the facade represent rapids, the church's literal and metaphorical foundation. *(Sendlinger Str. 32.)*

RESIDENZ. The richly decorated rooms of the Residenz (Palace), built from the 14th to 19th centuries, form the material vestiges of the Wittelsbach dynasty. The grounds now house several museums. The beautifully landscaped **Hofgarten** behind the Residenz houses the lovely temple of Diana. The **Schatzkammer** (treasury) contains jeweled baubles, crowns, swords, china, ivorywork, and other trinkets from the 10th century on. *(Open Tu-Su 10am-4:30pm. Last admission 4pm. DM6, students with ID, seniors, and group members DM4, children under 15 free with adult.)* The **Residenzmuseum** comprises the former Wittelsbach apartments and State Rooms, a collection of European porcelain, and a 17th-century court chapel. German tours of the Residenzmuseum meet just outside the museum entrance. The walls of the **Ahnengalerie,** hung with 120 "family portraits," trace the royal lineage in an unusual manner. Charlemagne would be surprised to find himself being held accountable for the genesis of the Wittelsbach family. *(Max-Joseph-Platz 3. Tel. 29 06 71. Take U-Bahn #3-6 to "Odeonsplatz." Open Tu-Su 10am-4:30pm. DM6, students and children DM4. Residenzmuseum tours Su and W 11am, Tu and Sa 2pm. DM8, Su DM10. Combination ticket to Schatzkammer and Residenzmuseum DM10, students and seniors DM8.)*

SCHLOSS NYMPHENBURG. After 10 years of trying for an heir, Ludwig I celebrated the birth of his son Maximilian in 1662 by erecting an elaborate summer playroom. Schloß Nymphenburg, in the northwest of town, is a handsome architectural symptom of Ludwig's dogged desire to copy King Louis XIV of France. A Baroque wonder set in a winsome park, the palace hides a number of treasures, including a two-story granite marble hall seasoned with stucco, frescoes, and a Chinese lacquer cabinet. Check out King Ludwig's "Gallery of Beauties"—whenever a woman caught his fancy, he would have her portrait painted (a scandalous hobby, considering that many of the women were commoners; as well as an ironic one, given that Ludwig grappled with an affection for men throughout his life). The palace contains a collection of antique porcelain, as well as the strange **Marstallmuseum** (carriage museum). *(Streetcar #17 (direction: "Amalienburgstr.") to "Schloß Nymphenburg." Palace open April-Sept. Tu-Su 9am-12:30pm and 1-5pm; Oct.-March 10am-12:30pm and 1:30-4pm. DM6, students DM4. Museum open Tu-Su 9am-noon and 1-5pm. Amalienburg open daily 9am-12:30pm and 1:30-5pm; Badenburg, Pagodenburg, and Magdalenen hermitage open Tu-Su 10am-12:30pm and 1:30-5pm. Entire complex DM8, students DM5, children under 15 with adult free. Grounds open until 9:30pm. Free.)*

BOTANISCHER GARTEN. Next door to Schloß Nymphenburg, the greenhouses of the immense Botanischer Garten shelter rare and wonderful growths from around the world. Check out the Indian and Bolivian water lily room, the eight-foot tall, 100-year-old cycadee, and the prickly cactus alcove. *(Tel. 17 86 13 10. Open daily 9am-8pm. Open 9-11:45am and 1-7:30pm. DM4, students DM2, under 15 DM0.50.)*

ENGLISCHER GARTEN. Abutting the city center is the vast Englischer Garten, one of Europe's oldest landscaped public parks. On sunny days, all of Munich turns out to bike, play badminton, ride horseback, or sunbathe. Nude sunbathing areas are designated FKK on signs and park maps. Consider yourself warned (or clued in, rather). Müncheners with aquatic derring-do surf the white-water rapids of the Eisbach, which flows artificially through the park; the stone bridge on Prinzregentenstr., close to the Staatsgalerie Moderner Kunst, is an excellent vantage point for witnessing these marine stunts.

OLYMPIC SPIRIT. An indoor sports and amusement park and Munich's newest nostalgic and interactive addition to its 1972 Olympic park, Olympic Spirit beckons sports buffs to check out its high-tech simulators that show various sports from the athlete's perspective, computer sports quizzes, booths to try out everything from bobsledding to basketball, videos of classic Olympic performances, and Sports Café, which broadcasts live sports events daily from 10am-12:30am. *(Tel. 30 63 86 26. Streetcar #21 (direction: "Westfriedhof") to "Olympic Spirit." Park open M-Th and Su 10am-7pm, F-Sa 10am-10pm. DM26, under 13 DM18.)*

NAZI SIGHTS. Mixed with Munich's Baroque elegance are visible traces of Germany's Nazi past. Buildings erected by Hitler and his cronies that survived the bombings of 1945 stand as grim memorials. The **Haus der Kunst,** built to enshrine Nazi principles of art, serves as a modern art museum; swastika patterns have been left on its porch as reminders of its origins (see **Museums,** below). The gloomy limestone building now housing the **music school** was built under Hitler's auspices and functioned as his Munich headquarters. From its balcony, he viewed the city's military parades; it was also here that Chamberlain signed away the Sudetenland in 1938.

🏛 MUSEUMS

Munich is a supreme museum city, and many of the city's offerings would require days for exhaustive perusal. The *Münchner Volksschule* (tel. 48 00 63 30) offers tours of many city museums for DM8. A day pass for entry to all of Munich's museums is sold at the tourist office and at many larger museums (DM30).

MUSEUMSINSEL

DEUTSCHES MUSEUM. One of the world's largest and best museums of science and technology. Fascinating exhibits of original models include the first telephone and the work bench upon which Otto Hahn split his first atom. Don't miss the mining exhibit, which winds through a labyrinth of recreated subterranean tunnels. A walk through the museum's 46 departments covers over 10km; grab an English guidebook (DM6). The planetarium (DM3) and electrical show will warm any physicist's heart. *(Tel. 217 91. S-Bahn #1-8 to "Isartor." Open daily 9am-5pm. DM10, seniors DM7, students and children under 15 DM4, children under 5 free.)*

KÖNIGSPLATZ

ALTE PINAKOTHEK. Contains Munich's most precious art. Commissioned in 1826 by King Ludwig I, the last of the passionate Wittelsbacher art collectors, this world-renowned hall houses works by Titian, da Vinci, Raphael, Dürer, Rembrandt, and Rubens. *(Barerstr. 27. Tel. 23 80 52 16. U-Bahn #2 to "Königsplatz." Open Tu-W and F-Su 10am-5pm, Th 10am-8pm. DM7, students DM4.)*

NEUE PINAKOTHEK. Sleek space for the 18th to 20th centuries: Van Gogh, Klimt, Cézanne, Manet, and more. *(Barerstr. 29. Tel. 23 80 51 95. Next to and with the same hours and prices as the Alte Pinakothek.)*

LENBACHHAUS. Munich cityscapes (useful if it's raining), along with works by Kandinsky, Klee, and the *Blaue Reiter* school. *(Luisenstr. 33. Tel. 23 33 20 00. U-Bahn #2 to "Königsplatz." Open Tu-Su 10am-6pm. DM8, students DM4.)*

GLYPTOTHEK. Assembled by Ludwig I in 1825 in pursuit of his Greek dream to turn Munich into a "cultural work of such sheer perfection as only few Germans have experienced." Features 2,400-year-old pediment figures from the Temple of Aphaea as well as Etruscan and Roman sculptures. *(Königsplatz 3. Tel. 28 61 00. Around the corner from the Lenbachhaus. U-Bahn #2 to "Königsplatz." Open Tu-W and F-Su 10am-5pm, Th 10am-8pm. DM6, students DM3.50.)*

ANTIKENSAMMLUNG. Flaunts a first-rate flock of vases and the other half of Munich's finest collection of ancient art; features Ancient Greek and Etruscan pottery and jewelry. *(Königsplatz 1. Tel. 59 83 59. Across Königsplatz from Glyptothek. U-Bahn #2 to "Königsplatz." Open Tu and Th-Su 10am-5pm, W 10am-8pm. DM6, students DM3.50. Joint admission with Glyptothek DM10, students DM5.)*

ELSEWHERE IN MUNICH

STAATSGALERIE MODERNER KUNST. In the **Haus der Kunst** at the southern tip of the Englischer Garten, this sterling gallery celebrates the vitality of 20th-century art, from the colorful palettes of the Expressionists to the spare canvases of the Minimalists. Showcases Beckmann, Kandinsky, Klee, Picasso, and Dalí. Constructed by the Nazis as the Museum of German Art, it opened with the famous *Entartete Kunst* (degenerate art) exhibit that included works of the Expressionists and Dadaists. Excellent visiting exhibits DM4-6 extra. *(Prinzregentenstr. 1. Tel. 21 12 71 37. U-Bahn #4 or 5 to "Lehel," then streetcar #17. Open Tu-W and F-Su 10am-5pm, Th 10am-8pm. DM6, students DM3.50.)*

MÜNCHENER STADTMUSEUM. A collection of whimsical museums, all with a Bavarian touch: film, fashion, musical instruments, weapons, and more. **Classic films** (DM8) roll every evening at 8pm. Foreign films shown with subtitles; call 23 32 55 86 for a program. *(St-Jakobs-Platz 1. Tel. 23 32 23 70. U-Bahn #3 or 6 or S-Bahn #1-8 to "Marienplatz." Open Tu and Th-Su 10am-5pm, W 10am-8:30pm. Open M 5pm-midnight, Tu-Su 11am-midnight. Museum DM5, students, seniors, and children DM2.50, under 6 free.)*

ZAM: ZENTRUM FÜR AUSSERGEWÖHNLICHE MUSEEN. Munich's Center for Unusual Museums, a brilliant place that brazenly corrals under one roof such treasures as the Corkscrew Museum, the Museum of Easter Rabbits, and the Chamberpot Museum. Fan of Empress Elizabeth of Austria? Sass on over to the Sisi Museum, sweetie. *(Westenriederstr. 41. Tel. 290 41 21. S-Bahn #1-8 to "Isartor" or streetcar #17 or 18. Open daily 10am-6pm. DM8, students, seniors, and children DM5.)*

MUSEUM FÜR EROTISCHE KUNST. For those lonely days when you're 5000km away from your beloved (or those uninspired days when you're right next to your beloved), this erotic art museum covers all 4 bases around the world and through time. Features a French book of sex-gags entitled *The Circus*, hot and heavy chess pieces, and a set of juicy Japanese illustrations. *(Odeonsplatz 8. Tel. 228 35 44. In same building as the Filmcasino. U-Bahn #3-6 to "Odeonsplatz." or bus #53. Open Tu-Su 11am-7pm. DM8, students DM6.)*

BMW-MUSEUM. The ultimate driving museum features a fetching display of past, present, and future products of Bavaria's second-favorite export. *(Petuelring 130. Tel. 38 22 33 07. U-Bahn #3 to "Olympiazentrum." Open daily 9am-5pm. Last entry 4pm. DM5.50, students DM4.)*

VALENTINMUSÄUM. Decidedly esoteric peek at the comical life of Karl Valentin, the German counterpart of Charlie Chaplin, and his partner Liesl Karlstadt. Valentin was Munich's quintessential comedian and social commentator. Curiosities include sham skeletons encased in the stone wall and a nail in the wall upon which Valentin hung up his first career as a carpenter. *(Isartorturm. Tel. 22 32 66. S-Bahn #1-8 to "Isartor." Open M-Tu and F-Sa 11:01am-5:29pm, Su 10:01am-5:29pm. 299Pfennig, students 149Pfennig.)*

SPIELZEUGMUSEUM. Two centuries of toys—compare the "futuristic" WWI figurines to the evolution of the slim, *schicki-micki* Barbie. *(Marienplatz. Tel 29 40 01. In the Altes Rathaus. Open daily 10am-5:30pm. DM5, children DM1, families DM10.)*

🎭 ENTERTAINMENT

THEATER AND OPERA

Munich's cultural cachet rivals the world's best. Its natives are great funlovers and hedonists, yet they reserve a place for folksy kitsch, cultivating a supreme and diverse *Szene* with something for everyone. Sixty theaters of various sizes are scattered throughout the city. Styles range from dramatic classics at the **Residenztheater** and **Volkstheater** to comic opera at the **Staatstheater am Gärtnerplatz** to experimental works at the **Theater im Marstall** in Nymphenburg. Standing tickets run around DM10. Munich's **opera festival** (in July) is held in the Bayerische Staatsoper (below) and accompanied by a concert series in the Nymphenburg and Schleißheim palaces. The *Monatsprogramm* (DM2.50) lists schedules for all of Munich's stages, museums, and festivals.

Munich shows its more bohemian face with scores of small fringe theaters, cabaret stages, art cinemas, and artsy pubs in **Schwabing. Leopoldstraße,** the main avenue leading up from the university, can be magical on a warm summer night in its own gaudy way—milling youthful crowds, art students hawking their work, and terrace-cafés create an exciting swarm. At the turn of the century this area was a distinguished center of European cultural and intellectual life, housing luminaries such as Brecht, Mann, Klee, Georgi, Kandinsky, Spengler, and Trotsky.

Gasteig Kulturzentrum, Rosenheimer Str. 5 (tel. 48 09 80). S-Bahn #1-8 to "Rosenheimer Platz" or streetcar #18 to "Am Gasteig." The most modern concert hall in Germany, the Kulturzentrum hosts musical performances ranging from classical to non-Western in its 3 concert halls and visual arts center. The hall rests on the former site of the Bürgerbräukeller, where Adolf Hitler launched his abortive Beer Hall Putsch. Features the **Munich Philharmonic** and a wide range of events, readings, and ballet. Box office in the Glashalle (tel. 54 89 89). Open M-F 10am-6pm, Sa 10am-2pm, and 1hr. before performances.

Bayerische Staatsoper, Max-Joseph-Platz 2 (tickets tel. 21 85 19 20; recorded information tel. 21 85 19 19). U-Bahn #3-6 to "Odeonsplatz" or streetcar #19 to "Nationaltheater." Standing-room and reduced-rate student tickets (DM6-20) to the numerous operas and ballets are sold at Maximilianstr. 11 (tel. 21 85 19 20), behind the opera house, or 1hr. before performance at the side entrance on Maximilianstr. Box office open M-F 10am-6pm, Sa 10am-1pm. No performances Aug. to mid-Sept.

Staatstheater, Gärtnerplatz 3 (tel. 201 67 67). U-Bahn #1 or 2 to "Fraunhoferstr." and follow Reichenbachstr. to Gärtnerplatz; or bus #52 or 56 to "Gärtnerplatz." Stages comic opera and musicals. Tickets available 4 weeks before each performance at the Staatstheater box office (tel. 20 24 11). Standing room tickets start at DM19. Open M-F 10am-6pm, Sa 10am-1pm, and 1hr. before performance.

Drehleier, Rosenheimer Str. 123 (tel. 48 27 42). S-Bahn #1-8 or bus #51 to "Rosenheimer Platz." A mixture of theater, cabaret, and performance art romps across this offbeat stage. One of the best cabaret scenes in Munich. Kitchen serves inexpensive salads and noodle dishes (DM6-15) until 10pm. Reservations required. Open Tu-Sa 6:30pm-1am. Performances Tu-Sa 10:30pm. Tickets DM20-30.

Münchner Kammerspiele, Maximilianstr. 26 (tickets tel. 233 37 00; recorded information tel. 23 72 13 26). Streetcar #19 to "Maxmonument." Exceptional modern theater and classics grace its two stages. The **Schauspielhaus,** Maximilianstr. 26, shows Goethe and Shakespeare (tickets DM11-59). The **Werkraum,** Hildegardstr. 1, features avant-garde and critical leftist pieces. Standing room tickets DM1.50. Tickets available 1 week in advance. Box office open M-F 10am-6pm, Sa 10am-1pm.

FILM

English films are often dubbed; search for the initials "OF" or "OmU" for screenings in the original language. Munich's **film festival** generally runs for a week in late June or early July. For schedules and information, contact **Internationale Filmwoche,** Türkenstr. 93, 80799 Munich (tel. 381 90 40). *In München* (free) lists movie screenings.

Museum Lichtspiele, Lilienstr. 2 (tel. 48 24 03), by the Ludwigsbrücke and part of the Deutsches Museum. S-Bahn #1-6 or streetcar #18 to "Isartor." Holds the world's record for most consecutive daily screenings of the *Rocky Horror Picture Show* (4pm); they do the Time Warp again at midnight. English-language films daily (DM11-13).

Türkendolch, Türkenstr. 74 (tel. 28 99 66 99), in the middle of the student district, has mini-film festivals dedicated to particular directors and themes.

◪ NIGHTLIFE

Munich's nightlife is a curious collision of Bavarian *Gemütlichkeit* and trendy cliquishness. Representatives of the latter trait are often referred to as *Schicki-Mickis,* loosely defined as club-going German yuppies—expensively dressed, coiffed and sprayed, beautiful, shapely, blonde specimens of both sexes. With a healthy mix of students and other less pretentious locals, the streets bustle with raucous beer halls, loud discos, and exclusive cafés every night of the week. The locals tend to tackle their nightlife as an epic voyage. The odyssey begins at one of Munich's beer gardens or beer halls (see **Beer, Beer, and More Beer,** below), which generally close before midnight and are most crowded in the early evening. The alcohol keeps flowing at cafés and bars, which, except for Friday and Saturday nights, shut off their taps at 1am. Then the discos and dance clubs, sedate before midnight, suddenly spark and throb relentlessly until 4am. The trendy bars, cafés, cabarets, and discos plugged into **Leopoldstr.** in **Schwabing** attract tourists from all over Europe (see **Entertainment,** p. 249). For easy access, dig the jaded hipsterwear out of your pack, or at least leave the white baseball hat and college T-shirt at home. A few more tips: no tennis shoes, no shorts, and no sandals (no, not even Birkenstocks—or haven't you noticed yet that you're the only person in Germany wearing them?). On weekends, though, you'll have to look like more money than your railpass costs.

The **Muffathalle,** Zellerstr. 4 (tel. 45 87 50 00), in Haidhausen, is a former power plant that generates hip student energy with techno, hip-hop, jazz, and dance performances. Take S-Bahn #1-8 to "Rosenheimerplatz" or streetcar #18 to "Deutsches Museum." (Open M-Sa 6pm-4am, Su 4pm-1am. Cover up to DM30.) Munich's alternative concert scene goes on at **Feierwerk,** Hansastr. 39-41 (tel. 769 36 00), which has seven stages and huge tents. Take S-Bahn #7 or U-Bahn #4 or 5 to "Heimeranplatz," then walk left down Hansastr. (10min.). In summer, there's lots of independent music, comedy, beer gardens, *Imbiße,* blues, and rock. Beer gardens open at 6pm; doors usually open at 8:30pm and concerts begin at 9pm. **Münchener Freiheit** is the most famous (and most touristy) bar/café district; more low-key is the southwestern section of Schwabing, directly behind the university on Amalienstr. and Türkenstr. (see **Food**, p. 243). When they close, hold-outs head for the late-night/early-morning cafés to nurse a last *Maß* or first cup of coffee.

Scads of culture and nightlife guides are available to help you sort out Munich's scene. Pick up *Munich Found, in München,* or *Prinz* (the hippest) at any newsstand to find out what's up. Big-name pop artists often perform at the **Olympiahalle,** while the **Olympia-Stadion** on the northern edge of town hosts mega-concerts. Check listings for dates and ticket information or call 30 67 24 24.

BEER, BEER, AND MORE BEER

The six great Munich labels are *Augustiner, Hacker-Pschorr, Hofbräu, Löwenbräu, Paulaner,* and *Spaten-Franziskaner,* yet most restaurants and *Gaststätte* will pick a side by only serving one brewery's beer. There are four main types of beer served in Munich: **Helles** and **Dunkles,** standard but delicious light and dark beers; **Weißbier,** a cloudy blond beer made from wheat instead of barley; and **Radler** (literally "cyclist's brew"), which is half beer and half lemon soda. Munich's beer typically has an alcohol content of 3.5%, though in *Starkbierzeit* (which runs two weeks, beginning with Lent), Müncheners traditionally drink *Salvator,* a strong, dark beer that is 5.5% alcohol. In May, art folk clean their palates with *Marbock,* a blond Bockbier. *Frühschoppen* is a morning beer-and-sausage ritual. *Prost! "Ein Bier, bitte"* will get you a liter, known as a *Maß* (DM8-11). If you want a half-*Maß* (DM4-6), you must specify it, though many establishments will only serve *Weißbier* in 0.5L sizes. Though some beer gardens offer non-meaty dishes, vegetarians may wish to eat elsewhere before proceeding to a beer garden for a post-meal swig. For an online guide to Munich's beer gardens, visit www.biergarten.com.

BEER GARDEN HISTORY 101 The official coat-of-arms of Munich depicts a monk holding a Bible in his right hand. Unofficially, the monk's left hand firmly clenches a large, frothy beer, raising it high and, with a twinkle in the eye, saying *"Prost."* Sacrilege? Not at all. In 1328, the Augustiner monks introduced *Bier* to unsuspecting Müncheners, who have since continued the 600-year-old trend. Bayern proudly holds the title as the largest producer *and* consumer of beer in Germany—in a mighty big way. Local breweries produce 123 million gallons of "liquid bread" per annum, 150,000 seats in Munich beer gardens beckon the thirsty, and every year, the average local imbibes more than 220 liters of the amber dew, more than twice the average drunk in the rest of Germany (though the figure does include the mighty Oktoberfest, during which locals and visitors together swig six million liters). The tradition of beer gardens in Bavaria is said to have begun with King Ludwig I, who allowed brewers to sell beer, but not food, in an outdoor restaurant setting. All citizens could afford to indulge in this yummy beverage by bringing their own meals to the gardens. Many of Munich's beer gardens today are shaded by large-leafed chestnut trees, planted before the invention of refrigeration to keep the ground above the storage cellars cool. Proudly honoring the Beer Purity Law *(Reinheitsgebot;* see p. 35*)* of 1516, Bavarians reaffirm their exalted and earned reputation as the ultimate, tried-and-true beer connoisseurs.

The longest beer festival in the world, Munich's **Oktoberfest** runs the last two weeks in September (Sept. 16-Oct. 1, 2000). The site of this uncontrolled revelry is the **Theresienwiese** or *"Wies'n"* (shortened perhaps after one *Maß* too many). Ride U-Bahn #4 or 5 to "Theresienwiese." The festivities began in 1810 when Prince Ludwig married Princess Therese von Sachsen-Hildburghausen; ironically, no alcohol was served at the original reception. The party was so much fun that Müncheners repeated the revelry the next year and every year following that, unable to resist a revival. The party kicks off with speeches, a parade of horse-drawn beer wagons, and the mayor's tapping of the ceremonial first *Faß* (barrel). The touristy *Hofbräu* tent is the rowdiest; fights often break out. Arrive early (by 4:30pm) to get a table—you must be seated to be served at Oktoberfest.

WITHIN MUNICH

Hirschgarten, Hirschgarten 1 (tel. 17 25 91). U-Bahn #1 to "Rotkreuzplatz," then streetcar #12 to "Romanplatz." Walk straight to the end of Guntherstr. and enter the Hirschgarten—literally, "deer garden." The largest beer garden in Europe is boisterous and pleasant, just as its name would suggest, but somewhat remote near Schloß Nymphenburg. Families head here for the grassy park and carousel. Entrees DM7-25. *Maß* DM8.60. Open daily 9am-midnight. Restaurant closed Mondays Nov.-Feb.

Augustinerkeller, Arnulfstr. 52 (tel. 59 43 93), at Zirkus-Krone-Str. S-Bahn #1-8 to "Hackerbrücke." Founded in 1824, Augustiner is viewed by most Müncheners as the finest beer garden in town. Lush grounds and dim lighting beneath 100-year-old chestnut trees and tasty, enormous *Brez'n* (pretzels; DM5.20) support their cause. The real attraction is the delicious, sharp Augustiner beer (*Maß* DM11), which entices locals, smart tourists, and scads of students. Food DM10-28. Open daily 10am-1am; hot food until 10pm. Beer garden open daily 10:30am-midnight or 1am, depending on weather.

Hofbräuhaus, Am Platzl 9 (tel. 22 16 76), 2 blocks from Marienplatz. Established in 1589, Munich's world-famous beer hall was originally reserved for royalty and invited guests; now it seems reserved for American frat boys and drunken tourists. 15,000-30,000L of beer are sold per day. It's a rite of passage to introduce backpackers from around the world to the joys of the Munich beer world. Hitler was proclaimed the first Nazi party chair in the *Festsaal*. Small beer garden out back under chestnut trees. *Maß* DM10.40. *Leberkäs* with spinach and potatoes DM9.90. Open daily 9:30am-midnight.

Augustiner Bräustuben, Landsberger Str. 19 (tel. 50 70 47). S-Bahn #1-8 to "Hackerbrücke." Relatively new beer hall in the Augustiner brewery's former horse stalls. DM4 for 0.5L. For the hungry horse, try the *Bräustüberl* (duck, two types of pork, *Kraut,* and two types of dumplings; DM14.60). Other delicious heaps of Bavarian food at excellent prices (DM6-20). Especially popular in winter. Open daily 10am-midnight.

Chinesischer Turm, (tel. 383 87 27), in the Englischer Garten next to the pagoda. U-Bahn #3 or 6 to "Giselastr." or bus #54 from Südbahnhof to "Chinesischer Turm." A fair-weather tourist favorite; lots of kids. *Maß* DM9.50. Pretzels DM5. Open daily in balmy weather 10am-11pm.

Augustiner, Neuhauser Str. 16 (tel. 55 19 92 57). Smaller manifestation of the *Keller* of the same name. Beer hall and sidewalk tables on the pedestrian zone between the station and Marienplatz. The restaurant on the right is pricier than the beer hall. Bavarian meals DM9-28. Beer hall *Maß* DM9.80; restaurant *Maß* DM10.90. Beer hall and restaurant open daily 10am-midnight. Kitchen open until 11pm.

Am Seehaus, Kleinhesselohe 3 (tel. 381 61 30). U-Bahn #6 to "Dietlindenstr.," then bus #44 to "Osterwaldgarten." Directly on the lovely Kleinhesseloher See in the Englischer Garten, and beloved by locals for the lack of tourists. *Maß* DM9.80. Open M-F 11am-midnight, Sa-Su 9am-midnight. Beer garden closes at 11pm.

Taxisgarten, Taxisstr. 12 (tel. 15 68 27). U-Bahn #1 to "Rotkreuzplatz," then bus #83 or 177 to "Klugstr." This beer garden is a gem—its small size has kept it a favorite of locals and students. Almost always full. Spare ribs, jumbo pretzels DM4.50. *Maß* DM9.50, *Weißbier* DM5. Open daily 11am-11pm.

Löwenbräukeller, Nymphenburger Str. 2 (tel. 52 60 21). U-Bahn #1 to "Stiglmaierplatz." Castle-like entrance, festive and loud cellar. Come here to taste the real *Löwenbräu,* if you dare: the bitter taste has a loyal core of local followers, despite general disapproval—it's considered by some to be the Budweiser of Munich beers. Ribs DM15, 0.5L beer DM4.90. Kitchen open 11am-midnight. Open daily 8am-1am.

Paulanerkeller, Hochstr. 77 (tel. 459 91 30). U-Bahn #1 or 2 to "Silberhornstr.," then bus #51 to "Ostfriedhof." Walk back down Bonifaziusstr. over the bridge and to the right. Also known as Salvatorkeller. It's big, old, and has strong beer. Remotely located on Nockherberg hill with a thirtysomething crowd. *Maß* DM10.80, 0.5L "Salvator" DM6.10. *Brez'n* and *Knödel* DM11.80. Open daily 9am-11pm.

Pschorr-Keller, Theresienhöhe 7 (tel. 50 10 88). U-Bahn #4 or 5 to "Theresienwiese." An outpost of the Hacker-Pschorr brewery along with the Hackerkeller down the street.

Good stuff. Come here for your breakfast beer, mostly with locals. *Maß* DM10.80. Meals DM10-20. Open daily 11am-11pm.

Parkrestaurant Tarock, Sophienstr. 7 (tel. 59 83 13), in the Alter Botanischer Garten, a block to the left from the train station. This peaceful outdoor beer garden, secluded from cars and trains by oodles of greenery, is good for a train layover. *Löwenbrau* DM8.50 per *Maß*. Most meals DM7-16. Open 10am-1am.

JUST OUTSIDE MUNICH

Waldwirtschaft Großhesselohe, Georg-Kalb-Str. 3 (tel. 79 50 88). S-Bahn #7 to "Großhesselohe Isartalbahnhof." From the train station, go down the stairs and turn right; head down Sollner Str. after passing Kreuzeckstr. and follow the signs (15min.). Relaxed beer garden with live music daily from noon (no cover). Classic and international jazz Sundays at noon. On a sunny day, schedule a *Frühschoppen* session for 11am or so. *Maß* DM9.80. Open daily 11am-11pm.

Forschungsbräuerei, Unterhachinger Str. 76 (tel. 670 11 69). Serves up some very strange brew—the name means "research brewery." Pleasant, comfortable tables under arching trees. Paradise for the connoisseur of obscure beers. *Maß* DM10.50. Open Tu-Sa 11am-11pm, Su 10am-10pm.

BARS

Many of the city's charming cafés (see **Food,** p. 243) double as hip nightly haunts. A few stalwarts only open the doors for drink after 5pm, and by 1am many squeeze revelers out into more late-night joints. Also see **Beer, Beer, and More Beer,** p. 251.

Reitschule, Königstr. 34. U-Bahn #3 or 6 to "Giselastr." Above a club, with windows overlooking a horseback-riding school. Marble tables and a sleek bar. Also a café with a beer garden out back. Very relaxed. Rumor has it this is where Boris Becker met his wife. *Weißbier* DM6. Breakfast served all day. Have your morning drink daily 9am-1am.

Master's Home, Frauenstr. 11 (tel. 22 99 09). U-Bahn #3 or 6 or S-Bahn #1-8 to "Marienplatz." A tremendous stuffed peacock greets visitors as they descend the gold painted staircase to the subterranean bar and *faux* private house. Lounge in the elegant living room with books and dusty velvet furniture, relax in the bedroom, or chill in the tub with a beer in hand. Eat gourmet Italian with the *Schicki-Mickis* in the restaurant (meals DM15-30), or chill with the more relaxed crowd in the bar. Mixed drinks DM11.50, other drinks similarly high-brow in price. Weekdays comfortable; weekends mobbed. Open daily 6:30pm-3am.

Günther Murphy's, Nikolaistr. 9a (tel. 39 89 11). U-Bahn #3 or 6 to "Giselastr." Cozy up in the "snuggle-box" with a Guinness (DM5-7.50). Good ol' Irish cheer accompanies each serving of scrumptious British and American food (DM9-30). You won't be able to find a seat, but it's more fun to mingle with the English-speaking crowd. All-day brunch buffet served on Sunday (DM15). "Limp in and leap out!" Open M-F 5pm-1am, Sa 2pm-3am, Su noon-1am.

Treznjewski, Theresienstr. 72 (tel. 22 23 49). U-Bahn #2 to "Theresienstr." Handsome dark-wooded bar with stylish frescoes. Good cocktails and chatty crowds until way late. Entrees DM15-30. Beer DM5. Open daily 8pm-3am.

MUSIC BARS

Nachtcafé, Maximiliansplatz 5 (tel. 59 59 00). U-Bahn #4 or 5 or S-Bahn #1-8 to "Karlsplatz." Live jazz, funk, soul, and blues until the wee hours. The chic and the wannabes rub shoulders in this modern jet-black bar. Things don't get rolling until midnight. Very *schicki-micki.* Breakfast served after 2am. No cover, but outrageous prices and a bouncer—easy-going weekdays, very picky on weekends when you'll have to look the part. On warm summer evenings the porch café is packed with elegant Müncheners drinking cocktails by moonlight. Karaoke on Sunday. Beer DM8 (0.3L).

Shamrock, Trautenwolfstr. 6 (tel. 33 10 81). U-Bahn #3 or 6 to "Giselastr." Live music runs the gamut from blues and soul to Irish fiddling to rock in this cozy Irish pub. Irish soccer highlights on Sundays. Guinness DM7.50. Pizza DM10-13. Open M-Th 5pm-1am, F 5pm-3am, Sa 2pm-3am, Su 2pm-1am.

Zur Unterfahrt Club 2, Kirchenstr. 96 (tel. 44 85 06 36). S-Bahn #1-8 or U-Bahn #5 to "Ostbahnhof." 30ish crowd. Alternative rock and jazz nights; offers 2-3 live performances per week. Open daily 7pm-1am. Cover for performances DM10 and up.

DANCE CLUBS

■ **Kunstpark Ost,** Grafinger Str. 6 (tel. 490 43 50). U-Bahn #5 or S-Bahn #1-8 to "Ostbahnhof." The newest and biggest addition to the Munich nightlife scene. A cultural "city within the city," this huge complex with 20 different venues swarms with young people hitting clubs, concerts, and bars—but most of all, dancing the night away. Try the psychedelic-trance **Natraj Temple** (open W and F-Sa), the alternative cocktail and disco joint **K41** (open Tu-Su), the stage/club **Babylon** (open W and F-Su), or concert hall **Incognito** (open M-Sa). Hours, cover, and themes vary—call 49 00 29 28 for information and tickets.

Nachtwerk and Club, Landesberger Str. 185 (tel. 578 38 00). Streetcar #18 or 19 or bus #83 to "Lautensackstr." The older, larger **Nachtwerk** spins mainstream dance tunes for sweaty mainstream crowds in a packed warehouse. Saturday is the beloved "Best of the 50s to the 90s" night. Its little sister **Club** offers a 2-level dance floor, just as tight and swinging as its next-door neighbor. Mixtures of rock, trip-hop, house, acid jazz, and rare grooves. Avoid Sunday night rehashing of German oldies-but-crappies. Beer DM4.50 at both places. Open daily 10pm-4am. Cover DM10 for both.

Reactor, Domagkstr. 33 (tel. 324 44 23), in the Alabamahalle. U-Bahn #6 to "Alte Heide." Situated along with three other discos on a former military base in Schwabing. Techno, house, and German oldies. Open F-Sa 9pm-4am. Try **Millennium Club** for techno highlights (Th-Su 9pm-6am; cover DM10-15), **Alabama** for German oldies (F-Sa 9pm-4am; drinks free until 1am), or **Schwabinger Ballhouse** for international jams (F-Sa 10pm-4am; cover DM15, all drinks DM1).

Backstage, Helmholtzstr. 18 (tel. 18 33 30). S-Bahn #1-8 to "Donnersberger Brücke." Wide range of music, but lots of "little Seattle," hip-hop, and techno. Mixed crowd, with lots of nose rings and green hair. Huge outdoor beer garden. Open W-Th 9pm-3am, F 10pm-5am, Sa 9pm-5am. No cover.

Pulverturm, Schleißheimer Str. 393 (tel. 351 99 99). U-Bahn #2 to "Harthof"; it's 15min. from the stop. A bit far out (geographically and otherwise), this dance club with beer garden lacks the pretension of Munich's other venues. Beer DM5.50. Anything from psychedelic to grunge; F is indie rock and Su kicks back with reggae. Open daily 10pm-4am. Cover DM10.

Opera, Helmholtzstr. 12 (tel. 129 79 69). S-Bahn #1-8 to "Donnersberger Brücke." A wacky warehouse disco offering some of the cheapest drinks in town (DM1-3). Sa acid jazz, M "spicy sounds from the swamps"—Swampy Spice? Tell me what you want. Open W-Sa 10pm-4am. Cover DM7.

GAY AND LESBIAN MUNICH

Although Bayern has the reputation of being intolerant of homosexuality, Munich sustains a respectably vibrant gay nightlife. The center of Munich's homosexual scene lies within the **"Golden Triangle"** defined by Sendlinger Tor, the Viktualien-markt/Gärtnerplatz area, and Isartor. Bars, cafés, and clubs of all atmospheres abound. Pick up the free, extensive booklet *Rosa Seiten* at **Max und Milian Book-store,** Ickstattstr. 2 (tel. 260 33 20; open M-F 10:30am-2pm, Sa 11am-4pm), or at any other gay locale for extensive listings of gay nightlife hotspots and services. The **Zentrum schwuler Männer** offers an array of telephone services for gay men. (General information tel. 260 30 56; violence hotline tel. 192 28; counseling tel. 194 46.) Some English is spoken, depending on the staff. (Open M-Th and Su 7-11pm, F-Sa

7pm-midnight.) For lesbian information, call **Lesbentelefon.** (Tel. 725 42 72. Open Tu 10:30am-1pm, W 2:30-5pm, and Th 7-10pm.) **Sapphovision,** a lesbian film center at the **Frauenzentrum Treibhaus,** Güllstr. 3 (tel. 77 40 41), shows films every second Friday of the month. **Lillemor's Frauenbuchladen** (see **Bookstores,** p. 238) provides information for lesbians. **Bei Carla,** Buttermelcherstr. 9 (tel. 22 79 01), is a café and meeting place for women.

Club Morizz, Klenzestr. 43 (tel. 201 67 76). U-Bahn #1 or 2 to "Fraunhofer Str." Reminiscent of certain Casablanca scenes, this relaxed café and bar is frequented by gay men. Settle into the low red sofa chairs and enjoy a cocktail (DM13.50-16). European and Thai dishes available until 12:30am; Thai curry DM19, pasta and other entrees DM18-26. Open M-Th and Su 7pm-2am, F-Sa 7pm-3am.

Soul City, Maximiliansplatz 5 (tel. 59 52 72), at the intersection with Max-Joseph-Str. Purportedly the biggest gay disco in Bayern. Beer DM7.50 (0.3L). Open M-Th and Su 10pm-4am, F-Sa 10pm-late. Cover DM10-25.

Fortuna Musikbar, Maximiliansplatz 5, (tel. 55 40 70). U-Bahn #4 or 5 or S-Bahn #1-8 to "Karlsplatz," then walk northeast along the Ring until you hit Maximiliansplatz. A hip and popular disco for lesbians. *The* place on Friday evenings for salsa. Open M and W-Su 10:30pm-6am. Cover DM10.

New York, Sonnenstr. 25 (tel. 59 10 56). U-Bahn #1-3 or 6 to "Sendlinger Tor." Fashionable gay men dance the night away. Laser show F-Su 11:30pm. Open daily 11pm-4am. Cover F-Su DM10 (includes drinks).

Café Nil, Hans-Sach-Str. 2 (tel. 26 55 45). U-Bahn #1 or 2 to "Fraunhofer Str." Take a right out of the U-Bahn down Klenzestr., a right on Ickstattstr., and a right on Hans-Sach-Str. Sleek café that's a day- and nighttime meeting place for gay men of all ages. Mobbed on weekends. Beer DM5 (0.4L), pasta DM13.50. Open daily 3pm-3am.

NEAR MUNICH: DACHAU

"Once they burn books, they will end up burning people," wrote German poet Heinrich Heine in 1820. His warning is posted at the Dachau concentration camp, next to a photograph of a Nazi book-burning. The walls, gates, gas chamber, and crematorium have been restored since 1962 in a chillingly sparse memorial to the victims of Dachau, the first German concentration camp and the model for the network of 3,000 work and concentration camps erected in Nazi-occupied Europe. Once tightly-packed barracks are now, for the most part, only foundations; survivors ensured, however, that at least two barracks would be reconstructed to teach future generations about the 206,000 prisoners who were interned here from 1933 to 1945. Residents of the city of Dachau—it is important to remember that there *is* a town here, which lives in the shadow of the camp every day—watch visitors with uncertainty, and even insecurity. Visitors should realize that while the concentration camp is treated as a tourist attraction by many, it is first and foremost a memorial; visitors come here for personal reasons, to grieve over the horrors of the Holocaust. Respectful behavior is imperative.

The wrought-iron gate at the **Jourhaus,** formerly the only entrance to the camp, reads *Arbeit Macht Frei* ("Work Sets One Free"); it was the first sight as prisoners entered the camp. There is also a Jewish memorial, a Protestant commemorative chapel, and the Catholic **Todesangst Christi-Kapelle** (Christ in Agony Church) on the grounds. (For more on the issues surrounding concentration camps, see **The Holocaust,** p. 16.) The museum, located in the former administrative buildings, examines pre-1930 anti-Semitism, the rise of Nazism, the establishment of the concentration camp system, and the lives of prisoners through photographs, documents, and artifacts. The thick guide (DM25, available in English) translates the propaganda posters, SS files, documents, and letters. Most exhibits are accompanied by short captions in English. Also on display are texts of the letters from prisoners to their families as well as internal SS memos. A short film (22min.) is screened in English at 11:30am and 3:30pm. The camp is open Tu-Su 9am-5pm.

BAYERN

Excellent two-hour **tours** in English leave from the museum. (July daily 12:30pm, Aug.-June Sa-Su, and holidays at 12:30pm. DM5 donation requested.) Call 17 41 for more information. To get there from Munich, take S-Bahn #2 (direction: "Peter-shausen") to "Dachau" (20min., DM7), then bus #724 (direction: "Kraütgarten") or 726 (direction: "Kopernikusstr.") from in front of the station to "KZ-Gedenkstätte" (20min., DM1.80).

In the mid-19th century, painters such as Carl Spitzweg and Max Liebermann traveled to Dachau. A 16th-century castle and a parish church built in the year 920 tops the Altstadt. Tours in German of the castle and the church leave from in front of the modern Rathaus, across the street from the tourist office. (Tours May-Oct. Sa 10:30am. DM6, children and students DM3. Castle and church open Sa-Su 2-5pm. DM3.) The tiny **tourist office,** Konrad-Adenauer-Str. 1 (tel. 845 66; fax 845 29), has information on the city of Dachau and sells maps for DM1. Take Alte Römel-str., turn right on Sudetenlandstr., which becomes Erich-Ollenhauer-Str., then turn left on Freisinger Str. and left on Konrad-Adenauer-Str. (Open M-F 9am-1pm and 3-6pm, Sa 9am-noon.) The **telephone code** is 08131.

ALLGÄU

Marketing offices have a ball with the Allgäu region; the spectacular lakes and snow-laced mountains have "glossy brochure material" written all over them. Stretching from the balmy shores of the Bodensee (Lake Constance) to the snow-capped peaks along the Austrian border, the region boasts inimitably charming villages, while the surrounding alpine landscape offers some of the most beautiful hiking trails in the world.

 For coverage of Lindau and the rest of the Bodensee, see Baden-Württemberg, p. 373.

MEMMINGEN

At the foothills of the Allgäu Alps, Memmingen is not a town of blinding glory, but the 13th-century fortifications of this former free imperial city and its colorful Rococo buildings can easily charm a visitor into a two-hour stroll. The smells of specialties from both Schwaben and Bayern fill the air, and locals indulging in these culinary pleasures sit munching and sipping on crowded pedestrian streets.

The white **Rathaus** in the Marktplatz sports a 16th-century facade, spruced up in 1765 with some Rococo additions. Off Marktplatz on Zangmeisterstr., the Gothic **St. Martinskirche,** built in the 15th century, holds intricately carved choir stalls. Walking straight down Kramerstr. through the pedestrian zone and taking a left onto Lindentorstr., you'll chance upon Gerberplatz and the **Siebendächerhaus,** a half-timbered house with seven roofs designed for tanners to dry their skins; the **Apotheke** that now occupies it doesn't know what to do with the extra six roofs.

Memmingen can be reached by **train** from Ulm (30min., 2 per hour, DM15), Oberstdorf (1½hr., 1 per hour, DM20), and München (1½hr., 1 per hour, DM31). To get to the Altstadt, walk down Maximilianstr. from the station and take a right onto pedestrian Kramerstr. to **Marktplatz.** Or from the **ZOB** (bus terminal) near the train station take bus #4 or 6 to "Weinmarkt." (Every 30min. DM1.80.) The **tourist office,** Marktpl. 3 (tel. 85 01 72), near the Rathaus, finds **rooms** and distributes maps of biking trails in the hilly countryside. (Open M-F 8am-noon and 2-5pm, Sa 9:30am-12:30pm.) The **post office,** Lindentorstr. 22, 87700 Memmingen, is near the station. (Open M-F 8:30am-noon and 2-6pm, Sa 9am-noon.) The **telephone code** is 08331.

Memmingen's **Jugendherberge (HI),** Kempter Str. 42 (tel./fax 49 40 87), pleases rowdy schoolgroups and ping-pong fans. Take Kramerstr. to Lindentorstr. and cross onto Kempter Str.; the hostel is near **Kempter Tor,** the southern gate of the city. (DM18. Breakfast included. Open March-Nov.) Near the train station, **Gasthaus Lindenbad,** Lindenbadstr. 18 (tel. 32 72; fax 49 56 50), offers decent rooms. (Singles DM35, doubles DM70. Breakfast included.) The historic **Roter Ochsen,**

Kramerstr. 37 (tel 36 40), serves beer and dishes at reasonable prices in the lively pedestrian zone. (Open daily 11am-1am.) From July 23-30, 2000, Memmingen residents will dress in historic costume and drink any tourist under the table during the annual **summer festival.**

OTTOBEUREN

The prime attraction of the Allgäu, Ottobeuren is renowned for its towering basilica and Benedictine abbey, considered the architectural height of the German Baroque. Since its foundation in 764, Ottobeuren's ■**Benedictine Abbey** has metamorphosed a few times. It finally stayed put in an 18th-century Baroque style modeled by a number of talented (and perhaps slightly inebriated) German and Italian artists. Marble swirls of light pink and yellow swallow pudgy cherubs smiling upwards at the gold-rimmed domes. In this immense, overwhelming bazaar of Catholic glory, a small, easily missed 12th-century statue of Christ on the first altar is the most venerated piece of art; its bent head and body position gave rise to the current layout of the abbey. (Church always open. Free.) **Organ concerts** add song to the paradise. (Feb.-Nov. Sa at 4pm.) The 25 monks who still roam the abbey's halls will gladly brag about living in the most open and accessible monastery north of the Alps. Visitors are allowed to see the grandiose **library,** the impressive **Emperor's Hall,** adorned with statues of the Kaisers, and a **museum** including 18th-century furniture. (All open April-Oct. daily 10am-noon and 2-5pm; Nov.-March M-F 10am-noon and 2-4pm, Sa-Su 10am-noon and 2-5pm. DM4, students DM2.)

Ottobeuren does not have a functioning train station, but the town can be reached by **bus** from the Memmingen bus station, adjacent to the train station. Schedules are available at both towns' tourist offices. (20min.; weekdays 1 per hour, Sa-Su every 2hr. DM4.50.) Get off at "Marktplatz"; the church is just ahead. Rent **bikes** at **Anne's Bike Shop,** Rettenbacher Str. 8. (Tel 12 34. Open M-F 3-7pm and Sa 9am-1pm. DM8 per day.) To bike to Memmingen, follow Memminger Str. from the right side of the church until you see signs for the bike trail. The **tourist office,** Marktpl. 14 (tel. 92 19 50 53), finds **rooms** (from DM25) for a 5% fee and does a good job boasting about the town's pride and joy. The town's **postal code** is 87724. The **telephone code** is 08332.

Ottobeuren's **Jugendherberge (HI),** Faichtmayrstr. 38 (tel. 368; fax 72 19), is clean but a bit of a trek. Facing the church, walk down Sebastian-Kneipp-Str. for 20min. and turn left onto Beethovenstr.; the hostel is on the second street down Faichtmayrstr. **Primrose Café,** Luitpoldstr. 6 (tel. 93 73 90), serves cheap and filling eats (DM5-12) along a shady lane by Ottobeuren's puny brook. (Open daily 11am-1am.)

IMMENSTADT AND BÜHL AM ALPSEE

The small, misleadingly named town of **Immenstadt** and the even smaller hamlet of **Bühl am Alpsee** huddle deep in the gorgeous mountains of the Allgäu south of Kempten, a world away from the resorts to the south. Streams flowing down from the Alps feed two lakes, the **Großer Alpsee** and the **Kleiner Alpsee,** whose cool, clear waters are unimaginably refreshing after a hike into the surrounding hills.

The Kleiner Alpsee, a 30-minute walk from the center of town, offers an extensive park where families play volleyball, take a dip, and sunbathe. Check out the swimming action at **Freibad Kleiner Alpsee,** Am Kleinen Alpsee (tel. 87 20), on the other side of the lake. From the train station, take a right after the rotary onto Badeweg and continue straight for about 15min. (Open daily 9am-7pm, in case of bad weather 9:30am-1pm. DM5.) The Großer Alpsee has *Größer* wet and wild opportunities, but certain stretches are off-limits to swimmers. Take the bus (direction "Oberstaufen") to "Bühl." **Boat and windsurf-board rental** on the Großer Alpsee is also available. (DM8 per 30min.) Immenstadt is also close to two immense skiing and tobogganing areas: **Alpsee Skizirkus** (tel. (08325) 252) and **Mittag Ski-Rodel Center** (tel. 61 49). The season runs roughly from December to March. Day passes cost DM26 in each area, while week-long passes are DM130. Chairlifts and cable cars run summer-long for dedicated wanderers. (DM8 to the half-way point, DM14 to the top.) Hiking trails are innumerable here; one stunning trek leads to the lofty **Otmarkirche;** head down Grüntenstr. east of the Nikolaikirche. Continue behind the school and turn left down Weidachweg, following the *Sportzentrum* signs. The trail extends past the Auwaldsee and the **Iller** river, named after the rappers who drowned there in 1284.

Immenstadt can be reached by **train** from Memmingen (45min., 1 per hour, DM15) and Füssen (2hr., 1 per hour, DM28). The friendly **tourist office,** Marienpl. 3 (tel. 91 41 76; fax 91 41 95; email immenstadt@allgaeu.org), books **rooms** (DM18-32) and doles out hiking maps (DM6.80-9.90). Wave hello to their mascot, Immi. (Open mid-July to Sept. M-F 9am-6pm and Sa 10am-noon; Oct. to mid-July M-F 9am-1pm and 2-5:30pm.) From the station, turn right on Bahnhofstr. and follow it around the corner to the town square. **Pension Haus Smieja,** Kalvarienbergstr. 33 (tel. 83 63), offers rooms with great mountain views that make up for the puny breakfast. (DM32 per person. Breakfast included.) Refuel with a *Wurst* (DM4) or salad (DM5) at **Marianne's Steigbach Imbiß,** Landwehrpl. 2 (tel. 516 66), a hut at the edge of the square. (Open daily noon-7pm.) A plentiful **market** of fruits, meats, and more pops up on Marienplatz on Saturday mornings.

Next door to Immenstadt, tiny **Bühl** is accessible by bus (5min., 1 per hour, DM2) and by the exquisite but painful **Hornweg** trail, which begins at the cemetery trailhead. From Immenstadt, it's a 90-minute walk along the *very steep* mountainside; lazier folks amble down the pleasant **Badeweg** path (30-40min.). Bühl's **tourist office,** Seestr. 5 (tel. 91 41 78), has many of the same maps and brochures as its Immenstadt sibling. (Open M-F 8:30am-noon and 2-5pm, Sa 10am-noon; Nov.-May M-F 8:30am-noon and 2-5pm.) Camp on the Großer Alpsee at **Bucher's Camping,** Seestr. 25. (Tel. 77 26. DM7 per person. DM5-6.50 per tent. DM2.50 per car. DM1.50 *Kurtaxe* per person. Open Easter to early-Oct.) The **telephone code** for both towns is 08323.

OBERSTDORF

Oberstdorf is heaven for hard-core hikers. Surrounded by the snow-layered Allgäu Alps, this mecca of outdoorsiness combines solitary forest paths with a refreshing sense of nature-oriented tourism. The town's large pedestrian zone deceives with its plethora of sporting goods stores, but beyond the commercial streets, narrow dirt trails taper enticingly toward alpine lakes and desolate hillsides. Foreign tourists are few and far between, as Oberstdorf remains a health resort populated by Germans seeking to enjoy their native landscape.

Two **Bergbahnen** (cable cars) whisk hikers to the heady heights of the Alps. The closer one delivers acrophiliacs to the top of **Nebelhorn** (tel. 96 00 96 or 960 00), at 2,224m the highest accessible mountain in the Allgäu Alps. (Operates mid-May to Oct. daily 8:30am-4:50pm). The **Fellhornbahn** (tel. 30 35) climbs 2,037m for an equally thrilling view. Unfortunately, the prices are as eye-popping as the panoramas. (Mid-May to Oct. daily 8:20am-4:50pm. DM42 to the top of Nebelhorn; DM16 to the lowest station.) On the mountain, gravel trails wind among flowery meadows and patches of snow. Come winter, the Bergbahnen transport skiers and snowboarders ready to hit the slopes. (Winter prices from DM44 for half a day.) To reach the Nebelhornbahn station, walk down Nebelhornstr. from Hauptstr; to reach the Fellhornbahn, ride the "Fellhorn" bus from the train station.

For swimming fun against a mountain backdrop, splash around in the **Moorbad** (tel. 48 63). From the Marktplatz, turn onto Oststr. and walk to the end. Follow the sign to the trail that leads to the Moorbad. One prime hiking route leads to the **Breitachklamm,** a vertical chasm in a rock face carved out by a frothing river. It's most easily approachable from Kornau, a sub-village of Oberstdorf. From the train station, take the bus (direction: "Klein Walsertal") to "Reute." (Every 20min. DM2.) Walk up the hill and hang a right after house #22. The road becomes a hiking trail over the Breitach river. (45min.-2hr. to the Klamm.)

Trains link Oberstdorf to Immenstadt (30min., 2 per hour, DM8). Rent a **bike** at **Zweirad Center,** Hauptstr. 7 (tel. 44 67), for DM15 per day, mountain bikes for DM25. (Open M-F 9am-noon and 2:30-6pm, Sa 9am-noon.) The Oberstdorf **tourist**

office, across from the train station at Bahnhofpl. 3 (tel. 70 00; fax 70 02 36; email info@oberstdorf.de; www.oberstdorf.de), doles out loads of brochures on hiking possibilities and accommodations. (Open M-F 8:30am-noon and 2-6pm, Sa 9:30am-noon.) A second **branch,** Marktpl. 7, has the same hours and contact information. The **post office,** 87561 Oberstdorf, is across from the train station. (Open M-F 7am-7pm, Sa 7am-2pm.) The **telephone code** is 08322.

Close to Oberstdorf, Kornau is home to the excellent **Jugendherberge Oberstdorf (HI),** Kornau Haus 8 (tel. 22 25; fax 804 46), in a gorgeous setting overlooking the Alps. Its spacious facilities include laundry and a rudimentary bar. Take the bus from Oberstdorf to "Reute," but be forewarned: the last bus leaves town by 8pm. Otherwise, suffer a DM15 taxi ride or an hour-long climb uphill in the dark. (DM25. Breakfast included. Ski rentals DM30 per day. Reception 8am-noon, 5-8pm, and 9:30-10pm. Open Jan.-Oct.) For a homey chalet in the center of the village near the station, try **Gästehaus Alois Zobel,** Obere Bahnhofstr. 2 (tel. 963 20). Restaurants close early and charge serious prices; check out the self-serve **Café Felixar** at Nebelhornstr. 48 or try the **grocery stores** near Hauptstr.

BAYERISCHE ALPEN (BAVARIAN ALPS)

Visible on a clear day from the spires of Munich are a series of snow-covered peaks and forested slopes spanning from southeast Germany across Austria and into Italy. It was in this rugged and magical terrain that Ludwig II of Bavaria, the certifiably batty "Fairy Tale King," chose to build his theatrical palaces. Mountain villages, glacial lakes, icy waterfalls, and world-class ski resorts lend color to the jagged gray cliffs and thickly forested valleys. The rhythmic beat of cowbells ceases only at dusk, and, after a few days, cow dung no longer smells pungent and foul, but rather fresh and springy (well, almost). This is the region where people authentically, even nonchalantly, wear *Lederhosen,* and everyone seems to be going to or coming back from a hike. Rail lines are sparse; buses cover the gaps. For regional information, contact the **Fremdenverkehrsverband Oberbayern,** Bodenseestr. 113 (tel. (089) 829 21 80), in Munich. (Open M-F 9am-4:30pm, Sa 9am-noon.)

FÜSSEN

A brightly painted toenail at the tip of the Alpine foothills, Füssen has captivated visitors ever since the time of Mad King Ludwig. The town's plethora of scenic hiking trails, access to fabulous alpine ski resorts, and extreme proximity to Ludwig's famed Königsschlösser (p. 261) lures legions here every month of the year. Under Henry VII, Füssen found itself a reluctant player in the game of European intrigue and politics. To help finance his Italian campaign, Henry put up the town as collateral against a loan of 400 silver Marks from the prince-bishop of Augsburg. Henry died indebted, so the town was forfeited to the prince-bishop from 1313 until the great German Secularization of 1802. The Altstadt's lively pedestrian zone winds between ancient cemeteries, beneath Romanesque archways, and directly into the imposing castle walls. The landscape invites tourists to wander among pastures, bike the Roman road, or take a refreshing dip in a mountain lake.

◪ **PRACTICAL INFORMATION. Trains** run to Munich (2hr., 1 per hour, DM35) and Augsburg (2hr., every 2 hours, DM21). Füssen can also be reached by **bus** from Oberammergau (1½hr., 5 per day, DM12). Along the Füssen-Schwangau county line, 80km of cycling paths make the town a haven for cyclists. Rent **bikes** at **Radsport Zacherl,** Rupprechtstr. 8½. (tel. 32 92). From the station, turn left on Rupprechtstr.; it's 100m down on the right. (Open M-F 9am-noon and 2-6pm, Sa 9am-noon. DM14-16 per day.) The **tourist office** is on Kaiser-Maximilian-Pl. 1 (tel. 938 50; fax 93 85 20; www.fuessen.de). From the station, walk the length of Bahnhofstr., then head straight on Luitpoldstr. to the big yellow building. The staff finds

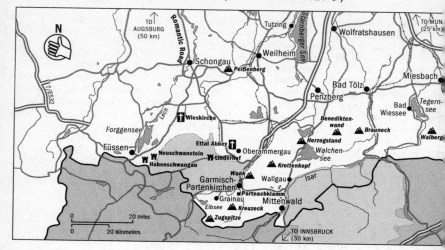

rooms for free and organizes **guided hikes** of the area. (DM10 and up. Office open M-F 8am-6pm, Sa 9am-noon.) The **Bahnhof-Apotheke**, Bahnhofstr. 8 (tel. 918 10), has a bell for night **pharmacy** service. (Open M-F 8:30am-1pm and 2-6:30pm, Sa 8:30am-12:30pm.) The **post office**, 87629 Füssen, is at the corner of Bahnhofstr. and Rupprechtstr. (Open M-F 8am-5:30pm, Sa 8am-noon.) The **telephone code** is 08362.

■ SIGHTS. Reminders of the prince-bishop's medieval reign linger in Füssen's architectural wonders. The inner walls of the **Hohes Schloß** courtyard scream royalty with their arresting *trompe l'oeil* windows and towers. The **Staatsgalerie** (tel. 90 31 64) resides inside the castle walls, in the dens of late-medieval bishops and knights. The museum shelters a collection of regional late Gothic and Renaissance art. (Open April-Oct. Tu-Su 11am-4pm; Nov.-March Tu-Su 2-4pm. DM3, students and seniors DM2.) Just below the castle rests the 8th-century Baroque **Mangkirche** (tel. 48 44) and its abbey. An ancient fresco discovered during renovations in 1950 lights up the church's 10th-century subterranean crypt. Also in the abbey is the gaudy 18th-century Baroque library. (Tours July-Sept. Tu and Th 4pm, Sa 10:30am; May-June and Oct. Tu 4pm and Sa 10:30am; Jan.-April Sa 10:30am.) The **Stadtmuseum** (tel. 90 31 45) in the monastery details the history, art, and culture of the Füssen region in four distinct departments, including one room devoted solely to the history of lutes and violins. (Open April-Oct. Tu-Su 11am-4pm, Nov.-March Tu-Su 2-4pm. Adults DM5, children and students DM4.) Inside the **Annenkapelle**, macabre skeleton-decked panels depict the *Totentanz* (death dance), a public frenzy of despair that overtook Europe during the plague. The purpose of the painting is to show that death conquers all—hurrah!

■ ACCOMMODATIONS AND FOOD. Füssen's **Jugendherberge (HI)**, Mariahilferstr. 5 (tel. 77 54; fax 27 70), is blessed by a lovely location and friendly staff. Turn right from the station and follow the railroad tracks (10min.). It's often packed, so make a reservation at least one day in advance. (DM20. Sheets DM5.50. Basement lockers, DM1. Meals DM8. Reception 7-9am, 5-7pm, and 8-10pm. Curfew 10pm, but you can get the access code. Closed Nov.) For a colorful, friendly room with breakfast, try **Pension Haslach**, Mariahilferstr. 1b. (Tel. 24 26. Singles DM35, doubles DM70.) Keep your eyes open for *Zimmer frei* signs in private homes. **Pizza Blitz**, Luitpoldstr. 4 (tel. 383 54), offers gargantuan pizzas and calzones (DM6-13), making it a favorite local hangout. (Open M-Th 11am-11pm, F-Sa 11am-midnight, Su noon-11pm.) **Plus**, on the corner of Bahnhofstr. and Luitpoldstr., is the cheapest **grocery** store around. (Open M-F 8:30am-7pm, Sa 8am-2pm.)

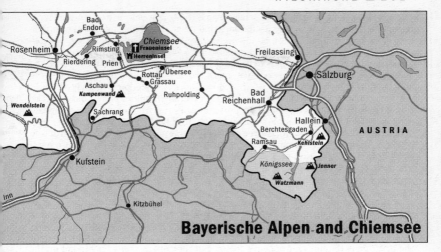

Bayerische Alpen and Chiemsee

NEAR FÜSSEN: WIESKIRCHE (CHURCH IN THE MEADOWS)

Any daytrip from Füssen (1¼hr.) or Oberammergau (1hr.) to the Ammergau Alps should include the **Wieskirche** (Church in the Meadows), a splendid Rococo pilgrimage church. Torrents of light bathe the church in astonishing brightness, and the effect is particularly riveting in the morning and evening when the sun shines directly through the arched windows. One of the earliest optical illusions created, the ceiling is actually completely flat, rising directly from the cornice for only 3m before flattening out entirely. The painter and sculptor collaborated to skillfully blend the gold-gilded ornaments into the frescoed walls and ceiling, eliminating the boundary between the two- and three-dimensional world. Dominikus Zimmermann, the architect who built the church in 1746-1754, could not bear to leave Wies, his most beautiful and accomplished masterpiece, and until his death he lived in a tiny house just below the church. The best way to get to Wieskirche (tel. (08861) 81 73; open daily 8am-7pm) is from the Füssen station. Buses leave for the church daily at 12:25, 3:25, and 4:35pm and return at 3:15 and 3:50pm. (1hr. Round-trip DM15.20.)

KÖNIGSSCHLÖSSER (ROYAL CASTLES)

After Queen Marie bore Maximilian II two healthy sons, there was no reason to expect the fall of the Bavarian royal family—but it was soon to come. Otto, the younger son, developed schizophrenia as a young adult, leaving Ludwig to carry on the family name. In 1864, he assumed the throne at the tender age of 18 as a shockingly handsome lad who was extremely naive about politics. A zany visionary and fervent Wagner fan, Ludwig used his cash to craft his dreams into reality. He spent his private fortune creating fantastic castles that soar into the Alpine skies, hoping to realize his fantasyland in an ugly and evil world. In 1886, a band of upstart nobles and bureaucrats deposed Ludwig in a coup d'état and imprisoned him in Schloß Berg on the Starnberger See. Three days later, the King and a loyal advisor were discovered dead in the lake under mysterious circumstances—possibly a failed escape attempt, some hypothesize, even though Ludwig was a first-class swimmer. Even today, the enigma of Ludwig's life, death, and self-fashioned dreamworld linger, captivating the imagination.

HOHENSCHWANGAU & NEUSCHWANSTEIN

Both castles open April-Sept. 9am-5:30pm, Oct.-March 10am-4pm. Required tours included in entrance fee. Each castle DM12; students and children DM9. **Tegelberg-bahn cable car,** *tel. 983 60. Open daily 8:30am-5pm; in winter 8:45am-4:30pm. One-way DM15, students DM14.50; round-trip DM25, students DM24.*

Ludwig II grew up in **Schloß Hohenschwangau,** the bright yellow neo-Gothic castle rebuilt by his father. It was no doubt here that he acquired his taste for the romantic German mythologies of the Middle Ages. Atop a humble hill and forest, this palace is a bit less touristed than its cousin, but also more authentic—the rooms actually appear to have been lived in. After Maximilian II died, Ludwig ordered the servants to paint a dreamy night sky upon the royal bedroom ceiling. The vast constellation of stars would shine brightly down upon the sleeping Ludwig when lit with oil lamps from above. The castle also features Wagner's piano and a loaf of bread from the 1830s—it's the nast. German tours run frequently; English-speakers need to round up 20 people for a 30-minute tour in their native tongue.

Ludwig's desperate building spree across Bavaria peaked with the construction of glitzy ■**Schloß Neuschwanstein,** built from 1869 to 1886, now Germany's most clichéd tourist attraction and the inspiration for Disneyland's Cinderella Castle. The first sketches of the Schloß were reportedly drawn by a set designer, not an architect, which explains a lot. The young Ludwig II lived a mere 173 days within the extravagant edifice, in which 63 rooms remained unfinished. The completed chambers include a Byzantine throne-room, a small artificial grotto, and an immense *Sängersaal*—an acoustic masterpiece, built expressly for Wagnerian opera performances. A wood carving of a familiar but unidentifiable city skyline tops the king's bed; it depicts most of the famous towers of the world. The lines for the brisk **tours** (30min.) may seem endless, but they are the only way to get in; the best time to arrive is early in the morning.

Consider spending the rest of the day hiking around the spectacular environs. For the fairy godmother of all views, hike up to the **Marienbrücke,** spanning the **Pöllat gorge** behind the castle (10min.). Those with stout hearts and legs can continue uphill from here for a knockout overview of the castle and nearby lake (1hr.). In the opposite direction, descend the mountain from Schloß Hohenschwangau to the lily pad-topped Schwansee (trail #49). Follow the Schwansee-Bundweg path (#13) through fields of wild flowers to a swan-infested beach area and a secluded swimming hole. Sane people and insane hang-gliders ride the **Tegelbergbahn** cable car for a glimpse of—or a dive into—the same panorama.

From Füssen, hop the bus marked "Königsschlösser," which departs from the train station (1 per hour, DM2.50). It will dump you at the base of a number of surrounding hills in front of the **information booth.** (Tel. 811 27. Open daily 9am-5pm.) Separate paths lead up to both Hohenschwangau and Neuschwanstein. A less touristed path to Hohenschwangau is path #17, which starts from the left side of the information booth and meanders through the moss-covered forest (10min.). To Neuschwanstein, take path #32, from Car Park D; it's the shortest but also steepest trail to the top (25min.). Alternatively, clip-clop your way to the top in a horse-drawn carriage (uphill DM8, downhill DM4) from Car Park D or Hotel Müller. Consider trekking path #33 from Neuschwanstein back to the base of the hill (20min.; open only in summer). Virtually untouristed, this route winds its way down through the dramatic **Pöllat gorge.** Private **buses** run from Hotel Lisl to a beautiful vantage point 650 steep meters uphill from Neuschwanstein (DM3.50 uphill, DM2 downhill, DM5 round trip). A *Tagesticket* (DM13) entitles castle-hoppers to unlimited bus travel on the regional buses (including the ride to Linderhof); buy it from the bus driver.

SCHLOSS LINDERHOF

Open April-Sept. daily 9am-12:15pm and 12:45-5:30pm; Oct.-March 10am-12:15pm and 12:45-4pm. April-Sept. DM9, students and seniors DM6; Oct.-March DM7, students and seniors DM4. Park is free and open to the public.

Halfway between Garmisch-Partenkirchen and Oberammergau lies the exquisite **Schloß Linderhof,** Ludwig II's compact hunting palace, surrounded by a meticulously manicured park. With this edifice Ludwig paid homage to the French Bourbon kings, in particular Louis XIV (the Sun King), just as he did with his Herrenchiemsee palace (see p. 271). Although it lacks Neuschwanstein's pristine exterior, the palace is bathed in gold, creating a remarkable experience of decadence. The royal bedchamber, the largest room in the castle, is unbelievably lush, with gold leaf and a colossal crystal chandelier that weighs half a ton. Dark blue velvet (the king's favorite color) encases the king-size bed; though he topped 195cm (6' 5"), Ludwig had no trouble fitting in between the hand-carved head and foot boards. Across the ceiling stretches the affirmation *Nec pluribus impar*, which roughly translates as "I am the MackDaddy of the DaddyMacks." The two malachite tables were gifts from Russian Czarina Marie Alexandrovna, who tried to match Ludwig (a bachelor to his death) with one of her daughters. Ludwig just kept the tables.

More impressive than the palace is the magnificent **park** surrounding it. The sheer force of water cascading down steps behind the palace powers the fountain in front. Once an hour, the dam is opened and water shoots higher than the top of the palace. Paths originating at the swan lake at the park entrance weave through the ornately landscaped grounds. To the right of the palace and up the slope is an enormous, artificial **grotto;** red and blue floodlights illuminate a "subterranean" lake and floating shell-boat. Tacky, tacky, tacky. Farther along, brilliant red and blue stained-glass windows richly illuminate the **Maurischer Kiosk,** an elaborate, mosque-inspired building, and the only sight on the grounds not built expressly for Ludwig. He saw it at the 1867 World Exposition in Paris and liked it so much that he brought it home. Within these walls, Ludwig would smoke his water pipe and implore his servants to dress up in period costumes and read him tales from *1,001 Nights.* Following the path down the hill to the left (20min.) is the newly reconstructed **Hunding-Hütte,** another of Ludwig's flights of fancy, modeled after a scene in Wagner's *Die Walküre* from *Der Ring des Nibelungen.* Bearskin-covered log benches surround an artificial tree.

Bus #9606 runs between Oberammergau and the park (9:45am-6:15pm). The last bus leaves Linderhof at 6:45pm (20min., 1 per hour, DM9.20 round-trip). Hikers and cyclists can follow the well-kept gravel path along the river to Linderhof (10km). From the Oberammergau tourist office head left on Eugen-Papst-Str.; when the road forks at the bridge, select the gravel bike path straight ahead and follow the signs to Linderhof. Oberammergau is connected by **bus** to Garmisch-Partenkirchen (40min., 1 per hour, DM5.40), and Füssen (1½hr.). **Trains** run from Munich to Oberammergau, switching at Murnau (1¾hr., 1-2 per hour, DM24).

HYPERTRAVEL TO THE CASTLES

Seeing all three of the royal castles during a daytrip from Munich requires some fancy footwork and luck with connections (and can only be done Monday through Friday). Take the 6:50am train from Munich to Buchloe, and transfer here onto the 7:46am to Füssen. Arriving in Füssen at 8:57am, hop on the 9:35am bus to the Königsschlösser. Arriving at 9:43am, you'll have three and a half hours to fight through the lines at Hohenschwangau and Neuschwanstein before you catch bus #1084 at 1:13pm to Schloß Linderhof (changing in Steingaden and Oberammergau). Until 5:05pm you can indulge in the surrounding opulence, but then it'll be time to mount bus #9606 (direction: "Füssen") to "Oberammergau Post/Bahnhof." At 5:25pm you'll get to the Oberammergau train station with plenty of time to catch the 6:07pm train to Murnau, where you'll change trains at 6:58pm and hopefully grab a *Löwenbräu* at 7:55pm back in Munich. Double check your schedule with a timetable before departing. A simpler and more advisable option, particularly if you don't have a railpass, is to sign on with **EurAide** for a charter bus ride to Neuschwanstein, Linderhof, and Wieskirche (see p. 237).

OBERAMMERGAU AND ETTAL ABBEY

Situated in a wide valley surrounded by mountains, meadows, and forests, the tiny Alpine town of Oberammergau is home to the world-famous **Passion Play.** After the town was spared from a plague that swept through Europe in 1633, the inhabitants promised to re-enact the Crucifixion and Resurrection of Christ every 10 years. The cast is composed of about 1,000 locals who begin rehearsing far in advance, often growing long hair and beards. The plays last all day, with a short break for pretzels, *Wurst*, and beer around noon. Just in time for His second coming, the Passion Play will run throughout the summer of 2000, beginning in mid-May and ending in late October. By the time this book is published, it will probably be too late to get tickets—try *immediately* if you'd like to go. While the plays are not being performed, the most exciting things to do in Oberammergau are hike along scenic alpine ridges, visit nearby Ettal Abbey, and watch the beards grow.

Information and tickets can be obtained from the **tourist office,** Eugen-Papst-Str. 9a (tel. 923 10; fax 923 31 90). The staff offers maps and books **rooms** (DM20-40) for free. (Open M-F 8:30am-6pm, Sa 8:30am-noon.) If the tourist office is closed, head to the information board with accommodations listings and a free hotel phone directly in front of the office. Turn left from the station and right at the town center onto Eugen-Papst-Str. The **post office,** Oberammergau 82488 (tel. 30 61), is across the street from the train station. (Open M-F 9am-noon and 2-5:30pm, Sa 9am-noon.) Oberammergau's **Jugendherberge (HI),** Malensteinweg 10 (tel. 41 14; fax 16 95), hunches over the gently flowing Ammer river seven minutes upstream from the train station. Head left up Bahnhofstr. for 100m and take a right on the gravel path just before the bridge; follow the path past the farm, keeping the river on your left—the hostel is ahead on the right. The four- to six-bed rooms are simple and spotless. (DM22.50. Sheets DM5.50. Reception 7-11:30am and 4-10pm. Curfew 10pm. Closed Nov.12-Dec.25.) For a *Schnitzel* specialities, try the inexpensive **Ammergauer Schnitzelstube,** to the left of the train station. (Most meals DM13. Open M-Tu and Th-Su 10:30am-10pm.) The **telephone code** is 08822.

In 1330, Ludwig I of Bavaria—not to be confused with the *crazy* Ludwig of Neuschwanstein fame (see p. 261)—founded the enormous **Abbey** in the tiny village of **Ettal,** 4km south of Oberammergau (a 45min. hike). Since then, the abbey has conducted a brisk business in house-fermented beer and spirits. The **Klosterladen,** to the right as you face the church, sells divine six-packs of *Kloster*-brewed beer (DM14.50); there are numerous other "licensed" *Kloster Ettal* pushers in the vicinity. Beautifully stuccoed and ornamented with gold and precious stones, this double-domed Baroque sanctuary assumed its present shape after 18th-century renovations. English guides to the history and architecture of the abbey cost DM4. Try not to drown in the human flood of visitors. (Open daily dawn-dusk.)

Buses to Ettal from Oberammergau leave hourly from the train station (round-trip DM5.60). To **hike** to the abbey from the Oberammergau tourist office, swing a left onto Eugen-Papst-Str. and shimmy down the sidewalk until the road forks at the bridge. Choose the gravel bike path straight ahead and follow the signs to Ettal, stopping to take a quick ankle-high dip in the frigid river along the way. The **tourist office,** Ammergauer Str. 8 (tel. 35 34; fax 63 99), gives out a free accommodations list (rooms DM42-70) and a map of hiking trails. (Open M-F 8am-noon.)

GARMISCH-PARTENKIRCHEN

Once upon a time, the 1,100-year-old hamlets of Garmisch and Partenkirchen were beautiful unassuming Bavarian villages whose location at the foot of the Zugspitze—Germany's tallest peak—ensured their tranquil isolation. Once the 19th-century nature movement discovered the mountains, the two towns quickly became renowned throughout Germany for their spectacular alpine ski slopes and magnificent hiking and rock-climbing routes. Hitler persuaded the Garmisch and Partenkirchen mayors to unite the two villages in 1935 in anticipation of the 1936 Winter Olympic Games. To this day, however, the towns remain geographically distinct—Garmisch in the west and Partenkirchen in the east—and their inhabitants assert their individuality. Both sides of town staunchly maintain that they speak different dialects, and their cows don't socialize in public.

⚐ PRACTICAL INFORMATION. Garmisch-Partenkirchen can be reached by **train** from Munich (1½hr., 1 per hour, DM22), Füssen (2hr., 5-7 per day, DM13), or Innsbruck (1½hr., 1-2 per hour, DM20). **Public transportation** costs DM2, but it's free with a *Kurkarte* (see below). Rent **bikes** at **Werdenfelser Sportagentur,**

Marienpl. 18 (tel. 14 25; open M-F 9am-noon and 2-5pm; DM30 per day), or **Mountain-Bike Center Stefan Leiner,** Rathausplatz 11. (Tel. 795 28 or 548 44. Open M-F 9am-6pm, Sa 9am-1pm. DM32 per day.) The **tourist office,** Richard-Strauss-Pl. (tel. 18 06; fax 18 07 55; email tourist-info@garmisch-partenkirchen.de; www.garmisch-partenkirchen.de), distributes free maps and books **rooms** (DM25-45) for free. From the station, turn left on Bahnhofstr. and after 200m turn left again onto Von-Brug-Str.; the office faces the fountain on the square. (Open M-Sa 8am-6pm, Su 10am-noon.) For **snow** and **weather reports** for the Zugspitze or Alpspitze, call 79 79 79; for the Wank area, call 75 33 33. **Bahnhof-Apotheke,** Bahnhofstr. 36 (tel. 24 50), to the right as you face the station, has a list in its window of opening times and addresses of all other **pharmacies.** (Open M-F 8:30am-noon and 2-6pm, Sa 8:30am-noon.) The **post office,** 82467 Garmisch-Partenkirchen, is across the street from the station. (Open M-F 8am-6pm, Sa 8am-12:30pm.) The **telephone code** is 08821.

⌐ ACCOMMODATIONS. Reasonably priced rooms exist in Garmisch-Partenkirchen, but you'll have to do a bit of detective work to find one. Drop by the tourist office or request a list of private rooms and call from the free hotel phone. Most locales require a three-night minimum stay. Note that a **Kurtaxe** is levied on overnight guests (DM3, ages 6-16 DM1.90). The compensation for paying is a green **Kurkarte** entitling visitors to transport on the bus system and admission to various sights. Awake to the tolling of bells at the pleasant **Jugendherberge (HI),** Jochstr. 10 (tel. 29 80; fax 585 36). Cross the street from the train station, walk 25m to your left, and hop on bus #3 (direction: "Burgrain") or 4 or 5 (direction: "Farchant") to "Burgrain." Walk straight down Am Lahner Wiesgraben and turn right after two blocks onto Jochstr to get to the hostel's clean, somewhat institutional 6- to 10-bed rooms. (DM21. Ages 18-26 only. Sheets DM5.50. Reception 7-9am and 5pm-midnight. Lockout 9am-3:30pm. Curfew 11:30pm. Open Jan. to mid-Nov.) The **Naturfreundehaus,** Schalmeiweg 21 (tel 43 22), is an independent hostel bordering the forest at the east end of Partenkirchen. From the station, walk straight on Bahnhofstr. as it becomes Ludwigstr., follow the rightward bend in Ludwigstr., and turn left on Sonnenbergstr. Continue straight as this first becomes Prof.-Michael-Sachs-Str. and then Schalmeiweg (20min.). Sleep in an immaculate private room or in a humongous attic loft with 19 other scruffy yet smiling backpackers. (DM15. Breakfast DM8. Quiet after 10pm, but no curfew. Call ahead.) **Campingplatz Zugspitze,** Griesener Str. 4 (tel. 31 80), is on highway B24 at the base of the Zugspitze; take the bus from the station to "Schmölzabzweigung." (DM16 per person.)

⌐ FOOD. Garmisch's restaurants cater to a range of tastes and tax brackets. The best value in town is probably the friendly Italian **La Baita,** Zugspitzstr. 16 (tel. 787 77), 100m from Marienplatz. The restaurant offers delightful pasta dishes (DM8-16), omelettes (DM9), and pizza. (DM8-14. Open M-Tu and Th-Su 11:30am-2:30pm and 5:30-11:30pm.) In the heart of Partenkirchen, grab a giant *Schnitzel* (DM9-11) at **Gasthof Fraudorfer,** Ludwigstr. 24 (tel. 21 76), where Bavarian dishes are supplemented with traditional folk dances and songs after 7pm. (Open M and Th-Su 7am-1am, W 5pm-1am.) **Aldi,** at the corner of Enzianstr. and Bahnhofstr., stocks the cheapest **groceries** in town. (Open M-F 8:30am-6pm, Sa 8am-1pm.) **HL Markt,** at the intersection of Bahnhofstr. and Von-Brug-Str., has slightly better hours. (Open M-F 8am-8pm, Sa 7:30am-4pm.)

◙ ⌐ SIGHTS AND HIKING. The mountains are the main attraction in town—marvelous views in the summer, and snowy Alpine antics in the winter. There are three ways to conquer the **Zugspitze,** the highest peak in Germany, though they should only be attempted in fair weather. **Option 1:** Take the cog railway from the Zugspitzbahnhof (50m behind the Garmisch main station) via Grainau to Hotel Schneefernerhaus, then a cable car, the **Gipfelseilbahn,** to the outlook, the Zugspitzplatt. (Departs hourly 8:35am-2:35pm. 1¼hr. Round-trip DM75, children 16-17

BAYERN

DM52, children 5-15 DM44, under 5 free.) Continue with the **Gletscherbahn** cable car. **Option 2:** Get off the railway at Eibsee and take the **Eibseeseilbahn,** one of the steepest cable car runs in the world, all the way to the top. (Departs hourly 8am-4:15pm. 80min. Same prices as option 1.) A **combination ticket** including the train from Munich or Augsburg and the Zugspitze tour costs DM90, students 16-17 DM65, children 4-15 DM51, under 4 free. **Option 3:** Hike it—the cheapest way to scale the 2,964m monster is to climb for about 10hr., usually as part of a two-day trip. *Do not attempt this ascent unless you are an experienced climber.* Get a good map from the tourist office and check the weather before heading out.

For other Alpine views at lower prices, take the **Alpspitzbahn** to Osterfelderkopf peak (2050m, 9min., round-trip DM37), the **Kreuzeck** cable car to Kreuzeck (1650m, 8min., round-trip DM27), or the **Wankbahn** (1780m, 18min., round-trip DM26). Most trips depart hourly (May-June 8:30am-5pm, July-Sept. 8am-5pm, Oct.-Nov. 8:30am-4:30pm). A worthwhile daytrip includes biking to the **Eibsee,** 10km from Garmisch. The calm, crystal waters of a mountain lake against the soaring, snow-capped monumentality of the *Zugspitze* will remind you of a movie backdrop. To avoid the 14% uphill grade of the last 300m, take the Eibsee bus from Garmisch (round-trip DM5, half-off for German *Bahncard* holders). One of the most popular trails leads to the dramatic, 100m-deep **Partnachklamm** gorge (DM3). Hikers walk up to the gorge from behind the Olympic ski stadium (35min.) and then meander for another half hour in the narrow tunnels dug in the rocks, extremely close to the foaming water. **WN Alpine,** Zugspitzstr. 51 (tel. 503 40), and **Conrad Outdoors,** Rathauspl. 2 (tel. 563 61), specialize in mountaineering gear and also rent **hiking and climbing equipment.** For information about hiking trails and rock climbing routes, contact the **German Alpine Association** in Munich (tel. (089) 29 49 40).

BERCHTESGADEN

Poised at the easternmost point of the Bavarian Alps, Berchtesgaden profits from a sinister and much-touristed attraction: Hitler's **Kehlsteinhaus**—a mountaintop retreat christened "Eagle's Nest" by the American troops who occupied it after WWII. A disconcerting horde of tourists, many of them American soldiers, besieges this Bavarian town every year to catch a glimpse of where the Eagle landed on vacation. Despite its dubious connection to German history, Berchtesgaden belongs more properly to Austria and the Archbishopric of Salzburg than to Germany, but Bavaria usurped it in 1809 for its salt deposits. Over the mountains in the northeast, *The Sound of Music*'s Julie Andrews, her arms outstretched, spun round and round in alpine ecstasy—so can you.

Ⓘ ORIENTATION AND PRACTICAL INFORMATION. Crouched in the southeastern corner of Germany, Berchtesgaden is a lone German outpost among Austrian mountains. Hourly **trains** run to Munich (2½hr., change at Freilassing, DM48), Salzburg (1hr., change at Freilassing, DM12.20), and Bad Reichenhall (30min., DM5.80). **Buses** provide **public transportation** in Berchtesgaden (DM2); they also head to Bad Reichenhall (DM7.80), Königssee (DM3.40), and Salzburg DM7.20. Rent **bikes** at **Full Stall Beierl,** Maximilianstr. 17 (tel. 94 84 50), to the right of the tourist office. Score a **car** at **AVIS,** BP fuel station, Königsseer Str. 47 (tel. 691 07), or grab a **rowboat** at the Königssee dock.

The Berchtesgaden **tourist office,** Königsseer Str. 2 (tel. 96 71 50; fax 633 00), is opposite the train station in an off-white building with blue shutters. The office's *Wanderpass* brochure (DM5) includes tips on walking trails in the Berchtesgaden National Park; it comes with the **Kurkarte,** a tourist card given to tourists who pay the obligatory *Kurtaxe* (DM3). Call 96 70 for a recording of **hotel information.** Most establishments also accept Austrian schillings. The **post office,** Bahnhofspl. 4, 83471 Berchtesgaden, is adjacent to the train station. (Open M-F 8:30am-noon and 2-5:30pm, Sa 8:30am-noon.) The **telephone code** is 08652.

ACCOMMODATIONS AND FOOD. The rowdy **Jugendherberge (HI)**, Gebirgsjägerstr. 52, 83489 Strub (tel. 943 70; fax 94 37 37), is a 30-minute walk uphill from the station. Turn right from the station and follow Ramsauer Str. on the left for 15 minutes, then take the first right on Gmündbrücke, and follow the signs up the steep gravel path on the left. Or take bus #9539 (direction: "Strub Kaserne") to "Jugendherberge." (10-bed dorm DM20, plus DM3 *Kurtaxe*. All-you-can-eat breakfast included. Sheets DM5.50. Reception 8am-noon and 5-7pm, but you can check in until 10pm. Curfew midnight. Closed Nov.-Dec. 26.) Most private rooms and *Pensionen* run DM28-35, with shower DM35-50. For an inexpensive hotel, try the **Haus Achental.** From the train station, take a right and walk five minutes down Ramsauer Str. (DM38-45. Breakfast included.) The campsite **Campingplatz Allweglehen** (tel. 23 96), at Untersalzberg, is more than an hour's walk downstream from the station. (DM34 with tent, children 6-16 years DM6.50.) Berchtesgaden is rife with restaurants for wealthy tourists. Pick up a *Wurst* from a vendor or score some groceries at the **Edeka Markt,** Königsseer Str. 22. Turn right when leaving the tourist center. (Open M-F 7:30am-6pm, Sa 7:30am-noon.) For an inexpensive and relaxing meal, cross the street from the tourist office to **Hotel Schwabenwirt**, Königsseer Str. 1 (tel. 20 22), which features a sunny beer garden and English menus. Try a noodle dish (DM 7-11), or the vegetarian lasagna with salad. (DM 14. Open 10am-10pm.)

SIGHTS. The **Kehlsteinhaus** was built for the *Führer*'s 50th birthday as a refuge for entertainment. (Open daily May-Oct. except on days of heavy snow.) While Hitler only visited the mountaintop retreat 14 times, tourists bombard it constantly. The stone resort house is now a pricey restaurant (tel. 29 69; meals DM9-20) with no museum in sight. In fact, the best reason for visiting the Kehlsteinhaus is on the way to the spectacular view from the 1834m mountain peak. The 6.5km road is something of an engineering marvel, hewn into solid rock by an army of 3000 men excused from conscription for health reasons—health reasons?! On the way back down, check out the 20+ buildings Hitler built for his officers and foreign dignitaries. They include an architectural studio, an experimental farm, a VIP hotel, and housing for SS officers.

To get to the Kehlsteinhaus, take bus #9538 (direction: "Obersalzberg, Kehlstein) from the covered platform to the right of the train station to "Obersalzberg, Hintereck." (June-Oct. roughly every 45min.; off-season much less regularly. Check with the tourist office for schedules. Round-trip DM5.80.) At Hintereck, while you're waiting for bus #9549 to "Kehlstein Parkpl., Eagle's Nest," buy your dual ticket for both the second leg of the bus ride and the elevator ride you'll take at the other end. (Every 30min. 9:30am-4pm. DM20, with Kurkarte DM19; children DM13, DM12.) At Kehlstein, reserve your spot on a return bus (we mean it) at the booth when you get off. Reserving a place on a bus leaving one hour after the time of your Kehlstein arrival will give you enough time to explore the mountaintop if you don't plan to stop for lunch at the summit. (Buses return to Hintereck every 30min., last one at 5:05pm.) From the parking lot, go through the tunnel and take the elevator to the Kehlsteinhaus. The elevator's golden mirrors are original, installed to quell Hitler's claustrophobia. Pack a jacket for the cool weather on the peak. A short English-language **tour** of the Eagle's Nest departs daily at 10:30 and 11:45am. (35min. DM6, children free. Meet at the tunnel entrance to the elevator.) To catch the 10:30 tour, take the 9:40am bus from the main post office to Kehlstein; for the 11:45 tour, hop the 10:40am bus. A 4-hour English-language tour must be reserved one day in advance from **Berchtesgaden Mini Bus Tours** (tel. 649 71 or 621 72) in the tourist office. (DM52, under 13 DM25, under 6 free. Meet at the tourist office M-Sa at 1:30pm.) The Bavarian hills are alive with the sound of minibuses; the same company also operates *Sound of Music* tours. Join English-speaking tour guides on a walk through the old city of Salzburg, Austria and a bus tour of the locations used in the film *The Sound of Music*. On the return to Berchtesgaden, sit back, relax, and listen to the "real-life" tale of the von Trapp family. (4hr. DM45, children under 12 DM25, children under 6 free. Tours leave M-Sa 8:30am from the Berchtesgaden tourist office. Passports and reservations required.)

The Berchtesgaden **Schloß** (tel. 20 85) was a monastic priory until Bavarian rulers took over the area and appropriated the property. It now houses a collection of art and weaponry. Bear right from the station, through the overhang labeled *Zentrum* on the right, and go up the covered staircase. Cross over the train tracks on the footbridge behind the station and follow the *zum Markt* signs to Bahnhofweg. Follow Bahnhofweg to Maximilianstr. and continue straight ahead; veer right at the cylindrical yellow parking garage, veer left by Gasthof Triembacher and then veer no more—follow the signs around the corner to the Schloß. (Open Su-F 10am-noon and 2-4pm; Oct.-Easter M-F 10am-1pm and 2-5pm; last entry 4pm. DM7, with Kurkarte DM6, students DM3.50, under 16 DM3.)

■■ **HIKING AND ENTERTAINMENT.** Wedged into extraordinary Alpine cliffs, the **Königssee** calmly mirrors the landscape on its blue-green surface. The walk from Berchtesgaden winds through fields and over brooks, and provides a breathtaking view of the Alps. From the train station, cross the street, turn right, and take a quick left over the bridge. Walk past the green-roofed building and take a left onto the gravel path near the stone wall. Follow the "Königssee" signs for a 5.5 km walk. Alternatively, take bus #9541 from the bus station near the train station (DM6.80 round trip) or the touristy **Alpenexpress train,** which departs from the Alpenexpress sign across the street from the train station and over the bridge. (Every hour from 10:20am to 5:25 pm. DM8, under 16 DM6.) By foot, bus, or train, you'll end up in the Königssee parking lot. Walk straight down Seestr. and look to your left for the **Nationalpark Informationsstelle**, which provides hiking information. At the end of Seestr. is the Königssee dock and the **Bayerische Seen Schiffahrt** counter (tel. 96 36 18), which offers cruises to other points along the Königssee. (Boats operate 7:50am-5:30pm. DM22.50, under 14 DM11.50. DM2.20 discount before 9am.) The best lake view is from the **Malerwinkel** (Painter's Outlook), around to the left of the lake, while the best aerial view is from the 1170m peak serviced by the **Jenner cable car** (tel. 958 10). Take bus #9541 (direction: "Königssee") from the train station to the end of the line. (Open in summer 8am-5:30pm; in winter 9am-4:30pm. DM26.)

At the **Salzbergwerke** (salt mines; tel. 600 20) near town, visitors dress up in old miner's outfits, toboggan down snaking passages in the dark, and raft on a salt lake in mines that have been operating since 1517. From the station, take bus #9548 to "Salzbergwerke." (1-2 per hr, 8:37am-7:40pm; DM2) or make the 30-minute trek across Königsseer Str. from the tourist office, through the parking lot and onto the gravel trail that runs along the river and eventually becomes a sidewalk. The tour lasts an hour, but allow two hours for purchasing tickets, dressing up, and touring. (Open May to mid-Oct. daily 9am-5pm; mid-Oct. to April M-Sa 12:30-3:30pm. DM21, children under 11 DM11.) To go **moonlight rafting,** call the Berchtesgaden Outdoor Club, Ludwig-Ganghofer-Str. 20½ (tel. 50 01).

NEAR BERCHTESGADEN: RAMSAU

Hiding among the alps 20km southwest of Berchtesgaden is the tiny village of Ramsau, a center for hikers, white-water kayakers, cyclists, and skiers. Dominated by the magnificent, snow-capped Waltzmann and Hochkalter mountains, Ramsau provides an ideal starting point for walks and mountain hikes in the **Berchtesgaden National Park.** In the winter, knicker-clad tourists take advantage of cross-country ski trails, sled runs, and ice skating on the Hintersee. The 16th-century **Pfarrkirche** (parish church), Im Tal 82 (tel. 988 60), dwells on a hill a couple sheep pastures down the road from the tourist office. To clear your sinuses, follow the white gravel-lined path across the road from the church to the **Kleingradierwerk Ramsau,** a small "outdoor brine inhalatorium" constructed out of hundreds of branches of mountain briar bushes. Even if your pains don't subside, a soothing 15 minutes of cool tranquility will dispel your hiking aches. Past the inhalatorium along a pebbly path is the **Kneippanlage**, a mountain stream wading pool built by a local doctor to improve circulation. The ice-cold water can prep feet for a day in the sun or cool them after hiking long trails. (Always open. Free.)

From Ramsau, a vast network of well-marked hiking trails radiates throughout the surrounding Alpine landscape. One short but excellent hike leads from the center of town, following the Ramsauer Ache, through the **Zauberwald** (magical forest) to the sparkling green **Hintersee**. Hitch up your *Lederhosen* and follow Im Tal from the tourist office past the Pfarrkirche, taking a left on Fendtenweg by Café Brotzeitstation. Cross the narrow foot bridge and, keeping the river on your right, follow the white-gravel trail to the Zauberwald and then on to the Hintersee. Weary legs make the return trip back to Ramsau by bus #9546 from Hintersee's bus station. (10min.; 1-2 per hour DM3.25.)

Ramsau can be reached by bus, bike, or foot from Berchtesgaden. Bus #9546 runs hourly from the Berchtesgaden bus station, to the right of the train station. (15min. DM3.80 one-way, DM6.50 round-trip.) Rent **mountain bikes** at **Sport Brandner,** Im Tal 64. (Tel. 790. Open M-F 9am-noon and 2-6pm, Sa 9am-noon. DM25 per day.) The friendly staff at the Ramsau **tourist office,** Im Tal 2 (tel. 98 89 20; fax 772), will shower you with trail maps and hiking information, and books rooms for free. (Open M-F 8am-noon and 1:15-5pm, Sa 9am-noon.) **Exchange money** and traveler's checks at **Raiffeisenbank,** Im Tal 89. (Tel. 390. Open M-Tu and Th-F 8:30am-noon and 2-4:30pm, W 8:30am-noon and 2-3:30pm. 24hr. **ATM.**) The **post office,** Im Tal 87, 83486 Ramsau (tel. 275), is across from Gasthof Oberwirt. (Open M-F 8am-12:30pm and 2:30-6:30pm, Sa 8am-12:30pm.) The **telephone code** is 08657.

Although there is no youth hostel, Ramsau sports a wide selection of fairly inexpensive *Pensionen* and *Gästehäuser*. (DM20-40, breakfast usually included.) **Gästehaus Marxen,** Hinterseer Str. 22 (tel. 213), is a quiet, friendly cottage two minutes from the "Marxenbrücke" bus stop. (DM23-28. Breakfast included.) **Campingplatz Simonhof,** Am Taubensee 19 (tel. 284), basks in a beautiful location on the Lattenbach river five minutes from the "Taubensee" bus stop. (DM8, cars DM9, children 3-16 DM4.) The colorful **Café Waldquelle,** Im Tal 62 (tel.291), offers seating on an outdoor patio with great opportunities for people-watching. Slurp down homemade buttermilk or fill up on bratwurst with sauerkraut and potatoes. (Open M-W and F-Su 11:30am-8pm. Most meals DM4-14.) Buy **groceries** at the **Edeka,** Im Tal 60. (Open M-F 8am-noon and 2:30-6pm, Sa 8am-noon.) The **Bäckerei-Konditorei,** Im Tal 3, sells fresh bread and pastries. (Open M-F 6:30-noon and 2-6pm, Sa 6:30-noon.) The **telephone code** is 08657.

BAD REICHENHALL

In Bad Reichenhall, it is considered vital to sit in front of a salt water fountain daily, cover oneself in mud, and then inhale oxygen from an intimidating apparatus. But even if you haven't come for the facials and cucumber eyepatches, the city's breathtaking views of the Austrian Alps and its "White Gold" (salt deposits) are just as pleasurable. The **Salzmuseum,** Alte Saline (tel. 70 02 51), is peppered with exhibits on the history and process of salt-making in the area. The obligatory tour in German winds through the damp underground passageways where brine (salt water) is pumped out of the mountain. (Tours April-Oct. daily 10, 11:30am, 2, and 4pm. DM8.50, with *Kurkarte* DM7, children 6-16 DM4.50.) At the museum's **Glashütte** (tel. 697 38), visitors experience the beauty of glass-blowing and glass-buying. (Tours M-F 9:30am-6pm, Sa 9am-1pm.) The **Glasofenwirtshaus** hosts a musical *Weißwurstfrühschoppen* (a Bavarian practice of getting plastered in the morning) every Saturday from 9am to 1pm. (Restaurant open M-F 9:30am-6pm, Sa 9am-1pm. Live music W-F 2:30-5pm.)

The center of the town's spa circuit is the palatial **Kurgarten.** From the train station, turn right and walk down Bahnhofstr. Take a left onto Kurstr. and continue until you reach the Kurgarten on the left. (Open April-Oct. daily 7am-10pm; Nov.-March 7am-6pm. Free.) The *Altes Kurhaus* in the garden offers a therapeutic blue theater, a music pavilion, and a chess set. At the salt spring fountain, buy a cup

(DM0.20) to drink from the *Trinksole* fountain. (Open M-Sa 8am-12:30pm and 3-5pm, Su 10am-12:30pm.) The 170m **Gradierwerk** out front is a bizarre wall known as an "open air inhalatorium." Built in 1912, it's covered with 250,000 *Dornbündel* (bundles of branches, briars, and thorns) through which salt-water mist trickles from April to October. For best results, sit and inhale for 30 minutes. The **Predigstuhl,** the oldest cable car of its kind in the world (1928), climbs 1614m of skiers' paradise. (1 per hour May-Sept. 9am-9pm; Oct.-April 9am-5pm. Round-trip DM24 if purchased at the tourist office, DM27 if purchased at the cable car. With *Kurkarte* DM26, under 16 DM12, under 6 free.)

Trains run to Munich (2½hr., 1 per hour, DM43) and Salzburg (20min., 1 per hour, DM7.60) with a change in Freilassing. Both trains and **buses** run to and from Berchtesgaden. (45min., 1 per hour, DM5.80.) Rent a **bike** at **Sport Müller,** Spitalgasse 3. (Tel. 37 76. Half-day rental DM12, full day DM15, children 20% off. Open M-F 9am-6:30pm, Sa 9am-1:30pm.) The **tourist office,** Wittelsbacherstr. 15 (tel. 606 303; fax 606 311), is to the right on the same road as the station, across from the Sparkasse bank. The staff provide maps and hiking tips. (Open M-F 8am-5:30pm, Sa 9am-noon.) **Club Aktiv** (tel. 672 38) offers **rafting** and **canyoning** tours. (DM60-85.) The **post office,** Bahnhofstr. 35, 83435 Bad Reichenhall, is to the right as you exit the station. (Open M-F 8am-5:30pm, Sa 8am-noon.) The **telephone code** is 08651.

There is no youth hostel in Bad Reichenhall and unfortunately most hotels are expensive. A small but very pleasant hotel is **Gästehaus Villa Fischer,** Adolf-Schmidt-Straße 4 (tel. 57 64), a short walk from the *Kurgarten.* (DM32-35. English and French spoken.) Endless cafes line the pedestrian zones of Salzburger Str. and Ludwigstr., where delectable *Mozartkugeln* (marzipan-and-chocolate balls) abound. At **Gasthof Bürgerbräu,** Waaggasse 2 (tel. 68 09), on Rathausplatz, traditionally dressed waiters serve local beer direct from the in-house brewery. (DM4.50 for 0.5L. Bavarian dishes run DM9.90-18.20. (Open daily 9am-11:30pm.) **Restaurant Fuchsbau,** Innsbrucker Str. 19, serves pizza (DM9-14) and Bavarian meals. (DM12.90-22.50. Open Tu-Su 7pm-3am.) For basics, head to the **grocery** store **HL Markt,** Bahnhofstr. 20, to the right of the station. (Open M-F 7am-8pm, Sa 7:30am-4pm.)

CHIEMSEE

For almost 2000 years, artists, architects, and musicians have chosen the Chiemsee as the setting for their masterpieces. With its picturesque islands, meadows, pastures, forests, marshland, and dramatic crescent of mountains, the region first lured the 9th-century builders of the **Fraueninsel cloisters.** Later, the eccentric King Ludwig II arrived to build **Königsschloß Herrenchiemsee,** his third and last fairy-tale castle, on the **Herreninsel.** The poet Maximilian Haushofer lived and died in **Prien,** and 11-year-old Mozart composed a mass in **Seeon** while on holiday. Most modern visitors to "The Bavarian Ocean" are artists of leisure; the area has been overrun by resorts and prices have risen. But don't expect to find many foreigners—Chiemsee is where the German *nouveaux riches* vacation. Prien, the largest lake town, offers easy access to the ski areas of the **Kampenwand,** the surrounding curtain of mountains, and to the resort paradises **Aschau** and **Sachrang.** For information on white-water **rafting,** call (08649) 243. Throughout the summer several **Trachtenfeste,** traditional festivals featuring parades, folklore, and pilgrimages, take place in different towns at the end of July and in mid-August; entrance fees run DM 5-7.

PRIEN AM CHIEMSEE

Without question, the best things about Prien are its idyllic Chiemsee coast and its highly frequented train station, which facilitates the use of the town as a base for sights elsewhere on the lake. To soothe that sore back, wade in the cold water of Prien's *Kneipp* water cure and then jump into a 90°F (32°C) thermal bath. Sitting on the Marktplatz is the canary yellow **Maria Himmelfahrt Church.** From the train station, take a right to Seestr. and walk left five minutes toward the steeple. The red-and-blue marble interior of the church boasts beautiful chandeliers and paintings. On the square behind the church rests the **Heimatmuseum.** With over 20 rooms decorated in 17th-century style, it houses enough clocks, fishing rods, and guns to fulfill any estate buyer's dreams. (Open April-Oct. Tu-F 10am-noon and 3-5pm, Sa 10am-noon, Nov.-March closed Sat.; DM3, students and children DM2.)

Located on the northwestern corner of the Chiemsee, Prien has **train** connections to Munich (1hr., 1 per hour, DM36) and Salzburg, Austria (40min., 1 per hour, DM26.40.) Call 28 74 for train information. Rent **bikes** at **Radsport Reischonböck,** Hochriesstr. 17 (tel. 46 31), 100m to your left after exiting the train station (DM12, open M-F 8am-12:30pm and 2-6pm, Sa 8am-noon), or hook up a set of **inline skates** from **Intersport Erhard,** Bernauer Str. 110 (tel. 626 57). Walk right out of the station, left onto Seestr., and left at the next intersection to Bernauer Str. (DM25 per day, knee and wrist pads included.) To paddle the Chiemsee, rent a **boat** from **Bootsverleih Stöffl** (tel. 20 00), at the red and white umbrella stand at the end of the footpath to the Chiemsee. (DM 17 per boat; open daily April-Oct.) The train station is a few blocks from the city center and a 20-minute walk north of the lake. To reach the Altstadt, turn right as you exit the station and then turn left on Seestr., which becomes Alte Rathausstr. The large, modern **tourist office,** Alte Rathausstr. 11 (tel. 690 50 or 69 05 55; fax 69 05 40), five minutes away on the left, is full of free maps and brochures, and books **private rooms** for free. (DM30-45 with breakfast. Office open M-F 8:30am-6pm, Sa 9am-noon.) Check out the **ticket booth** outside the train station for all your entertainment needs. (Open M-F 6:40am-7pm, Sa 8am-6pm, and Sun 8am-12:30pm and 1:20pm-6pm.) Putt around at **Minigolf Prien,** Seestr. 100 (DM 4.30, students DM4, children under 16 DM3), or dance the night away on the 3hr. **Chiemsee Schiffahrt river cruise** (tel. 690 50), leaving every Friday at 7:30pm from the Prien dock (DM25). Phone 10 37 to find out which **pharmacy** is open on any given night. The **telephone code** is 08051.

The cheapest bed in town is at the **Jugendherberge (HI),** Carl-Braun-Str. 66 (tel. 687 70; fax 68 77 15), a 15min. walk from the station and 10 min. from the lake. From the station, go right on Seestr. and under the train overpass. After two blocks, take a left on Staudenstr., which curves right and turns into Carl-Braun-Str. (6-bed rooms DM25. Showers, lockers, and breakfast included. Sheets DM5.50. Reception 8-9am, 5-7pm, and 9:30-10pm. Lockout 9am-1pm. Curfew 10pm. Open early Feb.-Nov.) An inexpensive hotel is **Pension Pellner,** Am Berg 11. From the train station, bear right onto Seestr. and walk about 10 min. Take another right on Jensenstr., walk for another 2 min. and take a left onto Am Berg. (DM30-36. Breakfast included. Open May-Oct.) **Campingplatz Hofbauer,** Bernauer Str. 110 (tel. 41 36; fax 626 57), is a 30min. stroll from the center of town. From the station, turn left at Seestr., left again at the next intersection, and follow Bernauer Str. out of town past the gas station and McDonald's. (DM10.50 per person, children 14 and under DM5.50, DM10 per tent and car. Showers included. Open April-Oct.) Most of the restaurants in Prien cater to the vacationing bourgeoisie. Try **Scherer SB Restaurant,** Alte Rathausstr. 1 (tel. 55 91), on the corner of Alte Rathausstr. and Bernauer Str. The self-serve restaurant cooks up hearty meals and filling salads. (DM9.50-23.50, daily specials DM6.90-8. Open M-F 9am-9pm, Sa 9am-3pm.) For a delicious Italian meal, descend into the green candlelight ambience of **La Piazza,** Seestr. 7 (tel. 56 52). The lively waitstaff serves savory pasta dishes (DM 11-13) and large, thin-crust pizzas (DM 9.80). Gather **groceries** from **HL Markt,** Seestr. 11 (open M-F 8am-8pm, Sa 8am-4pm.)

HERRENINSEL AND FRAUENINSEL

Ferries float across the waters of the Chiemsee from Prien to the **Herreninsel** (Gentlemen's Island), the **Fraueninsel** (Ladies' Island), and towns on the other side of the lake. (Roughly hourly departures from 6:40am-7:30pm. Round-trip to Herreninsel DM10, under 15 DM5; to Fraueninsel or to both islands DM12.50, under 15 DM6.) Both islands are now co-ed, although this wasn't always the case—a monastery on Herreninsel once complemented the still-extant nunnery on Fraueninsel in religious chastity and isolation. Supposedly, mischievous members of the cloth (of both sexes) met up on **Krautinsel** (Herb Island) and practiced the eyebrow-raising act of gardening; nowadays, the island remains uninhabited and unferried. For more information on passage to the islands, call Chiemsee-Schiffahrt (tel. 60 90). To get to the dock, hang a right from the Prien train station's main entrance and follow Seestr. for about 20 minutes. Alternatively, a slow 19th-century green steam train takes visitors from the train station to the dock roughly hourly; to get there, follow the *Chiemseebahn* sign. (Departs 9:40am-6:15pm. One-way DM3.50, round-trip DM5.50; children under 15 DM 1.50, DM 2.50. Total package, including train shuttle and ship passage, DM17.) The train station **information booth,** though central, has very limited hours. (Open July to mid-Sept. M-F 12:45-5:45pm.)

SCHLOSS HERRENCHIEMSEE

"Never can as unsuitable a location have been chosen for something as tasteless as this unfortunate copy of the palace at Versailles," Bavarian poet Ludwig Thomas pouted. Although some join Thomas in scowling at the Königsschloß's extravagance, year after year thousands of tourists faithfully flock to the Herreninsel to stroll the halls of this excessively furnished palace. To get to the palace from the ferry landing, either walk along the paved footpath (20min.) or take one of the horse-drawn carriages that run every 15 minutes. (DM4, children DM2.50.) The architecture of **Königsschloß Herrenchiemsee** (tel. 30 69) is fabulously overwrought as only King Ludwig II could manage. (Open April-Sept. daily 9am-5pm; Oct.-March10am-4pm. Admission and obligatory tour DM8, seniors, students, and disabled persons DM5, under 16 free with adult. German tours every 10min.; English tours 10:30 and 11:30am, 2, 3, and 4pm.) Ludwig bankrupted Bayern while building the palace, resulting in an odd juxtaposition of starkly barren rooms and the 20 overadorned chambers which were completed. The entire U-shaped palace is a shameless attempt to be larger, better, and more extravagant than Versailles. Ludwig II was so obsessed with the "Sun King" that he commissioned exact replicas of Versailles originals to grace the walls of his palace. There's even a **Hall of Mirrors,** only Ludwig's is longer than Louis's (hmm...); it took 25 people half an hour to light the more than 500 candles in this room when Ludwig decided to tour his palace. Candle-lit concerts are hosted here throughout the summer. For a more supernatural glow, check out the purple nightlight Ludwig had installed in his bedroom to mitigate his fear of the dark. None of Ludwig's other castles so well reflect his obsessive qualities or his relentless insistence on creating an alternate reality. A **museum** documenting Ludwig's life lies just inside the castle entrance. (Open April-Sept. 9am-5pm; Oct.-March 10am-4pm. DM4, students DM2.) For Herrenchiemsee **tourist information,** call (08051) 30 69.

THE WOEFUL DECLINE OF THE ß The story of the ess-tset ("ß") begins hundreds of years ago with the Goths, who devised a letter that efficiently did the work of a cumbersome double S with only one stroke, freeing more time for pillage and plunder. As time passed, the letter gained fame and renown, featuring prominently in the works of Goethe and Schiller. Yet the ess-tset may soon be a fugitive in its own land. It is only the most visible victim of a recent series of planned language and spelling reforms concocted by representatives of all the German-speaking states of Europe as "a systematic dismantling of anomalies." Other reforms standardize and Germanize the spelling of assimilated foreign words and other eclectically spelled words. Thus far, opposition in Germany has been vocal; in a recent referendum, voters in Schleswig-Holstein soundly rejected the proposed changes. In Austria, however, all systems still appear to go for the switch, and *Kinder* are already learning to spell ketchup *"ketschup."* If the ess-tset is exterminated as planned, there will be no way of knowing whether somebody is drinking within limits *(in Maßen)* or excessively *(in Massen)*—so why not opt for the latter?

FRAUENINSEL

Despite its proximity to Ludwig's material world, the Fraueninsel is no material girl. In fact, it's quite the opposite: a small realm of hard-working nuns and fishermen that shuns the most material of all possessions—the automobile; only footpaths wind through this subdued village. From the dock, a marked path curls toward the **island cloister,** passing its medicinal herb garden. (Open mid-June to Sept. daily 11am-6pm; Oct. to mid-June M-Sa 11am-6pm. DM4, students DM1.50.) The nuns make their own marzipan, beeswax candles, and five kinds of liqueurs, for sale in the convent shop. (0.2L *Klosterlikör* DM8.50.) The abbey dates back to at least 866. St. Irmengard, the great-granddaughter of Charlemagne and earliest known abbess of the cloister, is memorialized in a **chapel** behind the main altar. Her sarcophagus was exhumed in the 17th century, and in 1928 her remains were encased in glass within the altar. They're not much to look at—that's what 1,000 years will do to you. More interesting are the countless messages written to Irmengard on the opposite wall in thanks for deliverance after prayer. The **Torhalle** (gate) is the oldest surviving part of the cloister; various artifacts, including the 8th-century Merovingian **Cross of Bischofhofen,** are displayed in the room above the gate. The entire island can be circumnavigated on foot in 45 minutes. There are quite a few *Gaststätte* scattered all over the island, but prices are high because owners know they have hungry tourists trapped. Bring some food or be prepared to splurge. If you are stranded and starving, try the food store next to the post office on the right sight of the island when you step off of the ferry. For **tourist information,** call (08054) 511 or 603, or fax 12 72.

ELSEWHERE NEAR THE CHIEMSEE

While Prien is considered the "metropolis of the Bavarian sea," countless other idyllic towns melt into the landscape, offering resort luxuries, nature hikes, and historical attractions. **Übersee,** a playground for bikers, sailors, and windsurfers, lies on the Chiemsee just past Prien on the Munich-Salzburg train line. Contact their **tourist office.** (Tel. (08642) 89 89 50; fax 621 14.) Just northwest of the Chiemsee lies **Bad Endorf,** famed for its thermal baths and popular with older Germans; call the *Kurverwaltung* for more information. (Tel. (08053) 30 08 22; fax 30 08 30.) Bad Endorf also has a **hostel (HI)** (tel. (08053) 509; fax 32 92) located 3km from the train station on Rankhamer Weg 11. Take a left onto Bahnhofstr. when you leave the train station and walk until you hit Traunsteiner Str.; go right and walk to Hauptstr., take a left and walk to Lederer Bergstr.; the *Jugendherberge* sign will be down on your left. The hostel is quiet, cheery, and cheap. (DM16.50. Closed Dec.-early Feb.) Little villages curl up at the foothills of the mountains: **Grassau Verkehrsamt** (tel. (08641) 23 40; fax 40 08 41), **Rimsting Verkehrsamt** (tel. (08051) 44 61; fax 616 94), and **Riedering Verkehrsamt** (tel. (08036) 34 48; fax 37 58) can supply more information. **Rottau,** just south of the Chiemsee, nestles in a mountain ridge; call its **Verkehrsamt,** at Grassauer Str. 9. (Tel. (08641) 27 73; fax 14 19.)

  Aschau, a beautiful mountain town southwest of the Chiemsee, offers everything from horseback riding to mountain gondola rides, as well as solaria, tobogganing, skiing, and sailing. Head first to the **tourist office,** Kampenwandstr. 38. (Tel. (08052) 90 49 37; fax 90 49 45.) From the train station, take a left on Bahnhofstr., which turns into Kampenwandstr. (Open May to mid-Oct. M-F 8am-noon and 2-6pm, Sa 9am-noon, Su 10am-noon; mid-Oct. to April M-F 8am-noon and 1:30-5pm.) The office is located in the middle of a small pond in front of the **Kurpark,** where weekly summer concerts are held. Ten minutes down Kampenwandstr. sits **Schloß Hohenaschau,** built atop Burg Hohenaschau as the erstwhile outlook and protection point for the Prien Valley in the 12th century. (Required tours given May-Sept. Tu-Fr at 9:30, 10:30, and 11:30am; April and October Th at 9:30, 10:30, and 11:30am.) Accommodations can be found down the street from the tourist office at **Gästehaus Kirchlechner,** Kampenwandstr. 30. (Tel. (08052) 761. DM27-30 per person. Three night minimum.) Most restaurants in Aschau are expensive, but **Penny Markt**, Kampenwandstr. 22 offers a medium-size selection of your basic four food groups. (Open M-F 8:30am-7pm, Sa 8am-2pm.) Aschau is easily reached by **train** from the Munich-Salzburg route via Prien, and **buses** link Aschau to Munich.

To reach the tiny town of **Sachrang**, an exquisite Alpine village on the Austrian border, take the bus from the stop in front of Aschau's train station. For more information on excellent skiing, mountain climbing, and walking tours, stop by the tourist office, **Sachrang Verkehrsamt**, Dorfstr. 20. (Tel. (08057) 378; fax 10 51. Open M-Tu and Th-F 8am-noon and 2-5pm, W 8am-noon, Sa 9am-noon.)

BURGHAUSEN

The proverbial castle-on-the-hill overshadows everything else in tiny Burghausen, a hamlet separated from Austria by the Salzach River. The town lies in the ice age sediment deposited from the Salzach glacier, which carved a deep valley into the surrounding cliff. In medieval times, the town was protected by the longest fortress in Europe, which continues to loom broodingly over the Altstadt.

🛈 ORIENTATION AND PRACTICAL INFORMATION. Burghausen is most easily reached by **train** from Munich (2hr., 1 per hour via Mühldorf until 8:30pm), and **buses** run from Mühldorf, the transportation hub of eastern Bayern. Stepping off the train, you'll find yourself smack in the middle of suburbia. Don't panic. One hundred meters to your left at the end of the parking lot is a city map. Follow Marktlerstr. (directly in front of you) to the right; it's a 30-minute hike to the Stadtplatz. Or take the bus on Marktlerstr. around the corner from the train station. It's four stops to "Stadtpl." (Every 30min. 8:12am-7pm; fewer on weekends. DM2.) For a **taxi**, call 22 33. The **tourist office**, Stadtpl. 112-114 (tel. 24 35; fax 88 71 55), is located in the peppermint green **Rathaus** at the far end of the Stadtplatz. (Open M-W and F 8am-noon and 1:30-5pm, Th 8am-noon and 1:30-6pm, Sa 10am-1pm.) To explore the Burghausen area by **boat,** join **Plättenfahrten** (tel. 24 35) on a 1½ hour tour down the Salzach River on an ancient open-air salt gondola. Tours leave from the dock at Tittmoning, 18km south of Burghausen, and land at the Salzach boat launching dock in Burghausen. (Tours leave May-Oct. daily at 2pm. DM12, children and disabled persons DM6.) The **post office,** In den Grüben 162, 84489 Burghausen, is one block down from the Rathaus. The **telephone code** is 08677.

📑 ACCOMMODATIONS AND FOOD. The **Jugendherberge Burghausen (HI)**, Kapuzinergasse 235 (tel. 41 87; fax 91 13 18), is a schlep from the train station but close to the café-heavy In den Grüben. From the station, take the city bus at Marktlerstr. through Stadtplatz to "Hl.-Geist-Spital." Walk straight and turn left onto Kapuzinergasse (45min.). Or from Stadtplatz, continue through the arch at the far side of the square onto In den Grüben. At the end, cross the intersection to the left of the church onto Spitalgasse and turn right onto Kapuzinergasse. The hostel offers immaculate, spacious four-bed dorms with private showers and an impressive view of the castle, and the staff speaks fluent English. (DM14, DM20 with a delicious breakfast. Sheets DM5.50. Reception M-F 8-10am and 5-7pm, Sa-Su 8-9am and 5-7pm.) If you're after Bavarian dishes, try **Hotel Post**, Stadtpl. 39 (tel. 30 43). After 450 years, it knows its *Würstchen*. (Most meals DM13.50-18, beer DM4.) For A-plus "I" cuisine, try **Taj Mahal,** In den Grüben 166, which serves a unique mix of Indian and Italian dishes. (Open Tu-Sa 11:30am-2pm and 5:30-11:30pm, Su 11:30am-11pm.) Buy **groceries** at **Edeka** on In den Grüben, across from the post office. (Open M-F 8am-6pm, Sa 7am-noon.)

🏰 SIGHTS. The 1034m **Burg,** the longest medieval fortress in Europe, was considered impregnable—and indeed, it was only breached once. In 1742, the Habsburg Empire, eager to extend its borders into Bayern, fell upon the border town of Burghausen. Cowed by the Austrian show of arms and lacking outside reinforcements, Burghausen opened its gates without a fight. Days later, on October 16,

1742, Burghausen's moment of glory came: the brash 26-year-old *Hofkaminkehrermeister* (Master Chimney Sweep) Karl Franz Cura recruited 40 grenadiers for the seemingly impossible task of breaking through the castle walls. In one fell swoop, Cura brilliantly freed the castle and the city. (Burg open April-Sept. M-F 9am-noon and 1-5pm; Oct.-March Tu-Su 9am-noon and 1-4pm. DM4, students DM2.) Burghausen remains a distinguished fortress town akin to Heidelberg and Rothenburg in its medieval glory, only much less trafficked.

These days, the **castle ramparts** can be walked without violent reprisals, and the town's **historical museum** (tel. 651 98) is in the upper halls. (Open May-Sept. daily 9am-6pm; mid-March to April and Oct.-Nov. 10am-4:30pm. DM2.50, children DM1.) For the price of lugging your picnic basket up the steep footpath, the castle offers a grassy park area with a ravishing view of the town's red-tiled roofs and colorful gables. The footpath starts behind the **St. Jakobskirche**, a 12th century church across from the Rathaus. The castle's eerie **torture chamber** (tel. 615 34) was used until 1918. (Open mid-March to Oct. daily 9am-6pm; Nov. to mid-March Sa-Su 9am-6pm. DM2.50, children DM1.) A peek out one of the upper story windows affords a view of the grassy banks of the Wöhrsee far below, a popular swimming hole in the hot summer months. The **Hexenturm** across the way held accused witches until 1751. Below the castle, the rows of pastel facades lining the **Stadtplatz** shimmer with such soft medieval splendor that you may suspect Burghausen to be a doll house city. At the far end of the Stadtplatz looms the magnificent Baroque **Studienkirche St. Joseph,** a 1630 Jesuit convent.

PASSAU

Baroque arches cast long shadows across the cobblestone alleyways of Passau, a 2000-year-old city situated at the confluence of the Danube, the Inn, and the Ilz Rivers. The heavily fortified medieval castle, musty Gothic Rathaus, and row of bishops' palaces bear witness to the fact that this *Dreiflüssestadt* (three-river city) was once a center both of secular and religious power. In 739, the Church awarded Passau the seat of a diocese. Centuries later the *Stephansdom*, originally a Gothic structure and rebuilt as a pink-columned Baroque cathedral after a destructive fire, inspired the construction of an offspring cathedral by the same name in Vienna. In the 13th century, enterprising local merchants monopolized the European salt trade—a very profitable achievement, given that people consumed six times more salt than they do today. Today *Eiscafés* and monasteries, shoe stores and art galleries line the streets of this ancient city.

▐ GETTING THERE AND GETTING AROUND

Trains: Station located west of downtown on Bahnhofstr. (tel. (0180) 599 66 33). Trains to Regensburg (1-2hr., every hr., DM32); Nürnberg (2hr., every 2hr., DM60); Munich (2hr., every hr., DM52); Frankfurt (4½hr., every 2 hr., DM74-131); and Vienna (3½hr., 1-2 per hour). The service point information counter at the train station has officials who will answer questions and provide information about train transportation. Open M-F 6am-9pm, Sa 7am-9pm. The ticket counter is open M-F 5:50am-7:25pm, Sa 5:50am-6:25pm, Su 7am-8:25pm. Dump your bags in **lockers** for DM2-4.

Buses: Service to various towns around Passau with a number of stops within the city. Single ticket DM2, 4 rides DM5, 8 rides DM9. For schedules call 56 02 72. The **City-Bus** runs from the station to the Rathaus. (M-F 6:30am-10:10pm, Sa 7:30am-4:15pm; every 10-30min.; DM0.50).

Ferries: Donau Schiffahrt (tel. 92 92 92) steamers chug along the Danube to **Linz,** Austria, May to Oct. daily at 9am (5hr.). To daytrip it, take the morning steamer to Linz and return to Passau by bus or train in the afternoon (round-trip bus DM46; train DM48). Or stay overnight in Linz and return with the steamer the next day at 2:15pm (returns to Passau at 8:40pm; round-trip DM42). The **"Three Rivers" tour** of the city runs daily March to Oct. (40min., on demand, 10am-4:30pm; DM11, under 15 DM5.50). For an

elegant evening of live music and dancing, take an **evening river cruise** among a coupled clientele on the *Tanzfahrten ab Passau* steamer (4¾hr., April-Oct. every Saturday
at 7pm; DM27). All ships depart from the docks along the Fritz-Schäffer-Promenade by
the Rathaus.

Bike Rental: At the Hauptbahnhof. Prices depend on whether you came to Passau by
train. The stunning **Donau Radweg** (bike path) begins in Donaueschingen and continues through Passau into Austria; ask at the tourist office for the *Raderlebnis zwischen
Donau, Inn & Salzach* brochure and for other cycling maps of the area.

◪ ORIENTATION AND PRACTICAL INFORMATION

To reach the city center from the train station, follow Bahnhofstr. to the right until
you reach **Ludwigsplatz.** Walk downhill across Ludwigsplatz to Ludwigstr., the
beginning of the pedestrian zone, which becomes Rindermarkt, Steinweg, and
finally Große Messergasse. Continuing straight onto Schustergasse when the
street ends, you will soon reach the **Altstadt;** hang a left on Schrottgasse and you'll
stumble upon the **Rathausplatz.** From there, a glance upwards yields a picturesque
view of the Danube and the steep hill, beyond which lies the **Schloß.** Heading farther east on the tip of the peninsula leads to the point where the three rivers converge. A little blue City-Bus bops around town (DM0.50); one stop is directly to the
right of the station as you exit.

Tourist Office: Tourist Information, Rathauspl. 3 (tel. 95 59 80; fax 351 07). On the
banks of the Danube next to the Rathaus (see directions above). Free brochures, schedules, and tour information as well as cycling maps and guides. The staff books rooms
for a DM5 fee and provides information on cheaper hotels and *Pensionen* in the surrounding area (DM35-60). *WasWannWo,* a free monthly guide, chronicles everything
going down in Passau. An **Automat** in front of the tourist office gives maps and a brochure (DM1). Office open April-Oct. M-F 8:30am-6pm, Sa-Su 10am-2pm; Nov.-March
M-Th 8:30am-5pm, F 8:30am-4pm. A smaller **branch,** directly across from the train station at Bahnhofstr. 36 (tel. 955 80; fax 572 98), has free maps and brochures stocked
outside in case you get into town after hours. Open mid-Oct. to Easter M-Th 9am-5pm,
F 9am-4pm, Sa-Su 10am-2pm.

Tours: German-language walking tours of the city (1hr.) meet at the *Königsdenkmal*
(monument) in front of the church at Domplatz. April-Oct. M-F 10:30am and 2:30pm,
Sa-Su 2:30pm. DM4.50, children DM2.

Budget Travel: ITO Reisebüro, Bahnhofstr. 28 (tel. 540 48), across the street from the
train station in the *Donau Passage,* a mall-type establishment. Open M-W and F 8am-
6pm, Th 9am-8pm, Sa 9am-4pm.

Currency Exchange: Take a right out of the train station down Bahnhofstr. until Ludwigsplatz; **Volksbank-Raiffeisenbank,** Ludwigspl. 1, cashes traveler's checks for a DM2 fee
per check. Open M-W and F 8am-noon and 1:15-4:15pm, Th 1:15-5pm.

Laundromat: Rent-Wash, Neuburger Str. 19. From Ludwigsplatz, walk up Dr.-Hans-
Kapfinger-Str. and bear left on Neuburger Str. Open daily 7am-midnight. Wash DM6,
soap DM1. Dry DM3. Fabric softener DM0.30.

Emergency: Tel. 110. **Police,** Nibelungenstr. 17. **Fire** and **Ambulance,** tel. 112.

Hospital: Klinikum Passau, Bischof-Pilgrim-Str. 1 (tel. 530 00).

Pharmacy: 24hr. service rotates among the city's pharmacies; check the listings in the
notices section of the daily newspapers, either the *Tagespresse* or the *Passauer Neue
Presse,* or in the window of the **Bahnhof Apotheke,** Bahnhofstr. 17, to the right of the
station. Open M-F 8am-6pm, Sa 9am-1pm.

Post Office: Bahnhofstr. 27 (tel. 50 50), 94032 Passau, to the right of the train station
as you exit. Changes money and cashes traveler's checks for DM6 per check. Open M-F
8am-6pm, Sa 8am-noon. Extra window open M-F 7am-6:30pm.

PHONE CODE	0851

ACCOMMODATIONS AND CAMPING

Most *pensions* run DM35-60, while vacation houses (2-6 beds) run DM30-75. The only youth hostel in town is usually swarming with German schoolchildren, especially during June and July.

Jugendherberge (HI), Veste Oberhaus 125 (tel. 413 51; fax 437 09), in the sentinel guard's living quarters above the main gate to the medieval castle perched high above the Danube. A 35-45min. walk from the train station and a 20-30min. uphill trek from the Rathaus. Cross the suspension bridge downstream from the Rathaus, then **ignore the misplaced sign** pointing up the steps straight ahead, instead continuing right along the curve, through the lefthand tunnel. (Skeptics who follow the signs will get there, too—they'll just pay an extra 20min. of steep hell for their disbelief.) On your left will be a steep (but more direct) cobblestone driveway leading up to the hostel; when the path forks take a left through the yellow house, then a right to the hostel. Or you can hop the shuttle *(Pendelbus)* from Rathausplatz bound for the museum adjacent to the hostel (Easter to mid.-Oct. every 30min. M-F 10:30am-5pm, Sa-Su 11:30am-6pm; DM3, round-trip DM4). The hostel has a fantastic location and is beautiful and clean, but the 8-bed rooms feel very cramped. DM22. Breakfast included. Sheets DM5.50. Reception 7-11:30am and 4-11:30pm. New arrivals after 4pm only. Curfew 11:30pm. Reservations recommended.

Rotel Inn (tel. 951 60; fax 951 61 00). From the train station, walk straight ahead down the steps, down Haissengaß 1, and through the tunnel to this outlandish hotel right on the river. Built in 1993 in the shape of a sleeping man to protest Europe's decade-long economic slumber, this self-proclaimed "Hotel of the Future" packs travelers into tight rooms bedecked with primary-color plastics. Inside, passionate graffiti depicts a monstrous Japanese auto industry trampling America and squashing Europe. Claustrophobes beware; each room has only three feet of walking space before your shins smash against the 4-by-8 foot wall-to-wall rug. Radios in every room. Singles DM30; doubles DM50. Breakfast DM8. 24hr. reception.

Pension Rößner, Bräugasse 19 (tel. 93 13 50; fax 931 35 55). From the Rathaus, walk downstream along the Danube. Right on the Danube, these homey rooms are among the cheapest in the Altstadt. Call upstairs if no one's at the reception. Singles DM60-85; doubles DM80-100. All rooms come with bath. Breakfast included.

Gasthof-Pension "Zur Brücke," Landrichterstr. 13 (tel. 434 75), on the Ilz river, 45min. from the *Rathaus;* from the *Veste Oberhaus* cross the Luitpoldbrücke bridge and continue right along the curve, through the left-hand tunnel. Follow Halser Str. to the right of the yellow house, which turns into Grafenleite, along the Ilz river for about 10min., then turn right on Pfarrer-Einberger-Weg and left on Pustetweg; take a right over the bridge and a quick right onto Landrichterstr. Even better, take bus #4 to "Hals." Quiet, sunny rooms are bargains for the idyllic location. Singles DM35; doubles with bath DM35 per person. Breakfast buffet included.

Camping: Zeltplatz Ilzstadt, Halser Str. 34 (tel. 414 57). Downhill from the youth hostel, 10min. from the Rathaus at a beautiful location on the riverbank. Walk down Halser Str. (see above) all the way to the riverbank; keep right when Halser Str. becomes Grafenleite. Or take buses #1, 2, 3, or 4 from Exerzierplatz. DM9, under 18 DM7, under 6 free. Showers included. Reception 5-10pm. No camping vehicles. Open May-Oct.

◖▣ FOOD AND NIGHTLIFE

The student district centers on **Innstraße** near the university. From Ludwigsplatz, head down Nikolastr. and turn right on Innstr., which runs parallel to the Inn River. The street is lined with good, cheap places to eat and, more important, drink; the night-time action kicks off as early as 7pm. **Tengelmann,** on Ludwigstr. at Grabengasse (open M-F 8am-8pm, Sa 7:30am-4pm), and **Spar,** Residenzpl. 13 (open M 7:30am-6:30pm, Tu-F 7:30am-6pm, Sa 7:30am-1pm), provide **supermarket** eats.

Mensa, Innstr. 29, offers cafeteria meals (DM2.40-4.50). From Ludwigsplatz, follow Niko-lastr., turn right onto Innstr., head under the bridge, and at #29 take the stairs up and turn right. Then head for the farthest entrance on the left (15min.). Or take bus #3 to "Universität" (every 20min. from Exerzierplatz). *Currywurst* with fries DM2.40. Salad buffet DM1.25 per 100 grams. Any student ID will do. Open M-F 11am-1:45pm, M-Th 5pm-6:30pm, F 5-6pm. The **Mensa-Café** upstairs (no ID required) is open M-Th 8am-4pm, F 8am-2:30pm during the semester.

🔲 **Café Kowalski,** Oberer Sand 1 (tel. 47 03). From Ludwigsplatz, walk down Nikolastr. toward the river; take a left on Gottfried-Schäffer-Str. and walk almost two blocks until you see the terrace on the left side of the street. Chic décor, a groovy bar, and a terrace with outdoor seating overlooking the Danube. Hordes of college students chill with ice cream specialties (DM5.80-8.50), funky drinks (DM4.50-6.90), fresh salads (DM12.80-14.80), and pasta (DM13.80-14.80) while they groove on Thursdays at the terrace party or to the omnipresent MTV. Open daily 10am-11pm.

Café Duft, Theresienstr. 22. Folksy indoor and outdoor café (make sure to visit the gar-den in back) with little lighted trees and an aquatic theme. Lip-smackin' fruit-topped yogurt (DM3.40) and breakfast combos (DM9-19). Soups hearty enough to be meals (DM5-6). Fantastic vegetarian options. Open M-F 9am-1am, Sa-Su 10am-1am. Kitchen open until 11pm.

Wirtshaus Bayerischer Löwe, Dr.-Hans-Kapfinger-Str. 3 (tel. 958 01 11). Authentic—or at least that's what the waves of tourists believe. For big German food and appetites, try their daily lunch specialty (DM9.90). Wolf down your soup or salad (DM6-10). Beer DM4-5.20. Open daily 9am-1am.

Ratskeller, Rathauspl. 2 (tel. 26 30). A bustling restaurant in the back of the Rathaus with picturesque outdoor seating overlooking the Danube. Salads DM4, main dishes DM11-29. Daily "local cuisine" specials DM8-17. Open daily 10am-11pm. Closed Su and M nights.

Innsteg Café Kneipe, Innstr. 13 (tel. 355 03), one block from Nikolastr. and popular with students from morning 'til night. Black-painted interior, and as inviting to Mozart devo-tees as to body-pierced revolutionaries. Nurse a beer (*Maß* DM7.80) on the balcony over the riverbank. Daily menu DM5-21. Salads DM5-17. Open daily 10am-1am.

Camera, Frauengasse 34320, around the corner from the McDonald's on Ludwigsplatz. The city center's grooviest dance lair's stark black exterior foreshadows an underground pit of student angst and inebriation. Beer DM4.50-5.50. Open daily 10pm-3am, week-ends and holidays until 4 am. Live music every Tuesday during spring, early summer, and fall; otherwise, get down to house oldies and chart music.

👁 SIGHTS

STEPHANSDOM. Passau's beautiful Baroque architecture reaches its zenith at this sublime cathedral. *(Open M-Sa 8am-11am and 12:30-6pm. Free.)* Hundreds of cherubs, sprawled across the ceiling, purse their lips as the **world's largest church organ** stands erect above the choir. Its 17,774 pipes can accommodate five organists at once. *(Organ concerts May-Oct. M-Sa noon. DM4, students and seniors DM2. Th at 7:30pm. DM10, students and seniors DM5. No concerts on holidays.)*

ALTSTADT. Behind the cathedral is the **Residenzplatz,** lined with former patrician dwellings, as well as the **Residenz,** erstwhile home of Passau's bishops. The **Dom-schatz** (cathedral treasury) within the *Residenz* houses an extravagant collection of gold and tapestries purchased by the bishops with the wealth they tithed from their flocks in the 12th through 16th centuries. *(Open May-Oct. M-Sa 10am-4pm. DM2, students and children DM1.)* Tours of the cathedral (in German) are given daily. *(May-Oct. M-F at 12:30pm, meet in front of the side aisle; Jan.-April and Nov.-Dec. M-F at noon, meet underneath the main organ. DM2.)*

Nearby stands the Baroque church of **St. Michael,** built and gilded by the Jesuits. *(Open Feb. and April-Oct. Tu-Su 9am-5pm; Nov.-Jan. and March 10am-4pm. DM3, students DM1.50.)* The less opulent, 13th-century Gothic **Rathaus** was appropriated from a wealthy merchant in 1298 to house the city government. *(Open April-Oct. and Christmas-time 10am-4pm. DM2, students DM1.)* The *Trunksaal* (Great Hall) is a masterpiece showcasing rich, wooden paneling and dark marble. In the heart of the Altstadt, bright, arched skylights shelter the **Museum Moderner Kunst,** Bräugasse 17 *(Tel. 383 87 90. Open Tu-Su 10am-6pm, Th until 8pm. DM10, students and children DM6.)* The renowned **Passauer Glasmuseum** (tel. 350 71), next to the Rathaus in the Wilder Mann Hotel, houses 30,000 pieces of glass documenting the last 300 years of glassmaking. *(Open daily 10am-4pm. DM5, students DM3, children under 10 free.)*

VESTE OBERHAUS. Over the Luitpoldbrücke bridge, across the river and up the footpath is the former palace of the bishopric. *(Open early April-Oct. Tu-Su 9am-5pm.)* Once a place of refuge for the bishop and a prison for various enemies of the cloth, the stronghold now contains the **Cultural History Museum,** whose 54 rooms of art and artifacts span the last 2000 years. *(Tel. 49 33 50. The same bus that goes to the hostel (see above) also stops in front of the Veste Oberhaus. Every 30min. from the Rathausplatz; last bus leaves the Oberhaus at 5:15pm. Open Tu-F 9am-5pm, Sa-Su 10am-6pm. Closed Feb. DM7, students DM4.)*

LANDSHUT

Residents of Landshut are quick to point out that the House of Wittelsbach did not always call Munich or any of the *Königsschlößer* home. Landshut served as the main seat of government for Max and Ludwig's ancestors until 1255, and even after that it remained the capital of Lower Bayern. Less than an hour away by train from Munich, the city straddles the swiftly moving Isar. Red-roofed houses, flower gardens, and pedestrian walkways frame the wide river, which is a popular stomping ground for cyclists, dog walkers, and landscape artists. The city frolics with style during the **Landshuter Hochzeit,** a three-week medieval orgy with authentic (read: excessive) feasting, jousting, dancing, and period plays. First celebrated in 1475 and resurrected in 1903, the festival, re-enacting the magnificent *Hochzeit* (wedding) that Duke Ludwig arranged for his son Georg and his bride Hedwig, takes place every four years. Modern-day knights and ladies will put on their best boots and wedding dresses, respectively, from June 29 to July 20 in 2001; information and tickets are available from the tourist office.

⚑ ORIENTATION AND PRACTICAL INFORMATION. Landshut is best reached by **train** from Munich (45min., 2-3 per hour, DM19.50), Regensburg (45min., 2 per hour, DM14), or Passau (1½hr., 1 per hour). From the station, it's a 25-minute walk into town. Walk straight on Luitpoldstr. for about 10 minutes; follow the curve left and cross the bridge. Go through the town gates to your left, then continue straight ahead on Theaterstr.; turn left on Altstadtstr. and the Rathaus will be ahead on the right. Or use **public transportation;** all buses that stop at the station run to the center of town (one-way DM2; day card DM2.70). Purchase tickets from the bus driver. The **tourist office** *(Verkehrsverein),* Altstadtstr. 315 (tel. 92 20 50; fax 892 75), in the Rathaus, has primitive city maps for free and better ones for DM2. There's no room-finding service, but they will provide a list of available rooms; prices plummet beyond the magical "20-minute radius" from the city center. Pick up the *Monatsprogramm,* a pamphlet listing all concerts, art shows, dances, and films showing in any given month. For the latest on the dance/disco scene in the Straubing/Landshut/Regensburg area, pick up a copy of *Bagpipes.* (Open M-F 9am-noon and 1:30-5pm, Sa 9am-noon.) **St. Michaels Apotheke,** Luitpoldstr. 58, lists on-call **pharmacies.** (Open M-Tu 8:30am-6:30pm, Th 8:30am-7pm, W and F 8:30am-6pm, Sa 8:30am-12:30pm, closed every day from 1-2pm for lunch.) The **post office,** 84028 Landshut, is just to the left of the station as you exit. (Open M-F 8am-6pm, Sa 8am-noon.) The **telephone code** is 0871.

⚐ ACCOMMODATIONS AND CAMPING. The **Jugendherberge (HI)** is at Richard-Schirrmann-Weg 6 (tel. 234 49; fax 27 49 47). From the tourist office, walk to the left up Altstadtstr. and turn left onto Alte Bergstr. at the "Burg Trausnitz" sign. Pass the stairs leading to the *Burg*, and a few steps farther on your right follow Richard-Schirrmann-Weg to the end. The elegant modern villa sits on quiet, green grounds overlooking the town and provides comfortable but simple four-bed dorm rooms with private showers. (DM18.50 with shower and toilet, DM15 without, doubles DM20. Breakfast included. Sheets DM5.50. Reception 8am-noon and 5-10pm. Closed Dec. 23-Jan. 7.) One of the more affordable places in town is the **Pfälzer Weinstube Heigl,** Herrngasse 385 (tel. 891 32; fax 67 01 56), in the city center. Walk right from the Rathaus and take the fourth right onto Herrngasse. The rooms are freshly painted, and the staff is polite and cheery. (Singles DM59, with bath DM69; doubles DM94, with bath DM104.) Halfway between the train station and the Altstadt, **Hotel Park Café,** Papierstr. 36 (tel. 693 39; fax 63 03 07), offers a friendly reception and the bare necessities of a room. From the station, walk straight on Luitpoldstr., take a left on Stethaimerstr., and a right onto Papierstr. (15min. Singles DM50-80, doubles DM130. Breakfast included.) **Campingplatz Landshut-Mitterwöhr,** Breslauer Str. 122 (tel. 533 66), is located just outside of town along the banks of the Isar. From the Rathaus walk right down Altstadtstr. and straight ahead over Heiliger-Geist-Brücke, then follow the sidewalk and gravel path directly to the right of the bridge along the river for about 20 minutes. At the second bridge, Adenauerbrücke, take the stairs up to the street and walk left down Adenauerstr.; turn right onto Breslauer Str. at the camping sign; the site is on your left. Minigolf, table tennis, and laundry machines are available. (DM9 per site; DM5 per tent; DM6 per person, children under 13 DM4. Showers DM1. Open April-Sept.)

⚑ FOOD. Café Cappuccino, Altstadtstr. 337 (tel. 270 92), right down the street from the Rathaus, has tasty daily specials (DM12.20), salads (DM7-14), pasta (DM12-13), and, of course, cappuccino (DM4. Open M-Th 9am-midnight, F-Sa 9am-1am, Su 2-11pm.) The more expensive **Wittman,** Alte Bergstr. 68 (tel. 253 37), off Alte Bergstr. to the right of the footpath to Burg Trausnitz, offers noodle soup (DM4) as well as three-course German meals (DM14.80-24.80) and beer (DM4.40). A fruit and vegetable market appears Monday through Thursday and Saturday mornings in the Altstadt, in front of the Rathaus (7am-noon), and Friday on Am alten Viehmarkt. **HL Markt,** Dreifaltigkeitspl. 177, provides **groceries.** (Open M-F 8am-8pm, Sa 7am-4pm.)

◉ SIGHTS. The Landshut Altstadt features rows of gabled Gothic and Baroque houses filled with glitzy shops and restaurants. The proud, greenish-beige **Rathaus** (tel. 88 12 15) stands at the center bearing Renaissance and neo-Gothic architectural facades. Fantastic murals inside the *Trunksaal* (main hall) upstairs depict Georg and Hedwig's wedding. (Open M-F 2-3pm. Free.) Across from the Rathaus stands the **Stadtresidenz,** the first Renaissance-style palace to be built in Germany (1533-37). Its gleaming white classical facade conceals a spacious courtyard with arcades of distinct Italian influence. The **museum** upstairs (tel. 92 41 10) offers a glimpse of gloriously decadent palace rooms from the 16th to the 18th century and also houses a regional collection of art with works from the 16th and 17th centuries. (45min. tours April-Sept. daily 9am-noon and 1-5pm, last tour 4:30pm; Oct.-March daily 9am-noon and 1-4pm, last tour 3:30pm. DM4, students DM3, children under 15 free.) Geometrically intriguing bricks zig-zag up the 130m spire of **St. Martinskirche,** the world's highest church tower of its kind. Inside check out the late-Gothic **Madonna and Child** elaborately carved by Hans Leinberger in 1518. (Open April-Sept. daily 7:30am-6:30pm; Oct.-March 7:30am-5pm.) Farther up Altstadtstr., a sign points to **Burg Trausnitz** (tel. 92 41 10). To the left and up the crooked brick stairway (5-10min.) sits the hefty brick and red-tiled fortress built in 1204. The hard, seemingly impenetrable exterior conceals a soft yellow courtyard with tiers of delicate arches. The castle was the luxurious abode of the Wittelsbacher princes of Bavaria-Landshut until 1503. The amusing *Narrentreppe* (fool's staircase) inside displays frescoed scenes from the famous Italian folk plays, the **Commedia dell'Arte.** The castle interior can only be seen with a German-language tour, but you can borrow an English translation of the guide's words. (Same times and tours as Stadtresidenz Museum. DM4, students and seniors DM3.) A free shuttle runs from the Burg to the Altstadt. (Sa-Su 1:20-6:50pm, every 30min.) The new **Skulpturenmuseum im Hofberg** (tel. 890 21) exhibits the modern sculptures and charcoal sketches of Fritz Koenig (1942-1997). (Open Tu-Su 10am-1pm and 2-5pm. DM6, students and children DM4.)

STRAUBING

Perched on the fringe of the Bayerischer Wald near the Danube, Straubing lets down its hair for the annual 10-day **Gäubodenvolksfest** (Aug. 11-21, 2000). The festival (what locals call the "Fifth Season"), which started as an agricultural fair in 1812 under King Max, has since evolved into a massive beer-guzzling phenomenon second in size only to Oktoberfest. Seven enormous beer tents welcome over a million revelers, who, after imbibing a few liters of the local brews, spend their week's earnings on a bevy of amusement park rides. Accompanying the *Volksfest* is the **Ostbayernschau** (East Bavaria Show), a regional trade and industry exhibition (read: more beer; Aug. 12-20, 2000). Both are held in "Am Hagen," the *Fest* area 10 minutes north of the Markt. When they aren't festing, Straubing's residents and visitors enjoy the city's striking architecture, colorful houses, and cobbled pedestrian zone, as well as its zoo, water park, museums, and churches. For information about hiking into the Bavarian Forest from Straubing, call the **Bayerischer Waldverein** (tel. 412 39).

⁊ ORIENTATION AND PRACTICAL INFORMATION. Straubing is easily reached by train from Regensburg (30min., 1-2 per hour, DM13), Passau (1 hr., 7 per day, DM20), Landshut (1 hr., 1-2 per hour, DM15), and Munich (2 per hour, DM37). The information counter (tel. (0180) 599 66 33) is at the **train station.** (Open M 5:30am-6:15pm, Tu-F 6am-6:15pm, Sa 7:30am-12:30pm, Su 9:45am-6:30pm). Rent **bikes** at **Bund Naturschutz,** Ludwigspl. 14, first floor. (Tel. 25 12. DM10 with a DM50 deposit. Open M-F 8am-5pm, Sa 9am-1pm.) The Altstadt lies northwest of the train station, five minutes away on foot. Cross the street in front of the station, and look left for the *Fußweg-Zentrum* sign that points you across a crosswalk and through a small park, at the end of which is another identical sign; follow it right down Bahnhofstr., through the pedestrian zone and the clock tower passage. The **tourist office,** Theresienpl. 20 (tel. 94 43 07; fax 94 41 03), is to the left outside the clock tower tunnel. The office has free maps and extensive brochures on Straubing and neighboring towns. (Open M-W and F 9am-5pm, Th 9am-6pm; May-Sept. also Sa 9am-noon.) A public rest room is in the small tunnel just to the left of the tourist office. The staff give German tours of the Altstadt. (1½hr. May 9-Oct. 3 W and Sa at 2pm. DM5, students and seniors DM3, under 6 free. Tours leave from the tourist office. English tours by appointment.) The city's **pharmacies** rotate 24-hour service; check the listing on the wall to the left of the window of the **Agnes-Bernauer-Apotheke,** Bahnhofstr. 16. (Tel. 806 75. Open M-F 8am-6pm, Sa 8am-noon.) The **post office,** Landshuter Str. 21, serves all your mail-type needs. Walk left out of the train station and take a left on Landshuter Str. (Open M-F 8:30am-6pm, Sa 8am-noon.)

⁊ ACCOMMODATIONS AND CAMPING. The **Jugendherberge (HI),** Friedhofstr. 12 (tel. 804 36; fax 120 94), is 15 minutes from the train station. Turn right from the front entrance of the station and follow the curve of Bahnhofsplatz left. Turn immediately right onto Schildhauerstr. as it turns into Äußere-Passauer-Str., by the "Passau" sign. A crosswalk and a *Jugendherberge* sign pointing left up Friedhofstr. follow; the hostel is on your right. The hostel features creaking hardwood floors, comfortable leather sofas in the hallways, and an affectionate house dog. Informality and cleanliness reign supreme. Doubles are available if you're lucky, but most rooms are 4-, 6-, or 8-beds. (DM16.50, over 27 DM21.50. Breakfast included. Sheets DM5.50. Reception 7-9am and 5-10pm. New arrivals after 5pm only. Lockout 9am-5pm. 10pm curfew, but keys available with DM10 deposit. Showers between 6-8am and 5-10pm. Open April-Oct.) Most hotels and *Pensionen* in Straubing begin at DM60; one small and tidy exception is **Weißes Rößl**, Landshuter Str. 65 (tel. 325 81). Walk left out of the train station and left again down Landshuter Str.; the building is on your left. (DM35 with shower. Breakfast included.) A **Campingplatz** is located at Wundermühlweg 9. (Tel. 897 94. DM15-DM40. Open May-Oct. 15.)

❖ FOOD. The restaurant in the **Hotel Bischershof**, Frauenhoferstr. 16, left out of the tourist office and another left down the third alleyway, serves salads (DM3-9), grill specialties (DM18-22), and super cheap beer (DM3.80-4.60). There's a *Biergarten* out back. (Open M-Sa 11am-2:30pm and 5:30pm-1am, Su 11am-1am.) **Metzgerei Königsbauer**, Ludwigspl. 6 (tel. 815 94), near the *Stadtturm*, serves a hefty lunch at its *Stehcafé* (standing café). Entrees are available for take-out, including *Wienerschnitzel*, *Wurst*, *Knödel*, and every other German meat specialty. (DM4-8. Open M-F 7:30am-6pm, Sa 7:30am-4pm.) Fresh fruits and vegetables are sold at the **market** on Ludwigsplatz. (Open M-Th and Sa 7am-1pm, F 7am-6pm.) A **farmer's market** is held on Saturdays on Theresienplatz. **Norma**, Bahnhofstr. 14, on the left as you walk into town, has cheap groceries. (Open M-F 8:30am-6pm, Sa 8am-1pm.)

☗ SIGHTS. The five-turreted Gothic **Stadtturm** (watchtower) in the middle of the market square is the city's symbol. (1hr. tours in German March 28-Oct. 25 Th at 2pm; Sa-Su at 10:30am. Th and Sa tours leave from the tourist office; Su tours leave from the entrance to the watchtower. DM5, students DM3, under 6 free.) Built in the 14th century, the teal-green structure with an inset gold figure of Mary splits the Marktplatz. The **St. Peter's** complex houses a medieval graveyard with wrought-iron crosses and gravestones from as far back as the 13th century, a Romanesque basilica from roughly 1180, and three Gothic chapels, including one with a red marble epitaph devoted to the memory of Agnes Bernauer (see below). Tours of St. Peter's depart from the tourist office. (1½hr. Su at 2pm, most summer and autumn weekends.) Tall, slender white columns and graceful sculptures of saints clothed in gold give the **Basilika St. Jakob**, Pfarrplatz 1a, a divine elegance. Two-story stained glass windows illustrating the Annunciation and the lives of the disciples shed a dusky color on the pews below. Throw in a sustained choral note and *voilà!*—enlightenment! The **Gäubodenmuseum**, Frauenhoferstr. 9 (tel. 818 11), houses exhibits from the early Bronze Age, as well as a collection of regional art and folklore. (Open Tu-Su 10am-4pm. DM4, under 19 DM3.) At the end of the street, turn right down Zollergasse and around to the late-Gothic **Karmelitenkirche**, Albrechtsgasse 21. Angels and disciples peer down from the lavish gold altar and stolid white column onto the church's stunning Baroque interior.

One block down on Burggasse, the **Ursulinenkirche** suffers behind an off-putting white stucco facade. Built from 1736 to 1741 by the renowned Asam brothers as their last joint endeavor, the interior exhibits all the opulent, overbearing kitsch of Rococo. Peach marble columns snake up to the ceiling, lavishly covered in flashy gold and fanatic frescoes. Down Fürstenstr. on the banks of the Danube, parts of the **Herzogsschloß** date from 1356. Most of the palace interior is closed to the public, its innards clogged with the cholesterol blockage of bureaucracy. A few renovated floors house a new **state museum** (tel. 211 14) with a rather bland exhibition of images of worship from the 17th to the 20th century. (Open April-Sept. Th-Su 10am-4pm. DM4, under 19 DM3.)

☗☗ ENTERTAINMENT AND NIGHTLIFE. For complete concert, live music, and club information, pick up the free magazine *in'said* at the tourist office or at local bars. Nocturnal activity oscillates between bad and disco. **Max**, Hebbelstr. 14 (tel. 34 31), hidden in the Gäubodenpark shopping complex, is the place to trot to techno, trance, rap, and funk. (Open W and F-Sa 10pm-3am. Cover DM10; beer

DM4.50.) From the train station, head left toward the post office. Follow the road to the left as it curves under the train overpass; the Gläuboden Park mall is ahead.

Straubing's enormous swimming pool complex, **AQUA-therm**, Wittelsbacherhöhe 50-52 (tel. 86 41 78 or 86 41 79), hosts an 80m waterslide, several massage parlors, an indoor pool, a steam sauna, and a warm salt-water pool. Follow the tunnel to the left of the *Bahnhof* down Landshuter Str. and turn right onto Dr.-Otto-Höchtl-Str., which becomes Wittelsbacherhöhe.; it's on the right. Or take bus #2 from Ludwigsplatz to "Aquatherm." (Open June-Aug.10 daily 8am-9pm; Aug. 11-Sept. 14 M-F 8am-8pm, Sa-Su 8am-7pm. DM5, after 5:30pm DM3; students, seniors, and under 16 DM2; under 6 free.) **Bowl** yourself over at **Keglerhalle am Sportzentrum Peterswöhrd** (tel. 802 48), 20 minutes from the center of town. Take a right out of the tourist office down Ludwigsplatz and then turn left on Stadtgraben; walk for five minutes. Take a right onto Donaugasse, then a quick left onto Uferstr., and after about ten minutes take a left onto Am Peterswöhrd.; the alley is on your right. (Open daily 10am-midnight.) Straubing is home to the only **zoo** in eastern Bavaria (tel. 212 77), with more than 1400 closely quartered animals and a large aquarium. From the tourist office walk right down Theresienplatz and follow the road as it becomes Regensburger Str.; continue for 20 minutes. Walk through the parking lot and follow the *Fußweg zum Tiergarten* sign. (Open March-Sept. 8:30am-7pm; Oct.-Feb. 9am-dark. DM8, students and children 6-18 DM5, children under 6 DM3.)

REGENSBURG

Located at the northernmost point of the Danube's passage to the Black Sea, Regensburg spills onto the islands engulfed by the sinuous river as it converges with the Regen. Originally a fortress built by Marcus Aurelius in AD 179, the city became the first capital of Bayern, then the seat of the Perpetual Imperial Diet (the parliament of the Holy Roman Empire; see **Worms**, p. 396), and finally the site of the first German parliament. The staid history makes for great sites, and it is students who now purchase a life for Regensburg, invading the beer gardens and bars tucked into the most remote corners of the Altstadt.

█ GETTING THERE AND GETTING AROUND

Trains: To Munich (1½hr., 1 per hour, DM38), Nürnberg (1-1½hr., 1-2 per hour, DM27), and Passau (1-1½hr., 1 per hour, DM32). Ticket office open M 5:30am-7:30pm, Tu-F 6am-7:30pm, Sa 6am-6:30pm, Su 7:30am-8:45pm.

Ferries: Regensburger Personenschiffahrt (tel. 553 59 or 553 59), on Thunerdorfstr. next to the Steinerne Brücke. The main ship of the fleet goes to Walhalla April-Oct. daily at 10:30am and 2pm. 45min. One-way DM11, children DM5, families DM26. Round-trip DM16, children DM7, families DM38.

Public Transportation: Routes and schedules of Regensburg's bus system are available at the *Presse & Buch* store in the train station (DM1). The transport hub is "Albertstr.," 1 block straight and to the right from the station. Single ride DM3.50. Buses run until about midnight.

Taxi: Tel. 194 10, 570 00 or 520 52.

Bike Rental: Rent a Bike by Bike Haus (tel. (0177) 831 12 34), in the left wing of the station. Open daily 9am-7pm. DM15-17 per day, children DM10.

█ ORIENTATION AND PRACTICAL INFORMATION

The Altstadt sprawls over a square-shaped cobblestoned mecca; the Danube is to the north, the train station and Bahnhofstr. to the south, Kumpfmühlerstr. to the west, and Maximilianstr. to the east. Maximilianstr. leads from the station into the heart of the city. The university lies behind the station in the opposite direction from the Danube.

BAYERN

TOURIST AND LOCAL SERVICES

Tourist Office: Rathauspl. (tel. 507 44 10; fax 507 44 19), in the Altes Rathaus. From the station, walk down Maximilianstr. to Grasgasse and take a left. Follow the street as it turns into Obermünsterstr., turn right at the end to Obere Bachgasse and follow it 5 blocks down Untere Bachgasse to Rathauspl. The office, to the left across the square, provides free maps and books **rooms** for a DM1.50 fee. Open M-F 8:30am-6pm, Sa 9am-4pm, Su 9:30am-2:30pm. From April-Oct. open on Su until 4pm.

Tours: 1½hr. English tours of the city depart from the tourist office May-Sept. W and Sa at 1:30pm. DM8, students DM4.

Lost and Found: At the Neues Rathaus (tel. 507 21 05).

Bookstore: Booox, Goldene-Bären-Str. 12 (tel. 56 70 14), entrance on Brückstr. near the Steinerne Brücke. Cluttered bookstore has tons of discount booox along with a 2nd-floor shelf of cheap classics (DM7). Ooopen M-F 9am-8pm, Sa 9am-4pm. The **university bookstore** (tel. 56 97 50) is on the main plaza of the university (see **Mensa,** p. 286), and has 3 shelves of English novels. Open M-F 8:30am-5pm.

Women's Resources: Frauengesundheitszentrum, Badstr. 6 (tel. 816 44). Open Tu 10am-1pm and 2-5pm, W 10am-1pm, Th 2-5pm.

EMERGENCY AND COMMUNICATIONS

Emergency: Tel. 110. **Police:** Minoritenweg (tel. 192 22). **Fire** and **Ambulance,** tel. 112.

Crisis Hotline: In case of rape or other trauma, contact **Caritas** (tel. 78 20).

Pharmacy: Maximilian-Apotheke, Maximilianstr. 29, 2 blocks from the train station, posts 24hr. emergency information to the left of the door. Open M-F 8:30am-6:30pm, Sa 8:30am-1pm.

Hospital: Evangelisches Krankenhaus, Obere Bachgasse (tel. 504 00), near the Thurn und Taxis Schloß, is the most centrally located.

Post Office: on Bahnhofstr., 93047 Regensburg, next door to the train station. Open M-F 8am-6pm, Sa 8am-12:30pm.

Internet: Internet Café, Am Römling 9 (tel. 599 97 02). Walk down Goldene-Bären-Str. away from the Steinerne Brücke and turn left on Am Römling. DM5 per 30min. Open Tu-Su 7pm-1am.

PHONE CODE	0941

◤ ACCOMMODATIONS AND CAMPING

Most of Regensburg's cheap lodgings are centrally located and fill up quickly in summer. Reserve, reserve, reserve. If the hotels and *Pensionen* are full, the tourist office might find a room in a private home. Otherwise, try the hotels in outlying parts of town—all are linked to the center by reliable bus service.

Jugendherberge (HI), Wöhrdstr. 60 (tel. 574 02; fax 524 11), on an island in the Danube. From the station, walk down Maximilianstr. to the end. Turn right at the *Apotheke* onto Pfluggasse and immediately left at the *Optik* sign on tiny Erhardigasse. At the end, take the steps down and walk left over the Eiserne Brücke, which becomes Wöhrdstr. on the other side. The hostel is on the right (25min.). Or take bus #3, 8, or 9 from the station to "Eisstadion." The hostel is a step ahead on the right. Carpeted, cray-ola-colored rooms. DM28. Breakfast and sheets included. Dinner DM9. Key deposit DM5.50. Reception 6am-11:30pm. 24hr. reception. Check-in until 1am. No curfew. Reservations encouraged. Partial wheelchair access.

Spitalgarten, St.-Katharinen-Platz 1 (tel./fax 847 74), inside a 13th-century hospital. Cross the Steinerne Brücke and go inside the gate to St. Katherinen on the left. Pass through another gate and go past the left side of the church. Or take bus #12 from the

BAYERN

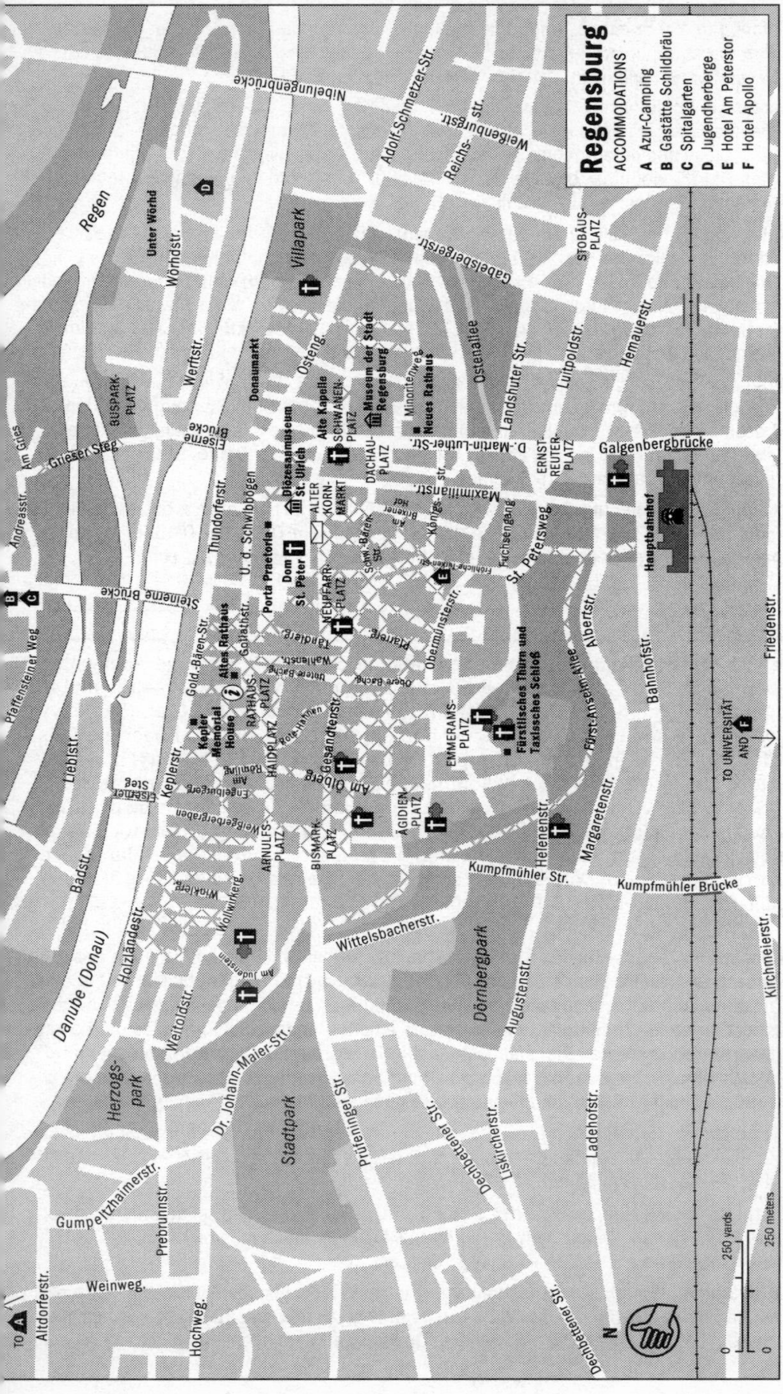

Regensburg
ACCOMMODATIONS
A Azur-Camping
B Gaststätte Schildbräu
C Spitalgarten
D Jugendherberge
E Hotel Am Peterstor
F Hotel Apollo
Regen
Danube (Donau)
Nibelungenbrücke
Steinerne Brücke
Eiserne Brücke
Griesersteg
Eiserner Steg
Unter Wöhrd
Villapark
Stadtpark
Dörnbergpark
Herzogspark
Ostenallee
Hauptbahnhof
Galgenbergbrücke
Kumpfmühler Brücke
Dom St. Peter
Porta Praetoria
Altes Rathaus
Kepler Memorial House
Diözesanmuseum St. Ulrich
Alte Kapelle
Museum der Stadt Regensburg
Neues Rathaus
Fürstliches Thurn und Taxissches Schloß
Donaumarkt
BUSPARKPLATZ
RATHAUSPLATZ
HAIDPLATZ
NEUPFARRPLATZ
ALTER KORNMARKT
SCHWANENPLATZ
DACHAUPLATZ
EMMERAMSPLATZ
ÄGIDIENPLATZ
BISMARKPLATZ
ARNULFSPLATZ
ERNST-REUTER-PLATZ
STOBÄUSPLATZ
D.-Martin-Luther-Str.
Maximilianstr.
St. Petersweg
Kumpfmühler Str.
Wittelsbacherstr.
Prüfeninger Str.
Dr. Johann-Maier-Str.
Gumpeltzhaimerstr.
Weinweg
Altdorferstr.
Hochweg
Prebrunnstr.
Liebigstr.
Badstr.
Holzländestr.
Weitoldstr.
Keplerstr.
Thundorferstr.
Landshuter Str.
Luitpoldstr.
Hemauerstr.
Bahnhofstr.
Friedenstr.
Kirchmeierstr.
Albertstr.
Margaretenstr.
Helenenstr.
Augustenstr.
Ladehofstr.
Liskircherstr.
Dechbettener Str.
Adolf-Schmetzer-Str.
Reichsstr.
Weißenburgstr.
Gabelsbergerstr.
Wöhrdstr.
Werftstr.
Osteng.
Andreasstr.
Am Gries
Pfaffensteiner Weg
Fürst-Anselm-Allee
Obermünsterstr.
Gesandtenstr.
Am Ölberg
Wollwirkerg.
Am Judenstein
TO UNIVERSITÄT AND F
TO A
250 yards
250 meters
N

BAYERN

station to "Stadtamhof." Head into the pink *Biergarten* and inquire about the *Pension* with the staff behind the counter. Singles DM40, doubles DM80. Breakfast included. Reception until midnight. Call, fax, or write well ahead.

Gaststätte Schildbräu, Stadtamhof 24 (tel. 857 24), is over the Steinerne Brücke; follow the street for 5min. and it's on the right. Or take bus #12 from the station to "Stadtamthof." Clean and orderly rooms, with bath and geraniums spilling from every window. Singles DM65, doubles DM110, triples DM150, quads DM190. Breakfast included. Reception 7:30am-midnight. Call ahead.

Hotel Apollo, Neuprüll 17 (tel. 910 50; fax 91 05 70). From the station, take bus #6 (direction: "Klinikum") to "Neuprüll" (15min.). Proximity to the university and the giant breakfast buffet make it worth the trip. Rooms have cable TV, radio, and phone, and hotel guests have access to a pool and sauna. Singles DM55, with shower DM70, with bath DM78; doubles DM99, with shower DM110, with bath DM140. Breakfast included. Reception M-Sa 6:30am-11pm.

Hotel Am Peterstor, Fröhliche-Türken-Str. 12 (tel. 545 45; fax 545 42), 5min. from the station. Head down Maximilianstr. and take the 2nd left onto St.-Peters-Weg, which becomes Fröhliche-Türken-Str. around the corner. Rooms are neat and simple, with bath and TV. Institutional, but fun anyway. Singles DM65, doubles DM75. Breakfast DM10. Reception 7-11am and 4-10:30pm.

Camping: Azur-Camping, Am Weinweg 40 (tel. 27 00 25). From station, bus #11 (direction: "Westbad") to "Westheim." DM10 per person. Tent DM7. Car DM6. Prices lower mid-Jan. to March and Sept. to mid-Dec. Reception 8am-1pm and 3-11pm.

🍴 FOOD

The 17th-century English dramatist and diplomat Sir George Etherege commented that Regensburg's "noble, serene air makes us hungry as hawks"—a laudable attempt to blame his swelling belly on the atmosphere rather than the heavy Bavarian fare and beer. A tantalizing number of cafés, bars, and beer gardens await to tempt the Imperial Diet. A plethora of **supermarkets** in the city, however, will mend the proverbial holes in your pockets: **Tengelmann,** Untere Brückgasse 2, on the way to the tourist office from the train station, is a good starting point for the makings of a lazy picnic. (Open M-F 8am-8pm, Sa 7:30am-4pm.) To stock up on fruit, vegetables, and other basics, head to the **market** on Dompl. (Open March-Oct. M-Sa 7am-6pm, Su 10:30am-6pm.) Otherwise, join the rest of Regensburg at a beer garden for a meal of *Würstchen*, pretzels, and of course, beer.

Mensa, on Albertus-Magnus-Str., in the park on the university campus. Take bus #6 (direction: "Klinikum") or #11 (direction: "Burgweinting") to "Universität Mensa," or turn right from the station and take the bridge over the tracks onto Galgenbergstr. Follow this street for about 20min. and take a right on Albertus-Magnus-Str. The stairs on the left lead up to the *Mensa*. The cheapest meal in Regensburg, with a lively student crowd. Meals DM3-6. Open M-Th 11:15am-1:45pm and 5-7pm, F 11:15am-1:45pm and 5-6:30pm. From Nov.-Feb. and May-July also open on Sa from 11:15am-1pm.

Hinterhaus, Rote-Hahnen-Gasse 2 (tel. 546 61), off Haidpl. down from Rathauspl. Crooked tables under dimly lit archways. Excellent vegetarian dishes and salads DM5-14. Open M-F 11am-1am, Sa-Su 6pm-1am.

Bistro Rosarium, Hoppestr. 3a (tel. 268 85). The gorgeous patio is set before the 7-hect-are Dörnbergpark. Surprisingly cheap for this location: lunch menu with drink is DM13, breakfasts start at DM7. Open daily 11am-1am.

Little Saigon, Dompl. 5. Nice indoor seating in central location ideal for taking out to picnic in one of the city's parks. Wide variety of vegetarian meals (DM9-11) and chicken dishes (DM13). English menu available. Open M-Sa 10am-midnight.

BEER GARDENS

Wurstküche, Thundorfer Str. (tel. 590 98), next to the Steinerne Brücke with a view of the river. A fun place to relax, sip a beer, and watch the ships drift by. The oldest operating fast food joint in Europe—the 12th-century workers who built the bridge broke for lunch here. Six small, delicious *Würste* from the smoky kitchen come with sauerkraut and bread (DM8.90). Open M-Sa 9am-6pm, Su 10am-6pm.

Goldene Ente, Badstr. 32 (tel. 854 55). Under magnificent chestnut trees on the banks of the Danube just across the Eiserner Steg footbridge, upstream from the Steinerne Brücke. The oldest inn in Regensburg; during the summer the beer garden is packed with well-pilsnered students. Steaks, *Würstchen,* and *Schnitzel* grilled at student-friendly prices (DM9-14). Open M-Sa 11am-2pm and 5pm-1am, Su 10am-1am.

Kneitinger Keller, Galgenbergstr. 18 (tel. 766 80), to the right from the station and over the tracks (10min.). Regensburg's largest beer garden, with 1,200 seats. Devoted locals, thirsty tourists, and intelligentsia-in-training alike follow their noses: the smell of beer has pervaded the entire area since the brewery was established in 1530. *Maß* DM7.80, six *Würstchen* with bread DM8.70. Open daily 9am-midnight.

🔎 SIGHTS

All-day museum passes admit bearers to the Reichstagsmuseum, Keplergedächt-nishaus, Stadtmuseum, and the town's modern art gallery; purchase them at the tourist office. (DM10, students and seniors DM5, families DM20.)

DOM ST. PETER

Cathedral tel. 597 10 02. Open April-Oct. daily 6:30am-6pm; Nov.-March 6:30am-5pm. Free. 1¾hr. tours May-Oct. M-Sa 10, 11am, and 2pm, Su noon and 2pm; Nov.-April M-Sa 11am, Su noon. DM4, students and children DM2. Museum tel. 516 88. Open April-Nov. Tu-Su 10am-5pm. DM3, students DM1.50, families DM7. Domschatz tel. 576 45. Open April-Nov. Tu-Sa 10am-5pm, Su noon-5pm; Dec.-March F-Sa 10am-4pm, Su noon-4pm. DM3, students DM1.50, families DM7. Ticket for Domschatz and Dom tour DM5. Wheelchair access to the Dom is via the cathedral's northern side, via the Eselturm.

The Domplatz provides a stable foundation for the soaring high-Gothic **Dom St. Peter** and the **Diözesanmuseum** adjacent to the church. Begun in 1276, the cathedral was finished in 1486, not counting the delicately carved 159m twin spires, which King Ludwig II added in characteristically grandiose style between 1859 and 1869. The collection of richly colored stained glass windows is dazzling. Inside the cathedral is the **Domschatz,** a priceless collection of gold and jewels purchased by the Regensburg bishops back in the days of indulgences and economic exploitation by the clergy.

PORTA PRAETORIA. A Roman gateway, the Porta Praetoria and ruins from its accompanying wall sketch a hazy outline of the city's original fortifications. They have been incorporated into a house located on Unter den Schwibbögen between the Dom and the Danube. One of the earliest documents of Regensburg's past is found on the front wall of the house—a flat foundation stone from the Roman fort of Castra Regina, inscribed in AD 179.

FÜRST THURN UND TAXIS SCHLOSS. Across from the station sits the Fürst Thurn und Taxis Schloß. Originally a Benedictine cloister, the 500-room compound has been the residence of the Prince of Thurn and Taxis since 1812; the new owners Baroque-ized the formerly Gothic buildings upon acquisition. The family earned their title from Kaiser Leopold I in 1695 in recognition of the booming postal business they had built. In recent times, with the nationalization of the post and the decline of nobility as a reliable profession, the royal family has fallen on hard times—hence the opening of the museum. In 1991, when the prince died, the princess had to sell the family jewels to pay the DM44million inheritance taxes. Luckily, the state bought the jewels and added them to the carriage museum in the castle to make the **Thurn und Taxis Museum.** 475 rooms of the private palace are still off-limits to the public, but the 25 other rooms are part of a tour that leaves from the main entrance. *(Tel. 504 81 33. Open M-F 11am-5pm, Sa-Su 10am-5pm. DM8, students DM6. Tours April-Oct. daily at 11am, 2, 3, and 4pm. Sa-Su additional tour at 10am; Nov.-March Sa-Su at 10 and 11am, 2 and 3pm.)*

WALHALLA. Down the river from Regensburg is Walhalla, an imitation Greek temple poised dramatically on the steep northern bank of the Danube. Ludwig I built the monument between 1830 and 1842 to honor Germans past and present whom he admired. Modeled after the Parthenon in Athens and named after the legendary resting place of Norse heroes, Walhalla stares imposingly down on the river as the boat from Regensburg approaches the dock (see p. 283). Ludwig called Walhalla "the child of my love." Hmm. The climb up the steep steps to the monument is tough going, but the view of the river and the opposite bank is stunning. In summer, the hallowed steps provide a lively evening hangout for students who venture here by bikes and car; probably not what poor Ludwig envisioned. Inside the monument are a series of busts of German leaders and military heroes, most of whom history left in oblivion. *(Tel. 96 16 80. Take bus #5 from the train station to "Donaustauf Wallhallastr." Open April-Sept. daily 9am-5:45pm; Oct. daily 9am-4:45pm; Nov.-March 10-11:45am and 1-4:45pm. DM3.)*

KEPLERGEDÄCHTNISHAUS. The iconoclastic astronomer and physicist Johannes Kepler died here of meningitis in 1630. Period furniture, portraits, and facsimiles of Kepler's work are on display. Up the street at Keplerstr. 2 is **Keplers Wohnhaus,** a colorful house where he hung his hat and spent time away from his gold-nosed patron and taskmaster, Tycho Brahe. It now houses a tanning salon.

ALTES RATHAUS. A few blocks away from the cathedral, the yellow Gothic town hall served as capital of the Holy Roman Empire until 1803. Four long iron rods are fastened on its side; these were the official measurement standards by which the merchants traded in the Middle Ages. The impotent Imperial Parliament, the first of many similar bodies in German history, lives on in the **Reichstagsmuseum** housed in the Rathaus. The differing heights of the chairs reflect the political hierarchy of the legislators. *(Tours in German April-Oct. every 30min. M-Sa 9:30am-noon and 2-4pm, Su 10am-noon and 2-4pm; Nov.-March tours hourly. English tours May-Sept. M-Sa at 3:15pm. DM5, students and seniors DM2.50.)*

◩ NIGHTLIFE

Many of the cafés and beer gardens listed above double as local nighttime haunts, and good bars raise inebriation to Walhallian heights. Ask at the tourist office for a free copy of *Logo* or *Stadtzeitung*—two monthly publications that list the liveliest events and addresses of the hippest bars and cafés in Regensburg.

Alte Mälzerei, Galgenbergstr. 20 (tel. 730 33 or for tickets 757 49). Regensburg's official cultural center is in an old malt factory that hosts a ramshackle bar with pop, jazz, funk, reggae, and blues. Beer DM4.20-4.90. Open daily 6pm-1am.

Wunderbar, Keplerstr. 11 (tel. 531 30). Young late-nighters pack into one of the only bars open after 1am, located just a few staggers from the Steinerne Brücke. Cocktails DM3. Open M-Th and Su 10pm-3am, F-Sa 9pm-3am.

Filmbühne, Hinter der Grieb 8 (tel. 579 26). Look for the staircase leading down within a green gate. Regensburg's funkiest scene attracts a diverse and bizarre crowd. Film posters and strange art are scattered everywhere. Open daily 9pm-1am.

Südhaus, Untere Bachgasse 8 (tel. 519 33). One of Regensburg's best discos. Tu "ultimate" alternative night; Th gay night. Beer DM5.50. Open M-Th 11pm-3am, F-Sa 11pm-4am. Cover M DM3, Tu-Th DM5, F-Sa DM6.

Scala, Gesandtenstr. 6 (tel. 522 93), in the Pustet-Passage between Rote-Hahnen-Gasse and Gesandtenstr. Fueled by 3 bars, hipsters work the dance floor all night long. Open W-Th and Su 11pm-3am, F-Sa 11pm-4am.

BAYERISCHER WALD (BAVARIAN FOREST)

A coddled national treasure, the Bayerischer Wald is the largest range of wooded mountains in central Europe. These 6000 square kilometers of peaks (60 of which are over 1000m high) and countless rivers and creeks stretch from the Danube to the Austrian and Czech borders to form a vast hook that lures hikers, campers, and cross-country skiers throughout the year. The **Naturpark Bayerischer Wald,** the first national park in Germany, strictly prohibits any activities that might alter the forest ecosystem—this includes camping and building fires outside of designated campgrounds. Clearly marked trails lace 8000 hectares (20,000 acres) of forest. You can trek it alone or sign up for free guided hiking tours, botanical tours, natural history tours, or tours of virgin woodlands. To sign up for one (at least a day in advance) or for information and schedules, contact the **Hans-Eisenmann-Haus,** Bömstr. 35, 94556 Neuschönau. (Tel. (08558) 961 50. Open daily Jan.-Oct. 9am-5pm.) For general information about the Bayerischer Wald, contact the **National-parkverwaltung Bayerischer Wald,** Freyunstr., 94481 Grafenau (tel. (08552) 960 00; fax 46 90). Pick up a copy of the forest newspaper *Informationsblatt Nationalpark Bayerischer Wald* for the latest news about the forest, or the free **encyclopedia** of the Bayerischer Wald, which is filled to the brim with phone numbers, maps, and listings. Both are available at any tourist office in the area.

The Bayerischer Wald is much more than just a verdant paradise; palaces, churches, and castle ruins are tucked away in tiny villages throughout the region. **Burgruine Hals,** an extensive castle ruin high on a woody cliff north of Passau, dates from the 12th century. The 18th-century **Wiesenfelden** gardens surround the ruins. For information contact the **tourist office,** 94344 Wiesenfelden. (Tel. (09966) 94 00 17.) **Frauenzell's** 15th-century Benedictine church is lavishly *barockisiert* and *funkisiert* (Baroquified and funkified), and parts of the **Annunciation Church** in **Cham** date from the 12th century.

The region is famous for its crafts, particularly **glass-blowing**. The glass produced here is prized (and dropped) throughout the world, particularly the dark green *Waldglas* (forest glass). Every little forest village seems to have its own *Glashütte*. For more information, contact the **Bergglashütte Weinfurter,** Ferienpark Geyersberg (tel. (08551) 60 66), in Freyung, or the **Freiherr von Poschinger Kristallglasfabrik,** Moosauhütte (tel. (09926) 940 10), in Frauenau.

The remoteness of the towns attracts few English-speaking visitors, but the park maintains a heavy flow of Germans seeking healthy, sedate vacations. Use the towns below as springboards from which to explore the nooks and crannies of this mountain region. An impressive 14 **HI youth hostels** dot the forest; Regensburg's tourist office (see p. 283) has a helpful brochure as well as current addresses.

ZWIESEL

The abundance of train connections running through Zwiesel makes it an excellent hub for scouting the heart of the Bayerischer Wald. A skier's paradise in the winter, in summer its focus flips to its 800-year history of glass-making, the modern-day incarnation of which is the production of postmodern wine glasses. Just north of town lies **Glas Park,** a village of glass-blowing houses that demonstrate to awed spectators how delicate fancies are created. Seven buses per day shuttle to the Glas Park from the Stadtplatz. (M-F beginning at 9:27am; last return at 6:37pm. DM 2.22.) The **Waldmuseum,** Stadtpl. 27 (tel. 608 88), behind the Rathaus, contains magical instruments and figurines and tells the tinkly tale of glass-making in the region. (Open May 15-Oct. 15 M-F 9am-5pm, Sa-Su 10am-noon and 2-4pm; Oct. 16-May 14 M-F 10am-noon and 2-5pm, Sa-Su 10am-noon. DM3, with *Kurkarte* DM2.50; disabled persons DM2, students DM1.) The **Spielzeugmuseum** (tel. 55 26), 20 meters behind the Waldmuseum, contains a large model train set, toys of all kinds, and teddy bears galore. (Open daily June-Aug. 9am-5pm, Sept.-May 10am-5pm.) For easy **hiking** near Zwiesel, head out of the Rathaus down Stadtplatz. Follow the street to the edge of the city and look for green *Fußwanderweg* signs on your left.

Trains run hourly from Plattling on the Nürnberg-Passau line (1hr., DM14.80). There is an information counter at the train station. (Open M 5:30am-12:10pm and 12:40-4:15pm, Tu-F 6:15am-12:10pm and 12:40-4:15pm, Sa 6:20am-12:40pm.) The **tourist office**, Stadtpl. 27 (tel. 84 05 23; fax 56 55), in the Rathaus, provides maps and hiking information and finds **private rooms** for free (DM25-90). From the station, turn right and walk downhill on Dr.-Schott-Str. After a few blocks, veer left onto Innenriederstr. and cross the bridge, then take a gentle left onto Stadtpl.; the Rathaus is on the left. (Open M-F 8:30am-5:30pm, Sa 10am-noon; Nov.-Dec. M-F 8:30am-5:30pm.) The **post office** is located at Dr.-Schott-Str. 55, 94227 Zwiesel. (Open M-F 8:30am-noon and 2-5:15pm, Sa 8:30-11am.) There is a large **wheelchair-accessible public telephone** booth directly in front of the post office. The **telephone code** is 09922.

The **Jugendherberge**, Hindenburgstr. 26 (tel. 10 61; fax 601 91), is a 30-minute walk from the station. Follow the directions to Stadtplatz, continue past the Rathaus, and turn right onto Frauenauer Str. Continue straight for 10 minutes and turn left on Hindenburgstr. (one block after the "AOK" sign); the hostel is just over the hill. Or take bus #1 from the station to "Jugendherberge" (DM2; 1 per hour). This clean hostel is the choicest accommodation in the Bayerischer Wald. *Klein aber fein* (tiny but shiny), repeats the proud hostel mother. (DM20. Spacious doubles available. Sheets DM5.50. Breakfast included. Reception daily 5-7pm. Curfew 10pm, but they'll give you a key.) For a quiet, small, inexpensive pension, try **Gästehaus Mühl** (tel. 18 21). From the train station walk left down Bahnhofstr. to the first intersection; take a left down Rabensteiner Str. and walk through the tunnel. Take the first left onto Badstr.; the house is on the left (10 min.). The inn features a common room with television and a balcony filled with flowers. (DM30. Breakfast included.) **Campingplatz TröpplKeller**, TröpplKeller 48 (tel. 17 09 or 603 91), is located on the Schwarzer Regen river, 2km from the center of town. From the train station, turn right and walk downhill on Dr.-Schott-Str. After a few blocks, right onto Schlachthofstr., then take another right onto Langdorfer Str. and walk about 800m to TröpplKeller on the left. (Campsite open year-round. DM8.50 plus DM1.50 *Kurtaxe*.)

The **Eiscafé-Pizzeria Rialto**, Stadtpl. 23, has outdoor seating on a busy street; feed the hungry beast with pizza (DM8-12.50), pasta (DM8-12), or an ice cream confection (DM6-11). Imbibe a beer (DM4) at the **Gasthaus MusicKantenKeller**, Stadtpl. 42, while feasting on a large bowl of goulash (DM8.50). Live music and dancing get the joint jivin' on the weekends. (Open M-Th and Su 9am-midnight, F-Sa 11am-1am.) **Lidl**, up the street from the tourist office at the intersection of Stadtplatz and Oberzwieselaner Str., is a convenient and extremely cheap supermarket. (Open M-F 8:30am-6pm, Sa 8am-1pm.) Amazingly enough, Zwiesel has an internet café! Walk right out of the Rathaus down Stadtplatz, which turns into Angerstr., and look for **Restaurant Piroschka;** the **Internet Treff**, Angerstr. 6 (tel. 62 54), is in the back. (DM1 per 6 minutes. Drinks DM4-8 and food DM8-12. Open M-Sa 11am-3pm and 6pm-1am.)

BODENMAIS

Bodenmais lies at the heart of the forest amid hills of velvet moss. The tourist-luring **Austen Glashütte** (tel. 70 06) on Bahnhofstr. across from the Rathaus, showcases and sells wine glasses, jewelry, and cheaper fragile trinkets. A skilled glass carver will engrave your name on every purchased item for free. You can view the glass being blown, then enjoy a local brew in a personally monogrammed souvenir *Stein* (DM3.90). **Hans und Hans'l,** two endearing Bavarians (complete with *Lederhosen*), sing and play the accordion on Fridays (1-5pm); please keep hands, feet, and objects to yourself. (*Glashütte* open M-F 9am-6pm, Sa 9am-4pm, Su 10am-4pm. Glass blown mid-May to mid-Oct. M-F 9am-noon and 1-6pm, Sa 9am-2pm, Su 10am-noon and 1-4pm; mid-Oct. to mid-May no glass blown on Sundays.)

Trains make the 20-minute journey between Zwiesel and Bodenmais roughly every hour (daily 6:25am-11:25pm to Bodenmais, 6am-10pm from Bodenmais; DM4.60). For a **taxi** call 484. Rent **bikes** at **Sport Weinberger,** Jahnstr. 20 (tel. 90 22 73), 10 minutes from the station left down Bahnhofstr. (Bikes DM25 per day. Inline skates DM15 per day with pads, DM10 without.) Arriving from Zwiesel, the **Wald-bahn** will drop you at the doorstep of the **tourist office,** Bahnhofstr. 56 (tel. 77 81 35; fax 77 81 50), in the modern Rathaus. The staff gives out a free book of accommodations and hiking trails, and offers a *Wanderpaß* (DM3) with tips and trails for hiking. (Open M-F 8am-6pm, Sa 9am-1pm, Su 9am-noon.) Outside the tourist office is an impressive information center with a free computerized room-finding service and a map of local alpine and nordic ski resorts. A public **fax** machine is located in the front of the tourist office lobby. The **post office,** Kötzinger Str. 25, 94249 Bodenmais, is a short walk from the station. Leaving the Rathaus, turn right on Bahnhofstr. and then veer right onto Kötzinger Str. (Open M-F 8:30am-noon and 2-5pm, Sa 8:30-11am.) The **telephone code** is 09924.

Bodenmais has 3,600 inhabitants and almost twice as many hotel beds. Even so, the town fills quickly in summer and winter; call ahead. The **Jugendherberge,** Am Kleinen Arber (tel. 281; fax 850), is 8km from town in the mountains, a whopping 1½-hour uphill hike through a very beautiful part of the forest. Follow Bahnhofstr. and turn right onto Scharebenstr. Hike up the narrow paved road for 15 minutes and then take a right on Gr. Arbor at the "Ortsverkehr Markt Bodenmais" bus stop. From there it's about an hour's climb—watch for the *Jugendherberge* signs. (Breakfast included. DM22.) For a small, bright, inexpensive room with a beautiful view of the entire town, head for **Pension Cornelia,** Scherau 22 (tel. 443). Exit left out of the train station on Bahnhofstr.; when the street curves right continue left onto Rißlochweg, then take a right on the steep Berggasse. Follow the sign pointing left to Scherau 22. (DM30. Breakfast included. Closed mid-Nov.-Dec. 25.) If you forgot your hiking boots at home, many of the private rooms and *Pensionen* in town are quite nice and fairly inexpensive (DM30-55). Try the 24hr. computerized room-finding service or attack the tourist office's accommodations booklet with gusto. The **Schmanterl Metzgerei Grillstube,** Bahnhofstr. 21, on the corner of Bergknappstr., serves *Leberkäs* with potato salad (DM8.90), *CurryWurst,* and fries. (Open M-F 7am-6pm.) **Dorf Stadt,** Bahnhofstr. 57 (tel. 74 03), cooks up Bavarian dishes (DM10.50-19.50) and vegetarian selections (DM12.50-14.50) to the tune of live, traditional music beginning at 8pm. Take a right down the street from the train station. (Open 11am until people are boogied out.) The **Penny Markt,** Bahnhofstr. 70, has cheap **groceries.** (Open M-F 8:30am-10pm, Sa 8am-4pm.)

REGEN

A nine-minute train trip from Zwiesel (1 train per hour, DM3), Regen offers a well-designed **Landwirtschaftsmuseum,** Schulgasse 2 (tel. 57 10 or 72 05). Displays of photos, tools, and a film present the history, farming, and development of the area. (Open daily 10am-5pm. DM3, children DM2.) The museum is adjacent to the **tourist office** (tel. 29 29) where the English-speaking staff boggles the mind with brochures. Head left out of the train station and take a left at the first stoplight on Bahnhofstr. At the next stoplight take a right over Ludwigsbrücke onto the Stadtplatz. Walk diagonally across the Platz and up the steps to the right of the Rathaus. (Open M-F 8am-5pm, Sa-Su and holidays 10am-5pm.) Regen also offers a calming **Kurgarten** with bizarre modern sculpture and fountains—turn into the park from Bahnhofstr., before the Ludwigsbrücke. The **Restaurant am Rathaus,** Stadtplatz 3 (tel. 22 20), directly downstairs and to the right of the tourist office, serves savory Bavarian cuisine (DM8-20) and offers a complete vegetarian menu (DM8-14), beer (DM4.50-5.50), and ice cream creations (DM5-8.50) in a large, relaxed space decorated with trophies and an assortment of liquor bottles. In case you haven't picked up on the differences between standard German and Bavarian dialect, they've spelled it out for you in chart form on the napkins. (Open daily 11am-9pm.) The **telephone code** is 09921.

B A Y E R N

EICHSTÄTT

Sheltered in the valley of the Altmühl river, Eichstätt doesn't make it onto many tourist itineraries. But unlike many well-preserved Bavarian towns, Eichstätt's buildings are actively in use today, serving as more than props put up every year for a stream of visitors. The town's university and position at the heart of the Altmühltal nature preserve make it both an environmental and intellectual center.

◪ ORIENTATION AND PRACTICAL INFORMATION. Trains run to Eichstätt from Ingolstadt (25min., 2 per hour, DM7.60) and Nürnberg (1¼hr., 1 per hour, DM25). A free **bus** shuttles the 5km between Eichstätt-Bahnhof and Eichstätt-Stadt stations, leaving from track 1. (10min., 1 bus after each arrival, 5am-11:30pm.) Rent **bikes** at **Fahrradgarage,** Herzoggasse 3 (tel. 21 10 or 899 87), in the tiny alley that leads from Marktpl. to the footbridge. (DM13 per day. Open daily 9-11:30am and 2:30-7pm.) **Heinz Glas,** Industrie 18 (tel. 30 55), rents **canoes** for trips down the Altmühl River. (M-F DM20 per day, Sa-Su DM25; under 12 50% off.) The **tourist office,** Kardinal-Preysing-Pl. 14 (tel. 988 00; fax 98 80 30), has free maps and books **rooms** (DM25-30) for free. From the Bahnhof, walk right and follow the information sign across the Spitalbrücke. Turn right on Residenzpl. and follow the bend left to Leonrodpl., then bear right until you reach Kardinal-Preysing-Pl. on the left; the tourist office is up the street on the right. (Open April-Oct. M-Sa 9am-6pm, Su 1-4pm; Nov.-March M-Th 9am-noon and 2-4pm, F 9am-noon.) **Tours** leave from the tourist office. (1½hr. April-Oct. Sa 1:30pm. DM5.) **Naturpark Altmühltal,** Notre Dame 1 (tel. 987 60), cloistered in a former monastery, also provides tourist information on trails and paths in the nature reserve. (Open May-Sept. M-Sa 9am-6pm, Su 10am-6pm; Oct. closes 1hr. earlier.) **Exchange money** at **Volksbank** on Marktpl. (Open M-Tu and Th 8:30am-noon and 2-4:30pm, W 8:30am-noon, F 8:30am-3pm. DM2 commission.) A convenient **pharmacy** is **Dom-Apotheke,** Dompl. 16. (Tel. 15 20. Open M-F 8am-6pm, Sa 8am-noon.) The **post office,** 85072 Eichstätt, is at Dompl. 7. (Open M-F 8:30am-5:30pm, Sa 9am-noon.) The **telephone code** is 08421.

◪◫ ACCOMMODATIONS AND FOOD. Eichstätt's **Jugendherberge (HI),** Reichenaustr. 15 (tel. 980 40; fax 98 04 15), is modern and comfortable. Follow directions to Willibaldsburg (see **Sights,** below), but turn right halfway up Burgstr. onto Reichenaustr. at the *Jugendherberge* sign. (6-bed dorm DM25. Breakfast included. Sheets DM5.50. Reception 8-9am and 5-7pm. Lockout 10am-5pm. Curfew 10pm, but they'll give you a key if you're over 18. Closed Dec.-Jan.) To get to the university **Mensa,** Universitätsallee 2 (tel. 93 14 60), walk toward the end of Ostenstr. and hang a right on Universitätsallee; it's on the right. Buy a card (DM3) from the cashier on the first floor. (Meals DM2-4.40. Cashier open noon-1:30pm. ID required. *Mensa* open during the semester M-F 11:30am-2pm; in summer 11:30am-1:30pm; closed Aug. to mid-Sept.) A relaxed **cafeteria** on the first floor has an outdoor garden. (Open M-Th 8:15am-7pm, F 8:15am-3pm; in summer M-F 8:15am-2:45pm.) **Schneller's Backstube,** Marktpl. 20a, provides inexpensive fresh bread and delicious pastries. (Open M-F 7am-6pm, Sa 8:30am-1pm.) In town, **Ammonit,** Luitpoldstr. 19 (tel. 29 29), is a student hangout with beer (DM4-8) and other snacks. (DM7-15. Open M-F 9:30am-1am, Sa-Su 9:30am-2am.) **L'Incontro,** Luitpoldstr. 21 (tel. 56 90) is a deluxe coffee bar. (Same hours as Ammonit.) **La Grotta,** Marktpl. 13 (tel. 72 80 or 15 07), has affordable pizzas (DM8.50-11) and pasta. (DM8-15. Open daily 11:30am-2pm and 5:30pm-1am. Kitchen open until 11pm.)

◪ SIGHTS. The **Willibaldsburg,** Burgstr. 19, conspicuously watches over the town from its high perch across the river. To reach the castle from the station, take a right; at the main intersection, turn right and follow the main street one block, then turn left on Burgstr. The 14th-century castle now houses the **Juramuseum** (tel. 29 56 or 47 30), Burgstr. 19, filled with fossils from the Jurassic period found in the Altmühltal Valley, once covered by a vast prehistoric sea. See the fossil of the earliest bird ever to catch a worm, the Archaeopteryx, who lived over 150 million years ago. Dinosaur movies (no Spielberg) are screened daily at 10:15am and 2:30pm. The **Museum für Ur- und Frühgeschichte** (tel. 894 50), also in the Willibaldsburg, picks up the story at the debut of *Homo sapiens* and continues through the era of Roman colonization. (Both museums open April-Sept. Tu-Su 9am-noon and 1-5pm; Oct.-March Tu-Su 10am-noon and 1-4pm. Juramuseum DM5, students DM4, children under 15 free. Museum für Ur- und Frühgeschichte DM10.)

Across the river, Eichstätt proper is built around the extravagant **Residenzplatz,** surrounded by Rococo Episcopal palaces. The west wing has a particularly magnificent portal, and the interior is just as richly decorated. Free German-language tours of the **Residenz** (tel. 702 20) begin here if there are at least five people. (Easter-Oct. M-Th at 11am and 3pm, F at 11am, Sa-Su every 30min. 10-11:30am and 2-3:30pm.) In a corner of Residenzpl., in the middle of a fountain, stands the **Mariensäule,** an elaborate column depicting the Virgin Mary. Behind the *Residenz* is the 14th-century **Hoher Dom,** an eclectic product of the Romanesque, Gothic, and Baroque eras. (Open M-Th 9:45am-1pm and 2:30-4pm, F 9:45am-3:30pm, Sa 9:45am-3pm, Su 12:30-5pm.) The east apse features richly colored stained glass, and the north aisle shelters the intricate 15th-century stone **Pappenheim altar.** On the other side of the altar is the entrance to the **Mortuarium,** resting place of Eichstätt's bishops, in which the Gothic **Schöne Säule** rises to meet the vault.

Also in the cathedral complex, the **Diözesanmuseum,** Residenzpl. 7 (tel. 502 79), examines the 1,200-year history of the diocese with statues, folk art, and paintings. (Open April-Oct. Tu-Sa 9:30am-1pm and 2-5pm, Su 11am-5pm. DM2.50, under 18 free.) Two blocks farther on Leonrodpl. is the Baroque **Schutzengelkirche,** built during the Thirty Years War, containing richly carved wooden pews and a striking golden sunburst above the high altar. Five hundred sixty-seven sculpted angels fly about the church's interior. Start counting.

INGOLSTADT

The site of the first Bavarian university from 1472 to 1800, the old Danube city of Ingolstadt is now best known as the home of Audi. The name of this luxury car company was originally *Horch*, the last name of auto innovator and entrepreneur August Horch, and German for "eavesdrop." After WWII it was changed to the Latin *Audi* (listen) to help exports in an international market resistant to German-sounding products. It would take much more than a name change, however, to shake the traditional look of this old town. The Stadtmitte remains a tightly packed collection of old school architecture, enclosed by lush greenery with no evidence of dirty industry in sight, and frequented by beaming university students.

🖪 **ORIENTATION AND PRACTICAL INFORMATION. Trains** roll from Ingolstadt to Munich (1hr., 2 per hour, DM22), Augsburg (1hr., 1 per hour, DM16), and Regensburg (1¼hr., 2 per hour, DM20). To reach the tourist office and the Altstadt from the distant train station, take bus #10, 11, 15, 16, or 44 to "Rathausplatz." Or follow Bahnhofstr. to Münchener Str. and head straight over the bridge down Donaustr. to Rathauspl. **Bus** routes center around the **Omnibusbahnhof,** located in the middle of the city. (Single ride DM2.70.) The **Mitfahrzentrale,** Harderstr. 14 (tel. 194 40), arranges ride shares. (Open M-F 2-6pm.) For a **taxi** call 877 88. **Radverleih Fahrradinsel,** Münchener Str. 2 (tel. 730 27), rents **bikes** for DM19 per day. (Open M-F 9am-12:30pm and 1:30-7pm, Sa 9am-4pm.) Ingolstadt's **tourist office,** Rathauspl. 4 (tel. 305 10 98; fax 305 10 99), in the Altes Rathaus, hands out maps and finds **rooms.** (Open M-F 8am-5pm, Sa 9am-noon.) Free **tours** in German leave from the office Saturdays at 2pm. **Exchange money** at **Volksbank,** Theresienstr. 32. (Open M-W 8am-4pm, Th 8am-5:30pm, F 8am-2pm.) **Franziskus-Apotheke,** Rathauspl. 13 (tel. 330 53), posts the latenight **pharmacy** information. (Open M-F 8am-6:30pm, Sa 8am-1pm.) The **post office,** 85024 Ingolstadt, is directly in front of the train station. (Open M-F 7:30am-6pm, Sa 8am-noon.) The **telephone code** is 0841.

▌ ACCOMMODATIONS AND CAMPING. Ingolstadt's superb **Jugendherberge (HI)**, Friedhofstr. 4 (tel. 341 77; fax 91 01 78), is in a renovated section of the old town fortifications. From the tourist office, take Moritzstr. and turn left on Theresienstr. to the Kreuztor. Walk through the gate and cross Auf der Schanz; the hostel is on the right (10min.). Large echoing rooms with private sinks, cavernous hallways, and a great location—hosteling rarely gets this good. (DM20-33. Sheets DM5.50. Reception 8am-11:30pm; inquire in the kitchen if no one's at the front desk. Curfew 11:30pm.) **Pension Lipp** (tel. 587 36), on Feldkirchener Str. down Schloßländestr. along the Danube and left up Frühlingstr., is pleasant if out of the way. (Singles DM40, with bath DM45; doubles DM75, with shower DM85.) Campers head to **Campingplatz am Auwaldsee** (tel. 961 16 16), but a car is a must. The site is off the E45/Autobahn A9, five minutes by car from the town center. (DM7.10 per person. Tent DM5.10. Car DM9.90. Open year-round.)

▐▌ FOOD AND NIGHTLIFE. The Kreuztor might be the symbol of the Altstadt, but it's also the epicenter of all that's hip and new in town. Local nightlife centers around **Kreuzstr.**, which turns into **Theresienstr.** toward the center of town. **Glock'n am Kreuztor,** Oberer Graben 1 (tel. 349 90), is the really loud beer garden in the park abutting the Kreuztor. Daily meat and pasta dishes run DM5-15. (Open daily 9am-2am. 18+.) **Sigi's Café und Bistro,** Kreuzstr. 6 (tel. 329 52), a few doors down, is small, and chic, with nice outdoor seating. *Wieners,* sandwiches, and salads are all under DM11. (Open M-F 9:30am-midnight, Sa 2pm-2am.) **Restaurant Mykonos,** Ludwigstr. 9, dishes Greek delights with a beer garden in back. Omelettes (DM8) and Greek specialities (DM9-13) grace the affordable lunch menu. (Open daily 11am-3pm and 5pm-1am.) **Tengelman,** Ludwigstr. 18, sells **groceries.** (Open M-F 8am-6pm, Sa 7:30am-2pm.)

Neue Welt, Griesbadgasse 7 (tel. 324 70), off Kreuzstr., is home to the local artist and music crowd with its own stage. Cabarets and alternative and R&B concerts premiere Mondays, Tuesdays, and Fridays. Try the chili, a *Tsatsiki* (DM5.50), or vegetarian rigatoni with "special sauce." (DM9. Beer DM5. Open daily 7pm-2am.) **Goldener Stern,** Griesbadgasse 2 (tel. 354 19), is in a light yellow house nearby. Self-proclaimed student-friendly prices are a joy, and an amicable staff sweetens the deal. Beer starts at DM4; chocolatey and fruity crepes run DM5-7. Relax in the beer garden. (Open daily 7pm-1am. 18+.)

▐▌ SIGHTS AND ENTERTAINMENT. The old city wall is magnificently represented by the turreted **Kreuztor,** topped by dainty stone ornamentations. Just beyond the gate outside the city wall is the **Stadtmuseum,** Auf der Schanz 45 (tel. 305 18 85), which explores the archaeological and cultural history of the area. (Open Tu-Sa 9am-5pm, Su 10am-5pm. DM4, students and seniors DM2; Su free.) Two blocks east of the Kreuztor stands the late Gothic **Liebfrauenmünster,** full of ornate altars and immense columns. A few blocks south on tantalizingly named Anatomiestr., the **Deutsches Medizinhistorisches Museum,** Anatomiestr. 18-20 (tel. 305 18 60) features an 18th-century "do-it-yourself" enema stool complete with a hand-operated water pump and padded seat with protruding 3-inch-long pipe. That was a little more information than anyone needed. The "skeleton room" displays skinned human corpses with dried-up muscles still attached and an eerie collection of shrivelled guts and limbs. The staff will lend you a thick English guidebook to interpret the German-only exhibits. (Open Tu-Su 10am-noon and 2-5pm. DM4, students and seniors DM2; Su free.) At the corner of Jesuitenstr. and Neubaustr. is the **Maria-de-Victoria-Kirche.** This once spare chapel for students of the nearby Catholic school was rococoed with a vengeance in 1732, and an awe-inspiring frescoco by Cosmos Damion Asam depicting Mary as queen of Heaven now adorns the ceiling. (Open Tu-Su 9am-noon and 1-5pm. DM2.50, students and children DM1.50.)

Across town on Paradeplatz is the 15th-century **Neues Schloß,** Paradepl. 4, a red-tiled castle that houses a band of pierced-and-tattooed *Szene* kids and the less fascinating **Bayerisches Armeemuseum** (tel. 350 67), an exhibit of military artifacts collected by King Ludwig "If-I-weren't-crazy-I'd-be-dangerous" II. (Open Tu-Su 8:45am-4:30pm. DM4, students DM2.; free on Su.) The brand-new **Museum für Konkrete Kunst,** Tränktorstr. 6-8 (tel. 305 18 06), is off Donaustr. near the Konrad-Adenauer-Brücke. The neon lights and funkadelic designs of the concrete art exhibits will make your head spin. (Open Tu and Th-Su 10am-6pm, W 10am-2pm and 5-9pm. DM4, students DM2, children under 10 free.) Have a burning fetish for automobiles? Call **Audi** for tour information (tel. 89 12 41).

AUGSBURG

Founded by Caesar Augustus in 15 BC, Augsburg was the financial center of the Holy Roman Empire and a major commercial city by the end of the 15th century. The town owed its success and prestige mainly to the Fuggers, an Augsburg family that virtually monopolized the banking industry; Jakob Fugger "the Rich" was personal financier to the Habsburg Emperors. The third-largest Bavarian city also went down in history as a focal point of the Reformation and the birthplace of Bertolt Brecht. Augsburg didn't fare well in WWII, however, and very little besides major monuments was reconstructed. Today its castles are scattered among modern office buildings, and industry is the main engine of Augsburg's economy.

🚩 ORIENTATION AND PRACTICAL INFORMATION. Augsburg is connected by **train** to Munich (30min., 3 per hour, DM25), Nürnberg (2hr., 2 per hour, DM45), Würzburg (2hr., 1 per hour, DM76), Stuttgart (1¾hr., 2 per hour, DM66), and Zürich (5hr., 2 per hour). The infamous **Europabus** line, canvassing the Romantische Straße route (see p. 296), stops at the Augsburg train station (northbound 10:30am; southbound 5:45pm). The **Mitfahrzentrale,** Barthof 3 (tel. 15 70 19), arranges ride-shares for a small fee. (Open daily noon-9pm.) The **tourist office,** Bahnhofstr. 7 (tel. 50 20 70; fax 502 07 45), off Königsplatz, about 300m from the station down Bahnhofstr., sells excellent maps and books **rooms** (DM30-40) for a DM3 fee. (Open M-F 9am-6pm.) A **branch** office (tel. 502 07 24) on Rathausplatz has longer hours. From the station, walk to the end of Bahnhofstr. and take a left at Königsplatz onto Annastr. Take the third right and Rathauspl. will be on the left; the branch office is on the right. (Open M-F 9am-6pm, Sa 10am-4pm, Su 10am-1pm.) Walking **tours** leave from the Rathaus (daily 2pm; DM12, students and children DM9), as do one-hour bus tours (daily 10:30am; DM14, students DM10). For a **pharmacy,** head to **Stern-Apotheke** on Marktplatz, behind the fountain. (Open M-F 8:30am-6:30pm, Sa 8:30am-1pm.) Augsburg's **post office,** Halderstr. 29, 86150 Augsburg, on the left as you face the station, **exchanges cash** (DM2 per transaction) and cashes traveler's checks. (DM6 per check. Open M-F 7am-8pm, Sa 8am-2pm, and Su 10am-noon.) The **telephone code** is 0821.

🚩 ACCOMMODATIONS AND CAMPING. Augsburg's **Jugendherberge (HI),** Beim Pfaffenkeller 3 (tel. 339 09; fax 15 11 49), has an inner courtyard that allows for a sense of seclusion, though it is seclusion in what feels like converted second-grade classrooms. From the station walk up Prinzregentenstr. as it curves to the right through town. Turn left at Karolinenstr. and then right at the cathedral on Innere Pfaffengasse. Bear left as it becomes Beim Pfaffenkeller. (DM20, over 27 DM25. Breakfast included. Sheets DM5.50. Key deposit DM20 or an ID. Reception 7-9am and 5-10pm. Curfew 1am. Closed Jan. Call ahead.) The cheapest privacy you'll find in a central location is at **Jakoberhof,** Jakoberstr. 39-41 (tel. 51 00 30; fax 15 08 44). From the station, follow Prinzregentenstr. until the intersection after Mittlerer Graben. (15min. Singles DM50, with bath DM75; doubles DM75, with bath DM105.) **Gasthof Lenzhalde,** Theolottstr. 2 (tel. 52 07 45; fax 52 87 61), is a 25-minute walk from the station. Bear right on Halderstr., take a sharp right onto Hermannstr., and cross the Gögginger Brücke. Take the first right onto Rosenaustr. and follow it for several blocks; when it curves right at the traffic light the Gasthof is straight ahead. Very simple, tidy rooms overlook a park on one side and train tracks on the other. (Singles DM42, with shower DM50; doubles DM78; triples DM110.) Pitch your tent at **Campingplatz Augusta,** ABA Augsburg-Ost, Am Autobahnsee (tel. 70 75 75). Take the bus (direction: "Neuburg") to "Autobahnsee" and follow the signs; the camp is about 400m away. (DM8 per person. Tent DM6. Car DM6.)

▣ FOOD. Myriad food stands line Maximilianstr. in the summer, but this *Imbiß* fare is surprisingly pricey. At **König von Flandern,** Karolinenstr. 12 (tel. 15 80 50), Augsburg's first *Gasthof*-brewery, the pleasing, rustic smell of the brewing wafts up to visitors. Large portions of soup (DM5-6), salad (DM5-10), and meat (DM10-14) will satisfy ravenous Bavarian food fiends. (Open M-Sa 11am-1am, Su 5pm-1am.) Stock up on **groceries** at **Penny Markt,** Maximilianstr. 71, to the left of the Rathaus (open M-F 8:30am-7pm, Sa 8am-2pm) or **Tengelmann,** at the corner of Alte Gasse and Jesuitengasse (open M-Th 8:30am-6:30pm, F 8am-6:30pm, Sa 8am-1pm).

◉ SIGHTS. Jakob Fugger, Augsburg's very own Daddy Warbucks, founded the **Fuggerei** quarter in 1519 as the first welfare housing project in the world. Still in use almost 500 years later, the narrow cobblestone streets and 53 gabled houses are a haven for the elderly, who earn their keep by praying for the departed souls of the Fuggers and pay only DM1.72 (the equivalent of a "Rhein Guilder") rent annually. Budget travelers need not apply. To reach the Fuggerei from the Rathaus, walk behind the Perlachturm tower on Perlachberg, which becomes Barfüßerstr. and finally Jakoberstr., and turn right under the archway. The gates close at 10pm. The **Fuggereimuseum** on Mittlergasse is in one of the only flats whose original construction survived the war, and is arranged to mimic the typical decoration of the homes, as well as the financial predilections of its owners. (Open March-Oct. daily 9am-6pm. DM1, students and seniors DM0.70.) Fugger was also responsible for building the **Fugger Haus,** Maximilianstr. 36-38, where the 1518 dispute between Martin Luther and Cardinal Cajetan ensured church schism. Luther stayed in the **St. Anna Kirche,** on Annastr. near Königsplatz, with Prior Frosch, and convinced him to pioneer the Reformation in Augsburg from this church.

Augsburg's medieval past unfolds at the brightly frescoed **Guildhaus,** down Bürgermeister-Fischer-Str. A left down Maximilianstr. leads to the huge Renaissance **Rathaus,** which encloses the **Goldener Saal** on its third floor. The wide rectangular room, richly ornamented with golden cherubs, recalls the importance of commerce in Augsburg's past (DM3). Down Hoher Weg to the left sits the **Hoher Dom,** the regional bishop's seat. Built in the 9th century, the cathedral was renovated in the 14th century in Gothic style and badly damaged in WWII. The chancel and high altar exemplify the Bauhaus-inspired design prevalent in German churches after the war. (Open M-Sa 6am-5pm.) Another cultural treasure destroyed during WWII and later rebuilt is the **Synagogue.** Turn right from the station on Halderstr.; the synagogue is on the left. Set back from the street by a gated courtyard, the early 20th-century synagogue is distinguished by its enormous Byzantine dome. (DM3. Open Tu-F 9am-4pm and Su 10am-5pm.)

Bertolt Brecht's birthplace was renovated in 1998, on the 100th anniversary of his birth. The museum does a good job of chronicling the life of one of the most influential 20th-century playwrights and poets through photographs, letters, and poetry. From the station head up Prinzregentenstr. to tiny Schmiedgasse on the right. (Open daily 10am-5pm. DM2.50, students and children DM1.50.)

ROMANTISCHE STRASSE (ROMANTIC ROAD)

Groomed fields of sunflowers and wheat checker the landscape between Würzburg and Füssen, which is spread like a mammoth picnic; dishy circular cities, castles in tasty shades of lemon and mint, and dense forests of healthy greenery seem laid out with the *Kitsch*-hungry traveler in mind. The region's pulchritude

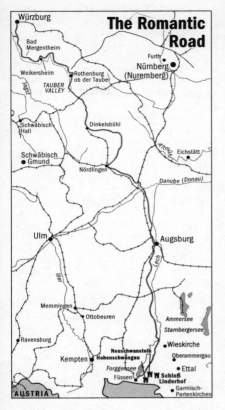

The Romantic Road

wasn't lost on the German tourism industry, which baptized it the **Romantische Straße** in 1950; the area has subsequently become the most heavily touristed region in Germany. Deutsche Bahn's **Europabus** transports throngs of American and Japanese tourists daily from Frankfurt to Munich and back. Though this is the most popular way to travel the Romantische Straße, it is also one of the most inflexible—there is only one bus in each direction per day. On the Frankfurt-Munich route, southbound buses leave Frankfurt daily at 8am, while northbound buses depart from Munich daily at 9am. Stops include Würzburg (southbound 10am/northbound 6:45pm), Rothenburg (2:30pm/4:15pm), Dinkelsbühl (4:15pm/2pm), Nördlingen (4:55pm/12:15pm), Augsburg (6:20pm/10:30am), and Munich (7:50pm/9am).

On the Dinkelsbühl-Füssen route, southbound buses leave Dinkelsbühl at 4:15pm, and northbound buses leave Füssen at 8am. Stops on this line include Augsburg (southbound 6pm/northbound 10:50am), Wieskirche (northbound only, 8:55am—with a 20min. stop for sightseeing), and Hohenschwangau and Neuschwan-

stein (8:33pm/8:07am). Check schedules with a tourist office before heading to the bus. The Europabus is relatively expensive. (Frankfurt to Rothenburg DM59, to Dinkelsbühl DM71, to Munich DM116. Dinkelsbühl to Hohenschwangau or Füssen DM66. Students and under 26 10% off, under 12 and over 60 50% off, under 4 free. Eurail and German Railpass holders get a 75% discount.)

A more economical way to see the Romantische Straße for those without rail-passes is to use the faster and much more frequent **trains,** which run to every town except Dinkelsbühl. Those traveling the Romantische Straße by **car** may have to park in lots outside the old city walls of some towns, but will have easy access to many suburban budget hotels, *Privatzimmer,* and campgrounds that lie outside the reach of pedestrian travelers. The Romantische Straße is an excellent opportunity for a leisurely **bike** journey, with campgrounds located 10 to 20km apart. Tourist offices offer excellent cycling maps and information on campgrounds along the road. For information or reservations, call **Deutsche Touring** in Frankfurt, Am Römerhof 17 (tel. (069) 790 32 81; fax 790 32 19). For general information, contact the **Romantische Straße Arbeitsgemeinschaft,** Marktplatz, 91550 Dinkelsbühl (tel. (09851) 902 71; fax 902 79).

ROTHENBURG OB DER TAUBER

Rothenburg ob der Tauber is *the* Romantic Roadstop, touched by everyone—and we mean *everyone*. While Rothenburg is busy enjoying the same commercialized fate as its favorite December holiday, don't knock all the touristic pomp; this small

BAYERN

town is probably your only chance to see a nearly intact medieval walled city in Bayern. At the end of the 19th century, locals set up strict preservation laws in order to preserve their 16th-century town. Unfortunately, Allied bombs destroyed 40% of Rothenburg in WWII. Fortunately, Rothenburg's legions of former tourists banded together to rebuild the Altstadt, which is a gorgeous reminder of Bayern's architectural past.

⊠ ORIENTATION AND PRACTICAL INFORMATION. Hourly **trains** run from Würzburg (40min, 1 per hour, DM15) and München (3hr., 1 per hour, DM60) to **Steinach,** where you can transfer for a quick trip to Rothenburg (15min.). **Buses** also serve the route, sometimes in place of the train in the evening. The **Europabus** leaves from the Hotel Rothenburg Hut across the street from the train station. For a **taxi** call 20 00 or 72 27. Rent **bikes** at **Herrmann Kat's,** Galgengasse 33 (tel. 61 11; open daily 8am-7pm; half-day DM10, full day DM15-18), or at **Rad und Tat,** Bensenstr. 17 (tel. 879 84; open daily 9am-6pm; DM20 per day). Rothenburg's **tourist office,** Marktplatz 2 (tel. 404 92; fax 868 07; email info@rothenburg.de), supplies maps in English and books **rooms** (DM35-60) for free or for a DM5 fee during the summer and Christmas. Walk left from the station, bear right on Ansbacher Str., and follow it straight to the Marktplatz (15min.); the office is on your right, across the square in the pink building with the clock on the upper storeys. (Open May-Sept. M-F 9am-12:30pm and 1-6pm, Sa-Su 10am-3pm; Nov.-April M-F 9am-12:30pm and 1-5pm, Sa 10am-1pm.) **Tours** in German depart daily from the steps of the Rathaus (90min.; April-Oct. and Dec. at 11am and 2pm; DM5), while tours in English meet daily at the Rathaus at 2pm (DM6). The ⊠"night watchman" leads a special tour with his candle-lit lantern and iron spear that is more entertaining than educating; meet at the Rathaus. (English at 8pm; DM6. German at 9:30pm; DM5.)

Wäscherei Then (tel. 27 75) is a **laundromat** located at Johannitergasse. (Wash and dry DM10. Open M-F 8am-6pm, Sa 8am-2pm.) **Löwen-Apotheke,** Markt 2 (tel. 84 10), has all your **pharmacy** phixins and a night bell for emergencies. (Open M-F 8am-6pm, Sa 8am-12:30 pm.) The **post office,** Bahnhofstr. 7, 91541 Rothenburg, is across from the station. (Open M-F 8:30am-noon and 2-5:30pm, Sa 8:30am-noon.) **Internet access** is at **Planet Internet,** Paradeisgasse 5 (tel. 93 44 15), to the right off Rödergasse. (Open M-Th noon-midnight, F-Sa 4pm-1am.) The **telephone code** is 09861.

⌐ ACCOMMODATIONS. An incredible number of **private rooms** (DM20-45) not registered with the tourist office are available; look for *Zimmer frei* signs. Just knock on doors bearing the signs to inquire. Despite their abundance, don't expect same-day availability in the summer or around Christmas. **Jugendherberge Rossmühle (HI),** Mühlacker 1 (tel. 941 60; fax 94 16 20; email jhrothen@aol.com), is in a former horse-powered mill that shelters modern two-to-six-bed rooms and a Calvin-Klein-ad-ready staff. Amenities include ping-pong and pool tables, a TV room where you can borrow movies, free storage lockers (DM5 deposit required), and washers and dryers—this is what all hostels should be like. Follow the directions to the tourist office, take a left down Obere Schmiedgasse, and go straight for about 10min. until you see the small, white *Jugendherberge* sign to the right. (DM22, with bath DM27. Tasty breakfast included. Sheets DM5.50. Dinner DM9. Reception 7am-midnight. Check-in until 10pm. Curfew midnight, but they'll give you an access code.) Rothenburg has an unbelievable number of *Pensionen* for a town its size, but most of them are expensive. For an exception, check out **Pension Raidel,** Wenggasse 3 (tel. 31 15), on the way to the hostel. Head down Obere Schmiedgasse and make a left on Wenggasse. Bright rooms and fluffy featherbeds, each one built and decorated by the owner, make this the most charming and authentic of the affordable *Pensionen* in the Altstadt. (Singles DM69, doubles DM89. Breakfast included. Call ahead.) **Pension Then,** Johannitergasse 8a (tel. 51 77; fax 860 14), has a very friendly staff. From the station, turn left, then right on Ansbacher Str. and right on Johannitergasse. (Singles DM40, doubles DM80-86. Apartment with kitchen DM25 per person with a 3-day minimum stay.)

❒ FOOD. With a cozy Christmas theme all year-round, it's not surprising that Rothenburg is famous for its heart-stopping *Schneeballen* (snowballs): large balls of sweet dough fried and then dipped in chocolate, nuts, and powdered sugar, with a sweet center of marzipan or amaretto. **Dillers,** Hofbronner Gasse 16 and Hafengasse 4 (tel. 866 23), offers these doughy concoctions at industrially produced rates. (DM3-5. Open daily 10am-6pm.) For fast food, try Rödergasse, off Marktpl., where *Döners* and hamburgers run DM5. **Roter Hahn,** Obere Schmiedgasse 21 (tel. 50 88), is the former home of the renowned wine-chugging Mayor Nusch whose tolerance for large doses of alcohol saved the town from destruction. The ancient restaurant caters to meat-lovers. Most meals cost less than DM14. (Open daily 11:30am-10pm.) **Fränkisches Haus,** Golgengasse 13 (tel. 34 39), offers regional specialties for DM10-17. (Open M-F 8am-6pm, Sa 8:30am-6pm, Su 9am-6pm.) **Pizzeria Roma,** Galgengasse 19 (tel. 45 40), serves pasta (DM8-13), pizzas (DM9-12), and fresh salads (DM8-13) in a dark interior with a small plastic fountain. (Open daily 11:30am-midnight.) Pick up fresh goods from vendors on the **Marktplatz** (W and Sa 7am-noon), or stop by **Kapsch** on Rödergassen, inside the city wall as you enter town, for **groceries.** (Open M-F 8:30am-6:30pm, Sa 8am-1pm.)

❒ SIGHTS. On the Marktplatz stands the Renaissance **Rathaus;** its 60m tower affords a nice view of the town. (Open daily 8am-6pm. Free. Tower open April-Oct. daily 9:30am-12:30pm and 1-5pm; Nov.-March M-F 9:30am-12:30pm, Sa-Su noon-3pm. DM1, children DM0.50.) In 1631, the conquering Catholic general Johann Tilly offered to spare the town from destruction if any local could chug a wine keg containing almost a gallon of wine. Mayor Georg Nusch successfully met the challenge, then passed out for several days. His saving **Meistertrunk** is reenacted with great fanfare each year. The town clock acts out a *slooow* motion version of the episode over the Marktplatz. (Hourly 11am-3pm and 8-10pm.) Inside the courtyard behind the Rathaus are the **Historien-Gewölbe,** which articulate the history of the Thirty Years War. (Open May-Sept. daily 9:30am-5:30pm; Oct.-Nov. and Jan.-April 10am-5pm; Dec. 1-4pm. DM3, students DM2.) Three gloomy stone cells lurk in the dungeon, where Mayor Heinrich Toppler and his son were once imprisoned by King Ruprecht. The **Jakobikirche,** Klostergasse 15, is famed for its altar by Tilman Riemenschneider, a 5,500-pipe organ, and its 14th-century stained glass windows. (Open April-Oct. M-F 9am-5:30pm, Su 10:30am-5:30pm; Dec. noon-2pm and 4-5pm. DM2.50, students DM1.) The **Reichsstadtmuseum,** Klosterhof 5 (tel. 404 58), housed in a restored 13th-century Dominican convent, displays implements used by medieval nuns and 13th-century Judaica. (Open April-Oct. daily 9:30am-5:30pm; Nov.-March 1-4pm. DM6, students DM4.) The town's **medieval crime museum,** Burggasse 3 (tel. 53 59), is definitely worth the entrance fee for anyone who can stomach the thought of iron-maiden justice. Take a picture of yourself in the stocks outside before heading into the dim, creepy basement housing the torture exhibits. Rooms upstairs continue the fun, with exhibits on "eye for an eye" jurisprudence and the special punishments once reserved for bad musicians, dishonest bakers, and frivolous gossips. (Open April-Oct. daily 9:30am-6pm; Nov. and Jan.-March 2-4pm; Dec. 10am-4pm. DM5, students DM4, children DM3.)

Camp holds brazen sway at Käthe Wohlfahrt's **Christkindlmarkt** (Christ Child Market), Herrngasse 2, and the more extensive **Weihnachtsdorf** (Christmas Village), Herrngasse 1 (tel. 40 90). Even if you *aren't* looking for a 4m-tall nutcracker or a pea-sized porcupine, head to the second floor to check out the discounted damaged items. (Open M-F 9am-6pm, Sa 10am-4pm; Easter-Dec. also Su 10am-6pm.)

DINKELSBÜHL

Forty kilometers south of Rothenburg, the historical town of Dinkelsbühl boasts a bevy of medieval half-timbered houses, a climbable 16th-century church tower, and a navigable town wall with gateways, towers, and moats. Sound familiar? It is, though locals claim their town's superiority lies in Dinkelsbühl's authenticity; the Altstadt corrals the largest number of original, unrestored structures on the

Romantische Straße (repainting, of course, doesn't count). The Gothic **St. Georgs-kirche**, which dominates the **Weinmarkt** at the center of town, sprouts a Romanesque tower and striking fan vaulting. A tale for tourists explains why the houses along **Nördlinger Straße** are oddly shaped—medieval superstition held that homes with right angles housed demons. Every summer the Dinkelsbühlers faithfully celebrate the salvation of their besieged town during the Thirty Years War with the **Kinderzeche festival** (July 14-23, 2000). The town tots' tears and the sweet voice of Kinderlore, the beautiful daughter of the town watchman, reputedly persuaded the invading colonel of Swedish King Gustavus Adolphus II to spare Dinkelsbühl. A recreation of the event accompanies parades, fireworks, dances, and, of course, crying kids—a strangely satisfying experience for hosteling travelers. (Tickets DM4-16.) The **Parkring** around the Altstadt separates the old and new parts of town, with a system of moats and dykes glorified by armies of ducks and willow trees. New to the old town is the spiffy **3-Dimensional Museum** (tel. 63 36), housed in the Nördlinger Tor of the town wall. The only such museum in the world, it encompasses all the different ways since the Middle Ages that people have represented thick stuff in thin ways. (Open April-Oct. daily 10am-6pm; Nov.-March Sa-Su 11am-4pm. DM10, with tourist office coupon DM9.)

When traveling by bus to and from Dinkelsbühl, plan ahead. Regional buses go to Rothenburg (9 per day, 1-3 per day on weekends; transfer buses at Dombühl or Feuchtwangen), and to Nördlingen (7 per day, 4-5 per day on weekends). Schedules are posted at the tourist office and at the town's main stop, **Am Stauferwall**. If you plan poorly, you might get stuck with the crowded and expensive **Europabus**, which takes tourists along the Romantische Straße (see p. 296). The **tourist office** (tel. 902 40; fax 902 79), on the Marktplatz, finds **rooms** for a DM3 fee. The office also rents **bikes** (DM7 per day). From the "Am Stauferwall" bus stop, walk right towards the city walls down the street of the same name. Take the first right on Nördlinger Str., which empties into the Marktplatz; the tourist office is in the rust-colored building with a bell tower on your right. (Open April-Oct. M-F 9am-noon and 2-6pm, Sa 10am-1pm and 2-6pm, Su 10am-1pm; Nov.-March M-F 9am-noon and 2-5pm, Sa 10am-1pm.) The **pharmacy** at Nördlinger Str. 7 (tel. 34 35), has a night bell for help at all hours. (Open M-F 8am-12:30pm and 2-6pm, Sa 8am-noon.) The **postal code** is 91550. The **telephone code** is 09851.

Built in 1508 as a grain store, the **Jugendherberge (HI)**, Koppengasse 10 (tel. 95 09; fax 48 74), is a huge, half-timbered fortress with wide wooden hallways garlanded with dried flowers. From the tourist office, head right up Nördlinger Str., and take a right on Bahnhofstr. after passing the Rathaus. At the first bus stop, swing left on Koppengasse; it's the large stucco building on the right. (2- to 8-bed rooms DM18. Breakfast included. Sheets DM5.50. Reception 5-10pm. Curfew 10pm. Open March-Oct.) **Gasthof Zur Sonne**, Weinmarkt 11 (tel. 576 70; fax 75 48), has airy rooms with stunning pastel color schemes. (Singles DM45-65, doubles DM75, triples DM102-120. Breakfast included.) Camp north of the city on Dürrwanger Str. at **DCC Campingpark Romantische Straße**. (Tel. 78 17. DM7.50 per person. DM16.50 per tent and car.)

Budget food is hard to find in touristy Dinkelsbühl. Head to **Ali Baba Imbiß**, Nördlinger Str. 8 (tel. 55 36 15), for *Döner* and salad. (DM3.50-8. Open M-Th 10am-midnight, F-Sa 11am-1am.) **Café Rossini**, Nördlinger Str. 17 (tel. 73 70), serves local cuisine (DM10-16), beer (DM3.40), and elaborate ice cream concoctions (DM8-10. Open M-Sa 9am-midnight, Su 1pm-midnight.) Buy **groceries** at **Tengelmann**, Nördlinger Str. 13. (Open M-F 8:30am-7pm, Sa 8am-2pm.)

NÖRDLINGEN IM RIES

The placid town of Nördlingen was created in the chaos and heat of a meteorite impact some 15 million years ago. Well, not exactly, but the plain it was built on during the Middle Ages was once a crater, created when the meteorite crashed, and then a prehistoric lake, before the sands of time caused it to fill up with mud. The wall surrounding this perfectly circular town was built entirely from "Rieser Moonstones"—stones which formed as a result of the collision. The only town in

Germany where the original walls are complete and can be navigated in their entirety, Nördlingen boasts a 90m Gothic bell tower nicknamed **"Daniel,"** from whose lofty height the town watchman has presided over the people below every evening for the last 500 years. Those who climb up the 350 steps to the keeper's chambers at the top of the "Daniel" are rewarded with a hawk's eye view of the town below. (Tower open daily April-Oct. 9am-8pm; Nov.-March 9am-5:30pm. DM3, under 17 DM2.) Elegant Gothic columns arch over the wide hall of **St. Georg,** dwarfing the people in the pews below. (Church open M-F 9:30am-12:30pm and 2-5pm, Sa-Su 9am-5pm.) Explore the history of this medieval town and the construction of its town wall in Nördlingen's **Stadtmauermuseum,** inside Löpsinger Tor. (Open daily 10am-4:30pm. DM2, under 17 DM1.)

Nördlingen can be reached by hourly **trains** from Augsburg (1hr., change at Donauwörth, DM20), Nürnberg (2hr., change at Donauwörth, DM35), and Ulm (2hr., change at Aalen, DM30). **Buses** also run from Dinkelsbühl to Nördlingen (45min., 8 per day, DM8). The **Europabus** (see p. 296) also stops daily at Nördlingen's Rathaus (southbound 4:55pm, northbound 12:15pm). The **tourist office** (tel. 43 80 or 841 16; fax 841 13) distributes maps and finds **rooms** for free. (Open M-Th 9am-6pm, F 9am-4:30pm, Sa 9:30am-12:30pm.) One-hour **tours** in German meet daily at the tourist office at 2pm (DM4). **Einhorn-Apotheke,** Polizeigasse 7, has a list of 24-hour pharmacies posted in the window. (Open M-F 8am-6pm, Sa 8:30am-noon.) The **post office,** 86720 Nördlingen, to the right of the train station as you exit, exchanges traveler's checks for a DM6 fee. (Open M-F 8:30am-5pm, Sa 9am-noon.) The **telephone code** is 09081.

Nördlingen's **Jugendherberge,** Kaiserwiese 1 (tel. 841 09, after 8pm 79 93 90), a small, friendly hostel with tidy rooms, is just outside the city walls on the north side of town. From Marktpl., follow Baldinger Str. out of the city walls; the hostel is on your right in the parking lot one cross street beyond the walls. (DM18. Reception 8-10am and 4:30-7pm.) **Drei Mohren Gasthof,** Reimlinger Str. 18 (tel. 31 13; fax 287 59), is just inside the town wall. From Marktpl., follow Schäfflesmarkt to Reimlinger Str; the hotel is on the right. (DM35 per person.) **Gasthof Walfisch,** Hallgasse 15 (tel. 31 07), is located in the center of town near Marktpl. Head left onto Windgasse and take a right on Hallgasse. (Singles DM30, with bath DM50; doubles DM60, with bath DM100.)

Nördlingen has numerous small restaurants and street cafés folded into its narrow alleyways, but the majority are expensive. An exception is the sprightly **Ciao Ciao Pizza Ristorante,** Luckengasse 15, which serves pizza (DM10-12) and pasta dishes. (DM11-14. Open Tu-Sa 6pm-midnight, Su 5-10pm.) For **groceries,** head to **Lidl,** Rübenmarkt 1, by the Rathaus. (Open M-F 8am-6pm, Sa 8am-1pm.)

WÜRZBURG

Würzburg's two great monuments, the Baroque Residenz, one of Germany's most ostentatious palaces, and the 13th-century Marienburg, stare at one another across two hills bisected by the Main River while tourists pass in and out of their ornate gates. As if this wasn't enough splendor for one town to handle, Würzburg is also the unofficial capital of the Franconian Wine Region, with vineyards lining the town's outskirts. Although the city has its origins as a religious center, Würzburg is now known as a university town. It was here in 1895 that Wilhelm Conrad Röntgen discovered X-rays and their medical applications, for which he was awarded the first Nobel Prize six years later. Today, more than 20,000 students attend the renowned Julius-Maximilians-Universität, which hosts six Nobel Prize winners among its faculty. Cyclists, streetcars, and skateboarders battle it out on the wide car-free pedestrian zone, paved with pigeon feathers and lined with cafés and Gothic cathedrals. Wartime bombings destroyed much of the town's 18th-century magnificence—all that remained intact in 1945 was the spire of the Marienkapelle—but its older giants remain unchanged, making Würzburg a scenic portal for Germany's great tourist trail, the Romantische Straße.

■★ ■ ORIENTATION AND TRANSPORTATION

To get to the city's center at the **Markt,** follow Kaiserstr. straight from the station, then take a right on Juliuspromenade, and hang a left on **Schönbornstr.,** the main pedestrian and streetcar road; the Markt is a few blocks down and to the right. Streetcars #1, 3, and 5 also run from the station to the Markt. The Main separates the rest of the city from the steep hills on which the fortress stands.

Trains: Depart to Rothenburg (1hr., 1 per hour, DM17), Nürnberg (1½hr., 2 per hour, DM28), Frankfurt (2hr., 1 per hour, DM38), and Munich (2½hr., 1 per hour, DM76).

Buses: Europabus traces the Romantic Road to Rothenburg (DM27) and Munich (DM84) daily at 9:45am, departing from bus platform #13 to the right of the station. The return bus to Frankfurt stops at Würzburg daily at 6:30pm. Reservations can be made 3 days in advance at **Deutsche Touring Büro,** Am Römerhof 17 (tel. (069) 790 32 81; fax (069) 790 32 19).

Public Transportation: Information tel. 36 13 52. **Streetcars** are the fastest and most convenient way around, but large sections are not covered. The **bus** network is comprehensive, though most routes do not run nights and weekends. Ask for **night bus** schedules at the WSB kiosk in front of the station. Single fare DM2.30, 24hr. ticket DM7.20.

Bike Rental: Fahrrad Station, Bahnhofpl. 4 (tel. 574 45), to the left of the station. DM17-20 per day, DM14-16 if you've traveled to Würzburg by train. Open Tu-F 9:30am-6:30pm, Sa 9:30am-1:30pm.

Mitfahrzentrale: Tel. 194 48 or 140 85, in the kiosk to the left of the train station exit. Ride shares to Frankfurt (DM8), Stuttgart (DM9), Munich (DM13), Berlin (DM17), and other cities. Open M-W 10am-4pm, Th-F 10am-6pm, Sa 10am-1pm, Su 11am-1pm.

⁊ PRACTICAL INFORMATION

Tourist Office: All 3 offices offer the same services. A branch in front of the **train station** (tel. 37 24 36) provides a packet with a free map and a hotel list for DM0.50; they also find **rooms** for DM5. Open M-Sa 10am-6pm. The **main office** (tel. 373 35), in the Palais am Kongresszentrum near the Friedensbrücke, where Röntgenring intersects the Main. Open M-Th 8:30am-5pm, F 8:30am-1pm. A 3rd office is located in **Haus zum Falken** (tel. 37 23 98), an ornamental yellow building on Marktplatz. Open M-F 10am-6pm, Sa 10am-2pm; April-Oct. also Su 10am-2pm.

Tours: 2hr. English-language tours depart from Haus zum Falken office and include entrance to the Residenzhof. Mid-April to Oct. Tu-Su at 11am. DM13, students DM10. A German-language tour without the Residenz departs April-Oct. daily at 10:30am. DM9, students DM7. Free 1½hr. **Rathaus tours** in German every Saturday at 10am and 4:30pm; Nov.-Dec. and Feb.-April 10am only. 2hr. **bus tours** in German depart from the bus station. M-Sa 2pm, Su 10:30am. DM15, students DM13.

Bookstore: Buchladen Neuer Weg, Sanderstr. 23-25 (tel. 355 90 18). Has a small but adequate selection of English-language novels. Open M-F 9am-8pm, Sa 9am-4pm.

Pharmacy: Engel-Apotheke, Marktpl. 36 (tel. 32 13 40), lists night pharmacies on the door. Open M-F 8:30am-6pm, Sa 8:30am-1pm.

Emergency: Police, tel. 110. **Fire,** tel. 112. **Medical Aid,** tel. 192 22.

Post Office: Bahnhofpl. 2, 97070 Würzburg. **Exchange money** (DM2 fee) and cash traveler's checks (DM6 fee per check). Open M-F 6am-7pm, Sa 8am-1pm.

BAYERN

| PHONE CODE | 0931 |

◤ ACCOMMODATIONS AND CAMPING

The one drawback to this otherwise excellent city is the lack of budget accommodations. Finding single rooms for less than DM45 is harder (much harder) than finding Waldo. Würzburg's least expensive beds are in the commercial zone around the station, near **Kaiserstr.** and **Bahnhofstr.**

Jugendgästehaus (HI), Bukarderstr. 44 (tel. 425 90; fax 41 68 62), across the river from downtown. Streetcar #3 (direction: "Heidingsfeld") or 5 (direction: "Heuchelhof") to "Löwenbrücke," then backtrack; go down the stairs with the *Jugendherberge/Kapelle* sign, turn right, walk past 2 streets and a Sparkasse on the left, go through the tunnel, and it's on the left. Enormous villa with views of the fortress and river. DM29. Breakfast and sheets included. Reception 8am-10pm. Check-in 2-5:15pm and 6:30-10pm. Curfew 1am.

Pension Spehnkuch, Röntgenring 7 (tel. 547 52; fax 547 60), to the right of the station down Röntgenring. Renovated rooms are very white and clean. Singles DM50; doubles DM92-94, with shower DM135. Breakfast included.

Gasthof Goldener Hahn, Marktgasse 7 (tel. 519 41; fax 519 61), in a little golden building with green-checkered stained glass windows directly off the Markt. Clean rooms with phone and TV. Singles DM40-50, with bath DM80; doubles with bath DM140. Hall shower DM3.

Camping Kanu-Club, Mergentheimer Str. 13b (tel. 725 36). Streetcar #3 or 5 (direction: "Heidingsfeld") to "Judenbühlweg." Go left as you exit the streetcar, take the first left, and follow the "C" signs to the building with an enormous canoe in front. Only 18 idyllic, riverside spots—call ahead. DM4 per person. Tents DM3. Reception noon-10pm.

◖♫ FOOD AND ENTERTAINMENT

To sample some of the Würzburg region's distinctive wines, try **Haus des Frankenweins Fränkischer Weinverband,** Krankenkai 1 (tel. 120 93). The city's sweeter answer to Munich's Oktoberfest, the lively **Kiliansfest** is held during the first two weeks in July. There is a farmer's **market** on the Markt. (Open Tu 6am-6pm, W 6am-4pm, F 6am-6pm, Sa 6am-2pm.) For inexpensive **groceries,** hit **Kapsch,** at the end of Kaiserstr. (Open M-F 8:30-8pm, Sa 8am-4pm.)

University Mensa, in the large, grey *Studentenhaus* on Am Exerzierplatz, through the doors to your left. Assembly-line eating. Würzburg University ID technically required for discounts, but even without one, it's cheap. Buy meal tickets at the machines outside the dining room. Meals DM2.25-4.50. Open mid-Oct. to mid-July M-F 11am-1:30pm, Sa 11:30am-1:30pm; dinner M-Th 5:30-7:30pm; Feb.-March closed Sa.

Le Clochard, Neubaustr. 20 (tel. 129 07). Crepes (DM5-8), sandwiches (DM7-11), and vegetarian dishes like *Jogurt-Kartoffeln* (potatoes topped with yogurt, cucumbers, and tomatoes; DM10.90) jive with the dark wood interior and plastic furniture outside. Come by in the late afternoon to gawk at the throng of caffeinated citizens enjoying "Happy Coffee-Crepe-Hour" (daily 3-5pm). Open daily 10am-1am.

Uni Café, Neubaustr. 2 (tel. 156 72), on the corner of Sanderstr. Relaxed student atmosphere and outdoor sidewalk seating with a great view of the Marienburg. Lunch specials DM7-11, breakfast DM3.50-9.50. Open M-Sa 8am-1am, Su 9am-1pm.

Kult, Landwehrstr. 10 (tel. 531 43), right off Sanderstr. toward the Ludwigsbrücke, keeps a low profile as a hip *Kneipe* for local customers. Salad and main dish DM8-10, spaghetti DM6.50. Mellow but crowded nights. Open daily 9am-1am.

Caféhaus Brückenbäck, Alte Mainbrücke (tel. 41 45 45). From the hostel, turn left on Saalgasse and walk 2 blocks to the far end of the bridge. Breezy atmosphere alongside the Main enhanced by a light natural menu of salads (DM7-16), fruit juices (DM4.50), and teas (DM5.50). Open M-F 8am-1am, Sa-Su 8:30am-1am.

👁 SIGHTS

RESIDENZ

Residenzplatz. Tel. 355 17 12. From the station, walk down Kaiserstr. and Theaterstr. Open Tu-Su April-Oct. 9am-5pm; Nov.-March 10am-4pm. DM8, students and seniors DM6. Painting gallery open Tu-Sa 9:30am-12:30pm. Greek collection open 2-5pm. The two galleries alternate being open Su 9:30am-12:30pm. Both free. Church open Tu-Su April-Oct. 9am-noon and 1-5pm; Nov.-March Tu-Su 10am-noon and 1-4pm. Free. Gardens open dawn-dusk. Free.

The Residenz was the base camp for Würzburg's prince-bishops during the Enlightenment. Towering over the sweeping Residenzplatz, the palace's vibrant ceiling fresco by Johannes Zick in the first-floor garden room has never been restored; in fact, his use of extravagant colors got him fired. The Italian painter Giovanni Tiepolo was hired to finish the job in a more sedate style. His ceiling fresco in the grand staircase is the largest in the world, and certainly among the most ostentatious. Crane your head and see if you can find an overweight officer in dress uniform. Too easy? See if you can spot the dead alligator, then. Also in the Residenz, the university's **Martin-von-Wagner-Museum** proudly displays a collection of Greek vases and fleshy Baroque paintings. The **Residenzhofkirche** is astounding—the gilded moldings and pink marble make this little church the apex of Baroque fantasy. Behind the complex is the **Hofgarten,** with cone-shaped evergreens and a vast maze of bushes perfect for a thrilling game of hide-and-seek.

KILIANSDOM. The 900-year-old cathedral was rebuilt in the mid-1960s after being obliterated in 1945, though it is debatable whether the reconstruction improved its overall appearance. Tilman Riemenschneider was responsible for the Gothic highlights of this large Romanesque cathedral. *(Kiliansplatz. Tel. 536 91. Open daily 8am-7pm. Tours April-Oct. M-Sa at noon, Su at 12:30pm. Free. Organ concerts M-Sa at noon.)*

FESTUNG MARIENBERG

Take bus #9 from the train station. Tours depart from the main courtyard Tu-F 11am, 2pm, and 3pm, Sa-Su hourly 10am-4pm. Fürstenbaumuseum tel. 438 38. Open April-Sept. Tu-Su 9am-12:30pm and 1-5pm; Oct.-March Tu-Su 10am-12:30pm and 1-4pm. DM4, students DM3. Mainfränkisches Museum tel. 430 16. Open Tu-Su 10am-5pm; Nov.-March closes 4pm. DM3.50, students DM2; pass to both museums DM6.

The striking symbol of the city has been keeping vigil high on a hillside over the Main since the 12th century. The footpath to the fortress starts a short distance from the **Alte Mainbrücke,** which is more than 500 years old and lined with statues of saints. Artifacts from the lives of the prince-bishops, a display on the destruction of Würzburg at the end of WWII, and *objets d'art* cluster in the **Fürstenbaumuseum.** Outside the walls of the main fortress is the castle arsenal, which now houses the **Mainfränkisches Museum.** The long hallways of the Baroque arsenal are lined primarily with religious statues featuring the work of Tilman Riemenschneider, the Master of Würzburg. A genius of Gothic styling, Riemenschneider sided with the peasants in their 16th-century revolts against Luther and the powers-that-were. When the insurrection was suppressed, the sculptor's fingers were broken as punishment, and he never worked again.

NÜRNBERG (NUREMBERG)

From the 14th until the 16th century, Nürnberg was a free city, answering to no one lower than the emperor. The city's days in the sun came to an end, however, as trade-routes shifted westward following the discovery of the Americas, and the Thirty Years War destroyed large parts of the city. Nürnberg took on a central role in German politics again in the 20th century, playing host to the massive Nazi Party rallies held between 1933 and 1938, and lent its name to the 1935 Racial Purity Laws. As Hitler's power grew, money started rolling in with the Nazis' armament industry. WWII took its toll, though, and 90% of the city was reduced to rubble in 1945. Because of Nürnberg's close ties to Nazi power, the Allies chose this city as

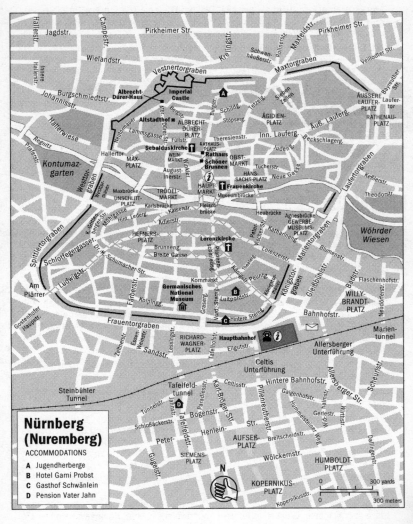

Nürnberg (Nuremberg)

ACCOMMODATIONS

A Jugendherberge
B Hotel Garni Probst
C Gasthof Schwänlein
D Pension Vater Jahn

the site for the war crimes tribunals. Today, Nürnberg jives with a steady German beat. Known for its toy fair and Christmas market, its sausages and gingerbread, and its association with former resident Albrecht Dürer as much as its ties to Nazism, the city persists in both the historical and contemporary consciousness of the German landscape.

⌐ GETTING THERE AND GETTING AROUND

Flights: Flughafenstr. 100 (tel. 937 00), 7km north of the city. **City-Airport-Express** (bus #20) runs every 30min. from U-Bahn #2 to "Hernnhütte" (DM6).

Trains: Trains chug to Würzburg (1hr., 2 per hour, DM28-42), Regensburg (1hr., 1 per hour, DM27-36), Munich (2hr., 2 per hour, DM54-74), Frankfurt (2hr., 1 per hour,

DM66-80), Stuttgart (2½hr., 6 per day, DM35-54), Berlin (6hr., every 2hr., DM149), and Prague (5hr., 2 per day). Computers outside the *Reisezentrum* help decipher schedules and sell tickets for travel within Germany.

Public Transportation: Choose from U-Bahn, streetcars, buses, regional trains (R-Bahn), and S-Bahn. Single-ride within the city DM3.30. *Kurzstrecke* (short distance) DM2.50. 10-ride ticket DM12.90. Day or weekend card DM7.80. The **VAG Verkehrszentrum,** downstairs in the train station (take the "Königstorpassage" escalator) offers free maps and transportation deals for tourists. Open M-F 7:30am-5:30pm.

Taxi: Tel. 194 10.

Bike Rental: Fahrradkiste, Knauerstr. 9 (tel. 287 90 64), outside the southwest corner of the Altstadt. Basic wheels DM9 per day with DM200 deposit. Mountain bikes DM15 per day with DM400 deposit. Open M-F 10am-7pm, Sa 10am-2pm.

Mitfahrzentrale: Strauchstr. 1 (tel. 194 44). Streetcar #4 to "Dutzendteich." Open M-F 9am-6pm, Sa 10am-1pm.

⑦ ORIENTATION AND PRACTICAL INFORMATION

The old city wall neatly circumscribes Nürnberg's thriving central district. From the train station, the main shopping district is across Frauentorgraben down **Königstr.,** which leads through the city walls. **Lorenzerplatz** and the **Hauptmarkt** lie just beyond this shopping district in the Altstadt's pedestrian zone. The **Burg** perches on a hill, overlooking the town from the northernmost part of the Altstadt.

TOURIST, FINANCIAL, AND LOCAL SERVICES

Tourist Offices: Verkehrsverein (tel. 233 60; fax 233 61 611; www.nuernberg.de), is in the train station near the main service desk. The staff offers free maps and a schedule of events and books **rooms** for a DM5 fee. Open M-Sa 9am-7pm. A **branch office** is on the Hauptmarkt near the golden fountain. Open May-Sept. M-Sa 9am-6pm, Su 10am-1 and 2-4pm; Oct.-April M-Sa 9am-6pm.

Tours: 2-5hr. English tours depart from the Hauptmarkt tourist office May-Oct. daily at 2pm. DM12, children under 14 free if accompanied by an adult.

Budget Travel: abr Reisebüro (tel. 201 00), on the Hauptmarkt, deciphers timetables and gives out information for a DM5 fee. Open M-F 9am-6:30pm, Sa 10am-1pm.

Currency Exchange: The **AmEx** office (below) is the cheapest option for those with or without The Card. Or head to the **post office** (below) or **Reisebank** (tel. 22 67 78). Facing the train station's central service desk walk left out the side door to the small beige trailer. DM5 commission for transactions under DM100, DM7.50 or 1% commission (whichever is higher) for transactions over DM100. Open M-Sa 7:45am-7:45pm, Su 9:15am-12:30pm and 1:30-5:15pm. Another good bet is the post office, below (DM2 commission).

American Express: Adlerstr. 2 (tel. 23 23 97), in the Hauptmarkt, at the corner of Tuchgasse and Winnerstr. Great rates for cash and traveler's checks. Nonmembers pay a 1% or DM2.50 fee. All AmEx services for cardholders or those with traveler's checks. Open M-F 9:30am-5:30pm, Sa 9:30am-12:30pm. Cashier closed noon-2pm.

Laundromat: SB Waschsalon, Spitzenbergstr. 2, near the University Mensa. Wash off the beer stains for DM6; suds run DM1. Open daily 6am-11pm.

EMERGENCY AND COMMUNICATIONS

Emergency: Tel. 110 or 192 22. **Police,** Jakobspl. 5. **Fire** and **Ambulance,** tel. 112.

Rape Crisis: Tel. 28 44 00. Counseling M 10am-noon, Tu 7-8pm, Th 4-6pm.

Pharmacy: City-Apotheke, Königstr. 29. Open M-F 8:30am-6:30pm, Sa 9am-4pm.

Hospital: Städtisches Klinikum, Flurstr. 17 (tel. 39 80). **Medical Assistance,** tel. 53 37 71.

Post Office: Bahnhofstr. 2, 90402 Nürnberg. **Exchanges money.** Open M-F 8am-7pm, Sa 9am-2pm, Su 11am-2pm.

Internet Access: Internetcafé M@x, Färberstr. 11 (tel. 23 23 84), at the corner of Frauengasse. Head up to the third floor of the complex; the café is on the right at the far end of the neon-lit hallway. Before 3pm 1hr. DM5; after 3pm 30min. DM5, 1hr. DM9. Open M-Sa noon-1am, Su 4pm-midnight.

PHONE CODE	0911

▐ ACCOMMODATIONS AND CAMPING

You don't have to trek outside the Altstadt walls to hang your hat in an inexpensive *Pension*, but it's best to call ahead in summer.

Jugendgästehaus (HI), Burg 2 (tel. 230 93 60; fax 23 09 36 11). From the station, cross Frauentorgraben, turn right, and walk along the outside of the city walls until you reach Königstor. Follow Königstr. through Lorenzerplatz over the bridge to the Hauptmarkt (10min.). Head in the direction of the golden fountain on the far left and bear right on Burgstr., then huff and puff up to the castle at the top of the hill in the direction of the sign pointing to Burgerstr. (about 20min.). Once a stable and grain storage for the imperial castle, the hostel's Romanesque arches, dizzying panorama over the city, and friendly desk staff (prone to playing with the loudspeakers) make for good hosteling fun. Doubles DM70, singles DM58. Reception 7am-1am. Curfew 1am. Reservations strongly recommended.

Jugend-Hotel Nürnberg, Rathsbergstr. 300 (tel. 521 60 92; fax 521 69 54). From the station, take U-Bahn #2 (direction: "Hernhütte") to the end, then bus #21 to "Zum Zelsenkeller." Rustic and cheerful, but far from the action. Nice surrounding grounds complement the dorm rooms, all with bath. Triples DM75, doubles DM58, singles DM37. Breakfast DM8. Reception 8am-10pm. Call ahead.

Hotel Garni Probst, Luitpoldstr. 9 (tel. 20 34 33; fax 205 93 36). From the station, follow the underground passage to Königsplatz past Burger King; turn left on Luitpoldstr. The block is seedy, the location central. The jolly family establishment is 3 floors up, with tiny, oddly shaped rooms. Singles DM40, with shower DM68, with bath DM80; doubles DM88, with shower DM100, with bath DM110-125. Breakfast included.

Gasthof Schwänlein, Hintere Sterngasse 11 (tel. 22 51 62; fax 241 90 08). From the station, take the underground passage to Königstr. and take an immediate left on Frauentormauerstr. Follow the town wall as it curves right; the hotel is about 200m down on the left. The quiet hallways of the *Pension* are soothing, although rooms are slightly cramped. Singles DM40, with shower DM50; doubles DM70, with shower DM80. Reservations by fax or mail only.

Pension Vater Jahn-Parma, Jahnstr. 13 (tel. 44 45 07; fax 431 52 36). From the south exit of the station, head down Eilgutstr. for 3 blocks (under the pedestrian underpass), then left under the heavily trafficked Tafelfeld tunnel (8min.). Gleaming rooms. Singles DM43, with bath DM63; doubles DM75, with shower DM85, with bath DM95. Breakfast included.

Camping: Campingplatz im Volkspark Dutzendteich, Hans-Kalb-Str. 56 (tel. 81 11 22), behind the soccer stadium. S-Bahn #2 (direction: "Freucht") to "Frankenstadion." DM9 per person. Tent DM5-10. Car DM5. Reception 2-10pm. Open May-Sept. Call ahead.

◖ FOOD

Nürnberg is famous for its cuisine: *Rostbratwurst* (rough but delectable grilled sausage), boiled *Sauerwurst*, and *Lebkuchen*, a candied variant of gingerbread, traditionally devoured at Christmas. For a super food, film, and beer extravaganza, bust a move to Cine Città (see **Entertainment and Nightlife,** p. 310). **Aldi,** near the station on Königstr., stocks cheap **groceries.** (Open M-F 8:30am-6pm, Sa 8am-2pm.)

BAYERN

Bratwurst Häusle, Rathauspl. 1, next to the Sebalduskirche, is the most famous and crowded *Bratwurst* spot in Nürnberg for good reason. 6 *Rostbratwürste* with sauerkraut or potato salad DM9.50. Beer DM5. Open M-Sa 10am-9:30pm.

Café Mohr, Färberstr. 3 (tel. 24 31 39), at the intersection with Karolinenstr. With an Art Deco atmosphere overlooking a lively square, the café is a fun meeting place. Crepes (DM5-9), salads (DM7-12), pineapple shakes (DM5.50), and cappuccino (DM4). Open M-Th 9am-midnight, F-Sa 9am-1am, Su 2pm-midnight.

Enchilada, Hauptmarkt (tel. 244 84 98), behind the Frauenkirche. A popular Mexican restaurant and bar with a variety of vegetarian options. Nachos (DM10), mexico salad (DM13), veggie quesadillas (DM16), and crazy cocktails (DM6-12). Open daily 11am-1am.

Bratwurst Röslein, Rathausplatz 6 (tel. 24 18 60), is a carnivorous paradise for flesh-eating monsters in an enormous beer hall with long wooden tables. Liver dumpling soup (DM4.50), roasted pig with dumplings smothered in dark beer sauce (DM11). No meal over DM11. Open daily 10am-midnight. Kitchen closes at 11pm.

■ SIGHTS

Allied bombing left little of old Nürnberg for posterity. The churches, castle, and buildings were all reconstructed after the war; most churches display post-war photos and feature empty pedestals where exterior statues were lost in the bombing. From the station, the closest part of the Altstadt is a walled-in area filled with cottages and shops; this is the **Handwerkhof,** a tourist trap masquerading as a historical attraction. The real sights lie farther up **Königstraße,** in the northwest corner of the Altstadt at the foot of the castle, around the Hauptmarkt.

KAISERBURG. Atop the hill, Nürnberg's symbol offers the best vantage point of the city. Over a period of five centuries, the Kaisers' fortress was added onto and subtracted from, making it Germany's most morphologically diverse castle. Originally erected in a much-reduced form in the 11th century, Germany's next emperor, Friedrich Barbarossa, expanded the Burg significantly. A war to defend the castle from the Hohenzollerns precipitated its near-total destruction in the 1300s, and the Gothic Kaiserburg extant today is largely a result of the 15th and 16th centuries. The spartan chambers housed every Holy Roman Emperor after Konrad III—it was law that every German Kaiser spend at least his first day in office here. Since the castle had no heating, however, the Kaisers usually spent their nights in the warm patrician homes of the Altstadt. Massive stone walls 13m tall and 7m thick surround the castle and the manicured gardens. Inside lurk the Romanesque chapel and the imperial living quarters. The obligatory 45-minute tour in German covers all parts and epochs of the Kaiserburg; the English-language tour offered by the tourist office also covers the castle (see p. 306). *(Tel. 22 57 26. Burg open daily April-Sept. 9am-noon and 12:45-5pm; Oct.-March 9:30am-noon and 12:45-4pm. Garden open daily 9am-8pm. Tours daily every 30min. Last morning tour noon; last afternoon tour April-Sept. 4:30pm; Oct.-March 3:30pm. DM9, students DM8.)*

AROUND THE ALTSTADT AND CASTLE

LORENZKIRCHE. Completely destroyed in WWII, the beautiful Gothic structure has been restored and once again displays perfectly preserved works covering every surface. Of particular interest is the 20m high **tabernacle,** and its delicate stone tendrils curling up into the roof vaulting. The large wooden carving hanging in front of the altar is Veit Stoß's 1517 masterpiece *Engelsgruß.* Free tours of the church meet at the entrance. *(On Lorenzpl. Open M-Sa 9am-5pm, Su 1-4pm. Tours in summer M-F 11am and 2pm; in winter M-F 2pm.)*

HAUPTMARKTPLATZ. The **Schöner Brunnen** (Beautiful Fountain) resembles nothing so much as the steeple of a Gothic church. Check out the 40 imaginatively carved figures, with Moses and the prophets up top. The main attraction of the small 14th-century **Frauenkirche** is its ornate facade, including the **Männleinlaufen,** the clock in the center of the facade. Crowds gather at noon when a small wooden band plays around the seated figure of Kaiser Karl, who commissioned the church in 1350. *(Open M-Th 8am-6pm, F 8am-5pm, Sa 8am-7:30pm, Su 10am-8pm. Free summer tours M 12:10pm and W 6pm.)*

RATHAUS. Built in early Baroque style and sprinkled with a little Renaissance Classicism, Nürnberg's Rathaus once held the largest council chamber in central Europe until it was destroyed by fire in 1945. Beneath the building hides the Lochgefängnisse (dungeons), exhibiting juicy medieval torture instruments. *(Tel. 231 26 90. Obligatory tour every 30min.; English translation available. Open April to mid-Oct. and Dec. M-F 10am-4:30pm, Sa-Su 10am-1pm. DM4, students DM2.)*

SEBALDUSKIRCHE. The Catholic church stands across from the Rathaus. Once a year on the feast day of St. Sebaldus, the saint's remains are taken from their resting spot in the bronze tomb in front of the altar for a parade around town. *(Open daily March-May and Sept.-Dec. 9:30am-6pm; June-Aug. 9:30am-8pm; Jan.-Feb. 9:30-4pm.)*

FELSENGÄNGE. This web of passageways and cellars below the Altstadt dates back more than 100 years. Bring a jacket; it's cold enough to store large barrels of beer. *(Bergstr. 19. Tel. 22 70 66. In the Altstadthof. 1hr. tours descend daily from Albrecht-Dürer-Platz at 11am, 1, 3, and 5pm. DM7, students DM5, children under 11 free.)*

RUINS OF THE THIRD REICH

DUTZENDTEICH. The ruins of the site of the Nazi Party Congress rallies of 1934 and 1935 possess a deserted disquiet and an unsettling non-presence to remind visitors of a terrifying moment in German history. The rallies drew more than 500,000 citizens annually. The park now holds the remains of Hitler's planned Nazi compound, which he proudly declared "the largest building site in the world"; the predominant building style represents the apogee of Nazi architecture—massive and harsh, mixing modernist straight lines with Neoclassical pretension. The litter strewn about and the overgrowth on the paths and buildings define the mood today. The **Zeppelinfield,** on the far side of the lake, contains the **Tribüne,** the massive marble platform from which Hitler addressed more than 100,000 inspired spectators. The faint remains of a swastika stained into the marble are visible on the central promontory despite attempts to efface it.

The poles spaced intermittently along the desolate field once stationed enormous banners, and were made infamous by Leni Riefenstahl's film **Triumph des Willens** (Triumph of the Will), which immortalized the 1935 Party rally in one of the most terrifying, enduring depictions of the Fascist aesthetic. On the other side of the lake are the remains of the congress center, designed to function as the party headquarters after the war. The overwhelming emotional power of Nazi events—injecting Wagnerian theater and Catholic ritual into Fascist grandiosity—can be seen in the exhibit **Faszination und Gewalt** (Fascination and Terror), accompanied by an excellent brochure; it's located inside the **Golden Hall,** at the rear of the Tribüne. The exhibits cover the rise of the Third Reich, Nürnberg's role in the growth of National Socialism, and the war crimes trials of 1946. The government has brainstormed uses for the abandoned structures; right now the wide steps of the Tribüne are used by skateboarders who pull their most daring stunts off the podium, while the congress hall is used for storage. *(Take S-Bahn #2 (direction: "Freucht") to "Dutzendteich," then take the middle of the three exits, head down the stairs and turn left. 200m down the highway is Strandcafé Wanner; turn left just after it and follow the paved path. Tel. 86 98 97. Golden Hall open mid-May to Oct. Tu-Su 10am-6pm. DM5, students DM4.)*

JUSTIZGEBÄUDE. On the other side of town, Nazi leaders faced Allied military judges during the infamous **Nürnberg war crimes trials** held in room 600 of the Justizgebäude. Soon after the trials, in October 1946, 10 men were hanged for their crimes against humanity. The building still serves as a courthouse, though it contains a small display on the trials. *(Fürtherstr. 22. Take U-Bahn #1 to "Bärenschanze" and continue farther on Furtherstr., walking away from the Altstadt.)*

🏛 MUSEUMS

GERMANISCHES NATIONALMUSEUM. This gleaming, modern building chronicles the last millennium of German art, with huge displays of medieval sculpture and a reconstructed cloister. Highlights include a few of Rembrandt's self-portrait etchings and paintings by Cranach, including a portrait of Martin Luther. *(Kartäusergasse 1. Tel. 133 10. From the Königstr. exit of the tunnel from the station turn left through the archway onto Frauentormauer and right on Kartäusergasse. Open Tu and Th-Su 10am-5pm, W 10am-9pm. DM6, students and seniors DM3.)*

FASZINATION UND GEWALT. One of Germany's foremost exhibitions on the Third Reich, located on the former Nazi Parade Grounds. See **Sights,** above.

ALBRECHT-DÜRER-HAUS. The residence of Nürnberg's favorite son and his long-suffering wife, the house contains period furniture along with a very few of Dürer's etchings and copies of his paintings (most originals are on display in Vienna, Munich, and Berlin), as well as an exhibit of less-than-masterful Dürer-derived works by modern artists. *(Albrecht-Dürer-Str. 29. Tel. 231 25 68. Uphill from the Sebalduskirche entrance. Open Tu-W and F-Su 10am-5pm, Th 10am-8pm. DM5, students DM2.50.)*

ALTSTADTHOF. The *Hof* houses a small historic brewery. No free samples, but tempting 0.2L bottles of house brew cost a mere DM2.50. *(Bergstr. 19. Tel. 22 43 27. Hourly tours M-F 2-7pm, Sa-Su 11am-5pm. DM4.50, children DM2.50.)*

🎵🎭 ENTERTAINMENT AND NIGHTLIFE

Nürnberg's nightspots run the gamut from ultra-traditional to hyper-modern. The Altstadt is packed with bars and clubs, the best of which reside in the west, near the river. Pick up the weekly *Plärrer* (DM4) at newsstands; the region's best magazine, it lists musical events, cultural happenings, and addresses of bars, discos, and cafés. The free guide *Doppelpunkt* is doled out at many bars and discos.

Cine Città, Gewerbemuseumspl. 3 (tel. 20 66 60), packs seven cafés, 12 cinemas, and a disco into its multimedia megaplex. The multi-cultural, constantly morphing restaurants offer affordable meals. (Open M-Th and Su until 3am, F-Sa until 4am.) Although most movies are dubbed into German, the weekly *Filmtips* provides a schedule of films in their original. **Roxy,** Julius-Loßman-Str. 16 (tel. 488 40), shows more current English-language flicks, from trashy horror movies to love-sick romances. **Planetarium,** Regiomontarsweg 1 (tel. 959 35 38), projects the heavens onto a cement dome. (Shows W 4 and 7:30pm, Th 7:30pm, and 2 weekends per month Sa 2:30pm, Su 11:30pm. Call for schedules. DM5, students DM3.50.)

BARS

Treibhaus, Karl-Grillenberger-Str. 28 (tel. 22 30 41), in the west part of the Altstadt, south of Westtor. Metal tables and dim lighting draw a well-heeled, older crowd trying to keep it real. Killer cocktails with snacks, salads, pastas, and breakfast (DM5-16.50). Their *Milchkaffee* gives "foam" a new meaning—be initiated. Open M-W 8am-1am, Th-F 8am-2am, Sa 9am-2am, Su 9am-1am. Kitchen open until 10pm.

Saigon, Lammsgasse 8 (tel. 244 86 57), off Albrecht-Dürer-Str. Enter through the industrial steel door in the passageway; the small bar swims in smoke and the croonings of Billy Holiday. You'd better know you're cool already—you wouldn't have come here otherwise. Espresso DM3, cocktails DM10.50-12. Open daily 9pm-3am.

Cartoon, An der Sparkasse 6 (tel. 22 71 70), is a popular gay bar off Theatergasse, near Lorenzplatz. Traditional *Kneipe* interior gets revamped by its patrons. Baguettes DM7. Beer DM4.30-4.50. Open M-Sa 11am-1am, Su 2pm-1am.

Starclub, Maxtorgraben 33 (tel. 55 16 82), entrance is in the back—follow the graffiti and the parade of slouching high schoolers. No *paparazzi*, but a relaxed ramshackle garden house with rooms bathed in cool blue lights. Diverse young crew creates a pocket of mischief in a residential area. Beer DM4. Open M-F 9:30am-1am, Sa-Su 2:30pm-1am.

Café Ruhestörung, Tetzelgasse 21 (tel. 22 19 21). From the Rathaus, head right on Theresienstr., then left on Tetzelgasse. Relaxed atmosphere, though quite a scene—people-watch with a vengeance. Outdoor seating with satanic red lighting. Serves breakfast, sandwiches, salads (DM5.50-12.50), and warm meals (DM8.50-13.50). Beer on tap DM5-7. Open M-W 7:30am-1am, Th-F 7:30am-2am, Sa 9am-2am, Su 9am-1am.

DANCE CLUBS

Mach 1, Kaiserstr. 1-9 (tel. 20 30 30), in the center of the Altstadt near Karlsbrücke. Grooving patrons change size, shape, and drapery depending on the day. Thursday attracts the mellow "Best of the 70s to 90s" crowd; Friday functions with "funk" and hip-hop; Saturday signifies house. Monday Mach 3, the sharpest yet. Open Th-F 10pm-4am, Sa 10pm-5am. Cover DM10.

Forum, Regensburger Str. 334. S-Bahn #2 to "Frankenstadion." Two dance floors assuage the musical needs of the cool. Hip-hop, trip-hop, and techno all represent. Some of the best bands around play at this joint. Open F-Sa and every 2nd Th 9pm-4am.

Tolerant, Königstr. 39. A mixed club frequented by queer and straight and everything in between. Some nights are men or women only—call ahead. Open M-Tu, Th, and Su 9pm-4am, W 8pm-4am, F-Sa 9pm-5am. Cover DM10.

BAYREUTH

Once you've turned off Tristanstr. onto Isoldenstr., walked past Walküregasse, and finally ducked into the Parsifal Pharmacy, there will be little doubt that you're in Bayreuth, the adopted home of Richard Wagner and the site of the annual *Festspiele*—a pilgrimage of BMW-driving devotees coming to bask in his operatic masterpieces. Wagner retreated to Bayreuth in 1872 to escape his creditors and other folks he had burned. The remote town promised privacy, an 18th-century opera house, and an enchanting ego-fluffing concept—fans would now have to trek great lengths to experience a true Wagner performance. The grandiosity of it all has left Bayreuth a treasure trove of gorgeous buildings. An affection for pomp (or a well-founded desire to mock Wagner groupies) makes Bayreuth worthwhile even for those less-than-enthralled with the man and his music.

🛈 PRACTICAL INFORMATION

Bayreuth is pronounced "buy-royt," *not* "bay ruth"; you will be scorched by lightning should you speak otherwise.

Trains: The train station lies 5min. north of the Altstadt; exit to the left and walk down Bahnhofstr. to reach the center. Trains zoom to Nürnberg (1hr., change at Lichtenfels, DM24.60), Bamberg (1½hr., DM24.60), and Regensburg (2hr., DM40).

Tourist Office: Luitpoldpl. 9 (tel. 885 88; fax 885 55), about four blocks to the left of the station. Offers maps, accommodation lists, a monthly calendar of events, and city **walking tours.** (DM8, students DM5. Tours May-Oct. Tu-Sa 10am; Nov.-April Sa only.) **Private rooms** are only available during the *Festspiele* (DM10 fee if the tourist office makes arrangements for you); at other times, the staff finds rooms in hotels and *Pensionen* for a DM5 fee. The office also sells tickets to Bayreuth's theater, opera, and musical venues. Open M-F 9am-6pm, Sa 9:30am-1pm.

Currency Exchange: Citibank, Maximilianstr. 46. Open M, Tu, Th 9am-1pm and 2-6pm, W 9am-1pm, and F 9am-1pm and 2-5pm.

Post Office: Bürgerreutherstr. 1, 95444 Bayreuth. Located across from the train station and to the right. Open M-F 8am-7pm, Sa 8am-1pm.

BAYERN

PHONE CODE	0921

ACCOMMODATIONS

If you visit during the *Festspiele* and forgot to book a room ahead, expect to shell out the cash if you want to stay in Bayreuth. Almost any other time, though, prices are reasonable and beds are available.

Jugendherberge (HI), Universitätsstr. 28 (tel. 25 12 62; fax 51 28 05). Bayreuth's brand-new hostel lies outside the city center past the Hofgarten near the university. Take bus #4 (DM2.70) from the Marktplatz to "Mensa," walk out of the *Uni* onto Universitätstr., and turn left. Or walk down Ludwigstr. from the city center, take a left onto Friedrichstr., then veer left onto Jean-Paul-Str., which merges with Universitätsstr. Friendly but a tad regimented: at 10pm, *everything* locks up. DM20. Breakfast included. Sheets DM5.50. Reception 7am-noon and 5-9:30pm. Lockout 9:30-11am. Curfew 10pm. Open March to mid-Dec.

Gasthof Hirsch, St. Georgen 26 (tel. 267 14 and 85 31 42). A 10min. walk behind the train station, on a corner with a rainbow of geraniums spilling out the windows. Exit the train station in the back, just beyond track five. Take a left as you exit, then right onto Brandenburger Str., and left on St. Georgen. Clean and crisp with 18 beds. Singles DM35-40; doubles DM70-80.

Gasthof zum Brandenburger, St. Georgen 9 (tel. 78 90 60; fax 78 90 62 40). The rooms are nice and sunny, as is the beer garden, and spiffy ivy wallpaper adorns the third floor. Singles DM35, with shower DM60; doubles DM60, with shower DM130.

Gasthof Schindler, Bahnhofstr. 9 (tel. 262 49). Close to the station. Clean rooms and a basement restaurant. Singles DM60; doubles DM95.

 FOOD

Bayreuth's abundance of traditional Bavarian fare will make your head (and stomach) spin. For cheaper eats, head to the **Norma** supermarket, Maximilianstr. 62 (open M-F 8:30am-7pm, Sa 8am-4pm), or check out the **market** in the Rotmainhal near Hindenburgstr. (Open W 7am-12:30pm and Sa 7am-1pm.)

Mensa (tel. 60 81). Fill 'er up at the university cafeteria for DM3-6; any student ID should do. Take bus #4 (DM2.70) from the Marktplatz to "Mensa," then walk past the buildings straight ahead. The enormous, low-roofed *Mensa* is to the right up the steps. Trade the cashier your ID and DM5 for a card, then put money on the card at the *Automaten* in the hall. After using the card to buy food, get your DM5, plus any balance left on the card, back from the cashier. Open March-April and Oct. 8am-6pm, May-July and Nov.-Feb. 8am-8:30pm.

Gaststätte Porsch, Maximilianstr. 63 (tel. 646 49). Enormous portions at great prices. *Schnitzel* and steak meals DM13-24. Open M-F 7am-8:30pm, Sa 7am-5pm.

Brauereischänke am Markt, Maximilianstr. 56 (tel. 649 19). The *bayerische Küche* comes up big with *Bratwurst* with potato salad or *Kraut* (DM8.80) and hearty steaks (DM17). Open M-Sa 9am-noon, Su 11:30am-6pm.

Hansl's Holzofen Pizzeria, Jean-Paul-Platz (tel. 543 44). An excellent, cheaper alternative to the local cuisine. Pizza DM7-15. Open daily 10am-10:30pm.

Café Wundertüte, Richard-Wagner-Str. 33 (tel. 51 47 48), has a cup of coffee and a slice of raspberry *Torte* with your name on it (DM5.80), served in a wood-paneled atmosphere. Delightful selection of small salads, sausages, and cheeses (DM4-10). Open M-F 10am-6:30pm, Sa 10am-5pm.

 SIGHTS

FESTSPIELHAUS. Wagner devotees visiting Bayreuth when the *Festspiele* are over console themselves with a tour of the **Festspielhaus.** From the train station, go right and up at the end of Siegfried-Wagner-Allee. To fund the 1872 construction,

BAYERN

the composer hit up sugar daddy Ludwig II, who was in the midst of his own ego-centric building spree. Ludwig responded with modest amounts of cash, resulting in a semi-spartan structure—Wagner fans must endure cushionless seats and precious little leg room to catch a show. *(Tel. 787 80. Tours Sept.-Oct. and Dec.-May at 10, 10:45am, 2:15, and 3pm. DM2.50.)*

RICHARD-WAGNER-MUSEUM. Haus Wahnfried was once home to Bayreuth's famed composer. It houses an inexhaustible and kitschy—yet valuable—collection of scores, costumes, and stage sets. See Wagner stamps, coins, and playing cards, as well as his spoons, mirror, and little *Wotan* and *Sieglinde* dolls (the Wagnerian Ken and Barbie). Three death masks provide morbid pleasure: Wagner's, composer Carl Maria von Weber's, and that of Wagner's friend Ludwig II. The thousands of exhibits are in German only—it might behoove you to pick up the melodramatic English guide-booklet (DM3). Those who fail to appreciate his *Gesamtkunstwerke* ("Total Works of Art," as he modestly referred to them) should recall Mark Twain's fiendishly accurate assessment of Wagner's music: "It's better than it sounds." Behind the house lie the graves of Wagner, his wife Cosima, and Russ, his big black dog. *(Richard-Wagner-Str. 48. Tel. 757 28 16. Open April-Oct. M, W, and F 9am-5pm, Tu and Th 9am-8pm; Nov.-March daily 10am-5pm. DM4, students DM2. 1-day passes for the Wagner Museum, the Jean-Paul-Museum, and Franz-Liszt-Museum available for DM6; 3-day passes to 6 museums for 1 adult and 2 children under 15 DM14.50. Wagner's compositions are played in the drawing room daily at 10am, noon, and 2pm; videos are shown at 11am and 3pm.)*

FRANZ-LISZT-MUSEUM. Just to the left of the haughty Wagner Museum, the **Franz-Liszt-Museum** exhibits the composer's pianos and music sheets and displays the room where he died (again, complete with death mask). In Bayreuth, Liszt is probably best known for fathering Wagner's wife—indeed, musical virtuosos also inbreed. For more on Liszt, see p. 31. *(Wahnfriedstr. 9. Tel. 757 28 18. Open daily 10am-noon and 2-5pm. DM3, students and seniors DM1.)*

JEAN-PAUL-MUSEUM. This museum celebrates the life of Bayreuth's greatest poet with an endless collection of notebooks and chairs. *(Wahnfriedstr. 1. Tel 757 28 17. Open daily 10am-noon and 2-5pm. DM3, students and seniors DM1. Ring to get in.)*

DEUTSCHES FREIMAURERMUSEUM. Inside the **Hofgarten,** an English-style park, sits the **Deutsches Freimaurermuseum.** If you've wondered what's inside those windowless Freemason temples, this museum of the world's oldest secular fraternity is the place for you. The rituals of masonic brotherhood have transpired in Bayreuth for 225 years. *(Hofgarten 1. Tel. 698 24. Open Tu-F 10am-noon and 2-4pm, Sa 10am-noon. DM2, students DM1. Ring to get in.)*

NEUES SCHLOSS. The 18th-century Baroque castle is the former residence of Friedrich the Great's sister, **Margravine Wilhelmine.** Considered one of Europe's most brilliant and cultured women, she married the Margrave of Bayreuth and ended up stuck in what must have seemed a provincial cow town. After a mysterious castle fire, she redecorated and rococoed like mad King Ludwig, and when she finished gilding the home furnishings, she swept her eyes across Bayreuth and strove to cosmopolitanize it. *(Tel. 759 69 21. Castle open April-Sept. Tu-Su 10am-5pm; Oct.-March Tu-Su 10am-3pm. DM4, students DM3.)*

MARKGRÄFLICHES OPERNHAUS. The lavishly ornate 1748 opera house is the tangible fruit of Wilhelmine's labours. Wagner originally thought this theater's pomp appropriate for his production, but its 500 seats and stage proved much too small for his grandiose needs. *(Opernstr. Tel. 759 69 22. Tours, including multimedia light show, every 45min. Open April- Sept. Tu-Su 10am-5pm; Oct.-March Tu-Su 10am-3pm. DM4.)*

KREUZSTEINBAD. If you're sweating from Bayreuth's palatial magnificence, make a splash in Bayreuth's fabulous outdoor pool, whose opulence proves that grand Wagnerian style is not limited to 18th-century opera houses. *(Universitätsstr. 20. Tel. 661 07. Open May-Sept. daily 7am-8pm. DM5, students DM2.50.)*

BAYERN

♫ THE WAGNER FESTSPIELE

For Wagnerians, a devotional visit to Bayreuth is like a pious pilgrimage to Mecca. Every summer from July 25 to August 28, thousands of visitors pour in for the **Bayreuth Festspiele**, a vast and bombastic—in a word, Wagnerian—celebration of the composer's works. The music fills the **Festspielhaus** theater that Wagner built for his "music of the future." The world's operatic darlings, directors, and conductors have been taking on *The Flying Dutchman, Der Ring des Nibelungen*, and *The Meistersinger* here since 1876. Judging from the number of German Wagner societies and clubs, the spectacle will probably continue for as long as the Holy Grail is old. Tickets for the festival (DM80-300, obstructed view DM40-50) go on sale several years in advance and sell out quickly. Wagnerophiles write to Bayreuther Festspiele, 95402 Bayreuth well before September *every year* and hope for the best. You'll be notified some time after mid-November. Reserve a room in town as soon as you get tickets.

COBURG

Coburg only joined Bayern in 1920 after centuries in Sachsen. This move fortuitously saved the city from inclusion in the GDR. The 1947 division of Germany shifted the town's geographical location from the heartland to the margins. Today, wealthy Coburg sits at the center again, but a brief trip north across the old GDR border reveals the vast incongruities the past 45 years have created. The 11th-century town has been beautifully preserved, thanks to an arbitrary line in the woods.

⚐ ORIENTATION AND PRACTICAL INFORMATION. Hourly **trains** go to Nürnberg (1½hr., DM39) and Erfurt (3hr., DM54). From the station, turn right on Lossaustr., left at the light on Mohrenstr., around the large, central Stadtcafé, and right on Spitalgasse to reach the Renaissance **Altstadt** (15min.). Coburg's **tourist office**, Herrngasse 4 (tel. 741 80; fax 74 18 29), off the Markt, offers free maps and books **rooms** (DM40-100) for free. (Open April-Oct. M-F 9am-6:30pm, Sa 9am-1pm; Nov.-March M-F 9am-5pm, Sa 9am-1pm.) **Tours** in German departs from the Markt. (Sa 3pm. DM5.) The **post office**, Hindenburgstr. 6, 96450 Coburg, is to the left off Mohrenstr. on the way to the Altstadt. (Open M-F 8am-6pm, Sa 8am-noon.) The **telephone code** is 09561.

⚑ ACCOMMODATIONS. Jugendherberge Schloß Ketschendorf (HI), Parkstr. 2 (tel. 153 30; fax 286 53), rests in a converted palace. The sight of play-school hostel furniture in the grand castle is a funny sight, but the modern rooms make spotless sense. Take bus #1 from the Markt to "DJH"; Parkstr. is up on the left. Or head down Ketschengasse to Ketschendorfer Str., and walk to Parkstr. (25min. DM22. Breakfast included. Sheets DM5.50. Reception 5-6pm and 8-9:30pm. Lockout 9am-noon. Curfew 10pm, but you can get a key.) **Gasthof Goldenes Kreuz**, Herrngasse 1 (tel. 904 73; fax 905 02), on Marktpl., offers clean, simple rooms and a restaurant downstairs. (Singles DM49, doubles DM99. Reception 11am-2:30pm and 5-11pm.) **Münchner Hofbräu**, Kleine Johannisgasse 8 (tel. 750 49; fax 904 34), is both a restaurant and *Pension*, two blocks from Marktpl. off Spitalgasse. (Singles with bath DM55, doubles with bath DM105. Breakfast included.)

⚑🍴 FOOD AND NIGHTLIFE. Two of Coburg's specialty foods are *Thüringer Klösser* (dumplings) and *Coburger Bratwurst*. Billowing clouds of smoke and the smell of grilled sausage hang thick in the air over the main square, home to a **farmer's market** (W and Sa 7am-1pm) and a **fruit market** (Tu 7am-noon). **Pizzeria Grillschorch**, Steinweg 46 (tel. 753 54), serves delicious pizzas (DM7-16) and pastas. (DM7.50-12. Open M-F 10am-11pm, Sa-Su 10am-midnight.) For **groceries**, head to **Norma** on Hindenburgstr., across from the post office. (Open M-F 8:30am-6:30pm, Sa 8am-2pm.) **Café Filou**, Bahnhofstr. 11 (tel. 900 70), offers a relaxed late-night atmosphere with funky round chairs and sepia-toned photographs. (Open M-

Sa 9:30am-1am, Su 10am-1am.) **Café-Floh,** Herrngasse 12, off Marktpl., attracts students with its dark-wood environment, conducive to late-night philosophizing over beer. Fresh baguettes run DM3-7. (Open Tu-Su 8pm-3am.)

◼ SIGHTS. The huge 16th-century building on Marktpl. is the frescoed **Rathaus.** The old **Stadthaus** across the square was once the abode of the Coburg dukes. The proud central statue is of **Prince Albert,** husband of Queen Victoria. To the right down Herrngasse towers the part-Renaissance, part-neo-Gothic **Schloß Ehrenburg** (tel. 808 80), the residence of the Coburg dukes from 1547 to 1918. (Tours April-Nov. Tu-Su 10am-4:30pm; Oct.-March Tu-Su 10am-3:30pm. DM4, students and seniors DM3.) Paved footpaths wind through the **Hofgarten,** a shaded, grassy expanse stretching from the Schloß to the 11th-century **Veste.** Allow 45 minutes to hike up the deceptively steep hill, or take bus #8 from the Rathaus to "Veste" (DM3.50) or the "Veste Express" which runs more often (DM3) and walk up about 50m. The 16th-century fortress, encircled by a double set of fortified walls, was inhabited until 1918, when Karl Eduard abdicated the dukedom. The **Kunstmuseum** (tel. 879 48) at the Veste houses all sorts of medieval goodies, from paintings by Cranach the Elder to a room once occupied by Martin Luther. (Open April-Oct. Tu-Su 10am-5pm; Nov.-March Tu-Su 1-4pm. DM6.) Back in town to the right off Herrngasse is the minty-green **Puppenmuseum,** Rückertstr. 2-3 (tel. 740 47). In one of its 32 chronologically ordered rooms following doll history from 1800 to 1955, spot Lilli, a curvy German doll from the 1950s intended for adults; the then-unknown American toy company Mattel bought the rights to her in 1958, and one year later young girls went Barbie-crazy, playing with an awkwardly shaped blonde. (Open April-Oct. daily 9am-5pm; Nov.-March Tu-Su 10am-5pm. DM3.50, students DM3.)

BAMBERG

Largely overlooked by travelers, Bamberg boasts a history spanning a thousand years. Emperor Henry II liked it so much that he made Bamberg the center of his empire and crowned it with a colossal cathedral. The magnificent building is but one shining example of the city's beauty—take time to behold the city's imperial palace, frescoes, and widely varied architecture. Bamberg's treasures owe a great deal to the city's sheer luck; unlike most German cities, it escaped two virulent wars relatively unscathed. In the Thirty Years War, the city survived two sieges by the formidable Swedish King Gustavus Adolphus; three centuries later, the city emerged from WWII with minor bruises. Today, Bamberg basks in its half-timbered splendor with an easy disposition not found in more touristed Bavarian cities.

✦ ▐▌ ORIENTATION AND TRANSPORTATION

The heart of Bamberg lies on an island between the **Rhein-Main-Danube** canal and the **Regnitz River** (named for its location at the confluence of the Regen and the Pegnitz Rivers). Across the Regnitz away from the train station and past the island lie the winding streets of the Altstadt. From the station, walk down Luitpoldstr., cross the canal, and walk straight on Willy-Lessing-Str. until it empties into Schönleinsplatz. Turn right onto Lange Str. and left up Obere Brückestr., which leads through the archway of the Rathaus and across the Regnitz (25-30min.). Or grab any city bus in front of the station to "ZOB" for a quick ride into town.

Trains: The main station is on Ludwigstr. Trains to Nürnberg (1hr., 3 per hour, DM8.20), Würzburg (1¼hr., 2 per hour, DM28), Munich (2½-4hr., 1-2 per hour, DM90), and Frankfurt (3¼hr., 1 per hour, DM81).

Public Transportation: An excellent transportation net centers around the large, yellow *ZOB* (Zentralomnibusbahnhof) on Promenadestr. off Schönleinspl. Single ride DM1.80. 5-ride ticket DM5. For information, head to **i Punkt.** Open M-F 7am-7pm, Sa 9am-2pm. All tickets and maps can be purchased from machines.

Taxi: Tel. 150 15 or 345 45.

Bike Rental: Fahrradhaus Griesmann, Kleberstr. 25 (tel. 229 67). Walk straight on Luit-poldstr. from the station, right on Heinrichsdamm after the bridge, left at the next bridge, and take the first right on Kleberstr. DM12 per day. ID required. Open M-F 9am-12:30pm and 2-5:45pm, Sa 9am-1pm.

▋ PRACTICAL INFORMATION

The **Bamberg Card,** valid for two days, gives great discounts on public transportation in the city, a walking tour, and admission to five museums (1 person DM13, 2 people DM24, 3 people DM35).

Tourist Office: Fremdenverkehrsamt, Geyerwörthstr. 3 (tel. 87 11 61; fax 87 19 60), on an island in the Regnitz. Follow the directions to the Altstadt, above. Once through the Rathaus, take two lefts and re-cross the Regnitz on the wooden footbridge; the tourist office is on the right under the arches. Avoid paying DM0.50 for a map by picking up a free hotel list, which has a better map. The staff books **rooms** for a DM5 fee. Open April-Oct. M-F 9am-6pm, Sa 9am-3pm., Su 10am-2pm; Nov.-March closed Su.

Tours: City tours meet in front of the tourist office April-Oct. M-Sa 10:30am and 2pm, Su 11am; Nov.-March M-Sa 2pm, Su 11am. DM8, students DM5. Tours of the cathedral and the Neue Residenz meet at the Neue Residenz and leave when there are "enough people." April-Sept. daily 9am-noon and 1:30-5pm; Oct.-March 9am-noon and 1:30-4pm. DM8, students DM6.

Currency Exchange: Citibank, on Schönleinspl. (tel. 332 21 11). Open M-Tu and Th 9am-1pm and 2-6pm, W 9am-1pm, F 9am-1pm and 2-5pm.

Bookstore: Görres Bücher, Lange Str. 24, stocks a good selection of contemporary novels in English and French on the top floor. Open M-F 9am-7pm, Sa 9am-2pm.

Laundromat: SB Waschsalon, in the 2nd floor of the Atrium mall to the left of the station. Wash DM8, dry DM1 per 8min. Open daily 7am-10pm.

Women's Resources: A woman's café pops up every Tuesday evening in **Café Jenseits,** Promenadestr. 5 (tel. 210 94), off Schönleinspl. The same building becomes a women's center M 9am-1pm.

Emergency: Tel. 110. **Police,** Schildstr. 81 (tel. 912 95 09). **Fire** and **Ambulance,** tel. 112.

Rape Crisis Line: Tel. 582 80.

Pharmacy: Martin-Apotheke, Grüner Markt 21, has a list of 24hr. pharmacies in the window. Open M-F 8:30am-6pm, Th 8:30am-7pm, Sa 8:30am-2pm.

Hospital: Klinikum Bamberg, Buger Str. 80 (tel. 50 30).

Post Office: Ludwigstr. 25, 96052 Bamberg, across from the train station. Open M-F 7:30am-6pm, Sa 8am-12:30pm.

PHONE CODE	0951

▋ ACCOMMODATIONS AND CAMPING

Most inexpensive lodgings can be found near **Luitpoldstraße,** the street that runs from in front of the train station.

Jugendherberge Wolfsschlucht (HI), Oberer Leinritt 70 (tel. 560 02 or 563 44; fax 552 11). Bus #18 to "Am Regnitzufer" (every 20min., DM1.50). Far from the city center, but rooms are tidy. DM20. Breakfast included. Sheets DM5.50. Reception 5-10pm. Curfew 10pm. Because it's the only hostel in Bamberg, it fills up quickly; call very early for summer reservations. If full, try the hostel in Coburg (see p. 314). Open Feb. to mid-Dec.

⬛ Maisel-Bräu-Stübl, Obere Königstr. 38 (tel./fax 255 03), 10min. from the station. Turn left off Luitpoldstr. before the river. Spacious, clean rooms with balconies overlook a pleasant courtyard. Singles DM39; doubles DM70, with shower DM80. Breakfast included. Delectable dinners from DM13. Reception 9am-midnight.

Hospiz, Promenadestr. 3 (tel. 98 12 60; fax 981 26 66). Central location off Schönlein-splatz. Balconies, sparkling white sheets, and generous breakfast allow for a night of luxury. Singles DM50, with bath DM70; doubles with shower DM80, with bath DM90-100; triples with shower DM108, with bath DM132. Reception 7am-9pm. Check-out 11am. Phone, fax, or mail reservations.

Fässla, Obere Königstr. 19-21 (tel. 265 16; fax 20 19 89). 10min. from the station. Go right off Luitpoldstr., above one of the most popular beer halls in town. All rooms have TVs, phones, and baths. Singles DM63, doubles DM98, triples DM130. Breakfast buffet included. Closed after 1pm on Sundays.

Camping: Campingplatz Insel, Am Campingpl. 1 (tel. 563 20). Bus #18 (direction: "Klinikum") to "Bug." Prime riverside locale. Showers, toilets, washing machines. DM6.50 per adult, DM4.50 per child, DM4.50 per tent, DM11 per car.

🌓🍺 FOOD AND NIGHTLIFE

Bamberg boasts several breweries, but its most unusual specialty is **Rauchbier** (smoke beer). The daring can try its sharp, smoky taste at **Schlenkerla,** Dominikan-erstr. 6 (tel. 560 60), Rauchbier's traditional home. The smoke brewery lies at the foot of the steps leading up to Dompl. **Der Beck,** Hauptwachstr. 16, at Hauptwacheck, offers scrumptious baked goods and pastries. (Open M-F 6:30am-6:30pm, Sa 6:30am-2pm.) **Tengelmann,** Lange Str. 14, sells **groceries.** (Open M-F 8:30am-6:30pm, Sa 7:30am-4pm.)

Mensa, Austr. 37, off Obstmarkt, serves the cheapest meals in town for under DM5. Dine on yellow plastic trays (or put your meal on one). Menu changes daily. Any student ID will do. Open daily 11:30am-2pm. **Snack hall** open until 7pm.

Ristorante Ferrari, Synagogenpl. 6. (tel. 282 77). In a garden that looks like the remains of Pompeii, only happier. Pricey but damn good Italian food. Spaghetti and salads DM15-17. Open daily noon-2pm and 5:30pm-midnight.

Café Zeitlos, Heinrichsdamm 7 (tel. 208 03 33). Coffee and cake on the 2nd floor of a building that survived the war. Step back into Germany's golden years. Coffee under DM4, salad DM10-14, baguette DM7. Open M-F 9:30am-1am, Sa 9am-1am, Su 2pm-1am.

Weinstube Zeis, Obstmarkt 3 (tel. 208 24 66). Cheap cheese *Spätzli* (DM11) and *Schnitzel* with french fries (DM14) on picnic tables that sprawl across a secluded pond-side site. Open daily 9am-3am.

Live Club, Obere Sandstr. 7 (tel. 50 04 58), offers varied disco to a very young crowd. Scene changes with the days, mixing everything from R&B to hip-hop to hardcore. Open M and W 9pm-1am, Sa 9pm-2am. Cover DM6 for live events.

Soul Food, Obere Sandstr. 20 (tel. 550 25). A more mature crowd of music lovers congregate to hear jazz, blues, and soul. Beer DM3. Open M-F 7pm-1am and Sa 7pm-2am.

📷 SIGHTS

ALTES RATHAUS. The old town hall guards the middle of the Regnitz, the left arm of the Main, like an anchored ship. Built in the 15th century, the Rathaus was strategically placed to keep up the appearance of equal preference of the church and state powers on either side of the river. Stand on one of the two bridges to gaze at its half-*Fachwerk*, half-Baroque facade with a Rococo tower in between. There are some strange visual effects in the frescoes—painted cherubs have three-dimensional dimpled legs and arms that jut from the wall where sculpted stone has been attached. The Rathaus also contains a faïence and porcelain exhibit in its **Glanz des Barock** galleries. Don't break anything—you'll deprive someone else of an extremely boring afternoon. (*Rathaus open Tu-Su 9:30am-4:30pm. Gallery open Tu-Su 9:30am-4:30pm. DM6, students DM4.*)

DOM. Founded by Emperor Henry II, the cathedral was consecrated in 1012, burned down twice, and was rebuilt in its present-day form in 1237. The most famous object within the Dom is the equestrian statue of the **Bamberger Reiter** (Bamberg Knight), which dates from the 13th century and depicts the chivalric ideal of the medieval warrior-king. Many stories have grown up around the statue over the years, including one that the statue was a prophecy of Hitler's rise to power. Just beneath the rider is the tomb of Heinrich II and Queen Kunigunde, with their life-size figures on the top and their histories carved into the side. Heinrich sponsored the construction of the cathedral and was later canonized. On the left side of the Dom is the entry to the **Diözesanmuseum,** which includes the **Domschatz** and the perfectly preserved garments of 10th- to 12th-century saints, popes, and Kaisers. *(Dom tel. 50 23 30. Across the river and up the hill from the Rathaus. Open April-Oct. daily 8am-6pm; Nov.-March daily 8am-5pm. Also 30min. Entry to museum DM4, students DM2. Organ concerts May-Oct. Sa noon. 1½hr. tours of Dom and Domschatz gather Tu-Sa 10:30am inside the main entrance of cathedral. DM5, students DM3.50.)*

NEUE RESIDENZ. The largest building in Bamberg, the **Neue Residenz** was built from 1600 to 1703. Only two hallways are open as a museum, holding art from the period of the palace's construction, but entry to the museum also includes a tour of the parade rooms of the palace. The highlight of the castle is the rose garden that lies beneath it. *(Dompl. 8. Tel. 563 51. Opposite the Dom. Open April-Sept. daily 9am-noon and 1:30-5pm; Oct.-March daily 9am-noon and 1:30-4pm; last entry 30min. before closing. DM5, students and seniors DM4. Tours meet at the cashier desk every 20min. April-Oct. daily.)*

PFAHLPLÄTZCHEN. The streets between the Rathaus and the Dom are lined with 18th-century Baroque houses, many of which are not yet renovated. At Pfahlplätzchen, the pink house on the corner of Judenstr., behold the bay window from which Hegel peered while editing the proofs of *Phenomenology of Spirit.* At the time, unable to find a university teaching position, the philosopher was serving as editor of the Bamberg newspaper.

E.T.A.-HOFFMANN-HAUS. The rickety house in which the author wrote his nightmarish *Der Sandmann* lies across the river. *(Schillerpl. 26. Open May-Oct. Tu-F 4-6pm, Sa-Su and holidays 10am-noon. DM2, students DM1.)*

ASCHAFFENBURG

Aschaffenburg calls itself "the town waiting to be discovered," and yet for nearly 1000 years plenty of powerful people—including Napoleon and the Bavarian king Ludwig I—have stopped by to visit, some deciding to stay. The city that served as a second residence for the electors of Mainz still retains much of its past charm. Not even the near-total destruction of the city during WWII and its subsequent military occupation have frustrated the hospitality of the locals. "Aschaffenburg likes you!" proclaims a glossy brochure—and it's not kidding.

⚑ ORIENTATION AND PRACTICAL INFORMATION. King Ludwig I's "Bavarian Nice" lies near the low, forested Spessart mountains on a high bank at a bend in the Main. Aschaffenburg is easily accessible by **train** from Frankfurt (1hr., every 20 min., DM12) or Würzburg (1hr., 2 per hour, DM22). To reach the castle and the **tourist office,** Schloßpl. 1 (tel. 39 58 00 or 39 58 01; fax 39 58 02) from the train station, cross Ludwigstr. in front of the station and turn left. Walk about 30m and turn right onto Frohsinnstr. Take the first right onto Eerthalstr., which brings you into the heart of the **pedestrian zone.** After another 300m, take a left onto Stickergasse. Located on the first floor of the town's ultra-modern library, the office books **rooms** for free and gives out excellent city maps. (Open M-F 9am-5pm, Sa 10am-1pm.) If the tourist office is closed, try the information desks across the square in the **Schloßmuseum** (open Tu-Su 11am-4pm), the **Weinstube** (open Tu-F 11am-midnight and Sa-Su 10am-midnight), or the **Galerie Jesuitenkirche** in the **Stadtgalerie.** (Open Tu 2-5pm, W-Su 10am-1pm and 2-5pm.) **Tours** of the town in German meet in front of the tourist office. (1½hr. Su at 2pm. DM4, under 12 free.) A **laundromat, SB Waschsalon,** Beckerstr. 26, is on the corner of Kneippstr. close to the hostel. (Open M-Sa 9am-9pm. Wash DM5, dry DM6, soap DM1.) Rent a **bike** at **ADFC,** Hohenweg 12. (Tel. 663 95. DM3.50 per hour, DM20 per day.) The **post office,** 63739 Aschaffenburg, left of the train station, **exchanges currency** and cashes traveler's checks for a DM6 fee. (Open M-F 7am-6pm, Sa 8am-noon.) The **telephone code** is 06021.

▚▙ ACCOMMODATIONS AND FOOD. Aschaffenburg's **Jugendherberge (HI)** is at Beckerstr. 47. (Tel. 93 07 63; fax 97 06 94.) From the train station, take bus #40 (direction: "Mespelbrunn"), #41 (direction: "Weibersbrunn"), or #45 (direction: "Dörrmorsbach") to "Schoberstr." Take the first left off Würzburger Str. onto Kneippstr. and then the first right onto Beckerstr.; the hostel is on the left. A friendly place run by die-hard *Fußball* fans. Serene running and cycling paths through woods and meadows surround the hostel. (DM18. Breakfast included. DM25 with breakfast and lunch, DM31 for all three meals. Sheets DM5.50. Closed Dec.-Jan. Reception 8-9am, noon-1pm, and 5-7pm. Curfew 10pm, though you can get a key at the desk.) Just outside the pedestrian zone and across from the Schöntal garden, the cheerful owner of **Hotel Pape Garni,** Würzburger Str. 16 (tel. 226 73; fax 226 22), provides a filling home-cooked breakfast with her rooms. From Schloßplatz, follow Schloßgasse or Pfaffengasse and turn left onto Dalbergstr., which turns into Sandgasse and then into Würzburger Str. (Singles DM50; doubles DM90. Hall bathrooms.) Hidden just inside the city wall, **Zum Roten Kopf** has mastered hearty food—strong enough for Bavarians, but pH-balanced for tourists hungry for *Schnitzel* with salad (DM15) and liver soup (DM4). From Schloßplatz, go down to the river by the castle parking lot, take a right onto Suicardusstr., and walk to the end of the street. (Open M and W-Su 10am-midnight.) Also convenient is **Stadtschänke,** a Bavarian restaurant and bar across the street and a little to the left of the train station. Daily menu options include spaghetti and salad. (DM8-13. Open M-F 9am-10pm, Sa 10am-7pm and Su 11am-7pm.)

▟ ENTERTAINMENT. For a trip to the disco the locals swear by, visit the **Colos-Saal,** Roßmarkt 19. (Tel. 272 39. Open 9pm-late.) Revellers also congregate at **Q-bar,** Sandgasse 53, a lively Cuban-themed *Kneipe.* (Open M-F 5pm-1am, Sa-Su 10am-1pm. Beer DM4.) Pick up *Fritz* magazine from the tourist office for a full listing of nightclubs in and around the city. After the annual winter hiatus, when *Fräulein* summer enters the stage, Aschaffenburg blossoms like a spring flower with a number of **festivals.** Locals and tourists indulge in the city's home-brewed pride and joy, **Heylands beer,** as they party with fireworks and merry-go-rounds for 11 days straight during the **Volksfest** (June 16-26, 2000). In July, the **Kippenburg** and **Schloß wine festivals** attract wine aficionados to the city. The annual **Carillion-Fest,** held the first weekend in August, brings renowned singers from around the globe as well as the tintinnabulating tourists who come to swim in the musical swell.

▣ SIGHTS. Schloß Johannisburg, the former domain of the Mainz bishops, is now an extensive museum of art filled with Dutch and German masters, and an amusing display of cork models of classical buildings such as the Colosseum. (Schloß open daily 9am-noon and 1-5pm; Nov.-March Tu-Su 11am-4pm. Museum open Tu-Su 9-11:30am and 1-4:30pm; Nov.-March Tu-Su 11am-4pm. Last entry 30min. before morning and afternoon closing. Museum admission DM5, students DM4.) A set of 48 chromatically tuned bronze bells rings across the landscape daily at 9:05am, 12:05, and 5:05pm. The **Schloßgarten** possesses intricate pathways, ivy-canopied benches, and old town walls, forming a secluded haven for romance. Sweetly tucked behind the *Schloßgarten* is the **Pompejanum,** a Pompeii-style structure built for Ludwig I in the mid-19th century. (Open mid-March to mid-Oct. Tu-Su 10am-12:30pm and 1:30-5pm. Last entry 30min. before morning and afternoon closing. DM3, students DM2.) Walking south on Schloßgasse, turn left at Dalbergstr. to find the famous **Stiftskirche St. Peter und Alexander,** whose style is a curious mix of

Gothic, Romanesque, and Baroque. The repository of a millennium of cultural history, the **Stiftmuseum** collection includes a 10th-century crucifix, Matthias Grünewald's painting *Beweinung Christi* (Mourning of Christ), and Vischer's *Magdalenenaltar*. (Tel. 33 04 63. Open M and W-Su 10am-1pm and 2-5pm. DM5, students DM2.) Continuing down Dalbergstr. as it becomes Sandgasse, beautiful half-timbered houses pepper the path to the **Sandkirche,** a carefully preserved 1756 Rococo church. (Open daily 8am-9pm.)

Just past the tightly packed Altstadt lie the famous **Schönbusch gardens** and their principal building, **Schloß Schönbusch,** a country house built between 1778 and 1780 for the archbishop of Mainz. From the train station, take bus #4 (direction: "Stockstadt") to "Schönbusch." The view from the **Chamber of Mirrors** (preserved from the original house and hence a bit distorted) reveals the city basking in the rich backdrop of the Spessart forests. The archbishop allowed no vegetation between his summer home and Schloß Johannisburg (3km away), and the two castles remain in that aristocratic see-you-see-me stance today. (Castle open mid-March to mid-Oct. Tu-Su 10am-12:30pm and 1:30-4:30pm. Admission and tour DM4, students DM3.) The park was built by Elector Friedrich Karl Joseph in 1775 as an experiment in English style landscape architecture. Embellished with artificial ponds, islands, and bridges, as well as tiny buildings like the **Freundschaftstempel** (friendship temple) and the **Philosophenhaus,** the park reeks of fairy tale fallacy. The 1829 **Irrgarten,** close to the restaurant at the park's entrance, is a maze formed by trimmed bushes. To hedge the fate of the minotaur, climb the wooden tower to gain an overhead view before tackling the labyrinth. (Open daily 9am-dusk. Free.)

BADEN-
WÜRTTEMBERG

Once upon a time, Baden, Württemberg-Hohenzollern, and Württemberg-Baden were three distinct states. When the Federal Republic was founded in 1951, the Allies masterminded a shotgun wedding, and the three became one: Baden-Württemburg. However, the Badeners and the Swabians (*never* "Württembergers") still proudly proclaim their distinct regional identities. Today, two powerful Ger-

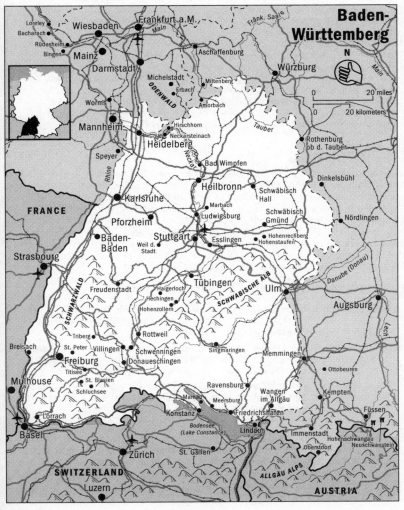

Baden-Württemberg

Loreley
Bacharach
Rüdesheim
Bingen
Wiesbaden
Frankfurt a.M.
Main
Fränk. Saale
Würzburg
Mainz
Darmstadt
Aschaffenburg
Michelstadt
Erbach
Miltenberg
ODENWALD
Worms
Amorbach
Mannheim
Hirschhorn
Neckarsteinach
Tauber
Rothenburg
ob d. Tauber
Heidelberg
Speyer
Bad Wimpfen
Rhine
Neckar
Dinkelsbühl
FRANCE
Heilbronn
Schwäbisch
Hall
Karlsruhe
Marbach
Schwäbisch
Gmünd
Nördlingen
Pforzheim
Ludwigsburg
Baden-
Baden
Stuttgart
Esslingen
Hohenrechberg
Hohenstaufen
Weil d.
Stadt
Strasbourg
SCHWARZWALD
Freudenstadt
Haigerloch
Tübingen
SCHWÄBISCHE ALB
Ulm
Danube (Donau)
Augsburg
Hechingen
Hohenzollern
Lech
Triberg
Rottweil
Breisach
St. Peter
Villingen
Schwenningen
Singmaringen
Memmingen
Freiburg
Donaueschingen
Titisee
Ottobeuren
Mulhouse
St. Blasien
Schluchsee
Ravensburg
Wangen
im Allgäu
Kempten
Lörrach
Mainau
Meersburg
Friedrichshafen
Füssen
Basel
Konstanz
Bodensee
(Lake Constance)
Lindau
Immenstadt
Hohenschwangau
Neuschwanstein
Zürich
St. Gallen
Oberstdorf
SWITZERLAND
ALLGÄU ALPS
AUSTRIA
Luzern

N

0   20 miles

0   20 kilometers

man stereotypes—the brooding romantic of the Brothers Grimm and the modern *homo economicus* exemplified by Mercedes-Benz—battle it out in Baden-Württemberg. Pretzels, cuckoo clocks, and cars were all invented here, and the region is as diverse as its homegrown products. Rural customs and traditions live on in the bucolic hinterlands of the Schwarzwald (Black Forest) and the Schwäbische Alb, while the modern capital city of Stuttgart celebrates the ascendancy of the German industrial machine. The province also hosts the ritzy millionaires' resort of Baden-Baden, the lovely vacation getaways of the exquisite Bodensee (Lake Constance), and the historic university towns of Freiburg, Tübingen, and Heidelberg.

HIGHLIGHTS OF BADEN-WÜRTTEMBERG

■ **Heidelberg's** cobblestone streets, literary past, historic buildings, and hopping nightlife draw droves of tourists. Ride the **cablecar** up to the crumbling Schloß or indulge in contemplative thought while strolling the **Philosophenweg** (p. 322).

■ A modern, corporate culture lies among lush greenery in **Stuttgart.** The **Schloßgarten** beautifies the city with fountains and flower gardens, while **mineral baths** provide hours of indulgent relaxation (p. 337).

■ Red-roofed **Tübingen** is known for its university and its **half-timbered houses.** The untouristed **Altstadt** showcases medieval German architecture at its finest (p. 345).

■ Hikers live out their fantasies in the **Schwarzwald** (p. 360). Stretches of pine forest and serene lakes cover the slopes of towering mountains from **Freiburg** (p. 353) in the south to **Baden-Baden** (p. 351) in the north.

■ About as tropical as Germany gets, the **Bodensee** boasts beautiful beaches with turquoise waters (p. 367). Gaze at the **Alps** from a boat or roam amid the animals made from flowers in the manicured gardens of **Mainau** (p. 371).

HEIDELBERG

The sunlight-coated town by the Neckar and its crumbling Schloß rising from the forest above have an eternal love affair with nature that has lured numerous writers and artists—Mark Twain, Wolfgang von Goethe, Friedrich Hölderlin, Victor Hugo, and Robert Schumann, to name a few. During summer, roughly 32,000 tourists *per day* also answer the call. Even in the off-season, legions of camera-toting fannypackers fill the length of Hauptstr., where postcards and T-shirts sell like hotcakes and every sign is in four languages. Yet the incessant buzz of mass tourism is worth enduring as Heidelberg's beautiful hillside setting, university, and lively nightlife live up to its well-known reputation.

☐ GETTING THERE AND GETTING AROUND

Trains: Frequent trains run from Mannheim (10min., 5 per hour, DM12.80), Stuttgart (40min., 1 per hour, DM38), and Frankfurt (1hr., 1 per hour, DM30). Other trains run regularly to towns in the Neckar Valley.

Public Transportation: Single ride tickets DM3.30. A day pass is valid from the time of purchase for up to 5 people on all streetcars and buses (DM10). Passes are available at the tourist office or at the HSB Kiosk across the street on Gneisenaustr.

Ferries: Rhein-Neckar-Fahrgastschiffahrt (tel. 201 81), on the southern bank in front of the *Kongresshaus,* runs Neckar cruises to Neckarsteinach (1¼hr., runs Easter-late Oct. 9:30am-3:30pm, round-trip DM16.50).

Taxi: Tel. 30 20 30.

Bike Rental: Per Bike, Bergheimer Str. 125 (tel. 16 11 48; fax 16 11 09). Half-day DM15, full day DM25, additional days DM20. Weekend special DM55. DM50 deposit or ID required. Open M-F 9am-6pm; April-Oct. also open Sa 9am-1pm.

Boat Rental: Rent paddleboats and rowboats on the north shore of the Neckar by the Theodor-Heuss-Brücke at **Bootsverleih Simon.** 3-person boat DM15 per hour. 4-person boat DM18. Open daily 10am-sundown.

BADEN-WÜRTTEMBERG

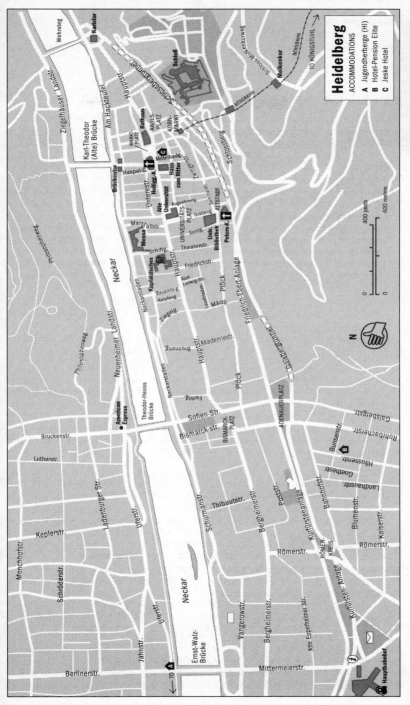

Heidelberg
ACCOMMODATIONS
A Jugendherberge (HI)
B Hotel-Pension Elite
C Jeske Hotel

N

0   400 yards
0   400 metres

Wehrsteg
Karlstor
Schloß-Wolfsbrunnenweg
Molkenkur
TO KÖNIGSTUHL
BERGBAHN
Schloß-Wolfsbrunnenweg
Schloßberg
Schloß
Hauptstr.
Ziegelhäuser Landstr.
Karl-Theodor (Alte) Brücke
Am Hackteufel
Brückentor
Haspel-G.
Rathaus
MARKT-PLATZ
KARLS-PLATZ
KORN-MARKT
Mittelbadg.
Haus zum Ritter
Unterstr.
Alte Heilig.-K.
Alte Universität
UNIVERSITÄTS-PLATZ
Augustinerg.
Grabeng.
Schulg.
ALTSTADT
Peters-K.
BERGBAHN
Plöck
Friedrich-Ebert-Anlage
Marstallstr.
Mensa
Schiffg.
Kupfälzisches
Hauptstr.
Theaterstr.
Univ. Bibliothek
Sandg.
Neckarstaden
Philosophenweg
Neckar
Neuenheimer Landstr.
Philosophenweg
Friedrichstr.
Karl-Ludwig-Str.
Bauamts-g.
Karpteng.
Ziegelg.
Brunneng.
Hauptstr.Akademiestr.
Plöck
Landfriedstr.
Märzg.
Farhtg.
ADENAUER-PLATZ
Gaisbergtunnel
Theodor-Heuss-Brücke
American Express
Bruckenstr.
Lutherstr.
Kepierstr.
Ladenburger Str.
Uferstr.
Schröderstr.
Mönchhofstr.
Jahnstr.
Ernst-Walz-Brücke
Neckar
Berlinerstr.
TO A
Vangerowstr.
Schurmanstr.
Thibautstr.
Bergheimerstr.
Sofien-Str.
Bismarck-str.
BISMARCK-PLATZ
Poststr.
Kurfürstenanlage
Alte Eppelheimer Str.
Bergheimerstr.
Mittermeierstr.
Bahnhofstr.
RÖMER-KREIS
Römerstr.
Kurfürsten-Anlage
Römerstr.
Kaiserstr.
Blumenstr.
Goethestr.
Landhausstr.
Häusserstr.
Blumenstr.
Rohrbacherstr.
Gaisbergstr.
Hauptbahnhof
Molkenkur

Hitchhiking: *Let's Go* does not recommend hitchhiking as a safe mode of transportation. Hitchers walk to the western end of Bergheimer Str. for all directions.

Mitfahrzentrale: Bergheimer Str. 125 (tel. 246 46; fax 14 59 59), matches riders and drivers. Freiburg DM24, Köln DM28, Hamburg DM54, Paris DM51. Open M-F 9am-5pm; April-Oct. also Sa 9am-noon.

🛈 ORIENTATION AND PRACTICAL INFORMATION

About 20km east of the Neckar's confluence with the Rhein, Heidelberg stretches along the river's shores for several kilometers, with almost all of the city's attractions clustered in the eastern quadrant on the southern shore. To get to the Altstadt from the train station, take any bus or street car to "Bismarckpl.," where **Hauptstraße** leads into the city's heart. Known as the longest pedestrian street in Germany, Hauptstr. is the city's backbone. To save money, buy the **Heidelberg Card** (valid two days), which includes use of public transit and admission to the Schloß and most sights, available at the tourist office (DM19.80).

Tourist Office: Tourist Information (tel. 142 20; fax 14 22 22; www.heidelberg.de/cvb), in front of the station. Pick up a copy of the mags *Meier* (DM2) and *Heidelberg Aktuell* (DM1) to see what's up. Books **rooms** with a 7% deposit for a DM5 fee. Office often steers guests toward more expensive places. Open March-Dec. M-Sa 9am-7pm, Su 10am-6pm; Jan.-Feb. closed Su. Additional tourist offices at the **Schloß** (tel. 211 44; open daily 9am-5pm; closed in winter) and at **Neckarmünzplatz.** Open daily 9am-6:30pm; closed in winter.

Currency Exchange: Change cash at the **Sparkassen** on Universitätspl. and Bismarckpl. Or try the exchange office in the train station. Open M-Sa 8am-8pm, Su 9am-1pm.

American Express: Brückenkopfstr. 1 (tel. 450 50; fax 41 03 33), at the north end of Theodor-Heuss-Brücke. Holds mail for members and owners of traveler's checks. Open M-F 10am-6pm, Sa 10am-1pm. A secondary office at **Kornmarkt** (tel. 60 18 16; fax 60 18 60) deals only with traveler's checks. Open M-F 10:30am-4:30 pm, Sa 10am-2pm.

Bookstores: Potter Books, Plöck 93 (tel. 18 30 01; fax 18 30 06), is an English-only bookstore that stocks a variety of new and used titles, from classics to trashy romances (DM30). Open M-F 10am-7pm, Sa 10am-4pm.

Emergency: Tel. 110. **Police:** Römerstr. 2-4 (tel. 990). **Fire** and **Ambulance,** tel. 112.

Women's Resources: Emergency hotline, tel. 18 36 43. **Buchhandlung Himmelheber,** Theaterstr. 16 (tel. 222 01; fax 230 52), stocks books by, for, and about women, and also hosts readings. Open M-W and F 9am-6:30pm, Th 9am-8pm, Sa 9am-2pm.

Aids Hotline: Tel. 194 11.

Post Office: Sofienstr. 6-10 (tel. 91 24 12), 69115 Heidelberg, off Bismarkpl. For Post Restante, include "Filiale Heidelberg 12." Open daily 9am-7:30pm.

Internet Access: Café Gecko, Bergheimer Str. 8 (tel. 60 45 20). Must order a drink to surf. DM4 per 30min. Open M-Th and Su 9am-1am, F 9am-2am, Sa 9am-3am.

PHONE CODE	06221

🛏 ACCOMMODATIONS AND CAMPING

Finding a bed in Heidelberg can be extremely taxing. During the summer, save yourself a major headache by arriving early in the day or, better yet, calling ahead. Possible options for those with some ingenuity and a railpass are the countless little towns and villages scattered around Heidelberg. There are **youth hostels** in: Neckargemünd (10min. away, tel. (06223) 21 33); Eberbach (25min., tel. (06271) 25 93); and Zwingenberg (35min., tel. (06251) 759 38). All these Neckar Valley towns lie along the Heidelberg-Heilbronn railroad; train service is reliable and regular between them. Better yet, the **Mannheim Jugendherberge** is only five minutes from Mannheim's train station, 15-20 minutes from Heidelberg (see p. 331).

Jugendherberge (HI), Tiergartenstr. 5 (tel. 41 20 66; fax 40 25 59). From Bismarckpl. or the station, bus #33 (direction: "Zoo-Sportzentrum") to "Jugendherberge." The "Jugendherberge is full today" sign on the tourist office door is practically permanent. Calling less than a week ahead rarely works; fax your reservation. Can be crowded and noisy, but its small **disco** is fun (open nightly). DM23, over 26 DM28. Sheets DM5.50. Reception until 11pm. Lockout 9am-1pm. Curfew 11:30pm; stragglers admitted at 1am. Partial wheelchair access. Members only.

Jeske Hotel, Mittelbadgasse 2 (tel. 237 33). From the station, bus #33 (direction: "Ziegelhausen") or 11 (direction: "Karlstor") to "Rathaus/Kornmark"; Mittelbadgasse is the second left off the square. English-speaking Euro-roamers fill this delightfully anti-quated Altstadt facility, and for good reason—it's the best value in Heidelberg. Unbeat-able location. Reservations only accepted an hour ahead of time. Doubles DM48. Breakfast DM10. Open Feb. to mid-Nov.

Hotel-Pension Elite, Bunsenstr. 15 (tel. 257 33 or 257 34; fax 16 39 49). From Bismark-tpl., follow Rohrbacher Str. away from the river and turn right on Bunsenstr.; the *Pension* is on the left. From the train station, take streetcar #1 to "Poststr."; the hotel is on the second street behind the Holiday Inn. Show your *Let's Go* guide to get these reduced rates. Nice rooms with high ceilings, bath, and TV. Single DM75; doubles for one person DM85; for two persons DM95-100; DM15 per extra person. Breakfast buffet included. DM5 credit card surcharge.

Camping Haide (tel. (06223) 21 11; email camping.haide@t-online.de), between Ziegel-hausen and Neckargemünd. Bus #35 to "Orthopädisches Klinik," then cross the river and turn right; the campground is on the right 10min. away. DM14.50-20 per person, DM6-12 per tent, DM2 per car. Cabins DM14.50-20. Reception 8am-noon and 4:30-7:30pm. Open April-Oct. **Camping Heidelberg-Schlierbach** is located on the other bank (tel. 80 25 06). Bus #35 (direction: "Neckargemünd") to "Im Grund." DM10 per per-son, DM4-12 per tent, DM2 per car.

◪ FOOD

Eating out tends to be depressingly expensive in Heidelberg; most of the restau-rants on and around Hauptstr. are exorbitantly priced. Just outside this central area, historic student pubs offer better values. Fill up a picnic basket at **Handelshof supermarket,** Kurfürsten-Anlage 60, 200m in front of the train station on the right. (Open M-F 7:30am-8pm, Sa 7:30am-4pm.) There is a **fruit market** on Marktpl. on Wednesdays and Saturdays.

Mensa, in the *Marstall* on Marstallstr. Bus #35 to "Marstallstr." Or, from the Alte Brücke, with your back to the old city, take a left along the river; it's the red fortress on the left. Must buy 5 tickets at a time (DM16.50); each gets you a main dish, 2 side portions, and soup. Lunch M-F 11:30am-2pm. Dinner M-Sa 6pm-10pm. A popular **café** next door serves coffee, snacks, and beer (DM3). Open M-F 9am-12:30am, Sa 11am-1am.

Großer Wok, Bergheimer Str. 1a (tel. 60 25 28), near Bismarckpl. Appetizing aromas whet your taste buds for Chinese specialties (DM4-12) served quickly to go or to eat atop bar stools. Open M-Th and Su 11am-11pm, F-Sa 11am-midnight.

Goldener Anker, Untere Neckar 52 (tel. 18 42 25), near the river and the Alte Brücke. Although most of the traditional German dishes are on the high end of the price scale, some are affordable (DM8-15). Open M-Sa 6pm-midnight.

Hemingway's Bar-Café-Meeting Point, Fahrtgasse 1 (tel. 16 50 53), at the corner of Neckarstaden. Things may not be immediately discernible in what a man writes, but eventually they are quite clear and by these and the degree of memorabilia decorating the walls, he will endure or be forgotten. Open daily 9am-1am.

Thanner, Bergheimer Str. 71 (tel. 252 34), is a swank café with an eclectic international menu, original artwork on the walls, and the only *Biergarten* in Heidelberg allowed to play music. Entrees DM7-25. Open M-Th and Su 9am-1am, F-Sa 9am-2am.

SIGHTS

HEIDELBERGER SCHLOSS. Presiding over Heidelberg's majestic elegance are the ramparts of the aging castle, the jewel in the crown of an already striking city. Its construction began early in the 14th century, and after 1329 it served as the home of the prince electors, whose statues decorate the facade in front of the entrance. Over a period of almost 400 years, the castle's dwellers commissioned their distinctive additions; the conglomeration of styles ranges from Gothic to High Renaissance. Thrice destroyed, twice by war (1622 and 1693) and once by nature (lightning in 1764), the castle's regal state of disrepair is best viewed from the **Philosophenweg** high above the northern bank of the Neckar. While walking around the castle grounds, visitors can cool off in the musty wine cellar. Its *Faß* is the largest wine barrel ever made, holding 220,000 liters. Local lore tells of a court jester and *Faß* guardian who drank nearly 18 bottles per day and finally perished after accidentally drinking a glass of water. The Schloß is easily accessible by an uphill path or by the **Bergbahn,** the world's oldest cable car, which runs from the "Bergbahn/Rathaus" bus stop to the castle. *(Castle tel. 53 84 14 or 538 40. Cable car round-trip DM4.70. Trams take off from the Kornmarkt parking lot next to the bus stop every 10 minutes from 9am to 7:45pm. Take bus #11 towards "Köpfel" or 33 towards "Karlstor." Getting inside the Schloß is possible only with a tour. DM4, students DM2. English tours daily at 11:30 am, 2, and 3:45pm. Grounds open daily 8am-dusk. DM3, students DM1.50, charged 8am-5:30pm only.)* The **Apothekenmuseum,** also in the castle, stopped dishing out the goods in 1693 but still features creepy displays on pre-modern pharmaceuticals and alchemy. *(Tel. 258 80. Open daily 10am-5:30pm. Free with entrance to castle grounds.)*

MARKTPLATZ. The Altstadt centers on the Marktplatz, a cobbled square where **Hercules' Fountain** stands, and where, in the 15th century, accused witches and heretics were burned at the stake; now tourists recline on a legion of plastic chairs. The two oldest structures in Heidelberg border the square. During Louis XIV's invasion of the town, terrified inhabitants scurried to the 14th-century **Heiliggeistkirche.** A wall dividing the church into Catholic and Protestant sections was torn down in 1936; now the church is used for Protestant worship. *(Open M-Th and Sa 11am-5pm, F 1-5pm, Su 1:30-5pm. Free. Church tower DM1, students DM0.50.)* Across from the church's southern face, the ornate facade of the **Haus zum Ritter** dates from the 16th century. The stately **Rathaus** overlooks the spectacle from the far end of the square.

UNIVERSITÄT. Heidelberg is home to Germany's oldest and perhaps most prestigious university, established in 1368. It was at Heidelberg that Clemens Brentano compiled *Des Knaben Wunderhorn,* a collection of folk poetry that led to the Brothers Grimm's own prose compilation. It was also here that sociology became a legitimate academic subject under the leadership of Max Weber. The oldest remaining buildings border the stone-lion fountain of the Universitätsplatz. Other university buildings dot the western Altstadt. Before 1914, in the aristocratic tradition, students were exempt from prosecution by civil authorities; instead, the crimes of naughty youths were tried and punished by the university faculty. Guilty students were jailed (at their leisure) in the **Studentenkarzer.** The walls are covered with graffiti—nothing can snuff the creativity of a willingly incarcerated college student (see p. 567). *(Augustinergasse 2. Tel. 54 23 34. Open April-Oct. Tu-F 10am-4pm. DM1.50, students DM1.)* After some time in jail, test your literacy skills on illegible manuscripts in the **Bibliothek,** with its collection of precious medieval manuscripts. *(Plöck 107-109. Tel. 54 23 80. Open M-Sa 10am-7pm. Free.)*

KURPFÄLZISCHES MUSEUM. The museum is crammed with artifacts such as the jawbone of an unfortunate *homo Heidelbergensis,* a.k.a. "Heidelberg man," one of the oldest (deceased) humans discovered. Elsewhere in the museum stand well-preserved works of art by Dürer and a spectacular archaeology exhibit. *(Hauptstr. 97. Tel. 58 34 02 or 58 34 00. Open Tu and Th-Su 10am-5pm, W 10am-9pm. DM5, students DM3; Su DM3, students DM2.)*

KARL-THEODOR-BRÜCKE. No trip to Heidelberg would be complete without a visit to the northern bank of the Neckar. Walk across the modern Karl-Theodor-Brücke; on the south side of the bridge stands a plump statue of the bridge's namesake prince elector, which he commissioned as a symbol of his modesty.

PHILOSOPHENWEG. If train schedules haven't given you enough time to contemplate the Other, or if you just need a romantic place to kiss the Other, take a walk on the "philosopher's path." A high path opposite the Neckar from the Altstadt, the Philosophenweg offers the best views of the city. It traverses the **Heiligenberg,** with its ruins of the 9th-century **St. Michael Basilika,** the 13th-century **Stefanskloster,** and an **amphitheater** built under Hitler in 1934 on the site of an ancient Celtic gathering place. *(To the right of the Karl-Theodor-Brücke, in the direction of the Marktplatz. Take streetcar #1 or 3 to "Tiefburg," a castle in neighboring Handschuhsheim, to begin the hike upwards.)*

🎵 🎭 ENTERTAINMENT AND NIGHTLIFE

The first Saturday in June and September, and the second in July, draw giant crowds to fireworks and pageants using the Schloß as a backdrop. The **Faschingsparade** (Carnival) struts through the city on Shrove Tuesday (March 7, 2000). The **Hand-Schuhsheim Fest** lures revelers across the river on the third weekend in June, while the **Schloßfestspiele Heidelberg** feature a series of concerts and plays at the castle for five weeks, beginning in late July. (Call 583 52 for tickets.) On September 30th, the **Heidelberger Herbst** brings a medieval market to the Altstadt, which later witnesses the **Weihnachtsmarkt** (Dec. 1-23).

The **Marktplatz** is the heart of the city's action; most popular nightspots fan out from here. **Unter Straße,** on the Neckar side of the Heiliggeistkirche, boasts the most prolific—and often congested—conglomeration of bars in the city. During fair weather, drunken revelers fill the narrow way until 1 or 2am. **Hauptstraße** also harbors a fair number of venues, and a few dot the north side of the river as well.

Zum Sepp'l, Hauptstr. 213 (tel. 230 85). Hosts a loud crowd that's been partying since 1634. Meals DM12-25. Beer DM4.80, "the Boot" (2L of beer) DM6.20. Get kicked. Open daily 11am-midnight.

Reichsapfel, Untere Str. 35 (tel. 279 50), is a popular bar with an older crowd. *Pils* DM4.60. Open daily 6pm-1am.

Cave 54, Krämergasse 2 (tel. 278 40), keeps a somewhat older crowd jumping with live jazz every Sunday. Other nights reggae, funk, and soul. Beer DM5. Open daily 10pm-3am. Cover DM5, Tu and Su DM12.

O'Reilly's (tel. 411 01 40), on the corner of Brückenkopfstr. and Uferstr. Cross Theodor-Heuss-Brücke, turn right, and follow the noise to this hopping Irish pub, where a young crowd drinks Guinness (DM5) by the liter. Open M-F 4pm-1am, Sa-Su noon-1am.

Schwimmbad Musikclub, Tiergartenstr. 13 (tel. 47 02 01), across the river. Conveniently located up the street from the hostel, but a trek otherwise, it's the city's main catwalk for bands with names like "Fatal Function." W Independent alternative; Th "Deutschrock." Open W-Th 8pm-3am, F-Sa 8pm-4am.

Little Heaven, Fahrtgasse 18 (tel. 226 61). Heidelberg's outpost of Euro-dance culture. Tu salsa and merengue, W hip-hop. Th all-you-can-guzzle beer for (DM12-15). Open daily 10pm-3am. Cover DM5-15.

VaterRhein, Untere Neckarstr. 20-22 (tel. 213 71), close to the river near the *Stadthalle.* College students converge after midnight to chill here among the vintage 1950s ads that decorate the wood-paneled walls. Cheap food and drinks. Goulash DM6, pizza DM11.50. *Pilsner* DM4.40. Open daily 8pm-3am.

Mata Hari (tel. 18 18 08), on Zwingerstr. near Oberbadgasse. Cramped, subdued gay and lesbian bar. Tu men only. Beer DM4. Open daily 11pm-3am.

NECKARTAL (NECKAR VALLEY)

The Neckartal—a stretch of the thickly forested Odenwald sliced by the Neckar—reaches from Heilbronn to Heidelberg. Centuries ago, a series of enterprising royals decided to build castles with the lofty goal of protecting merchants from pirates as well as the not-so-lofty goal of charging tolls for their services. Today, their trail of medieval castles dot the hilltops of the Neckartal and form part of the **Burgenstraße** (the Castle Road) that stretches from Mannheim to Prague. Largely unspoiled by tourism, the Neckartal is an excellent daytrip from Heidelberg.

Two train lines connect Heidelberg and Heilbronn, with stops in the small towns along both sides of the valley. One of the best ways to explore the valley is by biking along the well-maintained 85km route. Rent **bikes** at **Bike & Fun,** Hauptstr. 4 (tel. 693), in Neckarsteinach. (Open M-Tu, Th-F, and Su 10am-7pm, W 10am-1pm, Sa 9am-2pm. M-F DM15 per day, Sa-Su DM25. ID required.) In Hirschhorn, **Josef Riedel,** Hainbrunnerstr. 6 (tel. (06272) 20 17), has them for DM5 per half-day, DM10 per day. Finally, there's the **train station** in Eberbach (tel. (06271) 22 20), 30 minutes from Heidelberg. The **Rhein-Neckar Fahrgastschiffahrt** (p. 322) runs **boat tours** from Easter through late-October between Heidelberg, Neckargemünd, Neckarsteinach, Hirschhorn, and Eberbach. Round-trips cost DM4-19.50. For information and departure times, call (06221) 201 81 or (06229) 526.

NECKARSTEINACH

At the north end of the valley 14km upstream from Heidelberg, Neckarsteinach is renowned for its four medieval **castles** that peek proudly out of the pine trees and dominate the fishing village below. All within three kilometers of one another along the north bank of the Neckar River, the castles were built by the Steinachs, feudal tenants of the Bishop of Worms, during the 12th and 13th centuries. The two westernmost castles stand in ruins, while the two to the east tower in splendor; they are privately occupied, however, and visitors are not allowed inside. All can be reached by foot via the **Burgenweg.** From the train station, turn right on Bahnhofstr. and follow it until you reach Hauptstr. Turn left and follow the bend in the road to Pizzeria Castello; the *Schloßsteige* begins at the brick path leading upward to the right and connects to the Burgenweg. (Open March-Oct. M-Sa 9am-8pm.) Fireworks will light the sky above the town on June 24 and July 29, 2000, for the **Vierburgenbeleuchtung** (four-castle lighting).

Neckarsteinach's **tourist office,** Hauptstr. 7 (tel. 920 00; fax 318), inside the Rathaus, is one block down from Bahnhofstr. in the same direction as the *Schloßsteige.* The office has a list of private **rooms.** (Open M-W 8am-noon and 1:30-3:30pm, Th 8am-noon and 1:30-5pm, F 8am-noon.) For lodging, try the only hotel in town: **Vierburgeneck,** Unterhalb der Ruine. (Tel. 542. DM65. TV, private bath, and breakfast included.) For **camping,** head across the river to **Unterm Dilsberg.** (Tel. (06223) 725 85. DM6 per person. Open April-Sept.) **Bistro Stadtgarten am Neckar,** Schiedweg 22 (tel. 24 34), serves crepes with an outstanding view of the valley. (Meals DM7-13. Open daily 10:30am-10pm.) The **postal code** is 69239. The **telephone code** is 06229.

HIRSCHHORN AND BURG GUTTENBERG

Just south of Neckarsteinach lounges Hirschhorn am Neckar, a town whose reconstructed medieval Altstadt from a distance appears to be floating on the river. The settlement was ruled for centuries by the Knights of Hirschhorn, who in 1200 built their castle on Stockelberg mountain, displacing a happy herd of reindeer. History repeated itself many hundreds of years later, when an enterprising young capitalist bought the knights out; the mountain is now a posh hotel/restaurant complex. Nevertheless, the surrounding countryside is excellent for hiking, and **Schloß Hirschhorn** is worth a peek. By foot, follow the gray brick of Schloßstr. upward from the *Bürgerhaus* intersection (15min.); unless you are in a car, do not follow the road signs. The castle's terraces offer a fine panorama, and an even better one can be had at the top of the tower (DM0.30). Stone stairs curl from the castle down to the Altstadt; along the way, they pass the 15th-century **Karmeliter Klosterkirche,** with its Gothic interior and graceful altar.

Maps of local hiking trails are available at the **tourist office,** Alleeweg 2 (tel. 17 42 or 92 31 40), which also books **rooms** for free. From the station, turn left on Neckarsteinacher Str. and follow it to the intersection as it curves to the right. Turn right and walk downhill toward the river past the hotel. The office is in the rear of the yellow building on the right. (Open M-F 8am-noon and 2-5pm; April-Oct. also Sa 9am-noon.) The same building also houses the **Langbenmuseum,** an art and natural history museum with a collection of 17th- and 18th-century wooden statues, weaponry, and a truly terrifying diorama that crams more than 100 native fauna into a space the size of a king-size bed. (Open Tu and Th-F 2-4pm, Su 10am-noon and 2-4pm. DM1, children DM0.50.) The **post office,** Hauptstr. 27, 69434 Hirschhorn, is on the main drag. (Open M-F 8:30am-noon and 2-5pm, Sa 8:30am-noon.) The **telephone code** is 06272.

For overnight accommodations, check the hotels and *Pensionen* along Hauptstr. and the board outside the tourist office. **Haus La Belle,** Hauptstr. 38 (tel. 14 00), has cushy rooms with bath and TV from DM35 per person, breakfast included. Camp at **Odenwald Camping,** Langenthaler Str. (tel. 809; fax 36 58), one kilometer outside of town in the direction of the castle; follow the signs from the tourist office. (DM7 per person. Open April to mid-Oct.)

Thirty kilometers south of Hirschhorn towers **Burg Guttenberg,** which houses a **museum** detailing its 800-year history. (Open April-Oct. daily 10am-6pm.) Also within the castle walls is an **aviary** for birds of prey, maintained by prominent ornithologist Claus Fentzloff. Twice per day (April-Nov. 11am and 3pm; March and Nov. 3pm only), Fentzloff sends eagles and vultures flying inches above the heads of the crowds, plucking poor little chickens out of the sky, while he launches into lengthy scientific diatribes. (Museum and castle DM5. Bird show DM12. All DM15.) To reach Burg Guttenberg by rail, get off at Gundelsheim, cross the big bridge past the camping site, and walk 2km following the signs along the road, past wheatfields and terraced hillsides (25min.).

BAD WIMPFEN

Downstream from Heilbronn reposes the village of Bad Wimpfen, whose fairy-tale demeanor was once one of the best-kept secrets in southwest Germany. The immaculately preserved Altstadt is a 10-minute walk from the ornately Gothic train station. Follow Karl-Ulrich-Str. or take the steep hiking trail to the right of the station. Laid out along the northern side of the old castle walls, easily accessible points on the ancient battlements offer incredible views of the valley and surrounding countryside. Next to the Roter Turm (open Sa-Su 10am-noon and 2-5pm), the **Pfalzkapelle** hosts the **Kirchenhistorisches Museum,** which exhibits ecclesiastical artifacts from the town's monastery and churches, including a Luther Bible. (Open April-Oct. Tu-Su 10am-noon and 2-4pm. DM2, students DM1.) The **Blauer Turm,** Burgviertel 9 (tel. 89 68), offers a stunning view to those willing to climb the 169 steps. The tower's dramatic 1984 decapitation by lightning is documented on the way up the stairs. (Open Tu-Su 10am-6pm. DM2.) Next door, the sandstone **Steinhaus** contains the **Historisches Museum,** a somewhat sparse collection of artifacts both ancient and medieval. (Open April-Oct. Tu-Su 10am-noon and 2-4:30pm. DM2, students DM1.) The **Galerie der Stadt** features a small exhibit on contemporary artwork, while the **Reichstädtisches Museum** recounts the history of Bad Wimpfen. (Both open daily 10am-noon and 2-5pm. Admission to the Galerie is free; to the museum DM3, students DM2.) The world's only **Pig Museum,** Kronengäßchen 2 (tel. 66 89), off Hauptstr. near the *Kulturamt,* details the history of swine (considered a good luck symbol in Germany) with collector's items and lucky charms. (Open daily 10am-5pm. DM5, students DM2.50.)

The friendly **tourist office** in the train station (tel. 972 00; fax 97 20 20) finds **rooms.** (DM25-30. Open M-F 9am-1pm and 2-5pm, Sa-Su 10am-noon and 2-4pm.) **Tours** depart Sunday at 2pm from the tourist office (DM3). The **telephone code** is 07063.

BADEN-WÜRTTEMBERG

Hotel Garni Neckarblick, Erich-Salier-Str. 48 (tel. 96 16 20; fax 85 48), offers affordable luxury with a capital "L," very hospitable management, and a stunning view of the valley. Call to be picked up from the train station, or follow Mathildenbadstr. from the pedestrian zone out to the street and hang a right. Proceed for 15 minutes along Erich-Salier-Str. as it curves around the hillside; the hotel is on the right. All rooms include TV, telephone, and bath. They also rent **bikes** (DM5 for guests, DM15 for non-guests) and offer to pick guests up at the end of a day of biking to bring them back to the hotel. (Singles DM80, doubles DM115-140, triples DM175. Breakfast included. Call ahead or fax reservations.) Closer to the station, **Pension zur Traube,** Hauptstr. 1 (tel. 95 05 21; fax 95 05 21), offers less cushy but comfortable rooms with showers. (Singles DM55, doubles DM105. Breakfast included.) For traditional German fare, try **Dobel's Maultaschen,** Hauptstr. 61 (tel. 82 12), where *Maultaschen* (DM9-16), and beer draw locals around the bar. The salad bar (DM7) is a rare source of green fiber in the Neckar Valley. (Open M-Sa 10am-midnight, Su 10am-10pm.) **Grocery** stores are located on the other side of the Altstadt along Rappenamerstr.

MANNHEIM

For nearly a thousand years, Mannheim existed merely as a simple fishing village. In 1720, however, history took a step forward, when Elector Karl Phillipp made the city the capital of Rheinland-Pfalz. Mannheim's heady days as capital came to an end a mere 57 years later when the court packed up and marched off to Munich, as Elector Karl Theodor bid farewell—*Auf Wiedersehen,* baby. The desertion appears to have had little effect on the city; today's Mannheim is one of the most urbanized locales in southwest Germany. Besides the many grand buildings which the nobility left behind, Mannheim flaunts a substantial cultural scene and is a shopper's paradise. The easily navigated streets and almost nonexistent tourist population make the city a worthy destination for city-loving travelers.

■ **ORIENTATION.** Mannheim perches on a peninsula partitioned by **Kaiserring** directly in front of the train station; the **Innenstadt** lies to the west and the rest of the city lies to the east. The center is divided into a grid of 144 blocks along a central axis, **Kurpfalzstraße,** which runs from the center of the Residenzschloß northward to the Kurpfalzbrücke on the Neckar. Each block is designated by a letter and a number. Streets to the west of Kurpfalzstr. are designated by the letters **A** through **K** (from A blocks in the south to K blocks in the north) while streets to the east are similarly lettered **L** through **U.** The blocks on the central axis are numbered; the number of the block increases moving away from Kurpfalzstr. The giant grid is bounded by Bismarckstr. to the south, Parkring to the west, Luisenring to the north, and Friedrichsring and Kaiserring to the east. East of Kaiserring, streets assume regular names; perhaps the Pfalz electors discovered a more poetic side, or saw that they were running out of letters. The **A** and **M** streets will keep you oriented.

◪ **PRACTICAL INFORMATION.** Trains run twice per hour to Stuttgart (40min., DM57) and Frankfurt (45min., DM40). Mannheim's **streetcars** costs DM1.20 per ride in the Innenstadt and DM3.20 for rides beyond that. The *Ticket 24 Plus,* valid 24hr., costs DM10. The **tourist office,** Willy-Brandt-Platz 3 (tel. 10 10 11; fax (0621) 241 41; www.tourist-mannheim.de), a block from the station, distributes maps and information on accommodations. (Open M-F 9am-7pm, Sa 9am-noon.) The office also offers a **Mitfahrzentrale** ride-share service. A **laundromat** awaits on block G7 on the Luisenring side. (Wash DM6. Dry DM1 per 15min. Open daily 6am-11pm, last entry 10pm.) A **pharmacy, Bahnhof-Apotheke** (tel. 12 01 80), dispenses therapeutic goods at block L15, across from the station and to the left. (Open M-F 7am-8pm, Sa 7:30am-4pm.) **Email,** caffeine, and alcohol cravings can be slaked at **Neworld Internetcafé,** S3, #11 (tel. 156 84 20), a two-floor complex that claims to be Europe's largest internet café. (Open daily 10am-5am. DM4 per 30min.) The **post office,** 68161 Mannheim, is one block east of the station. (Open M-F 8am-8pm, Sa 8am-noon.) The **telephone code** is 0621.

ACCOMMODATIONS. Mannheim's **Jugendherberge (HI)**, Rheinpromenade 21 (tel. 82 27 18; fax 82 40 73), provides somewhat cramped rooms, but its delectable deluxe breakfast and super-convenient location, 10 minutes from the station, more than make up for the aging facilities. Walk through the underground passage (toward track 10), exit at the back of the station, and take a right. Follow Joseph-Kellner-Str., cross the tracks, and take a left; with the park on your right, continue down for about a block, and enter at the first entrance by the yellow mailbox. Or take streetcar #7 (direction: "Neckarau") to "Lindenhofplatz." (DM21, over 26 DM26. Breakfast buffet DM2. Sheets DM6. Reception 1-2pm, 4-6pm, 7-10pm. Curfew 12:30am. Members only.) The next best value is the spotless and conveniently located **Pension Arabella,** block M2, #12 (tel. 230 50; fax 156 45 27), two blocks north of the Schloß. (Singles DM40-45, doubles DM70-80, triples DM100. Breakfast DM7.50.) **Goldene Gans,** Tattersallstr. 19 (tel. 10 52 77; fax 422 02 60), two blocks northwest of the train station, has its entrance under ivy covering on Bismarkpl. during the day, but after midnight it's around the corner. Pleasant rooms are marred by noise on street-side suites. (Singles DM60-70, with shower DM75-85; doubles DM105-150. Breakfast included. Reception M-Sa 6am-midnight, Su 7am-8pm.)

FOOD AND NIGHTLIFE. The cheapest meals in town are at the government-subsidized **Studentenwerk Mannheim Mensa** (open M-F 11:30am-2pm and 5-7pm) and the adjacent, slightly more expensive **cafeteria** (open July-Aug. M-F 8:30am-5pm; Sept.-June M-Th 8:30am-7pm). The *Mensa* is located behind the Residenzschloß in the southwest corner. DM3.90 buys a *Schnitzel* with fries or a big salad. Antiques fill **Harlekin,** Kaiserring 40 (tel. 10 33 54), on the corner of Moltkestr. Sandwiches, pasta, and *Maultaschen* usually cost less than DM16. (Open M-F 9am-1am, Su 5pm-1am.) Folks of all ages congregate at **Stonehenge Irish Pub,** M4, #8-9 (tel. 122 39 49), which offers live Irish music a few times a week and Irish breakfasts every Sunday for DM11. (Open M-Th and Su 12:30am-1am, F-Sa til 3am.) Blocks **G7** and **H7** teem with lots of busy bars. Butchers, bakers, and grocers gather at the **market** in the square at the intersection of Kurpfalzstr. and Kirchstr. at the center of the city grid. (Open Tu, Th, and Sa 7am-2:30pm.)

SIGHTS. Mannheim's real attraction is its bustling commercial area, which centers around **Paradeplatz** at block O1 and extends for several teeming blocks in all directions, though most densely north and east. Restaurants, department stores, cafés, and movie theaters combine with the city's funky layout to form an urban space of an intensity rarely found in European roads. If the milieu of metropolitan Mannheim leaves you feeling guilty for not taking in enough Old Europe, the city has several substantial offerings, beginning with its emblematic masterpiece, the **Wasserturm** and surrounding gardens on **Friedrichsplatz**. Restored to its original glory in 1956, the elegant sandstone tower topped by a statue of Amphitrite almost lives up to its billing as "the most beautiful water tower in the world." On the south side of the manicured foliage and crystalline fountains of Friedrichspl. crouches the **Kunsthalle,** Friedrichspl. 4 (tel. 293 64 13), a museum surveying art from the mid-19th century to modern times, including works by Manet, Monet, Cézanne, and Beckmann. From the station, walk north on Kaiserring. (Open Tu-W and F-Su 10am-5pm, Th noon-5pm. DM4, students DM2.)

Along with a bizarre street-naming scheme, the electors left the giant **Residenzschloß**. The largest palace of the Baroque period, it now houses the **Universität Mannheim**. In the oddly gaudy **Schloßkirche** (tel. 292 28 90), the sleek coffer of the crypt holds Karl Phillip's third wife, Violante von Thurn und Taxis. Even odder, a Masonic symbol and a post horn decorate the altar, suggesting a bizarre link between efficient mail and eventual Masonic world domination. (Tours April-Oct. Tu-Su 10am-1pm and 2-5pm; Nov.-March. Sa-Su 10am-1pm and 2-5pm. DM4, students DM2.50.) The extensive **Reißmuseum** (tel. 293 31 50) consists of three buildings around block C5, northwest of the Schloß, which contain exhibits on archaeology, ethnology, and natural science. (Open Tu-W and F-Su 10am-5pm, Th noon-5pm. DM4, students DM2, free on Thursday afternoons.) Between the museum and the Schloß at block A4 stands the **Jesuitenkirche**, built as a symbol of the Pfalz court's reconversion to Catholicism. (Open daily 8am-noon and 2-6:30pm.) The poet Friedrich Hölderlin called it "the most splendid building I have encountered during my travels." This is perhaps poetically licentious, but the church is fantastic.

On the other side of the Innenstadt, several blocks northeast of the Wasserturm, the 100-acre **Luisenpark** (tel. 41 00 50) sprouts away. (Open daily May-Aug. 9am-9pm; Sept.-April 9am-dusk. DM5, students DM4.) The greenhouses, flower gardens, aviary, zoo, water sports, mini-golf, and frequent afternoon concerts offer something for everyone. South of Luisenpark, due east of Friedrichspl. on the **Augustanlage,** lies the terrific **Landesmuseum der Technik und Arbeit,** Museumstr. 1 (tel. 429 89), which displays the inner workings of big, creaky, rusty things through fun hands-on exhibits. In its six stories connected by tunnels and ramps, the museum covers "250 years of technical and social change and industrialization in southwest Germany." There's a working waterwheel, printing press, and BMWs galore. Take streetcar #6 (direction: "Neuostheim") to "Landesmuseum." (Open Tu and Th 9am-5pm, W 9am-8pm, F 9am-1pm, Sa 10am-5pm, Su 10am-6pm. DM5, students DM3, families DM7.) Nearby is the **world's first planetarium** (tel. 41 56 92), still projecting spacey visions. (Shows Tu 10am and 3pm, W and F 3pm and 8pm, Th 3pm, Sa-Su 5 and 7pm. DM8, students DM6.50.) The **Museumsschiff "Mannheim"** (tel. 156 57 56) floats in the Neckar, just by the Kurpfalzbrücke. Once the steamer Mainz, which sank in 1956, it has been retrieved from the Rhein's murky depths and offers a history of navigation. (Open Tu-Su 10am-4pm. DM2.)

SCHWÄBISCHE ALB (SWABIAN JURA)

The limestone plateaus, sharp ridges, and pine-forested valleys that stretch from Tübingen in the north to the Bodensee in the south are collectively known as the Schwäbische Alb, a region often considered an ugly cousin of the adjacent Schwarzwald. Its rough-hewn landscape is scenic yet stubborn, with a harsh climate that often vents its wrath on travelers. But the periphery is colored by the brush of the exotic and a bit of the uncanny. The powerful medieval dynasties that held the area found the Swabian peaks perfect sites for fortification, and big-time families like the Hohenstaufens filled the region with castles and abbeys. Now some placid herds of sheep, lofty castle ruins, and the region's name—Staufenland—are all that remain of the their legacy. The **Schwäbische Albstraße** (Swabian Jura Road) bisects the plateau, intersecting the Romantische Straße at Nördlingen (p. 300). A web of trails serves hikers; maps are available at regional tourist offices in most towns. Train service to many points is roundabout and often incomplete, but bus routes pick up the slack.

SCHWÄBISCH HALL

Riding into the Schwäbisch Hall station from Heilbronn is like entering the Twilight Zone. After nearly an hour of monotonous German countryside, the windows suddenly fill with hundreds of red-tiled roofs, soaring cathedral towers, and crumbling stone walls. The town was built near a salt well that served as its gold mine until the Dukes of Württemberg took possession of Hall and its main resource in 1802. Virtually ignored during the World Wars, Schwäbisch Hall's steeply sloping Altstadt is one of the most expansive and well preserved in Germany. Although tourism is present, it has yet to reach large proportions, leaving the city almost entirely to its residents and the few travelers who wander the ancient streets.

◪ ORIENTATION AND PRACTICAL INFORMATION. Schwäbisch Hall has two **train** stations. The **Hauptbahnhof** is close to town, but the and more important station is in **Schwäbisch Hall-Hessental,** on the main rail line to Stuttgart (1¼hr., 1 per hour, DM20). Bus #1 and 4B connect the station to Schwäbisch Hall proper (2-3 per hour; DM2, Sa-Su DM1). All bus lines at "Am Spitalbach" stop one block west and a few blocks down from the tourist office. On board, buy a *Tageskarte*, a day pass valid on all buses (DM5). Rent **bikes** at **2-Rad Zügel**, Johanniterstr. 55 (tel. 97 14 00), or closer to the Hessental area, **Radsport Fiedler**, Kirchstr. 4 (tel. 93 02 40). Prices start at DM10 a day. For a **taxi** call 61 17. Schwäbisch Hall's **tourist office,** Am Markt 9 (tel. 75 16 00; fax 75 13 97), has maps and books **rooms** for free. (Open May-Sept. M-F 9am-6pm, Sa-Su 10am-3pm; Oct.-April M-F 9am-5pm.) The **post office,** Hafenmarkt 2, 74523 Schwäbisch Hall, hides behind the Rathaus. (Open M-F 8:30am-12:30pm and 2:30-5:30pm, Sa 8:30am-noon.) The **telephone code** is 0791.

▐⬚ ACCOMMODATIONS AND FOOD. Schwäbisch Hall's **Jugendherberge (HI),** Langenfelder Weg 5 (tel. 410 50; fax 479 98), is past Marktpl. on the Galgenberg. Follow Crailsheimer Str. up and take a left onto Langenfelder Weg. A legion of couches decks the halls of the clean and homey hostel. (DM23, over 26 DM28. Breakfast buffet included. Sheets DM5.50. Reception 4:30-7pm. Curfew 10pm. Members only.) **Gasthof Krone Semir,** Klosterstr. 1 (tel./fax 60 22), offers basic, clean rooms. Follow the street to the right of Michaelskirche all the way up and around the corner on the right. TV in every room. (Singles DM40, doubles DM80. Breakfast included.) There is a **Campingplatz** (tel. 29 84) at Steinbacher See. Take bus #4 to "Steinbach/Mitte," then backtrack and follow the signs. (DM7 per person, under 16 DM5. Tent DM9.) **Taverne bei Vangeli,** Bahnhofstr. 15 (tel. 67 43), serves a bewildering array of Grecian specialities with a sizable vegetarian section. (Entrees DM9-15. Open daily 11:30am-2pm and 5pm-midnight.) **Warsteiner Ilge,** Im Weiler 2 (tel. 716 84) is where twentysomethings go to drink delicious yogurt shakes (DM4-6) and beer.

◪ SIGHTS. Three times charred by flames, Hall's half-timbered center was built in the 18th century. From the Schwäbisch Hall train station, cross Bahnhofstr. and head down the stone steps and footpath toward the river. Turn left on Mauerstr., cross the wooden footbridges that connect the islands in the Kocher, and follow the winding cobblestone streets to the **Marktplatz.** Use the church tower as a beacon. From the Schwäbisch Hall-Hessental train station, take bus #1 to "Spitalbach Ost," the last stop (20min.; DM2). The convex Baroque **Rathaus** confronts the Romanesque tower and Gothic nave of the **Michaelskirche,** which perches precariously atop a steep set of stone stairs. The church is Lutheran due to the town's pride and joy, Johannes Brenz, the reformer who converted Hall to Protestantism in the 1520s. Organ music often echoes in the church, rattling the pile of human bones and skulls in the medieval **ossuary,** an underground room behind the altar. The **Turmzimmer** atop the church's tower provides an incredible view of the town. (Open March to mid-Nov. M 2-5pm, Tu-Sa 9am-noon and 2-5pm, Su 11am-noon and 2-5pm; mid-Nov. to Feb. Tu-Su 11am-noon and 2-3pm. Tower DM1.)

A number of narrow, half-timbered alleys wind their way outwards from Marktpl. To the east, Obere Herrngasse leads to the eight-story Romanesque **Keckenturm,** on Keckenhof, which houses the **Hällisch-Fränkisches Museum** (tel. 75 12 89). Located in the medieval tower, the museum contains a smashing Baroque room and extensive exhibits on the history of Schwäbisch Hall. (Open Tu-Su 10am-5pm, W 10am-8pm. Tours in German W 6:30pm and Su 11am. Free.) The covered **Henkersbrücke,** down Neue Str., delivers a view of Schwäbisch Hall's Kocher River. In the northern part of the Altstadt, the **Gelbinger Gasse** is the town's most beautiful section. For a relaxing walk along the river, the gardens of the **Ackeranlage** back the tremendous architectural vista with tall, shady trees.

Above town, Steinbach, the only suburb of Hall that remained Catholic during the Reformation, appropriately holds **Kloster Großcomburg** (tel. 93 81 85), a former castle and Benedictine monastery dating from the 11th century. The 460m wall provides peep holes for views of the valley, but you must take a tour (in German only) to see the museum and impressive interior of the Baroque church, reconstructed in the 18th century. Take bus #4B to "Steinbach/Mitte," cross the street, and head left around Bildersteige. (Tours April-Oct. Tu-F at 10, 11am, 2, 3, and 4pm, Sa-Su at 2, 3, and 4pm; Nov.-March call ahead. DM4.)

The **Hohenloher Freilandmuseum** in Museumsdorf Wackers-hofen (tel. 97 10 10) reenacts the life of an old German agricultural village with 50 authentic low-ceilinged houses in the middle of scenic countryside. Let the fumes from the haystacks guide you to pigs, sheep, and cows. Watch Schnapps being made. *Prost!* Ride bus #7 to "Wackershofen," take a left down the path slightly before the stop, and follow the signs. (Open July-Aug. daily 9am-6pm; May-June and Sept. Tu-Su 9am-6pm; April and Oct. Tu-Su 10am-5:30pm. DM9, students DM5.)

🎭 **ENTERTAINMENT.** On summer evenings between mid-June and mid-August, the **Freilichtspiele**, a series of plays running the gamut from Shakespeare to Brecht, are performed on the steps of the Michaelskirche. Contact the tourist office (DM20-45, student discounts DM6-10). On the Saturday, Sunday, and Monday of Pentecost (June 10-12, 2000), Schwäbisch Hall celebrates the **Kuchen- und Brunnenfest,** during which locals don 16th-century costumes to dance traditional jigs. During the **Sommernachtsfest** (August 26, 2000), 30,000 little candles light patterns along the Ackeranlage.

SCHWÄBISCH GMÜND

On the northern cusp of the range, Schwäbisch Gmünd provides a base for excursions into the region. Billed as the oldest town in the Staufenland, it's been a center for gold and silversmithing since the 14th century. Beautifully wrought jewelry and ornaments can be found in many shops in the town center, which bristles with Baroque plaster facades and half-timbered buildings dating from the 15th and 16th centuries.

To reach the café-filled Marktplatz from the train station, turn left onto Lorchenstr., which becomes Ledergasse and eventually leads to the square. Farther southwest, Münsterplatz hosts the 14th-century **Heiligkreuzmünster** (Holy Cross Cathedral), the oldest church with a Gothic nave in Southern Germany. The architect Peter Parler, born in Gmünd in 1330, designed one wing and later replicated it in his plan of Prague's principal cathedral. An engineer must have fallen asleep at the drafting table, however, because in the late 1400s, the towers of the church collapsed, and the boxy compromise renders the building decidedly non-ecclesiastic in appearance. Perhaps to compensate for this shortcoming, the powers-that-be have covered the exterior with frightening statues that protrude horizontally in every direction. The bizarre collection ranges from screaming, tortured human figures to fanged beasts. The **Silberwaren- und Bijouteriemuseum** (tel. 389 10), across from the tourist office, features silversmiths tooling silver in the traditional style. Exhibits cover the history of the silver trade, the Silver Age, and silver arts. (Open W and Sa 2-5pm, Su 11am-5pm. Tour 2pm in German. DM5, students DM2.) The 16th-century **Kornhaus,** an old grain storage building off Marktpl., two blocks behind the Rathaus, now houses the **tourist office** (tel. 60 34 55; fax 60 34 59). The staff books **rooms** for a 5% fee and offer a large selection of maps. (Open M-F 9am-5:30pm, Sa 8am-noon.) The **post office**, 73525 Schwäbisch Gmünd, is opposite the train station. (Open M-F 8am-noon and 2:30-5:30pm.) The **telephone code** is 07171.

Sadly, Schwäbisch Gmünd has no hostel, though there is one nearby in Hohenstaufen (see below). **Gasthof Weißer Ochsen**, Parlerstr. 47 (tel. 28 12), has decent singles (DM35) and one double (DM65). **Gasthaus Zum Lamm**, Rinderbacher Gasse 19 (tel. 26 61), has a daily menu of Swabian specialties. (DM8.50-20. Open M 5pm-midnight, Tu-Sa 10am-2pm and 5:30pm-midnight, Su 11am-2pm.) An open-air **market** fills Münsterpl. on Wednesday and Saturday (7am-noon), while **supermarkets** can be found a block north along Bocksgasse.

THE KAISERBERGE

South of Schwäbisch Gmünd lie the three conical peaks, **Hohenstaufen, Hohenrechberg,** and **Stuifen,** which make up the **Dreikaiserberge.** Hohenstaufen was named after the castle that once graced its summit, built by the Hohenstaufen family. The castle is gone, but the view of the other two Kaiserberge peaks is spectacular. To reach Hohenstaufen from Schwäbisch Gmünd, take bus #12 to "Göppingen ZOB," then transfer to bus #13 and get off at "Hohenstaufen Jugendherberge" (1 per hour; last bus leaves at 7pm). Bus #13 goes directly there on Sundays and holidays, but the second and final bus rolls away at 12:30pm. If you catch it, get off at "Juhe" and put yourself right in the middle of hill action around **Jugendherberge Hohenstaufen,** Schottengasse 45 (tel. (07165) 438; fax 14 18), which has six- and eight-bed rooms on a gently sloping plain. (DM23, over 26 DM28. Breakfast included. Sheets DM5.50. Call ahead.)

Another prime hiking trail winds around **Hohenrechberg** to the east, and boasts a mysterious **castle ruin** and a Baroque **Wallfahrtskirche** (pilgrimage church) at its summit. The **Burgruine** is halfway up; pay DM1 to catch a breathtaking glimpse of the Schwäbische Alb from the castle's crumbled walls. To reach Hohenrechberg, take bus #4 (direction: "Wißgoblingen") to "Rechberg Gasthof Rad." Walk up Hohenstaufenstr.; the trail starts between the Volksbank and Jägerhof. The last bus to Schwäbisch Gmünd leaves around 6pm. The **tourist office** in Schwäbisch Gmünd (see p. 334) has a guide to the hiking trails. All buses to the Kaiserberge depart from Schwäbisch Gmünd's train station, though most also stop at Marktpl.

ULM

When Napoleon designated the Danube as the border between Württemberg and Bavaria, Ulm was split into two distinct cities, Ulm and Neu-Ulm. Brochures claim that they are Siamese twins, but it's pretty clear from a tourist's perspective that Ulm got the good end of the deal. Residents of both cities may proudly whistle the "Blue Danube" as they promenade along their mighty river, but only those in Ulm can brag about living in the city with the tallest church steeple in the world. The towering peak reveals itself from every corner of town and inspires a lively pedestrian district crowded with shoppers and beer-drinking people-watchers. Scientific genius also gravitates to Ulm; Einstein was born here, as was the slightly less famous "Tailor of Ulm." Albrecht Berblinger, tailor by day, inventor by night, made one of the first serious attempts at human flight in 1811 when he tried to cross the Danube on his "kite-wings" and nearly drowned. Perhaps to discourage any other residents from such ventures, the city constructed many charming bridges over the Venetian canals leading from the river. These, the proud *Münster*, and the joyful feel in the streets make Ulm a very pleasant excursion.

🔁 ORIENTATION AND PRACTICAL INFORMATION. Ulm is connected by **train** to all of southern Germany, with trains to Munich (1¼hr., 1 per hour, DM40) and Stuttgart (1hr., 2 per hour, DM32). Rent **bikes** from **Ralf Reich,** Frauenstr. 34. (Tel. 211 79. DM15 per day, DM30 per weekend, DM80 per week; 15% discount with BahnCard.) The contrast between the strikingly voluptuous white building that houses the **tourist office,** Münsterpl. 50 (tel. 161 28 30; fax 161 16 41; www.ulm.de), and the towering, ornate spire of the adjacent *Münster* epitomizes Ulm's strange unity of past and present. The office sells maps (DM0.50), the comprehensive and helpful *Gästemagazin* (DM2), and a do-it-yourself cardboard *Münster* sculpture kit (DM54.80); they also find **rooms** for free. (Open M-F 9am-6pm, Sa 9am-1pm.) The *Automat* outside sells a list of accommodations (DM1). Satisfy pharmaceutical fancies at the **Neue Apotheke,** Bahnhofstr. 13 (tel. 600 74), or check the posted list there to find out which **pharmacies** in town are open after hours. (Open M-F 8am-7pm, Sa 8am-2pm.) The **post office,** Bahnhofpl. 2, 89073 Ulm, is left of the station. (Open M-F 8am-6pm, Sa 8am-1pm.) The **telephone code** is 0731.

ACCOMMODATIONS AND FOOD. Ulm's **Jugendherberge Geschwister Scholl (HI)**, Grimmelfinger Weg 45 (tel. 38 44 55; fax 38 45 11), looks like a high school, only with sparkling facilities, communal showers, and four- to eight-bed rooms. Take any bus from the train station to "Ehinger Tor," and change to bus #4 or 8 (direction: "Kuhlberg"). Walk through the underpass just up the road and follow the *Sport-Gaststätte* signs to a set of stairs on the right side of the building. Descend. Cut through the grass to the right of the tennis courts, and turn left on the paved path. Follow the lone *Jugendherberge* sign. The hostel is named in memory of a brother and sister who were executed in 1943 for conspiring against Hitler. (DM23, over 26 DM28. Breakfast included. Sheets DM5.50. Reception 5-9:45pm. Curfew 10pm.) **Münster-Hotel**, Münsterpl. 14 (tel./fax 641 62), is located (surprise!) to the left of the *Münster*. Relish small rooms tackily decorated with maps of Germany on every desk. Beware the early morning bells. (Singles DM45, with shower DM65; doubles with shower DM90, with bath DM110. Breakfast included.) Across the river in Neu-Ulm, **Gasthof Rose**, Kasernstr. 42a (tel. 778 03), has lovely rooms in a quiet district. (Singles from DM30, doubles from DM70. Breakfast included.)

Ulm's restaurants reflect the culinary influences of both Schwaben and Bayern, including the unusual *Schupfnudel*, a half-potato, half-wheat noodle. Cheap and greasy *Imbiß* fare lines the way to the *Münster* along **Bahnhofstr.** and **Hirschstr.** For the most variety and the densest collection of restaurants, the territory between **Neue Str.** and the river is prime grazing ground. Across from the Rathaus, the **Erstes Ulmer Weizenbierhaus**, Kronengasse 12 (tel. 624 96), pours more than 20 varieties of *Weizenbier* and serves a number of decent dishes (DM5.50-12.80). A synthetic tree and red tiling give the restaurant an interesting ambience. (Open daily 4pm-3am.) Inside the Rathaus, **Dinea Restaurant**, Marktpl. 1 (tel. 66 11 26), offers a dazzling self-service buffet of fresh salads, pasta, and fish. (Daily specials DM6-12. Local brews from the tap DM2.90. Open daily in summer 8am-10pm, in winter 8am-9pm.) **Restaurant zur Zill**, Schwörhausgasse 19 (tel. 659 77), serves regional specialties in an inviting local-joint atmosphere. Meals run DM9-14. (Open M-F 11am-2pm and 5pm-midnight, Sa 11am-2pm and 5pm-1am.) A **farmer's market** springs up on Münsterplatz on Wednesday and Saturday mornings.

SIGHTS. At 161m, the steeple topping the **Münster** (tel. 15 11 39) is the tallest in the world. During the Middle Ages, members of guilds and other wealthy men decided to fund the building of a cathedral in their city, and so in 1377 the foundation stone was laid. Unfortunately, its conceivers and many successive generations passed away before the enormous steeple was completed 513 years later in 1890. When Ulm converted to Protestantism in 1530, many altars and ornate decorations were destroyed. Of those saved is *The Man of Sorrows*, a famous representation of Christ by 15th-century sculptor Hans Multscher, situated next to the front portal of the cathedral. Inside the looming Gothic walls, choir stalls carved out of wood by Jörg Syrlin the Elder form a community of emotional busts. Climb the 768 dizzying corkscrew steps of the spire on a clear day to see the Alps. (Church open daily April-June and Sept. 8am-6:45pm; July-Aug. 8am-7:45pm; Oct. 8am-5:45pm; Nov.-Jan. 9am-4:45pm; March 9am-5:45pm. Tower closes 1hr. earlier; DM3.50, children DM2.50. Free summer organ concerts M-Sa 11am, Su 11:30am.)

Nearby, the white building that houses the tourist office is also home to the **Stadthaus.** Designed by New York architect Richard Meier, its postmodern style, in conspicuous contrast to the Gothic *Münster*, raised great controversy among Ulm's residents. The basement holds interesting archaeological and historical exhibits on the Münsterplatz and the painstakingly slow construction of the *Münster*. (Open M-W and F-Sa 9am-6pm, Th 9am-8pm, Su 11am-6pm.) Towards the river on Neue Str., the **Rathaus,** built in 1370, is decorated with brilliantly colored murals and an elaborate astronomical clock, both from 1540. The old **Fischerviertel** (fishermen's quarter), down Kronengasse from the Rathaus, sports classical half-timbered houses, narrow cobblestoned streets, and canal-spanning footbridges.

Don't miss the **Schiefes Haus** (crooked house) at Schwörhausgasse 6. One of the oldest houses in Ulm, it now serves as a hotel as it slowly slides into the canal.

On the other side of the Rathaus is the **Ulmer Museum,** Marktpl. 9 (tel. 161 43 00), which features outstanding exhibits on both contemporary art and the archaeological past of the region. (Open Tu-W and F-Su 11am-5pm, Th 11am-8pm. DM5, students DM3. Free on F. Special exhibits DM8, students and seniors DM5.) The **Deutsches Brotmuseum,** Salzstadelgasse 10 (tel. 699 55), documents 6,000 years of bread-making and waxes philosophical about "the *Leitmotiv* of Man and Bread." (Open Tu and Th-Su 11am-5pm, W 10am-8:30pm. Last entrance 1hr. before closing. DM5, students DM3.50.) Well curated, it's a cultural history fan's dream come true. Don't miss "Cake—the pride of the housewife" or "Corn and bread in arts and crafts." One can easily overlook the tiny monument marking **Albert Einstein's birthplace,** donated to Ulm by India. It's in front of the train station, next to the McDonald's. Einstein's home long ago gave way to a glass-and-chrome bank. Every year on the penultimate Monday in July (July 24, 2000), the mayor of Ulm takes the stand at the **Schwörhaus** (Oath House) to carry on a centuries-old tradition by swearing allegiance to the town's 1397 constitution. The whole affair is accompanied by excessive drinking on the Danube.

STUTTGART

Surrounded by forested hills, criss-crossed by leafy parks and laced by vineyards, Stuttgart boasts the most verdant setting of any major German city. The ground also proved fertile for the seeds of a number of small start-ups which quickly bloomed into highly successful businesses; Porsche, Daimler-Benz, and a host of other corporate thoroughbreds call Stuttgart home. The former seat of the kings of Württemberg was blown to bits in WWII and was rebuilt in an uninspiring, functional style. Still, as the capital of Baden-Württemberg, Stuttgart maintains a thriving cultural scene, promoting an aura of tranquility in a very livable metropolis.

⌐ GETTING THERE AND GETTING AROUND

Flights: Flughafen Stuttgart (tel. 948 33 88). Take S-Bahn #2 or 3 to get to the city (30min.; one-way DM4.70).

Trains: The transportation hub of southwestern Germany, Stuttgart has direct rail links to most major German cities. Trains roll to Frankfurt (1½hr., 1 per hour, DM88), Munich (2½hr., 1 per hour, DM73), Berlin (5½hr., every 2hr., DM249), Basel (3hr., 1 per hour), and Paris (6hr., 3 direct trains per day). Call (0180) 599 66 33 for 24hr. schedule information.

Ferries: Neckar-Personen-Schiffahrt (tel. 54 99 70 60). Boats leave from the Bad Cannstatt dock, by Wilhelma zoo. Take U-Bahn #14 (direction "Remseck") to "Wilhelma." Ships cruise to towns along the Neckar (1-2 per day) from May to late Oct. Round-trip DM8-50. Watch out for older folks dancing the polka on board; bring your accordion or your earplugs. **Harbor tours** daily at 11am, 2, and 4:15pm (2hr., DM16).

Public Transportation: Find the name of the stop you're going to in the alphabetical list of stations and punch the corresponding number to receive a ticket. Single ride DM3.20-9.60. A 4-ride *Mehrfahrkarte* (DM10.40-36.40) saves 10% off single-ride rates. A *Kurzstrecke* (DM2) covers distances of under 2km, a good value when travelling between two points in the city center. Or buy a *Tageskarte,* valid on all trains and buses for 24hr. (DM12). **Nachtbus** (night bus) stops are marked with purple and yellow signs. The best deal for visitors is a 3-day **tourist pass,** valid on the U-Bahn (DM13) or the entire transit system (DM20); purchase these at the tourist office. There is an **information desk** (tel. 194 49) at the tourist office near the Hauptbahnhof; look for the desk under the *VVS* sign.

Car Rental: All have offices in the station near track 16. **Hertz,** tel. 226 29 21. Open M-F 7:30am-9pm, Sa 8am-5pm, Su 11am-7pm. **Europcar,** tel. 224 46 30. Open M-Sa 7:30am-9pm, Su 8:30am-9pm. **Sixt/Budget,** tel. 223 78 22. Open M-F 7:30am-9pm, Sa 8am-5pm, Su 10am-6pm. **Avis,** tel. 223 72 58. Open M-F 7am-9pm, Sa 8am-4pm.

Bike Rental: Rent a Bike, Kronenstr. 17 (tel. 209 90), in Hotel Unger. DM8 per hour, DM25 per day. Bikes are allowed on the U- and S-Bahn M-F 8:30am-4pm and 6:30pm until closing and Sa-Su all day; they're forbidden on buses and streetcars.

Mitfahrzentrale: Two locations. **Stuttgart West,** Lerchenstr. 65 (tel. 636 80 36). Bus #42 (direction: "Schreiberstr.") to "Rosenberg/Johannesstr." **Hauptstätter Str. 154** (tel. 60 36 06). U-Bahn #14 (direction: "Heslach/Vogelrain") to "Marienplatz." Both open M-F 9am-6pm, Sa 9am-2pm, Su 11am-2pm.

 ## ORIENTATION

At the heart of Stuttgart lies an enormous pedestrian zone where shops and restaurants stretch as far as the eye can see. **Königstraße** and **Calwerstraße** are the main pedestrian thoroughfares; from the train station, both are accessible through the underground **Arnulf-Klett-Passage.** To the left lies the tranquil castle gardens, to the right the thriving business sector. A number of discount packages and passes are available to tourists; among these is the **Stuttcard** (DM25), which offers three days of inner city transportation; admission to seven museums; and bargains for guided tours, theaters, the zoo, mineral baths, and other sights. Also available is the **Stuttgart Night Pass** (DM16) which covers entrance to various clubs and free drinks at others. Call the tourist office for more information.

ⓘ PRACTICAL INFORMATION

TOURIST SERVICES

Tourist Offices: I-Punkt, Königstr. 1 (tel. 222 80; fax 222 82 53; www.stuttgart-tourist.de), directly in front of the down escalator into the Klett-Passage. They may be busy, but they book **rooms** for free, sell excellent maps (DM1), and distribute bus and train schedules. The *Monatsspiegel* (DM3.50) lists museum hours, cultural events, and musical performances, and includes a guide to food and nightlife. Open May-Oct. M-F 9:30am-8:30pm, Sa 9:30am-6pm, Su and public holidays 11am-6pm; Nov.-April same hours but Su and holidays 1-6pm. **tips 'n' trips,** Rotebühlpl. 26-27 (tel. 222 27 30; fax 222 27 33; email jugendinformation@tips-n-trips.shuttle.de; www.shuttle.de/tips-n-trips), in the underground U-Bahn passage at Theodor-Heuss-Str. and Fritz-Elsas-Str. The with-it, ultra-helpful staff reams out reams of youth-oriented pamphlets about travel and the Stuttgart scene. A great resource. Open M-F noon-7pm, Sa 10am-4pm.

Consulates: South Africa, Erich-Herion-Str. 27 (tel. 58 64 41). **U.K.,** Breite Str. 2 (tel. 16 26 90).

American Express: Schillerpl. 4 (tel. 162 49 20; fax 162 49 22), near Schloßplatz. Holds mail, cashes traveler's checks, and doubles as a travel agency for members. A **second branch,** Arnulf-Klett-Platz 1 (tel. 226 92 67; fax 223 95 44) holds mail and cashes checks. Open M-F 9:30am-1:30pm and 2:30-6pm, Sa 9:30am-12:30pm.

LOCAL SERVICES

Lost and Found: Fundsachenstelle, Eberhardstr. 61f (tel. 216 20 16). Open M-W 8:30am-1pm, Th 8:30am-3:30pm, F 8:30am-12:30pm.

Bookstore: English Shop, Schellingstr. 11 (tel. 226 09 02). Specializes in all things British, offers classics and current best-sellers, and rents English-language videos. **Buchhaus Wittwer,** Königstr. 30 (tel. 250 70), also has books in English.

Gay and Lesbian Resources: Weißenburg, Weißenburgstr. 28a (tel. 640 44 94), is Stuttgart's gay and lesbian center. Office open M-F 7:30-9:30pm. Café open 3-10pm. **Erlkönig,** Nesenbachstr. 52 (tel. 63 91 39), is a popular gay and lesbian bookstore. Open M-F 10am-1:30pm and 3-8pm, Sa 10am-4pm.

Women's Resources: Fraueninformationzentrum, Landhausstr. 62 (tel. 26 18 91).

AIDS Resources: Hölderlinpl. 5a (tel. 224 69 00). Open M-F 10am-noon and M-Th 2-5pm. Anonymous hotline (tel. 194 11) open M and Th-F 6:30-9:30pm.

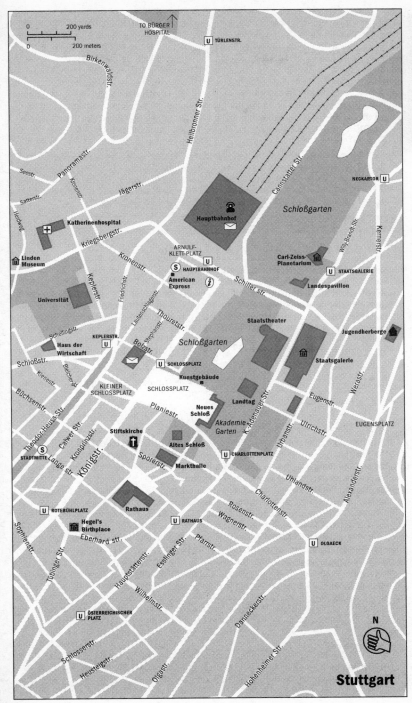

0   200 yards
0   200 meters

TO BÜRGER HOSPITAL

U TÜRLENSTR.

Birkenwaldstr.

Heilbronner Str.

Cannstatter Str.

NECKARTOR U

Schloßgarten

Seestr.

Panoramastr.

Kronenstr.

Jägerstr.

Sattelstr.

Hachweg

Katherinenhospital

Hauptbahnhof

Kernerstr.

Willy-Brandt-Str.

Carl-Zeiss-Planetarium

Linden Museum

Kriegsbergstr.

Kronenstr.

ARNULF-KLETT-PLATZ

U

S HAUPTBAHNHOF

American Express

Schiller Str.

U STAATSGALERIE

Landespavillon

Keplerstr.

Friedrichstr.

Universität

Lautenschlagerstr.

Thouretstr.

Stephanstr.

Staatstheater

Jugendherberge

Schellingstr.

KEPLERSTR.

U

Bolzstr.

Schloßgarten

Staatsgalerie

Haus der Wirtschaft

Schloßstr.

Kienestr.

Büchsenstr.

Theodor-Heuss-Str.

Büchsenstr.

U SCHLOSSPLATZ

KLEINER SCHLOSSPLATZ

Kunstgebäude

SCHLOSSPLATZ

Planiestr.

Neues Schloß

Landtag

Adenauer-Str.

Urbanstr.

Eugenstr.

Ulrichstr.

Werastr.

EUGENSPLATZ

Calwer Str.

Konpinzstr.

Stiftskirche

Akademie Garten

Alexanderstr.

S STADTMITTE

Lange Str.

Königstr.

Sporerstr.

Altes Schloß

Markthalle

U CHARLOTTENPLATZ

Uhlandstr.

Charlottenstr.

U ROTEBÜHLPLATZ

Rathaus

Rosenstr.

Wagnerstr.

Sophienstr.

Hegel's Birthplace

U RATHAUS

U OLGAECK

Eberhard str.

Tübinger Str.

Hauptstätterstr.

Esslinger Str.

Pfarrstr.

Wilhelmstr.

Danneckerstr.

U ÖSTERREICHISCHER PLATZ

N

Schlosserstr.

Heusteigstr.

Olgastr.

Hohenheimer Str.

Stuttgart

Laundromat: SB Waschsalon, Kienbachstr. 16. S-Bahn #13 to "Kienbachstr." Wash DM8, dry DM2 per 10min. Open daily 8am-10pm.

EMERGENCY AND COMMUNICATIONS

Emergency: Tel. 110. **Police,** Hahnemannstr. 1 (tel. 899 01). **Fire,** tel. 112.

Hospital: Bürgerhospital, Tunzhofer Str. 14-16 (tel. 253 00).

Pharmacy: Internationale, Königstr. 70 (tel. 22 47 80). Open M-W and F 8:30am-6:30pm, Th 8:30am-8:30pm, Sa 8:30am-2pm.

Post Office: At the **Hauptbahnhof,** 70001 Stuttgart. Open M-F 8am-8pm, Sa 8am-2pm, Su 10am-2pm. The post office at **Bolzstr. 3** does not hold mail. Open M-F 9am-8pm, Sa 9am-2pm.

Internet Access: tips 'n' trips offers the best deal in town at DM5 per hour (See **Tourist Offices,** above). If you don't want to stand in line for their lone computer, check out the top floor of the **Kaufhof** department store near the train station. DM3 per 30min.; open M-F 9:30am-9pm, Sa 9am-4pm. Or try the 3rd floor of the **Karstadt** department store across the way. DM5 per 30min. Open M-F 9am-8pm, Sa 9am-4pm.

PHONE CODE	0711

▌ ACCOMMODATIONS AND CAMPING

Most of Stuttgart's budget beds are located on the two ridges surrounding the downtown area and are easily accessible by streetcar. Hotels around the pedestrian zone and train station cater to customers used to paying top Mark—call ahead for better deals. Contact tips 'n' trips (see **Tourist Offices,** above) for information on cheap accommodation in Stuttgart. Though a commute away, the hostel in Ludwigsburg is a good alternative (see p. 345).

Jugendgästehaus Stuttgart, Richard-Wagner-Str. 2 (tel. 24 11 32 and 248 97 30). Streetcar #15 (direction: "Heumaden") to "Bubenbad." Continue in the direction of the streetcar on the right side of the street and veer right immediately; the place is on the right. Right. An excellent hostel situated in a quiet residential neighborhood. Spotless rooms with a great view, though the ones in the basement are slightly less spectacular. Singles DM35, with bath DM45, with bath and shower DM55; DM35 per additional person, with bath and shower DM10 more. Breakfast included. Dinner DM8. Key deposit DM20. Reception M-F 9am-8pm, Sa-Su 11am-8pm. No curfew.

Jugendherberge Stuttgart (HI), Haußmannstr. 27 (tel. 24 15 83; fax 236 10 41). Take the "ZOB" exit from the Klett-Passage, continue through the Schloßgarten, and follow the signs leading uphill along the paved path. Or take streetcar #15 (direction: "Heumaden") to "Eugensplatz" and go down Kernerstr., the street starting at the Apotheke; the entrance is about 5min. down Kernerstr. A lively mix of nationalities shacks up in slightly crowded 6-bed rooms, most offering spectacular city views. The 220 beds are often full; always call ahead. DM23, over 26 DM28. Breakfast included. Sheets DM5.50. Reception 7-9am and noon-11pm. Lockout 9am-noon. Strict curfew 11:30pm. Doors open briefly at 1am and 5am for hard-core children of the night.

Tramper Point Stuttgart, Wiener Str. 317 (tel. 817 74 76; fax 231 28 10). Take U-Bahn #6 (direction: "Gehrlingen") to "Sportpark Feuerbach," then cross the tracks, walking toward the sport park. Despite its name, this bizarre mural-covered wooden structure is not a gathering place for women of ill repute, but the funkiest and cheapest place to stay in Stuttgart. Cozy up on one of 25 cots in a crescent-shaped room, or an Iso-matte in case of overflow. DM13. Breakfast and shower included. Wool blanket DM1.50, or bring your own sleeping bag. Cooking facilities. Reception 5-11pm. Ages 16-27 only. Open late June to early Sept. for individuals, April-Nov. for groups with reservations.

Hotel Espenlaub, Charlottenstr. 27 (tel. 21 09 10; fax 210 91 55). Take U-Bahn #5 or 6 or streetcar #15 or 16 to "Olgaeck." High on the price scale, but a great location and nice accommodations. Singles start at DM60; doubles DM100. Breakfast, TV, phone, and bath included.

Camping: Campingplatz Cannstatter Wasen, Mercedesstr. 40 (tel. 55 66 96; fax 55 74 54), on the river in Bad Cannstatt. S-Bahn #1, 2, or 3 to "Bad Cannstatt." Exit through the back of the station, and follow the signs for "Wasen." After the tunnel, head diagonally left across the never-ending parking lot. DM8 per person; DM4 per child. Tent DM6-8. Car DM4. Reception 7am-noon and 2-10pm.

FOOD

Due to a sizable contingent of guest workers, Stuttgart's culinary scene is heartily spiced up by Greek, Turkish, African, and Asian restaurants. But the cuisine of the Schwaben region is itself one of the most appealing varieties of German food. *Spätzle* (thick noodles) and *Maultaschen* (pasta pockets filled with meat and spinach) are especially popular. For basic fruits and veggies as well as staples like bread and cheese, head to the **Wochenmarkt** on Marktplatz and Schillerplatz. (Open Th and Sa 8am-3pm.) For **groceries,** try the basement of **Kaufhof,** two blocks from the station. (Open M-F 9am-8pm, Sa 9am-4pm.)

Mensa, Holzgartenstr. 11. From the train station, take Kriegsbergstr. to Holzgartenstr. Turn left and go down the right side of the street over the underpass; the restaurant is on the right. A plain but functional place where quantity compensates for quality. Meals DM4-5. Open during the semester M-F 11:15am-2:30pm.; the rest of the year M-F 11:15am-1:30pm. The **Mensastüble** downstairs offers restaurant fare at slightly higher prices. Open M-F 11:15am-1:45pm.

Iden, Eberhardstr. 1 (tel. 23 59 89). U-Bahn to "Rathaus." Good vegetarian fare served cafeteria-style. Fifty kinds of salads (DM2.70 per 100g, which adds up quickly), noodles, and potatoes, served in a bright atmosphere with lots of Nordic furniture. More desserts than you can imagine. Open M-F 11am-9pm, Sa 10am-5pm.

Weinhaus Stetter, Rosenstr. 32 (tel. 24 01 63). U-Bahn to "Charlottenplatz," walk down Esslinger Str., and take a left onto Rosenstr. This local favorite offers intriguing Swabian specialties (DM7-9), all to be washed down with an incredible wine selection (DM5-7). Open M-F 3-11pm, Sa 10am-3am. Kitchen open M-Sa 3-11pm.

Waschsalon, Charlottenstr. 27 (tel. 236 98 96), at the corner of Charlottenstr. and Alexanderstr. U-Bahn #5 or 6 or streetcar #15 or 16 to "Olgaeck." A cool *Kneipe* with an identity crisis (it thinks it's a laundromat). Swabian specialities and crepes adorn the tables, while metallic pants grace the walls. Wild potatoes with herbs and a garlic sauce DM6.90. Open M-F and Su 10am-1am, Sa 4pm-2am.

UDO-Snack, Calwerstr. 23. Bills itself as "Stuttgart's *Kult-Imbiß* for over 20 years." Strolling through the pedestrian zone late at night, appease your growling stomach with cheap, greasy favorites like *Pommes Frites* and *Currywurst* (DM2.80-5.80) over rap music. Open M-Tu 11am-11pm, W-Th 11am-midnight, F-Sa 11am-1am, Su 3-11pm.

Akademie der schönsten Künste, Charlottenstr. 5 (tel. 24 24 36). U-Bahn to "Charlottenplatz." High ceilings, art-covered walls, a garden, and fewer seats than necessary at such a paragon of European sophistication. Considered the perfect date restaurant among trendy Stuttgarters; you'll understand why. Light fare isn't the cheapest (DM4-15), but the ambience makes up for it. Open M-F 7am-midnight, Sa-Su 9am-4pm.

SIGHTS

SCHLOSSGARTEN. Almost 20% of Stuttgart is under a land preservation order, resulting in something known as "the green U," much of which contains the **Schloß-garten,** Stuttgart's main municipal park. Running from the station southward to the Neues Schloß and northeast to the Neckar, the Schloßgarten is crammed with fountains and beautifully tended flower gardens. An 8km-long pedestrian bridge beginning at the Schloßgarten weaves a path above the city without ever leaving the parks. The north end of the Schloßgarten contains the expansive **Rosenstein-park,** which also holds the **Wilhelma,** a large zoological and botanical garden that claims 9,000 species of animals and plants. *(Tel. 540 20. Take U-Bahn #14 or Bus #52, 55, or 56 to "Wilhelma." Open daily March-Oct. 8:15am-5pm; Nov.-Feb. 8:15am-4pm. DM14, students DM7; after 4pm and from Nov.-Feb. DM9, students DM4.50.)*

SCHLOSSPLATZ. The Schloßgarten runs to **Schloßplatz,** off Königstr., upon which reposes the elegant, Baroque **Neues Schloß,** now home to stodgy bureaucrats and the 40 or so mythological statues that vogue on its roof. The 16th-century **Altes Schloß,** across the street on Schillerplatz, offers a graceful, colonnaded Renaissance courtyard.

HEGEL'S BIRTHPLACE. To interface with the *Weltgeist* (world-spirit), head to Hegel's birthplace, which is a few doors down from a busy porn shop. The house provides a thorough exegesis of the philosopher's life through letters, manuscripts, and notes. *(Eberhardstr. 53, a couple blocks east from the end of Königstr. Tel. 216 67 33. Take S-Bahn #1, 2, 3, 4, 5, or 6, U-Bahn #14, or streetcar #2 or 4 to "Rotebühlplatz (Stadtmitte)." Open Tu and F 10am-5:30pm, Th 10am-6:30pm.)*

MINERALBÄDER. Stuttgart harbors amazing **mineral baths,** formed from the most productive mineral springs in Western Europe. The 22 million liters of spring water pumped out *every day* contain chemical combinations with curative capabilities. All baths offer a spectacular array of pools, saunas, and showers—the perfect remedy for budget traveler exhaustion. Loll in the **Mineralbad Leuze,** an official health care facility. *(Am Leuzebad 2-6. Tel. 216 42 10. Open daily 6am-9pm. Day card DM15.50, students DM10.50; 2½hr. soak DM9.50, students DM6.50; 1¼hr. DM8, students DM5.50. Massage DM36.)* **Mineralbad Berg** is a little less posh. *(Am Schwanenplatz 9. Tel. 26 10 60. U-Bahn #1 or 14 or streetcar #2 to "Mineralbäder," then walk towards the river and the volcano-like fountains directly across from the U-Bahn station. Open M-F 6am-8pm, Sa 6am-7pm, Su 6am-1pm. Day card DM10. Massage DM30.)* A bit farther away, **Mineralbad Cannstatt** is better outfitted. *(Sulzerrainstr. 2. Tel. 216 92 41. Ride streetcar #2 to "Kursaal." Open M-F 9am-9:30pm, Sa 9am-9pm, Su 9am-5pm.)*

KARL-ZEISS-PLANETARIUM. Stuttgart stargazers get their fix at the Karl-Zeiss-Planetarium, enjoying shows with informative German voice-overs, cool visual effects (comets shooting, black holes sucking), and clichéd background music. Karl Zeiss is perhaps the most famous telescope manufacturer in the galaxy. *(Willy-Brandt-Str. 25. Tel. 162 92 15. U-Bahn #1, 9, or 14 or streetcar #2 or 4 to "Staatsgalerie," or walk from the south exit of the train station into the Schloßgarten for about 200m. Shows Tu and Th 10am and 3pm; W and F 10am, 3, and 8pm; Sa-Su 2, 4, and 6pm. DM9, students DM5.)*

🏛 MUSEUMS

A plethora of outstanding and diverse museums compensates for Stuttgart's paucity of monumental history. In addition to the magnificent art galleries and archaeology exhibits, the city offers displays on some of the more hedonistic aspects of everyday life: beer, cars, and playing cards. For once, and only once, drinking and driving mix quite well. The monthly *Monatsspiegel*, available at the tourist office, lists information on all museums.

▧ STAATSGALERIE STUTTGART. An absolutely superb collection housed in two wings: the stately paintings in the **old wing** date from the Middle Ages to the 19th century, while the **new wing,** a colorful stroke of postmodern daring, contains an essential collection of moderns including Picasso, Kandinsky, Beckmann, and Dalí. *(Konrad-Adenauer-Str. 30-32. Tel. 212 40 50. Open W and F-Su 10am-5pm, Tu and Th 10am-8pm. DM5, students DM3.)*

WÜRTTEMBERGISCHES LANDESMUSEUM. Located in the Altes Schloß, the museum details the Swabian region and people, with an emphasis on the abundant local archaeology. Excellent exhibits on Bronze Age Celtic metalwork, along with a number of fascinating skulls, crown jewels, and Roman pillars. *(Schillerpl. 6. Tel. 279 34 00. Open Tu 10am-1pm, W-Su 10am-5pm. DM5, students DM3. Wheelchair accessible.)*

LINDENMUSEUM STUTTGART. The museum features in-depth ethnological collections from America, the South Seas, Africa, and Asia. Western hegemonists can satisfy their curiosity about the exotic Other with accompanying films, lectures, and discussions. *(Hegelpl. 1. Tel. 202 24 56. 10 min. west of the train station along Kriegsbergstr. Take bus #40, 42, or 43 to "Hegelplatz." Open Tu, Th, and Sa-Su 10am-5pm, W 10am-8pm, F 10am-1pm. Free, except for special exhibits.)*

MERCEDES-BENZ-MUSEUM. A must for car-lovers. The original workshop, where Herr Daimler built the first generation of Mercedes-Benzes, now houses an elaborately modern exhibit; visitors ooh and aah at a century's worth of gleaming models. Hold high-tech "soundsticks" to your ear and learn all about the little German engine that could. Tight security weeds out BMW spies; you even need to take a special bus from the parking lot to the entrance. *(Mercedesstr. 137, in Stuttgart-Untertürkheim. Tel. 172 25 78. S-Bahn #1 to "Neckarstadion"; walk left under the bridge and turn left at the next intersection. Open Tu-Su 9am-5pm. Free.)*

PORSCHEMUSEUM. Tells much the same story as the Mercedes museum, but with sexier curves and an even greater *schicki-micki* factor. Vroom! *(Porschestr. 42, in Stuttgart-Zuffauhausen. Tel. 827 56 85. S-Bahn #6 (direction: "Weil der Stadt") to "Neuwirtshaus"; exit the station to the right (don't go under the tracks). Open M-F 9am-4pm, Sa-Su 9am-5pm. Free.)*

KUNSTGEBÄUDE. Houses both the **Württembergischer Kunstverein** (tel. 22 33 70) and the **Galerie der Stadt** (tel. 216 21 88). Both concern themselves with contemporary art in a variety of media. Each year, 8-10 intriguing exhibits feature local and international work. *(Schloßpl. 2, directly across from the Altes Schloß. Both museums open Tu and Th-Su 11am-6pm, W 11am-8pm. Free, but special exhibits usually DM8, students DM5.*

SCHWÄBISCHES BRAUEREIMUSEUM. Only in Germany could an entire museum be devoted to beer. Five millennia of the beverage's history culminate in a brew-it-yourself exhibit of current beer production. Everything's free but the samples. *(DM3.50-4 per beer. Robert-Koch-Str. 12, in Stuttgart-Vaihingen. Tel. 737 02 01. U-Bahn #1, 3, or 6 or S-Bahn #1, 2, or 3 to "Vaihingen Bahnhof." Walk along Vollmoellerstr. and turn right onto Robert-Koch-Str. Open Th-Su 10:30am-5:30pm.)*

DEUTSCHES SPIELKARTENMUSEUM. The most extensive playing card museum in Europe, it reveals only select specimens of its 400,000 card collection spanning six centuries and five continents in a series of small but fascinating exhibits. *(Schönbuschstr. 32. Tel. 756 01 20. U-Bahn #5 to "Leinfelden." From the train station, walk down Marktstr. and take a left onto Stuttgartstr. which becomes Schönbuschstr.; it's in the basement of the grammar school. Open Th-Sa 2-5pm, Su 11am-4pm.)*

🎵 🎭 ENTERTAINMENT AND NIGHTLIFE

The **Staatstheater,** across the plaza from the Neues Schloß, is Stuttgart's most famous theater, with operas, ballets, plays, and concerts by the dozen. (24hr. ticket information tel. 197 03 or 01 15 17; reservations tel. 20 20 90. Box office open M-F 10am-6pm, Sa 9am-1pm, and 1hr. before performance. DM16-90.) There are 25 other local theaters, and tickets for them are usually much cheaper (DM10-25, students DM5-15). The tourist office provides schedules and sells tickets, which can also be purchased at the **Kartenhäusle,** Geißstr. 4 at Hans-im-Glück-Brunnen. (Tel. 210 40 12. Open M-F 9am-6pm, Sa 9am-2pm; order by phone 9am-noon and 2-5pm.) **Corso Kino,** Hauptstr. 6 (tel. 73 49 16), shows films in their original language, with frequent special festivals and revivals. Take U-Bahn #1 to "Schillerpl." Schedules in English are available at the tourist office.

Stuttgart also offers a vibrant selection of annual festivals to please camera-toting tourists and liquored-up locals. The **Stuttgarter Weindorf** (wine village) is the largest wine festival in Germany. For 10 days starting on August 24, 2000, wine lovers will descend upon Schillerplatz and Marktplatz to sample more than 350 kinds of wine as well as scrumptious Swabian specialties. Beer gets 16 days of its own adulation in the **Cannstatter Volksfest** (Sept. 23-Oct. 8, 2000).

From pleasant chats over fine Italian coffee to hypnotic, techno-fueled hysteria, Stuttgart offers a full spectrum of nightlife nastiness. Serious prowlers should pick up either *Prinz* (DM5) or *Stuttgart Lift* (DM4.50) at any city newsstand; both contain detailed information on what's happening. **Tips 'n' trips** (see **Tourist Offices,** p. 338) also publishes up-to-date guides to the evening scene in German and English. Be assured, Dionysus never sleeps in this city. The area along Königstr. and Calwerstr. gets going in the early evenings with chatter and beer spilling from numerous cafés; later on, the nightlife clusters around Eberhardstr., Rotebühl-platz, and Kleines Schloßplatz. To appease sin-seeking tourists, there's the **Stuttgart Night Pass,** good for three nights' admission and free second drinks at various clubs, bars, and discos; ask at the tourist office for details.

Palast der Republik, Friedrichstr. 27 (tel. 226 48 87). This wooden bungalow emanates loud music as stylish after-hours aficionados congregate outside to down reasonably priced drinks (DM4-6). There's food, too. Open M-W 11am-2am, Th-Sa 11am-3am, Su 3pm-2am; in winter M-W and Su 11am-1am, Th-Sa 11am-2am.

Radio Bar, Rotebühlpl. 23 (tel. 62 87 09). Popular among a young preppy crowd, this place offers drinks (DM4-10), a lively dance floor, and pulsating house music 'til late. Open M-Th and Su 11:20am-2am, F-Sa 11:30am-4am. No cover.

Oblomow, Torstr. 20 (tel. 236 79 24). A café that throws open its doors late at night so passersby can hear its upbeat music. Foozball and pinball games. Vegetarians accommodated. Food DM4-8. Open daily 4pm-5am.

Café Stella, Hauptstätter Str. 57 (tel. 640 25 83). Polished postmodern café where a mellow crowd smokes and reads tarot cards. Occasional jazz performances. Pool table upstairs. Open M-Th 9am-1am, F 9am-2am, Sa 10am-2am, Su 10am-1am.

Zap, Hauptstätter Str. 40 (tel. 23 52 27), in the Schwabenzentrum. This glitzy social mecca is a thriving cesspool of fun. Hip-hop, house, and soul. Open Tu 9pm-3am, W-Su 10pm-4am. Cover DM8-15.

Lauras Club, Rotebühlpl. 4. Gay club blasts house and techno while S&M mannequins pose in cages. Open Th-Su 10pm-5am. No cover.

Kings, Calwerstr. 21 (tel. 226 45 58). Gays and lesbians groove to spiced-up 80s music beneath black lights and red velvet walls. Private, but open to non-members. Open W-Sa 10am-6am. Cover F DM10 and Sa DM15; includes 2 drinks.

NEAR STUTTGART: LUDWIGSBURG

Ludwigsburg popped out of the blue in the early 18th century, the narcissistic love child of Duke Eberhard of Ludwig. His modest idea: to erect a residential castle in the duchy's new capital bearing his own name. Unfortunately, Eberhard died before his playground was born, and although his successors finished decorating the castle, they preferred to live in Stuttgart. Even without the aristocratic element, Ludwigsburg became a lively Baroque city with a luxurious trio of palaces.

The opulent Baroque **Residenzschloß** is definitely worth seeing, even if you find yourself lost among German office fieldtrips. The 1¼-hour guided journey is the only way to see Ludwig's 3m-long bed (he was larger than life: almost 7 ft. tall) and the rest of the lavish gold, marble, and velvet interior. (Open mid-March to Nov. daily 9am-noon and 1-5pm. Tours in English at 1:30pm; German tours Nov. to mid-March M-F 10:30am and 3pm. DM8, students DM4.) The "Swabian Versailles" is situated in an expansive 30-hectare garden that earned Ludwig's complex the tourist brochure epithet **Blühendes Barock,** or "blooming Baroque." (Open mid-March to early Dec. daily 7:30am-8:30pm. Main entrance on Schondorfer Str. open 9am-6pm.) Inside, a perennial **Märchengarten** recreates scenes from major fairy tales in a large park of wild vegetation. (Open 9am-6pm. Adults DM12, students DM5.) Join 100 kids shouting *Rapunzel, Rapunzel, laß deinen Zopf herunter.* ("Rapunzel, Rapunzel, let down your hair!") The **Favoritschloß** (tel. 18 64 40) is an excellent destination for a stroll or picnic. The smaller Baroque gem was built as a hunting lodge and big-time party venue for Duke Carl Engler. (Open mid-March to Oct. daily 9am-noon and 1:30-5pm; Nov. to mid-March 10am-noon and 1:30-4pm. Frequent guided tours mid-March to Nov. daily 9am-noon and 1:30-5pm; Nov. to mid-March Tu-Su 10am-noon and 1-4pm. DM4.) If you're not all *Schloßed*-out by this point, continue for 30 minutes up the alley through the **Favoritenpark** and marvel at the third Ludwig palace—the Rococo **Monrepos** (tel. 225 50). Unfortunately, the castle is now a luxury hotel and is closed to visitors, but you can calm your frustrations by renting a **boat** and rowing on the peaceful lake nearby.

All three palaces host the annual **Ludwigsburger Schloßfestspiele,** a series of open-air concerts and performances that runs from early June to late September. For information on tickets, call the Forum am Schloßpark. (Tel. 91 71 00. Open M-F 8:30am-6:30pm, Sa 9am-1pm.) Even without renowned musicians in the neighborhood, Ludwigsburg offers a sense of refined, classy tranquility. No bumpy medieval cobblestone to be found here: the **Marktplatz** is smooth and spacious, with cotton-candy churches contemplating one another across an aristocratic divide.

To reach Ludwigsburg from Stuttgart, hop on S-Bahn #4 or 5 (direction: "Marbach" or "Bietigheim"; 20min.; DM4.30), or take the **boat** run by Neckar-Personen-Schiffahrt (see p. 337). The **tourist office,** across from the Rathaus at Wilhelmstr. 10 (tel. 910 26 36 or 910 22 52), books **rooms** for free. (Open M-F 9am-6pm, Sa 9am-2pm.) The only cheap lodging in town is the **Jugendherberge Ludwigsburg (HI),** Gemsenbergstr. 21 (tel. 515 64; fax 594 40). Take bus #422 to "Schlößlesfeld" (DM2.80). It's quite far from town, but the hostel's pastoral setting and nice balconies lend it a resort-like tranquility. (DM22, over 26 DM28. Huge breakfast DM5. Members only. Cold meal DM7.50, warm meal DM9. Reception 9am-1pm and 5-7pm. Curfew 10pm.) There are several restaurants on **Holzmarkt,** near Marktplatz. **Corfu,** Holzmarktstr. 2 (tel. 92 08 24), serves daily Greek specials, including a giant bean salad (DM6) and vegetarian entrees. (DM8.50-20. Open daily 11:30am-2:30pm and 5pm-midnight.) **Grocery stores** and bakeries run rampant along Myluisstr. and Arsenalstr. The **telephone code** is 07141.

NEAR STUTTGART: MARBACH

Friedrich Schiller was born in Marbach, a fact that is difficult to ignore. From drug stores to hair salons, the name of the prominently nosed poet is ubiquitous. The stately **Schiller-Nationalmuseum,** Schillerhöhe 8-10 (tel. 60 61), offers a detailed account of Schiller's life and work, and also looks at his Swabian contemporaries. Follow the signs from the train station. (Open daily 9am-5pm. DM4, students DM2.) Adjacent to the museum is the **German literature archive** (tel. 60 61), one of the largest of its kind in the country. Call ahead if you plan to visit. Die-hard Schiller devotees also visit the **Schiller-Geburtshaus,** Niklastorstr. 31 (tel. 175 67), where the author was born in 1759. Not an astounding amount to see here, except some Schiller artifacts and an animated video on the man. To get there, follow the signs through town. (Open daily 9am-5pm. DM3, students DM1.50.) From the Schiller-Nationalmuseum, you'll pass through the half-timbered **Bürgerturm** and **Marktplatz.** The nearby **Rathaus,** Marktstr. 23, has information on walking tours, hotels, and restaurants. (Open M 9-11am and 4-6pm, Tu and Th-F 9-11am, W 2-4pm.) Most of Marbach's **restaurants** are located along Marktstr. To reach Marbach from Stuttgart, take S-Bahn #4 until the end. The city's **telephone code** is 07144.

TÜBINGEN

With nearly half its residents affiliated with its 500-year-old university, Tübingen is academic and proud of it. The university has been a source of unrest from the Middle Ages to the student uprisings of the late 60s and beyond; students have boycotted classes to protest everything from the educational system and the Nazi past of many politicians to the Vietnam War. The compact Altstadt, a snail shell sheltering a lively student life, earned Tübingen the distinction of "highest quality of life" in a recent magazine poll.

⚡ ORIENTATION AND PRACTICAL INFORMATION

Thirty kilometers south of Stuttgart, Tübingen straddles the Neckar on the edge of the Schwarzwald. Easily reached by rail, it is one of the larger cities in the area, and it is connected by bus and train to many small towns in the Schwäbische Alb.

Trains: Chug daily to Stuttgart (1hr., 2 per hour, DM17).

Taxis: Taxizentrale, tel. 243 01.

Bike Rental: RADlager, Lazarettgasse 19-21 (tel. 55 16 51; fax 55 17 51), in the Altstadt. DM14 per day. Open M-Tu and Th-F 9:30am-1pm and 2-6:30pm, W 2-6pm, Sa 9:30am-2:30pm.

Boat Rental: Bootsverleih Märkle (tel. 31 52 29), on the river under the tourist office. Rowboats DM12 per hour. Pedalboats DM16 per hour. Open Apr.-Sept. daily 11am-8pm.

Mitfahrzentrale: Münzgasse 6 (tel. 194 40). Matches riders and drivers. Munich DM24, Frankfurt DM24, Köln DM39, Berlin DM62. Open M-F 10am-1pm and 3pm-7pm, Sa-Su 11am-2pm. Call 1-2 days in advance.

Tourist Office: Verkehrsverein (tel. 913 60; fax 350 70; www.tuebingen.de), on the Neckarbrücke. From the front of the station, turn right and walk to Karlstr., turn left and walk to the river. The office books **rooms** (DM30-100) for free and sells maps. Open M-F 9am-7pm, Sa 9am-5pm, Su 2-5pm; Oct.-April closed Su.

Tours: Leave from the tourist office April-Oct. W 10am, Sa-Su 2:30pm. DM5.

Mitwohnzentrale: Wilhelmstr. 2-3 (tel. 194 45; fax 55 10 70). Arranges apartments for stays of 1 month or longer. Open M-Th 10am-noon and 2-5pm, F 10am-3pm, Sa 10am-1pm.

Bookstores: The venerable, 400-year-old **Osiandersche Buchhandlung,** Wilhelmstr. 12 (tel. 920 10), carries a large selection of English and American literature. Open M-F 9am-8pm, Sa 9am-4pm. **Bücherkabinett Antiquariat,** Bachgasse 13 (tel. 55 12 23), houses 20,000 used books, 5% in English. Open M-F 10am-6:30pm, Sa 10am-3pm.

Cultural Center: German-American Institute, Karlstr. 3 (tel. 340 71).

Laundromat: Student Waschsalon, on the corner of Rappstr. and Herrenberger Str., across from Marquardtei (see **Food,** below). Open M-Sa 8am-11pm, DM5 wash.

Women's Resources: Frauencafé, Karlstr. 13 (tel. 328 62), in the magenta house a block from the station, is a hopping, women-only night spot/safe zone. Open Sept.-June M-F 8pm-midnight. **Frauenbuchladen Thalestris,** Bursagasse 2 (tel. 265 90 or 511 90), is a women's bookstore. Open M-F 10am-7pm, Sa 10am-2pm.

Rape Crisis Hotline: Frauenhaus, tel. 666 04.

Emergency: Police, tel. 110. **Fire and Ambulance,** tel. 112.

Post Office: Europapl. 2, 72072 Tübingen, 100m to the right of the station. Open M-F 7:30am-6:30pm, Sa 7:30am-12:30pm.

PHONE CODE	07071

▚ ACCOMMODATIONS AND CAMPING

Most of the lodgings in the city are not priced to please; ask about **private rooms** at the tourist office.

Jugendherberge (HI), Gartenstr. 22/2 (tel. 230 02; fax 250 61). Cross the bridge past the tourist office and make a right. Recently renovated; a terrace overlooks the Neckar. DM23, over 26 DM28. Breakfast included. Reception 5-8pm and 10-11pm. Lockout 9am-5pm. Curfew 10pm. Lockers DM5 deposit. Wheelchair access. Members only.

Hotel am Schloß, Burgsteige 18 (tel. 929 40; fax 92 94 10), on the hill leading to the Schloß. 3-star lodgings in a picturesque location. All rooms have phone and TV. Singles DM55, with shower DM72, with bath DM99-130; doubles with bath DM124-148. Breakfast included. Reserve by fax.

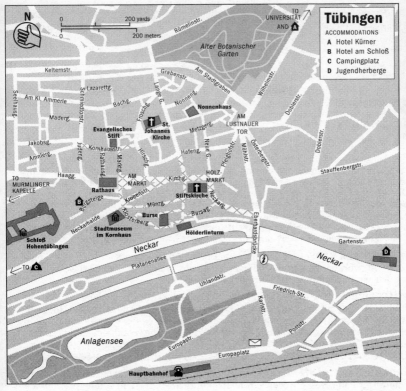

Hotel Kürner, Weizsäckerstr. 1 (tel. 227 35; fax 279 20), 20min. from the Altstadt. Follow Wilhelmstr. past the university and go right on Weizsäckerstr. Or bus #1, 2, 6, 7, or 15 to "Lothar-Meyer-Bau." Friendly management, 70s decor, and restaurant. All rooms have phone and TV. Singles DM58-68, doubles DM108. Breakfast included.

Camping: Rappenberghalde (tel. 431 45; fax 350 70). Go upstream from the Altstadt or left from the station; cross the river at the Alleenbrücke and turn left (25min.). Follow the blue signs. Or take bus #9 to "Rappenberg" (shout out to Iller, p. 257) and follow the river to your left. DM9.50 per person. Tent DM5.50-7. Bike rental DM15 per day. Laundry DM7.50. Reception daily 8am-12:30pm and 2:30-10pm. Open March-Oct.15.

📷 FOOD

With the smell of pungent herbs and fresh bread in the air, Tübingen's superb restaurants seduce student and tourist alike. Most inexpensive eating establishments cluster around **Metzgergasse** and **Am Lutznauer Tor.** Buy **groceries** at **Pfannkuch,** Karlstr. 3, next to the tourist office on the Neckarbrücke. (Open M-F 8:30am-7:30pm, Sa 8am-2pm.) The Altstadt bristles with grocery stores and bakeries.

Ratskeller, Haaggasse 4 (tel. 213 91). Entrance on Rathausgasse. Serves Swabian specialties and vegetarian platters (DM12-16) to loud locals and the occasional tourist (that's you). English menu available. Open M-Sa 6-11:30pm, Su 6-11pm.

Mensa, on Wilhelmstr. between Gmelinstr. and Keplerstr. Meals DM3.80 for Tübingen students, DM8.70 for guests. Salad bar DM0.85 for 100g. Open M-Th 11am-2pm and

6-8:15pm, F noon-2pm, Sa 11:45am-1:15pm. The **cafeteria** downstairs has cold food and dessert under DM5. Open M-Th 8am-8pm, F 8am-7pm. Both closed the mid-Aug.

Marquardtei, Herrenberger Str. 34 (tel. 433 86). Bus #8, 16, or 30 to "Rappstr." Run by enterprising students, it serves pizzas, *Schwäbisch* specialties, and vegetarian dishes (DM10-14). Open M-Sa 11:30am-12:30am, Su 10am-12:30am.

Da Pino, Mühlstr 20 (tel. 55 10 86), is a small but eminently delicious eatery. Pizzas DM7-10. Take out available. Open daily 11:30am-2:30pm and 4:30pm-12:30am.

■ SIGHTS

SCHLOSS HOHENTÜBINGEN. Atop the hill that rudely isolates the university from the rest of the city stands the castle, dating from 1078. Check out the dark tunnel and the staircase on the far side of the courtyard; both lead through the castle wall to breathtaking views of the surrounding valleys. *(Castle grounds open daily 7am-8pm. Free.)* Occupied by various university institutes, the Schloß is also home to the excellent **Museum Schloß Hohentübingen,** the largest university museum in Germany, which features an extensive collection of ethnographic and archaeological artifacts. Don't miss what is purported to be the **oldest surviving example of handwork** (an ivory horse sculpture that's 35,000 years old) or the ethereal hall with plaster casts of classical sculptures. *(Burgsteigell. Tel. 297 73 84. Open May-Sept. W-Su 10am-6pm; Oct.-April W-Su 10am-5pm. Tours Su at 3pm. DM4, students DM2.)*

WURMLINGER KAPELLE. The simple but beautiful chapel sits atop an idyllic pastoral hill, worlds away from Tübingen's crunchy academia. Follow the red-blaze signs from the Schloß to the Wurmlinger Kapelle trail.

STIFTSKIRCHE. The 15th-century church serves as the focal point of the Altstadt's winding alleys. In the chancel lie the tombs of 14 members of the House of Württemberg. Life-size stone sculptures of the deceased top the tombs. The church tower offers a rewarding view for those who survive the climb. *(Open daily 9am-5pm. Chancel and tower open April-July and Oct. F-Su 10:30am-5pm; Aug.-Sept. daily 10:30am-5pm. DM2, students DM1. Organ concerts July-Aug. Th at 6pm, Sept. Sa at 8pm.)*

AROUND MARKTPLATZ. On the square is **Buchhandlung Heckenhauer Antiquariat,** where Hermann Hesse worked from 1895 until 1899. It's still selling rare books. *(Holzmarkt 5. Tel. 230 18.)* Nearby, the **Kornhaus** contains the **Stadtmuseum,** with exhibits on the city's history. *(Kornhausstr. 10. Tel. 20 43 82. Open Tu-Sa 3-6pm, Su 11am-1pm and 3-6pm.)* A few blocks below Marktpl., on Kronenstr. dwells the **Evangelisches Stift.** Once a monastery, now a dorm for theology students, its alumni include such academic luminaries as Kepler, Hölderlin, and Hegel. *(Klosterberg 2. Tel. 56 10.)*

HÖLDERLINTURM. The great 18th- and 19th-century poet Friedrich Hölderlin lived out the final 36 years of his life in the nearby **Hölderlinturm** in a state of clinical insanity, spending his days writing neat quatrains on the four seasons. The tower now contains a museum dedicated to his life. *(Open Tu-F 10am-noon and 3-5pm, Sa-Su 2-5pm. Tours Sa-Su 5pm. DM3, students DM2.)*

PLATENALLEE. The buildings of the **Neckarfront** are best viewed from this tree-lined avenue that runs the length of the man-made island on the Neckar. Rumor has it that the university fraternities located on the riverfront will give free punting trips down the Neckar to those who ask.

■ ENTERTAINMENT AND NIGHTLIFE

Tübingen's nightlife is laid-back, mostly revolving around cafés in the Altstadt that begin brewing quiet cups of coffee at 10am and stay open into the night, serving beer to groups of students. Tübingen also has two major theaters: the progressive **Zimmertheater,** Bursagasse 16 (tel. 927 30; open M-F 10am-1pm and 3pm-6pm), and the larger, more conservative **Landestheater,** Eberhardstr. 8 (tel. 931 31 49). Tickets and schedules are available at the tourist office and at the box office at Eberhardstr. 6. (Open Tu-F 3:30-7pm, Sa 10am-1pm.) For **gay and lesbian nightlife,** head to **Südhaus** (below) on Wednesday nights for a mixed bar; gay afternoons are held on Sundays at **Luscht Café,** Herrenberger Str. 9, while a women's disco rips it up Saturday nights at **Club Voltaire,** Haaggasse 266.

Jazzkeller, Haaggasse 15/2 (tel. 55 09 06; fax 221 63), moves from jazz to funk to salsa and back again. Open M 7pm-2am, Tu-Th and Su 7pm-1am, F and Sa 7pm-3am. Opens 1hr. later July and Aug.

Südhaus, Hechinger Str. 203 (tel. 746 96). Take bus #3 or 5 to "Fuchsstr.," or night bus N9. A "socio-cultural center" featuring wacky art films, dance parties, and live acts. Schedules are plastered all over town. Cover DM10-25.

Tangente-Night, Pfleghofstr. 10 (tel. 230 07), by the Lustnauer Tor corner. Not to be confused with the less cool *Tangente-Jour.* A premier student hangout for beer at night or a book and cappuccino in the morning (0.3L *Pils* DM3.50; coffee DM3). Most fun Sept.-April Th-Su, when a DJ spins house, acid jazz, and techno. Open daily 10am-3am.

Neckarmüller, Gartenstr. 4 (tel. 278 48), is close to the youth hostel. Young and old alike drink and schmooze at picnic tables under shady trees. The only way to get closer to the Neckar is to rent your own boat. Try the house brew; light or dark DM3.90 for 0.3L. Open daily 10am-1am.

O'Donovan's Irish Pub, Burgsteige 7 (tel. 236 98), near the Schloß. With occasional live music acts and bar quizzes, this bit o' Eire keeps students flushed and happy, especially in the winter. Su Irish breakfast. Open M-F 5pm-1am, Sa 2pm-1am, Su 11am-1am.

Marktschenke, Am Markt 11 (tel. 220 35). With a few drinks, the cartoons on the walls are sure to amuse you. 0.5L *Hefeweizen* DM5.20. Open daily 9am-1am.

KARLSRUHE

By European standards, Karlsruhe was born yesterday. In 1715, Margrave Karl Wilhelm built a castle retreat for himself and his mistresses (hence the name, meaning "Karl's rest"). He then designed a planned city radiating out from the castle in the shape of a fan. It has been an architectural sensation ever since, perhaps due to the refreshingly spacious and navigable streets. Karlsruhe is home to Germany's two highest courts, the Federal Supreme Court and the Federal Constitutional Court. For travelers, the city offers a break from the burden of antiquity. For residents, Karlsruhe offers something even better—more than 1,700 hours of sun per year, earning it the title of "Sun City."

⚥ ORIENTATION AND PRACTICAL INFORMATION. From the station, the town center is a 25-minute walk from the train tracks along Ettlinger Str. and Karl-Friedrich-Str., or you can take any streetcar to "Marktplatz" or "Europaplatz." The **S-Bahn** costs DM3.50 per ride within the city, DM8 for a 24-hour ticket. For a **taxi** call 94 41 44. The **tourist office,** Bahnhofpl. 6 (tel. 355 30; fax 35 53 43 99; www.karlsruhe.de), across the street from the station, books **rooms** for free. The staff gives out the amazing *Karlsruhe Extra,* an annually updated guide (in English) with great maps. (Office open M-F 9am-6pm, Sa 9am-1pm.) A **branch office,** Karl-Friedrich-Str. 22 (tel. 35 53 43 76), is the same but closer to the Schloß. (Open M-F 9am-6pm, Sa 9am-12:30pm.) **Braunsche Universitätsbuchhandlung,** Kaiserstr. 120 (tel. 232 96; fax 291 16), has a small, top-notch selection of English-language books. (Open M-F 8:30am-8pm, Sa 9am-5pm.) **Waschsalon** resides at the corner of Scheffelstr. and Sophienstr. (Open M-Sa 8am-11pm. Wash DM7, dry DM1 per 10min.) The **post office,** 76133 Karlsruhe, sprawls near Europapl. (Open M-F 8:30am-6:30pm, Sa 8:30am-1pm.) The **telephone code** is 0721.

⌐ ACCOMMODATIONS. Karlsruhe's **Jugendherberge (HI),** Moltkestr. 24 (tel. 282 48; fax 276 47), is convenient to the Schloß and university, although it's far from the train station. Take the S-Bahn to "Europapl.," then follow Karlstr. until it ends.

Turn left onto Seminarstr. and turn left again on Moltkestr.; it's on the right. (DM22, over 26 DM28. Breakfast included. Sheets DM5.50. Reception briefly at 5, 7, and 9:30pm. Strict curfew 11:30pm. Lockout 9am-5pm. Members only.) **Hotel Augustiner,** Sophienstr. 73 (tel. 84 55 80; fax 85 33 20), offers the most affordable rooms in the city near the sights. (Single DM50, with shower DM65, doubles DM100. Breakfast included.) Camp at **Turmbergblick,** Tiengererstr. 40 (tel. 49 72 36; fax 49 72 37), in Durlach. Take S-Bahn #2 from the station to "Durlach Turmberg." (DM7-10 per person. Tents DM7. Reception 8am-1pm and 3-9pm. Open March-Sept.)

☐▟ FOOD AND NIGHTLIFE. A trade school's **Mensa** is located near the youth hostel. From the hostel's front door, walk straight ahead across the lawn between two buildings to the large, nondescript building. (Open M-Th 8:30am-4pm, F 8:30am-2pm.) **Krokodil,** Waldstr. 63 (tel. 273 31), offers salads, *Schnitzel*, breakfasts, and pastas (DM5-17) served in a mirrored bar and beer garden. (Open daily 8am-1am.) For traditional German fare, try **Goldenes Kreuz,** Karlstr. 21a (tel. 220 54), around the corner from Ludwigspl., where entrees run DM10-20. (Open daily 11am-10pm.) Buy produce at the **market** on Marktpl. (Open M-Sa 7:30am-12:30pm.) Many cafés on Ludwigspl. stay open until 1am. **Harmonie,** Kaiserstr. 57 (tel. 37 42 09), is a pub offering cheap eats (sausages and pasta DM7-12; beer DM3.50-6) and live music. (Open M-F 8am-1am, Sa 10am-1am, Su 9:30am-1am.)

▧ SIGHTS. The most spectacular sight in Karlsruhe is the locus of the city—all roads lead to the classical yellow **Schloß.** The **Schloßgarten,** with its impeccably maintained swathes of green and inviting benches, stretches out behind the castle for nearly half a kilometer. (Open until 10pm daily. Free.) The Schloß houses the **Badisches Landesmuseum** (tel. 926 65 14), with elaborate special exhibits and a permanent collection of antiques including the flashy **Türkenbeute** (Turkish booty). Watch out for the timely Y2K exhibit. (Take any train to "Marktpl." Open Tu and Th-Su 10am-5pm, W 10am-8pm. DM5, students DM3.) The **Museum beim Markt,** Karl-Friedrich-Str. 6 (tel. 926 64 94), dedicated to design and illustration, has a particularly fascinating Art Deco collection. (Open Tu and Th-Su 10am-5pm, W 1:30-8pm. DM3.) Around the corner are the **Kunsthalle,** Hans-Thoma-Str. 2 (tel. 926 33 55), and **Kunsthalle Orangerie,** Hans-Thoma-Str. 6, two top-notch art museums. European masterpieces from the 15th to the 19th centuries adorn the Kunsthalle—don't miss Grünewald's *Crucifixion*—while the Orangerie contains a smaller collection of modern art. (Take any train to "Europapl." Both open Tu-F 10am-5pm, Sa-Su 10am-6pm. DM5, students DM3.) The **Kunstverein,** Waldstr. 3, exhibits a smaller, more modern collection and an artsy café. (Take any train except #2 to "Herrenstr." Open Tu-W and F-Su 10am-1pm and 2-6pm; Th 10am-1pm, 2-6pm, and 7-9pm. DM4, students DM2.)

Occupying the upper floors of a former mansion, the recently renovated **Prinz-Max-Palais,** Karlstr. 10 (tel. 133 44 01 or 133 42 30), has a local history display that includes the purported **first bicycle in the world.** Check with the tourist office for current exhibits. (Open Tu and Th-Su 10am-5pm, W 11am-8pm. DM5, students DM3.50.) The quirkiest of Karlsruhe's museums is indisputably the **Oberrheinisches Dichtermuseum** (tel. 84 38 18), in the same building and dedicated to poets such as von Scheffel and Hebel. (Open Tu and Th-F 11am-5pm, W 11am-9pm. Free.) Beyond the Schloß and flanked on the west by the shopping district stretches the placid **Marktplatz.** To one side stands the rose-colored **Rathaus;** to the other, the imposing columns of the **Stadtkirche.** The red sandstone pyramid in the center of the square is the symbol of the city and Karl's final resting place.

The unremarkable **Bundesverfassungsgericht** (Federal Constitutional Court) stands next to the Schloß. It may be ugly, but give it some respect: it houses Germany's strongest legal safeguard against the return of totalitarian rule. Near Friedrichspl., the **Bundesgerichtshof** (Federal Supreme Court) is pumped with a formidable security apparatus.

Perhaps to balance all this heavy-duty legal responsibility, Karlsruhe relaxes to the max with a number of huge cultural festivals. Every February, Karlsruhe hosts the **Händel-Festspiele,** a 10-day series of performances of Händel's works (Feb. 23-March 4, 2000). The appetizing **Brigande-Feschd** takes place in late May, bringing a huge display of dishes from local restaurants. Local breweries play an essential role in the reveling **Unifest** in late July. The 10-day orgy of live music, food stands, and roaming students clutching mugs of beer takes place at the end of Günther-Klatz-Anlage and is the largest free open-air concert in Germany.

BADEN-BADEN

Anyone who ever wanted to lead the life of a pampered Old World aristocrat can have a ball in Baden-Baden. In its 19th-century heyday, Baden-Baden's guest list read like a *Who's Who* of European nobility. Although its status has declined, the spa town on the northern fringes of the Schwarzwald remains primarily a playground for the well-to-do; minor royalty, nouveaux riches, and the like gather here year-round to bathe in the mineral spas and drop fat sums of money in the elegant casino. The ritzy atmosphere is worth tolerating for the chance to experience the incredible baths and to stroll down the luxurious tree-lined boulevards of the chic downtown area.

🛈 **ORIENTATION AND PRACTICAL INFORMATION.** Baden-Baden's **train station** is inconveniently located 7km from town. If you're not up for the 90-minute walk along the park path, take bus #204, 205, or 216 (direction: "Stadtmitte") or #201 (direction "Oberbeuren") from the station to "Leopoldspl." or "Augustapl." (DM3.50). For a **taxi** call 381 11 or 621 10. A **branch** of the **tourist office** is located at the city entrance at Schwarzwaldstr. 52, a few blocks from the train station toward town. The **main office** is at Augustaplatz 8 (tel. 27 52 00; fax 27 52 02; www.baden-baden.de), in the flagrantly postmodern building next to the Kongresshaus. The staff offers free maps and a hotel list. (Open May-Oct. M-F 9:30am-6pm, Sa 9:30am-3pm, Nov.-April M-F 9:30am-5pm, Sa 9:30am-3pm.) Dig up your Armani for a night on the town at the **Waschsalon,** Scheiberstr. 14. (Tel. 248 19. Open M-Sa 7:30am-10pm.) The **main post office,** 76486 Baden-Baden, is located in the Wagener department store in the pedestrian zone below the Rathaus. (Open M-F 9am-7pm, Sa 9am-4pm.) Check your **email** at **Café Contact,** Eichstr. 5 (tel. 26 07 19), near Augustapl. (Open M and W-Su 2pm-midnight.) The **telephone code** is 07221.

🛏🍴 **ACCOMMODATIONS AND FOOD.** The cheapest bed in town is at the modern **Werner-Dietz-Jugendherberge (HI),** Hardenbergstr. 34 (tel. 522 23; fax 600 12), between the station and the town center. Take bus #201, 205, or 216 to "Grosse-Dollen-Str." and follow the signs uphill. The hostel's strange lack of showers is offset by the town's main attractions. (DM23, over 26 DM28. Sheets DM5.50. Reception 5-11pm. Curfew 11:30pm. Wheelchair accessible. Call ahead. Members only.) Rooms in the center of town are expensive with few exceptions. **Hotel am Markt,** Marktplatz 18 (tel. 270 40; fax 27 04 44), is next to the Friedrichsbad and the Stiftskirche. (Singles DM54-56, with shower DM78-90; doubles DM110-115, DM135-145. *Kurtaxe* DM5. Breakfast included. Dinner DM8-15. Reception 7am-10pm.) The unassuming **Hotel Löhr,** Adlerstr. 2 (tel. 262 04 or 313 70; fax 383 08), has its reception a block and a half away at **Café Löhr,** Lichtentaler Str. 19, across the street and back toward the station from the "Augustaplatz" bus stop. The rooms are spotless but small. (Singles DM35-70; doubles DM80-120.) Most restaurants in Baden-Baden aren't compatible with budget travel. **Pizzeria Roma,** Gernsbacher Str. 14, offers affordable pasta (DM10-15) in a prime location below the Rathaus. For **groceries** head to **Pennymarkt,** at the "Grosse-Dollen-Str." bus stop near the hostel. (Open M-W 8:30am-6:30pm, Th-F 8:30am-7pm, Sa 8:30am-2pm.)

◪ SPAS. Baden-Baden's history as a resort goes back nearly two millennia to the time when the Romans started soaking themselves in the area's **thermal baths.** The ▨**Friedrichsbad,** Römerpl. 1 (tel. 27 59 20), is a beautiful 19th-century bathing palace where visitors are parched, steamed, soaked, scrubbed, doused, and pummeled by trained professionals for three hours. There are 15 tubs of varying temperatures that await the nude, and at the end everyone gets wrapped up like mummies in pink blankets for a 30-minute nap. It's a marvelous experience, and not a stitch of clothing is permitted. (Open M-Sa 9am-10pm, Su noon-8pm. Last entry 3hr. before closing. Baths are co-ed Tu and F 4-10pm, and all day W and Sa-Su. Standard Roman bath DM36, with soap and brush massage DM48. DM6 discount with hotel coupon.) More modest or budget-minded cure-seekers should try next door at the astounding **Caracalla-Thermen,** Römerpl. 1 (tel. 27 59 40), which is cheaper, more public, and allows bathing suits except in the saunas upstairs. Indoor and outdoor pools, whirlpools, and solaria of varying sizes and temperatures pamper the weary traveler at a very reasonable price. Whichever bath you choose, the experience will be unforgettable. (Open daily 8am-10pm. 3hr. DM19, 4hr. DM25, 5hr. DM29. Discount with hotel or hostel coupon.) The large public **swimming pool** next to the hostel has a curvy slide and is the cheapest way to bathe in Baden-Baden. (Open 10am-8pm in good weather. Last entry 7pm. DM4.50, students DM3.)

▨ ◪ SIGHTS AND ENTERTAINMENT. When they're not busy pruning themselves at the baths, Baden-Baden's affluent guests head to the oldest **casino** in Germany (tel. 210 60), which, according to Marlene Dietrich, is the "most beautiful casino in the world." Modeled after Versailles, it prompts oohs and aahs from even the most well-traveled aristocrat. In earlier days, no citizens of Baden-Baden were allowed inside. These rules no longer apply, but a slew of others still do: you must be 21 in order to gamble here, and men must wear a coat and tie while women must have a dress or suit. The minimum bet is DM5, maximum bet DM20,000. (Open M-Th and Su 2-11pm, F-Sa 2pm-midnight. DM5. Tours April-Sept. 9:30am-noon, Oct.-March 10am-noon. English language tours by special arrangement. DM6.) There is no dress code for the slot machine wing, located in the Alter Bahnhof on Lange Str. (Open M-Th and Su 2pm-midnight, F-Sa 2pm-1am. DM2.) Next to the casino is the massive Neoclassical **Trinkhalle,** which contains a gold-plated fountain, souvenir shop, and a gallery of murals immortalizing local folktales. The free *Heilwasser* (healing water) tastes like it's good for you: warm and saline. Bring it on. (Open daily 10am-6pm. Free.) A few blocks in the opposite direction, down the paths of the verdant Lichtentaler Allee, the **Kunsthalle** (tel. 232 50) houses modern art exhibits. (Open Tu and Th-Su 11am-6pm, W 11am-8pm. Admission usually DM8, students DM4.) For a stunning view of the surrounding valleys, head up the steep stairwell from Marktplatz to the **Neues Schloß**. Once the home of the Margraves of Baden, the castle now hosts the **Stadtgeschichtliche Sammlungen,** which houses exhibits on the wet and wild history of Baden-Baden. (Open Tu-Su 10am-12:30pm and 2-5pm. DM2, students and seniors DM1.) For an even more exquisite view extending all the way to the French frontier, head to the 12th-century **Altes Schloß** (tel. 269 48). Its majestic ruins, the **Ruine Hohenbaden,** are a long and baffling hike from behind the Neues Schloß. Prepare to venture cluelessly through the Schwarzwald hills. In general, follow signs that point to *Kellerskreuz* and *Altes Schloß*. The view is undeniably worth it. Or take bus #214 (direction: "Ebersteinburg") to the end of the line and follow the signs. Alternatively, bus #215 makes two loops on Sundays and holidays at 1:15pm and 4:15pm between Augustaplatz and the Schloß. (Open April-Oct. Tu-Su 10am-8pm, Nov.-March Tu-Su 10am-7pm. Free.)

◪ HIKING. To rise above the decadence, escape to the nearby hills. The best place for immediate hiking is at the 668m **Merkur** peak east of town. Take bus #204 or 205 from Leopoldplatz to "Merkurwald," then ride the *Bergbahn* to the top, where a slew of trails plunge into the Schwarzwald. (Bergbahn runs daily 10am-

10pm, every 15min. DM4 one-way, DM7 round-trip.) The *Bergbahn* station at the bottom is crossed by the **Panoramaweg**. Marked by white signs with a green circle, the Panoramaweg connects the best look-out points near Baden-Baden. Pick up a map at the tourist office (DM3).

FREIBURG IM BREISGAU

When German Luftwaffe pilots mistakenly bombed their own city of Freiburg in May 1940, it wasn't difficult to see why. Freiburg, tucked in the far southwest corner of Germany, enjoys a persistent French influence, which has helped its genial, humor-loving citizens to flout the dour German stereotype. Similarly, this "metropolis" of the Schwarzwald has yet to succumb to the hectic rhythms of city life. The surrounding hills brim with greenery and fantastic hiking trails, paths link the medieval Schwabentor to the German trail network, and all traces of urbanity dissolve into serene countryside a few kilometers from the city center. The atmosphere is correspondingly relaxed, with many student-populated cafés scattered throughout cobblestoned streets filled with Birkenstocked bicyclists.

▆ GETTING THERE AND GETTING AROUND

Trains: To Karlsruhe (1hr., 2 per hour, DM44), Stuttgart (1½hr., 1 per hour, DM67), Straßbourg (1¾hr., 1 per hour), and Basel, Switzerland (45min., 1-2 per hour).

Public Transportation: Single fare on Freiburg's many bus and streetcar lines DM3.50. Day pass DM8; for 2 people DM10. Get the scoop on regional travel at **PlusPunkt,**

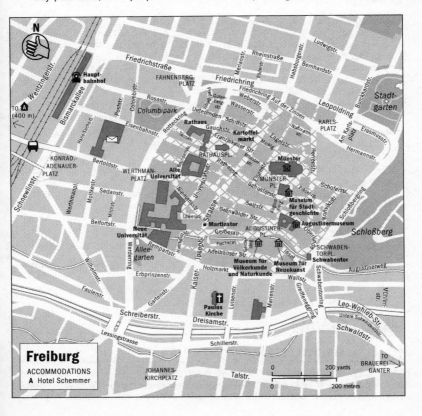

Salzstr. 3 (tel. 451 15 00), in the Altstadt, which serves your every transportation need. Open M-F 8am-7pm, Sa 8am-2pm. Another **branch** is below the S-Bahn platform at the train station. Most public transportation stops running around 12:30am, but a system of night buses (named after the planets) covers most major stops through the wee hours. (DM7 per ride; DM4 with Day-Card.)

Taxis: Tel. 444 44. Four you.

Mitfahrzentrale: Belfortstr. 55 (tel. 194 44), south of the station, just off Schnewlingstr. You're going to vacation in Germany without riding on the *Autobahn?* No, no. Get a chauffeur. Munich DM38, Paris DM46, Zurich DM17. Open M-F 9am-7pm, Sa 9am-1pm, Su 10am-1pm.

Bike Rental: Velo Doctor, Eschholzstr. 64 (tel. 27 64 77). DM15 per day, DM25 per weekend, DM48 per week. Open M-F 9am-7pm, Sa 9am-2pm.

Hitchhiking: *Let's Go* does not recommend hitchhiking as a safe means of transportation. Hitchers take public transit to departure points. For points north, take S-Bahn #5 (direction: "Zähringen") to "Reutebachgasse" and walk back 50m. West: S-Bahn #1 to "Padua-Allee," then bus #31 or 32 to "Hauptstr." East: S-Bahn #1 (direction: "Littenweiler") to "Lassbergstr.," then bus #18 (direction: "Langmatten") to "Strombad."

🛈 ORIENTATION AND PRACTICAL INFORMATION

Most of the city's sights and restaurants lie within walking distance from one another in the Altstadt, a 15-minute walk from the main train station, down tree-lined Eisenbahnstr. to Rathauspl.

Tourist Office: Rotteckring 14 (tel. 388 18 82; fax 388 18 87), 2 blocks down Eisenbahnstr. from the station. The staff finds **rooms** for DM5, and has free maps, but prefers to sell the comprehensive *Freiburg Official Guide* (in German or English) for DM6 or a small guide for DM1. 24hr. automated displays in front of the office and the train station can help you find accommodations if the staff is too busy. Open June-Sept. M-F 9:30am-8pm, Sa 9:30am-2pm, Su 10am-noon; Oct.-May M-F 9:30am-8pm, Sa 9:30am-2pm, Su 10am-noon.

Currency Exchange: The closest to the main train station is the **Volksbank** across the street and to the right. Open M-F 9am-6:30pm and Sa 9:30am-2pm. **24hr. ATM.**

Bookstore: Walthari, Bertoldstr. 28 (tel. 38 77 70). A fairly large collection of English-language paperbacks. Carries guides to the Schwarzwald region. Open M-F 9:30am-7pm, Sa 9:30am-4pm.

Laundromat: Café Fleck, Predigerstr. 3 (tel. 268 29). S-Bahn #5 or 6 (direction: "Reutebachgasse") to "Siegesdenkmal." Laundro-café—the truly efficient get a sandwich while they wash. Wash DM7, soap included. Dry DM1 per 10min. Laundromat open M-Sa 7am-1am. Café open M-F 7am-6:30pm, Sa 7am-5pm.

Emergency: Police, tel. 110. **Fire and Ambulance,** tel. 112.

Rape Crisis Hotline: tel. 333 39.

Gay Resources: Rosa Hilfe, tel. 251 61.

Internet Access: WebSPIDERcafe, Moltkestr. 28 (tel. 202 09 82). DM2.50 per 15min. Open M-Sa 9am-8pm.

Post Office: Eisenbahnstr. 60, 79098 Freiburg, 1 block straight ahead of the train station. Open M-F 8:30am-6:30pm, Sa 8:30am-2pm.

PHONE CODE	0761

🏠 ACCOMMODATIONS AND CAMPING

Most of Freiburg's hotels and *Pensionen* are expensive and located outside the city center. The tourist office books cheaper rooms (singles DM25-45, doubles DM45-80) in private homes, but a stay of at least three nights is usually required.

Freiburg's youth hostel is large, nondescript, and far from the Altstadt. If your accommodation is far away, purchase the transportation daypass to save money (see **Public Transportation,** above).

Jugendherberge (HI), Kartäuserstr. 151 (tel. 676 56; fax 603 67). S-Bahn #1 (direction: "Littenweiler") to "Römerhof," cross the tracks and backtrack 20m, then walk left down Fritz-Geiges-Str., cross the stream, and follow the footpath for about 10min. to the right. Schoolchildren sleep in brightly-colored rooms. Feels more like a dorm than most hostels. DM24, over 26 DM29. Sheets DM6. *Gästehaus* DM38, sheets included. Members only. Reception 7-9am and 1-10pm. Curfew 1am.

🐌 **Hotel Zum Löwen,** Breisgauer Str. 62 (tel. 809 72 20; fax 840 23), up the street from Gästehaus Hirschen (see below). A great deal. The staff will suggest Black Forest routes and even packs snacks for the trail. With the marble floors and white stucco walls it sure doesn't feel like budget travel. A brand-spanking new wing has just been added. Enter in the parking lot; the front door of the building is also labeled "Löwen" but leads into a more expensive place. All rooms have TV. Singles DM50, with shower DM60; doubles DM90, with shower from DM110. Breakfast included.

Hotel Schemmer, Eschholzstr. 63 (tel. 27 24 24; fax 220 10). From the train station, take the overpass at the end of track 1, go past the church and turn left. Friendly management and about the best location available. Looks like grandpa's den circa 1965 in bright blue and orange. Singles DM65, with bath DM75; doubles DM90, with bath DM95. Breakfast included.

Gästehaus Hirschen, Breisgauer Str. 47 (tel. 821 18). S-Bahn #1 to "Padua-Allee," backtrack 30m along the tracks, and walk down Breisgauer Str. for 5min. Be careful: this *Gästehaus* is on the other side of town from the hotel of the same name; also, it isn't the same as Hirschengarten-Hotel, which is right next door. Old house in a quiet farm neighborhood with rooms as cozy as the exterior would lead you to believe. Singles DM50, with shower DM80; doubles DM85, with shower DM110; triples DM120. Reception M-W and F-Su. TV and breakfast included.

Pension Gisela, Am Vogelbach 27 (tel. 824 72; fax 811 52). Bus #10 (direction: "Padua-Allee") to "Hofackerstr.," then double back 1 block and turn left, walk 250m, and turn right on Hasenweg before the train tracks. The tacky Schwarzwald-themed mural on the outside wall conceals large, hotel-quality rooms in a quiet residential neighborhood. Singles DM48-55, doubles DM85-105. Breakfast included. Apartments available for long-term guests.

Haus Lydia Kalchtaler, Peterhof 11 (tel. 671 19). S-Bahn #1 (direction: "Littenweiler") to "Lassbergstr.," then bus #17 (direction: "Kappel") to "Kleintalstr." Turn around and follow Peterhof up and to the left to the large wooden farmhouse with the water trough in front. Operated by the tireless and loquacious Lydia Kalchtaler, this *Pension* is a rest from institutional living at an unbeatable price. A rustic, idyllic atmosphere and available kitchen counter with the inconvenience of a 45min. commute to the center. DM25 per person. Sheets included. Make your own breakfast.

Camping: Hirzberg, Kartäuserstr. 99 (tel. 350 54; fax 28 92 12), has sparkling new camping facilities 20min. by foot from the Altstadt. Endlessly helpful English-speaking staff. S-Bahn #1 to "Stadthalle", then cross the street to the left via the underpass and walk straight (north) on Hirzbergstr. Cross the river at Max-Miller-Steg, keep going till you reach the busy street, then go 30m to the left. Near a quiet residential area. DM8 per person, DM5 per child. DM5-7 per tent. Summer tent rentals DM10-15 per day. Bikes DM15 per day. Laundry DM5. Reception 9am-10pm.

Camping: Mosle Park, Waldseestr. 77 (tel. 729 38; fax 775 78). S-Bahn #1 to "Hasemannstr." Backtrack to Jahnstr. and turn left. Follow Jahnstr. until it ends, then go left on Hammerschmiedstr. Follow that, cross the train tracks, and turn right on Littenweilerstr (about 15 min.). Beautiful forested location, ideally situated for hiking. DM8 per person; DM5 per child. DM4 per tent. DM9 per car. Wash and dry laundry DM13. Reception 8am-noon and 3-10pm. Open April-Oct.

◘ FOOD

In the early 15th century, the humanist Dietrich von Nieheim noted admiringly that in Freiburg "the supply of victuals is good and readily available." With more than 23,000 university students to feed, Freiburg's budget eateries carry on the fine tradition. During the daytime, the **Freiburger Markthalle** (tel. 38 11 11), next to the Martinstor, is home to food stands serving ethnic specialties for less than DM15. (Open M-F 7am-5pm, Sa 9am-2pm.) The **open-air market** on Münsterplatz sells everything from fresh radishes to an offer to etch your name onto a grain of rice. (Open M-Sa 7am-1pm.) Get **groceries** at **Edeka ActivMarkt,** Eisenbahnstr. 39, across from the post office. (Open M-F 7:30am-8pm, Sa 8am-4pm.)

Mensa: Two university *Mensen*—the blue-trimmed building on **Rempartstr.** in the Altstadt (lunch only) and **Hebelstr.** on the main campus north of the city center (lunch and dinner). It's true you need a Freiburg student ID to buy *Menukarten* (5 for DM19.50; each gets you a hot meal) and *Eintopfkarten* (5 for DM13.50; each gets you a bowl of stew or fries), but local students are willing to help out. One flavor fits all. Rempartstr. location open M-F 11:30am-2pm, Sa 11:30am-1:30pm. Hebelstr. location open M-F 11am-2pm and 5:30-7:30pm.

Brennessel, Eschholzstr. 17 (tel. 28 11 87). A plucky student tavern that fills the student gullet without emptying the student wallet. Funk and jazz abound. Don't miss the spaghetti *bolognese* (DM3.50) from 6-8pm, or *Pfannkuchen* (pancakes; DM5). Open M-Sa 6pm-1am, Su 5pm-1am. Kitchen open until 12:30am.

Milano, Schusterstr. 7 (tel. 337 35), 1 block from Münsterplatz.. With its salmon-leather interior and prime location, feels more high-brow than the prices might suggest. Authentic, delicious pizza (DM7-18) and pasta (DM7.50-15.50). Try the pasta marinara...mmm. Service with Italian flair. Open daily 11am-midnight.

Freiburger Salatstuben, Löwenstr. 1 (tel. 351 55), near Martinstor. A health-food haven with an array of imaginatively smart salads (100g DM2.20) belies the absence of vegetarian pretension. Even the desserts (DM4-5) are smart. Open M-F 11am-8pm, Sa 11am-4pm, 1st Saturday of the month 11am-6pm.

Hausbrauerei Feierling, Gerberau 46 (tel. 266 78). 2 gleaming copper vats form the centerpiece of this airy Freiburg institution. Across the way, the *Biergarten* sports thick-shadey chestnut trees. Wheat beer produced from ecologically-sound ingredients (0.5L DM5.80) beats traditional German fare (DM10-26). The place is packed at night, keeping the student waitresses on their toes. Open Su-F 11am-midnight, Sa 11am-1am. Kitchen noon-2pm and 6-10pm.

Greiffenegg-Schlößle, Schloßbergring 3 (tel. 327 28). Drink, eat, and look down over Freiburg from a terrace above the city. This mellow, chatty restaurant boasts a faaabulous view. Seats 800 and fills up when the weather cooperates. Beer DM5-7. Half-price salad buffet, happy hour on weekdays 11am-1pm. Entrance through the Schwabentor. Open year-round daily 11am-midnight.

◘ SIGHTS

What buildings the errant *Luftwaffe* bombers didn't hit, the Allies decisively finished off one night in 1944, obliterating most of the old city. Since then, the citizens of Freiburg have painstakingly recreated the city's architecture and public spaces.

MÜNSTER. Freiburg's pride and joy is its majestic cathedral, which towers 116m above camera-wielding hordes of tourists. With sections constructed between the 13th and 16th centuries, this architectural melange immortalizes in stained glass the different medieval guilds that financed its construction. Stumble up more than 300 steps to ascend the tower, from which you can watch the **oldest bell in Germany** (her name's Hosanna) and 26 others swing into motion. Protect your eardrums when the hour strikes. "One cannot conceive of a more beautiful view than the blue heaven peeking through the thousand openings of this cupola." So said philosopher Wilhelm von Humboldt after the harrowingly claustrophobic climb upwards. *(Open M-Sa 10am-6pm, Su 1-6pm. Tower open M-F 9:30am-5pm, Su 1-5pm; Nov.-April Tu-Sa 9:30am-5pm, Su 1-5pm. DM2.50, students DM1.50. Summer organ concerts Tu at 8:15pm. Free. Call 20 27 90 for more information.)*

SCHWABENTOR AND MARTINSTOR. On the south side of Münsterplatz wobbles the pink-tinted **Kaufhaus,** a merchants' hall dating from the 1500s. Two medieval gates—the Schwabentor and the Martinstor—stand within blocks of each other in the southeast corner of the Altstadt. The Martinstor, which served as a revolutionary barricade in the politically tumultuous year of 1848, has since been indelibly profaned by a set of golden arches. Now that's progress, Ronald.

SCHLOSSBERG. From the Schwabentor, take the pedestrian overpass across the heavily trafficked Schloßbergring and climb the glorified Schloßberg for a superb view of the city. From there, a number of hiking trails explore the forested hills. Try the **Langbuckweg** or its alternate, the **Waldfahrtstr.-Hirzberg-St. Ottilien** trail.

AUGUSTINERMUSEUM. A good bet for those who dig lots of medieval art, the Augustiner really shines because of its heartwarming depictions of Schwarzwald life. Included is admission to the **Wentzingerhaus Museum für Stadtgeschichte,** which displays paraphernalia related to Freiburg's colorful history. *(Augustiner at Salzstr. 32. Tel. 201 25 31. Housed in a former monastery 2 blocks south of the Münster. Wentzingerhaus tel. 201 25 15. On Münsterplatz. Both open Tu-Su 10am-5pm. DM4, students DM2; free 1st Sunday of every month.)*

MUSEUM FÜR NEUE KUNST. Freiburg's Museum of Modern Art displays the works of 20th-century German artists such as Otto Dix in a clean-lined, modern building. Borrow the extremely helpful English language guide for an enlightening lesson on modern German art. *(Marienstr. 10a. Tel. 201 25 81. Open Tu-Su 10am-5pm. Tours Sa 3pm and Su 11am. Free; special exhibits DM5.)*

MUSEUM FÜR UR- UND FRÜHGESCHICHTE. An immaculate, early Victorian Schloß sits atop a hill of vineyards and wildflowers; inside is a museum of ancient history. Myriad crumbling odds and ends illuminate the fascinating prehistory of the South Baden region. *(Tel. 201 25 71. Along Eisenbahnstr. between the station and the tourist office. Open Tu-Su 10am-5pm. Technically free, but DM3.50 donation requested, students DM2.)*

ADELHAUSERMUSEUM NATUR- UND VÖLKERKUNDE. The museum of natural history satisfies dinosaur and other fixations, in that order. Look for the 2000 exhibit on Australia, celebrating the 2000 Olympic summer games in Sydney. *(Gerberau 32. Tel. 201 25 66. Open Tu-Su 10am-5pm. General admission free; special exhibits DM5, students DM3.)*

BRAUEREI GANTER. The brewery conducts tours tracking the production of their malt beverage. The grand finale of the one-hour tour consists of a portion of *Fleischkäse*, bread, potato salad, and lots of beer atop one of the factory buildings. The view of the factory, the food finale, and the beer bash are all free (hint, hint). Call ahead to get in on the group tours. *(Schwarzwaldstr. 43. Tel. 218 51 81. S-Bahn #1 to "Brauerei Ganter." Tours Tu and Th at 1:30pm.)*

BÄCHLE. Unique to Freiburg is a system of narrow streams—known as Bächle—that run through the city. During medieval times, these swift-flowing gutters, fed by the Dreisam river, served as open-air sewers. Today they are the bane of any tourist studying a map *too* hard. But there are compensations for sodden footwear; legend has it that any visitor whose feet are wetted by them will one day marry a resident of Freiburg.

OTHER SITES. Tucked away in the blocks between the *Münster* and the tourist office are the **Rathaus,** an amalgam of older buildings whose bells chime daily at noon, and the oddly named **Haus zum Walfisch** (House of the Whale), where Erasmus of Rotterdam lived in exile from Basel for two years following the Reformation. This gold-trimmed wonder is a careful recreation of the original, which was destroyed in WWII.

BADEN-WÜRTTEMBERG

♪ ▓ ENTERTAINMENT AND NIGHTLIFE

Freiburg claims to be a city of wine and music, and, true to its word, it is awash with *Weinstuben* and *Kneipen*, though club offerings are less abundant. For the current events listings, pick up a free copy of *Freiburg Aktuell* from the tourist office or drop by the *Badische Zeitung* office (tel. 49 64 67) at Martinstor, where you can buy tickets for upcoming shin-digs. (Open M-Th 9am-5:30pm, F 9am-4:30pm, Sa 9am-1pm.) The **Freiburger Weinfest** is a weekend-long festival held on Münsterplatz the first weekend in July. Stagger around and sample some 300 different vintages (DM3-6 per glass) while a swing band plays. The annual three-week **Zeltmusikfestival** (June 29, 2000) brings big-name classical, rock, and jazz performers to two circus tents pitched at the city's edge. Tickets (DM15-40) sell surprisingly fast and can be bought by calling 50 40 30 or at the *Badische Zeitung* office. Take S-Bahn #5 to "Bissierstr." and catch the free shuttle bus to the site. In addition, the **Narrenfest** (Fools' Festival) is held the weekend before Ash Wednesday, and the **Weihnachtsmarkt** (Christmas market) runs from late November until just a few days before Christmas.

Freiburg's nightlife keeps pace with its students—afternoon cafés become pubs and discos by night. The streets around the university (**Niemensstr., Löwenstr., Humboldtstr.,** and the accompanying alleyways) form the hub of the city's scene.

Exit, Kaiser-Josef-Str. 248 (tel. 365 36). Despite its inhospitable name, thousands pour in and stay. Open M and W-Th 10pm-3am, F-Sa 10pm-4am. No cover Th and Sa with student ID. 18+.

Papalapub, Moltkestr. 30. (tel. 28 64 10), near the *Stadttheater*. A place to be for the ever-alternative students of Freiburg. Beer (of course), rock 'n' roll on the radio, and the rise and fall of conversation accompany the excellent pastas and pizzas (DM6-10). Open M-Sa noon-1am, Su 10am-1am.

Zum Schlappen, Löwenstr. 2 (tel. 334 94), near Martinstor. Serious beer drinkers head here. For DM15 you can flex your mettle by polishing off the 2L *Stiefel,* a fearsome vessel known to English-speakers as "The Boot" (DM23-32). Lots of posters, rather on the alternative side. Pizza DM6-10. Pasta DM7-12. Open M-Th 11:30am-1am, F-Sa 11:30am-2am, Su 3pm-1am.

Jazzhaus, Schnewlingstr. 1 (tel. 349 73), across from the train station and to the right. Featuring live performance almost every night, this spacious underground grotto has become a mainstay of the Freiburg cultural scene. Open M-Th and Su 8pm-2am, F-Sa 8pm-3am. Cover under DM10 for small acts, DM10-25 for more well-known performers. Call for tickets or show up after 6pm.

Dampfross, Löwenstr. 7 (tel. 259 39). The small *Kneipe* with big beer. Tiny student bar, with dark wood and American movie posters. Pils DM3.60 for 0.3L; salads and pasta DM7-13. The most popular dish is *Pommes mit Kräutercreme* (fries with herb cream; DM5.50). Divine. Connected through the back door to the café **Savo,** Löwenstr. 3-5 (same tel.), which plays stylish and mod to Dampfross's earthy and traditional. Drinks and food a bit more upscale. More room, too. Both open M-F 10am-2am, Sa from 11am, Su 5pm-1am. Food until 11pm, F and Sa until midnight.

Café Atlantik, Schwabentorring 7 (tel. 330 33). Spacious pub that grooves to American alternative tunes amidst pinball machines and Christmas lights. Daily happy "hour" noon-8pm. Packed in the winter, when the beer gardens close and live music acts abound. Cheap spaghetti DM5-8.50. Open daily noon-1am. Cover DM15-25 for live acts; otherwise free.

Agar, Löwenstr. 8 (tel. 38 06 50), next to Martinstor. Get down with Flower Power and the '80s.Lots of attitude. See or be seen, pick up or be picked up. Open Su, Tu, and Th for '80s night 10pm-2:30am, F-Sa house music 10pm-4am. Tu free with student ID. Last entry 2hr. before closing.

NEAR FREIBURG: BREISACH AND THE KAISERSTUHL

Twenty-five kilometers east of Freiburg, Breisach is separated from French Alsace by the Rhein and a few meters of beach on either side. The town's exquisite location comes replete with a beautiful Altstadt surrounded by unending hills of vineyards. Breisach's **Münster** dramatically crowns a steep riverfront promontory crowded with clapboard houses. Constructed between the 12th and 15th centuries, the church is plain compared to nearby cathedrals. Only the writhing, twisting wooden altar, the work of the mysterious 16th-century rap artist known only as Master H.L., comes close to flamboyance. From the church's promenade, the view stretches east and south to the rolling hills of the Schwarzwald and westward into France.

Continuing northward along Radbrunnenallee, a walled hilltop **fortress** boasting well-preserved medieval gates and excellent views of the countryside culminates in the garden atop the **Schloßberg.** In summer, the garden becomes a theater for the annual **Festspiele,** hosting several plays every weekend between mid-June and mid-September. (DM12, students DM10.) Breisach also hosts the **Weinfest Kaiserstuhl und Tuniburg,** where local wines are sampled, sprayed, and supped on the banks of the Rhein during the last weekend in Aug. Close by in the 17th-century Rheintor, the **Museum für Stadtgeschichte,** Rheintorpl. 1 (tel. 70 89), contains a large collection of city artifacts, including 3,000-year-old ceramics and chain-link undergarments from the 15th century—kinky stuff. (Open Tu-F 2-5pm, Sa 11:30am-5pm, Su 11:30am-6pm. Free).

Wine connoisseurs can register for a tour of **Badischer Winzerkeller** (tel. 90 00), one of the largest wine cellars in Europe; English speakers should call the tourist office in advance for a tour (3-7 samples DM5-9.50). The cellar is a 1km walk east of town. From the train station, go right on Bahnhofstr. and keep truckin' on Im Gelbstein. Closer by are the two cellars specializing in sparkling wine. The **Geldarmann Privatsektkellerei,** Am Schloßberg 1 (tel. 83 42 58; fax 83 43 51), pours bubbly alcohol from Baden, as does the **Gräflich von Kageneck'sche Wein & Sektkellerei,** Kupfertorstr. 35 (tel. 90 11 37; fax 90 11 99). Jaunts along the Rhein in big white ships are available through **Breisacher Fahrgastschiffahrt,** on the Marktplatz (tel. 94 20 10; fax 94 20 30). Two-hour joyrides run DM15; the company also runs ships to Strasbourg and Basel that can be used for one-way travel when not fully booked. Buy tickets at the dock or tourist office.

Near Breisach is the **Kaiserstuhl,** a clump of lush green hills that were volcanoes in their heyday. Now they attract hikers and bikers who come to see the flora and fauna, many of which are normally found only in warmer climates. The Freiburg-Breisach **train** stops at the towns of Ihringen and Wasenweiler, both located on the range's southern fringes. **Buses** handle the route straight into the hills; check the schedule at the Breisach Hauptbahnhof. Rent **bikes** at **Firma Schweizer,** Neutorstr. 31 (tel. 76 01), on the main pedestrian thoroughfare. (Open M-F 9am-12:30pm and 2-6:30pm. DM15 per day.) The most famous of the Kaiserstuhl trails is the **Kaiserstuhl Nord-Südweg,** which braves the densely vegetated hills and valleys, forging 16km from Ihringen northward to Endingen. From the Ihringen train station, walk straight down Eisenbahnstr. for 5 minutes; once past the church, turn right; the trail begins a block later at an alley on your left. The Nord-Südweg is marked by a blue diamond on a yellow field. For hiking maps, visit the Breisach **tourist office** (tel. 94 01 55; fax 94 01 58, email breisach-touristik@breisach.de; www.breisach.de), on the Marktplatz. The staff books **rooms** for a DM1 fee. From the train station, turn left on Bahnhofstr, keep the fountain with the huge spinning globe on your right, and go down Rheinstr. into the Marktplatz. (Open May-Oct. M-F 9am-6pm, Sa 10am-1pm, Su 1-4pm; Nov.-April M-F 9am-12:30pm and 1:30-5pm, Sa 1-4pm; Jan.-March closed weekends.) The **post office** is one block from the train station. (Open M-F 8am-noon and 2:30-5:30pm, Sa 8:30am-noon.) The **telephone code** is 07667.

Breisach's superb, modern **Jugendherberge,** Rheinuferstr. 12 (tel. 76 65; fax 18 47), boasts a stunning riverside location. From the train station, take a left and then left again at the intersection. After 20m, take the path leading under the main road. Cross the bridge to turn right and walk along the river. Turn left at the hostel sign. (DM23, over 26 DM28. Sheets DM6. Meals DM8.70. Reception 5-10pm. Curfew 11:30pm. Members only.) There is a **market** next door to the train station. (Open M-F 9am-6pm, Sa 9am-4pm.)

SCHWARZWALD (BLACK FOREST)

It might be a bit of an overstatement to say that Germans are obsessed with the dark, but from the earliest fairy tales to Franz Kafka's disturbing fiction, a sense of the uncanny and the sinister has long lurked in the German cultural consciousness. Nowhere is this collective dream of the dark more at home than in the Schwarzwald, a tangled expanse of evergreen covering the southwest corner of Baden-Württemberg. While the Schwarzwald owes its foreboding name to the eerie darkness that prevails under its canopy of vegetation, it is also the source of inspiration for the most quintessential German fairy tales, including the adventures of Hänsel and Gretel, as well as a slew of poetry and folk traditions. Many of these regional quirks are now exploited at the pervasive cuckoo-clock-*Lederhosen-Bratwurst*-keychain-and-ice-cream kiosks, which conspire, along with the devastating effects of acid rain, to erode the region's authenticity. Hordes of tourists are easily avoided, however, as innumerable trails wind through the region, leading willing hikers into more secluded parts of the forest. Skiing is also available in the area; the longest slope is at Feldberg (near Titisee).

The main entry points to the Schwarzwald are Freiburg, in the center; Baden-Baden to the northwest; Stuttgart to the east; and Basel, Switzerland, to the southwest. Most visitors cruise around in (or on) their own set of wheels, as public transportation is sparse. Rail lines encircle the perimeter, with only one **train** penetrating the region. **Bus** service is more thorough, albeit slow and less frequent. The **Freiburg tourist office** (p. 354) is the best place to gather information about the Schwarzwald.

NO BREAD CRUMBS THIS TIME The Schwarzwald
may be a hiker's paradise, but with its labyrinth of twisting trails it can easily become a tangled hell for novices. Even the trail markers are baffling: red diamonds, blue dots, green circles...purple horseshoes, anyone? Thankfully, the **Schwarzwaldverein** (Black Forest Association) has set up a system of markers for the major trails in the area. These trails are always marked by a diamond and are at least 10km of intense hiking each. These odysseys include the **Freiburg-Bodensee Querweg** (half-red, half-white diamond on a yellow field) and the 280km **Pforzheim-Basel Westweg** (always marked by a red diamond). Blue diamonds often mark trails with lots of uphill climbing and rewarding panoramas. **Terrain-Kurwege**, or TK, are well-marked trails that explore the local territory and are rarely longer than 10km. They are numbered in order of difficulty. A **Rundweg** is a connect-the-dots loop; a **Seerundweg**, which follows the shoreline of a lake, will be less taxing. A **Panoramaweg**, most popular with tourists, offers stunning views of the surrounding landscape.

HOCHSCHWARZWALD (HIGH BLACK FOREST)

Arguably the most enthralling neck of the woods, the Hochschwarzwald is so named for its high, pine-carpeted mountains, towering dramatically above lonely lakes and remote villages. The best source of information for the area is the **Freiburg tourist office**, Rotteckring 14 (tel. (0761) 368 90 90; fax 37 00 37).

At 1493m, **Feldberg** is the Schwarzwald's tallest mountain. The ski lift runs in summer and winter (round-trip DM5). Call the **tourist office** (tel. (07655) 80 19; fax 801 43; www.feldberg-schwarzwald.de) for information about Feldberg and 16 other ski slopes in the area. (Open M-Tu and Th-F 10am-noon and 3-5pm, W 10am-

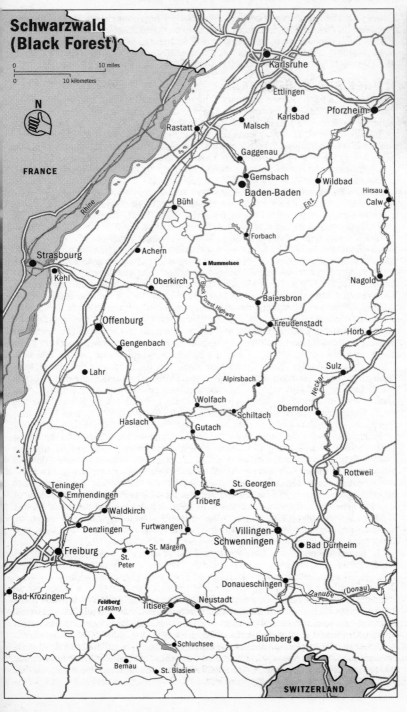

Schwarzwald
(Black Forest)

0   10 miles
0   10 kilometers

N

FRANCE

Karlsruhe

Ettlingen

Karlsbad

Pforzheim

Rastatt   Malsch

Gaggenau

Gernsbach   Wildbad

Baden-Baden   Hirsau

Bühl   Calw

Forbach

Rhine

Achern   Mummelsee

Strasbourg   Oberkirch   Nagold

Kehl   Baiersbron

Black Forest Highway

Offenburg   Freudenstadt

Gengenbach   Horb

Lahr   Sulz

Alpirsbach

Wolfach   Oberndorf

Haslach   Schiltach

Gutach   Neckar

Rottweil

St. Georgen

Teningen   Triberg

Emmendingen   Villingen-

Waldkirch   Furtwangen   Schwenningen

Denzlingen   Bad Dürrheim

Freiburg   St. Märgen

St.   Donaueschingen

Peter   Danube   (Donau)

Bad-Krozingen   Neustadt

Feldberg   Titisee

(1493m)

Schluchsee   Blumberg

Bernau   St. Blasien

SWITZERLAND

noon.) At 1234m above sea level, Feldberg's **Jugendherberge Hebelhof (HI)**, Passhöhe 14 (tel. (07676) 221; fax 12 32), may be the highest in Germany. Take the Titisee-Schluchsee train to Feldberg-Bärental, then the bus to "Hebelhof." (DM26, over 26 DM31. Reception 8am-10pm. Curfew 10:45pm. Reservations for winter. Members only.) For a **ski report**, call (07676) 12 14.

TITISEE AND SCHLUCHSEE

The Titisee and Schluchsee are two of the most beautiful lakes in the region. The more touristed Titisee (pronounced: TEE-tee-zay) is mobbed by Germans on hot summer days, and its lakeside pedestrian zone is a cheesy strip of souvenir shops and *Imbiß* stands. The 30-minute train from Freiburg glides through the scenic Höllental (Hell's Valley). Watch out for the Hirschsprung, a regal statue of a stag that crowns the cliff in a harrowingly narrow part of the valley. According to legend, a deer once narrowly escaped a hunter's arrow by making the impossible leap across the chasm.

Titisee's **tourist office**, Strandbadstr. 4 (tel. 980 40; fax 98 04 40; www.titisee.de), books **rooms** for a DM4 fee and rents **bikes** for DM15 per day; they also dispense maps of the 130km of nearby hiking trails (DM1-15). From the station, hang a right on Parkstr., take a left, and then a quick right around a pink house. The office is behind a set of flags. (Open July-Sept. M-F 8am-6pm, Sa 9am-noon and 3-5pm, Su 10am-noon; Oct.-June M-F 9am-noon and 1:30-5:30pm.) Hiking trails start in front of the office. Consider the placid **Seeweg**, or keep going along Strandbadstr. and turn right on Alte Poststr. for more challenging trails. Rent **paddleboats** from vendors along Seestr. (DM7 per 30min.) Guided **boat tours** depart from the same area, run by **Bootsverleih Winterhalder.** (Tel. 82 14. 25min. DM6.) Titisee's **telephone code** is 07651.

If the tourist density in Titisee is too great, head south to the **Schluchsee**, home to a slew of first-rate hiking trails. The simple **Seerundweg** circumvents the lake (18km, about 4hr.). More difficult and rewarding trails depart from the **Sportplatz** parking lot, a 15-minute walk up Dresselbacher Str. past the huge resort hotel. For an 18km, 6-hour trek, follow TK6 to the **Vogelhaus,** which houses a folk museum. (Open Tu and Su after 2pm.) Then follow signs for Hingerhäuser, Fischbach, Bildstein, and Aha before returning to Schluchsee. Cruise around the lake on the **Gisele Seerundfahrten** (tel. 449), which runs **boat trips** between Schluchsee, Seebrugg, Aha, and Blasiwald. (June-Sept. daily every hour 10am-5pm. DM4-7.) In Schluchsee, the boats depart from the beach near the **Aqua Fun Spaßbad** (tel. 77 32), which has several pools, water slides, and a sandy beach. (Open May-Sept. daily 9am-7pm. DM6.)

Hourly double-decker trains make the 30-minute jaunt from Titisee to the towns of Schluchsee and Seebrugg. Rent **bikes** at the gas station on Freiburger Str. towards Titisee. Schluchsee's **tourist office** (tel. 77 32; fax 77 59; www.schluchsee.de) is a block into the pedestrian zone in the *Kurhaus.* From the train station, turn right, walk through the underpass, and turn left up the brick sidewalk of Kirchsteige. The office sits at the corner of Fischbacher Str. and Lindenstr. The staff books **rooms** for free and offers a *Wanderwochenende* deal, by which you can get three nights' stay in a private room and hiking maps galore for DM99. (Open July-Aug. M-F 8am-6pm, Sa 10am-noon and 4-6pm, Su 10am-noon; Sept.-Oct. and May-June M-F 8am-noon and 2-6pm, Sa 10am-noon; Nov.-April same hours, except closed Sa.)

The **Jugendherberge Schluchsee-Wolfsgrund (HI)**, Seeweg 28 (tel. 329; fax 92 37), is ideally situated on the shore with a stunning lake view and comfortable facilities. From the station, cross the tracks and hop the fence, then follow the path right, over the bridge parallel to the tracks, to the hostel's front door. (DM23, over 26 DM28. May-Oct. DM1-2 *Kurtaxe*. Dinner DM8.70. Laundry DM6. Reception closed 2-5pm. Curfew 11pm.) **Haus Bergfrieden**, Dresselbacher Str. 23 (tel. 309), is uphill from the village center. Its tidy rooms are a steal. (DM25-28 per person. Breakfast included.) Pitch a tent at **Campingplatz Wolfsgrund** (tel. 77 32 or 77 33; fax 77 59). Walk left up Bahnhofstr. and continue onto Freiburger Str., take a left on Sägackerweg, follow it past Am Waldrain, and take another left. (DM8.50 per person. Tent DM10.) Stock up on **groceries** at **Schmidt's Markt,** Im Rappennest 2 (tel. 15 54). Schluchsee's **telephone code** is 07656.

Three kilometers down the lake at the end of the train line, the town of **Seebrugg** consists of nothing but a train station, a beach, and the **Jugendherberge Schluchsee-Seebrugg (HI),** Seebrugg 9 (tel. 494; fax 18 89). Then again, what more could you want? The splendid, renovated building couched among pine trees is a five-minute walk along the paved path from the train station. (DM23, over 26 DM28. Sheets DM6. May-Oct. *Kurtaxe* DM1.60. Reception 12:30-1pm, 5-6pm, and 6:30-10pm. Curfew 10pm. Members only.) Next to the hostel, a red diamond **hiking trail** darts into the forest, heading for the neighboring village of Blasiwald and its hillside cottages. This trail connects to the easier red dot **Seerundweg,** both crossing the admirable dam that spans a narrow neck of the lake. Debut your dental floss thong at the **Strandbad** beach to the left of the station. (Open daily May-Sept. DM2.50.) Rent **boats** here. (DM6 per 30 min., DM10 per hour.) Seebrugg's **telephone code** is 07656.

ST. BLASIEN

Were it not for its towering cathedral, St. Blasien would be an average town tucked into the southern mountains of the Black Forest. Third in size only to St. Peter's in Rome and Les Invalides in Paris, the **Dom**'s dome is constructed in a monumental classical style, rising above a charming Altstadt and immaculate white **Rathaus.** The origin of the cathedral stretches back to the 9th century, when the relics of St. Blasius were to be brought from Rome to Rheinau. On the way, the Benedectine monks chose to settle the well-protected Alb valley. Since then, the monastery has weathered a peasant's revolt and four fires, resulting in its late 18th-century neo-classical resurrection. The former abbey's green copper dome hides a false copula. (Open May-Sept. daily 8am-6:30pm, Oct.-April 8:30am-5:30pm. Free concerts July-Aug. Tu and Sa 8:15pm.) In the same building as the tourist office sits the **Museum St. Blasien** with exhibits on the Dom's past and town history. (Open Tu-Su 2:30-5pm. DM3, students DM1.) Every two years, St. Blasien hosts an international wood-carving contest, directing its attention for one week in late August to the army of chainsaws and sandpaper. The next face-off will take place in 2000.

No trip to St. Blasien is complete without a hike up the northern hillside for an unparalleled glimpse of the Dom. Stick to Todtmooser Str. in the pedestrian zone, cross the river and head straight uphill. Cross Luisenstr., continue onto Dr.-Determann-Weg; after turning the corner, a set of stone stairs to the left will leads to the forest. From there a number of trails offer excellent views of the Dom. Particularly popular is Unterer Philosophenweg; turn left. Or turn right on Blasiwalder Weg for its famous vista and **Windberg** waterfall. On the other side of town, more trails scale the idyllic **Holzberg** (Wood Mountain). Or facing the right side of the Dom, take Tuskulumweg and follow it through the pedestrian tunnel, following signs for **TK1.** A plethora of trailheads await on the other side of the highway.

A sublime 20-minute **bus** ride (#7319) connects St. Blasien with Seebrugg and the train system (1 per hour, DM6.20). The **tourist office,** Am Kurgarten 1-3 (tel. 414 30; fax 414 38; www.st-blasien-menzenschwand.de), has hiking maps and a catalog of **rooms.** From the main bus station, cross Umgehungsstr., enter the pedestrian zone, and bear right under the orange-trimmed gate. The tourist office is on the left. (Open M-F 10am-noon and 3-5pm and Sa 10am-noon, Oct.-May closed Sa.)

Most accommodations are in Menzenschwand (see **bus,** above). The **Jugendherberge Menzenschwand (HI),** Vorderdorfstr. 10 (tel. 326; fax 1435), offers the cheapest lodgings in the area. (DM21, over 26 DM26. Bedsheets DM6. Breakfast included. Call ahead.) **Private rooms** in Menzenschwand run from DM22 per night, considerably cheaper than in St. Blasien. Contact the Menzenschwand **tourist office,** Hinterdorfstr. 15 (tel. 930 90; fax 17 09), near the "Hirschen/Hintertor" bus stop. (Same hours as the St. Blasien tourist office.) If you miss the last bus to Menzenschwand, the cheapest night's stay in St. Blasien is **Hotel Garni Kurgarten,** Fürstabt-Gerbert-Str. 12 (tel. 527), across the street from the tourist office. (Singles from DM30, doubles DM70.)**Edeka,** across from the Dom, has **groceries.** St. Blasien's **telephone code** is 07672. Menzenschwand's is 07675.

ST. PETER AND ST. MÄRGEN

Sunk deep into a valley of cow-speckled hills 17km from Freiburg, St. Peter and St. Märgen exude an air of balmy tranquility. **Bus** #7216 runs from Freiburg to St. Märgen via St. Peter, but the more common route requires a **train** ride along the Freiburg-Neustadt line to "Kirchzarten" (3rd stop), where bus #7216 heads to St. Peter. Only half the buses continue on to St. Märgen; always check with the driver.

St. Peter, closer to Freiburg and surrounded by cherry orchards, juts high in the curative air, breaking through a crust of dark pine. Its **Klosterkirche** (tel. (07660) 910 10) rises above the otherwise uneventful skyline, egging the rest of town on with a gaudy interior of turquoise and mauve. (Open 24hr. Tours Su 11:30am, Tu 11am, Th 2:30pm. DM5. Organ concerts July-Sept. Su 5pm. DM10, students DM7.) The **tourist office** (tel. (07660) 91 02 24; fax 91 02 44) is in the Klosterhof. Get off the bus at "Zähringer Eck"; the office is right in front of the church under the *Kurverwaltung* sign. The staff has a list of affordable **rooms** starting at DM25. (Open M-F 8am-noon and 2-5pm; June-Oct. Sa 11am-1pm.) Many hiking paths—most of them well marked—begin at the tourist office and abbey. A relatively easy, but very scenic 8km path leads to **St. Märgen;** follow the blue diamonds of the **Panoramaweg.** From the abbey, make a sharp right alongside the Klosterkirche (do not cross the stream and main road), heading for the *Jägerhaus;* then cross the highway.

With links to all major Schwarzwald trails and a number of gorgeous day hikes, St. Märgen rightfully calls itself a *Wanderparadies.* One of the more challenging local trails leads to the **Zweibach waterfall;** follow signs with a black dot on a yellow field (16km, 4hr.). To reach the trail from the town center, walk downhill along Feldbergstr., turn left onto Landfeldweg, and follow signs for *Rankmühle.* The **tourist office** (tel. (07669) 91 18 17; fax 91 18 40) sits in the Rathaus 100m from the "Post" bus stop. The staff provides good hiking and biking maps (DM5) and finds **rooms** for free. (Open M-F 8am-noon and 2-5pm; June-Aug. also Sa 10am-noon; Nov.-Dec. closed afternoons.)

CENTRAL BLACK FOREST

More than hiking and biking, the thing that makes the central Black Forest tick is clocks. In 1667, the first wooden **Waaguhr** came into existence in Waldau. Since then, the Black Forest has become a breeding ground of ticking timepieces, with 12,000 clockmakers churning out 60 million clocks a year. The **Deutsche Uhrenstraße** (German clock route) winds its way through a number of towns, connecting glitzy clock museums and historic clock factories with tourist-hungry shops. Along the way, hikers haul past the Neckar and Danube rivers, and the famed **Schwarzwaldbahn** chugs through tunnels and over steep chasms.

DONAUESCHINGEN

A ten-year-old Mozart stopped in Donaueschingen on his way from Vienna to Paris and played three concerts in the castle. Since then, Donaueschingen has cultivated its status as a rest-stop for musical luminaries and the average traveler alike. Located on the Baar Plateau between the Schwarzwald and the Schwäbische Alb, its location makes it an ideal starting place for forays into the **Schwarzwald,** the **Lake Konstanz** region, and the **Wutach Schlucht** (Wutach Gorge) 15km to the south.

Donaueschingen's spurious claim to fame is its status as the "source" of the 2,840km Danube, the second-longest river in Europe and the only major one to flow west to east. Actually, the Danube begins where the Brigach and Brey Rivers converge, but the townsfolk decided to overlook this minor detail and build a monument to the river anyway. The **Donauquelle** (source of the Danube) is a shallow, rock-bottomed basin encased by mossy 19th-century stonework in the garden of **Schloß Fürstenberg,** located (by some inexplicable coincidence) right next to the Fürstenberg souvenir booth. The tapestries in the Schloß are spectacular, as is the bathroom—a shining marble cave with a massage-shower (no, you don't get to try it). The obligatory tour departs hourly. (Open Easter-Sept. M and W-Su 9am-noon and 2-5pm. DM5, students DM4. Garden always open.) Across the street from the Schloß the **Fürstenberg Sammlungen,** Karlspl. 7 (tel. 865 63), is a museum cluttered with former possessions of the princes of Fürstenberg. Diversity is the key with a room of clocks, the oldest known medieval manuscript of the epic **Nibelungenlied,** and the thoroughly horrifying skeleton(s) of infant Siamese twins. (Open Tu-Sa 10am-1pm and 2-5pm, Su 10am-5pm.) The museum, the Schloß, and the adjacent puddle are all within a 10-minute walk of the train station. Take a right in front of the station and walk one block before turning left at Josefstr., then cross the bridge and walk about 10min. more.

If the Fürstenberg decor leaves you covetous you can at least get royally smashed on free samples of the family beer at the **Fürstliche Fürstenberger Brauerei** (tel. 860), between Haldenstr. and Poststr. (Brewery tours DM7; arrange in advance.) Bike fiends rejoice: Donaueschingen is a terminus of the Danube **bicycle trail,** which skirts the river all the way to Vienna. The tourist office sells a map (DM18.80). Take Josefstr. from the station and turn right on Prinz-Fritzi-Allee into the **Fürstenberg Park,** where bicycle trails abound. Hikers can also take heart: parts of the Schwarzwald ring the western edge of town. Follow Karlstr. left to the blue **Rathaus,** then take Villinger Str. up away from town, making a left at the *Jägerhaus* signs. From there, a few trails venture into the forest.

Trains connect Donaueschingen to Freiburg (1½hr., 1 per hour, DM20), Triberg (30min., 1 per hour, DM12), and Rottweil (30min., 1 per hour, DM12). Rent **bikes** at **Zweiradhaus Rothweiler,** Max-Egon-Str. 11 (tel. 131 48; fax 127 95) for DM10-20 per day, depending on the length of your cycling trip. (Open March-Sept. M-Tu and Th-F 9:30am-12:30pm and 2:30-6pm, W and Sa 9:30am-1pm.) The **tourist office,** Karlstr. 58 (tel. 85 72 21; fax 85 72 28), books **rooms** for free. Veer right up the hill past the Schloß and turn left at Karlstr. (Open June-Aug. M-F 9am-6pm, Sa 10am-12:30pm; Sept.-May M-F 8am-noon and 2-5pm.) The office provides information about Donaueschingen's annual **Musiktage** in mid-October, a modern music festival. The **post office,** 78166 Donaueschingen, on the corner of Schulstr. and Kronenstr., is near the tourist office. (Open M-F 8am-noon and 2-6pm, Sa 8:30am-noon.) The **telephone code** is 0771.

Rest your weary feet at **Hotel Bären,** Josefstr. 7-9 (tel. 25 18), on the street directly in front of the train station. Singles with same-floor shower DM45, doubles DM90. Breakfast buffet included. Donaueschingen offers many pricey restaurants along Josefstr., although most have specials running DM10-14. **Pizzeria da Alfredo,** Villinger Str. 6, near the Rathaus, satisfies Italian cravings for DM6-20. (Open daily 11am-2:30pm and 5:30pm-midnight.)

TRIBERG

Tucked in a lofty valley 800m above sea level, the touristy whistle stop of **Triberg** has attitude about its altitude. The inhabitants brag in superlatives about the Gutacher Wasserfall—the **highest waterfall in Germany**—a series of bright cascades tumbling over moss-covered rocks for 163 vertical meters. Swarming with more than 400,000 visitors every year, these falls are tame by Niagara standards; however, the idyllic hike through the lush, towering pine trees makes up for the unimpressive trickle. The somewhat steep climb dissuades the less-than-fit from ascending. (Park admission DM2.50, students DM2.) The signs within the park for the **Wallfahrtskirche** point to a trail leading to the small **Pilgrim Church,** where pious ones have, according to legend, been miraculously cured since the 17th century. Keep going along Kroneckweg and follow the *Panoramaweg* signs for some hiking with an excellent view of the Schwarzwald valley. The **Schwarzwaldmuseum,** Wallfahrtsstr. 4 (tel. 44 34), back in town, is directly across the street from the waterfalls. The museum is packed with Schwarzwald paraphernalia of every imaginable variety, from re-enactments of the daily life of the *Schwarzwald Volk* (complete with slimy wax people) to a Schwarzwald model railroad that chugs away along a highly detailed cardboard landscape. (DM1 to watch it go. Open daily 9am-6pm; Nov.-April 10am-5pm; mid-Nov. to mid-Dec. weekends only. DM5, students DM3.) Beyond these attractions, the region's splendid natural surroundings promise some scrumptious hiking. Numerous trail signs on the outskirts of town point the way to a portion of the Pforzheim-Basel **Westweg.** The tourist office sells hiking maps (DM5.50); more detailed guides are available at the town's bookstores and souvenir shops.

Trains chug from Triberg to Freiburg (1¾hr., 1 per hour, DM32) and Rottweil (1½hr., 1 per hour, DM15). Triberg's **tourist office** (tel. 95 32 30; fax 95 32 36) hides on the ground floor of the local *Kurhaus.* Their staff gives out brochures, sells town maps (DM1), and dispenses a mammoth catalog of all hotels, *Pensionen,* and private rooms in the region. From the train station, cross the bridge, go under it, and bear right up steep Féjusstr., which turns into Hauptstr. Pass the Marktplatz (10min.) and a little farther up at Hotel Pfaff take a left; the office is in the *Kurhaus*—the building behind the flags past the Marktplatz. (Open M-F 9am-5pm; May-Sept. also Sa 10am-noon.) The town's sparkling, modern **Jugendherberge (HI),** Rohrbacher Str. 35 (tel. 41 10; fax 66 62), requires a masochistic 30-minute climb up Friedrichstr. (which turns into Rohrbacher Str.) from the tourist office. The sleek facilities and amazing view are quite luxurious. (DM22, over 26 DM27. Sheets DM5.50. Reception 5-7pm and at 9:45pm. Call ahead.) For those apprehensive about the climb, the **Hotel Zum Bären,** Hauptstr. 10 (tel. 44 93), offers worn-in rooms, most with showers, closer to the town center and the waterfall entrance. The jolly staff has been accommodating students for decades. (Singles DM37, with shower and toilet DM45; doubles with sink DM66, with shower and toilet DM84. Breakfast included.) Look for cuckoos at **Tick-Tack Stube,** Marktpl. 5 (tel. 68 19), while you wait for traditional German fare (DM10-20)—the restaurant is littered with clocks. (Open daily 11am-2pm and 5-10pm.) The **telephone code** is 07722.

ROTTWEIL

High up on a plateau with a view of the Swabian Alps, Rottweil bears the distinction of being the oldest city in Baden-Württemberg. An independent city under the Holy Roman Empire, Rottweil's contributions to the world's well-being have included both flameless gunpowder (the unfortunate brainchild of one Herr Duttenhofer) and certain pernicious canines. It comes as no surprise that the city is a bustling, ferocious little village that knows how to party. Chief among its shindigs is Rottweil's famous Fasnet celebration, which draws gawkers from all over Germany to watch 4,000 *Narren* (fools) storm through town in wooden masks and expensive costumes in a festive attempt to expel winter; the next outbreak is March 6-7, 2000. The Fronleichnam (feast of Corpus Christi) ceremony (June 22, 2000) reignites old Protestant-Catholic feuds in an innocent re-enactment.

⚑ ORIENTATION AND PRACTICAL INFORMATION. Lying on the Stuttgart-Zürich rail line, Rottweil is easily accessible by hourly **trains** to Stuttgart (1½hr., DM30). The train station lies in the valley below the town center, which translates into an unfortunate 20-minute uphill climb. Turn right upon leaving the station and head upward. When you reach the bridge, take another right to cross it. Hauptstr., the cross-street at the second block on your left, is the center of the town's action. Or take one of the frequent buses from the train station to "Stadtmitte." Halfway up the street on the right-hand side is the **tourist office,** Hauptstr. 23 (tel. 49 42 80 or 49 42 81; fax 49 43 73). The office books **rooms** for free and offers maps, an English guide to the city, and *Freizeit Spiegel*—a free publication detailing artistic, theatrical, and musical offerings. (Open April-Sept. M-F 10am-6pm, Sa 10am-noon; Oct.-March M-F 10am-1pm and 2-5pm.) Free 90-minute **tours** depart from the tourist office every Saturday at 2:30pm (May-Oct.). Rent **bikes** at **Alfred Kaiser,** Balingerstr. 9 (tel. 89 19), at the end of the bridge leading out of town from Hauptstr. (DM20 per day, mountain bikes DM30.) The **post office,** 78628 Rottweil, is at Königstr. 12. (Open M-F 8am-noon and 2-6pm, Sa 8am-noon). The **telephone code** is 0741.

⌐⌐ ACCOMMODATIONS AND FOOD. Inexpensive accommodations are difficult to find in the summer months; call early. To find the small and homey **Jugendherberge (HI)**, Lorenzgasse 8 (tel. 76 64), turn left on Lorenzgasse off Hauptstr., go right at the ivy-covered building, and left at the faded *Jugendherberge* sign. Many of the six- to eight-bed rooms in this half-timbered house face out onto the terrifically steep plunge into the Neckar. (DM22, over 26 DM27. Breakfast included. Sheets DM4. Reception 5-10:30pm. Open mid-Jan. to mid-Dec.) The *Pension* **Goldenes Rad,** Hauptstr. 38 (tel. 74 12), is often booked solid several weeks in advance. (Singles DM38, doubles DM70. Reception M-Sa 11:30am-2pm and 5pm-1am, Su 11:30am-2pm and 6pm-midnight.) For traditional regional cooking, head to **Zum goldenen Becher,** Hochbrücktorstr. 17 (tel. 76 85), a family restaurant where meals run DM12-30. (Open Tu-Su 11am-midnight.) At **Rotuvilla,** Hauptstr. 63 (tel. 416 95), feast on many incarnations of wood-oven pizza (DM9-16) in a half-timbered dining room. (Open M and W-Su 11:30am-2pm and 5pm-midnight.)

◉ SIGHTS. Rottweil's fanatic adherence to old traditions is not limited to celebrations. The town is a living architecture museum, its buildings graced with historic murals and meticulously crafted windows. At the summit of the hill looms the 13th-century **Schwarzes Tor,** built in 1289 and enlarged in 1571 and 1650. Higher yet stands the ancient **Hochturm,** which offers a stunning view of the Swabian Alps from its top. To scale it, pick up the key to the tower from the tourist office in exchange for DM2 and an ID. On weekends, the key is available next door at Café Schädle. Across Hauptstr. from the tourist office and the Gothic **Altes Rathaus** stands the **Stadtmuseum,** Hauptstr. 20 (tel. 49 42 56), which houses a 15th-century treaty between Rottweil and nine Swiss cantons—still valid to this day—and a collection of wooden masks from the *Fasnet* celebrations. (Open Tu-Sa 10am-noon and 2-5pm, Su 10am-noon. DM1.)

Behind the Altes Rathaus, the Gothic **Heilig-Kreuz-Münster** (Cathedral of the Holy Cross) houses an interesting array of gilded lanterns that are carried through town annually in the **Corpus Christi** procession. Subject to the winds of architectural fashion, this cathedral flip-flopped from 12th-century Romanesque to 15th-century Gothic to 17th-century Baroque and back to 19th-century Gothic revivalism. The refreshingly modern **Dominikanermuseum** (tel. 78 62; fax 49 43 77), on Kriegsdamm, is home to a collection of medieval sculptures of saints and, more important, an excellent exhibit on Rottweil's Roman past, highlighted by a 570,000-tile second-century mosaic. (Open Tu-Su 10am-1pm and 2-5pm. DM3.) For medieval stone sculptures, drop by the neighboring art collection in the **Lorenzkapelle,** Lorenzgasse 17. (Tel. 49 42 98. Open Tu-Su 2-5pm. DM1.)

BODENSEE (LAKE CONSTANCE)

Nearly land-locked Germany has long suffered from something of a Mediterranean complex. For this cold grey country, there are no white sand beaches of the Riviera, no sparkling waters of the Greek islands, none of the sun-bleached stucco of Italy—except for a strip of land on the **Bodensee.** This stretch of southern Baden-Württemberg provides opportunity for Italian fantasies to be enacted and Grecian longings (you know the kind) to be satisfied. Potted palms line the streets, public beaches are filled with sunbathers tanning to a melanomic crisp, and daily business is conducted with a thoroughly un-German casualness. Looking out across the lake, it's easy to see how the deception works so smoothly, as the surprisingly warm waters glow an intense turquoise blue more typically found in the Caribbean than in European lakes. With the snow-capped Swiss and Austrian Alps soaring in the background, the Bodensee is one of Germany's most stunning destinations.

Getting to the region by **train** is easy; **Konstanz** and **Friedrichshafen** have direct connections to many cities in southern Germany. Transport within the region requires long rides and tricky connections due to the absence of a single route that fully encircles the lake. In many instances, the bright white boats of the **BSB**

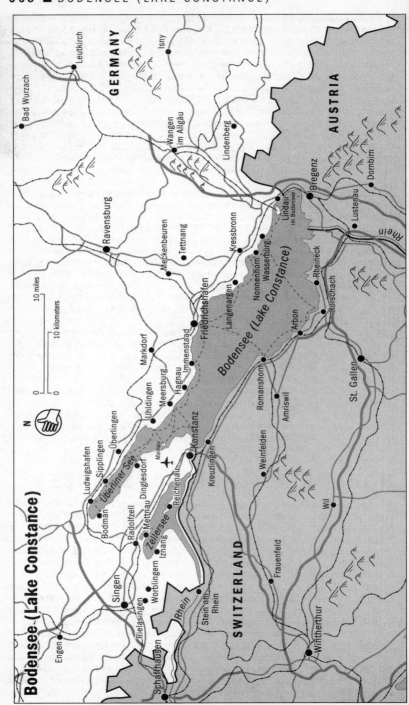

(Bodensee-Schiffsbetriebe) and other smaller lines, known collectively as the **Weiße Flotte,** are a quicker and more therapeutic alternative. Ships leave hourly from Konstanz and Friedrichshafen for all ports around the lake, departing every 1-3 hours. Those who plan to spend at least a week here should invest in the 7-day **Bodensee-Pass,** which includes one day of free ship travel and a 50% discount on all rail, bus, and gondola-lift tickets (DM57). If you want it that way, contact the BSB office in Konstanz (tel. 28 13 98; fax 28 13 73).

KONSTANZ (CONSTANCE)

Spanning the Rhein's exit from the Bodensee, the elegant university city of Konstanz has never been bombed. Part of the city extends into neighboring Switzerland, and the Allies were leery of accidentally striking neutral territory. The proximity of Switzerland and Austria gives the city an open, international flair. Its narrow streets wind around beautifully painted Baroque and Renaissance facades in the central part of town, while along the river promenades, gabled and turreted 19th-century houses gleam with a confident gentility. The waters of the Bodensee lap the beaches and harbors, and a palpable jubilation fills the streets.

▨ ORIENTATION AND PRACTICAL INFORMATION. Tickets for the **Weiße Flotte** ship line to Meersburg and Mainau are on sale in the building behind the train station. (Open March to mid-Oct. daily 7:40am-6:35pm.) Follow the underground passage near the tourist office to the harbor; otherwise, buy your tickets on the ship. The tourist office offers a two-day pass (DM34) including transportation on buses, the ferry, the Weiße Flotte, a city tour, and admission to Mainau (see p. 371). **Giess Personenschiffahrt** (tel. (07533) 21 77; fax (07533) 986 66) runs private boats hourly from behind the train station to **Freizeitbad Jakob** and **Freibad Horn** and leads tours of the Bodensee. (45min. June-Aug. daily 10:50am-5:50pm; May and Sept. Su only. DM8, children DM4.) **Buses** in Konstanz cost DM2.40 per ride, DM10 for a five-ride ticket, and DM7 for a one-day ticket for two adults and three children. The **Gästekarte,** available at any place of accommodation in the city for a stay of two nights or more (including the youth hostel) costs DM1.50 per day and gives you public transit within Konstanz, free or discounted admission to some sights, and one free dunk in the Jakobsbad. Rent **paddleboats and rowboats** at Am Gondelhafen. (Tel. 218 81. Open April-Oct. daily 10am-dusk. DM12-16 per hour.) Rent **bikes** from **Kultur-Rädle,** Blarerstr. 19. (Tel. 273 10. DM10 per half day, DM17 full day.) The tiny but spunky **Mitfahrzentrale,** Münzgasse 22 (tel. 194 40; fax 792 59), finds rides. (Munich DM23, Freiburg DM16, Stuttgart DM20. Open M 2-6pm, Tu-F 9:30am-12:30pm and 2-6pm, Sa 10am-2pm.) For a **taxi,** call 222 22.

The **tourist office,** Bahnhofspl. 13 (tel. 13 30 30; fax 13 30 60; email info@tourist information.stadt.konstanz.de), in the arcade to the right of the train station, provides an excellent walking map (DM0.50) and lots of information about the area. The staff finds **rooms** for a DM5 fee in private homes (three-night minimum stay), or in hotels for shorter stays. (Open May-Oct. M-F 9am-8pm, Sa 9am-4pm, Su 10am-1pm; Nov.-March M-F 9:30am-12:30pm and 2-6pm.) City **tours** (DM10) depart from the office as well. (April-Oct. M-Sa at 10:30am and Su at 2:30pm). Clean your clothes at **Waschsalon und Mehr,** Hofhalde 3. (Wash DM7, dry DM5 per 10min. Open M-F 10am-7pm, Sa 10am-4pm.) Some establishments list prices in Swiss Francs (SFr); see p. 44 for **exchange rates.** The **post office,** 78462 Konstanz, Markstatte 4, is near the train station. (Open M-F 8:30am-6pm, Sa 8:30am-noon.) Check **email** at **Schulze & Schultze Internet Café,** Pfauengasse 2 (tel. 152 74), near the Schnetztor in the southwest corner of the Altstadt. (Open until 1am. DM7.50 per 30min.) The **telephone code** is 07531.

▨ ACCOMMODATIONS AND CAMPING. Finding lodging in popular Konstanz can induce some massive migraines. Two words: call ahead! That way, you can secure a place at the marvelous **▨Jugendherberge Kreuzlingen (HI),** Promenadenstr. 7 (tel. from Germany (00 41 71) 688 26 63, from Switzerland (071) 688 26 63; fax

688 47 61). South of the border in Kreuzlingen, Switzerland, but actually closer to downtown Konstanz than the Konstanz hostel, it commands the tip of a small lakefront hill and features cushy leather furniture and a multilingual staff practically breaking their necks to serve you. From May-June, however, the hostel is almost always booked by school groups on vacation, so call ahead. The best way there is by foot (20min.). From the train station, turn left, cross the metal bridge over the tracks, turn right, and go through the parking lot to the checkpoint "Klein Venedig." Keep walking along Seestr. until the sharp right curve. Instead of following the street, continue straight ahead on the gravel path through the gate, past the billy goats, right through the Seeburg castle parking lot, and right up the hill to the building with a flag on top. (SFr23, or about DM28—both currencies accepted.) Breakfast and sheets included. Rents mountain bikes for SFr15 per day, kayaks for SFr12 per 2hr. Reception 8-9am and 5-9pm. Curfew 11pm. Open March-Nov.)

Jugendherberge "Otto-Moericke-Turm" (HI), Zur Allmannshöhe 18 (tel. 322 60; fax 311 63), is considerably less luxurious, with small rooms in a former water tower next to a graveyard. However, it has a terrific view. Take bus #4 from the train station to "Jugendherberge" (7th stop); backtrack and head straight up the hill. (DM30, over 26 DM35. Members only. Breakfast and dinner included. Sheets DM5.50. Reception April-Oct. 3-10pm; Nov.-March 5-10pm. Curfew 10pm. Lock-out 9:30am-noon. Call ahead.) **Jugendwohnheim Don Bosco,** Salesianerweg 5 (tel. 622 52; fax 606 88), is also cheap. From the station, take bus #1 to "Salzberg." Walk toward the intersection along Mainaustr. and keep on going. Or take bus #4, 9B, or 15 to the same stop, but cross Mainaustr. at the intersection and turn left. Walk 200m past the intersection, and follow the sign down the path to the right. Choose from 39 channels in the lively dayroom. (DM28 per person. Breakfast included. Sheets DM6.50. Curfew 10pm). **Campingplatz Konstanz-Bruderhofer,** Fohrenbühlweg 50 (tel. 313 88 or 313 92), is even cheaper. Take bus #1 to "Staad." The campground is along the waterfront. Call ahead, as it also fills up fast. (DM6.50 per person; DM5.50-8.50 per tent.)

🍴 **FOOD.** The **Mensa** dishes out Konstanz's cheapest food. Lunches, including dessert and a view of the lake, cost DM8-9. (Open M-F 11:15am-1:30pm.) The **cafeteria** on floor K6 has lighter fare and doesn't require ID. (DM2-5. Open M-Th 7:45am-6:30pm, F 7:45am-5pm; Aug. M-F 11am-2pm.) Take bus #9 from the train station to "Universität." The **Fachhochschule Mensa** also comes with a view. An international student ID is required for a changecard; ask the attendant. The hassle is worth it—meals cost DM4.40. (Open M-F 8:30am-4pm.) Stroll through the small streets surrounding the *Münster's* northern side: it is the oldest part of Konstanz, and now the center of its vibrant alternative scene, with health-food stores, left-wing graffiti, and student cafés. It's hard to get a seat in the very popular and dimly lit **Sedir,** Hofhaldestr. 11 (tel. 293 52). Choose from meat or vegetarian Turkish dishes DM8-12. Open M-F 11:30am-2pm and 6pm-1am, Sa noon-3pm and 6pm-1am, Su 6pm-1am. Kitchen open until 1:45pm and 11:30pm.) For **groceries,** head to **Tengelmann** at the corner of Münzgasse and Brotlaube. (Open M-F 8:30am-8pm, Sa 8am-4pm.)

📷 **SIGHTS.** Konstanz's **Münster,** built over the course of 600 years, has a 76m soaring Gothic spire and a display of ancient religious objects. Alas, the tower is subject to renovation until 2003. (Church open daily 10am-5pm. Free.) The **Rathaus** tells the tale of Konstanz's history with its elaborate frescoes. Wander down **Seestraße,** near the yacht harbor on the lake, or down **Rheinsteig** along the Rhein, to two picturesque waterside promenades. The tree-filled **Stadtgarten,** next to Konstanz's main harbor, provides an unbroken view of the Bodensee and of the statue of the voluptuous *Imperia* who guards the harbor. Across the Rhein from the Altstadt, near the "Sternenplatz" bus stop, is the **Archäologisches Landesmuseum,** Benediktinerpl. 5 (tel. 510 38 39; fax 684 52), a three-floor assemblage of all things ancient from Baden-Württemberg—jewels, spearheads, and re-assembled skeletons. (Open Tu-Su 10am-6pm. DM4, students DM3.) Get your fill of fossils, minerals, and ecological enlightenment at the **Bodensee-Naturmuseum,** Katzgasse 5-7. (Tel. 91 42 58; fax 258 64. Open May-Aug. 10am-8pm; Sept.-April 10am-6pm.)

Konstanz boasts a number of **public beaches;** all are free and open May to September. Take bus #5 **Strandbad Horn** (tel. 635 50), the largest and most crowded; it sports a nude sunbathing section modestly enclosed by hedges. In inclement weather, head next door to **Freizeitbad Jakob,** Wilhelm-von-Scholz-Weg 2 (tel. 611 63), a modern indoor-outdoor pool complex with thermal baths and sun lamps. Walk 30 minutes along the waterfront from the train station, or take bus #5 to "Freizeitbad Jakob." (Open daily 9am-9pm. DM8, students DM5.) **Strandbad Konstanz-Litzelstetten** and **Strandbad Konstanz-Wallhausen** can both be reached via bus #4. The twentysomething set frolics on the beach at the university. Take bus #4 to "Egg" and walk past the *Sporthalle* and playing fields, or take a 10-minute walk down through the fields from the Konstanz youth hostel.

NEAR KONSTANZ: MAINAU

The island of **Mainau** (tel. 30 30; fax 30 32 48), a 15-minute bus ride from Konstanz, is a rich and magnificently manicured garden, the result of the horticultural prowess of generations of Baden princes and the Swedish royal family. A lush arboretum, exotic birds, and huge animals made of flowers surround the pink Baroque palace built by the Knights of the Teutonic Order, who lived here from the 13th to the 18th century. Now thousands of happy little tourists scamper across the foot bridge from Konstanz to pose with the blooming elephants and take in the unparalleled view of the Bodensee amidst 30 different varieties of butterflies and a near-tropical setting. Amazingly, dozens of palm trees thrive here year-round thanks to the lake's moderating effect on the climate and the magic green thumbs of the island's massive gardening army. In summer, preserve your rapidly diminishing D-marks by waiting until after 6pm, when students get in for free and the island is tranquil and swathed with sunsets. From the Konstanz train station, take bus #4 (direction: "Bettingen") to "Mainau" (2 per hour). If the idea of going to a garden island by bus strikes you as plebeian, take a boat trip from behind the train station. (One-way DM5.40, round-trip DM9. Island open mid-March to Oct. 7am-8pm; Nov. to mid-March 9am-5pm. DM17, students DM9, seniors DM13.50, children DM5.50; after 6pm and Nov. to mid-March DM9, students and children free.)

MEERSBURG

Overlooking the Bodensee, the massive medieval fortress of **Burg Meersburg** (tel. 800 00) towers above the gorgeous town of Meersburg. Begun in the 7th century, Germany's **oldest inhabited castle** now houses deer antlers, rusting armor, and a very deep dungeon. (Open March-Oct. daily 9am-6:30pm; Nov.-Feb. 10am-6pm. DM9, students DM7, children DM5.50.) In the 18th century, a prince bishop had declared the **Altes Schloß** unfit to house his regal self, so he commissioned the sherbet-pink Baroque **Neues Schloß** (tel. 41 40 71). Elaborately frescoed, it now houses the town's art collection, the **Schloßmuseum,** and the **Dorniermuseum,** with models of Dornier airplanes. (Open April-Oct. daily 10am-1pm and 2-6pm. DM5, students DM4.) Meersburg's quirky, crowdy **Zeppelinmuseum,** Schloßpl. (tel. 79 09), between the two castles, presents anything remotely connected with zeppelins, including two full-sized zeppelin flight attendant mannequins and a 30-minute film on the history of the flying cigars. (Open April-Oct. daily 10am-6pm. DM5, students DM4.50.) To catch a view of the Bodensee against an alpine backdrop, trek up past the Altstadt, cross the intersection at Stettenerstr., and turn left onto Droste-Hülshoff-Weg, just before the orange house. Follow the signs for "Alpenblick." Or stroll the leisurely **Uferpromenade** along the harbor.

Meersburg is 30 minutes from Konstanz by **boat** (2 per hour, DM5.20). The town has no train station but the nearest accessible one is in **Überlingen,** 30 minutes away via bus #7395 (DM5, every 30min.). The **tourist office,** Kirschstr. 4 (tel. 43 11 10; fax 43 11 20; www.meersburg.de), provides free city maps, useful for the tangled Altstadt, and a list of accommodations. Climb the stairs from the sea-level Unterstadtstr., past the castle and the half-timbered houses, and continue through the Marktplatz towards the church; it's on the right. (Open May-Sept. M-F 9am-6:30pm, Sa 10am-2pm; Oct.-April M-F 9am-noon and 2-5pm.) The office also offers city **tours** every Wednesday at 10:30am and Saturday at 2pm (summer only; DM5). To reserve **rooms,** consult the **Zimmervermittlung,** Untere Stadtstr. 13 (tel. 804 40; fax 804 48), at the bottom of the stairs. (Open M-F 8:30am-noon and 2-6pm, Sa 9am-12:30pm. DM2 fee.) **Haus Mayer Bartsch,** Stettenerstr. 53 (tel./fax 60 50), has rooms with TV and balcony. From Marktpl., go up Obertorstr. through the gate, then head straight and bear right onto Stettenerstr. Keep on truckin'; it's on the left past the gas station. (Singles DM45, with bath DM60; doubles DM85, with bath DM135.) For tasty and honestly priced pizza and spaghetti (DM9-16.50, slices DM3) in this city of sky-high prices, **Da Nico,** Untere Stadtstr. 39 (tel. 64 48), provides a view of the lake and speedy pasta service. (Open daily 11am-11:30pm.) The **telephone code** is 07532.

FRIEDRICHSHAFEN

A former construction base for Zeppelins, Friedrichshafen had trouble getting back up off the ground after Allied bombing in 1944. The current town was rebuilt with sweeping, wide promenades and tree-lined boulevards that open up onto breathtaking panoramas of the Alps across the water. The city's flagship attraction is the superb **Zeppelinmuseum,** Seestr. 22 (tel. 380 10), which details the history of the flying dirigibles and their inventor. The fleet of 16 scale models is overshadowed by a 33m reconstruction of a section of the unfortunate *Hindenburg,* which went up in flames in Lakehurst, New Jersey in 1937. Climb aboard and check out the recreated passenger cabins. (Open May-Oct. Tu-Su 10am-6pm; Nov.-April 10am-5pm. Last admission 1hr. before closing. DM12, students DM6.) The **Schulmuseum,** Friedrichstr. 14 (tel. 326 22), documents school life in Germany as it has grown and flourished over the last 12 centuries; unfortunately, it does feature hordes of schoolchildren from this century. Don't miss the "punishment" exhibit or the Third Reich room. (Open April-Oct. daily 10am-5pm; Nov.-March Tu-Su 2-5pm. DM2.) The 17th-century **Schloßkirche,** on Friedrichstr. to the right of the station, almost burned to the ground in 1944. Today it stands in its rebuilt glory, despite the imitation marble high altar. (Open daily mid-April to late-Sept. 9am-6pm; Oct. 9am-5pm. Closes W 2:30pm.) The beach is at the **Strandbad,** Königsweg 11 (tel. 280 78). Take the hedged path to the right of the Schloßkirche entrance. (15min. Open daily mid-May to mid-Sept. 9am-8pm. DM2.50.)

Popular among avid cyclists, Friedrichshafen provides direct access to a number of **biking paths,** including the much-beloved **Bodensee-Radweg,** which whisks spandex the entire 260km around the Bodensee. The *Bodensee-Radweg* is marked by signs with a cyclist whose back tire is filled in blue (for the lake, get it?). The less hard-core can follow any of the other clearly marked routes, accessible from Friedrichstr.

There are two train stations in Friedrichshafen: the larger **Stadtbahnhof** and the easterly **Hafenbahnhof,** behind the Zeppelinmuseum and near the harbor and Buchhornpl. **Trains** connect the two stations (2-4 times per hr). Trains run to Munich (3 hr., 1 per hour, DM67) and Lindau (30min., 1 per hour, DM7.60). Friedrichshafen is also connected by frequent **buses** and **boats** to Lindau and Meersburg. The boat from Konstanz (1½hr.) costs DM12. Buy boat tickets on board or at the ticket counter next to the Zeppelinmuseum. (Open M-F 8:10am-5:45pm, Sa-Su 9am-5:45pm.) Rent your own boat (though don't attempt to get to Konstanz with 'em) at the **Gondelhafen** by Seestr. (Tel. 217 46. Open May-Sept. daily 9am-8pm. Rowboats and paddleboats DM7-11 per 30min., motor boats DM28-30.) Rent **bikes** from the *Fahrkartenausgabe* counter of the Stadtbahnhof (DM10-15 per day). The **tourist office,** Bahnhofpl. 2 (tel. 300 10; fax 725 88), across the square to the left of the city train station, sells maps (DM0.50), details biking routes, and reserves **rooms** for a DM5 fee. (Open Oct.-March M-F 9am-noon and 2-5pm; May-Sept. M-F 9am-5pm, Sa 10am-2pm.) The **post office,** Friedrichshafen 88045, is next to the Stadtbahnhof. (Open M-F 8:30am-6pm and Sa 8:30am-1pm.) The **telephone code** is 07541.

Friedrichshafen's quality **Jugendherberge Graf Zeppelin (HI),** Lindauer Str. 3 (tel. 724 04; fax 749 86), is clean, renovated, and 50m from the water's edge. Call ahead; this place fills up fast, especially in summer; from the Hafenbahnhof, walk down Eckenerstr. away from Buchhornplatz (5min.). From the Stadtbahnhof, walk left down Friedrichstr., and turn down Eckenerstr. (20min.) Or take bus #7587 (direction: "Kressbronn") to "Jugendherberge." (DM25, over 26 DM30. Breakfast included. Sheets DM5.50. Laundry facilities. Reception 7-9am, 2-7:30pm, and 8-10pm. Curfew for guests under 18 10pm. Lockout 9am-noon.) Well-touristed Friedrichshafen has very few affordable restaurants, so *Imbiß* stands, located along Friedrichstr., are your best bet. **Naturkost am Buchhornplatz,** Buchhornpl. 1 (tel. 243 35), serves home-cooked vegetarian food and offers take-out. For **groceries,** head to **Lebensmittel Fehl** on Seestr. (Open M-F 8am-6:30pm, Sa 8am-2pm.)

LINDAU IM BODENSEE

When geological forces crunched their way through southern Germany during the last Ice Age, Mother Nature decided that Lindau should be a resort. Connected to the lakeshore by a narrow causeway, the island sits cupped in aquamarine waters, enjoying a view of the Alps that's almost the same as the one you see on good chocolates. Tourists started floating in by steamship in 1835, and now close to a million come every year to soak in the balmy climate and wander among 14th-century gabled houses on **Maximilianstr.,** which forms the central part of town. Halfway along Maximilianstr., the **Altes Rathaus** is a fruity blend of frescoes. The **Cavazzen-Haus** in the Marktpl. houses the **Stadtmuseum** (tel. 94 40 73), which displays a collection of musical instruments and art ranging from fine French porcelain to 17th-century portraits of ugly German bluebloods. (Open April-Oct. Tu-Su 10am-noon and 2-5pm. DM5, students DM3.) A walk down **In der Grub**—the less touristed equivalent of Maximilianstr.—leads to the ivy-covered **Diebsturm** (robbers' tower), which looks more like Rapunzel's tower than the prison it once was. For properly dressed adults, the **Spielbank** (casino) by the Seebrücke offers the regular spinning of roulette wheels and thinning of wallets. The bet ceiling is DM12,000, so don't worry about losing too much money. (Open 3pm-4am. Admission DM5 and a passport—please daaarling, no jeans. 21+.)

Lindau has three beaches. **Römerbad** (tel. 68 30) is the smallest and most familial, located left of the harbor on the island. (Open M-F 10:30am-7:30pm and Sa-Su 10am-8pm. DM4, students DM3.) To reach the quieter **Lindenhofbad** (tel. 66 37), take bus #1 or 2 to "Anheggerstr." and then bus #4 to "Alwind." (Open M-F 10:30am-7:30pm, Sa-Su 10am-8pm. DM4, students DM3.) Lindau's biggest beach is **Eichwald** (tel. 55 39), a 30 min. walk to the right facing the harbor along Uferweg. Alternatively, take bus #1 or 2 to "Anheggerstr.," then bus #3 to "Karmelbuckel." (Open M-F 9:30am-7:30pm, Sa-Su 9am-8pm. DM5.)

Ferries link Lindau with Konstanz, stopping at Meersburg, Mainau, and Friedrichshafen along the way (3hr., 3-6 per day. DM18.80, under 24 DM11.20.) The **train** to Konstanz takes two hours (DM13). Fun-lovers rent **boats** 50m to the left of the casino, next to the bridge. (Tel. 55 14. Open mid.-March to mid.-Sept. daily 9am-9pm. Rowboats DM10-18, paddleboats DM14-18 per hour, motor boat DM45.) One-hour excursions (tel./fax 781 94) leave from the dock behind the casino at 11:30am, 1, 2:30, and 6pm (DM12, children DM6). Rent **bikes** (tel. 212 61) at the train station. (Open March to late Dec. M-F 9am-1pm and 3:20-6pm, Sa 9:30am-1pm, Su 9am-noon. DM13 per day.) Alternatively, **Fahrradies,** In der Grub 5 (tel. 235 39), will rent you wheels. (Open M-F 9:30am-1pm and 2:30-6pm, Sa 9:30am-1pm. DM12 per day, mountain bikes DM20.) The **tourist office,** Ludwigstr. 68 (tel. 26 00 30; fax 26 00 26), across from the train station, finds **rooms** for a DM5 fee. (Open mid-June to early Sept. M-Sa 9am-1pm and 2-7pm; May to mid-June and Sept. M-F 9am-1pm and 2-6pm, Sa 9am-1pm; April and Oct. M-F 9am-1pm and 2-5pm, Sa 9am-1pm; Nov.-March M-F 9am-noon and 2-5pm.) **Tours** leave from the office at 10am. (Tu and F in German, M in English. DM6, students and overnight guests DM4.) The **post office,** 88131 Lindau im Bodensee, is 50m to the right of the train station.

(Open M-F 8am-6pm, Sa 8:30am-noon.) Check **e-mail** at **Bamboo's Internet Café,** Dammsteggasse 4. (Tel. 94 27 67. DM10 per hour.) The **telephone code** is 08382.

The spectacular **Jugendherberge,** Herbergsweg 11 (tel. 967 10; fax 496 71 50), lies across the Seebrücke off Bregenzer Str. Walk (20min.) or take bus #1 or 2 from the train station to "Anheggerstr.", then transfer to Bus #3 (direction: "Zech") to "Jugendherberge." (DM28. Under 27 and families with small children only. Break-fast, sheets, and *Kurtaxe* included. Reception 7am-midnight. Curfew midnight. Call ahead.) Eat off the floor in the rooms at **Gästehaus Holdereggen,** Näherweg 4 (tel. 65 74). Follow the railroad tracks across the causeway to the mainland; turn right onto Holdereggengasse and left onto Jungfernburgstr. Näherweg is on the left (20min.). (Singles DM38, doubles DM76. DM3 *Kurtaxe* per person for one-night stands. Showers DM2.) **Campingplatz Lindau-Zech,** Frauenhofer Str. 20 (tel. 722 36; fax 26 00 26), is 3km south of the island on the mainland. It's within spitting distance of the Austrian border. *Let's Go* does not recommend spitting at either. Take bus #1 or 2 to "Anheggerstr.," then bus #3 (direction: "Zech") to the end. (DM9.50 per person. DM4 per tent. *Kurtaxe* DM1.50. Showers included. Open May-Oct.) Brush up your Greek with the *text*ured napkins at **Taverna Pita Gyros,** Paradiespl. 16 (tel. 237 02), while eating a *gyro*. (DM10. Open daily 10am-9pm.) For **groceries** try **Plus,** in the basement of the department store at the intersection of In der Grub and Cramergasse. (Open M-F 8:30am-6:30pm, Sa 8am-1pm.)

RHEINLAND-PFALZ

AND SAARLAND

The valleys, castles, and wine towns of Rheinland-Pfalz make the region a visual feast, as the Mosel curls downstream to the soft, castle-backed shores of the Rhein Valley. Centuries of literature attest to its beauty as well, from the *Nibelungenlied* to the Lorelei revelry. The Rheinland also provides a literal feast: a rich agricultural tradition keeps produce in abundance, and the many vineyards in the Rhein and Mosel Valleys produce sweet, delicious wines. Trier is a millennia-old collage of Roman sights, while the medieval towns of Mainz, Worms, and Speyer bow down to glorious cathedrals. The Rheinland has been politically potent since the days when its electors were the king-makers of the Holy Roman Empire. Saarland, on the other hand, has long been the locus of political contention; the little *Land*'s mineral wealth has been making both Germany and France covetous for centuries.

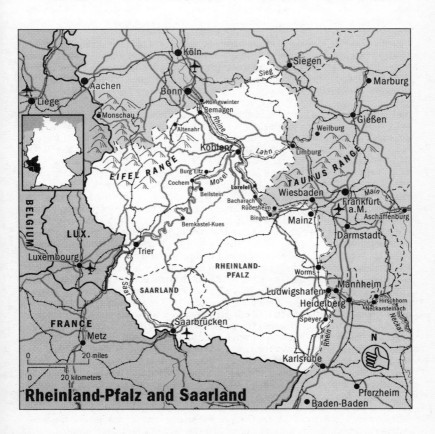

Rheinland-Pfalz and Saarland

> ## HIGHLIGHTS OF RHEINLAND-PFALZ
>
> ■ The **Rheintal** is a poet's dream come true. From its mystical **Lorelei cliffs** to its majestic castles and famous wineries, the Valley cannot fail to impress (p. 381).
> ■ For *really* old sights, head to **Trier,** where 2,000-year-old Roman ruins make the typical German Schloß seem like a sandcastle (p. 390).
> ■ Tiny hamlets with half-timbered houses abound in the **Moseltal.** The many well-touristed towns in the region keep up the German tradition of gorgeous, ubiquitous castles and are surrounded by endless vineyards (p. 386).
> ■ **Mainz** was once home to Johannes Gutenberg, inventor of the printing press, who celebrates his 600th birthday this year. Copies of his famous Bibles are on display at the Gutenberg Museum, while the fantastic Dom draws the devout (p. 384).

AHRTAL (AHR VALLEY)

The string of tiny hamlets that dots the serene Ahr River refers to itself as *Rotwein Paradies Deutschlands* (Germany's red wine paradise). Unlike most cheesy tourist bureau slogans, the Ahrtal lives up to its claims; in many picturesque places the vineyards climb up and *over* the area's craggy hills, continuing straight down the other side. Wine cellars and tiny family-owned wineries abound, and the bulk of information in the valley's tourist offices helps guide those in search of vinic pleasures (the *Erlebnis Ahrwein* pamphlet is the oenophile's bible).

Trains travel into the region from **Remagen,** halfway between Bonn and Koblenz. Trains depart from Remagen to the town of **Altenahr** approximately once every hour (45min., DM7.60). As the train chugs west, the hills become more rocky and steep, culminating in the violent, craggy peaks that surround Altenahr. Developed to supply peasants for the royalty of the local castle, **Burg Ahr** (reached by a trail across from the Rathaus), the town today caters to a different ruling force—the tourist industry. The **Sommer-Rodelbahn** (tel. 23 21) resembles a luge, without the cold, snow, or embarrassingly tight suits. Cables pull your sled to the summit and then let you rip down a 500m slippery steel track. A brake is provided for the meek. (Open April-Oct. M-F and Su 10am-6pm, Sa 10am-sundown; Nov.-March Sa-Su 11am-4pm, with sufficient demand. DM3.50 per ride, DM5 for two.) The well-heeled take the **taxi** from the station (DM3 per person, 4-person minimum). Another example of the strange interaction between cheesy technology and mountainsides is the **Seilbahn** (tel. 83 83), an 8-minute walk to the left from the train station (follow the signs). The lift will haul you up to mountaintop trails. (Open Easter-Oct. M-F 10am-6pm, Sa-Su 10am-7pm. DM3.50, children DM2; round-trip DM6, children DM3.) For less mechanical pleasures, sample the sweet juices of the Ahr through a *Weinprobe* (local wine tasting) at **Mayschoß-Altenahr,** on Tunnelstr. (Tel. 16 13. Open M-Sa 8am-noon and 1-6pm, Su 10am-6pm).

Information on hikes, lodgings, and train tickets is available at the **tourist office,** Altenburger 1a (tel. 84 48; fax 45 34), located in the train station. (Open M-W 10am-4pm, Th-F 10am-6pm, Su 11am-4pm.) The 24km *Rottweinwanderweg* begins here; follow the red grapes for a comprehensive tour of the valley. The **Jugendherberge Altenahr,** Langfigtal 8 (tel. 18 80), is in a nature reserve 20 minutes from town by foot. From the station, cross the bridge and turn right on Brückenstr., which becomes Tunnelstr. Don't go through the tunnel; as if on your way to grandmother's house, just go over the river and through the woods. Really. (DM21.30. Breakfast included. Reception daily 8am-10pm. Curfew 10pm, but you can get a key. Members only. Call ahead.) On the Ahr, the **Camping Schulz campground** (tel. 85 03) offers its bosom to your tired sole. Head right as you face the tracks, follow them on the footpath, and take a left when you come to the first road. The campground is on your right across the river. (DM7, children DM5. Tent DM5. Reception 8-10am and 3-5pm. Open Easter-Oct.) Altenahr is a virtual paradise for the wine imbiber and traditional food *bon vivant.* To stay within your budget without using a plastic *Imbiß* fork, visit **Ristorante Pizzeria Da Enzo,** Brückenstr. 9 (tel. 10 90). This friendly Italian joint sells great pizza (from DM7.50) and pasta (from DM8. Open M and W-Su 11:30am-2:30pm and 5-11pm.) Another option is **Im Weinhäuschen,** Brückenstr. 27 (tel. 31 15), a homely restaurant that serves savory specials for less than DM10, and potato pancakes with ambrosial apple sauce for a mere DM7. (Open daily 11am until bedtime.) The **telephone code** is 02643.

KOBLENZ

The etymology of "Koblenz," a corruption of Latin for "confluence," symbolizes the city's volatile history. Over the past 2,000 years, Rome, France, Prussia and Germany all fought to control this lovely city for its coveted location at the merger of the Mosel and the Rhein. Although wars of conquest have died down in recent years, the frenetic activity has not. Trains rattle along both sides of the river, and barges ringed by flirtatious speedboats plow through the water. For tourists, the rivers may be shining paths of history and legend, but they also serve as the conduits of modern German industry. Before reunification, the city served as the Republic's largest munitions dump; today, the pyrotechnics that light up the city are decorative, not destructive. During the annual **Rhein in Flammen** (Rhine in Flames) on August 12, 2000, the city is transformed into a fabulous flaming fiesta.

⛤ ORIENTATION AND PRACTICAL INFORMATION

Koblenz's sights cluster in the strip of Altstadt near the Mosel River between the **Deutsches Eck** (a spit of land jutting into the confluence of the Mosel and the Rhein, and the **Markt.** The train station lies far inland from either of the rivers, but busy **Löhrstr.** runs from it to the Markt, lined with shops, groceries, hotels, and eateries.

Trains: Koblenz lies along the line that connects Frankfurt to Köln. To Köln (1hr., 3-4 per hour, DM25), Mainz (1hr., 3 per hour, DM25), Trier (2hr., 1 per hour, DM30), and Frankfurt (2hr., 2 per hour, DM36).

Public Transportation: 10 main lines bus around the city and into the 'burbs for DM2.20-4.80 per ride. Day pass DM9. Tickets available from the driver. **Zentralplatz** offers the most convenient access to the Altstadt.

Taxi: Funk Taxi (tel. 330 55 or 194 10). Bring in da noise, bring in da...taxi.

Bike Rental: Biking the Rhein and Mosel is more satisfying than traveling by boat or train. See the pamphlet *Rund ums Rad,* sold in many bookstores, for detailed information. **Fahrradhaus Zangmeister,** Am Löhrrondell (tel. 323 63), offers bikes for DM10 per day. ID required. **Fahrrad Franz,** Hohenfelder Str. 7 (tel. 91 50 50), rents bikes for DM20 per day. Open M-F 9:30am-7pm, Sa 9:30am-4pm. **Vélo,** Konrad-Adenauer-Ufer 1 (tel. 151 02), and **Campingplatz Rhein Mosel** will outfit you for DM15 and DM10 per day, respectively.

Tourist Offices: The **main office,** Löhrstr. 141 (tel. 313 04; fax 100 43 88), a sharp left as you exit the train station, hands out boat schedules and city maps with hotel, restaurant, and pub listings. They find **rooms** (from DM60) for a steep 10% commission, so it may be better to check their free hotel listing yourself. Open M-F 9am-8pm, Sa-Su 10am-8pm. The **branch** located in the Rathaus offers the same services. (Tel. 13 09 20; fax 130 92 11. Open M-F 9am-8pm, Sa-Su 10am-8pm.)

Bookstore: Reuffel, Löhrstr. 90-92 (tel. 30 30 70), has lots of English paperbacks. Open M-W and F 9am-7pm, Th 9am-8pm, Sa 9am-4pm.

Laundromat: Wasch Center, on the corner of Rizzastr. and Löhrstr. Wash DM6, dry DM2 per 15min. Soap included. Open M-Sa 6am-midnight, last wash 11pm.

Emergency: Police, tel. 110. **Fire** and **Ambulance,** tel. 112.

Pharmacy: Rosen-Apotheke, Löhrstr. 139 (tel. 361 35), to the left when leaving the train station, posts a list in its front window of other pharmacies providing emergency services. Open M-F 8am-6:30pm, Sa 8:30am-1pm.

Post Office: Hauptpostamt, 65068 Koblenz, to the right of the train station exit. Open M-F 7am-7pm, Sa 7am-2pm.

PHONE CODE	0261

◤ ACCOMMODATIONS AND CAMPING

Since private rooms and most hotels in Koblenz are expensive, it may be worthwhile to trek across the river to the hostel. The difficult hike deters few, so call a day or two ahead.

Jugendherberge Koblenz (HI) (tel. 97 28 70; fax 972 87 30), in the *Festung* (see **Festung Ehrenbreitstein,** p. 380). For spectacular locations this hostel wins the prize; it yields a perfect view of Koblenz and much of the Rhein and Mosel valleys. Since inaccessibility was the fortress's *raison d'être,* however, getting there is less than half the fun, and may be a deterent for the travel-weary. Take bus #7, 8, or 8A from the stop across the street from the tourist office (direction: "Vallendar") to "Ehrenbreitstein Bf." if you intend to hike uphill. Continue along the Rhein side of the mountain on the main road following the *DJH* signs. Within minutes you'll come to a footpath leading to the *Festung* (20 min.). To ride the chairlift, take bus #9 or 10 from the tourist office to "Obertal." (Chairlift daily March-Sept. 9am-5:50pm. DM4, round-trip DM6; DM9 for non-hostel guests; includes *Festung* fee.) Fortunately, the hostel is friendly, clean, and worth the hike. DM24. Breakfast included. Dinner or lunch DM9, both DM15. Reception 7:30am-11:30pm. Curfew 11:30pm.

Hotel Jan van Werth, Van-Werth-Str. 9 (tel. 365 00; fax 365 06). This classy family-run establishment is among the best values in Koblenz. From the station, walk through Bahnhofplatz to Emil-Schuller-Str. on your left. At the end, take a left onto Hohenzollernstr. and then another left onto Van-Werth-Str. Singles from DM40, with shower and toilet DM75; doubles DM85-100, with shower and toilet DM120. Gummi bears and large breakfast buffet included. Reception 6:30am-10pm.

Hotel Sessellift, Obertal 22 (tel. 752 56; fax 768 72), directly across from the "Obertal" bus stop. Friendly staff and bright, clean rooms. DM40 per person. Breakfast included.

Camping: Campingplatz Rhein-Mosel, Am Neuendorfer Eck (tel. 827 19), across the Mosel from the Deutsches Eck. A ferry crosses the river in the day (DM0.60). DM6.50 per person. DM5 per tent. Reception 8am-noon and 2-8pm. Open April-Oct. 15.

◖▨ FOOD AND NIGHTLIFE

Koblenz's multinational origins found culinary expression as well, and the city is never at a loss for dining options. For **groceries,** head to **Plus,** Roonstr. 49-51. (Open M-F 8:30am-7pm and Sa 8am-2pm.) **Theater tickets** can be purchased from the box office in the Rathaus branch of the tourist office. (Tel. 129 16 10. Open M-F 9am-8pm, Sa-Su 10am-8pm.)

Marktstübchen, Am Markt 220 (tel. 755 65), at the bottom of the hill from the hostel, though the clientele seems to have never seen a hosteler. Authenticity's last stand, this joint serves *real* German food for *real* budget prices. Most entrees under DM11. Open M-Tu, Th, and Sa-Su 11am-midnight, W 11am-2pm, F 4pm-1am.

Salatgarten (tel. 364 55), where Casinostr. becomes Gymnasialstr. in the Altstadt just off Zentralplatz. Arteries (and taste buds) cry out for the vegetarian wonders that crop up here. Good salad bar. Self-service keeps prices low. Daily specials DM8-9. Open M-F 9:30am-6pm, Sa 9:30am-4pm.

RHEINLAND-PFALZ

Altes Brauhaus, Braugasse 4 (tel. 15 10 01), in the shadow of the Liebfrauenkirche. Popular with locals and tourists, the pub dishes out German food (around DM15) and home brew. Open M-Sa 10:30am-10pm. Kitchen open 11:30am-2:30pm and 5:30-10pm.

Rizza Obst & Gemüse, Rizzastr. 49, has an assortment of drinks, fresh fruit, and veggies. Open M-F 7:30am-7pm, Sa 7:30am-4pm.

Café Galleria Bistro & Pizzeria, Bahnhofplatz (tel. 337 58), near Hohenstaufenstr. Delicious pizzas and pastas from DM7. Open daily 10am-midnight.

Tatort, Münzplatz 15 (tel. 42 19). Grungy rock and roll bar that occasionally usurps Münzplatz as a stage for local bands. Open daily 6pm-late.

Atelier Filmtheater, Löhrstr. 88 (tel. 311 88), has weekly English-language screenings. DM12, students DM9.

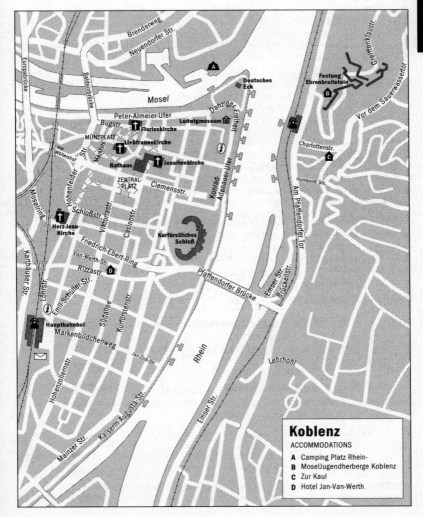

Koblenz

ACCOMMODATIONS

A Camping Platz Rhein-
B Mosel Jugendherberge Koblenz
C Zur Kaul
D Hotel Jan-Van-Werth

RHEINLAND-PFALZ

SIGHTS

DEUTSCHES ECK. German nationalism, along with Germany's two greatest rivers, converges at the Deutsches Eck (German Corner). A peninsula at the confluence of the Rhein and Mosel, it purportedly witnessed the birth of the German nation in 1216 when the Teutonic Order of Knights settled here. Today, the **Mahnmal der Deutschen Einheit** (Monument to German Unity) stands on the right, commemorating a rather different sort of union. Erected in 1897, it stands in tribute to Kaiser Wilhelm I for forcibly reconciling the internal conflicts of the German Empire (though the Kaiser played second fiddle to Bismarck; see p. 10). The 14m-tall equestrian statue of the Kaiser that once topped the monument was toppled in 1945. In a move that raised questions about German aesthetic sensibilities, not to mention resurgent nationalism, the statue was replaced by a duplicate in 1993.

BLUMENHOF. Behind the Mahnmal, in the beautiful, unassuming flower garden, lurks more blatant national *braggadocio*, though this time not on the Germans' part. Napoleon erected the fountain to commemorate the "certain impending victory" in his Russian campaign. The Russians, after routing the French army, added the mocking inscription "seen and approved."

CHURCHES. Attractions of a less fervent sort can be found in the many churches of Koblenz's Altstadt, within a few blocks of the Markt, many of which were restored after WWII. The 12th-century **Florinskirche** lost some of its luster in the 19th-century wars when Napoleon used it as a military encampment. *(Open daily 11am-5pm.)* The oval Baroque towers of the **Liebfrauenkirche** rise nearby. The church's emerald and sapphire stained glass and intricate ceiling latticework are stunning; the choir windows document the role of women in the Passion and Salvation of Christ. *(Open M-Sa 8am-6pm, Su 9am-12:30pm and 6pm-8pm.)* The masterful *Rheinisch* facade of the **Jesuitenkirche** on the Marktplatz conceals a startlingly modern interior. *(Open daily 7am-6pm.)* Koblenz's most mischievous monument lurks outside; the **Schängelbrunnen,** a statue of a boy that spits water on passersby, drives kids into frenzied glee.

FESTUNG EHRENBREITSTEIN. If ground-level viewing has got you down, head to Festung Ehrenbreitstein, a fortress at the highest point in the city. The Prussians used it to accommodate French troops in past centuries; today, the German state uses it to accommodate *you* (see **Jugendherberge Koblenz,** p. 378). *(Non-hostel guests DM2; students DM1.)*

MUSEUMS

MUSEUM LUDWIG IM DEUTSCHHERRENHAUS. The hilarious bronze sculpture in the courtyard gives this collection a well-deserved thumbs up! Mostly contemporary French art, but expect anything and everything in their continuously changing special exhibits. *(Danziger Freiheit 1. Tel. 30 40 40. Behind the Mahnmal. Open Tu-Sa 10:30am-5pm, Su 11am-6pm. DM5, students DM3.)*

MITTELRHEINMUSEUM. Contains three floors of art, much of which focuses on the painterly landscapes of the Rhein Gorge. *(Next door to the Florinskirche. Open Tu-Sa 10:30am-5pm, Su 11am-6pm. DM5, students DM3.)*

LANDESMUSEUM KOBLENZ. Exhibits include antique automobiles, cannons, wine, tobacco, and guns. A dangerous combination. Alas, no live ammo or tasty samples. *(Hohe Ostfront, in Festung Ehrenbreitstein. Tel. 970 30. Open mid-March to mid-Nov. M-Sa 9am-5pm, Su 10am-5:30 pm. Last entrance 15min. before closing. DM3, students DM2.)*

RHEINMUSEUM. A private museum devoted to all things *Rheinisch,* four floors of maritime history including old boats, engines, and fish. *(Charlottenstr. 53a. Tel. 70 34 50. Bus #9 or 10 to "Charlottenstr." Open daily 10am-5pm. DM5, children DM3.)*

RHEINTAL (RHINE VALLEY)

At present, the sun and moon alone cast their light upon these old buildings famed in story and gnawed by time, whose walls are falling stone by stone into the Rhein, and whose history is fast fading into oblivion. O noble tower! O poor, paralyzed giants! A steamboat packed with travelers now spews its smoke in your faces!

—Victor Hugo

Though the Rhein River runs all the way from Switzerland to the North Sea, the Rhein of the imagination exists only in the 80km of the gorge stretching from Bonn to north of Mainz. As the river rolls out to sea, treacherous whirlpools and craggy shores surround the castles of aristocrats. This is the Rhein of sailors' nightmares, poets' dreams, and the rhetorical storms of nationalism. From the famed Lorelei cliffs, legendary sirens lured passing sailors to their deaths on the rocks below. Heinrich Heine immortalized the spot with his 1823 poem "Die Lorelei," but he can hardly claim sole credit for the literary resonance felt along the river. The renown of Rhein wines from the hillside vineyards have inspired many a lesser illusion.

Two different train lines (one on each bank) traverse this fabled stretch; the line on the west bank that runs between Koblenz and Mainz sticks closer to the water and provides superior views. If you're willing to put up with lots of tourists, the best way to see the sights is probably by boat. **Köln-Düsseldorfer (KD) Line** (p. 429) covers the Mainz-Koblenz stretch three times per day during the summer, while more frequent excursions travel along shorter stretches of the river.

LORELEI CLIFFS AND CASTLES

The mythic distortion of the Rhein explodes into rocky frenzy along the cliffs of the **Lorelei.** This section of the river, with its switchbacks and boulders, was so difficult to navigate that a sailors' song, immortalized by the poet Heinrich Heine, developed about the siren *Lorelei*, who seduced sailors with her intoxicating song and drew them into the rocks. Protected by the plush interiors and tinted windows of the ubiquitous *Loreley Express* tour buses, most of today's Rhein travelers avoid such grim fates. Near the cliffs and the beloved statue of the maiden siren are the towns **St. Goarshausen** and **St. Goar,** on either side of the Rhein. **St. Goarshausen,** on the east bank, provides access by foot to the statue and the infamous cliffs. Facing the Rhein, follow Rheinstr. left past the last houses and to the peninsula on which the statue rests. To reach the cliffs, take the stairs across the street from the beginning of the peninsula (45min.).

Directly above St. Goarshausen, the fierce **Burg Katz** (Cat Castle) eternally stalks its prey, the smaller **Burg Maus** (Mouse Castle). Fortunately, the mouse escapes a Kafka-esque fate by hiding away upstream in the Wellmich district of Goarshausen. Though neither castle's interior is open to tourists, Burg Maus offers spectacular falconry demonstrations daily at 11am and 2:30pm. Call 76 69 for information, or visit St. Goarshausen's **tourist office,** Bahnhofstr. 8. (Tel. 91 00; fax 910 15. Open M-F 9am-1pm and 2-5:30pm, Sa 9:30am-noon.) Two minutes from the Lorelei Cliffs, the hostel **Jugendheim Loreley** (tel. 26 19; fax 81 89) lures travelers in with the friendly ditties of hip hostelers, only to drown them in crashing waves of schoolchildren. From the cliffs, walk past the red and white parking gate down the road a few hundred meters and take a left. (DM23.50. Breakfast included. Curfew 10pm.) Back in town, face the Rhein and go right on Rheinstr. and then Rheinpromenade to get to **Campingplatz Loreleystadt** (tel. 25 92), an eight-minute walk from the station. (DM8.50. Tent DM5.) The **telephone code** is 06771.

A ferry crosses the river to and from **St. Goar** (7 per hour, last ferry 11pm, round-trip DM2.50.), which provides a pleasant base for Lorelei explorations. The view from the cliffs on the eastern side is spectacular, and **Burg Rheinfels** (tel. 383) is dazzling. Tour the sprawling, half-ruined castle and its underground passageways by flashlight (DM5)—it doesn't get more *romantisch* than this. (Open daily 9am-6pm; last entrance 5pm. DM5, students and children DM3. Candle rental DM1.) St.

Goar's **tourist office,** Heerstr. 6 (tel. 383; fax 72 09), is in the pedestrian zone. (Open M–F 8am-12:30pm and 2-5pm, Sa 10am-noon.) The town has a convenient **Jugendherberge (HI),** Bismarckweg 17 (tel. 388; fax 28 69), 10 minutes from the station. With your back to the tracks, follow Oberstr. left and veer left on Schloßberg; Bismarckweg is the next right. (DM22. Breakfast and sheets included. Reception 5-6pm and 7-8pm. Curfew 10pm, but you can get a key.) **Hotel Hauser** (tel. 333; fax 14 64), on Marktpl., offers spotless, relaxing rooms at cheap prices. (Singles DM44, with bath DM55-75; doubles DM88-130. Breakfast included.) St. Goar's **postal code** is 56329. The **telephone code** is 06741.

BACHARACH

Bounded by a lush park on the river, a resilient town wall, and dramatically sloping vineyards, Bacharach maintains the kind of low profile coveted by glamour queens, B-movie has-beens, and royalty. All the sequestering has paid off—this hidden gem retains an irrepressible sense of identity in the face of increasing tourist traffic—exactly what the world needs now. The village's name is derived from the fact that it was once home to an altar stone to Bacchus. Like any holy city, Bacharach fills with pilgrims who come from near and far to worship dutifully at the town's numerous **Weinkeller** and **Weinstuben** (wine cellars and pubs), scattered throughout the impeccably preserved original half-timbered houses. Find love, sweet love, at **Die Weinstube,** behind the stunning **Altes Haus** in the center of town on Oberstr. Also accessible from Oberstr. is the 14th-century **Wernerkapelle,** ghost-like remains of a red sandstone chapel that took 140 years to build but only a few hours to destroy in the Palatinate War of Succession in 1689. It's a short climb up the steps next to the late-Romanesque **Peterskirche.**

The **tourist office,** Oberstr. 45 (tel. 91 93 13; fax 91 93 14), in the post office, a five-minute walk up to the right from the station, provides hiking maps. (Open April-Sept. M-F 9am-5pm, Sa 10am-1pm; Oct.-March M-F 9am-12:30pm and 1:30-5pm, Sa 10am-1pm.) Hostels get *no* better than the unbelievable **Jugendherberge Stahleck (HI)** (tel. 12 66; fax 26 84), a gorgeous 12th-century castle that provides an unbeatable panoramic view of the Rhein Valley for its 40,000 yearly visitors. Painstaking thought has gone into the minutest details of the hostel, from the individually named rooms (you might stay in *Falcon's Nest* or *Castle View*) to the great selection of local wines in the bar downstairs and the cheerful plaid sheets on your bed. The steep, exhausting 20-minute hike to the hostel is worth every step. Call ahead; they're usually full by 6pm. From the station, turn left at the Peterskirche and take any of the marked paths leading up the hill. (DM25.20. Breakfast included. Dinner buffet DM9.50. Curfew 10pm.) For those weary of uphill treks, the dynamic mother and son Dettmar duo run two centrally located pensions. Frau Dettmar runs clean **Haus Dettmar,** on Oberstr. 8. (tel./fax 26 61). Son Jürgen operates **Pension Ferienwohnungen** (tel. 17 15; fax 29 79) in an even better location. (It's all in the family; rates are the same at both Dettmar outposts. Singles DM55, doubles DM50-70.) Turn right from the station (heading downhill towards the river), then walk south for 10 minutes to reach **Campingplatz Bacharach** (tel. 17 52), to camp directly on the Rhein. (DM8 per person. Tent DM5.) The price is right at the uniquely named **Café Restaurant,** on Oberstr. 40, where three-course meals go for DM12-20, while smaller meals are DM5-12.50. The **telephone code** is 06743.

RÜDESHEIM

Seen from opposite the Rhein, Rüdesheim is a romantic's dream come true. Terraced vineyards stretch steeply up from the tiny town framed by two stone castles. Across the river, however, commercialism has found a home in the heart of town. Rüdesheim's location in the center of the Rheingau wine-producing region has made the town a tourist magnet. The picturesque 12th-century **Brömserburg,** Rheinstr. 2, like the rest of Rüdesheim, now succumbs to Bacchanalian indulgence—it's a **wine museum** (tel. 23 48) five minutes from the station and the ferry docks toward town along Rheinstr. (Open daily March to Nov. 9am-6pm. Last admission 5:15pm. DM5, students and children DM3.) The fortress boasts an eclectic architecture from the Middle Ages through Art Deco. Servings of kitsch are available along nearby **Drosselgasse,** a tiny alley where merchants peddle fake cuckoo clocks, lots of wine, and plenty of "authenticity." Up Drosselgasse to the left are signs for **Siegfrieds Mechanisches Musikkabinett,** Oberstr. 29 (tel. 492 17), a museum of automatic musical instruments with one of the largest collections of music boxes and player pianos in the world. (Open March-Nov. daily 10am-10pm. Obligatory tours every 15min. DM9, students DM5.) The **Mittelalterliches Foltermuseum,** Grabenstr. 13 (tel. 475 10), displays medieval devices prisoners endured to "salvage" their souls. (Open daily April-Nov. 10am-6pm. DM7, students DM6.) Eighty instruments as well as paintings and drawings provide a grisly exhibition.

The **Niederwalddenkmal,** a 38m monument crowned by the unnervingly nationalistic figure of *Germania* wielding a 1400kg sword, looms high above town. Erected to commemorate the establishment of the Second Reich in 1871, the central frieze features legions of 19th-century aristocrats pledging loyalty to the Kaiser flanked by winged emblems of war and peace. A **chairlift** *(Seilbahn)* runs from the top of Christoffelstr. (Open mid-March to mid-Nov. daily 9:30am-5:30pm. DM6.50, round-trip DM10.) Take a left directly before the tourist office. To reach the monument by foot, take Oberstr. from the station to a parking lot, then follow Kuhweg into the vineyards and any desired path towards the memorial.

The **tourist office,** Rheinstr. 16 (tel. 29 62; fax 34 85), is perched along the river. The staff books **rooms** (DM40-50) for a 10-12% fee. The **post office,** towards Brömserburg on Rheinstr., has an **ATM.** (Open M-F 8:30am-noon and 2:30 5pm, Sa 8:30-11:30am.) The **telephone code** is 06722. The **Jugendherberge (HI),** Am Kreuzberg (tel. 27 11; fax 482 84), is in the vineyards high above the town, but the

The Rhine

TO DÜSSELDORF

Köln (Cologne)

Bonn

THE RHINE

Sieg

Königswinter

Drachenfels

Altenahr

Bad Neuenahr

Bad Honnef

Remagen

Unkel

Ahrweiler

Erpel

Ahr

Linz

Ahrenfels

Bad Hönningen

Rhein

Neuwied

Koblenz

Deutsches Eck

Burg Eltz

Moselkern

Mosel

Lahnstein

Braubach

Lahn

LAHN VALLEY

Boppard

Bad Salzig

Burg Maus

GORGE

Burg Rheinfels

St. Goarshausen

St. Goar

Burg Katz

Lorelei

Burg Stahleck

Bacharach

Lorch

Burg Rheinstein

Assmannshausen

Burg Klopp

Rüdesheim

Wiesbaden

Bingen

Rhein

N

0   10 miles

0   10 kilometers

Mainz

25-minute walk through flowers, vines, and silence is aesthetically rewarding. Call ahead—they're often booked solid. From the station, walk down Rheinstr. and make a left on any street that catches your fancy. At Oberstr., turn right and bear left at the fork onto Germaniastr. and follow it to Kuhweg and the *Jugendherberge* signs. (DM22, over 26 DM27. Sheets DM6. Breakfast included. Reception 8-9am, 1-2pm, and 5-9pm. Curfew 11:30pm. Members only.) **Campingplatz am Rhein** (tel. 25 28) has prime riverside real estate for those with portable roofs. From the station, walk past town along the Rhein to the campsite. (DM7 per person. Tents DM8.40. Reception 8am-10pm. Open May-Sept.)

BINGEN

Caught at the junction between the Nahe and the Rhein, this little hillside town and one-time home of cult figure **Hildegard von Bingen** has long been overshadowed by its neighbor Rüdesheim. For those weary of tourists, however, Bingen offers a calm respite. On an island near the village of Bingen, downstream from Rüdesheim, the **Mäuseturm** (Mouse Tower) leans over the winding Rhein. According to legend, during a famine Archbishop (and arch-villain) **Hatto II** of Mainz was threatened by starving peasants demanding the food he hoarded. He proceeded to lock them up in a barn and set it on fire. Hearing their shrieks of pain, the sadistic Hatto cackled, "listen to my mice squeaking." Suddenly, a horde of mice rushed out of the barn, chased him into the tower, and ate him alive. The town's main daytime attraction, **Burg Klopp** (tel. 18 40), is five minutes from the tourist office through maze-like streets. The Burg hosts the **Heimatmuseum** (tel. 18 41 10), displaying third-century Roman milestones and a view from the top of its tower. (Open April-Oct. Tu-Su 9am-noon and 2-5pm. DM1, students DM0.50.)

The **tourist office**, Rheinkai 21 (tel. 18 42 05; fax 162 75), books **rooms** (from DM31) for a DM3 fee and offers a wealth of information on the 20km of hiking through the surrounding **Bingerwald**. From the station, stick by the tracks as they head east to Rheinkai, or get off at the Bingen station and head toward town for five minutes. (Open April-Nov. M-F 9am-6pm, Sa 9am-12:30pm; Dec.-March M-Th 9am-12:30pm and 1:30-4pm, F 9am-1pm.) Several **ferries** cross the river to Rüdesheim. (Every 40min.; DM2, round-trip DM3.) The ubiquitous **Kölner-Düsseldorfer** ferry sails to Koblenz (4 per day, DM42.40) and Bacharach (5 per day, DM18.80). The **Bingen-Rüdesheimer** ferry offers the best buy on Rhein cruises to Bacharach (DM12, students DM8.40) and St. Goar (DM19, students DM13.30). For a **taxi** call 356 49. The **telephone code** is 06721.

To get to the **Jugendherberge Bingen-Bingerbrück**, Herterstr. 51 (tel. 321 63; fax 340 12), follow the signs from the station (10min.). The hostel perches high on a hill and offers a great view, clean bedrooms, and a helpful staff. (DM21.30, with 2 meals DM30, with 3 meals DM34.50. Breakfast and sheets included. Check-in 5-10pm. Curfew 10pm.) **Hotel Hans Clara**, Rheinkai 3 (tel./fax 92 18 80), offers clean rooms in the middle of town. (Singles from DM50, doubles from DM90. Closed W.) **Prina's Pizzeria**, Fruchtmarktstr. 8, serves pizza and pasta for less than DM7. (Open M and W-Su 11:30am-2pm and 5pm-midnight.) **Pallazzo**, Rheinufer (tel. 100 32), Bingen's renowned mega-disco, resembles a yellow train station, attracting revelers from all along the Valley. The disco is right on the river—you can't miss it. Hours often change, but the party's always pumping Friday and Saturday from 9pm to 7am. (Cover from DM15.)

MAINZ

As the capital of Rheinland-Pfalz, Mainz has metamorphosed into a modern metropolis, but the monumental Dom and the maze of minuscule streets in the Altstadt are still the center of the city. Mainz seamlessly meshes its concrete and cobblestone; since the 1450s, when native son Johannes Gutenberg invented the printing press, Mainz has been at the center of Germany's media industry. Throughout 2000, Mainz offers events and exhibitions to celebrate the 600th anniversary of the famed printer's birth.

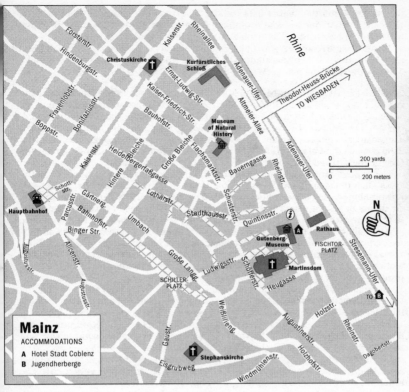

Mainz

ACCOMMODATIONS

A Hotel Stadt Coblenz
B Jugendherberge

🔼 **ORIENTATION AND PRACTICAL INFORMATION.** Streets running parallel to the Rhein sport blue nameplates, while streets running perpendicular to the river bear red ones. Mainz shares a transportation system with Wiesbaden, making daytrips easy. (To Wiesbaden, streetcar #8 runs 3 per hour on weekdays, 2 per hour on weekends.) The **Köln-Düsseldorf ferries** (tel. 23 28 00; fax 23 28 60) dock in Mainz and depart from the wharfs on the other side of the Rathaus. The **tourist office** (tel. 28 62 10; fax 286 21 55) doles out free maps and reserves **rooms** (from DM50) for a DM5 fee. (Open M-F 9am-6pm, Sa 9am-1pm.) **Tours** leave from the Markt near the Dom. (1½hr., July-Aug. daily 2pm, DM10.) The tourist office also sells the **Mainzcard**, which offers museum admission, public transportation, and hotel discounts for one day (DM10). Mainz's **AIDS-Hilfe** hotline (tel. 22 22 75) has the scoop on gay and lesbian life in the city. The **post office**, 55001 Mainz, is down Bahnhofstr. from the station. (Open M-F 8am-6pm, Sa 8:30am-12:30pm.) The **telephone code** is 06131.

📷🛏 **ACCOMMODATIONS AND FOOD.** Mainz's **Jugendgästehaus (HI)**, Otto-Brunfels-Schneise 4 (tel. 853 32; fax 824 22), is in Weisenau in a corner of the Volkspark. Take bus #22 to "Jugendherberge/Viktorstift." The renovated model hostel has clean rooms with private bath. (Doubles DM39; quads DM29. Reception 7am-midnight. Wheelchair accessible.) **Hotel Stadt Koblenz**, Rheinstr. 49 (tel. 22 76 02), has inexpensive, finely furnished rooms across the street from the Rathaus and within sight of the Dom. Take your choice of several buses to "Rheingoldhalle." (Singles DM75, with shower and bathroom DM100; doubles DM100, which shower and bathroom DM130; triples DM150. Breakfast included.)

Near the Dom, the **Central Café** (tel. 22 56 66), on the corner of Rheinstr. and Heugasse, cooks burgers and traditional German fare for less than DM15. (Open M-Th and Su 10am-1am, F-Sa 10am-2am). **Taverne Academica** (tel. 38 58 50), the university's "friendly bar," lives up to its slogan, serving good, cheap food and drink to a student crowd. All entrees under DM10. Take the bus to "Universität" and make a left. (Open M-F 10am-late, Sa noon-3pm and 7pm-late.)

⚅ **SIGHTS.** At the heart of Mainz lies the colossal sandstone **Martinsdom**, the resting place of the archbishops of Mainz whose extravagant tombstones line the walls. (Open April-Sept. M-F 9am-6:30pm, Sa 9am-4pm, Su 12:45-3pm and 4-6:30pm; Oct.-March M-F 9am-5pm, Sa 9am-4pm, Su 12:45-3pm and 4-5pm. Free.) The adjacent **Diözesanmuseum** houses changing exhibitions, though until April 15, 2000 it holds the **Gutenberg** exhibit due to construction on the Gutenberg museum (see below). (Open Tu-Sa 9am-5pm, Su 11am-6pm. Prices vary.)

The Altstadt stretches behind the Dom for a few blocks in and around Augustinerstr. On a hill several blocks south stands the Gothic **Stephanskirche**, notable for its stunning stained-glass windows created by Russian artist-in-exile **Marc Chagall**. On sunny days, the windows bathe the church in eerie blue light.From the Dom, take Ludwigstr. until it ends at Schillerpl. and follow Gaustr. up to the church. (Open daily 10am-noon and 2-5pm. Free.) Johannes Gutenberg, the father of movable type, is immortalized at the **Gutenbergmuseum**, Liebfrauenpl. 5. (tel. 12 26 40), contains several **Gutenberg Bibles**, a replica of his original press, an impressive collection of text art, early Asian calligraphy, and several other relics of the early printing industry. (Exhibit housed in Diözesanmuseum until April 15. Open Tu-Sa 10am-6pm, Su 10am-1pm. DM5, students DM2.50; Su free.) Near the museum, the very cool **experimental print shop**, Fischtorstr. 2 (tel. 12 26 86), lets visitors try their luck at Gutenberg's craft by setting and printing their own designs. (Open M-F 10am-5pm, Sa 11am-2pm. Free.) North of the museum on Rheinstr. is the **Brückenturm-Galerie** (tel. 12 25 22), a modern art museum that displays the works of regional artists. (Open Tu-F 11am-6pm, Sa-Su 11am-2pm.)

North of Marktpl. on Christophstr. is the **Pfarrkirche St. Christoph**, a half-ruined church that brings a poignant reminder of war to an otherwise gilded city. The reputed site of Gutenberg's baptism, the church was seriously damaged in WWII; the tower is still used for services, but the main body lies in ruins. (Open M-F 8:30am-4:30pm.) Along the river near the Theodor-Heuss-Brücke rests the **Kurfürstliches Schloß**, former palace of the archbishop. A comprehensive collection of art and archaeology, including a Judaica division and enormous Roman arches, awaits in the **Landesmuseum**, up the street at Große Bleiche 49-51. (Open Tu 10am-8pm, W-Su 10am-5pm. DM5, students DM3; Sa free.)

◩ **NIGHTLIFE. KUZ (Kulturzentrum)**, Dagobertstr. 20b (tel. 28 68 60), is Mainz's standard, eternally hip disco. Take bus #1 or 37 to "Holzturm/Fort-Malakoff-Park," face the shopping center across the street, and turn right. Walk one and a half blocks and turn left on Dagobertstr. (Open W 9pm-3am and F-Sa 10pm-4am. Cover DM8.) **Lindenbaum**, Holzstr. 32 (tel. 22 71 31), pleases with diverse dance tunes for the multi-aged crowd. Oldies on Mondays and classic rock on Wednesdays attract disco-dinosaurs, while the younger divas make appearances on all other days (grunge, indie, punk, industrial). Take bus #1 or 37 to "Holzturm/Fort-Malakoff-Park." Turn right on Holzstr. (Open Su-W 8pm-3am, Th 8pm-4am, F-Sa 8pm-5am.) During the third weekend in June, Mainz celebrates **Johannisnacht**—three days of old-fashioned revelry dedicated to Gutenberg (June 24-26, 2000). Movable type and Bacchanalian revelry do not easily combine, but Mainz manages it in high style.

MOSELTAL (MOSEL VALLEY)

Trying to avoid its inevitable surrender to the Rhein at Koblenz, the Mosel River slowly meanders past the sun-drenched hills, pretty towns, and ancient castles of the softly cut Moseltal. The headwaters of the Mosel flow from the Vosges Mountains of France, following a northeasterly course that winds over 200km of German territory from Trier to Koblenz. The slopes aren't quite as steep as the Rhein's narrow gorge, but the countless less-touristed vineyards of the gentle hillsides have been pressing quality vintages since the Romans first cultivated the vines 2,000 years ago. The only local complaints heard about the region is that summers are too dry (the least of worries for a visitor) and the winters too wet. For a few days, the mellow Mosel goes berserk, flooding and making the valley Venetian.

The best way to view the valley's scenery is by boat, bus, or bicycle; the train line between Koblenz and Trier strays frequently from the course of the river, cutting through the unremarkable countryside. Although passenger boats no longer make the complete Koblenz-Trier run, several companies run daily trips along shorter stretches in summer.

COCHEM

Like so many German wine-making villages, the hamlet of Cochem has become a repository of German nostalgia, its quintessential quaintness voraciously eaten up by busloads of elderly German city-dwellers. Despite their presence, Cochem's impressive vineyard-covered hills and sparkling **Reichsburg** (tel. 255) simply can't be cheapened into run-of-the-mill tourist fodder. Perched high atop a hill adjacent to the village, the castle's elaborately painted turrets lend the town a pleasant fairy tale quality enhanced by gnarled streets lined with clapboard houses.

Originally built in the 11th century, the castle was destroyed in 1689 by French troops under Louis XIV; in 1868, a wealthy Berlin merchant rebuilt it in neo-Gothic style. The view from the castle grounds alone warrants the 15-minute climb along Schloßstr. from the Marktplatz. Unfortunately, a peek into the castle's opulent interior can be taken today only as part of a guided tour. (Open daily mid-March to Oct. 9am-5pm. Frequent 40min. tours; written English translations available. DM7, students DM6, children DM3.) Take the tiny lane to the left as you walk down from the castle to the 15th-century **Peterskapelle**, enclosed by high walls and the ubiquitous vine-covered trellises. The other popular hillside attraction in town is the **Sesselbahn** (tel. 98 90 63) on Edenstr., a chair lift that runs to the **Pinnerkreuz**, a lone cross standing on a high peak illuminated by 10,000-watt bulbs at night. (Lift runs daily April to mid-Nov. 9:30am-dusk. One-way DM7, round-trip DM9.50; children DM3.20 and DM4.50, respectively). For even more theme-park style thrills 'n' spills, head across the river and follow the *Freizeitzentrum* signs to reach the gigantic **Moselbad** (tel. 979 90), a sprawling complex of pools, saunas, jacuzzis, and waterslides located five minutes north of the Nordbrücke, the bridge near the train station. (Open M 2-10pm, Tu and Th 9am-10pm, W and F 10am-10pm, Sa-Su 10am-7pm. Day ticket DM21, students DM15, ages 6-11 DM10.60, under 6 free. Outdoor pool only DM5, students DM3.)

Unlike much of the Mosel Valley, Cochem is easily accessible by **train** from Koblenz (1hr., 2 per hour, DM12), and Trier (1hr., 2 per hour, DM17). Although Cochem is equidistant to the two cities, the route to Koblenz hugs the Mosel, making for some spectacular views; the trip to Trier traverses serene but non-fantastic countryside. The Moselbahn **bus** service links DB trains to the rest of the Mosel Valley in **Bullay**, a town one stop away from Cochem (10min., 2 per hour, DM4.60). The **tourist office,** Endertplatz 1 (tel. 600 40; fax 60 04 44), next to the bridge, books **rooms** (from DM30) for free. From the train station, go to the river and turn right. (Open May-June M-Th and Sa 10am-5pm, F 10am-7pm; July-Oct. M-Th and Sa 10am-5pm, F 10am-7pm, Su 10am-noon; Nov.-April M-Th 10am-5pm, F 10am-7pm.) Along the way, you'll pass **Fahrrad-Shop Kreutz** (tel. 911 31), behind the Shell gas station along the river, which rents an array of **bikes.** (DM14 per day, DM70 per week. Open M-F 9am-6pm, Sa 9am-1pm. Passport required.) The **post office** is at the corner of Ravenestr. and Josefstr., one block from Endenplatz. (Open M-F 8am-5pm, Sa 8am-noon.) The **telephone code** is 02671.

Cochem's friendly, basic **Jugendherberge (HI),** Klottener Str. 9 (tel. 86 33; fax 85 68), is 15 minutes from the train station on the opposite shore. Cross the Nordbrücke to the left as you exit the station; the youth hostel is next to the bridge on the right. Beware the echoes that make schoolchildren seem much louder than usual. (DM22, with dinner DM32. Breakfast and sheets included. Reception daily noon-1pm and 5-10pm. Curfew 10pm, but they'll give you a key with a DM10 deposit.) If you've got your own portable party palace, walk down the path below the hostel to the **Campingplatz am Freizeitzentrum** (tel. 44 09) on Stadionstr. (DM6.50 per person, DM6-12 per tent. Wash and dry DM1.50. Bike rental DM14 per day. Reception 8am-10pm. Open Easter-Oct.) At the cheesy, good-hearted **Weinhexenkeller** (tel. 977 60), on Hafenstr. across the Moselbrücke, indulge in food (DM8-14) and divine Mosel wine. Local legend says that guests who imbibe too much fall under a witch's spell. Modern science says they become drunk. Either way, you'll have a perfect excuse to go nuts when the live music kicks in at 7pm. (Open daily 11am-2am.) **La Baia Ristorante Pizzeria,** Liniusstr. 4 (tel. 80 40), on the train station side of the Mosel near the Moselbrücke, serves excellent pizza (from DM6.50) and pasta (from DM7.50) on a nice second-floor terrace. The **Weinwoche** begins a week and a half after Pentecostal Monday and features some of the Mosel's finest vintages (DM1-2 per 100ml taste). During the last weekend in August, the **Heimat-und-Weinfest** culminates in a dramatic fireworks display.

BURG ELTZ

Originally constructed in the 11th and 12th centuries, **Burg Eltz** (tel. (02672) 95 05 00; fax 950 50 50; www.burg-eltz.de) is one of the only remaining intact Medieval castles in the Rheinland. The Burg rests on a small hill in a lush valley, belying its function as a fortress for the three branches of the Eltz family. Nature conspired in the defense: the Eltz brook flows on either side of the Burg's hill, providing a natural moat, while the sheltering woods were once favored hunting grounds. The Eltz party was crashed, however, in the 1330s by Baldwin, Elector of Trier, Eltz being the only thing between him and the Rhein. Two years and a lot of rock-slinging later, the Eltz family surrendered to Baldwin's terms: they retained possession of the castle as his minions…uh, vassals. But the arrangement was successful, because what now exists of the Burg was constructed mostly during the 15th century.

The castle's interior can only be seen by tour. Two 15th-century Flemish tapestries, called *verdures* for their dominant greenish hues, give the artist's fantastical rendering of the new animals described by explorers of the Americas and Africa. Sharing the room with these glorified rugs is Lucas Cranach the Elder's *Madonna with Grapes.* Various ornate and dazzling gold and silver pieces both functional and decorative are locked away in the **Schatzkammer** (treasure room), which is not part of the tour. (Open daily April-Oct. 9:30am-5:30pm. Tours every 15min.; English tours are given only upon sufficient demand, typically once an hour. DM9, students DM6, *Schatzkammer* DM4.) A café with outdoor patio sells generous, German-style snacks.

The nearest town to Burg Eltz accessible by **train** is **Moselkern.** Trains from Cochem run hourly (15min., DM5.80). From the town, the Burg is a pleasant one-hour walk. With your back to the train station, head right on Oberstr. through town until it passes under a bridge and becomes a slightly winding backwoods road along the Eltz brook. The road ends at **Ringelsteiner Mühle**—from here the path through the woods is well marked. The train station information center stores luggage. (Open M-F 5am-10pm, Sa-Su 5:40am-10pm.)

BEILSTEIN

A tiny hamlet of half-timbered houses, crooked cobblestone streets, and about 170 residents, Beilstein takes pride in being the smallest official town in Germany (it received town rights in 1319). Spared in WWII, Beilstein's untarnished beauty has made it the idyllic backdrop of several movies and political summits. Once upon a time, Adenauer and DeGespari created the European Economic Community (now the European Union) here. By day, Beilstein's natural charm draws a tourist crowd that exponentially increases its population, yet after 6pm, the spell breaks, and the peaceful town is yours. **Burg Metternich** is the resident castle; the French sacked it in 1689, but the view is still spectacular. (Open daily April-Oct. 9am-6pm. DM3, students DM2, children DM1.) Also worth a look is the Baroque **Karmelitenkirche,** with its intricately carved wooden altar and the famous **Schwarze Madonna von Beilstein,** a 16th-century Montserrat sculpture left behind by Spanish troops reintroducing Catholicism to the region. (Open daily 9am-8pm.)

The town can be reached by **bus** #8060, which departs from both Endertplatz and the station in Cochem. (10min.; M-F 12 per day, Sa 6 per day, Su 3 per day; DM4.80.) The **boats** of **Personnenschiffahrt Kolb** (tel. 15 15) also float to Belstein. (1hr.; May-Oct. 4 per day; one-way DM13, round-trip DM18). **Café Klapperburg,** uphill a block on the left from the bus stop, is the home of Beilsteins's **tourist office** (tel./fax 90 01 91). Lay down your sleepy head at **Pension Erna Burg,** Moselstr. 2 (tel. 14 24), next to the highway along the river. Clean rooms and down-home comfort. (DM26-32 per person. Breakfast included. Reception 9am-6pm; call if you're arriving later.) The **Klostercafé** outside the church (tel. 16 74) serves outstanding traditional food (DM10-15), fantastic Mosel wine, and a view that beats them both. (Open M-Sa 10am-7:30pm.) The **telephone code** is 02673.

BERNKASTEL-KUES

Of this pair of towns separated by the Mosel, Bernkastel has the sights: Burg ruins, a piece of gate from the Middle Ages, and a little pointy house. But it also has the tourists and tourist prices. Kues is mellower: its attractions include a wine museum and a beautiful chapel. The **Bernkastel Marktplatz,** located one block from the bridge, is a 400-year-old, half-timbered beauty. Around the corner, the narrow, steep-roofed **Spitzhäuschen** ("little pointy house") leans to one side; it looks to be straight out of a children's book. A scenic but grueling 20-minute climb along a vine-laden path leads to the ruins of **Burg Landshut** above the town and valley. A summer home for the archbishops of Trier until it was gutted by fire in 1693, the ruins have since been rudely usurped by an outdoor café-restaurant. The gorgeous view remains the same, especially from the tower (DM0.50). Back in town, walk north from the Marktplatz onto Graacher Str. to reach the **Graacher Tor,** the only preserved gate from the city wall of 1300.

Across the river lounges **Kues.** A few stately 19th-century mansions tower along the river and the **Cusanusstift** reposes next to the bridge. Also known as the **St. Nikolaus-Hospital,** this nursing home was founded in the 15th century by a local philanthropist and includes an elaborately decorated chapel. (Chapel open M-F 9am-noon and 2-6pm, Sa-Su 9am-noon.) Next door, the **Moselweinmuseum,** Cusanusstr. 1, pays tribute to the tools of the wine-making trade. (Open mid-April to Oct. daily 10am-5pm; Nov. to mid-April 2-5pm. DM3, students DM1.50.)

Rail service no longer connects Bernkastel-Kues to the world; instead, Moselbahn operates a bus service from Bullay to Trier, stopping in Bernkastel-Kues. **Buses** depart across the street from the defunct train station in Bernkastel to Trier (1½hr.; M-Sa 1-2 per hour, Su 4 per day; DM13). By some freak of nature (or provincial engineering), the road connecting Traben-Trarbach and Bernkastel-Kues curls around the Mosel for some 24km, but a footpath makes a bee-line between the two towns in 5.5km. The path is too steep to trek with a heavy backpack, but it's otherwise an easy and gorgeous hike. **Personenschiffahrt Kolb** (tel. 47 19) makes the trip by **boat** to and from Traben-Trarbach five times a day. (One-way DM15, round-trip DM22.) The **tourist office,** Am Gestade 5 (tel. 40 23; fax 79 53), across the street from the bus stop in Bernkastel, finds **rooms** (from DM40-50) for a DM3-5 fee. (Open May-Oct. M-F 8:30am-12:30pm and 1-5pm, Sa 10am-4pm; closed Sa Nov.-April.) The **telephone code** is 06531.

Bernkastel's **Jugendherberge,** Jugendherbergstr. 1 (tel. 23 95; fax 15 29), is actually better positioned to defend the valley than its neighbor **Burg Landshut**—it's actually *uphill* from the castle. Despite the traumatic 30-minute hike, the hostel offers classy, clean facilities and an incredible view. (DM22. Breakfast and sheets included. Reception 8am-10pm. Curfew 10pm.) Otherwise, snuggle in at **Campingplatz Kueser Werth,** Am Hafen 2 (tel. 82 00), on the Kues side of the river. From the bridge, turn left and follow the road along the river for 1.5km. (DM8 per person. DM5 per tent. Reception 8am-noon and 3-7pm. Open April-Oct.) **Kapuzinerstübchen,** Römerstr. 35 (tel. 23 53), on the Bernkastel side, serves German soups (DM3-5.50) and entrees (DM10-24. Open Tu-Su 11:30am-2pm and 5:45-9pm.) Thousands arrive in town for Bernkastel-Kues's **Weinfest** the first week of September.

TRIER

Older than any other German town, Trier has weathered more than two millennia in the western end of the Mosel Valley. Founded by the Romans during the reign of Augustus, Trier reached the height of its prominence in the early 4th century as the capital of the Western Roman Empire, becoming an important center for Christianity in Europe. Today the town is a patchwork quilt of uncommon design and grace, having seen an eclectic range of architectural styles. The vitality of Trier's visitors and students blends harmoniously with the dignity and beauty of its incredible Roman ruins and well-preserved Altstadt.

◪ ORIENTATION AND PRACTICAL INFORMATION

Trier lies less than 50km from the Luxembourg border on the Mosel. Most of the sights sit in the vicinity of the compact Altstadt. The gate to the Altstadt, **Porta Nigra,** is a 10-minute walk from the train station down Theodor-Heuss-Allee or Christophstr. Although most sights are within walking distance, the bus system can carry you anywhere for DM3. A **Trier Card,** available at the tourist office, offers admission to six museums and discounts on the Roman ruins, tours, and theater performances over a 3-day period (DM17). A **Trier Card Plus** also includes public transportation (DM25).

Trains: Depart to Saarbrücken (1½hr., 2 per hour, DM23), Koblenz (1¾hr., 2 per hour, DM30), and Luxembourg (45min., 1 per hour; DM15).

Ferries: Personen-Schiffahrt (tel. 263 17) sails to Bernkastel-Kues from the Kaiser-Wilhelm-Brücke. May-Oct. daily at 9:15am. Round-trip DM45.

Taxi: Taxi-Funk (tel. 330 30).

Bike Rental: Tel. 14 88 56, on track 11 at the train station. DM10 per day. Open April-Oct. daily 9am-7pm.

Tourist Office: Tourist-Information (tel. 97 80 80; fax 447 59 or 70 00 48; email info@tit.de; www.trier.de), in the shadow of the Porta Nigra, offers daily **tours** in English at 1:30pm (DM9). Open Jan.-Feb. M-Sa 9am-5pm; March M-Sa 9am-6pm, Su 9am-1pm; April-Oct. M-Sa 9am-6:30pm, Su 9am-3:30pm; Nov.-Dec. M-Sa 9am-6pm, Su 9am-3:30pm. Whew! During these constantly fluctuating hours, the staff hands out free maps and books **rooms** for free.

Bookstore: Akademische Buchhandlung, Fleischstr. 62 (tel. 97 99 01). Small selection of English paperbacks. Open M-F 9am-7pm, Sa 9am-4pm.

Wine Information: Margaritengässchen 2a (tel. 994 05 40), near the Porta Nigra. Staff advises on **wine tasting** in the Mosel region (and the office). Open daily 10am-7pm.

Laundry: Wasch Center, Brückenstr. 19-21, down the street from Karl Marx's old house. Wash DM8, dry DM3 per 25min. Open M-Sa 8am-10pm.

Gay and Lesbian Resources: Rosatelefon (tel. 194 46).

Post Office: 54292 Trier, on Bahnhofpl. Open M-F 8am-7pm, Sa 8am-1pm.

PHONE CODE	0651

ACCOMMODATIONS AND CAMPING

Jugendhotel/Jugendgästehaus Kolpinghaus, Dietrichstr. 42 (tel. 97 52 50; fax 975 25 40), one block off the Hauptmarkt. Dorms DM27, singles DM39, doubles DM78. Breakfast included. Reception 8am-11pm. Call as far ahead as possible.

Jugendgästehaus (HI), An der Jugendherberge 4 (tel. 14 66 20; fax 146 62 30). Bus #2 or 87 (direction: "Trierweilerweg" or "Pfalzel/Quint") to "Zur Laubener Ufer," and walk 10min. downstream along the river embankment. Or from the station follow Theodor-Heuss-Allee as it becomes Nordallee, forks right onto Lindenstr., and ends at the bank of the Mosel (30min.). Quads DM27, doubles DM36.50, singles DM57 (per person). Breakfast and sheets included. Reception open sporadically 7am-midnight.

Hotel Haus Runne, Engelstr. 35 (tel. 289 22). Follow Theodor-Heuss-Allee from the station and turn right on Engelstr. after the Porta Nigra. Large 70s-style rooms with TV. Singles DM45, doubles DM90, quads DM160. Breakfast included.

Camping: Trier City Campingplatz, Luxemburger Str. 81 (tel. 869 21). From Hauptmarkt, follow Fleischstr. to Bruckenstr. to Karl-Marx-Str. to the Römerbrücke. Cross the bridge, head left on Luxemburger Str., and then left at the camping sign. DM8. Tent DM5. Reception daily 8am-10pm. Open April-Oct.

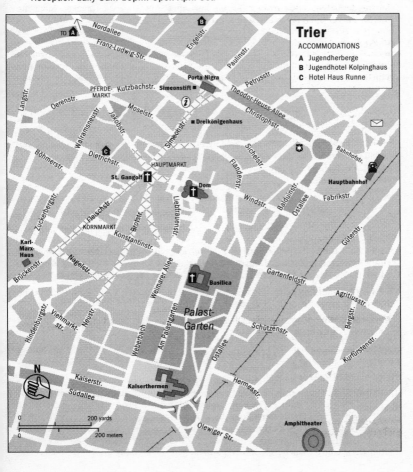

RHEINLAND-PFALZ

Trier

ACCOMMODATIONS

A   Jugendherberge
B   Jugendhotel Kolpinghaus
C   Hotel Haus Runne

◐ FOOD

For **groceries,** head to **Kaufmarkt,** at the corner of Brückenstr. and Stresemannstr. (Open M-F 8am-8pm, Sa 8am-4pm.)

🔉 Astarix, Karl-Marx-Str. 11 (tel. 722 39), is squeezed in a passageway next to Miss Marple's. If you get to the dreadfully tasteful sex shops, you've gone too far. Excellent, aesthetic food in an aesthetic atmosphere at unbelievable prices. Hip waitstaff without the attitude. Tortellini DM7.50, pizzas from DM9. Open M-Th 11am-1am, F-Sa 11:30am-2am, Su 6pm-1am. Kitchen closes M-Th and Su 11:30pm, F-Sa 12:30am.

Warsberger Hof, Dietrichstr. 42 (tel. 97 52 50), in the Kolpinghaus Hotel (above). Walk from Porta Nigra to the Hauptmarkt and turn right. Lunch specials and vegetarian fare from DM10. Open daily 11am-midnight. Kitchen closes at 11:30pm. **Cafeteria** in the back serves cheaper meals (DM7-9). Open M-F 11:30am-2:15pm.

Woorscht & Kneissjen, on Fleischstr. off the Hauptmarkt. Combined bakery and butcher shop sells tasty sandwiches on one side (DM3-5) and *Wurst* on the other (DM3.50).

Bierakademie, Bahnhofstr. 28 (tel. 994 31 95), half a block from the station. Today's geography lesson: around the world in 100 beers! For those who foolishly insist that man cannot live on beer alone, simple baguettes, hot dogs, and chicken wings are under DM10. Open M-Sa 11am-1am, Su 3pm-1am.

◐ SIGHTS

To save money, buy a one-day combination ticket valid at all Roman monuments. (Palm Sunday to Sept. DM9, Oct.-Nov. and Jan. to Palm Sunday DM4.50, Dec. DM4.)

PORTA NIGRA. Trier has its belly full of its Roman past, the most impressive of which is the Porta Nigra (Black Gate). Built in the 2nd century, the massive stone gate gained its name from the centuries of grime that metamorphosed its originally light yellow sandstone face into uneven sallow shades of gray. In the past, the gate served as the strongest line of defense against attacks on the city; now, throngs of tourists penetrate the barrier every day. *(Open daily Palm Sunday to Sept. 9am-6pm; Oct.-Nov. and Jan. to Palm Sunday 9am-5pm; Dec. 10am-4pm. DM4, students DM2. Last entry 30min. before closing.)*

SIMEONSTIFT. An 11th-century monastery enveloped by the Porta Nigra's courtyard the Simeonstift holds the **Städtisches Museum,** which has regular special exhibitions and a permanent collection of oils and sculptures. *(Tel. 718 14 50. Open April-Oct. daily 9am-5pm; Nov.-March Tu-F 9am-5pm, Sa-Su 9am-3pm. DM6, students DM5.)*

KAISERTHERMEN. The ruins of the Roman baths where Constantine once scrubbed himself still retain long, dark underground passages that make it easy to get lost. *(At the southeast corner of the walls. Same hours and admission as Porta Nigra.)*

AMPHITHEATER. Leave the Altstadt for an imaginary concert at the remains of the 2nd-century Amphitheater. Had the Rolling Stones toured in 169 (and they probably did), this 20,000-seat venue, one of the largest in the Roman Empire, certainly would have been on the itinerary. Instead, it held a spectacle even more appalling than an aged Mick Jagger: the theater hosted demonstrations of the most spectacular and gruesome ways of inflicting pain (and death) on humans and animals. *(A 5min. walk uphill from the Kaiserthermen along Olewiger Str. Admission and times same as Porta Nigra, but closed Dec.)*

HAUPTMARKT. Fruit stalls, florists, and ice cream vendors crowd the Hauptmarkt in central Trier. The colorful Gothic **Dreikönigenhaus,** on the left hand side of the Hauptmarkt as you walk away from the Porta Nigra, bears eloquent testimony to class antagonisms in old Europe. The front door of the merchant's home is located on the second story above street level, accessible only by a ladder, and was pulled inside when angry *Lumpenproletariat* besieged the lavishly adorned house.

KARL-MARX-HAUS. Growing up in this neighborhood, it's no surprise that young Karl Marx was inspired to write his theory of class conflict. The Karl-Marx-Haus, where young Karl first walked, talked, and dreamed of labor alienation, still stands and is a must-see for indefatigable Marxists. Busts and copies of the *Manifesto* abound. *(Brückenstr. 10. Tel. 430 11. Open April-Oct. M 1-6pm; Tu-Su 10am-6pm; Nov.-March M 3-6pm, Tu-Su 10am-1pm and 3-6pm. DM3, students DM2.)*

SPIELZEUGMUSEUM. Placate your inner child at the **Spielzeugmuseum** with two centuries of dolls, teddy bears, and automata. *(Nagelstr. 4-5. Tel. 75 850. Open April-Oct. daily 11am-5pm; Nov.-March Tu-Su noon-4pm. DM7.50, ages 10-18 DM4, under 10 DM3.)*

DOM

Dom open April-Oct. daily 6:30am-6pm; Nov.-March daily 6:30am-5:30pm. Daily tours at 2pm. Free. Schatzkammer open April-Oct. M-Sa 10am-5pm, Su 2-5pm; Nov.-March F-Sa 11am-4pm, Su 1:30-4pm. DM2, students and children DM1.30. Diözesanmuseum, Windstr. 6-8. Tel. 710 52 55. Open M-Sa 9am-5pm, Su 1-5pm. DM4, students DM2.

With a delightfully impressive interior design, the 11th-century cathedral's many nooks and crannies pleasantly shelter the tombs of archbishops. What is reputedly the **Tunica Christi** (Holy Robe of Christ) is enshrined at the eastern end of the cathedral. Tradition holds that this relic was brought from Jerusalem to Trier around 300 by St. Helena, mother of Emperor Constantine. It was last shown to the public in 1996. If you didn't see it, don't worry; it's *so* two millennia ago. Also in the Dom, the **Schatzkammer** touts a treasury of religious artifacts. Next to the Dom is the **Bischöfliches Dom- und Diözesanmuseum,** a surprisingly modern building showcasing holy art of all types. The museum also boasts one of the largest archaeological collections of any diocesan museum.

LIEBFRAUENKIRCHE. Adjacent to the Dom is the magnificent Gothic Liebfrauenkirche. Unlike the stained glass in most churches, which remains a pretty but peripheral decoration, the angular and stylized red and blue patterned windows of this basilika dominate its interior.

AROUND THE BASILIKA. The Basilika was originally the location of Emperor Constantine's throne room. *(Open M-Sa 9am-6pm, Su 11:30am-6pm. Free.)* Next door lies the bubble-gum pink **Kurfürstliches Palais,** a former residence of the archbishop-electors of Trier that today houses municipal government offices. It overlooks the well-kept **Palastgarten** where the statues have abnormally elongated toes. Along the eastern edge of the garden lies the **Landesmuseum,** an impressive collection of Roman stonework, sculpture, and mosaics, as well as a few other random relics, including a 2,700-year-old Egyptian mummy. *(Ostallee 44. Open Tu-F 9:30am-5pm, Sa-Su 10:30am-5pm. DM7, children DM3.)*

SCHWEBELBAHN. If you're simply not impressed with the above, ride the Schwebelbahn (gondola) across the Mosel to the Stadtwald and admire the primeval forest, the murmuring pines, and the hemlocks. *(Tel. 14 72 30. Open M-F 9am-6pm, Sa-Su 9am-7pm. DM4.50, children DM3; round-trip DM8, children DM4.)*

♫ ▥ ENTERTAINMENT AND NIGHTLIFE

Several annual festivals spice up Trier's atmosphere. The **Altstadtfest** brings live music, wine, and beer to the streets during the fourth weekend in June. The second weekend in July welcomes the **Moselfest,** with Saturday night fireworks over the water. The first weekend in August brings on the **Weinfest** in the nearby town of Olewig, kicked off by Friday fireworks.

Pubs, clubs, and *Kneipen* of all flavors fan out from the Hauptmarkt, with dense collections on **Judengasse** and the **Pferdemarkt.** Check posters and the free weekly *Der kleine Dicke* for parties and concerts.

Palais Walderdorff, (tel. 410 62), across from the Dom. By day a mellow café, by night a disco bright. Beautifully advertised themes. Café open daily 10am-10pm. Bar and disco daily 10pm-3am. Cover DM5-6.

The Dive, Judengasse 21 (tel. 444 24). Descending into the first subterranean bar, you feel like you're on a surreal beach, replete with plastic bamboo and wooden parrots. Keep going—the disco downstairs caters to a happy crowd with high-intensity dance music. Open M and F-Sa 9pm-3am, Th 9am-2am. Cover DM5.

Blaues Blut, Pferdemarkt (tel. 412 57). Mellow blue lighting and tiles on the bar evoke the floor of a swimming pool. Instead of getting an eyeful of chlorine, look out of your aquarium at the biped ravers. Open M-Th 9:30am-1am, F-Sa 9:30am-2am, Su 9:30am-1am.

SAARBRÜCKEN

Once again, Saarbrücken is in shambles. For centuries, the city's proximity to the French border has made it a center of one violent conflict after another, leaving virtually none of its Altstadt intact and clearing the way for rampant industrial development. Fortunately, today's destructive forces are much less pernicious—legions of bulldozers and jackhammer-wielding construction workers are tearing the city's streets apart to build a slick new DM500 million rail transit system, scheduled for completion by 2000. Focus on the future is found everywhere in Saarbrücken: postmodern architecture, countless factories and power plants, and a downtown area that beats with a cosmopolitan pulse. If you're looking for history, Saarbrücken isn't the place, but with a surprisingly urban atmosphere and a plethora of punks and other young progressives, The city may be one of the least touristed centers of the modern European cultural scene.

🔽 ORIENTATION AND PRACTICAL INFORMATION. Saarbrücken is connected twice hourly by train to Trier (1½hr., DM30) and Mannheim (1½hr., DM36). **Der Fahrradladen,** Nauwieser Str. 19 (tel. 370 98), rents **bikes.** (Open M 2-7pm, Tu-F 10am-7pm, Sa 10am-2pm.) The **Mitfahrzentrale,** Großherzog-Friedrich-Str. 59 (tel. 631 91), matches riders with drivers. (Open M-F 10am-6pm, Sa 10am-2pm, Su noon-3pm.) The **tourist office,** Am Hauptbahnhof 4 (tel. 365 15; fax 905 33 00; www.saarbruecken.de), is to the left of the station. The staff finds **rooms** for a DM3 fee. (Open M-F 9am-6pm, Sa 9am-3pm.) The handy **Saarbrücken Card** (DM13 for 2 days) provides transportation, free entrance to several sights, and theater discounts. Do your **laundry** at Eisenbahnstr. 8, across the bridge and a block behind the Ludwigskirche. (Wash DM6, dry DM1 per 10min. Open M-Sa 7am-10pm. Last wash 8:30pm.) The **post office,** 66111 Saarbrücken, is to the right of the station. (Open M-F 7am-6:30pm, Sa 7am-2pm, Su 9am-3pm.) Get **internet access** at the **inter@ctive café,** Ufergasse 2 (tel. 320 80), to the right off Bahnhofstr. (DM4 per 30min. Open M-Th and Su 4-11pm, F-Sa 3pm-1am.) The **telephone code** is 0681.

🛏 ACCOMMODATIONS AND CAMPING. The **Jugendgästehaus Europa (HI),** Meerwiesertalweg 31 (tel. 330 40; fax 37 49 11), is a 25-minute walk from the station. Head downhill and to the left; at the intersection veer left on Ursulinenstr., take a left at the Hela supermarket, and cross the parking lot. Or take bus #19 to "Prinzenweiher" and backtrack to the hostel. It's modern and hopping with young peeps. (Quads DM28 per person, doubles DM37 per person. Breakfast and sheets included. Reception 7:30am-1am. Curfew 1am.) **Gästehaus Weller,** Neugrabenweg 8 (tel. 37 19 03; fax 37 55 65), offers huge rooms with bath, phone, TV, and amazing color coordination. Go down Ursulinenstr, right on Mozartstr., carry on to Schumannstr., left on Fichtestr., and cross the bridge to Neugrabenweg. (Singles DM59-79; doubles DM89-105. Reception M-Sa 8am-11pm, Su 6-11pm. Call ahead.) **Hotel Schloßkrug,** Schmollerstr. 14 (tel. 354 48; fax 37 50 22), at the corner of Bruchwiesenstr., is 15 minutes from the station in a quiet, hip, location. Go left onto Ursulinenstr., right on Richard-Wagner-Str., and right on Schmollerstr. (Singles with shower and bath DM65; doubles with shower DM120, with bath DM145; triples with bath DM170.) **Campingplatz Saarbrücken,** Am Spicherer Berg (tel. 517 80), is far from the station. Take bus #42 to "Spicherer Weg," then cross Untertürkheimstr. and head uphill on Spicherer Weg. (DM6 per person. Tent DM8. Reception 7am-1pm and 3-10pm. Open March-Oct.)

🗭 **FOOD.** The streets around **St.-Johanner-Markt** brim with bistros, beer gardens, and ethnic restaurants. Walk down Reichstr. and turn left on Bahnhofstr. The buzzing **Schnokeloch,** Kappenstr. 6 (tel. 333 97), serves pizza and pasta for DM9-11. (Open M-F noon-3pm and 6pm-1am, Sa noon-1am, Su 6pm-1am.) Traditional German food (DM8-15) is served at the mellower **Spaten am Alten Brunnen,** Türkenstr., before the church. (Open M-F noon-2pm and 5pm-midnight, Sa-Su 5pm-midnight.) **Blue Moon** (tel. 317 80), on the corner of Schmollerstr. and Martin-Luther-Str., serves eclectic entrees (DM9-14) and boasts a funky ambience. (Open M-F 10am-3pm and 6pm-1am, Sa 6pm-1am, Su 10am-1am.) Come nightfall, students fill *Kneipen* in the **Chinesenviertel** a few blocks further, between Rotenbergstr., Richard-Wagner-Str., Dudweilerstr., and Großherzog-Friedrich-Str. **Hela,** at the end of Ursulinenstr., gives you yo' **groceries,** bee-atch. (Open M-F 8am-8pm, Sa 8am-4pm.)

🏛🎭 **SIGHTS AND ENTERTAINMENT.** While Saarbrücken is mainly remarkable for its super-modern commercial district, **St.-Johanner-Markt** does boast some pretty pieces of old Europe. Since the details on the bronze doors of the **Basilika St. Johann** have faded since its 1754 construction, it's difficult to tell whether the engraved figures are writhing in hell-fire or heavenly ecstatic bliss. (Open daily 9am-5pm. Free.) Take Kappenstr. from the market and then turn right at the intersection with Katherinenstr.; the church is on the left. The massive mustard **Staatstheater** stands south of the market next to the Alte Brücke; it was presented to Hitler after the Saarland was re-integrated into Germany in 1935. A walk along Am Stadtgarten leads to the **Moderne Galerie,** Bismarckstr. 11-19 (tel. 996 40). The gallery features such superstar modern art mofos as Picasso, Beuys, and Beckmann. Part two, the **Alte Sammlung,** Karlstr. 1, is across the street; medieval Madonnas, French porcelain, and antique jewelry are all here. Attached is the **Landesgalerie,** introducing some of the more promising regional artists. (Both museums open Tu and Th-Su 10am-6pm, W noon-8pm. DM3, students and children DM1.50.)

The **Saarbrücker Schloß** (tel. 50 62 47), on the other side of the Saar river, has morphed many times since the 9th century and now has tall sparkling glass columns on either side of its entrance. (Tours in German given Sa-Su at 4pm. Free.) The Schloßplatz is officially the **Platz des unsichtbaren Mahnmals** (Place of the Invisible Reminder) and home to one of the most interesting monuments you'll never see. In 1990, students at a nearby art school, under cover of darkness, dug up 2146 stones in the plaza and carved the names of former Jewish cemeteries on their undersides; this thoughtful memorial was the result. Three museums surround the plaza. To the south, adjacent to the Schloß, the **Historisches Museum** (tel. 50 65 49) includes cars, chairs from the 70s, and a disturbing collection of war propaganda. (Open Tu-W, F, and Su 10am-6pm, Th 10am-8pm, Sa noon-6pm. DM4, students DM2; Th after 5pm free.) To the north, the **Museum für Vor- und Frühgeschichte,** Schloßpl. 16 (tel. 95 40 50), has finds that include a Celtic countess's grave and jewelry from the 4th century BC. (Open Tu-Sa 9am-5pm, Su 10am-6pm. Free.) The 1498 **Rathaus** west of the Schloß hosts the wacky **Abenteuermuseum** (tel. 517 47), which crams a lot of anthropological loot into a few rooms, all of it collected by the original globe trotter Heinz Rox Schulz on his rampages through Asia, New Guinea, Africa, and South America. (Open Tu-W 9am-1pm, Th-F 3-7pm. DM3, children DM2.) The **Ludwigskirche** is an architectural gem five minutes down Schloßstr. and to the right. Its bright white interior is a refreshing departure from the usual Gothic gloom. (Open Tu 3-5pm, W 10am-noon, Sa 4-6pm, Su 11am-noon.)

WORMS

Of course you've heard of Worms. It was in European history class, when an unfortunate student (maybe it was you) raised his hand and asked what the whole class was thinking: "What's a diet of worms?" The teacher chuckled for a little longer than necessary and replied with characteristic wit, "I don't know what a diet of worms is, but the DEE-ATE of VOHRMS *(the Diet of Worms)* was the imperial council that sent Martin Luther into exile for refusing to renounce his heretical doctrines." Remember how funny that was? No? No matter—a visit to Worms will certainly refresh your memory, especially since little else of comparable import has happened here in the centuries since the famous gathering. Today's Worms is a fairly modern conglomerate of businesses with several fantastic historical and architectural sites scattered throughout. Although the city lacks any sort of core, the many churches, monuments, and puny museums warrant a daytrip.

7 ORIENTATION AND PRACTICAL INFORMATION. Worms is 45 minutes from Mainz by **train** (45min., 1 per hour, DM13). The **tourist office,** Neumarkt 14 (tel. 250 45; fax 263 28; www.worms.de), is in a small shopping complex across the street from the Dom St. Peter. (Office open M-F 9am-6pm, Sa 9am-noon; Nov.-March closed Sa.) Walking **tours** in German meet at the south portal of the Dom (2hr., April-Oct. Sa at 10am and Su at 3pm, DM5). **Exchange money** at the *Deutsche Bank* down Wilhelm-Leuschner-Str. from the station. (Open M-W 8:30am-12:30pm and 2-4pm, Th until 6pm, F until 3:30pm.) The **post office,** Kämmerstr. 44, 67547 Worms, is at the northern end of the pedestrian zone. (Open M-F 8am-6pm, Sa 8:30am-12:30pm.) The **telephone code** is 06241.

ACCOMMODATIONS, FOOD, AND ENTERTAINMENT. To get to the **Jugendgästehaus (HI),** Dechaneigasse 1 (tel. 257 80; fax 273 94), follow Bahnhofstr. right from the station to Andreasstr., turn left and walk until the Dom is on your left; the hostel is on your right. The hostel has bright two- to six-bed rooms, each with private bath. (DM27.80. Breakfast and sheets included. Reception 7am-11:30pm. Strict curfew 11:30pm.) A relaxed staff runs **Weinhaus Weis** (a *Pension,* not a drinking establishment), Färbergasse 19 (tel. 235 00), supplying soft beds in spacious rooms. (Singles DM38, doubles DM68. Breakfast included.)

The university **Mensa** is your ticket to cheap food—tastier than the notorious diet of worms. Travelers technically need an ID, but they often get by with language ability. Turn right as you exit the station, go right across the bridge, walk down Friedrich-Ebert-Str., and turn left on Erenburger Str. It's a block and a half up on your right, past the U.S. Army barracks. (Open M-Th 9am-4:30pm, F until 4pm.) The sounds of intense haggling at the **farmer's market** echo across Marktpl. (M, Th, and Sa mornings.)

In the basement of the building opposite the *Mensa* is the **Taberna,** a groovy *Studentenkneipe* with a weekly disco. (Open M-Th 3pm-1am. Disco open Th 9pm-late. Often closed July-Sept.) A swank young crowd swims in colorful tropical drinks at **Ohne Gleich,** Kriemhildenstr. 11 (tel. 41 11 77), down Bahnhofstr. to the right of the station. You'll feel like you've stepped into a Magritte painting. (W all cocktails DM7. Open M-Th and Su 9am-1am, F-Sa 9am-2am.) The Worms open-air **jazz festival** takes place each year at the beginning of July., while the **Backfischfest** brings a wine-drenched party of 70,000 people to Worms for nine days beginning the last weekend in August.

SIGHTS. The site of Luther's confrontation with the *Diet,* during which he shocked the membership by declaring, *"Ich stehe hier. Ich kann kein anders"* ("Here I stand, I can do no other"), is memorialized at the **Lutherdenkmal,** a larger-than-life statue erected in 1868 three blocks southeast of the station along Wilhelm-Leuschner-Str. Across the intersection stands the **Kunsthaus Heylshof,** which showcases a small collection of late Gothic and Renaissance art including Rubens'

Madonna with Child. (Open May-Sept. Tu-Sa 11am-5pm, Su 10am-5pm; Oct.-Dec. and Feb.-April Tu-Sa 2-4pm, Su 10am-noon and 2-4pm. DM3, students DM2.) The inviting greenery and deserted paths of the **Heylshofgarten** surround the museum.

Chief among Worms's architectural treasures is the **Dom St. Peter,** a magnificent Romanesque cathedral with a spooky crypt. Let your vampire fantasies run wild or stand and face the hounds of hell. According to the *Nibelungenlied,* Siegfried's wife Kriemhilde had a spat with her sister-in-law Brunhilde in the square in front of the Dom. (Open daily 9am-5:45pm. Donation requested.) Nearby stands the **Museum der Stadt Worms,** (tel. 946 39 11), with a bevy of artifacts dating from the Stone Age to the present. (Open Tu-Su 10am-5pm. DM4, students DM2.)

The 900-year-old **Heiliger Sand,** the oldest Jewish cemetery in Europe, is the resting ground for sundry rabbis, martyrs, and celebrities. Enter the cemetery through the gate on Willy-Brandt-Ring, just south of Andreasstr. and the main train station. On the opposite end of the Altstadt, the area around **Judengasse** stands witness to the thousand-year legacy of Worms's substantial Jewish community (once known as "Little Jerusalem"), which prospered during the Middle Ages but was wiped out in the Holocaust. The **Synagoge,** just off Judengasse, houses the *yeshiva* of the famous Talmudic commentator Rabbi Shlomo Ben-Yitzhak, better known as Rashi. (Open daily 10am-noon and 2-5pm.) Behind the synagogue is the **Jüdisches Museum** (tel. 85 33 45 and 85 33 70) in the **Raschi-Haus,** which traces the history of Worms's Jews. (Open Tu-Su 10am-noon and 2-5pm. DM3, students DM1.50.)

SPEYER

Speyer's political star rose and fell early. During the reign of the mighty Salian emperors in the 11th century, the town served as a principal meeting place for the Imperial Diets. As the emperors' power waned, Speyer slipped in significance, until ultimately the entire city was burned to the ground during the Palatinate War of Succession. By the time the two World Wars rolled around, Speyer didn't merit destruction; its gracefully ramshackle **Altstadt** and several glorious churches, until recently well off the beaten path of mass tourism, were spared from the bombings.

ⓘ ORIENTATION AND PRACTICAL INFORMATION. Speyer is easily reached by **train** from Mannheim (30min., 2 per hour) and Heidelberg (1hr., 2 per hour, DM20). **Bus** #7007 from Heidelberg (1½hr.) deposits passengers at the steps of the Kaiserdom. The helpful **tourist office,** Maximilianstr. 11 (tel. 14 23 92; fax 14 23 32; www.speyer.de), two blocks before Dom, distributes maps and has a list of accomodations. From the station, take the city shuttle to "Maximilianstr." (Open May-Oct. M-F 9am-5pm, Sa 10am-4pm, Su 11am-3pm; Nov.-April closed Su.) **Tours** of the city depart from in front of the tourist office. (April-Oct. Sa-Su 11am. DM5.) The **shuttle bus** runs the length of the city every 10 minutes (1-day ticket DM1). The **post office,** 67346 Speyer, is on Postpl., next to the Altpörtel. (Open M-F 8am-6pm, Sa 8am-12:30pm.) The **telephone code** is 06232.

▐▐ ACCOMMODATIONS AND FOOD. Speyer is blessed with its incredible new **Jugendgästehaus Speyer (HI),** Geibstr. 5 (tel. 615 97; fax 615 96), where fun is guaranteed by the nearby pool and the hostel's indoor ball pit. (Dorms DM27.80, doubles DM36.50, singles DM51.30. Reception daily 5-7pm and 9:30-10pm. Lockout 9-11am. Curfew 10pm. Members only.) **Pension Grüne Au,** Grüner Winkel 28 (tel./fax 721 96), has comfortable rooms with gleaming sinks. From Maximilianstr., go left on Salzgasse, continue to St. Georggasse. Walk in the same direction as the fish statue faces to the end of the square and take a right onto Salzturmgasse, which turns into Grüner Winkel; the hotel is on the right. (Singles DM50-75, doubles DM75-90.) North of Maximilianstr., **Korngasse** and **Große Himmelsgasse** shelter excellent restaurants. The **Gaststätte Zum Goldenen Hirsch,** Maximilianstr. 90a (tel. 726 94), offers traditional German fare. (Open M-F and Su 11am-1am, Sa 11am-

2am.) The second weekend in July (July 7-11, 2000) hosts the **Bretzelfest** (pretzel festival); the festivities involve concerts and parades. In early August, the **Kaisertafel Speyer** takes place—tables are set up along the streets and visitors are herded along and stuffed full of regional specialties.

■ **SIGHTS.** Since its construction in the 12th century, the **Kaiserdom** has been the symbol of Speyer. The immense Romanesque cathedral is noted for its main portals, flanked by seven statues on each side recounting the Crucifixion. The crypt under the east end coddles the remains of eight Holy Roman Emperors and their wives. (Open April-Oct. M-F 9am-7pm, Sa-Su 9am-6pm; Nov.-March M-Sa 9am-5pm, Su 1:30pm-5pm.) South of the Dom, the excellent **Historisches Museum der Pfalz,** Dompl. (tel. 132 50), offers a comprehensive presentation on Palatinate history and hosts highly-touted special exhibits on anything from pop art to Napoleon. Also included are the exquisite **Domschatzkammer** and the **oldest bottle of wine in the world**—a slimy leftover from some wild Roman blowout in the 3rd century. (Open Tu and Th-Su 10am-6pm, W 10am-8pm. DM8, students and children DM5; Tu after 4pm free. Free tours Su at 11am.) A left on Große Pfaffengasse and a right down Judengasse lead to the **Judenbad** (tel. 772 88), a Jewish *mikwe* (ritual bathhouse) from the 12th century. (Open April-Oct. M-F 10am-noon and 2-5pm, Sa-Su 10am-5pm. DM1.50.)

Maximilianstr., Speyer's main thoroughfare, spreads westward from the Dom, culminating in the medieval **Altpörtel,** an exquisitely preserved four-story village gate. Climb it for a great view. (Tower open April-Oct. M-F 10am-noon and 2-4pm, Sa-Su 10am-5pm. DM1.50.) From the Altpörtel, a southward jaunt on Gilgenstr. leads to the **Josefskirche** and its sister across the street, the **Gedächtniskirche.** (Both open May-Oct. daily 10am-6pm; Nov.-April M-Sa 10am-noon and 2-5pm, Su 2-5pm.) For those seeking something slightly more up-to-the-minute, the **Technikmuseum,** Geibstr. 2 (tel. 670 80; fax 67 08 20), fills a gigantic warehouse with 30,000 cubic meters of trains, planes, and automobiles, as well as an **IMAX theater** (tel. 67 08 50) and the "Adventure-simulator." (Take the city shuttle to "Technikmuseum." Museum open daily 9am-6pm. DM12, children DM8. IMAX DM12, children DM8. Combination ticket DM22, children DM15.)

HESSEN

Prior to the 20th century, Hessen was known for exporting mercenary soldiers to rulers such as King George III, who sent them off to put down an unruly gang of colonials on the other side of the Atlantic in 1776. Hessen ceased to exist as a political entity when it was absorbed by Bismarck's Prussia in 1866, until the Allies reinstated its *Land* status in 1945. Today, the region is the busiest commercial center in the country, led by the banking metropolis of Frankfurt. Overshadowed by this transit and commerce metropolis, the rest of Hessen attracts little attention from tourists, leaving the medieval delights of Marburg's *Uni*-culture and the fascination of Kassel blessedly off the beaten path.

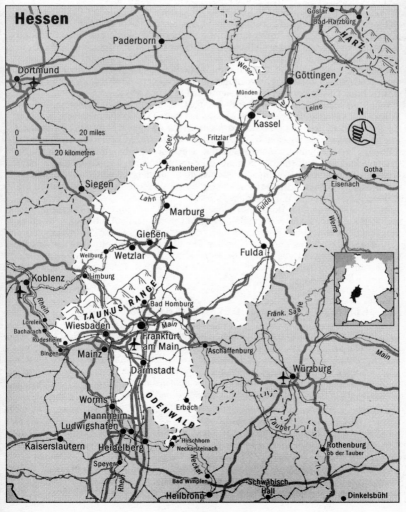

Hessen

HIGHLIGHTS OF HESSEN

■ With its historical **Römerberg,** happening nightlife scene, and superb museums, **Frankfurt** is a fast-paced city, respectable for much more than its central high-traffic airport and train station (p. 400).

■ The **Lahntal** is a treasure trove of outdoor fun (p. 413), and **Weilburg's** 14th-century Schloß and **crystal caves** are not to be missed (p. 414).

■ The university town of **Marburg** influenced the writings of the **Brothers Grimm** and has spawned a hip youth culture (p. 415).

■ The fairy-tale castles and waterfalls of **Wilhelmshöhe Park** and the cutting-edge **documenta** modern art exhibitions successfully merge in the curiously cosmopolitan city of **Kassel** (p. 419).

FRANKFURT AM MAIN

Skyscrapers loom over crowded streets, investment bankers scurry to and fro—it's not hard to see how Frankfurt acquired the derisive nicknames "Bankfurt" and "Mainhattan." Many visitors view Frankfurt as the most Americanized city in Europe, a claim quickly verified by the flashy McDonald's on every street corner and the city's unusually high crime rate. While lacking the architectural beauty of more traditional German cities, Frankfurt's integral economic role as home to the central bank of the European Union lends it a glitzy vitality.

Frankfurt made its first appearance when Charlemagne first put the "Ford of the Franks" on the map in 794. In 1356, the **Golden Bull** of imperial law (see p. 9) made the trade center the election and coronation site of the emperors until the Holy Roman Empire's dissolution. Since then, hordes of Frankfurters have gone on to influence western culture. **Anne Frank** and **Goethe** lived here, families such as the Oppenheims and Rothschilds influenced Frankfurt's economic development, and **Frankfurt School** members **Theodor Adorno, Max Horkheimer,** and **Walter Benjamin** elaborated their theories of art and society despite their temporary eviction to the United States during WWII (see p. 29).

After Allied bombers destroyed close to 100% of the city in 1944, Frankfurt received a complete concrete makeover paid for, ironically, by the same country that had demolished it a decade earlier. Today the city government spends more on cultural attractions and tourism than any other German city, and an equally rich *Kulturszene* thrives under the city's patronage. If all this isn't enough to make you visit, the likelihood of arriving in Germany at Frankfurt's Rhein-Main Airport probably is.

◧ GETTING THERE AND GETTING AROUND

Flights: The ultra-modern Frankfurt airport, **Flughafen Rhein-Main** (tel. 69 01), welcomes hundreds of airplanes and thousands of businesspeople from all over the world. From the airport, S-Bahn #14 and 15 travel to the Hauptbahnhof every 15min. Buy tickets (DM5.80) from the green *Automaten* marked *Fahrkarten* before boarding or face a stiff fine (DM20-80). Eurailpass valid. Most public transportation departs from Terminal 1; a free streetcar runs between the terminals every 15min.

Trains: Trains from most of Europe frequently roll in and out of Frankfurt's Hauptbahnhof to Köln (2½hr.; 2 per hour; DM70, under 26 DM56), Munich (3½-4½hr.; 2 per hour; DM212), Berlin (5-6hr.; 2 per hour; DM207, under 26 DM166), Hamburg (6hr.; 2 per hour; DM 191, under 26 DM153), Amsterdam (5hr.; every 2 hours; DM120, under 26 DM110), Paris (6-8hr.; every 2 hours; DM140, under 26 DM108), Rome (15hr.; 1 per hour; DM279). Call (0180) 599 66 33 for schedules, reservations, and information. Remember that some trains also depart from Terminal 1 of the airport.

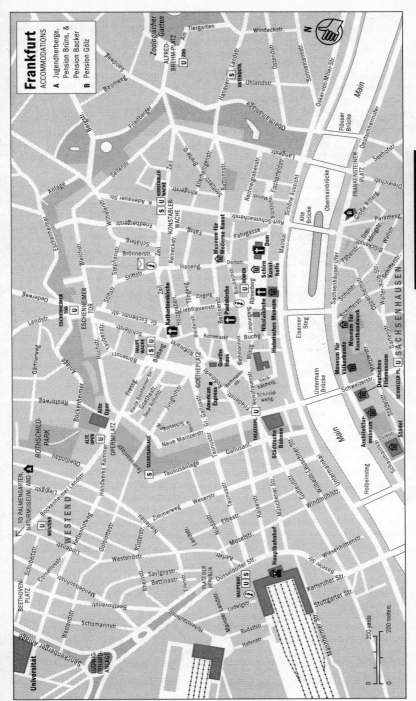

Frankfurt
ACCOMMODATIONS

A Jugendherberge,
   Pension Brüns, &
   Pension Backer
B Pension Gölz

HESSEN

HESSEN

Public Transportation: Refer to the subway map in the inside covers of this guide. For unlimited access to the S-Bahn, U-Bahn, streetcars, and buses, the *Tageskarte,* a pass valid until midnight of the day of purchase is available from machines in every station (DM8.20, children DM5). Single-ride tickets are valid for 1hr. in one direction, transfers permitted (DM3, rush hour DM3.60). Eurail passes valid only on S-Bahn trains. Some hotels offer a 2-day transportation pass (DM10) as well. *Passengers without tickets face a DM60 fine.* At the Hauptbahnhof, the S-Bahn and U-Bahn depart from the level below the long distance trains. Streetcars #10, 11, 16, 19, and 21 pass by the island platform directly outside the main (west) entrance, while buses #35, 37, and 46 leave from just outside and to the right of the main entrance. This system is certainly intimidating if not outright confusing; bring questions to the **Verkehrsinsel,** An der Hauptwache, near the Katharinenkirche and across from the *Kaufhof* department store. Open M-F 9am-8pm, Sa 9am-4pm. Watch out: the public transportation system shuts down around 1am every night. After 1am, walk or take a . . .

Taxi: Call 23 00 01 or 25 00 01, or show some leg to flag one down.

Mitfahrzentrale: Baseler Str. 7 (tel. 23 64 44 or 23 61 27). Take a right on Baseler Str. at the side exit of the Hauptbahnhof (track 1), and walk 2 blocks. Connects riders with drivers for a fee. Arranges rides to Berlin (DM32), Barcelona (DM88), and everywhere in between. Open M-F 8am-6:30pm, Sa 8am-2pm.

Bike Rental: Most convenient is the **Handgepäckaufbewahrung** counter (tel. 26 53 48 31) in the Hauptbahnhof, in the corridor across from the tourist information desk and next to a flower shop. Open daily 6am-midnight. Passport required.

Boat Rides: The city offers tours on the Mainkai, departing near the Römerberg (1¾hr., 2 per hour, DM12).

Hitchhiking: *Let's Go* does not recommend hitchhiking as a safe mode of transport. Hitching on the highway itself is strictly forbidden. Masochists heading to München from Konstablerwache south take buses #36 or 960 to the *Autobahn* interchange. To Köln or Düsseldorf, take S-Bahn #1 or 8 to "Wiesbaden Hauptbahnhof," then S-Bahn #21 (direction: "Niedernhausen") to "Auringen-Medenbach." Turn right, walk 800m, proceed under the *Autobahn,* and take the access road to the *Autobahn* rest stop.

■ ORIENTATION

A sprawling conglomeration of steel, concrete, glass, and scaffolding, Germany's fifth-largest city bridges the **Main** (pronounced MINE) 35km east of its confluence with the Rhein. Frankfurt's airport and train station are among the busiest in Europe. The station lies at the end of Frankfurt's red light district, which in typical Frankfurt fashion brings together international airline offices, sex bars, and banks. From the station, the town center is a 20-minute walk down Kaiserstr. or Münchener Str., which lead from the newer part of the city to the Altstadt. Located just north of the Main, the Altstadt contains the **Römerberg,** the well-touristed domain of old German kitsch. Take U-Bahn #4 (direction: "Seckbacher Landstr.") to "Römer." A few blocks north lies the commercial heart of Frankfurt, an expanse of department stores and ice cream vendors that stretches along Zeil from **Hauptwache** (S-Bahn #1, 2, 3, 4, 5, 6, or 8, two stops from the Hauptbahnhof) to **Konstablerwache** (one stop farther). Students, cafes, stores, and services cluster in **Bockenheim.** Take U-Bahn #6 or 7 to "Bockenheimer Warte." Across the Main, **Sachsenhausen** draws the *Ebbelwei*-lovers, the pub-crawlers, and the museum-goers. Take U-Bahn #1, 2, or 3 to "Schweizer Pl."

The **Frankfurt Card,** available at tourist offices and in most travel agencies, allows unlimited travel on all trains and buses, including the airport line; it also gets you 50% off admission to 15 museums, the *Palmengarten,* the zoo, and that veritable carnival funhouse, the airport visitors' terrace. (One day DM12, two days DM19.)

7 PRACTICAL INFORMATION

TOURIST AND FINANCIAL SERVICES

Tourist Office: Tel. 21 23 88 49; www.frankfurt.de. In the Hauptbahnhof, on the right side of the reception hall as you go through the main exit. Maps (DM1-2), brochures, souvenirs, tours, and lots more. Books rooms for a DM5 fee, or call ahead to reserve a room for free (tel. 21 23 08 08). Open M-F 8am-9pm, Sa-Su and holidays 9am-6pm. **Another branch** borders Römerplatz at Römerberg 27 (tel. 21 23 87 08), but the staff doesn't book rooms. Open M-F 9:30am-5:30pm, Sa-Su 10am-4pm. **City-Info,** Zeil 94a, is an information stand in the center of the commercial district. Open M-F 10am-6pm, Sa 10am-4pm.

Tours: Depart daily from the Römerberg tourist office and from the Hauptbahnhof tourist office 15min. later. 10am and 2pm; in winter only 2pm. DM44, students DM22.

Consulates: Australia, Gutleutstr. 85 (tel. 273 90 90; fax 23 26 31). Open M-Th 8:30am-1pm and 2-5pm, F 8:30am-1pm and 2-4:15pm. **South Africa,** Ulmenstr. 37 (tel. 719 11 30). Open M-F 8am-noon. **U.K.,** Bockenheimer Landstr. 42 (tel. 170 00 20; fax 72 95 53). Open M-F 9am-noon and 2-4pm; phone hours M-Th 8:30am-1pm and 2-5pm, F 8:30am-1pm and 2-4:30pm. **U.S.,** Siesmayerstr. 21 (tel. 753 50; fax 74 89 38). Open to the public M-F 8-11am; phone hours M-F 8am-4pm.

Currency Exchange: In Airport Hall B (open daily 7:30am-9pm) or the Hauptbahnhof (open daily 6:30am-10pm). Better rates, however, are available at any bank.

American Express: Kaiserstr. 8 (tel. 21 05 01 11, 24hr. hotline (0180) 523 23 77; fax 210 52 70). Does not hold mail. Exchanges foreign currency, handles traveler's checks, and arranges hotel reservations and car rentals. Services are free for cardholders or traveler's check customers. Open M-F 9:30am-6pm, Sa 9:30am-12:30pm.

LOCAL SERVICES

Budget travel: STA Travel, Bockenheimer Landstr. 133 (tel. 70 30 35), near the university. Books flights and sells ISICs. Open M-F 10am-6pm.

Bookstores: Süssman's Presse und Buch, Zeil 127 (tel. 131 07 51). Mostly English titles for those who need their Shakespeare or Clancy. Open M-W and F 9am-7pm, Th 9am-8pm, Sa 9am-4pm. **British Book Shop,** Börsenstr. 17 (tel. 28 04 92). Classics and popular novels in English. Open M-F 9:30am-7pm, Sa 9:30am-4pm.

Laundromat: Schnell & Sauber, Wallstr. 8, near the hostel in Sachsenhausen. Wash DM6, dry DM1 per 15min., soap included. Change machine. Open daily 6am-11pm. **Miele Washworld,** Moselstr. 17. Wash DM7, dry DM3. Open daily 8am-11pm.

EMERGENCY AND COMMUNICATIONS

Emergency: Tel. 110. **Fire** and **Ambulance:** Tel. 112.

Gay and lesbian hotline: Rosa Hilfe Frankfurt (tel 194 46). Open Su 6-9pm. In an emergency, call (0171) 174 57 21.

AIDS hotline: Tel. 405 86 80.

Women's Helpline: Tel. 70 94 94.

Disabled travelers: Frankfurt Forum, Römerberg 32 (tel. 21 24 00 00), publishes a guide to handicap-accessible locations in Frankfurt. Ask for Mr. Schmidt. Open M and W 10am-4:30pm, Tu 10am-6pm, and Th-F 10 am-2pm.

Pharmacy: Tel. 23 30 47; fax 24 27 19 16. In the basement of the train station by the subway entrances. Open M-F 6:30am-9pm, Sa 8am-9pm, Su and holidays 9am-8pm. If pharmacies are closed, call 192 92 for emergency prescriptions.

Post Office: Main branch, Zeil 90, 60001 Frankfurt (tel. 13 81 26 21; fax 13 81 26 24), inside the *Hertie* department store. Follow the yellow *Post* signs. U- or S-Bahn to "Hauptwache." Send and be sent. Fax and be faxed. Open M-F 9:30am-8pm, Sa 9am-4pm. **Branch office,** 60036 Frankfurt, on the upper level of the Hauptbahnhof. Open M-F 6:30am-9pm, Sa 8am-6pm, Su 11am-6pm.

Internet Access: Alpha, in the Hauptbahnhof's gambling salon, past track 24 on the north side of the station. DM1 per 4min. Satisfy further e-mail withdrawal at **CybeRyder Internet Café,** Töngesgasse 31 (tel. 92 08 40 10). DM5 per 30min. Open M-Th 10am-11pm, F-Sa 10am-1am, Su 3pm-11pm. Or try **Cyber's: the Inter-n-Active Café,** Zeil 112-114 (tel. 29 49 64), on the 7th floor of the ZeilGalerie. DM6 per 30min. Open M-F 11am-1am, Sa 10am-1am, Su noon-midnight.

PHONE CODE	069

▐ ACCOMMODATIONS

The hotel industry has no doubt decided to follow the city motto "show me the money." There are, however, a few cheap and charming options in the Westend/University area. A trade fair May 22-27, 2000 may make bargain rooms scarce. If all else fails, there are three other hostels less than 45 minutes away: Darmstadt (S-Bahn #12; see p. 411), Mainz (S-Bahn #14; see p. 384), and Wiesbaden (S-Bahn #1 or 14; see p. 409).

Jugendherberge (HI), Deutschherrnufer 12 (tel. 610 01 50; fax 61 00 15 99; www.jugendherberge_frankfurt.de). Take Bus #46 from the main train station (DM3, rush hours DM3.60) to "Frankensteiner Pl." Turn left along the river; the hostel sits at the end of the block. After 7:30pm M-F, 5:45pm Sa, and 5pm Su, hop on S-Bahn #2, 3, 4, 5, or 6 to "Lokalbahnhof"; make sure to walk down Darmstädter Landstr. with your back to the train bridge above. Walk on the right side of the street and take a right before the *Commerzbank* onto Dreieichstr.; continue on until you reach the Main River and the intersection with Deutschherrnufer. Take a left and the hostel will be on your left. In the midst of the Sachsenhausen pub and museum district, the hostel is occasionally loud and lively with inebriated locals and antsy schoolkids. Breakfast with unlimited buffet included; lunch and dinner also available. Lunch 12:30-2pm, dinner 6-7:30pm. DM8.70. Vegetarian meals available. DM26, over 26 DM33. Singles DM53 and doubles DM43 per person, but they are *very rarely* available. Required sheet deposit DM10. 24hr. reception. Check-in after 11am. Check-out 9:30am. No lockout. Curfew 2am. Reservations by phone or fax.

▧ **Pension Bruns,** Mendelssohnstr. 42 (tel. 74 88 96; fax 74 88 46). From the Hauptbahnhof, take a left onto Düsseldorfer Str. and walk north. After 2 blocks veer right on Beethovenstr. At the circle, go right on Mendelssohnstr. (10-15min.) Located in the wealthy Westend area near the university, 9 spacious Victorian rooms with high ceilings, hardwood floors, phones, and cable TV earn Pension Bruns the much-coveted *Let's Go* thumb. Ring the bell; it's on the second floor. Doubles DM79; triples DM105; quads DM140. Free breakfast in bed! Showers DM2. Call ahead.

▧ **Pension Backer,** Mendelssohnstr. 92 (tel. 74 79 92). Two subway stops from the city center, the *Pension* offers the best deal in town. Take U-Bahn #6 (direction: "Heerstr.") or 7 (direction: "Hausen") to "Westend." The cheapest of these well-lit, impeccable rooms are on the fifth floor (no elevator!). Singles DM25-50; doubles DM60; triples DM78. Breakfast included. Showers 7am-10pm (DM3). Reservations with deposit only.

Hotel an der Galluswarte, Hufnagelstr. 4 (tel. 73 39 93; fax 73 05 33). Run by the same folks as the Pension Bruns. Offers rooms at comparable prices available only to *Let's Go* readers: mention the guide and live in luxury on the cheap! Take S-Bahn #3 (direction: "Hohenmark"), 4 (direction: "Kronberg"), 5 (direction: "Friedrichsdorf"), or 6 (direction: "Galluswarte") to "Galluswarte." Exit under the sign marked "Mainzer Landstr.", take a right, walk a bit, and then take another right onto Hufnagelstr. *Let's Go* prices: singles DM70; doubles DM90. Includes breakfast, private shower, TV, and phone.

Hotel-Pension Gölz, Beethovenstr. 44 (tel. 74 67 35; fax 74 61 42; email hotel-goelz@aol.com). One street north of Pensions Backer and Bruns. U-Bahn #6 or 7 to "Westend." Quiet and beautiful rooms with all the amenities of an apartment: TV, phone, couch, and some with balconies. Singles DM65, with shower DM79-94; doubles with shower DM135-158; triples with shower DM165-188. Big breakfast included. Reservations recommended.

Fennisfuchser, Mainzer Landstr. 95 (tel. 25 38 55). Located near the Hauptbahnhof in the red light district, the hotel is a convenient place to crash. From the train station, take a left on Düsseldorfer Str., walk two blocks, and take a right onto Mainzer Landstr.; the hotel is one block down on the right. Enter through the restaurant downstairs. Singles DM55; doubles DM85; triples DM120. Special rates for stays longer than 1 night.

◖ FOOD

While cheap eats in Frankfurt are not nearly as rare as cheap beds, light eats may prove harder to come by, especially if you stick to the local culinary gems. Traditional German sausages and beer are popular in Frankfurt, but the region also treasures some dishes of its own: *Handkäse mit Musik* (cheese curd with raw onions), Goethe's favorite; *grüne Sosse* (a green sauce with various herbs, usually served over boiled eggs or potatoes); and *Ebbelwei*. Ah, *Ebbelwei*. Large mugs of this apple wine (also called *Ebbelwei*, or *Äpfelwein* up north) should never top DM3. Don't expect anything akin to the sharp sweetness of cider or the dryness of chardonnay; this isn't a wine to be sipped. Non-German foods abound; tasty crepes and even T-bone steaks are right at your fingertips, as are samosas, lo mein, and those omnipresent *Döner*.

For those on a tight budget, **supermarkets** are in plentiful supply. Just a few blocks from the youth hostel is a fully-stocked **HL Markt,** Dreieichstr. 56 (open M-F 8am-8pm, Sa 8am-4pm) while a **Tengelmann,** Münchener Str. 37, is close to the Hauptbahnhof. (Open M-F 8:30am-7:30pm, Su 8am-2pm.) The most reasonably priced kitchens surround the university in Bockenheim and nearby parts of Westend (U-Bahn #6 or 7 to "Bockenheimer Warte"), and many of the pubs in Sachsenhausen serve food at a decent price. Take U-Bahn #1, 2, or 3 to "Schweizer Pl." Bockenheim, the Zeil, and Römerplatz attract carts and stands.

SACHSENHAUSEN

▨ Adolf Wagner, Schweizer Str. 71 (tel. 61 25 65). Filling plates of sauce-soaked German dishes (DM8-27) and liters of *Äpfelwein* (DM2.50 per 0.3L) keep the patrons of this famous corner of old-world Frankfurt jolly, rowdy, and coming back for years. Open daily 11am-midnight.

Zum Gemalten Haus, Schweizer Str. 67 (tel. 61 45 59), four doors down from Adolf Wagner. The long wooden tables of this Sachsenhausen institution have seen generations of talkative locals treat their bellies to a quick *Wurst, Kraut,* and home-brewed wine (DM13). Groups can split the hefty *Frankfurter Platte* and sit outdoors in the *Gartenlokal* (garden restaurant). Open W-Su 10am-midnight.

Borsalino, Kleine Rittergasse 14-20 (tel. 61 13 98). When in Frankfurt, do as the Romans...*mangia la pasta* (DM7-10) outside and people-watch. Music and flirting until 4am daily.

Lorsbacher Taf, Große Rittergasse 49-51 (tel. 61 64 59). A family restaurant tucked in the cobblestoned streets of Alt-Sachsenhausen whose flower pots and ivy-covered walls create a village ambience. Traditional German entrees around DM12, soups DM5. Open Tu-Sa 4pm-midnight and Su noon-11pm. Beer garden open until 11pm.

WESTEND/UNIVERSITY

Mensa, U-Bahn #6 (direction: "Heerstr.") or 7 (direction: "Hausen") to "Bockenheimer Warte," then follow the "Mensa" signs. Your best bet for a filling, hot meal (DM5) with some collegiate attitude. Open M-F 11am-3pm.

Ban Thai Imbiß und Restaurant, Leipziger Str. 26 (tel. 77 26 75; 70 43 10 for takeout). Sizzling Thai dishes for those on the fly. Vegetarian options. Open daily 11:30am-10pm. Seating only after 7pm.

Pizzeria da Romeo, Mendelssohnstr. 83 (tel. 74 95 01). Typical Italian dishes (DM6-12) cooked by the real McCoy. Open M-F 10:30am-3pm and 4-9:30pm.

CITY CENTER

Kleinmarkthalle, on Hasengasse between Berliner Str. and Töngesgasse, is a 3-story warehouse with several bakeries, butchers, fruit and vegetable stands, and more. Cutthroat competition between the many vendors pushes prices way down. Innumerable varieties of cheese for sale, not to mention skinned rabbits. Open M-F 7:30am-6pm, Sa 7:30am-3pm.

SIGHTS

Much of Frankfurt's historic splendor lives on only in memories and in accurately reconstructed monuments nostalgic for the time before the bombing of 1944. Industrious Frankfurters, well aware that the same city could not be built twice, engineered its resurrection as a combined testament to pre- and postmodern times. A walk through the city center quickly reveals this architectural eclecticism.

RÖMERBERG. A pedestrian's voyage through Frankfurt should begin among the reconstructed half-timbered architecture and medieval fountain that grace most postcards of Frankfurt. To celebrate the 13 coronations of German emperors that were held in the city, the statue of Justice in the center of the square once sprouted wine; unfortunately for all she has since sobered up.

RÖMER. Standing at the west end of the Römerberg, the gables of Römer have marked the site of Frankfurt's city hall since 1405; it's also where the merchants who began the city's trade tradition stopped on the Main to sell their goods. Only the building's upper floors are open to the public. These include the **Kaisersaal,** a former imperial banquet hall adorned with portraits of the 52 German emperors from Charlemagne to Franz II. *(Open daily 10am-1pm and 2-5pm. Obligatory hourly tour DM3, students DM1.)*

DOM. East of the reconstructed Römerberg stands the only building in the city that survived the bombings. The red sandstone Gothic cathedral contains several splendidly elaborate altarpieces. The seven electors of the Holy Roman Empire selected the emperors here, and the Dom served as the site of coronation ceremonies between 1562 and 1792. A viewing tower atop the Dom is currently undergoing reconstruction and is slated to reopen in 2001. *(Open daily 9am-noon and 2-6pm.)* The **Dom Museum** inside the main entrance contains architectural studies of the Dom, intricate chalices, and the venerated robes of the imperial electors. *(Open Tu-F 10am-5pm, Sa-Su 11am-5pm. DM3, students DM1.)*

ALTE NIKOLAIKIRCHE. South of the Römerberg, this church raises its considerably more modest spires. The minimalist interior is home to occasional fits of organ music. *(Open daily April-Sept. 10am-8pm; Oct.-March 10am-6pm. Free.)*

PAULSKIRCHE. St. Paul's Church stands directly across Braubachstr. from the Römerberg. Now used as a political memorial and conference venue, the unusually round church served as the gathering place for Germany's first democratic National Assembly when it convened to draft a constitution for the fledgling German republic in the wake of the revolutionary tremors that swept through Europe in 1848-49 (see p. 10). Cognizant that Germany could not unify without the assent of powerful Prussia, the assembly attempted to cajole Prussia's Friedrich Wilhelm IV into accepting the crown of a constitutional monarchy. The king replied that he ruled by the grace of God, and the whole episode ended with the bloody repression of the democratic movement. *(Open daily 10am-5pm.)*

GOETHEHAUS. Of the half-dozen or so German cities that claim Goethe as their native son, Frankfurt legitimately possesses his early years. The master was born in Frankfurt in 1749, found his first love (a girl named Gretchen, said to be the inspiration for Marguerite in *Faust*), and penned some of his best-known works here, including *The Sorrows of Young Werther*. Unless you're a huge Goethe fan, the house is little more than a typical 18th-century showroom for a well-to-do family. It was one of the first buildings to be reconstructed after the war and refurnished with the family's original belongings, many of which the renowned author hated. *(Großer Hirschgraben 23-25, a few blocks northwest of the Römer. Tel. 13 88 00. Open April-Sept. M-F 9am-6pm, Sa-Su 10am-4pm; Oct.-March M-F 9am-4pm, Sa-Su 10am-4pm. Tours must be arranged in advance. DM7, students DM3.)*

HISTORISCHER GARTEN. Between the Dom and the rest of the Römerberg lie the Schirn Kunsthalle (see **Museums,** p. 407) and the plantless "garden" dating back to the 2000-year-old Roman settlement discovered when workers were digging a sewer line. Ahhhh, the miasma of history.

PALMENGARTEN. Tourists, children, businesspeople, and an extensive variety of native and exotic birds take refuge in the sprawling grounds of this garden in the northwest part of town. Rent a wooden boat and pretend you're rowing on the Main (DM4 per 30min.). The garden's greenhouses contain seven different "worlds," from the tropics to the plains. In summer, the grounds host a number of performances and exhibitions. *(Siesmayerstr. 61. Tel. 21 23 39 39. U-Bahn #6 or 7 to "Bockenheimer Warte." Open daily March-Oct. 9am-6pm; Nov.-Jan. 9am-4pm; Feb. 9am-5pm. Admission DM7, students DM3.)*

ZOO. For animal lovers, over 650 species ranging from the commonplace to the exotic are represented east of the city center. The daily feeding times of the apes (4:30pm; winter 4pm) and piranhas (Su and W at 11am) excite a certain bloodthirsty pleasure. *(Alfred-Brehm-Platz. Tel. 21 23 37 35. U-Bahn #6 or 7 to "Zoo." Open mid-March to Sept. M-F 9am-7pm, Sa-Su 8am-7pm; Oct. to mid-March daily 9am-5pm. DM11, students DM5; with U-Bahn ticket DM9, students DM4. Last Saturday of every month DM5.50, students DM2.50; with U-Bahn ticket DM4, students DM2.)*

MUSEUMS

Pick up a **Frankfurt Card** (see p. 402) for big savings on museum visits; or visit on Wednesdays, when most museums are free.

MUSEUMSUFER

The **Museumsufer** hosts an eclectic collection of museums. Located on the Schaumainkai along the south bank of the Main between the Eiserner Steg and the Friedensbrücke, the museums are housed in opulent 19th-century mansions as well as in more modern buildings designed by contemporary architects. The Museumsufer is also home to Frankfurt's weekly **flea market** (open Sa 9am-2pm during the warm months), and the **Museumsuferfest,** a huge cultural jamboree that draws more than a million visitors over three days in late August. Frankfurt also has nearly 50 spectacular commercial art galleries clustered around Braubachstr. and Saalgasse.

MUSEUM FÜR KUNSTHANDWERK. Arts and crafts imagined by human minds and made by human hands from Europe and the Near and Far East. *(Schaumainkai 17. Tel. 21 23 40 37 or 21 23 85 30. Open Tu and Th-Su 10am-5pm, W 10am-8pm. DM8, students DM4. Free on Wednesdays.)*

MUSEUM FÜR VÖLKERKUNDE. The Museum of Ethnology holds rare collections from the Pacific, Indonesia, Africa, and America. *(Schaumainkai 29. Tel. 21 23 15 10. Open Tu-Su 10am-5pm, W 10am-8pm. DM6, students DM3.)*

GALERIE 37. The only portion of the Museum für Völkerkunde open during renovations. Interesting, but very small. *(Schaumainkai 37. Tel. 212 57 55. Museum with gallery DM8, students DM4. Same hours as its parent.)*

HESSEN

DEUTSCHES FILMMUSEUM. Exhibits the development of filmmaking in an entertaining, interactive style. Film yourself flying on a carpet above the Frankfurt skyline, or take in an old movie on the 3rd floor. *(Schaumainkai 41. Tel. 21 23 88 30. Museum and adjoining café open Tu, Th-F, and Su 10am-5pm, W 10am-8pm, Sa 2-8pm. Tours Su 3pm. DM5, students DM2.50. Films DM8, students DM6.)*

ARCHITEKTURMUSEUM. A 3-floor survey of the last 10 years in European architecture in a beautifully designed space of white surfaces and right angles. *(Schaumainkai 43. Tel. 21 23 88 44. Open Tu and Th-Su 10am-5pm, W 10am-8pm. Tours Su 3pm. DM8, students DM4.)*

DEUTSCHES POSTMUSEUM. To remind you that Grandma didn't have email and that cell phones weren't ringing in restaurants 10 years ago, the museum exhibits the history of German communication and travel. Interactive video displays in German; English audio tours available. *(Schaumainkai 53. Tel. 606 00. Open Tu-Su 10am-5pm. The **Funkstation,** an amateur radio booth on the top floor, is open W 10am-5pm, Th 10am-1pm, and the first Sunday of each month 1-5pm. Museum and radio booth free.)*

STÄDEL. One of Germany's leading art museums, with an excellent collection of Old Masters, housed in a stately mansion. *(Schaumainkai 63, between Dürerstr. and Holbeinstr. Tel. 605 09 80. Open Tu and Th-Su 10am-5pm, W 10am-8pm. DM8, students DM4.)*

LIEBIEGHAUS. The castle-like building and gardens contain a fine collection of Asian and Egyptian art and sculptures from the medieval, Renaissance, Baroque, Rococo, and Classical periods. Hungry art lovers chill in the café on the patio. *(Schaumainkai 71. Tel. 21 21 86 17. Open Tu and Th-Su 10am-5pm, W 10am-8pm. Tours W 6:30pm and Su 11am. DM5, students DM2.50. Café open in the summer Tu-F 11am-10pm, Sa 11am-6:30pm, Su 10am-8pm.)*

ELSEWHERE IN FRANKFURT

■MUSEUM FÜR MODERNE KUNST. Not to be missed. Just a few blocks up the street from the Dom, the triangular building's interior (the "slice of cake") is an ideal setting for the stunning modern art housed within, including impressive works by Claes Oldenburg, Roy Liechtenstein, and Jasper Johns. Art in every medium imaginable, guaranteed to push the borders of your mind. The basement shows films and slides. *(Domstr. 10. Tel. 21 23 04 47. Open Tu and Th-Su 10am-5pm, W 10am-8pm. DM7, students DM3.50.)*

SCHIRN KUNSTHALLE. A postmodern art gallery hosting visiting exhibits in wide open spaces. *(Next to the Dom, entrance in a narrow alley. Tel. 299 88 20. Open Tu and F-Su 10am-7pm, W-Th 10am-10pm. DM9, students DM7. DM6 and DM4 on Sundays.)*

HISTORISCHES MUSEUM. A series of exhibitions on the history of Frankfurt, including a permanent *Äpfelweinmuseum,* an exhibit of Frankfurt porcelain, and a comparative display of the city before and after the WWII bombing. *(Saalgasse 19. Tel. 21 23 55 99. Open Tu and Th-Su 10am-5pm, W 10am-8pm. DM8, students DM3.)*

NATURMUSEUM. Features several fully mounted dinosaur skeletons, impressive works of taxidermy, and some big whales thrown in for kicks. The largest natural history museum in Germany attracts the largest school groups in Frankfurt. *(Senckenberganlage 25. Tel. 754 20. U-Bahn #6 or 7 to "Bockenheimer Warte." Open M-Tu and Th-F 9am-5pm, W 9am-8pm, Sa-Su 9am-6pm. DM7, students DM3.)*

🎵 🎭 ENTERTAINMENT AND NIGHTLIFE

Frankfurt might be lacking in other areas, but when it comes to nightlife it can run to the head of the class. Its ballet, theater, and opera receive massive endowments from the city to ensure that performances are first-rate. There are two major theaters: the **Alte Oper,** Opernpl. (tel. 134 04 00; U-Bahn #6 or 7 to "Alte Oper"), a magnificent classical building reconstructed in the 1980s, offers a full range of classical music. The **Städtische Bühne,** Untermainanlage 11 (tel. 21 23 79 99; U-

Bahn #1, 2, 3, or 4 to "Willy-Brandt-Pl."), mounts ballets and operas as well as experimental renditions of traditional German plays. For productions in English, the **English Theater,** Kaiserstr. 52 (tel. 24 23 16 20) near the Hauptbahnhof, puts on comedies and musicals. Shows and schedules of the city's stages are detailed in several publications, including *Fritz* and *Strandgut* (free at the tourist office), and the *Journal Frankfurt* (DM3.30), available at any newsstand. Students can often buy leftover tickets at reduced prices one hour before performance. Regular prices for these events range from DM10 for a youth orchestra performance to DM210 for a prime opera seat. For information, call **Frankfurt Ticket** (tel. 134 04 00). The jazz clubs that reinvigorated the city after WWII by drawing such legends as Duke Ellington and Ella Fitzgerald can be found on Kleine Bockenheimer Str., known as the **Jazzgasse** (Jazz Alley).

For a night out drinking, head to the **Alt-Sachsenhausen** district between Brückenstr. and Dreieichstr., home to a huge number of rowdy pubs and taverns specializing in *Äpfelwein.* The complex of narrow cobblestoned streets centering on **Grosse** and **Kleine Rittergasse** teems with canopied cafes, bars, and restaurants; gregarious Irish pubs also abound.

Frankfurt has a number of thriving discos and prominent techno DJs, mostly in the commercial district between Zeil and Bleichstr. Wear something dressier than jeans—unless they're *really* hip jeans—if you plan to try your luck with the neurotic bouncers. Most clubs are for folks 18 or older; cover charges run DM10-15. Don't think you'll escape these, either—most clubs make you pay upon exiting.

U60311, Roßmarkt. A recent addition to the techno scene sponsored by the well-known DJ Sven Väth. Popular hangout of the ultra-trendy. Open M-Th and Su 11pm-4am, F-Sa 10pm-6am. Cover DM15-30.

Nachtleben, Kurt-Schumacher-Str. 45 (tel. 206 50). On the corner of Kurt-Schumacher-Str. and Zeil, this chic place serves as a postmodern café by day and hosts hordes of rocking twentysomethings on its red velour-draped dance floor at night. Th means reggae, while F features hip-hop and R&B. Open M-W and Su 11pm-2am. Live concerts Th-Sa 11pm-4am. Cover DM7-9.

Dorian Gray, (tel. 69 02 21 21) in terminal 1 at the airport, right outside the U-Bahn exit (see p. 400). Don't plan on coming here until 1am. The far-out location explains the late hours of this expansive, sumptuous club. Young crowd, techno galore. Open Th 10pm-4am, F-Sa 10pm-8am. Cover DM15. Special guests on Saturdays and free breakfast at 5am on weekday mornings. Strict dress code.

The Cave, Brönnerstr. 11. Hosts mostly independent punk rock concerts as well as some reggae and ska in a speakeasy-style underground locale. Open M-Th 10pm-4am. Sa-Su 10pm-6am. Cover DM5.

Der Jazzkeller, Kleine Bockenheimer Str. 18a (tel. 28 85 37). An older crowd swings and swigs in this grotto-like mainstay of the Frankfurt jazz scene. Live music Th and Sa. Open Tu-Su 9pm-3am. Cover W and F DM8, varies other nights.

Blue Angel, Brönnerstr. 17 (tel. 28 27 72). A Frankfurt institution and one of the liveliest gay men's clubs around. Techno music, flashing lights and police whistles dominate the interior. Open daily 11pm-4am. Cover DM11, including drinks F and Sa.

Cooky's, Am Salzhaus 4 (tel. 28 76 62), off Goetheplatz. Not quite as chic as its club peers, Cooky's hosts a less sophisticated crowd in a basement pumped up by a fog machine and flashing lights. Cover DM8-10. Open M-Th and Su 11pm-4am, F-Sa 10pm-6am.

Sinkkasten, Brönnerstr. 5 (tel. 28 03 85). Mostly disco in a traditional nightclub atmosphere. Occasional live bands. Cover DM10-30, Sa DM8. Opening hours vary.

WIESBADEN

While most German cities flaunt their castles and cathedrals, Wiesbaden's center of gravity is a ritzy Monte-Carlo-esque casino. The city's designer boutiques and hip citizens still pay homage to the heady years of the 19th century when Europe's aristocracy came to frolic away its time and money. And despite the large American presence due to the nearby military base, a bit of the old Wiesbaden is here for the taking; you can still take the hydraulic funicular to the top of the Neroberg and, provided that you're formally attired, gamble away your life's savings at the casino.

◪ PRACTICAL INFORMATION. Wiesbaden's **tourist office**, Marktstr. 6 (tel. 172 97 80; fax 172 97 98), down Bahnhofstr. from the train station, books **rooms** (from DM70) for a DM6 fee. (Open M-F 9am-6pm, Sa-Su 9am-3pm.) Wiesbaden makes a good daytrip from Mainz (p. 384), as the two cities share a **public transportation** system. Ask about the day pass for buses. The **Mitfahrzentrale**, Bahnhofstr. 49-53 (tel. 33 35 55 or 194 40), in a camper halfway between the pedestrian zone and the station, arranges ride shares. (Open M-F 9am-6pm, Sa 9am-noon.) The **post office**, Kaiser-Friedrich-Ring 81, is to the left as you come out of the station. (Open M-F 8am-6pm, Sa 8am-noon.) The **telephone code** is 0611.

▟▐◻ ACCOMMODATIONS AND FOOD. Wiesbaden's selection of inexpensive accommodations is slim. The **Jugendherberge (HI)**, Blücherstr. 66 (tel. 486 57; fax 44 11 19), provides cheap beds, high-quality facilities, and a friendly staff. Take bus #14 (direction: "Klarental") to "Gneisenaustr." The bus lets you off on Blücherstr. Turn left, cross Gneisenaustr. and continue to the end of the street. (DM24, over 26 DM29. Sheets DM6. Breakfast included. Reception until midnight. Check-in after 2pm. Curfew midnight.) The pedestrian zone is brimming with pubs and restaurants, and spice abounds in the ethnic joints around **Schwalbacher Str.** between Pl. der Deutschen Einheit and Einserstr. **Kebab House**, Schwalbacher Str. 61 (tel. 30 63 45), dishes out gigantic servings of ready-made Turkish food for unbeatable prices. (DM5-8. Open daily 10am-1am.) **The Irish Pub**, Michelsberg 15 (tel. 30 08 49), rocks with live music every evening, offers enormous Irish breakfasts on Sundays (11am-3pm; DM14), and serves beer, wine, and coffee until the wee hours. (Open M-Th 6pm-1am, F 6pm-2am, Sa 7pm-2am, Su noon-1am.) **Setzkasten**, Wagemannstr. 33 (tel. 30 64 75), serves up scrumptious Bavarian specials for under DM16. (Open daily 4pm-4am. Kitchen closes at 3am.) **Victuals** can be obtained at **HL Markt**, 46-48 Friedrichstr. (Tel. 99 91 70. Open M-F 8am-8pm, Sa 8am-4pm.)

◙ ◨ SIGHTS AND ENTERTAINMENT. The patrons of the **Spielbank** (casino; tel. 53 61 00) gambol about within a large, posh compound alternately used for business conferences, parades, and local art exhibitions (as well as gambling). Situated off Wilhelmstr., the complex is bordered on two sides by the expansive **Kurpark**, where locals unwind under century-old willow trees during the summer. Take bus #1 or 8 to "Kurhaus/Theater." Compulsive gambler Fyodor Dostoevsky squandered the last 30 rubles that stood between him and destitution while visiting Wiesbaden, and so can you. (Coat and tie rental DM10. Open daily 3pm-3am. 21+.) Or flout the dress code and get down and dirty with the slots next door at **Kleines Spiel**. (Open daily 2pm-2am. DM2. 21+.) Opposite Kleines Spiel, on the other side of the *Kurhaus* is the stately **Staatstheater** (tel. 13 23 25), inscribed with the ominous instruction *Der Menscheit Würde ist in Eure Hand gegeben, bewahret Sie.* ("The dignity of mankind is in your hands, preserve it.") The Staatstheater and neighboring **Kleines Haus** present traditional and modern ballets, operas, and plays; tickets occasionally sell for as little as DM9-15. (Box office for Staatstheater and Kleines Haus open Tu-F 11am-6pm, Sa-Su 11am-1pm, and 1hr. before performance.) On Burgstr. west of the Staatstheater warbles the **world's biggest cuckoo clock**, topped by a giant moosehead. The birds strut every half hour from 8am to 8pm. Toward the train station on Friedrich-Ebert-Allee, the **Museum Wiesbaden** (tel. 368 21 70), reminiscent of a train station, houses temporary exhibits of modern German art. (Open Tu 10am-8pm, W-F 10am-4pm, Sa-Su 10am-5pm. DM5, students and seniors DM2.50.) The angular, red-brick **Marktkirche** is on the Markt near the tourist office. (Open Tu and F-Sa 10:30am-12:30pm, W 10:30am-noon, Th 3:30-5:30pm.)

Neroberg, a low hill at the north end of town, provides an alternative to Wiesbaden's bustle. The hill is crowned by the **Russisch-Griechische Kapelle,** the most impressive monument in the city. The painstakingly decorated Russian Orthodox chapel, modelled after the Cathedral of Christ the Redeemer in Moscow, was built in 1855 as a mausoleum for Princess Elizabeth of Nassau, the niece of a Russian Czar who was married to a local duke and died in childbirth at age 19. Her tomb dominates the chapel's inspiring interior. Take bus #1 to "Nerotal," and walk or take the **Nerobergbahn** (hydraulic funicular) to the summit of the 254m hill. (Funicular open May-Aug. daily 9:30am-8pm; April and Sept. W and Sa noon-7pm, Su 10am-7pm; Oct. W and Sa-Su noon-6pm. DM2; round-trip DM3. Kapelle open daily April-Oct. 11am-5pm. DM1, students and children DM0.50.)

DARMSTADT

Despite the fact that German speakers may translate Darmstadt as "intestine city," the town is actually quite lovely. Home to the venerable German Academy of Language and Literature, which annually awards the most prestigious honor in German letters, one would expect Darmstadt to be staid and reserved. But its other great distinction—a collection of superb pieces of late 19th-century *Jugendstil* (art nouveau) architecture—graces the city with its lighthearted, colorful appearance. Darmstadt's cultural traditions are complemented by its lively, bazaar-like streets, making it a surprisingly diverse, largely untouristed little place that's a short trip from Frankfurt.

▶ ORIENTATION AND PRACTICAL INFORMATION. Darmstadt is accessible from Frankfurt by frequent **trains** (30min., 3 per hour) or by S-Bahn #3 (both DM10.50). **S-Bahn** and **bus** tickets cost DM2.20, DM5.10 for 1 day, or DM30.60 for a 7-day ticket (students DM23). For a **taxi,** call **Funk** (tel. 194 10) any time of the day or night. The **tourist office** (tel. 13 27 82) in front of the main train station provides city maps and hotel guides and finds rooms. (Open M-F 9am-6pm, Sa 9am-noon.) A **branch office,** at Luisenpl. 5 (tel. 13 27 81), is located in a glass tower in the Luisencenter; they expect to be closed at some point in 2000 for renovations. (Open M-F 9am-6pm, Sa 10am-1pm.) Rent **bikes** at **Prinz-Emil-Garten,** Heidelberger Str. 56. Take S-Bahn #1 to "Prinz-Emil-Garten." Or rent at the *Minigolfplatz* (tel. 66 48 90), up the hill and to the left. (Open M-F 8am-8pm, Sa-Su 2-8pm; both locations DM7 per day.) For easy reading, visit **Duckbill & Gooseberry's British Shop,** Alexanderstr. 26 (tel. 753 80), on the corner of Mauerstr. (Open M-F 10am-7pm, Sa 10am-4pm.) **Louisetta,** Mauerstr. 4, a **gay and lesbian cultural center,** shows movies (M, Tu, and Su at 8pm) and serves drinks (Su from 7pm). Take Bus F or K to "Alexanderstr./TU." Send an **e-mail** to everyone back home from **Cantina y Bar Mexicano,** Luisenpl. 5, on the second floor (DM10 per hour). The **post office,** 64283 Darmstadt, sends telegrams and faxes. There are two branches: **Postamt 1,** to your left as you exit the main train station, and **Postamt 11,** at Luisenpl. 3. (Both open M-F 9am-6pm, Sa 9am-noon.) The **telephone code** is 06151.

▶▶▶ ACCOMMODATIONS, FOOD, AND ENTERTAINMENT. The **Jugendherberge (HI),** Landgraf-Georg-Str. 119 (tel. 452 93; fax 42 25 35), offers spotless 3-bed rooms and friendly service. Take Bus D (direction: "Ostbahnhof") to "Großer Woog." (DM24, over 26 DM29. Breakfast included. Reception until 1am. Lockout 1-6am. Members only.) The hostel overlooks **Großer Woog** (tel. 13 23 93), an artificial lake and swimming hole. (Open daily mid-May to mid-Sept. 8am-8pm. DM3.50, students DM2. Boats DM6 per hour) **Zentral Hotel,** Schuchardstr. 6 (tel. 264 11; fax 268 58), offers a great bargain for its extremely convenient location, well-appointed rooms, and breakfast. From Luisenplatz, walk along Luisenstr. with the Luisencenter mall on your right before turning left onto Schuchardstr. (Singles DM60, with shower DM90; doubles DM120, with shower DM150.)

Eating in Darmstadt can be pricey. Try **Plus,** the **grocery** store across from the Schloß on Marktpl. (Open M-F 8:30am-7pm, Sa 8am-4pm.) Every morning except Sunday fresh fruits and cold cuts crowd the Marktplatz for the outdoor **Markt.** Most of the city's inexpensive dining can be found in **Martinsviertel,** a student area northeast of the city center. The university **Mensa** dishes out cheap meals. With your back to the northern side of the Schloß, cross Alexanderstr., then take a right and walk past the yellow *Staatsarchiv* and gray five-story building on your left. Once past these, turn left down the stairs, then right and head upstairs into the University's *Otto-Bernd-Halle.* A decent selection of generous sandwiches (DM1) and light fare runs DM3-6. **Efendi's,** Landgraf-Georg-Str. 13 (tel. 29 38 09), has generous, spicy portions of Mediterranean dishes, including vegetarian options and large salads (DM3-9). Take a right when facing the gilded archway of the southern side of the Schloß and walk straight. Cross the intersection and Efendi's will be on the right. (Open M-Tu and Su 11am-midnight.) Locals recommend **Nachrichten-Treff,** 20 Elisabethenstr. (tel. 238 23), where beers (DM4) are served and live music is heard every day. (Open 11:45am-11:30pm.) From Luisenpl. take Luisenstr. and the first right onto Elisabethenstr. Pool action can be found at **Kuckucksnest,** a happening after-hours establishment a little farther up Landgraf-Georg-Str. The music is loud and beer runs DM3-7. (Cover M-Tu DM0.55, W-Su DM5.99. Open daily 8pm-3am.) For *Kneipe*-hopping late at night, the Martinsviertel, always full of college students, is best. Make sure to pick up *Journal Frankfurt* (DM3.30), a magazine that reports on nightlife in Darmstadt as well. The first week in July every year Darmstadt parties during **Heinerfest** with beer, music, fireworks, and rides in the city's center.

🔆 **SIGHTS.** The mecca of Damstadt's *Jugendstil* architecture (see p. 26) is **Mathildenhöhe,** an artists' colony on a hill west of the city center founded by Grand Duke Ernst Ludwig in 1899. The Duke fell in love with *Jugendstil* and invited seven artists to build a "living and working world" of art, giving them a huge budget to transform the urban landscape with this nature-friendly predecessor to Art Deco. The result was this startling architectural complex, heavy on flowered trellises and somber fountains. Check out the five-fingered **Hochzeitsturm** (wedding tower), the city's wedding present to Grand Duke Ernst Ludwig in 1908. (Open March-Oct. Tu-Su 10am-6pm. DM3, students DM1.) Rising like a monstrous jukebox against the German sky, the 48m tower offers a scenic view of Darmstadt. To reach the tower and all of Mathildenhöhe, walk east from the Luisenplatz along Erich-Ollenhauer-Promenade, or take bus F to "Lucasweg/Mathild," then take a right onto Lucasweg. Look out for events celebrating the colony's centenary birthday in 2000. The Mathildenhöhe also hosts the **Museum der Künstlerkolonie,** Alexandraweg 26 (tel. 13 27 78), which houses Art Nouveau furniture and rotating exhibits of modern art (Open Tu-Su 10am-5pm. Tours 11am on the first Su of each month. DM5, students DM3.) A gilded, three-domed Russian Orthodox Church, the **Russische Kapelle** (Russian Chapel), Nikolaiweg 18 (tel. 42 42 35), also rests on the Mathildenhöhe. (Open April-Sept. 9am-6pm, Oct.-March 9:30am-5pm. DM1.50, students DM1.) The chapel was imported stone by stone from Russia at the behest of Czar Nicholas II upon his marriage to Darmstadt's Princess Alexandra.

Right off of Alexandraweg near Mathildenhöhe, the **Institut für Neue Technische Form,** Eugen-Bracht-Weg 6 (tel. 480 08), enshrines the Braun design collection, which showcases the evolution of the company's renowned electrical appliances since 1955—everything from Aunt Sally's prized blender to Uncle Jörg's cutting-edge electric razor. (Open Tu-Sa 10am-6pm, Su 10am-1pm. Free.) A few blocks farther east at the corner of Seitersweg and Wolfskehlstr. lies the entrance to **Rosenhöhe,** a lively park that houses a rose garden and a mausoleum of the city's deceased dukes. The garden was planted in 1810 at the request of Grand Duchess Wilhelmine, who wanted a garden that breathed "the free, noble Spirit of Nature." With its overgrown lawns, hulking evergreens, and cemetery-like serenity, it seems to fulfill Wilhelmine's wish.

The gigantic coral and white **Schloß** is smack-dab in the middle of the city. Built between 1716 and 1727, it was modeled by a wistful Frenchman after Versailles. Since WWII, the Schloß has served as a public university library and police station. A small **museum** (tel. 240 35) tucked in the eastern wing holds 17th- to 19th-century ducal clothing and furniture. (Open M-Th 10am-1pm and 2-5pm, Sa-Su 10am-1pm. Obligatory 1hr. guided tour; last tour begins 1hr. before closing. DM5, students DM3.) What's a Schloß without a *Garten?* **Herrngarten,** a lush expanse of well-maintained greenery north of the Schloß, provides space for loafing students, gamboling dogs, and ducks (which you can't feed). Even more exquisite is the **Prinz-Georg-Garten,** arranged in Rococo style and maintained by a brigade of six gardeners. (Open April-Sept. 7am-7:30pm; Oct.-March 8am-dark.) Next to it, the recently renovated **Porzellanschlößchen** (little porcelain castle), Schloßgartenstr. 7 (tel. 78 85 47), flaunts an extensive collection of porcelain. (Open M-Th 10am-1pm and 2-5pm, Sa-Su 10am-1pm.) Those with a geological, paleontological, or zoological bent will appreciate the **Landesmuseum,** Friedenspl. 1 (tel. 16 57 03), at the southern end of the Herrngarten across from the Schloß, its doors framed by two lions. (Open Tu-Sa 10am-5pm, also W 7-9pm, Su 11am-5pm. DM5, students DM2.50.)

LAHNTAL (LAHN VALLEY)

The peaceful Lahn River flows through verdant hills, bounteous vineyards, and delightful *Dörfer*. As such, the valley is a very popular destination for German families wishing to enjoy the great outdoors. Every spring and summer, campgrounds and hostels fill with people who have come to take advantage of the hiking, biking, and kayaking along the Lahn. Rail service runs regularly between Koblenz in the West and Gießen at the eastern end of the valley, as well as between Frankfurt and Limburg.

LIMBURG AN DER LAHN

Limburg an der Lahn flourished during the Middle Ages as a bridge for merchants and journeymen traveling from Köln to Frankfurt. Today, it serves much the same function, but for a different reason—as the most important train station between Koblenz and Gießen, Limburg is an excellent base from which to explore the Upper Lahn Valley. Largely unscathed by WWII, Limburg prides itself on its well-preserved medieval town houses scattered throughout the Altstadt. Often confused with a notoriously cheesy Dutch city of the same name, Limburg an der Lahn is known for **St. Georg-Dom,** a majestic cathedral that rests on the peak of the Altstadt. In addition to serving as the seat for the bishop of the Limburg diocese, this architectural hybrid of Romanesque and Gothic styles shelters a series of galleries

THE OSMONDS OF CENTRAL EUROPE Although most of today's young people have had regretfully little exposure to the phenomenon of singing-and-dancing, vaguely Christian, large-littered rock 'n' roll families, **the Kelly Family,** enormously popular in Germany and the rest of central Europe, can provide a quick (and addictive) fix. Composed of nine long-haired gender-neutral siblings, the family members are American expats who outfit themselves in a weird mixture of 60s hippy headbands and bell-bottoms, medieval robes, and the latest Eurotrash fashions (including some mongo red platforms). Their message is similarly bizarre; their repertoire includes everything from gospel songs to catchy little ditties like "Papa Cool" and "Fell in Love with an Alien." While some may find the family's aesthetics unappealing, Europeans go ga-ga for the Kelly kids, with their latest album selling a whopping four million copies in Central Europe. While traveling through Germany, keep your eyes peeled for their colorful posters emblazoned with their bubbly, 60s-style logo; if you see one, that means the Family—double-decker bus and all—is coming to town. Buy a ticket if you can; shows sell out fast.

and carefully restored frescoes. From the train station, follow Bahnhofstr. until it ends in the Altstadt and take a left on Salzgasse. Take a sharp right onto the Fischmarkt and from there follow Domstr. all the way up to the Dom. Next to the cathedral the **Diözesanmuseum und Domschatz**, Domstr. 12 (tel. 29 52 33), display a small but significant collection of medieval religious artifacts dating back to the 12th century. (Open mid-March to mid-Nov. Tu-Sa 10am-1pm and 2-5pm, Su 11am-5pm. DM3, students DM1.)

The **tourist office**, Hospitalstr. 2 (tel. 61 66; fax 32 93), books **rooms** (from DM35) for free if you stop by (DM1 to book by phone). Turn left on the street in front of the station and make a quick right on Hospitalstr. The office also provides details about the local **Oktoberfest**, which begins the third week of October. (Open April-Oct. M-F 8am-12:30pm and 2-6pm, Sa 10am-noon; Nov.-March M-Th 8am-12:30pm and 2-5pm, F 8am-1pm.) The **Jugendherberge (HI)**, Auf dem Guckucksberg (tel. 414 93; fax 438 73), in Eduard-Horn-Park, has fuzzy green beds and a really friendly staff. From the station, go right through the underpass and take the left exit toward Frankfurter Str. Follow Im Schlenkert right until it empties onto a larger road, and take this right until it branches with Frankfurter Str. on the left; the hostel is on the right along Frankfurter Str. Or take bus #603 from Hospitalstr. (direction: "Am Hammerberg"; runs every hour on the hour from 8am-6pm) to "Jugendherberge." (DM23.50, over 26 DM28. Breakfast included. Sheets DM6. Reception 5-10pm. Curfew 11:30pm.) There's a **Campingplatz** (tel. 226 10) in a riverside location on the far side of the Lahn. Follow directions to the Dom until the Fischmarkt, then bear left (instead of right on Domstr.) downhill to Brückengasse and the Lahnbrücke. On the other side of the Lahn, turn right onto Schleusenweg and walk 10 minutes along the Lahn to the campground. (DM5.80 per person. DM4.50 per tent. Reception 8am-1pm and 3-10pm. Open May to mid-Oct.) **Café Bassin**, Bahnhofstr. 8a (tel. 66 70), has excellent small meals from DM5-9 and daily specials from DM5-12. (Open M-Sa 7am-7pm, Su 10am-7pm.) The **telephone code** is 06431.

WEILBURG

As the Lahn passes through the Taunus hills and the Wester forest, the river bends itself around Weilburg into a shape resembling Gumby's head. Sprawled across a high ridge, the town's 14th-century **Schloß** and its terraced surroundings dominate the valley below. The residence of the counts and dukes of Nassau from 1355 to 1816, the castle now houses the **Schloßmuseum** (tel. 22 36), which flaunts a 10th-century Frankish foundation, a Romanesque interior, and a princely Baroque garden. To reach the Schloß from Mauerstr., walk up Neugasse to Schloßplatz. (Open May-Sept. M-F 10am-5pm, Sa-Su 10am-6pm; March-April and Oct. Tu-Su 10am-5pm; Nov.-Feb. Tu-Su 10am-4pm. DM6, children DM4; includes a 1hr. tour; last tour 1hr. before closing.) Across the Schloßplatz you'll find the **Bergbau- und Stadtmuseum**, Schloßpl. 1 (tel. 314 59), where you can gawk at the Weilburg mineshafts (active until the 1950s) and speed through the city's economic and social history. (Open April-Oct. Tu-F 10am-noon and 2-5pm, Sa-Su 10am-5pm; Nov.-March M-F 10am-noon and 2-5pm. DM4, students DM2.) The **Weilburger Schloßkonzerte** bring a dizzying array of international musicians to Weilburg every June and July. For schedules and tickets call 410 42. Weilburg is very proud of its magnificent crystal caves, actually located in Kubach, 4km away. Even if castles and churches a few centuries old don't impress you, the 350 million year-old limestone chunks of the **Kubacher Kristallhöhle** (tel. 940 00), Germany's highest crystal caves, might do the trick. To reach the caves, take bus #660 from the station to "Kubach/Abzweig Edelsberg." (Open M-F 2-4pm, Sa-Su 10am-5pm. DM5, students DM4.)

The **tourist office**, Mauerstr. 6 (tel. 76 71; fax 76 75), rents **bikes** (DM15 per day) and reserves **rooms** (from DM35) for free. From the bus station in front of the train station, take bus #671 (direction: "Oberbrechen") to "Landtor" and walk uphill along Vorstadtstr., which becomes Mauerstr. From the train station, walk left along the tracks and over the bridge, then veer right at the yellow restaurant. When you reach the 18th-century Landtor gate, turn right and walk up Vorstadtstr. (Open M-F 9am-1pm and 2-4:30pm, Sa 10am-noon.) The newly renovated

Jugendherberge Weilburg-Odersbach (HI), Am Steinbühl (tel. 71 16; fax 15 42), is comfortable, spacious, and clean. From the bus station, take bus #656 (direction: "Waldernbach") to "Am Steinbühl," and walk up the path. (DM23.50, over 26 DM28.50. Breakfast included. Sheets DM6. Reception 5-10pm.) Eating well on a budget is difficult in Weilburg. The Markt has some restaurants serving regional fare, but your best bet are the inexpensive *gyro* and *Döner* stands (DM6-8) immediately across from the train station. The **telephone code** is 06471.

MARBURG

Almost two centuries ago the Brothers Grimm spun their tales around these rolling hills, and from a distance, Marburg an der Lahn seems more of their world than ours. The city's isolation in the Lahn Valley allowed Landgrave Philipp to found the first Protestant university here in 1527. Its alumni list now reads like an intellectual history course syllabus: Martin Heidegger, Boris Pasternak, T.S. Eliot, Richard Bunsen (of burner fame), and the Spanish philosopher José Ortega y Gasset, to name a few. Those less familiar with Nobel Prize-winners will recognize graduates **Jakob** and **Wilhelm Grimm,** whose philological studies led them to collect the fairy tales that brought them fame. Today 15,000 students pore over books, conversation, and one another on the banks of the Lahn.

ℹ ORIENTATION AND PRACTICAL INFORMATION

Marburg is served by frequent trains from Frankfurt and Kassel. **Rudolphsplatz** lies at the foot of the elevated **Oberstadt,** which is the heart of the city. From the train station, take buses #1, 2, 3, 5 or 6 or follow Bahnhofstr. over the Lahn until it ends. Take a left on Elizabethstr., which becomes Pilgrimstein and eventually merges with Biegenstr., shortly thereafter bringing you to Rudolphspl. (25min.). Along Pilgrimstein narrow staircases and steep alleys lead to the Oberstadt, as does the *Oberstadt-Aufzug* elevator. (Operates daily 6am-2am. Free.)

Trains: Trains go to Frankfurt (1hr., 1 per hour, DM20.30), Hamburg (3½hr., 6 per day, DM46), Kassel (1½hr., 1 per hour, DM27), and Köln (3¼hr., 1 per hour, DM55).

Public Transportation: A single ticket gets you anywhere in the city (DM2.20).

Taxi: Funkzentrale, tel. 477 77 or **Minicar,** tel. 144 44.

Bike Rental: Velociped, Alte Kasseler Straße 43 (tel. 245 11). DM15 per day. Open M-F 10am-4pm.

Tourist Office: Pilgrimstein 26 (tel. 991 20; fax 99 12 12), 150m from Rudolphsplatz. Bus #1, 2, 3, 5 or 6 to "Rudolphspl.," and exit to the north along Pilgrimstein; the office is on the left. Sells maps and books **rooms** (from DM35) for free. Open M-F 9am-6pm, Sa 10am-2pm.

Bookstore: N.G. Elwert, Pilgrimstein 30 (tel. 17 09 34), one block from Rudolphspl., has a selection of English books. There is an annex of the store at Reitgasse 7. Open M-F 9:30am-7pm, Sa 9:30am-4pm.

Laundromat: Wasch Center, at the corner of Gutenbergstr. and Jägerstr. Sip a beer (DM3-5.50) in the adjacent **Bistro Waschbrett** during rinse cycle. Wash DM6, dry DM1 per 15min. Open M-F 8am-10pm, Sa 8am-9pm, Su 2-9pm.

Women's Resources: Autonomes Frauenhaus, Alter Kirchainer Weg 5 (tel. 16 15 16). Open M and W 10am-1pm, Th 4-7pm.

Emergency: Police, tel. 110. **Fire,** tel. 112. **Ambulance,** tel. 192 92.

Post Office: Bahnhofstr. 6, 35037 Marburg, a 5min. walk from the train station on the right. Open M-F 9am-6pm, Sa 9am-noon.

PHONE CODE	06421

HESSEN

ACCOMMODATIONS AND CAMPING

Although small, Marburg boasts more than 30 hotels and *Pensionen;* however, competition hasn't done too much to keep prices down. Plan ahead if you intend to spend less than DM60.

Jugendherberge (HI), Jahnstr. 1 (tel. 234 61; fax 121 91). From the train station walk down Bahnhofstr. and make a left on Elizabethstr., which becomes Pilgrimstein. after the church. This leads to Rudolphspl.; cross the bridge and turn right onto the riverside path. Continue to the small wooden bridge. Clean, spacious rooms, some with bath. Call ahead; the hostel fills with school groups. DM24.50, over 26 DM29.50. Sheets DM6. Breakfast included. Reception 9am-noon and 1:30-11:30pm, but house keys available with ID or DM50 deposit.

Tusculum-Art-Hotel, Gutenbergstr. 25 (tel. 227 78; fax 153 04). Follow Universitätsstr. from Rudolphspl. and take the first left on Gutenbergstr. You might confuse this bright, well-kept hotel with an art gallery—each room is individually designed in the style of a modern artist. Singles DM55-70, with shower DM75-90; doubles DM100-120, with shower DM125-140. Reception 10am-6pm. Kitchen open 24hr.

Camping: Camping Lahnaue, Trojedamm 47 (tel. 213 31), on the Lahn River. Follow directions to the hostel and continue down-river for another 5min. DM7 per person. Tent DM5. Open April-Oct. Call ahead.

FOOD

Marburg's cuisine caters to its large student population; most establishments offer *Würste* or hefty pots of pasta. The streets surrounding the **Markt** are full of standing-room only cafés serving sandwiches for around DM5. **Aldi,** Gutenbergstr. 19, caters to your **grocery** needs. (Open M-F 9am-6:30pm, Sa 8am-2pm.)

Mensa, Erlenring 5. Cross the bridge at Rudolphspl. and make the 2nd left on Erlenring. Satisfy your hearty appetite with the university crowd. 3-course meals DM3-6. Open during the semester M-F 8:15am-10pm, Sa noon-2pm; during breaks M-F 8:15am-7:30pm, Sa noon-2pm.

Bistro-Café Phönix, Am Grün 1 (tel. 16 49 69). Tucked in a short alley between Rudolphspl. and Universitätsstr., the bistro serves traditional dishes as well as lighter fare. Ice-cold piña coladas (DM9) are a nice break from the omnipresent *Marburger Bier.* Open M-Th 10am-2am, F-Sa 10am-3am.

Café Barfuß, Barfüßerstr. 33 (tel. 253 49), is packed with locals. Big breakfast menu (DM5.50-12.50) served until 3pm. Amusing menu with very funny cartoons helps digest any of the 5 beers on tap (DM2.80-6.50). Open daily 10am-1am.

Café Vetter, Reitgasse 4 (tel. 258 88), is a traditional café proud of its terrace on the edge of the Oberstadt. Cake and coffee runs DM8. Open M and W-Sa 8:30am-6:30pm, Tu 11am-6:30pm, Su 9:30am-6:30pm.

SIGHTS

LANDGRAFENSCHLOSS. The former haunt of the infamous Teutonic knights looks today nearly as it did in 1500. Count Philip brought rival Protestant reformers Martin Luther and Ulrich Zwingli to his court in 1529 to convince them to kiss and make up; he was on the verge of success when an epidemic made everyone grumpy and uncooperative. The Schloß houses the **Museum für Kulturgeschichte,** which exhibits Hessian history and religious art, as well as the recently unearthed 9th-century wall remnants in the west wing. *(From Rudolphspl. or Markt take bus #16 (direction: "Schloß") to the end, or hike up the 250 steps from the Markt. Open April-Oct. Tu-Su 10am-6pm; Nov.-March Tu-Su 11am-5pm. Last entry 30min. before closing. DM3, students DM2.)*

ELISABETHKIRCHE. Save some ecclesiastical awe for the oldest Gothic church in Germany, modeled on the French cathedral at Rheims. The name of the church honors the town patroness, a widowed child-bride (engaged at four, married at 14) who took refuge in Marburg, founded a hospital, and snagged sainthood four years after she died. The **reliquary** for her bones is so overdone, it's glorious. *(Elisabethstr. 3. Tel. 655 73. With your back to the train station, walk down Bahnhofstr. 5min. and turn left on Elisabethstr. Open daily April-Sept. 9am-6pm; Oct. 9am-5pm; Nov.-March M-Sa 10am-4pm, Su after 11am. Church free; reliquary DM3, students DM2.)* Walk up the little hill across from the Elisabethkirche to the 13th-century **St. Michaelskapelle,** built as a funereal home to the many admirers of Elisabeth's shrine.

RUDOLPHSPLATZ. Today's university building was erected in 1871, but the original **Alte Universität** on Rudolphsplatz was built on the rubble of a monastery conveniently vacated when Reformation-minded Marburgers ejected the resident monks. As the central point on campus, the **Aula** bears frescos illustrating Marburg's history. The nearby houses with technicolor flags are former **fraternities.**

UNIVERSITÄTSMUSEUM FÜR BILDENDE KUNST. The university's impressive collection of 19th-and 20th-century painting and sculpture is housed in a banal-looking building surrounded by parking lots and a mini-mall. The variety of paintings includes masterpieces by Cranach, Picasso, and Kandinsky. The section on Expressive Realism depicts the lost generation of artists who matured during the Nazi period. *(Biegenstr. 11. Tel. 28 23 55. Open Tu-Su 11am-1pm and 2-5pm. Free.)*

MARKT. Greeting you in front of the 16th-century Gothic **Rathaus** is a horseman slaying a figure that tragically resembles Puff the Magic Dragon. For a glance at some really modern art, check out the **Kunstverein.** The gallery displays special exhibits by modern artists and, in August, pieces by local talent. *(Markt 16. Tel. 258 82. Open Tu-Th and Sa 10am-1pm and 2-5pm, F 10am-1pm and 2-8pm, Su 11am-1pm. Free.)*

OTHER SIGHTS. The 13th-century **Lutherische Pfarrkirche St. Marien** features amber-colored stained glass and an elaborate organ. *(Lutherische Kirchhof 1. Tel. 252 43. Open daily 9am-5pm. Free organ concerts Oct.-July Sa at 6:30pm.)* Down Kugelgasse the 15th-century **Kugelkirche** (sphere church) owes its peculiar name not to its shape but to the *cuculla* (hats) worn by the religious order that founded it.

🎵🎭 ENTERTAINMENT AND NIGHTLIFE

Bars and pubs in Marburg breed faster than rabbits; in the Oberstadt alone there are more than 60 fine establishments. Live music, concert, theater, and movie options are listed in the weekly *Marburger Express,* available at many bars and pubs. Things get hopping on the first Sunday in July, when costumed citizens parade onto the Markt for the rowdy **Frühschoppenfest.** Drinking officially kicks off at 11am when the brass rooster on top of the 1851 Rathaus flaps its wings. Unofficially, however, the barrels of *Alt Marburger Pils* are tapped at 10am when the ribald old Marburger *Trinklieder* (drinking ballads) commence.

🏛 **Barfly/Café News/Hollywood Stars/Down Under Dance Club,** Reitgasse 5 (tel. 212 05 or 26). All your nightlife needs in one convenient location. **Barfly** is a bistro and terrace café. Open daily 11am-1am. **Café News** is a trendy spot with a mesmerizing view of the Lahn Valley. Open daily 9am-1am. **Hollywood Stars,** down the spiral staircase, serves special drinks and American fare. Happy "hour" daily 6-7:30pm. Open daily 6pm-1am. **Down Under** raves on weekends—a dance mecca. Open F-Sa 9pm-1am.

Diskothek Kult, Temmlerstr. 7 (tel. 941 83). Bus #A1 (direction: "Pommernweg") or A2 (direction: "Cappeler Gleiche") to "Frauenbergstr." The only disco in town, this place gets 'em all, bringing in DJs from England and the U.S. with mad skillz. Open Tu-W 9pm-3am, F-Sa 9pm-4am. Cover DM3-5.

Bolschoi Café, Ketzerbach (tel. 622 24). From Rudolfsplatz, walk up Pilgrimstein until you reach the Elizabethkirche and turn left on Ketzerbach; it's at the end of the block. The Communist kitsch here will warm the cockles of any Cold Warrior's heart with its red candles, red walls, red foil ceiling, and 20 brands of domestic and imported vodka (DM3-6). Lenin's bust is stenciled on the wall. Open M-W and Su 8pm-1am, F-Sa 8pm-2am.

Hinkelstein, Markt 18 (tel. 242 10), a classic hangout for dart-playing locals listening to Hendrix and Jackson Brown. A respite from the techno scene. Open daily 7pm-1am.

Kulturladen KFZ, Schulstr. 6 (tel. 138 98), hosts an impressive array of events, including concerts, cabarets, and gay and lesbian happenings. Cover varies.

FULDA

In the grim days of the Cold War division, Fulda gained notoriety as the most likely target for a Warsaw Pact invasion, earning it the undesirable nickname "Fulda Gap." The city's central location between Hamburg, Berlin, Munich, and Köln changed from burden to asset as reunification turned Fulda into a transportation hub. Today Fulda is rich in culture and serves as the economic and political center of eastern Hessen. The result of this unsteady evolution is a strange contrast: in startling proximity to the marvelous historical treasures are rows of fast-food restaurants, boutiques, and mini-malls which support a steady flow of local teens.

⁊ ORIENTATION AND PRACTICAL INFORMATION. Due to its strategic location, Fulda offers good rail connections. **Trains** head to Frankfurt (1½hr., 2-3 every hr., DM47), Kassel (1hr., 2 per hour, DM47), Weimar (2hr., 1 per hour, DM48), Nürnberg (1½hr., every 2 hr., DM59), and Hamburg (3hr., 1 per hour, DM147). The **tourist office** (tel. 10 23 45; fax 10 27 75) lies through the courtyard of the Schloß. It offers free maps and books **rooms** for free. The office also sponsors guided walks through the city. (Open M-F 8:30am-6pm, Sa 9:30am-4pm, Su 10am-2pm. Tours April-Oct. M-Th 11:30am, F-Su 11:30am and 2pm; Nov.-March Sa 11:30am and 2pm, Su 11:30am. DM5-7, students DM2.50-5.) At **Die Wäscheleine,** Kanalstr. 6. (tel. 24 06 57), have your sundries washed for you. (Wash DM9, wash and dry DM15. Open M-F 10am-12:30pm and 1:30-5pm.) The **post office,** 36037 Fulda, is at Heinrich-von-Bebra-Pl. The **telephone code** is 0661.

⌜ ACCOMMODATIONS AND FOOD. Fulda's **Jugendherberge (HI),** Schirmannstr. 31 (tel. 733 89; fax 748 11) can be reached from the train station with bus #1B or #5052 to "Stadion"; proceed two minutes up the hill—it will be on your left. Cheery vistas, purple hallways, a friendly staff, and clean rooms make for an overall pleasant experience. (DM23.50, over 27 DM28.50. Breakfast included. Sheets DM6. Curfew 11:30pm, but you can ask for the combination.) Frau Kremer runs a spartan but delightfully inexpensive ship at the **Gasthaus Kronhof,** Am Kronhof 2 (tel. 741 47), behind the Dom just outside the old city walls. From the Schloß, cross the street and walk downhill on Kastanienallee, which becomes Wilhelmstr. after the Dom. Take a right along the city wall on Kronhofstr. and look for a raspberry-pink building three blocks down on the left. (Singles DM35; doubles DM70, with shower DM90. Breakfast included.)

Marktstücke, Gemüsemarkt 12 (tel. 762 90), sells a delicious Turkish *Fladenbrot* sandwich with either turkey or goat cheese (DM6), as well as fresh soups (DM5) and waffles (DM4. Open M-Sa 8am-7pm, Su 10am-7pm.) **Vollwertimbiß Radieschen,** Gemüsemarkt 15 (tel. 229 88), offers a different vegetarian meal everyday (DM8.50) as well as staple items like *Rhönburger* (veggie burger). (DM5; Open M-F 10am-6pm, in winter also open Sa 10am-2pm.) To get to the Gemüsemarkt from the Stadtschloß, follow Friedrichstr. past the Stadtpfarrkirche and take the first right adjacent to a parking garage. Follow the walkway to the Gemüsemarkt.

◙ SIGHTS. The Fulda prince-abbots who dominated the city's spiritual and secular life for almost 700 years commissioned the construction of the compact Baroque quarter. Built as the centerpiece of the quarter and the residence of the

Prince-Abbots, the **Stadtschloß**'s numerous exquisite historical rooms now share space with the offices of Fulda's city hall. Particularly striking are the **Spiegelsäle** (mirror rooms) and the **Fürstensaal** ("festivity hall"). Adorning the Baroque ceiling of the former dining hall is an expansive painting of Greek gods devouring Fulda specialties, while a tiny corner room is equipped with fully 420 mirrors and 46 tiny paintings. Every Friday all of Fulda's wedding ceremonies are held here, since the Schloß serves as the *de facto* city hall. The room leading into the enormous Fürstensaal is covered with 17th-century tapestries depicting scenes from the Old Testament, and the Fürstensaal itself is ringed with paintings from Greek mythology and portraits of 16 Habsburg emperors. Entrance to the castle also includes access to the **Schloßturm** (tower). On the way up to the panoramic view of Fulda and its lush greenery, you'll pass an array of more recent historical items including various mechanical and electrical inventions. (Castle open M-Th and Sa-Su 10am-6pm, F 2pm-6pm. DM4, students DM3. Guided tour DM0.50 extra. Tours in German April-Oct. M-Th and Sa-Su 10:30am and 2:30pm, F only at 2:30pm; Nov.-March M-F 2:30pm, Sa-Su 10:30am and 2:30pm. Entrance to Schloßturm only DM2, students DM1.) To reach this yellow behemoth from the train station, head down Bahnhofstr., turn right in front of the church onto Rabanus, and follow signs to the Schloß. Behind the palace lies a luxurious **park** lined with terraces and home to the 18th-century **Orangerie,** a striking piece of architecture originally built to house the royal garden of imported orange and lemon trees; it now houses a ritzy café and a convention center. The **Floravase,** one of the most treasured Baroque sculptures in Germany, graces the front steps of the *Orangerie.*

Across the street from the Schloß stands the enormous 18th-century **Dom,** which houses the tomb of St. Boniface. An 8th-century English monk and missionary known as "the apostle of Germany," Boniface founded the Fulda abbey. An alabaster Baroque memorial edged with black marble depicts St. Boniface surrounded by angels lifting his coffin lid on Judgment Day, though it looks more like the cherubs are trying to stuff him back in. (Open April-Oct. M-F 10am-6pm, Sa 10am-3pm, Su and holidays 1-6pm; Nov.-March M-F 10am-5pm, Sa 10am-3pm, Su and holidays 1-6pm. Free. Organ concerts May-June and Sept.-Oct. Sa at noon. Free.) The **Dom-museum,** accessible through the courtyard, displays the dagger with which the head of St. Boniface was severed in 754, as well as Lucas Cranach's *Christ and the Adulteress.* (Open April-Oct. Tu-Sa 10am-5:30pm, Su 12:30-5:30pm; Feb.-March and Nov.-Dec. Tu-Sa 10am-12:30pm and 1:30-4pm, Su 12:30-4pm. DM4, students DM2.50.) Directly to the right of the Dom is **St. Michaelskirche.** (Open daily April to Oct. 10am-6pm; Nov. to March 2-4pm. Free.)

KASSEL

After Napoleon III and his soldiers were trounced by Prussian troops at the Battle of Sedan in 1870, the unlucky French emperor was captured. While crossing the Franco-German border on his way to the Schloß Wilhelmshöhe prison, Aacheners jeered *Ab nach Kassel* ("off to Kassel") at the crestfallen monarch. The slogan echoed throughout Germany. Today, hordes of travelers still answer the call, coming to see the many treasures Kassel has to offer. The steeped traditions of Wilhelmshöhe and the grand hillside parks that inspired the Brothers Grimm to record their famous fairy tales complement the cutting-edge thinking of the documenta contemporary art exhibitions and a pulsating *Uni*-setting.

⚐ ORIENTATION AND PRACTICAL INFORMATION

Kassel is a diffuse city, the product of a nightmarish building boom that followed the postwar housing shortage. Get a free map of the city at the tourist office or at the hostel to navigate the more remote parts of the city. Deutsche Bahn chose Kassel to be an InterCity Express connection and rebuilt **Bahnhof Wilhelmshöhe-Kassel** to streamlined contemporary specs. The Wilhelmshöhe station is the point of entry to Kassel's ancient castles and immense parks on the west side; the older **Hauptbahnhof** is the gateway to the tightly packed and entirely modernized Alt-

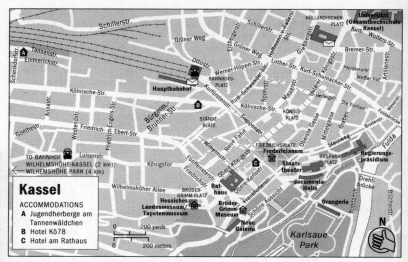

Kassel

ACCOMMODATIONS
A Jugendherberge am
  Tannenwäldchen
B Hotel Kö78
C Hotel am Rathaus

HESSEN

stadt. The Hauptbahnhof is now a model of extravagant hipness; its remodeling in the past year saturated it with postmodern adornments and one of the documenta exhibitions, the **caricatura.** IC, ICE, and most IR trains only stop at Wilhelmshöhe. Frequent trains, city buses, and streetcars shuttle between the stations; catch most other bus and streetcar lines at either the "Rathaus" or "Am Stern" stops. From the Hauptbahnhof, take streetcar #7 or 9 to "Rathaus," and streetcar #4, 7, or 9 to "Am Stern"; from Wilhelmshöhe, take streetcar #1, 4, or 6 to "Rathaus" or "Am Stern." The underground walkway in front of the Hauptbahnhof is often full of shady-looking types; don't walk there alone after dark. **Treppenstraße,** Kassel's original pedestrian zone and the first in all of Germany, and **Königsstraße,** the current pedestrian zone, are areas worth exploring.

Trains: To Frankfurt (2½hr., 2 per hour, DM54), Hamburg (2½hr., 2 per hour, DM99), Düsseldorf (3½hr., 1 per hour, DM145), and Munich (5hr., 1 per hour, DM172).

Ferries: Personenschiffahrt Söllner, Die Schlagd/Rondell (tel. 77 46 70; fax 77 77 76), at the Fuldabrücke near the Altmarkt, offers Fulda Valley tours (3hr.) mid-June to Aug. daily 2pm, May to mid-June and Sept. W and Sa-Su 2pm. One-way DM10, round-trip DM16, children half-price.

Public Transportation: Kassel's sophisticated system of buses and streetcars is integrated into the **NVV** (Nordhessischer Verkehrsverbund). Tickets priced by distance; single tickets range from DM2.50 (up to 4 stops) to DM43.70 (anywhere in the area). The **Multiticket** (DM8.50) is valid for 2 adults and 3 kids for a weekday or weekend. Ask questions at the **NVV-Center,** Königsplatz 366 (tel. 70 75 80).

Taxi: Tel. 881 11.

Car Rental: City-Rent Autofairmietung, Kurt-Schumacher-Str. 25 (tel. 77 08 21).

Bike Rental: FahrradHof, Wilhelmshöher Allee 253 (tel. 31 30 83), in the Wilhelmshöhe train station. Bikes from DM20 per day, DM80 per week. Open M-F 9am-1pm and 2-6pm, Sa 9am-3pm.

Tourist Office: Tourist-Information (tel. 340 54; fax 31 52 16), in Kassel-Wilhelmshöhe train station, sells maps (DM0.50). Ask about the **Kassel Service Card,** which provides access to public transportation and other discounts. 24hr. card DM12, 3-day card DM19. The staff also books **rooms** for a DM5 fee. Open M-F 9am-1pm and 2-6pm, Sa 9am-1pm.

Bookstore: Buchladung Vaternahm, Obere Königsstr. 7 (tel. 78 98 40). Broad selection of paperbacks in English. Open M-F 9:30am-8pm, Su 9am-4pm.

Laundromat: Schnell & Sauber, Friedrich-Ebert-Str. 83, near the hostel. Wash DM6. Dry DM1 per 11min. Soap included. Open M-Sa 5am-midnight.

Women's Resources: Frauenhaus Kassel, Frankfurter Str. 65 (tel. 89 88 89). **Beratungsstelle Schwarzer Winkel,** Goethestr. 44 (tel. 10 70 25).

AIDS Hotline: Frankfurter Str. 65 (tel. 28 39 07). Open daily 10am-1pm.

Emergency: Police, tel. 110. **Fire** and **Ambulance,** tel. 112.

Hospital: Städtische Klinik, Möncherbergstr. 41-43 (tel. 98 00).

Post Office: Hauptpostamt, Untere Königsstr. 95, 34117 Kassel, between Königsplatz and the university. Open M-F 8am-6pm, Sa 8am-noon.

Internet Access: InterDock Mediencafé, Untere Karlsstr. 4 (tel. 316 12 05,), in Dock 4 cultural center, behind Museum Friedricianum. DM8 per hour. Open Th-Sa 2-9pm.

PHONE CODE	0561

ACCOMMODATIONS AND CAMPING

Hotels in Kassel actively seek conventioneers and business crowds, but the large accommodations industry generally has a surplus of moderately priced rooms.

Jugendherberge am Tannenwäldchen (HI), Schenkendorfstr. 18 (tel. 77 64 55; fax 77 68 32). Streetcar #4 or 6 from the Rathaus or Bahnhof Wilhelmshöhe (direction: "Ottostr." or "Lindenberg") to "Annastr." Continue walking up Friedrich-Ebert-Str., and make a right on Schenkendorfstr. Or walk from the Hauptbahnhof: leave from the *Südausgang,* turn right on Kölnische Str., and turn right again onto Schenkendorfstr. Your window might overlook train tracks, but you also might get your own bathroom. DM24.50, over 26 DM29.50. Sheets DM6. Breakfast included. Reception 9am-11:30pm. Usually no curfew, but sometimes at midnight, depending on staff.

Hotel Kö78, Kölnische Str. 78 (tel. 716 14; fax 179 82). From the Hauptbahnhof, exit through the *Südausgang,* walk up the stairs, and follow Kölnische Str. uphill and to the right. From Bahnhof Wilhelmshöhe, follow the directions to the Jugendherberge, and from the train stop walk up Annastr. Turn right onto Kölnische Str. Handsome exterior shelters tastefully furnished rooms decorated with *documenta*-related artwork. Singles with shower from DM59, doubles from DM93. Breakfast included. All rooms have cable TV. Reception M-F 6am-10pm, Sa-Su 8am-10pm.

Hotel-Restaurant Palmenbad, Kurhausstr. 27 (tel./fax 326 91). Streetcar #3 (direction: "Ihringshäuser Str.") to "Wigandstr.," then 5min. uphill on An den Eichen. Or walk from Bahnhof Wilhelmshöhe up Wilhelmshöher Allee (towards Herkules), left on Baunsbergstr., and right on Kurhausstr. Cozy quarters, friendly staff. Singles DM49; doubles DM90, with shower DM95. Reception M-F 5:30-11pm, Sa 10am-11pm, Su 10am-3pm.

Hotel Am Rathaus, Wilhelmsstr. 29 (tel. 97 88 50; fax 978 85 30). From the Rathaus, make a left on Fünffensterstr., a left down Obere Karlsstr., and another left by the statue of Landgraf Karl striking a pose. Snug rooms and a central location. Singles DM61, with shower and TV DM70, with bath DM75; doubles with shower DM110-120. Hall toilets. Breakfast included. Reception 6am-10pm.

Camping: Kurhessen-Kassel, Giesenallee 7 (tel. 224 33). Bus #16 (direction: "Auestadion") or bus #25 (direction: "Bebelplatz") to "Damaschkebrücke." The campground boasts a stunning spot on the Fulda close to Karlsaue park. DM5 per adult, DM2 per child. Tents DM10-20. Reception 8am-1pm and 3-10pm. Open March-Oct.

◐ FOOD

Many of Kassel's culinary offerings take a bite out of the budget. **Friedrich-Ebert-Str.,** the upper part of **Wilhelmshöher Allee,** and the area around **Königsplatz** have supermarkets and cafés sprinkled among department stores and fashion boutiques. The **okay!** supermarket chain, with a branch at Bahnhof Wilhelmshöhe and another at Friedrich-Ebert-Str. 27, function as **grocery** stores, fruit stands, and bakeries rolled into one. (Open M-F 8:30am-8pm, Sa 8am-2pm.) Or pick through goodies at the **Markt** on Königsplatz. Inexpensive meals await in the university complex. From Bahnhof Wilhelmshöhe, take streetcar #1 to "Holländischer Pl.," cross through the underground passage, and continue in the same direction; walk along the left side of the university to the back and hang a right onto Arnold-Bode-Str. As in most large German cities, Kassel's Altstadt has food stands, bakeries, and *Imbiße.*

Mensa (tel. 804 25 87), on Arnold-Bode-Str. in the back left corner of the University, 100m across a gorge from the big red brick tower. Look for the *Mensa* sign—it's the only way to tell this brick building from the 50-odd others. Students with ID DM3-5, others tack on DM2. Lunch M-F 11:45am-2:15pm. The **Moritz-Restaurant** in the same building serves a more elaborate lunch with much shorter lines. Students DM5, others DM7. Open M-F 11am-2:30pm. Just around the corner, the **Studentwerke-Pavillon,** Diagonale 13, slaps together meals later in the day for the same prices. Open M-F 5-9pm. The café downstairs sells the cheapest ice cream around (DM0.80 per scoop).

Lohmann Biergarten, Königstor 8 (tel. 122 90). From the Rathaus, walk up Fünffensterstr. and make a left on Königstor. The only outdoor *Biergarten* in Kassel open late. One of Kassel's oldest and largest beer gardens, it serves tasty food at great prices. Spaghetti bolognese DM8, huge baguettes DM7, Greek salad DM8. Wash your meal down with beer (DM5 for 0.5L) or *Äpfelwein* (DM3). Open daily noon-2am.

Bistro & Restaurant Eckstein, Obere Königstr. 4 (tel. 71 33 00), at the corner of Fünffensterstr. The selection here is as large as the portions. Pizza DM6-13, veggie meals DM12. Lunch M-F noon-5pm, DM9. Open M-Th and Su 11am-1am, F-Sa 11am-2am.

Da Zhang, Kurfürstenstr. 8 (tel. 739 88 53), between the Hauptbahnhof and Treppenstr. Chinese specialties served in a classical Chinese-restaurant interior, complete with little fountains. Though main courses cost DM10-20, the *Schnellmenü* offers entrees for DM7.80 M-F 11am-2:30pm. Open daily 11am-2:30pm and 5:30-11pm.

◉ SIGHTS

Kassel's sights fall into three categories: those associated with documenta, those at Wilhelmshöhe, and those near the Rathaus. The museums and galleries of documenta are scattered downhill of Königsstr. between the Rathaus and Königsplatz towards the Fulda river. The sights at Wilhelmshöhe Park lie at one end of the long Wilhelmshöher Allee. At the other end stands the Rathaus, just after Wilhelmshöher Allee becomes Obere Königsstr. The latter road runs through Königsplatz to the *Uni.* Most of the museums—Schloß Wilhelmshöhe, Ballhaus, Hessisches Landesmuseum, Neue Galerie, and Orangerie—belong to **Staatliche Museen Kassel** and are covered by a package deal: the **Verbundkarte** offers admission to and is for sale at all of these museums (DM15, students DM10).

DOCUMENTA

In 1997, the Kassel hosted documenta for the 10th time since 1955. Several of the past documentas have become permanent exhibitions: visit Claes Oldenburg's *Pick-axe* on the banks of the Fulda near the Orangerie and Joseph Beuys' *7,000 oak trees,* both from documenta VII in 1982.

DOCUMENTA Hordes of art-lovers, dilettantes, and camera-toting curiosity-seekers descended upon Kassel in the summer of 1997 to take part in the world's pre-eminent exhibition of contemporary art, **documenta X.** Over the last 50 years, the consistency with which the documenta exhibitions have been challenging preconceptions of the political role of artistic expression serves as the best proof of its validity. Viewing contemporary art as a means of "social regulation or indeed control through the aestheticization of information and forms of debate that paralyze any act of judgment in the immediacy of raw seduction or emotion," the contributors emphasized the soul-searching and democratic potential of new media that subvert traditional notions of artistic form. Amid collections of giant Chia Pets and ironic images of "ideal" cityscapes, the show included a bevy of internet pieces which were broadcast worldwide in real-time (www.documenta.de). With memories of the recent exhibition still fresh, Kassel is preparing to launch documenta into the new millennium. Documenta XI will take place in Kassel from June 8 to September 15, 2002.

MUSEUM FRIEDRICIANUM. The enormous building is the oldest museum building on the Continent and houses the lion's share of documenta-related exhibitions. *(Friedrichspl. 18. Tel. 707 27 70. Open W and F-Su 10am-6pm, Th 10am-8pm. Single exhibition DM8, students DM5; entire museum DM12, students DM8.)*

DOCUMENTA-HALLE. Located between Museum Friedricianum and the Orangerie, the newest edition to the growing world of documenta houses changing exhibitions of modern art. *(Du-Ry-Str. Tel. 70 72 70. Open Tu-Su 10am-5pm. DM5, students DM3.)*

CARICATURA. Even the Hauptbahnhof has gotten in on the documenta action. Renamed **KulturBahnhof,** it houses the self-proclaimed "gallery for bizarre art." Changing exhibitions try relentlessly to convince skeptics that Germans *do* have a sense of humor. *(Bahnhofspl. 1. Tel. 77 64 99. Open Tu-F 2-8pm, Sa-Su noon-8pm.)*

DOCUMENTA-ARCHIVES. In Dock 4 cultural center, behind Museum Friedricanum. For those who can never get enough of documenta. Still not enough? Don't sulk; Kassel will host documenta XI from June 8 to September 15, 2002. *(Untere Karlsstr. 4. Tel 787 40 22. Open M-F 10am-2pm.)*

WILHELMSHÖHE

Wilhelmshöhe is a hillside park with one giant Greek hero, two castles, three museums, and five waterfalls, all punctuated with rock gardens, mountain streams, and innumerable hiking trails. The whole park experience—a cross between the halls of Montezuma and a Baroque theme park—takes up half a day; approach it with humor, cynicism, or a bicycle. From Bahnhof Wilhelmshöhe, take bus #43 (direction: "Herkules") to the last stop at the northern tip of the park.

HERKULES. A mighty **Riesenschloß** lurks near the bus stop. The octagonal, 33m structure is topped by a 30m tall pyramid and an 8m sculpture of Herkules, Kassel's emblem. The excessively masculine Greek hero jeers at his conquered foe, the giant Encelades, whose head pokes out of the rocks at the top of the cascades. An English author traveling in the 18th century described it as "one of the most splendid structures in all of Europe, not excluding those in Versailles, Frascati, or Tivoli." Visitors can climb up onto Herkules's pedestal and, if they're brave enough, into his club. *(Access to the base of the statue free. Pedestal and club open mid-March to mid-Nov. Tu-Su 10am-6pm. DM3, students DM2.)*

CASCADES. Climb down the right-hand side steps along the cascades—some are for humans and some for giants. Be warned: when there isn't enough water, the cascades aren't quite "cascading." If you arrive at the top of Herkules on a Sunday or Wednesday, check out the **fountain displays** at 2:30pm; they're timed so that a walk down the clearly designated path lands you at the next waterfall as the show begins (Easter-Sept. only). The grand finale comes at 3:45pm when the displays end in a grand 52m-high gush. Stake out a vantage point early. *(Veer off on the path to your right to get to the Steinhöfer Wasserfall. When the path and road split, stay on the path.)*

SCHLOSS LÖWENBURG. The castle is an amazing piece of architectural fantasy. It was built by Wilhelm in the 18th century with stones deliberately missing to achieve the effect of a crumbling medieval castle; to add to the ancient look, the material used was a rapidly deteriorating basalt. For some reason this Teutonic Don Quixote was obsessed with the year 1495 and fancied himself a time-displaced knight. In order to supplement the credibility of this pretense, he even built a Catholic chapel on the Schloß to date it before the Reformation, even though he himself was Protestant. Despite his claims of chivalry, the castle was built as a bedroom for his favorite concubine, who bore him 15 children—13 more than his wife. *(Tel. 935 72 00. Follow the directions above to the Steinhöfer Wasserfall; at the waterfall, turn onto the path to your left. When you reach the road make a right–the castle is 15min. ahead. Or catch bus #23 from the road at the bottom of the cascades. Open March-Oct. Tu-Su 10am-5pm; Nov.-Feb. Tu-Su 10am-4pm. Entry only with a tour. Tours every hour; last tour one hour before closing. DM6, students DM4.)*

SCHLOSS WILHELMSHÖHE. The building is the mammoth former home of the rulers of Kassel. Napoleon III was imprisoned here after being captured in the Battle of Sedan. The **Schloßmuseum,** records the extravagant royal lifestyle. *(Tel. 937 77. Exit Löwenburg on the same road that led you to it, and you'll see a footpath to your right. It's a 20min. walk to the Schloß along this path. Open March-Oct. Tu-Su 10am-5pm; Nov.-Feb. Tu-Su 10am-4pm. Tours of private suites leave when there are enough people. DM6, students DM4.)*

NEAR THE RATHAUS

KARLSAUE. The English Garden of Karlsaue sprawls along the Fulda. At its southern tip is the **Insel Siebenbergen**—Karlsaue's unique "Island of Flowers." From Königsplatz, hop on bus #16 (direction: "Auestadion") to "Siebenbergen." The **Orangerie,** Karlsaue 20c (tel. 705 43), located at the north end of the park in a bright yellow manor house, is home to the **astronomy and technology museum**. Inside you'll find mechanical and optical marvels as well as a planetarium. *(Open Tu-Sa 10am-5pm. DM5, students DM3. Free on Fridays. Planetarium shows Tu and Sa 2pm, W and F 3pm, Th 2pm and 8pm, Su 3pm. DM7, students DM3.)*

BRÜDER-GRIMM-MUSEUM. Exhibits the brothers' handwritten copy of *Kinder- und Hausmärchen,* their fabled collection of fairy tales, and translations into dozens of languages. *(Schöne Aussicht 2. Tel. 787 20 33. In Palais Bellevue near the Orangerie. Walk toward the Fulda from Friedrichspl. and turn right on Schöne Aussicht. Open daily 10am-5pm. DM3, students DM2.)*

DEUTSCHES TAPETENMUSEUM. The only wallpaper museum in the world, this place is wall-to-wall, floor-to-ceiling fun! Surprises include 16th-century embossed leather-and-gold Spanish hangings, a rare depiction of the battle of Austerlitz, a six-color wallpaper printer, and a letter from Goethe to Schiller mentioning an order of wallpaper. *(Brüder-Grimm-Pl. 5. Tel. 784 60. In the yellow Landesmuseum near the Rathaus. Open Tu-Su 10am-5pm. DM5, students DM3;F free.)*

🎵🎭 ENTERTAINMENT AND NIGHTLIFE

Dozens of music bars, pubs, cafés, and discos spice up Kassel's Altstadt. The stretch along **Ebertstr.** and **Goethestr.** between Bebelplatz and Königsplatz, and extending south along Rathenauallee toward the Rathaus, packs in the party

Geist. The free magazines *Fritz* and *Xcentric*, available at the tourist office, list an indispensable schedule of parties at the city's clubs. Kassel also fosters a lively **film** culture. Theaters cluster around the Altstadt; **Bali** (tel. 70 15 50) in the Hauptbahnhof shows movies in their original language. Kassel hosts an **outdoor film festival** every summer behind the Museum Friedricianum at the theater **dock 4** (tel. 787 20 67). Take Streetcar #1 or 3 to "Friedrichspl." Shows range from the artsy pretense of Godard to the authentic power of *Star Wars* (DM10). The **Staatstheater** (tel. 109 42 22) on Friedrichspl. hosts plays, concerts, operas, and ballet performances from mid-September to early July.

Salzmanns Factory, Sandershäuser Str. 31 (tel. 57 25 42), pumps it up with house and techno tracks Fridays from 10:30pm. Saturdays host a variety of parties starting around 10:30pm—check *Fritz* for details. Their recent addition is *Labor Ost*—an experimental theater and dance room. Cover DM10.

Musiktheater, Angersbachstr. 10 (tel. 840 44). Bus #27 to "Angersbachstr." A disco-party mecca. 3 humongous dance floors occupying 2 city blocks host techno, house, and pop. Open F-Sa after 8:30pm, sometimes also Th. Cover DM5.

Mr. Jones, Goethestr. 31 (tel. 71 08 18). Walking distance from the hostel at the corner of Querallee. Every city should have a hip bar and restaurant flaunting giant fluorescent insects. Excellent food of the Tex-Mex variety DM8-12. Open M-Th and Su 10am-1am, F-Sa 10am-midnight.

Café-Bar Suspekt, Fünffensterstr. 14 (tel. 10 45 22). Popular gay and lesbian pub belies its name with a laid-back and friendly ambience. During the day a pleasant café (Tu-Su 1-8pm), at night a bar (M-Th and Su 8pm-1am, F-Sa 8pm-2am).

Knösel, Goethestr. 26 (tel. 77 06 08). Genuine Kassel townies hang out in this classic beer-drinking environment. They love their beer and their *Fußball*. Open M-Th 4pm-1am, F-Sa 4pm-3am, Su 5pm-1am.

NEAR KASSEL: FRITZLAR

The birth of the town of Fritzlar as *Frideslar* (Place of Peace) dates to a not-so-peaceful act of St. Boniface, who, in 723, chopped down the huge **Donar's Oak,** the pagan religious symbol of the tribal Chats. The "Apostle of the Germans" used the timber to build his own wooden church, which today is the beautiful Petersdom. It was also here that Heinrich I was proclaimed king in 915, inaugurating the medieval incarnation of the Holy Roman Empire. Since then this diminutive medieval town has become isolated from the main routes of buzzing commerce and affluence. Nevertheless, having survived both WWII and the zeal of the post-war building projects unscathed, Fritzlar is content with its role as a postcard-perfect town of half-timbered houses) on the **Märchenstraße,** the German fairy tale road.

The gem of Fritzlar is the 12th-century **Petersdom,** with its two massive red sandstone towers and sizeable treasury, which includes the diamond and pearl-covered **Heinrichkreuz** as well as numerous precious robes and relics. (Open May-Oct. M-Sa 10am-noon and 2-5pm, Su 2-5pm; Nov.-April M-Sa 10am-noon and 2-4pm, Su 2-4pm. DM5, students DM2. Tours DM5, children DM2.) On the western extremity of the still-standing medieval city wall, the 39m **Grauer Turm** is the tallest defense tower in Germany. Though it no longer serves its original purpose, you can still climb it and enjoy the spectacular view (DM0.50). The **Hochzeitshaus** (tel. 98 86 28), on Burggrabenstr., has hosted weddings and festivals since the 16th century. It also houses the **Regionalmuseum,** which does its best to reflect all aspects and stages of Fritzlar's bumpy history. (Open March-Nov. M-F and Su 10am-noon and 3-5pm; Dec.-Feb. M-F 10am-noon and 3-5pm. DM3, children DM1.) Little towns spawn big festivals, and Fritzlar's *Wunderkinder* are no exception: the **Pferdemarkt** (July 13-15, 2000) and the **Altstadtfest** (Aug. 18-19, 2000) draw out *Lederhosen,* traditional music, and beer goggles.

Fritzlar is an ideal daytrip. It can be reached from either of the main train stations in Kassel by **train** (40min., 1 per hour, DM10) or bus (40min.). The **tourist office,** Zwischen den Krämen 5 (tel. 98 86 43; fax 98 86 38), sits in Fritzlar's Rathaus, the oldest official building in Germany, built in 1109. Make a left out of the train station and a quick right onto Gießener Str. After the bridge, make a left onto Fraumünsterstr., and then a right onto Georgengasse. At the top of the hill you'll find Gießener Str. (again). Hang a left, walk through the Marktplatz, and make a left onto Zwischen den Krämen. The office has a list of **rooms** (from DM25), but makes no reservations. (Open M 10am-6pm, Tu-Th 10am-5pm, F 10am-4pm, Sa-Su 10am-noon.) **Tours** (1½hr.) leave from the Rathaus, but only if there is a minimum of five people. (May-Sept. M-Sa 10am, Su 11am. DM5.) The **post office,** 34560 Fritzlar, is at the corner of Nikolausstr. and Gießener Str., near the Markt. (Open M-F 9am-noon and 2:30-5:30pm, Sa 9am-noon.) The **telephone code** is 05622.

HESSEN

NORDRHEIN-WESTFALEN
(NORTH RHINE-WESTPHALIA)

In 1946, the victorious Allies attempted to speed Germany's recovery by merging the traditionally distinct regions of Westphalia, Lippe, and the Rhineland to unify the economic and industrial nucleus of post-war Germany. The resulting *Land*, Nordrhein-Westfalen, meets no typical German stereotype. The region's dense concentration of highways and rail lines form the infrastructure of the most heavily populated (17 million inhabitants) and economically powerful area in Germany. The industrial boom of the late 19th century sparked social democracy, trade unionism, and revolutionary communism—the popular moniker "Red Ruhr" didn't refer to the color of the water. Despite downturns in heavy industry and persistently high unemployment, the great industrial wealth of the region continues to support a multitude of cultural offerings for the citizens and visitors of its lively

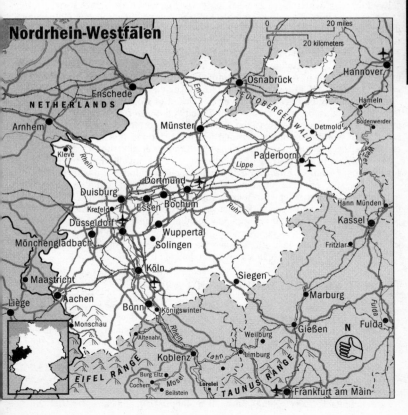

Nordrhein-Westfalen

towns and beautiful river valleys. While the region's industrial squalor may have inspired the philosophy of Karl Marx and Friedrich Engels, the natural beauty of the Teutoburg and Eifel mountains and the intellectual energy of Köln, Aachen, and Düsseldorf have spurred the muses of writers from Goethe to Heine to Böll.

HIGHLIGHTS OF NORDRHEIN-WESTFALEN

■ The crowning glory of German piety, **Köln's** Dom is the largest example of High Gothic architecture in the world. Köln shines beyond its cathedral, however, with a collection of world-class museums, great nightlife—including a burgeoning gay scene—and a fountain that gushes forth perfume (p. 428).

■ **Düsseldorf** is a wealthy, wealthy city, with a glitzy strip of designer boutiques (the "Kö") and a palpably cosmopolitan air. Budget travelers enjoy the exceptional Kunst-sammlung Nordrhein-Westfalen and the city's shrine to hometown writer-hero Heinrich Heine (p. 449).

■ Bordering Belgium and the Netherlands, beautiful **Aachen** exudes internationalism in a sophisticated university town atmosphere (p. 444).

■ See Germany's erstwhile capital, **Bonn,** in its new, bureaucrat-free incarnation (p. 438).

KÖLN (COLOGNE)

Founded as a Roman colony (*colonia*, hence Köln) in AD 48, Köln was Petrarch's "city of dreams" when the rest of Germany was just wilderness. The city's location at the intersection of several international trade routes ushered in a Golden Age during the Middle Ages and the Renaissance, bolstering Köln's present status as Germany's commercial, technical, and communications center *par excellence*. Today, nearly a million citizens call the city home.

Köln's major attraction is the majestic and legendary Dom. Designed to exceed all other churches in splendor, the Gothic structure took an amazing 632 years to build. During WWII, at least 14 bombs struck the cathedral, which somehow survived and has since become a powerful symbol of Köln's miraculous recovery from the Allied raids, which left 90% of the city center in ruins. Today, Köln is the largest city in Nordrhein-Westfalen and its most important cultural center, with a full plate of world-class museums and theatrical offerings. It is a prosperous, modern city with a penchant for bibulous celebrations (March 2-March 7, 2000).

Modern Köln is also the city of Nobel Prize-winning novelist Heinrich Böll, who set *The Lost Honor of Katharina Blum* and the scandalous *Clown* here. The novels concern the venom of press slander and the violation of civil liberties—topics appropriate to a city steeped in literary and journalistic tradition. Köln is the base for many national media networks, just as it was during the days of Karl Marx, who began his revolutionary career here as a local newspaper editor. Although Köln's citizens conduct their own communications in the impenetrable *Kölsch* dialect, the locally brewed *Kölsch* beer offers a savory experience that brings to the taste buds the kind of euphoria that the heavenly Dom delivers to the eyes.

▐ GETTING THERE AND GETTING AROUND

Flights: Flights depart from **Köln-Bonn Flughafen;** a shuttle to Berlin leaves 24 times per day. Call (01803) 80 38 03 for flight information. Bus #170 leaves stop #3 at the train station daily at 5:30, 6, and 6:30am, and then every 15min. 7am-8pm, and every 30min. 8-11pm; it stops at Köln-Deutz 5min. before proceeding to the airport (20min., DM8.70, children DM4.50).

Trains: Direct train lines connect Köln with Düsseldorf (30min., 6 per hour, DM12.20), Frankfurt (2½hr., 1 per hour, DM69), Hamburg (4hr., 1 per hour, DM130), Berlin (5½hr., every 2hr., DM190), Munich (6-8hr., 1 per hour, DM180). Trains also run every 2hr. to Brussels (2½hr., DM54), Amsterdam (4hr., DM79), and Paris (4hr., DM128).

Ferries: Köln-Düsseldorfer, (tel. 258 30 11; fax 208 82 38), begins its ever-popular Rhein cruises here. Sail upstream to Koblenz and fairy-tale castle-land in the Rhein Gorge. Students and children ages 4-12 half-price, seniors half-price on M and F. Most trips (excluding hydrofoils) covered by Eurail and German railpasses.

Public Transportation: VRS *(Verkehrsverbund Rhein-Sieg)* offices have free maps of the S- and U-Bahn, bus, and streetcar lines; one is downstairs in the train station near the U-Bahn. Major convergence points include the train station, **Neumarkt, Appellhofplatz,** and **Barbarossaplatz.** Single ride tickets DM2.20-14.20, depending on distance traveled. Day pass DM9.50. The *Minigruppen-Ticket* allows up to 5 people to ride all day after 9am for DM13-36.

Gondola: Rheinseilbahn (tel. 547 41 84), U-Bahn #16 (direction: "Ebertplatz/Mülheim") to "Zoo/Flora." Float over the Rhein from the Zoo to the Rheinpark. DM6.50, children DM3.50; round-trip DM10, children DM5. Open daily 10am-5:45pm.

Taxi: Funkzentrale, tel. 28 82. Cold medinas not available.

Car Rental: Avis, Clemensstr. 29 (tel. 23 43 33); **Hertz,** Bismarckstr. 19-21 (tel. 51 50 84).

Bike Rental: Kölner Fahrradverleihservice, Markmannsgasse (tel. 0171 629 87 96), in the Altstadt. DM4 per hour, DM20 per day. Open daily 9am-6pm. Daily 3hr. city **tour** in German and English at 1:30pm DM29.

Mitfahrzentrale: Citynetz Mitfahrzentrale, Maximinstr. 2 (tel. 194 40), to the left of the train station, matches riders and drivers. Open daily 9am-7pm.

Hitchhiking: *Let's Go* does not recommend hitchhiking. For all destinations, hitchers take bus #132 to the last stop.

▮ ORIENTATION AND PRACTICAL INFORMATION

Eight bridges carry Köln across the Rhein, but nearly all sights can be found on the western side. The train station is in the northern part of the **Innenstadt.** The Altstadt is split into two districts; **Altstadt-Nord** is near the station, and **Altstadt-Süd** is just south of the Severinsbrücke. Many high-end hotels in the Innenstadt sell the unbeatable **Köln Tourismus Card,** a packet of vouchers entitling the bearer to a city tour, discounts on Rhein cruises, a three-day pass to all city museums, and use of the public transportation system (DM30).

TOURIST AND FINANCIAL SERVICES

Tourist Office: Verkehrsamt, Unter Fettenhennen 19 (tel. 221 33 45 or 194 33; fax 22 12 33 20; www.koeln.org/koelntourismus), across from the main entrance to the Dom, provides a free city map and books **rooms** for a DM6 fee. Pick up the *Monatsvorschau* (DM2), a booklet with essential information and a complete monthly schedule of events. Open May-Oct. M-Sa 8am-10:30pm, Su 9am-10:30pm; Nov.-April M-Sa 8am-9pm, Su 9:30am-7pm.

Budget Travel: STA Travel, Zülpicher Str. 178 (tel. 44 20 11). Open M and Th 10am-8pm, Tu-W and F 10am-6pm.

Currency Exchange: An office at the **train station** is open daily 7am-9pm, but the service charges are lower at the **post office** (see below).

American Express: Burgmauerstr. 14 (tel. 925 90 10), near the Dom. **24hr. ATM.** Members' mail held 4 weeks. Open M-F 9am-5:30pm, Sa 10am-1pm.

LOCAL SERVICES

Bookstore: Mayrische Buchhandlung, Neumarkt 2 (tel. 20 30 70), has a fabulous paperback selection including books in English. Open M-F 9am-8pm, Sa 9am-4pm.

Cultural Centers: Amerika Haus, Aposteinkloster 13-15 (tel. 20 90 10; fax 25 55 43), offers English cultural activities. English language **library** open Tu-F 2-5pm. The **British Council,** Hahnenstr. 6 (tel. 20 64 40), on Neumarkt, offers the same services with a better Monty Python collection. Open Tu 2-7pm, W-F 1-5pm. Closed July 20-Aug.20.

Gay and Lesbian Resources: Schulz Schwulen-und Lesbenzentrum, Kartäuserwall 18 (tel. 93 18 80 80), near Chlodwigplatz. Information, advice, movies, youth activities, library, and popular café.

Women's Resources: Frauenamt, Markmansgasse 7 (tel. 22 12 64 82), fields questions on cultural services. Open M-Th 8:30am-1pm and 2-4pm, F 8:30am-12:30pm, but it's best to make an appointment. **Women's crisis hotline,** tel. 420 16 20.

Laundry: Eco-Express, at the corner of Richard-Wagner-Str. Wash DM6, dry DM1 per 10min. Soap included. Open M-Sa 6am-11pm.

EMERGENCY AND COMMUNICATIONS

Emergency: Police, tel. 110. **Fire** and **Ambulance,** tel. 112.

Pharmacy: Dom-Apotheke, Komödienstr. 5 (tel. 257 67 54), near the station, posts a list of after-hours pharmacies outside. English spoken. Open M-F 8am-6:30pm, Sa 9am-1pm.

Post Office: Hauptpostamt, 50667 Köln, at the corner of Breite Str. and Auf der Ruhr. From the Dom, head down Hohe Str. and take a right on Minoritenstr. The post office is on the right in the WDR-Arkaden shopping gallery. Open M-F 8am-8pm, Sa 8am-4pm.

Internet Access: In **FuturePoint** (see **Food,** p. 433).

PHONE CODE	0221

▚ ACCOMMODATIONS AND CAMPING

The brisk convention and tour business in Köln produces a wealth of rooms; the trick is pinning one down. Hotels fill up (and prices set sail) in the spring and fall when trade winds blow conventioneers into town. Summer is high season for Köln's two hostels, both of which brim to the beams from June to September. The main hotel haven centers around **Brandenburger Str.,** on the less interesting side of the train station. The **Mitwohnzentrale,** An der Bottmühle 16 (tel. 194 45), finds apartments for longer stays. (Open M-F 9am-1pm and 2-4pm.) Scrounging for a last minute room during *Karneval* is futile—most people book a year in advance for the festivities.

▨ **Station Hostel for Backpackers,** Marzellenstr. 44-48 (tel. 912 53 01; fax 912 53 03; email station@t-online.de; http://home.t-online.de/home/station). From the station walk 1 block along Dompropst-Ketzer-Str. and take the first right on Marzellenstr. The independent hostel has impeccable rooms, a chill atmosphere, and friendly staff. It's gay/lesbian-friendly and the location could only be more central if it was in the Dom. Dorms DM27, doubles DM35, singles DM40 (prices per person). Sheets DM3. Wash DM3, dry DM3. Internet access DM4 per 30min. 24hr. reception. No curfew. Call by 3pm on the day of arrival to confirm reservations.

Jugendherberge Köln-Deutz (HI), Siegesstr. 5a (tel. 81 47 11; fax 88 44 25), just over the Hohenzollernbrücke. Take S-Bahn #6, 11, or 12 to "Köln-Deutz." From the main exit of the S-Bahn station, walk down Neuhöfferstr. and take the first right; the hostel is in a tree-lined courtyard. Small but clean rooms in a good location, with two pinball machines and free access to washing machines (soap DM1). DM33, over 26 DM37. Breakfast and sheets included. Lunch or dinner DM7. Reception 11am-1am. Curfew 1am. Call ahead.

Jugendgästehaus Köln-Riehl (HI), An der Schanz 14 (tel. 76 70 81; fax 76 15 55), on the Rhein north of the zoo. U-Bahn #16 (direction: "Ebertplatz/Mülheim") to "Boltensternstr." Or walk along the Rhein on Konrad-Adenauer-Ufer until it becomes Niederländer Ufer and finally An der Schanz (40min.). Big common areas and lockers big enough to hide in. 4- to 6-bed rooms DM38.50, singles DM63.50. Breakfast and sheets included. Reception 24hr. No curfew. Call ahead.

▨ **Jansen Pension,** Richard-Wagner-Str. 18 (tel. 25 18 75). U-Bahn #1, 6, 7, 15, 17, or 19, to "Rudolfplatz" and follow Richard-Wagner-Str. nearly 2 blocks. The *Pension* is just before the intersection with Brüsseler Str. Infinitely charming rooms in a Victorian row-house. Singles DM50-60, doubles DM100. Breakfast included.

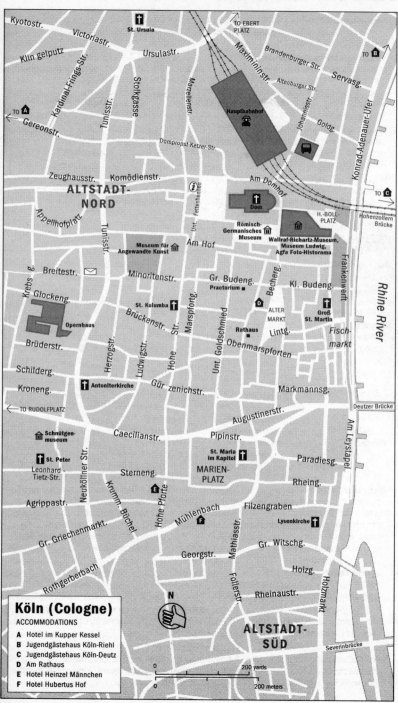

NORDRHEIN-WESTFALEN

Köln (Cologne)

ACCOMMODATIONS

A Hotel im Kupper Kessel
B Jugendgästehaus Köln-Riehl
C Jugendgästehaus Köln-Deutz
D Am Rathaus
E Hotel Heinzel Männchen
F Hotel Hubertus Hof

Hotel Im Kupferkessel, Probsteigasse 6 (tel. 13 53 38; fax 12 51 21). From the Dom, follow Dompropst-Ketzer-Str. as it becomes An der Dominikan, Unter Sachenhausen, Gereonstr., and finally Christophstr.; Probsteigasse is on the right. Well decorated, clean rooms. Singles from DM55, doubles from DM120. Breakfast included. Call ahead.

Hotel Heinzelmännchen, Hohe Pforte 5-7 (tel. 21 12 17; fax 21 57 12). Bus #132 (direction: "Frankenstr.") to "Waidmarkt," or walk down the Hohe Str. shopping zone until it becomes Hohe Pforte. Bright hallways and firm mattresses. Singles DM62, with bath DM70; doubles DM95, with bath DM110; triples DM135. Less for stays over 2 days. Breakfast included. Reception 6am-11pm; call if you're arriving later.

Hotel Hubertus Hof, Mühlenbach 30 (tel. 21 73 86; fax 21 89 55). Follow the directions above to Hohe Pforte and turn left on Mühlenbach. This gay-friendly hotel has fuzzy carpets and monster-sized rooms. Showers and toilets off the hall. Singles DM60, doubles DM85. Breakfast included. Reception 7am-9pm.

Hotel Berg, Brandenburger Str. 6 (tel. 12 11 24; fax 139 00 11). Bear left on Johannisstr. from the back exit of the train station and take the third left on Brandenburger Str. A standout for its well-kept rooms and homey breakfast area. Singles DM60, with shower DM90; doubles DM85, with shower DM160. Breakfast included. 24hr. reception.

Am Rathaus, Burgstr. 6 (tel. 257 76 24; 258 28 29). Standing on the front porch of the Rathaus, Am Rathaus is immediately on your right. This place is all about location. Singles DM75, doubles DM120. Breakfast included.

Das Kleine Stapelhäuschen, Fischmarkt 1-3 (tel. 257 78 62; fax 257 42 32). Cross the Altenmarkt from the back of the Rathaus and take Lintgasse to the Fischmarkt. An elegant *Rheinisch* inn replete with oak furnishings and a stunning circular staircase. Singles DM74-87, with shower DM98-125, with bath DM125-135; doubles DM125-135, with shower DM167-185, with bath DM195-225. Breakfast included.

Camping: Campingplatz Poll, Weidenweg (tel. 83 19 66), on the Rhein, southeast of the Altstadt. U-Bahn #16 to "Marienburg" and cross the Rodenkirchener Brücke. DM8 per person. DM4 per tent. DM4 per car. Reception 8am-noon and 5-8pm. Open April-Oct.

◖ FOOD

Small cafés packed with students and cheap restaurants line **Zülpicher Straße.** Take U-Bahn #7 or 9 to "Zülpicher Platz." Mid-priced restaurants with a fine selection of ethnic cuisine are concentrated around the perimeter of the Altstadt, particularly from **Hohenzollernring** to **Hohenstaufenring.** For glitzy cafés, the city's wealthy head to **Neumarkt.** Köln offers hungry visitors scrumptious *Rievekoochen* (potato pancakes), slabs of fried potato dunked in *Apfelmus* (apple sauce). Don't pass through Köln without sampling the city's smooth **Kölsch** beer. Local brews of the delightful stuff include *Sion, Küppers, Früh,* and the devout *Dom.* An open-air **market** on **Wilhelmsplatz** takes over the northern **Nippes** neighborhood to offer farm-fresh joys. (Open M-Sa 7am-noon.) A number of authentic German eateries surround the **Domplatz.** The city's best inexpensive eats are found in the Turkish district on **Weidengasse. HL,** Hohenzollernring 20 (tel. 257 29 66), sells **groceries.** (Open M-F 9am-8pm, Sa-Su 8:30am-4pm.) There's a bigger selection at **Mini-Mal,** Hohenstaufenring 30. (Tel. 923 36 57. Open M-F 8am-8pm, Sa 8am-4pm.)

▨ Café Waschsalon, Ehrenstr. 77 (tel. 13 33 78). Filled with decorative washing machines; turn on the spin cycle in your head with their fine drink assortment. Breakfast served until 4pm from DM5.50, lunch from DM8. Open M-Th 8am-1am, F 8am-3am, Sa 10am-3am, Su 10am-1am.

▨ Sushi Nara, Friesenstr. 70 (tel. 12 01 70). Excellent sushi at unbeatable prices. Meals from DM10. Open M-Th noon-3:30pm and 5:30pm-midnight, F-Sa noon-midnight, Su 6pm-11pm.

Café Magnus, Zülpicherstr. 48 (tel. 24 16 69). Beautifully presented meals at low prices, with a perfect location for watching the attractive university crowd. Pizzas and salads from DM6, pasta from DM10. Open daily 8am-3pm.

La Piazza, Maximinenstr. 4 (tel. 13 68 48), near Breslauer Platz. Directly behind the train station, the restaurant serves cheap and tasty Italian food close to the Dom. Open M-F 11:30am-2:30pm and 6-11:30pm, Sa-Su 6-11:30pm.

Sasmus Island, Heinsberg 11a (tel. 23 34 98), at the corner of Heinsberg and Zülpicherstr. Serves Spanish, Creole, Cajun, and South American dishes in a bright decor. Meals DM10. Open daily 8am-1am.

FuturePoint, Richmodstr. 13 (tel. 206 72 06), gives its sleek clientele just what it wants: a huge drink menu, esoteric snacks, and cheap **internet access** (DM2 per 15min.) in a chic café straight out of *The Jetsons*. Open daily 9am-1am.

Brauhaus Früh am Dom, Am Hof 12-14 (tel. 258 03 97). Offers the best *Kölsch* in town. Patrons enjoy a number of Kölner and German specialties while basking in the warm glow of the lit Dom and lit Germans in the outdoor *Biergarten*. Meals DM9-22. Open daily 8am-midnight.

Ganesha, on the corner of Händelstr. and Richard-Wagner-Str. Dinner prices at this Indian restaurant are good (DM12-19), but the lunch menu is a steal at DM8.50-10. Open M and Su 6-11pm, Tu-Sa noon-2:30pm.

Joe Champs, Hohenzollemring 1-3 (tel. 257 28 54). A 2-story sports bar serving huge burgers, both veggie and meat, and motley cocktails. Shows major U.S. sporting events. Open M-Th and Su noon-1am, F-Sa noon-2am.

◉ SIGHTS

DOM

Tel. 52 19 77. Directly across from the train station. Open daily 6am-7pm. Free. Tours in German M-Sa 11am and 12:30, 2 and 3:30pm, Su 2 and 3:30pm. DM6, students and children DM3. Tours in English M-Sa 10:30am and 2:30pm, Su 2:30pm. DM7, children DM4. Organ concerts mid-June to Aug. Tu 8pm. Free. Tower open March-Oct. 9am-5pm; Nov.-Feb. 9am-dusk. DM3, students DM1.50. Domschatzkammer open April-Oct. M-Sa 9am-5pm, Su 1-4pm; Nov.-March M-Sa 9am-4pm, Su 1-4pm. DM3, students DM1.50. Diözesanmuseum open M-W and F-Su 10am-5pm. Free.

When sight-seeing in Köln, it's impossible to save the best for last. Most train stations offer only drunks, beggars, and transients, but visitors exiting Köln's station are immediately treated to the beauty, power, and sorrow that emanate from the colossal ◼**Dom,** Germany's greatest cathedral. Visually overwhelming in intricacy and scale, the edifice took six centuries to build before being completed in 1880. The Dom is a pure example of High Gothic style, the largest of its kind in the world. For 500 years, the giant wooden crane, now kept inside, was as much Köln's trademark as the two massive towers. The stunning stained glass windows—enough to cover the floor twice—casts a harlequin display of colored light over the interior. Moving toward the front, the section to the right of the center altar bears the **Dombild triptych,** a masterful 15th-century painting and gilded altarpiece. The enormous sculpture shining brilliantly is the **Shrine of the Magi,** a reliquary of the Three Kings in blinding gold, brought to the city in 1164. The Magi are the town's holy patrons; they stand behind the altar in a magnificent 1531 woodcut of the town by Anton Woensam, and their three crowns grace Köln's heraldic shield. Tapestries of Rubens' *Triumph of the Eucharist* line the central nave. Look for the 976 **Gero crucifix,** the oldest intact sculpture of **Christus patiens** (depicting a crucified Christ with eyes shut), as well as Ruben's *Crucifixion of St. Peter.*

Five hundred and nine steps and 15 minutes are all it takes to scale the **Südturm** and peer down at the river below. Catch your breath at the *Glockenstube* (400 steps up), a chamber for the tower's nine bells. Four of the bells date from the Middle Ages, but the 19th-century upstart known affectionately as **Der große Peter** (at 24 tons, the world's heaviest swinging bell) rings loudest. Hailed as "Germany's Bell on the Rhein," it bears an engraved call for national unity. The **Domschatzkammer** in a corner of the cathedral holds the requisite clerical artwork and reliquaries:

thorn, cross, and nail bits, as well as pieces of 18 saints. Find more ecclesiastical favors in the **Diözesanmuseum,** just outside the south portal in the red building.

The allure of the cathedral illuminated from dusk to midnight is irresistible, drawing natives and tourists to the expansive **Domvorplatz** for a daily carnival of relaxation, art, and activism. Since time and acid rain have corroded much of the Dom's original detail, every piece is gradually being reproduced and replaced with new, treated stone. To expedite this task, play the "Dom lottery" at posts around the plaza and save a statue's fingernail. *(DM1-2.)*

INNENSTADT

In the shadow of the cathedral, the **Hohenzollernbrücke** crosses the Rhein. The majestic bridge empties out onto a promenade guarded by equestrian statues of the imperial family. A monumental flight of stairs leads to **Heinrich-Böll-Platz** and its cultural center (see **Museums,** p. 435), a complex of modern architecture that succeeds in complementing the Dom. Farther on, the squares and crooked streets of the old **Fischmarkt** district open onto paths along the Rhein; the café patios give way to an expanse of grass along the river, perfect for a picnic serenaded by musicians.

RATHAUS. Bombed in WWII, Köln's city hall has been reconstructed in its original mongrel style. The Gothic **tower** stands guard over Baroque cherubs flying around an ornate 1570 Renaissance arcade called the *loggia,* the only section to survive the war. The tower is adorned with a diverse array of historical and cultural figures; Marx and Rubens loom above rows of popes and emperors. A **Glockenspiel** offers a titillatingly tintinnabulary experience daily at noon and 5pm. *(Open M-Th 7:30am-4pm, F 7:30am-2pm. Tours W at 3pm. Free.)*

RÖMISCHES PRAETORIUM UND KANAL. Classical historians and *Ben Hur* fans will be impressed by the excavated ruins of the former Roman military headquarters. Looking like an abandoned set from a gladiator movie, the museum displays remains of Roman gods and a befuddling array of rocks left by the city's early inhabitants. *(From the Rathaus, take a right towards the swarm of hotels and then a left onto Kleine Budengasse. Open Tu-F 10am-4pm, Sa-Su 11am-4pm. DM3, students DM1.50.)*

HOUSE #4711. In the 18th-century, Goethe noted "How grateful the women are for the fragrance of **Eau de Cologne.**" This magic water, once prescribed as a drinkable curative, made the town (via the oft-mimicked export) a household name. If you're after the authentic article, be sure your bottle says *Echt kölnisch Wasser* (real Köln water); or look for the world-renowned "4711" label. Its name comes from the Mühlens family house, labeled House #4711 by the Napoleonic system that abolished street names. It has been converted into a boutique, with a small fountain continually dispensing the famous scented water. Visit and be torn apart by worshipping throngs. *(Glockengasse, at the intersection with Tunisstr. From Hohe Str., turn right on Brückenstr., which becomes Glockengasse. Open M-F 9am-8pm, Sa 9am-4pm.)*

MIKWE JUDENBAD. The glass pyramid to the left as you exit the Rathaus shelters the 12th-century Jewish ritual bath that burrows 15m down to groundwater. Medieval bathers generally went in naked, but you'll need at least a passport (ooohh...sexy moneybelt, stud) to obtain a key from the Rathaus. *(Open M-Th 9am-5pm, F 9am-1pm, Su 11am-1pm. Free.)*

OTHER SIGHTS. Köln-Riehl's **Zoo, aquarium,** and **botanical garden.** *(Tel. 778 51 22. Take a gondola (see Rheinseilbahn, p. 429) to "Zoo," or U-Bahn #16 to "Zoo/Flora." Zoo open daily April-Oct. 9am-6pm; Nov.-March 9am-5pm. Aquarium open daily 9am-6pm. Garden open daily 8am-dusk. Combined admission DM15, students DM8.50, children DM7.50.)*

CHURCHES

Köln's success in building awe-inspiring churches began hundreds of years before the idea for the Dom was conceived. The Romanesque period from the 10th to mid-13th century saw the construction of 12 churches roughly in the shape of a semi-circle around the Altstadt, using the holy bones of the saints to protect the city. The churches attest to the sacred glory and tremendous wealth of what was, at the time, the most important city north of the Alps. The city's piety even received poetic embodiment in a Samuel Taylor Coleridge poem: "In Köln, a town of monks and bones/And pavements fanged with murderous stones/And rags, and hags, and hideous wenches/I counted two-and-seventy stenches...." Probably the perfume.

ST. GEREON. One of the first medieval structures to use the unique decagon layout, St. Gereon houses a floor mosaic of David hacking off Goliath's head. *(Gereonsdriesch 2-4. Tel. 13 49 22. Open M-Sa 9am-12:30pm and 1:30-6pm, Su 1:30-6pm.)*

GROSS ST. MARTIN. Along with the Dom, Groß St. Martin defines the legendary Rhein panorama of Köln. The renovated church was reopened in 1985 after near destruction in WWII. Crypts downstairs house an esoteric collection of stones and diagrams. *(An Groß St. Martin 9. Tel. 257 79 24. Open M-Sa 10am-6pm, Su 2-4pm. Church free. Crypt DM1, students and children DM0.50.)*

ST. MARIA IM KAPITOL. Visitors are treated to amazingly ornate carved wooden panels detailing the life of Christ. *(Marienplatz 19. Tel. 21 46 15. Open daily 9:30am-6pm.)*

ST. CÄCILIEN. On the portal behind the church stands "Death"—the masterpiece of a professional sprayer, not drunken vandals. *(Cäcilienstr. 29. Tel. 221 23 10. Accessible only through Schnütgenmuseum, p. 436.)*

ST. URSULA. North of the Dom, the church commemorates Ursula's attempts to maintain celibacy despite her betrothal. She and 11 virgins under her tutelage were mistaken for Roman legionnaires and burned at sea. The Latin record of the tale indicated "11M," meaning 11 martyrs, but was later misread as 11 thousand virgins. More than 700 skulls and innumerable reliquaries line the walls of the **Goldene Kammer.** *(Ursulaplatz 24. Tel. 13 34 00. Open M 9am-noon and 1-5pm, W-Sa 9:30am-noon and 1-5pm. Church free. Kammer DM2, children DM1.)*

ALT ST. ALBAN. Behind the Rathaus, inside the overgrown ruins of the bombed church, parents mourn the children lost in war in a statue created by Käthe Kollwitz.

▥ MUSEUMS

Köln's cultural, religious and economic significance in Europe stocks this rich city's museums with a vast and impressive array of holdings. The main museums are free with the **Köln Tourismus Card.** (See p. 429.)

NEAR THE DOM

▨HEINRICH-BÖLL-PLATZ. Designed to maximize natural light, the unusual building houses three complementary collections. The **Wallraf-Richartz Museum** features crackly masterpieces from the 13th to the 19th century, from the Italian Renaissance through the French Impressionists. The **Museum Ludwig** spans Impressionism through Picasso, Dalí, Lichtenstein, Warhol, and to art where the glue and paint have yet to dry. The **Agfa Foto-Historama** chronicles chemical art of the last 150 years, including a rotating display of Man Ray's works. *(Bischofsgartenstr. 1. Tel. 22 12 23 82. Behind the Römisch-Germanisches Museum. Open Tu 10am-8pm, W-F 10am-6pm, Sa-Su 11am-6pm. Tours Tu 6pm, W 4:30pm, Sa 11:30am, and Su 11:30am and 3pm. DM10, students DM5.)*

RÖMISCH-GERMANISCHES MUSEUM. Built on the ruins of a Roman villa, the displays include the world-famous Dionysus mosaic, the tomb of Publicus, an intimidating six-breasted sphinx, and some naughty candle-holders. *(Roncallipl. 4. Tel. 22 12 44 28. Open Tu-Su 10am-5pm. DM5, students and children DM2.50.)*

MUSEUM FÜR ANGEWANDTE KUNST. A giant arts-and-crafts fair spanning seven centuries with a fabulous 20th-century design display and helpful English captions. *(An der Rechtschule. Tel. 22 12 67 14. West of the Dom across Wallrafplatz. Open Tu and Th-Su 11am-5pm, W 11am-8pm. Tours W 6pm, Sa-Su 2:30pm. DM5, students and children DM2.50.)*

NORDRHEIN-WESTFALEN

ELSEWHERE IN KÖLN

▓SCHOKOLADENMUSEUM. Better than Willy Wonka's Chocolate Factory. Salivate at every step of chocolate production from the rainforests to the gold fountain that spurts streams of silky, heavenly, creamy... Resist the urge to drool and wait for the free petite samples. *(Rheinauhafen 1a. Tel. 931 88 80. Near the Severinsbrücke. From the train station, walk along the Rhein and head right. Proceed under the Deutzer Brücke and take the first footbridge across to the small bit of land jutting into the Rhein. Open Tu-F 10am-6pm, Sa-Su 11am-7pm. Last entry 1hr. before closing. DM10, students, seniors, and children DM5. Tours Sa at 2 and 4pm, Su at 11:30am, 2, and 4pm. DM3.)*

NS-DOKUMENTATIONS-ZENTRUM. Once Köln's Gestapo headquarters, the museum now portrays Köln as it was during the Nazi regime and displays the 1,200 wall inscriptions made by political prisoners who were kept in the building. All informational plaques and film clips in German. *(Am Appellhofpl. 23-25. Tel. 22 12 63 31. On the far side from the Dom. Open Tu-F 10am-5pm, Sa-Su 11am-4pm. Tours first Sa of the month at 2pm. DM5, students DM2.)*

KÄTHE-KOLLWITZ-MUSEUM. The world's largest collection of sketches, sculptures, and prints by the brilliant artist and activist (see p. 24). Her images are dark and deeply moving, chronicling early 20th-century Berlin in stark black-and-white. *(Neumarkt 18-24. Tel. 227 23 63. In the Neumarkt-Passage. U-Bahn #9, 12, 14, 16, or 18 to "Neumarkt." Open Tu-F 10am-6pm, Sa-Su 11am-6pm. Tours Su at 3pm. DM5, students DM2.)*

SCHNÜTGENMUSEUM. The collection showcases ecclesiastical art from the Middle Ages to the Baroque, including tapestries and priestly fashions. *(Cäcilienstr. 29. Tel. 22 12 36 20. In St. Cäcilien, p. 435. Open Tu-F 10am-5pm, Sa-Su 11am-5pm. Tours Su at 11am, W at 2:30pm. DM5, students DM2.50.)*

🎵 ENTERTAINMENT

Köln explodes in celebration during **Karneval,** a week-long pre-Lenten festival. Celebrated in the hedonistic spirit of the city's Roman past, Karneval is made up of 50 major and minor neighborhood processions in the weeks before Ash Wednesday. **Weiberfastnacht,** March 1, 2000, is the first major to-do; the mayor mounts the platform at Alter Markt and abdicates leadership of the city to the city's *Weiber* (an archaic and not-too-politically-correct term for women). In the afternoon, the first of the big parades begins at Severinstor. The weekend builds up to the out-of-control parade on **Rosenmontag,** the last Monday before Lent (March 6, 2000). Everyone's in costume and gets and gives a couple dozen *Bützchen* (Kölsch dialect for a kiss on a stranger's cheek). Arrive early, get a map of the route, and don't stand anywhere near the station or cathedral—you'll be pulverized by the crowds. While most revelers nurse their hangovers on Shrove Tuesday, pubs and restaurants set fire to the straw scarecrows hanging out their windows. For more information on the festival and tickets to events, inquire at the **Festkomitee des Kölner Karnevals,** Antwerpener Str. 55 (tel. 57 40 00), or pick up the *Karneval* booklet at the tourist office.

Köln's traditional entertainment is a site of fierce competition with more than 30 theaters, including the **Oper der Stadt Köln** and **Kölner Schauspielhaus** near Schildergasse on Offenbachplatz. The **box office** (tel. 84 00) for the Schauspielhaus sells tickets for both. (Open M-Sa 9am-2pm.) **Köln Ticket** (tel. 28 01), a ticket agent located in the same building as the Römisch-Germanisches Museum (p. 435), sells tickets for everything else—Köln's world-class **Philharmonie,** open-air rock concerts, and everything in between. (Open M-W and F 9am-6:30pm, Th 9am-8pm, and Sa 9am-4pm.) For more on Köln's theaters, check the *Monatsvorschau,* available at the tourist office. The **Cinemathek** (tel. 257 59 21) entrance is on the ground floor of the three-museum building in Heinrich-Böll-Platz; current movies are screened almost daily, with most films in the original language. **Metropolis** (tel. 72 24 36), on Ebertplatz, shows mostly English language movies. From April to October, catch the **craft market** the last weekend of every month in the Altstadt, around Groß St. Martin church (see p. 435).

INSULTS FOR SALE The concept of free speech in Germany does not imply *cost-free* speech. While doling out compliments requires no budget, dropping insults will unload your wallet in no time. Public humiliation in Germany carries such destructive force that officials have created an insult price list; offended or drunk budget travelers should beware. The heaviest fines are incurred by mouth-flappers who put down a police officer's respectability: belting out *Trottel in Uniform* (fool in uniform) costs DM3000, while the lesser insult *Dumme Kuh* (dumb cow) requires a mere DM1200 payoff. Call any uniformed official *Idiot* (idiot), and you'll be out a whopping DM3000. The budget traveler's insult, *Holzkopf* (wood-headed), goes for DM1500. Equivalent insults in English are not exempt; stories abound of policemen who've doled out thousands of *Marks* in fines to tourists who think that Germans don't understand what "asshole" means. We tell you this merely as a warning—and prices, of course, are subject to change, you idiot.

⬛ NIGHTLIFE

Celebrating with lavish festivities has long been a tradition in Köln. Roman mosaics dating back to AD 3 record the wild excesses of the city's early residents. But instead of grape-feeding and fig-wearing, modern life in Köln now focuses on house music and a more sophisticated bump-and-grind. The closer to the Rhein or Dom you venture, the more quickly your wallet gets emptied. Students congregate in the *Bermuda-Dreieck* (triangle). The area is bounded by **Zülpicherstr., Zülpicherplatz, Roonstr.,** and **Luxemburgstr.** The center of gay nightlife runs up **Matthiasstr.** to **Mühlenbach, Hohe Pforte, Marienplatz,** and up to the **Heumarkt** area by Deutzer Brücke. Radiating westward from Friesenpl., the **Belgisches Viertel** is spiced with slightly more expensive bars and cafés.

Worshippers of Bacchus boozed themselves into stupors here, and the tradition of getting plastered is still highly practiced in Köln. At the various *Brauhäuser,* where the original *Kölsch* is brewed, waiters will bring one glass after another until you fall under the table unless you place your coaster over your glass. Make sure that the lines on your coaster correspond to the number of beers you actually drank—it's said they might count on the fact that you won't be able to count.

Papa Joe's Jazzlokal, Buttermarkt 37 (tel. 257 79 31), defines Köln's jazz scene with traditional, high-caliber live jazz and oodles of New Orleans atmosphere. For diehards, "Non-Stop Jazz" M-Sa after 8pm, Su after 3:30pm. Open M-Sa 7pm-2am, Su 3:30pm-1am. No cover.

Das Ding, Hohenstaufenring 25-27 (tel. 24 63 48). Popular, smoky, and very *noir*. Techno and other flavors. No severed hands. Open M and W 9pm-2am, Tu and Th-Su 9pm-3am. Cover DM7.

MTC, Zülpicherstr. 10 (tel. 240 41 88). A veritable smörgåsbord of olfactory and ol' factory fun. Schizophrenic musical offerings, alternating between punk/grunge, live concerts, and recorded bar tunes. Open M, W, and Su 9pm-2am, Tu and Th-Sa 9pm-3am. Cover DM6, including one drink.

Taco Loco, Zülpicherstr. 4a (tel. 25 14 16). With a daily happy "hour" from 6-8pm and tasty margaritas, it's not just the tacos that get crazy here. Generous nacho dishes satisfy late-night hunger. Livin' la...ah, shyat up. Open M-Th and Su 10am-2am, F-Sa 10am-3am.

Broadway, Ehrenstr. 11 (tel. 25 52 14). Appropriately located in a gutted theater box-office, the funky café is haunted by Köln's hippest artists and intellectuals. Open M-Sa 10am-12:30am, Su 3pm-12:30am.

Päffgen-Brauerei, Friesenstr. 64-66 (tel. 13 54 61). A local favorite since 1883. Legendary *Kölsch* is brewed on the premises and consumed in cavernous halls or in the *Biergarten.* Open daily 10am-midnight. Kitchen open 11am-11pm.

Café Stövchen, Ursulakloster 4-6 (tel. 13 17 12), in the shadow of the Ursulakirche. Sink into a swank couch, beer in hand, and dish out a schoolin' to some suckas at Jenga or Othello. Local flavor. Open M-F 11am-1am, Su 10am-1am.

Museum, Zülpicherpl. 9 (tel. 23 20 98). No temple of science is complete without a two-story dinosaur looking out over blood-alcohol experiments. Order your own 10L mini keg of *Kölsch.* A popular university field trip. Open M-Th and Su 7pm-1am, F-Sa 7pm-3am.

The Corkonian, Alter Markt 51 (tel. 257 69 31). Not a *Biergarten,* a *Bierstube,* or a *Kneipe,* the authentic Irish corner is pure pub. Trade your lager for dark beer topped with a clover. Open M-Th noon-1am, F-Sa noon-3am, and Su 11am-1am. After 8pm 20+.

GAY AND LESBIAN VENUES

■**Vampire,** Rathenauplatz 5 (tel. 240 12 11). The gay and lesbian bar has such a chill atmosphere and dark, soothing interior that anyone should come to enjoy a delicious holy water, and another... Happy hour 8-9pm. Disco F and Sa. Open Tu-Th and Su 8pm-1am, F-Sa 8pm-3am. No garlic.

Gloria, Apostelnstr. 11 (tel. 258 36 56). Crowded, popular, and plastered with cellophane wall-coverings, the café and occasional club is at the nexus of Köln's trendy gay and lesbian scene. Open M-Th 9am-1am, Su 10am-1am. Cover around DM15.

Star-Treff, Alte Wallgasse (tel. 25 50 63), at the corner of Ehrenstr. This schmaltzy gay-friendly cabaret shines with lavish drag shows in an ocean of cigarette smoke and red velvet. Showtimes W-Th and Su 8pm, F-Sa 7pm and 10:10pm.

BONN

No longer Germany's capital, Bonn can finally go back to just being Bonn instead of being pointedly *not* Berlin. Known derisively for the past 50 years as the *Hauptdorf* (capital village), Bonn was a nonentity before falling into the limelight by chance. Konrad Adenauer, the Federal Republic's first chancellor, resided in the suburbs, and the ever-considerate occupying powers made Bonn the "provisional capital" of the Western Occupation Zone before they baptized it as the capital of the fledgling Republic. The summer of 1991 brought headlines of "Chaos in Bonn" as Berlin fought for the right to reclaim the seat of government in a political catfight that cleaved every party from the CDU to the Greens. By the narrowest of margins, Berlin won; in 1999, the Bundestag packed up and moved on. Bonners have taken the loss well. Although Berliners joke that Bonn is "half the size of a Chicago cemetery and twice as dead," the sparkling streets of the Altstadt bustle with notable energy and eclecticism. The well-respected university and excellent museums bolster a thriving cultural scene.

█ GETTING THERE AND GETTING AROUND

The **Bonncard,** available in the tourist office for DM24 per day, covers transportation costs after 9am (all day Sa-Su) and admission to more than 20 museums in Bonn and the surrounding area.

Flights: Köln-Bonn Flughafen (tel. (02203) 40 40 01 02). Bus #670 runs from the train station. Every 20min. 5am-10pm. DM12.60, children DM6.30.

Trains: Trains depart for Köln (30min., 6 per hour, DM8.90), Koblenz (1hr., 3 per hour, DM14.80), and Frankfurt (1½hr., 1 per hour, DM59).

Public Transportation: Bonn is linked to Köln and other riverside cities by the massive **VRS** (Verkehrsverbund Rhein-Sieg) S-Bahn and U-Bahn network. Areas are divided into **Tarifzonen;** the farther you go, the more you pay. Single tickets (DM2.20-14.20), 4-ride tickets (DM8-12.80), and day tickets (DM9.50-35) are available at *Automaten* and designated vending stations. With the *Minigruppenkarte* (DM13-36 per day) 5 people can ride M-F after 9am and all day on weekends. Stop by the **Reisezentrum** under the train station to pick up a network map. Open M-Sa 5:30am-10pm, Su 6:30am-10pm.

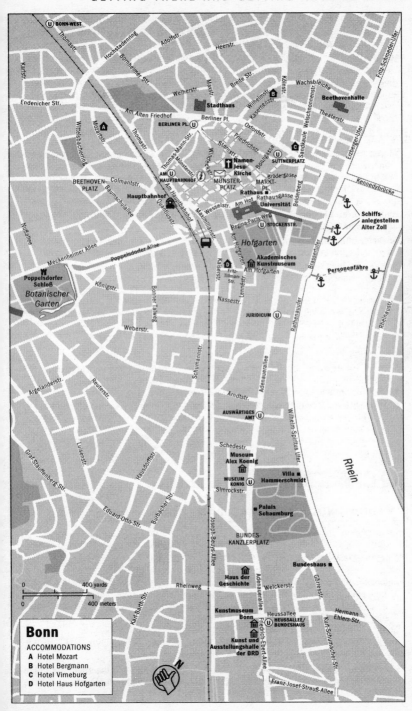

Bonn

ACCOMMODATIONS
A Hotel Mozart
B Hotel Bergmann
C Hotel Virneburg
D Hotel Haus Hofgarten

Taxi: Funkzentrale, tel. 55 55 55. The funk never grows old. (But this joke might.)

Car Rental: Hertz, Avis, InterRent Europcar, and **Alamo** have airport offices. **Kurscheid** (see **Bike Rental,** below) also rents cars.

Mitfahrzentrale: Herwarthstr. 11 (tel. 69 30 30), behind the train station, matches riders and drivers. Open M-F 10am-6pm, Sa 10am-2pm, Su for phone calls only 11am-2pm.

Bike Rental: Kurscheid, Römerstr. 4 (tel. 63 14 33), charges DM15 per day and offers a DM20 weekend special. Also rents cars. ID required for both. Open M-Sa 7am-7pm, Su 9am-1pm and 3-7pm.

ℹ PRACTICAL INFORMATION

Tourist Office: Münsterstr. 20 (tel. 77 34 66; fax 69 03 68), in a passageway near the train station in the pedestrian zone. Take the "Stadtmitte" exit from the station, walk 60m up Poststr. to Münsterstr. and turn left; the office is to the right. The helpful staff doles out fantastic maps (DM1) and books **rooms** for a DM3-5 fee. Open M-F 9am-6:30pm, Sa 9am-4pm, Su 10am-2pm.

Budget Travel: STA Travel, Nassestr. 11 (tel. 22 55 79), inside the Mensa building. Open M-Th 10am-7:30pm, F 10am-4pm.

Bookstore: The mammoth **Bouvier,** Am Hof 28 (tel. 729 01 64), has a wide range of foreign books on the top floor. Open M-F 9:30am-8pm, Sa 9:30am-4pm.

Gay and Lesbian Resources: Schwulen- und Lesbenzentrum, Am Frankenbad 5 (tel. 63 00 39), is located in a Mobil Autoöl parking lot. From Münsterplatz, follow Windeckstr., which becomes Sternstr., to Berliner Platz. Cross Berliner Pl. to Bornheimer Str. and after about 3 blocks take a right on Adolfstr.; Am Frankenbad is 2 blocks down the street and to the left (about 15min.). For **counseling** call 194 46; **gay assault hotline** 192 28. Open M-Tu and Th 8pm-midnight, W 9pm-midnight.

Women's Resources: Frauenberatungstelle, Kölnstr. 69 (tel. 65 95 00). Open M and Th 5-7:30pm, W and F 10am-noon.

Laundromat: Eco-Express Waschsalon, Bornheimer Str. 58. Wash DM6, dry DM1 per 10min. Open 6am-11pm.

Emergency: Police, tel. 110. **Fire** and **Ambulance,** tel. 112.

Pharmacy: Bahnhof-Apotheke dispenses the goods next to the tourist office. A list of night pharmacies is posted on the door. Open M-W and F 8:30am-7pm, Th 8:30am-7pm, Sa 9am-4pm.

Post Office: Münsterplatz 17, 53111 Bonn. Big. Yellow. Different. Walk down Poststr. from the station. Open M-F 8am-8pm, Sa 8am-4pm.

PHONE CODE	0228

⌂ ACCOMMODATIONS AND CAMPING

Most hotels in Bonn are tailored to wealthy tax-subsidized politicians, a vestige of its capital days. With one *Jugendgästehaus* but no *Jugendherberge,* even hosteling gets financially taxing in Bonn.

Jugendgästehaus Bonn-Venusberg (HI), Haager Weg 42 (tel. 28 99 70; fax 289 97 14; email jgh-bonn@t-online.de), is far from the center of town. Take bus #621 (direction: "Ippendorf Altenheim") to "Jugendgästehaus," or bus #620 (direction "Venusberg/Klinikum") to "Sertürnerstr.," turn left on Haager Weg and walk for 10min. A sparkling, super-modern place in the suburbs; it even has glass doors that slide open automatically and a nightly bar. DM39. Breakfast and sheets included. Laundry DM10. Reception 9am-1am. Curfew 1am. Wheelchair accessible.

Hotel Mozart, Mozartstr. 1 (tel. 65 90 71 74; fax 65 90 75). From the south exit of the station turn right onto Herwarthstr., left on Bachstr., then right on Mozartstr. Just the kind of Viennese elegance you'd expect in such a classical neighborhood. Large, trim rooms. Conveniently located. Singles DM75-88, with bath DM135-150; doubles DM105-115, with bath DM165-185. Breakfast included.

Hotel Bergmann, Kasernenstr. 13 (tel. 63 38 91; fax 63 50 57). From the station follow Poststr., turn left at Münsterplatz on Vivatsgasse, then right on Kasernenstr.; after 10min., the hotel is on the left. Cozy, elegant rooms. *Very* pink bathrooms in the hall. Singles DM60, doubles DM95. Reception hours sporadic—call ahead.

Hotel Virneburg, Sandkaule 3a (tel. 63 63 66). Walk up Poststr. and bear right on Acherstr. at the north end of Münsterplatz. Turn left on Rathausgasse and left again on Belderberg, which runs into Sandkaule. Or take U-Bahn #62, 66, or 67 to "Bertha-von-Suttner-Platz." Functional rooms, unbeatable price and location. Singles DM35-45, with shower DM55-65; doubles DM65-70, with shower DM90-95. Breakfast included.

Hotel Hofgarten, Fritz-Tillman-Str. 7 (tel. 22 34 82 or 22 34 72; fax 21 39 02). From the station turn right onto Maximilianstr., continue on Kaiserstr., and then turn left on Fritz-Tillman-Str. Live like an ambassador in this stately hotel. A fabulous splurge. Singles DM75-140; doubles DM125-185. Breakfast included. Call ahead.

Camping: Campingplatz Genienaue, Im Frankenkeller 49 (tel. 34 49 49). U-Bahn #16 or 63 to "Rheinallee," then bus #613 (direction: "Giselherstr.") to "Guntherstr." Turn left on Guntherstr. and right on Frankenkeller. Rhein-side camping in the suburb of Mehlem. DM8 per person. Tent DM5-8. Reception 9am-noon and 3-10pm.

🖸 FOOD

The **market** on Münsterplatz teems with haggling vendors and determined customers trying to get the best meat, fruit, and vegetables at the lowest prices. At the end of the day voices rise and prices plummet. (M-Sa 9am-6pm.) There is also a **supermarket** located in the basement of the Kaufhof department store on Münsterpl. (Open M-F 9:30am-8pm, Sa 9am-4pm.)

Mensa, Nassestr. 11, a 15min. walk from the station along Kaiserstr. In Bonn's glory days it swung with cosmopolitan flair. Reagan would sip *Dom Perignon* out of Maggie Thatcher's stilleto heels, and Helmut Kohl would lead the crowd in a round of bawdy German drinking songs. Now, it's just another *Mensa.* Cheap meals DM2-5.50. DM1 extra for non-students. Lunch M-Th 11:30am-2:15pm, F 11:30am-2pm, Sa noon-1:45pm. Dinner M-F 5:30-7:30pm. No dinner served July 5 to Oct. 9.

🖾 Carl's Mensa-Bistro, Nassestr. 15, has restaurant-quality meals served cafeteria-style at a price only slightly more expensive than the *Mensa.* Chili and burritos DM6-7, steaks DM6-11, salad DM1.20 per 100g. Open M-Th 10:30am-10pm, F 10:30am-3pm.

Cassius-Garten, Maximilianstr. 28d, at the edge of the Altstadt facing the station, with a back entrance in the court of the tourist office. A veggie bar where zealous disciples of health consume 50 kinds of salads, noodles, and whole-grain baked goods in a futuristic, white-glossed atrium. DM2.70 per 100g. Careful on your first time through: the weight really adds up. Open M-F 9am-8pm, Sa 9am-4pm.

Pizzeria la Piccola, Bonngasse 4 (tel. 63 78 16), a few steps from the *Beethovenhaus* and Marktplatz. The insidious scent curls out and drags in the unsuspecting. Pizzas from DM7.50. Open daily 11am-1am.

Café Blau, Franziskanerstr. 5 (tel. 65 07 17), across from the university. Serves light meals (breakfast DM2.50-6, salads DM5-11, crepes DM7-8), and fills up with loud crowds of students in the evening. Open daily 9am-1am.

Brauhaus Bönnsch, Sterntorbrücke 4 (tel. 65 06 10), pours its own highly civilized *Bönnsch,* the smooth-as-butter illegitimate son of Köln's *Kölsch* (DM2.50 for 0.2L). The delicious *Bönnsche Flammkuchen,* made from a 250-year-old Alsatian recipe, comes in many vegetarian (and non-vegetarian) varieties (DM13-17). Open M-Th and Su 11am-1am, F-Sa 11am-3am.

SIGHTS

The postwar architectural mandate to turn this small city into a world-class capital produced goofy results. While most of Bonn's bureaucracy has been packed up and shipped out, the hulls remain; most of the governmental buildings now serve as ministries, easing the transition from capital to government-lite. These erstwhile seats of power have a historical and novelty factor, but the castles, palaces, and museums that lend Bonn its cultural wealth lie just outside the city center.

BEETHOVENHAUS. Attracting music aficionados of all sorts, this museum located in the house of Beethoven's birth hosts a fantastic collection of the composer's personal effects—from his primitive hearing aids to his first violin. The symphonic ghost haunts Bonn annually during the **Beethoven festival** (Sept. 23-Oct. 16, 2000). The first fête, in 1845, was a riot, with Franz Liszt brawling with French nationalist Berlioz while King Ludwig's mistress Lola Montez table-danced. Call the tourist office for information. (*Bonngasse 18-20. Tel. 981 75 25. Open April-Sept. M-Sa 10am-6pm, Su 11am-4pm; Oct.-March M-Sa 10am-5pm, Su 11am-4pm. DM8, students DM6.*)

RATHAUS. Reminiscent of a voluptuous birthday cake, the town hall presides over the Marktplatz; in the similarly colorful 60s, de Gaulle, Kennedy, and Elizabeth II visited together for a photo-op.

MÜNSTER. The cathedral holds three stories of arches within arches that finally yield a gorgeous gold-leaf mosaic; a 12th-century cloister laced with crossways and latticed passages branches off under the doorway labeled "Kreuzgang." Keep an eye out for the incongruous blue-red Expressionist windows. (*Münsterplatz. Cloister open M-Sa 9am-5:30pm, Su 1:30-6pm.*)

BUNDESTAG. In its governmental heyday, the vaguely Bauhaus structure earned the title of "least prepossessing parliament building" in the world. It's possible to believe that Berlin was declared Germany's capital based on architectural grounds. (*Take U-Bahn #16, 63, or 66 to "Heussallee/Bundeshaus" or bus #610 to "Bundeshaus."*)

PALAIS SCHAUMBURG. Come see the former home of the German president! The less majestic **Denkmal** outside the Palais was erected in honor of Konrad Adenauer, one of Germany's and Bonn's most prominent personas. Nicknamed *der Alte* (the old guy), the postwar chancellor was Bonn's guiding light, but the 3m hollow-cheeked bust looks like a skull lifted from a pirate flag. Engraved into his cranium are allegorical figures—various animals, a pair of bound hands, and two French cathedrals. (*Adenauerallee 135-141.*)

OTHER SIGHTS. Forty thousand students study within the **Kurfürstliches Schloß,** the huge 18th-century palace now serving as the center of Bonn's **Friedrich-Wilhelms-Universität.** The Schloß is the gateway to the refreshing **Hofgarten** and **Stadtgarten,** forever filled with students and punks. To uncover Bonn's "other" palace, stroll down Poppelsdorfer Allee to the 18th-century **Poppelsdorfer Schloß.** The palace touts a French facade and an Italian courtyard, as well as beautifully manicured **botanical gardens.** (*Gardens open May-Sept. M-F 9am-6pm, Su 9am-1pm; Oct.-April M-F 9am-4pm. Su 9am-1pm. Free M-F, DM1 Su. Greenhouses open M-F 10:30am-noon and 2-4pm. Free.*)

 MUSEUMS

Bonn's museums are superb. The city enjoyed nearly 50 years of generous federal funding, and much of this wealth has been channeled into more than 20 museums in Bonn and the surrounding region. The **"Museum Mile"** begins at the **Museum Alexander Koenig.** Take U-Bahn #16, 63, or 66 to "Heussallee" or "Museum Koenig." The **Bonncard** provides free admission to most museums.

MUSEUM MILE

KUNSTMUSEUM BONN. A stunning contemporary building houses a superb selection of Expressionist and modern German art. *(Friedrich-Ebert-Allee 2. Tel. 77 62 60. Open Tu and Th-Su 10am-6pm, W 10am-7pm. DM5, students DM3.)*

■HAUS DER GESCHICHTE. A futuristic museum dedicated to critical and "interactive" German history. Thoughtful exhibits are highlighted by some antique VWs and a black enclosure with the scrolling names of Holocaust victims. *(Adenauerallee 250. Tel. 916 50. 1 block from the Kunstmuseum Bonn. Open Tu-Su 9am-7pm. Free.)*

KUNST-UND AUSSTELLUNGSHALLE DER BRD. The art here is so new you can smell the paint; check out the ultra-modern media-art room. The 16 columns flanking the *Ausstellungshalle* represent the 16 federal states of united Germany. *(Friedrich-Ebert-Allee 4. Tel. 917 12 00. Open Tu-W 10am-9pm, Th-Su 10am-7pm. DM10, students DM5.)*

MUSEUM ALEXANDER KOENIG. If taxidermy has a Louvre, this is it. Realistic and not at all creepy, the specimens in the exhibit are intriguing for anyone interested in animals. *(Adenauerallee 160. Tel. 912 22 15 or 912 22 19. Open Tu-F 9am-5pm, Sa 9am-12:30pm, Su 9:30am-5pm. DM4, students DM2.)*

ELSEWHERE IN BONN

FRAUENMUSEUM. The vast galleries glitter with interactive, modern art pieces by women. The second floor covers medieval art. Peculiar pieces on the roof and a Yoko Ono room provide more thought-provoking works. *(Tel. 69 13 44. U-Bahn #61 to "Rosental/Herrstr." Open Tu-Sa 2-6pm, Su 11am-6pm. DM8, students DM5.)*

AKADEMISCHES KUNSTMUSEUM. Lazy sculpture fans can forget about going abroad to see the masterpieces because they're all here, in the largest collection of plaster casts in Germany. Exhibits include Venus de Milo, the Colossus of Samos, and Laocöon. Better than the real thing. *(Tel. 73 77 38. On the far side of the Hofgarten. Open M-W, F, and Su 10am-1pm, Th 10am-1pm and 4-6pm. DM1, students free.)*

◤ NIGHTLIFE

Bonn's bombastic and versatile nightlife forcefully debunks myths suggesting that the city is boring. Of Bonn's monthly glossies, *Schnüss* is unbeatable; it's more complete than the free *Bonner Gästeführer* and *Szene Bonn*.

Schicht N8, Bornheimer Str. 20-22. (tel. 963 83 08). Quirkiest club in Bonn. Themed evenings range from Brit pop parties to Gothic-industrial "funerals." Open daily 10pm-5am. Cover Sa-Su DM5.

The Jazz Galerie, Oxfordstr. 24 (tel. 65 06 62). A hub for jazz and rock concerts. Open daily M-Th and Su 9pm-3am, F-Sa 9pm-4am. On concert nights opens at 8pm, but shows begin around 9:15pm. Cover for concerts DM10-20, for discos DM5.

Sharon, Oxfordstr. 20-21, is a soul discotheque for those who just can't get enough. Soul and funk F-Sa 10pm-5am. Cover DM10. 21+.

Pantheon, Bundeskanzlerplatz (tel. 21 25 21), in the shadow of an enormous Mercedes logo. The popular disco hosts concerts, stand-up comedy, and art exhibits. Open M-Sa 8pm-3am. Cover DM10.

Café Gottlich (tel 65 99 69), on tiny Fürstenstr. near the university. Serves drinks into the wee hours of the morning. Open M-Sa 9am-4am, Su noon-2am.

Café Z, in the **Schwulen- und Lesbenzentrum** (see p. 440), hosts gay night Tu, youth-group (ages 16-27) W, and mixed gay-lesbian Th. Lesbian party 2nd Sa in the month. Open M-Tu and Th 8pm-midnight, W 9pm-midnight.

Sharlies, Theaterstr. 2 (tel. 69 07 61), at the corner of Theaterstr. and Kölner Str. Hopping gay and lesbian bar. Open M-Th 9pm-4am, F-Sa 9pm-5am, Su 9pm-3am.

NEAR BONN: KÖNIGSWINTER AND DRACHENFELS

"The castled crag of Drachenfels frowns o'er the wide and winding Rhein," wrote Lord Byron in *Childe Harold's Pilgrimage*. According to the *Nibelungenlied* and to local lore, epic hero Siegfried slew a dragon who once haunted the crag. Siegfried then bathed in the dragon's blood and would have been invincible if not for the bare spot left by a leaf on his back. The ruins and the incredible view of the **Drachenfels** can be reached from Bonn and **Königswinter,** the town in the valley below the ruins. From Bonn, take U-Bahn #66 (direction: "Königswinter/Bad Honnef") to "Königswinter Fähre" (30min., every 20min., DM5.30). From Königswinter, follow Drachenfelsstr. (about 45min.). The less energetic take the **Drachenfelsbahn,** Drachenfelsstr. 53 (tel. (02223) 920 90), a railway leading to the top. (DM10 up, DM9 down, DM13 round-trip.) The **Nibelungshalle,** where the dragon once munched on tasty young virgins, is now a **reptile zoo** and **museum** (tel. (02223) 241 50) with more than 150 live reptiles. (Open mid-March to mid-Nov. daily 10am-7pm; mid-Nov. to mid-March Sa-Su 10am-7pm. DM6, students DM5.) The Drachenfels' little brother **Schloß Drachenburg** (tel. 261 55) raises its ornate turrets halfway between the museum and the ruin. Tours through the castle's fine interior depart hourly. (Open April-Oct. Tu-Su 11am-6pm. DM4, students and children DM3.)

AACHEN

Aachen jives day and night in four different languages, exuding a youthful internationalism in spite of its old age. Charlemagne sang the mantra of multiculturalism when he made the city the capital of his Frankish empire in the 8th century, and the tunes are still heard today—a flux of students and international travelers continually renew the vibrant atmosphere. Though it has been tossed back and forth among empires for centuries, Aachen has held onto its historical treasures while also nurturing modernity: the city's internationalism is expressed as a forum for up-and-coming European artists. Despite this dynamism, Aachen maintains strong ties to its Roman, medieval, and Renaissance past.

⚡ ORIENTATION AND PRACTICAL INFORMATION

Aachen is at the crossroads between Germany, Belgium, and the Netherlands. Many travelers cross the Dutch border to stock up on cheese.

Trains: Chug from Aachen to Köln (1hr., 2-3 per hour, DM20), Brussels (2hr., 1 per hour, DM51), and Amsterdam (4hr., 1-2 per hour, DM102).

Public Transportation: The main bus station is on the corner of Peterskirchhof and Peterstr. Tickets are priced by distance, with one-way trips running DM2.30-9.30. *24-Stunden* tickets provide a full day of unlimited travel within Aachen for DM8. For those under 21, a weekend pass for all buses can be purchased on Saturdays for DM5. Some hotels also offer a DM7 *Hotelgastkarte* good for 2 days of unlimited travel.

Mitfahrzentrale: Roermonder Str. 4 (tel. 194 40). Matches riders and drivers. Open M-Sa 10am-6pm; phone lines open 9am-9pm.

Bike Rental: Bike Shop, Pontstr. 141-149 (tel. 401 33 60). DM12 per day.

Tourist Office: Tel. 180 29 60; fax 180 29 31. In the Atrium Elisenbrunnen on Friedrich-Wilhelm-Platz, the office dispenses literature, runs **tours,** and finds **rooms** from DM35. From the train station, cross the street and head up Bahnhofstr., turn left onto Theaterstr., which becomes Theaterplatz, then right onto Kapuzinergraben, which becomes Friedrich-Wilhelm-Platz; the atrium is to the left. Open M-F 9am-6pm, Sa 9am-2pm.

Currency Exchange: At the post office in the train station. Open M-F 9am-6pm, Sa 9am-1pm, Su 10am-noon. Also at the **Hauptpostamt** near the tourist office.

Bookstore: Mayersche Buchhandlung, Ursulinerstr. 17-19 (tel. 477 70), at the corner of Buchkremerstr. Decent English section. Open M-W and F 9:30am-6:30pm, Th 9:30am-8:30pm, Sa 9:30am-2pm.

Gay and Lesbian Resources: Schwulenreferat, Kasinostr. 37 (tel. 346 32). Hosts a weekly café Tu after 8pm. Office open Tu 8-9pm, Th noon-2pm.

Laundromat: SB Waschsalon, Jülicher Str. 3. Wash DM5, DM4 on Wednesday. Dry DM1 per 10min. Open M-Sa 8:30am-10pm.

Emergency: Police, tel. 110. **Fire** and **Ambulance,** tel. 112.

Post Office: Hauptpostamt, Kapuzinergraben, 52064 Aachen, to the left of the train station. Walk down Lagerhausstr., right down Franzstr., and then right on Kapuzinergraben. Open M-F 9am-6pm, Sa 9am-1pm.

Internet Access: Öffentliche Bibliothek, Couverstr. 15. Open Tu-W and F 11am-5:45pm, Th 1:15-8pm, Sa 10am-1pm. DM6 per hour. **The Web,** Kleinmarschierstr. 6. Open M-F 10am-11pm, Sa 10am-midnight, Su noon-8pm. DM8 per hour.

PHONE CODE	0241

ACCOMMODATIONS AND CAMPING

Aachen has too much history for a town of its size, and the oodles of visitors push the lodging prices up. The **Mitwohnzentrale,** Süsterfeldstr. 24 (tel. 87 53 46), sets up lodging for longer stays. Take bus #7 (direction: "Siedlung Schönau") or 33 (direction: "Vaals") to "Westbahnhof." (Open M-F 9am-1pm and 3-6pm.)

Euroregionales Jugendgästehaus, Maria-Theresia-Allee 260 (tel. 711 01; fax 70 82 19). Two buses go to the hostel leaving from the "Finanzamt" bus stop. To get to this

Aachen
ACCOMMODATIONS
A ETAP Hotel
B Hotel Am Tivoli
C Hotel Cortis
D Hotel Marx
E Jugendgästehaus

departure point from the station, walk left on Lagerhausstr. until it intersects Karmeliterstr. and Mozartstr.; the bus stop will be on the other side of the street. Bus #2 (direction: "Preusswald") to "Ronheide" or 12 (direction: "Diepenbenden") to "Colynshof." With interior decorating that would please Armani and completely renovated facilities (including a bar with projection TV), this feels more like an expensive convention center than a youth hostel. DM38.50. Curfew 1am.

ETAP-Hotel, Strangenhäuschen 15 (tel. 91 19 29; fax 15 53 04). From the bus station, take bus #5 to "Strangenhäuschen." A chain budget hotel with rooms that follow a cookie-cutter pattern, but sanitary. Singles DM62, doubles DM74. F-Su all rooms DM62. Breakfast DM8.50. Reception 6:30-10am and 5-11pm. Checkout noon.

Hotel Marx, Hubertusstr. 33-35 (tel. 375 41; fax 267 05). Just a hop, skip, and jump from the station. Hop left on Lagerhausstr. which becomes Boxgraben, skip right on Stephanstr., and jump left on Hubertusstr. Friendly hotel with a small park in the backyard and in a great location 2 blocks from the Altstadt. Singles with bath DM85; doubles DM110, with bath DM140. Breakfast included.

Hotel Cortis, Krefelder Str. 52 (tel. 15 60 11; fax 15 60 12). From the central bus station, take bus #51 to "Tivoli." Backtrack down Krefelder Str. about 300m. Located outside Aachen proper, this hotel offers bright, comfortable rooms above a small bar. Singles from DM50, with shower DM67; doubles DM75-89, with shower DM110-114. Breakfast included. 24hr. reception.

Hotel Am Tivoli, Krefelder Str. 86 (tel./fax 91 95 20 or 91 95 21). Bus #51 to "Tivoli"; backtrack 100m on Krefelder Str. and the hostel will be on your left. A small inn with local flavor. Singles with bath DM65, doubles with bath DM100. Breakfast included.

FOOD

Much of **Pontstraße** seems to be an exercise in creating the perfect 90s café—Euro-simplistic furniture and signs cut from sheet metal and lit by fluorescent light are separated by more traditional *Imbiße* and cheap Italian pizza places. But beware—this region is also the prowling ground of the *Bahkauv*, a fearsome mythical blend of dog, puma, and dragon, which pounces on drunken revelers, inducing head-splitting hangovers. While in Aachen, be sure to try the native *Printen*, a tremendously appetizing spicy gingerbread biscuit refined from an old Belgian recipe. It's now a world-famous snack with an annual production of 4,500 tons. For the budget traveler, **Plus,** Marienbongard 27, off Pontstr., has an erratic selection of very cheap **groceries.** (Open M-F 8am-8pm, Sa 8am-4pm.)

Mensa (tel. 80 37 92), in the green-trimmed building on Pontwall, near the Ponttor. Meals DM3-7.50. Open M-Th 11:30am-2pm, F 11:30am-2pm.

Katakomben Studentenzentrum, Pontstr. 74-76 (tel. 470 01 41), encloses **Café Chico Mendes,** a vegetarian co-op café of the Catholic College. Entrees DM8-12. Half-off a very long list of drinks during the rare happy hour (Su 8:30-9:30pm). Open M-F 4:30pm-1am, Sa 6pm-1am.

Pera, Marienbongard 2, on the corner of Pontstr. Is it a Swedish furniture exhibition or a café? Minimalism reaches new heights here, but not on the drink list, which is as long as the bar stools are high. Open daily 11am-1am.

Tam-Phat, Pontstr. 100 (tel. 250 80), a family-run restaurant offering primarily Thai and Chinese dishes. Even slim budgets can afford their phat meals, including numerous vegetarian options (DM7-14). Open M-F 11am-3pm and 5-11pm, Sa-Su noon-11pm.

Egmont, Pontstr. 1 (tel. 40 60 44). Just off the Rathaus. This mildly expensive, upscale café attracts students and older types alike, who come to wine and dine in the updated elegant decor. Bring student ID for discounts. Open daily 9am-3am.

Van den Daele, Büchel 18 (tel. 357 24), just off the Markt. The finest selection of baked goods in Aachen's oldest house. Built in 1655, this *Printen* factory was made famous by artist/baker Leo van den Daele. The atmosphere is pure 18th century, and the house speciality is *Reisfladden* (rice pudding)—DM4 buys you one huge slice. Open M-W 9am-7pm, Th-Sa 9am-9pm, Su noon-6pm.

👁 SIGHTS

In 765, the Frankish King Pepin the Short took a dip in the hot springs north of Aachen's present city center. When his son **Charlemagne** (Karl der Große) assumed power, he made the family's former vacation spot the capital of the rapidly expanding kingdom, and later of the Holy Roman Empire.

DOM. The emperor's presence still dominates the city, in part through a local legend that claims that in WWII, a bomb aimed at the cathedral was deflected by a statue of Charlemagne. The 8th-century dome at its center tops three tiers of marble arches that separate the gilded roof from the mosaic floor. The neo-Byzantine structure demonstrates Charlemagne's attempt to transplant the grandeur of Constantinople to his own capital. His throne on the second level is a simple chair of marble slabs. Stained glass rings the 15th-century Gothic choir, and beneath the chancel lie some of the bones of the big guy himself in a sparkling gold and jewelled casket. *(Open daily 10am-7pm. Tours M 11am and noon; Tu-F 11am, noon, 2:30, and 3:30pm; Sa-Su 12:30, 2:30, and 3:30pm. DM3.)*

SCHATZKAMMER. Old Karl cuts more of a figure in the Schatzkammer. The most famous likeness of the emperor, a gold-plated solid silver bust, as well as the crown jewels shine brightly in this exceptionally rich treasury, just around the corner from a gigantic golden arm statue that holds his radius and ulna bones. Really. Other reliquaries hold bits and pieces of famous Jerusalemites—look for the remains of the Cross, nails, Christ's scourging robe, and John the Baptist's hair and ribs. *(Around the corner to the right from the Dom, tucked into the Klostergasse. Open M 10am-1pm, Tu-W and F-Su 10am-6:30pm, Th 10am-9pm. Last entrance 30min. before closing. DM5, students, seniors, and children DM3.)*

MARKTPLATZ. The 14th-century stone **Rathaus,** built on the ruins of Charlemagne's palace, looms over the wide Marktplatz beside the cathedral. Seventeenth-century citizens with a decorative obsession added Baroque flourishes to the facade. On the northern face stand 50 statues of former German sovereigns, 31 of whom were crowned in Aachen (not to mention the 12 queens who were also coronated here but didn't make the Rathaus cut). *(Tel. 432 73 10. Open daily 10am-1pm and 2-5pm. DM3, students and children DM1.50.)* A copy of the famed **Charlemagne statue** draws a picnicking, multi-colored-hair crowd who sit on the square talking on cell phones and playing cards. The **Puppenbrunnen,** a fountain whose lovable characters represent Aachen's clever townspeople, spews forth at the intersection of Krämerstr. and Hofstr.

🏛 MUSEUMS

Although the range of museums in Aachen is limited, the streets, especially in the Altstadt, shelter numerous little galleries worth browsing.

▇LUDWIGFORUM FÜR INTERNATIONALE KUNST. It's the building with the large clown in drag in front. The *Forum* follows a contemporary trend of scorning the title "museum," and its collection is cutting-edge. In the converted Bauhaus umbrella factory works of the current greats (Jeff Koons' gigantic sex dolls) are exhibited next to the soon-to-be-greats (a three-foot Marge Simpson stone fertility doll). **The Space,** underneath the museum, is yet another *Forum*—for dance, music, and theatre, that is. *(Jülicher Str. 97-109. Tel. 180 70. Open Tu and Th 10am-5pm, W and F 10am-8pm, Sa-Su 11am-5pm. Tours Su 11:30am and 3pm. Last entrance 30min. before closing. DM6, students DM3.)*

INTERNATIONALES ZEITUNGSMUSEUM. "What's black and white and re(a)d all over?" This classy museum houses more than 120,000 different international newspapers, including press from the revolutions of 1848, the World Wars, the day Hitler died, and reunification. *(Just up the street from the Markt. Pontstr. 13 Tel. 432 45 08. Open Tu-F 9:30am-1pm and 2:30-5pm, Sa 9:30am-1pm. Last entry 30min. before closing. Free.)*

NORDRHEIN-WESTFALEN

SUERMONDT-LUDWIG-MUSEUM. The 14th-century statues placed in the distinctly contemporary interior are slightly disconcerting, but this recently expanded museum holds 44 galleries of sculptures, paintings, engravings, and crafts, starting with the modern and ending with the medieval. *(Wilhelmstr. 18. Tel. 47 98 00. Open Tu and Th-F 11am-7pm, W 11am-9pm, Sa-Su 11am-5pm. Last entry 30min. before closing. DM6, students and children DM3.)*

🎵 🎭 ENTERTAINMENT AND NIGHTLIFE

Aachen has a lively theater scene, beginning with the **Stadttheater** (tel. 478 42 44), on Theaterplatz in the central city. (Box office open M-Sa 9am-1pm, 5-7pm, and 30min. before performance.) A small strip of newer, unconventional theaters line **Gasborn,** spearheaded by the **Aachener Kultur-und Theaterinitiative,** Gasborn 9-11 (tel. 274 58). At night, the streets come alive as swarms of students hit the cafés and pubs for a study break with the *Bahkauv* (see **Food,** p. 446). *Klenkes Magazin* (DM4), available at most newsstands, offers readers movies and music listings galore. *Stonewall TAC*, available in most cafés near the university and some newsstands, has a thorough listing of gay and lesbian events.

Atlantis, Pontstr. 141 (tel. 242 41), fills *all* entertainment needs with a multi-screen cinema that shows popular releases, a mellow terrace café, a space-age underground *Kneipe*, and a grab-and-go bar outside the cinema for the requisite pre-movie beer run. Café and *Kneipe* open M-Th and Su 10am-1am, F-Sa 10am-3am. Movie times vary—check out their weekly schedule.

B9, Blondelstr. 9. A fairly run-of-the-mill disco that fills nightly with students and Gen-Xers getting down to a diverse selection of music. Check any of the multi-colored party posters all over town. Open daily M-Th 11pm-3am, F-Sa 11pm-5am.

Café Kittel, Pontstr. 39 (tel. 365 60). Posters smother the walls with announcements for live music, parties, and special events in this café that is ever-so-slightly grittier than its neighbors. Enjoy bowls of coffee in the outdoor *Biergarten* or in the greenhouse. Vegetable quiche DM5.20. Open M-Th 10am-2am, F-Sa 10am-3am, Su 11am-2am.

Zum Eulenspiegel, Pontstr. 114 (tel. 373 97). Named after the mischievous German elf, this bar is proud of its laminated Ted Nugent album adorning the wall. On Thursday nights locals and tourists alike revel in *Kölsch* (DM2), Hefeweizen (DM3), Guinness (DM3), and a *really* inexpensive drink menu. Open daily 6pm-3am (or later).

MONSCHAU

The tiny town of Monschau subtly blends the French with the *Rheinisch*. In the 17th century, a deluge of Huguenots fleeing Catholic persecution settled in this region, plying their traditional skills to stimulate a thriving cloth industry. In 1794, Napoleon captured the town, kicking off 12 years of occupation. After some international horse-trading, Monschau again became part of Germany, and now the tourist invasion hits daily and with full force. Many residents still have French names, and the local cuisine offers treats from Germany's friendly neighbor to the west. Monschau still *looks* distinctly *deutsch*. In a narrow, secluded valley cut by the swift-flowing Ruhr about 30km south of Aachen, the town is a visual compendium of gray slate roofs, cobblestones, and brickwork, while the surrounding hills are filled with hiking trails.

The 19th-century Romantic landscape atmosphere is completed by the **Burg,** the ruins of a massive castle perched above Monschau. A steep set of stairs leads to the castle from the town center. A maze of tunnels and narrow stairways to high stone towers make the castle a playground for anyone who fancies being king for a day. Between the Burg and the town, the elegiac gray 1649 **Alte Pfarrkirche** stands with its shingled onion-turret. The **Glashütte,** Burgau 15 (tel. 024 72 32), at the end of the main road, has tourist-packed glass-blowing demonstrations every hour on the half-hour between 10:30am and 5:30pm. (Open daily 10am-6pm. DM3, students and children DM2.) On the path leading down from the Burg, the **Rotes Haus,**

Laufenstr. 10 (tel. 50 71), opens its bright pink doors into a stunningly well-preserved 18th-century cloth merchant's house. (Tours Easter-Nov. Tu-Su 10 and 11am, and 2, 3, and 4 pm. DM5, students and children DM3.) Across the bridge stands the **Evangelische Pfarrkirche,** another of the town's delicately-cut churches. On the other end of town, the authentic 19th-century **Senfmühle** (mustard mill), Laufenstr. 18 (tel. 22 45), can leave you delirious with desire for Monschau's famous mustard. (Demonstrations March-Oct. W 11am and 2pm. DM4, students and children DM2.)

Monschau is accessible from Aachen by bus #SB63, which leaves hourly from the Hauptbahnhof on weekdays and less frequently on weekends. Take the bus to the end, then transfer to bus #82 (1½hr., DM9). Getting back is easier: bus #166 runs hourly to Aachen (1¼hr., DM6). The **tourist office,** Stadtstr. 1 (tel. 33 00; fax 45 34), sits across from the steps leading to the Burg. (Open M-F 9am-noon and 1-4pm, Sa 11am-3pm, Su 11am-2pm; Oct.-Easter M-F 9am-noon and 1-4pm.) To help you recover from the mustard shock, the amicable staff book **rooms** (from DM25) for a DM5 deposit and sell hiking maps for the Eifel region. The **Jugendherberge Monschau (HI),** Auf dem Schloß 4 (tel. 23 14; fax 43 91), is built inside the courtyard of the Burg. Oddly appropriate for a budget honeymoon. (DM26, over 26 DM31. Breakfast included. Sheets DM6. Reception 8:30-9am, 12:30-1pm, and 5:30-7:30pm, or check for staff upstairs in the kitchen. Curfew 10pm, but keys are available.) The larger, more modern **Jugendherberge Monschau-Hargard (HI),** Hargardsgasse 5 (tel. 21 80; fax 45 27), lies outside of town. Take bus #82 or 166 (direction: "Hargard") from in front of the post office to the end, backtrack 100m, and follow the sign. (DM25, over 26 DM30. Breakfast included. Sheets DM6. Reception until 9pm. Curfew 10pm.) **Hotel Zum Stern,** Eschenbachstr. 21, offers gorgeous, brook-side rooms just off the Marktplatz. The antique furniture and charmingly curving floors attest to the house's 360 years. (Singles from DM68, doubles from DM129.) To satisfy the royal appetite without emptying the royal treasury, feast on pizzas and crepes (DM4.50-9) at **Tavola Calda,** Stadtstr. 42. (Tel. 72 17 63. Open daily 10am-9pm.) The **telephone code** is 02472.

DÜSSELDORF

As Germany's modish fashion hub, advertising center, and multinational corporation base, as well as capital of the densely populated Nordrhein-Westfalen, Düsseldorf crawls with German patricians and wanna-be aristocrats. Founded in the 13th century, the city has endured a series of terrific pummelings. Düsseldorf rebounded after suffering calamitous destruction during the Thirty Years War, the War of Spanish Succession, and WWII, each time with an indefatigable independence that translates into fierce pride among the city's residents. Set on the majestic Rhein, Germany's "Hautstadt" (a pun on *Hauptstadt,* meaning capital, and the French *haute,* as in *haute culture*) is a stately, modern metropolis. Some residents claim that Düsseldorf is not on the Rhein but on the Königsallee (also known as the Kö), a kilometer-long catwalk that sweeps down both sides of the old town moat. At night, propriety (and sobriety) are cast aside as thousands of Düsseldorfers flock to the 500 pubs in the Altstadt, trading their monocles and Rolexes for beer goggles and a damn good time.

▐ GETTING THERE AND GETTING AROUND

Flights: Frequent S-Bahn trains and a Lufthansa shuttle travel from the station to **Flughafen Düsseldorf.** Call 421 22 23 for flight information. Open 5am-12:30am.

Trains: Düsseldorf is connected by train to Frankfurt (3hr., 2 per hour, DM79), Hamburg (3½hr., 1 per hour, DM116), Berlin (4hr., 1 per hour, DM103), Munich (4hr., 3 per hour, DM191), Amsterdam (3hr., 1 per hour, DM55), Brussels (3¼hr., 1 per hour, DM59), and Paris (4½hr., 7 per day, DM140). It's cheaper to take the S-Bahn to Aachen, Dortmund, and Köln.

NORDRHEIN-WESTFALEN

Public Transportation: The **Rheinbahn** includes subways, streetcars, buses, and the S-Bahn. Single tickets, DM2.10-12, depending on distance traveled. The *Tagesticket* (DM11; higher prices for longer distances) is the best value—up to 5 people can travel 24hr. on any line. Tickets are sold by vending machine; pick up the *Fahrausweis* brochure in the tourist office for instructions. Düsseldorf's S-Bahn is integrated into the mammoth regional **VRR** *(Verkehrsverbund Rhein-Ruhr)* system, which connects most surrounding cities. For **schedule information,** call 582 28.

Taxi: Tel. 21 21 21.

Car Rental: Hertz, Immermannstr. 65 (tel. 35 70 25). Open M-F 7am-5pm, Sa 8am-noon. Rates start at DM400 per week.

Mitfahrzentrale: Konrad-Adenauer-Platz 13 (tel. 37 60 81), to the left as you exit the train station, and upstairs over a tiny travel office. Arranges ride shares. Open daily 9am-6pm. **City-Netz Mitfahrzentrale,** Kruppstr. 102 (tel. 194 44), is a chain with slightly higher prices. Open M-F 9am-7pm, Sa 9am-2pm, Su 11am-2pm.

Bike Rental: Zweirad Egert, Ackerstr. 143 (tel. 66 21 34). S-Bahn #6 (direction "Essen") to "Wehrbahn," turn right from the exit on Birkenstr., then right onto Ackerstr. and walk 10min. Call ahead to check availability. Bikes DM23.30 per day, DM100 per week. DM50 deposit and ID required. Open M-F 9:30am-6:30pm, Sa 10am-2pm.

⑦ PRACTICAL INFORMATION

Tourist Office: Konrad-Adenauer-Pl. (tel. 17 20 20; fax 35 04 04; www.duesseldorf.de). Walk up and to the right from the train station and look for the towering Immermanhof building. This shiny office with friendly staff is a bastion of information, and its free monthly *Düsseldorfer Monatsprogramm* details all goings-on about town. Open for concert and theater ticket sales (12% fee) and general services M-F 8:30am-6pm, Sa 9am-12:30pm; books **rooms** (DM55 and up) for a DM5 fee M-Sa 8am-8pm, Su 4-10pm. The **branch office,** Heinrich-Heine-Allee 24 (tel. 899 23 46), specializes in cultural listings. Open M-F 9am-5pm.

Budget Travel: Council Travel, Graf-Adolf-Str. 64 (tel. 36 30 30). Open M-F 10am-6pm, Sa 10:30am-1pm.

Consulates: Canada and **U.K.,** Yorckstr. 19 (tel. 944 80). Open M-F 8:30am-noon. **U.S.,** Kennedydamm 15-17 (tel. 47 06 10).

Currency Exchange: Deutsche Verkehrsbank, in the train station and the airport. Open M-Sa 7am-9pm, Su 8am-9pm.

American Express: Benzenbergstr. 39-47 (tel. 90 13 50). Mail held up to 4 weeks for card members. Open M-F 9am-6pm, Sa 10am-6pm, Su 9am-1pm.

Bookstore: Stern-Verlag, Friedrichstr. 24-26 (tel. 388 10). A good selection of paperbacks in many languages. Open M-F 9:30am-8pm, Sa 9:30am-4pm.

Women's Resources: Frauenbüro, Mühlenstr. 29 (tel. 899 36 03), 2nd floor. Walk-ins M-Th 8am-4pm, F 8am-1pm.

Gay and Lesbian Resources: Oberbilker Allee 310 (tel. 99 23 77). S-Bahn #6 to "Oberbilk" or U-Bahn #74 or 77 to "S-Bhf. Oberbilk." Open M-Th 10am-6pm, F 10am-4pm.

Laundromat: Wasch Center, Friedrichstr. 92, down the street from the Kirchpl. S-Bahn. Wash DM6. Dry DM1 per 15min. Soap included. Open M-Sa 6am-11pm.

Emergency: Police, tel. 110. **Ambulance** and **Fire,** tel. 112.

Pharmacy: Apotheke im Hauptbahnhof, open M-F 7am-8pm, Sa 8am-4pm. Staff speaks English. Closed pharmacies post lists of nearby open ones. **Emergency pharmacy,** tel. 115 00. **Emergency doctor,** tel. 192 92.

Post Office: Hauptpostamt, Konrad-Adenauer-Pl., 40210, a stone's throw to the right of the tourist office. Open M-F 8am-6pm, Sa 9am-2pm. Limited service M-F 6pm-8pm. **Branch office** in Hauptbahnhof open M-F 8am-6pm, Sa-Su 2pm-midnight.

Internet Access: See **g@rden** (p. 456) or **Ratin Gate** (p. 453).

PHONE CODE	0211

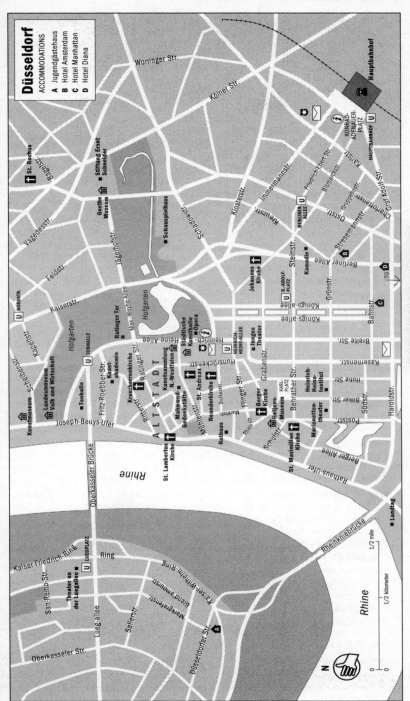

Düsseldorf

ACCOMMODATIONS

A Jugendgästehaus
B Hotel Amsterdam
C Hotel Manhattan
D Hotel Diana

C'MON RIDE THE TRAIN Riding the Düsseldorf subway is half practicality and half entertainment. Brand-new, huge high-definition television screens line the walls of the stations, displaying everything from weather forecasts to remarkably accurate horoscopes. Even cartoon shorts grace the screens, proving that the German travel authorities do indeed have a sense of humor—who knew? Nearby, Aachen's Hauptbahnhof subway station, lit entirely with fluorescent blue lights, is similarly entertaining, projecting cheery yellow streetcars that move back and forth while you wait for the real one to come along. If you're truly enjoying yourself in the station, gather your friends and stay all night—Deutsche Bahn's "Party Bahn" option allows devoted customers to rent a train car filled with drinks and music for an evening (tel. 194 40; conductors not included).

ACCOMMODATIONS AND CAMPING

Düsseldorf is a hugely popular international convention city where corporate crowds make rooms scarce and costly; it's not unusual for hotels to double their prices during a convention. Call at least a month ahead if possible. For a budget hotel stay, call the tourist office for trade fair dates and show up during a lull. Most rooms go for at least DM50 per person even in the off season. Fairly cheap hotels populate the seedy train station neighborhood.

Jugendgästehaus Düsseldorf (HI), Düsseldorfer Str. 1 (tel. 55 73 10; fax 57 25 13), is conveniently located just over the Rheinkniebrücke from the Altstadt. U-Bahn #70, 74, 75, 76, or 77 to "Luegplatz," then walk 500m down the BMW-lined Kaiser-Wilhelm-Ring. The hostel fills with whirlwind-tour-of-Europe groups making a pit stop in Düsseldorf. An unbeatable location makes up for moderately clean facilities and moderately high prices. DM37.50, over 26 DM41.50. Reception 7am-1am. Curfew 1am, but doors open every hour on the hour 2-6am.

Jugendherberge Duisburg-Wedau, Kalkweg 148e (tel. (0203) 72 41 64; fax 72 08 34). S-Bahn #1 or 21 to "Duisburg Hauptbahnhof," then bus #934 to "Jugendherberge." Quite far from the city, the neighboring town of Duisburg is accessible by a frequent streetcar (40min.), but public transportation closes by 1am and the hostel is too far for a taxi. Old but clean rooms. DM23.20, over 26 DM31. Wash and dry DM5. Reception 8am-10pm. Closed mid-Dec. to mid-Jan.

Hotel Amsterdam, Stresemannstr. 20 (tel. 840 58; fax 840 50), between Oststr. and Berliner Allee. From the station, start up Graf-Adolf-Str. and turn right at Stresemannplatz Recently renovated; now each room has a different color scheme. No-frills singles DM65, with TV and breakfast DM90; doubles from DM145. Reception 7am-midnight.

Hotel Manhattan, Graf-Adolf-Str. 39 (tel. 37 71 38; fax 37 02 47), 2 blocks from the station. The ghost of mid-1980s consumer America—the mirror-plated reception hallway reflects Coca-Cola posters into infinity. The rooms are less glitzy, but no less chintzy. A young, lively hotel. Singles DM68-105; doubles DM100-150, depending on ritziness and whether it's convention time. Breakfast buffet included. 24hr. reception.

Hotel Diana, Jahnstr. 31 (tel. 37 50 71; fax 36 49 43), 5 blocks from the station. Head left down Graf-Adolf-Str., left on Hüttenstr., and then a quick jog to the right on Jahnstr. Worn carpet, ugly tile, and questionable tapestry art, but it's all clean. Singles DM65; doubles DM95, with bath DM135. Breakfast included. 24hr. reception.

Hotel Bristol, Aderstr. 8 (tel. 37 07 50; fax 37 37 54), 1 block south of Graf-Adolf-Str. at the bottom tip of Königsallee. The well-appointed hotel offers elegance in profusion—even by the Kö's standards. Singles DM70, with shower DM95, with bath DM130; doubles DM120. Breakfast included.

Camping: Kleiner Torfbruch (tel. 899 20 38). S-Bahn to "Düsseldorf Geresheim," then bus #735 (direction: "Stamesberg") to "Seeweg." Pitch your palace and live like a king. DM7.50 per person, children DM4.50. DM10 per tent.

FOOD

For a cheap meal, the endless eateries in the **Altstadt** can't be beat. Rows of pizzerias, *Döner* stands, and Chinese diners reach from Heinrich-Heine-Allee to the banks of the Rhein, supplying standing meals by day and standing beers by night. The **Markt** on Karlsplatz offers shoppers plenty of foreign fruits and a local favorite, *Sauerbraten* (pickled beef). To watch well-dressed Beautiful People pay high prices for mediocre food, enjoy a cup of espresso on the **Kö. Olto Mess,** a popular **grocery** chain, should satisfy all your DIY needs. The most convenient location is at the eastern corner of Karlsplatz in the Altstadt. (Open M-F 8am-8pm, Sa 8am-4pm.)

Schnabelewojski, Bolkerstr. 53 (tel. 13 32 00), housed in Heinrich Heine's birthplace, has a smattering of café food and inexpensive wine, but its real draw is the "poetry café" at 8pm, the first Tuesday of each month, when customers read original or published poetry in many languages. Open M 4-11pm, Tu-F 3pm-midnight, Sa noon-1am, Su 11am-11pm.

Ratin Gate, Ratinger Str. 8 (tel. 32 20 40), is an internet café of the genuine variety; where food and drink accompany web-surfing. During happy "hour" (11pm-1am), it's not only the drinks, but also the web that's half-price. Internet access DM9. Open M-Th and Su 1pm-1am, F-Sa 1pm-3am.

Zum Uerige, Bergerstr. 1 (tel. 86 69 90). Some pheromone in the air inexplicably draws cool Germans to this seemingly average, heavy-wood, heavy-food restaurant. Try house specialties of *Blutwurst* (blood sausages; DM4) and Mainz cheese (DM4). When (if) you finish eating, settle down with a *Schlösser Alt* beer and soak up the crisp *Rheinisch* zephyrs. Open daily 10am-midnight. Kitchen open M-F 6-9pm, Sa 11am-4pm.

Galerie Burghof, Burgallee 1-3 (tel. 40 14 23), in Kaiserwerth next to Friedrich's Rhein ruins. U-Bahn #79 to "Klemensplatz." Walk down Kaiserwerther Markt and turn left on the Rhein promenade. Somewhat touristy, but delicious pancakes, a marvelous view of the Rhein and the Kaiserwerth ruins, as well as a 1932 Rolls Royce filled with stuffed chickens and a wedding-gowned mannequin covered with butterflies make eating here an oddly visual experience. Open daily 11am-1am. Pancakes served M-F 6-10:45pm, Sa 2-10:45pm, Su 2-11pm.

Marché, Königsallee 60 (tel. 32 06 81), in the Kö-Galerie mall. If you *must* dine on the Kö, Marché, safely hidden in a corner far from Armani's gaze, is one of the few places you can eat without blowing a week's budget. Entrees from DM7. Open M-Th and Su 9am-9pm, F-Sa 9am-10pm.

La Copa, Bergerstr. 4 (tel. 323 84 58). Sammy, Deano, and Barry Manilow have left the building, but not without bequeathing their beloved Copa with 50 tasty dishes (DM8-15). Wash it down with sangría. Open M-Th and Su noon-1am, F-Sa noon-late.

Zum Csikos, Andreasstr. 9 (tel. 32 97 71). This colorful little *Kneipe* is bursting with character and Hungarian food and drink. Try the *Gulyassuppe* (DM9) and watch out for famous *Düsseldorfers*. Open Tu-Su 6pm-3am.

 SIGHTS

KÖNIGSALLEE. The glitzy Kö, located just outside the Altstadt, embodies the vitality and glamour of Düsseldorf. While it doesn't have the fashion-center status of Milan or New York, it's twice as pretentious. So if you don't get runwayed over by models, you too can window-shop at Armani or ogle the Beemer parked outside. Head down Graf-Adolf-Str. from the train station (10min.). Properly called the Königsallee, the *belle époque* expanse was laid out over a century ago. Stone bridges span the little river that runs down the middle to trickle at the toes of a decadent statue of the sea god Triton. Midway up is the awesome **Kö-Galerie,** a gaudy marble-and-copper complex of one haughty store after another. Items *start* at US$100, and even the mannequins have attitude.

NORDRHEIN-WESTFALEN

HOFGARTEN. At the upper end of the Kö, the Hofgarten park is an oasis of green inside urban Düsseldorf and is the oldest public park in Germany. At the eastern end of the garden, the 18th-century **Schloß Jägerhof** houses the **Goethemuseum** (see **Museums,** see p. 455) behind its pink facade and white iron gates. The Hofgarten meets the Rhein at the Ehrendorf, museum plaza. The Neoclassical **Ratinger Tor** gatehouse leads into the garden from Heinrich-Heine-Allee. Twilight walks along the east bank of the Rhein are breathtaking.

HEINRICH-HEINE-INSTITUT. Beloved poet **Heinrich Heine** is Düsseldorf's melancholic son. His birthplace and homestead are marked by plaques, and every third restaurant and fast-food stand on his Bolkerstr. block bears his name. The institute is the official shrine, with a collection of manuscripts and an unsettling death mask. *(Bilker Str. 12-14. Tel. 899 55 71. Open Tu-Su 11am-5pm. DM4, students DM2.)*

BURGPLATZ. Farther up the Altstadt on the Rhein, Burgplatz used to be the site of a glorious castle, but tired citizens have saved only a single tower. The castle was built in 1324, burnt in 1490, rebuilt in 1559, razed in 1794, rebuilt in 1851, and flattened in 1872, at which point the townsfolk gave up—only the tower was reconstructed in 1900, and *that* was bombed to rubble in WWII. The pessimistic citizens waited until 1984 to rebuild the tower. Tread carefully—rumor has it that the cartwheel was invented in Düsseldorf, and the *Radschlager*, the legendary "somersaulting boys," grace every manhole cover, even topping a fountain on Burgplatz. In early June, the Kö *Let's Go* of its image just a little bit and holds a (highly competitive) cartwheeling tournament.

KAISERWERTH. North on the Rhein but still within Düsseldorf dwell the **ruins** of Emperor Friedrich's palace in the tiny town of Kaiserwerth. Built in 1184, the palace was destroyed in 1702 in the War of Spanish Succession, but the gloomy *Kaiserpfalz* frame remains. Take U-Bahn #79 to "Klemensplatz," then follow Kaiserwerther Markt to the Rhein, and walk left another 150m. In case you're curious, the seemingly out-of-place **tower** with the blinking lights visible from the Rhein at night is actually a clock called the **Rheinturm.** From bottom to top, the dots represent one second, 10 seconds, one minute, 10 minutes, one hour, and 10 hours.

EKO-HOUSE. Düsseldorf has the largest Japanese population of any European city. The EKO-House, across the Rhein from the Altstadt, is a beautiful garden and cultural center with frequent tea ceremonies and readings from Buddhist texts. *(Brüggener Weg 6. Take U-Bahn #70 or 74-77 to "Belsenplatz." Follow Quirinstr. to Comeniusplatz and turn left again on Niederkasseler Str. Tel. 57 40 71. Open Tu-Su 1-5pm. DM5, students DM3.)*

SCHLOSS BENRATH. The castle sits in the suburbs of Düsseldorf, a monument to the inadequacy complexes of the aristocracy. The architect used strategically placed mirrors and false exterior windows to make the squat, pink castle appear larger than it is, but the enormous, neurotically geometrical garden tempers the effect. *(S-Bahn #6 (direction: "Köln") to "Benrath." Castle open Tu-Su 10am-5pm. Tours every 30min. DM7, students and children DM3.50.)*

🏛 MUSEUMS

Düsseldorf's museums are numerous, large, and good—not only are the Top 40 of the art world well represented, but so is anybody who ever influenced them. Art clusters around Ehrenhof above the Altstadt and Grabbeplatz near the city center. The **ArtTicket** (DM20) includes entrance to all museums, and can be purchased at the tourist office or any museum.

ALTSTADT

KUNSTSAMMLUNG NORDRHEIN-WESTFALEN. The art museum is the black, reflecting, glass edifice west of the Hofgarten. Skylights lavish sunshine on Matisse, Picasso, Surrealists, and Expressionists. The collection of works by hometown boy Paul Klee is one of the most extensive in the world. *(Grabbepl. 5. Tel. 838*

10. U-Bahn #70, 75, 76, 78, or 79 to "Heinrich-Heine-Allee." Walk north 2 blocks, or bus #725 to "Grabbeplatz." Open Tu-Th and Sa-Su 10am-6pm, F 10am-8pm. Tours Su 11am and W 3:30pm. DM5, students DM3. Special exhibits DM10, students DM8.)

KUNSTHALLE. Across the square from the Kunstsammlung Nordrhein-Westfalen, it's not a museum, mind you, but a forum for modern exhibits of every shape and size. Open your mind and step inside. The stove-pipe on the museum is an art piece by Joseph Beuys intended to symbolize the link between art and the real world. Breathe deeply as you pass. *(Grabbeplatz. 4. Tel. 889 62 40. Admission depends on the exhibit; usually DM10, students and children DM7. Open Tu-Su 11am-6pm.)*

KUNSTMUSEUM DÜSSELDORF. A strong collection of Baroque and Romantic art in one wing balances an early 20th-century and contemporary collection in the other. On the ground floor, glassware, tapestries, dishes, and some astonishingly intricate locks memorialize 11 centuries of aristocratic decor. The **Kunstpalast** is an extension of the Kunstmuseum devoted to rotating contemporary exhibits. *(Ehrenhof 5. Tel. 899 62 40; fax 899 24 60. Open Tu-Su 11am-6pm. Tours Su 11am. DM5, students and children DM2.50.)*

GOETHEMUSEUM. The museum makes up for its lack of hometown advantage with a massive collection—30,000 souvenirs memorialize the poet and his friends. Everything in the mini-palace is furnished as Goethe would have wished it: to evoke his character. *(Jakobistr. 2. Tel. 899 62 62. In Schloß Jägerhof, at the east end of the garden. Streetcar #707 or bus #752 to "Schloß Jägerhof." Open Tu-F and Su 11am-5pm, Sa 1-5pm. Library open Tu-F 10am-noon and 2-4pm. DM4, students and children DM2.)*

ELSEWHERE IN DÜSSELDORF

FILMMUSEUM AND HETJENSMUSEUM. The film museum displays everything from shadow plays and hand-puppets (learn how to make Shakespeare's silhouette) to German-dubbed clips from the master directors. The connected Hetjens museum fills four floors with 8,000 years of pottery and ceramics. The **Black Box** theater, a cinema specializing in art-house flicks, is in the same complex. See **Entertainment,** p. 455. *(Schulstr. 4. Tel. 899 42 00. South of the Schloßturm on Rheinuferstr. Both open Tu and Th-Su 11am-5pm, W 11am-9pm. Admission to each DM6, students DM3.)*

STADTMUSEUM. The building clashes with its 18th-century neighbors, but it's exhibits aptly summarize the city's consumer history. *(Berger Allee 2. Tel. 899 61 70. By the Rheinkniebrücke. Open Tu and Th-Su 11am-5pm, W 11am-9pm. DM5, students DM2.50.)*

MAHN- UND GEDENKSTÄTTE. A small museum and document collection commemorates victims of the Third Reich, and displays artwork by children returning from concentration camps. *(Mühlenstr. 29. Tel. 899 62 06. Open Tu-F and Su 11am-5pm, Sa 1-5pm. Free.)*

NEANDERTHALMUSEUM. A museum where low-brows, thick-skulls, and knuckle-draggers can feel comfortable. The first remains of an entity identified as Neanderthal Man were found here; the museum introduces you to his 60,000-year-old relatives. *(Thekhauser Quall, in the suburb of Erkrath. Tel. (02104) 311 49. S-Bahn #8 to "Hochdahl," then bus #741 to "Neanderthal." Open Tu-Su 10am-6pm. DM2, students DM1.)*

🎵🎭 ENTERTAINMENT AND NIGHTLIFE

Folklore holds that Düsseldorf's 500 pubs make up *die längste Theke der Welt* ("the longest bar in the world"). Pubs in the Altstadt are standing-room-only by 6pm, and foot traffic is shoulder-to-shoulder by nightfall, when it is nearly impossible to see where one pub ends and the next begins. **Bolkerstr.** is jam-packed nightly with street performers of the musical and beer-olympic varieties. *Prinz* (DM5) is Düsseldorf's fashion cop and scene detective; it's often given out free at the youth hostel. *Facolte* (DM4) is the gay and lesbian nightlife magazine and is available at most newsstands. The free cultural guides *Coolibri* and *Biograph* are less complete but more than sufficient to hit you baby all night long. **Das Kommödchen** (tel. 32 94 43) is a tiny, extraordinarily popular theater behind the Kunsthalle at Grabbeplatz. (Box office open M-Sa 1-8pm, Su 3-8pm. Tickets DM38, students and children DM28.) Ballet and opera tickets are best bought (without service charge) at the **Opernhaus**, Heinrich-Heine-Allee 16a. (Tel. 890 82 11. Box office open M-F 11am-6:30pm, Sa 11am-1pm, and 1hr. before performance.) **Black Box,** Schulstr. 4 (tel. 899 24 90), off Rathausufer along the Rhein, serves the art-film aficionado with unadulterated foreign flicks. (DM8, students DM6.)

Stahlwerk, Ronsdorfer Str. 134 (tel. 73 03 86 81). U-Bahn #75 to "Ronsdorfer Str." This classic factory-turned-disco in one of Düsseldorf's grittier areas packs in 1,500(!) of the city's most divine. Open F-Sa and last Su of every month after 10pm. Cover DM10.

La Pocca, Grünstr. 8 (tel. 83 67 10). Just off the Kö, the club serves as a showcase for purchases made during the day. A mostly 20-something crowd dances the night away to house. Open F-Sa from 10pm, sometimes during the week. Cover DM8.

g@rden, Rathansufer 8 (tel. 86 61 60). In addition to **internet access** and a great view of the Rhein, the futuristic café and bar hosts DJs who spin everything from funk to R&B to techno. Café open after 11am, club after 9pm. Cover around DM15.

Engelchen, Kurze Str. 11 (tel. 32 73 56). Papered with posters and emanating Seattle grunge, the café offers Gen X types an atmosphere a lot less bombastic than the 300 or so Altstadt bars around the corner. Open M-F 9am-1am, Sa-Su 10am-3am.

Unique, Bolkerstr. 30 (tel. 323 09 90). Lives up to its name, at least in the context of Düsseldorf's Altstadt. Surrounded by an endless beerfest, the red-walled club draws a younger, trendier crowd. Open daily 10pm-late. Cover DM10.

Zum Uel, Ratinger Str. 16 (tel. 32 53 69). The crowd in front of Zum Uel renders the street impassable. Stop at the hugely popular pub for a glass of *Schlösser Alt,* (DM2.80 for 0.2L.). Open M-Tu, Th, and Su 10am-1am, W and F 10am-3am.

Café Rosa, Oberbilker Allee 310 (tel. 77 52 42). The socio-cultural mecca of Düsseldorf's gay community, this do-it-all *Kulturzentrum* offers self-defense classes and throws killer parties. Tu men only; F lesbians only. Open Tu-Sa 8pm-1am, later on weekends.

NEAR DÜSSELDORF: MÖNCHENGLADBACH

Mönchengladbach, known to all as MG (em-gay), has always stayed way ahead of the times. Their pre-Neanderthal ancestors set up one of the largest communities in the region over 300,000 years ago. In 974, Archbishop Gero founded a prominent Benedictine monastery and intellectual center, **Abteiberg,** a structure that still dominates the skyline. About 800 years later, the French kicked the monks out, and since then the deserted monastery has served as the **Rathaus.** Next door towers the 11th-century **Münster,** a church whose ecclesiastical treasures include a portable altar and a bust of the Saxon St. Vitus, the city's guardian. (Church open M-Sa 8am-6pm, Su noon-6pm. Museum open Tu-Sa 2-6pm, Su noon-6pm.) Around the corner, the mirrored **Städtisches Museum Abteiberg,** Abteistr. 27 (tel. 25 26 37), just beyond the Rathaus, houses a collection of 20th-century art including pieces by Andy Warhol, Roy Lichtenstein, and George Segal. (Open Tu-Su 10am-6pm; DM5, students and children DM2.50). Also at the top of the Abteiberg is the **Alter Markt,** an old cobblestone square now studded by small diners and craft shops. To reach the Alter Markt, turn left out of the train station and head up Hindenburgstr. past the mutant shopping district, or take bus #13 or 23 up the hill. Gaze down at the residential district, a dense blanket of pastel decorated houses with flowers spilling out of windows. Five **parks**—Geropark, Brundespark, Kaiserpark, Hardtor Wald, and Volksgarten—lie within MG proper, but most affecting is the **Bunter Garten** (Garden of Colors), in the center of town, accessible from Alter Markt by following Sandvadstr. for ten minutes. The park includes a botanical garden within its maze of forested paths.

Just outside of town stands the majestic **Schloß Rheydt** (tel. 66 92 89 00). From the station, take bus #6 to "Bonnenbroich" and then bus #16 to "Schloß Rheydt" (30min., but worth it). This pristine Renaissance palace is upstaged only by its own beautiful grounds, prize peacocks, and a tranquil, Monet-esque lily-padded moat. The museum inside houses rotating art and historical exhibits. (Open April-Sept. Tu-Su 11am-7pm, Oct.-March Tu-Sa 11am-4pm, Su 11am-6pm. DM5, kids DM2.50.)

Mönchengladbach is best seen as a day trip from Düsseldorf, about 30 minutes away by train. Nevertheless, the **tourist office,** Bismarckstr. 23-27 (tel. 220 01; fax 27 42 22), located in the *First Reisebüro* (travel agency) one block to the left of the train station, finds rooms (from DM45) for free. (Open M-F 9:30am-8:30pm, Sa 9:30am-1pm.) The **Jugendherberge Hardter Wald,** Brahmstr. 156 (tel. 56 09 00), lies at the boundary of a wheat field and a forest. From the station, take bus #13 or 23 to "Hardtmarkt" (20min.), walk straight and make a left at the *Jugendherberge* sign onto Brahmstr. (1.2km). The facilities are excellent but the hostel's bucolic location far from Mönchengladbach and really, really far from Düsseldorf rules out nasty nightlife action. (DM26, over 26 DM31. Breakfast included. Sheets DM6. Reception 8am-10pm; last check-in 6pm.) The **telephone code** is 02161.

RUHRGEBIET (RUHR REGION)

Germany's modern wealth and working class were forged from the coal and steel of the Ruhr Valley. After 1850, the Ruhr was the source of railroad expansion and the immense manufacturing demands of a newly unified (and bellicose) Germany, quickly becoming the foremost industrial region in Europe. Not everything ran smoothly in this era, however; the growing proletarianization and exploitation of the workers led to numerous strikes and strong socialist leanings. Nevertheless, the workers remained loyal to the government, and the Ruhr was torn apart not by Marxist revolution but by Allied bombers in WWII. The reconstruction program in the following years yielded numerous parks and gardens to brighten the region's smoggy visage; and due to a strong cultural initiative, travelers weary of the bleak landscape can get their aesthetic fix at many of the region's excellent museums and cultural centers. At the same time, the Ruhr's sprawling conglomeration of the streetcar, bus, and U-Bahn systems, linking many of the region's cities, offers the densest concentration of rail lines in the world, providing a snapshot of the industrial past.

NORDRHEIN-WESTFALEN

ESSEN

For a millennium, Essen was just another German cathedral town. By the eve of WWI, however, Essen had advanced to become the industrial capital of Germany, thanks to its seemingly limitless deposits of coal and iron. After its destruction in WWII, the city reformed its image as a soot-belching monstrosity by returning to an emphasis on its religious and cultural faces. As a result, the city is alive with concerts and museums, but huge department stores and office buildings dominate the city's atmosphere. At the same time, Essen's high-tech factories remain the industrial cornerstone of the Ruhr.

🗓️📻 PRACTICAL INFORMATION AND ACCOMMODATIONS. Trains run from Essen to Düsseldorf (½hr., 5 per hour, DM20) and Dortmund (20min., 4 per hour, DM20). Essen's **U-Bahn** and **streetcar** lines cost DM2.10 per ride. The spiffy new **tourist office,** Am Hauptbahnhof 2 (tel. 194 33; email touristikzentrale@essen.de, www.essen.de), across from the station, books **rooms.** (Open M-F 9am-5:30pm, Sa 10am-1pm.) The **Jugendherberge (HI),** Pastoratsberg 2 (tel. 49 11 63; fax 49 25 05), sits in the middle of a quiet forest in Werden, a suburb notable for its 8th-century **Abteikirche** and **Luciuskirche,** the oldest parishes north of the Alps. Take S-Bahn #6 to "Werden" (25min.) and bus #190 to "Jugendherberge." Rooms are standard but far from the city. (DM24, over 26 DM29. Breakfast included. Sheets DM6. Reception 7am-11:30pm. Curfew 11:30pm.) The basic, comfortable **Hotel Kessing,**

Hachestr. 30 (tel. 23 99 88; fax 23 02 89), is close to the train station. (Singles DM59, with bath DM85; doubles DM118, with bath DM138. Breakfast included. Prices go up when conferences are in town.) Camp at **Stadt-Camping Essen-Werden,** Im Löwental 67 (tel. 49 29 78), on the west bank of the Ruhr. Take the S-Bahn to "Essen-Werden" and continue south along the river. (DM7.50 per person, Tent DM15. Reception 7am-1pm and 3-9pm.) The **telephone code** is 0201.

📖 **FOOD.** The maze of stairs and escalators at **Porscheplatz,** near the Rathaus, crawls with vendors of cheap mall food. Take the U-Bahn to "Porscheplatz." The **Mensa** (tel. 18 31) is in the yellow-trimmed cafeteria building at the university. Take the U-Bahn to "Universität" and follow the signs to the building. (Open M-F 7:30am-4pm, Sa 7:30am-3:30pm.) Just across the street, **Beaulongerie,** on Segerothstr. (tel. 32 62 12), is a French store run by German Indians, offering hugely delicious baguettes (DM4.50) with a variety of fillings and sauces. (Open M-Th 11am-11pm, F-Sa 11am-1am.) The **Drospa** in the train station meets basic **grocery** needs. (Open M-Sa 6:30am-9:30pm, Su 9am-9:30pm.)

🏛 **SIGHTS.** The **Museumszentrum** at Goethestr. 41 houses three museums. Take streetcar #101, 107, or 127 or U-Bahn #11 to "Rüttenscheider Stern." Follow signs to the Museumzentrum and continue (north) on Rüttenscheiderstr., then turn left on Kuhrstr., and right onto Goethestr. The internationally-renowned **Museum Folkwang** (tel. 884 53 00) drops all the big names in modern art from Courbet to Pollack and hosts superstar special exhibits. The Folkwang's **Fotographische Sammlung,** takes on camera work from the early days. (Both open Tu-Th and Sa-Su 10am-6pm, F 10am-midnight. The photography collection is closed during summer holidays. Combined admission DM5, students and children DM3.) Infamous 19th-century arms and railroad mogul **Alfred Krupp** perfected steel-casting in industrial Essen. **Villa Hügel** (tel. 48 37), the Krupp family home (read: palace) for decades, was given to the city in the 1950s in order to brighten the company's image, which was tarnished by its Nazi affiliation. Even the gargantuan mahogany staircases and intricate carvings pale in comparison to the **Korea exhibit,** which fills the main building with all things bright and beautiful from the East. (Take S-Bahn #6 to "Essen-Hügel." Open M and W-Su 10am-7pm, Tu 10am-9pm. DM12, children and seniors DM8.50.)

Essen's **Münsterkirche,** close to the city center on Burgplatz, is an ancient, cloistered string of flowering courtyards and hexagonal crypts. The 1,000-year-old, doll-like *Goldene Madonna* stands beside the nave. (Open daily 7:30am-6:30pm.) Although Nazis gutted Essen's **Alte Synagoge** (tel. 84 52 18) in 1938, it stands today as the largest synagogue north of the Alps. Take the U-Bahn to "Porscheplatz" and follow the signs to the Schützenbahn; as you head south on the Schützenbahn, the synagogue is on your left. Inside, slides and pictures from the Third Reich era make up the Dokumentationsforum, a monument to the Jews of Essen. (Open Tu-Su 10am-6pm. Free.) The **Deutsches Plakatmuseum** sits on the third floor of the shopping mall at the intersection of Rathenaustr. and Am Glockenspiel. The poster museum features everything from the unusual (elephants in elephant-suits) to the downright bizarre (two pig heads eating a human heart), as well as a Gutenberg press. (Take U-Bahn #17 or 18 to "Bismarckplatz." Open Tu-Su noon-8pm. Free.) The **Ruhrlandmuseum,** Goethestr. 41 (tel. 884 51 28), exhibits the Ruhr in its industrial heyday. Experience the miner's life in the Weimar Republic without dirtying your hands. (Open Tu-W and F-Su 10am-6pm, Th 10am-9pm. DM5, students DM3.)

DORTMUND

With the exception of its American soul-twin, Milwaukee, Dortmund annually produces more beer than any other city in the world: 1,000L for each of its 600,000 citizens (you do the math). The best known of Dortmund's sudsy brood is the ubiquitous *Dortmunder Union* beer. As part of Germany's industrial backbone, Dortmund was a tempting target for Allied bombers, and 93% of the city center was leveled in WWII. Today, the city is still largely industrial. But there is more to this town than brewing and drunken bowling—Dortmund nurtures significant cultural offerings, and the post-war greening outside the city center has added a new zest to this classic trade city. Dortmund gleefully follows its soccer team, BVB09 (one of the best in Europe), with a passion: walk down any street, and when you hear the gnashing of teeth, the BVB has just given up a rare goal.

◪ ORIENTATION AND PRACTICAL INFORMATION. Dortmund is on the eastern edge of the tangle of cities in the Ruhr River area. The **S-Bahn** (#1 and 21) connects with Essen and Düsseldorf. **Trains** run to Köln (1½hr., 2 per hour, DM29) and Münster (1hr., every 20min., DM15). **ADFC,** Hausmannstr. 22 (tel. 13 66 85), rents **bikes** for DM10 per day. (Open M and W-Su 10am-6pm.) The **tourist office,** Königswall 18a (tel. 502 56 66, room booking 14 03 41; fax 16 35 93; email tourist-info@dortmund.de), across from the station, books **rooms** (DM55 and up) for a DM3 fee. (Open M-F 9am-6pm, Sa-Su 9am-1pm.) The **post office,** 44137 Dortmund (tel. 98 40), is located outside the north entrance of the train station. (Open M-F 8am-7pm, Sa 8am-1pm.) The **telephone code** is 0231.

▟▣ ACCOMMODATIONS AND FOOD. Hotel prices in Dortmund are high (singles from DM50), and there is no hostel or campground, but hostelers can easily jump the train to nearby Essen (p. 457); take S-Bahn #6 to Essen's hostel. Close to the station, **Hotel-Garni Carlton,** Lütge Brückstr. 5-7 (tel. 52 50 30; fax 52 50 20), has an elegant interior that is in sharp contrast to its decidedly un-elegant exterior in Dortmund's tiny red-light district. Head left on Königswall as you exit the station, taking a right on Gnadenort and then another right on Lütge Brückstr. (Singles DM55, with bath DM80; doubles DM120, with bath DM140. Breakfast included. Reception M-F 7am-4am, Sa 7am-2pm and 6:30pm-4am, Su 6:30pm-4am.) After satisfying your curiosity about beer mechanics at the Brauerei-Museum, head for some interactive experience at **Hövels Hausbrauerei,** Höherwall 8 (tel. 914 54 70), whose light brew, one among 11 on tap, is a town favorite. (Open daily 11am-1am. Kitchen open 11am-12:30am.) **Platzhirsch,** Brückstr. 62 (tel. 55 82 33) is cultivating record-breaking coats of wax on its candles. Sit at a funky triangle-shaped table and indulge in the massive drink list. (Open daily 7pm-1am.)

◪ SIGHTS. Museum am Ostwall, Ostwall 7 (tel. 502 32 47), was built in 1947 on the ruins of the Altstadt in order to make room for modern art, especially the kind suppressed by the Third Reich. Along with a Picasso and a Miró, much of the museum's collection is in line with the injunction "Everything is art!"—a phrase which actually graces one or two of the museum's paintings. (Open Tu-Su 10am-5pm. DM4, students and seniors DM1.) The Lennies and Squiggies of the world will be more comfortable in the **Brauerei-Museum,** Märkisch Str. 81 (tel. 541 32 89), located in the Kronen brewery, southeast of the city center. Take U-Bahn #41, 45, or 47 to "Markgrafenstr." and walk along Landgrafenstr. in the direction of the tower. It's four floors of German art in the form of kegs, steins, and 5,000 years of brewing history. (Open Tu-Su 10am-5pm. Free, but no samples.) The lonely, white-washed **Adlerturm,** at Kleppingstr. and Südwall, near the Rathaus, is the last remaining section of the old city walls. The tower has been bisected to show the layers of foundation. (Open Tu-Su 10am-5pm. DM2, students and seniors DM1). Dortmund's 12th-century **Marienkirche,** also in the city center, has an artistically brilliant altar and an enthroned figure of Christ. (Open Tu-F 10am-noon and 2-4pm, Sa 10am-5pm.) The **Dortmunder Tierpark** (tel. 502 85 81) houses more than 2,500 animals, including a special South American exhibit in the three-tiered Amazon house, where birds and rodents mingle with the visitors. Take U-Bahn #49 to "Hacheney." Pet a kiwi. (Open daily 9am-6:30pm. DM8, children DM4.)

DETMOLD

Worlds away from the industry of the Ruhrgebiet crouches Detmold, the premier city of the Teutoburger Wald. Until 1918 the royal seat of the Lippe-Detmold principality, Detmold has since been raking in the tourists.

◪ ORIENTATION AND PRACTICAL INFORMATION. Detmold's location makes it an ideal base for exploring the Teutoburger Wald. **Trains** run from Detmold to Osnabrück (1¼hr., 1 per hour, DM23), Hannover (2hr., 2 per hour, DM35), Köln (3½hr., 3 per hour, DM80). Though infrequently open, **Fahrradbüro Detmold,** Richtenhofstr. 14 (tel. 97 74 01; fax 30 02 01) rents out old **bikes.** (Open April-Oct. Tu and Th 5-7pm, Sa 10am–1pm. DM6 per day, DM30 per week. Passport or ID and DM50 deposit required.) The **tourist office,** Rathaus am Markt (tel. 97 73 28; fax 97 74 47; email info@detmold.de), is stocked with everything you need. From the station, head left on Bahnhofstr., turn right on Paulinenstr., then left on Bruchstr. into the pedestrian zone; walk another five minutes to the Rathaus. The tourist office is on the right side of the building. The city brochure is excellent, with a map detailed enough for hikes to the *Denkmal* and the surrounding area (DM1). The staff books **rooms** (from DM35) for free, and posts an accommodations list outside the building. (Open M-Th 9am-noon and 1-5pm, F 9am-4pm, Sa 10am-1pm; Nov.-March M-Th 9am-noon and 1-5pm, F 9am-noon.) **Tours** of the Altstadt take off from the main entrance of the Residenzschloß. (April-Oct. Sa at 10am, Su at 11am. DM4, students DM2.) The **telephone code** is 05231.

◪◪ ACCOMMODATIONS AND FOOD. In addition to the regular pack of wild school children, the **Jugendherberge Schanze (HI),** Schirrmannstr. 49 (tel. 247 39; fax 289 27), features its own mule. From *Bussteig* 3 at the train station, take bus #704 (direction: "Hiddesen") to "Auf den Klippen," and walk 10 minutes down the trail. By foot from the station, make a right on Paulinenstr., and a right on Freiligrathstr. (which becomes Bandelstr.), then a left on Bülowstr., followed by a right onto Schützenberg. (45min. DM22.60, over 26 DM27.60. Sheets DM6.50. Breakfast included. Lunch DM7.40. Dinner DM6.40. Reception until 10pm. Curfew 10pm, but guests are provided with keys.) Enjoy delicious crepes (DM3-6), baked potatoes (DM2-7), and salads (DM5) at **Knollchen,** Lange Str. 21 (tel. 283 99), where blue picket fences hang from the ceiling. (Open M-F 11am-7pm, Sa 10am-4pm.) **Kaiser's,** Bruchstr. 18-20, provides **groceries.** (Open M-F 8am-7pm, Sa 8am-2pm.)

◪ SIGHTS. Towering over the dense forest, the striking **Hermannsdenkmal** commemorates the Teutonic chief Hermann, proclaiming him liberator of the German people. Over-eager nationalists erected Hermann's monolithic likeness on an old encampment in 1875, and Kaiser Wilhelm I came to cut the ribbon. Complete with winged helmet, the statue wields a 7m sword with the disconcerting inscription, "German unity is my power, my power is Germany's might." The memorial also serves as a source of Germanic historical confusion: research continually relocates the battle to other hills. The only consensus reached is that the colossus does *not* mark the spot of the battle. (Open March-Oct. daily 9am-6:30pm; Nov.-Feb. 9:30am-4pm. DM2.50, children DM1.) The hike is beautiful but rather steep for the inexperienced (or lazy) hiker and like most of Detmold's attractions, it lies far from the city. Bus #792, which leaves from the train station, makes the ascent easier. (April-Oct. M-F 8:10, 9:10am, and 3:10pm; Sa 9:10am and 3:10pm; Su and holidays 10am and 1:10pm.) No less impressive and far more exhilarating is the **Adlerwarte** (tel. 471 71), featuring more than 80 birds of prey. Time your arrival with bus #701 from Detmold (direction: "Weidmüller") to "Adlerwarte" to catch a free flight exhibition. The falcons buzz the crowd, passing inches above startled faces and causing children and adults alike to shriek. (Open daily mid-March to Oct. 9:30am-5:30pm; Nov. to mid-March 10am-4pm. Displays mid-March to Oct. 11am, 3, and 4:30pm; Nov. to mid-March 11am and 2:30pm. DM7, children DM3.50.) Save money with the tourist office's combination ticket, **der Fliegende Hermann.** The ticket is valid at the Hermannsdenkmal, Adlerwarte, and the **Vogel- und Blumenpark.** (Bird and flower park. Tel. 474 39. Open April-Nov. daily 9am-6pm.) On weekends, the ticket also lets you ride the shuttle connecting the three sights for free. (DM11, children DM4.50.)

Detmold's **Westfälisches Freilichtmuseum,** (tel. 706 105) is less touristy, more original, and just plain cooler than most of Detmold's sights. Spread over 80 hectare,
this outdoor museum consists of more than 100 restored and rebuilt 17th- to 19th-
century German farm buildings as well as a village where blacksmiths still smith
and milk-churners still churn. A horse-drawn carriage takes you from the entrance
to the far end of the museum, where the central village is located (DM3, children
DM2). Take bus #701 (direction: "Weidmüller") to "Freilichtmuseum." (Open April-
Oct. Tu-Su 9am-6pm. DM7, children DM3.) In the Altstadt, cannons still arm the
courtyard of the **Fürstliches Residenzschloß** (tel. 700 20), a Renaissance castle in the
town's central park. (Tours daily April-Oct. on the hour 10am-5pm; Nov.-March no
5pm tour. DM6, children DM3.)

MÜNSTER

Perhaps even more than other tranquil, medium-sized German cities, Münster
maintains a level of repose and dignity that reflects its history as a place of peaceful reconciliation. As the capital of the Kingdom of Westphalia, Münster presided
over the 1648 peace that brought the Thirty Years War to an end, defining the borders of scores of German mini-states for centuries and casting the city as a place
for peaceful resolution. But the Münster of today offers much more than conscien-
tious objection and historic checkpoints: the 45,000 students of the Wilhelmsuniversität know how to put those 9th-century reveling monks to shame. Still, the
monks do their damnedest to keep the students in line, with the unenforced 1am
curfew providing a silent reminder of the ecclesiastic legacy.

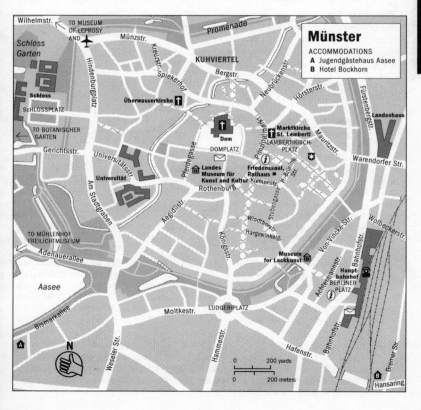

⑦ ORIENTATION AND PRACTICAL INFORMATION

Münster is located at the confluence of the lower channels of the Ems River, in the midst of the Münsterland plain. The magnificent promenade surrounds the Altstadt, which lies west of the train station.

Flights: Flughafen Münster-Osnabrück, located to the northeast of the city, has flights to major European cities. Bus #S50 shuttles between the train station and the airport. For **flight information,** call (02571) 940.

Trains: To Düsseldorf (1½hr., 3 per hour, DM35), Köln (2hr., 3 per hour, DM50), and Bremen (1¼hr., 1 per hour, DM54).

Car Rental: Hertz, Hammerstr. 186 (tel. 773 78). Open M-F 7:30am-6pm, Sa 7:30am-1pm, Su 9:30-11:30am.

Bike Rental: Münster's train station has an impressive bike rental service (tel. 484 01 70), with hundreds of bikes and amazingly long hours. DM11, DM7 for Deutsche Bahn customers. Open M-F 5:30am-11pm, Sa-Su 7am-11pm.

Mitfahrzentrale: AStA, Schloßplatz 1 (tel. 405 05). Open M-F 8:30am-4pm.

Tourist Office: Klemensstr. 10 (tel. 492 27 10; fax 492 77 43). Just off the Marktplatz. From the station, cross Bahnhofstr. and head left, taking a sharp right onto Windthorstr., and veer right onto Stubengasse; the office is on your left as Stubengasse crosses Klemenstr. and becomes H.-Bruning-Str. Staff books **rooms** (from DM50) for free and offers **tours** and theater tickets. Open M-F 9am-6pm, Sa 9am-1pm.

Laundromat: Wasch Center, Moltkestr. 5-7. Wash DM7. Dry DM1. Open M-F 6am-11pm.

Emergency: Police, tel. 110. **Fire** and **Ambulance,** tel. 112.

Post Office: Berliner Str. 37, 48143 Münster 1. Located directly to the left of the train station. Open M-F 8am-6pm, Sa 8am-5pm.

Internet Access: Universitäts Bibliothek, Krummer Timpen 3-5. From the entrance, turn right into the computer catalog room. Free. Open M-F 8am-9pm, Sa 9am-5pm.

PHONE CODE	0251

⌂ ACCOMMODATIONS AND CAMPING

Münster's accommodations are less than adequate. The shiny *Jugendgästehaus* is no steal, and hotels fill up quickly, so be sure to call several days ahead. In a pinch, there's a hostel in **Nottuln,** a 50-minute bus ride away (tel. (02502) 78 78; fax 96 19). Take bus #560 or 561 to "Rodeplatz," then follow the signs. (DM24, over 26 DM29. Breakfast included. Sheets DM6. Reception 8am-10pm.)

Jugendgästehaus Aasee, Bismarckallee 31 (tel. 53 24 70; fax 52 12 71). Bus #10 or 34 to "Hoppendamm." A huge brick hostel sitting on the river, newly renovated. Bike rental DM10 per day. Toilet and bath in each room. Quads DM39 per person, doubles DM49. Breakfast buffet and sheets included. Reception 7am-1am. Lockout 1am.

Haus vom Guten Hirten, Lindenweg 61 (tel. 378 70; fax 37 45 44). Bus #14 to "Mauritz Friedhof." Or take a long (40min.) walk—from the rear entrance of the train station, turn left on Bremer Str., right on Wolbecker Str., left on Hohenzollernring, right on Manfred-von-Richthofen-Str., and finally left on Lindenweg. Run by the Church, this hotel offers huge, comfy suites that debunk the myth that monks and nuns mustn't indulge. But you'll feel naughty anyway. Singles DM58, doubles DM98, triples DM138. Breakfast included. Reception 6am-9pm.

Hotel Bockhorn, Bremer Str. 24 (tel. 655 10), a 5min. walk from the station. From the rear exit of the train station, walk right on Bremer Str. 400m. Tidy, no-frills rooms are convenient to the Altstadt and to the train. The breakfast room is decorated with a piece of 17th-century furniture somehow borrowed from the Schloß. Singles DM60, doubles DM120. Breakfast included. 24hr. reception.

Hotel An'n Schlagbaum, Weseler Str. 269 (tel./fax 79 21 80). Bus #7, 15, or 16 to "Kappenberger Damm." 11 affordable rooms above a faded restaurant. Singles DM55, doubles DM90. Breakfast included.

Camping: Campingplatz Münster, Auf der Laer 7 (tel. 31 19 82). Bus #320 to "Wersewinkel." DM7 per person; DM4 per tent. Reception 8am-midnight.

🖸🗟 FOOD AND NIGHTLIFE

On Wednesdays and Saturdays, a **farmer's market** takes over the plaza in front of the Dom, offering fresh fruit, fresh meat, and not-so-"fresh" clothes. (Open daily 7am-2pm.) Fridays at 1pm brings the **biomarkt,** the politically correct, organically grown version of the regular market. The student district, **Kuhviertel** (literally, "cow quarter"—gives you an idea of how much Münster loves its students), is dotted with fairly inexpensive eateries and cafés. Bars line the streets across from the Schloß in the student quarter, and discos abound father southwest between the train station and the harbor. Free in university buildings, **Gig** provides monthly print coverage of nightlife and art openings in Münster and the surrounding area.

Cavete Akademische Bieranstalt, Kreuzstr. 38 (tel. 457 00). Founded by students for students in 1959, the first student pub in Westfalen serves homemade spinach noodles in thick sauces (DM12) in a dark, carnivalesque atmosphere. Open daily 7pm-1am. Kitchen closes M-Th and Su 11pm, F-Sa midnight.

Gaststätte Pinkus Müller, Kreuzstr. 7 (tel. 451 51). About as hip as an elbow and filled with tourists, but one of Germany's most acute joys is drinking beer in the house where it's brewed. Open M-Sa 11:30am-midnight.

🖎 **C.u.b.a.,** Achtermannstr. 10-12 (tel. 582 17). A hotspot for Münster's alternative crowd. This cultural center, disco, and *Kneipe* throws a massive Cuba-*fête* every 1st, 3rd, and 4th Saturday of the month (9pm-3am). Open daily 5pm-1am, but the cool kids don't come out to play until 11pm.

Diesel, Harsewinkelgasse 1-4 (tel. 57 96), in the Altstadt, at the intersection of Windhorststr., Stubengasse, and Loerstr. Fuel pumps, Keith Haring artwork, a red neon shrine filled with plastic flowers, and funky bossa nova music surround the pool table that takes up most of the café. Daily specials DM6-12. Open daily 10am-1am.

Zinc, Mauritzstr. 30, hums with odd neon lighting and clientele. Minimalist. Open 7pm-3am daily.

Le Différent, Hörsterstr. 10 (tel. 51 12 39), is the center of Münster's gay nightlife. Techno and charts on 2 dance floors. Open Tu and F-Sa 10pm-5am.

👁 SIGHTS

PROMENADE. When Goethe's carriage turned onto the huge tree-lined Promenade encircling the Münster Altstadt, he would slow it and smell the flowers. The Promenade is idyllic all the way around with couples licking ice cream and strolling in droves. In the west, the Promenade meets the Schloßgarten, where 19th-century trees are still growing, moss-covered and majestic. *(Open 6am-10pm.)* The **botanical gardens,** on the campus of the **Wilhelmsuniversität,** are especially inspiring. *(Open March-Oct. daily 8am-7pm; Nov.-Feb. 8am-4pm.)*

DOM. The heartbeat of Münster's religious life echoes through the huge **St. Paulus-Dom** on Domplatz in the center of the Altstadt. Though bombed in WWII, this cathedral has been beautifully restored. The Bishop's peaceful inner courtyard is open to the public. A stone from the similarly bombed Cathedral of Coventry stands in the entrance-way, carrying a wish for mutual forgiveness between Britain and Germany. From his pulpit in the cathedral, Bishop Clemens von Galen delivered a courageous sermon against the Nazi program of euthanasia for so-called "incurables." After wide distribution of the sermon, pressure from the church prompted a rare partial retreat by Hitler. Also inside the church, a statue of

St. Christopher points its massive toes to the 16th-century **astronomical clock,** which recreates the movements of the planets and plays a merry *Glockenspiel* tune. *(M-Sa noon, Su 12:30pm. Church open Tu-Sa 10am-noon and 2-6pm, Su 2-6pm. DM2.)* The remnants of past papal fashions are on display in the basement where an exhibit of splendid robes could make Armani jealous. *(Dom open M-Sa 6am-6pm, Su 6:30am-7:30pm. Courtyard open Tu-Sa 10am-noon and 2-6pm, Su 2-6pm.)*

MARKTKIRCHE ST LAMBERTI. Münster's piety takes a turn towards the macabre at the Marktkirche St. Lamberti, where three cages hang above the clock face. The cages were used to display the dead bodies of rebel anabaptists in the 16th century and still hang as a "reminder." Also suspended here is Germany's only free-hanging organ. *(Off the Prinzipalmarkt. Free concerts are given the first Saturday of every month at noon.)*

FRIEDENSSAAL. Next door to the church, the Friedenssaal (Hall of Peace), which kept one unknown woodcarver very busy for a very long time, commemorates the end of the Thirty Years War. Inside, a centuries-old human hand is on display. Nobody knows who it's from or what it's for, so don't ask. *(Open M-F 9am-5pm, Sa 9am-4pm, Su 10am-1pm. DM1.50, children and students DM0.80.)*

🏛 MUSEUMS

Münster treasures its historical and cultural artifacts in a well-maintained **Landesmuseum,** but its real gems are the small collections that celebrate the random. Ask the tourist office for information about all of the city's offerings, including its **railway museum, carnival museum,** and **museum of organs** (unrelated to the Leprosy Museum), all located in the suburbs.

MUSEUM OF LEPROSY. A little far away, but you should definitely drop by. The exhibits, including playful little leper-puppets, are strictly hands-off. *(Kinderhauser Str. 15. Tel. 285 10. To the northwest of the Altstadt. Open Su 3-5pm. Free. Call for an appointment on other days.)*

LANDESMUSEUM FÜR KUNST UND KULTUR. Contains modern sculptures and ancient paintings, arranged on 3 floors around a central atrium. *(Domplatz 10. Tel. 59 07 01. Open Tu-Su 10am-6pm. DM5, students and children DM2, family pass DM10. F free.)*

MÜHLENHOF-FREILICHTMUSEUM. The museum is a reconstructed 18th-century farm town. Have a picnic lunch on a millstone from 1868, pick up a loaf of indestructible *Schwarzbrot* (DM2) or some authentic wooden clogs (DM20). *(Sentruper Str. 225. Tel. 820 74. Open April-Oct. daily 10am-6pm, Nov.-March Tu-Sa 1-4:30pm and Su 11am-4:30pm. DM5, students and seniors DM3, children DM2.)*

MUSEUM FÜR LACKKUNST. The world's only exhibition of all things lacquered. Highlights from shiny empires of the past fill perfectly polished cases, while videos tell you how to make your living room the shiniest on the block. Visiting modern exhibits glisten in the basement. *(Windthorststr. 26, just off the Promenade. Tel. 41 85 10. Open Tu noon-8pm, W-Su noon-6pm. DM3, students DM1.50. Free on Tu.)*

Global
connection
with the AT&T
Network

AT&T
direct
service

Exploring the corners of the earth? We're with you. With the world's most powerful network, **AT&T Direct®** Service gives you fast, clear connections from more countries than anyone,* and the option of an English-speaking operator. All it takes is your AT&T Calling Card. And the planet is yours.

For a list of AT&T Access Numbers, take the attached wallet guide.

*Comparison to major U.S.-based carriers.

AT&T Direct® Service

AT&T Access Numbers

Austria ●	0800-200-288	Egypt ●(Cairo)	510-0200
Albania ●	00-800-0010	(Outside Cairo)	02-510-0200
Armenia ● ▲	8◆10111	Estonia	800-800-1001
Bahrain	800-000	Finland ●	9800-100-10
Belgium ●	0-800-100-10	France	0-800-99-0011
Bulgaria ▲	00-800-0010	Germany	0800-2255-288
Croatia	0800-220111	Greece ●	00-800-1311
Czech Rep. ▲	00-42-000-101	Hungary ●	00-800-01111
Cyprus ●	080-90010	Ireland ✓	1-800-550-000
Denmark	8001-0010	Israel	1-800-94-94-949

Italy ●	172-1011	Russia ● ▲	
Luxembourg †	0-800-0111	(Moscow) ▶	755-5042
Macedonia, F.Y.R. of ○		(St. Petersburg) ▶	325-5042
	99-800-4288	Saudi Arabia ◇	1-800-10
Malta	0800-890-110	South Africa	0-800-99-0123
Monaco ●	800-90-288	Spain	900-99-00-11
Morocco	002-11-0011	Sweden	020-799-111
Netherlands ●	0800-022-9111	Switzerland ●	0-800-89-0011
Norway	800-190-11	Turkey ●	00-800-12277
Poland ● ▲	00-800-111-1111	U.K. ▲ ✧	0800-89-0011
Portugal ▲	0800-800-128	U.K. ▲ ✧	0500-89-0011
Romania ●	01-800-4288	U.A. Emirates ●	800-121

FOR EASY CALLING WORLDWIDE

1. Just dial the AT&T Access Number for the country you are calling from.
2. Dial the phone number you're calling. *3.* Dial your card number.

For access numbers not listed ask any operator for **AT&T Direct®** Service. In the U.S. call 1-800-331-1140 for a wallet guide listing all worldwide AT&T Access Numbers.
Visit our Web site at: www.att.com/traveler
Bold-faced countries permit country-to-country calling outside the U.S.
- ●   Public phones require coin or card deposit.
- ▲   May not be available from every phone/payphone.
- ▶   Additional charges apply outside the city.
- ◇   Calling available to most countries.
- ✦   Await second dial tone.
- ✓   Use U.K. access number in N. Ireland.
- ✧   If call does not complete. use 0800-013-0011.
- †   Collect calling from public phones.
- ○   Public phones require local coin payment through the call duration.

When placing an international call *from* the U.S., dial 1 800 CALL ATT.

© 1999 AT&T

It's a **big world.**

And we've got the **network** to cover it.

Use **AT&T Direct®** Service
when you're out exploring the world.

NIEDERSACHSEN
(LOWER SAXONY) AND BREMEN

Niedersachsen extends from the Ems River to the Harz Mountains and from the North Sea to the hills of central Germany. Within its relatively small cities, Germans strive for economic success and contact with contemporary international culture—everything has a web address, and cultural and arts events are over-advertised in public transportation, phone booths, and the door of the scummiest restroom. Most towns as well as the spectacular East Frisian islands resist this trend, holding to traditional professions and ways of life. Topographically, Niedersachsen has two distinct flavors: old hills in the east; and flatlands in the west. The mainland is used almost exclusively for agricultural purposes; a train ride through the region often becomes a blur of green corn, barley, windmills, and bovine rumps. Since the Middle Ages, the region has been the seat of intense individualism. Niedersachsen still treasures its autonomy, harkening back to the Hanseatic traders who made the coast's fortune. A pocket of the region belongs to Bremen and Bremerhaven, two seafaring cities united in a unique case of state federalism to form Germany's smallest *Land*.

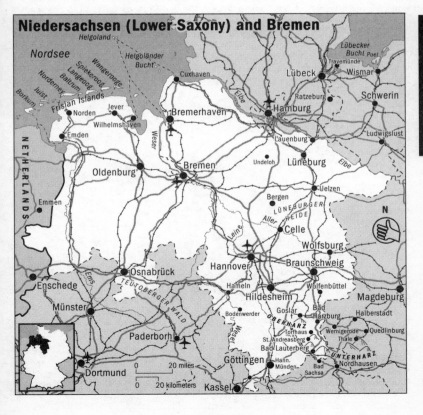

Niedersachsen (Lower Saxony) and Bremen

HANNOVER (HANOVER)

Despite its relatively small size, Hannover puts on a show of culture and cosmopolitan charm to rival cities twice as large. As the most important railway center in northwestern Germany, the city's myriad attractions lure travelers out of the Berlin-Hamburg-Köln triangle. But Hannover has seen darker times. Because of an unusual marriage that bound the Hanoverian royalty to the United Kingdom, the city found itself repeatedly attacked by foreign powers striking at the British throne. When the city later came under Prussian control, it benefitted from that empire's prosperity, but WWII put a stop to the good run, as 60% of the city was

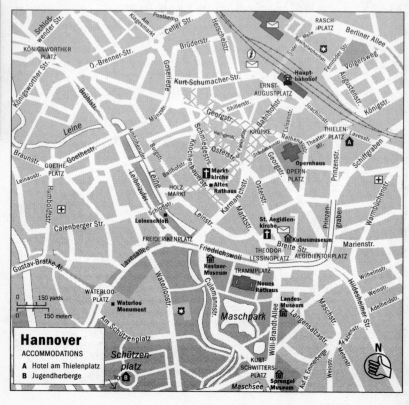

flattened. Yet resilient Hannover, accustomed to severe poundings, emerged like a happy Phoenix, leaping joyfully from the ashes. Today, with great economic vigor, a wealth of museums, a supreme opera hall, and a tradition of outdoor festivals, Hannover reigns as Niedersachsen's cultural and political capital.

⊏ GETTING THERE AND GETTING AROUND

Available at youth hostels and **ÜSTRA** offices, the **Hannover Card** provides public transportation within the city and to the airport, as well as admission or discounts at several museums. (DM14 for 1 day, DM23 for 3 days; group ticket for up to 5 people DM30 for one day, DM50 for 3 days.) Cards must be purchased by 7pm on the day before you plan to use them.

Flights: Hannover's airport is 20-30min. from the Altstadt. *Schnellbuslinie* (express bus) #60 runs from the Hauptbahnhof to the airport (M-F 5am-7pm, every 20min.; 7-10:30pm, every 30 min.; Sa-Su 5:30am-10:30pm, every 30min.; DM9). Flights depart to most German and many European cities. For flight information, call 977 12 23 or 977 12 24.

Trains: Hannover is well connected to cities in Northern Europe, especially within Germany. Trains leave at least one every hour for Hamburg (1½hr., DM50-67), Berlin (2½hr., DM78-101), Köln (3hr., DM104), Frankfurt (3½hr., DM140), Munich (4½hr., DM215), and Amsterdam (4½-5hr.).

Public Transportation: ÜSTRA, Hannover's mass-transit system, is extremely thorough and fast. From the station, walk to the lime-green stand in front of King August or at the "Raschpl." bus stop behind the station, and pick up the free map of the U-Bahn and bus lines (open M-F 8:30am-3:30pm, Sa 9am-1:30pm). Tickets can be bought at machines or from drivers. Hannover has 3 zones, so prices vary. *Kurzstrecke*, 3 stops, DM2; single ride DM3-5, children 6-11 DM1.50; day ticket DM6-10; group ticket for up to 5 people DM12-18. The Mitte and Altstadt are both in Zone 1; check list for other streets. *Remember to punch your ticket at the blue machines, or risk a DM60 fine!* A **Schüler-Wochenkarte** opens up the magical world of public transportation to students for 1 week; you'll need a student ID and a passport-sized photo to hand over (DM17.50). For more info and maps, call the **ÜSTRA customer service office** (tel. 16 68 22 38) in the Kröpcke station. Open M-W and F 8am-6pm, Th 8am-7pm, Sa 9am-2pm. The **Hannover Card** provides more comprehensive savings (see above).

Bike Rental: Radgeber Linden, Kötnerholzweg 43 (tel. 210 97 60). U-Bahn #10 to "Leinaustr." DM10 per day. Open M-Tu, Th-F 10am-1pm and 3-6pm, W and Sa 10am-1pm.

Taxi: Taxi Ruf, tel. 38 11.

EXPO 2000 As the sight of **EXPO 2000,** the first world exposition held in Germany (June 1-Oct. 31, 2000), Hannover will be one of the hottest tourist destinations in Europe this year. Hundreds of countries from the around the world have constructed pavilions on the 160-hectar site, highlighting the cultural, technological, and economic achievements of the past decade. The opening ceremonies (June 1) promise to be a "major multimedia event," with artists from around the world joining together to herald the Apocalypse...er, the new millennium. The literally thousands of events are too numerous to print—inquire at the tourist office when you arrive, or check out EXPO 2000's English website (www.expo2000.de/englisch). To get to the exposition site from the Hauptbahnhof, take the special "D" train or U-Bahn #11, 14, or 18 to "Expo-Ost." Or take U-Bahn #8 to "Messegelände." Be aware, however, that you won't be the only one taking a peek at the future: the exposition's planners are expecting upwards of 40 million visitors—that's about 260,000 a day! To avoid being stranded upon arrival, **reserve a room well in advance.**

☀ ORIENTATION

The old Saxon *"Hon overe"* means "high bank," referring to the city's position on the river **Leine**. In the heart of Hannover, the **Mitte,** lies the Hauptbahnhof, where a statue of Ernst August, first king of Hannover, beams from the saddle of his horse, surveying the city he founded. Bahnhofstraße extends from the horse's hooves, leading to the landmark **Kröpcke Café**. Below the statue's feet sprawls the underground **Passerelle,** a bizarre conglomeration of cheap diners and souvenir shops. Behind the station is **Raschplatz,** home to a disco and club scene. A pedestrian zone connects most of the center, including the shopping districts along **Georgstraße** and the Altstadt. The most interesting area for budget travelers is the student quarter surrounding the university.

ℹ PRACTICAL INFORMATION

Tourist Office: Hannover Information, Ernst-August-Pl. 2 (tel. 30 14 20). Outside the main entrance of the train station, facing the large rear of the king's splendid steed, turn right. In the same building as the post office. The superb staff finds **rooms** for any budget for a steep DM10 fee (**reservation line** tel. 811 35 00; fax 811 35 41), provides maps and information on cultural events, sells tickets to concerts and exhibits (tel. 30 14 30), and runs a full travel agency. Free hotel list available. Open M-F 9am-7pm, Sa 9:30am-3pm.

Tours: The **tourist office** offers 24 theme tours—"Animal Magic" or "Artistic Hannover," for example. Tel. 30 14 12. DM10-20, students DM7.50-15. To fully experience Hannover, follow the **Red Thread,** a 4km walking tour guided by a painted red line connecting all the major, and minor, sites. The accompanying Red Thread Guide (DM3), available from the tourist office, details the tour in English.

Student Travel Office: RDS, Fortunastr. 28 (tel. 44 60 37), off Limmerstr. The basics for the budget traveler. Flights and train packages. Open M-F 9am-6pm.

Consulate: U.K. Berliner Allee 5 (tel. 388 38 08). Behind the train station, across Raschpl., inside the triangular DG-Bank building. Open 8:30am-12:30pm and 1-2pm.

Currency Exchange: ReiseBank, just outside the train station, is the most convenient with the longest hours and decent commissions. Open M-F 7:30am-7pm, Sa 7:30am-5pm, Su 9am-12:45pm and 1:30-4:30pm.

American Express: Georgstr. 54, (tel. 36 34 28; 24hr. refund assistance, 85 31 00), across from the opera house. Travel agency and full cardmember services. Mail held for a maximum of 4 weeks for cardmembers, traveler's check clients, and travel agency customers. Open M-F 9am-6pm, Sa 10am-1pm.

Bookstores: Schmorl und von Seefeld, Bahnhofstr. 14 (tel. 367 50; fax 32 56 25), has English-language novels downstairs. Open M-F 9:30am-8pm, Sa 9:30am-4pm.

Laundromat: Wasch Center, at the corner of Hildesheimer Str. and Siemensstr. Take U-Bahn #1 (direction: "Sarstedt"), 2 (direction: "Rethen"), or 8 (direction: "Laatzen") to "Altenbekener Damm." Wash DM6, dry DM1 per 15min. Open daily 6am-11pm.

Emergency: Police, tel. 110 or 10 90. **Fire,** tel. 112. **Ambulance,** tel. 192 22.

Medical Assistance: EMS, tel. 31 40 44. **Medical Information,** tel. 31 40 44.

Gay and Lesbian Resources: tel. 194 11.

Women's Resources: Rape Crisis Line, tel. 33 21 12. **Shelter,** tel. 66 44 77.

Pharmacy: Georg-Apotheke, Georgstr. 19 (tel. 16 79 70; fax 131 99 94), near the train station. English spoken. Open M-F 8am-8pm, Sa 8am-4pm. Emergency information posted when closed, or call the **Emergency Pharmacy Service** (tel. 011 41).

Post Office: 30159 Hannover, in the same building as the tourist office. Open M-F 9am-8pm, Sa 9am-4pm, Su 10am-noon. Mail held above on first floor.

Internet Access: In Daily Planet (see **Nightlife,** p. 472).

PHONE CODE	0511

NIEDERSACHSEN

ACCOMMODATIONS

Finding budget accommodations in Hannover is difficult but not impossible. The youth hostel and two *Naturfreundehäuser* (similar to hostels, but not part of HI) provide affordable respites, as do private accommodations through the tourist office. Call the **reservation hotline** (tel. 811 35 00; fax 811 35 41). Should all else fail, traveling to the hostels in nearby Braunschweig or Celle may be cheaper than bedding down in one of Hannover's royally priced hotels.

> **!** **Safety Warning:** Hannover's hostel and *Naturfreundehäuser* are situated in parks and woods on the outskirts of town. Walkways in these areas are deserted and poorly lit at night; anyone planning to stay out past curfew should use caution.

Jugendherberge Hannover (HI), Ferdinand-Wilhelm-Fricke-Weg 1 (tel. 131 76 74; fax 185 55). U-Bahn #3 or 7 (direction: "Wehbergen") to "Fischerhof/Fachhochschule." From the station, cross the tracks and walk on the path through the school's parking lot; follow the path as it curves, and cross the street. Go over the enormous red footbridge and turn right. The hostel is 50m down on the right, within walking distance of the Maschsee and Schützenfestplatz. The 6- to 12-bed rooms are a bit tight. Major renovations and additions promise greater comfort and 9 new rooms. DM23, over 26 DM28. Sheets DM5.70. Reception 7:30-9am and 2-11:30pm. Curfew 11:30pm.

Naturfreundehaus Stadtheim, Hermann-Bahlsen-Allee 8 (tel. 69 14 93; fax 69 06 52). U-Bahn #3 (direction: "Lahe") or 7 (direction: "Fasanenkrug") to "Spannhagengarten." Walk 15m back to the intersection and follow Hermann-Bahlsen-Allee to the left for about 5min.; follow the sign to your right down the paved road 200m to the hostel. Tiny rooms, pretty blue bed linen, and a superior breakfast. DM43.80 per night. Breakfast included. Reception 8am-noon and 3-10pm. No curfew.

Naturfreundehaus Misburg, Am Fahrhorstfelde 50 (tel. 58 05 37; fax 958 58 36). Take U-Bahn #3 (direction: "Lahe") to the end. Then hop aboard bus #124 to "Misburg Garten"; once there, switch to bus #631 to "Waldfriedhof." Stroll up Am Fahrhorstfelde to the very end, go 10m straight ahead on the trail, and follow the sign. At least an hour's travel from the Hauptbahnhof. On a beautiful lake brimming with ducks. 4- to 6-bed rooms decked out in homey brown. DM30. Breakfast DM8.50. Sheets DM7.50 Reception Tu-Su 2-8pm. No curfew. The 30 beds fill quickly—reservations are necessary.

Hotel am Thielenplatz, Thielenpl. 2 (tel. 32 76 91 93; fax 32 51 88). Luxurious furnishings in a miniature lobby filled with all types—watch yourself, kid—and 150 beds in well-maintained rooms, all with TV. Rooms on the top floor (number 279 and higher) have panoramic views of the city. Singles with shower DM78-190; doubles with shower DM140-300, cheaper on weekdays. Breakfast buffet included. Check-out 11:30am.

 FOOD

Kröpcke, the once-renowned food court-café at the center of the pedestrian zone, now owned by Mövenpick, a restaurant chain, can hook you up with small snacks (from DM2.50) or nice sit-down meals (from DM13.50). The **Mövenpick Café** has reasonably-priced lunch specials and an all-you-can-eat salad bar (weekdays, 11:30am-11pm), sandwiches (DM3.20-6.50), and delicious ice cream treats (DM3-10.80). The **Lister Meile** area behind and inside the train station also offers cafés with pleasant seating options but not much going on in the way of interesting food (pizza, or, um, pizza), and more fast-food stands than you can count. **Spar supermarkets** sit by the Lister Meile and Kröpcke U-Bahn stops. (Open M-F 8am-7pm, Sa 8am-2pm.) An **Edeka**, at the corner of Pfarrlandstr. and Limmerstr. (U-Bahn #10 to "Leinaustr."), gets in on the **grocery** action. (Open M-F 8am-8pm, Sa 8am-4pm.) For a more international flavor, ride on down to the **Markthalle,** where a variety of snacks, meals, and booze awaits. (Open M-F 7am-6pm, Sa 7am-1pm.)

NIEDERSACHSEN

Mensa, Callinstr. 23 (tel. 768 80 35). U-Bahn #4 or 5 to "Schneiderberg." Take a right up Schneiderbergstr., just past the small bridge in the green-trimmed building. DM3 gets you the card on which you can deposit however much you want to spend. Meals DM2.20-3.70, DM6-8.50 for guests. If you miss the tight lunch hours, turn right off Schneiderbergstr. onto Callinstr., where several inexpensive cafés wait, most with outdoor seating. Open M-F 11:40am-2:30pm.

■ **Uwe's Hannenfaß Hannover,** Knochenhauerstr. 36 (tel. 326 16). Located in the center of the Altstadt, in the timber-framed house where the master brewer of Hannover once lived. The steaming *Niedersachsenschmaus* (DM7.50), a potato casserole, steadies the stomach while a *Bowle* of the house-brewed *Hannen Alt* lightens the head (DM5.40). Foot-long sandwiches DM9.50, salad bar DM5.50, prepared salads DM8.90. Daily specials served noon-3:30pm. Open M-Sa noon-2am, Su 3pm-2am.

■ **Jalda,** Limmerstr. 97 (tel. 21 23 26), serves a delightful combination of Italian, Greek, and Arabic dishes. Lunch specials M-F noon-4pm (DM10-11). Pizzas DM6-13, veggie fare DM5-11, meaty chow DM13-18. Take out or eat in with candlelight and funk in the background (funk music, that is). Diverse crowd—students at one table, grandma and grandpa in the corner booth. Open M-Th and Su noon-midnight, F-Sa noon-1am.

Peach Pit, Lister Meile 5 (tel. 34 34 32). A late night/early morning haven for the drunk, tired, and hungry. Although you won't run into Brenda or Brandon, you will likely see happy inebriates (Hi, Dylan!) looking for a sandwich (DM2.80-7), milkshake (DM3.50), or more beer. Open W 8pm-2am, Th 6am-2am, and F 6am until Su at 2pm—that's 56 continuous hours of 90210 antics!

⊙ SIGHTS

HERRENHAUSEN. In 1714, George I, the son of Electoral Princess Sophie, ascended the throne of the United Kingdom. His descendents continued as the rulers of Hannover and the United Kingdom until 1837, when the Hanoverians refused to accept an English queen—Sophie's great-great-great-great-granddaughter, Victoria. The city owes much to Princess Sophie, who furnished the three paradisiacal **Herrenhausen gardens.** The centerpiece is the Baroque **Großer Garten.** Its **Herrenhausen palace,** built in the 18th century and bombed to ruins in 1943, opens onto a garden roofed by topiary trees and populated by copies of Renaissance sculptures of mythical heroes and heroines. During the "illuminations," geyser-like fountains shoot from the ground to glow in the warm backlighting—gushing in their midst is Europe's highest garden fountain, the **Große Fontäne.** Originally 32m high, it has been gradually built up to 80m. Not as large as the **Großer Garten,** the smaller **Georgengarten** and **Berggarten** offer greenhouses bursting with orchids and other exciting vegetation. The fireworks contests held in summer provide dazzling displays. *(Take U-Bahn #4 (direction: "Garbsen") or 5 (direction: Stöcken") to "Herrenhäuser Gärten." Georgengarten open 24hr. Free. Großer Garten and Berggarten open Apr.-Oct. M-Tu 8am-8pm, W-Su 8am-10pm; daily Nov.-Mar. 8am-dusk. DM3. Light show W 5-7:30pm. DM5. Fountains M-F 11am-noon and 3-5pm, Sa-Su 11am-noon and 2-5pm. DM3.)*

ALTSTADT. Many "old buildings," a.k.a. sights, stand in Hannover's otherwisemodern **Altstadt,** a 15-minute walk from the train station. Walk down Bahnhofstr. and continue along as it becomes Karmarschstr.; take a right on Knochenhauer Str.—an old 14th-century cathedral, the **Marktkirche,** will be on your left. *(Hans-Lilje-Pl. Open daily 10am-4pm; check for concerts.)* Used for official purposes until 1913, Hannover's former **Rathaus** has become, in a final burst of glory…a shopping area and café. Best to gawk at the lovely exterior; inside it's expensive and dull.

LEIBNIZHAUS. A beautifully restored Baroque mansion, the house was home to brilliant mathematician, philosopher, man of letters, and royal advisor Gottfried Wilhelm Leibniz until his death in 1716. Tread carefully—this site cost DM22 million to restore. *(Holzmarkt 5. Tel. 62 44 50. Open Su 10am-1pm and 1:30-6pm.)*

TWIPSY KOMMT! As the site of the 2000 world exposition, Hannover has been preparing for its summer of glory by sending a large, multi-colored felt character named "Twipsy" out into the world to prophesy the fun to come. When this moon-headed puppet (modeled after a bizarre post-modernist painting) returns to Germany, he'll bring with him lots of robots, technology companies looking to make a buck, mystics, and superstars (like Bono, in full *POP* form); it promises to be the party of the millennium in little old Hannover.

ST. ÄGIDIENKIRCHE. A jog down Leinstr. brings you past the magnificent **Leineschloß**, seat of the Diet of Niedersachsen, to the ivy-covered shell of the **Ägidienkirche.** The massive damage suffered by the church during WWII was intentionally left untouched and memorial plaques were put up as reminders of the folly of war.

NEUES RATHAUS. Against the ruined remains of Hannover's medieval fortifications, the **Friedrichswall**, stands the more modern, spectacular Neues Rathaus. Hanoverians painstakingly recreated this palatial turn-of-the-century complex after WWII. Step inside to see models of the city in 1689, 1939, 1945, and today. Take the slanted elevator up the tower to behold the real thing. From up high, you can scout out Hannover's many parks, including the **Maschsee,** a 2km long lake just south of the Rathaus that's covered with sailboats and rowboats during the summer and ice skaters in winter. *(Rathaus Open April-Oct. M-F 9:30am-5:30pm, Sa-Su 10am-5pm. Elevator DM3, students DM2.)*

WATERLOO MONUMENT. Hannover's links with Britain are symbolized by a high column commemorating the Niedersachsen citizens who fought with the Brits, Russians, Austrians, and Prussians against Napoleon. *(From the Neues Rathaus, cross the Leine River bridge or walk through the tunnel near the subway.)*

🏛 MUSEUMS

🖼SPRENGEL MUSEUM. A 20th-century art lover's dream: James Turrell, Henry Moore, Dalí, Picasso, Magritte, and Horst Antes. Check out the light experiments by Turrell on the ground floor—the results will enlighten you. Good bistro. *(Kurt-Schwitters-Pl. Tel. 16 84 38 75. At the corner of the Maschsee and Maschpark, near the Neues Rathaus. Open Tu 10am-8pm, W-Su 10am-6pm. Permanent collection DM8.50; excellent special exhibits DM4.50.)*

🖼KESTNER-MUSEUM. Decorative arts of Medieval and Renaissance Europe, ancient Egypt, Greece, and Rome arranged creatively on three floors. Eat at the cafeteria on the second floor surrounded by 18th-century porcelain and 20th-century furniture. *(Trammpl. 3. Tel. 16 84 21 20. Next to the Neues Rathaus. Open Tu and Th-Su 11am-6pm, W 11am-8pm. DM5, students DM3; free on F.)*

WILHELM-BUSCH-MUSEUM. This is a cartoon museum—see wit and sarcasm channeled onto paper in vivid colors. Closed for architectural improvements until June 16, 2000. Grand opening? A show of cartoons from America's own *New Yorker*. *(Georgengarten 1. Tel. 71 40 76. U-Bahn #4, direction: "Gorbsen," or 5, direction: "Stöcken," to "Schneiderberg.")*

KUBUSMUSEUM. Hanoverian artists' co-op: a single room on the second floor shows the best (and weirdest) of the best. *(Theodor-Lessing-Pl. 2, near the Ägidienkirche. Tel. 16 84 57 90. Open Tu-F 11am-6pm, Sa-Su 11am-4pm. Free.)*

LANDESMUSEUM. Cultural museum with an outdoor bistro that hosts concerts. Mostly lame ground floor, with an aquarium, non-European "cultural" exhibit (read: jumble of African masks and Inuit huts), and Neanderthal skulls. A few worthwhile paintings on the top floor, including Rubens and the unusual 17th-century "Picture of a Moor" by Gerrit Dou. *(Willy-Brandt-Allee 5. Tel. 980 75. DM3, students free. Open Tu-Sa 10am-5pm, Th 10am-7pm.)*

HISTORISCHES MUSEUM AM HOHEN UFER. Sits in a 1960s "replica" of a 10th-century fortress. A very thorough exposition of Hannover's history and its cultural links with Britain. Also houses a huge collection of dioramas depicting scenes from battlefields. *(On Burgstr. next to the Leibnizhaus. Tel. 16 84 30 52. Open Tu 10am-8pm, W-F 10am-4pm, Sa-Su 10am-6pm. DM5, students and children DM3.)*

🎭 ENTERTAINMENT

More than 20 theaters make their homes in Hannover, supplying ballet, opera, dramas, and Broadway musicals. The **Opernhaus,** Opernpl. 1, the **Ballhof,** Ballhofstr. 5, the **Schauspielhaus,** on Theaterpl., and the **Theater am Aegi,** on Ägidientorpl., are the four largest. Tickets for most of the theaters (from DM12) are sold at the tourist office; call their ticket line at 30 14 30. ▲dvance tickets for the opera and the *Schauspielhaus* are also sold at the Opernhaus M-F 11am-7:30pm, Sa 11am-1pm, or by calling 16 84 61 40 for the opera or 16 84 67 10 for the *Schauspielhaus* one hour after the box office opens. Most theaters offer student tickets 30 minutes before each show at a 25% discount. For the official line on theater listings, festival dates, and other items of interest, pick up the monthly *Hannover Vorschau* from the tourist office (DM3) or the free *Hannover Live*. The Opernhaus provides its own thick guide to opera and ballet (free). The **UFA-Arthouse Thielenplatz,** Lavesstr. 2 (tel. 32 18 79), shows movies in English. The enormous **Cinemaxx,** Nikolaistr. 8 (tel. 130 93; tickets 126 32 00), and the **Palast Filmtheater,** Bahnhofstr. 5 (tel. 32 28 73), show dubbed American blockbusters.

If you're within a 100km radius of Hannover between July 2 and July 7, 2000, detour to its **Schützenfest** (marksmanship festival), the largest such *fête* in the world. Every summer since 1539, Hanoverians have congregated—weapons in hand—to test their marksmanship and retreat to the beer gardens to get *Schützen*-faced. In that order. The 10-day festival comes complete with parade, fireworks, chintzy stuffed animals, and rickety amusement park rides, but its main attraction is the *Lüttje Lage*, a feisty traditional drink. Without spilling, you must down the contents of two shot glasses simultaneously, holding them side by side in one hand; one glass contains *Weißbier*, the other *Schnapps*. For more information, contact the **Hannoversches Schützenfest** (tel. 161 18 54; fax 161 18 55). And if this isn't enough fun for you, Hannover delivers a nifty one-two punch. After giving the liver a brief respite, the **Maschseefest** (late July-early Aug.) hits you with another wild combination of concerts, masked balls, and street performances. For anyone left standing, the knockout blow falls with the **Altstadtfest** in the first or second weekend in August. All the big *Kneipen* and cafés convene for one last hurrah until next year. And for those folks who feel they must drop some cash in the streets every weekend, the **Flohmarkt** (flea market) on the **Leibnizufer** hits town every Saturday from 7am to 2pm.

⭐ NIGHTLIFE

When the sun goes down, Hannover lets 'em rip with an impressive array of packed cafés and pumping discos. The happening university crowds swarm the area of Linden-Nord, between Goetheplatz and Leinaustr., filling the cafés and *Kneipen*. For parties, snoop around the Mensa for signs (see **Food,** p. 470), or check either *Prinz* (DM4.50) or *Schädelspalter* (DM5), outstanding guides to nightlife in the city. The free *MagaScene* lists dance clubs and concerts. For live music, check out **The Capitol** (see below) or **Altro Mondo,** Bahnhofstr. 8 (tel. 32 33 27), in the City-Passage. Tickets are available by phone at 41 99 99 40.

🏚 **The Loft,** Georgstr. 50b (tel. 363 13 76). Right near Kröpcke, this hip joint is packed with students and smoke on the weekends. Open M-Th 9pm-2am, F-Sa 9pm-5am, Su 8pm-2am. Go through the back door to enter the alternative bistro-bar **Masa.** Enjoy falafel (DM6.50) and milkshakes (DM5.50) by candlelight. Masa open Sa-Su noon-5am, M-F noon-2am.

NIEDERSACHSEN

The Capitol, Schwarzer Bär 2 (tel. 44 40 66), sets the floor thumping with dance hits. Loosen up in a sea of bumping bodies. Next to the bar, a smaller floor for hard rock gets heads banging. Open F-Sa 10pm. Cover around DM8. Also houses the **Balou Music Club,** open W-Sa at 9pm. Call for a schedule.

Osho Disco, Raschpl. 7L (tel. 34 22 17), caters to a similar crowd as The Capitol. A lounge area surrounding the dance floor is a great place to meet (read: pick up) folks. Every Wednesday is "over 30-night"—no cover for survivors of the "Stayin' Alive" years. Open W-Su at 10pm. Cover W-Th and Su DM5, F-Sa DM8.

Daily Planet, Ägidientorpl. 1 (tel. 32 30 02). Jump out of your phone booth and stop the friggin' presses. A cool news bar with **internet access,** burgers, beers, and a wealth of hard liquor (DM3.30). Open M-Sa 10am-midnight.

Finnegan's Wake, Theaterstr. 6 (tel. 32 97 11). A place to chill with real Dubliners, where everybody knows *Ulysses's* name. Heats up early (9pm) even on weeknights; a good place to practice speaking English. Daily happy hour (4-6pm) and live Irish music (F-Su 9pm) liven the scene. Open M-F 4pm-2am, Sa-Su noon-2am.

Café-Kneipe Zaub, Königsworther Str. 32 (tel. 186 20). U-Bahn #10 to "Glocksee." Billiards, beer and Italian fare. Open daily 5pm-late.

Schwule Sau, Schaufeldstr. 38 (tel. 700 05 25). U-Bahn #6 or 11: "Kopernikusstr." One of the most popular gay and lesbian bars in Hannover, located in the university district. On good nights, the 3-person sofa in the corner seats 15. Tu ladies only. W men only. Sunday afternoons are teatime. Open Tu, W, and F 8pm-3am, Sa 9pm-7am, Su 3pm-2am. Cover DM6.

GÖTTINGEN

Home to Europe's first free university, Göttingen remains a college town to the core. The Georg-August-Universität boasts Otto von Bismarck as an alumnus and the Brothers Grimm as faculty members, but its real fame comes from its spectacular track record in hard science. Forty-one Nobel laureates have been students or faculty members, including Max Planck (the father of quantum mechanics) and Werner Heisenberg (author of the famous Uncertainty Principle). Heisenberg was the head of the German A-Bomb project, but a fundamental mistake in calculations lead his research teams down fruitless paths and kept the Bomb out of Hitler's hands. Political activism is a Göttingen tradition—in the years after its founding in 1734, the university was one of the most liberal in the German lands. By the 1920s, however, it degenerated into a hotbed of reactionary nationalism. After WWII, the pendulum briefly swung the other way as Göttingen earned a reputation as a *rote Uni* (red university). The ideological sparks have now subsided and the town exudes a serene, cosmopolitan air for its students and visitors.

🛈 ORIENTATION AND PRACTICAL INFORMATION

The Altstadt lies within the confines of a horseshoe-shaped ring road. At its center lie the **Altes Rathaus** and **Wilhelmsplatz,** site of the original university building.

Trains: Frequent trains to Berlin (2½hr., 1 per hour, DM100), Frankfurt (2hr., 1 per hour, DM66), Hannover (1hr., 2 per hour, DM30), and Hamburg (2hr., 2 per hour, DM80).

Public Transportation: Almost all city buses depart from the "Markt" and "Kornmarkt" stops. Single ride DM2.70, one transfer permitted.

Taxis: Hallo Taxi, "Göttingen's friendly taxis." Call 340 34 and say hallo.

Car Rental: Sixt, Groner Landstr. 33b (tel. 54 75 70). Open M-F 8am-6pm, Sa 8am-1pm.

Mitfahrzentrale: Mitfahrbüro Cheltenham House, Friedrichstr. 1 (tel. 48 59 88), hooks up riders and drivers. To Frankfurt DM25, Berlin DM30, Munich DM44. Open M-F 10am-6pm, Sa 10am-1:30pm.

Bike Rental: Fahrrad-Parkhaus (tel. 599 94), to the right of the station's main exit. Bikes from DM15 per day. Open M-Sa 5:30am-10pm, Su 8am-11pm.

Tourist Office: Tourist-Information, Markt 9 (tel. 540 00; fax 400 29 98; email tourismus@goettingen.de), in the Altes Rathaus. From the station, cross Berliner Str. to perpendicular Goetheallee. Follow it several blocks as it becomes Prinzenstr. and turn right onto Weender Str., which runs into the Markt. The staff books **rooms** (from DM30) for free. Open April-Oct. M-F 9:30am-6pm, Sa-Su 10am-4pm; Nov.-March M-F 9:30am-1pm and 2-6pm, Sa 10am-1pm. A smaller **Tourist-Center,** Bahnhofspl. 5 (tel. 560 00; fax 531 29 28), is at the train station. Open M-F 9am-6pm, Sa 9am-2pm.

Tours: Depart from the main hall of the Rathaus daily at 11:30am if 5 or more people attend. DM7. Tours in English available for large groups only.

Currency Exchange: Commerzbank, Prinzenstr. 2 (tel. 40 80), has the best rates in town. Open M-W 8:30am-4pm, Th 8:30am-6pm, F 8:30am-3:30pm.

American Express: Goetheallee 4a (tel. 52 20 70). Open M-F 9am-6pm, Sa 9:30am-12:30pm.

Bookstore: Deuerlich, Weender Str. 33 (tel. 49 50 00). Smaller branches at Weender Landstr. 6 and Theaterstr. 25. Open M-W and F 9am-7pm, Th 9am-8pm, Sa 9am-4pm.

Laundromat: Wasch-Salon, Ritterplan 4, opposite the Städtisches Museum. Wash DM4, soap DM1. Dry DM1 per 12min. Open M-Sa 7am-10pm.

Pharmacy: Goethe-Apotheke, Goetheallee 17-18 (tel. 563 64). Open M-F 8am-6:15pm, W 8am-4pm, and Sa 9am-1pm.

Emergency: Tel. 110. **Police,** Am Steingraben 19 (tel. 49 11). **Fire,** tel. 112. **Ambulance,** tel. 192 22.

Women's Resources: Frauenhaus (tel. 483 20). Open 24hr. Some English spoken.

AIDS Hotline: AIDS-Beratung, tel. 400 48 31.

Post Office: Heinrich-von-Stephan-Str. 1, 37073 Göttingen, to the left of the train station. Open M-F 7am-6:30pm, Sa 8am-1pm.

PHONE CODE	0551

ACCOMMODATIONS

The abundance of students and visitors in Göttingen makes the housing market tight but not unreasonable. Fortunately, the hostel is excellent and generally has rooms available, while those wishing to stay a few days or even a few months can check the **Mitwohnzentrale,** Rasenweg 8a (tel. 194 30), which matches up potential roommates. (Open M-F 10am-6pm, Sa 10am-2pm.)

Jugendherberge (HI), Habichtsweg 2 (tel. 576 22; fax 438 87). From the station, turn left onto Berliner Str., which becomes Nikolausberger Weg; it's a long trek down this street, but Habichtsweg eventually appears on the left (45min.). Or take bus #8, 10, 11, 15, or 18 to "Kornmarkt," then bus #6 (direction: "Klausberg") to "Jugendherberge." The hostel puts most *hotels* to shame with immaculate rooms and many singles. DM27, over 26 DM32. Breakfast and sheets included. Room keys require DM20 deposit. Reception 6:30am-11:30pm. Curfew midnight, or get a key with a DM30 deposit.

Hotel-Gaststätte Berliner Hof, Weender Landstr. 43 (tel. 38 33 20; fax 383 32 32). Neatly tucked next to the university. Take bus #20 or 24 to "Kreuzbergring." Floral comforters will put you to sleep on the spot. Singles DM60, with shower DM75; doubles with the works DM100. Reception 3-11pm.

Hotel Garni Gräfin Holtzendorff, Ernst-Ruhstrat-Str. 4 (tel. 639 87; fax 63 29 85). Remotely located in an industrial area, the hotel is worth considering if everything else is booked. From the station, take bus #13 (direction: "Harrenacher") to "Florenz-Sautorius-Str." Continue walking in the direction of the bus and take the second left. Comfortable singles DM49, with shower DM70; doubles DM85, with shower DM95.

◘ FOOD

Göttingen is blessed with a high-quality **Mensa** and vegetable **Markt.** An impressive array of peddlers haggle in the area between Lange and Kurze Geismarstr., including at a **fruit market** adjacent to the Deutsches Junges Theater (Tu, Th, and Sa 7am-1pm) and in the square in front of the Rathaus (Th 2-8pm). The most central **supermarket** is **Plus,** Prinzenstr. 13, across from the library. (Open M-F 8am-7:30pm, Sa 8am-4pm.) **Goetheallee,** running from the station to the city center, has late-night Greek, Italian, and Turkish restaurants. Bakeries and other places good for a quick snack line **Weender Str.** and **Jüdenstr.**

Zentral-Mensa, Pl. der Göttinger Sieben 4 (tel. 39 51 51). Follow Weender Landstr. onto Pl. der Göttinger Sieben, turn right into the university complex, and walk through the central plain to the cavernous *Studentenwerk* building on the left. Swarming with people and plastered with events listings, the cafeteria serves meals for DM5-6. Tickets sold downstairs—buy one or you can't eat. Open M-F 11:30am-2:15pm, Sa 11:30am-2pm. The **Central Café** sells baguettes and snacks. Open M-Th 9am-8pm, F 9am-7pm.

◪ **Shucan,** Weender Str. 11 (tel. 48 62 44). Just follow your nose to the friendly-looking toucan out front. A hip café and bar with hundreds of outdoor seats overlooking the Marktpl. behind the Rathaus. Baguettes (DM5-7) run a paltry second to the ornate ice cream creations (from DM5). No Froot Loops. Open M-Th and Su 9am-2am, F-Sa 10am-3am.

Nudelhaus, Rotestr. 13 (tel. 442 63). Oodles of noodles (27 different varieties), most DM8-15. A beer garden in back facilitates merry slurping. Open daily noon-11:30pm.

Göttingen

ACCOMMODATIONS
A Hotel Gräfin Holtzendorff
B Hotel-Gaststätte Berliner Hof
C Jugendherberge

Asia Mai Anh, Goetheallee 16 (tel. 479 24), serves fried rice (DM10-12) and your favorite Chinese dishes à la Deutschland. Most meals DM10-15. Lunch specials daily 11am-3pm (DM8-12). Open M and W-F 11am-3pm and 5-10pm, Sa-Su noon-10pm.

Pizzeria Sorrento, Jüdenstr. 13a (tel. 550 20). With Göttingen's plethora of gyro-joints, how does one choose? This one is popular with the locals—great selection, dirt cheap. Gyros DM6-10, pizzas DM7-13. They deliver. Open M-Th and Su 11am-2am, F-Sa 11am-3am.

◉ SIGHTS

ALTES RATHAUS. The courtyard of the Altes Rathaus serves as the meeting place for the whole town: punk, professor, and panhandler alike. The meter-tall **Gänseliesel** (goose-girl) on the fountain in front of the Rathaus is Göttingen's symbol, edging out Maya as "the most-kissed girl in the world"; graduating students, particularly budding doctors, line up to kiss the promiscuous bronze nymphet after receiving their diplomas. The repressed city council imposed a "kissing ban" in 1926, prompting one incensed (or perhaps just, uh, frustrated) student to sue. He lost, but town officials now turn a blind eye to extracurricular fountain activities. The bronze lion-head doorknob on the south portal of the **Rathaus** was crafted in 1300, making it the oldest town hall door knob in Germany. (So it's not the Pyramids. Deal.) Inside, elaborate murals depict 19th-century life in Göttingen.

GEORG-AUGUST-UNIVERSITÄT. The renowned university's campus fills an area bounded by Weender Landstr. and Nikolausberger Weg. Göttingen's student body is diverse, representing many styles, outlooks, and nationalities; still, you won't meet the cast from *Animal House* here.

BISMARCK SIGHTS. The **Bismarckhäuschen,** outside the city wall, is a tiny stone cottage built in 1459 where 17-year-old law student Otto von Bismarck took up residence after authorities expelled him from the inner city for boozing it up. *(Tel. 48 62 47. Open Tu 10am-1pm, Th and Sa 3-5pm. Free.)* The **Bismarckturm** commemorates the larger-scale trouble-making of his later career (see **Bismarck and the Second Reich,** p. 10). From the top of the old stone tower, there's a Göttingen-wide view. *(Im Hainberg. Tel. 561 28. Take bus A to "Bismarckstr./Reitsaal." Open Sa-Su 11am-6pm. Free.)*

MEDIEVAL CHURCHES. Göttingen hosts a number of notable churches. The **Jakobikirche's** 72m tower rises up next to the stone lambada sculpture called *Der Tanz.* Inside, it's fun to play with the miniature model of the impressive 1402 altar triptych. *(Tel. 575 96. At the corner of Prinzenstr. and Weender Str. Open daily 10am-5pm. Tower open Sa from 11am. Free organ concerts F at 6pm.)* Down Weender Str. behind the Altes Rathaus stands the fortress-like **Kirche St. Johannis.** The interior is unexceptional, but the tower in which students have lived since 1921 is more interesting. *(Tel. 48 62 41. Open daily 10:30am-12:30pm. Tower open Sa 2-4pm.)*

STÄDTISCHES MUSEUM. The municipal museum gives a detailed examination of the city over the last several millennia or so. The second floor holds the compelling history wing; the limited scope tells the story well. Hostelers will get a strange chill from a display of *Hitlerjugend* memorabilia which includes a number of *Deutsche Jugendherbergswerk* pins complete with swastikas on them. There's also a display of dozens of cover pages from Göttingen's Nazi-run local newspaper that presents a rather distorted view of history. The museum makes much of Göttingen's intellectual distinction and liberal sentiments: in 1837, on the 100th anniversary of the university's founding, a group of professors known as the Göttingen Seven made German history by sending a public letter of protest to King Ernst August, who had revoked the liberal constitution established four years earlier by his predecessor. Courageous signers included the Brothers Grimm, then well-known professors of literature; as expected, the Seven were all removed from office. *(Ritterplan 7. Tel. 400 28 43. One block north from the Jakobikirche on Jüdenstr. Open Tu-Su 10am-5pm. Permanent exhibit DM3, students DM1; temporary exhibits DM3, students DM2.)*

SYNAGOGUE MEMORIAL. On Untere Maschstr. stands a spiraling pyramid erected to commemorate the Göttingen synagogue that was razed in 1938. Viewed from above, the structure spirals into a monumental Star of David.

🎵 🎭 ENTERTAINMENT AND NIGHTLIFE

Göttingen's entertainment industry covers the entirety of the theatrical spectrum. For world-class performances, the renowned **Deutsches Theater,** Theaterpl. 11 (tel. 49 69 11), puts on the classics with tickets as low as DM11. Check out the slick *DT* catalogue for the schedule, available at the box office. (Open M-F 10am-1:30pm and 5-7pm, Sa 10am-noon, and 1hr. before performance.) To sample the youthful perspective, head down to the **Junges Theater,** Hospitalstr. 6 (tel. 49 50 15), which presents both the classic and the innovative. (Tickets DM19, students DM12.) All theaters close for the summer from July to mid-September. The Junges Theater also houses the **KAZ-Keller** (tel. 471 45), a pleasant *Kneipe* that hosts concerts and dances. (Open daily 8pm-2am.) Film buffs can indulge in the perverse pleasure of ruthlessly dubbed blockbusters and German-language flicks at **Capitol 3 Cinema,** Prinzenstr. 13 (tel. 48 48 84), or at the nine screens of the gigantic **Cinemaxx** (tel. 521 22 00) complex behind the train station. The artsy **Lumière,** Geismarer Landstr. 19 (tel. 48 45 23), is more cosmopolitan (DM9, students DM8).

Although Göttingen's disco and pub scene centers on the Altstadt, a few popular clubs perch on the outskirts of the university. The aptly named **Outpost,** Königsallee 243 (tel. 662 51), reputedly the best dance club in the city, keeps up a frenzied pace but closes rather early. (Open Tu and F-Sa 9pm-1am.) The best place to hear music and hang with students in the Altstadt is **Blue Note,** Wilhelmspl. 3 (tel. 469 07), under the *Alte Mensa* in Wilhelmsplatz. There's a different musical theme each day of the week, and live bands at least once a week. Jazz, reggae, and African pop are well represented. (Open daily from 8pm. Cover for concerts DM8-30.) **Nörgelbuff Musik-Kneipe,** Groner Str. 23 (tel. 438 85), located next to the "Kornmarkt" bus stop, has an impressive venue and live music—including the occasional "rock concert"—several times a week. (Open M-Sa after 7pm, Su after 8pm. Happy "hour" M-Sa 7-9pm. Concerts usually F-Sa.) **Irish Pub,** Mühlenstr. 4 (tel. 456 64), is one of the most popular student watering holes, with a seemingly infinite supply of Guinness and a ton of Gaelic *Gemütlichkeit.* (Open daily 6pm-2am.)

GOSLAR

Goslar won the national tourism lottery, with an Altstadt congested by immaculate half-timbered houses and winding narrow streets, and encircled by the divinely lush Harz Mountains. During WWII, Goslar's citizens proclaimed it neutral and free of soldiers, painting red crosses atop their homes. Under the Geneva convention, this act rendered the town a non-target for bombing, saving it from destruction. Exciting museums and provocative sculptures, designed and crafted by artists such as Henry Moore and Botero, are scattered throughout the village, enchanting the most jaded aesthete. In addition, as the hub of an extensive bus network, Goslar can spin you to any part of the region. Goslar's postcard perfection and its perch at the edge of the peaceful and popular Harz mountains has, however, turned it into something of a tourist trap. Beware.

🚩 ORIENTATION AND PRACTICAL INFORMATION. Trains roll hourly to Hannover (1½hr., 1 per hour, DM23) and Göttingen (1¼hr., 1 per hour, DM23). Goslar is a good base for a bus or hiking tour of the Harz Mountains. **Harz Bike,** Bornhardtstr. 3-5 (tel. 820 11), rents **bikes** for DM50 per day. (Open M-F 10am-5pm, Sa 10am-4pm.) The **tourist office,** Markt 7 (tel. 780 60; fax 230 05), across from the Rathaus, books **rooms** (from DM30) for free and offers maps of the Harz. **Tours** (DM8) depart regularly from the Marktplatz. (Open May-Oct. M-F 9:15am-6pm, Sa 9:30am-4pm, Su 9:30am-2pm; Nov.-April M-F 9:15am-5pm, Sa 9:30am-2pm.) **Harzer Verkehrsverband,** Marktstr. 45 (tel. 340 40; fax 34 94 66), inside the Industrie- und Handelskammer building, handles regional tourism and provides information on the Harz. (Open M-F 8am-4pm.) The **Frauenzentrum Goslar**, Breite Str. 15a (tel. 422 55), provides counseling for women. The entrance is on Bolzenstr. (Open M 9am-noon and 3-5pm, W 9am-noon, and F 9-11am.) The **post office** is at Klubgartenstr. 10, 38640 Goslar. (Open M-F 8am-5:30pm, Sa 9am-noon.) The **telephone code** is 05321.

 While the Oberharz Mountains loom over Niedersachsen and Thüringen, information about the entire Harz region can be found in Sachsen-Anhalt (see **Harz Mountains,** p. 196).

ACCOMMODATIONS AND CAMPING. The half-timbered Goslar **Jugendherberge (HI),** Rammelsberger Str. 25 (tel. 222 40; fax 413 76), wins the prize for being the most confusingly located hostel in the book. From Marktpl., take twisty Bergstr. southwest until it ends at Clausthaler Str. Directly across the street, between the trees, a stairway marked with a *Wanderweg* sign awaits. Take this pleasant path through the pines and head right at the fork at the path's midpoint to end up in the hostel's backyard (20min.). Or, take bus C from the train station (direction: "Bergbaumuseum") to "Theresienwall"; continue along in the same direction as the bus, and take a sharp left up the hill at the big white *Jugendherberge* sign (10 min.). The path is poorly lit at night. The hostel features smallish two- and six-bed rooms with new furniture. (DM21, over 26 DM26. Breakfast included. Reception 8:30am-2:30pm and 3-10pm. Curfew midnight. Members only.) **Gästehaus Elisabeth Möller,** Schiefer Weg 6 (tel. 230 98), features a large, shady garden and a patio perfect for afternoon naps. From the station, take a right on Klubgartenstr., which becomes Am Heiligen Grabe; cross Von-Garssen-Str., and turn right on Schiefer Weg. (Singles DM40, with shower DM50, with full bath DM60; doubles DM80-110.) **Campingplatz Sennhütte,** Clausthaler Str. 28 (tel. 224 98), is 3km from town along the B241. (Tel. 225 02. DM5.50 per person. Tent DM4. Car DM3.)

FOOD AND ENTERTAINMENT. The town's mountain **Markt** yodels every Tuesday and Friday (open 8am-1pm). The beautiful market square is ringed with restaurants, though cheaper bistros and cafés can be found along Hokenstr., where *Imbiß* stands provide meals for DM4-8. If for no other reason than its great name and special sauce, grab a bite to eat at **Mac Döner,** Marktstr. 36 (tel. 12 30). Fast Turkish food, under 5 billion served. (Open M-Th 11am-11pm, F-Sa 11am-1pm.) Music, beer, and the local crowd converge at **Kö Musik-Kneipe,** Marktstr. 30. (Tel. 268 10. Open M-Th and Su 4pm-2am, F-Sa 4pm-3am.)

SIGHTS. Guarded by a pair of bronze Braunschweig lions, the austere **Kaiserpfalz,** Kaiserbleek 6 (tel. 70 43 58), is a massive Romanesque palace that served as the ruling seat for 11th- and 12th-century emperors. The palace fell into sad decay by the 19th century but was extensively restored by Prussian aristocrats. The interior of the **Reichssaal** is plastered with murals; the huge paintings display carefully selected historical incidents in the mythic, pompous manner that only 19th-century Germans could properly pull off. In the palace's **Ulrichskapelle,** Heinrich III's heart lies tucked away inside a massive sarcophagus. (Museum and tomb open Jan.-Oct. daily 9:15am-5pm; Nov.-Dec. 10am-4pm. Last entry 30min. before closing. DM2.50, children under 11 free.) Below the palace is the **Domvorhalle,** Kaiserbleek 10, the sad remains of a 12th-century imperial cathedral destroyed 170 years ago.

The central **Marktplatz** is a delightful blend of ornate woodwork and trellises. The **Hotel Kaiserworth,** a former guild house, was for many years an eccentric, but striking addition to the square, with its superb gable spires and wooden statues of emperors gracing the facade. Recently, however, its elegant white front has been repainted a vulgar red. The hotel's statues have been painted up, too, in full comic-book color; it's now easier to see the coarsely humorous smaller figures on the corners. Each day in the market square, small **Glocken- und Figurenspiel** figures of court nobles and the miners whose work made the region prosperous dance to the chime on the treasury roof (9am, noon, 3, and 6pm). The Rathaus's **Huldigungssaal** is coated with early 16th-century depictions of the prophesying of Christ's return. The twin towers of the reconstructed 12th-century **Marktkirche** (tel. 229 22) loom behind the Rathaus. The church hosts the stained-glass saga of St. Cosmas and St. Damian, third-century twin doctors and martyrs. In a classic instance of the Roman empire's overkill, the saints were disciplined and punished by drowning, burning at the stake, stoning, and crucifixion. (Open April-Sept. Tu-Th and Sa 10:30am-3:30pm, F 10:30am-2pm, Su noon-3:30pm; Oct.-March Sa 10:30am-3:30pm.) The **Mönchehaus**, Mönchestr. 3, exhibits a grand modern art collection, including Anselm Kiefer, Calder, Miró, and Joseph Beuys. (Open Tu-Sa 10am-1pm and 3-5pm, Su 10am-1pm. Donation requested.) On the way back from the Kaiserpfalz, the fantastic **Musikinstrumente- und Puppenmuseum**, Hoher Weg 5 (tel. 269 45), is not to be missed. The owner has spent more than 40 years assembling the largest private instrument collection in Germany, including one of the **world's first accordions** and a 50s Wurlitzer jukebox. Visit the museum tucked inside, billed as the "smallest musical instrument museum in the world." (Open daily 11am-5pm. DM5, children DM2.50.) Goslar gets funky from August 30 to September 1 with its **Altstadtfest**—a watered-down version of Oktoberfest.

HAMELN (HAMELIN)

In the 700 years since the Pied Piper first strolled out of town, Hameln has transformed from a rat trap to a tourist trap. The original story was sordid enough: after Hameln failed to pay the piper his rat-removal fee, on June 26, 1284, he walked off with 130 children in thrall. But today the legend of the *Rattenfänger*, as he is known in German, draws tourists as mysteriously as his flute drew rodents seven centuries ago. With so much rat and piper paraphernalia crowding the streets, it's easy to forget about Hameln's residents. Apart from the costumed tourist-office officials, most do their best to avoid the legend altogether. Making your way through the souvenirchoked streets, you can almost hear the mayor consoling grieving parents, "You haven't lost a child, you've gained a lucrative tourist industry."

🔁 **ORIENTATION AND PRACTICAL INFORMATION.** Hameln bridges the Weser, 45 minutes from Hannover by **train** (2 per hour, DM15). For a **taxi**, call 74 77. **Oberweser-Dampfschiffahrt**, Inselstr. 3 (tel. 93 99 99; fax 230 40), runs **ferries** up and down the Weser to Bodenwerder, Holzminden, and Hannoversch Münden, and offers a complete package of tours. (1hr. expedition DM8, kids DM4, students DM5.50; 2½hr. DM16, students DM11, children DM8. Call for a schedule. Operates March-Oct.) Rent **bikes** from **Fahrradverleih Troche**, Kreuzstr. 7. (Tel. 136 70. Open M-F 9:30am-1pm and 2:30-6pm, Sa 9:30am-12:30pm. DM20 per day.) The hostel (see below) also has a few old bikes to rent to guests (DM8 per day). The **tourist office**, Deisterallee 3 (tel. 20 26 17 or 20 26 19; fax 20 25 00), on the Bürgergarten, tracks down **rooms** (from DM25) for free. They also give out a very comprehensive list of hotels and *Pensionen*. All while wearing silly 🔁Pied Piper costumes. These are people who love their work. From the station, cross Bahnhofplatz, make a right onto Bahnhofstr., and turn left onto Deisterstr., which becomes Deisterallee. (Open May-Sept. M-F 9am-1pm and 2-6pm, Sa 9:30am-12:30pm and 2-4pm, Su 9:30am-12:30pm; Oct.-April M-F 9am-1pm and 2-5pm.) A smaller booth in the **Hochzeithaus** is open in summer. (Open mid-April to Oct. Tu-F 11am-2pm and 2:30-4:30pm, Sa-Su 10am-2pm.) **Buchhandlung Matthias**, Bäckerstr. 56 (tel. 947 00), has a limited selection of English paperbacks. (Open M-F 9-6:30pm, Sa 9am-4pm; May-Sept. also open Su 12:30-4pm.) The **post office** is at Am Posthof 1, 31785 Hameln. (Open M-F 8am-6pm, Sa 8am-1pm.) The **telephone code** is 05151.

📛 **ACCOMMODATIONS AND CAMPING.** The beautifully located but regrettably Piper-festooned **Jugendherberge (HI)**, Fischbeckerstr. 33 (tel. 34 25; fax 423 16), sits on a dreamy bend in the Weser. From the station, take bus #2 to "Wehler Weg," and turn right onto Fischbeckerstr. Cross Bahnhofplatz, make a right onto Bahnhofstr., turn left on Deisterallee, and then go right around 164-er Ring (along the Hamel rivulet) to Erichstr. as it bends into Fischbeckerstr (about 40min.). German school kids *love* dreamy bends in rivers, so call a couple of months in advance if possible. Crowded rooms, but there's a piper-free view from the outdoor patio. (DM20, over 26 DM25. Breakfast included; magic flute to lure away schoolkids is not. Sheets DM5.70. Reception 12:30-1:30pm and 5-10pm. Curfew 10pm, but key available with DM30 deposit.)

Hameln's tourist boom has resulted in a large number of *Pensionen*. The **Gästehaus Alte Post,** Hummenstr. 23 (tel. 434 44; fax 414 89) is centrally located and kid-friendly. Colorful rooms complete with Picasso prints, television, telephone, and clock radio. A coffee maker and refrigerator are available for use. (DM34.50-55. Breakfast included. Checkout 11am.) Southeast of the city center, on gracious shores of Tönebon lake, lies **Campground Jugendzeltplatz,** Tönebonweg 8 (tel. 262 23), equipped with a sauna and warm showers. Take bus #44 or 51 to "Sädbad." (DM5 per person. Reception M-F until 10pm, Sa-Su until 11pm. Open May-Sept.)

◖ FOOD. The streets of the Altstadt around Osterstr. and Pferdemarkt are lined with restaurants and cafes, but the chances of finding a bargain are slim. A few good deals loom along Bäckerstr. near the *Münster*. Duck into **Julia's Restaurant,** Bäckerstr. 57 (tel. 444 32), a dimly lit cafeteria which serves spaghetti (DM8.50) various sorts of *Schnitzel* and *Wurst*, and crispy salads (DM3.50-8. Open M-F 10am-8pm, Sa 10am-4pm; May-Sept. also Su 11:30am-5pm.) **Mexcal,** Osterstr. 15 (tel. 428 06), serves excellent Mexican meals, and the lunch specials are a good deal (burritos DM9.90). Daily happy "hour" (noon-6pm) gets you cheap drinks (DM8.90—they're BIG. Open daily noon-midnight.) If you dare venture from the Altstadt, **Tandir,** Deisterstr. 38 (tel. 222 01), an elegant, *cheap* Turkish restaurant, will receive you with open arms and stuff you full of *Döner* (DM5-14), pizza (DM9-15), and other house specialties. Open brick oven and tables with spotless white linen. (Open M-Th 11am-midnight, F-Sa 11am-1am, Su 11am-11pm.) *Hamelners* flock for fruit, vegetables, and other treats to the open-air **market** on the Bürgergarten (W and Sa 8am-1pm). Hameln boasts an impressive array of edible rodents (if you swallow them whole, the fur will tickle your throat…mmm!). To catch these rats, pay to the tune of DM0.35 for tiny marzipan critters and up to DM6 for a jumbo pastry rat. Little crusty bread-rats cost DM3 at the excellent bakery in the **Schnelz Reformhaus,** Osterstr. 18, in the Altstadt. It also sells all-natural foodstuffs of every sort, a delight for the vegetarian. (Open M-W 8:30am-6pm, Th-F 8:30am-6:30pm, Sa 8:30am-2pm.) **Plus supermarket,** Bahnhofstr. 34-36, sells the basics. (Open M-F 8am-7pm, Sa 8am-2pm.)

◼ SIGHTS. If you cringe at the thought of small rodents or little flute players in motley capes, Hameln is probably not the best vacation spot; the Piper motif is inescapable. One of the few buildings unadorned is the gray, modern **Rathaus** (did we say RAT Haus?). In the courtyard out front, however, several elfin children with bowl cuts hang suspended in mid-air, following a 1975 piper statue by Karl-Ulrich Nuss to the **Rattenfängerbrunnen** (the "Piper fountain"). The **Bürgergarten,** across Rathausplatz, lends small but soothing relief to the tourist rat race. (Open daily 7am-10pm; fountains run daily April-Oct. 11am-noon, 3-4pm, and 7:30-8:30pm.) Walk back down Kastanienwall and turn right into the massive auto-free Altstadt. Also at Rathausplatz is the **Theater Hameln,** where a musical about the piper plays—along with some genuine theater, opera, and dance. (Call for information on 91 62 22, for tickets 91 62 20. Box office open Tu-F 10am-7pm and Sa 10am-1pm.) Off to the left, the **Rattenfängerhaus,** built in 1603, is decked out with startled-looking figureheads and a sad inscription recalling the sudden surge in the average age of townsfolk. Trek down another 100m to the **Leiesthaus,** Osterstr. 8-9 (tel. 20 22 15), where the **Museum Hameln** exhibits the Piper in 20 poses and 20,000 books. (Open Tu-Su 10am-4:30pm. DM3, students and children DM1.) The grim

Rattenfänger tale is re-enacted each Sunday at noon in a **Freilichtspiel** (open-air show) at the 1610 **Hochzeithaus.** (May-Sept., weather permitting. Free.) Small children dressed as rats chase a man with a large wooden instrument in his mouth wearing a multicolored suit and tight pants; it's simply saucy. At 9:35am, the **Glockenspiel** on the *Hochzeithaus* plays the *Rattenfängerlied* (Pied Piper song); at 11:45am you're serenaded by the *Weserlied;* and at 1:05, 3:35, and 5:35pm, a tiny stage emerges from the *Hochzeithaus,* and "rats" circle around a peculiar wooden flautist. After a fill of *Ratfänger* time, head to the **Glashütten Hameln,** Pulverturm 1 (tel. 272 39, fax 272 40), where you can watch people who don't care about rats or multi-colored tights fill their cheeks with air and blow molten glass into shape. (DM2, children DM1.50, under 6 free. Open M-F 9:30am-1pm and 2pm-6pm, Sa 9:30am-4pm, Su 10am-5pm.)

HANNOVERSCH MÜNDEN

Hannoversch Münden lies between the forested hills where the Fulda and the Werra combine—with the newborn Weser River popping out as a result of the consummation. Alexander von Humboldt called it "one of the seven most beautifully located cities in the world." With more than 700 preserved *Fachwerkhäuser,* this is one of the most attractive of Germany's six zillion half-timbered towns. The impeccable Altstadt remains refreshingly free of tourists despite its picture-book setting at the foot of the *Deutsche Märchenstraße* (German fairy tale route). To taste the flavor of the town, strolling aimlessly through the Altstadt might offer a richer palate than dragging yourself between sights. Either way, Münden offers a tiny world of architectural beauty and authenticity.

■ **ORIENTATION AND PRACTICAL INFORMATION.** Münden is easily accessible by **train** from Göttingen (40min., 1 per hour, DM10) and Kassel (30min., 2 per hour, DM8). **Ferries** navigate the Fulda and Weser rivers with **water tours** of the town (DM10-12). Ask for information at the tourist office (see below), or walk to **Weserstein** at the tip of the island "Unterer Tanzwerder" and hop on a ferry. The **tourist office** (tel. 753 13; fax 754 04) in the Rathaus books **rooms** (from DM25) for free. (Open June-Sept. M-F 9am-6pm, Sa 9am-1pm, Su 10am-1pm; Oct.-May Su-F 9am-4pm.) Help is also on hand from the information counter (tel. 750) in the same building after the office closes. (Open daily May-Sept. until 9pm; Oct.-April until 8pm.) **Tours** of the Altstadt leave from the tourist office. (June-Sept. M-Sa 10:30am, Su 2pm. DM4, children DM2.) Rent **bikes** and **boats** at **Busch Freizeit** (tel. 66 07 77), located at **Campingplatz Münden.** (See below. Open 8am-6pm. Bikes DM13, boats DM25 per day.) The **telephone code** is 05541.

■ **ACCOMMODATIONS AND FOOD.** The **Jugendherberge (HI),** Prof.-Oelkers-Str. 10 (tel. 88 53; fax 734 39), sits just outside the town limits on the banks of the Weser. From the station, walk down Beethovenstr., turn left at Wallstr., cross the Pionierbrücke, and turn right along Veckerhäger Str.; when the road makes a left turn, turn with it (40min.). Or take bus #135 from the train station (direction: "Veckerhäger-/Kasseler Str.") to "Jugendherberge." (Hostel DM21, over 26 DM26. Breakfast included. Sheets DM5.70. Reception 5-7pm and 9:45-10pm. Curfew 10pm, but a key to the front door is available. Call ahead. Closed 2 random weekends per month June-Sept.) Pitch your tent in view of the city walls at **Campingplatz Münden,** Oberer Tanzwerder (tel. 122 57; fax 66 07 78), 10 minutes from the train station on an island in the Fulda River off Pionierbrücke. Follow Kasseler Schlagd along the city walls and turn left on Tanzwerder. A bridge leads over to the island. (DM7.50 per person, DM5 per child. DM5.50 per tent. Reception 7am-10pm.)

The cheapest eats can be found at bakeries along **Lange Str.** or at the **Markt** behind the Rathaus (W and Sa 7am-1pm). Restaurants of all sorts abound in the area around the **Altmarkt,** but they tend to be pricey. For something affordable, try **Zeus** (tel. 26 08), at the corner of Loh-Str. and Mühlenstr. near the Rathaus, which sells Greek food (DM5-14) in a classy *Imbiß* setting. **Pizza Eck,** Rosenstr. 14 (tel. 20 94), serves hefty pizza and pasta plates. (DM6-9. Open M-Sa 11am-11pm, Su 5-11pm.) **Plus,** Marktplatz 5, stocks **groceries.** (Open M-F 8am-6:30pm, Sa 8am-2pm.)

⬛ **SIGHTS.** Weave through the angled side streets to admire the 14th-century *Fachwerkhäuser;* some of the oldest and most impressive are tucked away on **Ziegelstraße.** The 16th-century **Hinter der Stadtmauer 23,** a Jewish school since 1796, was gutted in 1938. A plaque stands outside in memoriam. Recent owners restored it and uncovered a *Mikwe* (ritual bath) in the basement. The ornate **Rathaus** is a prime example of the Weser Renaissance style that originated in the area around 1550. To reach the **Rathaus** from the station, cross the street and walk down Beethovenstr.; make a right onto Burgstr. and a left on Marktstr.; the Rathaus will be on the left immediately after Lange Str. Centuries-old markings of Weser flood heights mark the Rathaus corner walls, and coloring book scenes from the city's past line the walls inside. Figurines appear in the upper windows of the Rathaus and dance, juggle, and hit each other with heavy hammers to the ringing of the bells daily at noon, 3, and 5pm. Also outside is the wagon of Münden's former resident and favorite tourist gimmick, **Doctor Eisenbart,** an 18th-century traveling physician whose ability to treat many illnesses was overshadowed by his reputation as a quack and a swindler. The story of his life is played out on the stage in front of the Rathaus (June-Aug. Su 11am. DM4, children DM2). The **Blasiuskirche,** opposite the Rathaus, is decked out in periwinkle and emerald, with ornate Solomonic columns surrounding the altar and 15th-century crucifix. (Open May-Oct. daily 1-6pm.)

Münden's three islands—**Doktorwerder, Unterer Tanzwerder,** and **Oberer Tanzwerder**—are all easily accessible by small bridges on the outskirts of the Altstadt. The U.K.'s hired guns, the famed Hessian mercenaries, took off from the islet's former pier to face off against the upstart American colonists. The best view of the valley is from across the Fulda atop the **Tillyschanze** tower (tel. 18 90), built in 1882 to commemorate May 30, 1626. On this day during the Thirty Years War, General Tilly stormed through Münden, slaughtering more than 2,000 citizens. (Open daily 9am-1pm, Tu-Su 9am-8pm. DM2, children DM1.) Cross the Pionierbrücke and hang a left. Make another left on Tillyschanzenweg and follow it to the tower. **Tillyhaus,** Marktstr. 15, is where the general lived during the five-year occupation of the town. On the banks of the Werra, the austere **Welfenschloß** proves that not all Weser Renaissance buildings look like over-iced birthday cakes. The gray parts of the building are remnants of the original Gothic structure that burned down in 1560. The interior can only be admired on a guided tour (May-Sept. Su 2:30 pm; meet in front of the Rathaus), but it's not worth the DM4. The Schloß also houses the **Städtisches Museum,** which boasts a sizable antique collection and several of Gustav Eberlein's neo-Baroque sculptures. (Open M-F 10am-noon and 2:30-5pm, Sa 10am-noon and 2:30-4pm, Su 10am-12:30pm.) The city walls still sport seven of the original defense towers as well as the **Alte Werrabrücke,** built in 1329, and the 12th-century **Ägidienkirche.** Another victim of Tilly, a nearby gun powder tower, exploded and ignited the church. Doctor Eisenbart's grave is here; shed a tear for the poor old quack.

HILDESHEIM

The *tausendjähriger Rosenstock* (Thousand-Year-Old Rose Bush) symbolizes the prosperity of the town of Hildesheim. According to legend, Emperor Ludwig der Fromme (the Pious) lost his way after a hunt and fastened his relic of the Virgin Mary to the branch of a conspicuous rose bush. He managed to find his way home, and the next day, remembering his relic, returned to find it frozen to the branch. Since it was the middle of summer, he interpreted this as a divine sign and erected a chapel on the site, around which grew the majestic Dom and the town of Hildesheim. As long as the bush flourishes, so will Hildesheim. On March 22, 1945, Allied bombers flattened the town, yet the remarkable bush survived. The collapsed ruins of the Dom sheltered the roots from the flames. Eight weeks later, 25 buds were growing strong.

🛈 ORIENTATION AND PRACTICAL INFORMATION. Hildesheim is 45km southeast of Hannover, with hourly **trains** to Hannover (30min., DM10) and Göttingen (30min., DM40). **Bus** tickets within the city cost DM2.20 and are valid for one hour; a *Tagesticket* (DM6.50) is valid all day. Rent **bikes** at **Räder-Emmel**, Dingworthstr. 20-22 (tel. 438 22); it's on your way down the mountain from the hostel. (Open M-F 9am-1pm and 3-6pm, Sa 9am-1pm. DM5-10 per day.) The **tourist office,** Am Ratsbauhof 1c (tel. 179 80; fax 17 98 88; email tourist-info@hildesheim.com), two blocks from the Rathaus, offers brochures, passes out maps and city guides, and also books rooms for free. From the Hauptbahnhof, walk straight up Bernwardstr., which becomes Almsstr., which in turn becomes Hoher Weg; turn left onto Rathausstr., and turn right down Ratsbauhof. (Open M-F 9am-6pm, Sa 9am-1pm.) The tourist office also offers two-hour city **tours.** (April-Oct. M-F 2pm, Sa 10am and 2pm, Su 2pm. DM5.) **Die Gerstenbergsche,** Hoher Weg 10 and Rathausstr. 20 (tel. 10 66), offers a limited selection of English-language novels and chairs to lounge in. (Open M-F 9am-7pm, Sa 9am-4pm.) **Internet access** awaits in **@ Il Giornale,** Judenstr. 3. (Open M-Sa 9am-11pm. 40min. connection DM5.) The **post office,** Bahnhofplatz 3-4, is diagonal from the train station. (Open M-F 8am-6pm, Sa 8am-1pm.) The **telephone code** is 05121.

⌨ ACCOMMODATIONS. Hildesheim's pastoral **Jugendherberge (HI),** Schirrmanweg 4 (tel. 427 17; fax 478 47), perches on the edge of a bucolic farm with a gorgeous view of the city. There's a backyard disco for the *Schulkinder,* and fruit candies will be placed on your blue and white bedding. Take bus #1 (direction: "Himmelsthür") to "Dammtor." There, switch to bus #4 (direction: "Bockfeld") to "Triftstr." Cross the street and climb uphill (10min.) to the hostel. (DM21, over 26 DM23. Sheets DM5.70. Breakfast included. Reception M-Sa 8-9:30am, 5-7pm, and 9:45-10pm, Su 6-7pm and 9:45-10pm. Check-out 10am. Curfew 10pm, but key available with an ID.) In a less picturesque residential neighborhood rests **Maria Schröder's Pension,** Bleckenstedter Str. 2 (tel. 434 21; fax 227 67 12 27 67). From the train station, take bus #3 (direction: "Hildesheimer Wald") to "Schützenwiese"; cross the street and you'll find Bleckenstedterstr. right across from the police station. Ample rooms with plush sofas will have you feeling like a million *Marks,* but you'll only spend DM55. (Breakfast included.)

▣▣▣ FOOD, ENTERTAINMENT, AND NIGHTLIFE. Hildesheim has a diverse culinary scene, with plenty of variety and reasonable prices. From Bahnhofplatz, to the far right, savvy shoppers enjoy **Plus Supermarkt,** Hannoversche Str. 28. (Open M-F 8am-7pm, Sa 8am-2pm.) The **Amsthausstuben,** Markt 7 (tel. 323 23), serves German dishes from DM14. (Open daily from 10am, kitchen 11:30am-10pm.) For fresh vegetarian fare, check out **Scheidemann's Salad & Toast Bar,** Osterstr. 18 (tel. 390 04), a stand-up café with over 20 salads to choose from, DM7.50-14.50. Sandwiches cost DM4-7, pizzas DM5-8. Meat dishes are available, too. (Open M-F 9am-9pm, Sa 10am-2pm.) **Paulaner im Kneip,** Marktstr. 4 (tel. 360 13), offers a piece of Munich in Hildesheim. Lunch dishes start at DM6.80, but the real draw is the beer—sweet *Münchener* Paulaner (0.5L DM5.80; *Maß* DM10.50). After happy hour (M-F 5-7pm; 0.3L beer DM2.50), some may want to take a quick swim in the nearby Rathaus fountain. *Some.* (Open daily 10am-midnight). Opened in 1999, the **Theaterhaus Hildesheim,** Ostertor 11 (542 76), hosts visiting theater and dance companies, plays artsy flics, and stages concerts. The students in the area get down at **Vier Linden,** Alfelder Str. 55b (tel. 252 55), a hip dance-mecca with a popular bar. The first Saturday of every month is "Independence Night": they won't play anything you can hear on the radio. What *do* they play? Cool man. It's cool. (Club open M and Th 10pm-3am; bar open W-Su 6pm-1am.) The Irish *Kneipe* **Limerick,** Klaperhagen 6 (tel. 13 38 76), has lunch specials (11am-4pm; DM9-13), omelettes (DM8-13) and British draughts. (Open M-Th and Su 11am-1am.) For more information on nightlife, check out the free magazine *Public.*

🔅 **SIGHTS.** Hildesheim is a city of many churches, and the best way to see all of them is to follow the **Rosenroute** (rose path), a do-it-yourself tour of spray-painted white blossoms that wends around town. The tourist office has an English guide (DM2). Ludwig's favorite chapel, the **Annenkapelle,** and the famous *Tausendjähriger Rosenstock* bush are featured in the Dom's courtyard. (Open M-Sa 9:30am-5pm, Su noon-5pm. Courtyard DM0.50, children and students DM0.30.) The **Dom-Museum** and **Domschatz** (tel. 17 91 63), around to your left as you exit the Dom, showcases the Marian relic of old Ludwig—it's #8 on the *Schlacht bei Dinklar* exhibit—and other ecclesiastical goodies. (Open Tu-Sa 10am-5pm, Su noon-5pm. DM4, students DM1.50.) The **Marktplatz** is a plaza of reconstructed half-timbered buildings and archways featuring the majestic **Knochenhaueramtshaus** (butcher's guild house), reputed to be the "most beautiful wooden structure in the world." The facade is lavishly decorated with colorful paintings and German proverbs (e.g., *Arm oder reich, der Tod macht alles gleich*—"poor or rich, death treats all the same"). South of the city center at the intersection of Gelber Stern (Yellow Star) and Lappenberg lie the remains of Hildesheim's **synagogue.** The temple was torched on *Kristallnacht* in 1938, and a memorial has been placed on the site.

Looping back around the western tip of the city by way of buses #1, 4, 5, 13, or 33 to "Museum," drop in at the **Römer- und Pelizaeus-Museum,** Am Steine 1 (tel. 936 90), featuring a colorful collection of Egyptian art and artifacts as well as frequent and extensive special exhibits related to ancient cultures. Renovations and special exhibits mean prices and hours are in constant flux; call for information. (Usually open Tu-Su 9am-4:30pm. DM12, students DM9.)

BODENWERDER

In the land of Baron von Münchhausen, the legendary King of Liars, you might not be sure what to believe. It is said that the baron first related his fabulous tales of flying to the moon and navigating an ocean of milk to a cheese isle here, on the banks of the Weser. And it would seem likely that the baron himself is an elaborate fabrication of Bodenwerder's tourist industry, an attempt to out-fable Hameln, except that the little town's church ledgers have birth and death listings for Baron Hieronymus Carolus Friedericus von Münchhausen.

🔃 **PRACTICAL INFORMATION.** Bodenwerder is best reached by bus from Stadtoldendorf, a town on the Altenbeken-Braunschweig train line. Take bus #520 (direction: "Bodenwerder/Hameln") or #523 (direction: "Kemnade") to "Weserbrücke, Bodenwerder." From Hameln, take bus #520 (direction: "Stadtoldendorf"). The BahnCard entitles you to a 50% discount on these routes. Rent **bikes** from **Karl-Heinz Greef,** Danziger Str. 20. (Tel. 33 34. Open March-Oct. daily 8:30am-6pm. DM10 per day.) The **tourist office,** Weserstr. 3 (tel. 405 41; fax 61 52) hands out *Weg und Fähre,* which lists events. (Open M-F 9am-12:30pm and 2:30-6pm, Sa 9am-1pm; closed Sa Nov.-March.) **Tours** meet in front of the office (May-Sept. W at 3pm. DM3). The **post office,** 37619 Bodenwerder, is located across the street from the Rathaus. (Open M-F 8:30am-noon and 2:30-5pm, Sa 8:30-11:30am.) The **telephone code** is 05533.

🔃 **ACCOMMODATIONS AND CAMPING.** The tourist office prints a list of hotels and **private rooms** available for rent (from DM25). Bodenwerder's **Jugendherberge (HI),** Richard-Schirmann-Weg (tel. 26 85; fax 62 03), is a 15-minute walk from the pedestrian zone, but the last 100m is steep, steep, steep. Walk across the Weser and turn left, then right on Siemensstr., and follow the signs up Unter dem Berge. The institutional exterior conceals a fun-filled interior brimming with *Fußball* and ping-pong. (6-bed dorms DM20, over 26 DM25. Breakfast included. Lunch DM8.70, dinner DM6.80. Sheets DM5.70. Reception 4-7pm and 9:30-10pm. Curfew 10pm, but you can get a key to the side door.) The **Campingplatz und Gasthaus Rühler Schweiz,** Großes Tal (tel. 28 27 or 28 23), are located on the Weser, south of the Altstadt on the opposite side of the river. Cross the Weserbrücke and make a right on the path by the river. All rooms have showers and bathrooms. (Reception daily 2-6pm. Open March-Oct.)

FOOD AND ENTERTAINMENT. Bodenwerder's culinary offerings are nothing shocking: pizza, baked goods, ice cream. **Café König**, Große Str. 32 (tel. 4855), serves it up with style and a great view of the pedestrian zone. Most entrees run DM6-10, beer DM2.20-5. (Open daily 7am-6pm). For **groceries** check out **Rewe**, just across the Weserbrücke from the post office. (Open M-F 8am-8pm, Sa 8am-4pm.) Once a month, a **play** in the spa gardens reenacts Münchhausen's exploits (May-Oct. First Su of the month at 3pm. Free). On the second Saturday of August, Bodenwerder sets the Weser ablaze with its pyrotechnic **festival of lights.**

SIGHTS. On Münchhausplatz, the mansion-turned-**Rathaus,** the Baron's birthplace, holds the **Münchhausenzimmer und Heimatmuseum** (tel. 405 41). Inside, you'll find color illustrations of his exploits along with the legendary pistol with which he shot his horse off a steeple. (Open after April, 10am-noon and 2-5pm. DM2, children DM1.20.) The streets lining the pedestrian zone are riddled with 114 half-timbered houses; the oldest dot Königstr, Homburgstr., and Große Str. Farther up the pedestrian zone is a beautiful fountain depicting three of the baron's most outrageous adventures.

BRAUNSCHWEIG

Now that Braunschweig's Cold War border town duties are over, this middleweight city is pumping up its cultural attractions. The history of Braunschweig (sometimes called "Brunswick" in English) began in 1166, when Heinrich der Löwe (Henry the Lion) settled here. After hanging up his hat, Heinrich set about building a kingdom: he erected the famous Braunschweig lion statue (now the city's emblem), built Burg Dankwarderode, the castle around it, and inaugurated Braunschweig's metamorphosis into a thriving religious and commercial center. The town is saturated with gargantuan cathedrals and other monuments that once marked the free city's economic importance to the Holy Roman Empire. A former member of the Hanseatic League, Braunschweig now boasts a robust economy, which, combined with its brash bids for tourism, make it one of Niedersachsen's most vital cities.

GETTING THERE AND GETTING AROUND

Trains: Braunschweig lies on the main line between Hannover and Berlin. Trains roll frequently to Hannover (45min., 2 per hour, DM16.40), Magdeburg (45min., 2 per hour, DM29), and Berlin (1¼hr., 1 per hour, DM84).

Public Transportation: A thorough system of **streetcars** and **buses** laces Braunschweig and its environs, which comprise 3 zones. Braunschweig proper is zone 1, Wolfenbüttel (see p. 491) and suburbs make up zone 2, and even farther out, suburbia comprises zone 3. For info on routes, call 194 49; for times and ticket prices, call 383 27 10. A 90-min. ticket, valid for any number of transfers, costs DM2.80, or buy two for DM5. A daypass costs DM7, and a family day ticket (valid for up to 2 adults and 3 kids) costs DM9. Pick up a free, credit card-sized **map** at the booth in front of the train station or at the tourist offices. Most buses make their final run around 10:30pm. Fortunately, a system of **night buses** (NachtExpress), 15 in all, centered at the Rathaus stop, will get your inebriated butt where it needs to go (2 per hour, M-Th 10:30pm-12:30am, F until 1:30am, Sa-Su until 2:30 am).

Bike Rental: Glockmann + Sohn, Ölschlägern 29-30 (tel. 469 23), in the Magniviertel, off of Am Magnitor. Open M-F 9am-6:30pm, Sa 9am-1pm.

Car Rental: Europcar, Berliner Pl. 3 (tel. 24 49 80; fax 244 98 66), across from the train station, under the pink *Hotel Mercure* sign on the left. Open M-F 7:30am-6pm, Sa 8am-noon, Su 9-11am.

Mitfahrbüro, Wollmarkt 3 (tel. 194 40), matches riders and drivers. Walk to the northern tip of the pedestrian zone and up Alte Waage, which turns into Wollmarkt. Open M-F 10am-6pm, Sa 10am-2pm.

Taxis: Tel. 555 55, 666 66, 59 91, or 621 21. Call 444 44 for **Frauennacht-Taxi** (women's taxi).

🔢 ORIENTATION AND PRACTICAL INFORMATION

Braunschweig hunkers like a dozing lion between the Lüneburger Heide and the Harz Mountains. The Hauptbahnhof sits southeast of the city center, which is essentially an island ringed by the **Oker** river. Walking straight from the train station brings you across Berliner Platz to **Kurt-Schumacher-Str,** with a major S-Bahn line cutting down its center. This street curves to the left to meet **John-F.-Kennedy-Platz,** a major crossroad at the southeast corner of the central city. Following Auguststr. northwest from JFK-Platz leads to **Ägidienmarkt,** which brings you to **Bohlweg,** the wide street that is the eastern boundary of the main pedestrian zone. Turn left at Langer Hof to get to the Rathaus. Braunschweig's downtown attractions are mostly within this great circle, formed by the branching Oker. Streetcars and buses criss-cross the city; most lines pass through either the "Rathaus/Bohlweg" stops (downtown) or "JFK-Platz/K.-Schumacher-Str." stops (a 10min. walk from the train station). Streetcars #1 and 2 from the station head to all these stops.

Tourist Office: There are 2 tourist offices in town; one is inside the train station (open M-F 8:30am-5pm, Sa 9am-noon), and the other sits a block from the Rathaus, on Bohlweg (tel. 273 55 30 or 273 55 31; fax 273 55 19; www.braunschweig.de). Open M-F 9:30am-6pm, Sa 9:30am-2pm, Su 9:30am-12:30pm. Both offices find **rooms** in hotels and *Pensionen* for free (DM39 and up), but you can also just get a free copy of the hotel list from them. A range of **tours** (DM4-27) depart from the Bohlweg branch.

Mitwohnbüro: Wollmarkt 3 (tel. 130 00; fax 152 52), in the same office as the Mitfahrbüro (see above). Finds apartments and arranges sublets. Open M-F 10am-6pm, Sa 10am-2pm.

Currency Exchange: Dresdner Bank, at the corner of Neue Str. and Gördelingerstr., near the Altstadtmarkt. **24-hr. ATM.** Open M and F 8:30am-4pm, Tu and Th 8:30am-6pm, W 8:30am-1pm.

Bookstore: Pressezentrum Salzman, in the Burgpassage near the stairs, sells paperback pulp novels, as well as a limited selection of English and American magazines and newspapers. Open M-F 9:30am-8pm, Sa 9am-4pm. Also in the Burgpassage, near the escalators, **Karl Pfannkuch,** Kleine Burg 10, has novels in English, as well as an excellent collection of German classics. Open M-F 9:30am-8pm, Sa 9:30am-4pm.

Library: Öffentliche Bücherei, Hintern Brüdern 23 (tel. 470 68 38), right off Lange Str. Main building open M-Tu and Th-F 10am-7pm, Sa 10am-2pm, but the **foreign language library** is only open Tu noon-6pm and F 11am-4pm.

Emergency: Police, tel. 110. **Ambulance:** 192 22. **Fire,** tel. 112.

Pharmacy: Apotheke am Kennedy-Platz, Auguststr. 19 (tel. 439 55). Open M-F 8:30am-6:30pm, Sa 9am-1pm. **Emergency service** *(Notdienst)* information posted on the door (tel. 440 33).

Post Office: The main office, 38106 Braunschweig, is in the 16-story building to the right of the train station. Open M-F 8am-6pm, Sa 8am-1pm.

Internet Access: In **The Pink Cadillac** (see **Nightlife,** p. 491).

PHONE CODE	0531

▰ ACCOMMODATIONS

Considering the city's size, Braunschweig's budget accommodation cupboard is pretty bare, but what's on the shelves is clean and decently situated. Most affordable *Pensionen* and private rooms require a 10- to 15-minute walk. Pick up a free copy of *Hotels und Gaststätten* at the tourist office; it includes a listing of accommodations and cafés with prices, phone numbers, and city maps.

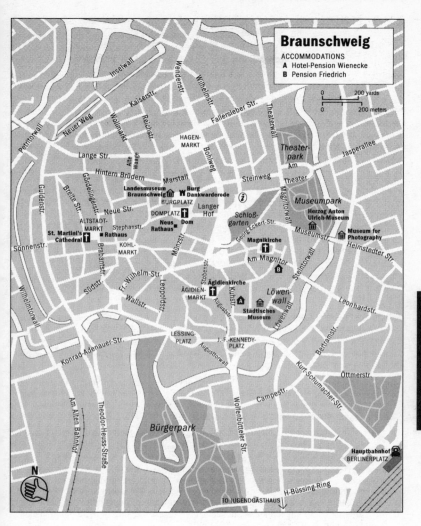

Braunschweig

ACCOMMODATIONS
A Hotel-Pension Wienecke
B Pension Friedrich

Jugendgästehaus (HI), Salzdahlumerstr. 170 (tel. 26 43 20; fax 264 32 70). From the station, take bus #11 (direction: "Mascherode"), or bus #19 (direction "Stöckheim") to "Klinikum Salzdahlumerstr." The hostel is across from the train station, on the left. By foot, walk left from the station on Berliner Pl. to H.-Büssing-Ring, turn left on Salzdahl-umerstr. and go under the overpass. Continue for 10min. A ways from town, the anti-septic buildings contain bright, spacious rooms, a huge backyard with little white pavilions, and kitchen facilities. DM18.50-37, depending on the number of bunks and bathroom facilities; over 26 DM22.50-37. Members only. Breakfast DM7. Sheets included. Key deposit DM30. Reception 7-10am and 4-10pm in the separate building on the left, through the little green metal gate.

Hotel-Pension Wienecke, Kuhstr. 14 (tel. 464 76; fax 464 64). From the station, walk up Kurt-Schumacher-Str. to JFK-Platz, bear right onto Auguststr. and then Kuhstr. (15min.).

Quiet, comfortable rooms on a pedestrian street near the city center with big windows, private bathrooms, and TVs. Singles DM79-86, with bath DM89-99; doubles with bath DM125-145; apartments for 1-4 people DM95-220. Breakfast buffet included.

Pension Friedrich, Am Magnitor 5 (tel. 417 28). In the Magniviertel, right by the Städtisches Museum. Cozy, with steep stairs in tight hallways. Singles are plain, but airy; doubles on the top floor are luxurious. TV and stereo in all rooms. DM60-80.

⬛ FOOD

A plethora of bars and *Imbiße* along **Bohlweg** proffer pizzas, salads, soups, and small sandwiches at reasonable prices. There's a produce market in the Altstadt every Wednesday and Saturday 8am-1:30pm. The **Kohlmarkt** area, southeast of the Altstadtmarkt in the city center, is a bustling, open space with many pleasant (though not terribly cheap) cafés and restaurants. The **Magniviertel's** winding streets, boutiques, and half-timbered houses provide a great setting for a meal or drink. Several malls—the **Burgpassage Galerie, Weltenhof,** and **City Point**—also have excellent food stands. **Atlantik's Früchtchen,** in the Burgpassage Galerie mall, is a fruit stand with frequent sales and unbelievably low prices (open M-F 10am-8pm, Sa 10am-4pm); and **Gemüse-Paradies,** in City Point, has delicious salads (DM2-5) and baked potatoes. (DM4.90-5.90. Open M-F 9am-8pm, Sa 9am-4pm, Su 11am-6pm.) Two supermarkets are at the ready on Porschestr. near the Ägidienmarkt: the run of the mill **Aldi,** Porschestr. 10 (open M-F 9am-6:30pm and Sa 8am-1pm); and next door, the more exotic **A. Chau,** an Asian specialty market that also has the basics. (Open M-F 9:30am-7pm, Sa 9am-4pm.)

Tolle Knolle, Stobenstr. 15-16 (tel. 437 33), near the "Bohlweg/Damm" stop. Potato soups (DM3.50-5.50), potato omelettes (DM8-9), potato salads (DM4-8), baked potatoes (DM4-14). Mr. Potato Head and his family appear on the menu, reminding you just who it is cheerfully sacrificing their lives to bring you lunch and dinner. Open M-F and Su 11:30am-3pm and 5:30-10pm.

Delicato, Münzstr. 9 (tel. 40 07 16), 3 blocks from Burgpl., protruding from the corner of Münzstr. and Kattreppeln. A top-notch Turkish specialty deli with colorful salads, hot lamb, vegetable dishes, and fresh-baked lasagna. Everything sold by weight; a plateful costs around DM10. Open M-F 9am-8pm, Sa 9am-4pm.

Vegetarisches Vollwert-Restaurant Brodocz, Stephanstr. 1 (tel. 422 36), across from the Karstadt perfume department, will help clear clogged arteries with vegetarian meals. Serves a delectable daily menu with salad, main course, and dessert (DM15). Daily specials DM8.50. Open M-Sa 11am-11pm, Su 3-10pm.

Café MM, Kuhstr. 6 (tel. 422 44), near Hotel-Pension Wienecke, offers omelettes (DM6.80-10.50), salads (DM6-11.50), and exciting pastabilities (DM6.80-10.50). The ritzy sidewalk bistro has Manet's café scenes recreated in a kind of meta-mural inside. Open M-Th and Su 9am-midnight, F-Sa 9am-2am.

TOUCHDOWN ON THE TENTH MERIDIAN

Braunschweig was the site of the first-ever European soccer match in 1874, and since then it's been an extremely vigorous and athletic town. Within the last decade, Braunschweig's seemingly endless sporting energy has been channeled into an American favorite: football. Yes, American football. In 1997, the Braunschweig *Lions* (name courtesy of Heinrich der Löwe) dominated the German bowl, bringing the coveted trophy home to their stadium north of the city. Encouraged by victory, they've been clashing shoulder pads even more fiercely ever since.

NIEDERSACHSEN

⚙ SIGHTS

All of Braunschweig was once crowded on a small island surrounded by offshoots of the Oker; the streams now form a slim moat around the Altstadt. Braunschweig's medieval sights ring the cobbled **Burgplatz,** at the center of which the city's (and Heinrich's) emblem, a **bronze lion,** stands guard. Heinrich's leonine symbol of regional dominance was first cast in 1166, as Braunschweig was positioning itself as a commercial center.

DOM ST. BLASI. One of Heinrich's architectural projects, the Dom looms at the southwest corner of the city center. In 1173, Heinrich oversaw the destruction of the tiny wooden church on the spot and the beginning of the Dom's construction, a project that would take another 22 years. The finished basilica shows only one telltale sign of its inheritance: a wooden crucifix above the Nave. Fast-fading frescoes color the ceiling and archways of the interior, illustrating the lives of Christ, Mary, John the Baptist, and Thomas of Canterbury. Below in the gloomy granite **crypt** rest the sarcophagi of Heinrich and his consort Mathilde. *(Dom open daily 10am-5pm. Crypt DM2.)*

DANKWARDERODE. The original Braunschweig lion has retreated to the castle's confines on the east side of Burgplatz. Originally Heinrich's 12th-century den, it now keeps priests' vestments and altar pieces (see **Museums,** below).

NEUES RATHAUS. A textbook example of the neo-Gothic style, the 1900 edifice boasts jutting spires, golden sandstone walls, russet roof tiles—the works. *(Take streetcar #1 or 2 to "Rathaus" from the train station; or walk (15min.) along Kurt-Schumacher-Str., then bear right at JFK-Platz. through Ägidienmarkt onto Bohlweg.)*

ALTSTADT-RATHAUS. The Burg and Dom lie at the eastern border of the pedestrian zone; at the western edge of the Altstadtmarkt the old town hall spreads its gray stone facade, peopled by statuettes of Braunschweig's sovereigns eternally surveying the marketplace.

DOM ST. MARTINI. Built concurrently with the Dom St. Blasi, the cathedral's magnificently ornamented interior includes an altar decorated with sculptures of the Wise and Foolish Virgins, who look like they carry larger than life Martini glasses. The story says that they were waiting for their grooms in the dark; the smarter bunch had enough lamp oil, and the less cerebrally gifted, well, didn't, and will thus continue to practice the safest form of safe sex. *(Next door to the Altstadt-Rathaus. Open Tu-F 10am-1pm and 3-5pm, Sa 10am-5pm, Su 10am-noon and 3-5pm. Free.)*

ST. ÄGIDIENKIRCHE. If your ecclesiastical hunger is not yet satiated, check out the spectacular St. Ägidien church and neighboring monastery, just up Auguststr. from JFK–Platz at the highest geographic spot in the Altstadt. The church of the former Benedictine monastery was built in the 13th century and is the only Gothic cathedral in town. The courtyard behind the church holds a trio of tall, mossy statues of Heinrich and some of his contemporaries, as well as some leaning tombstones. The monastery has been converted into the Jüdisches Museum (see **Museums,** below).

LÖWENWALL. Possibly the most relaxing place in Braunschweig, the Löwenwall is an oval-shaped park in the eastern part of the Innenstadt, near the Städtisches Museum. The obelisk, flanked by lions and two splashing fountains, is a monument to the city nobles who died in the Napoleonic Wars. *(Walk up Kurt-Schumacher-Str. from the train station; the Löwenwall will be on your right just before you reach JFK-Platz.)*

MAGNIVIERTEL. Braunschweig's friendliest social center is lined with pale cobblestoned streets and cafés centered around the **Magnikirche.** The quarter features the only half-timbered houses in Braunschweig, which escaped destruction in WWII and have been well-preserved since.

🏛 MUSEUMS

If you're planning to do a run of Braunschweig's museums in one day, you may want to purchase a **Braunschweiger Museumsverbund Tageskarte,** a day pass valid at all museums that is available at all museum desks and tourist offices (DM10).

HERZOG-ANTON-ULRICH-MUSEUM. This was the first European museum to open its doors to the general public. Its galleries are papered with Dutch masterpieces, including works by van Dyck, Vermeer, Rubens, and Rembrandt. Also holds a large collection of etchings and European decorative art. *(Museumstr. 1. Tel. 484 24 00. From the pedestrian zone, walk across Bohlweg and down Georg-Eckert-Str., which turns into Museumstr.; or ride streetcar #5 to "Museumstr." Open Tu and Th-Su 10am-5pm, W 1-8pm. DM5, students DM3.)*

DANKWARDERODE. Contains a museum which houses medieval goodies from Ulrich's collection and the original Braunschweig lion (see p. 489). The newly renovated **Rittersaal** (knights' hall) dazzles with its golden technicolor paintings. *(Burgpl. Tel. 484 24 00. Museum open Tu and Th-Su 11am-5pm, W 1-2:30pm and 4-8pm. Rittersaal open Tu and Th-Su 10-11am, W 2:30-4pm. DM5, students DM2.50.)*

🖼LANDESMUSEUM BRAUNSCHWEIG. This museum has several branches in town, and one in neighboring Wolfenbüttel. The main collection is here in the **Vieweg-Haus.** Among its treasures are another copy of the bronze lion (surprise!), an entire room full of Biedermaier furniture, love letters from the 1880s, little Nazi toy soldiers (including an angry man with a puny dark mustache), and a 1960s living room rimmed with avocados. *(Burgpl. 1. Tel. 484 26 02. To the left of the Dom. Open Tu-W and F-Su 10am-5pm, Th 10am-8pm. DM5, students DM2.50.)*

JÜDISCHES MUSEUM. Another branch of the Landesmuseum, the Jewish museum's reconstruction of the main room of the old synagogue is a disturbing complement to memorials to victims of the Holocaust. The synagogue's furniture and altar are authentic, rescued from the deteriorating building. *(Hinter Ägidien. Tel. 484 25 59. Open Tu-W and F-Su 10am-5pm, Th 10am-8pm. DM5, students DM3.50; free entry with ticket from main museum, and vice versa.)*

STÄDTISCHES MUSEUM. A specialized "domestic museum"; holdings include historical originals of furniture, appliances, living room bric-a-brac, and the world's first motorcycle. *(Löwenwall 16. Tel. 470 45 05. Open Tu-F and Su 10am-1pm.)*

🖼MUSEUM FOR PHOTOGRAPHY. The collection of photographs is small but diverse and hosts exhibitions featuring a single artist's work almost every month. Nifty old cameras and photo albums are also on display. *(Helmstedter Str. 1. Tel. 750 00. Just down Museumstr. from the Ulrich museum, or take bus #13 or 43 to "Steintor". Open Tu-F 1-6pm, Sa-Su 2-6pm. DM5, students DM3.)*

🎵🎭 ENTERTAINMENT AND NIGHTLIFE

The high-water marks of Braunschweig's theatrical scene were stained in 1772 with the first performance of Lessing's *Emilia Galotti*, and in 1829 with the premiere of Goethe's *Faust*. The monumental **Staatstheater** (tel. 123 40) built in the Florentine Renaissance style, was erected in 1861 to replace the old theater hall. The **Großes Haus,** Am Theater (tel. 484 28 00) is only one of three stages run by the state theater; the other two are the **Kleines Haus,** Magnitorwall 18 (tel. 484 28 00), and the **Theaterspielplatz,** Hinter der Magnikirche 6a (tel. 484 27 97). The Großes Haus plays big-name operas, ballets and musicals (DM8-51) and orchestral concerts (DM19-45); the Kleines Haus and Theaterspielplatz have everything from Goethe to David Mamet to modern dance (DM6-35). Call 500 01 41 for information. (Tickets at the Großes Haus available M-F 10am-6:30pm, Sa 10am-1pm.) The **LOT Theater,** Kaffeetwete 4a (tel. 173 03), is the home of the local avant-garde theater company. Walk up Gördelingerstr. from the Altstadtmarkt. (Box office open M-F

11am-2pm. Tickets DM13-20.) The **Stadthalle**, Leonhardpl. (tel. 707 07), is home to the **Braunschweiger Staatsorchester,** the city orchestra. There are a lot of movie theaters in Braunschweig; **Lupe,** Gördelingerstr. 7 (tel. 493 11), and **Broadway,** Kalenwall 3 (tel. 455 42), show artsy films. Pick up a copy of the free magazine *Filmtips* for a movie schedule.

Braunschweig has several free monthly magazines offering the skinny on local events: *Subway, Da Capo,* and *Cocktail.* It's telling that these magazines sometimes direct readers to cities as far away as Hamburg; still, the Braunschweig scene heats up to a steady simmer on weekends. The most lively area is the square formed by the intersection of **Sack, Vor der Burg,** and **Schuhstr.,** as well as **Neue Str.** nearby. The **Magniviertel** brims with cafés, bars, and genuine Braunschweig charm.

Movie, Neue Str. 2 (tel. 437 26), is a pop music-themed bar. Lots of beer on tap, cheap food (2 *Wieners* DM4.50), and rock and blues constitute the "feature presentation." Open daily 9am-2am.

Pupasch-Kneipe, Neue Str. 10-12 (tel. 445 61), just down the street from Movie. They're *die total verrückte Kneipe* ("the totally crazy bar"). Friendly service, lots of beer, and menus with space cut out for your nose, eyes, and mouth—don the happy mask and become a new person for the night! Open M-Th and Su noon-midnight, F-Sa noon-4am.

The Jolly Joker, Broitzemerstr. 220 (tel. 281 46 60). Bus #5, 6, or 19 to "Broitzemerstr." This titanic joint holds a large dance floor, six bars, a *Biergarten,* a cheap restaurant (fast-food meals DM5), and a Brechtian movie theater that offers a bar and pop flicks. W and Sa disco nights. Open M 9:30pm-2am, Tu and Th 9:30pm-2:30am, F-Sa 9pm-4am. Cover DM3; movies free.

The Pink Cadillac, Breite Str. 23 (tel. 416 61), just off the Altstadt Markt, has pool tables, a pink interior, and sporadic **internet access** (DM15 per hour). Open M-Th 6pm-midnight, F-Sa 6pm-2am, Su 4pm-midnight.

Flexx Treff, Leopoldstr. 38 (tel. 240 49 50). A place with a jukebox for the young, the hip, and the economically savvy. Mixed drinks DM3.50; 2-for-1 cocktails W 7-9pm. Breakfast from 6am (DM5). Open M-Th 4pm-2am, F 4pm-3am, Sa 6am-late, Su 6am-2pm.

WOLFENBÜTTEL

Just a few kilometers from Braunschweig lies Wolfenbüttel, its pretty little sister city. Hop on bus #21 from Braunschweig's Hauptbahnhof, or take a 10min. train ride. Most of Wolfenbüttel's Baroque-era architecture remains intact. Though a few of the city's old half-timbered houses show their age, the dominant aura is one of well-kept prosperity; welcoming vibes swell from the Schloßplatz, the riverside enclave within the city that features shady lawns and a circle of brightly colored historical attractions. Wolfenbüttel's medieval streets, red-tiled houses, and the occasional canal provide the quintessential German experience. And although the town attracts plenty of visitors, it retains a feeling of authenticity.

🖪 **PRACTICAL INFORMATION.** The Wolfenbüttel **tourist office** is at Rosenwall 1 (tel. 29 83 46; fax 29 83 47). From the station, head left on Bahnhofstr., and make a left onto Schulwall. Turn right onto Löwenstr., and bear left on Krambuden, going over the little bridge; the street straight ahead is Rosenwall, and the tourist office is around the corner, on the right. They lack a private room-finding service, but they book **rooms** in hotels for free and lead **tours** from the gateway of the Schloß. (DM5, under 14 free. Office open M-F 9am-12:30pm and 2-4pm, April-Oct. also Sa 9am-1pm. Tours April-Dec. Sa 2:30pm and Su 11am; Oct.-March Su 11am.) A **branch** of the tourist office is located at Stadtmarkt 9, open the same hours. Wolfenbüttel's **postal code** is 38300. The **telephone code** is 05331.

🖪🖪 **ACCOMMODATIONS AND FOOD.** Wolfenbüttel has a first-rate **Jugendgästehaus,** Jägerstr. 17 (tel. 271 89; fax 90 24 45). From the train station, go right and then head left on Bahnhofstr. and take a left at Schulwall. Continue on the same street when you reach Schloßplatz; you'll cross a little river and end up on Dr.-Heinrich-Jasper-Str. Make a left at Jägerstr (10 min.). The *Haus* has stellar rooms with lots of space and new furniture. (DM24, over 25 DM30. Full pension DM33, over 25 DM44. Breakfast included. Sheets DM3. Bikes DM5 per day or DM10 per week. Free canoe rental.) **Krambuden** and **Lange Herzogstr.**, just off the center of the Stadtmarkt, have many fruit stands and bakeries. The **Altstadt-Bistro**, Okerstr. 8 (tel. 10 88) serves lasagna (DM6), "Hawaii-Pizza" (DM4), and lots of other goodies. They deliver, too. (Open daily 10:30am-10pm.) Down the street, a **Kaiser's supermarket** sells inexpensive foodstuffs. (Open M-W 8:30am-7pm, Th-F 8:30am-8pm, Sa 8am-4pm.) While in Wolfenbüttel, don't miss the delicious coconut macaroons (DM1.20) served in bakeries around town. Resist the temptation to chew on the houses, though.

■ **SIGHTS.** The board game "Candyland" was clearly inspired by some sugar-obsessed American's visit to Wolfenbüttel—the pink **Trinitatiskirche** in the Holzmarkt (open Tu 11am-1pm, W 11am-1pm and 2-4pm, Th 3-5pm, Sa 11am-4pm), the wildly tilting half-timbered houses of the inner city, and the chancellery look like the results of architects fighting over the gingerbread man. The **Kanzlei**, Kanzleistr. 3 (tel. 270 71), which extends from the Stadtmarkt, can only be described as an absurd castle. With red walls and a bizarre metal statue perched outside, it defies architectural jargon. The chancellery houses the pre-history collection of the **Landesmuseum Braunschweig**—rocks, fossils, primitive tools, and the like. (Open Tu-F and Su 10am-5pm. DM5, students DM2.50.)

Once a stately, pure-white vision, the ducal **Schloß** (tel. 57 13) has been repainted in crimson with gray trim. The castle has the foundation of a 13th-century fortress of the Guelphs, but its current appearance is pure Baroque with a beautifully proportioned 17th-century clock tower and a ring of nymphs around it. The **Schloßmuseum** displays restored rooms from the ducal living quarters; be sure to view the ceilings. (Museum and castle interior open Tu-Sa 10am-5pm, Su 10am-1pm. Museum DM3.) Open-air performances take place in the Schloß's enclosed courtyard nearly every day from mid-June to mid-July; musicals, choral performances, chamber music concerts, jazz shows, and ballets are all on offer. Tickets are available at the *Braunschweiger Zeitung* office in Wolfenbüttel, Löwenstr. 6 (tel. 800 10).

Across the street from the Schloß is the yellow **Lessinghaus** (tel. 80 80), a compact mansion that was the local duke's gift to big-time *litterateur* **Gotthold Ephraim Lessing,** the court librarian of the nearby August-Bibliothek. The **museum** inside recalls Lessing's life and work through manuscripts, letters, and paintings, but beautiful moldings are what make it worthwhile. (Open Tu-Su 10am-5pm.) Behind the Lessinghaus, the stern **Herzog-August-Bibliothek** (tel. 80 82 14) guards a priceless collection of medieval and Renaissance books. Under the loving care of bookworm Duke August, the library became the largest in Europe. A series of medieval manuscripts culminates with a facsimile of the famous **Braunschweiger Evangelier,** a kaleidoscopically illuminated gospel drawn up in the late 12th century at the request of Henry the Lion; the state of Niedersachsen shelled out millions for the manuscript in 1983. The original is locked safely away. Also worth checking out are miniature oil portraits of Martin Luther and his wife, Katharin von Bora. (Open Tu-Su 10am-5pm.) Across from the castle is the 17th-century **Zeughaus,** whose high-gabled facade belies its former role as an armory. It now serves as a library annex holding the other half of the Herzog-August collection. (Open M-F 8am-8pm, Sa 9am-1pm.) The two libraries and the Lessinghaus sell combination tickets valid at all three sights. (DM6, students DM4, under 19 DM2, family DM12.) The city's other major sight, the **Hauptkirche Beate Mariae Virgins,** raises its spires across town in the Heinrichstadt section. A jutting four-faced clock tower and life-sized statues of saints grace the church's exterior. (Open Tu-Sa 10am-noon and 2-4pm. Suggested donation DM1.)

LÜNEBURGER HEIDE (LÜNEBURG HEATH)

Between the Elbe and Aller rivers stretches the shrub-covered Lüneburger Heide. The symbolic power of the heath is evidenced by many German literary greats: the delicate *Heideröslein* (wild rose) found a role in one of Goethe's *Lieder*, while Heine charmingly compared one lady's bosom to the "flat and bleakly desolate" landscape of the *Heide*. The undulating countryside moves quickly back and forth from farm to forest; green gives way to purple from July to September, when the bushes flower. If you want to see the grassy *Heide* during the flowering season, but would prefer not to sleep on it, put down the book and make reservations now. All of Germany comes here to bike, hike, motor, and otherwise frolic in the late summer. The most important regional towns are **Lüneburg** and **Celle**. In Lüneburg, the **Fremdenverkehrsverband Lüneburger Heide**, Barckhausenstr. 35 (tel. (04131) 737 30; fax 426 06), finds rooms in remote hamlets barely on the map. The staff also provide information on the Heide's *Heu-Hotels* (hay hotels), functioning barns with rooms that farmers rent out to travelers for around DM20. They're called hay hotels because that's where you sleep (bring a sleeping bag). But all have showers and toilets, and many are surprisingly luxurious. Extensive and detailed maps outline the *Heide's* 10 major bike tours. Tour 5, the 350km **Heide-Rundtour,** is the most comprehensive, passing through both Celle and Lüneburg.

LÜNEBURG

Perhaps because there is no salt-god, or perhaps because the name Salzburg was already taken, Lüneburg derives its name from the moon-goddess Luna. Regardless, this is a city built literally and figuratively on salt. The city made a 13th-century fortune with its stores of "white gold." The citizens' salt monopoly held Northern Europe in an iron grip until plague and war struck the town in the 1620s. Although "salt shocks" no longer pose a threat to the world economy, and Lüneburg's wealth and power have faded, neither the salt nor the town are obsolete. The salt is channeled into the city's famed rejuvenating baths, and the town, with its Gothic brick Altstadt and elegant half-timbered houses, retains its ancient grace. It was in Lüneburg that native poet Heinrich Heine penned one of Germany's greatest and most melancholic Romantic poems, the *Lorelei*.

🛈 ORIENTATION AND PRACTICAL INFORMATION. Lüneburg serves as the transportation center of the Heide. By train, the city lies between Hamburg (40min., 4 per hour, DM14.80) and Hannover (1hr., 1 per hour, DM35). Rent **bikes** at **Zweirad Altendorf** (tel. 557 77), next to the train station. (Open daily 9am-6pm. DM10 per day. DM200 deposit and ID required.) The **tourist office,** Am Markt (tel. 30 95 93 or 322 00; fax 30 95 98; www.lueneburg.de), in the Rathaus, books **rooms.** From the train station, head downhill away from the post office, take a left on Lünertorstr., and turn left on Bardowicker Str. at the end. (Open July-Aug. M-F 9am-7pm, Sa-Su 9am-4pm; May-June M-F 9am-6pm, Sa-Su 9am-1pm; Oct.-April M-F 9am-5pm, Sa-Su 9am-4pm.) Daily **tours** of the Altstadt leave M-F at 11am and Sa-Su at 2pm. (DM5, children DM2.50.) The **post office,** 21332 Lüneburg, is on the corner of Soltauer Str. and Saltztorstr. (Open M-F 8am-6pm, Sa 8am-noon.) **Internet access** is available at Lünestr. 6-7 (tel. 38 04 84) for DM10 per hour. (Open M-F 10am-7pm, Sa 10am-1pm.) The **telephone code** is 04131.

🛏 ACCOMMODATIONS. Hotels fill up rather quickly when the Heide blooms in July through September. At **Jugendherberge Lüneburg (HI),** Soltauer Str. 133 (tel. 418 64; fax 457 47), cheap and charming walk hand in hand. Small rooms have new furnishings and clean floors. Until 7pm during the week and Sunday after 1pm, bus #11 (direction "Rettmer/Hecklingen") runs from the train station to the hostel; get off at

"Scharnhorststr./DJH." During off hours, take bus #7 from "Auf dem Klosterhof" behind the Rathaus to "Ginsterweg," and walk 200m farther along Soltauer Str. Or brace yourself for a long haul from the station (30min.): turn left on Bahnhofstr., right at the bottom onto Altenbrückentorstr., then left onto the very long Berliner Str. Follow the street as it turns into Uelzener Str., make a right at Scharnhorststr., and continue until you meet Soltauer Str. (DM21, over 26 DM26. Breakfast included. Sheets DM5.70. Laundry DM5. Reception until 10pm. Curfew 10pm, but pocket a house key with DM20 deposit. Call ahead.) **Hotel Stadt Hamburg,** Am Sande 25 (tel. 444 38; fax 40 41 98), will put a grin on your face, unlike the dour visages of famous Lüneburgers whose portraits line the staircase. (Singles DM50, with shower DM55; doubles DM80, with shower DM90. Breakfast included. 24hr. reception. Call ahead.)

◨▣▣ **FOOD, ENTERTAINMENT, AND NIGHTLIFE.** The overabundance of salt makes Lüneburgers thirsty—at one time the tiny city was padded with 80 breweries. At **Kronen-Brauerei,** Heiligengeiststr. 39-41 (tel. 71 32 00), imbibe Lüneburg's own Pilsner (DM3.80) in a late 15th-century beer hall. (Open daily 11:30am-10pm.) For cheap food, try the **Mensa** on the university campus next to the hostel, which serves hot breakfasts and dinners. (Open 8:45-10:45am and 11:15am-2:15pm.) The adjacent café, **Building 26,** features live music. (Open M-Th 10am-7pm, F 10am-7pm and from 8pm, Sa only if there's a party, Su 11am-3pm.) Many cafés and nicer restaurants line Schröderstr. During the week, nightlife piles up around the Lünertor bridge, while locals pack the cafés along Am Stintmarkt. Strike it up at **Garage,** Auf der Hude 72 (tel. 358 79). Frequent live acts, raves, and theme parties complement the regular dance scene. (Open W and F-Sa after 10pm. Cover W DM2; F DM2 before 11pm, DM6 thereafter; Sa DM2 before 11pm, DM8 after.) Along with the rest of Germany, Lüneburg celebrates the 250th anniversary of the death of Bach with a **Bach Festival Week** (July 24-30, 2000), featuring concerts and exhibitions.

▨ **SIGHTS.** Legend has it that Lüneburg's salt stores were discovered when a wild boar fell into a pit and, clawing his way out, shook salt loose from his bristles. The **Deutsches Salzmuseum,** Sülfmeisterstr. 1 (tel. 450 65), presents much, *much* more than you ever wanted to know about salt. Did you get the necessary 19 grams today? (Open May-Sept. M-F 9am-5pm, Sa-Su 10am-5pm; Oct.-April daily 10am-5pm. DM6, students and children DM4. Tours M-F at 11am, 12:30, and 3pm; Sa-Su at 11:30am and 3pm. DM1.50, students DM1.) From the Rathaus, take Neue Sülze to Salzstr.; at Lambertiplatz, take the path behind the supermarket. Dine among salt-caked rafters in the attached **salt café.** The **Kloster Lüne** (tel. 523 18), on Domänehof, just over the Lünertor bridge, proudly displays its 15th-century face. (Open April-Oct. M-Sa 10am-12:30pm and 2:30-5pm, Su 11:30am-12:30pm and 2-5pm. DM5.) Side streets with old, ivy-covered houses and boutiques lead to the Gothic **Michaeliskirche** (tel. 314 00), on Johann-Sebastian-Bach-Platz in the Altstadt. The imposing brick, wood, and ceramic church was built in 1418 on a foundation of salt; the massive pillars have warped somewhat since then. Bach was a regular visitor to the church between 1700 and 1702. (Open M-Sa 10am-5pm.) The spire of the **Johanniskirche,** Am Sande (tel. 445 42), soars over the gables of the streets. Late 13th-century walls shelter a Gothic altar and Baroque organ. (Open M-Th 10am-5pm, F 10am-5:30pm, Sa 10am-6pm, Su 9am-5pm.) Lüneburg's other offbeat museums should be taken with a grain of...nevermind. The **Brauereimuseum,** Heiligengeiststr. 39-41 (tel. 410 21), was a working brewery for 500 years until its copper vats became museum pieces in 1985. The museum explains exactly how hops, malt barley, and water make the magic potion that keeps Germany going, going, and gone. (Going Tu-Su 1-4:30pm. Free.)

CELLE

The powerful prince electors of Lüneburg moved to Celle in 1398 after the Lüneburg War of Succession and remained here until 1705 when the last duke croaked. During those 307 years, the royalty lavished funds on their residence, building a massive castle and promoting the city's growth. The well-maintained half-timbered houses that line the streets used to be taxed by the number of crossed diagonal beams on their houses; the beams quickly became coveted status symbols—until the advent of the Mercedes-Benz logo.

7 ORIENTATION AND PRACTICAL INFORMATION. Celle is connected by frequent **trains** to Hannover (35min., 4 per hour, DM12) and Braunschweig (1½hr., 2 per hour, DM30). Rent a **bike** from **Fahrrad Werner,** Kanzielstr. 14 (tel 211 79), near the tourist office. (DM10 per day, ID required. Open M-F 9am-1pm and 3-6pm, Sa 9am-1pm). **The tourist office,** Markt 6 (tel. 12 12; fax 124 59), reserves **rooms** for free and distributes a list of concerts and musical productions. From the train station, walk up Bahnhofstr. as it becomes Westcellertorstr., turn left onto Schloßpl., then take the second right onto Stechbahn, and take the second left onto Markt. Or bus #2 or 3 to "Schloßpl." and follow the signs. (Open May-Oct. M-F 9am-7pm, Sa 10am-4pm, Su 11am-2pm; Nov.-April M-F 9am-5pm, Sa 10am-noon.) **Tours** start from the bridge in front of the Schloß. (April-Oct. W and Sa 2:30pm, Su 11am. Free.) **Bike tours** of the countryside leave Saturdays at 10:30am, call the tourist office for reservations. (June-Sept. DM5.) The **post office,** 03100 Celle, is on Schloßplatz. (Open M-F 8am-6pm, Sa 8am-1pm.) **Internet access** is available for DM5 per 30min. at **Spiel-Treff,** Am Heiligen Kreuz 7. (Open M-Sa 8am-11pm, Su 11am-11pm.) The **telephone code** is 05141.

▌▐ ACCOMMODATIONS AND FOOD. The **Jugendherberge (HI),** Weghausstr. (tel. 532 08; fax 530 05), covered with sky-blue siding (making it hard to see) and conveniently located near an aromatic cow pasture, reaches new levels in barn-chic. From the train station, take bus #3 (direction: "Boye") to "Jugendherberge." Turn left out of the station, walk up the pedestrian path as it becomes Biermannstr., turn left on Bremer Weg, and turn up the first right onto Petersburgstr. (DM21, over 26 DM26. Breakfast included. Sheets DM5.70. Reception until 10pm, but best time for check-in is 5-7pm. Curfew 10pm; house keys available with a DM50 deposit.) Next door at **Pension Luhmannshof,** Dorfstr. 8 (tel. 530 94), a little chocolate on each bed adds a touch of elegance, while rusty farm equipment gives the yard a country image. From Petersburgstr., it's the first building on the right after Weghausstr. (DM55 per person. Breakfast included. Reception until 9pm. Reservations recommended.) **Hotel Blühende Schiffahrt,** Fritzenwiese 39 (tel. 227 61), is considerably closer to the Altstadt. (DM60 per person. Breakfast included. Call ahead.) **Campingplatz Silbersee** (tel. 312 23) lies 7km northeast of the town. Take bus #6 (direction: "Vorwerk") to "Silbersee." (DM5.50 per person.) **Café Fricke,** Neue Str. 14 (tel. 21 49 18), at the intersection with Brandplatz, sets a merry table with Victorian decorations and cooks up crepes from DM5. (Open daily 10:30am-6pm.) **Alex's Antikcafé,** Schuhstr. 6 (tel. 21 75 40) makes its home in a secluded patio off the street, offering cheap, simple food (soup and sandwich combo DM10), and a spectrum of alcohol and coffee. (Open M-Su 9am-6pm.)

◪ SIGHTS. Some of the city's finest half-timbered houses are tucked away on side streets; to find them, wander down any of the smaller streets radiating from Schloßplatz or Großer Platz in the Altstadt. The **oldest house** in the area is at Am Heiligen Kreuz 26. The **Stadtkirche** stands just outside the massive pedestrian zone that dominates the Altstadt. The church tower provides a view of red- and brown-shingled roofs fading into the countryside. (Tower open April-Oct. Tu-Su 10am-noon and 2-4pm. DM2, children DM1.) In the Altstadt, the **Rathaus** is richly wrought in the Weser Renaissance style. Directly across the road, fine figures out of Celle's colorful history mark the hour on the **Glockenspiel.** (Daily at 10, 11am, noon, 3, 4, and 5pm.)

The **Herzogschloß,** Schloßpl. 13 (tel. 123 73), just west of the Altstadt, flaunts foundations that date back to 1292. One of the most renowned residents of the castle was Caroline-Mathilde; she was granted asylum here in 1772 after her politically expedient marriage to the King of Denmark collapsed when her affair with the King's minister was exposed. (Open Tu-Su 10am-5pm. Tours Tu-Su April-Oct. 10am-4pm on the hour; Nov.-March 11am and 3pm. DM4, students DM2.) Caroline-Mathilde's weeping likeness is found in the **Französischer Garten,** south of the Altstadt; guess why she's crying, Mr. "I've got a headache" King of Denmark. The 1740 Baroque **Synagoge,** Im Kriese 24, is one of the oldest standing places of Jewish worship in Germany and a memorial to Celle's once-thriving Jewish community. (Open Tu-Th 3-5pm, F 9-11am, Su 11am-1pm. Free.)

BERGEN-BELSEN

The Bergen-Belsen concentration camp was founded in 1940 as a "labor camp" for prisoners of war. For five years, about 20,000 Soviet prisoners were held there, performing futile, torturous "labor," like rolling heavy stones up and down hills, or digging ditches only to refill them. In January 1945, the POW camp was dissolved and the SS took over, bringing in thousands of Jews, homosexuals, and political dissidents who were evacuated from Auschwitz and other concentration camps. For four unimaginable months, tens of thousands of people lived in cramped conditions and suffered the mindless torture of the Nazis. Over 35,000 died of hunger and typhoid fever, including **Anne Frank,** whose symbolic gravestone is near the Jewish memorial. In total, Bergen-Belsen claimed more than 100,000 lives. In the documents building, a permanent exhibit displays the history of the camp and a film taken by British liberation forces. The grounds of the camp contain no original buildings; these were burned after liberation to prevent the spread of disease. Instead, a cemetery of mass graves stands on the site. A somber stone obelisk commemorates the 30,000 Jewish victims and a wall is inscribed with memorial phrases in the languages of the victims. The memorial (tel. (05051) 60 11) is open daily from 9am to 6pm. Take bus #9 from the Celle train station to "Belsen-Gedenkstätte." (1hr., daily 10:45am and 1:45pm, return at 4:56pm. DM8.20.)

BREMEN

Much like Hamburg, its Hanseatic sister city to the north, Bremen has given over its once famed medieval ambience to a thriving cosmopolitan swirl in which churches compete with video art for tourists' attention. The donkey, dog, cat, and rooster of the Brothers Grimm's fairy tale *Die Bremer Stadtmusikanten* (The Musicians of Bremen) were en route to Bremen when they terrified a band of robbers with their singing. The transients singing for attention at the city's train station maintain the tradition, and the tourist office pushes the theme whenever it can, much to the chagrin of those who would turn Bremen into a center for contemporary German art. The city's most enduring trait is a strong desire for independence: despite continuing struggles, Bremen and its daughter city Bremerhaven remain their own tiny, autonomous *Land* surrounded by Niedersachsen. This feisty streak has helped foster a liberal political climate that erupted into violent battles between police and demonstrators in 1980.

▐ GETTING THERE AND GETTING AROUND

Flights: Bremen's international airport (tel. 559 50) is 3.5km from the city center; take S-Bahn #5 (10min.). Frequent flights to major German cities, the East Frisian Islands, and other European countries.

Trains: Roll to Hannover (1hr., 2 per hour, DM34), Hamburg (1hr., 2 per hour, DM33), Bremerhaven (45min., 1 per hour, DM17), and Osnabrück (1hr., 2-3 per hour, DM33).

Public Transportation: An integrated system of streetcars and buses centered on the train station covers the city and suburbs. The best deal by far is the **Bremer Kärtchen,** with unlimited rides for 2 adults for 1 calendar day *(not* 24hr. from time of purchase; DM8). Single rides DM3.20, children under 16 DM1.60. 4-ride ticket DM9.60. Across from the Hauptbahnhof is a **VBN** information center with tickets and transportation maps (DM1). Open daily 6am-9pm.

Ferries: Schreiber Reederei (tel. 32 12 29) shuttles to the suburbs and towns along the Weser and ends up at Bremerhaven. 3½ hr.; May 16-Nov. 16 W-Th and Sa at 8:30am. One-way to Bremerhaven DM21, round-trip DM34.

Taxi: Pick up a taxi waiting at the back or front exit of the Hauptbahnhof or call 140 14. **Frauen Nachtaxi** (tel. 133 34) operates a women's taxi service daily 7pm-4am.

Car Rental: Avis, Kirchbachstr. 200 (tel. 21 10 77). Open M-F 7am-6pm, Sa 8am-1pm.

Bike Rental: Leave a DM50 security deposit and a photo ID, and pedal away from the **Fahrrad Station** (tel. 30 21 14), a bright red stand on your right as you exit the train station. DM15 per day, children DM9; DM60 per week, children DM45. Open March-May and Oct.-Dec. M-F 10am-5pm; June-Sept. M and W-F 10am-5pm, Sa-Su 10am-noon and 5-5:30pm.

■ ORIENTATION AND PRACTICAL INFORMATION

Bremen lies south of the mouth of the Weser River on the North Sea, making the city perfect for meandering, but take care on the blocks surrounding Ostertor-steinweg and Am Dobben late at night; as you move out of the Altstadt, the city's anthropomorphic patrons won't follow. Bremen has four distinct neighborhoods: the tourist-filled **Altstadt,** where most of the sights and the oldest architecture are; the **Alte Neustadt,** a residential neighborhood south of the Weser river; the **Schnoor,** an old neighborhood turned shopping village; and the **Viertel,** a student quarter filled with hip kids, clubs, and cheap food.

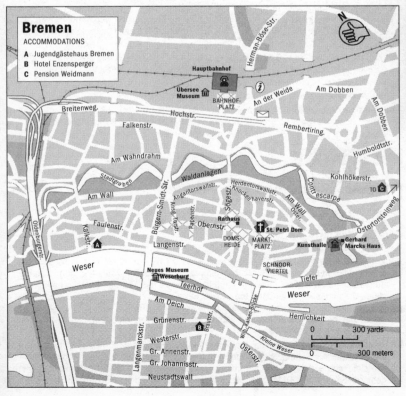

A **Tourist Card Bremen,** available at the tourist office, provides free travel on city transportation, 20% discounts to theater shows and city tours, and 50% off the cost of admission at many of Bremen's museums. (2-day card for 1 adult and 1 child DM19.50, 3-day card DM26; 2-day group card for up to 5 people DM35, 3-day DM46.)

Tourist Office: The souvenir-jammed **central office** (tel. 308 00 51; fax 308 00 30), across from the Hauptbahnhof, offers room listings. It also provides guides to museum exhibits and theater schedules, and sells tickets for concerts and festivals. A smaller **kiosk** next to the Rathaus performs the same tasks during the same hours. Open M-W 9:30am-6:30pm, Th-F 9:30am-8pm, Sa-Su 9:30am-4pm.

Consulate: U.K., Herrlichkeit 6 (tel. 590 90). Open M-Th 8:30am-12:30pm and 2:30-3:30pm, F 8:30am-12:30pm.

Currency Exchange: DVB, in the train station, exchanges currency and cashes traveler's checks for a DM5 fee. Open M-F 7:30am-7pm, Sa 8am-12:15pm and 1-4pm.

American Express: Am Wall 116 (tel. 17 46 00). Open M-F 9am-12pm and 1-5:30pm. 24hr. refund assistance: (0130) 853 100.

Bookstores: Storm, Langenstr. 10 (tel. 32 15 23). Some English books, dictionaries, and travel guides. Open M-F 9am-7pm, Sa 10am-3pm.

Gay Resources: Tel. 70 41 70. Provides information about gay events and services. Open M-W and F 10am-1pm, Th 4-5pm.

Women's Resources: Am Hulsberg 11 (streetcar: "Am Hulsberg"). Info pertinent to travelers is available in the lobby. **Frauenbuchladen Hagazussa,** Friesenstr. 12 (tel. 741 40), stocks over 3000 books of particular interest to women. Only women are admitted. Open M 10am-2pm, Tu-F 10am-6pm, Sa 10am-2pm.

Laundromat: Wasch Center, Vor dem Steintor. Follow Ostertorsteinweg to the bitter end—it's there. DM6 for wash, soap, and spin dry; another DM1 per 10min. to dry in a standard machine. Open daily 6am-11pm.

Pharmacy: Päs Apotheke, Bahnhofspl. 5-7 (tel. 144 15). Stated hours M-F 8am-6:30pm, Sa 8am-2pm, though there may be someone around later, or on Sunday, to help if you call or pass by.

Emergency: Police, tel. 110. **Fire and Ambulance,** tel. 112.

Post Office: Main office at Domsheide 15, 28195 Bremen (tel. 367 33 66), near the Markt. Open M-F 8am-7pm, Sa 9am-1pm. Another office is on Bahnhofspl. 21, by the train station. Open M-F 9am-8pm, Sa 9am-2pm.

PHONE CODE	0421

▟ ACCOMMODATIONS AND CAMPING

The key phrase is "call ahead." Inexpensive hotels exist, but they fill fast. The tourist office's free *Hotel-Liste* lists a few rooms in the DM20-40 range, but prices quickly rocket up to DM100.

Jugendgästehaus Bremen (HI), Kalkstr. 6 (tel. 17 13 69; fax 17 11 02). From the train station, take Bahnhofstr. to Herdentorsteinweg, go right at Am Wall, then turn left on to Bürgermeister-Smidt-Str. and right along the water to the 162-bed hostel. The linen is clean, the ping pong is fun, and the glowing Beck's Brewery sign across the Weser lulls you to sleep with visions of malt dancing in your head. DM27, over 27 DM34, family DM29 per person. Breakfast and sheets included. 24hr. reception. Check-in 2pm. Check-out 10am. No curfew.

Hotel-Pension Garni Weidmann, Am Schwarzen Meer 35 (tel. 498 44 55). Ostertorsteinweg becomes Am Schwarzen Meer: follow it. The plush comforters and cavernous rooms—complete with coffee-makers—are fit for royalty. Such pampering at bargain prices is in demand. Singles from DM40; doubles from DM80. Reservations recommended.

Hotel Enzensperger, Brautstr. 9 (tel. 50 32 24). From the Markt, cross the Wilhelm-Kaisen-Brücke over the Weser, turn right on Osterstr., and right on Brautstr. Clean, no-frills accommodations. Rooms have TV, telephones. Restaurant and bar downstairs. Singles DM48; doubles DM90. Breakfast included. Call a few days ahead.

Hotel Weltevreden, Am Dobben 62 (tel. 780 15; fax 70 40 91), just off Ostertorsteinweg. Comfortable rooms, good prices, close to Bremen nightlife. Singles DM60; doubles DM100, with shower DM120. Breakfast included. Reception open M-Sa 7am-10pm, Su 7:30am-1pm and 5-10pm. Call a few days ahead.

Camping: Am Stadtwaldsee 1 (tel. 21 20 02). S-Bahn #5 or #8 to "Külen Campf," then Bus #28 to the door. 2-person tent DM7.50, 3-person tent DM9.50, 4 or more DM11. DM4.50 per child. Washers and dryers DM4 each. Free showers and electrical hookup. Open all year.

FOOD

In the Rathaus, Bremen's renowned **Ratskeller** (tel. 32 16 76) is worth a visit. Dating back to 1405, it's one of the oldest wine bars in Germany. Settle in a cozy leather-and-wood booth or among huge barrels to enjoy one of 600 German wines; most are moderately priced (DM7-8 per 0.2L glass), but the meals run around DM40. (Always open; kitchen open noon-2:30pm and 6-11pm.) A cheaper way to eat well is in the open-air **market.** (Open daily 8am-2pm.) In the Marktplatz, bronze pigs herd pedestrians into take-out cafes on **Sögerstraße,** where shops sell everything from chocolate truffles to fish sandwiches. The restaurants of the **Schnoorviertel** are sweetly styled as old-fashioned German inns—this means they're overpriced. Student pubs proliferate farther east in the **Viertel,** and on and around **Ostertorsteinweg** (see **Nightlife,** p. 501). **Comet,** at the corner of Vor dem Steintor and Friesenstr., brings grocery shopping to the heart of the hip Viertel. Posters for parties and concerts line the walls.

Moto, Schlachte 22 (tel. 30 21 13), is a cheap pan-Asian place beside the Weser in a row of expensive cafés, all with good views of the water and the people. Try the soup or noodle dishes (DM5.50-17.50).

Basilikum, Langemarckstr. 129 (tel. 59 25 57). From the Altstadt the Bürgermeister-Smidt-Br. becomes Langemarckstr. Fresh banana, orange, tomato, and apple juice alongside soups (DM5), immense gyros (DM9.50-12.50), pizza (DM8-15), and salads (DM3-10) fill students and old men in a candlelit atmosphere.

Café Harlekin Bookshop, Lahnstr. 65b (tel. 50 19 11). From Langemarckstr. walk away from Beck's Brewery along Lahnstr. Bremen's best breakfast selection (served all day) is flanked by an alternative bookstore. The generous *Türkisches Frühstück* ("Turkish Breakfast," *Fladenbrot*, feta, olives, and cucumbers, DM7.50) makes a filling lunch. Open daily 10am-6:30pm.

Engel, Ostertorsteinweg 31-33 (tel. 766 15). Enjoy simple, elegant dining and people-watching in both the art nouveau interior and the leafy terrace outside. Lunch specials (DM10.50) include dessert. Other artful entrees DM10-19. Concerts on the terrace on summer weekends. Open daily from 9am.

BELOW THE BELT SHOPPING Bremen's Altstadt is crammed with stuffed animal wagons and mug shops, but there is a more exciting (and less expensive) way to buy *Bremisch*. The city has many second-hand stores (centered around **Am Dobben** and **Lahnstraße**) and two flea markets, one along the Weser on **Schlachte** on Saturdays (8am-5pm), and one on **Bürgerweide** on Sundays (8am-5pm). Bremen is also full of sex shops near the Hauptbahnhof and along Am Dobben. Inside? Delights only the flesh (and rubber) can know.

Café Torno, Am Dobben 71 (tel. 70 06 11). Relax nerves to American pop music. Hefty gyros (DM5-12), pasta dinners (DM9-12), and *cheap* drinks (from DM1.80). Open M-Th 11:30am-1am, F-Sa 11:30am-3am, Su 11:30am-1am.

Mensa Academia, Dechanatstr. 13-15 (tel. 364 91 67), at the *Hochschule für Künste.* Eat, drink, and "be" a student (necessary, but *how* is up to you) under ivy trellises in a stone courtyard while listening to the opera ingenues.

Ada, Ostertorsteinweg 99 (tel. 783 57). Subtitle: "Ardor." Try a tzatziki salad (DM4) and chase it down with a Turkish mocha (DM3). Always open.

👁 SIGHTS

RATHAUS. Bremen's Altstadt centers around the **Rathaus** and its 15th-century base decorated by an ornate Renaissance facade. It survived WWII only because the English pilot who bombed the area deliberately missed this target. *(Adults DM5, children DM2.50.)* Just left of the town hall is Gerhard Marcks's 1951 sculpture *Die Musikanten,* which shows the Grimms' donkey, dog, cat, and rooster in their model-mugging, robber-foiling stance.

ST. PETRI-DOM. Also a war survivor, the **St. Petri-Dom,** Sandstr. 10-12 (tel. 36 50 40), next to the Rathaus, has a mosaic exterior depicting the crucifixion. Below are stone saints; at their feet, lions and griffons gnaw on squirming victims. It's a pretty building—really. Inside, tourists herd and bray, but those other visitors who choose to see only the frescoed ceilings won't mind. The foundation dates to 798, when Charlemagne had the first stone placed here. *(Cathedral open M-F 10am-5pm, Sa 10am-1:45pm, Su 2-5pm. Free. Tower, all 265 steps, open May-Oct. M-F 10-11:20am and 12:20-4:30pm, Sa 10am-noon, Su 2-5pm. DM1.)* In a corner of the cathedral is the **Dom Museum** (tel. 365 04 11), housed in part of the original foundation with frescoes dating back 500 years. *(Open April-Nov. M-F 10am-5pm, Sa 10am-noon, Su 2-5pm; Dec.-March M-F 1-4:30pm, Sa 10am-noon, Su 2-5pm. DM3, students and children DM2.)* Your museum ticket is good for a DM1 discount on an entrance to the macabre **Bleikeller,** in the basement of the Dom. The mummified corpses of workers who fell from the roof of the cathedral were discovered here in 1695 and have been on exhibit for three centuries. *(Open May-Oct. M-F 10am-5pm, Sa 10am-2pm, Su 2-5pm; Nov.-Apr. daily 1-5pm. DM2, children DM1. Admission ticket likewise good for DM1 discount at the Dom museum above.)*

OTHER SIGHTS. Just past the *Domshof,* turn left on Domsheide for the **Schnoorviertel,** a district of red-roofed gingerbread houses, dainty shops, and dog salons. Between the Marktplatz and the Weser lies the narrow cobblestone **Böttcherstraße.** Once a crowded artisans' quarter, the street offers gilded archways, stained-glass windows, boutiques, and craft shops. It's worth standing with all the tourists at noon, 3, or 6pm for the magic of the Böttcherstr. **Glockenspiel.** Bells ring and part of the building swings open to deliver a performance by mechanical figurines, re-enacting wild sea and air exploits from the building's early memory. Come early— the prime gawking spots fill up quickly. The smell of the brew lures the helpless lush across the Weser to the **Beck's Brewery,** Am Deich 18/19 (tel. 50 94 55 55). Pilgrims can visit the inner sanctum for a paltry DM5 (and bring the kids for free!). Unlike its exported counterparts, homegrown Beck's offers the famous full bouquet expected in a German beer. *(Hourly tours Tu-Sa 10am-5pm, Su 10am-3pm. English tours at 1:30pm.)*

🏛 MUSEUMS

The persistence of the four traveling animals theme throughout the Altstadt might lead you to believe otherwise, but Bremen is a city of high culture. The city's sophistication and intelligence are most notably on display in Bremen's museums.

■**NEUES MUSEUM WESERBURG BREMEN.** Between the Klein Weser and the Weser, the museum crouches on the island in four red brick buildings that once served as warehouses. Inside is a new universe: white rooms on five floors filled with strange and beautiful installations of modern works by international artists. *(Terrhofstr. 20. Tel. 598390. Open Tu-F 10am-6pm, Sa-Su 11am-6pm. DM8, students and children DM5. Tours daily in German; DM11, students and children DM8. Free CD listening tour.)*

ÜBERSEE MUSEUM. Promises a *"Weltreise im Minutentakt"* ("a trip around the world in a matter of minutes"). With animals stuffed into tasteful poses in life-like "habitats" and displays of cultural artifacts in still life, it does just that...sort of. Exhibits ranging from a Shinto garden to a South Sea fishing village attempt to show the world outside Germany's borders. *(Bahnhofsplatz 13, next to the train station on the right. Tel. 361 91 76. Open Tu-Su 10am-6pm. DM6, students and children DM3, family pass DM12, under 6 free. Café-restaurant open M 5pm-2am and Tu-Su 10am-2am.)*

GERHARD-MARCKS-HAUS. An indoor and outdoor sculpture garden of works by the sculptor of *Die Musikanten* with display rooms and an outdoor house. Changing exhibitions of modern sculpture and graphic art. *(Am Wall 208, next to the Kunsthalle. Tel. 32 72 00. Open Tu-Su 10am-6pm. Tours Th at 5pm. DM6, students and children DM4.)*

KUNSTHALLE. Bremen's main collection includes Impressionist, Expressionist, and contemporary works, all bizarrely organized. *(Am Wall 207. Tel. 32 90 80. Open Tu 10am-9pm, W-Su 10am-5pm. DM8, students DM4.)*

♪▒ ENTERTAINMENT AND NIGHTLIFE

You want singing barnyard animals? Bremen delivers. Plus there's opera in the **Theater am Goetheplatz,** Am Goethepl. 1-3 (tel. 365 33 33), new drama in the **Schauspielhaus,** Ostertorsteinweg 57a (tel. 365 33 33), and auldies but goodies in the **Bremer Shakespeare Company,** Theater am Leibnizplatz (tel. 50 03 33). The **Theater im Schnoor,** Wüste Stätte 11 (tel. 32 60 54), does cabarets and revues, from postmodern Shakespeare (nothing is sacred) to parodies of the *Wehrmacht.* Summertime brings performances to parks around the city. Discount tickets are usually held for students. Check the tourist office, the theaters, or the publication *Bremer Umschau* (DM3) for schedules and prices, as well as information on free performances. *Foyer,* free at many museums, lists theater, music, film, and art openings. The tourist office also has a booklet with these listings that has an excellent map of the city attached. *Belladonna* lists cultural events of special interest to women. *Prinz,* a monthly entertainment mag, has comprehensive nightlife listings and the full scoop on the Bremen *Szene* (DM4.50 at the tourist office and newsstands). *Partysan,* a 'zine based in Hamburg, also lists big parties in Bremen (free at Engel and other cafes).

During the last two weeks of October, Bremen drinks beer and eats tubs of yummy lard cakes in honor of its trading heritage and freedom as a *Land* with the colorful **Freimarkt** fair, an annual event since 1095. And Bremen rocks—big concerts are often held in the **Weserstadion** (tel. 43 45 00) behind the train station. Tickets and information for small- and large-scale events are available at the tourist office. **Modernes Complex,** Neustadtswall 28 (tel 50 55 53), hosts films, plays, concerts, and dancing. Times and cover charges vary.

Bremen offers a well-developed and raucous pub culture, and the *Viertel* is the place to be. Find the true pulse of the nightlife on the densely populated **Ostertorsteinweg.** A lively gay and lesbian scene is scattered around the city, with centers at the edge of the *Viertel* on Am Dobben and Humboldtstr.

▒ **Moments,** Vor dem Steintor 65 (tel. 780 07). A wildly popular disco with well-advertised and well-attended parties. The music invariably improves during happy hour (10-11pm) with half-price drinks. Open daily 10pm-late.

Litfass, Ostertorsteinweg 22 (tel. 70 32 92). An all-day, all-night bastion of alternative chic that poses as a bar. As the eyes of the supermodel on the wall cast flirting glances toward you, coolly take down one of their piping hot coffees (from DM2.90). The extensive outdoor terrace and open facade make it the place to see and be seen. Open M-Th and Su 10am-2am, F-Sa 10am-4am.

Café Engel, Ostertorsteinweg 31-33 (tel. 766 15). A hip bar and restaurant whose patrons lack nothing in style, sophistication, or libations. Open daily 9am-late.

Confession, Humboldtstr. 156 (tel. 738 22). A swingin' gay and lesbian club featuring live blues, jazz, and alternative bands. Sit outside at the red picnic tables and stare at the yellow nipples on the front of the building. Is this fun or what? Open M-Th and Su 7pm-2am, F-Sa 9pm-late. Saturday women only.

TheaLit, Im Krummen Arm 1 (tel. 70 16 32). An evening club and center for women's and lesbian events. Bar, buffet dinners (DM38), salads (DM16), and "fingerfood" (DM3.50 a piece). Women only. Office open Tu-F 10am-12pm. Bar open Tu-Sa 7pm-12:30am.

BREMERHAVEN

The sea calls Bremerhaven—Bremen's younger, saltier sister city—but these days, no one is home. The city's residents would rather pack the **Columbus Center** mall than crowd the decks of any of the town's numerous antique (and land-locked) vessels. Men in drag may demonstrate in front of the beautiful **Große Kirche** (Great Church), which sits across the street from the Columbus Center. To get here from the train station take bus #505 or #506 to "Columbus Center"; the mall is across the street when you step off. Avoid the crowded, commercial **Bürgersmidt Str.** unless you need an ATM or a McDonald's. The **Alter Hafen** (Old Harbor) is a place of many delights and many, many German grandparents with their grandchildren; take bus #526 from the Hauptbahnhof to "Alter Hafen." Ferries sail daily for Helgoland, Germany's own Fantasy Island, at 9am (see below). The **Deutsches Schiffahrtsmuseum** has scurvy, cabin-fever, and whatever other boat-related psychoses you can think of. It's crazy for ships, with models and relics inside the building and real full-scale museum ships outside. (Open Apr.-Oct. daily 10am-6pm; Nov.-Mar. Tu-Su 10am-6pm. Admission DM5, students, seniors, and children DM2.50.) Docked nearby, but with separate admission, the **Museumschiffe U-Boot Wilhelm Bauer** is one of the only German submarines from WWII that was neither sunk nor scrapped (Open Apr.-Oct. daily 10am-6pm. DM4, under 18 DM3.) The other boats on display are more expensive, and the view from the shore is probably enough. At the **Zoo am Meer,** farther up the harbor, German schoolchildren scream and careen through the garden, while animals on the other side of the bars (polar bears, sea lions, monkeys) sit calmly and watch. If the babes jangle your nerves, there is a soothing aquarium downstairs. (Open May-Aug. daily 8am-7pm; Apr. and Sept. 8am-6:30pm; Oct.-Mar. 8am-5pm. DM4, students and children DM2. Free tours available with prior reservation.) Between August 31 and September 3, 2000, some of the best sailors in the world will flock to Bremerhaven for the "Sail Bremerhaven 2000" windjammer race.

Bremerhaven is 45 minutes from Bremen by **trains** that leave and arrive at least hourly; a **ferry** leaves Bremen each morning at 8:30am (see Bremen, p. 496). The **tourist office** (tel. 430 00), on the second floor of the Columbus Center to the far left of the escalators, finds rooms from DM30 for free. (Open M-W 9:30am-6pm, Th-F 9:30am-8pm, Sa 9:30am-4pm.) The **Verkehrsamt,** Van-Ronzelenstr. 2 (tel. 94 64 60; fax 460 65), does the same with different hours. (Open M-F 8am-4pm.) The **post office,** 27570 Bremerhaven, directly to the left as you leave the Hauptbahnhof, offers **currency exchange** and cashes traveler's checks for a DM6 fee. (Open M-F 8am-6pm, Sa 8am-1pm.) The **telephone code** is 0471.

Bremerhaven's number one combo platter, the **Jugendgästehaus-Jugendherberge (HI) two-for-one,** at Gaußstr. 54-56 (tel. 856 52; fax 874 26), offers a dazzling array of conveniences. Take bus #511 to "Gesundheitsamt." Work out in the mini-gym or visit their Volkswagen-sized spa. (Hostel DM28, over 26 DM31.50. *Jugendgästehaus* DM29.90. Breakfast and sheets included. Reception 7am-6pm.) Make reservations a week in advance.

HELGOLAND

Seduced by duty-free prices, German tourists endure a two- to four-hour ferry ride, jump into tiny skiffs to row ashore, and then run all over the island, snatching up as many cartons of cigarettes, meter-tall bottles of liquor, and cheese as they can legally carry before the ship departs at 4pm. A different kind of mayhem reigned at the conclusion of WWII, when the British navy evacuated the strategically valuable island and attempted to obliterate it with thousands of tons of dynamite. The island bears battle scars, including concrete docks that extend into the ocean, but the glitz and glam of consumption gild this historical blight with a flashy veneer.

When the weather is less than perfect, don't make Helgoland a daytrip—a ferry ride on the high seas will not put you in a cheese-eating mood—since the best way to enjoy the island is to go for a walk under the wide, wide sky. The three hours the ferry allows is plenty of time to buy a lunch at one of the carry-out places near the dock and climb or take the **elevator** to the top of the dunes, where fields of Queen Anne's lace, red paths, red cliffs, and a view out to sea await. (Daily until 9pm; one-way DM1, round-trip DM1.50.) There's also the beach to comb, and ferries leaving every half-hour for **Dünne**, Helgoland's little sister island, which is one big beach. (Ferries run 8am-8pm. Buy a *Fahrkarte* from machines on the dock.) Helgoland's **museum, aquarium, swimming pool, mini-golf,** and **tennis courts** aren't as exciting as its cliffs, but if you plan to stay more than one day, they might be of interest. Hours and prices vary; check the notices in the glass cases on the dock.

The cheapest and most reliable way to get to Helgoland is through Norddeich, Bremerhaven, or Cuxhaven. The **MS Frisia III,** operating from Norddeich, offers a lower fare but a longer ride (4hr.) and a skimpier schedule. (Departs May-June Tu 8am; July-Aug. Tu and F 8am. Daytrips DM43, under 13 DM27.) Ferry company **Reederei Warrings** (tel. (04464) 949 50; fax (04464) 94 95 30) sends the less than luxurious **MS Helgoland** from Bremerhaven. (4hr. Daily at 9am. Daytrip DM57, ages 11-18 DM38, 4-11 DM30. Open-ended return DM70, ages 11-18 DM40, 4-11 DM36.) The **MS Wappen von Hamburg** (tel. (04721) 55 48 95), which sails via Cuxhaven, is quickest (2hr. May-Sept. daily 10:30am. Daytrips DM55, ages 12-18 DM36; open-ended return DM68, ages 12-18 DM40.) The **telephone code** is 04725.

With thousands of visitors each year, Helgoland's **tourist office** (tel. 813 711; fax 81 37 25) greets travelers as they step off the skiff. Their free brochure offers a wealth of information, including a list of accommodations. (Open M-F 9am-5pm, Sa-Su 11:30am-5pm.) Helgoland's **Jugendherberge (HI),** Postfach 580 (tel./fax 341), sits right on the beach, a 10-minute walk from the ferry dock. Follow the maps and signs. (1-3 nights, DM40 each, 4 nights DM37 each; kids and families DM24 per person. Lunch DM8.50, dinner DM8. Sheets DM10. Reception Apr.-Oct. 10am-2pm and 5-7pm. Curfew 10pm. Call or fax 4-6 weeks ahead.)

OSNABRÜCK

Around 1300 the ancestors of Osnabrück's present-day citizens built a wall around two villages that had been developing for centuries; they called the unified town Osnabrück. It quickly developed into a commercial center, and when the warring parties sat down in 1648 to end the Thirty Years War, it was at Osnabrück. On October 25 of that year, the peace was announced to the town's citizens. They stood incredulous for a few minutes, then broke out in song. The townspeople eventually finished their song and went home, but a spirit of peacefulness remained. Three-hundred and fifty years after the Peace of Westphalia, Osnabrück is as tranquil as ever. Its pedestrian shopping areas contain glamorous fashion shops, expensive cafés, and overpriced art galleries, all in well-kept buildings.

◪ PRACTICAL INFORMATION. Trains run from Osnabrück to Hannover (1½hr., 1 per hour, DM36), Münster (½hr., 2 per hour, DM20), and Düsseldorf (2hr., 1 per hour, DM60). **Buses** travel around the city center (DM1.30) and to the outer zones (DM2.20), but the best deal is a *Tagesticket* (DM4), good for a day of unlimited travel after 9am. Rent **bikes** at the **Fahrradverleih** (tel. 25 91 31) in the train station. (Open M-F 6am-8pm, Sa 7am-2pm. DM8 per day, DM35 per week. ID and DM20 deposit required.) The **tourist office,** Krahnstr. 58 (tel. 323 22 02; fax 323 27 09; email tourinfo@osnabrueck.de), is just off the Rathaus. From the station, walk up Möserstr. as it turns into Herrenteich Str., follow the curve around, and turn onto Krahnstr. The staff books **rooms** (from DM30 per person) for free. (Open M-F 9:30am-6pm, Sa 9:30am-1pm.) Launder your duds at **Wasch Center,** on the corner of Kommenderiestr. and Petersburger-Wall. (Open daily 6am-11pm. Wash DM7, dry DM1.) The **telephone code** is 0541.

▓▓ ACCOMMODATIONS AND FOOD. South of the city center is the newly outfitted **Jugendgästehaus Osnabrück,** Iburger Str. 183a (tel. 542 84; fax 542 94). From the station, take bus #62 (direction: "Zoo") to "Kinderhospital." (DM26, over 26 DM31. Breakfast included. Sheets DM4. Reception 4-5pm and 8-10pm. Wheelchair accessible. Call ahead.) Clean rooms fill the **Hotel Jägerheim,** Johannistorwall 19a (tel. 216 35). From the station, turn left on Konrad-Adenauer-Ring, which becomes Petersburgerwall and then Johannistorwall. (Singles DM40, with bath DM64; doubles DM80, with bath DM104. Reception until 9pm.) For **camping,** try **Freizeitpark Attersee,** Zum Attersee 50 (tel. 12 41 47). From the station, take bus #22 to "Attersee." (DM6.50 per person.) The new **Pub'lic,** Markt 25 (tel. 205 18 18), takes trendiness to entirely new levels. Recline in the shadow of the Marienkirche and indulge in the creative drink menu. (Open M-Th noon-1am, F-Su 10am-2am.) **Lagerhalle,** Rolandsmauer 26 (tel. 33 87 40), is the town's one-stop nightlife center, with a popular *Kneipe*, a restaurant with international and vegetarian specials from DM5, an art-house film theater, and frequent rock concerts and dance parties. (Open Tu-Th 6pm-1am, F 6pm-2am, Sa 7pm-2am, Su 6:30-11pm.) A number of discount **supermarkets** line Johannisstr.

▓ SIGHTS. Osnabrück's stunning **Friedenssaal** (Hall of Peace) hides inside the perfectly preserved **Rathaus.** (Open M-F 8:30am-6pm, Sa-Su 10am-1pm. Tours Su 10:30am. Free.) Next to the Rathaus stands the **Marienkirche,** completely destroyed during the war, and fully rebuilt thereafter. (Open April-Sept. M-Sa 10am-noon and 3-5pm; Oct.-March M-Sa 10:30am-noon and 2:30-4pm.) The **tower** can be toured Sundays from 11:30am to 1pm. (DM2, children DM1.) The immense **Dom,** Kleine Domsfreiheit 24, has been collecting priceless religious relics since the 14th century. (Open Tu-F 10am-1pm and 3-5pm, Sa-Su 11am-2pm. Tours Su 10:30am.) The warm afterglow of Westphalia quickly fades amidst the permanent Felix Nussbaum exhibit at the **Kulturgeschichtliche Museum;** Nussbaum's paintings symbolically depict the tragedy of the Holocaust. (Open Tu-Th 11am-6pm, F 11am-8pm, Sa-Su 11am-6pm. DM3, students DM1.50.) Osnabrück's most famous son is **Erich Maria Remarque,** the acclaimed author of *Im Westen nichts Neues (All Quiet on the Western Front)*. Though Allied bombing completely destroyed his house on Hafenstr., literary travelers (that's you, sport!) can tour the **Erich-Maria-Zentrum,** Am Markt 6 (tel. 969 45 11), which documents his life and work. (Open Jan.-Nov. Tu-F 10am-1pm and 3-5pm, Sa 10am-1pm, 1st Sunday of the month 11am-5pm.) The Osnabrück **zoo,** Am Waldzoo 2-3 (tel. 95 10 50), is fantastic. Take bus #62 to "Zoo." Watch the tigers and bears frolic. Squeal with pleasure. (Open daily April-Oct. 8am-6:30pm; Nov.-March 9am-dark.)

OLDENBURG

Founded in 1108, the city of Oldenburg was spared the destruction of the Thirty Years War largely because its count at the time, Anton Günther, raised the most beautiful horses in Germany. Today's Oldenburg is much more than a one-trick pony—the unique Frisian culture runs deep in this city, and all its residents are actively involved in its preservation. The Altstadt flashes boutiques and bars at the visitor, and more museums exist than there is art to fill them. Most tourists will miss the beautiful residential neighborhood west of Alexanderstr., the cemetery, and the green, green *Schloßgarten*, which doesn't bother Oldenburgers, who are friendly, but not about to divulge all their secrets.

◪ ORIENTATION AND PRACTICAL INFORMATION. Oldenburg is easily accessible by **train** from Bremen (35min., 2 per hour, DM15.20), Osnabrück (1¾hr., 1 per hour, DM31), and Jever (1¼hr., every 2 hours, DM14.80). The old, moated city lies along an offshoot of the Weser river, and serves as a take-off point for excursions to East Frisia. The **tourist office,** Wallstr. 14 (tel. 157 44; fax 248 92 09), finds **rooms** for a DM4 fee (from DM30; call ahead) and piles visitors with numerous North Sea brochures. (Open M-F 10am-5pm, Sa 10am-1pm). **Rent bikes** at the **Fahrradstation** (tel. 163 45) on Neuesstr., across the street from the tourist office. (Open M-Th 7am-11pm, Sa 8am-11pm. DM12 per day, DM42 per week.) **Oldenburgische AIDS-Hilfe,** Bahnhofstr. 23 (hotline tel. 194 11), offers information on AIDS and gay resources, and has English-speaking counselors. (Open M 9am-noon and 2-4pm, W 9am-noon and 2-6pm, Tu and Th-F 9am-noon.) Oldenburg's **postal code** is 26123. The **telephone code** is 0441.

▐▐ ACCOMMODATIONS AND FOOD. The city's modern **Jugendherberge (HI),** Alexanderstr. 65 (tel. 871 35), is 1.5km from the station. From the train station, turn right on Molestr. At the post office, look to your right: take the walkway over the station, and turn left onto Karlstr. Follow it as it becomes Milchstr. and go left on Lindenstr. Alexanderstr. is to the left of the cemetery; walk 3min. to your new home. Humbly ask for crash-course in *Plattdeutsch. Moin!* Or take bus #7, 9, or 12 to "Lappen"; then, across the street, catch bus #2 or 3 to "Von Finckstr." (DM22, over 26 DM28.20. Breakfast included. Reception 5-11pm. Curfew 10pm, but you can get a key. The hostel fills quickly, so call several days ahead.) The **Hotel Hegeler,** Donnerschweerstr. 27 (tel. 875 61; fax 885 03 59), has clean rooms and a bowling alley—really! From the station, cross the walkway over the tracks and follow the road to Donnerschweerstr., then turn left and walk 150m. They have clean, spacious rooms with wooden desks and down comforters. (Singles DM45, with bath DM75; doubles DM90, with shower DM130. Call ahead.)

Picknick, Markt 6 (tel. 273 76), serves up regional specialties like potato pancakes with apple sauce (DM9) and baguettes. (From DM7. Open M-Sa 10am-late.) **Marvin's Biergarten,** Rosenstr. 8, is as laid-back as it gets. Interesting art, inside and out. You'll know you've found the right place when you see the eyes painted between the second floor windows. "Beer on tab" (DM2.20-5.80). From the train station, head up Bahnhofstr. and go left on Rosenstr. (Open M-Th and Su 7pm-2am, F-Sa 8pm-3am.) At the **Zauberkessel,** Kurwickstr. 6, parallel to Wallstr., patrons get medieval with live bards and not-so-medieval with an ample vegetarian menu. (Most meals DM7-17. Open M-Th and Su noon-1am, F-Sa noon-3am.) **Tandoor,** Staustr. 18 (tel. 170 75), serves gyros (DM11), pasta (DM9-14), and lunch specials (DM10). The *bunter Salatteller* ("colorful salad plate") will restore your faith in mankind. Scribble your order on the scraps of paper provided at the tables, then hand it to the man behind the counter; he knows what to do. (Open 24hr.)

▣ ♫ SIGHTS AND ENTERTAINMENT. Every morning, the city's residents jockey for position with hundreds of tourists as **daily markets** bustle in two different squares: one on the **Pferdemarkt,** an erstwhile horse-showing arena near the yellow brick state library, the other on the main square surrounding the 1887 **Rathaus.** The adjacent 13th-century **Lambertikirche** has endured Baroque and Neoclassical additions to its Gothic structure, which have rendered its interior shockingly...nondescript. (Open Tu-F 11am-12:30pm and 2:30-5pm, Sa 11am-12:30pm. Free.) A well-organized meetingplace for the 15th and 20th centuries, the **Landesmuseum,** Schloßpl. 26, in the lemon-yellow castle with white and mint icing, er, copper trim, houses Oldenburg's best collection. The city's history is told through

NIEDERSACHSEN

decorative and religious art displayed in rooms with individual soundtracks and videos. (Open Tu-F 9am-5pm, Sa-Su 10am-5pm. DM4, students, seniors, and children DM2.) The **Augusteum,** Elisabethstr. 1 (tel. 220 26 00), is an extension of the *Landesmuseum.* The lower floor showcases special exhibitions, while upstairs is home to Kirchner's Expressionist street scenes (see p. 24) and groggy Surrealist dreamscapes. (Open Tu-F 9am-5pm, Sa-Su 10am-5pm. German tours Su at 11am. DM4, students, children, and seniors DM2.) For slightly less esoteric action, walk another 300m to the **Naturkunde und Vorgeschichte Museum** (natural and prehistory museum), Damm 40-44 (tel. 924 43 00). Displays of Jewish life in the early 20th century are informative—except for the strange omission of the Holocaust. Also check out the spearheads and mastodons upstairs. (Open Tu-Th 9am-5pm, Sa-Su 10am-5pm. DM3, students and children DM1.50.) Down Lappen and across the street, the **Stadtmuseum,** Am Stadtmuseum 4-8, holds printing presses, stamps, and postcards from the city's history. (Open Tu-F 9am-5pm, Sa 9am-noon, Su 10am-5pm. Free.) Where Alexanderstr. and Nadorstr. diverge, the **Getrudenfriedhof,** Oldenburg's ancient cemetery, stretches its mausoleum- and headstone-covered lawn.

Oldenburg's nightlife centers around a curious man named "Popeye" who runs the club **JFK's** on Wallstr. Despite the campy and strangely morbid motif, Popeye injects some pulse into Oldenburg after hours, organizing numerous raves, dance parties, and beach parties. Just ask him what's goin' on. Oldenburg also offers **Pulverfass,** Kaiserstr. 24 (tel. 126 01), a popular, cruisey men-only gay disco. (Open F-Sa 11pm-5am. Cover DM5.) Another beer garden with live music on weekends is **Der Schwann,** (tel. 261 89), on Stau across from Kaiserstr. Watch the pretty boats sail across the harbor while downing cheap beer. (Open evenings until late.)

OSTFRIESLAND (EAST FRISIA)

Germany's North Sea shoreline and the seven sandy islands that hug the coast may as well belong to an entirely different country. The flat landscape, dotted with windmills, dramatic cloud scenes, and apocalyptic seascapes, seems to bear no relationship to the rest of the country's cheerful river valleys and bustling cities. Caught up in such dramatic scenery, it's easy to forget that people actually live here, but Frisian culture is still quite apparent. That Frisians are seafarers is clear from the popularity of maritime fashion, especially the omnipresent blue sailor's hat worn by almost every man in sight. Frisians treasure their delicious tea, which is often served with sugar candies called *Kluntje* in elaborate porcelain tea sets. The Frisian dialect is actually the closest linguistic relative to English; the musical

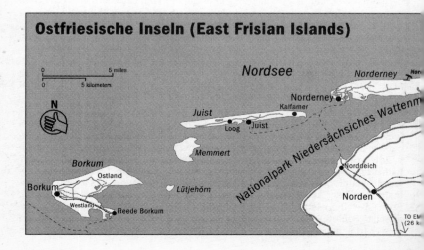

Ostfriesische Inseln (East Frisian Islands)

accent is nearly incomprehensible to Germans, but makes it easier on Anglophone tourists whose English accent is better understood here. Frisians greet one another by saying *Moin!*, the North German word for hello.

Twice a day, the tide goes out on the Frisian coast, exposing the ocean floor—called the **Watt**—between the mainland and the islands. Guides, called *Watt-führer*, are numerous and well advertised; check at the tourist office or on posters everywhere for a schedule of *Watt* tours.

 Never venture onto the Watt without a guide—quicksand pits abound, and the tide's rapid return is extremely dangerous.

Although the region has a number of HI youth hostels, don't expect to stay there unless you have a reservation; Ostfriesland is as popular with school groups as it is with tourists. The best bet for the budget traveler is a **private room,** booked through a tourist office, which start at DM25-30. If you plan on staying longer than a few days, and especially if you're traveling in a group, renting a **vacation apartment** (*Ferienwohnung*) is the best option. These apartments usually include a kitchen and start at about DM60 per night. Fortunately, miles of breathtaking beaches, green fields, and rolling dunes more than compensate for all the pre-planning.

JEVER

Four hundred fifty years ago, Jever received city rights from its patroness, Lady Mary, who ensured its culture by commissioning art and building fortifications and a school. Now the local brewery, famous throughout Germany, is its insurance. Located on Elisathufer north of the Altstadt, the **Fresisches Brauhaus** (tel. 137 11) offers a **tour** of the futuristic glass brewing complex that puts Jever on the map—and on tap—all over northern Germany. (Tours April-Oct. every 30min. M-F 9:30am-12:30pm; Nov.-March Tu-Th 10:30am only. DM10, including a souvenir mug, pretzel, and two glasses of beer. Call ahead.)

Jever's other industry is tourism, though this market is maintained in a slightly more subtle style than that of the Brauhaus. Most Jeverians dismiss their famed barley fetish, claiming that their finest offering is the castle located across from the tourist office at Alter Markt 18. The salmon-colored, 15th-century **Schloß** houses an engaging museum filled with art and trinkets dating back 500 years. (Open March to mid-Jan. Tu-Su 10am-6pm. DM4, students DM2, children DM1.50.) The Renaissance **Rathaus** cowers in the main square behind a mask of scaffolding. On Kirchplatz, the **Stadtkirche** is Jever's monument to persistence; after being

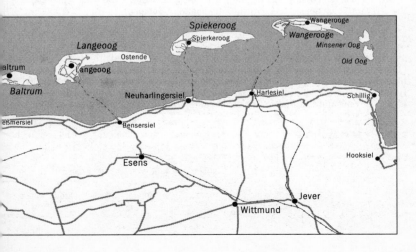

burned down it was reconstructed and modernized. Adjacent to the church is a **Glockenspiel,** which goes off at 11am, noon, 3, 4, 5, and 6pm, releasing figurines from Jever's history through its trap doors. The little people extend their hands to you in welcome; as the tourist office will tell you, you're meant to take it personally. Teetotalers take the bus to Hooksiel (every 2 hours), a small coastal port northwest of Jever, to indulge in its **beaches** and cozy campgrounds.

Getting to Jever can be tricky; let Deutsche Bahn do the work for you at one of their information desks. They'll give you a ticket that works for both **trains** and **buses** in the Jever region. The **tourist office,** Alter Markt 18 (tel. 710 10; fax 93 92 99), across from the Schloß, books **rooms** for free and directs brew-seeking visitors to their Shangri-La. (Open May to mid-Sept. M-F 10am-6pm, Sa 10am-2pm; mid-Sept. to April M-Th 9am-5pm, F 9am-1pm.) For a **taxi** call 30 30. The **telephone code** is 04461.

The **Jugendherberge Jever (HI),** Mooshütterweg 12 (tel. 35 90; fax 35 65), idles on a small street behind the Schloß. Rooms and facilities are standard. Unlike most other hostels in the region, rooms are generally available. (DM19, over 26 DM24. Breakfast included. Sheets DM5. Ring at the front desk to be let in. Curfew 10pm. Open April-Oct.)

PORT TOWNS

Only two mainland ports are accessible by train: **Emden,** the ferry port for Borkum, and **Norddeich,** ferry port for Norderney and Juist. The departure points for all other islands lie in a string of tiny ports on the coast—all connected by the overpriced **Bäderbus,** which runs from **Norden.** The ferry companies servicing **Baltrum** runs a separate bus from the train area which is conveniently timed with the ship. Beware: *the Bäderbus is not scheduled to connect with departing ferries*—and its driver is not concerned with getting you to your specific port on time. Keep your eye peeled for new ferry services and specials; companies often run inter-island trips or excursions to the duty-free haven of Helgoland (see p. 503). **Trains** run from Bremen to Emden (2hr., 1 per hour, DM34), Norden (2-2½hr., every 2hr., DM42), and Norddeich (2½hr., 1 per hour, DM43). They also head from Oldenburg to Emden (1¼hr., 1 per hour, DM22), Norden (1½-2hr., every 2 hr., DM30), and Norddeich (1½-2hr., 1 per hour, DM31).

EMDEN

A large seaport, Emden has a history as a thriving trading center. It survived the severe firebombings of WWII which destroyed 85% of the town, and today the reconstructed town is important chiefly because of its Volkswagen plant and the ferry port that sees travelers off to the island of **Borkum.**

Emden has two main squares: the **Neuer Markt,** a daily flower, meat, and produce market; and the **Stadtgarten,** home to the harbor, the **Rathaus,** and cafés frequented by musicians in the evenings. Both squares are located in the center of town and can be reached by taking Großestr., to the right as you exit the train station (15min.). Or take bus #3001 to "Rathaus." Also easily accesible from the train station (follow the signs) is Emden's most well-publicized museum, the **Kunsthalle,** Hinter dem Rahmen 13 (tel. 97 50 50). The permanent collection includes works by Picasso, Franz Marc, and an impressive exemplars from *Neue Sachlichkeit* artists

WINDPARKS The port towns of the Frisian islands are outwardly all about sea and sand, but behind every green *Deich* are miles of wheat fields which are used by the wiley Frisians for a second purpose: generating electricity. Instead of sails, enormous white propellers atop giant poles harness the wind's energy—you can see row upon row of them along the horizon. Bike and hiking trails have thoughtfully been provided in the wheat fields where the generators stand, making for adventurous journeys under their gale. Every town has its own *Windpark:* inquire at the local bike rental shop or tourist office for its location.

(see p. 24). (Open Tu 10am-8pm, W-F 10am-5pm, Sa-Su 11am-5pm. DM8, students and seniors DM5.) It also hosts great special exhibits, and the rooms atop the museum's spiral staircases offer a crash course in 20th-century art. The highly-acclaimed ▓**Bunkermuseum,** Holzsägerstr. 6 (tel. 322 25), off Großestr. near the Alter Markt, is the newest museum in town. The six floors of an old air-raid shelter trace the sad fate of Emden's population from 1941 to 1944, when the city was fire-bombed. Ask to see the film presentation (in English and German)—it's beautifully made and quite powerful. (Open May-Oct. Tu-F 10am-1pm and 3-5pm, Sa-Su 10am-1pm. DM3, students DM1.)

For a more light-hearted adventure, a visit to the charming **Dat Otto Huus** (tel. 12 21 21) is in order. The three-story edifice is a shrine to comedian, children's entertainer, and living legend **Otto Waalkes,** a native Emdener. The first floor is free; see kissing elephants (Otto's symbol) and buy images of Otto on everything from rubber to silicon. To see the second and third floors, featuring photos of Otto clowning with Boris Becker and Steffi Graf and other madcap antics, pilgrims must pay. (Open April-Oct. M-F 9:30am-6pm, Sa 9:30am-1pm and 3-6pm, Su 10am-4pm; Nov.-March M-F 9:30am-1pm and 3-6pm. Admission to the second and third floors DM4, children DM1.50.) The **Ostfriesisches Landesmuseum** (tel. 87 20 57), in the Rathaus, offers a menacing display of 16th- and 17th-century weapons. (Open April-Sept. M-F and Su 11am-5pm; Oct.-March Tu-F and Su 11am-4pm, Sa 1-4pm. DM6, students DM3, family card DM12.) The magnificent, 16th-century town church was all but destroyed during WWII, but the main hall remains; it now houses the **Johannes-Lasko-Bibliothek,** Kirchstr. 22 (tel. 915 00). Inside, the cavernous walls hold portraits, dusty books, and what's left of the statuary; hear jazz and classical music on the weekends. With the advent of the new Bug, some might want to tour the town's mammoth **Volkswagen plant.** (Tel. 86 23 90. Open M-Th 9:30am-1:30pm.)

Emden is located near the island of Borkum. Ferries leave daily from the Emden *Außenhaven;* take bus #3002 to "Borkumkai." The **tourist office,** Am Stadtgarten (tel. 974 00; fax 974 09), across from the Rathaus, books **rooms** for free and sells a bargain ticket that lets you into four of the city's museums. (DM9, under 18 DM4.50. Open May-Sept. M-F 9am-6pm, Sa 10am-1pm, Su 11am-1pm; Jan.-April M-F 9am-1pm and 3-5:30pm, Sa 10am-1pm.) The **postal code** is 26723. The **telephone code** is 04921.

The **Jugendherberge Emden (HI),** An der Kesselschleuse 5 (tel. 237 97; fax 321 61), overlooks a small stream and offers bikes and canoes for rent. If you miss bus #3003 to "Herrentor" (runs hourly M-Sa), it's a 20-minute walk from the Rathaus along Am Herrentor. The hostel caters to the kiddies, with comical paintings of cartoon animals in some of the bedrooms. (DM21.20, over 26 DM26.10. Breakfast included. Sheets DM6. Reception 5-10pm. Curfew 10pm.)

NORDEN AND NORDDEICH

Norden is the transportation polestar for any excursion around Ostfriesland. By train, it connects to Emden and Norddeich (1 per hour, DM3-5), and as the anchor of the **Bäderbus,** it provides easy access to every other port town. Call or visit the **tourist office** (tel. 98 62 01; fax 98 62 90), next to the Rathaus, for specific transportation information or to book **rooms** (from DM25) for free. (Open M-F 8:30am-12:30pm, Sa 9am-1pm.)

From the Rathaus, it's impossible to miss the gigantic tower on the other side of the market belonging to the 15th-century **Ludgerkirche.** (Open April-Sept. M 10am-12:30pm, Tu-Sa 10am-12:30pm and 3-5pm. Organ concerts mid-June to mid-Sept. W at 8pm.) Experience the church's **Glockenspiel** at 9am, noon, 3, or 6pm: at each hour the bells tinkle out a line from a German song about our hearts and our friends. If you are so moved, stay the whole day and sing along—the words are printed on the church bulletin board. If you're any good, the swells drinking in the square may throw you a beer. The great East Frisian fascination with tea is explained at the **Tee-museum** (tel. 121 00), Wesserstr. 1, in the town square. For DM1 on Wednesdays (May-Aug. only), participate in an East Frisian tea ceremony. Be careful: if you raise your pinky when you drink, someone may cut it off—play it cool, Anglophiles. The ceremony takes place at tea time (2 and 3pm), of course. (Open March-Oct. Tu-Sa

10am-4pm. DM4, children DM1.50, family card DM12.) In the same building is the **Heimatmuseum,** which explains the early culture of Ostfriesland, including dike construction and shoemaking. (Same admission and hours as tea museum.)

Often passed through only en route to Norderney or Juist, the suburban port **Norddeich** actually offers spectacular land- and seascapes well worth an extra look. The town's **Jugendherberge (HI),** Sandstr. 1 (tel. 80 64; fax 818 28), is an excellent base for exploring the region. From the Hauptbahnhof (*not* Norddeich-Mole), walk towards the ship masts visible through the bushes; once you have a clear view of the ocean, turn left and walk on the land side of the **Deich,** the green grass hump between the surf and the turf. Past the Hotel Regina Maris, you'll come upon a little white way; turn left on it and the hostel will be on the next corner on the left. The main hostel compound is almost always filled with schoolchildren, but the newly built pine cabins *(Blockhütten)* in the backyard allow you to escape the shrill *Schulkinder* and the 10pm curfew. (DM14, over 26 DM19. DM14 for a bed in a cabin. DM15 to pitch your own tent in the backyard. Reception 5-8pm.) **Nordsee-Camp,** Deichstr. 21 (tel. 80 73; fax 80 74), is 20 minutes farther down Badestr., which turns into Deichstr. It has impressive views, but dike-side camping gets chilly. (DM5 per day, DM8.25 per person. *Kurtaxe* DM3. Open mid-March to Oct.).

Ferries leave Norddeich daily for Norderney and Juist. The Norddeich **tourist office,** Dörper Weg 22 (tel. 986 02; fax 98 62 90), at the very end of the street, which opens off of Badestr. The staff finds **rooms** in *Pensionen* (DM23-35) for free, doles out ferry schedules, and arranges **Watt tours.** (Open M-Th 9am-1pm and 2-5pm, F-Sa 9am-4pm.) Numerous **bike** rental shops line Dörper Weg. Take advantage of the bike trails criss-crossing the fields around Norden and Norddeich. (DM10 per day, DM40 per week. Passport required.) For a **taxi,** call 800. The **postal code** is 26506. The **telephone code** for both cities is 04931.

WATT IS WATT? The North Sea draws back several kilometers from the shore, revealing the moist brownish-blue mud of the sea floor, crawling and gurgling with life. This squishy plain is called the **Watt** (pronounced VAHT), and visitors may tread upon it out to the middle of the sea—a little bit like Jesus. However, the miraculous walking of the *Watt should never (never ever) be attempted alone*—the sticky sea-bottom gets especially sticky with quicksand and other life-endangering traps. Instead, all would-be *Watt* wanderers should enlist the services of a *Wattführer,* a trained guide, who advertise their services on most islands and in the port towns. After selecting a guide, here's what to wear: thick socks and sneakers or rubber boots, available at souvenir shops everywhere; and something warm on top. Mushing your toes in the mud can be fun, but a tour barefoot could cause them to freeze and fall off. *Viel Spaß!*

OSTFRIESISCHE INSELN (EAST FRISIAN ISLANDS)

The East Frisian islands are seven in number and float in the southernmost part of the North Sea. They begin to warm up in early June, and every summer thousands of Germans vacation here, shrieking and shouting as they jump into the frigid waters. Six or seven ferry companies have set up shop on the mainland, making for dependable transportation to all the islands, but no main transit hub exists. Unless you want to take a tiny, vibrating plane for upwards of DM100, you can't travel between islands—you always have to return to the mainland. Fortunately, the **Bäderbus** runs from **Norden** to all the ferry ports, meaning that a 9am departure from the bus stop should have you on your island by noon. To comprehend all the ins and outs of your chosen island, buy its brochure at a tourist office in the region. These pamphlets contain extensive accommodation listings and everything you ever wanted to know about each particular piece of sand.

◪ BORKUM

Lodged in an inlet halfway between Germany and the Netherlands, Borkum is where the ever-industrious Germans go to do *nothing*. The island is festive and laid-back; witness the tiny, brightly painted train that carts vacationers through a serene, flower-filled landscape to the shiny happy town at the far end of the island. The town centers on a 19th-century **lighthouse,** a lovely structure that provides all the aforementioned brightness and a great view of the island from the top.

EMS (tel. (04921) 89 07 22; fax (04921) 89 07 42) runs a ferry service from Emden's *Außenhaven* (see p. 509). The ferry ships out to the island four times a day, returning twice to the mainland. (2hr. Same-day round-trip DM25, children DM12.50. Ticket window opens 1hr. before departure.) For more money, you can get to the island in half the time on the wicked cool **catamaran.** (DM39.50, children DM24.50). On the island, rent **bikes** at the **Fahrradverleih** at the train station. (DM3 per hour, DM8 per day. Open M-F 7am-6pm; Sa 7-8am, 9am-noon, 1-2pm, and 3-5pm; Su 7-8am, 9am-noon, 1-2pm, and 4-6pm.) Borkum's **tourist office,** Am-Georg-Schütte-Pl. 5 (tel. 93 30; fax 93 31 22), at the train station in town, books **rooms** for free, and sells the island's brochure (DM1) and maps. (Open M-F 9am-6pm, Sa 10am-noon). The **telephone code** is 04922.

Borkum's **Jugendherberge (HI),** Reedestr. 231 (tel. 579; fax 71 24), a five-minute walk from the dock, fills up quickly. A written request one month in advance is necessary in order to secure a room. (DM40.70, over 26 DM45.70. Three meals included. Curfew 10:30pm, but house keys are available.) **Insel-Camping,** Hindenburgstr. 114 (tel. 10 88), is 15 minutes from the train station by foot. (DM20 per person, tent included. Open March to Oct.)

◪ NORDERNEY

More "civilized" than the mainland, the island of Norderney is Germany's oldest North Sea spa. Once visited by the likes of Bismarck and Heinrich Heine, today the island provides a retreat for hustling hordes of bourgeois tourists. The town at the western tip of the island has numerous white turn-of-the-century hotels and lots of postcard and beach-bucket shops: it's fast on its way to becoming a big town! One spot of peace is the town's tiny **church,** built in 1578, and its equally tiny **graveyard.** The church is covered with roses and ivy; inside, model ships hang from the ceiling, and the local priest plays the organ all day long. (Open during daylight hours. Free.) Away from town, the dunes and beaches of the eastern two-thirds of the island are part of the **Wattenmeer national park.** To get to the spa or surrounding nature wonderland, you'll need the services of **Ferry Company Frisia** (tel. in Norden (04931) 98 71 24, fax 98 71 31; in Norderney (04932) 913 13, fax 913 10), which runs a ferry reminiscent of the Titanic from Norddeich. (1hr. day-trip DM27, open-ended return DM38. Call or check with the tourist office for schedules.) On Norderney, two **bike** rental shops are conveniently located just beyond the harbor. **Dicki Verleih** (tel. 33 78) is on Gorch-Fock-Weg. (Open daily 9am-6:30pm. DM3 per hour, DM12 per day.) Or try the **Fahrradverleih am Hafen** (tel. 13 26), 300m down Hafenstr. as you step off the ferry. (Open daily 9am-6pm. Same prices as Dicki.) For **groceries,** head to **Comet,** across the street from Dicki on Gorch-Fock-Weg. (Open M-F 8am-1pm and 3-6pm, Sa 8am-1pm.) For a **taxi,** call 23 45 or 33 33. To spend the night, check in with the friendly folks at the **tourist office,** Bülowallee 5 (tel. 918 50; fax 824 94), at the end of Hafenstr. The staff finds **rooms** in *Pensionen* or private homes from DM26 for a DM7.50 fee. (Open M-F 9am-6pm, Sa 10am-12:30pm and 2-4pm, Su 10am-12:30pm.) The **telephone code** is 04932.

Norderney has two **youth hostels,** both of which are full of German school children and expensive as hell; guests must pay for three meals a day for the duration of their stay. However, the owner of the hostel at **Südstraße** (tel. 24 51; fax 836 00) takes pains to provide a haven for stranded travelers. Follow Zum Fähranleger to Deichstr., then turn onto Südstr. (DM37.50, including both the *Kurtaxe* and full board. Sheets DM5. Reception 8:30-9am, 5:15-6pm, and 9:45-10pm. HI members only. Open March-Oct.) Somewhat less inviting due to its inconvenient location in the middle of the island is the hostel **Am Dünensender 3** (tel. 25 74; fax 832 66). If you miss the hourly bus to "Leuchtturm," you'll have to rent a **bike** in town or suffer the 1½- to 2-hour walk. Follow Deichstr. to its end, and head left on Karl-Reger-Weg, where signs point you to the hostel. (DM37.50, over 26 DM42.50. Full board included. Reception 8:30-10am. Open March-Oct.) **Camping** (tel. 16 14) is available in summer for HI members only (DM11 per person with breakfast). **Haus Westend,** Friedrichstr. 40 (tel. 26 85; fax 832 61), offers elegant rooms across the street from the beach for surprisingly low prices. Those on the top floor have ocean views. (Singles from DM55, doubles from DM60.) Another slightly less classy option is the nearby **Hotel Adriatic,** Friedrichstr. 8. (Tel. 26 62; fax 841 54. Singles and doubles from DM65.) The main camp site on the island is **Camping Booken,** Waldweg 2 (tel. 448), the next best thing to the hostels. Call ahead. (DM12 per person, DM12 per tent. Warm showers included. Wash DM6, dry DM5. Reception 10am-noon.)

◪ JUIST AND BALTRUM

Juist is 17km long, 500m wide, and famous for its birds. First settled in 1398, it's a bit tough to settle there now unless your "tent" is made of twigs and dried leaves. **Ferries** leave from the port at Norddeich at odd times, depending on tides and season; call the **Frisia** ferry service at (04931) 98 70 in Norden or (04935) 910 10 (fax 91 01 34) on Juist. (Ferries roughly 2 per day June-Oct. Same-day round-trip DM30. Open-ended return, valid for four days, DM40. Open-ended return, valid for 12 months, DM42.) You can also walk to Juist across the *Watt* from Norddeich, but *only with a guide* (DM6, children DM5). Check with the tourist office for schedules. The rental shop **Germania,** Wilhelmstr. 17 (tel. 297), has over 600 **bikes** for lease. (DM6-15 per day. Open daily 9am-6pm.) The **tourist office,** Friesenstr. 18 (tel. 80 90; fax 80 92 23; email juist@t-online.de), has maps and books **rooms** (DM29 and up) for free. (Open May-Sept. M-F 8:30am-noon and 3-5pm, Sa 10am-noon; Oct.-April M-F 3-6pm.) There is even a **Jugendherberge (HI),** Loogster Pad 20. (Tel. 929 10; fax 82 94. DM30, over 26 DM35. Breakfast and dinner included. Reception 8-10pm or whenever a boat arrives. Open March-Dec.) The **telephone code** is 04935.

The smallest of the Frisian Islands, with a population of 500, **Baltrum** is the ideal escape from civilization. The island prides itself on its silence (due to an absolute ban on motor vehicles) and its wilderness. Horses graze everywhere, and only a small (but well-provisioned) town interrupts the pristine landscape. **Watt tours** are available here; call the local *Wattführer*, Hans-Jürgen Broul, at 918 20. (1½hr. tours DM4, children DM2. 2½hr. tour DM5, children DM3.)

To reach **Baltrum,** take the bus from the Norden train station (one short stop from Norddeich; DM4, children DM2) to **Neßmersiel** to catch the ferry. (Open-ended return DM36, children DM18. Daytrip DM24, children DM11.) Train, bus (30min.), and boat (30min.) are all timed for a convenient rendezvous. (June-Nov. 2-3 per day. Last ferry to the island does not have a corresponding ferry back.) Note that daytripping visitors must pay a DM2 *Kurtaxe*. Transportation on Baltrum is provided by a **horse-drawn "taxi"** (tel. 316). You are not welcome to bring a bike over, nor can you rent one on arrival, but the island is small enough to traverse on foot. For more information, call the ferry company, **Reederei Baltrum Linie** (tel. 913 00; fax 91 30 40) or visit the **tourist office** (tel. 91 40 03; fax 91 40 05), on the left as you leave the harbor. The office also offers hotel information and books private **rooms** for free. (Open M-F 8:30am-12:30pm and 1:30-5pm.) Sorry HI fans: **no hostel** here; the tourist office is your best bet. The **telephone code** is 04939.

◪ LANGEOOG, SPIEKEROOG, AND WANGEROOGE

LANGEOOG. The **Bäderbus** from Norden (DM7.50) or from Esens (DM3.50) travels to **Bensersiel,** the departure point for ferries to Langeoog, an island first colonized by pirates. (May-Sept. 9 departures per day; Oct.-April 5 per day. Same-day round-trip DM30, children DM18. Open-ended return, valid for four days, DM34.) Contact the ferry service, **Schiffahrt der Inselgemeinde Langeoog,** on Langeoog (tel. 69 32 60; fax 69 32 63), or at Bensersiel. (Tel. (04971) 928 90; fax (04971) 92 89 23.) Rent a **bike** on Hauptstr. at the **Fahrradverleih.** (Tel. 14 14. Open daily 9am-1:30pm and 3-6pm. DM4 per hour, DM10 per day, DM40 per week.) For more information or to book a **room** (DM25 and up), visit the **tourist office,** Hauptstr. 28 (tel. 69 30; fax 69 31 16), in front of the *Inselbahnhof.* (Open M-F 9am-6:30pm, Sa-Su 10am-2pm and 4-6:30pm, and whenever a ferry arrives.) There are a number of **supermarkets** along Hauptstr. The **telephone code** is 04972.

Langeoog's **Jugendherberge Domäne Melkhörn (HI)** (tel. 276; fax 66 94) is smack-dab in the middle of the island, 4.5km from the train station. The hostel is only accesible by foot, bike, or horse and buggy—motor vehicles are prohibited. (DM36.90, over 26 DM38.90. Members only. Full board included.) The hostel also runs a **campground.** (DM33, over 26 DM35. Full board included. Reservation required. Curfew 10pm, but if you're 18 or older, you can get a key. Members only. Open April-Sept.)

SPIEKEROOG. "No festivals celebrated here," brags the official brochure for Spiekeroog, the island that takes pride in its natural silence and shipwrecks. The **Bäderbus** out of Norden travels to **Neuharlingersiel,** the departure point for Spieker-oog. The island's **tourist office,** Noorderpad 25 (tel. 919 30; for room reservations call 91 93 25), has information on ferries, **rooms** for as little as DM17, and hiking trails. (Open March-Oct. M-F 9am-5pm, Sa 9am-noon; Nov.-Feb. M-F 9am-12:30pm and 2-5pm.) Spiekeroog's **Jugendherberge (HI),** Bid Utkiek 1 (tel. 329), is a trifling 10-minute walk from either the port or the beach. (DM36.90 per person. Full board included. Written reservations are required one year in advance! Open April-Oct.) The **telephone code** is 04976.

WANGEROOGE. The journey to **Wangerooge** is a Herculean labor, but worth it if you're desperate to avoid the crowds that plague the other islands. From Norden, take a 90-minute ride on the *Bäderbus* (DM11) to the town of **Harlesiel.** Boats leave the dock two to four times daily from April to November; exact times vary. (1½hr. Same-day return DM29. Open-ended return DM44, children 4-11 DM22.) The *Bäderbus* often does not connect directly with the ferries here; if you have problems, go to the **DB information desk** in the harbor—they can arrange **flights** if necessary. Once on the island, take the **Inselbahn,** a tiny choo-choo train (free with a ferry ticket) to the main town, or make the 30min. trek on foot along the grassy dunes. Wangerooge's **tourist office** (tel. 990; for rooms call 948 80; fax 991 14), on the Strandpromenade right outside the *Inselbahn* station, has ferry information and books **rooms.** (Open M-F 9am-noon and 2-5pm, Sa-Su whenever a ferry arrives.) They can also direct you to the haunting **Westturm,** a landmark that's been converted into a striking **Jugendherberge (HI),** a 30-minute walk from both the ferry and train stations. Look for the stone tower. (Tel. 439; fax 85 78. DM34.10, over 26 DM38.10. Full board included. Reception 7-9am, 1-3pm, and 5-7pm. Curfew 10pm for those under 18. Open May-Sept. Call several weeks in advance.) The **telephone code** is 04469.

HAMBURG

The largest port city in Germany, Hamburg radiates an inimitable recklessness. Calling its atmosphere "liberal" or "alternative" does not do the city justice. With a fiercely activist population of squatters and a thriving sex industry comparable only to Amsterdam's, the city is a crazy coupling of the progressive and the perverse. As a busy port, Hamburg gracefully grew over the centuries into an industrial center of nearly two million inhabitants. Straddling several rivers, it was an early hub for overland trade from the Baltic Sea, and the first German stock exchange convened here in 1558. In 1618, Hamburg gained the status of Free Imperial City, a proud tradition of autonomy that endures to this day, as it wields considerable political power as one of Germany's sixteen *Länder*.

Poised on the crest of Germany's breakneck industrialization and naval construction drive, Hamburg became one of Europe's wealthiest cities by WWI. The *Hamburg-Amerika Linie* ruled the oceans of industry as the largest shipping firm in the world. At the outset of WWII, the city suffered a severe pummeling as the first stop on Royal Air Force bombing raids. The port was a primary target for the Allies; a single air raid killed 50,000 civilians, many of whom lived in crowded tenements along the waterfront. The conflagration in the streets reached temperatures of 1,000°C, leaving nearly half of the city's buildings in ruins. Fortunately, Germany's richest city could afford the reconstruction of much of its copper-roofed architecture. Since the late 1960s, an active conservation movement has steadily lobbied for the restoration of historic buildings, including museums, hotels, and houses. In the early 80s, however, violent riots erupted when police attempted to evacuate warehouses occupied by anarchists and left-wing intellectuals who were protesting property speculators' acquisition of the real estate. Today, Hamburg expresses its restlessness less violently, by exuding the energy of a city that has become a center of contemporary artists and intellectuals as well as reveling party-goers who live it up in Germany's self-declared "capital of lust."

HIGHLIGHTS OF HAMBURG

■ Befitting the second-largest city in Germany, Hamburg's museums are world-class: the **Hamburger Kunsthalle** displays a huge collection of art from medieval times to the present, while the **Deichtorhallen** hosts contemporary creations, and the **Museum für Kunst und Gewerbe** specializes in decorative arts (p. 524).

■ Hamburg is also damn sexy, with its **Reeperbahn red-light district** (p. 515), second only to Amsterdam's, and its **Erotic Art Museum** (p. 524).

■ A staggering **nightlife** scene will make you dance, fool, dance (p. 525).

▐ GETTING THERE AND GETTING AROUND

Flights: Jasper (tel. 227 10 60) makes the 25min. trip from the Kirchenallee exit of the Hauptbahnhof to **Fuhlsbüttel Airport** (tel. 507 50) every 20min. daily 5am-9:20pm. DM8.50, under 13 DM4. Or take U-Bahn #1 or S-Bahn #1 to "Ohlsdorf," then take an **express bus** to the airport, which runs every 10min. (daily 5:30am-11pm). DM3.90. **Lufthansa** (tel. (0180) 380 38 03) and **Air France** (tel. 50 75 24 59) are the two heavy hitters that fly to Hamburg.

Trains: The **Hauptbahnhof** handles most traffic with hourly connections to Berlin (2¾hr., DM93), Frankfurt (3¾hr., DM182), and Munich (6hr., DM256). Further trips to Hannover (1½hr., 3 per hour, DM67), Copenhagen (6hr., 3 per day, DM102), and Amsterdam (5½hr., 3 per day, DM105). The efficient staff at the **DB Reisezentrum** sells tickets and books vacation packages. Open daily 5:30am-11pm. **Dammtor** station is near the university, and **Altona** station is in the west of the city. Most trains to and from

Schleswig-Holstein stop only at Altona. Frequent trains and the S-Bahn connect the 3 stations. **Lockers** are available 24hr. for DM2-4 per day.

Buses: The **ZOB** (you down with ZOB? Yeah you know me!) is located across Steintorpl. from the Hauptbahnhof. To Berlin (8 per day, DM41), Paris (15hr., daily, DM115), Copenhagen (6hr., 2 per day, DM63). **Polenreisen** has good deals to Poland. Open M-F 9am-8pm, Sa 9:30am-1:30pm and 4-8pm, Su 4-8pm. **Lockers** are located in the main hall but cannot be accessed between 9pm and 5:30am (DM2).

Ferries: Scandinavian Seaways, Van-der-Smissen-Str. 4 (tel. 389 03 71; fax 38 90 31 41), about 1km west of the Fischmarkt (S-Bahn #1 or 3 to "Königstr."), sets sail to England and Ireland. Overnight ferries run to Harwich, England (20hr.), every other day. The cheapest tickets cost DM152, F-Sa DM182; students receive a 25% discount. Other destinations include Copenhagen, Oslo, and Amsterdam. Open M-F 10am-4:30pm; phone reservations M-F 9am-6pm, Sa 9am-2pm.

Public Transportation: HVV operates an efficient U-Bahn, S-Bahn, and bus network. Single tickets within the downtown area cost DM1.80. There are also 1- and 3-day tickets (DM9.50 and 23.30); consider buying a **Hamburg Card** instead (see below). All tickets can be bought at orange *Automaten*.

Taxis: Taxiruf, tel. 44 10 11.

Car Rental: Hertz has an office in the Hauptbahnhof's ReiseBank (see **Currency Exchange,** below; tel. 28 01 20 13; fax 24 53 78). Rates start at DM400 per week.

Mitfahrzentrale: City Netz Mitfahrzentrale, Ernst-Merk-Str. 8 (tel. 194 40). Ride-sharing deals. Berlin DM31, Köln DM45, Amsterdam DM59, Paris DM89. Open daily 7am-9pm.

Boat Rental: Rent sailboats, paddleboats and rowboats on the Außenalster from **Segelschule Kpt. Pieper,** An der Alster (tel. 24 75 78), directly across from the Hotel Atlantic at the foot of the Kennedybrücke. Sailboats DM27 per hour for 1-2 people (additional skippers DM3 per person), paddleboats and rowboats DM19 per hour. Sailing license required to rent sailboats. Open daily 10am-9pm.

Hitchhiking: *Let's Go* does not recommend hitchhiking as a safe mode of transportation. Those headed to Berlin, Copenhagen, or Lübeck take U-Bahn #3 to "Rauhes Haus" then walk up Mettlerkampsweg and turn right on Sievekingsallee to Hamburg Horn (a treacherous traffic rotary at the base of the *Autobahn*). Hitchers aiming for points south take S-Bahn #3 to "Wilhelmsburg" and wait at Raststätte Stillhorn.

ORIENTATION

Hamburg's fame as a North Sea port relies upon its huge harbor 100km inland, on the north bank of the **Elbe.** The city center sits between the river and the two city lakes, **Außenalster** and **Binnenalster,** formed by the confluence of the Alster and Bille with the Elbe. Most major sights lie between the **St. Pauli Landungsbrücken** port area in the west and the Hauptbahnhof in the east. Both the **Nordbahnhof** and **Südbahnhof** U-Bahn stations exit onto the Hauptbahnhof.

The **Hanseviertel** is a quarter thick with banks, shops, art galleries, and auction houses. The area's glamour turns window-shopping into an aesthetic pleasure, while the nearby shipping canals manage to give the quarter a pseudo-Venetian charm. North of the downtown, the **university** dominates the **Dammtor** area and sustains a vibrant community of students and intellectuals. To the west of the university, the **Sternschanze** neighborhood is a politically active community home to artists, squatters, and a sizeable Turkish population. The **Altona** district, with its own major train station, was once an independent city ruled by Denmark; as Hamburg grew, the Danes were ousted. At the south end of town, an entirely different atmosphere reigns in **St. Pauli,** whose raucous **Fischmarkt** (fish market) is juxtaposed by the equally wild (and no less smelly) **Reeperbahn,** home to Hamburg's infamous sex trade.

HAMBURG

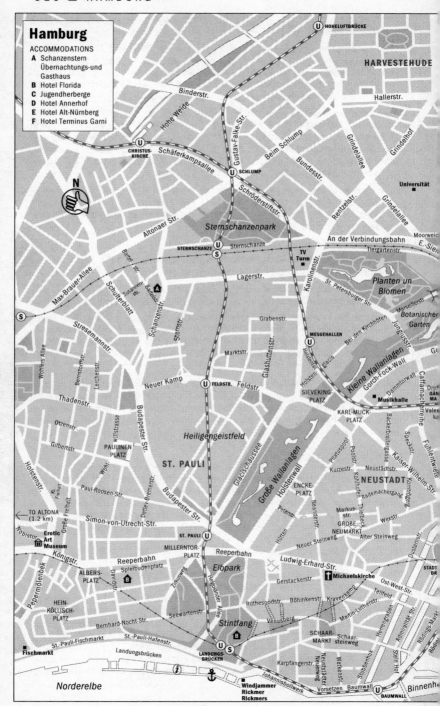

Hamburg

ACCOMMODATIONS

A Schanzenstern
Übernachtungs-und
Gasthaus
B Hotel Florida
C Jugendherberge
D Hotel Annerhof
E Hotel Alt-Nürnberg
F Hotel Terminus Garni

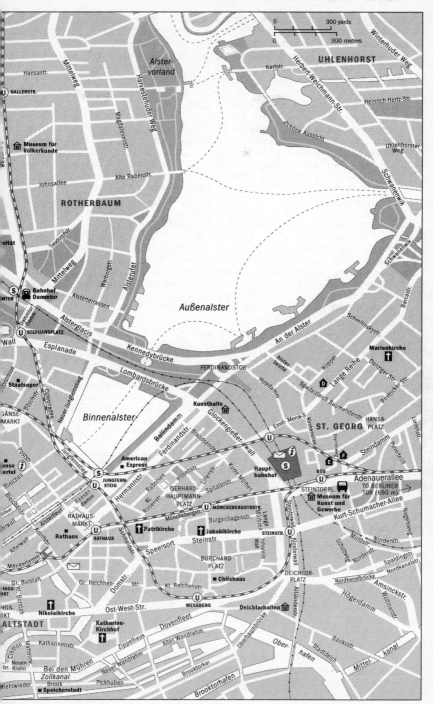

7 PRACTICAL INFORMATION

TOURIST AND FINANCIAL SERVICES

Tourist Offices: Hamburg's two main tourist offices supply free maps and pamphlets. The **Hauptbahnhof office**, near the Kirchenallee exit (tel. 30 05 12 01; fax 30 05 13 33; email info@hamburg-tourism.de; www.hamburg-tourism.de), books **rooms** for a DM6 fee. Open daily 7am-11pm. The less crowded **St. Pauli Landungsbrücken office** is located between piers 4 and 5 (tel. 30 05 12 00). Open daily 10am-7pm. A third office is in the **Hanseviertel** mall. Open daily 9am-6pm. For advanced reservations and information, call the **Hamburg Hotline** (tel. 30 05 13 00; open daily 8am-8pm). The offices all sell the **Hamburg Card,** a great means of exploring the city. For a fairly low price, it provides unlimited access to public transportation, admission to most museums, and discounts on bus and boat tours. 1 day DM12.50; 3 days DM26, without transportation DM10. An even better deal is the **Group Card,** which provides the same deals for up to five people. 1 day DM24; 3 days DM42, without transportation DM21.

Tours: Top-Tour-Hamburg (tel. 227 10 60) operates sight-seeing tours leaving every 20 minutes from 9:30am to 5pm from the Kirchenallee exit of the Hauptbahnhof and the St. Pauli Landungsbrücken. Adults DM22, children DM11; with Hamburg Card DM4 and DM2. **Hamburg Vision** (tel. 31 79 01 27) offers a similar tour with additional stops at the Rathaus and Michaeliskirche. DM25, students DM19, under 12 free. Tours last between 1¼hr. and 2hr. **O'Neil Bikes,** Beethovenstr. 37 (tel. 22 12 16), offers German-language bike tours of the city and environs. Prices from DM49 for a 3-4hr. tour. **Alster-Touristik** (tel. 347 42 40), across from Hotel Atlantic on the Außenalster (two blocks north of the Hauptbahnhof), leads a 1hr. jaunts around the lakes. Daily on the quarter hour 10am-5pm. DM13, seniors DM9, children DM6.50.

Consulates: Ireland, Feldbrunnenstr. 43 (tel. 44 18 62 13). U-Bahn #1 to "Hallerstr." Open M-F 9am-1pm. **New Zealand,** Heimhuder Str. 56 (tel. 442 55 50). Open M-Th 9am-5:30pm, F 9am-4:30pm. **U.K.,** Harvestehuder Weg 8a (tel./fax 448 03 20). U-Bahn #1 to "Hallerstr." Open M-F 9am-noon and 2-4pm. **U.S.,** Alsterufer 27 (tel. 41 17 10), on the Außenalster's west side. Open M-F 9am-noon.

Currency Exchange: ReiseBank, on the second floor of the Hauptbahnhof near the Kirchenallee exit, arranges money transfers for Western Union, cashes traveler's checks, and exchanges money for a DM5 fee. Amuse yourself with their computerized business card maker (DM2-10). Open daily 7:30am-10pm. Otherwise, try one of the dozens of banks downtown. Generally open M-W and F 9am-1pm and 2:30-4pm, Th 9am-1pm and 2:30-6pm. There's also a **ReiseBank branch** in the Altona train station.

American Express: Ballindamm 39, 20095 Hamburg (tel. 30 39 38 11 12; fax 30 90 81 30). Mail held for cardmembers up to 4 weeks; all banking services. Open M-F 9am-6pm, Sa 10am-1pm.

LOCAL SERVICES

Bookstores: Heine Buch, Grindelallee 24-28 (tel. 441 13 30), in the university district, has a superb selection of German literature. It also has an impressively comprehensive English-language section. Open M-F 9:30am-7pm, Sa 10am-4pm.

Library: Staats- und Universitätsbibliothek, Von-Melle-Park 3 (tel. 428 38 22 33). Hamburg's university library holds 2.75 million volumes, including a fine English-language collection. Open M-F 9am-9pm, Sa 10am-1pm; Aug. only M-F 9am-7:30pm, Sa 10am-1pm.

Gay and Lesbian Resources: Hein und Fiete (tel. 24 03 33), Pulverteich 21, in the rainbow-striped building. Open M-F 4-9pm, Sa 4-7pm. **Magnus-Hirschfeld-Centrum,** Borgweg 8 (tel. 279 00 69). U-Bahn #3 or bus #108 to "Borgweg." Daily films and counseling sessions. Evening café open daily 5pm-midnight. Center open M and F 2-6pm, Tu-W 7-10pm.

Women's Resources: See **Frauenbuchladen und Café,** p. 521

Laundromat: Schnell und Sauber, Grindelallee 158, in the university district. S-Bahn #21 or 31 to "Dammtor." Wash 6kg DM6, soap included. Dry DM1 for 15min. Open daily 7am-10:30pm. There are also several laundromats on Simon-von-Utrecht-Str., heading towards the Altona station from St. Pauli.

EMERGENCY AND COMMUNICATIONS

Emergency: Police, tel. 110. From the Kirchenallee exit of the Hauptbahnhof, turn left and follow the signs for "BGS/Bahnpolizei." There's also a police station on the **Reeperbahn** at the corner of Davidstr. and Spielbudenplatz. **Fire** and **Ambulance,** tel. 112.

Rape Crisis Line: Tel. 25 55 66. Open M and Th 10am-1pm and 3-7pm, Tu 9:30am-1pm and 3-4pm, W 3-4pm, F 10am-1pm. Staff speaks English.

Pharmacy: Exit the Hauptbahnhof on Kirchenallee and turn right. The staff of the **Senator-Apotheke** speaks English. Open M-F 7am-8pm, Sa 8am-4pm.

Post Office: Branch at the Kirchenallee exit of the Hauptbahnhof, 20097 Hamburg. Open M-F 8am-8pm, Sa 9am-6pm, Su 10am-4pm. **Poste Restante,** 20099 Hamburg, in the main branch on Grosser Burstah 3. Open M-F 8am-6pm, Sa 8am-12pm.

Internet Access: In the **Staats- und Universitätsbibliothek** (see **Library,** above). Head to the 2nd floor and look for the "Bibliografien" section. Open M-F 10am-7pm, Sa 10am-1pm. Free. Note that there are only six PCs, and the wait can be long. To avoid the lines, head to **Cyberb@r,** located on the 3rd floor of the gigantic **Karstadt** department store on Mönckebergstr. DM5 per 30min.

PHONE CODE	040

ACCOMMODATIONS AND CAMPING

Hamburg's single rooms, from DM60, reflect the price of the city's accommodations. Many establishments are tawdry with few comforts. A slew of small, relatively cheap *Pensionen* line **Steindamm, Steintorweg, Bremer Weg,** and **Bremer Reihe,** around the Hauptbahnhof. While the area is filled with drug addicts and wannabe-*mafiosi*, the hotels are for the most part safe. The tourist office's free *Hotelführer* aids in navigating past the filth. For stays longer than four weeks, try the **Mitwohnzentrale** at Schulterblatt 112. (Tel. 194 45. Open M-F 9am-1pm and 2-6pm, Sa 9am-1pm.) Take S-Bahn #21 or 31 or U-Bahn #3 to "Sternschanze." A passport is required, as well as a deposit of either DM100 cash or DM50 and a bank account number.

HOSTELS AND CAMPING

Schanzenstern Übernachtungs-und Gasthaus, Bartelsstr. 12 (tel. 439 84 41; fax 439 34 13; email info@schanzerstern.de; www.schanzenstern.de). S-Bahn #21 and #3 or U-Bahn #3 to "Sternschanze." Left onto Schanzenstr., right on Susannenstr., and left to Bartelsstr. Located in the middle of an electrifying neighborhood of students, working-class Turks, and left-wing dissenters, the Schanzenstern is managed by a politically and ecologically progressive cooperative. Situated on the upper floors of a renovated fountain pen factory, the hotel's 50 rooms are clean, quiet, bright, and tastefully decorated with Swedish wood furniture, plants, and cheerfully painted walls. Prices per person: dorm beds DM33, quints DM35, quads DM35, triples DM38, doubles DM45, singles DM60. Breakfast buffet DM11. Reception 6:30-2am. Wheelchair accessible. Reservations are a must in the summer and at New Year's.

Instant Sleep, Max-Brauer-Allee 277 (tel. 43 18 23 10; fax 43 18 23 11; email backpackerhostel@instantsleep.de; www.instantsleep.de). S-Bahn #21, 3 or 31 or U-Bahn #3 to "Sternschanze." From the station go straight on Schanzenstr., turn left on Altonaer Str. and follow it until it becomes Max-Brauer-Allee. This brand-new, spic-and-span hostel overlooks the progressive Schanzenstern neighborhood. Each room is painted with a different brightly-colored design. Email and internet access available. Prices per person: dorm beds DM29, triples DM35, doubles DM38, singles DM45. Sheets DM3. Reception 9am-2pm. No curfew. Call ahead.

Jugendherberge auf dem Stintfang (HI), Alfred-Wegener-Weg 5 (tel. 31 34 88; fax 31 54 07; email jh-stintfang@t-online.de; www.schoelzel.com/jh-hamburg/index.shtml). S-Bahn #1, 2, or 3, or U-Bahn #3 to "Landungsbrücke." A great location near the Reeperbahn and the subway and a beautiful view of the harbor compensate for the regimental house rules. Very clean rooms, showers, and kitchen. All halls same-sex. The hostel also features a high-tech email, internet, fax, phone, and word-processing facility. DM27, over 26 DM32. Sheets and breakfast included. Non-members pay a DM6 surcharge. Private rooms available for couples and families. Lunch and dinner DM8.50. Reception 12:30pm-1am. Lockout 9:30-11:30am. Curfew 1am. Call ahead.

Jugendgästehaus und Gästehaus Horner-Rennbahn (HI), Rennbahnstr. 100 (tel. 651 16 71; fax 655 65 16; email jgh-hamburg@t-online.de), U-Bahn #3 to "Horner-Rennbahn" or bus #160 from Berliner Tor. From the main exit of the station, turn right—the hostel is about 10min. by foot, at the corner of Tribünenweg. Inconveniently far from the center, located next to a horse-racing track. Extremely clean and secure. DM31.50, over 26 DM37; slightly less for longer stays. Members only. Family rooms available. Reception 7-9:30am and 12:30pm-1am. Curfew 1am, stragglers admitted at 2am.

Camping: Campingplatz Rosemarie Buchholz, Kieler Str. 374 (tel. 540 45 32). From Altona train station, take bus #182 or #183 to "Basselweg" (10 min.), then walk 100m in the same direction as traffic. Leafy setting near a very busy road. DM7 per person. Tents DM12.50 per night. Showers DM1.50. Reception 8am-10pm. Quiet hours 10pm-7am. Check-out noon. Call ahead.

HOTELS

Hotel Alt-Nürnberg, Steintorweg 15 (tel. 24 60 24; fax 280 46 34). From the station, go right on Kirchenallee and left onto Steintorweg. Heidi-themed decor in the heart of Hamburg's somewhat sketchy Hauptbahnhof neighborhood. Very convenient to trains. Each clean and smallish room features a telephone, some with TV. Singles DM60, with shower DM90; double DM90, with shower DM130. Call ahead.

Hotel Florida, Spielbudenpl. 22 (tel. 31 43 94). U-Bahn #3 to "St.Pauli," or S-Bahn #1 or 3 to "Reeperbahn." Located in the heart of Hamburg's thriving nightlife and sex industry, Hotel Florida offers small but clean rooms adjacent to Hamburg's biggest clubs. Singles DM60, doubles DM95, triples DM135. Breakfast included.

Hotel Terminus Garni, Steindamm 5 (tel. 280 31 44; fax 24 15 18). From the Hauptbahnhof's Kirchenallee exit, turn right. Doubles DM45, with shower DM60; triples with bath DM165. Breakfast included. 24hr. reception.

Hotel Annerhof, Lange Reihe 23 (tel. 24 34 26; fax 24 55 69). From the train station's Kirchenallee exit take the 2nd left. Singles DM48, doubles DM82. Call ahead.

⬛ FOOD

The most interesting part of town from a culinary standpoint is **Sternschanze,** where Turkish fruit stands, Asian *Imbiße*, and avant-garde cafés entice the hungry passersby with good food and (equally important!) atmosphere. **Schulterblatt, Susannenstr.** and **Schanzenstr.** host a slew of funky cafés and restaurants. Slightly cheaper establishments abound in the **university** area, especially along **Rentzelstr., Grindelhof,** and **Grindelallee.** In **Altona,** the pedestrian zone leading up to the train station is packed with ethnic food stands and produce shops. Check out the market inside Altona's massive **Mercado** mall, which includes everything from sushi bars to Portuguese fast-food. There's even a **Safeway.** (Open M-F 10am-8pm, Sa 9am-4pm.) In a pinch, the shopping arcade at the **Hauptbahnhof** has about a dozen fast food joints. (Open daily 6am-11pm.)

STERNSCHANZE

Take S-Bahn #21 or 31 or U-Bahn #3 to "Sternschanze."

⬛ **Noodles,** Schanzenstr. 2-4 (tel. 439 28 40). Along with innovative pasta creations, Noodles serves up veggie entrees alongside a full bar. Trippy ambient music provides an appropriate acoustic background for the alternative community of Sternschanze. Try the tortellini with broccoli and ham (DM10.50, small portion DM8) or one of their generous salads. Breakfast from DM7.50. Beer DM5. Open M-Th and Su 10am-1am, F-Sa 10am-3am.

Machwitz, Schanzenstr. 121 (tel. 43 81 77). Join the hip student crowd in the funky angular interior or people-watch outside. The CD collection is even better stocked than the bar. Creamy soups DM6, entrees DM10-15. Occasional concerts from local bands. Open daily from 10am until everyone leaves.

Asia Imbiß Bok, Bartelstr. 29. *Imbiß* is a misnomer here—this joint serves real restaurant food. Try the spicy Thai noodles or some of the other savory Korean and Chinese options (DM8-16). Full Korean dinner DM25. Open daily 11:30am-11:30pm.

Falafel-König, Schanzenstr. 113. As the name implies, this tiny Lebanese *Imbiß* is indeed the seat of the "Falafel-King." Basic falafel DM5, with one of half a dozen toppings (mmm...cauliflower!) DM6. Open M-Th and Su 11:30am-midnight, F-Sa 11:30am-3am.

UNIVERSITY

Mensa, Schlüterstr. 7. S-Bahn #21 or 31 to "Dammtor," then head left on Rothenbaumchaussee, left on Moorweidenstr., then right onto Schlüterstr. Check bulletin boards for special events. Meals DM2-7 with student ID, more for non-students. Open daily 10am-7:30pm; serves lunch M-F 11am-2pm and dinner 4-7pm.

Geo Pizza aus dem Holzbackofen, Beim Schlump 27 (tel. 45 79 29). U-Bahn #2 or 3 to "Schlump." Delectable pizzas (DM9-16) and a large vegetarian selection. The Inferno Pizza (DM11.80-13.80), topped with an incendiary blend of jalapeños, red peppers, beef, onions, salsa, and corn, transforms humans into fire-belching beasts. Open M-F from 9am, Sa-Su from 10:30am.

ALTONA

Café Gasoline, on Bahrenfelder Str. near the Altona train station, caffeinates its customers as they relax in comfy wicker chairs. The carefully spray-painted exterior is just as artistic as the chic candlelit interior. Open daily from 11am until the java runs out.

Duschbar, on A.-Wartenburg-Pl. Attracts a lively 20-something crowd with its ultra-90s decor and drink menu. Open daily 11am-late; happy "hour" 6-9pm.

Indian Tandoori, Ottenser Hauptstr. 20, in the pedestrian zone near Altona train station. Whether you eat inside or outdoors in the *Fußgängerzone*, Indian Tandoori's food is sure to jump-start your Teutonically impaired taste buds. If you're in a hurry, grab an order of samosas (DM6); otherwise, feast on their namesake tandoori chicken (DM11) or chicken tikka masala (DM10). There are also a number of vegetarian options; try the palak paneer (DM13.50).

ELSEWHERE IN HAMBURG

Frauenbuchladen und Café, Bismarckstr. 98 (tel. 420 47 48). U-Bahn #3 to "Hoheluftbrücke" A primarily lesbian, women-only establishment. Pick up the *Hamburger Frauenzeitung* (DM6) if you read German. Open M-F 10am-7pm, Sa 10am-3pm.

◼ SIGHTS

ALTSTADT

GROSSE MICHAELSKIRCHE. The gargantuan 18th-century Michaelskirche is the grand-daddy of all Hamburg churches. It is affectionately and somewhat fearfully referred to as *"der Michael."* While the exterior is a bit imposing—the statue of St. Michael above the doorway mischievously grins at the passing tourists—with its scalloped walls, the inside looks like a concert hall. *Der Michael*'s bulbous Baroque tower is the official emblem of Hamburg; it's also the only one of the city's six spires that can be ascended—by foot or by elevator. On weekends, the tower is used to project a multimedia presentation about Hamburg's millennial

HAMBURG

existence onto a five-meter-high screen. *(Tel. 37 67 81 00. Open April-Sept. M-Sa 9am-6pm, Su 11:30am-5:30pm; Oct.-March M-Sa 10am-4:30pm, Su 11:30am-4:30pm. DM1. Screenings Th-Su hourly 12:30-3:30pm. DM5, students, children, and Hamburg Card holders DM2.50. Organ music April-Aug. daily at noon and 5pm. Tower DM4.50, students and children DM2. Crypt DM2.50 for the living.)*

RATHAUS. The copper spires of the town hall, a richly ornamented, neo-Renaissance monstrosity that serves as the political center of Hamburg, rises above the city center. The Rathausmarkt in front of it is the place for constant festivities, ranging from demonstrations to medieval fairs. *(Tel. 428 31 20 64. Tours of the Rathaus in German every 30min. M-Th 10am-3pm, F-Su 10am-1pm. Tours in English and French every hour M-Th 10:15am-3:15pm, F-Su 10:15am-1:15pm.)*

NIKOLAIKIRCHE. In the city center rests somber ruins of the old Nikolaikirche, a reminder of Hamburg's time as an Allied bombing target. A 1943 air raid flattened this example of early neo-Gothic architecture. City officials have left the ruins unrestored as a memorial to the horrors of war. In front of its bombed-out hull lies the **Hopfenmarkt,** home to a motley melange of *Imbiße*, book, and clothing stands. *(Just south of the Rathaus, off Ost-West-Str.)* Behind the church ruins is a zig-zagging maze of canals and bridges centered on the **Alte Börse** (old stock market). The buildings along nearby **Trostbrücke** sport huge copper models of clipper ships on their spires—a reminder of the place of sea-trade in making Hamburg's wealth.

SPEICHERSTADT. East of the docks near the copper dome of the **St. Katherinenkirche** *(open daily 9am-5pm; free organ concerts W at 12:30pm)* lies the historic warehouse district Speicherstadt. These elegant, late 19th-century brick storehouses are filled with cargo, spices, and swarms of stevedores.

KONTORHAUSVIERTEL. At the corner of Burchardstr. and Pumpen, the **Chilehaus** showcases architecture of a different generation. Designed to look like the sails of a ship when viewed from the plaza to the east, this striking *trompe l'oeil* office building is the work of Expressionist architect Fritz Höger, who also designed the **Sprinkenhof** building across the street. The Great Fire of 1842 unfortunately consumed many of the quarter's 17th- to 19th-century office buildings, some of which are carefully restored. On summer afternoons, locals gather in the sidewalk cafes.

MÖNKEBERGSTRASSE. The pedestrian shopping zone, which stretches from the Rathaus to the Hauptbahnhof along Mönckebergstr., is punctuated by two spires. The first belongs to the **St. Petrikirche,** site of the oldest church in Hamburg. Free concerts resonate through its Gothic arches every Wednesday evening at 5:15pm. *(Open M-Tu and F 10am-6:30pm, W-Th 10am-7pm, Sa 10am-5pm, Su 9am-6pm.)* The second church in the area is the **St. Jakobikirche,** known for its 14th-century Arp-Schnittger organ. *(Tel. 536 60 79. Open daily 10am-5pm.)*

OTHER SIGHTS

ST. PAULI LANDUNGSBRÜCKEN. Hamburg's harbor, the largest port in Germany, lights up at night with ships from all over the world. More than 100,000 dockers and sailors work the ports, and their presence permeates Hamburg. Numerous companies offer harbor cruises: **Kapitän Prüsse** departs every 30 min. from Pier 3. *(Tel. 31 31 30. DM15, children DM7.50.)* **HADAG** offers more elaborate cruises of outlying areas from Pier 2. *(Tel. 311 70 70. Every 30min. 9:30am-6pm. DM15, children DM7.50.)* After sailing the East Indies, the 19th-century **Windjammer Rickmer Rickmers** was docked at Pier 1 and restored as a museum ship. Old navigation equipment, all brass and polish, is juxtaposed with modern nautical technology. *(Tel. 35 69 31 19. Open daily 10am-6pm. DM6, students DM5, children under 12 DM4.)* The elevator to the **old Elbe tunnel** protrudes through the floor of the building behind Pier 6. With all of its machinery exposed, the building looks like a nautilus machine built for the gods.

PLANTEN UN BLOMEN. To the west of the Alster near the university area, the park features dozens of obsessively well-planned and -trimmed flower beds surrounding two lakes and a handful of outdoor cafés. From May to September, daily performances ranging from Irish step-dancing to Hamburg's police orchestra shake the outdoor **Musikpavillon;** there are also nightly **Wasserlichtkonzerte,** lighted fountain arrangements put to music. *(May-Aug. 10pm, Sept. 9pm).*

ALSTER LAKES. To the north of the city center, the two Alster lakes are bordered by tree-lined paths. Elegant promenades and commercial facades surround **Binnenalster,** while windsurfers, sailboats, and paddleboats dominate the larger **Außenalster.** Ferries, more personal than the bigger Hamburg boats, sail from here (see **Tours,** p. 518).

FISHMARKT. Veritable anarchy reigns as charismatic vendors haul in and hawk huge amounts of fish, produce, and other goods. The market fascinates in the morning, as early risers mix with flashy revelers trying to rally and keep the night going. Listen for cries of *"Ohne Geld!"* ("No Money!") and keep your head up—to grab attention, the fruit vendors toss free pineapples into the crowd. *(U- or S-Bahn to "Landungsbrücken" or S-Bahn to "Königstr." Market open Su 6-10am, off-season 7-10am.)*

BEYOND THE CENTER

GEDENKSTÄTTE JANUSZ-KORCZAK-SCHULE. In the midst of warehouses, the school serves as a memorial to 20 Jewish children brought here from Auschwitz for "testing" and murdered by the S.S. only hours before Allied troops arrived. Visitors are invited to plant a rose for the children in the flower garden behind the school, where plaques with the children's photographs line the fence. *(Bullenhuser Damm 92. Tel. 78 32 95. S-Bahn #21 to "Rothenburgsort." Walk north from the station and make a right on Bullenhuser Damm; the school is 200m down. Open daily 10am-5pm. Free.)*

ERNST-THÄLMANN-GEDENKSTÄTTE. In 1923, Communist leader Ernst Thälmann led a march on the police headquarters, setting off a riot that resulted in the death of 61 protestors and 17 police officers. Thälmann was later murdered by the Nazis at Buchenwald and subsequently became the first martyr of the GDR. His life and times are chronicled in this small museum. *(Ernst-Thälmann-Platz. Tel. 47 41 84. Open Tu-F 10am-5pm, Sa-Su 10am-1pm. Donation requested.)*

KZ NEUENGAMME. An idyllic agricultural village east of Hamburg provided the backdrop for the Neuengamme concentration camp. Here the Nazis killed 55,000 prisoners through slave labor. In 1948, Hamburg prison authorities took over the camp and demolished all of the buildings to construct a German prison on the site; the mayor at that time believed that the facility would cleanse Neuengamme's sullied reputation. In 1989, the Hamburg senate moved the prison in order to build a more appropriate memorial on the site. Banners inscribed with the names and death-dates of the victims, along with four 500-page books listing their names, hang in the **Haus des Gedenkens.** *(Jean-Doldier-Weg. Tel. 723 10 31. Take S-Bahn #21 to "Bergedorf," then bus #227, which runs hourly on the :40. About 1hr. from Hamburg to "Jean-Doldier-Weg." Open May-Oct. Tu-Su 10am-6pm, Sept.-April 10am-5pm.)*

🏛 MUSEUMS

Hamburg's many museums are filled with everything from African war masks to 18th-century pornography. The one- or three-day **Hamburg Card** (see p. 518) provides access to most of these museums, with the exception of the Deichtorhallen and the Erotic Art Museum. Hamburg also has a thriving and exciting contemporary art scene; pick up a list of the city's galleries and their current exhibits at either tourist office. At noon on Wednesdays, most museums offer a short presentation or lecture on topics ranging from Cézanne to Korean shamanism; the free newspaper *Die Museen* lists topics and current exhibits.

HAMBURGER KUNSTHALLE. This first-rate art museum is three-pronged: the first part of the collection contains a superb exhibition of German and Dutch art, from the medieval era through the 19th century. The next assortment contains works by 19th-century French painters such as Millet, Courbet, Manet, and Monet. The newly built **Galerie der Gegenwart** displays Warhols, Picassos, and a pair of Levi's nailed to the wall. *(Glockengießerwall 1. Turn left from the "City" exit of the Hauptbahnhof and cross the street. Tel. 428 54 26 12. Open Tu-W and F-Su 10am-6pm, Th 10am-9pm. DM15, students DM12, family pass DM21.)*

DEICHTORHALLEN HAMBURG. Hamburg's contemporary art scene resides here in two buildings that were former fruit market halls. New exhibits each season showcase up-and-coming artists. Outstanding, but expensive. *(Deichtorstr. 1-2. U-Bahn #1 to "Steinstr." Follow signs from the subway station; look for two entwined iron circles. Tel. 32 10 30. Open Tu-Su 11am-6pm, Sa-Su 10am-6pm. DM10, students each building DM8.)*

MUSEUM FÜR KUNST UND GEWERBE. A fantastic, rich collection of handicrafts, china, and furnishings ranging from ancient Egyptian and Roman to Asian and *Jugendstil*. Sure to inspire you to new heights of interior decoration. The museum also has an extensive photography collection, from daguerreotypes to digital images. *(Steintorpl. 1. Tel. 428 54 27 32. One block south of the Hauptbahnhof. Open Tu-W and F-Su 10am-6pm, Th 10am-9pm. DM8, students and seniors DM4, under 16 DM3.)*

EROTIC ART MUSEUM. Follow the silver sperm painted on the floor as they lead you through four floors of tactful iniquity. The first two floors examine postcard-sized sketches of assorted aristocrats and their voluptuous maids, while the top two levels focus on the art of bondage. The Reeperbahn location is home to the permanent collection, while the building at Bernhard-Nocht-Str. entertains exhibits that are just passing through. The museum is in surprisingly good taste, as evidenced by the Haring originals on the fourth floor and the sonorous classical music. The Reeperbahn peep-show crowd tends to head elsewhere. *(Nobistor 12 and Bernhard-Nocht-Str. 69. Tel. 31 78 41 26. S-Bahn #1 or 3 to "Reeperbahn." Open Tu-Su 10am-midnight. DM15, students DM10.)*

HAMBURGISCHES MUSEUM FÜR VÖLKERKUNDE. With two floors of glass cases brimming with weapons, clothing, and cooking utensils, the exhibit is a treasure trove of imperial plunder. *(Rothenbaumchaussee 64. Tel. 428 48 25 24. U-Bahn #1 to "Hallerstr." Open Tu-W and F-Su 10am-6pm, Th 10am-9pm. DM7, family card DM14, students and seniors DM3.50, under 16 DM2. Half-price on Fridays.)*

HERZLICHEN GLÜCKWUNSCH!

Need a place to celebrate your birthday while on vacation? For DM75-100, the **Museum für Kunst und Gewerbe** will lead you and your friends around its hallowed halls on appropriately themed tours. Topics include *amor vincit omnia* (depictions of love) or the indubitably more popular *in vino veritas*, which traces the importance of wine and is, of course, followed by ample samplings of the "devil's elixir." *Zum wohl!*

♫ ENTERTAINMENT

As the cultural capital of the North, Hamburg patronizes the arts with money and attention. Federal and municipal subsidies of high culture in Germany lower ticket prices significantly; in addition, most box offices and concert halls offer generous student discounts. The **Staatsoper,** Dammtorstr. 28 (tel. 35 17 21), houses one of the best opera companies in Germany, tending toward the modern, but also playing a steady stream of Bizet and Puccini. Tickets start at DM7. (Take U-Bahn #1 to "Stephansplatz." Open M-F 10am-6:30pm, Sa 10am-2pm.) For the past decade, John Neumeier has directed the associated **ballet company,** transforming it into the acknowledged dance powerhouse of the nation. **Orchestras** abound—the Philharmonie, the Norddeutscher Rundfunk Symphony, and Hamburg Symphonia, the big three, all perform at the **Musikhalle** on Karl-Muck-Platz. (Tel. 34 69 20.) Take U-Bahn #2 to "Gänsemarkt" or "Messehallen." The Musikhalle also hosts **chamber music** concerts on a regular basis, as well as the odd jazz performance. Call 41 80 68 for tickets. Hamburg's many churches offer a wide variety of classical concerts (usually free)—see **Sights** above. The German **cabaret** tradition is still alive and kicking at a number of venues, including **Das Schiff** (tel. 36 47 65), on Holzbrück-estr. (U-Bahn #3 to "Rödingsmarkt") and the drag theater **Pulverfass**, Pulverteich 12 (tel. 24 97 91), off of Steindamm, near the Hauptbahnhof. (Shows daily at 8:30 and 11:30pm, Friday and Saturday also at 2:30am. DM20 minimum.)

The **Deutsches Schauspielhaus**, Kirchenallee 39 (tel. 24 87 13), is located across from the Hauptbahnhof. The theater presents a full venue—Ibsen, Brecht, Fass-binder—and *Rent.* (Box office open 10am-showtime. Student tickets as low as DM10.) The **English Theater,** Lerchenfeld 14 (tel. 227 70 89), entertains both natives and tourists with its English-language productions. (U-Bahn #2 to "Mundsgurg." Performances M-Sa at 7:30pm; matinees Tu and F at 11am.) **Thalia,** Alstertor 1 (tel. 32 26 66), sets up adventurous avant-garde musicals, plays, and staged readings. (S-Bahn #1 or 3 or U-Bahn #1 or 2 to "Jungfernstieg.") They also have regular per-formances in the **Hamburger Kunsthalle** (see **Museums,** p. 524). Most theaters sell half-price tickets to students at the regular box office as well as at the evening box office, which generally opens one hour before performances. In July and August, many theaters close down, but only to make way for the **Hamburger Sommer** arts festival; pick up a schedule at any kiosk. This year, **Carmen 2000** will grace the Hagenbeck's Tierpark stage from June to October; for information on the "mod-ernized" Bizet opera, call 35 71 85 36. The **West Port** jazz festival, Germany's largest, runs July 15-24, 2000. Call 44 64 21 for tickets.

The movie scene in Hamburg is dauntingly diverse, ranging from the latest American blockbusters to independent film projects by university students. The **Kommunales Kino Metropolis,** Dammtorstr. 30a (tel. 34 23 53), a non-profit cinema, features new independent films and revivals from all corners of the globe, focus-ing on pieces from the U.S., France, Germany, and Italy. **Kino 3001,** Schanzenstr. 75 (tel. 43 76 79), shows artsy alternative flicks.

Live music prospers in Hamburg, satisfying all tastes. Superb traditional jazz swing at the **Cotton Club** and **Indra** (see **Nightlife,** below). On Sunday mornings, good and bad alike play at the **Fischmarkt** (see p. 523). Rock groups jam at **Große Freiheit,** Große Freiheit 36 (tel. 31 42 63), and at **Docks,** Spielbudenpl. 19 (tel. 31 78 83 11). The renowned **Fabrik,** Barnerstr. 36 (tel. 39 10 70), in Altona, features every-thing from funk to punk. Cover runs about DM12. For more information, check the magazine *Szene* (DM5), which has an exhaustive listing of what's going on.

The **Hafengeburtstag,** or "harbor birthday," is the city's biggest bash. Hamburg owes its prosperity to May 7, 1189, when Friedrich Barbarossa granted the town the right to open a port. The city still celebrates the anniversary for a weekend in early May, featuring music and other events. In 2000, the party runs May 5-7. Dur-ing April, August, and November, the **Heiligengeistfeld** north of the Reeperbahn metamorphoses into the **Dom,** a titanic amusement park with fun-booths, kiosks, and merry-go-rounds. The festival's offerings of beer and wild parties have sub-merged its historical connection to the church.

 # NIGHTLIFE

Sternschanze, St. Pauli, and Altona areas monopolize Hamburg's crazy nightlife scene. The infamous **Reeperbahn,** a long boulevard which makes Las Vegas look like Sunday church, is the spinal cord of St. Pauli; sex shops, strip joints, peep shows, and other establishments seeking to satisfy every libidinal desire compete for space along the sidewalks. Crowds meander up and down the Reeperbahn like ants, occasionally crossing the street to peek into a shop window or dodge one of the many greaseballs who beckon passersby to enter the "erotic" interiors of their strip clubs. Though the Reeperbahn is reasonably safe for both men and women, it is not recommended for women to venture to the adjacent streets. Herbertstr.,

Hamburg's only remaining legalized prostitution strip, runs parallel to the Reeperbahn, and is open only to men over 18. The prostitutes flaunting their flesh on Herbertstr. are licensed professionals required to undergo health inspections, while the streetwalkers are venereal roulette wheels. Needless to say, men (mostly) and women flock to this district to revel all night long in an atmosphere simmering with sultry energy. Although the sleaze peddlers commodify women, they have failed to stifle the vital spark of the many clubs that cater to those not seeking sex for sale. Between the sex shops and prostitutes, many of Hamburg's best bars and clubs fill with a young crowd that leaves debauchery and degradation outside.

Students trying to avoid the hypersexed Reeperbahn head north to the spiffy streets of **Sternschanze**. Unlike St. Pauli, these areas are centered around cafés and weekend extravaganzas of an alternative flavor. Filled with spectacular graffiti that crosses the boundary into "public art" and posters that could easily be the products of high-end design schools, the neighborhood hums with creative energy and creatively-dressed people. Much of Hamburg's **gay scene** is located in the **St. Georg** area of the city, near Berliner Tor. Gay and straight bars in this area are more welcoming and classier than those in the Reeperbahn. In general, clubs open late and close late, with some techno and trance clubs remaining open until noon the following day. *Szene*, available at newsstands (DM5), lists events and parties. *Hinnerk* lists gay and lesbian events.

STERNSCHANZE

Rote Flora, Schulterblatt 71 (tel. 439 54 13). Held together both figuratively and literally by the graffiti and posters that cover all its vertical surfaces, this graffiti-covered mansion serves as the nucleus of the Sternschanze scene. A café (and motorbike repair shop) during the week, the Flora lights up on weekends, with huge dub and drum 'n' bass parties inside the spooky and decrepit ruin; political films, such as the wittily titled "Trainstopping" (about efforts to stop the shipment of nuclear waste via Germany's railway), are also shown in this squatter's community center. Café open M-F 6-10pm. Opening times vary. Weekend cover DM8 or more. Motorbike repair M 6-8:30pm.

Logo, Grindelallee 5 (tel. 410 56 58). If you can play it live (and loud), you can play it at Logo. Nightly live music at this friendly club near the university gives locals a chance to be rock stars. Very jeans and t-shirt. Open nightly from 9:30pm. Cover varies.

Frauenkneipe, Stresemannstr. 60 (tel. 43 63 77), S-Bahn #21 or 3 to "Holstenstr." A bar and meeting place for women. Visitors who are disconcerted by the Reeperbahn and drunken-sailor scene will find another Hamburg here. For women only, gay or straight. Open Tu-F from 8pm, Sa from 9pm, Su from 6pm.

ST. PAULI

Mojo Club, Reeperbahn 1 (tel. 43 52 32), has more attitude than it knows what to do with; Mojo takes its address literally. Called the best club in Germany by MTV. The attached **Jazz Café** attracts the trendy and features acid jazz. Usually open 11pm-4am. DM12 cover on weekends.

La Cage, Reeperbahn 136. If you're rich and pretty, make an appearance at the prettiest club in Hamburg, where glitz drips from cascades of hanging beads and two big silver cages dominate the dance floor. The club sends out special invitations to modeling agencies in order to fill the floor with faces whose perfection matches the decor. Open F-Sa 11pm. Cover DM18.

Absolute, Hans-Albers-Pl. 15 (tel. 317 34 00), hosts the gay scene Sa nights as it spins unrelenting house to a younger crowd that grooves (and cruises) until well after the sun is up. Open after 11pm. Cover DM10.

Cave, Reeperbahn 6. Hamburg's house for "house" (meta-house!). Descend into the smoky neon Cave, where nothing but wild, raving techno at 100bpm spins out with enough bass to turn your eardrums inside out. More than a great club, Cave is also one of Hamburg's best accommodation deals. In exchange for a DM15 cover charge, you can stay from opening time at 1am until the close at noon without having to worry about any curfew. Breakfast not included.

Indra, Große Freiheit 64 (tel. 31 79 63 08), is a haven of calm live jazz just off the adrenaline-powered Reeperbahn. Cool cats talk quietly in low light over a million cigarettes. Open W-Su from 9pm; music starts around 11pm. Cover DM5-10.

Molotow, Spielbudenpl. 5 (tel. 31 08 45), parallel to the Reeperbahn. This basement lives at the fringes of Hamburg's club scene. While mildly committed to funk, the club's DJ spins an eclectic mix of hip-hop, garage, salsa, and industrial Th-Sa from 10pm onwards. Cover DM10.

Große Freiheit 36/Kaiser Keller, Große Freiheit 36 (tel. 31 42 63). The Beatles played on the small stage downstairs during their early years. Today the Wu-Tang Clan stomp about on the big stage upstairs. Go figure. Call for show times and ticket prices (DM20-30). Open daily.

Cotton Club, Alter Steinweg 10 (tel. 34 38 78; fax 348 01 23); U-Bahn #3 to "Rödingsmarkt." Gives a different jazz, swing, or skittle band a chance every night. Smoky atmosphere, mostly older crowd, great jazz. Open M-Sa 8pm-midnight. Shows start at 8:30pm. Cover around DM12.

SCHLESWIG-HOLSTEIN

The only *Land* to border two seas, Schleswig-Holstein's past and present livelihood is based on the trade generated at its port towns. In between the coasts, verdant plains, populated mainly by sheep and plump bales of hay, produce much of northern Germany's agricultural goods. Although Schleswig-Holstein became a Prussian province in 1867 following Bismarck's defeat of Denmark, the region retains close cultural and commercial ties with Scandinavia. Linguistically, Schleswig-Holstein is also isolated from its southern neighbors by its various dialects of *Plattdeutsch* and, to a lesser extent, the Frisian spoken within its borders. The most noticeable difference is the local greeting *Moin*, a *Plattdeutsch* salutation used throughout the day.

HIGHLIGHTS OF SCHLESWIG-HOLSTEIN

■ Spiky with medieval spires and sugary with marzipan, **Lübeck** takes visitors back—*way* back—to the days when it was capital of the Hanseatic League. Hear the strains of the **largest mechanical organ in the world** and tour Thomas Mann's former home and literary inspiration, the **Buddenbrookhaus** (p. 528).
■ The **Holsteinische Schweiz** may not be Switzerland, but it sure is pretty. Stroll around its two lake towns, **Plön** and **Eutin**, to explore its forests and castles (p. 536).
■ **Schleswig** has an ancient fishing village, excellent museums, and a Dom whose tower provides a view of half the *Land* (p. 541).
■ Bear all on the barren dunes of **Sylt**, Germany's favorite beach spot (p. 545.).

LÜBECK

Lübeck wears its skyline of neo-classical townhouses and copper 13th-century spires so well, you would never guess that the greater part of the city was razed in WWII. The town's present appearance is thanks to a painstaking reconstruction undertaken in the 1950s. In its heyday, Lübeck was the capital of the Hanseatic League, carrying a big stick on account of its control of trade across Northern Europe. Though no longer a center of political and commercial influence, Lübeck was home to literary giants Heinrich and Thomas Mann and retains the pulse and energy of a bustling city beyond the glitz of marzipan and the sheen of tour buses.

⊏ GETTING THERE AND GETTING AROUND

Trains: Frequent departures for Hamburg (45min., 2 per hour, DM17), Kiel (1¼hr., 1 per hour, DM23), Schwerin (1¼hr., 1 per hour, DM20), Rostock (1¾hr., 1 per hour, DM37), and Berlin (3¼hr., 1 per hour, DM87).

Public Transportation: Although the Altstadt is easily seen on foot, Lübeck has an excellent bus network. The **ZOB** (central bus station) is across from the train station. Single ride DM3.20, children DM1.70. **Mehrfahrtkarten** (books of 6 tickets) DM15.50. The best value is the **Lübeck Card**—it's valid on all local buses, including those going to Travemünde, allows the bearer to take 2 children along for free on weekends and holidays, and offers significant discounts at most museums (1 day DM9). Direct questions to **Service Center am ZOB**, tel. 888 28 28. Open M-F 6am-8pm, Sa 9am-1pm.

Ferries: Quandt-Linie, An der Untertrave 114 (tel. 706 38 59), has cruises around the Altstadt and harbor every 30min. 10am to 6pm daily from the bridge in front of the Holstentor. DM10, students DM8.

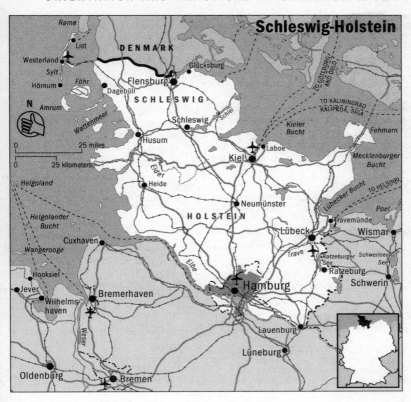

Taxi: Lübeck Funk-Taxi, tel. 811 22. Available 24hr., but best to call at least 30min. ahead. **Behindertentaxi,** tel. 811 21, has wheelchair-accessible taxis.

Car Rental: Hertz, Willy-Brandt-Allee 1 (tel. 33 33 35), by the train station, next to the Mövenpick hotel. Open M-F 7am-6pm, Sa 7am-1pm, Su 9-10am.

Bike Rental: Buy Cycle, Mühlenbrücke 1 (tel. 757 57; fax 757 56), rents bikes, despite the name. DM12 per day. ID required. Open M-Sa 10am-6:30pm. **Konrad Renta-Bike,** in a white trailer on Adenauerstr. near the station. DM1 per hour, DM8 per day. Open M-F 10am-7pm, Sa 10am-4pm, Su noon-4pm.

Mitfahrzentrale: Hinter der Burg 1a (tel. 707 14 70), arranges ride shares.

🛈 ORIENTATION AND PRACTICAL INFORMATION

Because water surrounds Lübeck, getting into serious navigational trouble requires getting wet first. Moving around the city can be a very Kafkaesque experience, particularly at night, when everything looks the same and you're never sure where you are or whether you've been there before. When confused, a good rule of thumb is to head uphill, towards **Königstr.** and **Breite Str.**, the two main streets which crest the ridge on which Lübeck stands.

Tourist Office: Avoid the tourist office in the train station (tel. 86 40 75; fax 86 30 24; open M-Sa 9am-1pm and 3pm-6pm); they charge DM4 for maps and high fees for booking a room (DM5 *plus* 10% of your hotel bill). Instead, head for the helpful office in the Altstadt at Breite Str. 62 (tel. 122 54 13 or 122 54 14; fax 122 54 19). They don't book rooms, but staff can point you in the right direction and give you a free map. Open M-F 9:30am-6pm, Sa-Su 10am-2pm.

Currency Exchange: In the station near the exit. Open M-Sa 9:30am-6:30pm, Su 9:30am-1pm.

Bookstore: Buchhandlung Weiland, Königstr. 67a (tel. 16 00 60), has a great stock of English-language paperbacks in the basement, including cheap versions of short classics. Upstairs there's a special Brothers Mann section (in German). Open M-W and F 9am-7pm, Th 9am-8pm, Sa 9am-4pm.

Laundromat: McWash, (tel. 702 03 57) on the corner of An der Mauer and Hüxterdamm. Wash 7kg DM7 (includes soap). Dry 10kg DM1.20 per 15min. Open M-Sa 6am-10pm.

Emergency: Police, tel. 110. **Fire,** tel. 112. **Ambulance,** tel. 192 22.

Rape Crisis Center: Marlegrube 9 (tel. 70 46 40). Open daily 5pm-7pm.

Women's Resources: Anarat, Steinrader Weg 1 (tel. 408 28 50). A center for women to share information about art, culture, and whatever else it is women get mixed up in these days. Open W 4-6pm, Th 5-7pm. **Mixed Pickles,** Kanalstr. 70 (tel. 702 16 40), is a center for girls and women, especially those who are disabled. Pick up a copy of *Zimtzicke,* a women's events calendar containing other important numbers and addresses, at the tourist office.

Pharmacies: Adler-Apotheke, Breite Str. 71 (tel. 798 85 15), across from the Marienkirche. Open M-F 8am-7pm, Sa 8:30am-4pm.

Post Office: Königstr. 44-46, 23552 Lübeck, across the street from the Katharinenkirche. **24hr. ATM.** Open M-W 8am-6pm, Th-F 8am-7pm, Sa 8am-2pm.

Internet Access: Cyberb@r, on the 4th floor of the *Karstadt* department store, across the street from the tourist office. DM3 per 15min., DM5 per 30min.

PHONE CODE	Fahrenheit 0451

◤ ACCOMMODATIONS AND CAMPING

Mitwohnzentrale Home Company, Glockengießerstr. 28 (tel. 194 45), arranges rooming situations and apartments for longer stays. (Open M-F 9am-1pm.)

■ **Rucksack Hotel,** Kanalstr. 70 (tel. 70 68 92 or 261 87 92; fax 707 34 26), on the north side of the Altstadt by the canal. From the station, walk past the Holstentor, left on An der Untertrave, right on Beckergrube, which becomes Pfaffstr. and then Glockengießerstr; the hostel is on the corner of Kanalstr. (20min.). Or take bus #1, 11, 13, 21, 31, 34, or 39 from the station to "Pfaffenstr.," and turn right at the church on Glockengießerstr. Bright, cheery rooms in a former factory-turned-alternative cooperative. 10-bed dorms DM24; 6-bed dorms DM26; quads DM28, with bath DM40; double with bath DM40 (all prices per person). Self-serve kitchen. Breakfast DM8, served in Café Affenbrot (see **Food,** below). Sheets DM6. Reception 9am-1pm and 3-10pm. Wheelchair accessible.

■ **Sleep-In (CVJM),** Große Petersgrube 11 (tel. 719 20; fax 789 97), near the Petrikirche in the Altstadt, 10min. from the station. Walk past the Holstentor, turn right on An der Obertrave, left on Große Petersgrube, and look to the right for the sign. "Lively" does not quite capture the time in the pub downstairs. Raucous. *Rowdy.* Sleep? What? These are good accommodations for travelers who prefer not to get up until late afternoon. 4- to 8-bed dorms DM15, doubles DM20-40. Apartments DM30-40 per person. Breakfast DM5. Sheets DM5. Reception M-F 8am-10pm, Sa-Su 8am-noon and 5-7:30pm.

Jugendgästehaus Lübeck (HI), Mengstr. 33 (tel. 702 03 99; fax 770 12). From the station head for the Holstentor, cross the river, make a left on An der Untertrave and turn right on Mengstr. The hostel is conveniently close to the sights in an historic building. Triples and quads 1st night DM30, over 26 DM38; additional nights DM27.50, over 26 DM36. Doubles DM32, over 26 DM41. Breakfast and sheets included. Lockout midnight, but guests over 18 can get a key. Reception 7:30am-noon and 1:15pm-midnight. Members only. Call ahead.

Baltic Hotel Priebe, Hansestr. 11 (tel. 855 75 or 812 71; fax 838 31), across the street from the *ZOB*. Small but clean rooms 2min. from the station and 5min. from the Altstadt. Telephone and TV in every room. Singles DM50-85, doubles DM100-130, triples from DM140. Filling breakfast buffet included. Reception 8am-10pm.

Camping: Campingplatz Lübeck-Schönbocken, Steinraderdamm 12 (tel. 89 30 90 or 89 22 87), on a distant site northwest of the city. Showers, washing machines, and cooking facilities available. From the *ZOB*, bus #8 (direction: "Bauernweg") to the end, then walk 300m along Steinraderdamm toward the city. DM7 per person. Tent DM6.

🦁 FOOD

While the rest of Germany swims in beer, Lübeck drowns in coffee, with no point more than a saucer's throw away from a caffeine fix. Of course this is still Germany, so Lübeck's cafés function as the nightlife venue of choice by staying open until the wee hours to serve beer. Hipper, more popular cafés lie along **Mühlenstr.** in the eastern part of the city. A local specialty is *Lübecker Marzipan*, a delectable candy made with sugar and almonds. The confectionery **I.G. Niederegger,** Breite Str. 89 (tel. 530 11 26), across from the Rathaus, is the place to purchase marzipan pigs, jellyfish, and even the town gate. A **Co-op supermarket** is at the corner of Sandstr. and Schmiedstr. (Open M-F 8:30am-7pm, Sa 9am-4pm.)

🍴 **Tipasa,** Schlumacherstr. 12-14 (tel. 706 04 51). The hip waitstaff leisurely weave through the candle-lit interior, carrying pizza, pasta, and vegetarian dishes to hungry

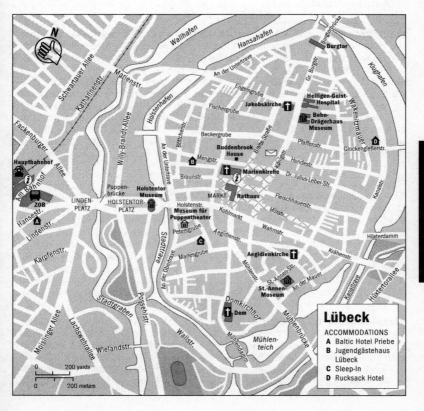

Lübeck

ACCOMMODATIONS
A Baltic Hotel Priebe
B Jugendgästehaus
   Lübeck
C Sleep-In
D Rucksack Hotel

SCHLESWIG-HOLSTEIN

students. Try the *Tipasa-Topf,* a spicy stew of tomatoes, beef, mushrooms, and peppers (DM11). Pizza DM6.50-11. *Biergarten* in back. Open M-Th and Su noon-1am, F-Sa noon-2am. Kitchen closes 30min. earlier.

Café Affenbrot, Kanalstr. 70 (tel. 721 93), on the corner of Glockengießerstr. A vegetarian café. Dine on monkey-bread burgers (pineapples, berries, salad, and cheese on whole wheat, DM8) at tables made from old-fashioned sewing machines. Meals DM8-11. Open daily 9am-midnight. Kitchen closes at 11:30pm.

Café Amadeus, Königstr. 26 (tel. 70 53 57). If the name conjures up images of a sophisticated café in Vienna, think again—cheesy plastic booths and cheesier techno beats fill the interior. Italian meals DM6-14. Open M-Th and Su 8am-12:30am, F-Sa 8am-2am.

Mädchen- und Frauencafé, An der Untertrave 97 (tel. 122 57 46), on the 2nd floor of the women's center. A friendly women-only café serving coffee, tea, and cake. Open Su 3-8pm. Breakfast W-Th 10am-1pm.

◉ SIGHTS

To see Lübeck from above, hop on the double-decker **LVG Open-Air-Stadtrundfahrt.** The red bus stops at all municipal bus stops in town and runs frequently every day. Prices same as regular public transportation.

RATHAUS. On the eve of Palm Sunday, 1942, Allied bombers flattened most of Lübeck. After the war, the city used Marshall Plan funds to begin the daunting task of renovating the leveled Altstadt. At its center lies the Rathaus, a striking 13th-century structure of glazed black and red bricks. *(Open M-F 9:30am-6pm, Sa-Su 10am-2pm. Tours M-F at 11am and noon. DM4, students DM2.)*

MARIENKIRCHE. Behind the pedestrian zone towers the Marienkirche, begun in the Romanesque style around 1200 but finished as a Gothic cathedral in 1350. Completely gutted in the 1942 raid, the church's interior has been carefully restored except for the rear, where a memorial chapel has been constructed around the remains of the great bell that dropped and smashed into the floor during the bombing. The church's music comes from the **largest mechanical organ in the world.** The saints literally come marching in at noon on the church's newly restored **astronomical clock.** The famous medieval **Totentanzbild** used to encircle the chapel opposite the astronomical clock, but it was destroyed in 1942; all that remains is a reproduction, including the *Kaiser* holding hands with two wooden skeletons representing the plague. *(Open daily in summer 10am-6pm; in winter 10am-4pm. Tours W and Sa 3:15pm. DM6, student DM4. Organ concerts daily at noon, Tu at 6:30pm, Th at 8pm, and Sa at 6:30pm. DM5, students DM3.)*

BUDDENBROOKHAUS. Literary giants **Heinrich** and **Thomas Mann** lived here as children. The house is now a museum dedicated to the life and works of both brothers. Thomas's works expressed his fierce opposition to Nazism and a profound ambivalence about German culture. While Thomas received the Nobel Prize for literature in 1929, his brother also wrote a number of important works, including *Professor Unrat,* on which the famous Marlene Dietrich film *Der blaue Engel (The Blue Angel)* is based. The house holds special summer events, including a "literary walk" through Lübeck on weekends from June to September. *(Mengstr. 4. Tel. 122 41 92. Opposite the Marienkirche. Open daily 10am-5pm. DM7, students DM4. Walks DM12, students DM10.)*

MUSEUM BEHN- UND DRÄGERHAUS. Modern art clashes beautifully with the neo-classical architecture of an 18th-century townhouse. The first floor features works by contemporary Lübeck artists, while the second houses a small collection with paintings by Edvard Munch, Max Liebermann, and Max Beckmann. The artists' cooperative in the **sculpture garden** outside showcases local artists. *(Königstr. 11. Tel. 122 41 48. Open Tu-Su April-Sept. 10am-5pm; Oct.-March 10am-4pm. DM5, students DM3. Free first Friday of every month. Sculpture garden free.)*

KATHARINENKIRCHE. A former 14th-century Franciscan monastery, the church now houses modern art exhibitions including lumpy terra cotta sculptures by Ernst Barlach. Note the cheerfully ornate depictions of misery and death. *(Königstr. 7. Tel. 122 41 80. Open Tu-Su 10am-1pm and 2pm-5pm. Free.)*

JAKOBIKIRCHE. Traditionally a church for seafarers, the whitewashed, high-ceilinged church contains a beautifully ornamented organ. *(North of the Rathaus on Breite Str., near Koberg. Open daily 10am-6pm. Organ concerts F 8pm. Free.)*

PETRIKIRCHE. An elevator climbs to the top of the 13th-century steeple for a sweeping view. *(East of the Rathaus on Schmiederstr. Church open daily noon-7pm. Tower open April-Oct. 9am-7pm. Admission DM3.50, students DM2.)*

HEILIGEN-GEIST-HOSPITAL. The long barn with rows of tiny cabins inside was built as a hospital in 1820 and served as an old-age home from 1851 to 1970. The **cloister** in front contains several medieval murals. *(Am Koberg 9. Open May-Sept. Tu-Su 10am-5pm; Oct.-April Tu-Su 10am-4pm. Free.)*

HOLSTENTOR. Between the Altstadt and the station is the massive Holstentor, one of Lübeck's four 15th-century gates and the symbol of the city. Inside, the **Museum Holstentor** displays exhibits on ship construction, trade, and quaint local implements of torture. *(Tel. 122 41 29. Open April-Sept. Tu-Su 10am-5pm; Oct.-March 10am-4pm. DM5, students DM3, under 19 DM1.)*

DOM. Founded by Henry the Lion in 1173, as evidenced by his trademark lion statue, the rather unremarkable cathedral features a late Gothic crucifix. *(Domkirchhof. Tel. 747 04. At the southernmost end of the inner island. Open April-Sept. 10am-6pm; March and Oct. 10am-5pm; Nov. 10am-4pm; Dec.-Feb. 10am-3pm. Free.)*

ST.-ANNEN-MUSEUM. Displays crosses, tablets, altars, and other paraphernalia of the opiate of the masses, as well as an exhibit upstairs recounting Lübeck's cultural history. *(St.-Annen-Str. 15. Tel. 122 41 37. Off Mühlenstr. Open April-Sept. Tu-Su 10am-5pm; Oct.-March Tu-Su 10am-4pm. DM5, students DM1. Free first Friday of every month.)*

MUSEUM FÜR PUPPENTHEATER. Thirteen rooms filled with more than 700 laughing, dancing little puppets made of wood. *(Kolk 16. Tel. 786 26. Just below the Petrikirche. Open daily 10am-6pm. DM6, students DM5, children DM3.)*

♫ 🎭 ENTERTAINMENT AND NIGHTLIFE

Lübeck is world-famous for its **organ concerts.** The **Jakobikirche** and **Dom** offer a joint program of concerts every Friday at 8pm (DM10, students DM6). The smaller **Propsteikirche Herz Jesu,** Parade 4, near the Dom, has free concerts Wednesdays at 8pm; call 328 58 for details. For entertainment listings, pick up *Piste, Szene, Zentrum,* or (for women) *Zimtzicke* from the tourist office. Lübeck's two major theaters offer generous student discounts. The huge **Theater Lübeck,** Beckergrube 10-14 (tel. 745 52 or 767 72), puts on operas, symphonies, and mainstream German and American plays. (Box office open Tu-Sa 10am-1pm, Th-F 4-6:30pm, and 30min. before performance. Tickets DM25-50.) The smaller **Theater Combinale,** Hüxstr. 115 (tel. 788 17), gets down with avant-garde works (tickets DM15-20).

Kandinsky, Fleischhauerstr. 89. More than 30 tables in the street, a mile-long drink list, and live jazz in the evenings. Open M-Tu and Su 1pm-1am, F-Sa 1pm-2am.

Finnegan, Mengstr. 42 (tel. 711 10). The Irish pub serves Guinness and other dark, yeasty beers (DM4-6) guaranteed to make you go *Bragh* the next morning. Very popular with locals. Open M-F 4pm-1am, Sa-Su 4pm-whenever.

Café Flou, Tünkenhagen 1. Not just a café with pool tables, it's a "Rock Café." Baguettes DM8-12, beer DM4-6.50. Open M-Th and Su 6pm-1am, F-Sa 6pm-2am.

Bad Taste, An der Untertrave 3a. Draws healthy crowds to watch local bands rock out under camouflage netting and disco balls. There's something enjoyably obnoxious every night, with weekends reserved for particularly vicious events like tattooing and piercing. Times and cover vary; check posters around town.

SCHLESWIG-HOLSTEIN

NEAR LÜBECK: TRAVEMÜNDE

Fifteen kilometers north of Lübeck, Travemünde's family-friendly beaches and casino are famed seducers of urbanized Germans. Boutiques line the streets, wicker chairs display their graceful rattan backs along the stretch of beach near the north pier, and the monolithic Hotel Maritim towers above it all. The **Aqua-Top**, Strandpromenade 1b (tel. 804 42), a fun-filled glass complex of spas and swimming pools, pampers guests with saunas, massages, and waterslides. (Open M-F 10am-9pm, Sa-Su 10am-6pm. Day pass DM16, children DM8; with sauna DM22, children DM16.) The four-mast trade ship **Passat** is moored across the inlet in **Priwall**. (Open May 13-Sept. 26 daily 10am-5pm. DM5, students and children DM2.50.) Take the **ferry** that leaves from near the corner of the Strandpromenade and Travepromenade (2min., every 15min., DM0.60, children DM0.30). **Travemündewoche,** a week of concerts and sailing, takes place the last week of July.

Travemünde is easily accessible from Lübeck by **train** (25min., 1 per hour) or **bus** #30 or 31 from the *ZOB* (45min., day pass valid); both the train and bus cost DM2.80. There are three train/bus stops: **Skandinavienkai** accesses the Scandinavia-bound ferries, **Travemünde-Hafen** is close to the town center, and **Travemünde-Strand** leads directly to the beach. **Quandt-Linie** (tel. (0451) 777 99) runs harbor tours hourly from the Travepromenade (DM14, children DM12). Another option is to go on a **duty-free cruise:** for DM2-3, several companies will chauffeur you around the Baltic for a few hours, all the while enticing you with tax-free shopping. **TT-Linie** (tel. 80 10) runs to Trelleborg, Sweden from the **Skandinavienkai**. (M-Th and Su 10am and 10pm. Round-trip DM69.) The **tourist office,** Strandpromenade 1b (tel. 804 30; fax 804 60), is located in the Aqua-Top. Walk from the Travemünde-Strand station down Bertlingstr. and turn right on Strandpromenade. The staff books **rooms** for free. (Open M-Sa 10am-6pm, Su 10am-1pm.) The **post office** on Rose has a **24hr. ATM.** (Open M-F 8:30am-12:30pm and 2:30-6pm, Sa 8:30am-noon.) The **telephone code** is 04502.

The **Jugend-Freizeitstätte Priwall,** Mecklenburger Landstr. 69 (tel. 25 76; fax 46 20), is across the inlet. Take the ferry to Priwall and walk along the path for 300m; it's on your right. Surrounded by a standing army of white tents, the hostel makes you feel like a member of the *Bundeswehr.* (DM15, over 26 DM20. *Kurtaxe* DM5. Breakfast DM6. Sheets DM6. Reception M-F and Su 4-10pm, Sa 7-9am and 2-10pm. Curfew midnight. Open April to mid-Oct. Call ahead.) Pitch your tent next door at **Strandcamping-Priwall,** Dünenweg 12. (Tel. 28 35. DM7 per person. Tent DM9. Reception 9am-noon and 3-7pm. Open April-Sept.). Hard-core *Deutsch* fast food and bakeries decorate the downtown beach path and **Dünenweg** in the Priwall.

NEAR LÜBECK: RATZEBURG

The island town of Ratzeburg, founded in the 11th century by Henry the Lion, swims in the Ratzeburger See, 24km from Lübeck. The natural beauty of the town's environs makes bikers and hikers rush to the lakeside, along with the German Olympic crew team, which trains daily on the huge *See.* Other than the scenery, Ratzeburg's main means of seduction is its art—two small but significant museums offer unique collections by 20th-century artists A. Paul Weber and Ernst Barlach, who lived in the town, as well as Günter Grass, who resided nearby.

Weber's astounding satirical lithographs and watercolors are on permanent display, along with the artist's workshop and printing press, at the ■A.-Paul-Weber-Haus, Domhof 5 (tel. 86 07 20). From the Markt, turn left (coming from Lüneburger Damm) onto Domhof, the second street exiting the square. (Open Tu-Su 10am-1pm and 2-5pm. DM3, students DM1.) Ratzeburg's **Dom,** down the street from the Weberhaus, was built by Henry the Lion soon after he colonized Schleswig-Holstein and houses galleries of religious works. (Open April-Sept. daily 10am-noon and 2-6pm; Oct.-March Tu-Su 10am-noon and 2-4pm.) Between the Weberhaus and the Dom lies the **Kreismuseum** (tel. 123 25) in the **Herrenhaus,** the summer residence of Duke Adolf Friedrich IV. The museum is filled with a random mishmash of Biedermeier furniture, art by Weber, Grass, and Barlach, and the obligatory pointy Prussian helmet display. (Open Tu-Su 10am-1pm and 2-5pm.

DM2, students DM1.) A larger collection of Barlach's work sits on the opposite side of the Marktplatz from the Dom in the **Ernst-Barlach-Gedenkstätte,** Barlachpl. 3 (tel. 37 89). Haunting, meditative bronzes and manuscripts are on display. (Open March-Nov. Tu-Su 10am-1pm and 2-5pm. DM3, students DM1.50.)

The **train station** is a 30-minute walk from Marktplatz. With your back to the station, turn right and follow Bahnhofsallee as it becomes Lüneburger Damm, Unter den Linden, and finally Herrenstr. Or take bus #2 to "Marktplatz." Hourly **trains** connect Ratzeburg with Lübeck (30min., DM7.60) and Lüneburg (40min., DM15). The **tourist office,** Schloßwiese 7 (tel. 80 00 80; fax 53 27), is between the train station and the Marktplatz. From the station, head down Bahnhofsallee until it becomes Lüneburger Damm (15min.) or take bus #2 to "Alter Zoll"; it's behind a small parking lot on the left. The staff books **rooms** (DM30-40) for free. (Open M-Th and F 9am-5pm, Sa-Su 10am-4pm.) Join the hordes of nature-lovers and rent a **bike** from **Fahrradverleih Schloßwiese** (tel. 44 66) on the lake, just past the tourist office. (Open daily 10am-6pm. DM15 per day.) The **post office,** 23909 Ratzeburg, is at Herrenstr. 12. (Open M-F 8am-noon and 2-6pm, Sa 8am-noon.) The **telephone code** is 04541.

To reach Ratzeburg's **Jugendherberge (HI),** Fischerstr. 20 (tel. 37 07; fax 847 80), take any bus from the train station to Marktplatz or follow the directions to the square above. Continuing straight through the Markt down Langenbrückenstr., turn right onto Schrongenstr. and follow it until it becomes Fischerstr.; it's at the end of the street. (DM21, over 26 DM26. Sheets DM6. Laundry DM6. Reception 7am-10pm. Curfew 10pm, but you can ring the bell until 11:30pm, or get a key.) **Groceries** await at **Edeka** on the corner of Herrenstr. and Barlachstr. (Open M-F 8am-7pm, Sa 7:30am-4pm.) **Pinocchio,** Herrenstr. 14, is just about the cheapest thing going in *Imbiß*-free Ratzeburg. The menu features pizza (DM8-20) and pasta (DM11-16) in lots of exciting Italian varieties. (Open daily noon-10:30pm.)

LAUENBURG AN DER ELBE

Lauenburg an der Elbe takes quintessential European quaintness to entirely new levels. The cobblestones are perfectly aligned, the streets are perfectly narrow, and the houses are perfectly medieval. Was that Mother Goose around the corner? Easy transport to Lauenburg is one of many remnants of the town's past; the town earned its bread as a stop on the great medieval canals connecting the mines of the Lüneburger Heide to the salt-starved towns of the Baltic coast. Lauenburg is still on the train route from Lüneburg to Lübeck, with connections to Hamburg and Berlin at either end. Lüneburg is a mere 15 minutes away, while the journey to Lübeck takes just under an hour.

The Lauenburg Altstadt consists of two halves—the **Unterstadt** down by the river, and the **Oberstadt** up above, joined by pathways of narrow steps. Most of the sights are located in the Unterstadt, an uninterrupted half-timbered strip built over the Sperrmauer, a stone embankment. The **Uferpromenade** is a narrow cobblestoned path (quaint, of course) between the houses and runs along the river's edge, ideal for walking or biking. Lauenburg's houses, many of which date back to the 16th century, are distinctive for their elaborately painted wood-and-brick framework. The **Mensingschehaus,** Elbstr. 49, off the Kirchplatz, is one of very few survivors of a catastrophic 1616 fire that charred the Duke, his young wife, and most of the posher houses in town. The former **Rathaus,** Elbstr. 59, now houses the **Elbschiffahrtsmuseum** (tel. 512 51), which documents the town's shipping industry. (Open March-Oct. daily 10am-1pm and 2-5pm; Nov.-Feb. W and F-Su 10am-1pm and 2-5pm. DM2.) The house at **Elbstr. 97** takes this cuteness thing a little bit too far. At about 6 ft. wide, it is one of the smallest in Germany. You can even rent it if you really want to live out your Grimms' fairy tale fantasies (tel. 522 20). In the center of the Altstadt, the **Maria-Magdalena-Kirche,** Kirchplatz 1, stands tall and solid over the city; the church tower was a signal to returning sailors that they were home at long last. (Open M-Sa 10am-5pm, Su 9am-5pm.) To the left of the church is a pretty 17th-century square, filled with sagging half-timbered houses whose beams are inscribed with religious messages. Above the church in the Oberstadt's

Amtsplatz is the **Schloßturm,** built between 1457 and 1477. After the town burned down in 1616, the tower served as a state-of-the-art vantage point from which vigilant watchdogs observed the town burn down six more times. Now the tower can be climbed for a view of Lauenburg that is only moderately better than the one from the hill. (Open same hours as the tourist office, below. Free.) Nothing remains from the **Schloß** except one wing, now used to house municipal offices.

Frequent trains run to Lüneburg (15min., 1 per hour, DM6) and Lübeck (1hr., 1 per hour, DM17). From Hamburg, **bus** #31 makes the 40-minute trip to Lüneburg from the "Bergedorf" S-Bahn stop. To reach the town from the train station, cross the bridge and turn left; the Altstadt will appear about 20m after you pass the giant **Hitzler** (don't forget the z!) **wharfs.** The **tourist office** (tel. 59 09 81; email info@lauenburg-elbe.de; www.lauenburg-elbe.de) sits across from the Schloßturm on Amtsplatz. (Open M-Tu and F 8:30am-12:30pm and 1:30-4:30pm, W 8:30am-12:30pm and 1-3pm, Th 8:30am-12:30pm and 1:30-7pm—got that?) The **Jugendherberge Lauenburg (HI),** Am Sportplatz 7 (tel. 25 98), is a pleasant hike—if a long one (20min.)—from the Altstadt. At the fork in the road at Elbstr. 20, follow the Radweg zur Jugendherberge sign left to the Uferpromenade. After about 10 minutes the paved promenade ends; make a right here onto Kuhgrund (unmarked). Turn left at the *Jugendherberge* sign and take the dirt path through the woods (5min.). The hostel is the big brick building at the top of the hill. The brightly colored hostel, packed with school groups, offers game rooms with ping pong and a TV. (DM21, over 26 DM26. Breakfast included. Sheets DM6. Closed Dec. 15-Jan. 15. Call ahead.) *Pensionen* abound in the Altstadt, mostly closer to the train station; look for *Zimmer frei* signs. Private rooms run DM25-55 per person.

The outdoor cafés on the waterfront tend to cater to the wealthier tourists who frequent the river cruises (fish dishes DM16-25). Cheaper eats can be had in the Oberstadt's pedestrian zone. There is also an **Aldi supermarket** there. (Open M-F 8am-6pm, Sa 8am-1pm.) The **telephone code** is 04153.

HOLSTEINISCHE SCHWEIZ (HOLSTEIN SWITZERLAND)

Spanning the countryside between Lübeck and Kiel, the Holsteinische Schweiz is the province's vacation playground. Placid lakes, lush forests, and moderately relaxed vacationing Germans populate the idyllic landscape alongside fish and fowl.

PLÖN

The small town of Plön balances on a narrow strip of land that runs between two gigantic lakes, the Kleiner Plöner See and the Großer Plöner See. Even as this natural "bridge" threatens to buckle under the weight of German and Scandinavian tourists and school groups, the town continues to hold weekly festivals during the summer and maintain a surprisingly large number of monuments. Plön didn't gain its current appearance until 1636, when Kaiser Wilhelm II built one of his vacation homes here, transforming it into a fashionable resort. These days, most tourists bypass the town for the surrounding lakes and tree-sheltered trails whose shady seduction once attracted the royal family.

⊓ PRACTICAL INFORMATION. Plön lies on the main rail line between Lübeck and Kiel. **Trains** travel hourly to Kiel (30min., DM12), Lübeck (40min., DM12), and Eutin (15min, DM4.60). For a **taxi,** call 66 66 or 35 35. Rent **bikes** at **Wittich,** Lange Str. 34. (Tel. 27 48. Open M-Sa 9:30am-6pm. DM10 per day.) Rent **boats** at the **Kanucenter,** Ascheberger Str. 76 (tel. 41 43), near the camp ground. (Kayaks DM8-10 per hour, DM25-40 per day; canoes DM10-40 per hour, DM40-120 per day.) **Großer Plöner Seerundfahrt** chugs around the lake from the dock on Strandweg. (10 minutes past the hour daily 10am-5pm. DM12, students under 20 DM7.) The **tourist office,** Am Lübschen Tor 1 (tel. 504 50; fax 50 95 20; email tour-info@ploen-am-see.de; www.ploen-am-see.de/tourist-info), lies between the station and the Markt. Follow the signs from the station. The staff sells a good map (DM4) and books **rooms** for free. (Open M-F 9am-6pm, Sa 10am-1pm.) The **post office**, 24306 Plön, is next to the station. (Open M-F 8:30am-noon and 3-6pm, Sa 8:30am-noon.) The **telephone code** is 04522.

⚆⚆ ACCOMMODATIONS AND FOOD. If you're staying for a week or longer, your best bet is a vacation home; otherwise, private rooms (DM21-52) are a good deal. Plön's **Jugendherberge (HI)**, Ascheberger Str. 67 (tel. 25 76; fax 21 66), is—brace yourself—brimming with Britney Spears-adoring *Schulkinder*. Walk left from the station along Bahnhofstr. as it becomes Lübecker Str. and then Lange Str. through the center of town. Keep going as Lange Str. becomes Hamburger Str., Ascheberger Chaussee, and finally Ascheberger Str; the hostel is on the left (45min.). Two- to six-bed rooms let you get to know your roommates *well*, though some have large windows that let a little air and light in. (DM21, over 26 DM26. Breakfast included. Sheets DM6. Front door locked 10pm-7am, but you can get a key. Checkout 9am. Members only.) **Hotel Zum Hirschen**, Bahnhofstr. 9 (tel. 24 23), across from the station, has small, clean rooms and a convenient location. (Singles DM50-55, doubles DM80-110.) **Campingplatz Spitzenart**, Strecke Neumünster B430 (tel. 27 69), is next to the hostel. (DM8 per person. Tents DM6-10. Open April-Oct.) Plön's restaurants are unexciting and expensive. The pedestrian zone around the **Markt** supports a healthy, if not particularly hip, café culture. **Spar**, Lübecker Str. 32, has the lowest prices and the longest hours of any **grocery store**. (Open M-F 8am-8pm, Sa 8am-4pm.) **Kochlöffel**, across from the Nikolaikirche on the Markt, sells delicious chicken dishes, all under DM5. (Open M-Sa 9am-10:30pm, Su 11am-10:30pm.) **Antalya-Grill**, Lange Str. 36 (tel. 39 82), offers grill platters (DM3-16) and spicy pizzas. (DM8-14. Open daily 11am-1am, Sa-Su until 2am.)

⬛ SIGHTS. Plön's main attraction is the late Renaissance **Schloß**. On top of the Schloßberg, the palace affords a spectacular view out over the surrounding lake. Further away from town is the lush **Lustgarten** and the modest **Prinzenhaus**. The brick 18th-century beauty was the private *Lusthaus* (heh, heh) of the last duke, who enjoyed participating in boyish sports. Down the eastern slop of the Schloßberg is Plön's small 19th-century **Rathaus**. From there, Schloßbergstr. dips down into the **Markt**, the current commercial center of Plön and the site of its many festivals, which often involve small carnival rides and *always* involve beer. The Markt is also Plön's religious center, hosting the heavenly **Nikolaikirche.** Some of its original 12th-century splendor was dumbed down in 1542 in response to the anti-pomp fashions of the Reformation; the church was later torn down and rebuilt because it was falling apart from old age. It then burnt to a crisp in June of 1864, necessitating yet another reconstruction. The final product (cross your fingers!) is on display daily from 10am-4pm for free.

The town's other archaic attraction is the **Museum des Krieges,** Johannisstr. 1 (tel. 74 32 69). The museum is housed in a former apothecary and displays 17th-century glassware, porcelain, and other goodies swiped from the Schloß. (Open mid-May to Sept. Tu-Sa 10am-noon and Tu-Su 3-6pm; Nov. to mid-May Tu-Sa 10am-noon. DM3, students DM1.) Next door to the museum is the **Johanniskirche,** on Johannisstr. The church was built in 1685 for the ducal couple, Johann Adolph and Dorothea Sophie, and has a small graveyard alongside it. (Open 10am-4pm. Free.) Far east of the town center on the ridge that runs between the two lakes, the **Parnaßturm,** a former lookout tower, provides an amazing view well worth the 20-minute climb up Rodomstorstr. from the Gänsemarkt, just west of the station. (Open Easter-Oct. 9am-7pm. Free.)West of the center, the **Prinzeninsel** stretches out from the mainland into the Großer Plöner See. A tiny canal spanned by a foot-bridge divides it from the shore. The island shelters a sandy beach complete with snack bar. The lake has quite a pungent odor, making a swim an *experience*. Perhaps walking the trails to get here is a nicer one.

EUTIN

Plön may pack more of an historical punch, but as the region's main shopping center, Eutin has the power of cash. The daily town market is more like a fair, with jewelry, sailor suits, and housewares mixed in with the usual fruit, vegetables, meat, and cheese. Like Plön, Eutin sits between two lakes: the Großer Eutiner See to the east and the Kleiner Eutiner See to the west. Like Plön, a series of dukes made the city more culturally attuned during the 17th century, and in the 18th century, composer Carl Maria von Weber provided it with a tourist industry to last for years to come (he wrote some music, too).

⚑ ORIENTATION AND PRACTICAL INFORMATION. Eutin lies on the rail line between Lübeck and Kiel. Hourly **trains** run to Lübeck (20min., DM9), Kiel (1hr., DM15), and Eutin (15min., DM4.60). Rent **bikes** at the stand at the tourist office. (DM10 per day. Open daily 9am-7pm.) The **tourist office,** Bleekergang 6 (tel. 709 70; fax 70 97 20), also provides an overwhelming array of brochures and books **rooms** for free. (Open May-Sept. M-F 9am-6pm, Sa-Su 10am-1pm; Oct.-April M-Su 9am-5pm.) From the station, turn left on Bahnhofstr. and right on Plöner Str. Follow the street to Voßpl. and head straight on tiny Rosengartenweg to the Strandpromenade. Turn left at the lake; the office will be on your left. The **post office,** Bahnhofstr. 6, 23701 Eutin, across from the station, **exchanges money.** (Open M-W 7am-6pm, Th-F 7am-7pm, Sa 7am-2pm.) The **telephone code** is 04521.

⚑◫▣ ACCOMMODATIONS, FOOD, AND ENTERTAINMENT. The **Jugendherberge (HI),** Jahnhöhe 6 (tel. 21 09; fax 746 02), often has space. Follow the directions to the tourist office (above) to Voßpl. Turn left on Riemannstr. and left again on Jahnhöhe; the hostel is on the right. The local swimming pool is only two minutes away. (DM21, over 26 DM26. Breakfast included. Sheets DM6. Lockout 11pm, but you can get a key.) The **Markt** offers a number of cafés as well as more hum-drum fast food joints. For **groceries,** try **Sky Market,** Benzstr. 10, off the Markt. (Open M-F 8am-7pm, Sa 8am-4pm.) Climb aboard a **lake cruise** with **Eutiner Seerundfahrten,** which leave the Strandpromenade daily at 12:15pm, 1:30pm, and 2:45pm (1hr., DM7), or expand your Romantic fantasies on the **Nachtwächterrundgang** ("the night watchman's rounds"), a role-playing tour of Eutin that meets at the Schloß gates. (Daily at 7:30pm. DM6.)

◲ SIGHTS. Two stone monkeys squat on the bridge leading across the moat to Eutin's central monument, the **Eutiner Schloß,** Schloßplatz (tel. 709 50). The austerity of the complex's sparse rooms and plain marble floors somehow inspire more vivid images of 16th-century nobility. (Obligatory tours daily on the hour 10am-4pm, except 1pm. DM7, students DM5, children DM3, family card DM15.) The landscaped **Eutiner Schloßgarten** has a few buildings hidden amidst its lush lawns. The **Seepavillon** pokes out of the Großer Eutiner See. The **Küchengarten,** south of the castle, has an **Orangerie** and other horticultural goodies. Farther from the Schloß, the **Tempelgarten** contains a "Chinese" bridge and the **Monopteros,** a faux ancient Greek temple. (Grounds open 24hr. Free.) Next door to the Schloß, the **Ostholstein-Museum,** Schloßplatz 1 (tel. 701 80), makes a valiant effort at filling its two floors with portraits of the town's dukes and Carl Maria von Weber. (Open April-Sept. Tu-Su 10am-1pm and 2pm-5pm; Oct.-Jan. and March Tu-Su 3-5pm. DM3, students DM2.)

KIEL

Site of the 1936 and 1972 Olympic sailing events, the waters around Kiel swim ceaselessly with brightly colored sails. These multiply in the last full week of June, when the annual Kieler Woche (tel. 901 24 16) takes place. An internationally renowned regatta, the festival enlivens the harbor and floods the town with music, food, and beer. Except for travelers with a fetish for nautical machinery, Kiel offers little to visitors besides ferry connections to Scandinavia and access to the world's busiest artificial waterway, the Nord-Ostsee-Kanal. Allied bombings here were unsurprisingly ruthless, destroying 80% of the city. Unfortunately, Kiel retained little of its historic beauty.

⚑ PRACTICAL INFORMATION. Hourly **trains** run daily from Kiel to Hamburg (1½hr.), Lübeck (1½hr.), and Flensburg (1hr.). The **Mitfahrzentrale,** Sophienblatt 52a (tel. 194 40; fax 67 67 42), two blocks south of the train station, matches riders and drivers for DM0.10 per km. (Open M-W and F 9am-7pm, Th 9am-8pm, Sa 10am-

3pm, Su 11am-3pm.) At DM3.10 per ride, Kiel's extensive **public transportation** system will quickly result in a massive cash hemorrhage. Avoid the fiscal bloodletting by investing in a **Kieler Karte,** which also offers discounts at many sights (1 day DM12, 3 days DM17). Most of Kiel's buses pass through the rows of stops outside the train station; the ones on the train station side of the street *generally* head north, while the ones on the Sophienhof side go south. All mixed up? Call 311 311 for a **taxi.** Rent **bikes** at **Radsport Center Kiel,** Kranshagener Weg 38 (tel. 170 10; fax 171 31). Kiel's **tourist office,** Andreas-Gayk-Str. 1 (tel. 76 09 01; fax 760 54 39), is located in the post office building, two blocks north of the train station. It finds **rooms** for free and books 'em for a DM3.50 fee. (Open M and F 9am-8pm, Tu-Th and Sa 9am-6:30pm, Su 9am-2pm.) Do **laundry** at **Die Waschmaschine,** Sophienblatt 47. (Open 10am-6pm, Sa 9am-1pm.) The **post office,** Stresemannpl. 1-3, 24044 Kiel, is on the other side of the bus station from the train station. (Open M-F 8am-7pm, Sa 8:30am-2pm.) **Exchange money** at the adjacent **Postbank** (same hours as the post office; closes at 1pm on Saturdays). The **telephone code** is 0431.

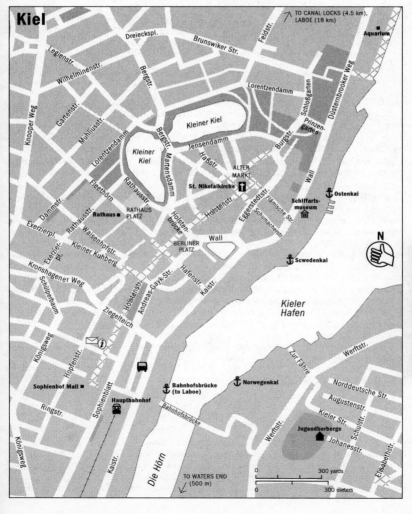

✍ FERRY CONNECTIONS. All **ferries** except those bound for Norway and the Baltics leave from the piers on the west side of the harbor. **Baltic Line,** on the west side near the station at **Schwedenkai** (tel. 20 97 60), will take you to Sweden. **Color Line** (tel. 730 03 00; fax 730 04 00) at **Norwegenkai,** on the opposite side of the harbor, sails to Oslo. (12½hrs. Departs daily at 2pm. Single cabin DM114-174, double DM150-202.) **Langeland-Kiel,** (tel. 97 41 50; fax 945 15), on the west side of **Ostenkai,** ships out to Bagenkop, Denmark (2½hr.; DM7, in July DM9). Boats bound for Kaliningrad and the Baltics leave from **Ostuferkai.**

⌂ ACCOMMODATIONS AND CAMPING. Kiel's boss hostel, **Jugendherberge Kiel (HI),** Johannesstr. 1 (tel. 73 14 88; fax 73 57 23), has uncrowded quads, each with its own shower and bathroom. Take bus #4 from the train station on the Sophienhof side to "Kieler Str.," and backtrack one block, then turn right on Johannesstr.; or take the Cinemaxx exit from the train station and walk toward the harbor. Take the bridge across and walk in the same direction through the construction site to the overpass. Turn left, following the small, white signs through the garden to the hostel. (15min. DM28, over 26 DM33. Sheets and breakfast included. Reception 7am-1am. Checkout 7am-9am. Curfew 1am. Members only.) **Campingplatz Falckenstein,** Palisadenweg 171 (tel. 39 20 78; fax 39 20 78), is a distant 13km from the center. Take bus #44 (direction: "Strand") to "Seekamp." Backtrack to Scheidekoppel and hike 20 minutes through wheat fields until Palisadenweg, then turn left down toward the beach. (DM7 per person. Tent DM6-12. Open April-Oct.)

⌕ FOOD. Sandwich, Holstenstr. 92, counts on tourists' thirst for expensive Coca-Cola; fight the power by bringing your own drink and enjoy the yummy little sandwiches noted in the appellation. (DM2.50-3.50. Open M-Sa 6:30am-6pm.) The Kieler Brauerei, Alter Markt 6 (tel. 90 62 90), has dark suds (DM3-6) and expensive breadbaskets (DM12-15), but at least this barley center is somewhat authentic. (Open M-Th and Su 11am-1am and F-Sa 11am-2am.) Get groceries at **Kaiser's** on the ground floor of the Sophienhof mall. (Open M-F 9am-8pm, Sa 8:30am-4pm.)

◉ SIGHTS. The sights and sounds of the harbor, the city's focal point, are omnipresent in stolid, modern Kiel. The highlight is the largest team of **canal locks** in the world. The view of the canal and the harbor is amazing. Take bus #4 to "Kanal," then the ferry that runs every 15 minutes (free). Walk right 10 minutes along Kanalstr. from the ferry dock to the *Schleuseninsel*. Alternatively, landlubbers can take bus #1 or 41 to "Schleuse." (30min. Obligatory tours daily 9am-3pm, every 2hr. DM3, students DM1.) Hugging the west coast of Kiel's harbor, the **Schiffahrtsmuseum,** Wall 65 (tel. 34 28), displays model ships. (Open mid-April to mid-Oct. daily 10am-6pm; mid-Oct. to mid-April Tu-Su 10am-5pm. Free.) North of the ship museum is the **Aquarium des Instituts für Meereskunde,** Düsternbrooker Weg 20 (tel. 597 38 57), home to a smallish collection of marine life. (Open daily April-Sept. 9am-7pm; Oct.-March 9am-5pm. DM2.50, students DM1, children DM0.50.) At the end of the Holstenstr. shopping district stands the 13th-century **Nikolaikirche,** Altermark (tel. 929 37). The church is frequently the site of free concerts. (Open M-F 10am-1pm and 2-6pm, Sa 10am-1pm.)

NEAR KIEL: LABOE

While some choose to mix it up with the tugboats and swim in the **Kieler Förde,** warmer water awaits in nearby **Laboe.** Use of the beaches requires a **Strandkarte** (DM4), which must be purchased at the *Automaten* to avoid a DM10 fine. Bus #100, from the *Sophienhof* side of the bus stop (direction: "Laboe"), will take you on a tour through the 'burbs to the beach (50min., DM5.40, *Kieler Karte* valid). A much more attractive way to get there is to take the **ferry** (1hr.), which costs the same as the bus and offers a spectacular tour of the *Förde*. From the station, walk toward the water and follow the *FSK* signs to the bridge. Laboe's harbor, which on weekends hops to the sound of jazz, is at the head of **Strandstraße,** a bucolic promenade lined with ice cream shops, fish restaurants, and the occasional flea market. The crowds thin out considerably about 300m down at the non-smoking section of the beach. A bit farther, **U-Boot 995,** with eight-person rooms the size of phone booths, is a tourist attraction, not a hostel. Used in WWII submarine campaigns, U-Boot 995 is now open to tourists. (Open daily mid-April to mid-Oct. 9:30am-6pm, mid-Oct. to mid-April 9:30am-4pm. DM3.50, under 18 DM2.50, free for German soldiers in uniform. *Let's Go* does not recommend enlisting in the German army as a means of obtaining discounts.) Across the street, winning no awards for architectural subtlety, stands the **Marine-Ehrenmal** (tel. 87 55), a 72m brick and concrete erection built commemorating "the sailors of all nations who died on the seas." The exhibits chronicle the maritime successes of the World Wars in a disturbingly unapologetic manner. Take the elevator to the 57m high observation deck for an incredible view of the *Förde* and Baltic Sea. (Same hours as the U-Boot. DM5, under 18 DM3, family card DM14.) Laboe's **tourist office,** Strandstr. 25 (tel. 42 75 53; room reservations 79 36), on the boardwalk, will hook you up with a **room** (DM30-40, breakfast included) for a 10% fee. Rent **bikes** at the **Fahrradverleih,** Strandstr. 14 (DM10 per day). The **telephone code** is 04343.

SCHLESWIG

At the southernmost point of the Schlei inlet, Schleswig bills itself as the "friendly city of culture," a title earned by its picture-perfect fishing settlements, 16th-century castle, and extensive museum collections. Originally settled by Vikings, Schleswig became an important fishing and trade center in the Middle Ages. The city was subsequently the seat of the Gottorfer dukes, small-time nobles who set themselves up in a showy castle on the banks of the Schlei. Today Schleswig's laid-back pace, beautiful surroundings, and millennium-long history provide visitors with a relaxing tour of an interesting cross-section of European history.

🔁 ORIENTATION AND PRACTICAL INFORMATION. Unlike most German towns, Schleswig centers around its **bus terminal** *(ZOB)* rather than its train station. The town center, part shopping mall, part conscientiously preserved Altstadt, sits on the north bank of the **Schlei,** while the train station lies 20 minutes south of town. **Stadtweg** is a major commercial and pedestrian zone; Schleswig's sights are south of it. To get to the train station, take bus #1, 2, 4, or 5 from the stop outside

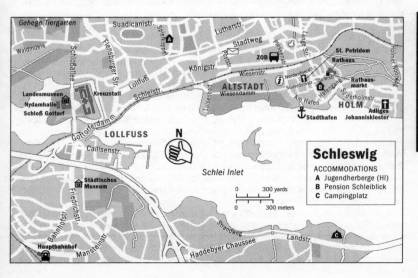

Schleswig

ACCOMMODATIONS
A Jugendherberge (HI)
B Pension Schleiblick
C Campingplatz

the *ZOB*, which is close to the Altstadt. **Trains** head hourly to Kiel, Flensburg, and Hamburg (via Neumünster). Single rides on Schleswig's **bus** network cost DM1.90. To avoid being stripped of cash and dignity, purchase a **Schleswig Card** (DM13), valid for three days of public transit and admission to most sights. Rent **bikes** at **Peters Fahrradverleih,** Bahnhofstr. 14a. (Tel. 376 88. DM10 per day.) The **tourist office,** Plessenstr. 7 (tel. 248 78; room reservations 248 32; fax 207 03), is up the street from the harbor; from the *ZOB*, walk down Plessenstr. toward the water. The staff books **rooms** (DM25-60) for a 10% fee. (Open May-Sept. M-F 9am-12:30pm and 1:30-5pm, Sa 9am-noon; Oct.-April M-Th 9am-12:30pm and 1:30-5pm, F 9am-12:30pm.) **Schnell und Sauber,** Stadtweg 70, washes 6kg of **laundry** for DM6. (Open M-Sa 6am-10pm.) The **post office,** Stadtweg 53-55, 24837 Schleswig, **exchanges money** at counter 5. (Open M-F 9am-12:30pm and 2:30-6pm, Sa 9am-noon.) The **postal code** is 24837.

▚▟ ACCOMMODATIONS AND FOOD. The **Jugendherberge (HI),** Spielkoppel 1 (tel. 238 93), is close to the center of town. Take bus #2 (direction: "Hühnhauser Schwimmhalle") from either the train station or the *ZOB* to "Schwimmhalle"; the hostel is across the street. For those shunning the bus, walk (with your back to the *ZOB*) right along Königstr. and turn right onto Poststr. Keep going in this direction as it changes to Moltkestr. and then turn left onto Bellmannstr. Follow this street to Spielkoppel, which will be on your left; the hostel is on the right across from the school. Great location and a view of the Schlei inlet. (DM21, over 26 DM26. Sheets DM7. Breakfast included. Reception 7am-1pm and 5-11pm. Curfew 11pm.) For a night in a former *Fischerhaus* overlooking the water (or for the TV in every room), try **Pension Schleiblick,** Hafengang 4 (tel. 234 68; fax 234 68). Follow Plessenstr. toward the harbor. Continue as it turns into Am Hafen, then bear left onto Hafengang. (Singles DM65, doubles DM110-130. Reception daily until 11pm. Breakfast included.) The **Wikinger Campingplatz,** Am Haithabu (tel. 324 50; fax 331 22), is across the inlet from the Altstadt. **Da Paolo,** Stadtweg 65 (tel. 298 97), serves traditional pizza and pasta on red-checkered tablecloths. (Open daily noon-3pm and 5:30pm-midnight.) Also try the seafood—fresh and cheap—at the *Imbiße* down by the **Stadthafen.** Schleswig's own **Asgaard-Brauerei,** Königstr. 27 (tel. 292 06), keeps the Viking tradition, looting and pillaging (at least metaphorically) with golden ale, though you must supply the hornèd headwear. Sandwiches are expensive (DM7.50-11.50), but—praise Odin—the beer's not (DM3-6)! (Open M-Th 5pm-midnight, F-Sa 11am-2am, Su 11am-midnight.)

◙ SIGHTS. Schleswig's Altstadt, located a few blocks up from the harbor, is stuffed to the gills with meandering cobblestoned streets leading along the town's unusually hilly terrain. **Stadtweg,** the main pedestrian zone, is lined with smart shops and a department store. Towering over it all is the copper steeple of the 12th-century **St. Petri-Dom,** renowned for its successful combination of Romanesque and high Gothic architecture, as well as for its intricately carved 16th-century **Bordesholmer Altar** by Brüggemann. Climb the 112m tower for DM2, children DM1. (Open May-Sept. M-Th and Sa 9am-5pm, F 9am-3pm, Su 1pm-5pm; Oct.-April M-Th and Sa 10am-4pm, F 10am-3pm, Su 1pm-4pm.) In the summer the church offers a choral and organ concert series on Wednesday evenings (DM10-15, students DM5-8). Two blocks beyond the Dom, the narrow alleys unfold onto the **Rathausmarkt,** a quiet square adjacent to the 15th-century **Rathaus.** From the square, follow Töpferstr. and turn right on Fischbrückestr. Beyond Knud-Laward-Str. begins the **Holm,** a small fishing village with a tiny church in the main square, which doubles as Holm's cemetery.

A 20-minute walk along the harbor from the Altstadt, 16th-century **Schloß Gottorf** (tel. 81 32 22) and its surrounding buildings house the **Landesmuseen,** a treasure trove of artwork and artifacts in six museums. The castle is home to most of the exhibits; the first floor consists of 16th- and 17th-century Dutch and Danish artwork, alongside tapestries, suits of armor, and the Gottorfs' apartments. Upstairs

MATJES *Matjes* (MAHT-yes), the Scandinavian word for herring, is all the rage in northern Germany during the first few weeks of June, which are officially dubbed the *Matjes-Wochen* (Herring Weeks). Several varieties exist: *niederländisch* (Dutch), with cream sauce and vegetables; *Hausfrauen-Art* (housewife), in sour cream with onion and apple; and sweet and sour, doused in sugared vinegar—but any restaurant worth its salt has its own secret recipe. Look for *Matjes* advertised everywhere, from the dives in the train station to the hip Schanzenstr. cafés. The fish has a very strong, sweet taste that is not acquired—you'll either love it or hate it. Wash it down with a glass of *Alsterwasser*—literally "water from the Alster" (one of Hamburg's lakes), but actually a gentle mix of beer and Sprite that tastes a lot better than it sounds.

the path leads to the incredibly ornate **Kapelle** (chapel), built in 1591. The grand finale is the appropriately named **Hirschsaal,** whose deer-endowed walls feature real antlers. The room itself houses an oddly out-of-place collection of Ottoman and Persian artifacts. The second floor is also home to the excellent **Jugendstilmuseum,** a collection of art deco paintings and furniture. Wipe your shoes before going in—even the carpets are part of the exhibit. One floor up are the main exhibits of the **Archäologisches Landesmuseum.** The rest of the museum is in the **Nydamhalle** adjacent to the castle, including a 4th-century fishing boat and an exhibit on the Saxon migration to England. On the other side of the castle, the **Kreuzstall** and the adjacent buildings house the **Museum des 20. Jahrhunderts,** an extensive collection devoted to the artists of the Brücke school, including Emil Nolde, Max Pechstein, and Ernst Ludwig Kirchner, as well as a well-rounded presentation of adherents to the *Neue Sachlichkeit.* Finally, the park surrounding the castle holds an **outdoor sculpture museum** featuring contemporary German sculptors. (All museums open daily March-Oct. 9am-5pm; Nov.-Feb. 9:30am-4pm. DM7, students DM3.)

If you find yourself longing to see the remains of a civilization of tall, attractive people who seem to have made a lot of combs and beautiful boats, ferries travel from the Stadthafen near the Dom to the **Wikinger Museum Haithabu.** The museum, next to an archaeological dig of a former **Viking settlement,** covers all aspects of Viking life in three huts. Despite the throngs of tourists, it's not a hokey place: the area around the museum has walking paths and a strikingly landscaped cemetery. (Open daily April-Oct. 9am-5pm; Nov.-March Tu-Su 9am-4pm. DM4, students DM2, families DM10.) About five minutes up the road heading to the station, the **Städtisches Museum,** Friedrichstr. 9-11 (tel. 93 68 20), houses documents and *objets trouvés* from Schleswig's history. (Open Tu-Su 10am-5pm.)

FLENSBURG

With the Danish border only a hop, skip, and a stumble away, Flensburg is Germany's northernmost city. You can't go anywhere in northern Germany without encountering Flensburger Pilsner on tap, and the town itself is swimming in it. The presence of a large international student population and so much locally brewed alcohol injects some pulse into the region's otherwise stasis-loving veins. While cheerfully commercial and mildly intellectual today, Flensburg's prosperity has in the past brought on bad times. Its success as a medieval port made it a target of envious 17th-century rivals. Slow reconstruction during the 18th century allowed Hamburg and Copenhagen to become the region's supreme port cities, but Lady Luck seemed to wink propitiously during WWII, when few Allied bombs fell on the town. However, Flensburg's good condition attracted the fleeing Nazi government, which named the town Germany's provisional capital and then surrendered it almost immediately afterwards on May 7, 1945.

⌧ PRACTICAL INFORMATION. Trains link the city to Schleswig (1hr.), Kiel (1hr.), and Hamburg (1½hr.) every hour, while others head north to Copenhagen (5hr., twice daily) and many other Danish cities. **Buses** also cross the border to the

Danish towns of Sønderborg (1¼hr.) and Aabenrå (50min.) from gate B4. Flensburg's **public transportation** system saves a lot of uphill walking in town; most buses circulate through the *ZOB* two blocks from Holm below the harbor (single ride DM1.90). From the west bank of the harbor, **Hansalinie**, Eckernförder Landstr. 2 (tel. 980 01; fax 989 01), runs five **ferries** a day between Flensburg and Glücksburg in Germany and Gravenstein and Kollund in Denmark (DM6, children 7-14 DM4). The **tourist office**, Speicherlinie 40 (tel. 230 90; fax 173 52), lies off Große Str.; follow the signs through the courtyard. The staff books **rooms** (DM20-35) for free and arranges summer tours of the brewery for DM5. (Open M-F 9am-6pm.) The **post office**, near the train station at Bahnhofstr. 40, 24939 Flensburg, **exchanges currency.** (Open M-F 8am-6pm, Sa 8am-1pm.) The **telephone code** is 0461.

■▣ **ORIENTATION AND SIGHTS.** Flensburg surrounds the natural harbor formed by the inland banks of the **Flensburger Förde;** streets run up from the water's edge into the hills. Heading straight down Bahnhofstr. from the station and zigzagging across Friedrich-Ebert-Str. will lead you on a 20 minute tour to the lively Altstadt and Flensburg's huge pedestrian zone along **Holm** and **Große Str.** On the way you'll pass the **Deutsches Haus**, on Neumarktstr., a Bauhaus-style concert hall donated to Flensburg in recognition of the city's loyalty in the 1920 referendum. In the **Südermarkt,** just up Rotestr., the beautiful 14th-century **Nikolaikirche** boasts a gargantuan organ, the *Organ Maximus*. The church is named after the patron saint of skippers ("What'cha doin', lil' buddy?") and scurvy sailors. (Open Tu-F 9am-5pm, Sa 10am-1pm. Free.) Beyond the **Nordermarkt** stands the **Marienkirche** with its bizarre 1950s-era stained-glass windows. (Open Tu and Th-F 10am-4pm, W and Sa 10am-1pm. Free.) The **Marientreppe**, Norderstr. 50, offers a glimpse of Denmark atop its 146 stairs. The **Schiffahrtsmuseum**, Schiffbrücke 39 (tel. 85 29 70), documents Flensburg's nautical history and role in Denmark's once-thriving Caribbean trade. (Open Tu-Sa 10am-5pm, Su 10am-1pm. DM5, students DM2.50.) The last weekend in May hosts the **Rum Regatta.**

▐▐ **ACCOMMODATIONS AND FOOD.** Flensburg's **Jugendherberge (HI)**, Fichtestr. 16 (tel. 377 42; fax 31 29 52), offers no escape from exercise, whether it be running laps on the nearby track or making the long walk into town. From the train station, take bus #1 (direction: "Lachsbach") or 4 (direction: "Klueshof") to "ZOB" and change to #3 or 7 (direction: "Twedter Plack") to "Stadion," then follow the signs. (DM21, over 26 DM26. Sheets DM7. Reception 8-8:45am, 5-6pm, and 9:30-10pm.) The **Nordermarkt** simmers with a slew of cafés and bars. For those itching to see what a metric hangover feels like, **Hansen's Brauerei**, Große Str. 83 (tel. 222 10), serves home-brewed beer by the meter for DM26 (12 drinks for the price of 10!) and German food in equally absurd quantities. Their whopping Sunday special bloats you with 1kg of ribs for DM14. (Open M-Th and Su 11am-midnight, F-Sa, 11am-2am.) For those in the market for something a little lighter, **Apfelsinchen**, Große Str. 33, whips up shakes (DM4), smoothies (DM5-6), and salads (DM4-6).

NEAR FLENSBURG: GLÜCKSBURG

Ten kilometers from Flensburg, **Glücksburg** boasts beautiful beaches (DM4) and a fairy-tale **Schloß** (tel. (04631) 22 13 or 22 43) surrounded by a looking-glass lake. Unlike Wonderland, Glücksburg can be reached by bus from gate B6 of the *ZOB* (35min., DM3.50) or by ferry via Kollund, Denmark (50min., 5 per day, DM3, passport required). From the Glücksburg bus station, backtrack a block towards the post office and follow the *Schloß* signs, or get off at the beach (one stop earlier) and follow the signs around the lake (2.5km). Portraits of pasty dukes and duchesses, along with their multiple chins, hang on every wall. Skate around the second floor in the slippers provided while discovering just how these inbred 16- to 19th-century royals were. On the third floor, Gobelin tapestries depict scenes from Ovid's *Metamorphoses*. Don't miss the "corpses" in the dungeon. (Open April-Oct. 10am-5pm; Nov.-March 10am-4:30pm. DM8, students DM6.)

SYLT

The sandy, windswept island of Sylt stretches far into the North Sea, culminating in Germany's northernmost point. The 10km long **Hindenburgdamm** connects Sylt—traditionally a favorite spot for government luminaries and other wealthy vacationers, but now a more democratic affair—to the mainland. The beauty of Sylt's undulating dunes and occasional pine forests attracts large crowds, especially to **Westerland**. The mother of all Kurtowns and the largest town on the island, Westerland is abuzz with bourgeois types traipsing down the boardwalk. Parts of the island are heinously overdeveloped; others are deserted.

7 PRACTICAL INFORMATION. Trains from Hamburg's **Altona** station travel to Westerland via Husum (2½hr., 1 per hour). **Public transportation** on the island is quite expensive but very thorough. (DM6.20 to reach either hostel from Westerland, day card DM20.) Buses leave from the *ZOB* terminal to the left of the train station. Rent a **bike** from **Fahrrad am Bahnhof** at the station, across from track 1. (DM9 per day, DM49 per week. Open daily 9am-1pm and 2pm-6:30pm.) Sylt levies a *Kurtaxe* on any easy riders hoping to hit the beaches. (June-Sept. DM6, May and Oct. DM5.50 per day, Nov.-April DM3; under 18 free.) **Ferries** run seven to 11 times a day from List harbor to **Havneby** on the Danish island of **Rømø**. (50min. One-way DM56, round-trip DM87, same-day return DM79.) Call **Rømø-Sylt Linie** (tel. 87 04 75) in List for reservations and information. **Adler-Schiffe**, Boysenstr. 13 (tel. 987 00), in Hörnum, runs daytrips to Amrum. The **tourist office** (tel. 99 88; fax 99 81 00) in the train station books **rooms** (DM35 and up) for a minimum DM10 fee or 8% of your bill. (Open daily in summer M-Th 9am-6pm, F-Sa 9am-10pm, Su 11am-4pm.) For rooms in List, call 952 00; in Hörnum, 96 26 26; in Kampen, 46 98 33. The **post office,** Kjeirstr. 17, 25992 Sylt, is near the non-*ZOB* exit of the train station. (Open M-F 8am-6pm, Sa 8am-noon.) The **telephone code** is 04651.

☎ ACCOMMODATIONS. Sylt offers two youth hostels. Those neither wayward nor lucky enough to earn a spot in Hörnum's reform school will have to settle for the adjacent **Jugendherberge Hörnum (HI)**, Friesenpl. 2 (tel. 88 02 94; fax 88 13 92). The hostel offers a convenient location next to a bus stop and a **SPAR grocery store** (open M-F 8am-noon and 2:30-6pm, Sa 8am-1pm), though more sensitive travelers may be put off by the barbed wire and watchtower-fortified yards of the reform school. From the *ZOB*, take bus #2 (direction: "Hörnum Hafen") to "Hörnum-Nord" and continue along Rantumer Str., turning left at the *Jugendherberge* sign. Behind the hostel, a secluded beach stretches for miles. (DM23, over 26 DM28. Sheets DM7. Reception noon-1pm and 5-10pm. Curfew 11pm. Reservations strongly recommended.) List's **Jugendherberge Mövenberg** (tel. 87 03 97; fax 87 10 39) lies near the northern tip of the island amid the dune trails. Catch bus #1 (direction: "List Hafen") from the Westerland *ZOB* and take it to the end of the line (DM6.20). If you're lucky you can change for the infrequent bus #5 to "Mövenberg"; otherwise, return to the second intersection from the bus stop, turn right and follow the *Jugendherberge* sign 3km, past the sheep and dunes. Be aware that school groups covet the hostel's proximity to the youth beach. (DM23, over 26 DM28. Breakfast included. Reception 7-9am, noon-2:30pm, and 4-10pm. Curfew 11pm. Reservations strongly advised. Open mid-March to Oct.)

☐☂ SIGHTS AND HIKING. From Westerland, the best way to explore the 39km-long island is by bicycle. The main bike path follows the highway, making it good for intertown travel, while the smaller dirt and gravel paths meander through the dunes, affording stunning views of the ocean. Outside the recreational chaos of the main town, where shopping is everyone's favorite summer sport, Sylt offers sparsely populated beaches, including the (in)famous **Bühne 16**, whose nude bathers reveal that water wings do not a swimsuit make. Sylt's beaches also provide the only locale in Germany where windsurfing is possible. While they're no Waikiki, the beaches at **Wellingstedt, Hörnum,** and **Strandhalle** all produce rideable surf.

While Westerland is a convenient starting-point for an island adventure, its rows of designer shops and overpriced restaurants can become claustrophobic in the high season. To avoid (most of) the crowds, head north; beyond Westerland's city limits, unpopulated dune trails and small vacation villages await. North of **Kampen** (one town north of Westerland), the main road leads through rolling grass-covered dunes and fields sparsely inhabited by cows and horses. **List,** Sylt's northernmost town, is an excellent base for hikers and bikers wishing to explore the trails leading into the remote dunes of **Ellenbogen,** the northernmost point in Germany.

AMRUM

The closest island to Sylt, **Amrum** draws (mostly wealthy) visitors with its cliff-sized dunes, fragrant pine forests, and miles of sandy beaches. Nine square kilometers of Amrum are sand; the other 20 square kilometers support five towns: **Wittdün,** the main town; **Steenodde; Süddorf; Nebel,** winner of the highest-percentage-roofs-thatched prize; and **Norddorf. Wittdün** has a pleasant main street, **Hauptstr.,** as well as a souvenir- and *Imbiß*-free **Strandpromenade.** But the island's main attraction is the **Kniepsand**—kilometers of the whitest sand bordering the North Sea. Between the *Kniepsand* and the towns lies a narrow strip of grassy dunes interspersed with lakes and hiking trails, crowned by the **Amrumer Leuchtturm,** the tallest lighthouse on Germany's North seacoast. (Open April-Oct. M-F 8:30am-noon.) Use the lighthouse as a lookout point, or climb to one of the **Aussichtsdünen** that dot the walkways through the dunes. Amrum has two museums, both of which are worth a once-over, even if only from the outside. Both are located in **Nebel.** The **Mühlenmuseum** (tel. 22 89), in a shaggy windmill, has exhibits on the history and prehistory of Amrum, the lighthouse, and some model boats. (Open M-W 10am-noon, Th-Su 3pm-6pm.) To learn more about Frisian culture, step inside the **Ömrang Hüüs** Waaswai 1 (tel. 41 53), an 18th-century captain's home. (Open M-F 10am-1pm and Saturday afternoons in summer.) **St. Clemens,** Nebel's church, is also worth a visit.

Getting to Amrum provides its own excitement as folks can **run** to the island across the **Wattenmeer** (see **Watt is Watt?,** p. 510) from Sylt at low tide. The path connecting the two islands contains a few **quicksand** pits, making it advisable to take a guided tour (tel. 21 75; DM6). For the less adventurous, **Adler-Schiffe** (tel. (04842) 268; fax 264) runs boats to Wittdün from Hörnum on Sylt. (50min. Departs 11am and 5:15pm. Round-trip DM35, children DM16.) Amrum has two **bus** lines: bus #1 services Norddorf, Nebel, Süddorf, and Wittdün, while bus #2 services Wittdün, Süddorf, Steenodde, and Nebel. (Single ride DM2-2.50. Day-card DM9). **Bikes** are available for rent *everywhere* on the island, but prices go up the closer you are to Wittdün and the ferry. (A good price is around DM6 per half-day, DM10 per day.) Amrum's transportation authorities would prefer that cyclists keep off the main road, and so two main paths running along either side of the island have been paved. The **green trail** goes through pine forests to the west, while the **yellow trail** rolls through the pastures and villages in the east. The **tourist office** (tel. 940 30; fax 94 03 20), near the ferry, books **rooms** for DM15 per person.

Although Amrum has nearly 1,000 guest beds available, they are almost all full in summer. Adventurers may have some luck in the mornings at the tourist office. The **Jugendherberge Wittdün,** Mittelstr. 1 (tel. 20 10), has large, clean rooms, some with beach views. From the ferry, walk straight away from the boat and turn right onto Mittelstr. Note that *Pensionen* of equivalent price and greater tranquility can be found. If you really want to stay here anyway, you'll need a reservation, unless there's a miracle. (DM23, over 26 DM28, plus *Kurtaxe.* Sheets DM7. Reception 11am-1pm and 4:30-9:30pm. Members only. Open April-Nov.) Restaurants in Wittdün tend to be fairly expensive, but fortunately there are two **SPAR supermarkets** on Hauptstr. (Open M-F 9am-6pm, Sa til 9am-1pm.) **Café Barfuß,** on Hauptstr. across from the post office, has a beer garden and a small *Imbiß.* (DM5-9. Open M-F and Su 9am-11pm.) The **post office** is on Hauptstr. 30. (Open M-F 9am-noon and 2:30-5pm, Sa 9am-noon.) Amrum's **telephone code** is 04682.

MECKLENBURG-VORPOMMERN

More than 1,700 lakes, the marshy coast of the Baltic Sea, and labyrinthine medieval towns make up the lonely landscape of Mecklenburg-Vorpommern. Once a favored vacation spot for East Germans, this sparsely populated northernmost province of the former GDR retains the sturdy, raw-boned natural beauty of the *Bundesboonies*. Cyclists and hikers flock to Mecklenburg's lakes and Rügen, which offer some of Germany's most spectacular scenery. And as restoration work in the region's main cities continues, dramatic Hanseatic architecture emerges from the rubble. Tourists are again beginning to fill seaside resorts that were the playground of the early 20th-century glitterati, and the area is gradually getting back on its feet. With an unemployment rate hovering around 20%, however, Mecklenburg-Vorpommern's cities remain economically and politically troubled, and the presence of neo-Nazis is, unfortunately, palpable.

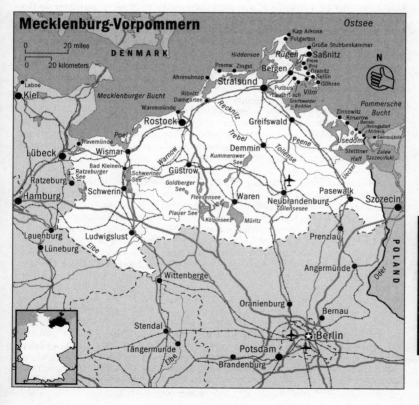

Mecklenburg-Vorpommern

SCHWERIN

First recognized in 1018, Schwerin is the grandfather of Mecklenburg-Vorpommern's cities, and with the *Wende*, the city regained its status as capital of the *Land*. Surrounded almost entirely by lakes and largely free of Communist "architectural innovations," Schwerin's Altstadt brims with well-preserved townhouses and remnants of its past life as an elegant spa town. A number of galleries and performance spaces house dozens of art festivals and concerts throughout the year, but *haute culture* isn't all the city has to offer. On weekends, the streets fill with chic club-hoppers, making it not impossible to take in an opera and a rave in the same night (and morning).

⚐ ORIENTATION AND PRACTICAL INFORMATION. Schwerin lies on the Magdeburg-Rostock rail line and is easily accessible from all major cities on the Baltic coast. **Trains** connect Schwerin to Rostock (1¼hr., 1 per hour, DM22) and Lübeck (1½hr., 1 per hour, DM20). The **tourist office,** Am Markt 1 (tel. 592 52 12; fax 55 50 94), books **rooms** (DM30-50) for free and has calendars of concerts and openings. From the train station, go right on Grundthalplatz and continue as it turns into Wismarsche Str.; take a left on Arsenal, a right on Mecklenburgstr., and another left on Schmiedestr. (Open M-F 10am-6pm, Sa-Su 10am-2pm.) The **Apotheke am Markt,** Puschkinstr. 61 (tel. 59 23 50), just off the Marktplatz, has an emergency bell. (Open M-F 8am-6pm, Sa 8:30am-1pm.) **Schnell & Sauber,** on Platz der Freiheit, keeps you clean. (Wash 6kg for DM4, soap included. Dry for DM0.50 for 12 minutes.) **Zweirad Nord,** Goethestr. 58 (tel. 557 44 22), rents **bikes** for DM10 per day with a DM50 deposit. The main **post office** resides at Mecklenburgstr. 6, 19053 Schwerin. From the Markt, go down Schmiedestr. and turn right. (Open M-F 8am-6pm, Sa 9am-noon.) The **telephone code** is 0385.

⚐⚐ ACCOMMODATIONS AND FOOD. The **Jugendherberge (HI),** Waldschulweg 3 (tel./fax 326 00 06), is located south of town in the woods by the lake. Take bus #14 to "Jugendherberge," get off at the last stop, and walk toward the zoo; the hostel is on the left. With Schwerin's increasing popularity, the friendly hostel frequently fills, so phone first. (DM23, over 26 DM28. Breakfast included. Sheets DM6. Reception 9am-noon and 4-10pm. Curfew 10pm.) The cheapest place to catch a bite to eat is at the **Edeka supermarket,** just off the Markt on Schmiedestr. (open M-F 8am-8pm, Sa 8am-4pm) or at a string of fast food joints in the **Wurm,** a mall on Marienplatz. (Open M-F 9:30am-8pm, Sa 9:30am-4pm, Su 11am-4pm.) The mephistophilean ambiance at **Café Faust,** at (of course) Goethestr. 101, may draw you in; pull up a barstool in the *Gestalt* of a pile of books and drink in the draughts of hell. (Open daily from 11am.) For a less jarring experience, wile away the night at the mustard-yellow **Bernstein Café,** Voßstr. 46, a 10-minute walk off the beaten path down Wallstr., which serves marvelous coffee and inexpensive but good breakfast. (DM4.50-8.50. Open daily from 11am.) An even cheaper breakfast can be found at **Café Antik,** at Schliemanstr. and Münzstr.: *Frühstück abgebrannt* (burned-down breakfast, DM3) consists of a cup of coffee and a cigarette. To pay for it, bring along an heirloom, as the store doubles as an antique shop. (Open daily 11am-midnight.)

■ **SIGHTS.** Schwerin's **Schloß** (tel. 520 29 20), located on an island just south of the city center, is everything your mother told you a castle should be; the building's ridiculous amalgamation of architectural styles is either majestic or gaudy. The castle served as the seat of the dukes of Mecklenburg, who ruled the area until the 1918 upheaval chased the monarch from power. The castle's gilded Baroque cupolas runneth over with luxury—the red silk wallpaper and mahogany floors pale in comparison to the sumptuous throne room with its gilt and marble columns. (Open Tu-Su 10am-6pm. DM6, students DM3.) Across from the Schloß, the **Alter Garten** was the site of mass demonstrations preceding the downfall of the GDR in 1989. Atop a cascade of stairs on the right sits the **Staatliches Museum,** which houses a good collection of 15th- to 19th-century Dutch and German art, including a few works by Rembrandt, Cranach the Elder, and Rubens. (Open Tu 10am-8pm, W-Su 10am-6pm. DM5, students DM2.) Looking uphill, the nearest spire belongs to the 13th-century Gothic **Dom.** (Open M-Sa 10am-5pm, Su noon-

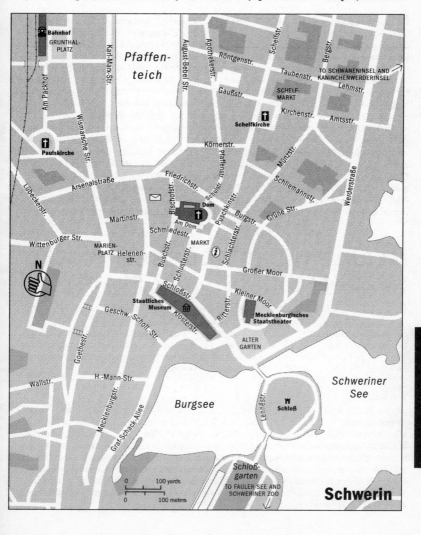

Schwerin

M.-VORPOMMERN

5pm.) For DM2, sweat your way up the 110m tower. Organ music can be caught every Monday at 2:30pm (free). At the **Schleswig-Holstein-Haus,** Puschkinstr. 12 (tel. 55 55 27), tickets to generally high-quality art exhibitions are DM6-8, students a few Marks less. Schwerin's former **synagogue** reposes silently at Schlachterstr. 3, off the Marktplatz; the temple was destroyed in a pogrom in 1938. The building used to house the region's memorial to its Jewish community, but closed several years ago after an interior looting by local skinheads.

Animals cavort at the **Schweriner Zoo** (tel. 39 55 10; fax 395 51 30), which borders the hostel adjoining the **Fauler See.** (Open April-Sept. M-F 9am-5pm, Sa-Su 9am-6pm; Oct.-March daily 10am-4pm. DM8, students and children DM5.) The zoo specializes in water fowl, but it has its share of ferocious mammals. Another option for nature lovers is the reserve on **Kaninchenwerder** island set in the Schweriner See. In summer, **ferries** leave at least once an hour from the docks to the left of the Schloß to visit the island's rabbits. (One-way DM9, children DM2.50.)

▣ ▤ ENTERTAINMENT AND NIGHTLIFE. The striking cream-pillared building next door to the museum (see above) is the **Mecklenburgisches Staatstheater** (tel. 530 00), currently in the midst of a dramatic revival (call for ticket service). **Kultursommer '00,** available from the tourist office, lists a selection of public sculptures, along with a guide to performances. Tickets for most shows can be bought through **Ticketservice Behnke,** Am Markt 10. (Tel. 56 05 00. Open M-F 10am-6pm, Sa 10am-noon.) Schwerin's best sights often double as performance spaces; each summer, the steps of the museum are converted into an opera stage, and in the nearby Schloß, the throne room is a grand venue for monthly concerts (DM39, students DM19). The **Schelfstadt** neighborhood houses a number of galleries and performance spaces; everything from literary readings to folk music concerts takes place in **Der Speider,** Röntgenstr. 22 (tel. 56 05 00). The **Kammerkino,** Röntgenstr. 12 (tel. 55 50 78), around the corner, shows international independent films. Loud crowds flock to **Louis,** Wittenburger Str. 50 (tel. 758 84 84), where frequent live bands keep the party going into the early morning. (Open Th-Sa from 9pm.) For those who get tired, respite can be found next door at **Pub-Pela;** the music is only a few decibels quieter, but chairs and tables replace sweaty dancing bodies.

MECKLENBURGISCHE SEENPLATTE (MECKLENBURG LAKE PLAIN)

When things got hectic in Berlin, Bismarck often found refuge among the reserved but sincere folk of the Mecklenburgische Seenplatte. The reminders of the GDR are not as painfully obvious here as in other regions of Eastern Germany, perhaps because the Socialist-era architects were wise enough to leave the forests and hills alone. A popular vacation area for more than a century, the Seenplatte attracts plenty of summer crowds; consider advance reservations.

WAREN

Conveniently located within an hour of Rostock and two hours of Berlin, Waren draws crowds to the northern edge of the Müritz, Germany's largest freshwater lake. The city fills with busloads of tourists in the summer; to avoid them, head for ▨Müritz national park, a unique preserve of rare birds and marshland. The Waren tourist office has tons of information about guided tours of this paradise for hikers and bikers, ranging from early-morning bird-watching jaunts to all-day canoeing, biking, and hiking triathlons. Especially useful is the Müritz-Nationalpark-Ticket, which is good for a day of travel on a combination of bus, rail, and ferry connections (DM10-30, students DM5-17.50).

⁊ ORIENTATION AND PRACTICAL INFORMATION. Waren is easily reached from Rostock (1hr., every 2hr., DM22), Berlin (1¾hr., every 2hr., DM51), and Güstrow (30min., 1 per hour, DM15). **Warener Schiffahrtsgesellschaft,** Am Stadthafen (tel. 12 56 24; fax 12 56 93), and **Müritzwind Personenschiffahrt,** Strandstr. (tel. 66 66 64; fax 66 58 79), both offer **boat tours** of the Müritz lake that vary in length from one to four hours (DM7-22, children half-price). Rent **bikes** around the corner from the train station at **Bureau Mobil,** Lloydstr. 2b. (Tel. 73 25 50. Open M-F 9am-6pm, Sa 9am-noon. DM10 per day.) **Waren Information,** Neuer Markt am Stadthafen (tel. 66 61 83; fax 66 43 30), in the town square, has maps of the park, brochures, and finds **rooms** (DM30) for a DM5 fee. The office runs both park and town tours in German. (M, W, and F 10am; Sa-Su 11am. DM5, students DM3.) From the train station, turn right onto the footpath and follow it over Schweriner Damm; go left on Friedenstr. and left again on Lange Str. (Open April-Oct. M-F 10am-noon and 2-6pm, Sa 10am-noon and 1-4pm; Nov.-March M-F 10am-4pm.) A **pharmacy, Fontane-Apotheke,** Lange Str. 55 (tel. 642 70) keeps you fit. (Open M-F 8am-6pm, Sa 8am-12:15pm.) Reach the **post office,** Güstrower Str. 24, 17192 Waren, by turning right as you exit the train station and following the road along the tracks. (Open M-F 9am-5:30pm, Sa 9am-noon.) The **telephone code** is 03991.

⌐⌐ ACCOMMODATIONS AND FOOD. The **Jugendherberge (HI),** Auf dem Nes-selberg 2 (tel./fax 66 76 06), dwells in the woods south of town. From the station's Schweriner Damm exit, go left on Schweriner Damm, bear right at the fork in the road, and then walk along the harbor down the successive streets Zur Steinmole, Strandstr., Müritzstr., and Am Seeufer. When you reach the wooded hill on the left, head straight up the path (25min. walk). Or walk 100m to the left as you leave the train station and take bus #3 (direction: "Ecktannen") to "Wasserwerk." The 60 beds book quickly, but the hostel boasts a lovely location, and the friendly man-agement will set up tents outside if they're full. (DM16, over 26 DM21. Breakfast DM7. Sheets DM7. Reception 4-6pm and 8pm, or ring the bell. Members only.) There is regular camping at **Azur,** on Fontanestr. (tel. 26 07). Follow the directions to the youth hostel (above), but keep going on Am Seeufer until you reach Fon-tanestr. Or take bus #3 or 5 (direction: "Ecktannen") to the last stop. (DM6 per per-son, DM3 per tent.) The **City Ristorante,** Friedenstr. 8 (tel. 66 87 03), offers large and small pizzas (DM5-12) and other dishes. (Open daily 10am-11pm.) A **Spar supermar-ket** is at Neuer Markt 23. (Open M-F 8am-8pm, Sa 8am-noon.)

◙ SIGHTS. Since Waren's primary attractions are nature-related, it's not surpris-ing that restoration of the former Altstadt is not a top priority. Sitting on the quiet **Alter Markt,** the weather-beaten 14th-century **Altes Rathaus,** the crumbling **Speicher** (granary) that presides over the harbor, and the 290-year-old **Altes Schulhaus** (old schoolhouse), have all seen better days. Next door, the **Georgenkirche** lost its roof to fire in 1699 and received only a modest, flat replacement. Müritz's modest **aquar-ium** and **aviary** lives under the Herrenseebrücke. (Open March-Sept. Tu-F 9am-6pm, Sa-Su 9am-noon and 2-5pm; Oct.-April Tu-F 10am-4pm, Sa-Su 10am-noon and 2-5pm. DM5, students DM3.)

GÜSTROW

Were it not home to a huge collection of works by the prolific 20th-century artist Ernst Barlach, Güstrow would be like most of Mecklenburg-Vorpommern's towns: a mass of crumbling buildings with satellite dishes and *Imbiße* poking out of the brickwork. A model city for Germany's EXPO 2000 urban renewal project, Güstrow has begun pulling itself out of its decrepit state. In addition to filling the city with pacifist sculptures, Barlach fiercely opposed German nationalism and fascism, causing the Nazis to condemn his work as *Entartete Kunst* (degenerate art). Güstrow is also the hometown of Uwe Johnson, the GDR author subjected to constant surveillance and forced into exile in 1959 for "subversive" writings that criticized the divisions between East and West—the town's only monument to the author is a street that bears his name.

⑦ ORIENTATION AND PRACTICAL INFORMATION. Central Güstrow lies south of the train station. To get there, follow Eisenbahnstr. until it becomes Lindenstr., then go about 45m farther on Lindenstr. before turning left onto Pferdemarkt. Güstrow is connected to Rostock (45min., 1 per hour, DM12) and Waren (30min., 1 per hour, DM15). **Fahrrad Dräger**, Langestr. 49 (tel. 68 40 10), rents **bikes** for DM8-10 per day. (Open M-F 9am-noon and 1-6pm, Sa 9am-noon.) **Güstrow Information**, Domstr. 9 (tel. 68 10 23; fax 68 20 79), finds **rooms** (DM30 and up) for a DM5 fee. (Open March-Sept. M-F 9am-6pm, Sa-Su 9:30am-1pm; Oct.-April closed Su.) The office offers city **tours** that leave from Franz-Parr-Pl. daily at 11am. (June-Sept. DM4, students DM2.) Do laundry at **SB Waschsalon**, Pferdemarkt 35. (Wash DM6, dry DM2. Open 7am-10pm.) The **post office** is at Pferdemarkt 52, 18271 Güstrow. (Open M-F 8am-6pm, Sa 9am-noon.) **Internet** access is available at **Die Zockergruft**, Greviner Str. 23 (tel. 68 26 11), for DM10 per hour; just don't hit your head on the chains. The **telephone code** is 03843.

⬛⬛ ACCOMMODATIONS AND FOOD. Güstrow's cute but distant **Jugendherberge (HI)**, Heidberg 33 (tel. 84 00 44), is 4km from town, and serviced by bus #224, that runs only 5 times a day. Take the same route as to the Barlach Atelierhaus (see **Sights**, below); stay on the path until it hits Heidberg and bear left. (DM27, over 26 DM33. Breakfast included. Curfew 10pm.) Also consider using the room-finding service at the tourist office (tel. 84 00 44). **Café Küpper**, on Domstr., serves sweets, pizza (DM7) and sandwiches. (Open M-F 8am-7pm, Sa 11am-7pm, Su 1-7pm.)

◨ SIGHTS. The Barlach tour of Güstrow begins on the southwest side of town with the **Dom**, which houses Barlach's most famous work, *Der schwebende Engel* (The Hovering Angel). Created as a testament to the horrors of war, the angel was originally designed to hang above the pews of the Dom but is now tucked away in a corner. The statue was originally cast in 1926, but was then publicly melted down and made into bullets by the Nazis in 1941. After WWII, a plaster cast of the statue was found buried in West Germany, and, in 1952, the angel was restored and rededicated to the war's victims. (Open M-Sa 10am-5pm, Su 2-4pm.)

Walking back to Domstr., the recently renovated **Schloß** towers ahead. A grand example of Renaissance architecture, it is complete with a cute **Schloßgarten** surrounded by an ingenious shrub wall, gates and windows included. The **Schloßmuseum** (tel. 75 20) is proud of its works by Barlach. (Open April-Oct. Tu-Su 9am-5pm; Nov.-March Tu-Su 10am-5pm. DM5, students DM2.) On the west side of town, the **Gertrudenkapelle**, Gertrudenpl. 1 (tel. 68 30 01), houses a collection of Barlachs in an octagonal white chapel and peaceful garden. (Open March-Oct. Tu-Su 10am-5pm; Nov.-Feb. Tu-Su 11am-4pm. DM3, students DM2.) The only church in town neglecting Barlach is the **Pfarrkirche St. Marien**. Sitting in the shadow of the Dom, the church displays a recently restored altarpiece from 1522, and over 180 sculpted figures by Brussels artist Jan Borman. Organ music echoes in the church on Wednesdays at 12:15pm. (Open M 10am-noon and 2-4pm, Tu-F 10am-5pm, Sa 10am-4pm, Su 2-4pm.)

Barlach's **Atelierhaus** (studio), Heidberg 15 (tel. 822 99), hosts the largest collection of his works in the house in which they were created. Though its setting is beautiful, Barlach was never happy working there, and the studio was functional for only a few years. (Open Tu-Su 10am-5pm.) It's a one-hour walk from the Altstadt, and bus #4a comes here every three to four hours, so renting a bike is the best way to visit. Head down Greviner Str. from the Marktplatz and follow it as it turns into Plauer Str. until you see the "Barlachweg" signs. Follow this path around the lake past the grassy beach; continue 100m through the woods and the museum will be on the left.

WISMAR

Wismar is rapidly recovering from a vicious one-two combination of war damage and 50 years of neglect. Today, money from busloads of German tourists fuels restoration of the city and construction of the two cathedrals that were almost completely destroyed in a 1945 bombing. The Gothic **St. Georgenkirche**, a five-minute walk west of the Marktplatz, was once the place of worship for craftsmen; now it is their place of work — scaffolding and hard-hat requirements make the church inaccessible to tourists. Across the street, the lonely 80m tower of the **Marien-kirche,** along with before-and-after photos, shows the irrevocable destruction of the 14th-century basilica. The **Nikolaikirche,** nearer the port on Hinter der Chor, provides a hint of the lost majesty of Wismar's churches. Budget travelers can pay homage to St. Mauritius; an altar devoted to the patron saint of grocery stands to the left of the entrance. (Open M-Sa 10am-noon and 1-3pm, Su 1-3pm. DM1 donation requested.) Closer to the Marktplatz, the **Heiliger Geist Kirche** contains medieval art and an adorable not-quite-life-size nativity scene. (Open M-Sa 10am-4pm.)

The Marktplatz's dizzying juxtaposition of architectural styles is a record of Wismar's history of destruction and reconstruction. The medieval **Rathaus** was rebuilt in 19th-century Neoclassical style after its roof collapsed in 1807 and destroyed most of the original building. The **Wasserkunst,** an ornate metal mushroom built in Dutch Renaissance style, was the village spigot for 300 years. Running downhill from the Marktplatz on ABC-Str., the **Schabbelhausmuseum** features the works of local artists and an extensive medical history museum. (Open Tu-Su 10am-8pm. DM3, students DM2.) Its gory centerpiece is a display case full of the most deformed teeth pulled by a local dentist. *Let's Go* recommends brushing your fangs at least twice a day.

Frequent **trains** connect Wismar to Rostock (1½hr., 1 per hour, DM22.20) and Schwerin via Bad Kleinen (30min., 1 per hour, DM9.80). From the train station, follow Bahnhofstr. right, make a left on Am Poeler Tor, and cross the Schweinsbrücke (pig-bridge—check out their reveling statues) toward the Marktplatz. Wismar has no youth hostel, so finding a place to sleep requires a visit to the **tourist office,** Stadthaus am Markt 11 (tel. 25 18 15; fax 28 29 58). The staff, which speaks little English, will recommend rooms (DM30-50) and provide helpful brochures and maps. (Open daily 9am-6pm.) For a bite to eat, head to **Das Kittchen** (slang for "prison"), Vor dem Fürstenhof 3 (tel. 259 43 20), just behind the Marienkirche. It's decorated with cheerfully black humor in a jailhouse motif. (Open Tu-Sa from 5pm, Su from 10am. Meals DM7-14.) The **Spar supermarket,** Lübschestr. 21, on the road behind the Rathaus, sells groceries. (Open M-F 8am-6pm, Sa 8am-noon.) The **post office,** Mecklenburger Str. 18, 23966 Wismar, is behind the Wasserkunst corner of the Marktplatz. The **telephone code** is 03841.

Cheap (DM2), uncrowded beaches stretch around the nearby island of **Poel.** Bus #430 (direction: "Timmendorf Strand") goes from Dr.-Leber-Str. to the beaches of Schwarzenbusch and Timmendorf (45min., 1 per hour, DM5). The rolling fields and sparkling sea are a welcome break from sometimes over-touristed Wismar.

ROSTOCK

East German schoolchildren were always taught to think of Rostock, the largest and most active port in Eastern Germany, as the GDR's "gateway to the world." After reunification, Rostock's booming business declined as industrial ships began to shift their home harbors to Hamburg. Then, eight years ago, an event occurred that would change the way the world viewed the city. The tension caused by a flood of immigrants finally caused the dam to break. On August 24, 1992, a hostel for foreigners seeking political asylum in Germany was attacked and set ablaze by neo-Nazi youths. Today, most Rostock natives would like to place this event in the past; many walls spray-painted with swastikas also carry the response *Nazis raus!* ("Nazis out!") added by a later hand, evidence of the city's considerable left-leaning student population, who lend the area a lively nightlife and cosmopolitan feel. Both psychologically and physically, people here have made an effort to move on. Reconstruction and restoration work can be seen in most quarters of the Altstadt, and the number of tourists flocking to the beaches is once again high. What happened in 1992 should not discourage you from visiting Rostock, but rather leave you aware of continuing problems in the new Germany. You might come to see the old church towers, or pass through on your way to Scandinavia; whatever the case may be, recall Günter Grass's words: "Since Rostock, Germany has changed."

M.-VORPOMMERN

☞ GETTING THERE AND GETTING AROUND

Trains: Call 493 44 54 for information. Hourly connections to Schwerin (1hr., DM22.20), Stralsund (1½hr., DM19.40), and Wismar (1¼hr., DM22.20). Numerous daily connections to Berlin (2½hr., DM53), Hamburg (3hr., DM75), and Dresden (7hr., DM118).

Public Transportation: Streetcars #11 and 12 shuttle from the main station to the Altstadt. A single ticket is DM2, but the *Tageskarte*, a one-day ticket for streetcar, bus, and S-Bahn, is worth it at DM5.50. The S-Bahn leaves from the main station for Warnemünde and the newer suburbs every 15min. To get to the bus station for lines to smaller towns, leave the train station through the Südstadt exit. Bus service thins out at night, leaving only the *Fledermaus* (bat) buses connecting a few central stops. Late night buses have blue circles with pictures of bats on them.

Ferries: Boats for **Scandinavia** leave from the **Überseehafen** docks. **TT-Linie,** Hansakai (tel. 67 07 90; fax 670 79 80) runs to Trelleborg, Sweden (5hr., 6 per day; one-way DM50, students and children DM25). **Scandlines Europa GT Links** (tel. 670 06 67; fax 670 66 71) sails to Gedser, Denmark (2hr., 8 per day; one-way DM8 Th-Su, DM5 M-Th, children DM2.50). Ferries also leave from the **Warnemünde** docks; **DFO** (tel. 514 06; fax 514 09) sails to Gedser, Denmark, and offers special trips to other Scandinavian ports (2hr., 8 per day; one-way DM10-16, children DM5-8; round-trip DM20-32, children DM10-16).

Bike Rental: Radstation, on your right as you exit the train station (tel. 240 11 53). DM12 per day, DM8 per day for 5 or more days. ID required. Open M-F 10am-6pm, Sa 10am-1pm.

☷ ORIENTATION AND PRACTICAL INFORMATION

The majority of Rostock's sights lie in the downtown area, with the exception of **Warnemünde,** a peaceful fishing village and resort town to the northwest. The city's suburbs consist of huge brick-and-concrete apartment blocks linked by long, wide roads. These areas are not well lit, and local thugs have been known to be hostile toward foreigners. *Single travelers, particularly women, should avoid these areas at night.* Rostock is served by an extensive network of S-Bahn trains, buses, and trams; they run less frequently during the late hours and at night, so check schedules before you set out.

Tourist Office: Schnickmannstr. 13/14 (tel. 194 33; fax 497 99 23). From the train station, take streetcar #11 or 12 to "Lange Str.," then follow the sign to the right. *Zimmervermittlung* finds **rooms** (DM30-40) for a DM5 fee. Staff also leads 1½hr. **tours** in German through the town (May-June and Sept. W and F-Su at 2pm. DM7, children DM5). Open M-F 10am-6pm, Sa-Su 10am-2:30pm. Oct.-Apr. closed one hour earlier on weekdays.

Currency Exchange: Citibank, on Kröpeliner Str. near Universitätsplatz, charges DM5 for exchanging cash. 24hr. ATM. Open M and W 9am-1pm and 2-4:45pm, Tu and Th 9am-1pm and 2-6pm, F 9am-1pm. **Deutsche Bank,** Kröpeliner Str. 84, exchanges cash without a fee and travelers checks for a DM5 fee. Open M, T, Th 9am-6pm, W 9am-1pm, F 9am-3pm.

Emergency: Police, tel. 110. **Ambulance and Fire,** tel. 112.

Gay and Lesbian Resources: rat + tat, Leonhardstr. 20 (tel. 45 31 56). Open M 10am-1pm and 3-5pm, Tu and Th 2-6pm.

Pharmacy: Rats-Apotheke, Neuer Markt 13 (tel. 493 47 47). Open M-F 8am-6pm, Sa 8am-1pm.

Post Office: Hauptpostamt, Neuer Markt, 18055 Rostock. Open M-F 8am-6pm, Sa 8am-1pm.

Internet Access: See **Riz Café,** p. 556.

PHONE CODE	0381

ACCOMMODATIONS

Because both of Rostock's hostels are quite far from town and in somewhat dangerous neighborhoods, your best bet is the tourist office.

Jugendgästeschiff Rostock-Schmarl (tel. 71 62 24; fax 71 40 14). Past travelers have complained of harassment by aggressive hooligans while walking to the hostel, but once inside, the kind staff will guide you around their hostel-boat-museum-bar. Take the S-Bahn (direction: "Warnemünde") to "Lütten Klein," then bus #35 (direction: "Schmarl Fähre") to the end. Follow the buoy-lined street to the *Traditionsschiff*; reception is on the 2nd fl. Unfortunately, the last #35 bus through the dangerous harbor area imposes an effective 8pm curfew.

Jugendherberge Rostock-Warnemünde (HI), Parkstr. 46 (tel. 54 81 70; email JH.Warne@t-online.de). Provides spacious, clean rooms and ping pong. Take the S-Bahn (direction: "Warnemünde") to the end, cross the bridge, and head straight on Kirchenstr. as it becomes Mühlenstr. and then Parkstr. (20-25min.). Or ride the S-Bahn to "Warnemünde Werft" and then bus #36 (direction: "Warnemünde-Strand") to Parkstr. Doubles DM23.50. Breakfast included. Sheets DM5, dinner DM8. 24hr. reception.

FOOD

While no one will ever accuse Rostock of being a gastronome's heaven, eating here doesn't necessarily mean choking on *ein Whopper* and *Pommes Frites*. **Neue Markt,** on Seinstr. across from the Rathaus, sprouts into a small market of

M.-VORPOMMERN

fruits and vegetables and various roasted meats (open M-F 8am-5pm, Sa 8am-1pm), while the bakeries on Kröpeliner Str. offer an array of cheap sandwiches and pastries. In Warnemünde, several restaurants along the beach fish up the bounties of the sea.

Mensa, on the corner of Südring and Albert-Einstein-Str. From the train station or the Altstadt, streetcar #11 (direction: "Neuer Friedhof") to the end and bus #27 (direction: "Biestow") or 39 (direction: "Stadthalle/ZOB") to "Mensa" (one stop). Or take bus #25 from the train station (direction: "Mensa") to the end. Upstairs, students load their trays; a full meal will run about DM8. (Open M-F 11:15am-2pm, Sa 12:30-4pm.) Downstairs, a bulletin board advertises all major parties and club shows, while on weekends the *Mensa* holds what students claim is the best **disco** in Rostock. Open Th-Su after 10pm. Call 459 12 48 for the program. Cover DM5 and up.

Mo Mo, Barnstorfer Weg 34. Streetcar #11 (direction: "Neuer Friedhof") to "Doberaner Platz." Serves Middle Eastern noodle dishes (DM8-14) along with tasty hip-hop. Word. Open daily 9am-2am.

Wespennest, Karlstr. 19 (tel. 492 21 93). A women-only café and women's center. Open Tu-Sa 7pm-midnight.

Riz Café, Wismarische Str. 44 (tel. 496 11 61), sports funky email kiosks with screens tilted below clear plastic tables. Mingle with the techno-savvy staff while sipping an espresso. Internet connection DM3 per hour. Open M-Sa 9am-10pm.

Café 28, Mühlenstr. 28 (tel. 524 67), in Warnemünde on the way to the hostel, is a shiny, happy hangout. Soups, salads, and small but tasty dishes run DM6-16. Open May-Oct. M-F noon-late, Sa-Su 10am-late.

👁 SIGHTS

MARIENKIRCHE. This 13th-century beast of a brick basilica is near the main square at the Steintor end of Kröpeliner Str. In the final days of the 1989 turmoil, the services here overflowed with political protesters who came to hear the inspiring sermons of Pastor Joachim Gauck. In one of his more heroic gestures, Pastor Gauck began to publicly chastise the secret police by calling out the names of those *Stasi* members whom he could identify from the pulpit. After reunification, Gauck was entrusted with the difficult job of overseeing the fate of the *Stasi* archives. The confusing 12m **astronomical clock** behind the faux-marble altar dates from 1472. At noon and midnight, mechanical apostles strut in a circular procession, but only 11 make it inside before the door closes. *(Open M-Sa 10am-5pm, Su 11am-noon. DM2 donation requested.)*

KRÖPELINER STRAßE. Relics of Rostock's past as a center of Hanseatic trade still stand. Although half of the city was destroyed in WWII, many of the half-timbered and glazed-brick houses have been restored. Kröpeliner Str. (or simply "Kröpe"), the main pedestrian mall, runs east to the **Kröpeliner Tor,** the former town gate. The main buildings of the **Universität Rostock,** one of the oldest universities in North Central Europe, are near the middle of Kröpeliner Str. Next to the university, along the remains of the city wall, sits the **Kloster zum heiligen Kreuz,** a restored cloister which was originally built by the Danish Queen Margaret in 1270. The museum contains medieval art, sculptures by the omnipresent Ernst Barlach, and special exhibits. *(Open Tu-Sa 10am-5pm. DM4, students DM2.)*

RATHAUS. A strawberry-pink wedding cake of a building, the town hall on the **Neuer Markt** was originally composed of three separate *Bürger* houses united by a Gothic wall with seven towers; elaborate detailing can still be seen above some of the portals. The **Steintor, Kuhtor,** and **Lagesbuschturm** sit in close proximity to Steinstr., connected by remnants of the recently renovated town wall.

ALTER MARKT. Rostock's commercial center before the war now buzzes with the hammering sounds of extensive restoration. Strike a Quasimodo pose as you ascend the reconstructed tower of the **Petrikirche,** from which you can see all of Rostock, including the ominous cooling towers of its nuclear power plant. *(Open M-F 9am-noon and 2-5pm, Sa-Su 11am-5pm. Tower DM2.)*

ZOO. Rostock's stunning zoo housed some of its animals in public offices during the war; the apes were guests of the police station. Now the extensive collection of animals lives on its own land. *(Take streetcar #11 (direction: "Neuer Friedhof") to "Zoo." Open April-Oct. daily 9am-7pm, Nov.-March 9am-5pm. DM9, students DM7, children DM5.)*

SCHIFFAHRTMUSEUM DER HANSESTADT. Displays tell tales of wild seafaring along the rocky Baltic coast. Amused guards look on as visitors try to copy ship knots at a hands-on exhibit. *(August-Bebel-Str. 1. Take streetcar #11 to "Steintor." Tel. 492 26 97. Open Tu-Su 10am-6pm. DM4, students DM2.)*

JEWISH ROSTOCK. Rostock was once home to a substantial Jewish population; little remains, however, of Rostock's Jewish community. The SA razed the synagogue on Augustenstr., and the SS began the deportations soon after. Only partially destroyed in the war, the **Jewish cemetery** still stands. In the 1970s, the government decided to embed the gravestones face-down into the earth in order to create the city's **Lindenpark.** Pressure from the international Jewish community forced the city to right most of the stones and add a memorial in 1988. *(Take streetcar #1, 3, or 11 to "Saarplatz," then go south through the park.)*

WARNEMÜNDE. To the north of Rostock and accessible by S-Bahn lies the beach town **Warnemünde.** The **Alter Strom** (old harbor), across the bridge from the train station, rings with the sounds of fishing boats, fish hawkers, and the shattering of teeth on rock candy. Warnemünde's sunny beach stretches far into the distance; walk long enough, and you can bare all (look for *FKK* signs at beach entrances). Near the Alter Strom toward the sea stands a **lighthouse** whose 30m tower can be scaled (DM1). For a comprehensive survey of those tiny, colorful *Pfister* houses, visit Warnemünde's **Heimatmuseum,** Alexandrinerstr. 31, just off the Kirchenplatz. *(Open W-Su 10am-6pm. DM4, students DM2.)*

■ NIGHTLIFE

At night, Rostock's student population of about 10,000 comes out to play, congregating along Kröpeliner Str. and around Wismarische Str. and Barnstorfer Weg. Check out *Rostock Szene,* which lists local clubs and performances, and *Nordost Eventguide,* a chic little booklet that covers clubs in all of Mecklenburg-Vorpommern. Both are available at the tourist office for free.

Studentenkeller (tel. 45 59 28), through the big yellow building on Universitätsplatz. *The* nighttime destination for scores of Rostock's students. Four rooms and an outdoor patio are packed with Euro fashion, cell phones, and fluorescent hair. Open M-Sa 10pm-late.

La Lupina, Leonhardstr. 20 (tel. 459 14 07), is a sleek café/bar with an alternative clientele and drink menu. Wear black. Open M-Sa 6pm-late.

Central, Leonhardstr. 22 (tel. 490 46 48), next door, hops with a twentysomething crowd that spills out into the street. Open M-Sa 2:30pm-2am, Su 10am-2am.

Mephisto, Seestr. 16 in Warnemünde, is where vacationing students satisfy their need for drink and music; stick around long enough and you might get breakfast (DM6). Open W-Su 7pm-late.

FISCHLAND, DARSS, AND ZINGST

The peninsula between Rostock and Stralsund draws thousands of tourists to bathe in its waters each year. Unlike many of northeast Germany's other seaside resorts, however, these beaches have humble roots as fishing villages that escaped the attention of the 19th-century glitterati who preferred to build their pompous villas on Rügen and Usedom. Towns nestle quietly in the forests near the sea, inviting nature lovers to hike or bike through the woods and families to stretch across the beaches. Though the three towns are populated more by tourists than residents, for the most part they have done well in their attempts to develop individual characters and avoid commercialization.

While there is no train service to the area, **VGN bus #210** shuttles hourly between **Ribnitz-Damgarten** in the west and **Barth** in the east. Bus service is slow and expensive (DM11.80 from Ribnitz-Damgarten to Zingst); most tourists come by car. The area is connected by **ferry** to Hiddensee (see p. 566).

FISCHLAND

Though Fischland's beaches are not as paradisiacal as those in Darß or Zingst, the area is more interesting culturally than its northern neighbors. **Ahrenshoop** is Fischland's highlight. In the early 20th century, it became a hangout for artists and intellectuals; when they figured out that everybody was painting the same thing over and over again, the colony scattered. Ahrenshoop held onto its legacy, however, and today it is an oasis of galleries in a land of beachside resorts. **Dünenhaus,** Am Schiffenberg, has a slew of early 1900s landscapes of the area that show just how repetitive painting the beach could be. (DM4, students DM2. Open M-F 2-6pm, Sa-Su 10am-6pm.) The more modern and interesting **studio,** Schiffenberg 70 (tel. 806 18), next door has a sprawling sculpture in the front yard, and contains art and art-in-progress. The area's best gallery, **Neues Kunsthaus Ahrenshoop,** Bernhard-Seitz-Weg 3a (tel. 807 26), has contemporary art from around the Baltic in four bright rooms as well as a sculpture garden. For a culinary experience, stop by the existentially (un)named **Café Namenlos** (no-name café), Am Schiffenberg, which serves mildly pretentious food at less pretentious prices. (Open daily from 11am.)

Ahrenshoop's **tourist office,** Kirchnersgang 2 (tel. 234; fax 300), books **rooms** and provides information on gallery showings. (Open M-F 9am-6pm, Sa 10am-4pm, Su 1-4pm.) Rent **bikes** at **Fahrradverleih-Gielow,** Dorfstr. 21. (Tel. 801 34. Open daily 10am-8pm. DM8 per day.) Ahrenshoop's **post office,** 18347 Ostseebad Ahrenshoop, is at Grenzenweg 17 in the **Spar supermarket,** so you can pick up a picnic lunch and mail home a postcard at the same time. (Tel. 389. Open M-F 8am-6pm, Sa-Su 8am-noon.) The **telephone code** is 038220.

DARSS

The northwest corner of the peninsula is barely touched by civilization and, therefore, a mecca for people trying to get away from it. The central attraction of the **Prerow,** the main settlement in the Darß, is the beach, which stretches 7km toward Zingst. Well-maintained bike paths crisscross the area; the **Kompass Wander- und Radtourenkarte** (DM12.80) is a detailed map of the area and its paths. The **Darß museum,** Waldstr. 48 (tel. 697 50), showcases the area's flora and fauna, but, more interestingly, many of the handcarved doors are from the day when Prerow made money from fish instead of tourists. Many of the historic doors are still on their hinges and in use—wander through the town to see the brightly colored doors that the museum hasn't appropriated yet. Prerow's other reminder of its history is the **Seemanskirche,** Kirchenort 2, which fishermen built in 1728 to celebrate the Big Fisher. The simple exterior of the church hides a wild Baroque altar. (Open M-Sa 10am-5pm.)

Prerow's **tourist office,** Gemeindeplatz 1 (tel. 61 00; fax 610 26), finds **rooms** for free. To get around, rent **bikes** at **Fahrradverleih Wittenburg,** Bebelstr. 18. (Tel 697 60. DM10 per day.) Prerow's **post office,** 18375 Ostseebad Prerow, is at Hafenstr. 8. (Tel. 220. Open M-F 9am-noon and 2-5pm, Sa 9am-noon.) Adventurous souls will opt for **Campingplatz Robinson,** Hagens Düne (tel. 601 98), whose shiny monkey bars and savings will attract campers of all ages. (DM6 per person; DM11 per tent.) Pick up **groceries** at **Edeka Markt,** Bersstr. 4. (Open M-F 8am-6pm, Sa-Su 8am-noon.) Prerow's **telephone code** is 038233.

ZINGST

Of the area's resort towns, Zingst is the best groomed and glossiest, but lacks much of the character of its neighbors. Still, the amazing beaches go far to make up for a touristy, glass-and-stucco atmosphere. Since it is the most popular resort town in the region, booking several months in advance is necessary for the summer months. Zingst's **tourist office,** Klosterstr. 21 (tel. 815 21; fax 815 25), gives out maps and lists of **rooms.** (Open M-Sa 9am-6pm, Su 9am-noon and 2-6pm.) Rent **bikes** at **Fahrradverleih Neumann,** Postplatz 8. (Tel. 189 37. Open daily 9am-6pm. DM10 per day.) The **Jugendherberge (HI),** Glebbe 14 (tel. 154 65), fills up months in advance, so call ahead. Rooms are basic, and it's a 10min. walk to the beach. (DM28 per night, over 26 DM34.50. Sheets DM6. Reception 9am-noon and 4-10pm.) Stock up for a day on the beach at **Jen's Markt** on Postplatz. (Open M-F 7:30am-6:30pm, Sa 7:30am-1pm.) Zingst's **telephone code** is 038232.

STRALSUND

Albrecht von Wallenstein, commander of the Catholic army during the Thirty Years War, lusted after Stralsund. "Even if it were chained to heaven, I'd want to have it," he panted, but Stralsund resisted his advances. After years of neglect, the city is gradually regaining its former beauty. The GDR years spent little money on Stralsund, causing priceless 13th-century buildings to fall into decay, but also preserving its skyline almost exactly as it appeared in 1293, when it helped to found the Hanseatic League and asserted itself as a trading and shipbuilding center. Today the key to Stralsund's charm is its unique geography; the hill of the Altstadt is bordered to the south and west by two natural ponds and slopes gently north toward the Strelasund, the strait that separates Rügen from the mainland.

⁊ ORIENTATION AND PRACTICAL INFORMATION

Stralsund's major sights and attractions are concentrated in the **Altstadt,** where the distinctive spires of the city's three churches make excellent navigational beacons. **Ossenreyerstraße,** which runs north-south, is the main pedestrian zone. Two of the city's former gates, the **Kutertor** and the **Kniepertor,** sit to the west and north, respectively. The train station squats across the bridge and down the street from the Kutertor.

Trains: Stralsund is connected to Rostock (1hr., 1 per hour, DM19.40), and to Binz (1hr., DM15) and Saßnitz on Rügen; several trains also leave daily for Berlin (3½hr., DM68) and Hamburg (4hr., DM73).

Buses: Intercity buses depart from Frankenwall, south of the train station.

Public Transportation: Bus lines #1, 2, 3, 4, 5, and 6 circle the Altstadt, serving the outskirts of town. Single ride DM2.50; day pass DM5.

Ferries: Reederei Hiddensee (tel. (0180) 321 21 50) runs 3 times per day to the ports of Kloster, Vitte, and Neuendorf on Hiddensee (round-trip DM24-26, children DM13-15, bikes DM10) and to Schaprode on Rügen's west coast (DM7, children DM3.50).

Bike Rental: Tel. 28 01 55. At the service desk in the train station. DM10 per day. Open M-F 6am-9pm, Sa 7am-2:30pm, Su 9am-4:30pm.

Tourist Office: Stralsund Information, Alter Markt 9 (tel. 246 90; fax 24 69 49; e-mail INFO-HST@t-online.de). From the station, head straight on Jungfernstieg, turn right onto the path at the intersection about 300m from the train station to transverse Knieper Teich; continue straight through the Kütertor, and turn left on Ossenreyerstr. Or take bus #4 or 5 to "Kütertor." The office distributes free maps, finds **private rooms** (DM25-100) for a DM5 fee, and sells tickets for **tours** through the Altstadt (DM7). They also offer a **tourist coupon** (DM1) that reduces admission prices for most of the city's sights and museums. Open June-Sept. M-F 9am-7pm, Sa 9am-2pm, Su 10am-2pm; Oct.-May M-F 10am-6pm, Sa 10am-2pm. The **branch office** in the train station (tel. 29 43 06) books **rooms** for a DM5 fee. Open M-F 9am-6pm, Sa 9am-1pm, but you can call until 8:30pm.

Women's Resources: Frauen in Not (tel. 29 51 12). 24hr. hotline.

Pharmacy: Bahnhofsapotheke, Tribseer Damm 6 (tel. 29 23 28), by the train station.

Emergency: Police, tel. 110. **Fire** and **Ambulance,** tel. 112.

Post Office: Neuer Markt, 18439 Stralsund, in the red-brick building opposite the Marienkirche. **Exchanges currency.** Open M-F 8:30am-6pm, Sa 8:30am-1pm.

PHONE CODE	03831

■ ACCOMMODATIONS

Jugendherberge Stralsund (HI), Am Kütertor 1 (tel. 29 21 60; fax 29 76 76). The hostel is a gorgeous 15min. walk from the train station. Follow the directions to the tourist office, but stop at Kütertor; the hostel shares a wall with the *Tor.* Located in a 17th-century town hall with a courtyard, the hostel is convenient, but watch those low ceilings. Many school groups in summer. DM23, over 26 DM26. Breakfast buffet included. Sheets DM6.50. Reception 7-9am and 3-10pm. Lockout 9am-3pm. Curfew 10pm, but you can ring the bell until 1am.

Jugendherberge Stralsund-Devin (HI), Strandstr. 21 (tel. 49 82 89 or 27 03 58). From the station, take bus #3 to "Devin" (25min., DM2.50), then walk straight into the woods. Take the trail on the left side of the dreary-looking *Kurhaus-Devin,* and turn left when you hit Strandstr. (5min.). Located in the nearby village of Devin, this hostel is bigger than the one in Stralsund, but much harder to reach. The 20 buildings are close to the beach, and spaces are sometimes generous even when full. DM19, over 26 DM25. Breakfast included. Sheets DM7. Bike rentals to guests DM10 per day. Reception 7:30-10am and 4-7pm. Curfew 10pm. Open March-Oct.

■ FOOD

Large portions and decent prices rarely keep company in Stralsund these days; even supermarket bills are pretty steep. Stock up on **groceries** at **Lebensmittel-Feinkost,** Ossenreyerstr. 49, in the Ost-West Passage. (Open M-F 8am-7pm, Sa 8am-1pm.) Or indulge in cake and coffee at **Stadtbäckerei und Café,** Ossenreyerstr. 43. (Tel. 29 40 82. Open M-F 7am-6pm, Sa 8am-5pm, Su 1-5pm.)

Al Porto, Seestr. 14 (tel. 28 06 20). Stralsund's beautiful people get their noodle fix at this mildly pretentious harbor restaurant and café. While much of the food is on the more expensive side, the pizza is decently priced (DM10-15). Open daily 11am-11pm.

Galerie Café, Badenstr. 44 (tel. 29 07 65), serves artistic food as well as a new vegetarian dish every day. The selection of international magazines is even greater than the selection of coffees. Open M-F 10am-7pm, Sa 2-7pm.

Hansekeller, Mönchstr. 48 (tel. 70 38 40) occupies an authentic Renaissance basement where customers down *Wurst* and guzzle *Bier.* Come hungry. Open 11am-midnight.

Essbar, Kleinschmeidstr. 22 (tel. 29 81 76), has a small but succulent Italian-French menu, and is a hangout for artists after the theater. Entrees around DM16.

Speicher-Café, Katherinenburg 34 (tel. 29 70 93), is the local teen hangout by day/club by night. Open 11am-late.

■ SIGHTS

ALTER MARKT. Stralsund's compact Altstadt island is free of GDR-era architecture. The Alter Markt, to the north, is surrounded by several of the town's oldest buildings. The remarkably well-preserved 14th-century red-brick facade of the Gothic **Rathaus** displays the coats-of-arms of the other major players in the Hanseatic League, as well as Stralsund's trademark green and gold 12-point stars.

St. Nikolaikirche, behind the Rathaus, is the oldest church in town, built in the same style as Lübeck's Marienkirche. *(Open Tu-F 10am-5pm, Sa 10am-4pm, Su 2-4pm.)*

NEUER MARKT. After the wealthier half of Stralsund built their church, merchants from the other side of the tracks responded by erecting the Gothic **Marienkirche** on Neuer Markt. The church houses a rare mid-17th-century Stellwagen organ as well as a rather phallic Soviet memorial in the front yard. Climb the church tower for the best view of Stralsund. Getting to the top is an adventure; after climbing the narrow, winding staircase, you have to ascend the last 150 feet on a ladder. *(Open daily 10am-5pm.)*

ST. JAKOBI. The third of Stralsund's monumental churches, on Böttcherstr., was heavily damaged in 1944 and further harmed during GDR days. Its organ's pipes were removed and used as rain gutters; the church is currently being restored.

DEUTSCHES MUSEUM FÜR MEERESKUNDE UND FISCHEREI. Between the Alter and Neuer Markt, Stralsund's two major museums have replaced the monks in the adjoining buildings of the **St. Katharinen** monastery. A good way to use the tourist coupon is to visit the most popular museum in northern Germany, which contains many tanks of tropical fish, a shark tank, and the mandatory collection of Baltic Sea fish. Bring a camera, as the gift shop doesn't sell any postcards of the five-foot-long whale penis on display. *(Katharinenberg 14. Tel. 265 00. Open May-June daily 10am-5pm; July-Aug. daily 9am-6pm; Nov.-April Tu-Su 10am-5pm. DM7, students DM3.50.)*

JOHANNISKLOSTER. An alternate route from the Alter Markt follows Külpstr. to Schillstr., ending at the Johanniskloster, a Franciscan monastery built in 1254—45 years after St. Francis of Assisi founded the order. The monastery is down by the harbor and is a glory of Gothic hallways, 14th-century mosaics, murals (rescued from 30 layers of peeling paint), roses, and red-brick walls. Next to the monastery is the former **Johanniskirche;** ruined in 1944, it now hosts occasional open-air concerts and theater. *(Church open Tu-Su 10am-6pm. DM4, students DM3, including a tour; free last Wednesday of every month.)* The quiet courtyard contains a dramatic Ernst Barlach *pietà*, as well as a **memorial** to Stralsund's lost Jewish community. The sculpture used to sit on the Apollonienmarkt, near the former site of the synagogue, but was placed in the cloister after it was vandalized by neo-Nazis in 1992; graffiti marks still remain.

OTHER SIGHTS. A stroll along the **Sundpromenade** at sunset reveals the rolling green hills of Rügen across the bay. Another beautiful walk runs along **Knieperwall,** the **Knieperteich** (pond), and the remains of the **town wall.** The **Knieper Tor** and **Küter Tor** date back to the 13th century.

RÜGEN

Bathing in the Baltic Sea northeast of Stralsund, Germany's largest island offers a varied landscape of white beaches, rugged chalk cliffs, farmland, beech forests, heaths, and swamps. Stone Age ruins and megalithic graves (easily identified piles of stones) are scattered about like enormous paperweights. Teutonic tribes were pushed out by Slavs during migrations in the 5th century; 500 years later, the rule of the pagan inhabitants was broken by invading Danes, who in turn bestowed the joys of Christianity upon the not-so-eager Slavs. In the 19th century, it was the nobility who invaded the island, transforming Rügen into a resort stacked with ritzy Neoclassical villas that are slowly being renovated after decades of neglect.

The most striking architectural achievement of the island is understandably understated in the official tourist literature. An important part of Hitler's racial purification plan was the **Kraft durch Freude** (*KdF;* strength through joy) initiative, intended to cultivate happy Aryans for the new Germany. As part of this plan, Nazi authorities designed a 5km complex of interconnected five-story buildings at **Prora** that was intended to provide seaside lodging for 20,000 German workers at the negligible cost of three *Reichsmarks* a day. After the war, the nearly finished complex fell into the hands of the Soviets, who intended to dynamite the place.

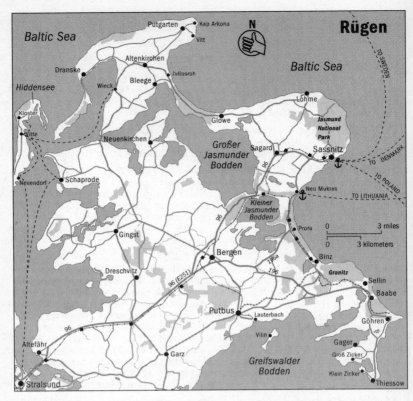

But after two unsuccessful attempts at demolition, the durability of the armored-concrete walls proved stronger than the will of East German authorities to purge the past. The buildings lodged the military until 1989. Except for a hotel, a youth hostel (see p. 13), a *Kindergarten*, and a sprawling museum that nervously recalls Prora's past, the long hallways are now empty.

Today, the tourist industry in Rügen is treading water. Once the prime vacation spot for East Germans, tourism has decreased somewhat as East Germans explore Western Germany's vacation spots. Still, summer months are busy. *Let's Go* strongly recommends booking a room in advance by phone or by writing ahead. For groups of three or more, a *Ferienwohnung* (vacation apartment) can be a surprisingly affordable option at DM20-30 per person. There are only two hostels, one in **Prora** and the other in **Binz,** and the latter is almost constantly booked.

Rügen is so close to Stralsund's coast that you could almost swim there; however, since **trains** leave hourly for Binz and Saßnitz, you can probably leave your water wings at home. It's only an hour from Stralsund to Saßnitz, which makes daytrips an option, especially if the hostels on Rügen are booked. **Buses** connect Stralsund with Rügen's largest towns, and a **ferry** runs to Schaprode, near Hiddensee, on Rügen's west coast.

Once on the island, public transportation is reliable but expensive and infrequent—most visitors come with cars. Trains connect Stralsund with Binz, Prora, and Saßnitz via **Bergen,** an unattractive town in the center of the island. To get to Kap Arkona in the north or Göhren in the south, however, you'll have to take an **RPNV** bus (which run every 1-2hr.); check schedules carefully, and make sure you know when the last bus leaves, lest you get stuck. The **Rasender Roland,** a narrow-gauge rail line, runs every two hours from Putbus to Göhren (DM 15) with stops in many spa towns; unfortunately, the railway is more of a tourist attraction than a means of practical transportation. Although the island is large, the major points of interest lie no more than 20km from one another. The best way to get around is by combining the train and buses with walking, hiking, and biking. Well-marked **trails** cover the entire island.

BINZ

"They paved paradise and put up a parking lot." Joni Mitchell's words ring painfully true in Binz, the main beach town on Rügen. The beat on the street here is the sound of jackhammers working furiously to resurrect Binz as Germany's "other Sylt." Recently restored seaside mansions, many of which are rapidly reopening as spiffed-up luxury hotels, hark back to Binz's former incarnation as a fashionable, aristocratic resort. While there isn't much to see in Binz, there is plenty to do, with miles of sandy beach perfect for swimming, sunbathing, windsurfing, or playing badminton with accountants from Düsseldorf. There are also two **nude beaches** tastefully situated at the far ends of the town beach, suitable for just hanging out. The **Historisches Museum,** Zeppelinstr. 8, displays everything from doorknobs to chamber pots from the area's old houses. (Open daily 10am-6pm. DM4, students DM2.) Down the street, take in the family entertainment at the outdoor stage, where crooners and oompah bands produce tunes that may leave you in tears. Luckily, Binz leaves a better taste in the mouth than in the ears, as it teems with restaurants, bars, and ice cream stands. The **Strandcafé Binz/Pizza Ristorante da Barbara,** Strandpromenade 29, serves pasta and herring specialties. Try the *gnocchi alla gorgonzola* (DM 12.50), or one of a dozen pizzas. (DM7-15. Open daily 11am-late.) More restaurants and a **crazy billiards** game (miniature golf with pool cues, DM2.90 for 18 holes) are in the **Vitarium,** a greenhouse-type building at the north end of the beach, for occupation on rainy days.

Accommodations in Binz fill up quickly and are DM10-15 more expensive than on other parts of the island. The **Zimmervermittlung,** Jasmunder Str. 2 (tel. 27 82), books **rooms** for free. (Open M-F 9am-5pm, Sa 9am-noon.) Equally plentiful in Binz are **tourist offices;** the most convenient is in the train station (tel. 22 15), which offers free maps and advice. (Open M-F 9am-5pm, Sa-Su 9am-1pm.) The **post office** is at Zeppeliastr. 3, 18609 Binz. (Open M-F 9am-noon and 2-6pm, Sa 9am-noon.) The **telephone code** is 038393.

The scarcity of rooms carries over to the better of Rügen's two youth hostels, **Jugendherberge Binz (HI),** Strandpromenade 35 (tel. 325 97; fax 325 96; e-mail Jugendherberge_Binz@t-online.de), which underwent a DM7.8 million renovation in 1997. (DM34; over 26 DM41.50. Breakfast included. Sheets DM7. Reception 8:15-9am and 6-9:30pm. Curfew 10:30pm, but you can get an access code.) More dependable but exponentially less attractive accommodations await in the **Jugendherberge Prora (HI)** (tel. 328 44; fax 328 45), a massive 400-bed hostel popular with school groups. To get there, take either the Bergen-Binz train or the Binz-Saßnitz bus to "Prora-Ost" (not "Prora"), cross the tracks and follow the signs. (DM25, over 26 DM30. Reception 7-9am and 4-10pm. Curfew 11pm. Call ahead or show up by 4pm.) The **Edeka supermarket,** at the corner of Schillerstr. and Zeppeliastr., boasts long hours and long lines. (Open M-W 8am-6:30pm, Th-F 8am-7pm, Sa 8am-1pm.)

SASSNITZ

Saßnitz has fallen hard since Prussian author Theodor Fontane penned in *Effi Briest:* "To travel to Rügen means to travel to Saßnitz." Today, the town consists of crumbling masses of apartment blocks interspersed with recently refurbished seaside villas. While Saßnitz is little more than an unpleasant enclave of GDR nostalgia, its proximity to the stark chalk cliffs and bucolic forests of **Jasmund national park** (see below) make it an attractive base for hikers and other nature-lovers.

Saßnitz also serves as Rügen's ferry station. **Ferries** leave for Sweden, Denmark, Russia, and Lithuania from the *Fährhafen* in **Mukran.** Take bus #414b from the train station to "Saßnitz Fährhafen" (15min.). Other companies send boats on

water tours around the national park and to Kap Arkona from the *Stadthafen* below the town. (Daily 9am-5pm, DM10-15.) Shorter hauls to the Danish island of Bornholm and to Świnoujście, Poland also depart from the *Stadthafen*. Rent a **bike** at Birkenweg 12 (tel. 350 75), about 500m right of the train station. (DM10-15 per day. Open M-F 9:30am-1pm and 2-5:30pm, Sa 10am-noon.) Saßnitz's **tourist office**, Seestr. 1 (tel. 51 60; fax 516 16), is in the 11-story Rügen Hotel. From the train station, walk down Bahnhofstr. and take a left on Hauptstr. The staff books rooms (DM30-40) for a DM8 fee. (Open April-Oct. M-F 9am-7pm, Sa 10am-7pm, Su 2-7pm; Nov.-March M-F 9am-5pm.) The **post office**, 18546 Saßnitz, is at Hauptstr. 34. (Open M-F 9am-1pm and 2-5pm, Sa 9am-noon.) The **telephone code** is 038392.

The closest campground is **Campground Nipmerow** (tel. (038302) 92 44), under ancient beech trees next to the national park, near the *Königstuhl*. Catch bus #408 (direction: "Stubbenkammer") from the train station and ask the driver to let you out at the camp. (DM8 per person. DM4-6 per tent. Wash DM5; no dryers. Reception 8am-10pm.) Pick up groceries for your hike at **Plus**, Bahnhofstr. 1. (Open M-W 8am-6:30pm, Th-F 8am-7pm, Sa 8am-1pm).

JASMUND NATIONAL PARK

The spectacular chalk cliffs rising just north of Saßnitz and culminating in the famous **Großer Stubbenkammer** were forged by massive glaciers 12,000 years ago; despite some erosion, they'll still give you the chills. There are a couple of options for approaching the cliffs. The most direct (but also the least fun) is to take bus #408 to "Stubbenkammer" from the stop outside the Saßnitz train station (DM2.50); it runs every half hour during the summer and lets you off about 10m away from the **Königstuhl** (king's chair), the most famous of the cliffs. To avoid the air-conditioned bus route, pick up the bike trail next to the church at the end of Hauptstr. in Saßnitz; a good vantage point can be found by following signs to "Waldhalle," then hiking about a kilometer south down the end of the bike trail steps will take you to a chalky beach. The path to the *Königstuhl* is also clearly marked. For the best views, take the **Hochuferweg** (high coastal trail) all the way from Saßnitz to the *Stubbenkammer*. Despite the intimidating name, the 8.5km trail (a 3hr. hike) is fairly easy and runs from one incredible scenic lookout to the next. To pick up the trail, follow the "Stubbenkammer" signs through Saßnitz up the hill until you reach the parking lot, where there's a detailed map of the park showing all the trails and their corresponding blazes—follow the ones for "Hochuferweg."

The trail leads first to the **Wissower Klinken** (3km), which you might recognize from Caspar David Friedrich's paintings—these were his favorite chalk cliffs. Even though they've lost about 3m to erosion since he painted them, their beauty still seems almost supernatural. Continuing for another 5km, you'll reach the **Victoriasicht** lookout, and then the famous *Königstuhl*, which is anticlimactic after all the beautiful views. If you follow the mob to the lookout area, you'll have to pay for the view, which isn't much better than what you've already seen for free. (DM2, students DM1.)

Look up to the left, and you'll see a small guard post once used by GDR authorities to make sure no one escaped by boat to Sweden. For a bit of solitude, walk down the steep and windy paths to the flint-covered beach. Another trail leads from the *Königstuhl* to the lovely **Herthasee**, a lake named after the German harvest goddess Hertha. According to myth, Hertha drowned her mortal servants in this lake, and their spirits supposedly still gather on the banks each night, although we didn't stick around to find out. Nearby, the **Herthaburg**, a U-shaped earth wall built by the Slavs in the 7th century, recalls the less peaceful periods of this violently beautiful landscape.

GRANITZ AND GÖHREN

The **Jagdschloß Granitz** is a silly, castle-like hunting lodge designed and built in 1836 by Prussian architect Friedrich Schinkel, whose unmistakable creations can be seen all over the island. Built atop the Tempelberg hill, its 38m tower offers a breathtaking panorama of the island. Faint of heart, beware: Bambi's family tree is mounted on the walls of the **Jagdmuseum** (hunting museum) inside the "castle." (Open Tu-Su 9am-6pm. DM5, students DM4.) The *Roland* stops at the Jagdschloß, as does the **Jagdschloßexpress,** which makes round-trips from the *Kurhaus* in Binz. (DM10, children DM6.) From the "Jagdschloß" *Roland* stop, head uphill on the trail off to the right to reach the castle. To walk or bike the 5km from Binz, pick up the trail near the "Binz Roland" station. Heading south from the *Roland* "Jagdschloß" stop to the village of Lancken-Granitz, you'll pass a bunch of huge prehistoric graves; one dates back to 2300 BC.

The *Roland's* final stop is **Göhren,** on the easternmost tip of the forested **Mönchgut peninsula,** which was settled in the 13th century by monks who believed in total self-sufficiency. Things move at a noticeably slower pace than on the rest of Rügen. The city sits on a hill, and from the church off Strandstr. one can look across the sea at Greifswald. Göhren, like every other town worth its salt on Rügen, has a nice beach; it's also the base of numerous **hiking and biking trails** leading through peaceful beaches, forests, and the rolling hills of the **Zickersche Alpen.** Göhren's main attraction is the **Mönchguter Museum,** composed of four tiny museums scattered about the town which display local history through exhibits housed in an old schoolhouse, a 17th-century cottage, a thatched-roof barn, and a ship. (All museums open May-June and Sept.-Oct. Tu-Su 10am-5pm; July-Aug. daily 10am-6pm. Each museum DM4, students DM3, with *Kurkarte* DM3, students DM2. Day card for all 4 museums DM14, students DM10, with *Kurkarte* DM10, students DM6.)

Navigating in Göhren requires little effort, as almost everything lies either on **Strandstraße** or right off it. To get to the center of town from the train station, follow Strandstr. up the hill. Frequent **buses** connect Göhren to Binz, Bergen, and Saßnitz to the north and Klein Zicker to the south (DM5-10). The **Fahrradverleih** Kastanienalle 8 (tel. 254 06), rents touring bikes (DM8) and mountain bikes. (DM10. Open daily 9-11am and 4-6pm.) The **tourist office,** Schulstr. 8 (tel. 21 50 or 259 10; fax 259 11; www.goehren.de), provides information and books **rooms** for a 10% fee. From the train station, follow Strandstr. up the hill and to the left, then go right on Waldstr., and right again onto Schulstr. (Open M-Th 8am-6pm, F 8am-12:30pm and 4-6pm, Sa-Su 4-6pm.) **Sparkasse Rügen,** on Strandstr., cashes traveler's checks for a 1% fee and has an **ATM.** (Open M-Tu and F 8:30am-1pm and 2-4pm, W 8:30am-1pm, Th 8:30am-1pm and 2-6pm.) The **post office,** 18586 Göhren, is inside the **Edeka grocery store** on Strandstr. (Open M-F 8am-7pm, Sa 8am-1pm, Su 8am-noon.) The **telephone code** is 038308.

The **campground** (tel. 901 20; fax 21 23) is near the train station and the beach. From the station, turn right and follow the signs. The staff **rents bikes** and runs a restaurant, cinema, and **laundromat.** (DM6 per person; DM4.50-8 per tent. Reception M-F 7am-1pm and 3-7pm, Sa-Su 9am-noon and 3-7pm.) **Ostseeresidenz Göhren** (tel. 912 55), on the beach down the hill from Strandstr., has slightly expensive fish and vegetarian entrees served in a pleasant ballroom overlooking the sea. Try the *Rotbarschfilet* (DM18.50).

KAP ARKONA AND VITT

At the northern tip of Rügen, Kap Arkona—Germany's only cape, flanked on either side by the villages of Putgarten and Vitt—stretches into the Baltic. The main attractions of the area, two lighthouses and Vitt itself, are beautiful but unfortunately infested with souvenir shops and busloads of tourists. **Buses** run hourly from Saßnitz (#419, 40min., DM7.40) and Bergen (#110, 50min., DM9) to Altenkirchen, where you can transfer to bus #403 to Putgarten (20min., DM2). **Putgarten** serves as the transportation hub and tourist center of Kap Arkona. The **Arkonabahn,** a humiliating motorized train, connects to Putgarten, Vitt, and the lighthouses for a modest cost. (30min., every 30min. DM3 each stop or DM8 round-trip; students DM2 per stop, DM5 round-trip.) **Horse-drawn carts** offer even less efficient transportation between Putgarten and the lighthouses for the same prices as the slightly faster *Arkonabahn*. Before reunification, the two lighthouses on Kap Arkona resided in a restricted area belonging to the GDR's National People's Army; the **Leuchtfener Arkona,** designed by Schinkel, has been open to the public since 1993. Built in 1826, it guarded the GDR's sea borders. Nearby, the **Marinepeilturm** was built in 1927 and rigged with a fancy electronic system that could eavesdrop on British radio communications. Now it houses archaeological finds from the **Tempelburg Arkana,** a Slavic fortification built in the 8th century and destroyed by the Danes in 1168. (Lighthouses open daily 11am-12:30pm and 1:30-5pm. Each lighthouse DM5, students DM4. Combination ticket DM9, students DM7.)

The combination souvenir shop and **tourist office** (tel. 419; fax 419 17), in the parking lot by Kap Arkona, 300m down the road from Putgarten's bus stop, books **rooms.** (Open Jan.-March daily 11am-5pm; March-May 9am-9pm; June-Oct. 10am-7pm.) Pick up a free guide or rent a **bike** to wheel around. (DM2.50 per hour, DM10 per day.) The **Drewoldke campground** (tel. 124 84) is east of Altenkirchen. (DM8.50 per person; DM9 per tent. Reception 8am-1pm and 3-10pm. Open April-Oct.) The **telephone code** is 038391.

NEAR RÜGEN: HIDDENSEE

West of Rügen lies the slender island of Hiddensee, known in the *Plattdeutsch* dialect as *dat söte Länneken* (the sweet island). Free of youth hostels, campgrounds, motor vehicles, and other sources of pollution, Hiddensee remains the same sliver of unadulterated natural beauty that drew Sigmund Freud, Albert Einstein, and Käthe Kollwitz to its shores. Ferries serve Hiddensee's three towns: Neuendorf, Vitte, and Kloster. Of the three, **Neuendorf** is the least spectacular; like the heath surrounding it, the town rests silently except in winter, when local plants are picked for *Sanddorn,* a rust-colored, honey-like drink, served hot or cold in most of the island's restaurants. (DM5 per bottle, DM15-25 for the alcoholic variant.) North of Neuendorf lies **Vitte,** the island's main town and home to Hiddensee's sandiest beach. As Hiddensee has neither a hostel nor a campground, visit the **tourist office,** Nordereude 162 (tel. 642 26; fax 642 25; e-mail inselinformation.hiddensee@t-online.de), which can be found by following signs to the Rathaus. (Open M-F 9am-5pm, Sa 10am-noon.) The island's beauty and action climax in **Kloster,** the northernmost town. The great naturalist author and social dramatist **Gerhardt Hauptmann** summered in Kloster from 1930 to 1943 and is buried here; there is a memorial to him and his work. The huge wine cellar reveals that Hauptmann loved the bottle nearly as much as the pen. (Kirchweg 13. Tel. 397. Open May-Oct. 10am-5pm; Nov.-April 11am-4pm. DM3, students DM 1.50.)

Kloster's museums and sandy beaches are mere appetizers for the hills above the town which make up the **Dornbusch,** an area so pristine that not even bikes are allowed. Follow the trails which run along the grassy hillsides carpeted with wildflowers to reach the **Leuchtturm,** from atop which you can see the entire island. (DM4, DM2.50 with *Kurkarte.* Open daily 10:30am-6pm.) Fully enjoying Hiddensee requires renting a **bike,** preferably a burly one with plenty of gears and nice fat tires, as the majority of the island's roads are either muddy country trails or sandy beach paths. Bike rentals *(Fahrradverleih)* are everywhere on the island; the standard rate is DM10 for a three-speed. Pick up fresh fruit and bread at **Spar supermarket,** Hattenweg 6 (open M-Sa 8am-6pm, Su 11am-6pm) and head for the hills; though ferries dump loads of tourists who crawl the mountains, the plethora of trails lets you pretend you're alone. For those seeking real solitude, spend a night on the island; the only ferry arrives in Vitte at 11:30am and leaves at 4:30pm.

Ferry connections are available to Hiddensee from Stralsund on the mainland (see Stralsund, p. 559) and Schaprode on Rügen's west coast. Ferries leave Schaprode approximately four times per day. (45min. DM8, children DM6; roundtrip DM12, children DM8.) The **telephone code** is 038300.

GREIFSWALD

Endowed with one of the oldest universities in Germany and an array of youth-oriented shops, Greifswald clearly belongs to its students. They zoom through the city on bikes, and their 543 years of professors are commemorated by scores of plaques around the city. The talented hands of Caspar David Friedrich (see p. 24) painted the skyline and nearby cloister ruins into art world fame in the late 19th century. Greifswald has managed to hold on to a few of his works, which are at least partially responsible for the German Romantics' obsession with man's insignificance; unfortunately, most of the paintings have been snatched up by bigger museums in Berlin and Düsseldorf.

◪ ORIENTATION AND PRACTICAL INFORMATION. Greifswald is the easternmost city on Germany's Baltic coast, lying 30km southeast of and 60km west of the Polish frontier. **Trains** chug to Stralsund (20min., 1 per hour), Rostock (2½hr., 8 per day, DM28), Schwerin (3½hr., 5 per day, DM52), and Berlin (3hr., 1 per hour, DM60). **Buses** cover the inner city and suburbs (single ticket DM2.30, day card DM5). There are **taxi** stands outside the train station and the Rathaus. The **tourist office**, Schuhagenstr. 22 (tel. 34 60; fax 37 88), offers free maps and guided tours in German (M, W, and F at 2pm; DM10). They also book **private rooms** (DM30-50) for free. (Open M-F 9am-6pm, Sa 9:30am-12:30pm.) Exchange **money** at the **Deutsche Bank** on the Markt. (Open M, W, and F 8:30am-4pm, Tu and Th 8:30am-6pm. 24hr. **ATM** available.) For **gay and lesbian services,** contact **Rosa Greif**, Lange Str. 49. (Tel. 89 70 34. Open Tu 3-5pm, Th 5-9pm.) There is a **women's center** at the **Frauenausbildungs- und Beratungszentrum Baltic,** Spiegeldorfer Wende 2 (tel. 82 03 43). The **Rats-Apotheke,** Am Markt 2, fills all your pharmaceutical needs. (Open M-F 8am-6pm, Sa noon-8pm, Su 8am-8pm.) The **post office** is at Am Markt 15-19, 17489 Greifswald. (Open M-F 8am-6pm, Sa 9am-noon.) Check **email** at **Billiard Café,** Wollweberstr. 22. (Open Tu-F 5:30-11pm, Sa-Su 2:30-11pm.) The **telephone code** is 03834.

▐▛▐ ACCOMMODATIONS, FOOD, AND NIGHTLIFE. Greifswald has no youth hostel; the *Zimmervermittlung* at the tourist office is your best bet. During the summer it's wise to call ahead, or you'll end up dishing out at least DM80-100 to stay in a hotel. While Greifswald's culinary options are scant, its club life is not. The **Mensa,** Am Schießwall (tel. 86 17 11), opens for breakfast at 8am and remains open for lunch through 3:30pm; buy a magnetic card outside the cafeteria (DM2-4). The Mensa reopens most nights as a club, though hours and programs vary; check out the posters on the first floor to see what's on. **Café Quark,** Karl-Marx-Platz 19 (tel. 50 22 35), at the end of Lange Str. in a building that combines Neoclassicism and a third-grade color scheme, is a popular hangout. (Open Tu-W 6pm-2am, Th-Sa 8pm-4am.) Another hotspot, open irregularly, is **Klex,** a youth center at Lange Str. 14 (tel. 89 83 30); it also doubles as a breakfast café. (Open M-F 9am-noon.) The most popular club among locals, **Fly-In,** Gaußstr. 12 (tel. 82 03 72), is a 35min. ride from the Altstadt. Take bus #30 to "Max-Planck-Str." In addition to the *Biergarten* that line Lange Str., Greifswald has a few hidden-away cafes. **Café Lichtblick,** Domstr. 13, serves inexpensive caffeinated beverages. (Open M-F 9am-5pm.) **Café mal Anders,** Lange Str. 49, serves it up in a well groomed patio-garden. (Open Tu-F 11:30am-5pm.) Cheap eats can be had at **City-Back Discount,** Lange Str. 87 (open M-F 6:30am-6pm, Sa 7-11am) or at the **Spar** supermarket inside the Altstadt's monstrous Dompassage shopping center. (Open M-F 8am-8pm, Sa 8am-4pm.)

◉ SIGHTS. Stretching high above the Greifswald skyline is the tower of the **Nikolaikirche.** A small viewing platform has been built around the tower of the 14th-century basilica; climb through a maze of wooden beams to the rickety heights of the building and survey Greifswald in all its glory (DM3, students DM1.50). The city has still not removed the cannonballs that were lodged in the east wall of the 13th-century **Marienkirche** by an angry elector of Brandenburg in 1678, but the early Gothic interior of the church is worth a look. (Open M-F 10am-noon and 2-4pm, Sa-Su 10am-noon.)

The unkindness of the university's professors has been memorialized in the **Karzer,** a prison where naughty students would endure several days of solitary confinement—bringing a whole new dimension to the repercussions of missed deadlines. Greifswald's Karzer is notable because students locked up there

M.-VORPOMMERN

maliciously painted beautiful coats-of-arms on the walls and carved their names in impeccable script on the doors. Greifswald's **Museum der Stadt,** Theodor-Pyl-Str. 1-2 (tel. 27 20), has an exhibit on Caspar David Friedrich, though it contains precious few of his works. (Open W-Su 10am-6pm.) Near the train station, the university's **botanical gardens,** Münterstr. 11 (tel. 86 11 30), are filled with domesticated plants and the plaques that describe them. (Open M-F 9am-3:45pm, Sa-Su 1-3pm.) Running around the city is a tree-lined pedestrian boulevard; when the town wall was razed in the late 1700s, kilometers of greenery replaced it. At 700 years old, the **house** at Markt 13 is the oldest (if not the prettiest) in Greifswald. Two doors down, a 15th-century residence competes in both garishness and age.

A few kilometers east of Greifswald, the coastal villages of **Wieck** and **Eldena** keep the city supplied with fresh fish. Make a trip to the carefully preserved **Klosterruine** in Eldena, across from Wolgaster Str. The remains of this 12th-century Cistercian monastery once housed Danish monks, but was in great part destroyed by Swedish soldiers plundering for raw materials. Friedrich immortalized the ruins in a series of Romantic images; stop by and contemplate your insignificance. In June, the cloisters become a venue for open-air Bach recitals. Take bus #60 (direction: "Wieck Brücke") to the end.

USEDOM

Usedom is probably more interesting for what it was than what it is. The late 19th century drew crowds of wealthy Berliners whose millions of Reichmarks built the beaches into an elitist playground, nicknamed "Berlin's bathtub." Depression and war sent them scattering, but their beach toys—enormously gaudy houses and long piers—remain, albeit in various states of decay. Today the island is the bathtub of the *petit bourgeoisie;* a less glittering crowd of middle-class families fills the beaches and rents rooms in a few of the restored palaces. An astonishing amount of the island has been neither restored nor destroyed, and the quiet, cavernous buildings lend the area a haunting atmosphere.

◪ ORIENTATION AND GETTING AROUND. Usedom is the northeasternmost point in Germany; the eastern part of the island is part of Poland. The island still fills up in July and August, when the beaches become crowded with *Strandkörbe* (people-baskets that block the sun), so it's a good idea to reserve accommodations in advance. Usedom is connected to mainland Germany at **Wolgast,** where hourly **trains** connect to **Züssow** and the rest of the national train system. Alternatively, **Adler-Schiffe** (tel. 038378/32583) runs **ferries** from the Usedom resorts to **Saßnitz** (p. 563) on the island of **Rügen** (4hr., 1 per day, DM43.50). On the island, **public transportation** takes the form of the **Usedomer Bäderbahn (UBB),** which runs from Wolgast to Ahlbeck (1hr., every 30min., DM10) and stops at most beach towns in between. From the Wolgast train station, cross the drawbridge and turn left to reach the UBB station. You'll have to buy a *Kurkarte* (DM4, students DM2) if your hotel doesn't provide you with one; these cards offer access to all beaches as well as discounts at many of Usedom's tourist spots.

ZINNOWITZ

Larger and less naturally striking than the other resorts on the island, Zinnowitz nonetheless benefits from a minimum of tourists and a plentiful supply of cheap accommodations. The sparkly new **Kurverwaltung** (tel. 49 20; fax 422 29), at the corner of Neue Strandstr. and Dünenstr., provides free maps of the island and books rooms (DM30-60) for free. (Open M-F 9am-8pm, Sa-Su 10am-5pm.) The tourist office also offers **bike tours** (M and W-Th at 10am; DM5, DM3 with *Kurkarte*). Rent **bikes** at the **Fahrradverleih**, Dr.-Wachsmann-Str. 5. (Tel. 428 69. Open daily 8am-noon and 1-7pm; DM6-10.) There is a **pharmacy** at Neue Strandstr. 39. (Tel. 20 24 62. Open M-F 8am-6pm, Sa 8:30am-noon.) The **post office**, 17454 Zinnowitz, is at Neue Strandstr. 22. (Open M-F 9am-6pm, Sa 9am-noon.) The **telephone code** is 038377.

If the *Zimmervermittlung* at the tourist office leaves you looking for cheaper accommodations, check out the **Sportschule**, Dr.-Wachsmann-Str. 30 (tel. 422 68; fax 422 80), which in addition to rooms also offers a large track, soccer field, handball court, and ping-pong tables. (DM35 per person; sheets DM5.) Just down the street, **Campingplatz Pommernland**, Dr.-Wachsmann-Str. 40 (tel. 403 48; fax 403 49), has several expensive but very new bungalows (doubles DM140, quads DM180) and rents camping places. (DM8.50, tents DM7-10. Reception open daily 8am-noon and 2-9pm.) Apart from a small village of fish huts (open daily from 10am until the fish run out), there is a **grocery store** next to the post office. (Open daily 9am-4pm.)

KOSEROW

Probably the best way to imagine Koserow is to play forest-and-beach relaxation tapes at full blast with your eyes closed. At the narrowest and highest part of Usedom (a staggering 58m), Koserow's remarkable forests of moss-covered trees fall sharply onto a surreally perfect sandy beach in what is, refreshingly, the least touristy of Usedom's resort towns. The **tourist office**, Hauptstr. 34 (tel. 204 15) offers free maps and hiking tips. (Open daily 8am-4pm.) You'll have to go to the **Zimmervermittlung** (tel. 210 62), in the same building as the tourist office, to get yourself a room. (DM30-60. Reservation service free, but call early in the year for the summer months.) Most services line Koserow's Hauptstraße, which leads conveniently to the train station. Buy your (legal) drugs at the **Vineta-Apotheke** at the corner of Schulstr. and Hauptstr. (Tel. 202 35. Open M-F 8am-6pm, Sa 8am-noon.) The **post office**, 17459 Koserow, is near the train station at Hauptstr. 49a. (Open M-F 9am-noon and 2:30-6pm, Sa 9am-noon.) Check **email** at **Hotel Nautic**, Hauptstr. 46e. (DM8 per hour. Open daily 10am-9pm.) The **telephone code** is 038371.

While nearly every house in the small town advertises rooms for rent, they are usually booked well in advance. **Wald und Meer**, perched in the woods on the west end of town at the end of Forster-Schrödter-Str. (tel. 26 20; fax 262 40), offers fairly spartan bungalow accommodations in 2-6 bed rooms. (DM26 per person. Breakfast included.) Pitch your tent at **Campingplatz Am Sandfeld** (tel. 207 59; fax 214 05) to enjoy the cheapest accommodations and best views on the island. (DM8 per person. Wash DM4. Beach access DM1.)

Like its neighboring towns, the best places to eat in Koserow are the bakeries and fish huts. Several places along Hauptstr. churn out fresh bread, and fresh fish is for sale just north of the pier. For **groceries**, stop by **Netto** on Hauptstr., next to the train station. (Open M-F 8am-8pm, Sa 8am-6pm, Su 11am-5pm.)

BANSIN, HERINGSDORF, AND AHLBECK

The resort towns of Bansin, Heringsdorf, and Ahlbeck (known as the "Kaiserly three") are connected by a long, well groomed beach promenade and a string of crumbling, eerily deserted mansions left from the glory days of the turn of the century. Splendid beaches and a fascinating history are good reasons to visit the towns; nightlife and fine dining are not. Most of the tourist crowds are comprised of young families and busloads of elderly Germans.

There are several ways to travel among the three towns; the most scenic is a walk or bike ride along the 8km **Strandpromenade**. Lazier sorts can hop on the

Kaiserbäder-Express, a dorky little motorized train which makes 45min. rounds of the three towns in all its choo-chooing blue-and-white glory (DM3). Those too cool for the miniature train can take the real one; the **Usedomer Bäderbahn** shuttles between the towns every half-hour. (17min.; DM2-10, depending on destination; day pass DM10.) The **telephone code** for all three towns is 038378.

Bansin is the smallest and most residential of the three cities and offers little else apart from the beach. However, it does have the best food in the area: just west of the pier, fishermen sell the day's catch as fish sandwiches (DM2-3). Come early; the huts open around 8am and close when the day's catch is sold (usually by 3-4pm). Bansin's **tourist office** is on the pier (tel. 470 50; fax 47 05 15), but they'll direct you to Ahlbeck's *Zimmervermittlung* (see below) if you call in search of a room. (Open M-F 9am-6pm, Sa-Su 10am-3pm.) Exchange **money** at the **Sparkasse,** Seestr. 5. (Open M, Tu, F 8:30am-noon and 1:30-4pm, W 8:30am-noon, Th 8:30am-noon and 1:30-6pm.) There is a **pharmacy, Fontane-Apotheke,** at Seestr. 4. (Tel. 293 04. Open M-F 8am-1pm and 2-6pm, Sa 8am-noon.) The **post office,** 17429 Bansin, is at Seestr. 8. (Open M-F 9:15am-noon and 2:30-6pm, Sa 9:15am-noon.)

Heringsdorf was once the most elite of the three resort towns; check out the abandoned abode of Kaiser Wilhelm II, Delbrückstr. 6, for a taste of the village's imperial past. The tourist industry is once again on the rise here; the shiny combination of the new pier, shopping center, and the glassy **Platz des Friedens** at the center of town are the result of many vacation Deutschmarks. To get to the Platz, turn left on Bülowstr. from the station, right on Friedenstr., and follow it to the end.

Heringsdorf's **tourist office** is at Kulmstr. 33, next to the Rathaus. (Tel. 24 51; fax 24 54. Open M-F 9am-6pm, Sa-Su 10am-3pm.) Most other services cluster around the Platz. The **Sparkasse** (tel. 23 60) exchanges money for DM3 or a 1% fee and has **24hr. ATMs.** (Open M, Tu, F 8:30am-noon and 1:30-4pm, W 8:30am-noon, Th 8:30am-noon and 1:30-6pm.) The **Apotheke** at Seestr. 40 (tel. 25 90) lists local doctors and their telephone numbers in the window. (Open M-F 8am-6pm, Sa 8am-noon.) For a **taxi,** call 225 26. The **post office,** 17424 Heringsdorf, is at Seestr. 17. (Open M-F 8:30am-noon and 2:30-5:30pm, Sa 9am-noon.)

During the high season (July and August), it is virtually impossible to find accommodations in Heringsdorf; most vacationers reserve early in the year for the summer months. The **Jugendherberge Heringsdorf (HI),** Puschkinstr. 7-9 (tel. 223 25; fax 323 01), has taken over a beach house between Heringsdorf and Ahlbeck. From the train station, turn right on Liehrstr. and follow the signs. (DM29, over 26 DM36. Beach tax May-Sept. DM3.80, Oct.-April DM1.90. Advanced reservations required. Breakfast included. Sheets DM7. Reception open 8-9am, noon-1pm, and 6-10pm. Curfew 10pm.) If the hostel is full, call the *Zimmervermittlung* in Ahlbeck (see below). Food in Heringsdorf is unremarkable. **Schwenn's,** in the Platz des Friedens, offers a small array of **groceries.** (Open M-F 7am-7pm, Sa 7am-noon and 3-6pm, Su 8am-noon and 3-6pm.)

The beach is obviously Heringsdorf's main attraction; the salty sea climes and clean air have survived a century of political struggle unharmed. They haven't gone unnoticed, however, and the beaches can get claustrophobically crowded in season. The **Villa Irmgard,** Maxim-Gorki-Str. 13, traces the rise and fall of 19th century Usedom resort life. This former home of Russian writer **Maxim Gorki** has been converted into a museum and now houses an exhibit of Gorki's personal possessions (probably interesting only to Gorki fanatics), as well as a more interesting collection of intricate swimsuits and everything else that the rich and famous needed at the beach. (Open Tu-Su 10am-6pm. DM4, with *Kurkarte* DM2.)

Ahlbeck blends into Heringsdorf geographically, yet has less of its neighbor's 20th-century shopping mall feel. Restored mansions give the town a 19th-century ambience. The center of Ahlbeck is at the intersection of Goethestr. and Seestr; walking along Goethestr. from Heringsdorf reveals some of the more decrepit mansions in the area. The piers of Ahlbeck and Heringsdorf highlight the differences between the villages: Ahlbeck's century-old red-and-white wooden structure contrasts sharply to the glitzy new pier in Heringsdorf. There is, however, little difference between the beaches, which remain fairly crowded in summer.

Just a few kilometers east of Ahlbeck is the Polish border town **Świnoujście** (Swinemünde in German). Though cars are not allowed across the border, you can follow the herd of German tourists in search of bargains and explore the Polish resort by bike or on foot—just remember to bring your passport.

Ahlbeck's **tourist office,** Dünenstr. 45 (tel. 24 51; fax 24 54), books **rooms** (DM30-50) in the tri-city area for free. (Open M-F 9am-6pm, Sa-Su 10am-3pm.) **Fahrradverleih Ziegler,** Dünenstr. 37 (tel. 305 40), is conveniently located on the main drag and rents **bikes** for DM10 per day. (Open daily 9am-6pm.) The **Sparkasse,** Seestr. 17 (tel. 23 70), exchanges **money** for DM3 or a 1% fee. (Open M, Tu, F 8:30am-noon and 1:30-4pm, W 8:30am-noon, Th 8:30am-noon and 1:30-6pm.) There is a **pharmacy, Marsson-Apotheke,** at Seestr. 13. (Tel. 23 40. Open M-F 8-6:30pm, Sa 8am-12:30pm.) The **post office,** 17419 Ahlbeck, is at Seestr. 25. (Open M-F 8:30am-noon and 2:30-5pm.) A couple of Italian restaurants battle it out above the pier—check out **Mamma Mia** (tel. 28 00), on the corner of Dünenstr. and Seestr. (Open daily 11:30am-12:30am.) Across the street, **Fischhandlung Werner Reimer** offers more substantial fish sandwiches. (DM2-5. Open M-F 9am-6pm, Sa 9am-5pm.) What little nightlife the family-oriented towns have is centered around the **Haus der Erlebnisse,** Dünenstr. 37 (tel. 303 45), which shows dubbed American movies and hosts the occasional disco.

M.-VORPOMMERN

APPENDIX

HOLIDAYS AND FESTIVALS

HOLIDAYS

DATE	HOLIDAY	ENGLISH
January 6	Heilige Drei Könige	Epiphany
March 8	Aschermittwoch	Ash Wednesday
April 21	Karfreitag	Good Friday
April 23	Ostersonntag	Easter Sunday
April 24	Ostermontag	Easter Monday
May 1	Tag der Arbeit	Labor Day
June 1	Christi Himmelfahrt	Ascension Day
June 11	Pfingstsonntag	Whit Sunday (Pentecost)
June 12	Pfingstmontag	Whit Monday
June 22	Fronleichnam	Corpus Christi
August 15	Maria Himmelfahrt	Assumption Day
October 3	Tag der deutschen Einheit	Day of German Unity
November 1	Reformationtag	Reformation Day
November 1	Allerheiligen	All Saint's Day
December 25-26	Weihnachtstag	Christmas

FESTIVALS

DATE	FESTIVAL	CITY
Jan. 7-March 7	Fasching (Carnival)	Munich
February 9-20	Berlinale film festival	Berlin
March 2-7	Karneval	Köln
May 5-7	Hafensgeburtstag	Hamburg
June-Oct.	Expo 2000	Hannover
Late June	International Film Festival	Munich
Late June/Early July	Christopher Street Day	Berlin and major cities
Early July	Love Parade	Berlin
July 21-30	Bach Festival	Leipzig
Late July	Unifest	Karlsruhe
July 25-Aug. 28	Wagner Festspiele	Bayreuth
Aug. 11-21	Gäubodenvolksfest	Straubing
Aug. 24-Sept. 3	Wine Festival	Stuttgart
Sept. 16-Oct. 1	Oktoberfest	Munich
Dec. 24-27	Christmas Market	Nürnberg

TIME ZONES

Germany uses West European time (abbreviated MEZ in German). Add six hours to Eastern Standard Time and one hour to Greenwich Mean Time. Subtract nine hours from Eastern Australia Time and 11 hours from New Zealand Time. Germany, like the rest of Western Europe, observes Daylight Savings Time.

TELEPHONE CODES

In Germany, dial 00 to get an international line, then dial the country code, the city or area code (*without* the first 0), and the number. **Germany's country code is 49.**

COUNTRY CODES

Australia	61	Ireland	353
Austria	43	Netherlands	31
Belgium	32	New Zealand	64
Czech Republic	420	Poland	48
Denmark	45	South Africa	27
France	33	Switzerland	41
Hungary	36	United Kingdom	44
Italy	39	U.S. and Canada	1

CITY CODES

Aachen	0241	Kassel	0561
Bayreuth	0921	Kiel	0431
Berlin	030	Köln	0221
Bonn	0228	Leipzig	0341
Braunschweig	0531	Lübeck	0451
Bremen	0421	München	089
Dessau	0340	Münster	0251
Dresden	0351	Nürnberg	0911
Düsseldorf	0211	Passau	0851
Erfurt	0361	Regensburg	0941
Frankfurt	069	Rostock	0381
Freiburg	0761	Stuttgart	0711
Göttingen	0551	Trier	0651
Hamburg	040	Tübingen	07071
Hannover	0511	Weimar	03643
Heidelberg	06221	Würzburg	0931

MEASUREMENTS

Like the rest of the rational world, Germany uses the metric system. Keep this in mind whenever you see a road sign or any other distance indicator—those are kilometers, not miles, so whatever distance is being described is not as far away as Americans and Britons might think. Also, all German recipe books use metric measurements. And, unfortunately, gasoline isn't as cheap as it looks to those used to gallons: prices are *per liter.*

MEASUREMENT CONVERSIONS

1 inch (in.) = 2.54cm	1 centimeter (cm) = 0.39 in.
1 foot (ft.) = 0.30m	1 meter (m) = 3.28 ft.
1 yard (yd.) = 0.914m	1 meter (m) = 1.09 yd.
1 mile = 1.61km	1 kilometer (km) = 0.62 mi.
1 ounce (oz.) = 28.35g	1 gram (g) = 0.035 oz.
1 pound (lb.) = 0.454kg	1 kilogram (kg) = 2.202 lb.
1 fluid ounce (fl. oz.) = 29.57ml	1 milliliter (ml) = 0.034 fl. oz.
1 gallon (gal.) = 3.785L	1 liter (L) = 0.264 gal.
1 acre (ac.) = 0.405ha	1 hectare (ha) = 2.47 ac.
1 square mile (sq. mi.) = 2.59km^2	1 square kilometer (km^2) = 0.386 sq. mi.

LANGUAGE

Although the majority of the post-World War II generations in Germany speak English, you'll have many real face-to-face encounters with people who don't, especially when traveling in Eastern Germany. German is a rigidly structured language, following strict grammatical rules. Mastering them is quite an accomplishment in itself—"Life," Thomas Love Peacock said, "is too short to learn German." Before asking someone a question in English, always preface your query with a polite *Sprechen Sie englisch?* (Do you speak English?).

PRONUNCIATION

Although you cannot hope to speak correct German without studying it, you can make yourself understood by learning only a little German. The first step is to master the pronunciation system. Unlike English, German pronunciation is for the most part consistent with spelling; there are no silent letters.

Consonants are pronounced as in English with the following exceptions: **J:** always pronounced as a Y. **K:** always pronounced, even before an N. **QU:** pronounced KV. **S:** pronounced as Z. **V:** pronounced as F. **W:** pronounced as V. **Z:** pronounced as TS. The hissing, aspirant **CH** sound, appearing in such basic words as *Ich* (I), *nicht* (not), and *sprechen* (to speak), is quite tricky for untrained English-speaking vocal cords. After A, O, U, or AU, it is pronounced as in the Scottish, "loch"; otherwise it sounds like a soft CH, as in "chivalry." If you can't hack it, use an SH sound instead. The diphthong **SCH,** found at the beginning of many German words, is pronounced SH, as in the word "shut," while **ST** and **SP** are pronounced "SHT" and "SHP," respectively.

German has one consonant that does not exist in English, **the "ß,"** which is alternately referred to as the *scharfes S* (sharp S) or the *Ess-tsett*. It is a shorthand symbol for a **double-S,** and is pronounced just like an English "ss." The letter appears only in lower case and shows up in two of the most important German words for travelers: *Straße*, "street," which is pronounced "SHTRAH-sseh" and abbreviated "Str."; and *Schloß*, "castle," pronounced "SHLOSS." Note that the use of the "ß" is being phased out in an effort to standardize spelling (see **The Woeful Decline of the ß,** p. 272).

German vowels and diphthongs also differ from their English counterparts: **A:** as in "father." **O:** as in "oh." **U:** as in "fondue." **AU:** as in "wow." **IE:** as in "thief." **EI:** like the I in "wine." **EU:** like the OI in "boil." An **umlaut** over a letter (e.g., ü) changes the pronunciation. An umlaut is sometimes replaced by an E following the vowel, so that "schön" becomes "schoen." An **Ä** sounds a lot like the short "e" in "effort," while an **Ö** is pronounced like the "e" in "perm." To make the **Ü** sound, round your lips to say "ooh," keep them in this position, and then try to say "ee" instead. Germans are very forgiving toward foreigners who butcher their mother tongue. There is, however, one important exception—place names. If you learn nothing else in German, learn to pronounce the names of cities properly. Berlin is "bare-LEEN," Hamburg is "HAHM-boorg," Munich (München) is "MEUWN-shen," and Bayreuth is "BUY-royt."

NUMBERS, DATES, AND TIMES

A space or period rather than a comma is used to indicate thousands, so 10,000 is written 10 000 or 10.000. Instead of a decimal point, Germans use a comma, e.g., 3.1415 is written 3,1415. Months and days are written in the reverse of the American manner, e.g., 10.11.92 is November 10. The numeral 7 is written with a slash through the vertical line, and the numeral 1 is written with an upswing, resembling an inverted "V." Note that the number in the ones place is pronounced before the number in the tens place; thus "fünfundsiebzig" (FUHNF-oont-ZEEB-tsish; literally "five and seventy") is 75, *not* 57. This can be hard to keep in mind.

The months in German are *Januar, Februar, März, April, Mai, Juni, Juli, August, September, Oktober, November, Dezember*. The days of the week are *Montag, Dienstag, Mittwoch, Donnerstag, Freitag, Samstag/Sonnabend*, and *Sonntag*. Germany uses the 24-hour clock for all official purposes: 20.00 equals 8pm. Thus, *fünfzehn Uhr* (15.00) is 3pm, etc. When Germans say "half eight" (*halb acht*), they mean 7:30; "three quarters eight" (*dreiviertel acht*) means 7:45 and "quarter eight" (*viertel acht*) means 7:15.

GERMAN-ENGLISH GLOSSARY

German nouns are always capitalized. Words separated by a slash indicate the male and female forms. For example, a male student would say *Ich bin Student*, while a female student would say *Ich bin Studentin*.

Abendessen: dinner
abfahren: to depart
Abfahrt: departure
Abteil: train compartment
Achtung: beware
Allee: avenue
Altstadt: old town, historic center
ankommen: to arrive
Ankunft: arrival
Apotheke: pharmacy
Arbeit: work
Ausgang: exit
Auskunft: information
Ausstellung: exhibit
Ausweis: ID
Auto: car
Autobahn: highway
Autobus: bus
Bad: bath, spa
Bahn: railway
Bahnhof: train station
Bahnsteig: train platform
Berg: mountain, hill
Bett: bed
Bibliothek: library
Bier: beer
Bundesrepublik Deutschland (BRD): Federal Republic of Germany (FRG)
Brot: bread
Brücke: bridge
Brunnen: fountain
Bundestag: parliament
Burg: fortress
Busbahnhof: bus station
Damen: ladies
Dennkmal: memorial
Dusche: shower
Dom: cathedral
Dorf: village
echt: real
ekelig: disgusting
Ehefrau: wife
Ehemann: husband
Einbahnstraße: one-way street
Eingang: entrance
Eintritt: admission
Essen: food
Fähre: ferry
Fahrplan: timetable
Fahrrad: bicycle
Fahrschein: train ticket
Feiertag: holiday
Fernseher: TV set

Festung: fortress
Flohmarkt: flea market
Flughafen: airport
Flugzeug: airplane
Fluß: river
Fremdenverkehrsamt: tourist office
Frühstück: breakfast
Fußgängerzone: pedestrian zone
Garten: garden
Gasse: alley, street
Gasthaus: guest house
Gaststätte: local bar with restaurant
Gedenkstätte: memorial
geil: cool OR horny
Hafen: harbor
Hauptbahnhof: main train station
Hauptpostamt: main post office
Herren: Gentlemen
Hof: court, courtyard
Innenstadt: city center
Imbiß: fast-food stand
Insel: island
Jugendgästehaus: youth hotel
Jugendherberge: youth hostel
Kaiser: emperor
Karte: ticket
Kino: cinema
Kiosk: newsstand
Kirche: church
Kneipe: bar
König: king
Königin: queen
Kreuz: cross, crucifix
Kunst: art
Kurort: spa town
Kurtaxe: overnight resort tax
Kurverwaltung: *Kurort* tourist office
Land: German state/province
Lesbe: lesbian (n.)
Markt: market
Marktplatz: market square
Mauer: wall
Meer: sea
Mensa: university cafeteria
Mitfahrzentrale: ride-share service office
Mitwohnzentrale: long-term accommodation service
Münster: cathedral
Museum: museum

Notausgang: emergency exit
Notfall: emergency
Notruf: emergency hotline
Party: party
Paß: passport
Pension: cheap hotel
Platz: square
Polizei: police
Postamt: post office
Privatzimmer: room in a private home
Quittung: receipt
Rathaus: town hall
Rechnung: bill, cheque
Reisebüro: travel agency
Reisezentrum: travel office in train stations
S-Bahn: commuter rail
Sammlung: collection
Schatzkammer: treasury
Scheiße!: shit!
Schiff: ship
Schloß: castle
Schule: school
schwul: gay (adj.)
See: lake
Speisekarte: menu
Stadt: city
Strand: beach
Straße: street
Straßenbahn: streetcar
Tal: valley
Tankstelle: gas/petrol station
Teich: pond
Tor: gate
Turm: tower
U-Bahn: subway
umsteigen: to make a transit connection
Universität: university
Veganer/in: vegan
Vegetarier/in: vegetarian
Viertel: quarter, district
Vorsicht: caution
Wald: forest
wandern: to hike
Wanderweg: hiking trail
Weg: road, way
Wein: wine
Wurst: sausage
Zeitung: newspaper
Zimmer: room
Zug: train

GERMAN PHRASEBOOK

The following phrasebook is meant to provide only the very rudimentary phrases you will need in your travels. Nothing can replace a full-fledged phrasebook or a pocket-sized English-German dictionary. The German numbering system is especially confusing; look in the **Language** section above for further explanation. German features both an informal and formal form of address (see p. 36); in the tables below, the polite form follows the familiar form in parentheses.

GREETINGS

ENGLISH	GERMAN	ENGLISH	GERMAN
Hello.	Hallo.	Good-bye.	Tschüß! (informal); Auf Wiedersehen! (formal)
Excuse me/sorry	Entschuldigung/ Verzeihung.	My name is...	Ich heiße...
Could you please help me?	Können Sie mir bitte helfen?	What is your name?	Wie heißt Du (heißen Sie)?
How old are you?	Wie alt bist Du (sind Sie)?	Where are you from?	Wo kommst Du (kommen Sie) her?
Good morning.	Guten Morgen.	How are you?	Wie geht's (geht es Ihnen)?
Good afternoon.	Guten Tag.	I'm fine.	Es geht mir gut.
Good evening.	Guten Abend.	Do you speak English?	Sprichst Du (sprechen Sie) englisch?
Good night.	Gute Nacht	I don't speak German.	Ich kann kein Deutsch.

USEFUL PHRASES

ENGLISH	GERMAN	ENGLISH	GERMAN
Thank you (very much).	Danke (schön).	Please.	Bitte.
What?	Was?	I am a student (male/ female).	Ich bin Student (m)/ Studentin (f).
When (what time)?	Wann?	Are there student discounts?	Gibt es Studentener- mäßigungen?
Why?	Warum?	No problem.	Kein Problem.
Where is...?	Wo ist?	I don't understand.	Ich verstehe nicht.
I'm from...	Ich komme aus...	Please speak slowly.	Sprechen Sie bitte langsam.
America/USA	Amerika/den USA	Please repeat.	Bitte wiederholen Sie.
Australia	Australien	Pardon? What was that?	Wie bitte?
Canada	Kanada	Yes/No	Ja/nein
Great Britain	Großbritannien	Maybe	Vielleicht
Ireland	Irland	I would like...	Ich möchte...
New Zealand	Neuseeland	I'm looking for...	Ich suche...
South Africa	Südafrika	I need...	Ich brauche...
I'm not feeling well.	Mir ist schlecht.	How much does that cost?	Wieviel kostet das?
I have a headache.	Ich habe Kopfweh.	Where is the phone?	Wo ist das Telefon?
I need a doctor.	Ich brauche einen Arzt.	I don't know.	Ich weiß nicht.
Leave me alone.	Laß mich in Ruhe.	Where is the toilet?	Wo ist die Toilette?
I'll call the police.	Ich rufe die Polizei.	I have potato salad in my Lederhosen.	Ich habe Kartoffelsalat in meine Lederhosen.
Help!	Hilfe!	What does that mean?	Was bedeutet das?
Do you have anything cheaper?	Haben Sie etwas billigeres?	Are there any vacancies?	Gibt es ein Zimmer frei?
No thanks.	Nein, danke.	How do you say that in German?	Wie sagt man das auf deutsch?

DIRECTIONS AND TRANSPORTATION

(to the) right	rechts	**(to the) left**	links
straight ahead	geradeaus	**Where is...?**	Wo ist...?
next to	neben	**opposite**	gegenüber
How do I find...?	Wie finde ich ...?	**It's nearby.**	Es ist in der Nähe.
How do I get to...?	Wie komme ich nach...?	**Is that far from here?**	Ist es weit weg?
Where is this train going?	Wohin fährt der Zug?	**When does the train leave?**	Wann fährt der Zug ab?

TIMES AND HOURS

open	geöffnet	**closed**	geschlossen
morning	Morgen	**opening hours**	Öffnungszeiten
afternoon	Nachmittag	**today**	heute
night	Nacht	**yesterday**	gestern
evening	Abend	**tomorrow**	morgen
What time is it?	Wie spät ist es?	**break time, rest day**	Ruhepause, Ruhetag
It's (seven) o'clock.	Es ist (sieben) Uhr.	**At what time?**	Um wieviel Uhr?

NUMBERS

one	eins	**two**	zwei
three	drei	**four**	vier
five	fünf	**six**	sechs
seven	sieben	**eight**	acht
nine	neun	**ten**	zehn
eleven	elf	**twelve**	zwölf
fifteen	fünfzehn	**twenty**	zwanzig
twenty-five	fünfundzwanzig	**thirty**	dreißig
forty	vierzig	**fifty**	fünfzig
sixty	sechsig	**seventy**	siebzig
eighty	achtzig	**ninety**	neunzig
one hundred	hundert	**one thousand**	tausend

FOOD AND RESTAURANT TERMS

bread	Brot	**rice**	Reis
meat	Fleisch	**water**	Wasser
vegetables	Gemüse	**tap water**	Leitungswasser
cheese	Käse	**roll**	Brötchen
wine	Wein	**beer**	Bier
sausage	Wurst	**pork**	Schweinefleisch
chicken	Huhn	**beef**	Rindfleisch
potatoes	Kartoffeln	**french fries**	Pommes frites
sauce	Soße	**coffee**	Kaffee
tea	Tee	**jelly**	Marmelade
It tastes good.	Es schmeckt gut.	**It tastes awful.**	Es schmeckt widerlich.
Check, please.	Rechnung, bitte.	**I would like to order...**	Ich hätte gern...
I'm a vegan.	Ich bin Veganer (m)/ Ich bin Veganerin (f).	**I'm a vegetarian.**	Ich bin Vegetarier/Vegetarierin.
Give me chocolate.	Gib (Geben Sie) mir Schokolade.	**Give me a nutella sandwich.**	Gib (Geben Sie) mir ein Nutellabrötchen.

OPPOSITES ATTRACT

together	zusammen	alone	allein/e
good	gut	bad	schlecht
happy	glücklich	sad	traurig
big	groß	small	klein
young	jung	old	alt
full	voll	empty	leer
hot	heiß	cold	kalt
safe	sicher, ungefährlich	dangerous	gefährlich
alive	lebendig	dead	tod
besonders	special	einfach	simple
mehr	more	weniger	less
vor	before	nach	after
pretty	schön	ugly	häßlich

NEVER, NEVER GONNA GET IT

You're cute	Du bist hübsch.	I'm...	Ich bin...
You're friend is cute.	Dein Freund/Deine Freundin ist hübsch.	drunk	betrunken
I have...	Ich habe...	bisexual	bi
a boyfriend/girlfriend	einen Freund/ eine Freundin	gay	schwul
a venereal disease	eine Geschlechtskrankheit	lesbian	Lesbe
no inhibitions	keine Hemmungen	straight	hetero
no money	kein Geld	not sure	mir nicht sicher
handcuffs	Handschellen	That'll be fifty Marks.	Das macht fünfzig Mark.
You're da bomb.	Du bist die Bombe.	Get lost.	Hau ab.
The hostel is close.	Die Jugendherberge ist in der Nähe.	Oops. The hostel just closed.	Huch. Die Jugendherberge hat gerade zugemacht.
What's your sign?	Was ist dein Sternzeichen?	Really? I'm a Cancer. Do you want to dance?	Wirklich? Ich bin Krebs. Willst Du tanzen?
Can I buy you a drink?	Kann ich Dir einen Drink kaufen?	My boyfriend would like to meet you.	Mein Freund möchte Dich kennenlernen.

CLIMATE

Germany's climate is temperate. Rain is common year-round, though it is especially prevalent in summer, when the weather can change with surprising disjointedness from one hour to the next. Temperatures typically range between -1 to 2 °C (30-36 °F) in deep winter to 12 to 25 °C (55-77 °F) in July and August.

To convert from °C to °F, multiply by 1.8 and add 32. For a rough approximation, double the Celsius and add 25. To convert from °F to °C, subtract 32 and multiply by 0.55. For a rough approximation, subtract 25 and cut it in half.

°CELSIUS	-5	0	5	10	15	20	25	30	35	40
°FAHRENHEIT	23	32	41	50	59	68	77	86	95	104

DISTANCES (KM) AND TRAVEL TIMES BY TRAIN

	Aachen	Berlin	Bonn	Bremen	Dresden	D-Dorf	Frank-furt	Freiburg	Hamburg	Hannover	Kassel	Köln	Leipzig	München	Nürnberg	Rostock	Stuttgart
Aachen		642	90	387	649	80	263	541	484	351	307	68	576	650	503	638	450
Berlin	5½hr.		608	390	214	565	564	827	285	285	388	583	192	587	431	219	652
Bonn	1½hr.	5hr.		349	570	78	181	422	450	317	273	26	497	588	399	604	357
Bremen	4hr.	4hr.	3½hr.		488	298	467	700	119	133	281	324	370	745	573	297	657
Dresden.	9hr.	3hr.	8hr.	6hr.		568	471	724	485	371	337	578	124	494	346	474	572
Düssel-dorf	1½hr.	4hr.	45min.	3hr.	7hr.		231	492	423	272	228	41	493	618	449	577	414
Frankfurt	3½hr.	4hr.	2hr.	4hr.	6hr.	3hr.		272	497	362	194	192	398	399	223	651	216
Freiburg	5hr.	6½hr.	4hr.	6hr.	9hr.	4½hr.	2hr.		755	613	454	443	661	340	369	994	179
Hamburg	5hr.	2½hr.	4½hr.	1hr.	5hr.	3hr.	3½hr.	6hr.		163	311	425	377	775	607	184	679
Hannover	4hr.	2hr.	3hr.	1hr.	4½hr.	3hr.	2½hr.	5hr.	1½hr.		176	292	263	640	478	338	565
Kassel	5hr.	3hr.	4hr.	2½hr.	5½hr.	4hr.	2hr.	4hr.	2½hr.	1hr.		248	276	479	304	465	397
Köln	1hr.	4½hr.	30min.	3hr.	7½hr.	30min.	2½hr.	4hr.	4hr.	3hr.	4hr.		505	579	432	579	379
Leipzig	7hr.	2hr.	6hr.	4hr.	1½hr.	6hr.	3¾hr.	7hr.	4½hr.	3hr.	3½hr.	6hr.		422	274	366	499
München	7½hr.	7hr.	5hr.	6hr.	7hr.	6hr.	3½hr.	4½hr.	6hr.	4½hr.	4hr.	5½hr.	6hr.		162	761	221
Nürnberg	6hr.	5hr.	4hr.	4hr.	5hr.	5hr.	2hr.	4½hr.	4½hr.	3hr.	2½hr.	4½hr.	4hr.	2hr.		618	247
Rostock	8hr.	3hr.	8hr.	4hr.	6hr.	7hr.	6hr.	9hr.	2hr.	4hr.	5hr.	7hr.	5½hr.	9hr.	7½hr.		833
Stuttgart	4½hr.	5½hr.	3hr.	5hr.	7hr.	4hr.	1½hr.	2hr.	5½hr.	4hr.	3hr.	3hr.	6hr.	2hr.	2½hr.	8hr.	

APPENDIX

INDEX

ABOUT LET'S GO

FORTY YEARS OF WISDOM

As a new millennium arrives, *Let's Go: Europe*, now in its 40th edition and translated into seven languages, reigns as the world's bestselling international travel guide. For four decades, travelers criss-crossing the Continent have relied on *Let's Go* for inside information on the hippest backstreet cafes, the most pristine secluded beaches, and the best routes from border to border. In the last 20 years, our rugged researchers have stretched the frontiers of backpacking and expanded our coverage into Asia, Africa, Australia, and the Americas. We're celebrating our 40th birthday with the release of *Let's Go: China*, blazing the traveler's trail from the Forbidden City to the Tibetan frontier; *Let's Go: Perú & Ecuador*, spanning the lands of the ancient Inca Empire; *Let's Go: Middle East*, with coverage from Istanbul to the Persian Gulf; and the maiden edition of *Let's Go: Israel*.

It all started in 1960 when a handful of well-traveled students at Harvard University handed out a 20-page mimeographed pamphlet offering a collection of their tips on budget travel to passengers on student charter flights to Europe. The following year, in response to the instant popularity of the first volume, students traveling to Europe researched the first full-fledged edition of *Let's Go: Europe*, a pocket-sized book featuring honest, practical advice, witty writing, and a decidedly youthful slant on the world. Throughout the 60s and 70s, our guides reflected the times. In 1969 we taught travelers how to get from Paris to Prague on "no dollars a day" by singing in the street. In the 80s and 90s, we looked beyond Europe and North America and set off to all corners of the earth. Meanwhile, we focused in on the world's most exciting urban areas to produce in-depth, fold-out map guides. Our new guides bring the total number of titles to 48, each infused with the spirit of adventure and voice of opinion that travelers around the world have come to count on. But some things never change: our guides are still researched, written, and produced entirely by students who know first-hand how to see the world on the cheap.

HOW WE DO IT

Each guide is completely revised and thoroughly updated every year by a well-traveled set of over 250 students. Every spring, we recruit over 180 researchers and 70 editors to overhaul every book. After several months of training, researcher-writers hit the road for seven weeks of exploration, from Anchorage to Adelaide, Estonia to El Salvador, Iceland to Indonesia. Hired for their rare combination of budget travel sense, writing ability, stamina, and courage, these adventurous travelers know that train strikes, stolen luggage, food poisoning, and marriage proposals are all part of a day's work. Back at our offices, editors work from spring to fall, massaging copy written on Himalayan bus rides into witty, informative prose. A student staff of typesetters, cartographers, publicists, and managers keeps our lively team together. In September, the collected efforts of the summer are delivered to our printer, which turns them into books in record time, so that you have the most up-to-date information available for your vacation. Even as you read this, work on next year's editions is well underway.

WHY WE DO IT

We don't think of budget travel as the last recourse of the destitute; we believe that it's the only way to travel. Living cheaply and simply brings you closer to the people and places you've been saving up to visit. Our books will ease your anxieties and answer your questions about the basics—so you can get off the beaten track and explore. Once you learn the ropes, we encourage you to put *Let's Go* down now and then to strike out on your own. You know as well as we that the best discoveries are often those you make yourself. When you find something worth sharing, please drop us a line. We're Let's Go Publications, 67 Mount Auburn St., Cambridge, MA 02138, USA (email: feedback@letsgo.com). For more info, visit our website, http://www.letsgo.com.

Next time, make your *own* hotel arrangements.

Yahoo! Travel

READER QUESTIONNAIRE

Let's Go

Name: _____

Address: _____

City: _____ **State:** _____ **Country:** _____

ZIP/Postal Code: _____ **E-mail:** _____ **How old are you?** ____

And you're...?   in high school   in college   in graduate school

              employed   retired   between jobs

Which book(s) have you used? _____

Where have you gone with Let's Go? _____

Have you traveled extensively before?   yes   no

Had you used Let's Go before?   yes   no   **Would you use it again?**   yes   no

How did you hear about Let's Go? friend   store clerk   television

                               review   bookstore display

                               ad/promotion   internet   other: _____

Why did you choose Let's Go? reputation   budget focus   annual updating

                          wit & incision   price   other: _____

Which guides have you used? Fodor's   Footprint Handbooks   Frommer's $-a-day

                        Lonely Planet   Moon Guides   Rick Steve's

                        Rough Guides   UpClose   other: _____

Which guide do you prefer? Why? _____

Please rank the following in your Let's Go guide: (1=needs improvement, 5=perfect)

packaging/cover	1 2 3 4 5	food	1 2 3 4 5	maps	1 2 3 4 5
cultural introduction	1 2 3 4 5	sights	1 2 3 4 5	directions	1 2 3 4 5
"Essentials"	1 2 3 4 5	entertainment	1 2 3 4 5	writing style	1 2 3 4 5
practical info	1 2 3 4 5	gay/lesbian info	1 2 3 4 5	budget resources	1 2 3 4 5
accommodations	1 2 3 4 5	up-to-date info	1 2 3 4 5	other: _____	1 2 3 4 5

How long was your trip?   one week   two wks.   three wks.   a month   2+ months

Why did you go? sightseeing   adventure travel   study abroad   other: _____

What was your average daily budget, not including flights? _____

Do you buy a separate map when you visit a foreign city?   yes   no

Have you used a Let's Go Map Guide?   yes   no   **If you have, which one?** _____

Would you recommend them to others?   yes   no

Have you visited Let's Go's website?   yes   no

What would you like to see included on Let's Go's website? _____

What percentage of your trip planning did you do on the web? _____

What kind of Let's Go guide would you like to see? recreation (e.g., skiing)   phrasebook

                 spring break   adventure/trekking   first-time travel info   Europe altas

Which of the following destinations would you like to see Let's Go cover?

      Argentina   Brazil   Canada   Caribbean   Chile   Costa Rica   Cuba

      Morocco   Nepal   Russia   Scandinavia   Southwest USA   other: _____

Where did you buy your guidebook?   independent bookstore   college bookstore

                travel store   Internet   chain bookstore   gift   other: _____

Please fill this out and return it to **Let's Go, St. Martin's Press,** 175 Fifth Ave., New York, NY 10010-7848. All respondents will receive a free subscription to *The Yellow-jacket*, the Let's Go Newsletter. You can find a more extensive version of this survey on the web at http://www.letsgo.com.

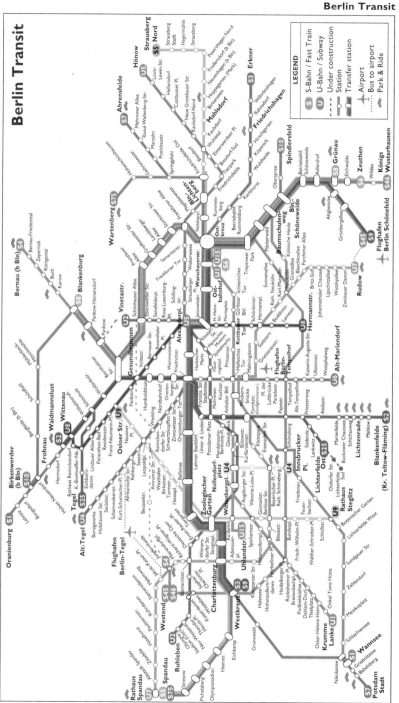

Berlin Transit

Munich Transit

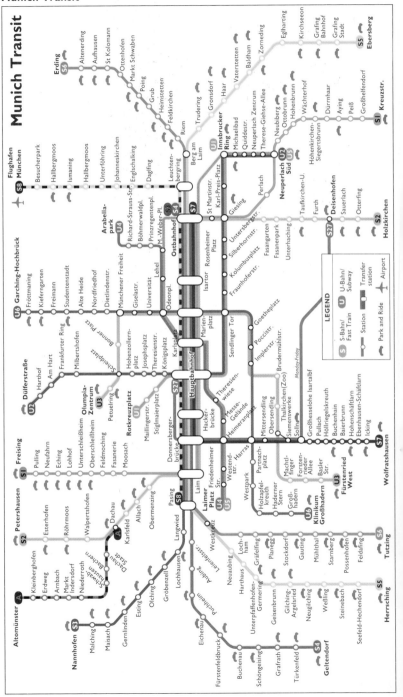

Hamburg Transit

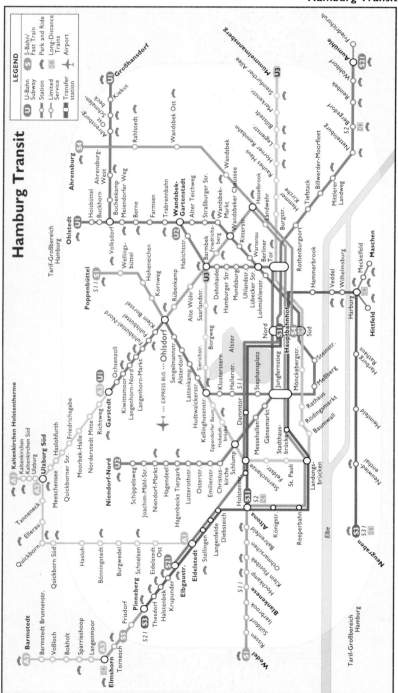

Frankfurt Transit

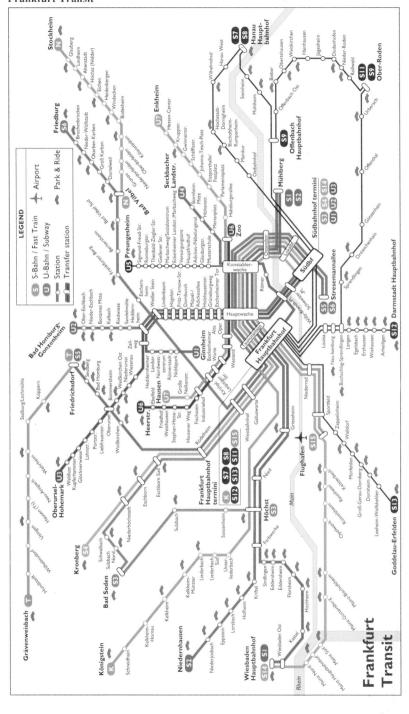

Frankfurt Transit